Health Education
Elementary and Middle School Applications

NINTH
EDITION

Susan K. Telljohann
University of Toledo

Cynthia W. Symons
Kent State University

Beth Pateman
University of Hawaii

Denise M. Seabert
University of West Florida

McGraw Hill Education

HEALTH EDUCATION

Published by McGraw-Hill Education, 2 Penn Plaza, New York, NY 10121. Copyright ©2020 by McGraw-Hill Education. All rights reserved. Printed in the United States of America. No part of this publication may be reproduced or distributed in any form or by any means, or stored in a database or retrieval system, without the prior written consent of McGraw-Hill Education, including, but not limited to, in any network or other electronic storage or transmission, or broadcast for distance learning.

Some ancillaries, including electronic and print components, may not be available to customers outside the United States.

This book is printed on acid-free paper.

1 2 3 4 5 6 7 8 9 LWI 21 20 19

ISBN 978-1-260-56627-7
MHID 1-260-56627-7

Cover Image: *Students eating: ©Monkey Business Images/Shutterstock; Kids in circle: ©serrnovik/123RF; Disabled children: ©FatCamera/Getty Images; Father with children: ©Chad Springer/Image Source*

mheducation.com/highered

BRIEF CONTENTS

CONTENTS

PREFACE

VISION AND GOALS

The ideas, concepts, and challenges presented in this text have developed out of many different experiences: teaching elementary and middle-level children; teaching a basic elementary/middle school health course to hundreds of pre-service elementary, early childhood, and special education majors; working with numerous student teachers; and serving on a variety of local, state, and national curriculum and standards committees. Authors and contributors are and have been engaged in teaching in K–8 settings, designing curriculum, developing instructional strategies, and collaborating with state and local educators to provide professional development. This has provided opportunities to use the content and strategies included in this ninth edition.

We have written this textbook with several groups in mind: (1) the elementary and middle-level education major who has little background or experience in health education but will be required to teach health education to her or his students in the future, (2) the health education major who will be the health specialist or coordinator in an elementary or middle school, (3) the school nurse who works in the elementary/middle school setting, and (4) those community health educators and nurses who increasingly must interact with elementary and/or middle school personnel. Our goal is to help ensure that elementary and middle school teachers and health specialists obtain the information, skills, and support they need to provide quality health instruction to students.

CONTENT AND ORGANIZATION

The ninth edition is divided into three sections. Section I, "Foundations of Health Education," includes Chapters 1 through 4. This section introduces the coordinated school health program, the relationship between health and learning, the national health initiatives, the development of the elementary/middle school health education curriculum, the concept of developmentally appropriate practice, lesson and unit planning, and assessment. The basics of effective health education and effective instruction approaches are provided, including a critical analysis of standards-based approaches to health education and strategies for creating a positive learning environment, managing time constraints, and handling controversial topics and issues.

Sections II and III reflect the Centers for Disease Control and Prevention's Health Education Curriculum Analysis Tool.

Section II, "Helping Students Develop Skills for Positive Health Habits," includes Chapters 5 through 9 and focuses on the positive health habits students can adopt and maintain to help them live a healthy life. The chapters in Section II cover mental and emotional health, healthy eating, physical activity, safety and unintentional injury prevention, and personal health and wellness. Section III, "Helping Students Translate Their Skills to Manage Health Risks," focuses on the health risks students need to avoid or reduce to promote health. These chapters (10 through 14) cover intentional injury prevention and violence; tobacco use; the use of alcohol and other drugs; sexual health; and managing loss, death, and grief.

Sections II and III present the content and the personal and social skills that comprise the National Health Education Standards. Each chapter in these sections begins by discussing the prevalence and cost of *not* practicing the positive health behavior, the relationship between healthy behaviors and academic performance, and relevant risk and protective factors. Readers then are provided with information about what schools are currently doing and what they should be doing in relation to the health behavior. Chapters in these sections also provide background information for the teacher, developmentally appropriate strategies for learning and assessment, sample student questions with suggested answers (Chapters 11–14), and additional recommended resources, including evaluated commercial curricula, children's literature, and websites.

CHAPTER-BY-CHAPTER CHANGES OF THE NINTH EDITION

The new edition includes updated statistics throughout. "Strategies for Learning and Assessment" have been revised to integrate more opportunities and to integrate technology into learning and assessment. Children's literature recommendations have been significantly revised including numerous new books in Chapters 5–14.

All references to YRBS and SHPPS data have been updated to include the most recently disseminated data.

Chapter 1: Whole School, Whole Community, Whole Child

- The Whole School, Whole Community, Whole Child section provides a current description of each component of the WSCC model.

Chapter 3: Standards-Based Planning, Teaching, and Assessment in Health Education

- Teacher's Toolboxes have been revised.

Chapter 4: Building and Managing the Safe and Positive Learning Environment

- Cooperative learning components have been updated to include new strategies and application ideas.
- Teacher's Toolbox focused on "Evaluation of Web-Based Resources" has been revised.

Chapter 6: Promoting Healthy Eating

- Dietary Guideline information has been updated.
- Food label information includes newest requirements.

Chapter 10: Preventing Intentional Injuries and Violence

- Significantly updated section on child maltreatment.

Chapter 11: Tobacco Use and Electronic Nicotine Systems Prevention

- Enhanced the chapter to include a new section on electronic nicotine systems, such as e-cigarettes and vaping.

Chapter 13: Promoting Sexual Health

- "Sample Student Questions and Suggested Answers about Sexuality" have been revised.

Chapter 14: Managing Loss, Death, and Grief

- Revised Teacher Toolbox, "Warning Signs for Suicide."

INSTRUCTOR AND STUDENT ONLINE RESOURCES

The 9th edition of *Health Education: Elementary and Middle School Applications* is now available as a SmartBook™—the first and only adaptive reading experience designed to change the way students read and learn.

SmartBook creates a personalized reading experience by highlighting the most impactful concepts a student needs to learn at that moment in time. As a student engages with SmartBook, the reading experience continuously adapts by highlighting content based on what the student knows and doesn't know. This ensures that the focus is on the content he or she needs to learn, while simultaneously promoting long-term retention of material. Use SmartBook's real-time reports to quickly identify the concepts that require more attention from individual students—or the entire class. The end result? Students are more engaged with course content, can better prioritize their time, and come to class ready to participate.

Key Student Benefits

- SmartBook engages the student in the reading process with a personalized reading experience that helps them study efficiently.
- SmartBook includes powerful reports that identify specific topics and learning objectives the student needs to study.
- Students can access SmartBook anytime via a computer and mobile devices.

Key Instructor Benefits

- Students will come to class better prepared because SmartBook personalizes the reading experience, allowing instructors to focus their valuable class time on higher level topics.
- SmartBook provides instructors with a comprehensive set of reports to help them quickly see how individual students are performing, identify class trends, and provide personalized feedback to students.

How Does SmartBook Work?

- *Preview:* Students start off by *Previewing* the content, where they are asked to browse the chapter content to get an idea of what concepts are covered.
- *Read:* Once they have *Previewed* the content, the student is prompted to *Read*. As he or she reads, SmartBook will introduce LearnSmart questions in order to identify what content the student knows and doesn't know.
- *Practice:* As the student answers the questions, SmartBook tracks their progress in order to determine when they are ready to *Practice*. As the students *Practice* in SmartBook, the program identifies what content they are most likely to forget and when.
- *Recharge:* That content is brought back for review during the *Recharge* process to ensure retention of the material.

Speak to your McGraw-Hill Learning Technology Consultants today to find out more about adopting SmartBook for *Health Education: Elementary and Middle School Applications, 9th edition*!

RESOURCES

Key teaching and learning resources are provided in an easy-to-use format for the ninth edition of Heath Education. The resources include the following teaching tools:

- *Instructor's Manual to Accompany Health Education: Elementary and Middle School Applications.*
- *PowerPoint slides.* A complete set of PowerPoint slides is available for download. Keyed to the major points in each chapter, these slide sets can be modified or expanded to better fit classroom lecture formats. Also included in the PowerPoint slides are many of the illustrations from the text, including the children's art.
- *Test bank.* The test bank includes true-false, multiple choice, short-answer, and essay questions. The test bank is also available with EZ Test computerized testing software. EZ Test provides a powerful, easy-to-use test maker to create printed quizzes and exams.

ACKNOWLEDGMENTS

I would like to express deep appreciation to my colleagues who significantly contributed to the revisions made in this edition.

Wendy S. Baker, MLS, K-5 STEAM Educator, Hudsonville Public Schools, Hudsonville, MI, significantly revised the children's literature recommendations provided with Chapters 5–14. She also updated many of the teaching and assessment strategies to effectively integrate technology.

Ryan G. Erbe, PhD, Minister, New York City Church of Christ, revised Chapter 4: Building and Managing the Safe and Positive Learning Environment; Chapter 5: Promoting Mental and Emotional Health; and Chapter 12: Alcohol and Other Drug Use Prevention.

Janet Kamiri, MPH, CHES, revised Chapter 6: Promoting Healthy Eating; Chapter 7: Promoting Physical Activity; Chapter 9: Promoting Personal Health and Wellness; and Chapter 13: Promoting Sexual Health.

Diana Ruschhaupt, MS, MCHES, Owner/Partner, Health Ed Pros, revised Chapter 3: Standards-Based Planning, Teaching, Assessment in Health Education; Chapter 11: Tobacco Use Prevention; and Chapter 14: Managing Loss, Death, and Grief.

Their expertise and experience have provided invaluable contributions to the ninth edition.

Finally, I would like to thank those who have made it possible for me to continue to share this resource with you. The vision, expertise, and dedication of Susan K. Telljohann, Cynthia W. Symons, and Beth Pateman will forever be captured throughout this textbook. These three school health educators have been vital in shaping school health education, mentoring the next generation of school health educators, and positively altering what we today know as school health education. Our profession and the work that has come from it are better because of these wise individuals.

We hope that you enjoy the changes and additions made in this ninth edition. We welcome any comments or suggestions for future editions. We wish all the best and success in teaching health education to children and preadolescents.

Denise M. Seabert on behalf of
Susan K. Telljohann
Cynthia W. Symons
Beth Pateman

 **Connect**®

Students—study more efficiently, retain more and achieve better outcomes. Instructors—focus on what you love—teaching.

SUCCESSFUL SEMESTERS INCLUDE CONNECT

FOR INSTRUCTORS

You're in the driver's seat.

Want to build your own course? No problem. Prefer to use our turnkey, prebuilt course? Easy. Want to make changes throughout the semester? Sure. And you'll save time with Connect's auto-grading too.

65%
Less Time Grading

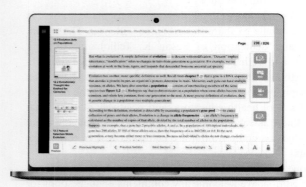

They'll thank you for it.

Adaptive study resources like SmartBook® help your students be better prepared in less time. You can transform your class time from dull definitions to dynamic debates. Hear from your peers about the benefits of Connect at **www.mheducation.com/highered/connect**

Make it simple, make it affordable.

Connect makes it easy with seamless integration using any of the major Learning Management Systems—Blackboard®, Canvas, and D2L, among others—to let you organize your course in one convenient location. Give your students access to digital materials at a discount with our inclusive access program. Ask your McGraw-Hill representative for more information.

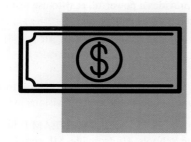

©Hill Street Studios/Tobin Rogers/Blend Images LLC

Solutions for your challenges.

A product isn't a solution. Real solutions are affordable, reliable, and come with training and ongoing support when you need it and how you want it. Our Customer Experience Group can also help you troubleshoot tech problems—although Connect's 99% uptime means you might not need to call them. See for yourself at **status.mheducation.com**

©Shutterstock/wavebreakmedia

Effective, efficient studying.

Connect helps you be more productive with your study time and get better grades using tools like SmartBook, which highlights key concepts and creates a personalized study plan. Connect sets you up for success, so you walk into class with confidence and walk out with better grades.

"I really liked this app—it made it easy to study when you don't have your text-book in front of you.**"**

- Jordan Cunningham, Eastern Washington University

Study anytime, anywhere.

Download the free ReadAnywhere app and access your online eBook when it's convenient, even if you're offline. And since the app automatically syncs with your eBook in Connect, all of your notes are available every time you open it. Find out more at **www.mheducation.com/readanywhere**

No surprises.

The Connect Calendar and Reports tools keep you on track with the work you need to get done and your assignment scores. Life gets busy; Connect tools help you keep learning through it all.

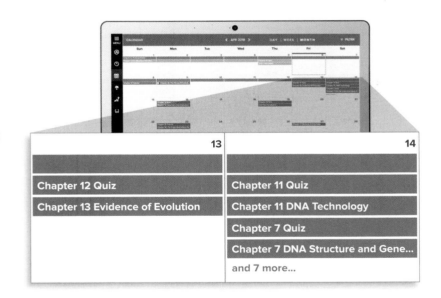

13	14
Chapter 12 Quiz	**Chapter 11 Quiz**
Chapter 13 Evidence of Evolution	**Chapter 11 DNA Technology**
	Chapter 7 Quiz
	Chapter 7 DNA Structure and Gene...
	and 7 more...

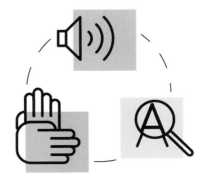

Learning for everyone.

McGraw-Hill works directly with Accessibility Services Departments and faculty to meet the learning needs of all students. Please contact your Accessibility Services office and ask them to email accessibility@mheducation.com, or visit **www.mheducation.com/about/accessibility.html** for more information.

©Monkey Business Images/Shutterstock

Foundations of Health Education

Section I begins with a review of important definitions and concepts that frame current understandings about health and health promotion. Next, a rationale for the importance of school health programming as a mechanism to reduce health risks and promote school success is discussed. With the foundation of the *Healthy People* agenda and findings from the most recent School Health Policies and Practices Study, this section contains a review of the ten critical components of the Whole School, Whole Community, Whole Child approach to health and learning. Teachers in elementary and middle schools will be enriched by examining the ways in which the broad science about brain function and learning have been translated into strategies for improving health instruction. Information about the value of using health education theory to inform practice is introduced, and a critical analysis of standards-based approaches to health education is provided. Finally, this section highlights strategies for creating a positive learning environment, promoting connectedness, managing time constraints, and dealing with controversial content and associated instructional issues in health education and promotion.

1

©FatCamera/iStock/Getty Images

Whole School, Whole Community, Whole Child

A Collaborative Approach to Learning and Health

DESIRED LEARNER OUTCOMES

After reading this chapter, you will be able to . . .

- **Define each of the domains of personal health.**

- **Identify behavioral risk factors that influence illness and death.**

- **Describe the link between student health and academic achievement.**

- **Discuss the influence of school health programs on improving school success.**

- **Summarize the role of each element of the Whole School, Whole Community, Whole Child model in improving the health of all stakeholders in the school community.**

- **Discuss the combined impact of the elements of the Whole School, Whole Community, Whole Child model on improving the health of all stakeholders in the school community.**

HEALTH: DEFINITIONS

A review of common understandings about health reveals that most people think in terms of physical well-being. As such, most people focus their thoughts and efforts on preventing or managing illnesses, participating in fitness activities, or modifying dietary behaviors. It is important, however, for teachers in elementary and middle schools to understand that health is a very broad concept that extends far beyond the limitations of the physical domain.

In 1947, the World Health Organization developed an informative definition of health defining it as "a state of complete physical, mental, and social well-being and not merely the absence of disease or infirmity."[1] This definition made a critical contribution by clarifying that health is influenced by a number of interrelated and influential factors.

Today, health is best understood as the capacity to function in effective and productive ways, influenced by complex personal, behavioral, and environmental variables that can change quickly. Bedworth and Bedworth have defined health as "the quality of people's physical, psychological, and sociological functioning that enables them to deal adequately with the self and others in a variety of personal and social situations."[2] Further, Carter and Wilson have clarified that "health is a dynamic status that results from an interaction between hereditary potential, environmental circumstance, and lifestyle selection."[3] These definitions confirm that, although a great deal of personal control can be exerted over some sources of influence over health, the capacity for a person to be in complete control of all such factors is limited. In summary, current definitions emphasize both the independent strength *and* the interactive effect of six influential domains of health: the physical, mental/intellectual, emotional, social, spiritual, and vocational.

Physical Health (Physical/Body)

The most easily observed domain of health is the physical. In addition to being influenced by infectious agents, physical well-being is influenced by the combined effects of hereditary potential, exposure to environmental toxins and pollutants, access to quality medical care, and the short- and long-term consequences of personal behaviors. As such, physical health results from a complex and changing set of personal, family, social, financial, and environmental variables.

Initial and often lasting impressions of the health of a friend or classmate are based on observed physical characteristics, including height, weight, energy level, and the extent to which the person appears to be rested. In addition, it is common to make judgments about health status based on observed behaviors. In this context, if friends participate in regular exercise or always wear a seatbelt, others are likely to conclude that they are healthy. Conversely, very different judgments often are made about the health of friends who are overweight or use tobacco products. Although a person's health outcomes might improve if they participated in fewer risky behaviors, such individuals might be very healthy in other influential domains.

Mental/Intellectual Health (Thinking/Mind)

The capacity to interpret, analyze, and act on information establishes the foundation of the mental or intellectual domain of health. Additional indicators of mental or intellectual health include the ability to recognize the sources of influence over personal beliefs and to evaluate their impact on decision making and behaviors. Observing the processes of reasoning, the capacity for short- and long-term memory, and expressions of curiosity, humor, logic, and creativity can provide clues about mental or intellectual health.[4]

Like the other domains, mental or intellectual health is important at every stage of life. In addition to exerting influence over all elements of well-being, positive mental health can contribute to the ability of people to:

- Realize their full potential.
- Manage stresses of daily living.
- Work productively.
- Make meaningful contributions.

Many factors, including those that are biological (e.g., genetics and brain chemistry) and life circumstances or experiences (e.g., trauma or abuse), can influence mental health. Importantly, positive mental health can be enriched by participating in enriching activities in the other domains of health including regular and vigorous physical activity, getting enough sleep, and maintaining positive relationships with others.

Mental health challenges are common, and help is available. However, even though most people are willing to seek professional help when they are physically ill, many unfortunately are hesitant or even refuse to pursue therapeutic interventions when confronted with mental health challenges. Importantly, when care is provided by a trained professional, many people feel improvement in their mental health status, and others can recover completely.[5]

Emotional Health (Feelings/Emotions)

The emotional domain of health is represented by the ways in which feelings are expressed. Emotionally healthy people communicate self-management and acceptance and express a full range of feelings in socially acceptable ways. Experiencing positive emotions and managing negative ones in productive ways contribute balance to emotional health. Importantly, emotionally robust individuals practice a range of coping skills that enable them to express negative feelings (sadness, anger, disappointment, etc.) in ways that are not self-destructive or threatening to others. In this way, emotional health contributes to and is reflected in perceived quality of life.

Many people who feel isolated, inadequate, or overwhelmed express feelings in excessive or abusive ways. Others suppress or bottle up strong emotions. Routinely attempting to cope with negative feelings by burying them has been demonstrated to contribute to stress-related illnesses, including susceptibility to infections and heart disease. Fortunately, counseling, support groups, and medical therapies can help people manage emotional problems of many types. An important starting resource for those attempting to manage such problems is their family doctor. This professional, with whom people are familiar and comfortable, can diagnose, treat, or make referrals for effective therapies to support and enrich emotional health.[6]

Social Health (Friends/Family)

Humans live and interact in a variety of social environments, including homes, schools, neighborhoods, and workplaces. Social health is characterized by practicing the requisite skills to navigate these diverse environments effectively. People with strength in the social domain of health maintain comfortable relationships characterized by strong connections, mutuality, and intimacy. In addition, socially healthy people communicate respect and acceptance of others and recognize that they can enrich and be enriched by their relationships.[7]

Unfortunately, many people are unable to function in comfortable and effective ways in the company of others. Such individuals can't integrate a range of important social skills into daily living. Often, this is a consequence of being self-absorbed. Such limited focus can compromise one's ability to recognize needs and issues of importance to others. As a consequence, poorly executed social skills and the associated behavioral consequences can place significant limitations on the ability to initiate and maintain healthy relationships. Such limitations compromise personal health and the quality of life of others.

Spiritual Health (Spiritual/Soul)

The spiritual domain of health is best understood in the context of a combination of three important elements:

- Comfort with self and the quality of interpersonal relationships with others.
- The strength of one's personal value system.
- The pursuit of meaning and purpose in life.[8]

Spiritually healthy people integrate positive moral and ethical standards such as integrity, honesty, and trust into their relationships. These individuals demonstrate strong concern for others regardless of gender, race, nationality, age, sexual orientation, or economic status. Although some people believe that spiritual well-being is enriched by their participation in formal religious activities, the definition of spiritual health is not confined to sacred terms or practices.

People with compromised spiritual health might not be guided by moral or ethical principles that are broadly accepted or believe that a higher being or something beyond themselves contributes meaning to their lives. Among such individuals, short-term economic objectives, self-interest, or personal gain at the expense of others could be of primary importance. People with compromised spiritual health are likely to feel isolated and have difficulty finding meaning in activities, making decisions about significant issues, or maintaining productive relationships with others.

Vocational Health (Work/School)

The vocational domain of health relates to the ability to collaborate with others on family, community, or professional projects. Vocationally healthy people are committed to contributing their fair share of effort to projects and activities. This commitment is demonstrated by the high degree of integrity with which individuals approach tasks. In addition to personal enrichment, the vocational domain of health is manifested in the degree to which a person's work makes a positive impact on others or in the community. The behaviors of people with compromised vocational health threaten personal work-related goals and have a negative impact on the productivity of professional associates and the collaborative community of the school or workplace.

Lōkahi: A Model of "Balance, Unity, and Harmony"

When evaluating the quality of a person's health, it is important to remember that balance across the domains is as important as maintaining an optimal level of functioning within each. In this context, a middle school student who uses a wheelchair because of a disabling condition might produce very high-quality academic work and have confident and effective relationships with classmates. Conversely, a person who is very healthy in the physical domain might be limited in the ability to express emotions productively or to behave in ways that confirm a poorly developed moral or ethical code.

All cultures have developed ways to communicate about shared beliefs, values, and norms that influence behaviors within the group. In Hawaiian culture the term *lōkahi*, meaning "balance, unity, and harmony," is used to express this ideal. Depicted in Figure 1–1, the Lōkahi Wheel is a culturally specific depiction of the domains of health.[9] Readers will note that names for each part of the Lōkahi Wheel have been linked to the corresponding name of each domain of health discussed. In addition, this illustration reinforces the importance of maintaining a solid balance

Thinking About Health in Hawai'i
The Lōkahi Wheel

Lōkahi
(Harmony, Balance, Unity)

Physical/Body	Spiritual/Soul
Friends/Family	Work/School
Thinking/Mind	Feelings/Emotions

FIGURE 1–1 | **The Lōkahi Wheel**

SOURCE: Native Hawaiian Safe and Drug-Free Schools Program, *E Ola Pono (Live the Proper Way): A Curriculum Developed in Support of Self-Identity and Cultural Pride as Positive Influences in the Prevention of Violence and Substance Abuse* (Honolulu, HI: Kamehameha Schools Extension Education Division, Health, Wellness, and Family Education Department, 1999).

across the domains as a foundation for maintaining personal, family, and community health.

With a focus on the health of students in elementary and middle schools, examination of the Lōkahi Wheel reinforces the negative impact that an imbalance in the health of one person can exert on the "balance, unity, and harmony" of their family, school, and community. In this way, a student who uses tobacco, alcohol, or other drugs is likely to face negative health, academic, family, and/or legal consequences. Simultaneously, such behaviors can threaten the health of family and friends. Also, the behavioral risks of one student will disrupt the functional "balance" at school, in the workplace, and in the community. As such, it is clear that unhealthy risk behaviors can have significant personal and far-reaching negative consequences.

Lōkahi serves as a foundation for the Hawaiian term *e ola pono*. Though this term has a number of related interpretations, generally it is translated as "living in the proper way" or "living in excellence." When students live their lives in a way that is orderly, successful, and true to what is in their best interest, the elements of their health are in balance and simultaneously enrich the well-being of their family, school, and community.[10]

As discussed in Chapter 2 of this text, to be effective, developmentally appropriate health education learning activities for students in elementary and middle schools must enable learners to translate general or abstract concepts into understandings or representations that have personal meaning or relevance. To enrich student understanding of the influence of each domain of health and the combined importance of a balance between them, teachers are encouraged to explore the learning activity described in Consider This 1.1.

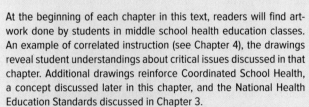

Consider This **1.1**

Health: A Personal Evaluation

At the beginning of each chapter in this text, readers will find artwork done by students in middle school health education classes. An example of correlated instruction (see Chapter 4), the drawings reveal student understandings about critical issues discussed in that chapter. Additional drawings reinforce Coordinated School Health, a concept discussed later in this chapter, and the National Health Education Standards discussed in Chapter 3.

Importantly, the artistic depiction at the beginning of Chapter 1 was done by a sixth grader. This Lōkahi Wheel provides a very personal view through the eyes of this middle school student of each domain of health and the balance of their combined effects. To enrich understanding and personalize the concept of health, teachers are encouraged to have students draw their own Lōkahi Wheels. The inclusion of color, personally meaningful depictions, and family characteristics should be encouraged. As a way to extend the learning activity, students could be asked to write a journal entry or share their "health story" with family members. In addition, the class could create a composite Lōkahi Wheel representing events, conditions, and circumstances that influence the health of the group as a whole. Finally, this learning activity could be correlated with social studies instruction as a way to explore ways in which people depict and communicate about issues of cultural and historical significance.

DETERMINANTS OF HEALTH

In 1979, the U.S. government embarked on a sweeping initiative to improve the health of all Americans. This multidecade agenda was launched with the publication of *Healthy People: The Surgeon General's Report on Health Promotion and Disease Prevention*. This document confirmed that the leading causes of illness and death among Americans had undergone dramatic change between the beginning and the end of the twentieth century. In the early 1900s, the greatest number of Americans died as a result of infectious or communicable diseases, including influenza and pneumonia, tuberculosis, and diarrhea and related disorders. Fortunately, due to measures such as improved sanitation and medical discoveries, Americans living just a century later enjoyed significantly longer, healthier lives.[11]

During the past century between 1900 and 2000, the average life span of Americans lengthened by greater than thirty years. Many factors contributed to such dramatic improvement in the health and life span of Americans during the twentieth century. In 1999, the Centers for Disease Control and Prevention (CDC) compiled a list of ten specific achievements that made a "great" impact on improving the nation's health during that 100-year period. These achievements are reviewed in Table 1-1.[12] It is important to recognize and celebrate the kinds of individual, community, and governmental activities that made these advancements possible. Such efforts continue to influence improvements in the health of all Americans today.

Although there were dramatic increases in the length and the quality of life of Americans since 1900, *Healthy People* reinforced the need to address factors that continue to cause premature death. This report confirmed that approximately 50 percent of premature morbidity (illness) and mortality (death) among Americans was linked to variables largely beyond personal control. These variables include heredity (20 percent); exposure to environmental hazards, toxins, and pollutants (20 percent); and inadequate access to quality medical care (10 percent).[13] It is significant to note, however, that *Healthy People* confirmed that the remainder of premature illness and death (approximately 50 percent) could be traced to participation in risky health behaviors.[14] Table 1-2[15, 16] contrasts past and current leading causes of death among Americans.

Examination of Table 1-2 contrasts the devastating impact of communicable/infectious diseases on previous generations with the consequences of chronic diseases (those that last a year or longer and require medical attention or limit daily activity) on the length and quality of life of Americans today. Conditions including heart disease, stroke, cancer, diabetes, and arthritis are among the most common, costly, and preventable of all health problems. The combined effects of two of these chronic conditions—heart disease and cancer—account for more than 45 percent of all American deaths each year. Importantly, the combined effects of chronic diseases account for seven of every ten American deaths every year.[17] Almost one of every two American adults has at least one chronic disease. In addition to their prevalence, such conditions cause limitations in the daily activities among people who are affected by them.[18] As a nation, more than 85 percent of health care spending goes to the

TABLE 1–1

Ten Great Public Health Achievements in the United States, 1900–1999

1. *Vaccination:* resulted in eradication of smallpox; elimination of polio in the Americas; and control of measles, rubella, tetanus, and other infections in the United States and around the world
2. *Improvements in motor-vehicle safety:* include engineering advancements in highways and vehicles, increased use of safety restraints and motorcycle helmets, and decreased drinking and driving
3. *Safer workplaces:* better control of environmental hazards and reduced injuries in mining, manufacturing, construction, and transportation jobs, contributing to a 40 percent decrease in fatal occupational injuries since 1980
4. *Control of infectious disease:* resulted from clean water, improved sanitation, and antibiotic therapies
5. *Decline in deaths due to heart disease and stroke:* a 51 percent decline in cardiovascular death since 1972—related to decreased smoking, management of elevated blood pressure, and increased access to early detection and better treatment
6. *Safer and healthier foods:* decreased microbe contamination, increased nutritional content, and food-fortification programs that have nearly eliminated diseases of nutritional deficiency
7. *Healthier moms and babies:* better hygiene and nutrition, available antibiotics, greater access to early prenatal care, and technological advances in maternal and neonatal medicine—since 1900, decreases in infant (90 percent) and maternal (99 percent) death rates
8. *Family planning:* improved and better access to contraception, resulting in changing economics and roles for women, smaller families, and longer intervals between births; some methods related to reduced transmission of human immunodeficiency virus (HIV) and other sexually transmitted diseases
9. *Fluoridation of drinking water:* tooth decay prevented regardless of socioeconomic status; reduced tooth loss in adults
10. *Recognition of the health risks of tobacco use:* reduced exposure to environmental tobacco smoke; declining smoking prevalence and associated deaths

While not ranked in order of significance or degree of contribution, the accomplishments on this list continue to help Americans live longer and healthier lives.

SOURCE: Centers for Disease Control and Prevention, "Ten Great Public Health Achievements—United States, 1900–1999," *MMWR* 48, no. 12 (1999): 241–43.

TABLE 1–2

Leading Causes of Death Among Americans in 1900 and Today
(ranked in order of prevalence)

1900	Today
Pneumonia	Heart disease
Tuberculosis	Cancer
Diarrhea/enteritis	Chronic respiratory diseases
Heart disease	Unintentional injuries
Liver disease	Stroke
Injuries	Alzheimer's disease
Cancer	Diabetes
Senility	Influenza and pneumonia
Diphtheria	Nephritis and other kidney disorders
	Suicide

SOURCES: U.S. Department of Health, Education and Welfare, Public Health Service, *Healthy People: The Surgeon General's Report on Health Promotion and Disease Prevention* (Washington, DC: U.S. Government Printing Office, 1979). National Center for Health Statistics, *Health, United States, 2016: With Chartbook on Long-term Trends in Health* (Hyattsville, MD, 2017).

NOTE: In 1900, the leading causes of death for most Americans were communicable or infectious conditions. Today, however, most Americans die as a result of chronic conditions.

treatment of chronic diseases. These persistent conditions are the causes of deaths that could have been prevented, lifelong disability, compromised quality of life, and an overwhelming burden of health care costs.[19]

An important first step to understand and address the complex burden of chronic diseases is to recognize that the majority of these conditions have been linked to participation in relatively few health-risk behaviors. Evidence suggests that four modifiable health-risk behaviors—lack of physical activity, poor nutrition, tobacco use, and excessive alcohol consumption—account for

much of the illness, suffering, cost, and early deaths related to chronic diseases.[20] Data in Table 1–3 identify the risk behaviors that undergird the actual causes of most American deaths.[21, 22] Consistent with the information found in this table, although a physician might indicate a clinical diagnosis of heart disease on a death certificate, the root cause of the heart disease could be traced to the cumulative effects of participation in any number of underlying risk behaviors.

It is important to remember that the greatest majority of adults who participate in risk behaviors initiated those health habits during their youth. Public health professionals at the CDC identified six priority health behaviors to guide educational programmers and intervention specialists. Owing to the demonstrated link between these behaviors and the leading causes of illness and death among Americans, curriculum developers and teachers should target educational strategies at reducing the risks associated with the following:

- Tobacco use.
- Poor eating habits.
- Alcohol and other drug risks.
- Behaviors that result in intentional or unintentional injuries.
- Physical inactivity.
- Sexual behaviors that result in HIV infection, other sexually transmitted diseases, or unintended pregnancy.[23]

In addition to addressing specific personal health risks, school-based professionals must remember that human behavior in general, and health behavior specifically, is influenced by complex sources. While it is important to equip students with the functional knowledge and essential skills to manage personal health risks, it is equally important to recognize that such

TABLE 1-3

Underlying Risk Behaviors—Actual Causes of Death in the United States in 2000

Risk Behavior	Approximate Number of Deaths	Approximate Percent of Annual Deaths
Tobacco	435,000	18.1
Poor diet and physical inactivity	365,000	15.2
Alcohol	85,000	3.5
Infections	75,000	3.1
Toxic agents	55,000	2.3
Motor vehicles	43,000	1.8
Firearms	29,000	1.2
Sexual behavior	20,000	0.8
Drug use	17,000	0.7

SOURCES: A. H. Mokdad et al., "Actual Causes of Death in the United States, 2000," *Journal of the American Medical Association* 291, no. 10 (March 10, 2004): 1238–45; Centers for Disease Control and Prevention, *Chronic Disease Overview* (https://www.cdc.gov/chronicdisease/overview/index.htm, 2017).

NOTE: It is important to exert influence over the common lifestyle risk behaviors linked to many of the causes of premature death. These health risks represent the actual leading causes, rather than the clinical diagnoses provided at the time of death for the majority of Americans.

behaviors do not happen in a vacuum. Public health researchers have identified five major sources of influence on American health. Similar to the causes of premature death identified in the 1979 *Healthy People* and those actions discussed in Table 1-1, today's influential variables include:

- *Biology and genetics:* Examples of such determinants of health include age, sex, and inherited conditions. Importantly, some biological and genetic factors affect some people more than others. In specific, older adults are more prone to poorer health outcomes than their adolescent counterparts and sickle-cell disease is most common among people with ancestors from West African nations.
- *Social factors:* The social determinants of health include physical conditions and other factors in the environment in which people are born, live, learn, play, and work. Examples of importance include the availability of resources to meet daily needs, prevalent and powerful social norms and attitudes, transportation options, public safety, and quality schools.
- *Health services:* Both access to and the quality of available health services influence health outcomes for all Americans. Examples of barriers to medical care include limited availability of specialized services in a local area, high cost, poor insurance coverage, and limited language access. In this context, if people don't have health insurance, research has demonstrated that they are less likely to participate in preventive care and to delay seeking medical treatment for illness or injury.
- *Public policy:* Local, state, and federal laws and policy initiatives have been demonstrated to influence the health of individuals and the population as a whole. For example, when taxes on tobacco sales are increased, the health of the people living in that region is improved by reducing the

number of people using tobacco products. Readers are encouraged to review the influence of the federal Affordable Care Act in this regard.

- *Individual behavior:* As discussed, positive changes in individual behaviors including reducing dietary risks, increasing physical activity, and reducing or eliminating the use of tobacco, alcohol, and other drugs, can reduce chronic diseases. In addition, the simple act of hand washing is one of the most important individual acts with the potential to reduce the short-term impact of infections.[24]

Although each of these factors exerts independent influence, the interaction among them is significant. In this context, it is clear that health is rooted in homes, schools, neighborhoods, workplaces, and communities. While individual behaviors such as eating well, staying active, not smoking, and seeing a doctor for preventive care or when sick can influence health, well-being also is influenced by their cumulative effects. Social determinants and environmental factors including access to quality schools, availability of clean water, air and healthy foods, and enriching social relationships help to clarify why some people are healthier than others. Only when people understand and can address the independent and combined effects of these sources of influence, will it be possible to achieve the highest quality of health for all. Given the complexity of this challenge, the coordinated efforts of individuals, families, schools, civic groups, faith-based organizations, and governmental agencies will be necessary to address the complex health challenges confronting youth.[25]

HEALTHY YOUTH, HEALTHY AMERICANS

Since the publication of *Healthy People* in 1979, local, state, and federal agencies have assumed leadership for a long-term broad and collaborative initiative to promote health and prevent disease among Americans. Every ten years, the U.S. Department of Health and Human Services (HHS) has gathered the latest data, analyzed accumulated information, and reviewed the best science about trends and innovations collected across the previous decade. Then, the best of this evidence is used to establish and monitor national health objectives targeting a broad range of health issues. These specific and measurable objectives establish a foundation to help individuals and communities make and act on informed health decisions.[26]

In addition to the focus on a range of critical health issues, this decades-long agenda has been organized around measurable objectives targeting diverse ages and groups of Americans. Among these targeted groups are children and youth. Since its inception, *Healthy People* has encouraged collaboration among influential stakeholders and institutions to protect and promote the health of this age group.[27]

Adolescence has been confirmed to be a period characterized by significant developmental transition. Youth between the ages of 10 and 19 are confronted with complex challenges associated with puberty and the task of cultivating skills to negotiate requisite developmental tasks. Although generally a healthy time of life, pertinent issues of significance can take root during adolescence. Tobacco and other substance use and abuse, sexual risks,

Quality health education can help empower children in all domains of health.

motor vehicle crashes, and suicidal thoughts or acts can determine current health status or influence the development of chronic diseases that will be manifested in adulthood. Research has demonstrated that adolescents particularly are sensitive to contextual influences in their environment. Factors including cues from family members, peers, those in their neighborhoods, and expectations and norms presented in the media can challenge or support their health. This is particularly true of the school environment in which policies, practices, and influential others can exert a powerful impact on the decision making and behaviors of youth.[28]

In addition to the developmental issues that challenge adolescents, a growing body of research has documented the importance of early childhood (birth to age 8) as a period in which the physical, cognitive, and social-emotional foundation for lifelong health and learning are established. During this developmental stage, the brain grows to 90 percent of its adult size and children learn to regulate their emotions, cultivate skills to form attachments, and develop language and critical motor skills. All of these milestones can be delayed if young children experience significant environmental stress or other risks that affect the brain or compromise physical, social-emotional, or cognitive growth.

More than any other stages of development, early and middle childhood (ages 6 to 12 years) set the stage for developing health literacy and practicing self-management, decision making, and the skills to negotiate conflicts with others. Typical and nonfatal conditions including asthma, obesity, and developmental and behavioral disorders can affect the health and education outcomes of those at this developmental stage. Importantly, health risks encountered during early and middle childhood can affect the well-being of the adolescents and adults who children will become.[29]

To review important health promotion targets for children and youth contained in *Healthy People 2020*, readers are encouraged to examine Table 1–4. Listed are the objectives that identify actions for many influential stakeholders in school communities designed to promote the health of youth.[30]

TABLE 1–4	HEALTHY PEOPLE

Healthy People 2020 Objectives That Specify Action for Advocates and Stakeholders in Schools

Adolescent Health (AH)

AH-5:	Increase educational achievement of adolescents and young adults.
AH-6:	Increase the proportion of schools with a school breakfast program.
AH-7:	Reduce the proportion of adolescents who have been offered, sold, or given an illegal drug on school property.
AH-8:	Increase the proportion of adolescents whose parents consider them to be safe at school.
AH-9:	Increase the proportion of middle and high schools that prohibit harassment based on a student's sexual orientation or gender identity.
AH-10:	Reduce the proportion of public schools with a serious violent incident.

Disability and Health (DH)

DH-14:	Increase the proportion of children and youth with disabilities who spend at least 80 percent of their time in regular education programs.

Early and Middle Childhood (EMC)

EMC-4:	Increase the proportion of elementary, middle, and senior high schools that require health education.

Educational and Community-Based Programs (ECBP)

ECBP-2:	Increase the proportion of elementary, middle, and senior high schools that provide comprehensive school health education to prevent health problems in the following areas: unintentional injury; violence; suicide; tobacco use and addiction; alcohol or other drug use; unintended pregnancy, HIV/AIDS, and STD infection; unhealthy dietary patterns; and inadequate physical activity.
ECBP-3:	Increase the proportion of elementary, middle, and senior high schools that have health education goals or objectives which address the knowledge and skills articulated in the National Health Education Standards (high school, middle, and elementary).
ECBP-4:	Increase the proportion of elementary, middle, and senior high schools that provide school health education to promote personal health and wellness in the following areas: hand washing or hand hygiene, oral health, growth and development, sun safety and skin cancer prevention, benefits of rest and sleep, ways to prevent vision and hearing loss, and the importance of health screenings and checkups.
ECBP-5:	Increase the proportion of elementary, middle, and senior high schools that have a full-time registered school nurse-to-student ratio of at least 1:750.

TABLE 1–4 *(continued)*

Environmental Health (EH)

EH-16:   Increase the proportion of the Nation's elementary, middle, and high schools that have official school policies and engage in practices that promote a healthy and safe physical school environment.

EH-23:   Reduce the number of public schools located within 150 meters of major highways in the United States.

Family Planning (FP)

FP-12:   Increase the proportion of adolescents who received formal instruction on reproductive health topics before they were 18 years old.

Hearing and Other Sensory or Communication Disorders (Ear, Nose, Throat-Voice, Speech, and Language) (ENT-VSL)

ENT-VSL-21:   Increase the proportion of young children with phonological disorders, language delay, or other developmental language problems who have participated in speech-language or other intervention services.

Injury and Violence Prevention (IVP)

IVP-27:   Increase the proportion of public and private schools that require students to wear appropriate protective gear when engaged in school-sponsored physical activities.

IVP-34:   Reduce physical fighting among adolescents.

IVP-35:   Reduce bullying among adolescents.

IVP-36:   Reduce weapon carrying by adolescents on school property.

Mental Health and Mental Disorders (MHMD)

MHMD-2:   Reduce suicide attempts by adolescents.

MHMD-4:   Reduce the proportion of adolescents who engage in disordered eating behaviors in an attempt to control their weight.

Nutrition and Weight Status (NWS)

NWS-2:   Reduce the proportion of children and adolescents who are considered obese.

NWS-10:   Increase the proportion of schools that offer nutritious foods and beverages outside of school meals.

NWS-11:   Prevent inappropriate weight gain in youth and adults.

NWS-12:   Eliminate very low food security among children.

Physical Activity (PA)

PA-3:   Increase the proportion of adolescents who meet current Federal physical activity guidelines for aerobic physical activity and for muscle-strengthening activity.

PA-4:   Increase the proportion of the Nation's public and private schools that require daily physical education for all students.

PA-5:   Increase the proportion of adolescents who participate in daily school physical education.

PA-6:   Increase regularly scheduled elementary school recess in the United States.

PA-7:   Increase the proportion of school districts that require or recommend elementary school recess for an appropriate period of time.

PA-10:   Increase the proportion of the Nation's public and private schools that provide access to their physical activity spaces and facilities for all persons outside of normal school hours (i.e., before and after the school day, on weekends, and during summer and other vacations).

PA-13:   Increase the proportion of trips made by walking.

PA-14:   Increase the proportion of trips made by bicycling.

Substance Abuse (SA)

SA-1:   Reduce the proportion of adolescents who report that they rode, during the previous 30 days, with a driver who had been drinking alcohol.

SA-2:   Increase the proportion of adolescents never using substances.

SA-18:   Reduce steroid use among adolescents.

SA-21:   Reduce the proportion of adolescents who use inhalants.

Tobacco Use (TU)

TU-2:   Reduce tobacco use by adolescents.

TU-3:   Reduce the initiation of tobacco use among children, adolescents, and young adults.

TU-7:   Increase smoking cessation attempts by adolescent smokers.

TU-15:   Increase tobacco-free environments in schools, including all school facilities, property, vehicles, and school events.

TU-18:   Reduce the proportion of adolescents and young adults in grades 6 through 12 who are exposed to tobacco marketing.

SOURCE: U.S. Department of Health and Human Services, *Healthy People 2020* (www.healthypeople.gov/2020/topics-objectives; 2018).

NOTE: Education professionals are encouraged to evaluate the extent to which their schools have established policies and practices that bring them into compliance with these national health objectives.

HEALTH IN THE ACADEMIC ENVIRONMENT

Today, youth are confronted with health, educational, and social challenges on a scale and at a pace not experienced by previous generations of young Americans. Violence, alcohol and other drug use, obesity, unintended pregnancy, and disrupted family situations can compromise both their short- and long-term health prospects.[31]

Educational institutions are in a unique and powerful position to improve health outcomes for youth. In the United States, nearly 60 million students are enrolled in more than 1,20,000 public and private elementary and secondary schools. In this context, schools have direct contact with more than 95 percent of American youth between the ages of 5 and 17 years. Sustained for over six hours every school day, this instructional engagement proceeds over a thirteen-year period, a time of significant social, psychological, physical, and intellectual development.[32-35] As such, schools represent the only social institution that can reach nearly all young people.

Beyond offering efficient access to the critical mass of youth, schools provide a setting in which friendship networks develop, socialization occurs, and norms that influence behavior are developed and reinforced.[36] Importantly, such social norms prevail in the school environment *before* specific health behaviors can become habitual for individual students. As a result, developmentally predictable experimentation with a range of health behaviors occurs in context of relationships with professional adult educators who are academically prepared to organize developmentally appropriate learning experiences to empower children to lead safer, healthier lives.

Unfortunately, advocates committed to promoting child and adolescent health in schools have been challenged by sweeping efforts to reform public education. Since the early 1980s, many research reports, position statements, and legislative initiatives have been directed at improving the quality of education for all students. The passionate commitment to reform the nation's education enterprise has taken many forms, including experimentation with strategies to improve teacher preparation, evaluation of student performance, and the U.S. Supreme Court decision supporting vouchers to promote school choice options for parents. Most school improvement plans have increased reliance on quantitative measures of student performance in the basic, or core, academic subjects including language arts, mathematics, social studies, and the physical sciences. In addition, significant efforts and financial resources have been mobilized to enrich instructional practices targeting the Common Core Standards, an agenda explored in Chapter 2.

Unfortunately, support for academic activities designed to address the complex health challenges confronting students are missing in most calls for education reform. *A Nation at Risk*, a report by the National Commission on Excellence in Education, included health education on a list of academic subjects identified as part of the "educational smorgasbord." This prestigious and powerful 1983 report, sponsored by the U.S. Department of Education, asserted that the American education curricula had become "diluted . . . and diffused" and recommended that educational programs in this "smorgasbord" category be either eliminated or significantly reduced in emphasis during the school day.[37] Echoes of this perspective remain in the federal No Child Left Behind and Race to the Top agendas discussed in Chapter 2.

Importantly, a growing body of science confirms that student health behaviors, academic outcomes, and school policies and practices designed to address them are "inextricably intertwined."[38] The American Cancer Society and representatives of more than forty national organizations concluded that "healthy children are in a better position to acquire knowledge" and cautioned that no curriculum is "brilliant enough to compensate for a hungry stomach or a distracted mind."[39] To reinforce this position, a recent and significant research agenda concluded that:

> No matter how well teachers are prepared to teach, no matter what accountability measures are put in place, no matter what governing structures are established for schools, educational progress will be profoundly limited if students are not motivated and able to learn. . . . Healthier students are better learners.[40]

In this context, the Council of Chief State School Officers (CCSSO), the professionals responsible for education programming and policy in each state, issued *Policy Statement on School Health*. Recognizing that "healthy kids make better learners and that better students make healthy communities," this policy statement urged education leaders "to recognize the enormous impact that health has on the academic achievement of our nation's youth." Further, the esteemed CCSSO urged all educators to "look beyond standards setting and systems of accountability and join with public and private sector mental health, health, and social services providers to address the widespread conditions that interfere with student learning and students' prospects for healthy adulthood."[41]

Beyond making this statement of advocacy, this important policy statement contained a number of recommendations for state and local education leaders. At the state level, education and legislative leaders were encouraged to demonstrate their commitment to acting on the evidence-based links between health and academic success by engaging in such activities as:

- Disseminating data that confirm the impact of health-promoting activities on academic achievement.
- Designating senior-level staff to oversee school health-related activities.
- Supporting policies that promote student health, including restricting vending machine sales, prohibiting tobacco use on school property, and ensuring health insurance coverage for all students and staff.
- Ensuring curricular compliance with the National Health Education Standards.
- Allocating adequate funding for school health promotion.[42]

In recognition that school-based activities to promote student health must occur in the context of, rather than in competition with, strategies to improve education outcomes, many professional and policy advocates have responded. Of note, ASCD convened a meeting of the Commission on the Whole Child. This group was charged with the important task of redefining the "successful learner."[43] Their specific responsibility was to reframe the understanding of a "successful learner" from a student whose achievement is measured only by scores on academic tests, to one who is knowledgeable, emotionally and physically healthy, engaged in civic activities and events, involved in the arts, prepared for work and for economic self-sufficiency, and ready for the world after completing formal schooling.[44]

The Position Statement on the Whole Child, developed by the Commission of the Whole Child, affirmed that academics remain essential, but are only one element of student learning and development. Rigorous testing can be only one part of a complete system of educational accountability. In an expansion of conventional thinking about education reform, the "new compact" established by ASCD calls on teachers, schools, and communities to collaborate to ensure that

- "Each student enters school healthy and learns about and practices a healthy lifestyle,
- Each student learns in an intellectually challenging environment that is physically and emotionally safe for students and adults,
- Each student is actively engaged in learning and is connected to the school and broader community,
- Each student has access to personalized learning and to qualified, caring adults, and
- Each graduate is prepared for success in college or further study and for employment in a global environment."[45]

Achieving these ambitious outcomes requires the establishment of coalitions of supportive and involved families, community volunteers, and advocates for health promotion networks and school health councils. In addition, ASCD has reinforced the importance of support provided by governmental, civic, and business organizations. Schools must develop challenging and engaging curricula, provide professional development and planning time for high-quality teachers and administrators, cultivate a safe, healthy, orderly, and trusting learning environment, promote strong relationships between adults and students, and support health promotion networks and school health councils. Finally, teachers were called on to use evidence-based instruction and assessment practices, engage learners in rich content, make connections with students and families, manage their classrooms effectively, and model healthy behaviors.[46]

Given the complex health and learning challenges facing today's students it is critical for educators, families, and other advocates to remember that children don't grow and learn in isolation. They grow physically, emotionally, ethically, expressively, and intellectually in networks of families, schools, neighborhoods, and communities. Educating the whole child won't happen with emphasis only on measures of academic achievement.[47]

As a result of the contributions of such powerful advocates, health promotion activities are gaining credibility as an effective and efficient way to promote student success as stakeholders learn that the choice of focusing on education outcomes *or* academic success is a false one. Mounting evidence has confirmed the destructive impact of student health risks on attendance, class grades, performance on standardized tests, and graduation rates.[48]

Due to the complexity of the health and academic problems confronting students, it is not reasonable nor realistic to expect that schools can address them without support. Such challenges will require the collaborative efforts of families, communities, health care providers, legislators, the media, and others. While there are no simple solutions, schools can provide a focal point for many such efforts.[49]

WHOLE SCHOOL, WHOLE COMMUNITY, WHOLE CHILD

A Foundation for Understanding

Each day, in schools across the United States, even the most talented students are confronted with risks for alcohol or other drug-related behaviors, pregnancy, or the negative outcomes of violence. In response to these and many other threats, it is common for well-intentioned but often misguided stakeholders to respond with crisis intervention approaches. Rather than developing stable, evidence-based, and sustained policies and practices, educators attend to such health issues only when there is a catastrophic, sensational, or newsworthy event. Importantly, such reactive approaches have been shown to meet the needs of only limited numbers of students and have been demonstrated to produce short-lived outcomes.

As discussed earlier in this chapter, *Healthy People* provided a starting point for organizing many kinds of targeted health initiatives, including those based in the nation's schools. Concerned advocates for children and youth would be wise to review the important definitions of medical care, disease prevention, and health promotion contained in this historic publication. Understanding these concepts can help to establish the boundaries of professional practice, identify realistic program expectations, and target key stakeholders with shared responsibility for the promoting and protecting health of students.

In *Healthy People,* "medical care" is defined with a primary focus on "the sick" and involves activities designed "to keep these individuals alive, make them well, or minimize their disability."[50] Each day, many students in America's schools receive medical care consistent with this definition. They have conditions that have been diagnosed and are being treated by trained clinicians. School-based education professionals are not equipped to provide such diagnostic and therapeutic intervention. Exceptions exist only in circumstances in which first aid or emergency care must be provided. Even in such cases, only trained individuals in the education community should render emergency care. The appropriate role for school-based professionals in managing students who need medical care includes referral, support, and compliance with the prescriptions and proscriptions made by attending clinicians. In this context, the appropriate role for educators is to support parents and trained others to carry out such care plans.

"Disease prevention" "begins with a threat to health—a disease or environmental hazard—and seeks to protect as many people as possible from the harmful consequences of that threat."[51] Disease prevention is best understood as the process of "reducing risks and alleviating disease to promote, preserve, and restore health and minimize suffering and distress."[52] Often, teachers emphasize hand washing and proper disposal of soiled tissues as part of daily classroom practice. Education professionals collaborate with school nurses, administrators, parents, and medical care providers to manage outbreaks of infections and other conditions including chicken pox, head lice, and the flu. School policymakers work with public health officials in screening and enforcing compliance with immunization policies. Whether working independently in the classroom or collaborating with others, teachers assume a much more active role in disease prevention than in the implementation of medical care delivery in the school setting.

Though there are circumstances in which medical care and disease prevention strategies are warranted, school-based professionals must be capable and comfortable with activities that focus on student health promotion. *Healthy People* defined all strategies that begin with "people who are basically healthy" as the target for health promotion activities. Health promotion "seeks the development of community and individual measures which can help [people] develop healthy lifestyles that can maintain and enhance the state of well-being."[53] More currently, health promotion is best understood as any "planned combination of educational, political, environmental, regulatory, or organizational mechanisms that support actions and conditions of living conducive to the health of individuals, groups, and communities."[54]

In this context, the primary task for educators working with students who are "basically healthy" is to implement health promotion activities at the school site. As concluded in *Healthy People,*

> Beginning in early childhood and throughout life, each of us makes decisions affecting our health. They are made, for the most part, without regard to, or contact with, the health care delivery system. Yet their cumulative impact has a greater effect on the length and quality of life than all the efforts of medical care combined.[55]

A commitment to health promotion at the school site provides a foundation for proactive collaboration by many stakeholders invested in both the health and school success of learners. The contrast between common school health practice and strategies based on sound health promotion research is highlighted in Consider This 1.2, "A Fence or an Ambulance." This poem, written in the 1800s, makes the value of a commitment to a health promotion philosophy based on prevention very clear.

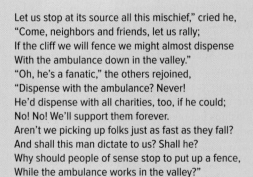

Consider This **1.2**

A Fence or an Ambulance   Joseph Malins

'Twas a dangerous cliff, as they freely confessed,
Though to walk near its crest was so pleasant;
But over its terrible edge there had slipped
A duke and full many a peasant.
So the people said something would have to be done,
But their projects did not at all tally;
Some said, "Put a fence around the edge of the cliff,"
Some, "An ambulance down in the valley."

But the cry for the ambulance carried the day,
For it spread through the neighboring city;
A fence may be useful or not, it is true,
But each heart became brimful of pity
For those who slipped over that dangerous cliff;
And the dwellers in highway and alley
Gave pounds or gave pence, not to put up a fence,
But an ambulance down in the valley.

"For the cliff is all right, if you're careful," they said,
"And, if folks even slip and are dropping,
It isn't the slipping that hurts them so much,
As the shock down below when they're stopping."
So day after day, as these mishaps occurred,
Quick forth would these rescuers sally
To pick up the victims who fell off the cliff,
With their ambulance down in the valley.

Then an old sage remarked: "It's a marvel to me
That people give far more attention
To repairing results than to stopping the cause,
When they'd much better aim at prevention.

Let us stop at its source all this mischief," cried he,
"Come, neighbors and friends, let us rally;
If the cliff we will fence we might almost dispense
With the ambulance down in the valley."
"Oh, he's a fanatic," the others rejoined,
"Dispense with the ambulance? Never!
He'd dispense with all charities, too, if he could;
No! No! We'll support them forever.
Aren't we picking up folks just as fast as they fall?
And shall this man dictate to us? Shall he?
Why should people of sense stop to put up a fence,
While the ambulance works in the valley?"

But a sensible few, who are practical too,
Will not bear with such nonsense much longer;
They believe that prevention is better than cure,
And their party will soon be the stronger.
Encourage them then, with your purse, voice, and pen,
And while other philanthropists dally,
They will scorn all pretense and put up a stout fence
On the cliff that hangs over the valley.

Better guide well the young than reclaim them when old,
For the voice of true wisdom is calling,
"To rescue the fallen is good, but 'tis best
To prevent other people from falling."
Better close up the source of temptation and crime
Than deliver from dungeon or galley;
Better put a strong fence round the top of the cliff
Than an ambulance down in the valley.

A Program Model for Best Practice

While it is true that most schools invest considerable time and expertise in managing a range of health problems, in most cases, these efforts are implemented as isolated or competing entities. In this context, it is common for school communities to organize categorical activities such as Red Ribbon Week campaigns to reduce drug risks, transportation safety activities at the start of the school year, physical education instruction, and free or reduced-cost lunches for children living in poverty, with little thought about their focus, coordination, or sustainability. It is easy to see that such school health activities are operating under a "more of anything" rather than a "better is better" philosophy. As a result, their effectiveness and sustainability are compromised severely.

By contrast, evidence suggests that it is far better to organize all school health activities around a framework in which the talents and efforts of many professionals and resources in the school and local community can be mobilized to promote health and school success for all students, not just those with episodic or demanding health challenges. Such a coordinated approach is a way for many school health promotion activities to be systematic and intentional.[56] In addition, health messages can be communicated with consistency and reinforced through multiple channels, the duplication of services can be reduced, resources funded by tax dollars can be maximized, and advocates are better able to focus their efforts.

For years, health educators implemented the Coordinated School Health (CSH) model in effort to collaboratively impact student health. In recent years, ASCD and the Centers for Disease Control and Prevention have collaborated to improve this model, resulting in the Whole School, Whole Community, Whole Child (WSCC) model. The WSCC model combines and builds on elements of the traditional Coordinated School Health model with a significant emphasis on raising academic achievement and improving learning by integrating a health and well-being focus.[57] The WSCC model "provides a framework that stakeholders—school districts, state boards of education, school and public health professionals, and community organizations—can use to coordinate the education and health policies, processes, and practices to serve each child."[58]

The WSCC model includes ten components, which are divided into four distinct components. The evolution of this model meets the need for greater emphasis on both the psychosocial and physical environment as well as critical roles that community agencies and families must play. The ten components include the following: health education; nutrition environment and services; employee wellness; social and emotional school climate; physical environment; health services; counseling, psychological, and social services; community involvement; family engagement; and physical education and physical activity.[59]

Consistent with the body of literature confirming links between student health and a range of measures of school success, Dr. Lloyd Kolbe, one of the architects of CSH, revisited his original work and concluded that the goals of the modern school health program are consistent with the agenda of educational reform. Consistent with the advocacy position taken by ASCD for education for the "whole child," Dr. Kolbe asserted that modern school health programs develop when the efforts of education, health, and social service professionals are integrated purposefully to tackle four overlapping and interdependent types of goals for students:

- Goals focused on improving health knowledge, attitudes, and skills.
- Goals focused on improving health behaviors and outcomes.
- Goals focused on improving educational outcomes.
- Goals focused on improving social outcomes among learners.[60]

In this way, the WSCC model puts both student health and academic achievement at the heart of the matter and provides an efficient and effective way to improve, protect, and promote school success *and* the well-being of students, families, and education professionals. When fully implemented in a school community, WSCC has the capacity to:

- Maximize the impact of all available expertise and resources directed toward risk reduction and health promotion.
- Conserve taxpayer dollars by reducing duplication of services for health issues.
- Maximize use of public facilities in the school and community to promote health.
- Enhance communication and collaboration across health promotion professionals in the school and community.
- Address student health risks in the context of, rather than in competition with, the academic mission of the school.

Student health advocates are encouraged to review Figure 1–2, a depiction of how the community, school, and families collaborate with focus on the student.

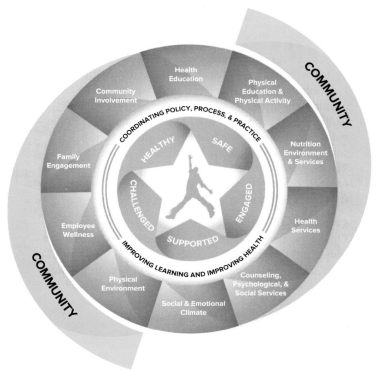

FIGURE 1-2 | **Whole School, Whole Community, Whole Child Model**
SOURCE: https://www.cdc.gov/healthyyouth/wscc/

Health Education: The Keys to Quality Health Instruction

The most familiar component of WSCC is its educational, or instructional, foundation: comprehensive school health education. This element of an effective school-based health promotion program is defined as the "development, delivery, and evaluation of planned, sequential, and developmentally appropriate pre-kindergarten through grade 12 instruction and learning experiences designed to promote the health literacy, knowledge, attitudes, skills, and well-being of students. The content taught is standards-based, includes multiple health topics, and addresses the physical, intellectual, emotional, and social dimensions of health."[61] As such, a program of quality health instruction is focused on enabling and empowering students to gather accurate functional health information, evaluate attitudes, beliefs, and perceptions that influence personal and community health, and practice the essential skills needed to integrate health-enhancing behaviors into daily living. To accomplish this, health education must be addressed with the same commitment and integrity as any other academic discipline of the school curriculum. Readers are encouraged to review selected findings from the School Health Policies and Practices Study (SHPPS 2016) concerning comprehensive school health education in the Chapter 1 "More Resources" section of the Online Learning Center.

Consistent with the current literature identifying evidence-based approaches to comprehensive school health education, antiquated thinking and strategies must be updated. In particular, instructional approaches grounded in information acquisition and content mastery alone are not likely to equip students to manage the complex health challenges confronting them. After a decade of evaluation, researchers from the World Health Organization revealed the following important findings about school health education:

- Health education that concentrates on developing health-related skills and increasing comprehension of health knowledge and attitudes is more likely to enable youth to practice healthy behaviors.
- Skill development is more likely to result in healthy behavior outcomes when skill practice is tied to specific health content, decisions, or behaviors.
- The most effective method of skill development is learning by doing—learners involved in active rather than passive learning experiences.[62]

Consistent with best-practice protocol identified in the education literature, quality health education is grounded in activities that bridge all three domains of learning: the (1) cognitive, (2) affective, and (3) psychomotor, or skill, domains. In addition, health education curricula must reflect the most current and accurate knowledge base and incorporate developmentally appropriate, ability centered, and culturally relevant learning materials and technological resources.

Consistent with such a best practice orientation to health instruction, the Joint Committee on National Health Education Standards, a collaborative group of professionals representing national health and advocacy organizations, published

National Health Education Standards: Achieving Excellence (2nd ed.) in 2007. This publication specified national standards developed to set ambitious goals for improving health education for all students. The developers also provided rationale for each standard and identified specific performance indicators to be achieved by students in grades 2, 5, 8, and 12. Elementary and middle school teachers should examine Appendix A, containing the health education performance indicators for students in grades pre-K–2, 3–5, and 6–8. Teacher's Toolbox 1.1 highlights the importance of functional knowledge and the essential skills that are the foundation of the National Health Education Standards. The standards provide a framework for developing a rigorous health education instructional scope and sequence and meaningful evaluation protocol for students in all grade levels.[63] Importantly, the School Health Policies and Programs Study (SHPPS) conducted in 2016 confirmed that nearly 82 percent of schools follow national, state, or district health education standards.[64] Readers are encouraged to review Chapter 3 of this text that contains an expanded discussion of the National Health Education Standards and their applicability for improving health education practice.

In addition to standards-based approaches, school districts use many ways to describe how much health education students at various grade levels are required to receive (minutes per week, hours per quarter, hours per school year). SHPPS 2016 confirms that nationwide, 32.0 percent of districts specify time requirements for health education for students in elementary schools, 52.3 percent had such requirements for students in the middle

---

Teacher's Toolbox 1.1

National Health Education Standards

1. Students will comprehend concepts related to health promotion and disease prevention to enhance health.
2. Students will analyze the influence of family, peers, culture, media, technology, and other factors on health behaviors.
3. Students will demonstrate the ability to access valid information and products and services to enhance health.
4. Students will demonstrate the ability to use interpersonal communication skills to enhance health and avoid or reduce health risks.
5. Students will demonstrate the ability to use decision-making skills to enhance health.
6. Students will demonstrate the ability to use goal-setting skills to enhance health.
7. Students will demonstrate the ability to practice health-enhancing behaviors and avoid or reduce risks.
8. Students will demonstrate the ability to advocate for personal, family, and community health.

SOURCE: National Health Education Standards: Achieving Excellence, 2nd ed. (Atlanta, GA: American Cancer Society, 2007). www.cancer.org/bookstore

NOTE: "This list of health education standards represents the work of the Joint Committee on National Health Education Standards. Copies of *National Health Education Standards: Achieving Excellence* can be obtained through the American School Health Association, the Association for the Advancement of Health Education, or the American Cancer Society."

grades, and 72.3 percent had such specified requirements for high school students. In this context, SHPPS 2016 revealed that nationwide, one-third of elementary schools mandate time be spent on teaching young people to develop healthy behaviors during a time when many young people confront a broad range of health risks.[65] Importantly, the Joint Committee on National Health Education Standards recommends that students pre-K to grade 2 receive a minimum of forty hours and that their counterparts in grades 3–12 receive a minimum of eighty hours of formal health instruction each school year.[66]

Across both the standards- and time-based models of health education, research has revealed that more hours of formal health instruction are necessary to produce changes in the affective domain than in either the cognitive or the psychomotor domain of learning. It is important to note that, forty to fifty hours of formal health education is necessary to produce stable improvements across all three domains of learning: functional knowledge, attitudes, and essential skills.[67]

In addition to differences in instructional time mandates, there is great variability in the health topics addressed in the curricula of local school districts. Choosing or developing the best possible health education curriculum is an important step in making sure that the program of instruction is effective at promoting healthy behaviors among all students. Unfortunately, in many districts, the process of curriculum selection or development lacks structure and focus. Such an approach can result in inadequate and ineffective health instruction.

To help address this matter, the CDC has developed the Health Education Curriculum Analysis Tool (HECAT) that contains guidance and resources for conducting a clear, complete, and consistent analysis of health education curricula. Districts that use HECAT will find help in selecting or developing evidence-based, appropriate, and effective health education courses of study. Further, with the help provided by this important resource, school-based professionals and other stakeholders can improve the delivery of evidence-based health education to students.[68]

This book is organized around HECAT curricular topics. In addition to an expanded discussion of HECAT in Chapter 2, curricular topics in this text are organized into two sections:

- Section II: Helping Students Develop Skills for Positive Health Habits
- Section III: Helping Students Translate Their Skills to Manage Health Risks

Teacher's Toolbox 1.2 highlights priority health issues that should be addressed in a developmentally appropriate way with all students in elementary and middle grades.[69]

Unlike secondary schools, in which content specialists are employed, elementary and middle school classroom teachers often are expected to deliver health education instruction. In such cases, it is common for the school nurse or community resource personnel to provide additional instructional support or supplemental expertise. Many elementary and middle school teachers report that they have inadequate academic preparation to teach complex or often controversial health education topics, and lack confidence or enthusiasm for health instruction. Often

Teacher's Toolbox 1.2

Sound Health Education: Instructional Topics for Which HECAT Tools Have Been Developed

- Alcohol and Other Drugs
- Healthy Eating
- Mental and Emotional Health
- Personal Health and Wellness
- Physical Activity
- Safety
- Sexual Health
- Tobacco
- Violence Prevention

SOURCE: Centers for Disease Control and Prevention, *Health Education Curriculum Analysis Tool* (www.cdc.gov/healthyyouth/HECAT/index.htm; 2017).

these deficiencies are related to residual limitations from their teacher preparation program. Unfortunately, state departments of education often specify only minimal requirements for teacher certification or licensure for those who will teach health education concepts to younger learners. As confirmation, SHPPS 2016 reveals that only 67.8 percent of districts require those teaching health at the middle school to be certified, licensed, or endorsed by the state to teach health education.[70]

To help address this matter, responsibilities and competencies have been developed for the professional preparation of elementary and middle school classroom teachers who assume the primary responsibility for teaching health education to young students. These responsibilities and competencies, developed by representatives of professional health education associations, are identified on Connect.[71, 72]

Readers are encouraged to use these competencies as a foundation for conducting a self-check of strengths and weaknesses in their own expertise. Classroom teachers who feel ill prepared or uncomfortable managing health education topics or a range of instructional activities are encouraged to participate in staff development or continuing education opportunities for in-service professionals. Such programs are designed to help teachers update content expertise and develop skills to improve classroom instruction.

In summary, SHPPS 2016 contains confirmation that 81.7 percent of districts follow national, state, or district health education standards.[73] Administrators, curriculum developers, and health teachers can review Table 1–5 for a checklist of important questions regarding the elements of a comprehensive school health education.[74] In addition, readers will find an expanded discussion about this important topic in Chapter 2 of this text.

Health Services

The practice of providing health services in the school setting began in the early twentieth century as a way to improve academic outcomes for students. Public health nurses began working in schools to reduce student absenteeism related to outbreaks of communicable diseases.[75] Today, although communicable diseases are still an issue for many students, there are many other complex health-related barriers to academic achievement. Asthma, child abuse and neglect, domestic and school violence, adolescent pregnancy and parenting, alcohol and other drug use, mental health concerns, and a lack of health insurance coverage are among the issues addressed by today's school health service providers.[76]

School health services include a range of policies and programs designed to assess the health status of children, as well as measures to protect the health of all children. Although various school personnel contribute to the school health service program, the school nurse assumes primary responsibility for leadership with this WSSC component. With the support of parents, teachers, administrators, support staff, community agency professionals, and a range of medical care providers, the school nurse leads the collaborative effort to:

- Provide direct health care to students and staff.
- Provide leadership for the provision of health services.
- Provide screening and referral for health conditions.
- Promote a healthy school environment.
- Promote health.

- Serve in a leadership role for health policies and programs.
- Coordinate care between school personnel, family, community, and health care providers.[77]

Effective and timely delivery of such services is influenced by the number of nurses available at the school site to respond to students' needs.[78] The National Association of School Nurses (NASN) has issued a powerful position statement in which it has asserted that to meet the health and safety needs of all students, the maximum ratio of nurse to student should be:

- One school health nurse to no more than 750 students in the healthy student population.
- One school health nurse to no more than 225 students who may require daily professional nursing services.
- One school health nurse to no more than 125 students in the severely chronically ill or developmentally disabled population (those with complex health care needs).
- A potential 1:1 ratio for individual students who need daily and continuous professional nursing services.

In this way, recommendations for best practice were quantified to equip school communities to meet the changing and often complex health needs of the student population attending American schools today. As confirmation of this requisite obligation, in 1999, the U.S. Supreme Court ruled that schools must provide all nursing services required by students to attend school, including one-on-one nursing care.[79] Unfortunately, SHPPS 2016 confirmed that the majority of schools fail to comply with this as only 10.9 percent of school districts nationwide have adopted a policy specifying a maximum school nurse to student ratio. Further, only 8.2 percent of districts confirmed that they have adopted a policy stating that each school will have a specified ratio of school nurses to meet the needs of students.[80]

Although debate continues about the types and amount of direct health services that should be provided at the school site, it is clear that school nurses must manage care plans for students with special health care needs. In addition, these service providers must institute policy and protocol approved by the board of education for administering medication to students. As the number of students with special needs attending schools continues to grow, new, expensive, and often labor-intensive demands are placed on school districts and their health service providers. School administrators have legal responsibility for the safety of all students enrolled in each public school district. This includes providing and supervising the program of health services. Unfortunately, many school districts have assigned these tasks to classroom teachers or support staff colleagues who have no training. Such practices are dangerous for the student, the school employee, and the school district.

The National Association of School Nurses has asserted that health services should be provided directly by a registered professional school nurse who has a minimum of a baccalaureate degree in nursing and is licensed through a board of nursing.[81] Consistent with this assertion, Teacher's Toolbox 1.3 identifies recommended policies and procedures to guide safe and effective administration of medications in schools.[82] Consistent with these minimum guidelines boards of education and district

Teacher's Toolbox 1.3

Safe and Effective Medication Administration in Schools: Policies and Procedures

The National Association of School Nurses developed a position statement providing guidance in the development of policies and procedures that ensure safe and effective medication administration in schools. The registered professional school nurse is responsible for medication administration and leading the development of policies and procedures that will ensure effective and safe medication administration. Policies and procedures, consistent with federal and state laws, should be established to address the following:

- Delegation (when permissible by state law), training, and supervision of unlicensed assistive personnel;
- Student confidentiality;
- Medication orders;
- Medication doses that exceed manufacturer's guidelines;
- Proper labeling, storage, disposal, and transportation of medication to and from school;
- Documentation of medication administration;
- Rescue and emergency medications;
- Off-label medications and investigational drugs;
- Prescription and over-the-counter medications;
- Complementary and alternative medications; and
- Psychotropic medications and controlled substances.

SOURCE: National Association of School Nurses, Position Statement: Medication Administration in Schools (www.nasn.org/nasn/advocacy/professional-practice-documents/position-statements/ps-medication; Revised February 2017).

administrators are encouraged to review local policies to confirm that they ensure the safety and legal protection of all concerned.

Although school nurses assume primary leadership for providing health services, many other educators and advocates are engaged in responding to student health issues that can compromise achievement. Classroom teachers are in an important position to participate in initial observation and referral of any conditions evident in students. Reports of such observations should be made to the school nurse or others specified in school district policy. In response, the coordinated team of health service providers can plan appropriate interventions to address the problem.

School nurses also collaborate with a range of allied health professionals in providing a formalized program of student health status assessments. In most school districts, a child must have a health examination before enrolling in school. Some school districts require additional periodic health examinations for students. These requirements vary from state to state. Most states also require vision and hearing screening at some point during the school life of each student. Often, vision and hearing difficulties are not identified until the child enters school. Scoliosis screening is a simple, but very effective, procedure to identify spinal curvatures among students in upper-elementary grades. During the elementary school years, the child's weight and height also are recorded. These measurements provide a record of basic childhood growth and development. Such growth data can

provide quick confirmation that a child's physical development is on pace with chronological age.

School health service professionals also coordinate disease prevention measures and participate in activities to protect the health of students, faculty, and staff. To this end, policies must be developed in collaboration with public health officials to exclude from school activities those children who are infected with contagious conditions. Classroom teachers must be informed about when and under what circumstances a child excluded from school due to a communicable disease can be permitted to return.

Every state has a legislative mandate requiring that children be immunized against certain communicable diseases before they can enroll in school. Although these state requirements differ slightly, immunization requirements for polio, diphtheria, pertussis, tetanus, measles (rubeola), German measles (rubella), and hepatitis are common. Accurate record keeping and communication with immunization providers can be very time-consuming, but important, roles of the school nurse.

Finally, it is imperative that school districts develop written policies for managing sick and injured students. In addition to a protocol for managing emergencies, staff development programs must ensure full compliance with universal precautions for handling body fluid spills in the educational environment. Such training should be extended to all school staff, including playground monitors, bus drivers, and other classified staff.

Clearly, the program of school health services fills a critical role in promoting student health and advancing the academic mission of schools. Table 1–6 provides a checklist of important questions to help guide the establishment of a quality program of health services in a school community.[83]

TABLE 1–6

Confirming a Commitment to a Quality Program of Health Services: A Checklist of Important Questions

Does your school have a full-time, registered school nurse responsible for health services all day, every day?

Are an adequate number of full-time school nurses available (at least one nurse per school)?

Does the school nurse or other health services provider promote the health and safety of students and their families by engaging in classroom and other activities about essential health topics (consistent with HECAT)?

Does your school implement a systematic approach for referring students, as needed, to appropriate school- or community-based health services?

Does your school have a system for collecting student health information prior to school entry and every year thereafter?

Is all pertinent health information communicated in writing to all appropriate staff members?

Does your school have access to and work with a consulting school health physician who assists with your school health programs?

Does the school nurse or other health services provider have a system for identifying and tracking students with chronic health conditions?

Does your school facilitate or provide case management for students with poorly controlled chronic health conditions?

SOURCE: Centers for Disease Control and Prevention, School Health Index: A Self-Assessment and Planning Guide—Elementary School (Atlanta, GA: CDC, 2017): Module 5.

Healthy School Environment

Like other elements of WSSC, the environment in which a student spends a large part of every day in the school year makes an impact on both their health status and academic achievement. The most conspicuous element of a healthy school environment is related to the physical condition of the buildings, vehicles, playgrounds, sport facilities, and other school district properties. Policies adopted by the local board of education govern safety and management of noise, temperature, lighting, and air and water quality in physical learning environments. In addition, administrators establish and implement policies that govern school start times, an issue that has been demonstrated to influence academic outcomes particularly among teens.[84] Finally, these leaders are in a position to establish policies including the establishment of "bully-free zones" that help maintain a healthy social and emotional environment in the school community.

In a broad agenda to establish healthy school communities, research has revealed that the role of school administrators, particularly building principals, is critical. By integrating policies and practices that promote health into the overall school improvement process, school leaders are able to take concrete steps to enrich all elements of the school environment.[85]

While it is the responsibility of school leaders to adopt and enforce policies to ensure health and safety in all school facilities and on all school grounds, it is the responsibility of all school personnel to ensure that children do not become injured in classrooms or during activities for which they are the designated supervisors. Although this does not mean that the classroom teacher must make necessary repairs to school equipment, it is important for all school employees to report potential health hazards to designated district personnel. To ensure that potential hazards are addressed quickly, teachers should make such reports in writing.

A primary source of concern for school environmental advocates is the management of specific physical hazards. Recent research has confirmed the importance of the relationship between the physical environment of a school and the health and academic achievement of learners. Leaky roofs, problems with heating and ventilation, lack of cleanliness, and the use of cleaning chemicals can trigger a range of health problems in students. Asthma and allergies that can increase absenteeism and reduce academic performance are among the most common of such negative consequences of threats in the school environment. Importantly, a growing body of research has confirmed that when an investment is made to improve the environment of a school, not only are student health and achievement influenced, but teacher and staff productivity and retention rates are improved.[86]

School districts also are responsible for the safety of students being transported on school buses and in other school vehicles. Because the potential for injury is always present, all school vehicles must be in safe operating condition. In addition, bus drivers should be provided with continuing education opportunities focused on the operation of the bus, the management of the behaviors of their young passengers, and compliance with universal precautions in the event of an emergency in which someone could be exposed to blood or other body fluids.

In addition, classroom teachers play a role in school district transportation matters by providing instruction for and supervision of students. Children need to learn appropriate ways to get on and off buses and safe and appropriate behavior when they are being transported. Also, students should receive information about safe places to wait for the bus along roadways and how and where to proceed from the bus after disembarking.

In cooperation with community police departments, teachers and other school district personnel participate in a range of safety programs. These programs, intended to meet the needs of students who attend schools within walking distance of their homes, are designed to teach pedestrian safety to students in elementary grades. In addition, many districts and local communities employ adults to monitor student safety at the busiest, or most hazardous, intersections in the district.

Another critical, but often overlooked, aspect of a healthy environment is the social and psychological climate of the school. Schools need to be places where all students and staff feel cared for, included, and personally valued.[87] School personnel must establish an inviting, safe, and nurturing learning environment that extends throughout the school campus. Research has confirmed that students who feel like they are welcomed and engaged citizens in their schools report greater enjoyment of their academic experience than their counterparts attending less healthy schools. In this context, engaged students also demonstrate patterns of higher academic achievement.[88]

Research involving fifth graders has revealed that the environment, or social context, of a school is related to a range of student attitudes and behaviors. In this study, social context was defined as a school environment that students perceived to be caring. Student participation in co-curricular activities, development of shared norms, and involvement in decision making concerning school matters all were shown to be important components of a healthier social context. In confirmation of the importance of health social context, those students who attended schools with a stronger sense of community tended to engage in less drug taking and delinquent behavior.[89]

Educators are reminded that the important elements of a healthy school environment are not limited to the maintenance of physical facilities and the establishment of a welcoming emotional climate. In addition, school professionals must enforce policies that manage the full range of student risk behaviors including bullying, weapon carrying, tobacco, alcohol, and other drug possession, and acting-out behaviors. Such policies must be enforced consistently for all students and personnel within the school community. Enforcement of tobacco-free campus policies during all school activities and elimination of fund-raising activities that threaten the nutritional health of students are examples of such policies under review in many school districts.

Creating and maintaining a safe and healthy school environment is consistent with WSSC.

All school personnel and child health advocates share a responsibility for maintaining the highest standards for a healthy, safe, and nurturing learning environment. Examine Table 1–7 for a review of important questions that when answered in the affirmative confirm a commitment to a healthy school environment.[90]

Nutrition Environment and Services

Schools are in a unique position to promote healthy dietary behaviors and help ensure sufficient nutrient intake among America's youth. A comprehensive program of school-based

TABLE 1-7

Confirming a Commitment to School Health and Safety Policies and Environment: A Checklist of Important Questions

Does your school or district have written comprehensive health and safety policies that they communicate broadly and through varied outlets?

Does your school foster a positive psychosocial school climate?

Has your school implemented all components of the district wellness policy?

Has the school established a climate that prevents harassment and bullying?

Do staff members actively supervise students everywhere on campus?

Does your school have a written crisis response plan that includes preparedness, response, and recovery elements?

Is the crisis response plan practiced regularly and updated as necessary?

Does the school provide and maintain a safe physical environment on all grounds and buildings?

Does your school consistently implement indoor air quality practices including for pest management?

SOURCE: Centers for Disease Control and Prevention, *School Health Index: A Self-Assessment and Planning Guide—Elementary School* (Atlanta, GA: CDC, 2017): Module 1.

nutrition services provides a variety of nutritious and appealing meals that meet the health and nutrition needs of all students. Since a national epidemic of childhood obesity and the associated costs and consequences have been documented, establishing a school nutrition program of consistent quality has become a top priority in many communities.

The dietary behaviors of elementary and middle school students have a significant impact on their physical development. In addition, a growing body of literature has confirmed the strong relationship between nutritional behaviors and student achievement. Researchers have noted that hungry children manifest behaviors such as apathy and shorter attention spans. These students often have lowered energy levels and a compromised ability to concentrate, factors that threaten attention to detail and the general quality of academic work. Hungry children are at increased risk for infections and tend to be absent from school more often than classmates who are well fed. There is little question that students who are absent frequently tend to fall behind in their studies.[91]

In response to the inadequate nutritional intake of many students, the national school lunch and breakfast programs were initiated by the federal government. Begun in 1946 with the enactment of the National School Lunch Act, local school districts were provided with surplus agricultural commodities and federal funds to defray the costs of providing nutritious meals delivered through the mechanism of a school-based lunch program. Today, management of this program is the responsibility of the U.S. Department of Agriculture.

Whereas the costs of operating school-based breakfast and lunch programs are significant, concern over such fiscal matters must be balanced against research that has demonstrated that such meals are a significant source of nutrition for many children. On school days, many children consume as many as half their daily calories at school.[92] Recent research

has confirmed that more than 90 percent of students eat lunch at school, with over 30 million kids participating in the National School Lunch Program and more than 14 million participating in the School Breakfast Program.[93]

To help manage the identified costs and to provide support for the nutritional enrichment of so many children, the *Healthy, Hunger-Free Kids Act* was passed by the federal government in 2010. This legislation authorizes funding and sets policy to guide the core child nutrition programs managed by the U.S. Department of Agriculture. As a consequence, for the first time in over thirty years, real reforms to the school breakfast and lunch programs will improve the critical nutrition and hunger safety net for millions of school-age children and youth.[94]

Beyond the amount and enriching nutritional density of foods made available to children through school-based programs, research has confirmed that student participants have greater class participation and greatly improved achievement than do hungry students.[95] Compared to children who skip it or those who eat breakfast at home, children who eat a school breakfast

Adequate nutrition is critical to the physical and emotional well-being of children and supports their academic success. School breakfast and lunch programs provide a key source of nutrition for many students.

©David Buffington/Getty Images

enjoy such improved health outcomes as eating more fruits, drinking more milk, and eating a wider variety of foods. In addition, offering a free breakfast to all students improves the learning environment for all. Research has demonstrated that in schools in which students are offered this nutritional enrichment, there are the following:

- Declines in reports of discipline and psychological problems.
- Reduced numbers of visits to school nurses that can interrupt critical instruction.
- Decreased incidents of tardiness.
- Increases in student attendance and attentiveness.[96]

In addition to schoolwide policies and practices, wise teachers have learned to collaborate with food service personnel to enrich the nutrition education curriculum. Food service personnel in some school districts provide nutrition education activities that are developmentally appropriate and meaningful for all students. Some schools have organized student/food service advisory councils, to collaborate on special meal planning and nutrition education activities. Special-event luncheons, nutrition newsletters, cafeteria bulletin boards or posters, food-tasting parties, and nutritional labeling of breakfast or lunch line food choices are activities intended to enrich and extend the nutrition education program of studies beyond the classroom.[97]

Beyond its use as a location for breakfast and lunch, the cafeteria in many middle schools is used only to accommodate large-group study halls. Wisely, some districts have developed ways to use this area for more academically enriching activities. Special mini-lectures on a range of topics can be targeted to particular students during their lunch meal. In addition, student organizations, teachers, and administrators can construct table tents to highlight important content matters or upcoming events on the school calendar.[98] In this way, nutrition education is enhanced without sacrificing valuable classroom instruction time, and the use of valuable instruction space is expanded.

In addition to using the cafeteria as a learning laboratory, classroom teachers are encouraged to engage students in a range of cross-curricular instructional activities that can extend healthy eating concepts across the school day. Using fruits and vegetables to teach younger students about colors, engaging middle school students in learning about weights and measures using foods grown in a school garden, and reinforcing math and health concepts through calorie counts and nutritional value charts are just a few examples of such extension activities.

Unfortunately, it has become more and more common for food industry marketers to invest in strategies to increase access of their products and messages to children. Experts in marketing to children realize that targeting adult policymakers in schools is sound short- and long-term practice. In return for needed funds and materials, marketers gain access to captive audiences of children who have money to spend, who can influence the purchasing patterns of their families, and who are the consumers of the future. Marketing strategies that focus on children in schools are very successful, as brand-name and less healthy foods are marketed in school cafeterias and hallways, products and coupons are distributed on holidays and as rewards for achievement, and students and their parents sell products to raise funds for their schools.[99]

Many elementary and middle schools provide access to less-than-healthy foods. For example, SHPPS 2016 findings revealed that approximately two-thirds of school districts have no policies which require schools to prohibit junk foods (foods or beverages that have low nutrient density) from being sold in vending machines, served at class parties, or made available in school stores or snack bars. Fewer than 10 percent of districts have policies that prohibit serving junk food at staff meetings, in concession stands, and during meetings attended by student family members.[100]

In light of growing concerns about childhood obesity and related negative health outcomes, administrators, parents, and child health advocates need to explore alternative funding options that do not compromise the health of enrolled students. To this end, Table 1–8 provides a checklist of important questions to guide school health advocates toward confirming a commitment to quality school nutrition services.[101] (Readers can find much more information about promoting healthy eating in Chapter 6 of this text.)

Counseling, Psychological, and Social Services

Mental, emotional, and behavioral problems among children and youth are real, prevalent, painful, and costly. Often referred to as "disorders," these problems are a source of stress for children, families, schools, and communities. Common disorders among children include anxiety, attention deficit hyperactivity disorder (ADHD), conduct disorders, autism, and severe depression. Importantly, the number of youth and families affected is significant. Research has estimated that as many as one in five school-age youth have a mental health disorder that can be diagnosed and requires treatment. Unfortunately, less than 20 percent of affected children and adolescents receive the treatment they need.[102]

Mental, emotional, and behavioral disorders in children and adolescents are caused by biological factors including genetics, chemical imbalances, and trauma to the central nervous system resulting from a head injury. Environmental factors, including exposure to violence, extreme stress, or the death or loss of a significant person, also can cause such disorders (see Chapter 14 for an expanded discussion). Despite the cause, schools are an ideal place for mental health promotion, prevention, and early intervention policies and practices for students. As such, it is clear why counselors, psychologists, and other social service providers play such an important role in WSCC.

While resources to promote and protect mental health often are limited in the school community, educators must not underestimate the impact of mental health challenges on academic success. Psychologist Dr. Howard Adelman has identified five related barriers to learning:

- Inadequate basic resources—food, clothing, housing, and a sense of security at home, at school, and in the neighborhood.
- Psychosocial problems—difficult relationships at home and at school; emotional upset; language problems; sexual, emotional, or physical abuse; substance abuse; delinquent or gang-related behavior; and psychopathology.
- Stressful situations—inability to meet the demands made at school or at home, inadequate support systems, and hostile conditions at school or in the neighborhood.
- Crises and emergencies—death of a classmate or relative, a shooting at school, or natural disasters such as earthquakes, floods, or tornadoes.
- Life transitions—onset of puberty, entering a new school, and changes in life circumstances (moving, immigration, loss of a parent through divorce or death).[103]

Although there are a number of models and approaches around which school-based mental health services are organized, three kinds of professionals most frequently offer such care: school counselors, psychologists, and social workers. Originally, school counselors were employed to provide vocational guidance for students. Today, their role has been expanded to include helping students solve relationship problems, make decisions to improve learning outcomes, and address developmental challenges. Their mental health colleagues—school psychologists—evaluate the psychological functioning and needs of students and coordinate referral networks and collaborative activities with other community service providers. In particular, school psychologists play a critical role in responding to learners with special needs. In addition, school psychologists provide individual and group counseling for students, and conduct informational sessions for parents, faculty, and staff. Finally, in many school communities, social workers bridge the school, the home, and the community, by offering case management, group counseling, home visits, advocacy, parent education, and coordination of programs for youth.[104]

In addition to intervention services for students and their families, counselors and social workers provide instruction in many elementary and middle schools. These resource professionals organize learning activities focused on nonviolent conflict resolution, problem solving, communication, and decision-making skill development. In addition, counselors, psychologists, and social workers collaborate in curriculum and staff development activities in some districts.

In summary, student assistance programs staffed by a range of providers offer services for students who experience personal or social problems that can influence school performance and health. SHPPS 2016 has confirmed that nearly 90 percent of school districts have adopted policies mandating such services for all students.[105]

TABLE 1-9
Confirming a Commitment to Quality School Counseling, Psychological, and Social Services: A Checklist of Important Questions
Are counseling, psychological, and social services provided by a full-time counselor, social worker, and psychologist?
Does the counseling, psychological, or social services provider promote the emotional, behavioral, and mental health of and provide treatment to students and families?
Does the counseling, psychological, or social services provider collaborate with other school staff members to promote student health and safety?
Does your school implement a systematic approach for referring students, as needed, to appropriate school- or community-based counseling, psychological, and social services?
Does your school aid students during school and life transitions (such as changing schools or changes in family structure)?
Does the counseling, psychological, or social services provider have a system for identifying students who have been involved in any type of violence and, if necessary, refer them to the most appropriate school-based or community-based services?

SOURCE: Centers for Disease Control and Prevention, *School Health Index: A Self-Assessment and Planning Guide—Elementary School* (Atlanta, GA: CDC, 2017): Module 6.

To evaluate the program of mental health services in local schools, readers are encouraged to review Table 1-9, a checklist of important questions that confirm a commitment to quality school counseling, psychological, and social services.[106] Further, readers can find additional information about promoting mental and emotional health among students in elementary and middle grades in Chapter 5.

Physical Education and Physical Activity

In 1996, the Surgeon General of the United States published a landmark report on physical activity and health. This document confirmed the following significant benefits of regular participation in physical activity: a reduced risk of premature death and a decreased likelihood of developing heart disease, diabetes, and colon cancer.[107] In addition, people who exercise on a regular basis are more likely to participate in other healthy behaviors including improved dietary behaviors, more effective stress management practices, and lower cigarette use.[108]

Importantly, the Surgeon General's report documented that the health benefits of physical activity are not limited to adults. Regular activity among children and youth helps build healthy bones, muscles, and joints; helps control weight; supports development of lean muscle mass; addresses risks for high blood pressure; and reduces feelings of depression and anxiety.[109]

In addition to numerous health benefits, emerging literature has established a link between participation in physical activity and enhanced academic outcomes for students. In particular, research has concluded that students engaged in a consistent, organized program of school-based physical activity experience increased concentration and improved scores on tests of math, reading, and writing skills.[110] In light of these findings, the American Association of School Administrators has concluded that "children need to be attentive to maximize the benefits of participation in learning tasks. Attention takes energy, and students who are physically fit, well-nourished, and stress-free have more energy."[111]

Given the amount of time spent there, schools are an ideal location for students to get the recommended sixty minutes of physical activity each day. Given the availability of facilities and trained professionals, school can pursue a combination of strategies to help children be more active. Among such steps, schools can:

- Create policies that increase access to and encourage physical activity for all students.
- Maintain strong physical education programs that engage students in moderate to vigorous activity at least 50 percent of their class time.
- Integrate physical activity into classroom practice so students can be active across the school day and not only in physical education class.
- Employ qualified and credentialed staff to teach physical education and to meet the activity needs of students with disabilities.[112]

Sound programs of physical education provide the backbone for school-based fitness activities. Such programs are developed to include a range of learning activities targeting cardiovascular health, muscular endurance, flexibility, strength, agility, balance, coordination, and good posture. Emphasis is placed on physical fitness and the development of skills that lead to lifelong habits of physical activity. As in other content areas, national physical education standards have been developed to provide guidelines for evidence-based program development.

The amount of time allotted for the physical education class varies from as little as fifteen to twenty minutes at some schools to as much as forty-five minutes to one hour at others. To address such variability, the National Association for Sport and Physical Education (NASPE) recommends that students in elementary schools receive a minimum of 150 minutes of physical education per week. Depending on the needs and maturation of students, this equals an approximate average of thirty minutes of formal physical education instruction per day.[113]

The amount of vigorous aerobic activity in which each student is a participant also is worthy of discussion. When observing an elementary physical education class, it is common to witness large blocks of time when many students are standing or sitting while a few are active or the teacher is instructing. Relays and team games tend to result in limited participation for the majority of students. A recent study of a county in Texas revealed that elementary school students were engaged in vigorous activity for only three minutes and twenty-four seconds in a typical forty-minute physical education class.[114] Clearly, this is not an acceptable level of participation if there is to be any positive impact on the physical fitness or achievement of students.

An important addition to the program of formal physical education is the provision of recess for most elementary school children. Unfortunately, many schools reduce recess time in favor of preparation for proficiency testing or count recess time periods toward compliance with state requirements for participation in physical education. This practice is unacceptable, as it implies

Daily physical activity for children—during physical education class and recess—enhances academic performance and sets the stage for lifelong healthy activity habits.

TABLE 1–10
Confirming a Commitment to Quality Physical Education and Physical Activity: A Checklist of Important Questions
Do all students in each grade receive physical education for at least 150 minutes per week throughout the school year?
Do physical education classes have a student/teacher ratio comparable to that of other classes?
Do all teachers of physical education use an age-appropriate, sequential physical education curriculum that is consistent with national or state standards for physical education?
Does the school prohibit exemptions or waivers for physical education?
Do teachers keep students moderately to vigorously active for at least 50 percent of the time during most or all physical education class sessions?
Are all physical education classes taught by teachers who are certified or licensed to teach physical education?
Does the physical education program consistently use practices as appropriate to include students with special health care needs?
Does your school promote or support walking and bicycling to school?
Does your school or district ensure that spaces and facilities for physical activity meet or exceed recommended safety standards for design, installation, and maintenance?

SOURCE: Centers for Disease Control and Prevention, *School Health Index: A Self-Assessment and Planning Guide—Elementary School* (Atlanta, GA: CDC, 2017): Module 3.

that physical education learning experiences are less important than experiences in other academic subjects. Unfortunately, SHPPS 2016 confirmed that only 64.8 percent of school districts required schools to provide regularly scheduled recess periods for students in the elementary grades.[115]

Table 1–10 reviews important questions that confirm a commitment to quality physical education and other physical activity programs.[116] Further findings are available for reader review in the Online Learning Center, and in Chapter 7.

Employee Wellness

Since the 1970s, corporate America has demonstrated an increased interest in health promotion initiatives for employees. Providing long-term hospitalization for an aging American public has led many businesses to seek ways to reduce costs for hospital, medical, and other types of insurance. Many in the health promotion and medical care professions are committed to the notion that, with appropriate health promotion and disease prevention initiatives, these costs can be reduced. Corporations with work-site health promotion programs formalize opportunities for employees and their families to assume more responsibility for their health and well-being. In turn, the employees tend to be more productive, are absent less frequently, and have improved attitudes and better morale.

Boards of education and administrators are faced with the same issues as their colleagues in corporate management positions. Schools represent one of the largest employers in the United States. On average, approximately 5 percent of the U.S. workforce is employed in schools doing jobs as teachers, administrators, nurses, counselors, social workers, food service workers, maintenance staff, and more.[117] A significant portion of a school district budget is earmarked for health insurance and related benefits for faculty and staff.

School districts are ideal locations for work-site health promotion programs. School buildings are constructed with a wide range of facilities, and school districts employ resource professionals skilled in planning and implementing quality health promotion programs. Screenings, health education, employee assistance programs, health care, immunizations, and policies that support safe and healthy lifestyles are among the formalized activities integrated into the employee contracts in some school districts.

School-based health promotion programs for faculty and staff have been shown to:

- Decrease absenteeism.
- Lower health care and insurance costs.
- Increase employee retention.
- Improve morale.
- Reduce the number of work-related injuries.
- Increase productivity.
- Increase motivation to practice healthy behaviors.
- Provide healthy role models for students.[118]

Healthy teachers, administrators, and support staff are less costly to taxpayers and have fewer absences that require temporary employment of substitute teachers. Better continuity of instruction for students is maintained and costs are contained. In support of such health and cost containment outcomes, SHPPS 2016 contains confirmation that 54 percent of school districts require schools to have employee wellness programs. Further, nearly one-quarter of districts provide preventative screenings such as body mass index, diabetes, and cholesterol.[119] Elementary and middle school teachers interested in exploring the advantages of such programs in their local district should review Table 1–11. This checklist reviews important questions that confirm a commitment to quality health promotion for staff.[120]

Family Engagement and Community Involvement

Today, many associate a range of student problems with shortcomings in the school program, yet there are many entities in every community with whom children and their families engage. Children who attend local schools also are influenced by practices in the neighborhoods, churches, and stores and by medical care providers with whom they have contact. No school district is solely responsible when a community is confronted with children who have developed problems with tobacco, alcohol or other drugs, or violence. Rather, every student who is at risk lives in some kind of family arrangement, resides in a neighborhood, shops in local stores, and might participate in religious celebrations. All student advocates must remember that the complexity of today's health and social problems require that no one agency or group be blamed or held responsible for intervening in the absence of other stakeholders. Student risk behaviors are influenced by a complex set of variables. Thus, effective prevention and intervention are based on collaborative approaches.

Key stakeholders in this collaboration are parents or custodial caregivers. By action and example, these adults shape the lives of their children from birth through adulthood. Whereas it is common for the influence of friends and peers to increase during adolescence, research has confirmed the continued significance of parents in shaping choices and behaviors of their children. Close parent–child relationships characterized by mature parenting skills, shared family activities, and positive role modeling have well-documented effects on the health and development of youth.[121]

As an important step in confronting such challenging issues, the school health literature has confirmed the need for local districts to establish a school health advisory council. Such organizations focus the efforts of school, medical, safety, and advocacy services on health promotion in the school community. Specifically, such coalitions or committees work to increase the quantity and quality of school-based health promotion efforts. Such groups also help reduce duplication of services and enhance

TABLE 1–12

Confirming a Commitment to Quality Family Engagement and Community Involvement: A Checklist of Important Questions

Does your school communicate with all families in a culturally and linguistically appropriate way, using a variety of communication methods, about school-sponsored activities and opportunities to participate in school health programs and other community-based health and safety programs?

Does your school's family education program address effective parenting strategies?

Do families and other community members help with school decision making?

Does your school or district have a formal process to recruit, train, and involve family and other community members as volunteers to enrich school health and safety programs?

Does your school provide opportunities for family members to reinforce learning at home?

Do family and community members have access to indoor and outdoor school facilities outside school hours to participate in or conduct health promotion and education programs?

Does your school work with local community organizations, businesses, or local hospitals to plan community events that promote health and wellness for students, families, and community members?

Does your school partner with community-based healthcare providers to link students and families to accessible community health services and resources?

SOURCE: Centers for Disease Control and Prevention, *School Health Index: A Self-Assessment and Planning Guide—Elementary School* (Atlanta, GA: CDC, 2017): Modules 10 & 11.

the visibility and potential impact of all participant agencies. With pooled resources, advocacy initiatives that are too large for any one agency become realistic health promotion options.[122]

In addition to addressing more global concerns, elementary and middle school classroom teachers would be wise to cultivate relationships with student health advocacy organizations and agencies in their communities. Many of these organizations offer support for classroom instruction by providing resource materials developed to focus on a broad range of health content matters.

Table 1–12 contains a checklist of important questions that confirm a commitment to quality family engagement and community involvement with the schools.[123] In addition, parent engagement is discussed in greater detail in Chapter 2 and throughout this text.

Pulling It All Together

The health status and academic achievement of students who attend elementary and middle schools are threatened by many complex health-related variables. While learning is threatened among students who are absent due to allergies or communicable infections, others have difficulty maintaining their attention to schoolwork because of dietary risks or bullying. The key to confronting such complex issues is to capitalize on the many resources and talents of professionals who are committed to promoting the health of students.

The Whole School, Whole Community, Whole Child (WSCC) model represents best practice in school health promotion. The successful integration of this model into the active life of the school community depends on several key elements. As a foundation, all school and community personnel with expertise in any aspect of student health should be engaged as active participants in this proactive health promotion agenda. The likelihood of successful implementation of the WSCC model in a local school community is related to the extent of cooperation, collaboration, and communication among the stakeholders. Adults with particular expertise representing the eight component programs must organize their efforts in a coordinated manner.

Many schools offer a range of programs designed to react to the health risks of students who are at risk. Additionally, other districts offer diverse activities to prevent participation in any number of health-risk behaviors. Importantly, activities must be offered in a coordinated and intentional manner to increase the probability of their longevity and success.

As an example of such a coordinated approach, nutritional health promotion is very different in a school community with the WSCC model than in one that has not embraced this model. Such a district, with an established school health council, might collaborate in planning proactive and well-organized activities, including the following:

- *Health education:* Provide a developmentally appropriate nutrition education curricular scope and sequence.
- *Health services:* Provide consultation and resources for planning a nutritional health week in which cross-curricular instruction focuses on healthy foods.
- *Healthy environment:* Review, by administrators and the board of education, all fund-raising policies and practices to make sure that none sabotage the district commitment to nutritional health promotion.
- *School food services:* Establish training tables for athletes, students involved in co-curricular activities, and interested others, including building faculty and staff.
- *Counseling:* Provide support groups and appropriate referral activities for students with eating disorders or other risky dietary behaviors.
- *Physical education:* Develop exercise prescriptions that feature healthy weight management practices for all students.
- *Faculty and staff:* Organize a "Healthy Nutrition for Life" support group open to all faculty and staff.
- *Family engagement:* Have students plan a healthy meal with their families.
- *Healthy community:* Organize "a taste of [name of your community]" event. Invite local restaurants and food outlets to the school campus to prepare samples of their healthy entrées for school district residents. Proceeds can support a range of health promotion activities.

Finally, many school health advocates have identified the need for a person or leadership group to coordinate and serve as "champions" for all activities of the school health program. The primary responsibility of this person or group is to translate the model components into specific programming activities to meet local needs. In particular, such program coordinators focus their professional time and energies on heading the school health advisory committee, maintaining the program budget, and organizing advocacy and liaison activities with district, community, and state agencies. The coordinator provides direct health promotion activities and services and organizes evaluation activities to ensure quality control of the many aspects of the WSCC model.[124]

The School Health Index (SHI), referenced in this chapter, is a very valuable tool developed by the CDC, and can help schools improve their health and safety policies and programs. Easy to use and completely confidential, the SHI has two activities that teams of representatives from school communities can complete. The self-assessment process structures a way for stakeholders to identify strengths and weaknesses in all eight components of CSH. After this self-assessment is completed, schools can use the planning tool in the SHI to identify and rank-order recommended actions for improving a collaborative approach to student health.[125]

ASCD, one of the nation's largest and most respected education organizations, has issued a *Position Statement on Health and Learning*. This important statement is based on the assertion that "successful learners are not only knowledgeable and productive but also emotionally and physically healthy, motivated, civically engaged, and prepared for work and economic self-sufficiency, and ready for the world beyond their own borders." Because both emotional and physical health are critical to accomplishing such short- and long-term goals for the educational process, ASCD concluded that health should be "fully embedded into the educational environment for all students." Consistent with the text in this chapter, this national organization concluded that both the health and the learning needs of children are best addressed when:

- Health is recognized as a multifaceted concept best enriched by supporting the intellectual, physical, civic, and mental attributes of learners.
- Health and learning are supported by coordinated and comprehensive teacher, school, family, community, and policy resources.
- Communities, families, schools, teachers, and policymakers assume reciprocal responsibility for enriching health and learning among students.[126]

In 2014, ASCD and the Centers for Disease Control and Prevention (CDC) collaborated in the development of the updated and expanded Whole School, Whole Community, Whole Child (WSCC) model. This contemporary approach combines and builds on the elements of the traditional coordinated school health approach from the CDC and the whole child framework from ASCD in exploiting the talents of many adults in positions of responsibility and authority to focus on promoting student health while maintaining a focus on the primary mission of schools: to maintain the highest standards of academic achievement.[127]

 ## INTERNET AND OTHER RESOURCES

WEBSITES

Action for Healthy Kids
www.actionforhealthykids.org

Alliance for a Healthier Generation
www.healthiergeneration.org

American Cancer Society
www.cancer.org

American School Health Association
www.ashaweb.org

Center for Health and Health Care in Schools
www.healthinschools.org

Centers for Disease Control and Prevention—Division of Adolescent and School Health
www.cdc.gov/healthyyouth/

Centers for Disease Control and Prevention—Health and Academic Achievement web page
www.cdc.gov/healthyyouth/health_and_academics/

National Association of School Nurses
www.nasn.org

Office of the Surgeon General
www.surgeongeneral.gov

School Health—Society for Public Health Education
www.sophe.org/focus-areas/school-health

U.S. Department of Agriculture's Team Nutrition Website
www.fns.usda.gov/tn/team-nutrition

U.S. Department of Education - Office of Safe and Healthy Students
www2.ed.gov/about/offices/list/oese/oshs/index.html

OTHER RESOURCES

ASCD. *Creating a Healthy School Using the Healthy School Report Card,* 2nd ed. (Alexandria, VA: ASCD, 2010).

ASCD. "Aligning Health and Education in Today's Economic Context." *Education Update* 55, no. 7 (2013): 1, 4–5.

Bradley, B. J., and A. C. Greene. "Do Health and Education Agencies in the United States Share Responsibility for Academic Achievement and Health? A Review of 25 Years of Evidence About the Relationship of Adolescents' Academic Achievement and Health Behaviors." *Journal of Adolescent Health* 52 (2013): 523–32.

Bushaw, W. J., and S. J. Lopez. "The 45th Annual PDK/Gallup Poll of the Public's Attitudes Toward the Public Schools—Which Way Do We Go?" *Phi Delta Kappan* 95, no. 1 (2013): 9–25.

Dillon, N. "RX for Health." *American School* 199, no. 6 (2012): 12–16.

Duchouquette, C. "One Size Fits No One." *American School* 200, no. 9 (2013): 32–33.

Institutes of Medicine. *Schools and Health: Our Nation's Investment* (Washington, DC: National Academy Press, 1997).

Lucarelli, J. F. et al. "Facilitators to Promoting Health in Schools: Is School Health Climate the Key?" *Journal of School Health* 84, no. 2 (2014): 133–40.

Navarro, V. "What We Mean by Social Determinants of Health." *International Journal of Health Services* 39, no. 3 (2009): 423–41.

Price, H. B. *Mobilizing the Community to Help Students Succeed* (Alexandria, VA: ASCD, 2008).

Rodriguez, E. et al. "School Nurses' Role in Asthma Management, School Absenteeism, and Cost Savings: A Demonstration Project." *Journal of School Health* 83, no. 12 (2013): 842–50.

Taras, H. et al. "Medications at School: Disposing of Pharmaceutical Waste." *Journal of School Health* 84, no. 2 (2014): 160–67.

The Education Alliance. *Positive Youth Development: Policy Implications and Best Practices* (Charleston, WV: The Education Alliance, 2007).

U.S. Department of Health and Human Services. *National Prevention Strategy: America's Plan for Better Health and Wellness* (Washington, DC: National Prevention, Health Promotion, and Public Health Council, 2011).

U.S. Environmental Protection Agency. *IAQ Tools for Schools Health and Achievement—Managing Asthma in Schools* (www.epa.gov/iaq/schools/asthma.html).

ENDNOTES

1. World Health Organization, "Constitution of the World Health Organization," *Chronicle of the World Health Organization* (1947): 1.
2. D. Bedworth and A. Bedworth, *The Profession and Practice of Health Education* (Dubuque, IA: Wm. C. Brown, 1992).
3. G. F. Carter and S. B. Wilson, *My Health Status* (Minneapolis, MN: Burgess Publishing, 1982), 5.
4. J. Thomas Butler, *Principles of Health Education and Health Promotion* (Belmont, CA: Wadsworth/Thomson Learning, 2001), 6.
5. U.S. Department of Health and Human Services, "What Is Mental Health?" (https://www.mentalhealth.gov/basics/what-is-mental-health; 2017).
6. American Academy of Family Physicians, "Mental Health: Keeping Your Emotional Health" (familydoctor.org/mental-health-keeping-your-emotional-health; 2018).
7. Butler, *Principles of Health Education and Promotion.*
8. B. L. Seaward, "Spiritual Wellbeing: A Health Education Model," *Journal of Health Education* 22, no. 3 (1991): 166–69.
9. Native Hawaiian Safe and Drug-Free Schools Program, *E Ola Pono (Live the Proper Way): A Curriculum Developed in Support of Self-Identity and Cultural Pride as Positive Influences in the Prevention of Violence and Substance Abuse* (Honolulu, HI: Kamehameha Schools Extension Education Division, Health, Wellness, and Family Education Department, 1999).
10. Ibid.
11. U.S. Department of Health, Education, and Welfare, Public Health Service, *Healthy People: The Surgeon General's Report on Health Promotion and Disease Prevention* (Washington, DC: U.S. Government Printing Office, 1979).
12. Centers for Disease Control and Prevention, "Ten Great Public Health Achievements—United States, 1900–1999," *MMWR* 48, no. 12 (1999): 241–43.
13. U.S. Department of Health, Education, and Welfare, Public Health Service, *Healthy People.*
14. Ibid.
15. Ibid.
16. National Center for Health Statistics, *Health, United States, 2016: With Chartbook on Long-term Trends in Health* (U.S. Department of Health and Human Services: Hyattsville, MD, 2017).
17. Centers for Disease Control and Prevention, *Chronic Disease Overview* (www.cdc.gov/chronicdisease/overview/index.htm; 2017).
18. Ibid.
19. Ibid.
20. Ibid.
21. A. H. Mokdad et al., "Actual Causes of Death in the United States, 2000," *Journal of the American Medical Association* 291, no. 10 (March 10, 2004): 1238–45.
22. Centers for Disease Control and Prevention, *Chronic Disease Overview.*
23. L. Kolbe, "An Epidemiological Surveillance System to Monitor the Prevalence of Youth Behaviors That Most Affect Health," *Health Education* 21, no. 3 (1990): 24–30.
24. U.S. Department of Health and Human Services, *Determinants of Health* (www.healthypeople.gov/2020/about/foundation-health-measures/determinants-of-health#health%20services; 2018).
25. U.S. Department of Health and Human Services, *Social Determinants of Health* (https://www.healthypeople.gov/2020/topics-objectives/topic/social-determinants-of-health; 2018).
26. U.S. Department of Health and Human Services, *Leading Health Indicators* (https://www.healthypeople.gov/2020/Leading-Health-Indicators; 2018).
27. Ibid.
28. U.S. Department of Health and Human Services, *Adolescent Health* (www.healthypeople.gov/2020/topics-objectives/topic/Adolescent-Health; 2018).
29. Ibid.
30. U.S. Department of Health and Human Services, *2020 Topics and Objectives—Objectives A-Z* (www.healthypeople.gov/2020/topics-objectives; 2018).
31. U.S. Department of Health and Human Services, *Healthy People 2010. Understanding and Improving Health, and Objectives for Improving Health,* 2nd ed. (Washington, DC: U.S. Government Printing Office, 2000).
32. National Center for Education Statistics, *Fast Facts. Enrollment Trends* (http://nces.ed.gov/fastfacts/display.asp?id=65; 2018).
33. National Center for Education Statistics, *Fast Facts. Educational Institutions* (http://nces.ed.gov/fastfacts/display.asp?id=84; 2018).
34. Centers for Disease Control and Prevention, *Healthy Schools: Whole School, Whole Community, Whole Child* (https://www.cdc.gov/healthyschools/wscc/index.htm; 2018).
35. National Center for Education Statistics, *Private School Universe Survey (PSS)* (https://nces.ed.gov/surveys/pss/tables1516.asp; 2018).
36. U.S. Department of Health and Human Services, *Healthy People 2010: Conference Edition, in Two Volumes,* 7–4.
37. National Commission on Excellence in Education, *A Nation at Risk: The Imperative for Educational Reform* (Washington, DC: U.S. Department of Education, 1983).
38. A. Novello et al., "Healthy Children Ready to Learn: An Essential Collaboration Between Health and Education," *Public Health Reports* 107, no. 1 (1992): 3–15.
39. American Cancer Society, *National Action Plan for Comprehensive School Health Education* (Atlanta, GA: American Cancer Society, 1992), 4–7.
40. Charles E. Basch, "Healthier Students Are Better Learners: A Missing Link in School Reforms to Close the Achievement Gap," *Equity Matters: Research Review,* no. 6 (New York: Campaign for Educational Equity, Teachers College, Columbia University, March 2010), 4.
41. Council of Chief State School Officers, *Policy Statement on School Health* (Washington, DC: CCSSO, July 17, 2004), 1.
42. Ibid., 7–8.
43. ASCD, *The Learning Compact Redefined: A Call to Action, A Report of the Commission on the Whole Child* (Alexandria, VA: ASCD, 2007), 43.
44. Ibid.
45. Ibid., 20.
46. Ibid., 3.
47. Ibid., 11.
48. C. Wolford Symons et al., "Bridging Student Health Risks and Academic Achievement Through Comprehensive School Health Programs," *Journal of School Health* 67, no. 6 (1997): 220–27.
49. Basch, *Healthier Students Are Better Learners,* 6.
50. U.S. Department of Health, Education, and Welfare, Public Health Service, *Healthy People,* 119.
51. Ibid.
52. "Report of the 2000 Joint Committee on Health Education and Promotion Terminology," *American Journal of Health Education* 32, no. 2 (2001): 90–103.
53. U.S. Department of Health, Education, and Welfare, Public Health Service, *Healthy People,* 119.
54. American Association for Health Education, "Report of the 2011 Joint Committee on Health Education and Promotion Terminology," *American Journal of Health Education* 43, no. 2 (March/April 2012): 19.
55. U.S. Department of Health, Education, and Welfare, Public Health Service, *Healthy People,* 119.
56. J. V. Fetro, C. Givins, and K. Carroll, "Coordinated School Health: Getting It All Together," in *Keeping The Whole Child Healthy and Safe,* ed. M. Scherer (Alexandria, VA: ASCD, 2010).
57. ASCD, *Whole School, Whole Community, Whole Child* (www.ascd.org/programs/learning-and-health/wscc-model.aspx; 2018).
58. Centers for Disease Control and Prevention, *Healthy Schools: Whole School, Whole Community, Whole Child* (www.cdc.gov/healthyschools/wscc/approach.htm; 2015).
59. Centers for Disease Control and Prevention, Healthy Schools: Components of the Whole School, Whole Community, Whole Child (WSCC) (www.cdc.gov/healthyschools/wscc/components.htm; 2015).
60. L. J. Kolbe, "Education Reform and the Goals of Modern School Health Programs," *The State Education Standard* 3, no. 4 (2002): 4–11.
61. American Association for Health Education, "Report of the 2011 Joint Committee on Health Education and Promotion Terminology," 16.
62. World Health Organization, *Information Series on School Health: Skills for Health; 2003* (www.who.int/school_youth_health/media/en/sch_skills4health_03.pdf; 2007).
63. Joint Committee on National Health Education Standards, *National Health Education Standards:*

Achieving Excellence, 2nd ed. (Atlanta, GA: American Cancer Society, 2007).

64. Centers for Disease Control and Prevention, *Results from the School Health Policies and Practices Study 2016* (www.cdc.gov/healthyyouth/data/shpps/pdf/shpps-results_2016.pdf; 2017).

65. Ibid.

66. Joint Committee on National Health Education Standards, *National Health Education Standards.*

67. D. B. Connell et al., "Summary of Findings of the School Health Education Evaluation: Health Promotion Effectiveness, Implementation, and Costs," *Journal of School Health* 55, no. 8 (1985): 316–22.

68. Centers for Disease Control and Prevention, *Health Education Curriculum Analysis Tool* (www.cdc.gov/healthyyouth/HECAT/index.htm; 2017).

69. Ibid.

70. Centers for Disease Control and Prevention, *Results from the School Health Policies and Practices Study 2016;* 2017.

71. American Association for Health Education, *Health Instruction Responsibilities and Competencies for Elementary (K–6) Classroom Teachers* (Reston, VA: AAHE, 1992).

72. American Association for Health Education, *2008 NCATE Health Education Teacher Preparation Standards* (http://caepnet.org/accreditation/caep-accreditation/spa-standards-and-report-forms/shape-health-ed; 2015).

73. Centers for Disease Control and Prevention, *Results from the School Health Policies and Practices Study 2016;* 2017.

74. Centers for Disease Control and Prevention, *School Health Index: A Self-Assessment and Planning Guide– Elementary School* (Atlanta, GA: CDC, 2017): Module 2.

75. C. M. Smith and F. A. Mauer, eds., *Community Health Nursing: Theory and Practice,* 2nd ed. (Philadelphia, PA: Saunders, 2000).

76. National Association of School Nurses (NASN), *The Role of the School Nurse* [brochure] (Scarborough, ME: NASN, 1999).

77. National Association of School Nurses, *Position Statement: The Role of the 21st Century School Nurse* (www.nasn.org/nasn/advocacy/professional-practice-documents/position-statements/ps-role; 2016).

78. National Association of School Nurses, *Position Statement: School Nurse Workload: Staffing for Safe Care* (www.nasn.org/nasn/advocacy/professional-practice-documents/position-statements/ps-workload; 2015).

79. *Cedar Rapids Community School District v. F. Garret,* 526 US 66, 1999.

80. Centers for Disease Control and Prevention, Health Services: Results from the School Health Policies and Practices Study 2016, 46.

81. National Association of School Nurses, *Position Statement: Education, Licensure, and Certification of School Nurses* (www.nasn.org/nasn/advocacy/professional-practice-documents/position-statements/ps-education; 2016).

82. National Association of School Nurses, *Position Statement: Medication Administration in Schools* (www.nasn.org/nasn/advocacy/professional-practice-documents/position-statements/ps-medication; 2017).

83. Centers for Disease Control and Prevention, *School Health Index: A Self-Assessment and Planning Guide– Elementary School:* Module 5.

84. K. Wahlstrom, "School Start Time and Sleepy Teens," *Arch Pediatr Adolesc Med.* 2010; 164(7): 676–677.

85. Association for Supervision and Curriculum Development, *Keeping the Whole Child Healthy and Safe* (Alexandria, VA: ASCD, 2010), 271–78.

86. U.S. Environmental Protection Agency, "Why Healthy School Environments are Important: Impact on Children's Health and Academic Performance"

(www.epa.gov/schools/why-healthy-school-environments-are-important; 2018).

87. J. F. Bogden, *Fit, Healthy, and Ready to Learn: A School Health Policy Guide* (Alexandria, VA: National Association of State Boards of Education, 2000).

88. V. Battistich et al., "Schools as Communities, Poverty Levels of Student Populations, and Students' Attitudes, Motives, and Performance: A Multilevel Analysis," *American Education Research Journal* 32 (1995): 627–58.

89. V. Battistich and A. Hom, "The Relationship Between Students' Sense of Their School as a Community and Their Involvement in Problem Behaviors," *American Journal of Public Health* 87, no. 12 (December 1997): 1997–2001.

90. Centers for Disease Control and Prevention, *School Health Index: A Self-Assessment and Planning Guide– Elementary School:* Module 1.

91. K. B. Troccoli, "Eat to Learn, Learn to Eat: The Link Between Nutrition and Learning in Children," *National Health/Education Consortium: Occasional Paper* 7 (April 1993): 1–33.

92. Kaiser Permanente, *The Weight of the Nation: Community Action Kit: Food in Schools* (https://share.kaiserpermanente.org/static/weightofthenation/docs/topics/WOTNCommActTopic_School%20Food_F.pdf).

93. School Nutrition Association, *School Meal Trends & Stats* (https://schoolnutrition.org/AboutSchoolMeals/SchoolMealTrendsStats; 2018).

94. U.S. Department of Agriculture, *School Meals: Healthy Hunger-Free Kids Act* (www.fns.usda.gov/school-meals/healthy-hunger-free-kids-act; 2017).

95. American School Food Service Association, "Impact of Hunger and Malnutrition on Student Achievement," *School Food Service Research Review* 13, no. 1 (1989): 17–21.

96. Food Research and Action Center, *School Breakfast Program* (http://frac.org/federal-foodnutrition-programs/school-breakfast-program; 2014).

97. D. Allensworth and C. Wolford, *Achieving the 1990 Health Objectives for the Nation: Agenda for the Schools* (Bloomington, IN: American School Health Association, 1988).

98. Ibid., 26.

99. J. Levine, "Food Industry Marketing in Elementary Schools: Implications for School Health Professionals," *Journal of School Health* 69, no. 7 (1999): 290–91.

100. Centers for Disease Control and Prevention, *Nutrition Environment and Services: Results from the School Health Policies and Practices Study 2016,* 25–35.

101. Centers for Disease Control and Prevention, *School Health Index: A Self-Assessment and Planning Guide– Elementary School* (Atlanta, GA: CDC, 2017): Module 4.

102. M. Sander, "Strengthening Children's Mental Health Services Through School-based Programs," *NAMI Beginnings* (Winter 2012): 3.

103. H. Adelman, "School Counseling, Psychological, and Social Services," in *Health Is Academic: A Guide to Coordinated School Health Programs,* eds. E. Marx, S. Wooley, and M. Northrop (New York: Teachers College Press, 1998).

104. N. Brener et al., "Mental Health and Social Services: Results from the School Health Policies and Programs Study 2000," *Journal of School Health* 71, no. 7 (2001): 305–12.

105. Centers for Disease Control and Prevention, *Health Services and Counseling, Psychological, and Social Services: Results from the School Health Policies and Practices Study 2016,* 36–52.

106. Centers for Disease Control and Prevention, *School Health Index: A Self-Assessment and Planning Guide– Elementary School* (Atlanta, GA: CDC, 2017): Module 6.

107. U.S. Department of Health and Human Services, *Physical Activity and Health: A Report of the Surgeon General* (Atlanta, GA: Centers for Disease Control and Prevention, 1996).

108. C. Bouchard et al., *Exercise, Fitness, and Health: A Consensus of Current Knowledge* (Champaign, IL: Human Kinetics Books, 1990).

109. U. S. Department of Health and Human Services, *Physical Activity and Health: A Report of the Surgeon General.*

110. L. Kolbe et al., "Appropriate Functions of Health Education in Schools: Improving Health and Cognitive Performance," in *Child Health Behavior: A Behavioral Pediatrics Perspective,* eds. N. Krairweger, J. Arasteli, and J. Cataldo (New York: John Wiley, 1986).

111. American Association of School Administrators, *Critical Issues Report: Promoting Health Education in Schools—Problems and Solutions* (Arlington, VA: American Association of School Administrators, 1985).

112. Centers for Disease Control and Prevention. *The Association between School Based Physical Activity, Including Physical Education, and Academic Performance* (Atlanta, GA: U.S. Department of Health and Human Services, 2010).

113. SHAPE America: Society of Health and Physical Educators, *The essential components of physical education: Guidance document* (Reston, VA, 2015).

114. J. Cawley, C. Meyerhoefer, and D. Newhouse, "Not Your Father's PE," *Education Next* 6, no. 8 (Fall 2006): 2.

115. S. M. Lee, A. J. Niliser, J. E. Fulton, B. Borgogna, and F. Zavacky, "Physical Education and Physical Activity: Results from the School Health Policies and Practices Study 2016," 16–24.

116. Centers for Disease Control and Prevention, *School Health Index: A Self-Assessment and Planning Guide– Elementary School:* Module 3.

117. Directors of Health Promotion and Education, *School Employee Wellness: A Guide for Protecting the Assets of Our Nation's Schools* (Washington, DC: Directors on Health Promotion and Education, 2010).

118. Ibid., 8.

119. Centers for Disease Control and Prevention, "Health Services and Counseling, Psychological, and Social Services: Results from the School Health Policies and Practices Study 2016," 51.

120. Centers for Disease Control and Prevention, *School Health Index: A Self-Assessment and Planning Guide– Elementary School:* Module 9.

121. D. Aufseeser, S. Jekielek, and B. Brown, *The Family Environment and Adolescent Well-being: Exposure to Positive and Negative Family Influences* (Washington, DC: Child Trends and San Francisco, CA: National Adolescent Health Information Center, 2006).

122. D. Allensworth and C. Wolford, *Achieving the 1990 Health Objectives for the Nation: Agenda for the Schools,* 26.

123. Centers for Disease Control and Prevention, *School Health Index: A Self-Assessment and Planning Guide– Elementary School:* Modules 10 & 11.

124. K. Resnicow and D. Allensworth, "Conducting a Comprehensive School Health Program," *Journal of School Health* 66, no. 2 (February 1996): 59–63.

125. Centers for Disease Control and Prevention, *School Health Index: A Self-Assessment and Planning Guide– Elementary School* (U.S. Department of Health and Human Services: Atlanta, GA, 2017).

126. ASCD, "All Adopted Positions," *Health and Learning* (http://www.ascd.org/news-media/ASCD-Policy-Positions/All-Adopted-Positions.aspx#health_and_learning; 2004).

127. ASCD, *Whole School, Whole, Community, Whole Child* (Alexandria, VA: ASCD, 2018).

2

(Shayna, age 12)

Comprehensive School Health Education

Applying the Science of Education to Improving Health Instruction

DESIRED LEARNER OUTCOMES

After reading this chapter, you will be able to . . .

- **Identify key policymakers and ways in which they influence education practice in the United States.**

- **Summarize ways in which findings from the growing body of brain science can be applied to improve teaching and learning.**

- **Describe the application of developmentally appropriate practice to improving health instruction for students in elementary and middle schools.**

- **Summarize characteristics of effective health education curricula.**

- **Describe effective strategies for engaging students in curriculum planning.**

INTRODUCTION

One important way to begin the process of developing effective health education curricula and instructional practices is to review important findings about learning from education literature. Health educators who understand how students learn and the developmental challenges confronting them are better equipped to develop and implement evidence-based and effective learning experiences. In addition, a review of literature about how schools function and current findings about educational effectiveness can inform the thinking of parents, teachers, and administrators involved in making decisions that affect local health education policy, practice, and curricula.

INFLUENTIAL POLICYMAKERS IN THE EDUCATION COMMUNITY

The education enterprise in the United States is grounded in a commitment to decentralization. Rather than being controlled by the federal government, the education of our youth is the responsibility of each state. State-specific mandates and recommendations are interpreted and applied by each local school district. As such, the system for educating American children is designed so that decisions about curricular topics and their boundaries, teacher licensure requirements, and the planning, development, implementation, and evaluation of instruction reflect the unique interests and education standards adopted by each state.

As the voice for education reform has become more powerful, experimental models for educating students have emerged and are being tested. Today's parents can choose from a range of schooling options for their children. This expansion has fulfilled the dreams of school choice advocates who entered the education reform conversation in the past century during the Reagan administration. Vouchers for public school students to attend private schools and proposals for the establishment of charter or community schools were offered. The belief that the competition provided by school choice would pressure poorly performing public schools to improve was the central argument among advocates for education reform at this early time.[1]

Today, positions represented by varied stakeholders and advocacy groups communicate strong, yet competing messages about what is best for schools and students. Shared by many educators and teachers' unions is the belief that schools alone can't eliminate achievement gaps and other education challenges. Supporters committed to the notion that the problems confronting schools result from such complex factors as socioeconomic disparities call for more government spending on the health of poor children, expanded preschool programming, supports for parents, and meaningful after-school activities for students. Others, including many politicians, place the blame for failing schools on teachers' unions that "protect ineffective teachers," rather than focusing on what is best for learners. Still others advocate for greater accountability for schools and their employees. Those supporting this commitment to increased and documented accountability, call for an urgent resistance of any forces that support what they consider to be the status quo.[2] Due to the range of complex challenges confronting the education enterprise, elements of all of these positions are true. Importantly, as vigorous debate continues and alternative models for educating youth are tested, it can be difficult to understand who controls the structure, policies, and practices governing schooling in the United States.

Exercised by an increasing number of parents, the education option of charter, or community, schools is being selected by caregivers for their children. Recent data from the National Center for Education Statistics confirm that nearly 2.8 million students attend more than 6,900 such schools in the United States.[3] Charter or community schools operate with public monies and must conform to state standards for health and safety. Charter schools also must operate in full compliance with federal civil rights laws. These schools, however, are granted considerable autonomy in developing policies, curricula, and programs.[4]

As another option, a growing number of students are being educated in their homes by parents or caregivers. Since 1999, when national prevalence data about home schooling were first collected, the estimated percentage of the school-age population being home schooled has risen to approximately 1.8 million or slightly more than 3 percent of American students.[5] Reasons offered for making this choice include the belief that a better education can be provided at home, the desire to provide religious or moral instruction, an objection to what local schools teach, or the capacity to respond to a child with a disability or special need.[6] In most states, adult family members in charge of educational activities must submit education plans and maintain records with their state department of education. Parents and caregivers who choose to home school their children can find an increasing amount and variety of educational materials, including Internet resources specifically developed to meet their needs.[7]

First tested in the cities of Milwaukee and Cleveland, tuition voucher programs were proposed by politicians and education reform advocates as a way to give economically disadvantaged families access to the widest range of school choice alternatives. Vouchers were challenged by many groups of professional educators who saw such programs as a drain on the limited allocations of public monies for public education. A Supreme Court decision in 2002 confirmed that states have the legal right to distribute public tax dollars to parents for use as tuition vouchers for their children to attend private schools.[8]

Ranging from the option to take online classes to complete graduation requirements to Internet-based high schools, virtual schools offer another education option for parents and their children. Since the first statewide public high school opened over a decade ago in Florida, many students have taken advantage of the flexibility of virtual learning options. Today, over 30 states run virtual schools and Alabama and Michigan require all students to participate in some form of online learning to graduate from high school. While challenges including financial confront this school choice option, if done well, virtual learning can be engaging, highly personalized, and make a significant contribution toward meeting the needs of learners.[9]

Private schools represent a more established and historically significant education alternative in the United States. More broadly available and widely accessed by parents and their children than other school choice options, private schools operate with a minimum of government influence or control. Recent data confirm that approximately 5.8 million students (about 10 percent) attend approximately 34,500 private schools (25 percent) across the United States.[10, 11] Importantly, great variability exists across states concerning government involvement in or oversight about such matters as curriculum, performance evaluation, and professional preparation requirements for teachers and administrators. Many private schools were established by religious organizations to meet the educational needs of the children of early settlers, whereas others were organized around secular unifying missions or goals. To this day, the largest private school enterprise in the United States operates under the auspices of the Catholic Church. In most cases, boards of directors or trustees comprised of prominent members of the community, volunteers, religious leaders, and/or alumni of the school are responsible for setting policies for individual schools or groups of schools. The majority of funding for private schools is generated from the tuition and fees charged to attendees.[12]

Attended by over 50 million or the majority of students, public schools in the United States must operate in full compliance with several layers of federal, state, and local laws.[13] In addition, public schools and their employees must respond to the expectations and concerns of parents and other taxpayers in the local community. As a result, many stakeholders have a voice in public school policy and practice.

Influence at the National Level

Throughout U.S. history, the federal government has exerted only narrow and limited influence over education policy. Contrary to the assertions of many that the governance of public schools is centralized in Washington, DC, Congress specified that the U.S. Department of Education would maintain a very broad role in public education by participating in activities such as the following:

- Enforcing civil rights laws, prohibiting discrimination, and ensuring equity.
- Exercising leadership by sponsoring research and evaluating policy strategies and pilot programs.
- Providing funds for activities to enrich economically disadvantaged students and children with special needs.
- Promoting educational effectiveness through support of state-developed tests of proficiency in core content areas.[14]

No Child Left Behind (NCLB)

With the reauthorization of the Elementary and Secondary Education Act in 2002, the influence of the federal government over public education in the United States was strengthened. This act, termed *No Child Left Behind (NCLB)*, established a multiyear national agenda intended to improve academic achievement among all students. As a result of this legislation, the federal government assumed leadership for specific activities in state

education agencies and local school districts across the nation with a focus on:

- Improving student performance on test scores in selected content areas.
- Eliminating achievement gaps among different racial, ethnic, income, and disability groups of learners.
- Upgrading the qualifications of teachers and paraprofessionals working in schools.

The original purpose of NCLB was a worthy one. This act was intended "to ensure that all children have a fair, equal, and significant opportunity to attain a high-quality education and reach, at a minimum, proficiency on challenging state academic achievement standards and state academic assessments."[15] This federal law affecting public education policy and practice in all schools was built with a focus on four key elements:

- Accountability for results.
- Emphasis on policies and instructional practices demonstrated by research to be effective.
- Expansion of options for parents.
- Extension of local control and flexibility in the management of schools.[16]

Findings about the effectiveness of this federal legislation confirmed that the results were mixed. Education officials in many states and school districts reported that scores on tests of math and reading went up, and achievement gaps narrowed or remained constant. In general, schools began to invest more energy in aligning curricula with standards and many started to use assessment data to inform decision making about school improvement. In addition, nearly 90 percent of teachers in core subjects met the NCLB definition of "highly qualified."

Importantly, NCLB was a federal mandate that was grossly underfunded. Federal funding to support NCLB implementation stagnated and nearly 80 percent of school districts reported that they had to use local tax dollars to cover the costs of mandated activities.[17] In addition, although the law requires that the Elementary and Secondary Education Act be reauthorized every five years, this funding process has been delayed in the U.S. Congress and is long overdue.

In addition to managing the financial burdens of NCLB compliance, school districts have had to change instructional time allocation to accommodate mandated testing.[18] A recent analysis of such costs in midsize school districts revealed the following:

- Students in heavily tested grades can spend as many as 50 hours per week taking tests.
- Students in high-stakes testing grades spend up to 110 hours per year engaged in such test-preparation activities as taking practice tests and learning test-taking strategies (110 hours equals approximately 1 month of school).
- The estimated annual cost of testing in heavily tested grades can exceed 10 percent of the annual per pupil expenditure amount in a typical state.

Although this study did not factor in the costs of test-prep materials and lost service from teachers assigned to administer the mandated tests, if the testing agenda were abandoned, instructional time could be increased by approximately 40 minutes each school day.[19]

Blueprint for Reform of the Elementary and Secondary Education Act

Given the failure of the U.S. Congress to reauthorize NCLB and the commitment to education reform made by the Obama administration, the White House released the *Blueprint for Reform of the Elementary and Secondary Act* in 2010. Grounded in the belief that NCLB created a system of incentives for states to lower standards and measure students' skills on "bubble tests," the *Blueprint* contained strategies to fix identified problems revealed in the law and to move the imperative of education reform forward with "common-sense strategies." Specifically, the *Blueprint*

- Acknowledged that the most effective teachers generally are not rewarded for doing a great job or for accepting additional responsibilities *and* reinforced the value of using multiple assessment strategies (not just student test scores) to evaluate teachers fairly and pay them for hard and successful work.
- Recognized that NCLB narrowed the focus of the curriculum and marginalized history, the arts, and other critical subjects *and* reformed the need to focus on year-to-year text scores so educators could focus on high-quality educational outcomes for all students in subjects such as the arts and foreign languages, as part of state accountability systems. In this way, teachers of subjects other than math and science would not be ignored.
- Eliminated the misuse of test data and teaching to the test *and* measured school performance both on achievement level and on growth in student performance.
- Refocused the punitive orientation of NCLB *and* empowered states to adopt high and rigorous standards for student performance and then to reward schools for both progress and achievement.[20]

Even though 80 percent of federal funding policies for core programs has remained relatively consistent, more than $4 billion has been awarded to states identified to be leading the way in education reform. This national competitive federal fund, titled "Race to the Top," has served as a catalyst for change in states to establish and maintain effective education strategies in four critical areas:

- Adopting internationally benchmarked standards and assessments designed to prepare students for success in college and the workplace and to compete in the global economy.
- Building data systems that measure student growth and success, and inform teachers and principals about how they can improve instruction.

©Realistic Reflections

Children with special needs increasingly are integrated into general education classrooms where instructional adaptations can be made to meet their needs.

- Recruiting, developing, rewarding, and retaining effective teachers and principals, especially where they are needed most.
- Turning around the lowest-achieving schools.

States that demonstrate readiness to meet benchmarks for reform in these critical areas have received federal grants not based on politics, ideology, or the preferences of a particular interest group. Rather, funding and implementation of the *Blueprint for Reform of the Elementary and Secondary Act* maintains a focus on improving education outcomes for children and so the U.S. economy and the nation as a whole.[21]

The Common Core State Standards Initiative

Consistent with the education reform movement of the 1990s, state departments of education across the United States began to develop instructional standards across a range of content areas. By the early 2000s, every state had developed and adopted its own learning standards specifying what students in each grade level should know and be able to do. In addition, each state defined "proficiency" of the level at which students were identified to be sufficiently educated at each grade level and by the time they graduated from high school. In the name of accountability—a key tenant of the federal NCLB legislation—states then developed and administered high-stakes assessments. Over time, an uneven patchwork of academic standards had been developed, and there was no agreement on what students should know and be able to do. Further, there was no consistency across the nation as to how outcomes should be measured among students at each grade level.[22]

Recognizing the value of and need for consistent learning goals across the states, state-level representatives from the Council of Chief State School Officers and governors representing the

National Governors Association coordinated a state-led effort to develop standards designed to provide a clear and consistent framework for educators. In collaboration with teachers, administrators, and other experts, the Common Core Standards published in 2010 provide a set of high-quality academic standards in Mathematics and English language arts and literacy (ELA) that identify what students should know and be able to do by the completion of each grade in school. In addition, these goals were created to ensure that all students would graduate from high school with the skills and knowledge necessary to succeed in college, career, and life, regardless of where they live. According to its mission statement, the Common Core Standards Initiative aims to:

> provide a consistent, clear understanding of what students are expected to learn, so teachers and parents know what they need to do to help them. The standards are designed to be robust and relevant to the real world, reflecting the knowledge and skills that our young people need for success in college and careers. With American students fully prepared for the future, our communities will be best positioned to compete successfully in the global economy.[23]

Consistent with this mission, the Common Core Standards are:

- Fewer, higher, and clearer to best drive effective policy and practice.
- Aligned with college and work expectations, so that all students are prepared for success upon graduating from high school.
- Inclusive of rigorous content and applications of knowledge through higher-order skills, so that all students are prepared for the twenty-first century.
- International benchmarks, so that all students are prepared for succeeding in our global economy and society.
- Research- and evidence-based.[24]

In this context, the Common Core is focused on developing higher-order, critical-thinking, problem-solving, and analytical skills that today's public school students will need to be successful. Although a number of concerns have been voiced about this national initiative, including those focused on threats to the historical tenant of local control and the "one-size-fits-all" orientation, forty-one states, the District of Columbia, four U.S. territories, and the Department of Defense Education Activity (DoDEA) have adopted and are moving forward with the Common Core Standards.[25]

Federal Monitoring and Supervision of School Health Activities

A number of federal agencies have been charged with the responsibility of monitoring and providing support for school-based health education and promotion activities. The Office of Safe and Healthy Students in the U.S. Department of Education provides financial and policy assistance for drug and violence-prevention activities in schools, and the U.S. Department of Agriculture oversees school food service activities, including the National School Breakfast and National School Lunch Programs.

Even though it has no direct policy or governing authority over state and local education agencies, the U.S. Department of Health and Human Services (USDHHS) manages a range of activities that support school health efforts. In particular, the Centers for Disease Control and Prevention, a subdivision of the USDHHS, manages funding programs to support prevention and control of diabetes, heart disease, obesity, and associated risk factors and the promotion of adolescent health through HIV/STD prevention and surveillance. Further, CDC's Division of Adolescent and School Health manages youth at-risk behavior surveillance activities and provides resources and support for the implementation of the Whole School, Whole Community, Whole Child model (described in Chapter 1) across the states. In addition, the Public Health Service of the USDHHS and the Office of the Surgeon General have produced a number of documents and reports focusing national attention and resources on the health issues confronting children and youth. As an example, *The Surgeon General's Vision for a Healthy and Fit Nation* was released in 2010. In addition to shining a spotlight on improving access to safe health and fitness activities in communities, childcare establishments, and work sites, recommendations are included for mobilizing the medical community. This report places a particular emphasis on the need to create healthy schools by making the assertion that to help students develop lifelong habits, "schools should provide appealing healthy food options including fresh fruit and vegetables, whole grains, and water and low fat beverages." In addition, this report recommends that school systems "require nutritional standards and daily physical activity for all students."[26]

Teaching Students with Exceptional Needs: A Brief Introduction

In context of recognized criteria, children with disabilities are defined as those who face persistent challenges when they try to participate in ordinary childhood activities. Specific challenges include those that are physical, behavioral, or emotional making it difficult for affected children to participate in strenuous activities, get along with others, communicate and learn, or participate in neighborhood or school activities with peers.[27] Among school-age children, the most common functional disabilities that limit participation in activities of daily living include speech or language impairments, health impairments, learning disabilities, and autism.[28]

To respond to the needs of children with disabilities, the reauthorization of the Individuals with Disabilities Education Act (IDEA) was passed into law in December 2004. The Individuals with Disabilities Education Improvement Act ensures that services will be provided for children with disabilities across the nation. To accomplish this, IDEA 2004 governs how states and public agencies provide early intervention and special education and related services for more than 6.5 million eligible infants, toddlers, children, and youth with disabilities between their birth and age 21.[29]

With particular focus on children and youth of school age, the law stipulates that a free appropriate public education in the least restrictive environment must be made available for students diagnosed with disabilities who require special education services. IDEA 2004 identifies specific disability categories that qualify students for special education and/or related services, including specific learning disability, serious emotional disturbance, mental retardation, autism, other health impairments, and orthopedic impairments. Students with disabilities also can access educational services under Section 504 of the federal Rehabilitation Act.[30]

Nearly 13 percent of U.S. school-age children have been diagnosed with a specific disability, and an increasing number of them are being integrated into general education classrooms.[31] In most cases, it is the classroom teacher who assumes instructional responsibility for students with disabilities. As such, regardless of their training, teachers must learn to adapt and accommodate all instruction to meet the educational needs of all learners. Typically teachers or other support staff with particular expertise in special education or related services are be identified to assist classroom teachers with necessary classroom assistance or instructional modifications. In this way, classroom teachers are an integral part of the multidisciplinary team engaged in decision making about best practice for each student with a disability. Then, these decisions are reflected in the specific Individualized Education Program (IEP) or 504 plan developed to meet the needs of each child.

Often overlooked is the critical need for educators and parents to collaborate in meeting both the academic and the health needs of students with disabilities. To support both school success and healthy behavioral outcomes for all students, teachers must be skilled at and comfortable with implementing a wide range of instructional strategies, including adapted learning centers, computer-assisted instruction, cooperative and peer-based learning activities, and skill development in self-management and other essential skills. All students benefit from diversified instruction complemented by instructional adaptations or accommodations when necessary. Most accommodations are simple and easily implemented (e.g., more time for completing tasks, adapted assignments, the use of special equipment). Other accommodations can be extensive. Having a large repertoire of strategies that support academic and health outcomes is the key to learning success for all.[32]

Influence at the State Level

The U.S. Constitution asserts that education is the responsibility of each state. At the state level, the governor is responsible for developing the state budget and proposing initiatives of importance. The state legislature, however, has final authority over state policies, state budgets, and the distribution of state funds. Across the United States, states contribute about 45 percent of the funds necessary to cover public education costs.[33] Many governors and legislators have found that it is politically wise to express their commitment to improving education outcomes as a way to generate support and popularity among constituents. Unfortunately, competing political pressures, budgetary realities, and turnover among officials in state government often challenge continuity and implementation of such intentions. As such, public school districts in most states are confronted with significant budgetary challenges.

Although the scope of influence varies from state to state, it is the state board of education (SBE) that is responsible for policy-making and enforcement and for governance of the public

schools. In some states, members of the SBE are elected. In others, they are appointed by the governor. In most states, a chief state school officer chairs the SBE. This professional, usually trained as an educator, holds the title of state superintendent, commissioner, secretary, or director of education. Typically, the SBE is responsible for maintaining a broad long-term vision for education. Further, this body must provide bipartisan leadership over matters such as decision making concerning engagement in the Common Core Standards initiative, graduation requirements, and teacher licensure.

In this way, the SBE sets many policies that influence school health programming in the local school districts of each state. This body has the power to require that all students receive nutrition education or daily physical education. In addition, many SBEs have wrestled with questions concerning the amount and type of sexuality education to be delivered within their state.

Under the guidance of the chief state school officer and the SBE, the state education agency (SEA) or state department of education enforces regulations governing federal and state programs, distributes funds to local school districts, and offers technical assistance and training for employees. In addition, the state department of education, sometimes referred to as department of public instruction, develops curricular guidelines, performance standards in specific content areas, and tests of student performance. This body also is responsible for evaluating school improvement plans. As such, SEA employees collaborate with community agencies and school leaders to support continuous improvement in local school districts.[34]

Influence at the Local Level

In each community, public school districts must comply with all federal and state education laws. Importantly, it is the local school board that is responsible for establishing policies and practices that define the day-to-day operations in the schools. This model of governance grew from a commitment to the belief that local citizens should control the policies and practices of the public schools in their communities. Currently, there are approximately 13,500 local public school boards operating in the United States. Their responsibilities include hiring personnel, approving the district curricula, selecting texts, managing the budget, and contracting for services.[35] Local tax dollars account for approximately 46 percent of local public education costs.[36]

With very few exceptions, local school boards are composed of elected members. The number of school board members varies from state to state, but there are three general eligibility requirements for candidates:

1. *Age.* In most states, those seeking a seat on the board must be at least 18 years of age.
2. *Residence.* Candidates must live within the geographic boundaries of the school district they will represent.
3. *Financial affiliation.* To avoid the potential for conflict of interest, persons running for a seat on the school board must not be employed by the school district.

In this context, a wide range of professional expertise and interest is reflected in the deliberations and decisions made by a local school board.

Every school board member has strong beliefs about what constitutes the best education for local children. Disagreements about how this ideal is translated into practice are common among members of local boards of education. In addition to personal passions about education issues, elected members must represent the values and interests of their constituents. As such, activist residents and special interest groups can exert a powerful influence over school district policies and practices.

To help bridge gaps that emerge between the education ideals of members of the board, concerned citizens, and the education needs of students, school districts employ a superintendent, or chief executive officer who is responsible for implementing policies and practices adopted by the local school board. Typically, the superintendent is supported by a number of professional assistants. Depending on the size and budget of the school district, a number of trained specialists serve as staff in the central office of the district. Collectively, these professionals oversee curriculum, budget, personnel, operations, transportation, and policy implementation.

Unions and other employee associations influence the budget and operations within school districts. Many school communities have organized unions for teachers (the National Education Association [NEA] and American Federation of Teachers [AFT]) and administrators. Local chapters of unions for noncertified or classified staff can be very active. These groups participate in activities such as contract negotiations, employee health and advocacy initiatives, and resolution of conflicts or grievances.

Within each school building, a variety of employees manage daily operations. The principal supervises the instructional program, maintains a safe and nurturing learning environment, evaluates teachers and other staff, and represents the school to parent and community groups. Assistant principals and "school improvement" or "site-based management" teams assist many principals. These teams are composed of teachers, coaches, custodial and school support staff, and parents or other community representatives.

A growing body of literature confirms the importance of engaging parents and concerned others in informing the health education programs and practices in local schools.[37] Teachers in elementary and middle schools who are challenged by curricular decisions and threats to student success and healthy behavior outcomes would be wise to identify committed stakeholders within their school community from whom they can seek counsel and support.

Understanding the organization and sources of influence over public schools is important for educators and other student advocates. Though the structure of the public education system appears to be cumbersome and inconsistencies between local policies and practices are common, it is designed to maximize input from taxpayers and other concerned stakeholders. With this sound philosophical underpinning, children can be educated in ways that reflect the best education practice mediated by parental concerns and community needs, values, and standards.

LESSONS FROM THE EDUCATION LITERATURE

As discussed, the sources of influence over school policy and practice are varied, and the call for education reform has been loud and persistent. All of this is happening at a time when student populations are becoming more diverse, and school communities are being asked to deliver more services to meet the broadest range of learner needs. As a result, education professionals are challenged to improve academic success while meeting social, emotional, occupational, and health needs among increasingly diverse learners.

A range of educational innovations, including school councils, parent involvement task forces, continuous improvement teams, and authentic assessment resource networks, have been proposed as ways to improve the quality of instruction to maximize academic success for all students.

Unfortunately, many proposals to reform education have a political, financial, procedural, or operational motivation. As a consequence, many strategies are not grounded in sound education theory or evaluated to confirm that they are evidence-based. The highest standards, the most rigorous achievement testing protocol, and the most creative curricula can undermine meaningful learning unless they are planned and implemented with specific attention to how students process information and learn.[38]

Connecting Brain Research with Learning

As a foundation for improving teaching and learning, educators have begun to explore ways to translate research from the neurological and cognitive sciences into effective classroom practices. Such brain research has begun to show promise for improving teaching and learning, particularly among students with diverse learning needs.[39]

Brain research has given educators a way to translate neuroimaging data into classroom activities that stimulate parts of the brain demonstrated to be active during information processing, memory, and recall. Research suggests that the most successful strategies are those that teach for meaning and understanding, and that learning is most likely to occur in classrooms in which students feel low levels of threat but reasonable degrees of challenge. In addition, research has confirmed that students who are active, engaged, and motivated devote more brain activity to learning than do their counterparts. Findings from this growing body of literature cluster into the following categories.[40]

Findings About Acquiring and Integrating Knowledge

Brain research has confirmed that learning must occur within the context of what the learner already knows, has experienced, or understands.[41] In addition, new information must be processed so that it can be retrieved for use across different situations or contexts. The more a student repeats a learning activity, the more nerve connections in the brain are stimulated. Further, different parts of the brain store different parts of a memory. For example, singing a song is the result of complex brain activity. One part of the brain stores the tune, while another area stores the song's lyrics. As a result, the brain must reconstruct the parts of that memory before the person can re-create the whole song.[42]

To promote learning, teachers are encouraged to:

- Present new information within the context of prior knowledge or previous experience.
- Structure opportunities for students to repeat learning activities as a way to cement information or skills in their memories.

- Use mnemonics to promote associations in memory tasks.
- Incorporate visually stimulating learning materials and hands-on manipulatives to activate the right hemisphere of the brain and incorporate text-based presentations to activate the left hemisphere.
- Integrate art, music, and movement into learning experiences to promote learning by activating different parts of the brain.[43]

In this context, Teacher's Toolbox 2.1 contains brain-friendly techniques for improving memory.[44]

Findings About Positive Attitudes Toward Learning

While teachers have long suspected that attitudes affect learning, a growing body of brain research has confirmed this link between the cognitive and affective domains of learning. Interestingly, the concept of "emotional intelligence" has been characterized as the best predictor of life success.[45] Though understandings of emotional intelligence have been debated, brain science has confirmed that nerve pathways connect the emotional and cognitive processing centers in the brain. For example, research has confirmed that hormones alter brain chemistry in students under stress. When students are stressed, chemicals are released into the brain that can impair memory and learning.[46] In this context, evidence suggests that teachers should consider the following emotionally supportive classroom practices as a foundation for promoting learning:

- Establish a challenging but supportive classroom environment that reduces stress associated with academic difficulties and peer conflicts. Pair students with a homework buddy, arrange for peer-based tutoring or practice sessions focusing on study skills, and conduct one-on-one meetings with students to reinforce trust.
- Structure learning experiences that enable students to practice social skills and peer acceptance. Hold class meetings and use literature- and history-based learning materials that celebrate diversity. Model appreciation for contributions of students with different learning styles and needs.
- Create and reinforce a climate of civility in the classroom. Model saying "please" and "thank you" for specific student behaviors.
- Use humor, movement, or the expressive arts to promote an engaging learning environment and ease instructional transitions. Such activities arouse emotional centers in the brain, a foundation for peak academic performance.[47]

Findings About Extending and Refining Knowledge

Like many skills, thinking must be practiced for students to be able to extend and refine knowledge. Classroom activities should require students to go beyond the lower-order tasks of recognizing or memorizing. Learning strategies must be constructed in such a way that students are challenged to explore information more deeply and analytically. Students must practice manipulating information by comparing, contrasting, deducing, analyzing errors, and analyzing perspective. Further, brain research supports activities in which students are engaged in classifying concepts and using complex retrieval and integration systems in the brain.[48] To this end, teachers are encouraged to consider the following classroom strategies:

- Design learning activities that require students to build on prior knowledge or experience.
- Structure opportunities for students to compare their work with model responses.
- Create rubrics that require students to develop models or visual representations of error patterns in their work.
- Structure learning experiences in which students identify patterns of events and compare or contrast characteristics or attributes among ideas.[49]

Findings About Meaningful Use of Knowledge

Learners are most successful when they believe that information is necessary to help them accomplish a goal. Evidence suggests that experiential learning activities that require students to make decisions, conduct experiments, and investigate ways to solve real-world problems activate those areas within the brain responsible for higher-order thinking. In this context, productive learning experiences extend beyond hands-on activities. When

---

Teacher's Toolbox 2.1

Brain-Friendly Techniques to Improve Memory

The body of research about the brain has the potential to enrich classroom practice for students with a variety of learning styles and abilities. In particular, the suggested strategies extend memory activities beyond the confines of repetitive drills. Such strategies are evidence-based and can be applied to all content areas.

Connect to prior knowledge, experience, or skill.	• Discuss common experiences. • Identify emotions in memory. • Review senses memories.
Develop personal relevance.	• Identify rationale for activities. • Associate family experience. • Clarify personal value of action. • Create mnemonics.
To go from short- to long-term memory, information must make sense.	• Integrate manipulatives. • Represent ideas with foods. • Map concepts visually. • Write associations in journals.
Elaborate and extend key concepts.	• Simulate concepts with gross-motor activities. • Depict ideas with sounds or verbalizations. • Represent ideas with the arts. • Reinforce concepts with play. • Create computer-based simulations. • Reinforce classroom work by going on field trips. • Interview family about topic.

SOURCE: J. King-Friedrichs, "Brain-Friendly Techniques for Improving Memory," *Educational Leadership* 59, no. 3 (November 2001): 76–79.

physical activities are paired with problem-solving tasks, memory and learning are enhanced.[50]

Examples of such strategies include the following:

- Assignments in which students are actively engaged in investigating, analyzing, and solving problems from the world around them.
- Learning activities that require students to demonstrate learning in multiple ways, including inventions, experiments, displays, and musical or oral presentations.[51]

Findings About the Learning Habits of the Mind

Learning is promoted for students who are able to establish and practice important habits, including goal setting, monitoring their own thinking, setting standards for self-evaluation, and regulating behaviors, including their own work habits. Research has confirmed the value of exploring, understanding, and applying concepts in the context of individual ways of thinking and interpreting.

In this context, researcher Howard Gardner has asserted that intelligence is difficult to reduce to a single number, or IQ score. In this spirit, teachers are encouraged to review the extensive bodies of research focused on learning styles and multiple intelligence theory as a context for translating brain research into teaching strategies.[52] Teacher's Toolbox 2.2 contains a checklist for identifying and responding to the range of intelligences represented in a group of learners.[53]

Pertinent classroom strategies include the following:

- Use thinking logs and reflective journals with students of varying abilities.
- Embed group discussions into cooperative learning structures.
- Model classroom habits that foster reflection about learning. Holding class discussions that reinforce reflection and recording important concepts and facts learned in a lesson are very productive strategies.[54]

Although researchers agree that exploration of brain function is an emerging science, the field of neurology and cognitive science has experienced an explosion in recent years. As the research matures, it will continue to shed light on thinking and learning patterns among the broadest range of learners. In addition, as more inroads are made in translating this body of research into meaningful classroom practice, decision making about reforming education in classrooms and schools will become easier for teachers, curriculum developers, and school administrators. Evidence gathered to this point has confirmed that brain-compatible instruction

1. Provides as much experiential learning as possible.
2. Structures ways for learners to build on prior knowledge.
3. Includes rehearsal strategies for students.
4. Enables students to revisit instruction over time.
5. Emphasizes concepts more than facts.
6. Clarifies when and how information could be used in the "real world."
7. Takes place in a safe and nurturing environment.
8. Includes positive emotional components to enhance learning and retention.[55]

A summary of brain research, implications for classroom practice, and examples for improving health education can be found in Teacher's Toolbox 2.3.[56, 57]

Authentic Instruction and Achievement

Once district curricula are updated and teachers have participated in staff development to increase their capacity to manage approaches to learning based on the growing body of brain science, the next step is to maximize the authenticity of all learning activities. Newmann and Wehlage describe *authentic learning* as that which has meaning and significance. This is contrasted with many conventional approaches to instruction and testing that are trivial or useless.[58] As a quick test, teachers can evaluate the extent to which current classroom practice is likely to result in authentic outcomes by asking themselves a few important questions as they plan and organize learning activities. Teachers are encouraged to reflect on the extent to which, as a result of their participation,

- Students will practice the construction of meaning as a foundation for producing knowledge.
- Students will be engaged in disciplined inquiry as a basis for constructing meaning.
- Students will produce work directed toward discussion, outcomes, and/or performances that have value or meaning beyond the confines of the classroom or school.[59]

Specifically, it is the responsibility of teachers to make sure that their approach to teaching is consistent with the following five criteria, or standards, of authentic instruction:

1. *To what degree are students encouraged to use higher-order thinking skills?* Lower-order thinking occurs when students are asked to memorize then recite facts. At this lower level, learners apply rules though repetitive experiences. By contrast, higher-order thinking requires students to manipulate, synthesize, explain, or draw conclusions about ideas. The goal of all instructional activities should be for students to transform the original meaning of an idea in some way. While higher-order thinking implies a challenge for students, it ensures that they will be engaged in solving problems and making meaning that has applicability or relevance. For example, student learning and violence risk reduction are enhanced when learners engage in translating district violence policies into meaningful classroom practice rather than simply reading or memorizing the local code of conduct.

2. *What is the depth of knowledge included in the lesson?* Depth of knowledge refers to the extent to which student work reflects their understanding of ideas that are substantial or important. Knowledge is characterized as thin or superficial if it does not deal with significant issues or ideas within a topic or content area. Superficiality is inevitable if students grasp only a trivial understanding of important concepts, or if they cover large amounts of fragmented information. Knowledge is characterized as deep when it focuses on developmentally appropriate ideas that are central to a topic or discipline. Students are engaged in work that is deep when they make distinctions, develop arguments, and construct explanations. Though fewer topics might be addressed within a specified time period, this approach is far more sound. By planning for deep instruction, teachers are better able to

LINGUISTIC INTELLIGENCE: SENSITIVITY TO THE SOUNDS, STRUCTURE, MEANINGS, AND FUNCTIONS OF WORDS AND LANGUAGE

Does the student:

- Write better than average for age?
- Have an advanced vocabulary for age?
- Enjoy reading books?
- Enjoy word games?
- Tell tall tales, stories, or jokes?
- Re-create tongue twisters and rhymes?
- Verbalize memories of names, dates, and other facts?

Planning question for teacher:

- How can I incorporate the written or spoken word into daily classroom practice?

Helpful teaching materials:

- Books, tape recorders, stamp sets, books on tape, walkie-talkies, comic books, word games

LOGICAL-MATHEMATICAL INTELLIGENCE: SENSITIVITY TO, AND CAPACITY TO DISCERN LOGICAL OR NUMERICAL PATTERNS; ABILITY TO HANDLE LONG CHAINS OF REASONING

Does the student:

- Enjoy logic puzzles or brainteasers?
- Enjoy math and science classes?
- Organize things into categories or hierarchies?
- Play chess or other strategy games?
- Compute math quickly in head?
- Ask questions about how things work?
- Enjoy experiments?

Planning question for teacher:

- How can I incorporate numbers, calculations, classification, or logic activities into daily classroom practice?

Helpful teaching materials:

- Calculators, computers, math manipulatives, number games, and equipment for experiments

SPATIAL INTELLIGENCE: CAPACITY TO PERCEIVE THE VISUAL-SPATIAL WORLD ACCURATELY AND TO PERFORM TRANSFORMATIONS BASED ON INITIAL PERCEPTIONS

Does the student:

- Report clear visual images?
- Read maps, charts, and diagrams more easily than text?
- Enjoy puzzles or mazes?
- Respond more positively to illustrations than to text?
- Enjoy art activities?
- Draw well?
- Doodle on learning materials?

Planning question for teacher:

- How can I use visual aids, color, art, or metaphor in daily classroom practice?

Helpful teaching materials:

- Graphs, maps, videos, cameras, optical illusions, art materials, and LEGO or block sets

BODY-KINESTHETIC INTELLIGENCE: THE ABILITY TO CONTROL BODY MOVEMENTS AND TO HANDLE OBJECTS WITH SKILL

Does the student:

- Excel in one or more sports?
- Mimic the gestures or mannerisms of others?
- Take things apart and put them back together?
- Move, tap, or fidget when seated for a period of time?
- Integrate fine-motor coordination or skill into a craft?
- Report physical sensations while thinking or working?
- Dramatically express ideas or feeling?

Planning question for teacher:

- How can I involve the whole body or integrate hands-on experiences and dramatic depictions into daily classroom practice?

Helpful teaching materials:

- Building tools, clay, sports equipment, manipulatives, theater props.

MUSICAL INTELLIGENCE: THE ABILITY TO PRODUCE AND APPRECIATE RHYTHM, PITCH, AND TIMBRE; APPRECIATION FOR THE FORMS OF MUSICAL EXPRESSION

Does the student:

- Have a good singing voice?
- Remember melodies of songs?
- Play a musical instrument?
- React to environmental noises or anomalies in music (off-key)?
- Unconsciously hum to self?
- Enjoy and work well while music is played in the classroom?
- Tap rhythmically while working?

Planning question for teacher:

- How can I integrate music, environmental sounds, rhythmic patterns, or melodic frameworks into daily classroom practice?

Helpful teaching materials:

- Musical instruments, tape recorders, CD players, improvised musical instruments

INTERPERSONAL INTELLIGENCE: THE CAPACITY TO RECOGNIZE AND RESPOND APPROPRIATELY TO THE MOODS, TEMPERAMENTS, MOTIVATIONS, AND DESIRES OF OTHERS

Does the student:

- Enjoy socializing with peers?
- Give advice to friends with problems?
- Demonstrate leadership skills?
- Have a strong sense of empathy for others?
- Have several close friends?
- Have others seek out his or her company?
- Appear to be street-smart?

Planning question for teacher:

- How can I engage students in peer sharing, cooperative learning, or large-group activities?

Helpful teaching materials:

- Board games, party supplies, props and costumes for role-playing.

INTRAPERSONAL INTELLIGENCE: AWARENESS OF PERSONAL FEELINGS AND THE ABILITY TO DISCRIMINATE AMONG EMOTIONS; KNOWLEDGE OF PERSONAL STRENGTHS AND WEAKNESSES

Does the student:

- Display a sense of independence and strong will?
- "March to the beat of a different drummer" in learning and living style?
- Play and work well alone?
- Have a strong sense of self-direction?
- Prefer working alone to collaboration?
- Accurately express feelings?
- Have strong and positive self-esteem?

Planning question for teacher:

- How can I evoke feelings and memories or give students more choices in daily classroom practice?

Helpful teaching materials:

- Journals, personal progress charts, materials to reinforce self-checking, equipment for projects.

NATURALISTIC INTELLIGENCE: CAPACITY TO DISTINGUISH MEMBERS OF SPECIES, RECOGNIZE DIFFERENT SPECIES, AND IDENTIFY RELATIONSHIPS AMONG SPECIES

Does the student:

- Bring insects, flowers, or other natural things to share with classmates?
- Recognize patterns in nature?
- Understand the characteristics of different species?
- Demonstrate interest and ability in classification of objects?
- Recognize and name natural things?
- Collect environmental artifacts?
- Care for classroom pets and plants?

Planning question for teacher:

- How can I incorporate living things, natural phenomena, or ecological exploration into daily classroom practice?

Helpful teaching materials:

- Plants, animals, binoculars, tools to explore and document the environment, gardening equipment

SOURCE: T. Armstrong, *Multiple Intelligences in the Classroom*, 3rd ed. (Alexandria, VA: ASCD, 2009). Used with permission.

Summarizing and Applying Brain Research to Health Promotion

Each number below highlights a research finding from the growing body of brain science. Each finding is interpreted for better understanding (A), general implications for improving classroom practice are discussed (B), and an example for improving student health promotion is provided (C).

1. *The brain is a complex parallel processor.*
   A. Thoughts, emotions, and imagination all operate simultaneously, allowing elements of the system to interact and to exchange input from the environment.
   B. Because no single teaching method or learning strategy can address all the variations of brain operation, teachers need to create learning environments that engage as many aspects of the brains of students as possible.
   C. To promote nutritional health, teachers would be wise to include pertinent music, visual depictions, menu planning, and food preparation and tasting into units of instruction.

2. *Learning involves the whole body and its processes.*
   A. Learning is natural for the brain, but it is a process that can be supported or influenced negatively by student health status.
   B. Classroom practice is enriched when teachers help minimize stress, threats, and boredom. Such states affect brain function differently than do peace, challenge, and contentment. In addition, teachers must recognize that health is not just an instructional class or body of information. Despite the fact that they might be the same chronological age, it is unrealistic to expect children of unequal health status to reach the same level of achievement. Healthy kids may differ by as much as five years in acquisition of basic skills.
   C. Regardless of the health unit of instruction, teachers should create health class practices that encourage children to drink enough water to keep their brains properly hydrated.

3. *The search for meaning is innate.*
   A. Making sense of our experiences is linked to survival and is a basic brain function. Our brains register the familiar while searching out and responding to novel stimulation.
   B. While teachers would be wise to establish classroom policies and routines that communicate stability and behavioral boundaries, they must balance the familiar with learning opportunities that satisfy curiosity, discovery, and challenge.
   C. The kinds of alcohol risk reduction activities developed to engage and challenge learners identified as gifted and talented should provide guidance for developing learning opportunities about this topic for all students.

4. *The brain searches for meaning by patterning.*
   A. The brain is designed to identify and generate patterns, to organize and categorize information into meaningful groupings.
   B. For learning activities to be effective, they must be based on or associated with things that make sense to students. Teachers should avoid basing lessons on elements of isolated or disconnected pieces of information.
   C. Tobacco lessons based on repetition of facts are far less successful than thematic units of instruction that require students to use math skills to calculate costs of tobacco use or to explore the history of tobacco as a cash crop in various states in the United States.

5. *Emotions are critical to patterning.*
   A. Emotions, expectations, and thoughts can shape one another and can't be separated in the brain.
   B. Teachers must remember that the degree to which students feel supported by them and their colleagues will affect student learning.
   C. When teachers model consistent communication patterns across the school day that convey respect and value for learners, students are more likely to practice similar communication skills with classmates and others when confronted with health issues.

6. *The brain processes parts and wholes simultaneously.*
   A. Research has demonstrated that there are significant differences between the left and right lobes of the brain. However, both hemispheres work to organize information by reducing it to parts and by working with wholes or series of whole sets of inputs.
   B. Learning is cumulative and developmental.
   C. As a way to address decision-making skill development, many teachers create units of instruction focused on practicing such skills outside the context of genuine experiences. It is far more effective to teach and practice decision-making skills in the context of daily dietary experiences or field trips to the grocery store.

7. *We understand and retain best when facts and skills are embedded in spatial memory.*
   A. Learning experiences are enriched by both internal processes and social interaction.
   B. To maximize learning experiences, teachers should connect them to real-life experiences as often as possible. Examples include field trips, stories, metaphors, drama, and meaningful homework experiences that connect learners with their families, neighborhood, and community.
   C. The impact and value of bullying risk reduction activities are enriched when students are immersed in complex and interactive learning experiences. Rather than only lecturing about the negative consequences of bullying, teachers should construct activities in which students read developmentally appropriate and pertinent stories, participate in dramatic play activities and simulations, and practice personal management and advocacy skills with others.

8. *Complex learning is enhanced by challenge but is inhibited by threat.*
   A. The brain is able to maximize connections when risk taking is encouraged within a safe context. Similarly, the brain processes stimulation less efficiently and effectively when the individual perceives threat.
   B. Creating a safe learning environment for relaxed alertness, thinking, and risk taking is critical for understanding and learning.
   C. While sexual health instruction should be regarded with as much academic rigor as other subject matter, the threat of failure or of a low grade might inhibit critical thinking and learning about developmentally appropriate sexual health issues.

SOURCE: R. N. Caine and G. Caine, *Unleashing the Power of Perceptual Change: The Potential of Brain-Based Teaching* (Alexandria, VA: ASCD, 1997); B. Samek and N. Samek, "It's a Brain Thing: Keeping Students Focused and Learning," a presentation at the 78th Annual Meeting of the American School Health Association, October 16, 2004.

help students make connections between topics.[60] Chapter 3 provides a discussion focused on applying this standard to promoting student health.

3. *To what extent do instructional activities and class content have meaning beyond the classroom?* Unfortunately, many common learning activities make no authentic contribution to learning. Some certify only that students have been compliant with the rules and norms of their school. Other such instructional activities provide evidence only that students have navigated systems in the school established to support efficiency rather than learning. Lessons gain authenticity when instruction is connected to the larger community in which students live. As a framework for understanding or applying knowledge, students must address real-world problems or incorporate experiences or events from outside the school into classroom learning experiences.[61] For example, student learning and nutritional health can be enriched when learning opportunities extend beyond content mastery about vitamins and minerals. Functional knowledge and decision-making skill development are supported by visiting local food producers, conducting product analyses at local grocery stores, or carrying out vitamin and mineral scavenger hunts in home kitchens.

4. *How much class time is involved in substantive conversation about the subject?* It is all too common for teachers to engage students in unsophisticated classroom conversation. Typically, classroom instruction is one-directional with a planned body of information delivered from teacher to students. Then it is common for part of the lesson to be followed by a recitation period in which students respond to predetermined questions in pursuit of predetermined answers. This process is the oral equivalent of true-false or short-answer written tests of content acquisition. By contrast, high-level, substantive conversation is framed by three characteristics:

- Conversation is focused on higher-order ideas about the topic, including making distinctions, applying ideas, and raising questions rather than simply reporting facts, definitions, or procedures.
- Ideas are shared in an unscripted forum—students are encouraged to explain their thinking, ask questions, and respond to the comments of classmates.
- Conversation builds improved collective understanding of lesson themes or topics.

For example, instruction about injury risk reduction is enriched when teachers make time to cultivate and extend discussions about ways to manage potentially dangerous play spaces at school, at home, and in local neighborhoods.

5. *Is there a high level of social support for the achievements of peers?* Low levels of social support for achievement are evident in classrooms in which the behaviors or comments of teachers and classmates discourage effort, experimentation, creativity, and engagement among all students. Conversely, high-level social support is evident when teachers and classmates reinforce norms of high expectations for all students with consistency. In such classrooms, everyone communicates mutual respect and celebrates risk taking and hard work when confronting challenging tasks.[62] To support cognitive enrichment and skill development about

Social support for achievement promotes positive learning experiences.

physical activity, opportunities should be provided for students to experience activities that feature group problem solving, celebrate the contribution of diverse skills, and eliminate rewards for selected "stars" who experience individual success.

Professionals are reminded that authentic instructional approaches are useful for all content areas and teaching methods. This approach is demonstrated when any instructional activity—new or old, in or out of school—engages students in using complex thinking skills to confront issues and solve problems that have meaning or value beyond simple written tests.

Developmentally Appropriate Practice

Regardless of the age of students or the focus of a lesson (increasing functional knowledge, helping students examine their health beliefs and attitudes, or practicing essential skills to live healthier lives), developmentally appropriate practice criteria should serve as the foundation for translating content recommendations contained in the district curriculum document into sound classroom practice. Researchers have found that "the use of developmentally appropriate practices is one of the best current strategies to ensure that individual children will have opportunities for engaging in meaningful and interesting learning on a daily basis."[63]

Developmentally appropriate practice requires teachers to meet students where they are, then to organize learning environments and experiences so learners can reach goals that are challenging yet achievable. To accomplish this, instruction is delivered in context of the age and developmental characteristics of learners and responds to the social and cultural contexts in which they live and go to school. Importantly, developmentally appropriate practice does not mean that instructional rigor is reduced. Rather, learning experiences are organized and delivered in a way that is contextual to student capacity while being challenging enough to promote engagement, growth, and progress.[64]

The National Association for the Education of Young Children reminds all teachers that planning developmentally appropriate learning activities for any content area has two important dimensions. These involve instructional practices that respond to:

- The age-appropriate attributes of learners.
- Individually appropriate characteristics of students.

Age-Appropriate Activities

Teachers in elementary and middle grades are advised to focus their lesson-planning energies on organizing age-appropriate learning activities for students. Age-appropriate practices are based on research in human development that confirms the universal and predictable sequences of growth and change that occur in the physical, emotional, social, and intellectual, or cognitive, dimensions of all children.[65] Appendix C of this text contains a summary of common growth and development characteristics and identifies the corresponding needs of students in kindergarten through grade 9 that can serve as a foundation for developing curricula and delivering instructional activities that are age-appropriate practice.[66]

Wise teachers will use this general information about typical or predictable development of students as a foundation for cultivating a productive learning environment and for planning instructional activities that correspond to the developmental attributes, needs, and abilities of students of a given age.[67] With the foundation of a developmental framework, teachers who have had no or only limited personal contact with a particular group of students, such as at the start of the school year, can maximize their planning time. Further, age-appropriate cues are helpful for teachers as they introduce new, potentially emotionally charged, or controversial health education topics.

Individually Appropriate Activities

As teachers have more contact with particular groups of students, they learn that students have different patterns and/or timing in their personal growth and development that can influence their ability to integrate education concepts into daily behavior.[68] With the advantage of such familiarity with their students, teachers are able to build lessons that respond to specific individual and group needs and characteristics. In this way, enrichment of the learning environment and instructional practice evolves as specific student characteristics become evident.

It is important to remember that there can be discrepancies between chronological age and ability. Whereas all students need structured opportunities to practice health-promoting skills, students with cognitive disabilities might need instructional adaptations or accommodations to learn age-relevant skills. By paying attention to individual learner attributes, teachers are better equipped to develop lessons that are both age and ability centered.

Conclusion

In relation to planning from either an age- or an individually appropriate practice perspective, teachers should begin their decision making and planning with a review of the following student characteristics:

- *Physical* abilities and limitations.
- *Mental*, or *cognitive*, attributes, including variables such as time on task, attention span, and interests.
- *Social* interaction patterns with family, friends, teachers, and influential others.
- *Emotional* characteristics and reaction patterns.
- *Language* skills and attributes as a foundation for understanding and communication.[69]

Such information about students can serve as a foundation for best practice when teachers integrate the following considerations into their curriculum development and lesson planning:

- *What is known about child development and learning, including:*
  1. Age-related human characteristics to support decisions about meaningful instruction.
  2. General age-related clues about activities, materials, interactions, or experiences that will be safe, healthy, interesting, achievable, and challenging to learners.
- *What is known about the strengths, interests, and needs of individual learners in a group, as a foundation for*
  1. Identifying individual variations in students.
  2. Adapting classroom policy, practice, and learning activities to respond to needs, interests, and abilities of diverse students.
- *What is known about the social, cultural, and family contexts in which children live, as a way to*
  1. Make sure that learning experiences are meaningful and relevant.
  2. Ensure that respect for the uniqueness among learners and their families is communicated.

The content and skills to be learned and how best to construct or organize the learning environment should be based on

- The body of literature confirming attributes of best practice about the topic (evidence-based practice guidelines).
- Family and community standards.
- Policy mandates of the state and the local board of education.
- Developmental characteristics and abilities of students.
- The relationship between previous learning experiences and the new content and/or skills to be mastered.[70]

To balance less sound approaches based on distractions including teacher comfort levels or preferences, antiquated textbook content, or community traditions that compromise learner health, the National Association for the Education of Young Children reminds health educators that developmental needs and characteristics of learners must serve as the guide for best practice. For this reason, tobacco, alcohol, and other drug–prevention instruction for primary-grade children should focus on developmentally appropriate concepts such as:

- Recognizing why household products are harmful if ingested or inhaled.
- Complying with rules about safe and adult-supervised use of medication.
- Identifying community health helpers who provide directions and prescriptions for medication.
- Recognizing that matches and lighters should be used only by grown-ups.
- Practicing fire prevention and safe escape strategies.

In this way, the needs and abilities of the learners, rather than other pressures, become the basis for planning and implementing lessons. Learner attributes, needs, and concerns must take center stage in lesson planning and curriculum development. To this end, the Riley Children's Hospital in Indianapolis has summarized important developmental missions, or tasks, that children will confront during the elementary and middle grades. Consider This 2.1 contains these reminders that can provide a foundation for creating developmentally appropriate curricula and lesson plans.[71]

When organizing learning strategies that are both age and individually appropriate, health educators of students in elementary and middle grades should remember the following:

- The most effective activities tend to be those that help students connect the health-promoting functional knowledge and essential skills addressed in class with other aspects of their lives in and out of school.
- The most effective lesson planning is based on a combination of developmental and/or observed characteristics of students, the body of literature in the content area, and teachers' best professional judgments.
- Learning, particularly about health-promoting behaviors, is rarely successful if teachers approach it as a spectator sport for students. Students of all ages learn best in an active learning environment that encourages exploration and interaction with materials, other children, teachers, and other adults.
- Learning activities and materials should be concrete, real, and relevant to the daily lives of the students, rather than focused on some possible negative long-term outcome.
- Flexibility, resourcefulness, and humor are important characteristics for teachers to cultivate. Children's interests and abilities often violate developmental expectations (think about young children and their fascination with the language and lore of dinosaurs), and even well-planned lessons sometimes flop. Teachers must be prepared to adapt, adjust, and think on their feet.
- Planning to celebrate human diversity is critical. Given the range of health beliefs and practices represented in every classroom, activities should be carefully structured to omit

sexist and culturally biased language, examples, and stereotypes (firefighters vs. firemen, mail carriers vs. mailmen, police officers vs. policemen, flight attendants vs. stewardesses, exclusive male references to physicians, exclusive female references to nurses).[72, 73]

Research-Based Strategies for Improving Achievement

Until recently, many people were convinced that achievement and learning were influenced exclusively by nonschool factors, including the home environment, socioeconomic status, and/or natural aptitude or ability of learners. Before the 1970s, teaching was regarded largely as an expression of individual passion or the manifestation of an artistic gift, rather than resting firmly on a foundation of scientific research. In this regard, the 1966 landmark Coleman Report asserted that the actions taken by schools contributed little to student achievement.[74]

By the late 1970s, however, researchers began to narrow their work to focus on analyzing the influence of teachers and their instructional practices on student success. Findings confirmed that classroom teachers have the potential to make a significant impact on student achievement. Research has documented that whereas effective teachers are successful with students of all ability levels, the students of ineffective teachers generally make less than adequate academic progress.[75]

To enrich understanding, researchers conducted a comprehensive study that identified those instructional strategies most likely to enhance student achievement among all students, in all grade levels, and across all subjects. Findings revealed nine categories of instructional strategies that have a strong and positive influence on student achievement.[76] Teachers planning lessons for students in elementary and middle grades are encouraged to

IDENTIFYING SIMILARITIES AND DIFFERENCES

Presenting students with explicit direction for identifying similarities and differences between and among objects or ideas enhances understanding and the ability to use knowledge. The following classroom strategies are suggested to support learning:

1. Comparison tasks
2. Classification tasks
3. Metaphors
4. Analogies

SUMMARIZING AND NOTE TAKING

The creation of a summary requires students to delete, substitute, and retain selected information. This requires students to analyze the organization, structure, and sequence of the information beyond the superficial level. The following classroom strategies are suggested to support learning:

1. Rule-based strategies for summarizing.
2. Summary frames (organizing summary by responding to a series of teacher-developed questions).
3. Teacher-prepared notes or outlines.
4. Webbing notes (visual "web" depictions of key concepts).
5. Narrative/visual note combinations.

REINFORCING EFFORT AND PROVIDING RECOGNITION

Although these strategies do not engage the cognitive skills of learners, they help students examine attitudes and beliefs they hold about themselves and others. In particular, reinforcement and recognition highlight the importance of investing effort in tasks and affirm accomplishments with meaningful rewards. The following classroom strategies are suggested to support learning:

1. Using literature, art, or other references to reinforce the value of investing effort when confronting tasks.
2. Charts or rubrics depicting effort and achievement.
3. Personalizing recognitions (e.g., "personal bests").
4. "Pause, prompt, then praise."
5. Verbal and concrete symbols of recognition (nothing that compromises student health—candy, pizza parties, etc.).

HOMEWORK AND PRACTICE

These familiar strategies enable students to deepen their understanding and to master requisite skills. The purpose of homework should be made clear to students and the volume of work should be variable as students get older. In addition, sufficient class time should be allocated for focused practice sessions. The following classroom strategies are suggested to support learning:

1. Establish, communicate, and reinforce homework policies.
2. Design assignments with clearly identified purposes and outcomes.
3. Vary feedback.
4. Chart accuracy, efficiency, and speed in using skills.
5. Segment complex skills.
6. Clarify the importance of skills or processes to be mastered.

NONLINGUISTIC REPRESENTATIONS (IMAGES OF IDEAS)

There are many ways for students to create images of ideas to reinforce their understanding. In all cases, these representations should clarify, refine, or elaborate on student knowledge. The following classroom strategies are suggested to support learning:

1. Graphic organizers
2. Physical models
3. Mental pictures
4. Movement representations or depictions

COOPERATIVE LEARNING

Please refer to Chapter 4 for an extensive discussion, recommendations, and examples of cooperative learning applications.

SETTING OBJECTIVES AND PROVIDING FEEDBACK

The skills associated with setting clear goals enable students to establish direction for their learning and help them realize both short- and long-term desires. Instructional goals help students narrow and refine the focus of their work and personalize tasks assigned by teachers. To be most meaningful, teacher feedback should be corrective, constructive, complimentary, and timely and should reinforce a specific task or goal specified by the teacher or the student. The following classroom strategies are suggested to support learning:

1. Contracts
2. Criterion-referenced feedback
3. Student-led feedback (peer-based or self-directed)
4. Progress monitoring

GENERATING AND TESTING HYPOTHESES

These processes require students to engage in higher-order thought. To accomplish such learning tasks, students must make predictions or draw conclusions about an event or an idea. Students should be encouraged to practice making clear explanations about their hunches and the outcomes they expect. The following classroom strategies are suggested to support learning:

1. Problem-solving tasks
2. Historical investigations
3. Inventions
4. Decision-making exercises
5. Templates and rubrics for reporting work

CUES, QUESTIONS, AND ADVANCE ORGANIZERS

This category of activities is intended to help students retrieve and activate what they already know about a topic. The activation of prior knowledge is critical to all types of learning, as it enables students to focus on important concepts and to reflect on issues from a higher-order perspective. The following classroom strategies are suggested to support learning:

1. Questions that elicit inferences
2. Questions that require analysis
3. Narratives as advance organizers
4. Skimming information prior to reading for depth
5. Graphic advance organizers

SOURCE: R. Marzano, D. Pickering, and J. Pollock, *Classroom Instruction That Works* (Alexandria, VA: ASCD, 2001). C. Dean et al., *Classroom Instruction That Works,* 2nd ed. (Alexandria, VA: ASCD, 2012).

examine related descriptions and recommendations contained in Teacher's Toolbox 2.4.[77, 78]

Drawn from the literature about learning theory and from the disciplines of behavioral psychology and neuroscience, the following summary should serve as a reminder to teachers, administrators, and parents that students learn best when

1. Information or skills seem relevant to them.
2. Students are actively involved in the learning process.
3. Learning experiences are organized.
4. Learning experiences enable students to derive their own conclusions.
5. Students become emotionally involved with or committed to the topic.
6. Students can interact with others.
7. Information can be put to immediate use or skills can be practiced rather than simply discussed.
8. Students recognize the reason for or value of the information or tasks to be mastered.
9. Positive teacher–learner relationships are cultivated.
10. A variety of teaching methods and learning strategies are used.[79]

THE STATE OF THE ART IN HEALTH EDUCATION

Health education is integral to the primary mission of schools. It provides students with functional knowledge and essential skills to be successful learners and to adopt, practice, and maintain healthy-enhancing behaviors.[80] By increasing the capacity of schools to provide state-of-the-art and developmentally appropriate health education, the critical need to improve the health of our nation can be addressed more efficiently and effectively.[81] In support of this assertion, a groundbreaking joint position statement was released by the American Cancer Society, the American Diabetes Association, and the American Heart Association. Readers are encouraged to review excerpts from this statement, developed collaboratively and endorsed by these preeminent national organizations, in Consider This 2.2.[82]

Grounded in the body of sound education research, the health education curriculum in local school districts must be organized into a scope and sequence that supports the development of and increasingly sophisticated body of functional knowledge, analysis of influential beliefs and attitudes, and practice of essential health-promoting skills. A Comprehensive Health Education Program is designed to promote healthy living and discourage health-risk behaviors among all students (Chapter 1). To reach these instructional goals, sound health education curricula include structured learning opportunities in which students are engaged as active learners. The foundation for effective practice is provided by the National Health Education Standards (Chapters 1 and 3) and reinforced for local school districts by state instructional standards.

It is important to remember that, regardless of local district practices, all health education classrooms include heterogeneous groups of students. In addition to intellectual ability, students vary with regard to interest, background, and health experiences. As such, the school district health education course of study must be developed to meet the highest standards, be regularly and rigorously evaluated, be consistent with community standards, and respond to the needs of the widest range of learners.

Supporting Sound Health Education Teaching Practice

The majority of people begin to experiment with all kinds of health-risk behaviors during their youth. Initial exposure to such risks occurs before most people participate in any formal and evidence-based health instruction. To address this obvious case of developmentally *inappropriate* practice, health education advocates have invested considerable energy in trying to make planned

---

Consider This 2.2

Health Education in Schools—The Importance of Establishing Healthy Behaviors in Our Nation's Youth

The American Cancer Society, the American Diabetes Association, and the American Heart Association believe that quality health education programs delivered in the nation's schools can improve the well-being and health of our children and youth. In the United States, chronic diseases are the leading causes of morbidity and mortality; however, engaging in healthy behaviors, such as participating in physical activity, eating healthy, and avoiding tobacco use, has been linked to prevention of chronic diseases.

The health and well-being of our nation's young people is not a matter of luck. It is not a chance or random event. It must be a planned outcome. The case for well-designed, well-resourced, and sustained health education in the nation's schools is compelling.

The American Cancer Society, the American Diabetes Association, and the American Heart Association encourage quality school health education within all schools in the United States through the use of strategies such as

- Utilizing school health education programs that adhere to the recommendations from the National Health Education Standards.
- Employing highly qualified and effective health educators.
- Ensuring recommended health education instruction time at the elementary and secondary levels.
- Having a national plan and budget to support school health education.

In conclusion, the potential for school health education to improve health and save lives is significant. If we as a nation want to keep children and adolescents healthy, it is important to find better ways to provide quality school health education.

SOURCE: American Cancer Society, "Health Education in Schools—The Importance of Establishing Healthy Behaviors in Our Nation's Youth" (*Health Educator*, Fall 2008, Vol. 40 Issue 2).

and intentional health education a more prominent and consistent part of the course of study in elementary schools.[83]

Evidence has emerged that supports a comprehensive approach to health education. Importantly, as years of sound health instruction increase, so do student knowledge, reflections of healthy attitudes, and practice of health-enhancing behaviors. Yet barriers continue to make it difficult to implement effective health education. Time limitations, policy constraints, teacher priorities, the pressure to focus on subjects included in high-stakes tests, and a general lack of reinforcement by state and local education policymakers are a few of the challenges faced. Though research has confirmed that teachers have an interest in addressing health issues with their students, many report feeling inadequately prepared to provide health instruction to their students. As a result of an emphasis on other matters in university teacher education programs, teachers have expressed that they were ill-equipped to plan developmentally appropriate health instruction for young learners. As a consequence of the combination of such factors, health education is relegated to a very low status in most elementary schools.[84]

Regardless of the professional preparation that they received, all in-service health teachers must participate in an ongoing program of staff development. Many school districts regard staff development as a responsibility to be managed within the district. Others collaborate with state or regional colleagues to plan meaningful and timely enrichment activities. In addition, it is common for teachers to attend conferences of state or national organizations to gain professional enrichment.

Regardless of where it is delivered, staff development programming should focus on specific issues that update and refine teacher expertise. It is important for all teachers to increase their comfort with interactive teaching methods across a range of health topics. Further, staff development activities must update teacher knowledge and help them cultivate the requisite skills to find credible and developmentally appropriate instructional resources. In conclusion, teachers are encouraged to enrich their capacity for:

- Using standards-based, theory-driven, and research-based approaches to health instruction.
- Identifying and collaborating with appropriate community and agency health-promotion resources.
- Cultivating meaningful parent engagement in health education.
- Evaluating and integrating sound web-based resources and other current materials into classroom practice.
- Practicing advocacy skills for student health promotion.[85]

Translating Health Education Theory into Practice

Although most elementary and middle school teachers believe that health education is important, it is difficult to dedicate sufficient instructional time to address all health education essential content and skills within the school day. As a result, teachers must use limited instructional time wisely. Because not all health education strategies are equally successful, teachers in the elementary and middle grades should remember the following when planning lessons targeting student health behaviors:

- What students know and think influences the health behaviors in which they participate (specific health behaviors are influenced by the functional knowledge base that students have about the health issues confronting them).
- Though knowledge is necessary, it is not enough to produce most changes in student health behavior.
- Health behavior does not occur in a vacuum, but is influenced by perceptions, motivations, skills, and the social environment in which it takes place.[86]

Research has confirmed that the most promising health education practice extends beyond the goal of content mastery to address the health determinants, social factors, attitudes, values, norms, and skills that influence specific health behaviors. Effective health educators acknowledge that health behaviors are complex and base their lessons on theoretical approaches.[87]

Theories present a systematic way to understand health behaviors by identifying and addressing the important factors that influence them. Most theories used to explain health behavior have come from other disciplines including psychology, sociology, anthropology, consumer behavior, and marketing. Theories equip teachers with tools to move beyond intuition or content, resources, and methodologies used with previous groups of students. Theories can help teachers understand why their students pursue common risky health behaviors and how to organize lessons that are most likely to be successful. Finally, theories can help teachers identify key times and factors to enrich student assessment or evaluation of lesson effectiveness.[88]

Health educators use many theories to guide their professional practice. When focused on the health behaviors of individuals, professionals often base programming and research on such theories as the health belief or stages of change models or the theory of planned behavior (TPB). Social cognitive theory can be useful when trying to understand the influence of family or friends on the health behaviors of a student, and the diffusion of innovations, communication theory, or community organization models can help guide health-promotion programming among larger and more diverse groups of people.[89]

While it is not important for classroom teachers in elementary and middle schools to understand the underpinnings of all health behavior theories, one way to enrich instruction with a theoretical foundation is to apply the theory of planned behavior. This theory is based on the belief that the most important factor that influences health behavior is behavioral intention. The theory of planned behavior asserts that behavioral intention is influenced by three major variables:

- *Attitudes toward the behavior.* This variable reflects the degree to which the student has made a favorable or an unfavorable evaluation of the behavior. This includes the individual's belief about what will happen if he or she participates in the behavior and the extent to which he or she cares about the outcome of engaging in the behavior.
- *Subjective norms.* The perceived social pressure to participate in or to refuse to participate in a behavior constitutes the

HealthSmart Theoretical Framework
(Producing Healthy Results)

What Students Believe (Attitudes Toward Healthy Behaviors)	**Influence of Others on Health Behaviors** (Healthy Norms)	**Students' Confidence to Act** (Perception of Control)
• Activities encourage students to value healthy behaviors. • Activities help students connect healthy behaviors with desired health outcomes.	• Activities help students understand that family and friends want them to act in healthy ways. • Activities increase students' motivation to comply with the wishes of family and friends.	• Activities offer opportunities for students to anticipate situations in which they will need to make healthy choices. • Activities develop knowledge, skills, and support to build students' confidence in their ability to practice healthy actions.

Students Express Intentions to Act in Healthy Ways

Students Think, Choose, and Act in Healthy Ways

FIGURE 2–1 | Theory of Planned Behavior in Practice

SOURCE: W. Kane, S. Telljohann, and ETR Associates. *HealthSmart Middle School Program Foundation: Standards, Theory, Results* (Santa Cruz, CA: ETR, 2012). Used with permission.

foundation of this variable. Norms reflect how much an individual's families and friends will approve of a behavior and how much motivation there is to comply with the wishes of family and friends.

- *Perceived behavioral control.* This variable includes the individual's belief about the ease or difficulty of performing a behavior, based on the individual's beliefs about his or her level of control over the behavior and perceived ability to do the behavior.[90]

Figure 2–1 illustrates the theory of planned behavior in practice. Following are some examples of how a teacher might apply each element of this theory in actual classroom practice:

1. Students express intentions to act in healthy ways.
   A. Teachers can encourage students to sign and post pledges (to wear safety belts, to drink plenty of water, to eat five fruits and vegetables a day).
   B. Teachers can ask students to stand or raise their hands if they intend to practice a healthy behavior.
2. Attitudes toward the behavior.
   A. Students can investigate the short-term effects of smoking and determine how those effects might influence their quality of life.
   B. Teachers can ask students to explain possible outcomes if they had a wreck on their bike while not wearing a bike helmet. Would they anticipate a different outcome if wearing a bike helmet?

3. Subjective norms.
   A. Teachers can help students clarify actual norms. (For example, students often overestimate the number of peers who practice unhealthy behaviors such as smoking. It is important that students understand that the majority of their peers do not smoke. Teachers can use local and state data to help students understand actual smoking rates.)
   B. Teachers can encourage students to write about or verbalize healthy behaviors in which they participate. (For example, ask students to identify their favorite fruit or vegetable. This will confirm the norm that most students eat fruits and vegetables.)
4. Perceived behavioral control.
   A. Encourage students to practice peer-resistance skills before they are pressured to engage in risky or unhealthy behaviors.
   B. Teach students how and where to access valid and reliable health information.
   C. Encourage students to participate in a health behavior change project.

With the foundation of a health behavior theory, teachers can focus their planning more directly on influencing health behavior. Sections II and III of this text offer a variety of teaching activities that feature parts of the theory of planned behavior in applied instructional practice.

Characteristics of Effective Health Education Curricula: Foundations for Decision Making and Best Practice

Informed by national and state content standards, a sound health education curriculum approved by the local board of education provides a foundation for instruction that is most likely to promote healthy behavior outcomes among students. As in other academic content areas, the term *curriculum* applied to health education can have several meanings:

- A written course of study that outlines broadly what students will know and be able to do (behavioral expectations and learning objectives) by the end of a single grade or multiple grades in a particular health content area or tobacco prevention education.
- An educational plan incorporating a structured, developmentally appropriate series of intended learning outcomes and associated learning experiences for students, generally organized as a detailed set of directions, strategies, lessons, and a related combination of school-based materials, content, and events.

Throughout this text, *curriculum* will apply to those health education teaching strategies and learning experiences that provide students with opportunities to acquire the attitudes, knowledge, and skills necessary for making health-promoting decisions, achieving health literacy, adopting health-enhancing behaviors, and promoting the health of others.[91]

Some school districts assemble teams of local professionals to develop curriculum materials with a specific focus on meeting learner needs in that district. Other school communities buy curriculum packages produced by for-profit companies, community agencies (American Cancer Society/American Lung Association tobacco risk–reduction curricula), government agencies, or other national groups with an interest in particular issues (DARE curricula offered by local police departments). Regardless of how it is developed, a common set of elements characterize a sound health education curriculum including:

- A set of intended learning outcomes or learning objectives that are directly related to students' acquisition of health-related knowledge, attitudes, and skills.
- A planned progression of developmentally appropriate lessons or learning experiences that lead to achieving these objectives.
- Continuity between lessons or learning experiences that clearly reinforce the adoption and maintenance of specific health-enhancing behaviors.
- Accompanying content or materials that correspond with the sequence of learning events and help teachers and students meet the learning objectives.
- Assessment strategies to determine if students achieved the desired learning outcomes.

Though some educators and advocates consider a textbook, a collection of activities, or a website to be a curriculum, these typically do not contain all of the important identified elements. They can, however, serve as potentially valuable resources or support materials.[92]

Selecting an effective prevention program from the range of those developed by corporate entities, community health or government agencies, or other advocacy groups can be challenging. Prevention programs should address the specific needs of a particular group and be able to produce similarly positive outcomes across different settings and populations. Various federal agencies have identified youth-targeted programs that they consider to be worthy of recommendation based on rigorous review. The list of websites at the end of this chapter identifies these resources.

Importantly, even curricula and other school–community partnership programs that have been shown to be effective do not always meet the needs of *local* schools. A number of barriers to implementing such programs in school-based instructional environments have been identified:

- Relatively few health curricula show evidence of effectiveness.
- Few identified curricula target multiple health-risk behaviors.
- Many health education curricula, including those that have been locally developed, have not been evaluated using rigorous research methods.
- For a number of reasons, schools cannot implement the curriculum (with fidelity) as it was implemented in evaluation studies.[93]

The Health Education Curriculum Analysis Tool (HECAT) developed by the Centers for Disease Control and Prevention contains guidance, tools, and valuable resources to conduct an analysis of health education curricula (Chapter 1). HECAT results can help local districts select or develop an appropriate and effective health education curricula and improve the delivery of health instruction. Based on scientifically demonstrated evidence of effective curricula and the National Health Education Standards (Chapters 1 and 3), HECAT reflects the importance of:

- Using science to improve health education practice.
- Engaging school personnel, parents, and community members in the review and selection of curriculum.
- Acknowledging the authority of local stakeholders in setting health education priorities, determining appropriate content, and making curriculum selection decisions.
- Flexibility in accommodating different values, priorities, and curriculum needs of communities and schools.

HECAT facilitates assessment of comprehensive curricula that address multiple topics and grade levels, a single-topic or single-grade focus, and the health education component of a more comprehensive intervention (part of a Whole School, Whole Community, Whole Child approach). Specifically, HECAT was developed to enable local school districts to assess comprehensive health education curricula and curricula developed to focus on the following:

- Alcohol and Other Drugs.
- Healthy Eating.
- Mental and Emotional Health.
- Personal Health and Wellness.
- Physical Activity.
- Safety.
- Sexual Health.
- Tobacco.
- Violence Prevention.[94]

HECAT is based on the body of research that confirms the value of teaching functional health information (essential knowledge), shaping personal values and beliefs that support healthy behaviors, shaping group norms that value a healthy lifestyle, and developing the essential health skills necessary to adopt, practice, and maintain healthy behaviors. Readers will find a summary of evidence-based characteristics of an effective health education curriculum in Table 2–1.[95]

Former president Jimmy Carter has asserted, "The bottom line of what needs to be done in improving American health is through the public elementary and secondary schools in our country. In the past, health has been a kind of appendage, a kind of novelty, forced upon quite often unwilling superintendents, teachers and administrators in the school system, and part of it is our own fault."[96] As parents, teachers, government agencies, and concerned health and education advocates demand accountability for all school-based activities, health educators must respond. Only when the local curriculum is research-based, theory-driven, and developmentally appropriate can health risks among students in elementary and middle schools be reduced. Using HECAT and integrating the lessons reviewed in this chapter into classroom practice will equip teachers to support health behavior risk reduction among the students in their care.

TABLE 2–1
Characteristics of an Effective Health Education Curriculum

Focuses on clear health goals and related behavioral outcomes
An effective curriculum has clear health-related goals and behavioral outcomes that are directly related to these goals. Instructional strategies and learning experiences are directly related to the behavioral outcomes.

Is research-based and theory-driven
An effective curriculum has instructional strategies and learning experiences built on theoretical approaches (e.g., social cognitive theory and social inoculation theory) that have effectively influenced health-related behaviors among youth. The most promising curriculum goes beyond the cognitive level and addresses health determinants, social factors, attitudes, values, norms, and skills that influence specific health-related behaviors.

Addresses individual values, attitudes, and beliefs
An effective curriculum fosters attitudes, values, and beliefs that support positive health behaviors. It provides instructional strategies and learning experiences that motivate students to critically examine personal perspectives, thoughtfully consider new arguments that support health-promoting attitudes and values, and generate positive perceptions about protective behaviors and negative perceptions about risk behaviors.

Addresses individual and group norms that support health-enhancing behaviors
An effective curriculum provides instructional strategies and learning experiences to help students accurately assess the level of risk-taking behavior among their peers (e.g., how many of their peers use illegal drugs), correct misperceptions of peer and social norms, emphasizes the value of good health, and reinforces health-enhancing attitudes and beliefs.

Focuses on reinforcing protective factors and increasing perceptions of personal risk and harmfulness of engaging in specific unhealthy practices and behaviors
An effective curriculum provides opportunities for students to validate positive health-promoting beliefs, intentions, and behaviors. It provides opportunities for students to assess their vulnerability to health problems, actual risk of engaging in harmful health behaviors, and exposure to unhealthy situations.

Addresses social pressures and influences
An effective curriculum provides opportunities for students to analyze personal and social pressures to engage in risky behaviors, such as media influence, peer pressure, and social barriers.

Builds personal competence, social competence, and self-efficacy by addressing skills
An effective curriculum builds essential skills—including communication, refusal, assessing accuracy of information, decision making, planning and goal-setting, self-control, and self-management—that enable students to build their personal confidence, deal with social pressures, and avoid or reduce risk behaviors. For each skill, students are guided through a series of developmental steps:

- Discussing the importance of the skill, its relevance, and relationship to other learned skills.
- Presenting steps for developing the skill.
- Modeling the skill.
- Practicing and rehearsing the skill using real-life scenarios.
- Providing feedback and reinforcement.

Provides functional health knowledge that is basic, accurate, and directly contributes to health-promoting decisions and behaviors
An effective curriculum provides accurate, reliable, and credible information for usable purposes so students can assess risk, clarify attitudes and beliefs, correct misperceptions about social norms, identify ways to avoid or minimize risky situations, examine internal and external influences, make behaviorally relevant decisions, and build personal and social competence. A curriculum that provides information for the sole purpose of improving knowledge of factual information will not change behavior.

(continued)

TABLE 2–1 (*continued*)

Uses strategies designed to personalize information and engage students

An effective curriculum includes instructional strategies and learning experiences that are student-centered, interactive, and experiential (e.g., group discussions, cooperative learning, problem solving, role playing, and peer-led activities). Learning experiences correspond with students' cognitive and emotional development, help them personalize information, and maintain their interest and motivation while accommodating diverse capabilities and learning styles. Instructional strategies and learning experiences include methods for:

- Addressing key health-related concepts.
- Encouraging creative expression.
- Sharing personal thoughts, feelings, and opinions.
- Thoughtfully considering new arguments.
- Developing critical thinking skills.

Provides age-appropriate and developmentally appropriate information, learning strategies, teaching methods, and materials

An effective curriculum addresses students' needs, interests, concerns, developmental and emotional maturity levels, experiences, and current knowledge and skill levels. Learning is relevant and applicable to students' daily lives. Concepts and skills are covered in a logical sequence.

Incorporates learning strategies, teaching methods, and materials that are culturally inclusive

An effective curriculum has materials that are free of culturally biased information but includes information, activities, and examples that are inclusive of diverse cultures and lifestyles (such as gender, race, ethnicity, religion, age, physical/mental ability, appearance, and sexual orientation). Strategies promote values, attitudes, and behaviors that acknowledge the cultural diversity of students; optimize relevance to students from multiple cultures in the school community; strengthen students' skills necessary to engage in intercultural interactions; and build on the cultural resources of families and communities.

Provides adequate time for instruction and learning

An effective curriculum provides enough time to promote understanding of key health concepts and practice skills. Behavior change requires an intensive and sustained effort. A short-term or "one shot" curriculum, delivered for a few hours at one grade level, is generally insufficient to support the adoption and maintenance of healthy behaviors.

Provides opportunities to reinforce skills and positive health behaviors

An effective curriculum builds on previously learned concepts and skills and provides opportunities to reinforce health-promoting skills across health topics and grade levels. This can include incorporating more than one practice application of a skill, adding "skill booster" sessions at subsequent grade levels, or integrating skill application opportunities in other academic areas. A curriculum that addresses age-appropriate determinants of behavior across grade levels and reinforces and builds on learning is more likely to achieve longer-lasting results.

Provides opportunities to make positive connections with influential others

An effective curriculum links students to other influential persons who affirm and reinforce health-promoting norms, attitudes, values, beliefs, and behaviors. Instructional strategies build on protective factors that promote healthy behaviors and enable students to avoid or reduce health risk behaviors by engaging peers, parents, families, and other positive adult role models in student learning.

Includes teacher information and plans for professional development and training that enhance effectiveness of instruction and student learning

An effective curriculum is implemented by teachers who have a personal interest in promoting positive health behaviors, believe in what they are teaching, are knowledgeable about the curriculum content, and are comfortable and skilled in implementing expected instructional strategies. Ongoing professional development and training is critical for helping teachers implement a new curriculum or implement strategies that require new skills in teaching or assessment.

SOURCE: Centers for Disease Control and Prevention, *Characteristics of an Effective Health Education Curriculum* (www.cdc.gov/healthyschools/sher/characteristics/; 2014).

INVOLVING CHILDREN IN CURRICULUM PLANNING

As an alternative to teacher-developed curricula, educators have been exploring the value of involving children in the planning process. Unfortunately, it is not a practice that is widely implemented in elementary and middle school classrooms. Although most administrators and teachers would not want to develop all health curricula this way, there are compelling reasons to supplement conventional instruction with instruction informed by the interests of students. When students are invited into the process of determining the focus of their learning activities, they become active in practicing communication skills. With teacher support, children are better able to connect health issues to other content areas, including language arts and social studies. A collaborative approach to planning also can bring richness to classroom instruction, because it is grounded in the identified interests of

a particular group of students. In this way, it capitalizes on the elements of individually appropriate practice.

Curriculum scholars recommend a four-step procedure for teachers interested in engaging students in a collaborative approach to planning. It is recommended that these steps be implemented after the teacher has identified potential instructional topics or themes. Themes can emerge from student comments.[97] The recommended sequence of steps involves students in seeking answers to four specific questions:

Step 1: *What do you wonder?* During this stage of planning, students are given the opportunity to express ideas, questions, or concerns about an identified topic. As questions about the topic emerge, teachers can gain insight into development, language skills, misconceptions, and thinking processes among students.

Step 2: *What can we do to find out?* This step in the collaborative process is based on the fundamental idea that learning is a social,

A collaborative approach to planning helps keep students energized and involved in learning.

methods that they identify to solve problems or answer questions and the materials they will need to achieve their goals. As students identify necessary materials, teachers are urged to clarify responses and reinforce the connection between problem-solving methods and materials.

Step 4: *What will you bring (do)? What would you like me to bring (do)?* As concepts, methods, and materials to be explored are clarified, specific contributions to the process are collected from volunteers. Consistent with the tenets of authentic instruction, students reinforce the connection between classroom topics and events or experiences from their own lives. This step also provides fertile opportunities for parent engagement, as "expert" consultation or support can be solicited from supportive adults.

or collaborative, process. As a result, activities in this phase of planning reinforce the importance not only of students' questions but also of their involvement in finding answers or solutions. In this context, the teacher and students brainstorm ways in which they can work together to "find out." As an outgrowth of this process, students practice brainstorming and problem-solving skills, and their creativity is reinforced when they help design learning activities.

Step 3: *What materials do we need?* In this step in the process, students are encouraged to make a connection between the

When children are involved in planning curricula for their classrooms, both teachers and students are rewarded. As curriculum and learning activities emerge from mutual interests, teachers are freed from the constraints of artificial time lines, students are energized by concepts and issues that are of interest to them, parent engagement can be formalized, and the benefits of integrated or cross-curricular instruction can be realized for everyone (Chapter 4). Although unconventional, such a collaborative model provides a vehicle for implementing a developmentally appropriate practice approach to health instruction.[98]

 INTERNET AND OTHER RESOURCES

WEBSITES

Various federal agencies have identified youth-related programs that they consider to be worthy of recommendation on the basis of expert opinion or a review of design and research evidence. These programs focus on different health topics, risk behaviors, and settings. A comprehensive list can be found at the Registries of Programs Effective in Reducing Youth Risk Behaviors (http://www.cdc.gov/healthyyouth/adolescenthealth/registries.htm; 2017). Following is a list of evaluated resources related to specific health topics and risk behaviors:

Center for the Study and Prevention of Violence:

Blueprints for Healthy Youth Development
 www.colorado.edu/cspv/blueprints/

Child Trends
 www.childtrends.org

National Registry of Evidence-Based Programs and Practices

(Sponsored by the Substance Abuse and Mental Health Services Administration, U.S. Department of Health and Human Services)
 http://nrepp.samhsa.gov/

Office of Juvenile Justice and Delinquency Prevention Model Programs

(Sponsored by the Office of Juvenile Justice and Delinquency Prevention, U.S. Department of Justice)
 www.ojjdp.gov/mpg/

Preventing Drug Use Among Children and Adolescents: A Research-Based Guide

(Sponsored by the National Institute on Drug Abuse, National Institutes of Health, U.S. Department of Health and Human Services)
 www.nida.nih.gov/Prevention/index.html

Research-Tested Intervention Programs

(Sponsored by the National Cancer Institute, National Institute of Health)
 http://rtips.cancer.gov/rtips/index.do

Teen Pregnancy Prevention Programs

(Sponsored by the Office of Adolescent Health, U.S. Department of Health and Human Services)
 www.hhs.gov/ash/oah/grant-programs/teen-pregnancy-prevention-program-tpp/index.html

What Works Clearinghouse

(Sponsored by the U.S. Department of Education, Institute of Education Sciences)

http://ies.ed.gov/ncee/wwc/

OTHER RESOURCES

Ferguson, M. *Will the Light Shine on Education?* (Washington, DC: Center on Education Policy, 2016).

Gardner, H. *Multiple Intelligences* (Los Angeles, CA: Into the Classroom Media, 2013).

Jensen, E. "How Poverty Affects Classroom Engagement." *Educational Leadership* (May 2013): 24–30.

Kendall, J. *Understanding Common Core State Standards* (Alexandria, VA: ASCD, 2011).

McTighe, J. and G. Wiggins. *Essential Questions: Opening Doors to Student Understanding* (Alexandria, VA: ASCD, 2013).

Saavedra, A. R. and V. D. Opfer. "Learning 21st-Century Skills Requires 21st-Century Teaching." *Kappan* (October 2012): 8–13.

Scholastic and Bill & Melinda Gates Foundation. *Primary Sources: America's Teachers on Teaching in an Era of Change* (Seattle, WA: Scholastic and the Bill & Melinda Gates Foundation, 2014).

Shanahan, T. "The Common Core Ate My Baby and Other Urban Legends." *Educational Leadership* (December 2012/January 2013): 11–16.

Slotnik, W. J. "Retool State-to-District Intervention for Better Outcomes." *Kappan* (March 2014): 39–43.

Tappe, M. K. and R. Galer-Unti. "U.S. Policies for School Health Education: Opportunities for Advocacy at the Local, State, and National Levels." *Health Promotion Practice* (May 2013): 328–33.

ENDNOTES

1. D. Stover, "The Choice Evolution," *American School Board Journal* 196, no. 11 (2009): 20.
2. American School Board Journal, "A New Direction," *Education Vital Signs 2009* (March 2009): 2–3.
3. National Center for Education Statistics, *Elementary and Secondary Enrollment* (https://nces.ed.gov/programs/coe/indicator_cga.asp; 2018).
4. J. F. Bogden, *Fit, Healthy, and Ready to Learn: A School Health Policy Guide* (Alexandria, VA: National Association of State Boards of Education, 2000).
5. National Center for Education Statistics, *NCES Blog: Measuring the Homeschool Population* (https://nces.ed.gov/blogs/nces/post/measuring-the-homeschool-population; 2017).
6. Statistic Brain, *Home School Statistics* (www.statisticbrain.com/home-school-statistics; 2014).
7. Bogden, *Fit, Healthy, and Ready to Learn.*
8. Ibid.
9. N. Dillon, "A Slow Build," *American School* 196, no. 11 (November 2009): 28–29.
10. National Center for Education Statistics, *Private School Enrollment* (https://nces.ed.gov/programs/coe/indicator_cgc.asp; 2018).
11. Council for American Private Education, *FAQs About Private Schools* (capenet.org/facts.html; 2014).
12. Bogden, *Fit, Healthy, and Ready to Learn.*
13. National Center for Education Statistics, *Fast Facts: Back to School Statistics* (https://nces.ed.gov/fastfacts/display.asp?id=372).
14. Bogden, *Fit, Healthy, and Ready to Learn.*
15. U.S. Congress, *No Child Left Behind Act of 2001: Conference Report to Accompany H.R. 1, Report 107–334* (Washington, DC: Government Printing Office, 2001).
16. U.S. Department of Education, *No Child Left Behind: A Parent's Guide* (Washington, DC: U.S. Department of Education, Office of the Secretary, Office of Public Affairs, 2003).
17. J. Jennings and D. S. Rentner, "Ten Big Effects of the No Child Left Behind Act on Public Schools," *Phi Delta Kappan* 88, no. 2 (October 2006): 110–13.
18. Ibid.
19. H. Nelson, *Testing More, Teaching Less: What America's Obsession with Student Testing Costs in Money and Lost Instructional Time* (Washington, DC: American Federation of Teachers) (www.aft.org/pdfs/teachers/testingmore2013.pdf; 2013).
20. U.S. Department of Education, *Built for Teachers: How the Blueprint for Reform Empowers Educators* (www2.ed.gov/policy/elsec/leg/blueprint/teachers/publication_pg3.html).
21. U.S. Department of Education, *Race to the Top Fund* (www2.ed.gov/programs/racetothetop/index.html; 2016).
22. Council of Chief State School Officers (CCSSO) and National Governors Association Center for Best Practices (NGACenter), *Common Core State Standards Initiative: Preparing America's Students for College and Career* (www.corestandards.org; 2018).
23. Ibid.
24. Ibid.
25. Ibid.
26. U.S. Department of Health and Human Services, *The Surgeon General's Vision for a Healthy and Fit Nation* (Washington, DC: U.S. Department of Health and Human Services, Office of the Surgeon General, 2010).
27. K. Tyler, N. Cook, and M. Macdonald. (2014). *Physical Activity and Children with Disabilities: Viable Resources Available for Community and Health Professionals,* PALAESTRA, 28(4), 17–22.
28. National Center for Education Statistics, *Students with Disabilities* (https://nces.ed.gov/fastfacts/display.asp?id=64; 2018).
29. U.S. Department of Education, *Building the Legacy: IDEA 2004* (http://idea.ed.gov; 2018).
30. U.S. Department of Education, *Individuals with Disabilities Education Improvement Act of 2004 (H.R. 1350),* December 2004.
31. National Center for Health Statistics, *Students with Disabilities* (https://nces.ed.gov/fastfacts/display.asp?id=64; 2018).
32. D. J. Bernert, "Educators Who Integrate Students with Disabilities into Sexuality Education Programs," in *Partners in Prevention: Whole School Approaches to Prevent Pregnancy and Sexually Transmitted Infections* (Kent, OH: American School Health Association, 2006).
33. L. Musu-Gillette and S. Cornman, *Financing education: National, state, and local funding and spending for public schools in 2013,* NCES Blog, January 25, 2016 (https://nces.ed.gov/blogs/nces/post/financing-education-national-state-and-local-funding-and-spending-for-public-schools-in-2013; 2018).
34. Bogden, *Fit, Healthy, and Ready to Learn.*
35. Ibid.
36. Musu-Gillette and Cornman, *Financing education.*
37. Bogden, *Fit, Healthy, and Ready to Learn.*
38. F. M. Newmann and G. G. Wehlage, "Five Standards of Authentic Instruction," *Educational Leadership* 50 no. 7 (April 1993): 8–12.
39. M. M. Hardiman, "Connecting Brain Research with Dimensions of Learning," *Educational Leadership* 59, no. 3 (November 2001): 52–55.
40. J. Willis, "Which Brain Research Can Educators Trust?" *Phi Delta Kappan* 88 no. 9 (May 2007): 697–99.
41. B. Perry, "How the Brain Learns Best," *Instructor* 11, no. 4 (2000): 34–35.
42. R. Leamnson, "Learning as Biological Brain Change," *Change* 32, no. 6 (2000): 34–40.
43. Hardiman, "Connecting Brain Research with Dimensions of Learning."
44. J. King-Friedrichs, "Brain-Friendly Techniques for Improving Memory," *Educational Leadership* 59, no. 3 (November 2001): 76–79.
45. D. Goleman, *Emotional Intelligence* (New York: Bantam Books, 1995).
46. E. Jensen, "How Julie's Brain Learns," *Educational Leadership* 56, no. 3 (1998): 41–45.
47. Hardiman, "Connecting Brain Research with Dimensions of Learning."
48. L. Lowery, "How New Science Curriculums Reflect Brain Research," *Educational Leadership* 56, no. 3 (1998): 26–30.
49. Hardiman, "Connecting Brain Research with Dimensions of Learning."
50. Leamnson, "Learning as Biological Brain Change."
51. Hardiman, "Connecting Brain Research with Dimensions of Learning."
52. T. Armstrong, *Multiple Intelligences in the Classroom,* 3rd ed. (Alexandria, VA: ASCD, 2009).
53. Ibid.
54. Hardiman, "Connecting Brain Research with Dimensions of Learning."
55. P. Wolfe, *Brain Matters: Translating Research into Classroom Practice,* 2nd ed. (Alexandria, VA: ASCD, 2010).
56. R. N. Caine and G. Caine, *Unleashing the Power of Perceptual Change: The Potential of Brain-Based Teaching* (Alexandria, VA: ASCD, 1997).
57. B. Samek and N. Samek, "It's a Brain Thing: Keeping Students Focused and Learning," a presentation at the 78th Annual Meeting of the American School Health Association (October 16, 2004).
58. Newmann and Wehlage, "Five Standards of Authentic Instruction."
59. D. Archbald and F. M. Newmann, *Beyond Standardized Testing: Assessing Authentic Academic Achievement in the Secondary School* (Reston, VA: National Association of Secondary School Principals, 1988).
60. Newmann and Wehlage, "Five Standards of Authentic Instruction."
61. Ibid.
62. Ibid.
63. S. L. Ramey and C. T. Ramey, "The Transition to School," *Phi Delta Kappan* 76, no. 3 (November 1994): 197.
64. C. Copple and S. Bredekamp, eds., *Developmentally Appropriate Practice in Early Childhood Programs Serving Children from Birth through Age 8,* 3rd ed. (Washington, DC: National Association for the Education of Young Children, 2009), xii.
65. S. Bredekamp, ed., *Developmentally Appropriate Practice in Early Childhood Programs Serving Children from Birth Through Age 8* (Washington, DC: National Association for the Education of Young Children, 1987), 1–2.
66. J. W. Lochner, "Growth and Developmental Characteristics," in *A Pocketguide to Health and Health Problems in School Physical Activity,* ed. B. Petrof (Kent, OH: ASHA, 1981), 4–9.
67. Bredekamp, *Developmentally Appropriate Practice,* 2.
68. Ibid.

69. Ibid., 1, 3, 5.

70. S. Bredekamp and C. Copple, eds., *Developmentally Appropriate Practice in Early Childhood Programs* (Washington, DC: National Association for the Education of Young Children, 1997), 8-15.

71. P. Keener, *Caring for Children: Useful Information and Hard-to-Find Facts About Child Health and Development* (Indianapolis, IN: James Whitcomb Riley Memorial Association, 2001), 106-8.

72. Bredekamp, *Developmentally Appropriate Practice*, 2-5.

73. Copple and Bredekamp, eds., *Developmentally Appropriate Practice*, 33-50.

74. J. S. Coleman et al., *Equality of Educational Opportunity* (Washington, DC: U.S. Government Printing Office, 1966).

75. S. P. Wright, S. Horn, and W. Sanders, "Teacher and Classroom Context Effects on Student Achievement: Implications for Teacher Evaluation," *Journal of Personnel Evaluation in Education* 11 (1997): 57-67.

76. R. J. Marzano, *A Theory-Based Meta-Analysis of Research on Instruction* (Aurora, CO: Mid-Continent Research for Education and Learning, 1998).

77. R. Marzano, D. Pickering, and J. Pollock, *Classroom Instruction That Works: Research-Based Strategies for Increasing Student Achievement* (Alexandria, VA: ASCD, 2001).

78. C. Dean, E. Hubbell, H. Pitler, B. Stone, *Classroom Instruction that Works: Research Based Strategies for Increasing Student Achievement,* 2nd ed. (Alexandria, VA: ASCD, 2012).

79. R. M. Pigg, "20 Concepts of Learning," *Journal of School Health* 63, no. 9 (November 1993): 375.

80. Centers for Disease Control and Prevention, *Characteristics of an Effective Health Education Curriculum* (www.cdc.gov/healthyschools/sher /characteristics/index.htm; 2015).

81. U.S. Department of Health and Human Services, *Healthy People 2020* (www.healthypeople.gov; 2018).

82. American Cancer Society, American Diabetes Association, and American Heart Association, Health Education in Schools—The *Importance of Establishing Healthy Behaviors in Our Nation's Youth* (*Health Educator,* Fall 2008, Vol. 40 Issue 2).

83. D. Wiley, "Elementary School Teachers' Perspectives on Health Instruction: A Commentary," *American Journal of Health Education* 33, no. 2 (March/April 2002): 83-85.

84. R. Thakery et al., "Elementary School Teachers' Perspectives on Health Instruction: Implications for Health Education," *American Journal of Health Education* 33, no. 2 (March/April 2002): 77-82.

85. D. Duffy, "The Right Stuff: Two Perspectives on What It Takes to Be an Effective Health Teacher," *RMC Health Educator* 2, no. 3 (Spring 2002): 1-4.

86. U.S. Department of Health and Human Services, *Theory at a Glance: A Guide for Health Promotion Practice* (Washington, DC: National Cancer Institute, 2005).

87. Centers for Disease Control and Prevention, *Health Education Curriculum Analysis Tool* (www.cdc.gov /healthyyouth/HECAT/index.htm; 2017).

88. U.S. Department of Health and Human Services, *Theory at a Glance: A Guide for Health Promotion Practice.*

89. Ibid.

90. I. Aizen, *Theory of Planned Behavior Diagram* (http:// people.umass.edu/aizen/tpb.html; 2002).

91. Centers for Disease Control and Prevention, *Health Education Curriculum Analysis Tool* (www.cdc.gov /healthyyouth/hecat/; 2017).

92. Ibid.

93. Ibid.

94. Ibid.

95. Centers for Disease Control and Prevention, *Characteristics of an Effective Health Education Curriculum.*

96. J. Carter, "The Challenge of Education for Health in America's Schools," *Journal of School Health* 60, no. 4 (April 1990): 129.

97. K. C. Williams, "What Do You Wonder? Involving Children in Curriculum Planning," *Young Children* 52 no. 6 (September 1997): 78-81.

98. Ibid.

3

(Jaime, age 13)

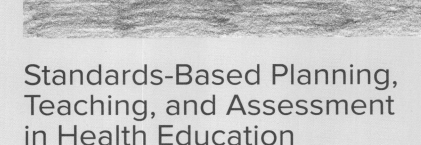

Standards-Based Planning, Teaching, and Assessment in Health Education

DESIRED LEARNER OUTCOMES

After reading this chapter, you will be able to . . .

- **Describe the focus of school health education reflected in the National Health Education Standards.**

- **Summarize the concepts and skills included in the National Health Education Standards.**

- **Describe the process of integrating standards, content areas, healthy behavior outcomes, and theoretical constructs for yearly, unit, and lesson planning.**

- **Summarize strategies for including students with diverse backgrounds, interests, and abilities in health education lessons.**

- **Explain the role of rubrics in health education assessment.**

- **Describe interactive, standards-based learning, and assessment strategies.**

- **Use the Internet and other resources for assistance in standards-based planning, assessment, and teaching.**

INTRODUCTION

When adults are asked what they remember about school health education in their own K–12 experience, they frequently reply, if they remember health education at all, that they mainly learned factual information about health topics. In contrast, today's school health education helps students develop the functional knowledge and skills they need to adopt, practice, and maintain health-enhancing behaviors.

The publication of the National Health Education Standards in 1995 marked this important change in focus for school health education.[1] Revised and updated in 2007 (Teacher's Toolbox 1.1), the standards identify important personal and social skills that elementary and middle school students can apply in the context of priority health content areas. For example, students learn to compare and contrast the best use of communication and refusal skills in different kinds of health-risk situations (e.g., declining a ride with a drinking driver) they might encounter.

This change from an information-based to a skills-based focus is grounded in promising curriculum evaluation research on programs that include a strong skills component. Various federal agencies have identified youth-related programs that they recommend on the basis of a review of design and research evidence or expert opinion.[2] Parents, teachers, administrators, and community members support school health efforts designed to increase healthy behaviors rather than merely to increase health knowledge. For example, schools want to prevent and reduce tobacco use on and off campus rather than ensure that students can name the carcinogens in tobacco smoke.

A skills-based approach helps students acquire tools for making sense of the enormous amount of health information generated each year. Rather than memorizing countless health facts, students learn to access valid health information and evaluate the quality of information sources for themselves. When students take an active role in acquiring information, they build their functional knowledge as astute investigators rather than passive receivers.

The National Health Education Standards and related performance indicators (Appendix A) focus on important health-promoting concepts and skills for students in grades kindergarten through 8. Many state and local education agencies used the standards as the basis for creating their own standards and curriculum documents. The personal and social skills reflected in the standards include the following:

1. *Core concepts*—learning functional knowledge, which is the most important information essential for health promotion and disease prevention.
2. *Analysis of internal and external influences*—examining internal influences (feelings, likes, dislikes, curiosity, values, beliefs, fears, moods) and external influences (family, peers, culture, technology, and media, such as advertising, social media, music, television, and movies) on health decisions and behaviors.
3. *Access to information, products, and services*—learning to locate and use the best sources of health information, products, and services to fulfill health needs.

4. *Interpersonal communication*—practicing and comparing verbal and nonverbal strategies for clear communication and peer resistance across priority health-risk areas.
5. *Decision making*—learning and applying age-appropriate processes for making health-promoting decisions.
6. *Goal setting*—learning and applying age-appropriate processes for setting and working toward health-related goals.
7. *Self-management*—learning to practice skills for healthy behaviors, such as stress management, anger and conflict management, injury and disease prevention, and personal health care.
8. *Advocacy*—learning to act in effective ways to promote personal, family, and community health.

This manner of referring to the National Health Education Standards (e.g., Standard 7: self-management) originated with the work of the Council of Chief State School Officers (CCSSO), the State Collaborative on Assessment and Student Standards (SCASS), and the Health Education Assessment Project (HEAP).[3] HEAP provided groundbreaking leadership in assessing the National Health Education Standards. RMC Health provided further leadership through the development of analytic rubrics and checklists for assessing the standards. The criteria used to assess standards in this text are adapted from the RMC Health rubrics (Appendix B).

Elementary and middle school students need many opportunities to practice health-related skills in the context of the content areas addressed in Chapters 5 through 14. Thus, each content chapter includes learning and assessment strategies organized by the National Health Education Standards and grade levels, and closely aligned with the Health Education Curriculum Analysis Tool (HECAT). To reinforce the standards, health educators Donna Rodenhurst and Jimmy Edwards had their seventh-grade health education classes make classroom posters to illustrate what the standards mean in "kid terms." The work of their students appears throughout this text.

MEETING THE NATIONAL HEALTH EDUCATION STANDARDS

The idea of meeting the health education standards is twofold in this chapter. Students in grades K–8 meet standards when they demonstrate the ability to apply essential concepts and skills to help keep themselves and others healthy and safe. The overall goal of health education is for students to adopt and maintain healthy behaviors. Thus, health education should contribute directly to a student's ability to engage in health-enhancing behaviors and to avoid or reduce behaviors that can lead to poor health.

Before educators can help their students meet standards, however, they must get to know the standards for themselves. This chapter provides an introduction to each of the National Health Education Standards followed by information on planning, assessment, and teaching with the standards. The chapter ends with example learning and assessment strategies that teachers can apply across content areas.

Standard 1: Core Concepts

Students Will Comprehend Concepts Related to Health Promotion and Disease Prevention to Enhance Health

Acquiring core concepts refers to learning functional knowledge, which is the information most essential to health promotion and disease prevention. Core concepts are the content knowledge of health education. Rather than being passive receivers, young people should be active seekers of information. Thus, National Health Education Standard (NHES) 1, core concepts, is closely linked to NHES 3, access to information, products, and services.

Given the overwhelming amount of health information generated each year and the limited time available for teaching about health, how can teachers make decisions about the content that is essential for students to acquire? They can consider the following guidelines:

NHES 1 | *Students will comprehend concepts related to health promotion and disease prevention to enhance health.* (Alyssa, age 12; Rochelle, age 12)

- *Focus first on the important content areas identified in this text.* Health education must share time with many other content areas in the elementary and middle school curriculum. Teachers must ensure that the most important public health priorities for children, described in Chapters 5 to 14, are the focus of health education lessons.
- *Build on what children already know and what they want to know.* The Know-Wonder-Learn (KWL) chart, described in the section "Strategies for Learning and Assessment," is a useful tool for assessing students' current knowledge and understanding their questions before proceeding with health instruction. How many children are taught about food groups each year as if they have never seen them before? Teachers model respect for students when they take the time to start where students are and provide opportunities for them to build their own content knowledge.
- *Articulate health instruction within and across grade levels.* Teachers spend a great deal of time articulating math and English Language Arts instruction. Ideally, teachers also should have time for articulation in the other important curriculum areas (science, social studies, health education, the arts, and physical education). What should the health education focus be at each grade level? What are students' interests? What topics belong in the health curriculum, compared to the science or physical education curriculum? How can teaching in other content areas support student learning about health?
- *Integrate health instruction into other content areas in deliberate ways.* Children in the elementary and middle grades read a variety of picture and chapter books related to personal and social health skills. Teachers can integrate health education by having their students discuss the goals, decisions, communication skills, and self-management strategies of the characters in the stories. To assist teachers, each content chapter includes ideas for children's literature for health education. Similarly, mathematics and science instruction can engage students in a "health problem of the day," such as calculating and comparing the percentage of calories from fat, salt, and sugar in various snack foods, exploring the physics of stopping on a skateboard, or planning and measuring a layout for a school garden.
- *Identify functional knowledge that is essential for health promotion and disease prevention.* Identifying the ways in which sexually transmitted diseases are and are not transmitted is functional knowledge essential for disease prevention. However, explaining how viruses and bacteria work is not essential for self-protection and might more appropriately be part of the science or biology curriculum. Similarly, learning to name the bones and muscles is not nearly as important for health promotion as learning the effects of healthy nutrition and regular physical activity on the skeletal and muscular systems. When setting priorities for health information, teachers should consider what students must know to stay healthy and safe.

The Health Education Curriculum Analysis Tool (HECAT) from the Centers for Disease Control and Prevention (CDC) identifies healthy behaviors in nine important topic areas for today's school health education (Teacher's Toolbox 3.1).[4] These topics mirror the content of Chapters 5 to 14 in this text.

The theory of planned behavior (Chapter 2) can help teachers focus lesson time in ways that are most likely to influence healthy behavior. Lessons related to core concepts can help students develop positive attitudes toward health by connecting healthy behaviors with positive results. Learning core concepts also can help students consider the consequences of their behaviors.

Health education lessons should engage students in scratching beneath the surface to discover how the concepts and skills they learn connect with their lives. A student might reason, "Breakfast is important because it helps people stay alert. I want to stay alert because I want to do well in school." On the other hand, a student might reason, "I know smoking is unhealthy for me, but it's more important right now to have friends, and some of my friends smoke." Health education can help students first make connections with their lives and then dig deeper to explore alternatives. For example, in the latter example, the student could explore new choices for maintaining important relationship with friends. The student might decide to spend time with these friends when they are involved in nonsmoking activities, such as sports or movies; try low-key refusals to smoking ("No thanks, not right now"); or give reasons for not wanting to smoke ("Nah—my mom will smell it on my clothes and I'll be so busted").

NHES 2 | *Students will analyze the influence of family, peers, culture, media, technology, and other factors on health behaviors.* (Kylie, age 12; Kimberly, age 12)

Standard 2: Analyze Influences

Students Will Analyze the Influence of Family, Peers, Culture, Media, Technology, and Other Factors on Health Behaviors

Students often find this standard to be a favorite. Working on this standard helps young people consider answers to the perplexing health behavior question "Why do we do what we do—especially when what we do doesn't always seem to be the smartest thing?" In practicing the skill of analyzing influences, students look at factors inside themselves (internal influences), such as feelings, likes, dislikes, curiosity, moods, needs, values, fears, and desires. How do these factors influence what we decide to do in terms of our health? Students also examine outside factors (external influences) in all their variety—friends, family, culture, technology, television, movies, advertising, and social media of all kinds. Are these influences real? In terms of advertising and media, who's working behind the scenes, and what do they want to persuade us to do?

Media, parents and family, peers, community, cultural and peer norms, and personal values and beliefs are important influences on health behavior that students should examine. The theory of planned behavior supports lessons that help students examine social pressures to participate or refuse to participate in health behaviors. Complex personal, family, religious, and sociocultural factors influence health-related decisions. Health education lessons can be structured to help students understand that family and friends want them to act in healthy ways and that most of their peers practice healthy behaviors. Teachers can use data from the national and local Youth Risk Behavior Surveillance System[5] and Global School-based Student Health Survey[6] for important reality checks on other students' health behaviors and norms among young people.

Although students may perceive that they and others are influenced by families, friends, feelings, and culture, they may be less willing to believe that they are influenced by advertisers ("Who, me?

Not!"). An interesting start to lessons on media influences is to have students identify and count the product logos on their clothes, shoes, book bags, and lunchboxes. In "How Advertising Targets Our Children," Perri Klass, MD, cited research showing that advertising does help push children and adolescents toward unhealthy behaviors.[7] At the same time, shielding young people is increasingly difficult as marketers exploit the Internet and social media. Klass spoke with Jennifer Harris, director of marketing initiatives at the Yale Rudd Center for Food Policy and Obesity, who said:

> The ways that foods are marketed to children through television advertising is important. Each day, on average in the United States, children and teenagers see 12 to 14 food ads on television. What parents may not realize is that their children are also exposed to messages from other sources such as Websites, social media, and mobile apps.[8]

Teachers can engage students in spotting and analyzing the media and marketing messages that bombard them every day. Teacher's Toolbox 3.2 provides a list of techniques that students can use to examine the strategies marketers employ to target their messages, including advertisements that students encounter online and through social media. Students also can use these techniques to create their own student-designed media messages.

Media literacy researcher Donna Grace suggests that educators think beyond the notion that students are passive victims of advertising. Dr. Grace works with students to help them purposefully produce their own media, rather than passively consuming messages in the environment. She states that in the process, students have the opportunity to think and talk about the images they have created and to construct their own critiques. The production process allows students to play with, mediate, and, in some cases, rework media messages rather than absorb them uncritically.[9]

Healthy Behavior Outcomes

A pre-K–12 school health education curriculum should enable students to do the following:

Promoting an Alcohol and Other Drug-Free Lifestyle (AOD)

1. *Avoid misuse and abuse of over-the-counter and prescription drugs.*
2. *Avoid experimentation with alcohol and other drugs.*
3. *Avoid the use of alcohol and illegal drugs.*
4. *Avoid driving while under the influence of alcohol and other drugs.*
5. *Avoid riding in a motor vehicle with a driver who is under the influence of alcohol or other drugs.*
6. *Quit using alcohol and other drugs if already using.*
7. *Support others to be alcohol- and other drug-free.*

Promoting Healthy Eating (HE)

1. *Eat the appropriate number of servings from each food group every day.*
2. *Eat a variety of foods within each food group every day.*
3. *Eat an abundance of fruits and vegetables every day.*
4. *Choose to eat whole grain products and fat-free or low-fat milk or equivalent milk products regularly.*
5. *Drink plenty of water every day.*
6. *Limit foods and beverages high in added sugars, solid fat, and sodium.*
7. *Eat breakfast every day.*
8. *Eat healthy snacks.*
9. *Eat healthy foods when dining out.*
10. *Prepare food in healthful ways.*
11. *Balance caloric intake with caloric expenditure.*
12. *Follow an eating plan for healthy growth and development.*
13. *Support others to eat healthy.*

Promoting Mental and Emotional Health (MEH)

1. *Express feelings in a healthy way.*
2. *Engage in activities that are mentally and emotionally healthy.*
3. *Prevent and manage interpersonal conflict in healthy ways.*
4. *Prevent and manage emotional stress and anxiety in healthy ways.*
5. *Use self-control and impulse-control strategies to promote health.*
6. *Get help for troublesome thoughts, feelings, or actions for self and others.*
7. *Show tolerance and acceptance of differences in others.*
8. *Establish and maintain healthy relationships.*

Promoting Physical Activity (PA)

1. *Engage in moderate to vigorous physical activity for at least 60 minutes every day.*
2. *Regularly engage in physical activities that enhance cardio-respiratory endurance, flexibility, muscle endurance, and muscle strength.*
3. *Engage in warm-up and cool-down activities before and after structured exercise.*
4. *Drink plenty of water before, during, and after physical activity.*
5. *Follow a physical activity plan for healthy growth and development.*
6. *Avoid injury during physical activity.*
7. *Support others to be physically active*

Promoting Personal Health and Wellness (PHW)

1. *Brush and floss teeth daily.*
2. *Practice appropriate hygiene habits.*
3. *Get an appropriate amount of sleep and rest.*
4. *Prevent vision and hearing loss.*

5. *Prevent damage from the sun.*
6. *Practice behaviors that prevent infectious diseases.*
7. *Practice behaviors that prevent chronic diseases.*
8. *Prevent serious health problems that result from common chronic diseases and conditions among youth, such as allergies, asthma, diabetes, and epilepsy.*
9. *Practice behaviors that prevent foodborne illnesses.*
10. *Seek out help for common infectious diseases and chronic diseases and conditions.*
11. *Seek out health care professionals for appropriate screenings and examinations.*
12. *Prevent health problems that result from fads or trends.*

Promoting Safety (S)

1. *Follow appropriate safety rules when riding in or on a motor vehicle.*
2. *Avoid driving a motor vehicle–or riding in a motor vehicle driven by someone–while under the influence of alcohol or other drugs.*
3. *Use safety equipment appropriately and correctly.*
4. *Apply safety rules and procedures to avoid risky behaviors and injury.*
5. *Avoid safety hazards in the home and community.*
6. *Recognize and avoid dangerous surroundings.*
7. *Get help for self or others when injured or suddenly ill.*
8. *Support others to avoid risky behaviors and be safe.*

Promoting Sexual Health (SH)

1. *Establish and maintain healthy relationships.*
2. *Be sexually abstinent.*
3. *Engage in behaviors that prevent or reduce sexually transmitted disease (STD), including HIV infection.*
4. *Engage in behaviors that prevent or reduce unintended pregnancy.*
5. *Avoid pressuring others to engage in sexual behaviors.*
6. *Support others to avoid or reduce sexual risk behaviors.*
7. *Treat others with courtesy and respect without regard to their sexuality.*
8. *Utilize appropriate health services to promote sexual health.*

Promote a Tobacco-Free Lifestyle (T)

1. *Avoid using (or experimenting with) any form of tobacco.*
2. *Avoid second-hand smoke.*
3. *Support a tobacco-free environment.*
4. *Support others to be tobacco-free.*
5. *Quit using tobacco, if already using.*

Prevent Violence (V)

1. *Manage interpersonal conflict in nonviolent ways.*
2. *Manage emotional distress in nonviolent ways.*
3. *Avoid bullying, being a bystander to bullying, or being a victim of bullying.*
4. *Avoid engaging in violence, including sexual harassment, coercion, exploitation, physical fighting, and rape.*
5. *Avoid situations where violence is likely to occur.*
6. *Avoid associating with others who are involved in or who encourage violence or criminal activity.*
7. *Get help to prevent or stop violence including harassment, abuse, bullying, hazing, fighting, and hate crimes.*
8. *Get help to prevent or stop inappropriate touching.*
9. *Get help to stop being subjected to violence or physical abuse.*
10. *Get help for oneself or others who are in danger of hurting themselves.*

SOURCE: Centers for Disease Control and Prevention, *Health Education Curriculum Analysis Tool* (Atlanta: Centers for Disease Control and Prevention, 2013) (www.cdc.gov/healthyyouth/hecat/).

Teacher's Toolbox 3.2

Advertising Techniques

1. *Bandwagon.* Everyone is using the product. Join the people who get it!
2. *Testimonials.* Famous people and experts endorse the product.
3. *Snob or cool appeal.* The coolest and most elite people use and talk about the product.
4. *Fun and friendship.* Friends have fun together using the product. This product can lead to new friendships.
5. *Just plain folks.* Ordinary people (the people next door) talk about the product as a good value that makes good sense.
6. *Humor.* Entertainment and laughter are used to sell the product.
7. *Emotion.* Strong emotional appeals are used to sell the product.
8. *Statistics.* Facts and figures that indicate consumers are making the best choice are used to sell the product.
9. *Romance.* Romantic situations are used to sell the product.
10. *Sex appeal.* Using this product will make you sexy like the spokespersons.
11. *Cultural or group pride and patriotism.* Pride in identity with a culture or group is used to sell the importance of belonging that comes with the product.
12. *Fear appeal.* Consumers should buy the product to prevent negative consequences (identity theft) or social consequences (bad breath).
13. *Exaggeration.* It's "the best ever!" It's "one of a kind!" "The solution is so simple!"
14. *Problem solvers.* This product will take care of everything and change your life.
15. *Repetition.* The same message or phrase is used over and over.
16. *First on the block.* The product will show that consumers are ahead of their time.
17. *Limited time offer.* Consumers are told they should buy the product now before the price goes up or the supply is all gone.

The theory of planned behavior is linked strongly to the skill of analyzing internal and external influences on health behaviors. As students examine social approval and pressures to participate or refuse to participate in a behavior, they are exploring the variable of subjective norms. The learning and assessment strategies in this text provide many hands-on opportunities to engage students in the process of taking direct action in understanding and responding to diverse influences.

Standard 3: Access Information, Products, and Services

Students Will Demonstrate the Ability to Access Valid Information and Products and Services to Enhance Health
NHES 1 and 3 are closely connected. Learning to access valid health information is as important as learning the information itself in promoting positive health behaviors. NHES 3 requires that students learn to identify, access, and evaluate the health-enhancing products and services they need.

Students make many health-related decisions in their day-to-day lives, often while being bombarded with incomplete and inaccurate information. Students must learn to identify credible sources of information and use that information to make healthy choices. Increasingly, students may find health sources through technology, such as the Internet. Other situations require students to seek advice from school and community health helpers.

Children are far more capable of conducting their own health investigations than many educators realize. Fourth-grade teacher Nadine Marchessault engaged her students in co-creating an integrated health and language arts curriculum, based on their questions and interests. The students worked in small groups to plan and complete research on topics such as building strength, divorce and resolving conflict, exercising, safety and first aid, food groups, learning strategies versus cheating, snacks and nutrition labels, and tobacco—a close match for the priority health topics addressed in this text. The students identified trustworthy information sources, interviewed knowledgeable adults, surveyed peers, compiled their research, and made oral presentations, which included developing visuals and handouts for the audience, extending formal invitations to other classes, and videotaping their presentations. Because the students selected their own topics, they worked tirelessly to complete their reports. As one student wrote in reflection, "It was scary, but we did good!" Perhaps most interesting, the students said at the beginning of the project that they were interested in learning new things but not so interested in school. At the end of the project, their interest increased in both categories. Working toward this standard provides opportunities for students to become questioning consumers of health information, products, and services. Questions such as "Who says?" and "What are their qualifications?" are part of NHES 3. Another important NHES 3 question is "Who benefits?"

Older individuals need these skills, too. To model their understanding of NHES 3, a group of teacher education students reported on Botox (botulinum toxin), used to temporarily paralyze facial muscles. Tiny amounts of injected Botox relax the facial muscles used in frowning and raise the eyebrows, temporarily removing wrinkles.[10] The students found striking before-and-after pictures on the Internet and excitedly recommended the Botox regimen to their peers, saying "Got wrinkles? Get Botox!" Questioning by their instructor revealed that the students had consulted only commercial (.com) websites for their report and had not ventured into education (.edu), professional organization (.org), or government (.gov) websites to critically evaluate the product. The students obviously did not meet NHES 3, and they conducted further investigations on the topic to report back to the class.

Teaching students to evaluate information, products, and services with a critical eye is consistent with the theory of planned behavior. As students explore information about and claims made for various products and services, they shape their attitudes toward health behaviors. For example, if the students in the preceding example had investigated Botox more thoroughly, they would have learned that repeated Botox treatments can result in drooping eyelids, headache, bruising, and other side effects such as reduced blinking, and weakness in the muscles of the face. In extreme cases, this muscle weakness can limit facial expressions.[11] Practicing skills—such as accessing valid information—can increase perceived behavioral control and self-efficacy as students gain confidence in their ability to practice healthy behaviors.

NHES 3 | *Students will demonstrate the ability to access valid information and products and services to enhance health.* (Keegan, age 12)

Standard 4: Interpersonal Communication

Students Will Demonstrate the Ability to Use Interpersonal Communication Skills to Enhance Health and Avoid or Reduce Health Risks

Students need to learn and practice communication skills in the context of their relationships with family, friends, and others. To become effective communicators, students need a wide variety of

realistic learning opportunities to try out their skills at resisting pressure, communicating empathy and support, managing conflicts, and asking for assistance. Practicing communication skills provides a natural link to language arts and performing arts as students engage in script writing, editing, rehearsing, and performing in various scenarios.

The theory of planned behavior supports communication lessons that provide the opportunity for students to express their intention to behave in a certain way, describe their attitudes, ascertain the position of others, and affirm their perceived ability to practice the behavior. For example, in dealing with a misunderstanding among friends, a student might state the intention to get the friends together to talk things out, explain why talking things out is a good idea, refer to others who use this practice successfully, and express confidence that the group of friends has the ability to come to a positive solution to the problem. The importance of teaching communication and peer resistance/refusal skills is explained further in the rest of this section.

Communication Skills

Effective communication includes many skills that do not come naturally—they must be learned. Just as athletes practice sport skills, young people need structured opportunities to practice effective communication skills.

Good communication skills are important in families, friendships, the classroom, and the workplace. The two main types of verbal communication skills are speaking and listening. Speaking skills include the ability to clearly convey a specific message. Many plans have been ruined because a person did not provide clear information to a listener (e.g., "We'll pick you up at 4:00 P.M. instead of 4:30."). Another important speaking skill is the use of I statements. Children can practice expressing their feelings by saying "I feel _____ when you _____." Most people receive I messages better than an accusatory "you" statement (e.g., "You always want to have it your way, and you make me sick!"). The way a person says something also is important. Changing one's tone of voice (soft or loud) or nonverbal cues (a wink or a stare) can completely change the message someone else receives.

NHES 4 | *Students will demonstrate the ability to use interpersonal communication skills to enhance health and avoid or reduce health risks.* (Kelli, age 13; Nicole, age 12)

1. Make eye contact with the speaker, when appropriate.
2. Give nonverbal cues, such as nodding and facing the speaker.
3. Don't interrupt. (Repeat: Don't interrupt.)
4. Paraphrase what the speaker says.
5. Ask appropriate questions.
6. Give feedback that is genuine and sincere.
7. Respond in an empathetic manner.

Listening is the second skill in oral communication. People feel good when they talk to a person who listens. On the other hand, they may feel discouraged when they try to have a conversation with someone who interrupts, never looks at them, or checks text messages throughout a conversation. "Empathic listening is a way of hearing what a person is feeling and responding to promote mutual understanding and trust." Teacher's Toolbox 3.3 identifies important strategies for listeners.

With the increasing use of social media, teachers also should address written communication skills. What is okay and not okay to post with regard to privacy, safety, and civility? What if the sender and recipient perceive a message very differently? What are the positive and negative uses of social media. Are kids sometimes hurt by social media? Teachers will have no problem engaging students in conversations about this topic, which is very much on the minds of young people.

Peer Resistance/Refusal Skills

Adolescents report that some of the most common reasons they initiate risky behaviors are that they believe that their friends do it, want to fit in with others, and need to belong to a group. Being accepted into a group is important at every age, but it is especially important during early adolescence. In contrast, lower-elementary children generally are egocentric and family-focused, which may result in a lack of attention toward other children. Upper-elementary children begin to extend beyond their family and to practice the important task of establishing their own identities. Although establishing an identity is developmentally appropriate and necessary, children may begin to participate in negative behaviors because of peer influence or because they want to be accepted by a group. For example, some children are influenced by friends to cheat on homework, lie to parents, or join in bullying another student.

Students benefit from participating in instructional activities that expose them to potential social pressures to participate in risky behaviors. These activities should be conducted in the safe and controlled environment of the classroom, under the supervision of a skilled teacher before students actually confront these pressures in real life. In this context, teachers can show video/movie/television clips about social pressures that young people experience or students can role-play the types of pressure situations they might encounter in or away from school. Teachers should follow with well-planned discussions and demonstrations

of how to get out of pressure situations and still maintain positive peer relationships. Because younger students (grades 3 to 5) admire "big kids," an excellent strategy is to have older students (grades 6–8) role-play pressure situations and demonstrate successful peer resistance skills.

Children need time to practice peer resistance skills in the classroom beginning around third grade. At this age, children show increased independence from adults and begin to rely more heavily on their peers. Teacher's Toolbox 3.4 provides peer pressure resistance techniques students can practice in the classroom.

Standard 5: Decision Making

Students Will Demonstrate the Ability to Use Decision-Making Skills to Enhance Health

NHES 5, decision making, is closely related to NHES 6, goal setting. The short- and long-term realistic goals that students set for themselves can provide important reasons to make good decisions for their health and future.

Thinking through decisions does not come naturally to most students. In fact, parents and teachers often are bewildered by the impulsivity of the young people in their care. R. E. Dahl indicated that, although adolescence generally is the healthiest and most resilient phase of the human life span, overall morbidity and mortality rates increase from childhood to adolescence, with the primary causes of death and disability in this age group related to problems with control of behavior and emotions.[12] These problems appear to be related to changes that occur in the brain before, during, and independently of adolescence.

Behaving as an adult requires the development of self-control over behavior and emotions. Adults change their behaviors to avoid negative future consequences, initiate and persist in certain courses of action, manage complex social situations even when strong emotions are involved, and self-regulate their feelings and behaviors to attain long-term goals. All these behaviors involve the prefrontal cortex of the brain, which is among the last regions of the brain to achieve full functional maturation. Dahl likened the challenge facing adolescents to starting the engines without a skilled driver. Today's adolescents experience earlier puberty, resulting in several years of living in a sexually mature body with sexually activated brain circuits—but with relatively immature neurobehavioral systems involved in self-control and emotional regulation.[13]

Adults want adolescents to demonstrate increasing self-control over their emotions and behavior, consider long-term consequences, abide by complex social rules, and use strategies and planning to move toward goals. Furthermore, parents and teachers want adolescents to accomplish these tasks during a time when they often experience strong and conflicting emotions. To complicate matters, many adolescents have a great deal of freedom but insufficient guidance as they try to navigate complex decision making. Thus, adolescents often show extremely poor decision making in real-life situations.[14]

In *Teenage Brain: A Work in Progress,* the National Institute of Mental Health (NIMH) reported that MRI studies show how

Peer Pressure Resistance Techniques

Give an excuse or a reason. This technique is familiar to most students, who use it in other types of situations, such as when they forget their homework or when they don't clean their room. Following are examples of reasons or excuses (here, for not smoking):

- I promised my dad I would come straight home after school.
- I'm allergic to smoke.
- I'm going to the movies with my older brother and his friends.

Avoid the situation or walk away. Have students think of ways to leave a situation to avoid being confronted with peer pressure to engage in an unhealthy behavior. For example, students may think that there will be alcohol at a party and choose not to go. If they find alcohol at a party when they get there, they may choose to leave. Following are examples of avoiding the situation or walking away:

- I can't right now—I have to finish my project by tomorrow morning.
- I can't go to the party because I'm grounded.
- I have to leave now—I'm supposed to be home in five minutes.

Change the subject. Students refuse an offer and then change the subject. For example, if a friend offers you a drink, say, "No, thanks. Say, where did you go last night after the ballgame?" Following are other examples of changing the subject:

- Are you going to Shelley's house to work on that science project?
- Let's go play some basketball.
- Let's stop by my house and get a snack.

Repeat the refusal. Students repeat the same response, with no additional response. Following are examples of repeated refusals:

- I don't want to.
- Not right now.
- No, thanks.

Strength in numbers, or recruit an ally. When students find friends who have the same values, they can find strength in numbers. Pressure situations become less difficult when friends support their decisions. Following are examples of strength in numbers:

- What would you do in this situation?
- What do you think I should do?
- Do you agree with what they want me to do?

Suggest alternatives. Students suggest healthy alternatives. Following are examples of alternatives:

- Let's go for a run.
- We can surprise Dad if we shovel the driveway before he gets home.
- Let's call Sherry and see if she's going to Sue's house.

NHES 5 | *Students will demonstrate the ability to use decision-making skills to enhance health.* (Brandy, age 12)

teens process emotions differently from adults.[15] Researchers scanned brain activity as subjects identified the emotions on pictures of faces displayed on a computer screen. Young teens, who characteristically perform poorly on the task, activated the amygdala, a brain center that mediates fear and other gut reactions, more than the frontal lobe. As teens grow older, their brain activity during this task tends to shift to the frontal lobe, leading to more reasoned perceptions and improved performance. The

NIMH concluded that while studies show remarkable changes occurring in the brain during the teen years, they also demonstrate what every parent can confirm: The teenage brain is a very complicated and dynamic arena that is not easily understood and definitely is in progress.

Continuing NIMH research reveals more on the striking changes taking place in the brain during the teen years. In key ways, the brain doesn't look like an adult's brain until the early 20s. The parts of the brain responsible for more "top-down" control, controlling impulses, and planning ahead—the hallmarks of adult behavior—are among the last to mature.[16]

Given the complexity of brain development and its relationship to emotional and behavioral control, the theory of planned behavior should be considered in its entirety. A simple one-shot approach (e.g., teaching a series of steps for decision making and then moving on to a new topic) is not sufficient for helping students develop their thought processes and skills. Identifying behavioral intentions, attitudes, subjective norms, and perceived behavioral control are all involved in thorough planning and teaching. Students need well-structured opportunities to identify the important issues for themselves and others inherent in the decisions they make. Health education can be planned to help them do this more thoughtfully.

Decision making is an important social skill that can empower students. Students, and even adults, often make decisions without really thinking about them. From a young age, children should be given opportunities and encouraged to make some decisions of their own, with the help of caring adults.

Children learn two important lessons when they are allowed to make some of their own choices. First, they learn that every choice is connected to a consequence. They learn that some choices produce results that are unpleasant or even dangerous. When children are allowed to experience minor unpleasant results, with adult support, they begin to understand decision making and its consequences in ways that serve them well as independent thinkers. Second, children learn that they will be held accountable for their choices. If parents, caregivers, and teachers hold children accountable for their decisions, children increasingly learn responsibility for their actions.

Johan Lehrer, author of *How We Decide*,[17] explains that both reason and emotion are necessary for good decision making. He recommends "thinking about thinking," saying, "Whenever you make a decision, be aware of the kind of decision you are making and the kind of thought process it requires. . . . The best way to make sure that you are using your brain properly is to study your brain at work, to listen to the argument inside your head."

Young children don't need to learn a formal decision-making model. Instead, children in the early elementary grades should be encouraged to make choices and then experience the resulting positive or negative outcomes of their choices. Children need opportunities to talk about their choices and the outcomes with caring adults. Upper-elementary and middle-level students are capable of using a formal decision-making model as a means of organizing their thoughts into a process for making the increasingly complex decisions that confront them. A variety of decision-making models can be found in health education curricula. Teacher's Toolbox 3.5 shows two models that work well with upper-elementary and middle-level students. Capture students' interest by asking them to think of themselves as pilots in a flight simulator.

Teachers must pay careful attention to the ideas and beliefs that students take away from their classroom when decision-making discussions end. Upper-elementary and middle-level students may use a decision-making model to rationalize exactly what they want to do, even if that behavior isn't healthy. Dr. Caryn Matsuoka[18] found that middle school students were adept at using the reasoning and inquiry skills they had learned in elementary school (i.e., Habits of the Mind,[19] Good Thinker's Toolkit[20]). Although most students were using their reasoning skills in positive ways to navigate their new middle school environments, at least one student indicated that he was using his reasoning skills to justify an action—stealing—that most of his peers and adults would consider harmful. Educators can use the theory of planned behavior to help students dig deeper into their thinking by linking their intentions and attitudes (in this case, potentially hurtful ones) to additional information to act in more health-enhancing ways. This information might involve subjective norms ("What do other classmates think? Do they think this is right or wrong? What do parents, teachers, and other family members think? Why? How would I feel if I made a

---

Teacher's Toolbox **3.5**

Example Decision-Making Models: Piloting the Flight Simulator

Ask students to think about practicing their decision-making skills like a pilot in a flight simulator. The problems they encounter require both reason and emotions to solve.

PRACTICE FLIGHTS FOR EARLY ELEMENTARY STUDENTS

1. *Problem.* Define the problem.
2. *Alternatives.* List alternative solutions.
3. *Pros and cons.* List the positive and negative consequences of each alternative, including thoughts and emotions.
4. *Choose.* Make a choice and try it.
5. *Evaluate.* How did it go? What would you do next time you fly?

PRACTICE FLIGHTS FOR UPPER-ELEMENTARY AND MIDDLE-LEVEL STUDENTS

1. *Define the problem.* Define the specific decision to be made.
2. *Identify a support group (co-pilots and flight crew).* Make a list of people who could help in making the decision. Include at least one adult on this list.
3. *List alternatives.* Brainstorm a list of all possible alternatives. Try to think of all the different ways this situation could be handled; come up with at least three. Questions for brainstorming include:

- What has worked in the past in a similar situation?
- What would an adult I respect do to solve this problem?
- What are some things I haven't tried that might work?

4. *Identify pros and cons.* List the pros and cons (positive and negative consequences) of each alternative. Consider both short- and long-term outcomes. Ask questions about each alternative:

- What would my family and friends think?
- What are my feelings and fears about each alternative?
- How does each alternative fit into my value system?

5. *Eliminate alternatives.* Cross out the alternatives that no longer seem acceptable. Consider your thoughts and emotions about each.
6. *Rank the remaining alternatives.* List the remaining solutions in the order you want to try them. (Eliminate this step if only one solution remains.)
7. *Try the chosen alternative.*
8. *Evaluate the choice.* What happened and why? Did you land the plane safely?

decision like this that went against their values and my values?") or perceived behavioral control ("How easy or difficult would it be for me to solve this problem?"). Teachers can ask other students to weigh in on perplexing issues by asking "What do others think about this? Is this a good decision for everyone involved? Why or why not? What could happen? What could happen after that? How could we look at this problem from another angle?" Students can help each other when they are encouraged to reason together in honest conversation within a safe environment.

Standard 6: Goal Setting

Students Will Demonstrate the Ability to Use Goal-Setting Skills to Enhance Health

NHES 6 calls for students to practice skills in goal setting. A goal is an aim related to something a person would like to do, have, or become. An achievable goal is within a person's power to accomplish in the short or long term. Without goals, children and adolescents, and even adults, may lose their sense of direction and make poor choices.

Health education lessons can help students assess their current health status and make plans to improve their health, taking into account variables such as their level of commitment, diverse alternatives, positive and negative consequences, barriers to progress, important steps toward their goals, and supports for their actions. Students also need to create ways to track their progress and evaluate their accomplishments—a tall order for most young people.

Health Educator Joyce Fetro states that without clear goals, students' personal efforts and hard work may not lead to the results they want. Conversely, learning to set achievable short- and long-term goals can help young people prioritize what's most important to them and work meaningfully toward getting where they want to go.[21] Teacher's Toolbox 3.6 provides a series of goal-setting steps for students.

Identifying supports for and barriers to achieving goals is an important part of the goal-setting process. Students can name family members and friends who want to see them succeed and can enlist their help in accomplishing their goals. Students need supporters who can provide a caring but honest appraisal. Similarly, students should think hard about attitudes, beliefs, experiences, or people ("Oh, one little piece of cake won't hurt you!") who might intentionally or unintentionally block their progress. Teachers and peers can help students plan strategies in advance to deal with barriers when they arise.

Learning to set a clear, achievable goal is a skill that young people need to master. Fetro recommends that students take time to perform a reality check on who and where they are and to

NHES 6 | *Students will demonstrate the ability to use goal-setting skills to enhance health.*
(Brittany, age 12; Chevante, age 12)

Teacher's Toolbox 3.6

Goal-Setting Steps

Set a long-term goal. What do you want to accomplish?

- Think about something specific you want to do or do better.
- Be sure your goal is SMART (specific, measurable, attainable, realistic, and time-bound).

Assess your situation. Where are you now, and where do you want to be in the future?

- How are you doing now?
- What do you want to change?

Make a plan. What steps do you need to take to achieve your goal?

- What resources will you need?
- Who will support your efforts?
- What short-term goals should you set to meet your long-term goal? How will you celebrate as you achieve them?
- What obstacles will you need to overcome? What will you do in case of setbacks?
- How long will it take to meet your goal? Develop a timeline.

Evaluate your progress. How did you do?

- If you reached your overall goal, celebrate your success and thank those who helped.
- If you have difficulty reaching your goal, rethink the goal-setting steps. Celebrate your successes along the way and make plans to try again.

develop a mental picture of where they want to go.[22] In terms of actually setting goals, students need practice in identifying aims that truly are important to them. For example, a young person who sets a goal of becoming a teacher mainly because his or her parents are teachers may find that teaching isn't the right career choice. Goals should be SMART (specific, measurable, attainable, realistic, and time-bound). How will a person know if steps toward the goal are having the desired effect? What would real progress look like?

Determining whether a goal is under a person's control is an essential step in the goal-setting process.[23] Health education lessons can help students realize that the only behavior they can manage is their own. For example, a student might enlist family support in collecting and taking bottles and cans from home to a recycling center in the neighborhood each Saturday. The student also can ask other families in the neighborhood to join the effort, but the decision to participate rests with each family. Thus, the goal that is within the student's control is to manage the recycling effort at home.

Making plans to track progress and evaluate how things are going is another important aspect of goal setting. Students can create personalized charts or graphs to provide a visual reminder of their goals. Students also can create their progress charts online. Students should make plans to celebrate progress along the way, by themselves or with others. The content chapters provide additional learning and assessment strategies for helping students learn and practice successful goal setting.

NHES 7 | *Students will demonstrate the ability to practice health-enhancing behaviors and avoid or reduce risks.* (Tisha, age 12; Janna, age 12; Kuulei, age 12)

Standard 7: Self-Management

Students Will Demonstrate the Ability to Practice Health-Enhancing Behaviors and Avoid or Reduce Risks

Having students adopt and maintain healthy behaviors is the goal of school health education. Providing opportunities for students to learn and practice a range of personal and social skills to promote health is the focus in the classroom. Ultimately, young people and adults choose their own courses of action in health-related matters. Teachers can ensure that children are prepared with a ready tool kit of health skills and knowledge to assist them in making the decisions and taking the actions that are best for them. Teachers don't assess students on the health behaviors they actually practice. Rather, teachers assess them on their ability to demonstrate personal and social skills to facilitate and promote healthy behavior.

The content chapters contain teaching strategies for helping children learn to be good self-managers. In many instances, self-management skills naturally overlap with other personal and social skills, such as communication and decision making. Teachers and students can think of self-management as the "doing" skill—the actions students actually take to keep themselves and others healthy and safe in real-life situations.

In the classroom, students can work together to create strategies to use in potentially challenging situations. For example, middle school students might plan to carry a cell phone or money for a cab with them whenever they are riding with others to social events, such as parties or ball games. If the person they are supposed to ride home with begins drinking, the students then have a way to call for a ride with a sober driver, whether a parent, older sibling, friend, or taxi driver. Performing healthy practices such as hand washing and flossing and learning to stop your own nosebleed are other examples of self-management.

Behavioral rehearsals are an important part of learning self-management. Practicing ways to deal with strong emotions (e.g., counting to ten) and stress (e.g., going for a walk, talking to a friend, listening to music) is helpful to students of all ages, even those in kindergarten. For example, when young children demonstrate alternatives such as walking away, saying "Stop it!" or asking a teacher for help when classmates persist in mean-spirited teasing, they are practicing self-management skills. Relieving stress during exam periods by taking deep breaths to calm the mind, standing for stretch breaks between testing sessions, or using positive self-talk also helps students build their tool kit of personal self-management strategies.

The intention to practice healthy behavior is an important component of the theory of planned behavior. However, intention by itself is not enough—it must work together with the other components of the model (attitudes, subjective norms, and perceived behavioral control).

The theory of planned behavior advocates using the whole model to create learning opportunities for students. To start, students need accurate and complete information (e.g., individuals can contract STDs from oral sex as well as from vaginal intercourse) to help them develop healthy attitudes and make informed decisions. Students also need to examine norms related to the behavior of their peers (e.g., most middle and high school students do not have intercourse) and explore the beliefs of their families and friends about sexuality. Finally, students need assistance in building their perceived behavioral control and self-efficacy with respect to decisions and actions related to sexuality. For example, health education lessons can provide opportunities for students to anticipate challenging situations (e.g., potential risks involved in going to someone's house when parents are not at home) and to practice peer resistance and other self-management skills before they face actual risk-taking situations. In summary, telling students the attitude that they "should" have (the familiar "just say no") without further education results in many students just not buying it.

NHES 8 | *Students will demonstrate the ability to advocate for personal, family, and community health.*
(Sterling, age 12; Taylor, age 12; Samantha, age 12)

Standard 8: Advocacy

Students Will Demonstrate the Ability to Advocate for Personal, Family, and Community Health

NHES 8 calls for students to learn the skills they need to advocate for personal, family, and community health. Becoming an advocate for health means learning to promote and encourage positive health choices and to take a stand to make a difference on a health-related issue.

Students must learn to declare their positions clearly when they try to educate and influence others about important issues. As advocates, students also assume the role of supporting others to promote healthy social norms. Any advocacy effort should have a healthy norms component. Advocacy campaigns can be especially effective when older students work with younger children. Students often believe that "everyone is doing it" in terms of health-risk behaviors. Well-planned advocacy efforts can help young people recognize that same-age and older peers are making healthy choices.

The theory of planned behavior supports health education lessons that help students understand that their family and friends want them to act in healthy ways. Students also gain perceived behavioral control when they see that their classmates and older students support and engage in healthy behaviors. Health education lessons about advocacy should be relevant to students' interests and development. If students aren't interested in an issue, advocacy efforts might be a shallow exercise. For example, social pressures to use tobacco usually begin in early adolescence.

Thus, upper-elementary and middle-level students will be more attuned to tobacco prevention campaigns than will lower-elementary students.

Educators can invite students to tackle health advocacy issues for their whole school by framing their efforts around the Whole School, Whole Community, Whole Child (WSCC) model (Chapter 1). How can students envision each WSCC component contributing to an advocacy effort? Upper-elementary and middle-level students might plan and carry out a campaign to promote daily physical activity in the following ways:

- *Health education:* Help design and teach hands-on lessons for younger students that help them learn about the health benefits of cardiorespiratory (aerobic) endurance, muscular strength and endurance, flexibility, and body composition.
- *Health services:* Consult with school health services personnel for guidelines on how individuals with asthma, allergies, or other chronic conditions can participate safely in physical activity.
- *Physical environment:* Work with administrators to ensure access to water fountains and bottled water. Ask school administrators for permission to design a walking trail on the school grounds.
- *Nutrition environment and services:* Work with school food service personnel to create gardens for growing food that can be served in the school cafeteria.
- *Counseling, psychological, and social services:* Ask school counselors to help students understand the social and emotional benefits of physical activity.
- *Physical education:* Help design and teach lessons for younger students that focus on ways to increase activity (three

students per long jump rope, alternating often as turners and jumpers, rather than one long line waiting for one jump rope) during physical education and recess periods.

- *Employee wellness:* Interview teachers and staff about the kinds of physical activity that interest them, and design opportunities that are student-led.
- *Community involvement and employee engagement:* Involve parents and community members in a campaign to increase physical activity by recording their activity on student-designed posters and charts. Ask community businesses to donate funds for Frisbees, jump ropes, and balls for recess periods.
- *Social and emotional climate:* Increase opportunities for physical activity during transition times throughout the day to boost prosocial behaviors and emotional health of students and staff.

PLANNING EFFECTIVE SCHOOL HEALTH EDUCATION

Building on Evaluation Research

"Healthy kids make better learners" is a reminder educators often use to stress the importance of effective health education in K–8 classrooms. As discussed in Chapter 1, research data indicate that school health education can contribute to students' well-being and school achievement.

The goal of health education is for students to adopt and maintain healthy behaviors. To this end, health education should contribute directly to students' ability to engage in health-enhancing behaviors and avoid behaviors that can lead to poor health. Unfortunately, common approaches to health education (having students take notes from lectures, memorize information for a test, or complete stacks of worksheets) show little or no evidence of being effective.

Chapter 2 described the characteristics of health education lessons that are consistent with evaluation research. These characteristics are the foundation of the recommendations and strategies for teaching health education in this text. The theory of planned behavior serves as a starting point for planning. The introductory and content chapters focus on teaching the most important concepts using a skills-based approach to achieve healthy behaviors. This chapter and the content chapters assist educators with planning health education that is effective, engages students, and fits naturally into the K–8 curriculum.

Working with the Big Picture in Mind

Earlier in this chapter, readers "met" the eight National Health Education Standards. A math educator asked during a health curriculum presentation, "What makes these standards unique to health education? Mathematics teachers also want students to communicate with each other, make good decisions, and learn core concepts as they engage in mathematics." The answer to this question lies in the priority health content areas (e.g., healthy eating, preventing violence) that provide the context for students to learn the health education standards.

How can the standards and content areas be integrated into a cohesive, manageable, and memorable approach to curriculum planning? Teacher's Toolbox 3.7 provides an example of an

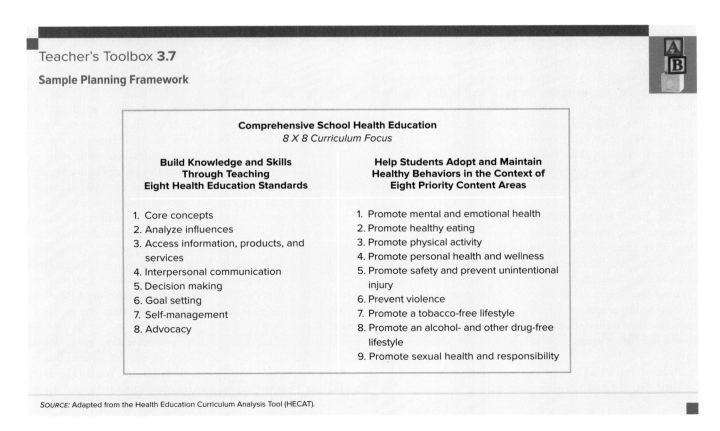

Teacher's Toolbox **3.7**

Sample Planning Framework

Comprehensive School Health Education	
8 X 8 Curriculum Focus	
Build Knowledge and Skills Through Teaching Eight Health Education Standards	**Help Students Adopt and Maintain Healthy Behaviors in the Context of Eight Priority Content Areas**
1. Core concepts	1. Promote mental and emotional health
2. Analyze influences	2. Promote healthy eating
3. Access information, products, and services	3. Promote physical activity
4. Interpersonal communication	4. Promote personal health and wellness
5. Decision making	5. Promote safety and prevent unintentional injury
6. Goal setting	6. Prevent violence
7. Self-management	7. Promote a tobacco-free lifestyle
8. Advocacy	8. Promote an alcohol- and other drug-free lifestyle
	9. Promote sexual health and responsibility

SOURCE: Adapted from the Health Education Curriculum Analysis Tool (HECAT).

eight-by-eight focus for the health curriculum. A grid of the standards and content areas can be created to pinpoint the emphasis at the elementary and middle school levels.

Teaching to Standards

What does it mean to teach to standards? For many educators, this is a new way of thinking. When teachers begin to plan around standards, they sometimes find that some of their long-used classroom approaches don't connect clearly to important learning. For example, middle school health educator Lynn Shoji stated that she realized she was spending so much time on content (facts) that she didn't have enough time for the personal and social skill development outlined in the health education standards. Still, the content was important. She solved this dilemma by teaching her students to conduct their own research (NHES 3) and share their findings with the rest of the class. Her students learned communication (NHES 4) and advocacy (NHES 8) skills in making their presentations. Having the courage to examine familiar teaching habits can lead to meaningful new ways to help students succeed.

Another challenge is rethinking activities that have become classroom favorites because students find them enjoyable. If the activity under scrutiny can be linked to standards, content areas, healthy behaviors, and theoretical constructs, it deserves a closer look. A learning activity called "Balloon-Up," found in Chapter 5, is engaging and interactive—and also links directly to standards-based teaching. Balloon-Up allows students to experience a simple decision-making model first-hand in the classroom, which helps in meeting NHES 5. The model then can be applied in the context of any content area to help students consider healthy behaviors, their intentions toward a behavior, what they believe their family and friends think about a behavior, and how successful they believe they would be at carrying out the behavior. Students can demonstrate learning through story or script writing about a decision they need to make, and demonstrate each step of the decision-making model in their writing. Used simply as an activity to fill class time, Balloon-Up has little relevance other than as a study break. However, if Balloon-Up is used to engage students in discussions about the decisions they encounter in and out of school, alternatives, and the consequences of their decisions, it becomes a teaching strategy with purpose in the curriculum.

This chapter and the content chapters (5–14) are filled with standards-based learning strategies. Thoughtful planning means more than choosing an activity for the day. Teachers should select strategies carefully to help students learn what they need to know and how to apply it.

Teachers can conduct an Internet search to compare and contrast the health education standards for local and state education agencies. How do the standards align with national standards? How do education agencies differ in terms of the topic areas they cover?

Readers also should locate the health education curriculum for their district education agency and school.

Yearly Planning

Teacher's Toolbox 3.8 provides an example of a yearly health education plan, based on the healthy behavior outcomes that serve as a basis for teaching concepts and skills across content areas. The healthy behavior outcomes build on one another and grow in complexity from one grade cluster to the next.

The sample yearly plan focuses each month on a particular content area. Lessons might or might not be taught daily, but they should at a minimum be taught weekly. Educators don't expect children to learn to read with occasional hit-or-miss language arts lessons. Similarly, devoting sufficient instructional time to health education increases the potential to help students develop healthy behaviors. Scheduling adjustments can be made as needed in middle schools, where semesters or quarters might be the norm.

Working from this broad yearly plan, educators at the local level can develop a more detailed weekly scope (concepts and skills) and sequence (order) appropriate for their students. For example, the healthy behavior outcome "practicing safety rules and procedures" in grades K–2 typically includes learning concepts and practicing skills related to fire, school bus, pedestrian, and playground safety. However, these curriculum decisions should be local. Children who live in coastal or island communities, for example, need to learn ocean and sun safety, whereas children who live in very cold climates need to learn how to protect themselves during winter conditions.

The Health Education Curriculum Analysis Tool provides information on developing scope and sequence in health education. The HECAT notes that scope and sequence should address the concepts and skills students need *before* they encounter health-risk situations, help coordinate instruction within standards and across grade levels, and show reinforcement of skills and concepts without excessive repetition.

Unit Planning

From a yearly plan, educators move to decisions about units of study related to a particular topic or theme. Units are more than a collection of daily lesson plans or health activities for the day. They address important questions and ideas that invite students' curiosity and engagement. Common threads of inquiry connect one lesson to the next and to children's lives. In health education, units can be created to answer important questions about a content area (What does it mean for elementary students to express feelings in healthy ways) or a skill (How can middle school students use social media in safe and healthy ways?). The authors encourage unit developers to focus on intriguing questions that students want to answer (e.g., How do we make all parts of our school safe from bullying?) rather than single-word topics or themes that likely are too broad to be covered in one unit (e.g., safety).

Teacher education programs and education agencies use a variety of unit formats. Educators should ask for information on local methods and sample units. Grant Wiggins and Jay McTighe have written extensively about their backward design

Sample Yearly Plan Based on Healthy Behaviors, Grades K–8

Month	Content Area (chapter)	Grades K–2* Build for 3–8 ⇒	Grades 3–5* Build ⇒	Grades 6–8* ⇒ Build from K–5
July–August	Promoting mental and emotional health (5)**	• Express feelings in a healthy way. • Engage in activities that are mentally and emotionally healthy. • Prevent and manage interpersonal conflict in healthy ways.	• Prevent and manage emotional stress and anxiety in healthy ways. • Use self-control and impulse-control strategies to promote health.	• Get help for troublesome thoughts, feelings, or actions for self and others. • Show tolerance and acceptance of differences in others. • Establish and maintain healthy relationships.
September	Promoting healthy eating (6)	• Eat the appropriate number of servings from each food group every day. • Eat a variety of foods within each food group every day. • Eat an abundance of fruits and vegetables every day. • Choose to eat whole grain products and fat-free or low-fat milk or equivalent milk products regularly. • Drink plenty of water every day.	• Limit foods and beverages high in added sugars, solid fat, and sodium. • Eat breakfast every day. • Eat healthy snacks. • Eat healthy foods when dining out.	• Prepare food in healthful ways. • Balance caloric intake with caloric expenditure. • Follow an eating plan for healthy growth and development. • Support others to eat healthy.
October	Promoting physical activity (7)	• Engage in moderate to vigorous physical activity for at least 60 minutes every day. • Drink plenty of water before, during, and after physical activity.	• Engage in warm-up and cool-down activities before and after structured exercise. • Avoid injury during physical activity. • Support others to be physically active	• Follow a physical activity plan for healthy growth and development. • Regularly engage in physical activities that enhance cardio-respiratory endurance, flexibility, muscle endurance, and muscle strength.
November	Promoting safety and preventing unintentional injury (8)	• Use safety equipment appropriately and correctly. • Apply safety rules and procedures to avoid risky behaviors and injury. • Avoid safety hazards in the home and community.	• Follow appropriate safety rules when riding in or on a motor vehicle. • Avoid driving a motor vehicle—or riding in a motor vehicle driven by someone—while under the influence of alcohol or other drugs.	• Recognize and avoid dangerous surroundings. • Get help for self or others when injured or suddenly ill. • Support others to avoid risky behaviors and be safe.
December	Promoting personal health and wellness (9)	• Brush and floss teeth daily. • Practice appropriate hygiene habits. • Get an appropriate amount of sleep and rest. • Prevent vision and hearing loss.	• Prevent damage from the sun. • Practice behaviors that prevent infectious diseases. • Practice behaviors that prevent chronic diseases. • Prevent serious health problems that result from common chronic diseases and conditions among youth, such as allergies, asthma, diabetes, and epilepsy.	• Practice behaviors that prevent foodborne illnesses. • Seek out help for common infectious diseases and chronic diseases and conditions. • Seek out healthcare professionals for appropriate screenings and examinations. • Prevent health problems that result from fads or trends.
January	Preventing violence (10)	• Manage interpersonal conflict in nonviolent ways. • Manage emotional distress in nonviolent ways. • Avoid bullying, being a bystander to bullying, or being a victim of bullying. • Get help to prevent or stop inappropriate touching.	• Get help to stop being subjected to violence or physical abuse. • Get help for one self or others who are in danger of hurting themselves. • Avoid situations where violence is likely to occur.	• Avoid engaging in violence, including sexual harassment, coercion, exploitation, physical fighting, and rape. • Avoid associating with others who are involved in or who encourage violence or criminal activity. • Get help to prevent or stop violence including harassment, abuse, bullying, hazing, fighting, and hate crimes.
February	Promoting a tobacco-free lifestyle (11)	• Avoid second-hand smoke.	• Avoid using (or experimenting with) any form of tobacco. • Support a tobacco-free environment.	• Support others to be tobacco-free. • Quit using tobacco, if already using.
March	Promoting an AOD-free lifestyle (12)	• Avoid misuse and abuse of over-the-counter and prescription drugs. • Support others to be alcohol- and other drug-free.	• Avoid experimentation with alcohol and other drugs. • Avoid the use of alcohol. • Avoid the use of illegal drugs.	• Avoid riding in a motor vehicle with a driver who is under the influence of alcohol or other drugs. • Quit using alcohol and other drugs if already using.
April	Promoting sexual health (13)	• Establish and maintain healthy relationships.	• Treat others with courtesy and respect without regard to their sexuality.	• Be sexually abstinent. • Avoid pressuring others to engage in sexual behaviors. • Support others to avoid or reduce sexual risk behaviors.
May–June	Revisiting mental and emotional health (5)	• Help students prepare for a healthy summer break!	• Help students prepare for a healthy summer break!	• Help students prepare for a healthy summer break!

SOURCE: *Adapted from the Centers for Disease Control and Prevention, *Health Education Curriculum Analysis Tool* (Atlanta: Centers for Disease Control and Prevention, 2013)
**Include material on managing loss, death, and grief here or later in the year (Chapter 14).

approach to unit planning known as Understanding by Design (UbD).[24] UbD units are planned in three stages:

1. Clarify desired results.
   - What content standards or goals will this unit address?
   - What habits of mind and cross-disciplinary goals will this unit address?
2. Determine needed evidence.
   - What criteria will be used in each assessment to evaluate attainment of the desired results?
   - What qualities of the evidence are most important?
3. Develop the learning plan.
   - What pre-assessments will be used to check students' prior knowledge, skill levels, and potential misconceptions?
   - Does the learning plan reflect principles of learning and best practices?
   - Is the learning plan tightly aligned with stages 1 and 2?
   - Is the plan likely to be engaging and effective for all students?[25]

In *Integrating Differentiated Instruction + Understanding by Design,* Carol Ann Tomlinson and Jay McTighe expand on the backward design process.[26] Teacher's Toolbox 3.9 provides a backward design template adapted for health education units or lessons. Readers may be especially interested in the health education unit "You Are What You Eat": A Unit Planned with Backward Design, included in the Tomlinson and McTighe text.

In addition to the HECAT, teachers can locate excellent Internet resources for health education unit and lesson planning. The following websites provide a good starting place:

BAM: Body and Mind (www.cdc.gov/bam)

HealthTeacher: Classroom tools to help kids live well (www.healthteacher.com)

PE Central (www.pecentral.org)

WebQuest.org (www.webquest.org)

CAST UDL Lesson Builder (www.lessonbuilder.cast.org)

Units offer many possibilities for curriculum integration with other subject areas. A unit on helping students express their feelings in healthy ways could explore the skills of interpersonal communication, decision making, and self-management within the content area of promoting mental and emotional health. Teaching through children's literature provides a natural link with language arts. Suggestions for children's literature are included in each content chapter; a combined list of recommended books can be found on the Online Learning Center.

Lesson Planning

The task of lesson planning can seem overwhelming to teacher education students, student teachers, and beginning teachers, especially when their mentor teachers and more experienced colleagues appear to work from notes jotted in their planning books.

Teaching about health through children's literature helps engage students and allows for curriculum integration with language arts.

Effective lesson planning is a skill that new teachers sharpen with experience and feedback from other educators.

Building on Wiggins and McTighe's backward design, this text offers a format that can be used for planning units or lessons.

Step 1: Focus on my students (Who are they? What are their learning needs?)

Step 2: Desired results (What do I want my students to understand and be able to do?)

Step 3: Assessment evidence (How will students show what they learn?)

Step 4: Active learning plan (How will I teach so all my students learn?)

Step 5: Reflection (What did we learn? How can I improve teaching and learning next time?)

Teacher's Toolbox 3.9 illustrates this format, customized for the health education standards and content areas discussed in this text. A step-by-step look at this lesson design process follows.

1: Focus on My Students

Planning starts with thinking about your students—their backgrounds, experiences, and the strengths they bring to the classroom. This section should include initial thoughts on differentiation for diverse learners.

2: Desired Results

The next step is to identify *desired results.* What do you want your students to understand and be able to do as a result of your plan? What end do you have in mind? Thinking through the following ideas can help you create a meaningful plan. This example focuses on interpersonal communication skills (NHES 4).

Standards: Health education standard(s) and performance indicator(s) Teachers begin by selecting standards and performance indicators to focus the lesson. A standard provides a broad target for the lesson (e.g., students demonstrate the ability to use interpersonal communication skills to enhance health).

Planning Template for Health Education

Title: _____

Developed by: _____ Grade level: _____ Date: _____

Step 1: Focus on My Students
- What do I know about my students?
- What are their learning needs?
- How will I modify or adapt my lessons so all of my students learn?

Step 2: Desired Results (What do I want my students to learn?)
- **Standards:** Health education standard(s) and performance indicator(s)
- **Context:** Health content area(s)
- **Behavior:** Healthy behavior(s)
- **Theory to Practice:** Theory of planned behavior construct(s)
- **Differentiation:** Enrichment, IEP objectives, or other plans for diverse learners

Step 3: Assessment Evidence (How will students show what they learn?)
- **Performance Task:** What will students *do* to demonstrate learning?
- **Criteria:** How good is good enough? (Show checklists, rubrics, or other criteria.)
- **Other Evidence:** Self-reflections, quizzes, tests, observations, journals, homework

Step 4: Active Learning Plan (How will I teach so all my students learn?)

• **Steps for Students:** What will students do during the lesson? (detailed sequence)	• **Reminders for Teachers:** What do I need to remember to say and do?

- **Materials:** What materials do I need to have ready?
- **Time:** Approximately how much time do I need?
- **Resources:** Where did I get my ideas?

Step 5: Reflection (What did we learn? How will I improve teaching and learning next time?)
- What happened during my lessons (what did the students and I say and do)? How effective was my lesson design and teaching?
- What evidence can I show that my students learned about health (e.g., student work or other response)? How effective was my assessment plan for getting information about what they learned?
- How did I do in meeting my desired results for these health lessons? What are my next steps to improve student learning for health?

SOURCE: Adapted from A.C. Tomlinson and J. McTighe, *Integrating Differentiated Instruction + Understanding by Design.* (Alexandria, VA: Association for Supervision and Curriculum Development, 2011).

Performance indicators give more detail about how the standard looks in practice and the purpose of the lesson (students demonstrate healthy ways to express needs, wants, and feelings). A unit or lesson based on this standard and performance indicator should help students learn to communicate openly and honestly in ways that are beneficial to everyone concerned. Focusing on one standard and performance indicator is perfectly acceptable, especially for those who are new to unit and lesson planning. However, units and lessons can focus on several standards at once, including standards from other content areas (e.g., an integrated lesson that addresses standards in both health education

and performing arts). See health standards and performance indicators in Appendix A.

Context: Health content area(s) The health content areas provide the context or backdrop for teaching communication skills that promote good health. For younger children, the content area of Promoting Mental and Emotional Health provides an excellent context for learning to communicate needs, wants, and feelings in ways that are helpful rather than hurtful. Elementary teachers can help children think through and practice the difference between tattling (trying to get someone in trouble) and helping (getting adult help when someone is in danger, upset, or might get hurt), both of which involve interpersonal communication. Upper-elementary students can learn to communicate needs, wants, and feelings in ways that promote calm rather than confrontational responses in tense situations. Middle-level students can compare and contrast communication skills in pressure situations across content areas. For example, although a student might say in response to pressure to smoke, "Nah, not now, let's go play basketball." The same response wouldn't work at all in a pressure situation to have sex! What could students say instead? Chapters 5 to 14 provide communication skill strategies across health content areas.

Behavior: Healthy behavior(s)

Identifying the healthy behavior focus for the unit or lesson provides the underlying reason for teaching. What healthy behaviors do educators want students to have the knowledge and skills to practice throughout their lives? In the content area of Safety or Promoting an Alcohol- and Other Drug-Free Lifestyle, units or lessons might focus on the healthy behavior of "Avoid riding in a car with a driver who is under the influence of alcohol or other drugs." The communication skills a young person needs to promote this healthy behavior can be tremendously complex. Children may have no choice about riding with an adult who is inebriated and might risk an abusive response if they protest. Respectfully asking to ride with someone else ("I'd like to ride with Auntie Lynn") or to stay behind ("Could I stay over at Sam's house tonight?") might be viable alternatives students could consider in the safe environment of the classroom. The healthy behaviors teachers are trying to promote over time are an important component of health units and lessons. See a summary of healthy behaviors in Teacher's Toolbox 3.1.

Theory to Practice: Theory of planned behavior construct(s)

Educators often speak of linking theory to practice. The Theory of Planned Behavior (Chapter 2) provides a guide to key factors that are most likely to influence students' health behavior. With limited time for health education in the K–8 curriculum, the constructs help in planning units and lessons that truly can make a difference. The constructs are

1. Intentions to act
2. Attitudes toward a behavior
3. Subjective norms (perceived social pressures related to a behavior)
4. Perceived behavioral control (perceived ease or difficulty of performing a behavior)

Educators can fine-tune units and lessons by thinking through which of these constructs they are trying to influence. A lesson on interpersonal communication within the context of Promoting a Tobacco-Free Lifestyle, designed to help students avoid using tobacco, could be drawn from the constructs *intention to act* ("I will use my words and actions to say no to tobacco, even if older kids pressure me after school") and perceived behavioral control ("I've practiced in lots of situations with my friends in the classroom, and I believe I can use repeated refusals without making a big deal out of it or losing my friends"). The teaching strategies in this textbook are aligned with one or more constructs, which can help educators think carefully about assessment. For example, older students

could interview family members and friends about their views on dating (subjective norms). To demonstrate their learning, students could design a questionnaire, conduct interviews, compile data, display results, and draw conclusions about the healthy ways in which their friends and families want them to act.

Differentiation: Enrichment, IEP objectives, or other plans for diverse learners

Differentiation means planning to ensure that all students have the opportunity to learn. Educators must consider the needs and characteristics of all the children in their classroom to make learning meaningful, rather than one size fits all. For example, the learning strategy *Punahele Bear: How Do We Talk to Each Other?* in Chapter 5 provides several considerations for differentiation. One is that some students may want to watch and listen rather than actually provide examples of words or actions that they hear or see at school. In particular, young children may not want to say "mean words" they've heard, even as part of a learning activity. Another consideration for differentiation might involve planning for children in the class who are unable to speak, hear, or walk. What modifications or adaptations can a teacher make to allow them to participate in the activity? Teachers also can provide differentiation by permitting students to choose one of several performance tasks to work on alone or with a partner.

To learn more about meeting the needs of diverse learners, teachers can investigate Universal Design for Learning (UDL). UDL is a framework for designing educational environments that enable all learners to gain knowledge, skills, and enthusiasm for learning. UDL helps reduce barriers to the curriculum and provide supports for learning. Teachers can learn more through the National Center on Universal Design for Learning at www.udlcenter.org/aboutudl/udlguidelines. In addition, the National Center on Response to Intervention (RTI) helps schools identify students at risk for poor learning outcomes, monitor student progress, provide evidence-based interventions and adjust the intensity and nature of those interventions depending on a student's responsiveness, and identify students with learning disabilities or other disabilities. Teachers can learn more at www.rti4success.org/.

3: Assessment Evidence

Assessment should have the same characteristics as instruction—it should be meaningful and significant for students and their families. Educators call this kind of assessment "authentic," which is another way of saying something is valued in school and the world outside the school.[27] Assessment should be planned concurrently with instruction, rather than as an afterthought when a grade is needed. Educators should think beyond pencil-and-paper testing for assessment. Teacher's Toolbox 3.10 provides an extensive list of strategies that allow students to demonstrate their knowledge and skills.

Performance Task: What will students do to demonstrate learning?

A performance task describes what students will do to show learning and meeting standards. As indicated in Teacher's Toolbox 3.10, tasks might include creating a marketing campaign, designing and implementing a research project, developing a presentation or exhibition, or participating in a service learning project. Educators should think of the word *do* in relation to designing

Assessment Strategies for Health Education Concepts and Skills

Students can complete many kinds of individual and group projects to demonstrate their understanding of the concepts and skills in the National Health Education Standards.

Written	Oral	Visual	Kinesthetic
Brochure	Debate	Advertisement	Dance
Journal	Discussion	Diagram	Field trip
Portfolio	Role-play	Image	Game
Poem	Song	Infographic	Play
Research report	Video	Poster	Simulations
Story		Slide show (Prezi, etc.)	Skits
		Website	Stations

performance tasks. What will students do to demonstrate their learning that others can read, see, hear, and feel? The key is to ensure that performance tasks fit well with the standards and performance indicators that students will demonstrate. Students become deeply involved in designing and demonstrating their knowledge and skills in engaging performance tasks.

Criteria: How good is good enough? (Show checklists, rubrics, or other criteria.) Students also enjoy collaborating to determine the qualities of a good performance. The question teachers and students want to answer in terms of criteria is, "How good is good enough?" To illustrate, there are many ways to create a presentation or exhibition that students can use to demonstrate the advanced communication skills required for advocacy (NHES 8). Criteria for creating a good presentation or exhibition as a performance task could require students to provide information from at least three valid sources, ensure that all their information is correct, make two or more connections between behaviors and health, and show evidence of targeting their message to a particular audience (classmates). Educators should note that criteria relating to technical matters such as layout, grammar, spelling, and use of computer graphics are not health related. If such procedural criteria are part of the overall assessment, they should be identified clearly and scored separately from the health criteria.

Other Evidence: Self-reflections, quizzes, tests, observations, journals, homework In addition to a performance task that is the culminating or *summative* assessment of a student's work, teachers should collect other evidence about a student's progress. Teachers can use quizzes, observations of how students work together, journals, homework, or self-reflections as additional evidence of learning. These in-progress checks on learning are called *formative* assessments. Formative assessment involves giving students meaningful feedback to help them improve their performance. Teachers can learn more about formative assessment in the excellent resource, *Checking for Understanding: Formative Assessment Techniques for Your Classroom,* by Douglas Fisher and Nancy Frey.[28] Fisher and Frey explore formative

assessment through oral language, questions, writing, projects and performances, tests, and common assessments and consensus scoring. Similarly, Connie Moss and Susan Brookhart explain in *Advancing Formative Assessment in Every Classroom* that teachers and students engage in formative assessment when they focus on learning goals, take stock of where current work is in relation to the goal, and take action to move closer to the goal.[29]

4: Active Learning Plan

Wiggins and McTighe describe the "twin sins" of typical instructional design in schools as coverage-focused teaching and activity-focused teaching.[30] Coverage-focused instruction, with an emphasis on learning factual material, has been typical of health education in the past. However, new and even experienced teachers sometimes find it tempting to plan by choosing activities that children think are "fun." Educators often see engaging hands-on teaching ideas at workshops and understandably are eager to try them with their students. In keeping with the recommendations of Wiggins and McTighe, however, educators should start with desired results and assessment evidence and then identify the active teaching strategies that will best help students learn and demonstrate learning.

There are many ways to structure learning plans. Teacher candidates should seek out the format used in their teacher education program. New teachers can talk with experienced teachers and the curriculum directors in their school or district to learn whether there is a preferred planning template.

A learning plan should begin with an introduction that grabs students' interest. Some educators refer to this "hook" as the anticipatory set or focusing event. For example, to start a lesson on interpersonal communication skills, a teacher might arrange for someone to call on a cell phone, at the beginning of the lesson. The teacher could use exaggerated words, tone, and facial expressions to heighten the students' interest in the call. In other words, teachers can do much more than simply state, "Today, boys and girls, we are going to learn about communication."

Interesting introductions are followed by a logical sequence of learning activities that flow one to another. In the learning plan featured in Teacher's Toolbox 3.9, the authors suggest thinking first in terms of what *students* will do, with notes alongside that provide important reminders for teachers. This procedure gets the focus where it should be—on the students and what they are doing to learn. In learning plans of this type, teachers might write, "Students will participate in the Lilo and Stitch learning strategy about pressure situations (Chapter 5) and then identify different ways they saw classmates use their words, voices, facial expressions, and body movements to communicate effectively." This approach moves from the teacher's role as, "I will explain, I will model, I will demonstrate," to one of facilitator and guide, as students explore a real-time situation in which they just participated. In any learning plan, teachers must keep the classroom environment safe and positive.

Good learning plans end with a closing that helps students think back on what they've learned. A new teacher illustrated the importance of helping children reflect on the reason for the lesson. Her second graders participated in a parachute activity for physical education, during which the children spontaneously chanted, "Shake, shake, shake!" They were flapping the parachute to toss lightweight plastic balls high in the air in hopes of sending them through the hole in the center of the chute, or bounce certain balls off the chute while keeping others aloft by adjusting their shakes as a group. The teacher, confident that the children had understood the importance of teamwork, asked a little boy what he had learned that day. To her chagrin and amusement, the student shrugged, scratched his head, and responded, "I don't know—shake your booty, I guess." What is clear to the lesson designer is not always clear to students. Thus, a closing time to reflect together is important. A thoughtful closing to lessons also helps prepare students for the question parents often ask: What did you learn in school today?

A plan should include sufficient detail for another teacher to follow it. Notes on materials to have ready, the approximate time needed, and resources used for the lesson are helpful. The Strategies for Learning and Assessment in each content chapter can be used to build standards-based learning plans.

5: Reflection

Charlotte Danielson and Thomas McGreal claim that few activities are more powerful for professional learning than reflection on classroom practice.[31] Teachers may learn as much from thinking, writing, and talking about their classroom experiences as from the experiences themselves. Educators find that taking the time to pause and systematically consider their work improves their teaching. To assist in a structured approach to reflection, educators can consider three questions at the conclusion of health education lessons:

1. What happened during my lessons (what did the students and I say and do)? How effective was my lesson design and teaching?
2. What evidence can I show that my students learned about health (student work or other responses)? How effective was my assessment plan for getting information about what they learned?
3. How did I do in meeting my desired results for these health lessons? What are my next steps to improve student learning for health?

Retelling the lesson helps teachers examine it for themselves and explain it to readers or listeners. Often the events are highly entertaining in the retelling, even if they didn't seem so at the time. A student teacher taught a well-planned lesson on dengue fever to her first-grade students, as requested by her mentor teacher. Dengue fever, spread by mosquitoes, was a concern in the community at the time. The student teacher finished reading a picture book about mosquitoes and was well into the lively discussion portion of her lesson when one of the children, who had been especially quiet that period, vomited on the carpet. The student teacher immediately had a number of challenges on her hands—contacting the custodian and the health aide, comforting the sick child, and keeping the other children from touching him or the carpet in their desire to help. One of the children suddenly made a connection to the lesson and cried, "Russell threw up. He must have dengue fever! Oh, nooooo!" Needless to say, a great deal of excitement ensued. In retelling the story, the student teacher understandably described it as "the worst hour of my life!" In this case, the student teacher was prepared for her lesson and handled the emergency well. In answer to what her students learned, she certainly could say that they knew the symptoms of dengue fever and made a connection right before her eyes. They also learned, after calming down, that Russell simply didn't feel well and might have eaten something that upset his stomach, and that not all vomiting indicates dengue fever. The student teacher learned that even the most brilliant educators can't anticipate every eventuality and that a cool, calm approach is valuable in a classroom filled with anxious first graders.

Including Learners with Diverse Backgrounds, Interests, and Abilities

Students differ in many ways—sex, gender role, culture, religion, race, ethnicity, age, national origin, ancestry, ability, learning needs, talents, interests, language, sexual orientation, socioeconomic status, home community, aspirations, desires, temperament, and physical characteristics, to name a few. Making the classroom a place where all students feel safe and welcome is one of the most important and challenging aspects of promoting child and adolescent health. Chapters 4 and 5 provide a variety of ideas for building classroom community for everyone. An excellent resource for learning to bring students together is Jeanne Gibb's book *Reaching All by Creating Tribes Learning Communities.*[32] *Tribes* describes an ongoing process—more than a series of activities—that teachers can use to engage all students in the life of the classroom.

In addition to helping all students feel safe and welcome, educators must do their utmost to help all students learn. Educators can make careful observations about students' needs and incorporate a variety of engaging approaches to learning into their lessons. Sometimes needed modifications are clear. Students with a visual impairment might need large-print pages to assist them in reading a research assignment. Other students might benefit from having a reading assignment recorded so they can listen as they read the printed pages.

Special education professor Rhonda Black provides the following suggestions, which she calls "just good teaching," for making instruction more effective for students with cognitive disabilities:

1. *Use visual aids.* Use realistic photos and simple diagrams. Complicated abstract charts can be confusing.

2. *Repeat key information.* Ask students for feedback to check their understanding. Reinforce important concepts and provide small amounts of information spaced out over time.

3. *Provide opportunities to practice interpersonal skills.* Behavioral rehearsals are an excellent technique to help young people prepare for situations they are likely to encounter.

4. *Use many approaches.* Use a variety of teaching methods—verbal discussions, movement, signs, colors, the senses.

5. *Use humor when appropriate.* Life is sometimes comical. Having a sense of humor (and helping students find their own sense of humor) is a valuable teaching asset.

Classrooms are diverse places. Making all students feel welcome and included sets the stage for successful learning.

6. *Encourage questions.* Set aside time for questions. Say to students, "I don't know the answer. How can we find out together?"

7. *Keep it simple.* Present ideas and their practical applications in logical ways.

8. *Be concrete.* Abstract reasoning is often difficult for students with cognitive disabilities. Don't use abstract metaphors and analogies (learning about the birds and the bees) or phrases that can be misunderstood (*cat got your tongue, in over my head*).

9. *Find out the words and terms that students know, and use those to make new connections.* A word like *cardio-respiratory* might be totally unknown to students, but they might be familiar with the idea of "aerobics."

10. *Check how the communication is going.* Teachers might be saying one thing and their students hearing something completely different. If a teacher says "vagina" and the students hear "China," confusion is inevitable.[33]

As educators get to know their students, they learn about the different cultures, beliefs, and circumstances that are part of students' home communities. Remaining open to listening, learning, and responding with genuineness and empathy is of paramount importance in drawing students together as a learning community.

Linking Health Education with Other Curriculum Areas

Planning for the elementary and middle grades provides many opportunities to link health education with other curriculum areas. Units of study related to a particular theme, such as "Staying Healthy in a Rapidly Changing World," could incorporate investigations related to social studies and geography, mathematics, science, physical activity, and health, with resulting student presentations building on visual and performing arts, language arts, and technology. These types of units take careful planning and collaboration among teachers in various subject areas.

Linking health education to other curriculum areas also can be done at a simpler level. Many children's books tell stories that deal with managing strong feelings, making a natural connection between health education and language arts. Teacher's Toolbox 3.11 provides examples of standards-based curriculum links between health education and other subject areas in the K–8 curriculum.

The Common Core State Standards (www.corestandards.org/), described in Chapter 2, provide new opportunities to link health education with learning in English Language Arts (ELA) and mathematics. In particular, key points in the ELA standards align well with the National Health Education Standards (NHES):

1. Reading—The CCSS call for increasing complexity in what students must be able to read and the progressive development of reading comprehension of literature and informational texts. NHES 1 (core concepts) and NHES 3 (accessing information) support reading in this manner.

2. Writing—An emphasis on research and the ability to write logical arguments based on substantive claims, sound reasoning, and relevant evidence align with NHES 2 (analyze influences), NHES 4 (interpersonal communication), and NHES 8 (advocacy).

3. Speaking and Listening—An important focus of the speaking and listening standards is academic discussion in one-on-one, small-group, and whole-class settings. NHES 4 (interpersonal communication) and NHES 8 (advocacy) support the development of students' skills in speaking and listening. These standards also require students to gain, evaluate, and present increasingly complex information, as indicated in NHES 3 (accessing information).

4. Language—The language standards require students to grow their academic vocabulary, which aligns with NHES 1 (core concepts) and NHES 3 (accessing information).

5. Media and Technology—Skills related to media use, both critical analysis and production of media, are integrated throughout the ELA standards. Similarly, NHES 2 (analyzing influences), NHES 4 (interpersonal communication), and NHES 8 (advocacy) provide opportunities for students to demonstrate their skills through media and technology.

Teacher's Toolbox 3.11

Sample Standards-Based Learning Opportunities That Link Health Education to Other Subjects in the K–8 Curriculum

Learning Opportunity	Subject Area	Health Education
Write and perform an original song or theater production that tells the story of resolving a difficult decision. Sponsor a showing of class drawings, paintings, and sculptures to promote various aspects of health.	Fine arts • Music • Theater • Visual arts	• Analyze influences • Decision making • Self-management • Interpersonal communication • Advocacy
Read child and adolescent literature to initiate discussions about mental, emotional, social, and physical health concepts and how they influence health behaviors.	Language arts • Reading	• Core concepts • Analyze influences
Conduct an original research project on a health issue, documenting resources and reporting in a written document.	• Writing	• Core concepts • Access information
Measure and record personal changes in physical growth over time.	Mathematics • Measurement and data	• Core concepts
Access and analyze public health statistics to establish the incidence and prevalence of various types of injuries and estimate the probability of injury related to specific risk behaviors.	• Statistics and probability	• Access information
Describe ways students can promote a physically active lifestyle for themselves and their families. Examine school physical activity facilities to ensure access for all participants.	Physical education • Maintain a health-enhancing level of physical activity • Exhibit responsible personal and social behavior that respects self and others	• Self-management • Advocacy • Access information • Interpersonal communication • Advocacy
Investigate the influence of various substances on the function of the body systems and use this information to advocate for a tobacco-, alcohol-, and other drug-free lifestyle.	Science • Life sciences	• Core concepts • Advocacy
Determine how research in earth and space science can contribute to improved health, quality of life, and longevity.	• Earth and space sciences	• Core concepts • Access information
Contrast the approaches that various cultures take in public health messages about preventing HIV infection. Determine the extent to which public health practices in one part of the world can affect health status in other parts of the world.	Social studies • Culture • Global connections	• Core concepts • Advocacy • Access information • Analyze influences
Access health-related information through the Internet and design a web page to communicate recommendations for personal health. Design a questionnaire on the STD knowledge of classmates, teachers, and parents. Organize and present data with a computer presentation application (PowerPoint).	Technology • Access and exchange information in a variety of ways • Compile, organize, analyze, and synthesize information	• Access information • Self-management • Advocacy • Access information • Analyze influences

ASSESSING STUDENT WORK

Many people think of state testing when they hear the term *assessment*. However, Wiggins and McTighe offer a much broader perspective:

> Assessment is the umbrella term for the deliberate use of *many* methods of gathering evidence of meeting desired results, whether those results are state content standards or local curricular objectives. The collected evidence we seek may well include observations and dialogues, traditional quizzes and tests, performance tasks and projects, as well as students' self-assessments gathered over time. Assessment is thus a more learning-focused term than evaluations, and the two should not be viewed as synonymous.[34]

Educators should consider a broad array of assessment strategies that allow students to demonstrate what they know, understand, and can do. Teacher's Toolbox 3.12 provides a framework of assessment approaches and methods, indicating those that are performance based. See Teacher's Toolbox 3.10 for a more detailed list of written, oral, visual, and kinesthetic strategies that educators can consider for assessing student work in health education.

Engaging Students in Assessment

One of the most important aspects of authentic assessment—that is, assessing what matters in life both in and beyond the classroom—is inviting students to participate in decisions about

Performance-Based Assessment				
Selected Response Items	**Constructed Responses**	**Products**	**Performances**	**Process-Focused Responses**
Matching	Fill-in	Artistic expression—drawing, painting, poem, song	Dramatization	Checklist
Multiple-choice	Short answer	Portfolio	Movie	Learning Log
True-false	Essay	Research Project	Play	Observation
		Story	Presentation	Process Description
		Website	Role-play	

what is of value and how it can be fairly assessed. Although the health education standards provide specific criteria for meeting standards, students can add their own ideas to build ownership and investment into their work.

To illustrate, meeting the health education standard of advocacy (NHES 8) involves stating a health-enhancing position, providing support for the position, demonstrating audience awareness, and showing strong conviction (Figure 3-1). To get students' input, teachers can pose these questions: "What do you think would make a great advocacy presentation? What do you want to see, hear, and do during your classmates' presentations?" Students might decide that they want presenters to choose topics that kids care about, involve them in active participation rather than having them just sit and listen, and explain topics with engaging media presentations. When students plan with these ideas in mind, they are better able to meet the NHES 8 criterion of demonstrating audience awareness and can target their presentation with greater precision.

Educators can involve their students in assessment by making sure students understand and have a say in what is required of them from the very beginning of a new unit of study. Most educators remember situations as students when they felt they needed to guess what the instructor wanted in terms of a research paper or test material. Involving students early in the assessment process leads to higher-quality work and minimizes misunderstandings.

Developing and Using Rubrics

Rubric is a term that educators hear often in relation to assessment. A rubric is simply a framework or scoring guide for assessing student work. Appendix B includes scoring rubrics developed by RMC Health for each National Health Education Standard. RMC Health developed these analytic rubrics in collaboration with respected education author Jay McTighe.

Teachers and students can practice using a rubric by scoring a familiar activity. For instance, what might people consider when assessing their last movie experience? If someone simply says that the experience was "great," "okay," or "a bummer," listeners don't know why. To paint a more analytic picture of their experience, moviegoers could design a rubric to allow a more informative assessment. Patrons could evaluate the quality of the story (*totally into it, somewhat interesting, boring*), the acting (*really believable, fairly convincing, lame*), the picture (*sharp and clear, mostly in focus, blurry or jumpy*), and the sound (*just right for my ears, sometimes a bit too loud or soft, annoyingly loud or soft*). In addition, the temperature of the theater (*very comfortable, mostly comfortable, too hot or too cold*) and the price of refreshments (*very reasonable, mostly affordable, a rip-off*) could be considered in the assessment of movie enjoyment.

The RMC Health rubrics show four possible scores for student work. As teachers and students look at the advocacy rubric (Figure 3-1), they will note scores of 3 and 4 meet and exceed standards, respectively, and that scores of 1 and 2 do not meet standards. This initial distinction is important in addressing the assessment question "How good is good enough?" The rubrics clearly describe performances that are acceptable (meet standards) and those that go beyond basic requirements (exceed standards) or do not measure up to requirements (does not meet standards). When teachers and students develop rubrics, they should designate clear distinctions related to the categories and descriptors they use. The first and most important distinction is between work that meets standards and work that does not. Figure 3-2 provides an example of a rubric stated in kid terms, with descriptors in language selected by students.

Rubistar (www.rubistar.4teachers.org) is a web-based tool to help teachers create quality rubrics for project-based teaching activities. Registration is free. Registered users can access their rubrics at any time, and save and edit them online. Rubistar contains templates for oral projects, multimedia, math, writing, products, reading, art, work skills, science, and music. Teachers can enter health-related keywords (health, nutrition, mental health, bully prevention) to search Rubistar by rubric titles, author's name, or author's e-mail address. Teachers can explore a variety of health-related rubrics posted online.

The content chapters provide a variety of learning strategies for standards-based health education. Each learning strategy is followed by simple suggestions for assessment. When learning strategies and assessment are planned together, teachers increase opportunities for both instructional improvement and student achievement.

	Health-Enhancing Position	Support for Position	Audience Awareness	Conviction
4 Exceeds standards	• Extremely clear, health-enhancing position	• Thoroughly supports position using relevant and accurate facts, data, and evidence	• Strong awareness of the target audience (e.g., the audience's perspective, interests, prior knowledge)	• Displays strong and passionate conviction for position
3 Meets standards	• Generally clear, health-enhancing position	• Adequately supports position using facts, data, evidence; support may be incomplete and/or contain minor inaccuracies	• Adequate awareness of audience	• Displays conviction for position
2 Does not meet standards	• Unclear or conflicting positions	• Inadequately supports position due to limited information and/or some inaccuracy, irrelevant facts, data, or evidence	• Some evidence of awareness of audience	• Displays minimal conviction for position
1 Does not meet standards	• No position stated OR position is not health-enhancing	• No accurate or relevant support for position provided	• No evidence of awareness of audience	• Conviction for position not evident

FIGURE 3–1 | **Analytic Rubric for National Health Education Standard 8, Advocacy**   Students will demonstrate the ability to advocate for personal, family, and community health

SOURCE: Adapted from and used with permission from RMC Health, Lakewood, CO (rmc.org).

Score	Standard: Advocacy	Self-Assessment
4	• Clearly stated health-enhancing position • Demonstrated how to influence and support others to make positive health choices • Used a communication technique and modified it for audience	
3	• Health-enhancing position mostly clear • Demonstrated how to influence and support others to make positive health choices fairly well • Used a communication technique and mostly modified it for audience	
2	• Health-enhancing position somewhat clear • Demonstrated how to influence and support others to make positive health choices somewhat • Used a communication technique and slightly modified it for audience	
1	• Health-enhancing position was unclear • Unable to influence and support others to make positive health choices • Did not use a communication technique/modify it for audience	

FIGURE 3–2 | **Student Rubric for National Health Education Standard 8, Advocacy**

Designing Performance Tasks

RMC Health conceptualizes assessment as a shift in thinking, from "teach and test" to the alignment and congruence of standards (concepts and skills), assessment, and instruction. Classroom assessment should (1) promote learning, (2) incorporate multiple sources of information, and (3) provide fair, valid, and reliable information. Similarly, the National Council of Teachers of Mathematics (NCTM) states, "Assessment should not merely be done *to* students; rather, it should also be done *for* students, to guide and enhance their learning."[35]

How can teachers design standards-based performance tasks that are linked to instruction? RMC Health provides a performance assessment template that includes three steps:

1. Select National Health Education Standards (or local standards) and content areas.
2. Construct a "prompt" or item for student response.

3. Determine criteria for success in terms of concepts (NHES 1) and skills (NHES 2–8).

Teacher's Toolbox 3.13 provides an example of a teacher-created performance task for upper-elementary and middle-level students based on NHES 4 and 8, interpersonal communication and advocacy, and the content area promoting a tobacco-free lifestyle.

Educators should note that the performance task emphasizes skills demonstration as well as conceptual knowledge.

Portfolio assessment is a type of performance task that is widely used in elementary and middle school classrooms. When students design portfolios, they select their best and most representative work to illustrate how they meet standards. For example, a

---

Teacher's Toolbox **3.13**

Sample Standards-Based Assessment Task

Communicating About the New Healthy Indoor Air Ordinance in Our Hometown
Upper Elementary and Middle School

Step 1: Identify standards and content areas
Standards: Interpersonal Communication (NHES 4) and Advocacy (NHES 8)
Content Area: Promoting a Tobacco-Free Lifestyle

Step 2: Construct the prompt
Instructions to Students:

Setting and role: You are a clothing store owner in Our Hometown. The city has updated its Healthy Indoor Air Ordinance, which bans smoking in public places, to include E (electronic) cigarettes. Your customers may or may not know about the rule change, and they may or may not agree with it. Your employees are concerned about explaining the new rule to customers.

Challenge: Your challenge is to model, for your employees, communication with customers who ask about, complain about, or break the E cigarette rule. You need to model positive communication that provides a clear and respectful message to customers in a way that helps you maintain positive relationships with them (so they will stay and shop in your store!). You also need to help customers understand why the new rule is healthy for employees and other customers. Remember that some customers merely will be asking about the rule, but others may be unhappy or angry about it.

Products and performance: Write a script for a scenario in your store that happens on the Friday night that the rules go into effect. During the scenario, you will have to deal with three different customers who (1) ask about the rules, (2) complain about the rules, and (3) light up E cigarettes. You must inform your customers about the new rule, modeling positive communication for your employees, and convince your customers that the new E cigarette rule is a positive change and that they should stay and shop in your store.

Scoring: Your work will be scored on two standards: Interpersonal Communication and Advocacy.

Step 3: Determine criteria for success and share with students

Interpersonal Communication	Advocacy
• Demonstrate appropriate verbal and nonverbal communication strategies. • Demonstrate appropriate communication skills. • Demonstrate appropriate communication behaviors.	• State a clear position. • Support the position with information. • Target the message to your customers. • Show strong conviction for your position.

SOURCE: Adapted with permission from the Hawaii Department of Education (content) and the Rocky Mountain Center for Health Promotion and Education (format).

portfolio related to the health education standards might require middle school students to select two samples of their work for each standard studied during their semester-long health education course. A further requirement might specify that at least four different content areas should be addressed in the student work samples. Students might present their portfolios during designated class times or during special parent nights at their schools.

Portfolios can be completed with file folders, notebooks, display boards, or other physical organizers. Students increasingly are learning to compile E (electronic) portfolios for assessment and presentation. E portfolios can be shared with teachers and fellow students online for editing, revision, and final presentation.

Providing Feedback to Promote Learning and Skill Development

Using teacher- and student-created rubrics provides far more information for students on their progress than do simple letter grades (B+) or general written phrases such as "Good job!" When a student receives feedback that he or she stated an extremely clear health-enhancing position and displayed strong and passionate conviction for the position but has not yet demonstrated a strong awareness of the target audience, he or she knows exactly where to fine-tune his or her upcoming advocacy presentation. Teachers can give meaningful feedback by communicating to students on the rubrics—circling the level of performance within a particular category, writing comments and suggestions at the bottom of the rubric, and attaching it to student work. Many educators find this way of providing feedback to be timely and time-saving.

In addition to providing feedback through rubrics, teachers should think about the way they interact with students as they observe them at work. Though praising children with generic phrases such as "Way to go!" and "Great!" often is sincere and well intended, students benefit from a more genuine and informative conversation about their work. For example, a teacher who is circulating around the classroom as children draw pictures to illustrate their self-management strategies for expressing strong feelings might say, "Tell me more about your picture and what you are thinking—I see you have three people in your drawing." This comment invites students to express their thought processes and intentions, knowing that their teacher is listening.

Another consideration in measuring students' progress is looking at the quality of their work over time. A chemistry major earned a score of only 9 percent out of a possible 100 percent on his or her first advanced calculus test. With hard work and group study sessions, his or her grades improved to the range of 90 to 95 percent by the end of the semester. In traditional grading—averaging—this student likely would fail the course, but an examination of the student's progress throughout the semester leads to a different decision.

Many educators say that they love teaching and dislike assigning grades. Assessing student performance and providing formative and summative feedback is important for learning, however. Applying the assessment strategies in this text and other resources and participating in professional development can place assessment in a new and inviting light for educators, students, and families alike.

The learning and assessment strategies presented here provide building blocks for standards-based lessons and units that can be tailored to local needs. Assessment criteria are used with permission from the RMC Health. See Appendix B for Scoring Rubrics.

STRATEGIES FOR LEARNING AND ASSESSMENT

This section provides an example of a standards-based learning and assessment strategy for each NHES standard. The examples in this chapter can be applied to any content area. Chapters 5 to 14 include content-specific learning and assessment strategies organized by standard and grade cluster (K–2, 3–5, and 6–8). Each set of strategies begins with a restatement of the standard and a reminder of the assessment criteria, drawn from the RMC Health rubrics in Appendix B. Strategies are written as directions for teachers and include applicable theory of planned behavior (TPB) constructs—intention to act in healthy ways, attitudes toward behavior, subjective norms, perceived behavioral control—in parentheses.

NHES 1 | Core Concepts

Students will comprehend concepts related to health promotion and disease prevention to enhance health.

ASSESSMENT CRITERIA
- Connections—Describe relationships between behavior and health; draw logical conclusions about connections between behavior and health.
- Comprehensiveness—Thoroughly cover health topic, showing breadth and depth; give accurate information.

Know-Wonder-Learn (KWL) Chart A KWL chart can be used with any curriculum topic. Using newsprint or a chalkboard, draw three columns labeled *Know*, *Wonder*, and *Learn*. For the given topic (e.g., bullying), have students list all the facts that they know or think they know. Record all information offered by students in the *Know* column—verification comes later. Some teachers write students' names next to the information they volunteer as a record of the class discussion. When the *Know* column is completed, go on to the *Wonder* column. What do students wonder and want to know about this topic? Record all questions, along with students' names.

To integrate this activity with NHES 3 (access information, products, and services) decide with the students how class members will verify their facts (*Know* column) and answer their questions (*Wonder* column). Who will be responsible for finding out about each fact or question? Learning the skill of accessing information can mean making trips to the library, inviting guest speakers to address the class, interviewing parents or community members, e-mailing an expert, reading resource books in the classroom, and using the Internet to investigate websites.

When the work is done, have students complete the *Learn* column to answer the question "What did we learn?" Help students focus on the core concepts they need to know to stay safe and healthy.

ASSESSMENT | Completing the KWL chart is an embedded assessment task as well as a record of what the class investigated and learned. Students also can write and draw in journals about what they learned. Criteria for assessing the KWL chart or journals include ensuring that all final information is accurate and that students can provide the breadth and depth of information appropriate for their grade level. In addition, students should be able to describe one or more relationships and make one or more connections between behaviors and health. (Construct: Attitudes toward behavior.)

NHES 2 | Analyze Influences

Students will analyze the influence of family, peers, culture, media, technology, and other factors on health behaviors.

ASSESSMENT CRITERIA

*   Identify both external and internal influences on health.
*   Explain how external and internal influences interact to impact health choices and behaviors.
*   Explain both positive and negative influences, as appropriate.

External Influences: Family Health Practices   Ask students to think about and list all the things their families do to stay healthy. The teacher or students can display the list on newsprint or a chalkboard. The class list might include eating healthy meals and snacks, drinking 1 percent or skim milk, exercising regularly, playing games or other activities together, practicing personal health care, and getting to bed early. Have children make a list of their family health practices to take home and share with their families. Ask students to discuss how their family's choices (choice of cereal or toothpaste) affect their preferences. Have students ask themselves, "How does my family influence my choices and my health?"

ASSESSMENT   As an assessment task, have students create posters depicting their family health practices. Have them take their poster home to share with their families. As assessment criteria, have students describe a minimum of three healthy family habits and explain how the family habits influence their own health actions. (Construct: Subjective norms.)

NHES 3 | Access Information, Products, and Services

Students will demonstrate the ability to access valid information and products and services to enhance health.

ASSESSMENT CRITERIA

*   Access health information—Locate specific sources of health information, products, or services relevant to enhancing health in a given situation.
*   Evaluate information sources—Explain the degree to which identified sources are valid, reliable, and appropriate as a result of evaluating each source.

Web Search for Health   Have students work with a partner or group of three to complete an online search of health topics. Students can brainstorm a list of questions they want to know more about and decide on a common set of questions for the class. Teachers must set ground rules and guide students in the types of sites to explore (.edu, .gov, .org). Students have a set amount of time to answer the questions (e.g., what's really in an energy drink?) and then share and compare their findings with the class. Teachers should be alert to helping students debate the validity of the information they find and dig deeper into the quality of their resources.

ASSESSMENT   Completing the web search questions is the assessment task. Assessment criteria include having students identify one or more appropriate resources for the questions after the class discussion. Students might also

identify counterexamples, or inappropriate resources, for various questions. For example, what differences do students note as they look at various kinds of websites ending in .edu, .org, .gov, and .com? (Construct: Perceived behavioral control.)

NHES 4 | Interpersonal Communication

Students will demonstrate the ability to use interpersonal communication skills to enhance health and avoid or reduce health risks.

ASSESSMENT CRITERIA

*   Use appropriate verbal/nonverbal communication strategies in an effective manner to enhance health or avoid/reduce health risks.
*   Use appropriate skills (negotiation skills, refusal skills) and behaviors (eye contact, body language, attentive listening).

Tableau: Pressure Points   Have students work in small groups to discuss times they have been pressured to participate in an uncomfortable or unwanted behavior. The situations do not have to be health related—students need peer resistance skills in a wide variety of situations. Ask students to share how they felt and how they responded. Ask students if they knew what to say or what to do. Ask what they wanted to say and do and whether they were able to do it. After gathering students' ideas, share the list of peer pressure resistance techniques from this chapter (see Teacher's Toolbox 3.4).

ASSESSMENT   For an assessment task, have students work in small groups to plan and perform a short scenario that demonstrates a realistic pressure situation. At the point where students need to use peer resistance skills, have the actors freeze in place to form a still picture or *tableau* (a new vocabulary word for most students). Ask class members to advise the actors on what to say or do to resist pressure in healthy ways. Have class members recommend a health-enhancing way to end the story, and have the actors act it out. For assessment criteria, agree with students that they will demonstrate at least two verbal and one nonverbal peer pressure resistance strategies to deal with the tableau situation in healthy ways. (Constructs: Perceived behavioral control, subjective norms.)

NHES 5 | Decision Making

Students will demonstrate the ability to use decision-making skills to enhance health.

ASSESSMENT CRITERIA

Reach a health enhancing decision using a process consisting of the following criteria:

*   Identify their personal values, purpose in life, goals, and connections with others.
*   Describe the decision they are facing.
*   Explain how the decision would affect their personal values, purpose in life, goals, and connections with others.
*   Decide and reflect on the decision.

Decision-Making Puzzle   Students identify their own purpose in life, goals, values, and personal connections with others (components of their own "Me Puzzle"). Ask students why these may be important factors when considering the decisions they make. Provide students with a health-related scenario where they need to make a decision. After students have identified the decision they are making, they will then consider the effect that decision would have on their purpose in life, goals, values, and personal connections. In other words, how would this decision fit into their "Me Puzzle." This may require further prompting/probing from the teacher.

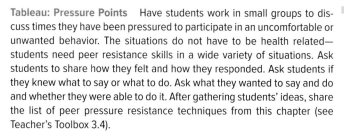

Students will then write down their ideas to help them make a decision. Once the decision has been made, students will write down the decision and a brief reflection describing why they made their decision and describe the process they used. As a post-lesson activity, students can create their own "Me Puzzle" with the components they explained during the lesson.[36]

ASSESSMENT | The assessment task is the reflection where students describe why they made the decision they made. For assessment criteria, check to see that the students have stated their decision and clearly explained why they made that decision and how easy or hard it was. Students should also clearly describe the decision-making process they used. Have students compare their reflections with others. (Construct: Perceived behavioral control.)

NHES 6 | Goal Setting

Students will demonstrate the ability to use goal-setting skills to enhance health.

ASSESSMENT CRITERIA

- Goal statement—Give goal statement that identifies health benefits; goal is achievable and will result in enhanced health.
- Goal setting plan—Show plan that is complete, logical and sequential, and includes a process to assess progress.

The Little Engine That Could: **A Closer Look at Goal Setting** Watty Piper's book *The Little Engine That Could* provides students with an opportunity to examine the steps involved in goal setting through a familiar story. Teachers can ask students to listen for evidence of the important goal-setting steps as the story is read: (1) a clear, achievable goal; (2) a plan that includes logical, sequential steps; (3) ways to build support and deal with obstacles; and (4) a process to assess progress. The goal is clear—the little train needs to deliver cars of wonderful things to boys and girls on the other side of the mountain. What was the little train's plan? What obstacles did she encounter, and how did she deal with them? Whose support did she need? What can students learn about providing support for themselves and others? How did the Little Blue Engine know she was making progress and reaching her goal? What is the most important lesson about reaching a goal in this story? Teachers can ask students to talk together to identify a goal they would like to reach as a class and to make a plan that includes the basic goal-setting steps. Examples include a "no-name-calling" week, a "saying please and thank you" week, or a "healthy snacks only" week.

ASSESSMENT | The assessment task is the class goal the students set. For assessment criteria, students should identify an achievable class goal, the steps to achieve it, plans to build support and deal with obstacles, and a process to assess class progress. (Construct: Perceived behavioral control.)

NHES 7 | Self-Management

Students will demonstrate the ability to practice health-enhancing behaviors and avoid or reduce risks.

ASSESSMENT CRITERIA

- Identify a healthy stress management strategy that their parent uses.
- Utilize the strategy with their parent.

Parent Stress Reducer Young people can learn from adults how to manage stress. At the end of a lesson on stress management, ask students to identify a stress reduction strategy that their parents use. For homework, students will ask their parent(s) what their favorite healthy stress reduction strategy is. Students will report back the next day in class what the stress reducing strategy is. After each classmate has shared, assign students homework that requires them to use the stress reduction strategy with their parent at some point over the next few days. Students will write a reflection describing the strategy, how much they enjoyed it, how easy or difficult it was to use, and what the process was like as they experienced the strategy with their parent(s).

ASSESSMENT | The assessment task is the reflection where students describe the healthy stress management strategy and the experience with their parent(s). For assessment criteria, check to see that the students have clearly described the strategy and the experience with their parents. Have students share their reflections with others. (Construct: Perceived behavioral control, subjective norms.)

NHES 8 | Advocacy

Students will demonstrate the ability to advocate for personal, family, and community health.

ASSESSMENT CRITERIA

- Health-enhancing position—Give clear, health-enhancing position.
- Support for position—Support position with facts, concepts, examples, and evidence.
- Audience awareness—Show awareness of target audience; choose words, tone, and examples to suit audience.
- Conviction—Display conviction for position.

What Do Kids Really Do? Establishing Social Norms by Using Data from the Youth Risk Behavior Survey and the Global School-based Student Health Survey Most states and many large cities conduct the Youth Risk Behavior Survey (YRBS), funded by the Centers for Disease Control and Prevention (CDC). Countries around the world conduct the Global School-based Student Health Survey (GSHS), also funded by the CDC. Students can type YRBS or GSHS into the search line at www.cdc.gov to locate data. Have students work in small groups to explore results for various states and cities (YRBS) and counties (GSHS). Students can prepare their data for a health advocacy presentation to classmates. Alternatively, teachers can print tables from the Internet in advance for students' use. An important way to use these data is to ask students to concentrate on the number and percentage of students who practice healthy behaviors. For example, what percentage of U.S. middle school students did not use an electronic vapor product during the past thirty days? Students can work on one topic (tobacco use) or a variety of topics (alcohol and other drug use, injury and violence, nutrition) to search for data on what "kids really do." This activity links with NHES 3 (accessing information, products, and services). Using and interpreting the YRBS and GSHS data tables make an excellent link with mathematics.

ASSESSMENT | The advocacy presentations that students make as a result of their research into YRBS and GSHS data are the assessment tasks. For assessment criteria, remind students to focus on advocacy by stating a clear, health-enhancing position; supporting the position with data; targeting the message to classmates; and showing strong conviction. (Construct: Subjective norms.)

WEBSITES

American School Health Association (ASHA)
www.ashaweb.org

Association for Supervision and Curriculum Development (ASCD)
www.ascd.org/Default.aspx

BAM! (Body and Mind)—Site for Students with Information for Teachers
www.cdc.gov/bam

CAST UDL Lesson Builder
lessonbuilder.cast.org

Global School-Based Student Health Survey GSHS
www.cdc.gov/gshs/index.htm

Health Education Curriculum Analysis Tool (HECAT)
www.cdc.gov/HealthyYouth/HECAT

HealthTeacher
www.healthteacher.com

Healthy Youth, Adolescent and School Health, CDC
www.cdc.gov/healthyyouth

KidsHealth
www.kidshealth.org

PE Central
www.pecentral.org

Registries of Programs Effective in Reducing Youth Risk Behaviors
www.cdc.gov/healthyyouth/adolescenthealth/registries.htm

Response to Intervention (RTI) Action Network
www.rtinetwork.org

RMC Health
rmc.org

Rubistar
http://rubistar.4teachers.org

Society for Health and Physical Educators
https://www.shapeamerica.org

WebQuest.org
www.webquest.org

Youth Risk Behavior Surveillance System (YRBSS), CDC
www.cdc.gov/HealthyYouth/yrbs/index.htm

OTHER RESOURCES

Fisher, D., and N. Frey. *Checking for Understanding: Formative Assessment Techniques for Your Classroom*, 2nd ed. (Alexandria, VA: Association for Supervision and Curriculum Development, 2014).

Gibbs, J. *Reaching All by Creating Tribes Learning Communities* (Windsor, CA: CenterSource Systems, LLC, 2006).

Moss, C. M., and Susan M. Brookhart. *Advancing Formative Assessment in Every Classroom* (Alexandria, VA: Association for Supervision and Curriculum Development, 2009).

Tomlinson, C. A., and J. McTighe. *Integrating Differentiated Instruction + Understanding by Design* (Alexandria, VA: Association for Supervision and Curriculum Development, 2006).

Tomlinson, C. A., and T. R. Moon. *Assessment and Success in a Differentiated Classroom* (Alexandria, VA: Association for Supervision and Curriculum Development, 2013).

Wiggins, G., and J. McTighe. *The Understanding by Design Guide to Creating High-Quality Units* (Alexandria, VA: Association for Supervision and Curriculum Development, 2011).

Wiggins, G., and J. McTighe. *Understanding by Design*, expanded 2nd ed. (Alexandria, VA: Association for Supervision and Curriculum Development, 2005).

ENDNOTES

1. Joint Commission on National Health Education Standards, *National Health Education Standards* (Atlanta, GA: American Cancer Society, 1995).

2. Centers for Disease Control and Prevention, *Registries of Programs Effective in Reducing Youth Risk Behaviors* (www.cdc.gov/healthyyouth/adolescenthealth/registries.htm).

3. Council of Chief State School Officers, *Assessing Health Literacy: Assessment Framework* (Soquel, CA: ToucanEd, 1998).

4. Centers for Disease Control and Prevention, *Health Education Curriculum Analysis Tool—HECAT* (www.cdc.gov/HealthyYouth/HECAT).

5. Centers for Disease Control and Prevention, *YRBSS: Youth Risk Behavior Surveillance System* (www.cdc.gov/HealthyYouth/yrbs/index.htm).

6. Centers for Disease Control and Prevention, *Global School-Based Student Health Survey GSHS* (www.cdc.gov/gshs/index.htm).

7. P. Klass, "How Advertising Targets Our Children," *The New York Times* (http://well.blogs.nytimes.com/2013/02/11/how-advertising-targets-our-children/?_r=0).

8. Ibid.

9. D. Grace, "Gender, Power and Pleasure: Integrating Student Video Production into the Elementary Literacy Curriculum," *Curriculum Perspectives* 23, no. 1 (2002): 21–27.

10. WebMD, *Botulism Toxin* [Botox] (www.webmd.com/beauty/botox/botulinum-toxin-botox).

11. Ibid.

12. R. E. Dahl, *Adolescent Brain Development: A Framework for Understanding Unique Vulnerabilities and Opportunities* (www.bluestemcenter.com/articles/Adolescent%20Brain%20Development.pdf).

13. Ibid.

14. Ibid.

15. National Institute of Mental Health, *Teenage Brain: A Work in Progress* (https://www.psychceu.com/Brain_Basics/teenbrain.pdf).

16. National Institute of Mental Health, *Teen Brain: 6 Things to Know* (https://infocenter.nimh.nih.gov/nimh/product/The-Teen-Brain-6-Things-to-Know/OM%2016-4307).

17. J. Lehrer, *How We Decide* (New York: First Mariner Books, 2010), 249.

18. C. N. Matsuoka, conversation with author, Honolulu: HI, March 2007.

19. A. L. Costa and B. Kallick, *Discovering and Exploring Habits of the Mind* (Alexandria, VA: Association for Supervision and Curriculum Development, 2000).

20. M. Lipman, *Philosophy Goes to School* (Philadelphia: Temple University Press, 1988).

21. J. Fetro, *Personal and Social Skills* (Santa Cruz, CA: ETR Associates, 2000).

22. Ibid.

23. Ibid.

24. G. Wiggins and J. McTighe, *Understanding by Design,* expanded 2nd ed. (Alexandria, VA: Association for Supervision and Curriculum Development, 2005).

25. G. Wiggins and J. McTighe, *The Understanding by Design Guide to Creating High-Quality Units* (Alexandria, VA: Association for Supervision and Curriculum Development, 2011).

26. C. A. Tomlinson and J. McTighe, *Integrating Differentiated Instruction + Understanding by Design* (Alexandria, VA: Association for Supervision and Curriculum Development, 2006).

27. Wiggins and McTighe, *Understanding by Design.*

28. D. Fisher and N. Frey, *Checking for Understanding: Formative Assessment Techniques for Your Classroom,* 2nd ed. (Alexandria, VA: Association for Supervision and Curriculum Development, 2014).

29. C. M. Moss and S. M. Brookhart, *Advancing Formative Assessment in Every Classroom* (Alexandria, VA: Association for Supervision and Curriculum Development, 2009).

30. Wiggins and McTighe, *Understanding by Design.*

31. C. Danielson and T. McGreal, *Teacher Evaluation to Enhance Professional Practice* (Alexandria, VA: Association for Supervision and Curriculum Development, 2000).

32. J. Gibbs, *Reaching All by Creating Tribes Learning Communities* (Windsor, CA: CenterSource Systems, LLC, 2006).

33. B. Pateman et al., "Promoting Sexual Health and Responsibility: Healthy Sexuality Education for Hawaii's Youth," *Educational Perspectives* 34, no. 2 (2001): 25–30.

34. Wiggins and McTighe, *Understanding by Design.*

35. National Council of Teachers of Mathematics (NCTM), *Principles and Standards for School Mathematics* (Reston, VA: NCTM, 2000).

36. R. Erbe, "Me Puzzle: Spiritual Decision-Making," *American Journal of Health Education* 38, no. 5 (2007): 304–307.

4

(Kiana, age 13)

Building and Managing the Safe and Positive Learning Environment

D E S I R E D   L E A R N E R   O U T C O M E S

After reading this chapter, you will be able to . . .

- **Describe the relationship between connectedness and academic achievement and improved student health outcomes.**

- **Describe activities that foster connectedness in the school, through engagement with parents and families, and in the classroom.**

- **Summarize a range of learning activities that enrich instruction with a direct focus on child and adolescent health issues.**

- **Discuss the strengths and weaknesses of interdisciplinary instructional approaches.**

- **Evaluate electronic resources to enhance health education practice.**

- **Develop an action plan for managing controversy in health education.**

INTRODUCTION

Although the structure and time frame of the school day have remained relatively stable, the knowledge base across all content areas has grown exponentially. As a result, teachers are challenged to fit an ever-expanding body of functional knowledge and essential skill development opportunities into the school day.[1] Elementary school teachers in self-contained classrooms must manage the allocation of time resources to accommodate effective instruction across diverse content areas including reading, mathematics, science, social studies, computer literacy, and health education. In addition, they must manage the physical transition of students to other learning environments for music, art, and physical education when such instruction is made available to students.

In middle schools, it is the norm for school districts to hire content specialists to provide health instruction for students. Health teachers in middle schools are confronted with the time constraints associated with a fixed "bell" schedule that segments the school day and signals students to move quickly and efficiently from one class to another. Thus, middle school health teachers have well-defined time periods in which to deliver meaningful and developmentally appropriate learning experiences for students.

All teachers, including those most highly motivated to implement effective instructional activities to address the health challenges confronting their students, are challenged by time constraints. In addition, such episodic events as mandated testing can interrupt the continuity of instruction and competing community priorities, and a reported lack of teacher comfort with health issues also threaten dedicated time for quality health instruction.

Learning about critical health issues can be disrupted for students in elementary grades by predetermined recess and lunch periods. Even when the health education course of study and instructional activities for young students are developmentally appropriate, evidence-based, and consistent with state and national standards (Chapters 2 and 3), competing demands on instruction time can exert a negative impact. As a consequence, it is all too common and unfortunate that important learning activities or even whole units of health education be sacrificed.

This chapter suggests practical ways to manage such challenges confronting teachers. Reminders of the importance of connecting with learners in effective ways have been included. In addition, suggested tools including learning activities that can be incorporated into a range of health education content areas and cooperative learning applications for health education lesson planning are suggested.

Beyond direct approaches to health issues, this chapter examines correlated and integrated health education strategies that extend health education across the curriculum. Suggestions for managing potentially controversial health topics are offered, and the importance of parent engagement in health promotion activities is reviewed. Specific ways to engage parents in student health promotion are suggested.

Most of the recommendations included in this chapter are strategies with which teachers in the elementary and middle grades are familiar. Importantly, however, the tools in this chapter are applied specifically to evidence-based Comprehensive School Health Education. These practical recommendations are offered to help teachers who feel that, though important, health promotion activities are just one more thing to add to an already overcrowded school day.

FOSTERING CONNECTEDNESS: STRATEGIES TO IMPROVE ACADEMIC ACHIEVEMENT AND STUDENT HEALTH

Historically, efforts to improve health have focused on reducing the risks associated with specific behaviors including tobacco, alcohol, and other drug use; early sexual initiation; physical inactivity; and bullying. Importantly, however, a growing body of evidence confirms that significant reductions in such risks can be achieved by supporting the development of *protective factors* that help children avoid behaviors that put them at risk for adverse health and educational outcomes.

As discussed in Chapter 5, research has demonstrated that protective factors include individual, social, or environmental characteristics or that help students reduce the effects of stress, increase their ability to avoid risks, and enrich their social and emotional competence.[2] Specific protective factors include such attributes as having a positive outlook about the future or resources including access to parents after school or at dinner time that serve as a buffer between youth and the harmful effects of negative situations and events including the exposure to violence.[3]

Cultivating School Connectedness

Among the most powerful protective factors identified in the education and health literature is *school connectedness*. Defined as the belief among students that adults and peers in the school care about their learning and about them as people, school connectedness has been shown to make a significant contribution to academic success and health risk reduction.[4] While many education reform advocates assert that schools should focus only on the acquisition of knowledge that can be evaluated, others express concern that schools are expected to do too much to respond to student needs. Importantly, current research has demonstrated that investing in the nonacademic but vital matter of school connectedness pays significant academic dividends. Specifically, students who report a strong sense of school connectedness are more likely to:

- Attend school more regularly.
- Stay in school longer without or before dropping out.
- Have better grades.
- Perform better on tests.[5]

While exerting such a positive influence on academic achievement, school connectedness has been demonstrated to exert a simultaneous influence on promoting healthy behaviors. In this context, students who feel more connected to their school are less likely to:

- Smoke cigarettes, drink alcohol, and participate in sexual intercourse.
- Carry weapons and become involved in violence.
- Be injured from dangerous activities such as drinking and driving or not wearing seat belts.
- Have emotional problems, suffer from eating disorders, and experience suicidal thoughts and attempts.[6]

Sometimes referred to as "school engagement" or "school bonding," students who report a strong attachment to their school are more likely to engage in extracurricular activities and invest in their academic progress. In addition, students with a stronger sense of school connectedness report feeling like they belong, they like school, they have friends, and that their teachers are supportive or caring. Finally, connected students confirm their belief that the discipline policies and practices in their school are fair and effective.[7]

A number of evidence-based strategies have been demonstrated to promote school connectedness. Research has confirmed that *people connect with people before they can connect with institutions*. As such, strong and positive relationships among students and their teachers, administrators, custodians, coaches, counselors, and other school personnel are the key to promoting school connectedness. When students believe that adults in the school are committed to creating a caring, well-structured learning environment in which expectations are high, clear, and fair, they are more likely to report that they are connected to their school. In this way, learning environments that are more personalized enrich the ability of students to respond and perform better.[8]

In addition to the importance of such adult support, belonging to a positive peer group has been demonstrated to increase school connectedness. Students who have cultivated stable networks with peers who are socially competent, engaged in school activities, complete homework, and help others tend to perform better in school and are more protected from being victimized and bullied. By contrast, if the norms of a peer group support

socially irresponsible behavior, those students are less likely to be involved in school activities and their achievement can be compromised. Students who report being highly connected to school report relationships with school-based friends whereas their counterparts report having more friends outside of school or that they feel socially isolated.[9]

School connectedness also is enhanced among students who demonstrate a commitment to education. Learners who believe that school is important to their future and who report that the adults in their school share their investment in education tend to achieve more and report engaging in fewer health risks.

Finally, connectedness is enhanced among students who attend schools in which a healthy and safe psychosocial environment is evident. In addition, a pleasant physical environment raises expectations for safety and sets the stage for positive relationships between adults and students that are characterized by mutual respect. School climate, and so connectedness, is enriched by specific factors including fair and consistently implemented discipline policies, opportunities for meaningful student participation in decision making, and implementation of effective classroom management practices.[10]

Consider This 4.1 contains a summary of evidence-based strategies and actions that teachers and other school staff can take to increase school connectedness.[11] Readers are encouraged to reflect on their own school experience and identify the extent to which such activities made an impact on their health-risk behaviors and academic achievement.

Cultivating Connectedness Through Parent Engagement

In addition to the important ways in which school-based professionals contribute to the protective factor of school connectedness, a growing body of literature has confirmed that parents, caregivers, and other significant family members make an additional protective contribution when they are engaged in the school life of their children. In specific, parent (the term used in this chapter to refer to the adult primary caregivers of children including biological parents and others) engagement in schools has been linked to productive student behavior, academic achievement, and strengthened social skills. In addition, when

---

Consider This 4.1

Strategies and Actions for Teachers and Other School Staff to Increase School Connectedness Among Students

1. Create processes that engage students, families, and communities and that facilitate academic achievement.
2. Provide opportunities for families to be actively involved in their children's academic and school life.
3. Provide students with the academic, emotional, and social skills necessary to be actively engaged in school.

4. Use effective classroom management and teaching methods to foster a positive learning environment.
5. Participate in professional development opportunities to enhance your abilities to meet the diverse needs of your students.
6. Promote open communication, trust, and caring among school staff, families, and community partners.

SOURCE: Centers for Disease Control and Prevention, *Fostering School Connectedness: Improving Student Health and Academic Achievement—Information for Teachers and Other School Staff* (www.cdc.gov; April 2016).

their parents are engaged, students are more likely to avoid a range of unhealthy behaviors.[12]

Defined as parents and school staff working together to support and improve the learning, development, and health of children and adolescents, parent engagement implies a shared responsibility. Meaningful and productive collaborations are cultivated when adults in schools, community agencies, and other organizations reach out to engage parents in meaningful ways while parents provide concurrent support for learning and development in their children. When significant adults are able to send consistent messages of support across the multiple settings in which children function, both health and learning are enriched.[13]

Given the significance of such findings, it is not surprising that education reform efforts have confirmed the important role to be played by parents. With a particular focus on improving achievement outcomes, positive effects have been demonstrated when parents engage in the strategies including the following:

- When families support learning in their homes, students experience higher achievement.
- Achievement gains occur regardless of socioeconomic status, ethnic/racial background, or the education level of parents.
- Children of parents who are engaged in their learning have higher grades and test scores, better attendance, and are more likely to complete homework assignments. In addition, these students have higher graduation rates and are more likely to enroll in postsecondary education.
- When parents fail to cultivate productive working relationships with school personnel, children are more likely to fall behind in their school performance.[14]

In addition to their role in influencing improved academic outcomes, parents can exert a strong and powerful influence over the health behaviors in which their children participate. In this context, research has demonstrated that family connectedness provides the strongest of all protective factors against emotional distress, disordered eating, and suicidal thoughts and attempts.[15]

The amount and quality of communication between caregivers and their children is particularly important in influencing sexual risks among youth. Research has confirmed that effective communication between parents and teens is likely to deter teens from participating in sexual experimentation at an early age. Such constructive communication also has been linked to the use on contraception among young people if, or when, they engage in sexual intercourse. Importantly, when teens and their mothers discuss contraception, such conversations *do not* cause or imply permission for teens to engage in risky sexual behavior.[16]

Finally, the health behaviors in which parents participate have been linked to the health risks of children. Although parents who use tobacco are more likely to have children who smoke, this factor is not causal. Due to many complex sources of influence over teen tobacco use, parents who smoke don't necessarily influence their children to smoke. The value that parents place on a tobacco-free lifestyle has been shown to be very influential over tobacco use in their children. Regardless of parental tobacco use, children who understand that their parents are negative about

Parents who are engaged in homework activities with their children communicate that they are committed to success in school.

their use of tobacco are less likely to smoke than the children of adults who communicate a more permissive attitude about the behavior.[17]

The key to achieving identified academic gains and health-risk reduction rests in implementing sound collaborative activities beyond those that exclusively occur between parents and their children. While further research is needed to provide insight into all factors that motivate parents to get involved in the school lives of their children, it is clear that engagement is more likely to happen when parents believe that their actions will make a direct contribution to improved learning outcomes.[18] Importantly, the kinds of activities linked to enriched academics extend beyond volunteering at the school site during the school day.[19] In this context, the author of an article in *American School Board Journal* asserted that "the cookie-baking, word-processing, candy-selling, paper-shuffling, showing-up activities are not likely to have much impact on achievement."[20] Importantly, research has identified several expressions of parental engagement in the educational process that have been linked consistently with improved academic performance.[21] These activities primarily are based in the home and reinforce the commitment students must make to their schoolwork. The kinds of behaviors most likely to improve academic outcomes for students include the following:

- *Managing and organizing children's use of time.* Parents of successful students help their children organize their schedules and check to see that their children are following routines.[22] In addition, parents would be wise to stay informed about school activities, performance, and assignments and to provide a place and time for homework to be completed. Finally, academic outcomes are improved for students whose parents know where they are, with whom they are spending time, and when they plan to come home. Engaged parents also supervise and exercise control over nonschool activities, including time devoted to television viewing.

- *Helping with homework.* Participating in homework provides parents with the opportunity to confirm their interest and take a direct role in their children's schooling. Specific suggestions for supporting academic success include making certain that assignments are completed, checking accuracy, and asking questions about the nature of assignments.
- *Discussing school matters with children.* It is important for children and their parents to talk regularly about school activities. The kind of conversation also is important: Parents should be willing to discuss problems as well as successes and reinforce persistence in confronting challenges. In addition, research supports developmentally appropriate collaborative decision making about matters such as participation in activities, projects undertaken, and, for older students, course selection.
- *Reading to and being read to by children.* A large body of research confirms the importance of reading activities for developing reading proficiency in younger learners. In addition, there is a connection between achieving school success and living in a home that is literacy-laden—that is, one that contains newspapers, books, magazines, and a computer or word processor.[23]

As with school connectedness, research has identified a range of activities in which parents and other caregivers can engage to establish or maintain productive relationships between themselves and school-based professionals.[24] Review of the contents of Consider This 4.2 will reveal examples of specific actions that can be taken by parents shown to reinforce protective factors, improve academic outcomes, and reduce health risks.

In addition to the value of believing that their efforts contribute to academic success, engagement is increased among parents who feel like their children and local school personnel expect and want them to be active participants in the education of their children. To reinforce such beliefs, all school staff must use varied means to communicate that parent engagement is wanted and expected.[25] While it is common for educators to express such expectations through verbal means, via e-mail blasts, or in district newsletters, three specific actions have been demonstrated to increase parent engagement particularly as it pertains to health promotion.

As a foundation, school district personnel must take steps to *connect* and build positive relationships with parents. To support connectedness among students and engagement among their parents, school staff and their community partners must identify and make the advantages of establishing productive collaborations very clear to all stakeholders.[26] A number of actions led by education professionals have been demonstrated to promote and sustain connections with parents. In specific, educators are encouraged to:

- Describe authentic parent engagement as a priority in the school mission statement.
- Establish a range of policies, practices, and programming that maximize parent engagement.
- Establish a sustained and welcoming environment for parents.
- Implement strategies to increase parent participation in school health activities, services, and programs (convenient timing of activities, providing child care, eliminating transportation and parking challenges, etc.).
- Provide enrichment and capacity-building activities for parents.
- Cultivate ways for parents to offer enrichment for school staff and community stakeholders.[27]

In addition to establishing connections with parents and cultivating a welcoming environment, schools must offer a range of activities that serve to *engage* parents in student learning and health promotion. To this end, six strategies have been demonstrated to increase such engagement, including:

- Providing parenting support through instructional seminars, workshops, and resource collaboratives in the school and community.
- Communicating with parents with consistency and effectiveness.
- Implementing varied opportunities and times for parents to provide voluntary service.
- Supporting learning at home.
- Encouraging parents to be part of decision making in their local schools.
- Cultivating community, school, and parent collaborations.[28]

Consider This 4.2

Parent Actions Demonstrated to Reinforce Protective Factors, Improve Academic Outcomes, and Reduce Health Risks

1. Encourage your children to talk openly with you, their teachers, and other school staff about their needs and worries.
2. Investigate school expectations for learning and behavior by talking with teachers and staff, attending school meetings, and reading information that is distributed.
3. Support school expectations for work and behavior in the home.
4. Communicate and meet regularly with teachers to discuss your child's academic progress, accomplishments, and targets for improvement.
5. Help your child with homework activities.
6. Provide a space and the tools for students to do school work at home.
7. Encourage your child to participate in school activities.

SOURCE: Centers for Disease Control and Prevention, *Helping Your Child Feel Connected to School—Information for Parents and Families* (Atlanta, GA: U.S. Department of Health and Human Services, April 2016). www.cdc.gov

Teachers are encouraged to invest time with each student every day and to use icebreaker and trigger activities to help build a sense of connectedness, engagement, and a positive learning environment.

inclusive. This is particularly important as today's students are increasingly diverse. To maximize academic productivity, all students must feel safe, be skilled at communicating both self-respect and respect for others, understand classroom rules and procedures, and celebrate the academic successes they and their classmates experience. To promote such an environment, teachers must structure policies, practices, and communication strategies in ways that enhance student engagement and a sense of connectedness with classroom learning experiences and with the larger school community.

In addition to making sure they communicate respect, enthusiasm, and an invitation to learn, teachers must implement learning activities that promote a safe and positive learning environment into regular classroom practice. Such activities, often referred to as "icebreakers," are designed to (1) reinforce an "inviting" learning environment, (2) cultivate connections between learners, and (3) foster approachability for students with their teachers. In addition, such learning activities can be planned to introduce a topic or particular content to follow. In this way, simple and efficient "trigger" activities can provide a bridge into the topic for the day or between days when content coverage is extended.

Following is a discussion of a number of icebreaker activities that can be used to communicate that the classroom environment is safe and engaging. Each activity is described for general classroom application, but teachers are encouraged to use them to respond to classroom circumstances or modify them so they can be used as trigger activities to enhance health instruction.

Finally, it is important to *sustain* parent engagement, a significant challenge especially as children grow into adolescence and progress through middle and high school. In this regard, it is important for education professionals to identify specific barriers that keep parents from engaging in school activities with consistency. Once challenges are identified, staff must work with parents to develop strategies to manage them.[29] Teacher's Toolbox 4.1 describes common challenges to get and keep parents engaged in school-related activities that support learning and promote student health. In addition, selected recommendations developed by the Centers for Disease Control and Prevention are offered to help reduce or eliminate identified impediments.[30]

Developing a strategy to engage these important caregivers in ways demonstrated to exert a positive influence on academic outcomes and health risk participation depends on a comprehensive approach implemented by all concerned stakeholders, not just educators *or* parents. While developing such a comprehensive plan is an important task for school staff, it must be noted that mutually rewarding relationships between parents and school personnel develop most commonly when all parties make an honest and authentic commitment to achieving the best outcomes for all learners.

Cultivating Classroom Connectedness

Although a great deal of time in professional education programs is devoted to helping educators learn to organize effective and meaningful ways to help students engage with learning materials (texts, curricula, online resources, etc.), how students interact with each other largely is ignored. Importantly, how teachers structure student–student interaction exerts significant influence over how they learn, feel about their classmates, their sense of connectedness with the adults at their school, and even their self-esteem.[31]

In this context, as a starting point for effective instruction in any content area, teachers must plan how they will cultivate a positive learning environment that is safe, engaging, and

Clustering

Clustering is a learning activity designed to enable students and teachers to talk with many people during a short period of time. The class will need enough space to walk around the room freely. Consider pushing desks and chairs toward the walls to allow space in the center of the room. Explain that you will call out categories to form small groups. When students cluster in groups, they introduce themselves to each other and try to learn every person's name. For younger students, teachers should select categories with limited choices (favorite season, number of siblings, eye color), designate an area of the room for each choice, and facilitate student movement to appropriate areas. Teachers could post pictures in assigned areas of the room to reduce confusion. For older students, have children write responses to categories on an index card, select students to share their choices, and then group students with like-minded peers. Repeat this process until all students are grouped. Teachers can participate in clustering as an icebreaker to help learn student names and to increase accessibility. When students return to the larger group, ask them, "What happened?" "How did you feel?" "What did you learn?"

Solutions for Six Common Challenges to Sustaining Parent Engagement

Challenge 1

Parents are unable to attend meetings or activities because of schedule conflicts (e.g., related to work, family, religious, or community activities). To help address this challenge:

- Schedule meetings and activities more likely to match varying parent schedules by the following:
  - Survey parents to identify times, dates, and days that work best for them.
  - Schedule more than one meeting or activity opportunity.
  - Host meetings and activities during the day for parents who work or are unable to attend at night.
  - Convene meetings after rush hours and at locations in the community rather than at the school site.
- Provide incentives to encourage parents to attend at-school meetings and events by the following:
  - Provide child care.
  - Provide food or refreshments.
  - Award door prizes provided by community sponsors.
  - Include icebreaker activities or other enjoyable activities in the meeting agenda.
- Provide alternative ways for parents to access information and communicate with school staff that supplement meetings and activities held at the school site by the following:
  - Establish an e-mail listserv for teachers and parents.
  - Create a 24-hour voice mail service to enable parents to express thoughts and concerns outside of regular school hours.
  - Hosting conference calls.
  - Establishing a school blog or online bulletin board.

Challenge 2

Parents can't attend meetings and activities due to a lack of transportation. To help address this challenge:

- Provide transportation by any of the following means:
  - Use school buses.
  - Create a shared school/community "ride board."
  - Provide bus tokens or other public transportation fares.
  - Arrange parent carpools.
- Hold events off-site or online via the following:
  - Meet in community locations where parents can easily gather, including parks, libraries, community centers, or churches.
  - Host webinars.
  - Create podcasts that are archived online.

Challenge 3

As a result of any negative experiences from when they were in school, a lack of familiarity with the school culture, or other factors, parents are uncomfortable at school meetings and activities. To help address this challenge:

- Provide opportunities for parents to get to know about the school and the school staff in nonthreatening ways by doing any of the following:
  - Host informal get-togethers *before* there is a problem with their child.
  - Provide continuing education opportunities for parents.
  - Host parent-only social events at the school site.
  - Have students serve as greeters at school-sponsored parent meetings and activities.
- Implement programs that are culturally sensitive and that reflect the social and environmental aspects of the community by the following means:
  - Host multicultural events that connect families.
  - Serve culturally diverse and healthy snacks at meetings and activities.
  - Ensure that diverse and multilingual staff or parent liaisons are in attendance at family meetings and activities.
  - Make the school a de facto community center for families.

Challenge 4

Due to language barriers or a lack a familiarity with terms used by school staff, parents don't comprehend information and communication, particularly about student health issues at activities and meetings. To help address this challenge:

- Provide translation services for non–English speaking parents by the following means:
  - Ask parents or students (if appropriate) to volunteer to provide translation services.
  - Offer educational programs translated into representative languages.
  - Provide school publications and Web resources in multiple languages.
  - Cultivate language-specific school telephone call lines for families.
- Reduce barriers to understanding information by the following:
  - Avoid use of education and health jargon with families.
  - Prepare informational materials at an eighth-grade or lower reading level.

Challenge 5

School staff that are not experienced or trained to work with parents have had trouble sustaining relationships and parent engagement efforts. To help address this challenge:

- Provide professional development opportunities for school staff that focus on strengthening parent engagement by doing the following:
  - Offer a variety of topics to meet a range of staff needs.
  - Schedule professional development activities at flexible times.
  - Cultivate partnerships with local universities for professional development services in return for research opportunities at the school site.
- Develop strategies to work through staff resistance to change, turf issues, and power struggles that might threaten parent–teacher interactions by either of the following:
  - Talk with school staff members about their concerns related to parent engagement.
  - Coach school staff about how to cultivate positive relationships with parents.

Challenge 6

There is difficulty sustaining school administrative or financial support for parent engagement. To help address this challenge:

- Share data with the principal that demonstrates parent interest and the positive impact parent engagement has on education and health outcomes by any of these means:
  - Share assessments of parent needs and interests.
  - Share data that demonstrated the efficacy of parent engagement.
  - Present health-related data from the Youth Risk Behavior Survey (YRBS) to highlight health issues confronting students in the state.
- Empower parents to speak with administrators about the positive impact of their having been engaged in the health of students and at the school by either of the following:
  - Ask the PTA to communicate with administrators about the benefits of parent engagement.
  - Invite school administrators, media, celebrities, and education and health officials to witness parent engagement in action.
- Seek opportunities for financial support by taking the following actions:
  - Respond to calls for grant proposals.
  - Develop strategies that require limited or no financial support.
  - Solicit funds and in-kind contributions from community partners.
  - Partner with the PTA or a local university to apply for external funding.

SOURCE: Centers for Disease Control and Prevention, *Parent Engagement: Strategies for Involving Parents in School Health* (Atlanta, GA: 2013), 20–23.

Whip Around

Whip Around helps students learn names quickly. Have the class sit or stand in a circle, so that everyone can see everyone else. Ask students to say their names and tell something about themselves as directed. Initially, the teacher can start the activity, followed by one of the students sitting to either side who takes a turn. Then, the activity progresses by engaging students around the circle. Topics can include such issues as students' favorite subject in school, or what they want to be when they grow up. A favorite topic of elementary students during Whip Around is their "claim to fame." In "claim to fame," students tell their name, followed by something for which they are or hope to be famous in the future. Students are encouraged to be creative during this activity. As discussed, Whip Around takes only a short time to complete and functions as an icebreaker activity, giving students and teachers the opportunity to learn names and other information about classmates. In addition, Whip Around can be modified into a trigger activity by using themes or questions about content covered previously.

Boundary Breaking

Boundary Breaking develops connectedness and communication skills. Ask students to stand or sit with a partner. If there is an odd number of students in the class, teachers should participate. Ask one student to be the "talker" and the other the "listener." Ask a question, then give the talker in the pair thirty seconds to answer the question while the listener attends quietly. If the talker runs out of things to say, the listener can ask questions. Call time after thirty seconds; talkers and listeners switch roles and repeat the activity, asking a new question. Have students choose a new partner after each pair of questions. Conduct Boundary Breaking throughout the year to help students get to know each other on a more personal level and to practice speaking and listening skills. Sample questions include:

> What was the title of the last book you read, and what was it about?
>
> What is your favorite hobby and why?
>
> What is your favorite subject and why?
>
> How do you select your friends, and what is the most important characteristic in a friend?
>
> If you could be any animal (other than a human), what animal would you choose and why?
>
> What is something about yourself that you are really proud of and why?

A good resource for questions is *The Kids' Book of Questions*, by Gregory Stock.[32] This book contains 260 questions that are developmentally appropriate for elementary and middle school youth. Students can also make up questions to use.

Four Corners

Put up large sheets of paper in the four corners of the classroom at the end of the school day or while students are out of the room. Each sheet of paper should have one word written on it that represents a category. Examples of categories that can be used include kinds of animals, colors, pizza toppings, sports or activities, and geometric shapes. To begin the activity, ask students to think about which of the four corners they prefer. On signal, have students go to the corner of their choice. Students will introduce themselves by name and tell why they chose that corner. By changing the focus to a pertinent health topic or issue, this activity can be used as a trigger for instruction or as a review or "exit" activity.

Snow Cones

Use brightly colored paper to represent the flavors of snow cones (crushed ice doused with flavored syrup in a paper cone). Have students sit in a circle. One uniquely colored sheet of paper in the center of the circle serves as the "target." Pass around paper of various colors, allowing students to choose their favorite. They'll need a pencil or marker and a hard surface on which to write. When everyone has a sheet of paper, have students fold their sheet in fourths and number the squares. In the upper-left-hand corner (vertical or horizontal—students choose), ask students to write their name. Then the teacher asks a question and students write their answer in that block. You can ask questions of all kinds or ones focused on a specific instructional topic. When students have finished, have them crumple their papers up in a ball and toss them at the target in the center of the circle. When all the colored balls of paper are in the center, ask students to get up and retrieve a piece of paper that is a different color than their own, without bumping anyone else. Students should go back to their place in the circle and read what is written on the paper they selected. Next, ask students to write their names in the upper-right-hand corner of the paper. Ask another question. Students write their answer, toss the papers in again, retrieve, read, and write names and the answer to a new question. Repeat until all four squares are filled. When applied as a trigger activity designed to enrich instruction, Snow Cones can provide an opportunity to review or assess student knowledge or attitudes. (This activity is adapted from Jeanne Gibbs's *Tribes*.)[33]

Time to Move!

Activities that include a gross-motor element provide an effective change of pace for classroom instruction. Have students start by sitting in a circle in chairs or at desks (that don't slide easily). Start by standing in the center of the room and having students get up on signal, walk across the circle, and sit at another chair. When students demonstrate that they can move without risk, start the activity. Say "It's time to move if..." and continue with a description of some of the students in the classroom—for example, "It's time to move if you are wearing blue" or "It's time to move if you like chocolate milk." When students get the idea, remove one chair as they are moving around the room. The student who is left without a seat goes to the center of the circle and continues the activity. To end the activity, simply slip the chair that was removed back into place and ask everyone to return to their original seats. (This activity is adapted from Jeanne Gibbs's *Tribes*.)[34]

Greetings Before School Begins

Before school begins for the year, teachers send a postcard to each student. Write a brief note that communicates your excitement about working with each child throughout the next school year. Students and their parents or caregivers will be surprised and pleased to receive this early and affirming message.

Positive Letters and Phone Calls

An excellent way to connect with parents or caregivers is to make contact with them when things are going well for their child. Teachers are encouraged to share improvements in behavior or performance in a certain subject, or communicate that they enjoy the creativity their child brings to the class. E-mail reinforcement or affirmation messages also can encourage parent engagement in school activities. Teachers must make sure that such "good news" communications are shared frequently and with the caregivers of all students.

The Appreciation Activity

This activity is enjoyable for students and can be accomplished in a relatively short amount of time. First, ask students what it means to appreciate someone or something. Then ask students for examples of statements that show appreciation ("I appreciate you because you help me with my homework"; "I appreciate you because you smile a lot"; "I appreciate you because you always say 'Good morning'?"). Next, have students help each other tape a piece of paper to their backs, with the following words at the top: "I appreciate you because you. . . ." Without signing their names, students move around the room and write an appreciation statement on the backs of as many classmates as possible in the allotted time. After time is called, have students return to their seats, take their papers off their backs, and read them, perhaps aloud.

Popcorn Appreciation

At the end of the school day, have students gather in a circle for Popcorn Appreciation. You or any student can start by saying "Today, I appreciated [student's name] for [reason]"—for example, "Today, I appreciated Neil for helping me on the computer"; "Today, I appreciated Lola and Cathy for helping me put away the art supplies"; or "Today, I appreciated Eric for sharing his snack with me." Allow students to volunteer their appreciations for the day, rather than going around the circle. Teachers should share their appreciation of children who may be overlooked or who are not affirmed by classmates to help reinforce a classroom norm of acceptance and respect for all in the classroom community. Popcorn Appreciation is a way to allow children to leave school with the positive aspects of the day ringing in their ears. The value in expressing appreciation provides students and teachers with the opportunity to recognize many kinds of efforts rather than praising only students who did especially well at academic tasks. Hearing and saying specific appreciations helps students and teachers improve both reflection and communication skills.[35]

Interviews

Conducting interviews can help students practice important oral and written communication skills. In addition, interviewing family members or neighbors can personalize academic content or enable students to learn about their heritage, culture, or community. Interviewing a classmate might help students make new friends.

Once completed, students are encouraged to share the results of their interviews with classmates by reporting something new that they learned.

Class Picture Inspection (for Teachers)

Teachers are encouraged to use a class picture or roster to ensure that they connect with every student each day. At the end of every day, look at the class picture and try to remember at least one positive comment you made to each student. For those students who did not receive a positive comment for the day, make sure to start the next day by making such a remark to them. Positive comments do not always have to relate to schoolwork or be expressed as praise. Positive comments and appreciations can relate to personalities and interests and can be expressed as questions and in conversation. Students feel valued and affirmed when their teachers show genuine interest in their lives ("How did your soccer team do yesterday?" "Have you been working on some of your drawings this week?" "Wow—how's it going being the new big sister in the family?").

Featured Student of the Week

Every week of the school year, select a different student as the Student of the Week. Teachers must make sure that every child has a turn to be honored in this way. Notify parents and caregivers in advance, so students can bring in items from home or prepare things to include on the Student of the Week bulletin board. Students might want to display pictures or information about their favorite food or sport, talents they have, lessons that they are taking outside of school, or other things they enjoy doing. Sometimes, students bring family or baby pictures to display. To support the development of the bulletin board, teachers can create a list of potential things to share. Such a display allows other students to learn more about the featured student and can provide an opportunity to discuss and honor unique family or cultural customs.

Student Collage (Cross-Curricular Activity)

Have students make a collage that represents things they like to do or do well. Students can draw, write, or cut pictures out of magazines to enrich their collages. Younger students might want to make their collage on an outline of their bodies (students can trace each other on butcher paper). Display the completed collages in the classroom and have students explain them to learn more about their classmates. This learning activity is cross-curricular with the content area of fine arts.

Graffiti or Word Wall

Cover a large bulletin board or wall in the classroom with butcher paper. Allow students to write or draw on the graffiti wall whenever they complete their work or during any free time. Teachers might want to identify specific themes for graffiti or word walls, including seasonal health issues, ways to be a friend, appreciations for classmates, favorite activities, or favorite foods. In addition, words added to the "wall" could be limited to those related to an instructional health topic as a way to reinforce pertinent vocabulary. Teachers are encouraged to make an agreement with students that they will write or draw only positive representations or comments on the graffiti or word wall. If negative comments or pictures are placed on the wall, use a class meeting to allow students to decide how to manage this or other problems.

Journal Writing

Have students keep a journal throughout the school year. Journaling reinforces a range of important writing skills. Ask students to respond to instructional activities or class events, write creative stories or poetry, or share their feelings about the day. Be sure to collect student journals frequently and respond to the entries. Although providing written responses takes time, teachers can model desired writing skills or enrich their relationships with students by making the time to provide a reply to journal entries.

Role-Playing

Role-playing is particularly effective with middle school students. Acting allows students to be creative while practicing a range of skills, including resistance, communication, affirmation, and decision making. Use scripted and half-scripted role-plays to help students get started. Then, turn the role-play design process over to students with open-ended scenarios.

Success of the Day

At the end of each school day, ask students to write down a success they experienced that day. Students should keep these successes in a journal or notebook to review when they need to lift their spirits. Students can share their successes with classmates or can write them on a teacher-developed form to share with family members.

Class Contracts

It is important for teachers to promote the idea that classrooms are communities of learners that are shared by students and teachers. Allowing students to have input in establishing the rules of the class, through a class or a personal positive behavior contract, helps reinforce this concept. Although there are several ways to develop a class contract, a suggested format follows. First, introduce the concept of a *contract* (an agreement in which everyone gives something and gets something back in return). Discuss circumstances or jobs for which people make and sign contracts. Next, ask students to discuss the meaning of the word *privilege*. Ask them to think of privileges they have liked having at school or at home. Explain that they will be able to gain such privileges by creating a class contract. List examples of privileges on the board or on newsprint under the heading "Students Get." Suggestions might include several five-minute activity breaks during the school day, additional time during which the teacher reads a book aloud, or extra library time each week.

Review the list and then negotiate which items can be given to the students. For instance, a student might suggest that there should be no tests. Although most teachers have to give tests, they might offer to not give any tests on Friday.

Next, remind students that very few things in life are free, and if they want privileges, they must give something in return. Ask students what they would be willing to give and write their suggestions on the board or on newsprint under the heading "Students Give." Suggestions from elementary students might include good effort, cooperation, attention, positive attitude, participation, and respect. Ask the students if they can live up to the items on the "Students Give" list. If students cannot live up to a certain item on this list,

then it must be removed. Remind students that this is a class contract for which everyone shares responsibility.

Next, share your list under "Teacher Gives." Preprint the list to save class time. Sample items from a "Teacher Gives" list could include attention, time, energy, knowledge, humor, kindness, fairness, and extra help. Students appreciate this part of the contract because they feel the teacher also is giving things to make the class run more fairly and successfully. Then share a preprinted list of "Nonnegotiables." These are the rules that must be followed—no negotiation is possible. Some "Nonnegotiables" are "Follow all school rules," "No tobacco use by anyone," "Never say I can't," and "No put-downs allowed." Next, discuss the consequences of breaking a rule in the contract or how to manage if anyone, teacher or student, does not live up to it. Most of the time, students will come up with stiffer consequences than the teacher.

Some consequences suggested by elementary students might include staying after school, apologizing to the class, and doing extra homework. It is important for teachers to make sure that consequences are developmentally appropriate. For example, doing extra homework as a consequence doesn't help students enjoy learning because homework is being used as a punishment. A more appropriate consequence is to have students write an explanation of what went wrong, why it happened, and how to behave more responsibly if the situation arises again.

In the last part of the contract, build in a plan for celebration. For example, when the class follows the contract they created for a week, have a celebration time that includes all class members, with healthy snacks, music, and time to participate in favorite activities. Help students think of these times as celebrations of cooperative achievement rather than as rewards. Rewards sometimes are used to exclude certain children and engender a sense of competition instead of collaboration.

After students agree on the contract, make a copy for everyone in the class with your signature and send it home to parents or caregivers. Have parents or caregivers and students sign the contract and return it to you. Post a large copy of the contract in the room. If there is a student in the class who does not agree with the contract, have an individual conversation with the student to discuss the benefits for all concerned. As a foundation for establishing classroom norms of safe, healthy, and productive behavior, it is important that all students abide by the contract despite potential disagreement with some element of it.

Students usually create class contracts with the rules most teachers would initiate without their input, but often are more willing to follow the rules if they can be participants in the development of them. Teachers who try making a class contract for the first time should remember that students might need a period of adjustment to it. If the contract is broken, use these incidents as an opportunity for teaching and learning rather than as a signal to abandon it. Some teachers might feel that it is easier to throw out the contract and come up with their own rules and consequences. Though this might seem efficient, as the school year progresses teachers find that it becomes increasingly difficult to use such a "top-down" approach as the foundation for effective classroom management.

Once students get accustomed to the idea that they can influence class rules and consequences, they begin to hold other students accountable to contract stipulations. Students can hold their teachers accountable as well. Health educator Lynn Shoji shares that she knows she needs to watch her comments when her middle school students remind her "Mrs. Shoji, that was a put-down."[36]

Contracts also provide an effective method for working with individual students on skill development or behavioral management. Teachers can develop specific contracts with students to work on goal setting, planning, time management, and other objectives. Such contracts can be used daily, weekly, or as needed. See Teacher's Toolbox 4.2, "Sample Contracts for a Third-Grade Class" for examples.

Class Jobs

Teachers and students can collaborate in brainstorming a list of class jobs. Then, teachers can allow students to apply as individuals or small groups for jobs that appeal to them. Class jobs could include serving as line leader, lunch money collector, chalkboard cleaner, trash can monitor, pencil sharpener monitor, bulletin board designer, calendar monitor, attendance taker, or as plant or animal caretaker. Be sure that all jobs are equal-opportunity—girls and boys should be able to hold any class job. Elementary teacher Diane Parker initiates the idea of "helper families" in her classroom.[37] Students work in groups to perform jobs for a given period of time. Then, jobs rotate among the "helper families" in the classroom.

Participation in Classroom Decisions

Although many decisions are made for elementary and middle school students, it is important to equip them with essential skills to make their own decisions when possible and appropriate. For example, students might get to decide where they will sit for a particular activity, which book they will read, which of two assignments they will complete first, or the format for a particular assignment (poster, skit, dance, or rap). As discussed in Chapter 3, decision making is complex and includes defining problems, generating and evaluating choices, and selecting and acting on best options. In addition to cultivating opportunities for students to practice decision-making skills, it is helpful to discuss positive and negative consequences that can result from them. For example, students could be encouraged to evaluate such things as, "What will happen if I choose to sit by my best friend during science? Will we both do our best work, or will we distract each other? What's the best decision for me and why?"

Class Meetings

Regular class meetings convened to discuss current class issues openly provide an important opportunity to increase student empowerment and self-management. Rules for class meeting might include:

- All students sit in a circle facing each other.
- Only one person speaks at a time.
- Stick to the topic.
- Be honest.
- Be thoughtful of the feelings of others.
- Speak only for yourself.

Sample Contracts for a Third-Grade Class

Class Contract

Students Get	*Students Give*
• Field trips	• Try hard
• No Friday tests	• Study
• Good grades	• No talking when others are talking
• Fun	• Pay attention
• Friends	• Be prepared
• Extra help	
• To learn	

Teacher Gives

Nonnegotiables
- Follow school rules
- No put-downs

- Fairness
- Understanding
- Extra help
- Humor
- Enthusiasm
- Praise
- Kindness
- Good explanations

Consequences
- Apology to class
- Stay after school
- Go to principal

I agree to this contract for the school year.

Student's signature: _____

Parent's/caregiver's signature: _____

Teacher's signature: _____

Individual Student Contract

My goal is to _____
                (state goal)

I can do this if I _____
                (plan of action)

If I do this, I will _____
                (reward)

If I don't do this, I will _____
                (consequence)

Student's signature: _____

Parent's/caregiver's signature: _____

Teacher's signature: _____

Teachers are encouraged to have students set class meeting rules and to review them and the meeting agenda before it is scheduled to take place. During the class meeting, teachers can act as facilitators by sitting outside the circle, answer questions or clarify comments when necessary, and summarize meeting content. In this scenario, students run the meeting themselves. Students might want to choose different student discussion leaders for each meeting. Alternatively, teachers can sit in the circle to participate as a class member who has an equal voice (but not the discussion leader, unless the children need assistance).

All kinds of topics are appropriate for class meetings. Students might want to discuss a specific class project or issue. If the class has conducted a health fair for parents, a class meeting could be used for students to express both the positive and negative outcomes or to make suggestions for improving the activity in the future. As an alternative, class meetings can be scheduled to enable students to plan for a special event, for example, "We are going on a field trip with our grade level. We have 103 students and four buses. Two buses hold 25 and two buses hold 45 students. How many students should go on each bus? How will we decide who goes on which bus?"

A good time to have a weekly class meeting is on Friday afternoons so students have the opportunity to evaluate activities, issues, or problems that arose over the week. Active participation in class meetings can take time, especially if students have never had this kind of voice before. Over time, and with practice, students begin to give useful feedback about activities and issues. Reinforce the notion that students will not be punished for discussing negative matters confronting their class. Rather, encourage students to suggest ways to improve a situation or manage challenges.

Question Box

Create a class question box to promote a positive learning environment. Students can write anonymous questions about topics discussed in class. Importantly, teachers must establish the boundary that all questions must be focused on student activities and interests, rather than personal questions about the teacher or other students. A question box allows students who are hesitant to speak in class to get answers to their questions. It is common for teachers to use this activity for sexuality questions, but the question box is a great classroom strategy to maintain across the year. Teachers must make it clear that any time a student reveals any danger to self or others, they must contact or make an official referral to parents or to an appropriate resource professional. Finally, it is vital for teachers who create question boxes to establish a consistent time each week to respond to student questions.

Guest Speakers

Expose students to careers, skills, and diverse talents by inviting respected individuals from the community to share their interests or areas of expertise as classroom guests. Hearing from community members or parents helps students to get to know people with unique skills or careers. Be sure you know any classroom guest and have reviewed his or her remarks before any adult from the community interacts with students.

"He-roes" and "She-roes" (Cross-Curricular Activity)

Correlate health education with social studies by having students investigate the lives of men ("he-roes") and women ("she-roes") who have made a difference for good in the world throughout history. To create a link with language arts, ask students to identify local he-roes and she-roes (parents, older brothers or sisters, community helpers) as the main characters of short stories they write to share with the class.

Peer Tutoring/Cross-Age Teaching

Have upper-elementary and middle-level students tutor or provide instructional reinforcement for their younger counterparts. It is common for older students to take their roles as models for younger students very seriously. Further, students of all age groups are enriched by such shared learning experiences. Some schools initiate "reading buddy" programs in which older students read with younger students and discuss books together. Finally, if your school has resource or special education classrooms, consider developing a collaborative peer tutoring program that involves students with special needs.

Community Service/Service Learning Projects

Ask students to brainstorm and then gather information about various community service projects in which they could participate. Service learning reinforces important values including helping and contributing to better the local community. Ideas include cleaning up parks or playgrounds, bringing or serving food to needy families, visiting and performing for residents of a nursing home, and raising money for a community project. Help students make arrangements to complete service learning projects by allowing them to take developmentally appropriate responsibility for planning, permissions, and implementation. Such experiential activities can be concluded by asking students to write and share written reflections about their experiences.

INSTRUCTION ORGANIZED WITH A SPECIFIC FOCUS ON HEALTH ISSUES

Once schools, families, and teachers have implemented strategies to promote connectedness, a common starting point is to organize content and instruction into discrete segments or disciplines. Many education researchers assert that each content area in the school curriculum represents a discrete form of knowledge. As such, academic disciplines or content areas have their foundation in unique sets of issues and questions. Developmental psychologist Jean Piaget defined a discipline as a specific body of teachable knowledge, with its own background of education, training, methods, and areas of focus.[38] In this context, the organization of instructional delivery into discrete academic disciplines in American middle and high schools is based on the goal of enhancing efficiency.[39]

Many local district curricula have been developed around strictly focused subjects or content areas. In response, it is common for elementary schools to organize instruction into focused content areas. Secondary schools that adopt such a time management approach organize instructional delivery into discrete and predetermined blocks of time and employ content specialists to deliver instruction.

Direct instruction delivered in this way represents the most common curricular and scheduling model in the U.S. education enterprise. It is associated with the following advantages for students, teachers, administrators, and parents:

- Parents, teachers, and students are familiar and comfortable with it.
- The approach is consistent with courses of study, standards, and testing protocol developed in most states.
- Textbooks and supplementary learning materials are readily available.
- Students are empowered with specialized information and skills.
- Secondary teachers academically prepared as content specialists are equipped with limited range but a great depth of expertise within a given discipline.
- All content areas, including those perceived to be of less importance, are afforded a portion of formal instructional time.

Supporters of such an approach to health education base their endorsement on the belief that health education is grounded in a discrete body of knowledge. As such, health education has its own philosophical underpinnings and content integrity, and it is worthy of specific and dedicated instructional time.[40]

Instructional Activities with Many Uses

It is not uncommon for teachers to associate a particular learning activity with a specific grade level, health issue, or unit of instruction. Teachers must remember, however, that there are countless instructional activities and learning strategies that can be adapted to address a wide range of health issues and diverse target audiences. Teachers interested in activities with applicability to meet the developmental needs of a range of ages and abilities of students and to manage diverse health topics are encouraged to examine Teacher's Toolbox 4.3. Suggested activities can be applied to all of the National Health Education Standards.

Teacher's Toolbox 4.3 provides a starting point for teachers to experiment with cross-topical application of learning activities. Recommendations for their use in context of specific health issues can be found in later chapters of this text. Finally, these activities can be applied across the curriculum to reinforce instruction in a range of academic subjects, including reading, social studies, math, and science.

Cooperative Learning: An Instructional Alternative

As teachers select effective learning strategies to respond to student needs, they must remember that the diversity of the student body in their classrooms is increasing each school year. Teachers will recognize this change in cultural, ethnic, racial, religious, economic, social, and language terms. Such diversity can manifest itself with positive or negative outcomes for students, teachers, and the learning process. If structured and managed with intention, diversity among students can result in increased achievement and productivity, creativity in problem solving, growth in cognitive and moral reasoning, and increased ability to recognize and accept the point of view of others. Unfortunately, diversity among students also has been associated with such negative outcomes as lowered achievement, closed-minded rejection

of new information, and increasingly negative relationships characterized by hostility, bullying, rejection, and racism; a prescription for student difficulties and classroom management problems for teachers and school leaders.[41]

Teachers play a critical role in structuring the learning environment and the kinds and quality of interactions that occur between students. Research has confirmed that there are three basic ways in which students interact during classroom learning experiences:

- The *competitive* model in which students vie for recognition as the "best" (spelling bees or races to see who gets a correct answer first during a review game).
- *Individualistic* approaches in which students work toward meeting set criteria, with their success depending only on their own performance without influence by other students (achievement tests of proficiency).
- *Cooperative* learning, in which interaction occurs in the context of learning in small groups within which students must collaborate to achieve shared goals while maintaining individual accountability.

The value systems that provide the foundation for each approach to learning exist as a "hidden curriculum" under the surface of the formal and intentional activities that permeate school life for students. Because everyone faces situations in which these engagement patterns are in operation, all students must learn to function effectively in each.[42]

Importantly, not all student engagement patterns have been demonstrated to be equally effective in helping learners to master concepts and skills. Cooperative learning has been demonstrated to have a powerful impact on learner outcomes in the areas of achievement, interpersonal relationships psychological health and social competence, and converting diversity into strength.[43] Numerous and significant studies have confirmed the following important and positive results:

- Working together to achieve a common goal results in higher achievement and greater productivity than working alone. Cooperative learning produces higher-level reasoning, more frequent generation of new ideas, and a greater ability to transfer what is learned across situations.
- When students work together to achieve a common goal, they care more about each other and are more committed to the success and well-being of classmates than when they work independently or compete to see who is the best.
- When students learn to value collaboration through accomplishing a shared success, they experience greater psychological health and higher self-esteem than when they compete with peers or work independently.
- When cooperative rather than competitive or individualistic approaches are used across the school day, diversity among students becomes a source of creative enrichment and increased productivity.[44]

Commonly used in upper-elementary and middle-school classrooms, cooperative learning is both a teaching philosophy and a collection of instructional strategies (structures). This approach has been incorporated into lessons in diverse content areas

Selected Activities with Applicability to a Range of Health Topics and Grade Levels

Anonymous Cards Strategy

The Anonymous Cards activity enables students to compare and contrast their knowledge, beliefs, and self-reported practices with classmates. This activity can be used to explore health issues across all three learning domains (cognitive, affective, psychomotor) while protecting students' anonymity. Nonwriters can use drawings, colors, or shapes to respond.

1. Each student receives an identical 3 × 5 inch card or piece of paper. All students must have similar writing implements.
2. Students are instructed to provide no personal identification on the card or paper.
3. Students respond to a series of teacher-developed questions on their card.
4. Questions are reviewed and cards are collected when all students have completed their responses.
5. The teacher shuffles the cards and redistributes them. Students receive a card that is not their own. Students who receive their own card in this process are encouraged to proceed with the activity as though the responses were provided by a classmate. It is important to assure the presumption of anonymity as cards are redistributed.
6. The teacher cues the discussion with the following: "Who has a card on which someone said . . .?" or "What did your classmate who wrote on the card that you received have to say about . . .?"

Human Scavenger Hunts/People Scrambles

This activity works well for any group of students with reading and writing skills. Developmentally appropriate accommodations must be made. The Human Scavenger Hunt is an effective trigger activity, or it can be used to summarize a unit of instruction.

1. Prior to class, teachers construct a handout asking students to conduct a self-assessment of their knowledge, attitudes, or self-reported practices about the health issue on which the unit is focused. Space is provided for student reflections on the handout.
2. One self-assessment sheet is distributed to each student.
3. Developmentally appropriate time limits are set for students to address all questions or items on the sheet.
4. When all students have completed this portion of the activity, they are encouraged to seek classmates with additional knowledge, different beliefs, or alternative health practices. Classmates from whom this information is gathered are asked to place their signature on the sheet confirming that they shared their alternative response.
5. Teachers are encouraged to place strict time limits on this final phase of the activity. In addition, the activity may be structured to limit the number of signatures that students may gather from any one classmate.

Carousel Activity

Structuring developmentally appropriate time blocks for all phases of this activity is imperative. The advantage of this activity is that each student responds to each item independently in relative anonymity to classmates outside their small group before small groups process the responses. This activity can be used to introduce, reinforce, or summarize units of health instruction.

1. Prior to the class, the teacher prepares a series of trigger questions, phrases, or words about the health topic. Each is placed at the top of a large sheet of newsprint paper.
2. Students are organized into appropriately sized groups. Each student has something with which to write. Each group receives a sheet of newsprint for consideration. For older students, the groups can assemble around sheets that have been taped to the wall. For younger students, working on the floor might be appropriate.

FIGURE 4–1 | The Fishbone Diagram

3. In carefully monitored time periods, all students are encouraged to provide written feedback to the question or issue on their large sheet of paper. As students respond concurrently, it must be reinforced that no student may write on top of the work provided by any other student.
4. When the time period has elapsed, all students are asked to stop writing. The groups of students are instructed to rotate to another issue or question to which they will respond. When they reach the next sheet, they are to provide as complete a response as possible in the available time. Teachers are urged to remind students to ignore the work of previous responders. This process continues until all students have responded to all items.
5. When groups return to the sheet on which they provided their original responses, they are to read all responses, tally and react to the comments, and prepare to share a summary of the remarks with the class as a whole.

Fishbone Diagrams

This activity can be part of an art or social studies correlation. Adapted from the body of literature on total quality management, it is also referred to as Ishikawa Charts, a tool for brainstorming. This brainstorming format has the advantage over its counterparts of enabling students to compare and contrast information, beliefs, or self-reported skills.

1. Prior to the lesson, the teacher prepares a blank fishbone diagram for each student or for each small group (Figure 4–1). In addition, the teacher identifies a theme with contrasting points of view.
2. Each student places the theme on which he or she is working in the "head" of the fishbone diagram. Then opposing viewpoints, conflicting information, or alternative practices are brainstormed. Contrasting responses are written on opposing "bones" of the diagram.
3. When completed, responses are shared with partners, small groups, or the whole class.

including language arts, math, social studies, and science.[45] Regardless of the context in which it is applied, cooperative learning makes each individual group member stronger by learning in collaboration with others.[46]

Cooperative learning involves much more than randomly arranging clusters of students into discussion groups.[47] Cooperative learning groups are intentionally organized to include students with a range of abilities. Consider This 4.3 reviews the differences between traditional approaches to group work and the cooperative learning group approach.[48] In addition, the work on multiple intelligences, discussed in Chapter 2, provides an interesting and effective way to organize students into cooperative learning groups.[49]

Cooperative learning requires students to be responsible for their own achievement and for that of their groupmates. This practice reinforces collaboration and encourages a more reciprocal status among group members.[50] Specifically, cooperative learning implies that students depend on one another for rewards by contributing to the achievement of the whole group through participation in peer-based learning.[51] Cooperative learning groups and activities are organized with consistency around the following common elements:

- *Positive interdependence* (sink or swim together): This is ensured through establishing a cooperative goal structure and distributing tasks and resources equitably among group members.
- *Face-to-face promotive interaction* (assist and encourage others to achieve): Students seated in close physical proximity are supported in mutual discussion of all aspects of the assignment. In addition, they learn about the importance of effort and how to recognize and acknowledge it in others.
- *Individual and group accountability* (individuals are responsible for doing their part): Although there is a focus on group outcomes, it is important that individual student achievement not be compromised. To this end, teachers can assess individual learning by assigning individuals to bring completed work to the group, picking random students to

answer questions, and assigning a challenging job or role to each student.
- *Interpersonal and small-group skills* (skills are required to be an effective group member): Rather than assuming that students possess social and collaborative skills (communication, decision making, conflict resolution, etc.), teachers must teach them as a foundation of cooperative learning. Reinforcement of these skills is enhanced by establishing the following expectations for groups: Everyone contributes and helps, everyone listens carefully to others, group members praise good work, and quiet voices are used unless otherwise specified.
- *Group processing* (discuss how well the group is functioning and make suggestions for improvement): Formal acknowledgment is provided by assessing group achievement and working relationships. This can be accomplished by having students identify at least three group members or specific things that enhanced collaborative success through use of learning logs, sentence stems, or other strategies that promote reflection. Such positive outcomes are supported when role assignments (recorder, timekeeper, etc.) are rotated within cooperative learning groups.[52]

Researchers and educators have developed a number of cooperative learning strategies or structures for use with diverse age groups of students and with a range of content areas. These structures make an effective contribution to instruction by supporting academic growth in the cognitive, affective, and psychomotor learning domains. Selected cooperative learning strategies, or structures, include Round-Robin, Corners, Numbered Heads Together, Pairs Check, Think-Pair-Share, Team Word Webbing, and Roundtable. A brief overview of these common structures is found in Table 4–1.[53]

Though there is a robust body of literature about uses and effectiveness of cooperative learning, little information confirms its effectiveness in enriching health education practice. The National Commission on the Role of the School and the Community in Improving Adolescent Health has asserted that a

Consider This **4.3**

Key Concepts of Cooperative Learning Groups

1. **Positive Interdependence**: Students need each other to complete the task or goal. Everyone commits to personal success and group success.
2. **Accountability**: Every member of the group is accountable for contributing work to the group goal. Student performance is assessed frequently.
3. **Interpersonal and Small Group Skills**: Team work skills such as leadership, decision making, trust-building, communication, and conflict management are needed to function effectively.

4. **Face-to-Face Promotive Interaction**: Students promote each other's learning by helping, sharing, and encouraging efforts to learn. Students promote each other's successes by sharing resources.
5. **Group Processing**: Students communicate openly with each other to express concerns and to celebrate accomplishments. They discuss how well they are achieving their goals and maintaining effective working relationships. Teachers monitor groups and give feedback to the groups and to the class as a whole.

SOURCES: IT Learning and Development, Penn State University, August 2017. Johnson, Johnson, and Holubec, *Cooperation in the Classroom*, Interaction Book Company, 1991.

TABLE 4–1

Examples of Cooperative Learning Strategies

Cooperative Graffiti: The teacher writes down a broad topic on the front board, and then students write down as many ideas as they can (in different colored pens/markers) that correlate with the topic written on the board. Once the time is up (about 5–10 minutes), then have students try and organize their colorful ideas into categories.

One-Minute Papers: This allows teachers to get feedback from students after a lesson is taught. Have students answer questions such as What was the most important thing you learned? What are you unsure about? What questions do you still have? What is one thing you'd like to know more about? Put students into groups to discuss their answers to these questions. What do they all have in common? Discuss with the entire class.

Three-Minute Review: This is used when the teachers stop any time during a lecture or discussion and allow teams three minutes to review what has been said with their group. Students in their groups can ask a clarifying question to the other members or answer questions of others.

Three-Step Interview: This is a strategy that is effective when students are solving problems that have no specific correct answers. The teacher presents an issue about which varying opinions exist and poses several questions for the class to address. The students in pairs become the interviewer and the interviewee. After the first interview has been completed, the students' roles are switched. After each student has had a turn, the pairs read their interviews to the class. After all interviews have been done, the class writes a summary report of the interview results.

SOURCES: Arizona State University: https://www.ode.state.or.us/opportunities/grants/nclb/title_iii/5cooperative-learning-strategies.pdf

new kind of health education should be developed, an approach focused on enriching student skills in making decisions, dealing with group pressure, avoiding fights, and working cooperatively.[54] Consistent with this call, early research has confirmed that cooperative learning has been associated with improving some health outcomes including content mastery of HIV/AIDS information and enhanced self-esteem, conflict resolution skills, and social and resiliency skills.[55, 56]

In an effort to expand health education applications of cooperative learning, readers will find a "jigsaw" structure developed to enrich a unit of instruction focused on promoting healthy eating in Teacher's Toolbox 4.4.[57] In this example, middle-grade students organized into cooperative learning groups increase their understanding of the Dietary Guidelines for Americans developed by the U.S. Departments of Agriculture and Health and Human Services, 2010. Group members are responsible for developing expertise in one segment of a similar body of information that is distributed to each group. Students then teach this information to group members.

Although cooperative learning requires teachers to do a different kind of preparation, impressive student outcomes can be achieved in context of rather than in place of instructional goals. Valuable instructional time is conserved without compromising academic goals.

Teachers are encouraged to explore the expansive body of literature about cooperative learning particularly as it relates to the Common Core Standards agenda discussed in Chapter 2. It is unlikely that this model will completely replace more traditional or competitive, classroom approaches, but cooperative learning has been demonstrated to enrich the learning experiences of diverse groups of students when used as an instructional supplement from one-third to one-half of the time.[58]

Individualized Instruction: An Important Alternative

Although the majority of health education curricula are developed around a discipline-specific focus that might include cooperative learning, individualized instructional approaches can

---

Teacher's Toolbox 4.4

Applying Cooperative Learning to Promoting Healthy Eating: Using a "Carousel"

- Students are broken into groups of three to four. Teacher places chart paper around the room with different questions on them related to healthy eating. Teachers are encouraged to review Chapter 6, "Promoting Healthy Eating," to help with their preparation for implementing this "carousel."
- This lesson can be done before starting a new unit to activate prior knowledge, during the unit, or at the end of review.
- Each group starts at a different poster and is given a different color marker to write with. The marker travels with the groups around the rooms, and each group has one to two minutes to answer the question on the chart paper.
- Students then rotate around the room to the next poster and repeat the process. Teachers may want to try to get each group member to write down their ideas on the paper so that each student's ideas are evident on the paper.
- When every group has written on each piece of paper, the class comes together for a whole class discussion and shares what is written on the posters.

SOURCE: Gray, Shelley, *How to Use the Cooperative Learning "Carousel" Strategy* (May 12, 2016). shelleygrayteaching.com/carousel/

provide significant enrichment to educational practice. This less common instructional format has enjoyed wide use in learning resource centers to meet the needs of students with learning or developmental disabilities. In addition, individualized instruction is used to provide remediation or as a supplement to more conventional educational approaches.[59]

Specific applications of individualized instruction that have particular potential to enrich health education practice include the use of learning centers located in the classroom and health fairs that serve larger target audiences. Learning centers and health fairs that focus on timely health issues add an important individualized dimension to elementary and middle school instructional practice.

Learning Centers

A learning center consists of an organized sequence of student-centered activities, each of which increases functional knowledge, helps students practice essential skills, or helps students examine their attitudes or beliefs about a health topic. While working at a learning center, students are active, independent, and can process information in the context of personal experiences or understandings. Learners work at their own pace, selecting from any number of interesting and multisensory activities organized to supplement more formal or larger-group instruction.

Typically, learning centers are arranged in a compact location in the classroom. To develop a learning center, teachers collect sets of materials, instructions, or complete activities in a designated, often separate, classroom space. The physical space of a learning center often is large enough for several students to work simultaneously but independently on self-selected tasks. This reinforces the notion of "parallel play," particularly appropriate for students in pre-primary and primary grades. Commonly, student work is displayed at the learning center as a way to stimulate thinking and reinforce creativity among classmates. Projects also can be shared with broader school audiences in hall, library, or lobby displays.

Learning centers designed to promote student health provide extended time for in-depth exploration of health concepts. As discussed earlier in this chapter, health education is not given the highest priority by many classroom teachers who must manage limited instructional time. Learning centers provide a way to both support and extend basic health instruction without taking time away from whole-group instruction. At learning centers, engaged students can move beyond mastery of basic content to explore beliefs and norms and practice health-promoting skills. Well-designed learning centers can:

- Organize resource materials for students.
- Encourage students to work independently.
- Respond to individual learning pace.
- Incorporate both independent and collaborative activities.
- Supplement or reinforce basic instruction.
- Provide opportunities for applying higher-order thinking skills and working in multiple learning domains.
- Combine a well-organized structure with freedom for independent thinking and creative expression.
- Provide opportunities for peer-based learning.

Though it is common for teachers to organize classroom interest areas that feature a range of materials and resources, learning centers must be instructionally sound. Planning should be focused on the following common elements:

- Developmentally appropriate learning objectives or organizing concepts.
- Directions for students working at the center.
- Samples or models of previously completed work.

- Media or computer applications.
- Strategies for introducing and sequencing activities.
- Evaluation protocol based on the identified objectives.

Learning center suggestions for promoting physical activity in safe play spaces targeting students in the upper-elementary grades can be found in Teacher's Toolbox 4.5.

Health Fairs

An interesting and effective alternative to conventional learning centers confined to a small space in the classroom is to organize multiple centers developed by students into a health fair. Often, students and teachers are familiar with the format of health fairs from having participated in such events at a hospital, shopping mall, or community center. A health fair or health carnival can be an exciting and useful trigger or reinforcement activity when incorporated into the district's approved health education graded course of study of the school district.

When describing a county or state fair, words such as *fun, excitement, noise, rides, food, booths, games, prizes, music, color,* and *exhibits* often come to mind. The same words have been used to describe health fairs or carnivals. Health fairs provide opportunities to teach health concepts in a hands-on, fun, creative, and developmentally appropriate way. Student-developed learning centers focus health instruction on topics as diverse as substance abuse prevention, disability awareness, the senses, and fire safety. Although health screenings (including vision and hearing testing, reaction-time testing, and blood typing) often are conducted at community health fairs for adults, such activities are not developmentally appropriate ways to enrich student understanding.

Although health fairs provide valuable supplemental health education learning experiences, they should not be perceived as the foundation for direct health instruction in any school. The purpose of a health fair is to stimulate interest in health issues and to expose participants to a variety of developmentally appropriate health issues in a compressed period of time. In addition, students gain in-depth understanding about a single health topic when they create a learning center for a health fair. The health fair also can serve as an effective organizational umbrella for collaborative activities among community groups, parents, teachers, and students. As such, health fairs can provide unique and memorable learning experiences for all who are involved.

Health fairs can be incorporated into an elementary and middle school health curriculum in a variety of ways. In one common example, college students enrolled in health education classes, junior or senior high school health classes, or community health professionals can organize a health fair to meet the needs of students in the elementary grades. Such collaboration between younger students and their secondary or university counterparts or local agency professionals are mutually enriching.

In addition, health fairs can be integrated into the academic program of studies of elementary and middle schools when students in the upper grades develop learning centers and organize

Teacher's Toolbox 4.5

Exploring Safe Play Spaces in My School, Neighborhood, and Community

Learning objectives/organizing concepts:

- Learners will identify safe and unsafe play spaces on their school campus.
- Learners will create a visual depiction of all the physical activities in which they could participate within walking or biking distance of their home.
- Learners will explore their community (Chamber of Commerce) website to evaluate the commitment to safe and noncompetitive physical activity for local children.
- Learners will serve as advocates for safe play spaces in their local community.

Materials needed for students working at the center:

- Laminated task lists with suggested procedures (creative expression should be encouraged).
- Rubrics clarifying task elements and evaluation criteria.
- School campus maps.
- Drawing materials (markers, paper, rulers, etc.).
- Poster board, scissors, magazines, glue sticks, and so on.
- Computer access to local Internet resources and/or text and visual material provided by city, Chamber of Commerce, local police department, and so on.
- Materials to write letters, samples of letters to the editor from the local newspaper, materials to make buttons or bumper stickers, contact information for local officials.

Resource samples or models to display in learning centers:

- Previous letters to the editor written by students.
- Samples of political or campaign buttons.
- Maps developed by students.
- Posters/collages assembled by students.
- Sample bumper stickers.

Strategies for introducing and/or sequencing activities:

- Teachers are encouraged to number task lists or organize materials in numbered packets if a developmental progression is important to successfully completing learning center tasks.
- While teachers are encouraged to be clear with directions, they are cautioned against being overly directive, because such an approach can compromise the positive independence fostered by learning centers.

Evaluation tools:

- Checksheets for self-evaluation (formative and summative).
- Rubrics.
- Bullet points to guide peer evaluation of work products.
- Presentations or opportunities to share work with classmates.
- Suggestions for ways to share work with parents, school administrators, and community leaders.

---

a health fair for their primary-grade counterparts. Teachers who supervise student planning for such cross-age approaches to learning should pay attention to developmentally appropriate practice concerns for younger students who will be invited to such a health fair.

Also, middle-grade students can organize a health fair for parents and the local community. When organizing a fair for parents, appropriate topics for adults—including diabetes prevention, tobacco use, cardiovascular disease prevention, and osteoporosis prevention—should be the focus. Such an activity allows students to learn more about the health concerns of grown-ups while promoting health in their community.

Finally, groups of students can organize a health fair to meet the health needs and interests of other students in their own school. For example, seventh graders can develop a health fair for sixth and eighth graders in their middle school. Such health fairs can be a very effective way to address timely and important matters in a school community.

Regardless of the format and target audience, such critical student skills as organizing, planning, implementing, and evaluating are practiced. To maximize the academic benefit of creating a learning center to contribute to a larger health fair, a sample organizational outline has been provided in Teacher's Toolbox 4.6. Although they are special events that supplement rather than replace effective and developmentally appropriate

Teacher's Toolbox 4.6

Sample Health Fair Outline

Following is a model of an outline that students can be asked to submit to the teacher clarifying plans and procedures for their health fair learning center:

- I. General health topic of the learning center
- II. Specific theme or concept on which the center is focused
- III. Learning center number
- IV. Organization or sequence of activities
    - A. How will your topic be introduced?
    - B. What functional information will be shared?
    - C. What multisensory activities have been planned?
    - D. What summary/closure activities have been planned?
- V. Diagram or drawing of the layout of the booth
- VI. List of equipment and materials needed
- VII. List of things to be distributed

comprehensive health education (discussed in Chapter 2), health fairs are an effective way to correlate or integrate health education concepts with a range of other content areas (approaches discussed later in this chapter).

Limitations of Direct Instructional Approaches

Although familiar and comfortable for many education stake-holders, discipline-specific approaches to teaching and learning present challenges for many. Regardless of content area, the major problem associated with direct instructional approaches rests with the fragmentation of time. In practical application, as students in secondary schools move from one subject to another, they also change rooms. As a consequence, teachers are forced to structure learning activities within designated time boundaries rather than in response to the developmental needs or pace of learning among students.

Because concepts and information are fragmented by necessity, an unrealistic and often inaccurate view of problems and issues is presented. Direct instruction implies that students must manage situations and questions one at a time or only within content categories. A review of the research on brain-based instruction from Chapter 2 reminds readers that learning is most likely to occur when students make connections between new concepts and preexisting knowledge. Direct instruction does not formalize learning experiences that will capitalize on students' abilities to draw relationships between or across issues. To be equipped to manage the tasks that confront them in their daily lives, students must participate in learning experiences in which they practice making connections within and between complex and disparate concepts.[60]

In addition, discipline-specific instruction can reinforce the value of competition. This common competitive teaching/learning philosophy is implemented in today's classrooms more than 90 percent of the time.[61] The underpinning of direct instruction implies that all students are expected to do their own work. As discussed earlier in this chapter, classmates are discouraged from seeking help from their peers and assisting a classmate usually is regarded as cheating. As a result of such intentional or unintentional expectations or norms, students are reinforced for working against one another to accomplish personal goals. In this way, the potential benefits of collaborative problem solving and decision making about academic challenges are not realized for many learners. Even under the best of circumstances, a hierarchy of student performance emerges that influences academic performance, classroom climate, and student interaction in negative ways.[62] Such negative consequences can be reduced with cross-curricular approaches.

INTERDISCIPLINARY INSTRUCTIONAL APPROACHES

In 1977, educator Lionel Elvin provided an analogy to help educators see the value of alternatives to direct instructional approaches. He suggested that, when we are walking outside, we are not confronted with fifty minutes of exclusive contact with flowers, followed by fifty minutes of contact with only one kind of animal.[63] As discussed in Chapter 2, research has confirmed that in the process of learning, the brain searches for patterns and interconnections as a way to make meaning about new concepts. If students learn by making connections, then educators must explore ways to teach through formalizing connections among concepts.[64]

Interdisciplinary instruction is defined as a view of knowledge (and, thus, a curriculum) that formally applies information, beliefs, and skills from more than one discipline to a problem, topic, theme, or experience.[65] Natural links between content areas serve as the foundation for implementing interdisciplinary instruction in classroom practice. For example, ideas for cross-curricular instruction might be stimulated among readers who review Teacher's Toolbox 3.11, which contains links between the National Health Education Standards and standards developed in other content areas.

Correlated Health Instruction

Although educators have identified a variety of interdisciplinary approaches to instruction, correlation is very common in health education practice. In correlated instructional approaches, complementary, discipline-specific units of study or related disciplines are brought together to answer common questions, solve problems, or address complex issues. The advantages of correlated instruction are evident for health education:

- Connections between previously unrelated content areas are formally reinforced.
- Realistic and complex health issues can be addressed.
- Complementary resource materials have begun to emerge.
- Time management problems can be eased with a correlated instruction approach.

Teachers who are interested in correlating health education with another content area are urged to examine the treatment of health concepts presented in texts written for other subjects. Such an examination offers a starting point for reducing repetition and expanding the use of correlated learning activities. Teachers are most likely to find such material in science textbooks. Though a useful starting place, teachers and administrators must not consider the text developed for science instruction or any other content area to be the primary source of information about health issues for students.

Among those who are skilled with conventional approaches to instruction, problems can be associated with correlated instructional approaches. Any change in organization and process that deviates from what is familiar might be met with resistance from parents, teachers, administrators, or students. In addition, scheduling problems, a lack of teacher training and capacity, and assessment challenges are common.

Teachers in self-contained classrooms who attempt correlated instruction can place unintentional emphasis on one content area over another. For example, if a teacher has greater expertise in language arts than in health education, it is unlikely that the health issue explored in a trade book, play, or poem will receive equal attention or emphasis. This imbalance can be exaggerated in response to topical emphasis on state tests of achievement.

Health-specific content areas serve as the organizational structure for the chapters in this text. Importantly, to reinforce the value of embracing interdisciplinary or cross-curricular approaches to learning, each content chapter features a list of recommended children's and adolescent books. In addition, as a way to enrich instruction, many learning activities include links to topic-specific, developmentally appropriate literature. Many of the books have been selected because they have been recognized with the Newbery Award for their literary merit. Others have received the Michael. L. Printz award for excellence in young adult literature, while still others have been suggested because they contain multicultural characters, themes, or illustrations. Some of the suggested books appear on the chapter and activity lists because they have received the Caldecott Award for noteworthy illustrations. Still others have been included because they have been recognized as noteworthy by the American Library Association (ALA). The ALA recognizes books as noteworthy because of their commendable quality, creativity, or because they have captured particular interest. Finally, other books have been suggested because they have been recommended by teachers who have had success in using them in applied learning activities with students.

These lists are not intended to serve as a complete catalog of all appropriate books that address health-related issues. Rather, they are intended to reinforce the value of sound correlated instructional approaches. These and other trade books can provide a starting place for integrating health education concepts into classrooms and districts exploring a whole-language approach to reading instruction. Teachers, parents, and concerned others are urged to examine Table 4–2 that contains a list of children's trade books with themes about or characters with disabilities or special needs. Consistent with the National Health Education Standards, the characters and stories in these books can open meaningful conversation, expand understanding of diversity, and provide context for practicing a range of health-promoting skills.

As is the case with all children's and adolescent literature, teachers must ensure that selected books are developmentally appropriate and have received thorough review. Readers who are concerned about the potential for controversy about this curricular approach or student health issue are urged to read the section "Controversy Management in Health Education" found later in this chapter.

Integrated Health Instruction: Thematic Units

In integrated approaches to instruction, multiple discrete content areas are collected into thematic units of instruction. Such thematic units of instruction can last a few days or can extend over longer periods of time. Thematic or integrated instruction is common in early childhood learning environments. The most compelling reason to incorporate integrated instruction into classroom practice in the upper grades is that it presents complex challenges and circumstances that are consistent with life outside the classroom. Consequently, it is stimulating and motivating for students and teachers.

Readers interested in thematic units of instruction are encouraged to review the example contained in Teacher's Toolbox 4.7. Caution is urged, as time, resource, and assessment challenges are common when attempting integrated instruction. Funding constraints, preparation time, and staff development are practical issues that compromise long-range integrated planning. In addition, parents often need to be educated about the value of integrated educational approaches if such approaches are to have widespread application and acceptance.[66]

As with cooperative learning, responding to the developmental needs of students should drive curricular decision making.

TABLE 4–2
Children's Literature with Themes or Characters with Disabilities or Special Needs

These books below can be added as more recent, available, and/or relevant books:

Ages 5–8
Aseltine, Lorraine, and Nancy Taut. *I'm Deaf and It's Okay.* Albert Whitman, 1991.
Bertrand, Diane Gonzales. *My Pal, Victor.* Raven Tree Press, 2004.
Cairo, Shelly, Jasmine Cairo, and Tara Cairo. *Our Brother Has Down's Syndrome.* Firefly Books, 1993.
Elliot, Rebecca. *Just Because.* Lion, UK, 2011.
Ely, Lesley. *Looking after Louis.* Frances Lincoln, 2004.
Goldin, Barbara Diamond. *Cake and Miracles: A Purim Tale.* Marshall Cavendish, 2010.
Graff, Lisa. *The Thing About Georgie.* Laura Geringer, 2007.
Hudson, Charlotte. *Dan and Diesel.* Red Fox, 2006.
Klise, Kate. *Stand Straight, Ella Kate.* Dial, 2010.
Lang, Glenna. *Looking Out for Sarah.* Charlesbridge Publishing, 2001.
Rodanas, Kristina. *The Blind Hunter.* Marshall Cavendish, 2003.
Seeger, Pete. *The Deaf Musicians.* Putnam, 2006.
Thomas, Pat. *Don't Call Me Special.* Barron's, 2012.
Tourville, Amanda Doering. *My Friend Has Autism.* Picture Window Books, 2010.
VanNiekerk, Clarabelle. *Understanding Sam and Asperger Syndrome.* Skeezel Press, 2008.

Ages 8–12
Attwood, Sarah. *Making Sense of Sex: A Forthright Guide to Puberty, Sex and Relationships for People with Asperger's.* Jessica Kingsley, 2008.
Draper, Sharon. *Out of My Mind.* Atheneum Books for Young Readers, 2010.
Estes, Eleanor. *The Hundred Dresses.* Harcourt Brace Jovanovich, 1944.
Herrera, Juan Felipe. *Featherless.* Children's Book Press, 2004.
Kent, Rose. *Rocky Road.* Alfred A. Knopf, 2010.
Konigsberg, E. L. *The View from Saturday.* Simon & Schuster, 1998. (Newbery Award).
Lord, Cynthia. *Rules.* Scholastic Press, 2006. (Newbery Honor Book).
Meyer, Donald J., ed. *View from Our Shoes: Growing Up with a Brother or Sister with Special Needs.* Woodbine House, 1997.
Palacio, R.J. *Wonder.* Alfred A. Knopf, 2012.
Polacco, Patricia. *Thank You, Mr. Falker.* Putnam, 1998.
Shaw, Beth Kobliner, and Jacob Shaw. *Jacob's Eye Patch.* Simon & Schuster, 2013.
Williams, Laura E. *The Can Man.* Lee & Low Books, 2010.
Wrobel, Mary. *Taking Care of Myself: A Hygiene, Puberty and Personal Curriculum for Young People with Autism.* Future Horizons, 2003.

Though teachers are not likely to abandon direct instruction, they might find that interdisciplinary approaches can enrich instruction about the complex health issues facing elementary and middle school students.

USING ELECTRONIC RESOURCES IN HEALTH EDUCATION

Anyone who has visited an elementary or middle school in recent years has noticed a changing learning landscape. Though many of the conventional approaches to teaching and learning remain,

In addition to other forms of technology, computers can open a door to challenging, developmentally appropriate, and enriching learning experiences that promote student health.

there is ever-increasing evidence of the use of instructional technologies. In classrooms, school-based learning labs, technology is being used to enrich learning and assessment (see the discussion about electronic portfolios and rubrics in Chapter 3). In many cases, computers provide access to challenging and enriching learning experiences for students of wide-ranging abilities. In addition, volumes of information are accessible to students, who have increasingly sophisticated computer expertise.

Given this rapid growth, it is not surprising that the technological literacy of students often surpasses that of their teachers, parents, and other significant adults. In fact, American users of technology have been given names that relate to the year of their birth, the kind of technology to which they had access while growing up, and the kind of learning environment in which they learned. People born between 1946 and 1964 are referred to as the "TV Generation." These adults learned in passive learning environments. Their counterparts who hold the highest education levels were born between 1965 and 1976 and are referred to as "Generation X." People born between 1977 and 1998 are referred to as "Generation Y" or the "Net Generation" because they grew up using computers. Finally, people born since 1999 are the first generation of Americans to have seen their parents embrace the technology that is so common in their lives. These people are referred to as "Generation Z."[67]

In context of health education technology is being used to enrich student capacity to live, learn, and work successfully in a world that is increasingly complex and media-rich. Research has confirmed that all instruction including that, which is enriched by technology, should parallel desired healthy behavior outcomes for learners. As such, the measure of the effectiveness of health education enriched by technology is based on the extent to which engaged learning and collaboration are promoted and supported. This suggests that the effective use of technology promotes the following:

- Engagement, meaningful learning, and collaboration with a focus on cultivating essential skills that can be used in the daily lives of students.
- The use of technology as a tool for learning, communication, and collaboration.[68]

In this context, the Centers for Disease Control and Prevention has confirmed that today's youth are the most ethnically diverse generation in U.S. history and that their health concerns range from cultivating productive relationships to managing stress and eating and exercising in healthy ways. They use technology to share information through social networking, blogging, e-mailing, and texting. Studies have confirmed that over 75 percent of teens use social networking sites with regularity.[69] In addition, more teens in the United States own a cell phone than a personal computer so it is not surprising that over 90 percent send or receive text messages regularly. In this context, youth are more likely to use this mode of communication than e-mail.[70] It is interesting to note that boys and girls use

Teacher's Toolbox 4.7

Promoting a Tobacco-Free Lifestyle Across the Curriculum

With tobacco risk reduction as a central theme, instructional activities in other content areas might be organized in the following way:

- *Integrated language arts.* Students dictate or write a newspaper story about examples and types of tobacco use that they have seen around their school. Younger students' stories could focus on the risk of playing with matches or lighters that a child might find in the home, school, or neighborhood.
- *Mathematics.* After gathering information about the costs of a pack of cigarettes in the local community, students calculate the costs of smoking for a week, a month, and a year. Following this activity, they create a list of healthy alternative purchases.
- *Geography.* Students map and graphically code locations of tobacco production, transportation, and sales in their region or state.
- *Science.* Students trace the path of cigarette smoke for primary smokers and for second-hand and side-stream tobacco exposure as smoke enters the body, passes through the lungs and bloodstream, and is exhaled.
- *Health education.* Students collect information about the location and types of tobacco advertising in their community. Following this collection of data, they analyze the types of messages and the intended target audiences of each message.
- *Art.* Students develop a "Tobacco-Free Me and We" campaign for the local school community.
- *Social studies.* Students examine the history and economic impact of tobacco production in the United States as a foundation for current local, state, and national policies and practices.

technology differently. While boys watch more television and share videos online, girls are more likely to blog, e-mail, and use messaging platforms.[71]

With this background in mind, it is critical for teachers and other school staff to use technology effectively when developing instructional strategies. To provide support for health educators who strive to reach this goal, the International Society for Technology in Education has developed six National Educational Technology Standards that share many skills that are consistent with those identified in the National Health education Standards. In context of these national standards, students will:

1. Demonstrate creative thinking, construct knowledge, and develop innovative products and processes using technology. (Creativity and Innovation)
2. Use digital media and environments to communicate and work collaboratively, including at a distance, to support individual learning and contribute to the learning of others. (Communication and Collaboration)
3. Apply digital tools to gather, evaluate, and use information. (Research and Information Fluency)
4. Use critical thinking skills to plan and conduct research, manage projects, solve problems, and make informed decisions using appropriate digital tools and resources. (Critical Thinking, Problem Solving, and Decision Making)

5. Understand human, cultural, and societal issues related to technology and practice legal and ethical behavior. (Digital Citizenship)
6. Demonstrate a sound understanding of technology concepts, systems, and operations. (Technology Operations and Concepts)[72]

Associated with these standards are critical performance indicators including a student focus on applying existing knowledge to generate new ideas, collaborating with peers to develop digital products and resources, and evaluating and selecting valid information sources and digital tools.

Given the open nature of the Internet, teachers are reminded that anyone can post anything on it without the content being subjected to evaluation or review for accuracy or quality. Consequently, teachers would be wise to help students cultivate specific skills to navigate it and other technologies effectively and safely. Among other skills, teachers must conduct scrupulous evaluation of all Internet resources and materials to be shared with students. In addition, Teacher's Toolbox 4.8 identifies important criteria for teachers and their older students to use to support informed decision making about the use and quality of web-based resources.[73] Readers are reminded that such issues as cybersafety and cyberbullying will be addressed in pertinent content chapters in this text.

Teacher's Toolbox 4.8

Accessing Health Information, Products, and Services

Students need guidance in determining if health information is accurate and reliable. Use the following questions to determine if the information accessed is reliable.

Purpose (The reason the information exists.)

- What is the purpose of the information? To inform? Teach? Sell? Persuade?
- Is the information a fact? Opinion?
- Does the point of view appear to be objective? Impartial?
- Are there any biases?

Authority (The source of the information.)

- Who is the author/publisher/source?
- Are the author's credentials or affiliations given?
- What are the author's qualifications?
- Is there any contact information?
- Does the URL reveal anything about the author or source? (IE) .com .edu .gov .org .net

Currency (The timeliness of the information.)

- When was the information published or posted?

- Has the information been revised or updated?
- Is the information current or out-of-date?
- Are the links functional?

Relevance (The importance of the information for your needs.)

- Does the information relate to your topic?
- Who is the intended audience?
- Have you looked at a variety of sources?
- Is the information at an appropriate level?

Accuracy (The reliability, truthfulness, and correctness of the informational content.)

- Where does the information come from?
- Is the information supported by evidence?
- Has the information been reviewed?
- Does the language or tone seem biased and free of emotion?
- Are there spelling, grammar, or other errors?

SOURCES: Kent State University, *Evaluation Criteria* (University Libraries, December 2016). https://libguides.library.kent.edu/hed32542 National Institutes of Health, *How to Evaluate Health Information on the Internet: Questions and Answers* (June 24, 2011). http://ods.od.nih.gov/Health_Information/How_To_Evaluate_Health_Information_on_the_Internet_Questions_and_Answers.aspx

Evidence confirming the effects of using instructional technology to enrich health-risk reduction has begun to emerge. Importantly, the value of integrating a range of technologies into health education practice has begun to show promise. Although more is known about crafting effective targeted health communications and ways to enrich learning about health for teens, little is known about such approaches for students in elementary and middle grades.

As computer access for all students increases and instruction is delivered that incorporates a range of technological enrichments, more developmentally appropriate resources that enrich higher-order thinking will be produced to meet the needs of younger learners. Although computers and other technological devices will never eliminate connectedness between students and effective teachers, they do offer a vehicle for exploring an increasingly sophisticated and cost-effective range of resources to enrich learning and classroom practice.

CONTROVERSY MANAGEMENT IN HEALTH EDUCATION

Controversy, a conflict of values, is an inevitable part of life in a pluralistic society. School-based professionals and programs are vulnerable targets of controversy because their primary source of funding is public tax dollars. In addition, the U.S. education enterprise is based on mandatory participation for all children and youth. Controversy about school policies and practices takes two common forms:

1. Conflict about what content and issues should be addressed.
2. Disagreement over implementation of the curriculum.[74]

In the context of such sources of conflict, the subject matter and curricular approaches that provide a foundation for sound health education practice can provide fertile ground for dispute. In some school districts, the notion of including Comprehensive School Health Education in the approved district curriculum is regarded as an inappropriate use of instructional time. Advocates for an approach to education focused only on core content often view attention to anything else as a waste of valuable academic time. Still others view any instructional attention to student health issues as an intrusion into family issues or as an attempt to usurp parents' rights.

Some health topics are likely to evoke little or no heated response, while others (sexual health promotion, stress management, death education, and some approaches to tobacco, alcohol, and other drug risk reduction) can serve as a lightning rod for parental and public concern. In addition, HECAT and the National School Health Education Standards imply that the primary focus of instruction should be skill development in potentially controversial areas.

Like education professionals, parents and taxpayers who express concern about curricular or policy matters in their schools are motivated by a commitment to creating the best possible learning environment for students. Consequently, the best way to avoid controversy is to formalize open and effective communication among all stakeholders.[75] Coordinated School Health provides a helpful starting place to anticipate and manage discrepancies in values and even formalizes a structure for community and parental review of all curricular and policy matters.

There is no guarantee that controversy can be avoided, but recommendations have been offered for the school community to manage any negative outcry in a way that will reduce its impact on the quality and continuity of health instruction. Though many such recommendations are taken from the body of research in human sexuality, school personnel might find them helpful when confronted with controversy about reading or math curricula or literature selections in the school library.

Anticipation: Strategies for School Leaders

The most effective strategy for managing controversy in a school district is to anticipate the potential for it. The following recommendations have been suggested by school health and education leaders and are offered to help in developing proactive, districtwide plans:

1. *Do your homework.* Knowledge of demographic facts about the community and state, as well as data about the health risks of children and youth, is critical. In addition, school administrators must be fluent in information about local health agencies, counseling services, medical facilities, and law enforcement agencies. Finally, it is vital for school personnel to have an accurate understanding of the social norms and standards in their school community.

2. *Engage a broad base of planners.* For best results, all planning groups must reflect the community. Efforts must include input from students, parents, advocates, opponents, and leaders of faith-based organizations in the school district.

3. *State goals clearly.* Standards and testing parameters developed by state departments of education are best regarded as a starting point for activities within local districts. Although potentially time-consuming, the investment in reaching consensus on goals will minimize controversy in the long run.

4. *Cultivate support networks.* Administrators would be wise to seek support from those community providers who see the result of myth and misinformation among youth. Public health professionals, medical care providers, youth counselors, the faith community, and senior citizen representatives often are aware of such negative consequences.

5. *Identify articulate spokespersons.* Regardless of profession, there are individuals within every community who can serve as respected and articulate advocates and respond to concerns about school-based health promotion programming.

6. *Create awareness within the community.* Often, controversy can be reduced if the community is aware of the needs of its students. Wise administrators cultivate the media, hold open forums, and provide presentations to civic and religious

organizations to provide information about health issues confronting local youth.

7. *Be positive.* Negativism on the part of administrators can become a self-fulfilling prophecy for controversy. All efforts must be made to manage each confrontation as it arises rather than to interpret activities as a conspiracy against health promotion activities.[76, 77]

School districts that have established school health advisory committees are far more able to manage controversy successfully than are their less proactive counterparts. The importance of well-planned, developmentally appropriate, board-approved health curricula cannot be overstated. School district officials must provide staff development activities for teachers delivering potentially controversial instructional activities. Finally, classroom-based professionals must be assured that they have administrative support at all times.

In the event that controversy surfaces, the following strategies are suggested for school leaders:

- Know your goals and be able to communicate them positively and effectively.
- Listen and find common ground.
- Don't get defensive.
- Keep supporters informed and involved.
- Step up an information campaign.
- Be honest and forthright.
- Respect differences.
- Remain positive.[78]

Recommendations for Teachers

Although most of the activities listed in "Anticipation: Strategies for School Leaders" are beyond the responsibility of classroom teachers, it is the teachers who must translate district policy into instructional practice. As a starting point, many teachers look to district-approved texts and instructional materials. Unfortunately, these materials rarely provide help in teaching potentially controversial topics. A review of currently available elementary and middle school health textbooks reveals a lack of coverage of certain subjects. Most common is the omission of information about human reproduction, sexuality, and childbirth.

As discussed earlier in this chapter, teachers must be prepared to create a safe and nurturing learning environment for all students about all subject matter in the district course of study. As a starting point, Chapter 13 provides guidelines for promoting sexual health that can be generalized to address any health education content area. In addition, teachers must be prepared to provide accurate and timely information about all content matters. To this end, participation in staff development opportunities is advised. Also, teachers must seek the support of their local administrators and would be wise to consult colleagues in professional associations to which they belong.

Finally, the following recommendations can help teachers respond to the many questions children have about their health. In general, the reaction to student questions can be as important as the response that is provided. In this context, teachers are encouraged to:

- Know local district policies and approved curricular parameters.
- Affirm and clarify questions.
- Separate personal emotions, values, and beliefs from responses.
- Maintain the lines of communication.

The following types of questions and corresponding response strategies are particularly relevant to questions about potentially controversial topics.[79]

Requests for Information

Many times, students will be very curious about a subject or will need something clarified. If the teacher thinks the question is appropriate for the grade level and knows the answer, then it is certainly appropriate to answer the question. The question should be answered age-appropriately and with proper terminology. If the teacher does not know the answer, he or she should tell the student so and should ask students to identify a strategy for finding the answer. In addition, it is important for the teacher to make sure student questions get correct, developmentally appropriate responses.

If the teacher feels the question is inappropriate for the grade level, the teacher should tell the class that he or she does not feel comfortable answering that question. However, it is important to find out from the student why he or she asked it. The teacher should try to find out more information about what motivated the question before answering it.

Finally, it is critical for teachers to know about any local policies concerning responding to student questions about selected issues (contraception, same-sex relationships). Some school districts have established a list of responses for teachers to read in addressing inquiries about these matters.

"Am I Normal?" Questions

"Am I normal?" questions generally focus on concerns about students' bodies and the physical and emotional changes that are occurring in them. It is important to validate their concerns by informing them that many young people of their age share those concerns. Next, the teacher should provide information about what students can expect as their bodies continue to change, grow, and develop over the next few years. In addition, it is appropriate to suggest that they can talk to parents, counselors, or clergy or consult other community resources if they need additional information.

Permission-Seeking/Personal Belief Questions

Generally, these questions are intended to ask permission to participate in a particular behavior. For example, "Is it normal for kids my age to . . . ??" "Did you participate in . . . activity when you were growing up?" or "Do you think it is okay to . . .??" are cues for parents and teachers that permission might be being sought. It is important to avoid using the word *normal* or *typical* when answering questions. Morality enters into these questions, and it is not up to teachers to decide what is right or wrong for students. The exception to this is something that is against the law. Also, it is important to establish ground rules at the beginning of the year and to emphasize that personal sexual behavior is not open for discussion. In particular, teachers are urged not to share personal experiences with students when such information can be construed as permission to act in a similar way.

Shock Questions

Sometimes, students ask questions to shock the teacher. Many questions are shocking because of the vocabulary used. To deal with this situation, the teacher should reword the question, using proper terminology. In any case, it is important for the teacher to stay calm and not act embarrassed. Finally, it might be necessary for teachers to remind students when questions are inappropriate and/or require a private conversation.

Conclusion

The key to managing potential controversy is to have a comprehensive plan in place to anticipate and manage negative community response to curricular matters. While maintaining fidelity to school policies and curricular boundaries, teachers can serve as advocates for change when student health needs are not being met. Successful implementation of controversy management lies in knowing parents and key stakeholders in the community. Increasing parental engagement in all aspects of the education process is an important goal for all school districts.

 INTERNET AND OTHER RESOURCES

WEBSITES

WEBSITES WITH A FOCUS ON HEALTH AND HEALTH PROMOTION

American Academy of Pediatrics
www.aap.org

CDC A-Z Index
www.cdc.gov/AZ/a.html

Healthfinder
healthfinder.gov

Mayo Clinic
www.mayoclinic.org

National Institutes of Health
health.nih.gov

Office of Disease Prevention and Health Promotion—U.S. Department of Health and Human Services
www.hhs.gov

WebMD
www.webmd.com

OTHER RESOURCES

COOPERATIVE LEARNING

Johnson, D., R. Johnson, and M. B. Stanne. *Cooperative Learning Methods: A Meta Analysis* (Minneapolis: University of Minnesota, 2000).

SCHOOL CONNECTEDNESS

Association for Supervision and Curriculum Development. *The Learning Compact Redefined: A Call to Action* (Alexandria, VA: ASCD, 2007).

Blum, R. *School Connectedness: Improving the Lives of Students* (Baltimore, MD: Johns Hopkins Bloomberg School of Public Health, 2005).

Henderson, N. "Havens of Resilience." *Educational Leadership* 71, no. 1 (September 2013): 22–27.

Jackson, R., and A. Zmuda. "Four (Secret) Keys to Student Engagement." *Educational Leadership* 72, no. 1 (September 2014): 18–24.

Weissberg, R. P., and J. Cascarino. "Academic Learning + Social-Emotional Learning = National Priority." *Phi Delta Kappan* 95, no. 2 (October 2013): 8–13.

Whitlock, J. *Research Facts and Findings: Fostering School Connectedness* (Ithaca, NY: ACT for Youth, Cornell University, November 2003).

Wilder Research. *Social Connectedness and Health* (St. Paul, MN: Wilder Research, March 2012).

EDUCATIONAL TECHNOLOGY

Association for Supervision and Curriculum Development. "Turning Blind Spots into Hotspots." *Education Update* (February 2014): 2, 3–6.

Bernhardt, J. M., J. D. Chaney, B. H. Chaney, and A. K. Hall. "New Media for Health Education: A Revolution in Progress." *Health Education and Behavior* (April 2013): 129–32.

Foundation for Excellence in Education. *Digital Learning Report Card 2013* (Tallahassee, FL: ExcelinEd, 2014).

Herrington, J., and L. Kervin. "Authentic Learning Supported by Technology: 10 Suggestions and Cases of Integration in Classrooms." *Educational Media International* 44, no. 3 (2007): 219–36.

Jacobs, H. H. *Curriculum 21: Essential Education for a Changing World* (Alexandria, VA: Association for Supervision and Curriculum Development, 2010).

Levin, B. B., and L. Schrum. "Technology-Rich Schools Up Close." *Educational Leadership* (March 2013): 50–55.

Lombardi, M. M. *Authentic Learning for the 21st Century: An Overview* (Louisville, CO: Educause Learning Initiative, 2007).

Scherer, M. "Transforming Education with Technology: A Conversation with Karen Cator." *Educational Leadership* (February 2011): 16–21.

Turner, K. H. "Digitalk: A New Literacy for a Digital Generation." *Kappan* (September 2010): 41–46.

SCHOOL AND FAMILY PARTNERSHIPS

Centers for Disease Control and Prevention. "Positive Parenting Practices" (www.cdc.gov/healthyyouth/protective/positiveparenting/index.htm).

Ferlazzo, L. "Involvement or Engagement." *Educational Leadership* (May 2011):10–14.

Hoerr, T. R. "What Are Parents Thinking?" *Educational Leadership* (December 2011/January 2013): 90–91.

Stover, D. "A Place at the Table." *American School Board Journal* (September 2012): 16–21.

U.S. Department of Education. "School Is Increasingly Viewed as a Family and Community Affair." *The Challenge: A Publication of the Office of Safe and Drug-Free Schools* (October 2008): 1–4.

U.S. Department of Health and Human Services. *Parents, Speak Up!: A Guide for Discussing Relationships and Waiting to Have Sex* (Washington, DC: USDHHS, 2007).

ENDNOTES

1. H. H. Jacobs, "On Interdisciplinary Curriculum: A Conversation with Heidi H. Jacobs," *Educational Leadership* (October 1991): 24.
2. M. Quackenbush, W. M. Kane, and S. K. Telljohann, *Teach and Reach: Emotional and Mental Health* (Santa Cruz, CA: ETR Associates, 2004).
3. M. Kipke, ed., *Risks and Opportunities: Synthesis of Studies on Adolescence* (Washington, DC: National Academies Press, 1999).
4. Centers for Disease Control and Prevention, *School Connectedness: Strategies for Increasing Protective Factors Among Youth* (Atlanta, GA: U.S. Department of Health and Human Services, 2009).
5. Centers for Disease Control and Prevention, *Fostering School Connectedness: Improving Student Health and Academic Achievement—Information for Teachers and Other School Staff* (www.cdc.gov/healthyyouth/protective/pdf/connectedness_teachers.pdf; May 2014).
6. Ibid.
7. R. Blum, *School Connectedness: Improving the Lives of Students* (Baltimore, MD: Johns Hopkins Bloomberg School of Public Health, 2005), 1.
8. Ibid., 4.
9. Centers for Disease Control and Prevention, *School Connectedness: Strategies for Increasing Protective Factors Among Youth.*
10. Ibid., 6–7.
11. Centers for Disease Control and Prevention, *Fostering School Connectedness: Improving Student Health and Academic Achievement—Information for Teachers and Other School Staff.*
12. C. L. Storr, N. S. Ialongo, S. G. Kellam, and J. C. Anthony, "A Randomized Controlled Trial of Two Primary School Intervention Strategies to Prevent Early Onset Tobacco Smoking," *Drug and Alcohol Dependence* 66 (2002): 51–60.
13. J. L. Epstein, *School, Family, and Community Partnerships: Preparing Educators and Improving Schools*, 2nd ed. (Boulder, CO: Westview Press, 2011).
14. A. Henderson, T. Mapp, and A. Averett, *A New Wave of Evidence: The Impact of School, Family, and Community Connections on Student Achievement* (Austin, TX: National Center for Family and Community Connections with Schools, 2002).
15. Centers for Disease Control and Prevention, *School Connectedness: Strategies for Increasing Protective Factors Among Youth*, 5.
16. C. Dailard, "Recent Findings from the 'Add Health' Survey: Teens and Sexual Activity," *Guttmacher Report on Public Policy* (August 2001): 9–16.
17. U.S. Department of Health and Human Services, *Got a Minute? Give It to Your Kid* (Atlanta: Centers for Disease Control and Prevention, Office on Smoking and Health, 2002).

18. K. V. Hoover-Dempsey, O. C. Bassler, and J. S. Brissie, "Explorations in Parent-School Relations," *Journal of Educational Research* 85 (1992): 287–94.
19. Centers for Disease Control and Prevention, *Parent Engagement: Strategies for Involving Parents in School Health* (Atlanta, GA: U.S. Department of Health and Human Services, 2013).
20. R. Jones, "How Parents Can Support Learning," *American School Board Journal* (September, 2001): 18–22.
21. Jeremy D. Finn, "Parental Engagement That Makes a Difference," *Educational Leadership* 55, no. 8 (May 1998): 20–24.
22. R. M. Clark, *Family Life and School Achievement* (Chicago: University of Chicago Press, 1983).
23. R. M. Wolf, "The Measurement of Environments," in *Invitational Conference on Testing Problems*, ed. A. Anastasi (Princeton, NJ: Educational Testing Service, 1964).
24. Centers for Disease Control and Prevention, *Helping Your Child Feel Connected to School: Information for Parents and Families* (www.cdc.gov/healthyyouth/protective/pdf/connectedness_parents.pdf; May 2014).
25. C. L. Green, J. M. T. Walker, K. V. Hoover-Dempsey, and H. M. Sandler, "Parents' Motivations for Involvement in Children's Education: An Empirical Test of a Theoretical Model of Parental Involvement," *Journal of Educational Psychology* 99, no. 3 (2007): 532–44.
26. J. L. Epstein, *School, Family, and Community Partnerships: Your Handbook for Action*, 3rd ed. (Thousand Oaks, CA: Corwin Press, 2009).
27. Centers for Disease Control and Prevention, *Parent Engagement.*
28. J. L. Epstein, *School Family and Community Partnerships.*
29. Centers for Disease Control and Prevention, *Parent Engagement*, 20.
30. Ibid, 20–23.
31. R. T. Johnson and D. W. Johnson, "An Overview of Cooperative Learning," in *Creative and Collaborative Learning*, eds. J. Thousand, A. Villa, and A. Nevin (Baltimore, MD: Brookes Press, 1994).
32. G. Stock, *The Kids' Book of Questions* (New York: Workman, 1988).
33. J. Gibbs, *Tribes: A New Way of Learning and Being Together* (Sausalito, CA: Center Source Systems, 1995).
34. Ibid.
35. Ibid.
36. L. Shoji, conversation with author, November 2001.
37. D. Parker, conversation with author, February 2001.
38. J. Piaget, *The Epistemology of Interdisciplinary Relationships* (Paris: Organization for Economic Cooperation and Development, 1972).

39. H. H. Jacobs, ed., *Interdisciplinary Curriculum: Design and Implementation* (Alexandria, VA: Association for Supervision and Curriculum Development, 1989), 7.
40. E. E. Ames et al., *Designing School Health Curriculum*, 2nd ed. (Dubuque, IA: Wm. C. Brown, 1995), 90.
41. D. Johnson and R. T Johnson, *Cooperation and Competition: Theory and Research* (Edina, MN: Interaction Book Company, 1989).
42. R. T. Johnson and D. W. Johnson, "An Overview of Cooperative Learning," in *Creativity and Collaborative Learning*, eds. J. Thousand, A. Villa, and A. Nevin (Baltimore, MD: Brookes Press, 1994).
43. S. Friedland, "Bridging the Gap," *Executive Educator* 16, no. 10 (October 1994): 27.
44. Johnson and Johnson, *Cooperation and Competition.*
45. B. Cinelli et al., "Applying Cooperative Learning in Health Education Practice," *Journal of School Health* 64, no. 3 (March 1994): 99–102.
46. R. Johnson and D. Johnson, *Cooperative Learning and Conflict Resolution* (www.newhorizons.org/strategies/cooperative/johnson.htm; 1997).
47. Cinelli et al., "Applying Cooperative Learning," 100.
48. Ibid.
49. Ibid., 101.
50. Friedland, "Bridging the Gap."
51. Cinelli et al., "Applying Cooperative Learning," 100.
52. C. B. Dean et al., *Classroom Instruction That Works: Research-Based Strategies for Increasing Student Achievement*, 2nd ed. (Alexandria, VA: Association for Supervision and Curriculum Development, 2012), 36.
53. Cinelli et al., "Applying Cooperative Learning," 103.
54. National Commission on the Role of the School and the Community in Improving Adolescent Health, *Code Blue: Uniting for Healthier Youth* (Alexandria, VA: National Association of State Boards of Education and AMA, 1990), 37–38.
55. Cinelli et al., "Applying Cooperative Learning," 99–100; Gist, "Problem-Based Learning," 12.
56. G. Tanaka, J. Warren, and L. Tritsch, "What's Real in Health Education?" *Journal of Health Education* 24, no. 6 (1993): 57–58.
57. Cinelli et al., "Applying Cooperative Learning," 102.
58. Friedland, "Bridging the Gap."
59. Ibid.
60. Jacobs, *Interdisciplinary Curriculum*, 1.
61. Friedland, "Bridging the Gap."
62. Ibid.
63. L. Elvin, *The Place of Common Sense in Educational Thought* (London: Unwin Educational Books, 1977).
64. Susan M. Drake, *Planning Integrated Curriculum* (Alexandria, VA: Association for Supervision and Curriculum Development, 1993), 3.

65. Jacobs, *Interdisciplinary Curriculum*, 8.

66. Drake, *Planning Integrated Curriculum*, 2.

67. M. Sprenger, *Brain-Based Teaching in the Digital Age* (Alexandria, VA: Association for Supervision and Curriculum Development, 2010), xiii.

68. Joint Committee on Health Education Standards, *National Health Education Standards: Achieving Excellence*, 2nd ed. (Atlanta, GA: The American Cancer Society, 2007), 61.

69. PEW/Internet, Teens, Social Media and Technology Overview 2015.

70. Ibid.

71. Centers for Disease Control and Prevention, Audience Insights: Communicating to Teens (Aged 12-17) (www.cdc.gov/healthmarketing/resources.htm#insights, 2009).

72. International Society for Technology in Education, National Educational Technology Standards (www.iste.org/standards/standards-for-students; 2014).

73. Kent State University, University Libraries, "Evaluation Criteria" (libguides.library.kent.edu/hed32542; 2014).

74. Loren B. Bensley and Elizabeth Harmon, "Addressing Controversy in Health Education," *Alliance Update* (May/June 1992): 9-10.

75. Ibid.

76. J. G. Sowers, *Guidelines for Dealing with Resistance to Comprehensive Health Education* (Hampton, NH: Sowers Associates, 1994).

77. J. Sowers, "Building Bridges to Common Ground," in *Partners in Prevention*, eds., M. Rubin and S. Wooley (Kent, OH: American School Health Association, 2006): 19-23.

78. J. G. Sowers, *Guidelines for Dealing with Resistance to Comprehensive Health Education*.

79. K. Middleton et al., *Contemporary Health Series: Making Health Education Comprehensive* (Santa Cruz, CA: ETR Associates, 1991), 31-33.

Helping Students Develop Skills for Positive Health Habits

This section focuses on the *positive health habits* students can adopt and maintain to help them live a healthy life. It contains the content and the personal and social skills found in the National Health Education Standards. Each chapter in this section begins with an introduction that provides information about the prevalence and cost of not practicing the positive health behavior, relationship between the healthy behavior and academic performance, and risk and protective factors related to the behavior. Readers learn what schools currently are doing and what they should be doing in relation to the health behavior. Each chapter also provides background information for the teacher, developmentally appropriate strategies for learning and assessment, and children's literature and Internet and other resources related to each content area.

5

(Joyce, age 12; Michelle, age 12)

Promoting Mental and Emotional Health

DESIRED LEARNER OUTCOMES

After reading this chapter, you will be able to . . .

- **Describe the prevalence and cost of mental and emotional health problems among youth.**

- **Explain the relationship between mental and emotional health problems and compromised academic performance.**

- **Identify factors that influence mental and emotional health.**

- **Summarize current guidelines and practices for schools and teachers related to mental and emotional health.**

- **Summarize developmentally appropriate mental and emotional concepts and skills for K–8 students in the context of the National Health Education Standards and target healthy behavior outcomes.**

- **Demonstrate developmentally appropriate learning strategies and assessment techniques that incorporate concepts and skills shown to promote mental and emotional health among youth.**

- **Identify effective, evaluated commercial mental and emotional health promotion curricula.**

- **Identify websites and children's literature that can be used in cross-curricular instructional activities promoting mental and emotional health.**

INTRODUCTION

Robi Kahakalau's beautiful song "Every Child a Promise" reminds us that great potential lies within each unique child and that our responsibility is to help children unlock and live their dream.[1] Although many educators are familiar with the extensive literature on children who are considered at risk for problems of many kinds, research in the field of positive psychology focuses on qualities such as hope, wisdom, creativity, future mindedness, courage, spirituality, responsibility, and perseverance rather than on the more limited perspective of problems and deficits.[2] In keeping with this focus, Mervlyn Kitashima, one of the participants in the Kauai Longitudinal Study of Resilience, encourages educators to think of all students as "at promise" rather than at risk.[3]

Longitudinal studies indicate that the majority of children who come from at-risk backgrounds become healthy, competent adults.[4] This chapter helps educators build on the qualities and strengths that allow children to build *resilience,* the term used to describe those who "bounce back" despite difficulties and who learn to "love well, work well, play well, and expect well."[5]

Mental and emotional health problems are growing among children and adolescents in the United States.[6] The world is a scary, uncertain, and even violent place for many young people. School needs to be a tremendously safe and dependable place—physically, emotionally, mentally, and socially—in their lives. Educators can work to encourage the positive capacities of young people as well as to facilitate access to the services they and their families need when problems arise. All students have strengths that can be put to productive use, and resilience efforts in schools can help students succeed. In the words of Martin Krovetz, educators can help all students learn to use their minds and hearts well.[7]

Prevalence and Cost of Mental Health Problems

Mental health in childhood and adolescence is characterized by the achievement of expected developmental cognitive, social, and emotional milestones and by secure attachments, satisfying social relationships, and effective coping skills. The Surgeon General's Report on Mental Health stated that mentally healthy children and adolescents enjoy a positive quality of life and function well at home, in school, and in their communities. The report cautioned that children are not little adults. They must be viewed in the context of their social environments, which include families, peer groups, and larger physical and cultural surroundings.[8]

Mental health disorders and illnesses are serious threats to the health of children in the United States. Health scientists have reported sharp declines in major infectious and medical problems among young people during the past century. In contrast, mental health problems appear to be increasing. Epidemiology studies have indicated that one in four or five youth in the United States meet criteria for a mental health disorder and very few receive the treatment they need.[9] The National Institute of Mental Health (NIMH) identified the following mental disorders that affect children and adolescents:

> Anxiety disorders
> Attention deficit hyperactivity disorder (ADHD)
> Autism spectrum disorders (pervasive developmental disorders)
> Bipolar disorder
> Borderline personality disorder
> Depression
> Eating disorders
> Childhood-onset schizophrenia[10]

See Table 5–1 for more information.

Mental health problems produce more impairment than almost any other condition among children and adolescents. In contrast to most disabling physical diseases, mental illnesses begin early in life with half of all lifetime cases beginning by age 14 and three-quarters by age 24. Thus, mental illnesses can be considered the chronic diseases of the young. Pervasive and long delays often occur between the onset of a mental disorder and the first treatment.[11]

Children's mental disorders affect many young people and their families. Boys and girls of all ages, backgrounds, and regions of the United States experience mental disorders. A 2009 National Research Council and Institute of Medicine report estimated that as many as 20 percent of children living in the United States experience a mental disorder in a given year, with approximately $247 billion spent annually on childhood mental disorders. Because of the impact on children, families, and communities, children's mental disorders are an important public health issue in the United States.[12]

The financial cost of unmet needs is just a small part of the price society pays. Failure to provide mental health services for children and families also causes unnecessary long-term suffering. When untreated, mental health disorders can lead to school failure, family conflicts, drug abuse, violence, and even suicide.[13] Intentional self-harm (suicide) was the third leading cause of death for children aged five to fourteen in 2015.[14]

Mental disorders increasingly are treatable. Students referred for mental health services significantly decrease absence from school, while those not referred increase both absenteeism and tardiness. For example, the expansion of knowledge in genetics, brain imaging, and behavioral research is leading to a better understanding of the causes of ADHD, how to prevent it, and how to develop more effective treatments for all age groups.[15] There is no known way to prevent ADHD. Therefore, early detection and treatment is the best strategy for minimizing the consequences of this common mental disorder.[16]

Results from National Comorbidity Study Adolescent Supplement indicated that only about 36 percent of youth with any lifetime mental disorder received services, and only half of these youth who were severely impaired by their mental disorder received professional mental health treatment. The majority (68 percent) of the children who did receive services had fewer than six visits with a provider over their lifetime. Despite recent programs designed to improve mental health services for youth,

TABLE 5–1

Mental Disorders Affecting Children and Adolescents

Anxiety Disorders

Anxiety is a normal reaction to stress that generally helps people deal with day-to-day situations that arise in life. However, when anxiety becomes an excessive, irrational dread of everyday situations, it has become a disabling disorder. The five major types of anxiety disorders are

- *Generalized Anxiety Disorder (GAD)*—Characterized by chronic anxiety and exaggerated worry and tension, even when there is little or nothing to provoke it.
- *Obsessive-Compulsive Disorder (OCD)*—Characterized by recurrent, unwanted thoughts (obsessions) and/or repetitive behaviors (compulsions). Repetitive behaviors (e.g., hand washing, counting) are often performed with the hope of preventing obsessive thoughts or making them go away, but these so-called rituals provide only temporary relief, and not performing them markedly increases anxiety.
- *Panic Disorder*—Characterized by unexpected and repeated episodes of intense fear accompanied by physical symptoms that may include chest pain, heart palpitations, shortness of breath, dizziness, or abdominal distress.
- *Post-Traumatic Stress Disorder (PTSD)*—Can develop after exposure to a terrifying event or ordeal in which grave physical harm occurred or was threatened. Traumatic events that may trigger PTSD in children include violent personal assaults, natural or human-caused disasters, or accidents.
- *Social Phobia (or Social Anxiety Disorder)*—Characterized by overwhelming anxiety and excessive self-consciousness in everyday social situations. Social phobia can be limited to only one type of situation (e.g., speaking in front of others) or, in its most severe form, may be so broad that people experience symptoms almost anytime they are around others.

Attention Deficit Hyperactivity Disorder (ADHD)

Attention deficit hyperactivity disorder, ADHD, is one of the most common mental disorders in children. Children with ADHD have impaired functioning in multiple settings, including home, school, and in relationships with peers. If untreated, the disorder can have long-term adverse effects into adolescence and adulthood. Symptoms of ADHD appear over the course of many months, and include

- *Impulsiveness*—A child who acts quickly without thinking first.
- *Hyperactivity*—A child who can't sit still, walks, runs, or climbs around when others are seated, talks when others are talking.
- *Inattention*—A child who daydreams, or seems to be in another world, is sidetracked by what is going on around him or her.

Autism Spectrum Disorders (Pervasive Developmental Disorders)

Autism spectrum disorders (ASDs), also known as pervasive developmental disorders (PDDs), cause severe and pervasive impairment in thinking, feeling, language, and the ability to relate to others. These disorders usually are first diagnosed in early childhood and vary from a severe form, called autistic disorder, through pervasive developmental disorder not otherwise specified (PDD-NOS), to a much milder form, Asperger syndrome. Parents are usually the first to notice unusual behaviors in their child. In some cases, the baby seemed "different" from birth. The first signs of an autism spectrum disorder also can appear in children who had been developing normally.

Bipolar Disorder

Bipolar disorder, also known as manic-depressive illness, is a serious medical condition that causes shifts in a person's mood, energy, and ability to function. Unlike the normal ups and downs that everyone goes through, the symptoms of bipolar disorder are severe. Dramatic mood swings go from overly "high" and/or irritable to sad and hopeless, and back again, often with periods of normal mood between. Severe changes in energy and behavior go along with these changes in mood. The periods of highs and lows are called episodes of mania and depression.

Borderline Personality Disorder

Borderline personality disorder (BPD) is a serious mental illness characterized by pervasive instability in moods, interpersonal relationships, self-image, and behavior. This instability often disrupts family and work life, long-term planning, and the individual's sense of self-identity. Originally thought to be at the "borderline" of psychosis, people with BPD suffer from a disorder of emotion regulation. Patients often need extensive mental health services. Yet, with help, many improve over time and eventually are able to lead productive lives.

Depression

Only in the past two decades has depression in children been taken very seriously. The depressed child may pretend to be sick, refuse to go to school, cling to a parent, or worry that the parent may die. Older children may sulk, get into trouble at school, be negative, grouchy, and feel misunderstood. Because normal behaviors vary from one childhood stage to another, it can be difficult to tell whether a child is just going through a temporary or is suffering from depression. If a visit to the child's pediatrician rules out physical symptoms, the doctor might suggest that the child be evaluated, preferably by a psychiatrist who specializes in treating children.

Eating Disorders

An eating disorder is marked by severe disturbances in eating behavior, such as extreme reduction of food intake or extreme overeating, or feelings of overwhelming distress or concern about body weight or shape. The types of eating disorders are

- *Anorexia Nervosa*—Anorexia nervosa is characterized by emaciation, a relentless pursuit of thinness and unwillingness to maintain a normal or healthy weight, a distortion of body image and intense fear of gaining weight, a lack of menstruation among girls and women, and extremely disturbed eating behavior.
- *Bulimia Nervosa*—Bulimia nervosa is characterized by recurrent and frequent episodes of eating unusually large amounts of food (binge eating) with a feeling of lack of control over the eating. This binge eating is followed by a type of behavior that compensates for the binge, such as purging (vomiting, excessive use of laxatives or diuretics), fasting, and/or excessive exercise.
- *Binge-Eating Disorder*—Binge-eating disorder is characterized by recurrent binge-eating episodes during which a person feels a loss of control over his or her eating. Unlike bulimia, binge-eating episodes are not followed by purging, excessive exercise, or fasting.

Schizophrenia

Schizophrenia is a chronic, severe, and disabling brain disorder. People with schizophrenia sometimes hear voices others don't hear, believe that others are broadcasting their thoughts to the world, or become convinced that others are plotting to harm them. These experiences can make them fearful and withdrawn and cause difficulties when they try to have relationships with others.

SOURCE: National Institute of Mental Health. www.nimh.nih.gov/health/publications/treatment-of-children-with-mental-illness-fact-sheet/index.shtml

TABLE 5-2

Youth Risk Behavior Survey Data Related to Mental and Emotional Health, 2017

Risk Behavior	Percent Reporting Behavior		
	Total	Females	Males
Felt so sad or hopeless almost every day for two or more weeks in a row that they stopped doing some usual activities during the past 12 months	31.5	41.1	21.4
Seriously considered attempting suicide during the past 12 months	17.2	22.1	11.9
Made a suicide plan during the past 12 months	13.6	17.1	9.7
Actually attempted suicide during the past 12 months	7.4	9.3	5.1
Suicide attempt resulted in an injury, poisoning, or overdose that had to be treated by a doctor or nurse during the past 12 months	2.4	3.1	1.5

SOURCE: Centers for Disease Control and Prevention. "Youth Risk Behavior Surveillance—United States, 2015." https://www.cdc.gov/healthyyouth/data/yrbs/pdf/2017/ss6708.pdf

such as the State Children's Health Insurance Program and the federal Children's Mental Health Initiative, many children in need of mental health care still do not receive it. In addition, the relatively low number of treatment visits suggests that the few who are getting treatment may not have sufficient professional follow-up. Ethnic disparities in mental health care, especially of mood and anxiety disorders, are still widespread.[17]

The Centers for Disease Control and Prevention (CDC) conducts the Youth Risk Behavior Survey (YRBS) in odd-numbered years to monitor priority health-risk behaviors among youth, including behaviors related to mental and emotional health. Table 5-2 provides data on risk behaviors reported by high school students across the United States related to depression and suicide.[18]

In *Healthy People 2020,* the U.S. Department of Health and Human Services identified major public health objectives for mental health among children and adolescents (Table 5-3).[19] This chapter addresses the ways families, schools, and communities can work together to promote mental and emotional health

©Creatas/PunchStock

Mental health is positively associated with academic achievement. Attachment to peers, emotional resiliency, and a belief in a positive future all promote mental and emotional health in young people.

TABLE 5-3

Healthy People 2020 Objectives Related to the Mental Health of Children and Adolescents

EMC-1	Increase the proportion of children who are ready for school in all five domains of healthy development: physical development, social-emotional development, and approaches to learning, language, and cognitive development.
AH-3	Increase the proportion of adolescents who are connected to a parent or other positive adult caregiver.
AH-3.1	Increase the proportion of adolescents who have an adult in their lives with whom they can talk about serious problems.
MHMD-2	Reduce suicide attempts by adolescents.
MHMD-3	Reduce the proportion of adolescents who engage in disordered eating behaviors in an attempt to control their weight.
MHMD-4.1	Reduce the proportion of adolescents aged 12 to 17 years who experience major depressive episodes (MDEs).
MHMD-6	Increase the proportion of children with mental health problems who receive treatment.
MHMD-11	Increase depression screening by primary care providers.
MHMD-11.2	Increase the proportion of primary care physician office visits that screen youth aged 12 to 18 years for depression.

SOURCE: U.S. Department of Health and Human Services. *Healthy People 2020.* www.healthypeople.gov/2020/topics-objectives

and to facilitate access to appropriate mental health services in a timely manner.

Mental and Emotional Health and Academic Performance

Mental health problems among young people often are recurrent illnesses that ebb and flow over time, with many children and adolescents experiencing problems that persist into adulthood. Adolescents miss more school as a result of emotional and behavioral symptoms than for any other condition. Young people with mental health problems are more likely to drop out of school and fail than any other group of children with disabilities.[20]

Health, Mental Health and Safety Guidelines for Schools, developed by more than three hundred health, education, and safety professionals from more than thirty national organizations and by parents and other supporters, states,

> Health, mental health, and safety . . . are inextricably linked to student achievement. . . . Substance abuse, anxiety about home life, anxiety about relations with peers, exposure to violence, and any unaddressed symptoms are examples of health and safety issues associated with less than optimal achievement in school.[21]

For U.S. children aged 1 to 19, the group of conditions that lowers quality of life and reduces life chances the most consists of emotional and behavioral problems and associated impairments. No other set of conditions comes close to the magnitude of deleterious effects on this age group. Children with these disorders have a greatly increased risk of dropping out of school and not being fully functional members of society in adulthood.[22]

The National Association of School Psychologists (NASP) identified the following mental health challenges as being among the problems children face that can affect their learning and behavior at school:

- Stress and anxiety
- Worries about being bullied
- Problems with family or friends
- Loneliness or rejection
- Disabilities
- Depression
- Thoughts of suicide or of hurting others
- Concerns about sexuality
- Academic difficulties
- Alcohol and substance abuse
- Fear of violence, terrorism, and war.[23]

Research conducted by the Collaborative for Social and Emotional Learning (CASEL) revealed that academics improve when schools expand the curriculum to teach students to manage their emotions and to practice empathy, caring, and cooperation. Children who participated in such programs were better behaved, more positive, less anxious, and measured higher on grades and test scores than children who did not participate. CASEL president Roger P. Weissberg stated, "When kids are disaffected or they're not motivated and engaged, improving academic test scores is a real challenge, and that can't be done unless you address students' social, emotional, and cognitive needs."[24] In keeping with these findings, the Illinois State Board of Education

TABLE 5–4

Illinois Learning Standards for Social and Emotional Learning (SEL)

Social and emotional learning (SEL) is the process through which children develop awareness and management of their emotions, set and achieve important personal and academic goals, use social awareness and interpersonal skills to establish and maintain positive relationships, and demonstrate decision making and responsible behaviors to achieve school and life success. A strong research base indicates that these SEL competencies improve students' social/emotional development, readiness to learn, classroom behavior, and academic performance.

Goal 1:
Develop self-awareness and self-management skills to achieve school and life success.

Goal 2:
Use social awareness and interpersonal skills to establish and maintain positive relationships.

Goal 3:
Demonstrate decision-making skills and responsible behavior in personal, school, and community contexts.

SOURCE: Illinois State Board of Education, Illinois Learning Standards, Social and Emotional Learning (SEL). https://www.isbe.net/pages/social-emotional-learning-standards.aspx

FIGURE 5–1 | Collaborative for Academic, Social, and Emotional Learning (®CASEL 2017) www.casel.org

identified three goals for social and emotional learning for students in grades K–12 (Table 5–4). Figure 5–1 shows CASEL's "Framework for Systemic Social and Emotional Learning" that identifies five core competencies.

The ways schools and classrooms operate can have a tremendous effect not only on the mental health and well-being of young people but also on their opportunities to achieve academically and to develop mentally, emotionally, socially, and physically. C. E. Basch, author of *Healthier Students Are Better Learners,* stated, "No matter how well teachers are prepared to teach, no matter what accountability measures are put in place, no matter what governing structures are established for schools, educational progress will be profoundly limited if students are not motivated and able to learn. Health-related problems play a major role in limiting the motivation and ability to learn of urban minority youth, and interventions to address those problems can improve educational as well as health outcomes."[25] A compilation of research linking health status, health behavior, and academic achievement, entitled *Making the Connection,* similarly stated, "[Children] . . . who face violence, hunger, substance abuse, unintended pregnancy, and despair cannot possibly focus on academic excellence. There is no curriculum brilliant enough to compensate for a hungry stomach or a distracted mind."[26]

NASP Director of Research Jeffrey Charvat has provided further evidence on the relationship between mental health and academic achievement. Among the findings, Charvat reported that

- K–12 students who participated in school-based social and emotional learning programs improved in grades and standardized test scores.
- Changes in school climate and connectedness for the better are associated with increases in student performance in reading, writing, and mathematics.
- Children's developmental competence is integral to their academic competence.
- Intervening to reduce anxiety in children with high anxiety predicts improved school performance and social functioning.
- School mental health programs improve educational outcomes by decreasing absences and discipline referrals and improving test scores.
- Healthy peer relationships predict students' grades concurrently and over time.[27]

School failure is a strong predictor of high-risk behaviors.

Recognizing this growing body of compelling research, the National Governors Association stated,

> Policymakers need to focus on eliminating the barriers that affect these lower-performing students' readiness to learn. Among these barriers are physical and mental health conditions that impact students' school attendance and their ability to pay attention in class, control their anger, and restrain self-destructive impulses.[28]

The intent of this chapter is to help educators support the mental and emotional health of students in all aspects of their school experience and facilitate timely access to the services students and their families need.

Factors That Influence Mental and Emotional Health

Untreated mental health problems can disrupt children's functioning at home, at school, and in the community. Without treatment, children with mental health issues are at increased risk of school failure, contact with the criminal justice system, dependence on social services, and even suicide. Parents, family members, teachers, and caregivers usually are the first to notice when a child has problems with emotions or behavior. Signs that may indicate the need for professional help are:

- Decline in school performance
- Poor grades despite strong efforts
- Constant worry or anxiety
- Repeated refusal to go to school or to take part in normal activities
- Hyperactivity or fidgeting
- Persistent nightmares
- Persistent disobedience or aggression
- Frequent temper tantrums
- Depression, sadness, or irritability[29]

Risk and Protective Factors

Risk factors are characteristics, variables, or hazards that, if present for a given individual, make it more likely that the individual will develop a disorder. Risk factors are not static but change in relation to a developmental phase or a new stressor in a person's life. Risk factors for developing a mental disorder or experiencing problems in social-emotional development include in most cases some combination of genetic and environmental factors.

In 2009, the Institute of Medicine (IOM) released *Preventing Mental, Emotional, and Behavioral Disorders Among Young People: Progress and Possibilities.*[30] The report updates a 1994 IOM book, *Reducing Risks for Mental Disorders,* focusing attention on research and program experience with younger populations. The report states that mental, emotional, and behavioral (MEB) disorders among young people, as well as the development of positive health, should be considered in the framework of the individual and contextual characteristics that shape their lives, as well as the risk and protective factors that are expressed in those contexts. The concept of risk and protective factors is central to framing and interpreting the research needed to develop and evaluate interventions.[31]

The IOM report indicated that risk factors can occur at multiple levels, including biological, psychological, family, community, and cultural levels. Risk factors, which may be associated with problem outcomes, can be fixed (e.g., ethnicity) or vary in an individual over time. Protective factors are characteristics at the individual, family, or community level that are associated with a lower likelihood of problem outcomes. However, distinguishing the effects of protective from risk factors often is difficult, because the same factor may be labeled either way (e.g., good parenting versus poor parenting, high or low academic performance).[32]

When potentially modifiable risk and protective factors are identified through research, preventive approaches can be developed to change those factors to prevent the development of mental, emotional, and behavioral problems. Other risk factors can help define populations that are potential candidates for prevention, such as children exposed to divorce, poverty, bereavement, a mentally ill or substance-abusing parent, abuse, or neglect. Although interventions aimed at these children typically do not target the risk factor itself (e.g., a divorce has already occurred), they can be designed to reduce the likelihood of problem outcomes given elevated risk.[33]

The effect of risk factors is complex and may be associated with multiple outcomes and other confounding risk factors. Many studies have attempted to tease apart specific versus general effects of childhood risk factors on mental, emotional, and behavioral problems. For example, parental divorce is associated with other risk factors, such as interparental conflict, parental mental health problems, and harsh and inconsistent parenting. It is also associated with multiple problem outcomes, including substance abuse problems, internalizing and externalizing problems, and academic problems. Risk and protective factors influence each other and the development of emotional and behavior problems over time.[34]

The IOM report stated that negative life events at the family, school or peer, and community levels have been associated with multiple psychopathological conditions, such as anxiety, depression, and disruptive disorders. Similarly, social support and problem-solving coping appear to have broad protective effects. IOM reiterated that these factors operate at multiple interrelated levels.[35]

Based on the voluminous and complex research on risk and protective factors related to mental, emotional, and behavioral disorders in young people, IOM drew three major conclusions:

1. Research has identified well-established risk and protective factors for MEB disorders at the individual, family, school, and community levels that are targets for preventive interventions. However, the pathways by which these factors influence each other to lead to the development of disorders are not well understood.
2. Specific risk and protective factors have been identified for many of the major disorders, such as specific thinking and behavioral patterns for depression or cognitive deficits for schizophrenia. In addition, nonspecific factors, such as poverty and aversive experiences in families (e.g., marital conflict, poor parenting), schools (e.g., school failure, poor peer relations), and communities (e.g., violence), have been shown to increase the risk for developing most MEB disorders and problems.

3. Interventions designed to prevent MEB disorders and problems and those designed to promote mental, emotional, and behavioral health both frequently involve directly strengthening children's competencies and positive mental health or strengthening families, schools, or communities. However, improved knowledge pertaining to the conceptualization and assessment of developmental competencies is needed to better inform interventions.[36]

GUIDELINES FOR SCHOOLS

State of the Practice

The CDC's Division of Adolescent and School Health (DASH) conducts the School Health Policies and Practices Study (SHPPS) every six years to monitor efforts to improve school health policies and programs.[37] Table 5–5 provides data on district policies and practices related to mental and emotional health.

In terms of mental and emotional health education at the state level, 43.1 percent of states developed, revised, or assisted in developing model policies, policy guidance, or other materials; 60.8 percent distributed or provided model policies, policy guidance, or other materials; and 70.6 percent provided technical assistance. In addition, 60.0 percent of states provided funding for professional development or offered professional development for those who teach health education during the two years before the study for mental and emotional health. In 2016, SHPPS included district-level data showing that 41.2 percent of districts adopted a policy requiring those who teach health education to receive professional development on emotional and mental health topics and 63.6 percent of districts provided funding for professional development. Some 56.9 percent of elementary schools, 74.2 percent of middle schools, and 82.2 percent of high schools adopted a policy stating that schools will teach specific health topics, by school level.[38]

TABLE 5–5

School Health Policies and Practices Study (SHPPS) 2016 Data Related to Counseling, Psychological, and Social Services

Percentage of districts with specific policies and practices related to health services and counseling, psychological, and social services

Policy or practice	Districts (%)
Has someone in the district who oversees or coordinates counseling, psychological, or social services	79.5
Has arrangements to provide health services or counseling, psychological, or social services to students in the district at other sites not on school property	48.4
Schools will maintain and keep an emotional or mental health history in any type of student record	45.7
Requires a newly hired school counselor to have as minimum a mater's degree in counseling	53.7

SOURCE: Centers for Disease Control and Prevention, *School Health Policies and Practices Study (SHPPS) 2016* (Atlanta, GA: CDC, 2017). www.cdc.gov/HealthyYouth/shpps/index.htm

Table 5-5 provides data on policies and practices related to mental health and social services. See the complete report at https://www.cdc.gov/healthyyouth/data/shpps/pdf/shpps-results_2016.pdf. As of July 2018, New York State became the first state to mandate the teaching of mental health instruction for all grades. Citation: New York State Department of Education. Mental Health: School Mental Health Education. http://www.nysed.gov/curriculum-instruction/mental-health

State of the Art

Promoting mental and emotional health is most effective when schools and communities work in partnership. Students, teachers, parents, school staff, and community members all play important roles.

The *Health, Mental Health and Safety Guidelines for Schools* provide definitions, information, and resources for a wide variety of mental and emotional health topics and issues, including abuse, ADHD, bullying, eating disorders, diversity, grief, parenting, relationships, sexual identity, social skills, substance abuse, suicide, and violence. Each community, with the help of its own health, safety, mental health, and educational experts and community members, should decide which guidelines are basic, which do not apply, and which to work toward. The guidelines can help community and school leaders determine the breadth of school health, mental health, and safety issues and set priorities for future action.[39]

The Centers for Disease Control and Prevention developed the Health Education Curriculum Analysis Tool (HECAT) to help educators achieve state-of-the-art practice in health education. The Mental and Emotional Health (MEH) module contains the tools to analyze and score curricula that are intended to promote mental and emotional health. The module uses the National Health Education Standards as the framework for determining the extent to which the curriculum is likely to enable students to master the essential knowledge and skills that promote mental and emotional health. This chapter includes the HECAT's healthy behavior outcomes and developmentally appropriate concepts and skills for promoting mental and emotional health. The HECAT is available at the Healthy Youth website of the Division of Adolescent and School Health (DASH) at CDC (www.cdc.gov/healthyyouth/HECAT/index.htm?s_cid=tw_eh443).

GUIDELINES FOR CLASSROOM APPLICATIONS

Important Background for K–8 Teachers

This section includes important topics for teachers to consider in establishing a mentally and emotionally healthy classroom environment. These considerations include:

- Creating safe and caring classroom communities.
- Examining self-esteem: what it is and what it's not.
- Fostering resilience: helping students use their minds and hearts well.
- Recognizing and helping students who have problems.
- Taking care means teachers, too.

Creating Safe and Positive Classroom Communities

Setting clear and consistent expectations for student behavior is an important foundation for caring classrooms that are physically, mentally, emotionally, and socially safe. Many teachers engage their students in creating a manageable number of easy-to-understand classroom agreements that children work toward throughout the school year. Examples include the four *Tribes* learning community agreements developed by Jeanne Gibbs:

1. Attentive listening
2. Appreciation/no put-downs
3. The right to pass
4. Mutual respect[40]

Schoolwide behavioral expectations across all grade levels are especially helpful, such as the three "take cares":

1. Take care of yourself.
2. Take care of each other.
3. Take care of this place.

Teachers can create a three-column ("double-t") chart with their students to give real-life examples of what each agreement looks like, sounds like, and feels like in practice. For example, "take care of yourself" sounds like no tattling or telling to get someone else in trouble. However, if someone is in danger or hurt, "take care of others" sounds like telling a teacher, "Shelley fell and skinned her knee, and we need your help."

Another idea for establishing classroom agreements is to have students write want-ads for "best possible teachers" and "best possible students" as the basis for how everyone will work together. Students usually are delighted to write their list of qualifications for great teachers. To their surprise, their list for great students often has similar characteristics.

In addition to expectations for student behavior, the way teachers work with students on a day-to-day basis is tremendously important for creating healthy classrooms. Barbara Landau, author of *The Art of Classroom Management: Building Equitable Learning Communities*, stated:

> Inclusive and welcoming management and curricular practices are a necessity. They are the most powerful means by which to ensure that all students have an equal opportunity to be successful regardless of the languages they speak, the beliefs they hold, the disabilities that challenge them, their gender, or the color of their skin.[41]

Bob Sornson, founder of the Early Learning Foundation, offered these twelve important tips for creating a positive classroom environment that can enhance student achievement:

1. **Build Connections Daily.** Greet students at the door. Use eye contact, smile, and call students by name. Show them you care enough to ask about their lives. Tell them your own story. Build the personal connection.
2. **Use Consistent Procedures and Routines.** Developing and consistently using classroom procedures helps students feel secure, teaches them which behaviors are appropriate for the classroom, and supports a shared purpose in the classroom.
3. **Respond Quickly to Misbehavior.** Nip misbehavior in the bud, not with anger and intimidation, but with a carefully honed set of responses that keep your classroom calm

and safe. Children will not learn optimally in an unsafe environment. As teachers, it is our job to model calm, emotionally appropriate behaviors and to ensure that no child is afraid of physical or emotional harm in the school.

4. **Notice Specific Positive Behaviors.** Spend five times more energy noticing good behavior than criticizing inappropriate behavior. Emphasize the use of specific positive noticing rather than general praise. Use phrases like "I noticed you were really concentrating today, and that you were one of the first students to get your work done. How did you learn to stay so focused?"

5. **Use Instructional Design for Success.** Be aware of the instructional levels and needs of your students, and make adjustments in your instructional design so students are working at their level of readiness as much as possible. Students learn optimally, stay motivated, give time to a task, and behave better when they are working with a high expectation of success.

6. **Neutralize Arguments.** Avoid getting sucked into difficult arguments with students. Learn the skills of responding with empathy rather than anger when students try to argue.

7. **Sometimes Delay Consequences.** When you are unsure how to respond, too angry to think straight, or are working with a child who is emotionally distraught, recognize that you do not have to solve every problem right that minute. Take a breath, calm yourself and the student, and in some cases give yourself some time to consider options before dealing with a problem.

8. **Develop an Empathetic Classroom Culture.** Empathy is the ability to identify with and understand somebody else's feelings. It may be the most important skill in your repertoire of behavior management skills. Build a classroom in which students feel empathy for each other and from their teacher.

9. **Build Connections with Families.** Be the teacher who sends home good news instead of only criticism and punishment. Reach out to parents and build connections that will help your students know that school and home are on the same team.

10. **Use Enforceable Statements.** Avoid using threats. Learn to use words carefully, describing those things you are willing to do or allow in your classroom; for example, "We'll be going out to recess as soon as all the tables are clean and the students are quiet."

11. **Offer Choices.** Sometimes share control, especially over the little things. Ask students questions such as, "Would you like to do the odd-numbered questions or the even-numbered questions today?"

12. **Teach Problem-Solving Skills.** As much as is reasonable, avoid telling students what they ought to do when they are capable of solving their own problems. Guide students to believe they have the capacity to think, learn, and solve problems on their own. Help students develop self-efficacy.[42]

One of the most important reminders for new teachers as well as for experienced educators who want to create more inclusive and caring classroom communities is *don't give up.* New ways of thinking and acting take time to teach and learn. Students in elementary and middle school truly are a work in progress. With caring and persistent teaching, revisited as needed, they can learn to act in respectful ways that are inviting to others and to themselves. Teaching children to feel empathy and value relationships is as important as any subject in the curriculum.

Examining Self-Esteem: What It Is and What It's Not

An education cartoon illustrating a common problem with understanding the role of self-esteem in school settings showed a young teacher talking with her principal. The caption read, "I didn't have time to teach them anything. I was too busy building their self-esteem." These words pinpoint what many educators, parents, and community members have come to believe about attempts to build self-esteem—it's an empty process consisting of puffing up children's ideas about themselves with no basis in reality that takes time away from the real work of schools, which is academics. This section looks into the research on self-esteem and suggests ways to put important concepts into practice in the classroom.

Robert Reasoner, writing for the National Association for Self-Esteem (www.self-esteem-nase.org/index.php), stated that, "Efforts to convey the significance and critical nature of self-esteem have been hampered by misconceptions and confusion over what is meant by the term self-esteem." The term is difficult to define because of its multiple dimensions, which include cognitive, affective, and behavioral elements. Reasoner cautioned, however, that the significance of self-esteem should not be lost in the confusion over what it means. The National Association for Self-Esteem defines *self-esteem* as "The experience of being capable of meeting life's challenges and being worthy of happiness. . . . This concept of self-esteem is founded on the premise that it is strongly connected to a sense of competence and worthiness and the relationship between the two as one lives life. . . . The value of this definition is that it is useful in making the distinction between authentic or healthy self-esteem and pseudo or unhealthy self-esteem. A sense of personal worth without competence is just as limiting as competence without worthiness."[43]

Martin Seligman spoke directly to concerns about self-esteem:

> Armies of American teachers, along with American parents, are straining to bolster children's self-esteem. That sounds innocuous enough, but the way they do it often erodes children's sense of worth. By emphasizing how a child feels, at the expense of what the child does—mastery, persistence, overcoming frustration and boredom, and meeting challenge—parents and teachers are making this generation of children more vulnerable to depression.[44]

Seligman goes on to say that children soon learn to ignore the puffery and constant flattery—often with no real basis—that they hear in some classrooms. Thus, teachers need to think carefully about how they talk with children. Many teachers have been trained to praise children constantly and to direct a comment to one child ("I like the way Neil is sitting up so straight and tall") to get other children to behave. Although praising Neil for sitting up straight certainly is better than yelling at the other students, and might get Joe and Sandy to sit up some of the time, it might also cost Neil socially in terms of friends, playmates, and name-calling. Quackenbush, Kane, and Telljohann summarized research showing that when troubled young people learn to feel unwarranted high self-esteem (when they are praised in the absence of anything exemplary about their performance), they are more likely to behave violently or aggressively when they receive criticism in the future. Thus, research indicates that self-esteem without foundation is not useful for young people and might even be detrimental.[45]

What can teachers do, then, to build children's sense of competence and self-efficacy as a genuine source of self-esteem? Seligman encourages teachers to think in terms of helping children "do well" rather than merely "feel good" about themselves. Seligman stated,

> Feelings of self-esteem in particular, and happiness in general, develop as side effects—of mastering challenges, working successfully, overcoming frustration and boredom. . . . The feeling of self-esteem is a byproduct of doing well. Once a child's self-esteem is in place, it kindles further success. . . . There is no question that feeling high self-esteem is a delightful state to be in, but trying to achieve the feeling side of self-esteem directly, before achieving good commerce with the world, confuses profoundly the means and the end.[46]

In talking with children about their work, teachers can stop to ask real questions and listen to children's answers rather than sweeping around the room saying "Good job!" to everyone they pass. To illustrate, a teacher education student shared that she hadn't really taken to heart the seminar discussions on engaging children in genuine conversations about their work. Instead, she said in passing to a little girl who was hard at work on a painting, "Good job—I like your boat!" The little girl looked up at her, looked down at the picture, and burst into tears. "It's not a boat!" she wailed. The teacher education student said ruefully that she wished she had said "Tell me about your picture" and waited to hear what the little girl would say.

Fostering Resilience: Helping Students Use Their Minds and Hearts Well

Martin Krovetz, author of *Fostering Resiliency: Expecting All Students to Use Their Minds and Hearts Well*, explained resiliency theory as the belief in the ability of every person to overcome adversity if important protective factors are present in that person's life. He expressed the belief that when the school community works to foster resiliency, alongside the efforts of family and community, a large number of students can overcome great adversity and achieve bright futures. To foster resilience for all students, schools must examine everything from how and what students are taught to the ways schools are organized and students are grouped. Teaching students such skills as persistence, impulse control, and empathy can be directly related to fostering resiliency.[47]

Bonnie Benard defined resiliency as the ability to bounce back successfully despite exposure to severe risks.[48] A resilient community focuses on the protective factors that foster resiliency for its members. These factors include caring, high expectations and purposeful support, and ongoing opportunities for meaningful participation.[49]

Judith Deiro, in her book *Teachers DO Make a Difference*, acknowledged that teachers face more intense challenges with students today than they did thirty years ago.[50] Teachers need effective ways to deal with the complicated human situations they encounter in today's classrooms. Deiro affirmed that teachers do not want to be social workers—they are teachers and want to act in a teacher's role. She described effective, role-appropriate ways for teachers to make a difference for their students, to help students who live in high-risk situations, without becoming social workers or adding more work to their busy schedules. Deiro stated that *the most powerful and effective way teachers can help students overcome the negative influences in their environment is by developing close and caring connections with them.* Research indicates that today's youth have too few pro-social adults (individuals who obey the laws of society, respect social norms, and care about the well-being of others) in their lives. The healthy development of children in today's society depends on having more caring adults meaningfully involved with them.[51]

Research on bonding also shows powerful ways teachers can make a positive change in students' lives. The Kauai Longitudinal Study on Resilience, which studied children born into adverse home conditions in Hawaii in 1955, documented factors that helped these children grow up to be successful, well-adjusted adults.[52] More often than not, the key factor was a caring, responsive teacher. The resilient adults these children grew up to be often mentioned a favorite teacher as the person who really made the difference for them. Other studies have found similar results.

How do teachers put these ideas into practice in the classroom? If the number one prerequisite for student learning is establishing caring, respectful, inviting relationships with young people, how do teachers structure their thinking, actions, and classrooms to go about doing this? Deiro studied the behaviors of teachers to learn how they established healthy, nurturing connections with students. She summarized the strategies the teachers used, often in combination[53]:

- *Creating one-to-one time with students.* Teachers did this by making themselves accessible to students before classes, between classes, and after school; opening their classrooms early and keeping them open after school; stationing themselves in the doorway between classes; encouraging and being open to personal conversations; getting involved in extracurricular activities; maximizing individual and small-group contact during lessons; interspersing personal talk during lectures; providing personally written comments on student papers; and using nonverbal communication, such as eye contact and standing close to students.

- *Using appropriate self-disclosure.* Deiro defined appropriate self-disclosure for student–teacher relationships as the act of sharing or disclosing the teacher's own feelings, attitudes, and experiences with students in ways that are helpful to the students and enhance their learning process. Appropriate disclosure can build a bridge between students and teachers on a common human level.

A caring teacher can make all the difference in helping children build resilience.

- *Having high expectations of students while conveying a belief in their capabilities.* A school culture of high expectations is a critical factor in increasing academic achievement. Students need adults in their lives who believe they can achieve. Students enjoy being around teachers who see them as bright and capable with bright futures in front of them. The key seems to be conveying a belief in student capabilities while holding high expectations. Teachers can help most by expressing their belief in students by problem-solving with them to help them achieve, even when they are struggling, rather than by expressing disappointment about what students haven't been able to do.
- *Networking with parents, family members, and friends of students.* In schools situated in functional communities, parents know the parents of their children's friends, and teachers know the family, friends, and neighbors of their students. These "intergenerational closures" provide a common circle of friends and acquaintances and create additional sources of information about students. Teachers can strengthen their connection with students by living in the communities where they work.
- *Building a sense of community among students within the classroom.* The word *community* refers to a relational association within which human interactions and social ties draw people together. A genuine sense of community comes after group members commit themselves to taking significant risks and sharing meaningful experiences. Group members are accepting and tolerant of one another, with a sense of belonging and relatedness extending to everyone in the group. *Inclusive* is another important word used to describe relational classroom communities.
- *Using rituals and traditions within the classroom.* Rituals and traditions bond individuals with their families, communities, institutions, or even countries. Rituals are activities that are performed the same way each time they are introduced, such as beginning each health lesson with a related news item brought in by a student. Traditions are customs, practices, or special events that are routinely acknowledged and honored, such as Martin Luther King Jr. Day. Rituals and traditions help build a sense of community.

This introduction to the important area of fostering resilience in children can provide a springboard for further study among interested teachers. In addition to the resources cited in this section, teachers can explore the books listed in "Internet and Other Resources" at the end of the chapter.

Recognizing and Helping Students Who Have Problems

Teachers who provide safe, caring, and resilience-building classrooms contribute enormously to the mental and emotional well-being of their students. However, in most school situations, individual students will need additional support due to mental, emotional, learning, or health difficulties. Some occurrences, such as a trauma at school or in the larger community, affect everyone in the school population and the community.

Quackenbush, Kane, and Telljohann advised that the two types of events most likely to call for teacher intervention are individual students with emotional problems (a student who is being bullied) and events that affect students as a group (a serious injury to a student in the school or community). Chapters 10 and 14 in this text, on preventing violence and on managing loss, death, and grief, provide guidance for teachers in responding to school and community events that affect students.[54]

Education on assisting children with specific disabilities is beyond the scope of this text. The authors strongly recommend that all teachers participate in professional development opportunities for learning to work with children who have special physical, mental, emotional, social, and other health needs and disabilities. In addition, teachers should avail themselves of all possible assistance from qualified special education teachers and resource staff at the school, district, and state levels. The need to provide a safe and welcoming environment applies to all students, including those with special learning needs and disabilities.

Mental Health America provides helpful information for teachers, parents, and community members seeking to understand and recognize signs and symptoms of mental and emotional health conditions among children and adolescents. Teachers must remember that they are neither counselors nor mental health professionals—they should not attempt to make diagnoses, interview children, or express opinions about diagnoses to parents and caregivers. The teacher's responsibility is to make appropriate referrals to help children and their families access the mental health services they need. Mental Health America provides an excellent Children's Mental Health Resource List. These resources are a great starting place for learning to help and get help for children who are experiencing difficulty. In particular, the role of stress and family stress in children's lives cannot be overstated. Examples from the Children's Mental Health Resource List (www.mentalhealthamerica.net/conditions/childrens-mental-health) include:

- ADHD and kids
- Autism

- Bipolar disorder
- Conduct disorder
- Depression
- Grief
- Suicide
- Substance use

Teachers need to know where to go to find more information on specific problems that arise in their classrooms. Teachers should identify those specialists in their schools, districts, and states who can provide the assistance they need. In addition, teachers can access valid and reliable resources on the Internet, including those listed at the end of this chapter in "Internet and Other Resources."

Taking Care Means Teachers, Too

Teachers want to help their students grow to become resilient people who demonstrate mental and emotional health, persist when work or life circumstances are challenging, and are justly proud of their hard-earned accomplishments. However, Deiro[55] acknowledged that consistently caring without achieving consistent returns creates an imbalance in the caring cycle—the mutual giving and receiving of caring—and is the root of emotional burnout among teachers. Teachers who are too exhausted mentally, emotionally, or physically to come to school and perform at their best are unlikely to be able to help anyone, including students. Teachers can practice the health education standard of self-management by taking care of themselves as well as their students. Ideas for a teacher's "take care of yourself" list include eating nutritiously, getting plenty of sleep, exercising regularly, and learning to manage stress in healthy ways.

A final recommendation is for teachers to spend time with other educators who value students and teaching as much as they do. Staying away from complainers, the teacher's lounge (if it's a negative place), and other people and places that disparage children, families, school administration, and the teaching profession is a great self-management strategy.

Recommendations for Concepts and Practice

The goal of health education is to help students adopt or maintain health-enhancing behaviors. School districts and teachers should identify the health-enhancing behaviors they would like their students to maintain or adopt. The list found in the Teacher's Toolbox 5.1 identifies possible healthy behavioral outcomes related to promoting mental and emotional health. Though not all these suggestions are developmentally appropriate for students in grades K–8, this list can help teachers understand how the learning activities they plan for their students support both short- and long-term desired behavior outcomes.

Teacher's Toolbox 5.1

Developmentally Appropriate Knowledge and Skill Expectations for Mental and Emotional Health

HEALTHY BEHAVIOR OUTCOMES (HBO) FOR MENTAL AND EMOTIONAL HEALTH

HBO 1. Express feelings in a healthy way.
HBO 2. Engage in activities that are mentally and emotionally healthy.
HBO 3. Prevent and manage interpersonal conflict, in healthy ways.
HBO 4. Prevent and manage emotional stress and anxiety in healthy ways.

HBO 5. Use self-control and impulse-control strategies to promote health.
HBO 6. Get help for troublesome thoughts, feelings, or actions for oneself and others.
HBO 7. Show tolerance and acceptance of differences in others.
HBO 8. Establish and maintain healthy relationships.

Grades K–2 Knowledge Expectations	Grades 3–5 Knowledge Expectations	Grades 6–8 Knowledge Expectations
NHES 1: Core Concepts		
MEH1.2.1 Explain the importance of talking with parents and other trusted adults about feelings. (HBO 1, 2 & 8)	MEH1.5.1 Identify characteristics of a mentally and emotionally healthy person. (HBO 1 & 2)	MEH1.8.1 Describe characteristics of a mentally and emotionally healthy person. (HBO 1 & 2)
MEH1.2.2 Identify appropriate ways to express and deal with feelings. (HBO 1, 2, 3 & 4)	MEH1.5.2 Explain what it means to be mentally or emotionally healthy. (HBO 1 & 2)	MEH1.8.2 Explain the interrelationship of physical, mental, emotional, social and spiritual health. (HBO 1 & 2)
MEH1.2.3 Explain the relationship between feelings and behavior. (HBO 1 & 5)	MEH1.5.3 Describe the relationship between feelings and behavior. (HBO 1 & 2)	MEH1.8.3 Discuss how emotions change during adolescence. (HBO 1 & 2)
	MEH1.5.4 Identify role models who demonstrate positive emotional health. (HBO 1, 2, 3, 4, 5, 7 & 8)	MEH1.8.4 Explain appropriate ways to express needs, wants, emotions, and feelings. (HBO 1, 2, 3, 4 & 5)
	MEH1.5.5 Describe appropriate ways to express and deal with emotions. (HBO 1, 2, 4 & 5)	MEH1.8.5 Describe role models that demonstrate positive mental and emotional health. (HBO 1, 2, 3, 5, 7 & 8)
	MEH1.5.6 Describe healthy ways to express affection, love, friendship, and concern. (HBO 1, 2 & 8)	MEH1.8.6 Summarize the benefits of talking with parents and other trusted adults about feelings. (HBO 1, 2 & 8)
		MEH1.8.7 Describe healthy ways to express affection, love, friendship, and concern. (HBO 1, 2 & 8)

(continued)

Grades K–2 Knowledge Expectations (*continued*)	**Grades 3–5 Knowledge Expectations** (*continued*)	**Grades 6–8 Knowledge Expectations** (*continued*)

MEH1.2.4 Describe the difference between bullying and teasing. (HBO 1, 3 & 7)

MEH1.2.5 Explain the importance of respecting the personal space and boundaries of others. (HBO 2, 3, 5 & 8)

MEH1.2.6 Explain why it is wrong to tease or bully others. (HBO 7)

MEH1.2.7 Identify the benefits of healthy family relationships. (HBO 8)

MEH1.2.8 Identify the benefits of healthy peer relationships. (HBO 8)

MEH1.5.7 Explain the importance of talking with parents and other trusted adults about feelings. (HBO 1, 2 & 8)

MEH1.5.8 Identify feelings and emotions associated with loss and grief. (HBO 1 & 4)

MEH1.5.9 Identify feelings of depression, sadness, and hopelessness for which someone should seek help. (HBO 1 & 6)

MEH1.5.10 Describe the importance of being aware of one's own feelings and of being sensitive to the feelings of others. (HBO 1, 7 & 8)

MEH1.5.11 Identify positive and negative ways of dealing with stress and anxiety. (HBO 2, 3, 4 & 5)

MEH1.5.12 Explain the importance of respecting the personal space and boundaries of others. (HBO 2, 3 & 8)

MEH1.5.13 Identify characteristics of someone who has self-respect. (HBO 2 & 7)

MEH1.5.14 Give examples of pro-social behaviors (e.g., helping others, being respectful of others, cooperation, consideration). (HBO 2, 7 & 8)

MEH1.5.15 Explain that anger is a normal emotion. (HBO 3)

MEH1.5.16 Identify personal stressors at home, in school, and with friends. (HBO 3 & 4)

MEH1.5.17 Identify characteristics of someone who has self-control. (HBO 3, 4 & 5)

MEH1.5.18 List physical and emotional reactions to stress. (HBO 4)

MEH1.5.19 Describe the value of others' talents and strengths. (HBO 7)

MEH1.5.20 Describe how people are similar and different. (HBO 7)

MEH1.5.21 Identify characteristics of healthy relationships. (HBO 8)

MEH1.5.22 Describe the benefits of healthy family relationships. (HBO 8)

MEH1.5.23 Describe the benefits of healthy peer relationships. (HBO 8)

MEH1.5.24 Identify characteristics of a responsible family member. (HBO 8)

MEH1.8.8 Describe a variety of appropriate ways to respond to stress when angry or upset. (HBO 1, 3, 4 & 8)

MEH1.8.9 Summarize feelings and emotions associated with loss and grief. (HBO 1 & 4)

MEH1.8.10 Explain the importance of a positive body image. (HBO 2)

MEH1.8.11 Describe how mental and emotional health can affect health-related behaviors. (HBO 2, 3 & 4)

MEH1.8.12 Describe how sharing or posting personal information electronically about self or others on social media sites (e.g., chat groups, e-mail, websites, phone and tablet applications) can negatively impact mental and emotional health. (HBO 2, 3 & 7)

MEH1.8.13 Explain the causes, symptoms, and effects of depression. (HBO 2, 3, 4 & 5)

MEH1.8.14 Explain the causes, symptoms, and effects of anxiety. (HBO 2, 3, 4 & 5)

MEH1.8.15 Describe the signs, symptoms, and consequences of common eating disorders. (HBO 2, 4 & 5)

MEH1.8.16 Describe pro-social behaviors that help prevent violence. (HBO 2, 7 & 8)

MEH1.8.17 Describe what it means to be a responsible person. (HBO 2 & 8)

MEH1.8.18 Describe characteristics of a responsible family member. (HBO 2 & 8)

MEH1.8.19 Describe examples of situations that require self-control. (HBO 3, 4 & 5)

MEH1.8.20 Describe how power and control differences in relationships can contribute to aggression and violence. (HBO 3, 5, 6 & 8)

MEH1.8.21 Describe ways to manage interpersonal conflict nonviolently. (HBO 3, 5 & 7)

MEH1.8.22 Explain why it is important to understand the perspectives of others in resolving interpersonal conflicts. (HBO 3 & 7)

MEH1.8.23 Explain causes and effects of stress. (HBO 4)

MEH1.8.24 Describe personal stressors at home, in school, and with friends. (HBO 4)

MEH1.8.25 Explain positive and negative ways of dealing with stress. (HBO 4)

MEH1.8.26 Analyze the risks of impulsive behaviors. (HBO 5)

MEH1.8.27 Explain how the expression of emotions or feelings can help or hurt oneself and others. (HBO 5 & 6)

MEH1.8.28 Explain why people with eating disorders need professional help. (HBO 6)

MEH1.8.29 Examine the importance of being aware of one's own feelings and of being sensitive to the feelings of others. (HBO 6 & 8)

MEH1.8.30 Explain how intolerance can affect others. (HBO 7)

MEH1.8.31 Explain the benefits of living in a diverse society. (HBO 7)

MEH1.8.32 Explain why it is wrong to tease or bully others based on personal characteristics (such as body type, gender, appearance, mannerisms, and the way one dresses or acts). (HBO 7)

MEH1.8.33 Describe characteristics of healthy relationships. (HBO 8)

MEH1.8.34 Explain the qualities of a healthy dating relationship. (HBO 8)

MEH1.8.35 Differentiate healthy and unhealthy relationships. (HBO 8)

Grades K–2 Skill Expectations	Grades 3–5 Skill Expectations	Grades 6–8 Skill Expectations

NHES 2: Analyze Influences

MEH2.2.1 Identify relevant influences of family on mental and emotional health practices and behaviors.

MEH2.2.2 Identify relevant influences of school on mental and emotional health practices and behaviors.

MEH2.2.3 Identify relevant influences of media and technology on mental and emotional health practices and behaviors.

MEH2.2.4 Describe positive influences on mental and emotional health practices and behaviors.

MEH2.2.5 Describe negative influences on mental and emotional health practices and behaviors.

MEH2.5.1 Identify relevant influences of culture on mental and emotional health practices and behaviors.

MEH2.5.2 Identify relevant influences of peers on mental emotional health practices and behaviors.

MEH2.5.3 Identify relevant influences of community on mental and emotional health practices and behaviors.

MEH2.5.4 Describe how relevant influences of family and culture affect mental and emotional health practices and behaviors.

MEH2.5.5 Describe how relevant influences of school and community affect mental and emotional health practices and behaviors.

MEH2.5.6 Describe how relevant influences of media and technology affect mental and emotional health practices and behaviors.

MEH2.5.7 Describe how relevant influences of peers affect mental and emotional health practices and behaviors.

MEH2.8.1 Explain the influence of school rules and community laws on mental and emotional health practices and behaviors.

MEH2.8.2 Explain how perceptions of norms influence healthy and unhealthy mental health practices and behaviors.

MEH2.8.3 Explain how social expectations influence healthy and unhealthy mental and emotional health practices and behaviors.

MEH2.8.4 Explain how personal values and beliefs influence personal mental and emotional health practices and behaviors.

MEH2.8.5 Describe how some health risk behaviors influence the likelihood of engaging in other unhealthy mental and emotional health behaviors (e.g., how alcohol and other drugs increase the risk of suicide and self-injury).

MEH2.8.6 Analyze how relevant influences of family and culture affect mental and emotional health practices and behaviors.

MEH2.8.7 Analyze how relevant influences of school and community affect mental and emotional health practices and behaviors.

MEH2.8.8 Analyze how relevant influences of media and technology affect mental and emotional health practices and behaviors.

MEH2.8.9 Analyze how relevant influences of peers affect mental and emotional health practices and behaviors.

NHES 3: Accessing Information, Products, and Services

MEH3.2.1 Identify trusted adults at home who can help promote mental and emotional health.

MEH3.2.2 Identify trusted adults and professionals in school who can help promote mental and emotional health (e.g., school nurse, school counselor).

MEH3.2.3 Identify trusted adults and professionals in the community who can help promote mental and emotional health (e.g., counselors, social workers, healthcare providers).

MEH3.2.4 Explain how to locate school health helpers who can help with mental and emotional health (e.g., school nurse, school counselor).

MEH3.2.5 Explain how to locate community health helpers who can help promote mental and emotional health (e.g., counselors, healthcare providers).

MEH3.2.6 Demonstrate how to locate school health helpers to enhance mental and emotional health.

MEH3.5.1 Describe characteristics of accurate mental and emotional health information.

MEH3.5.2 Describe characteristics of appropriate and reliable mental and emotional health products.

MEH3.5.3 Describe characteristics of appropriate and trustworthy mental and emotional health services.

MEH3.5.4 Demonstrate how to locate sources of accurate mental and emotional health information.

MEH3.8.1 Analyze the validity and reliability of mental and emotional health information.

MEH3.8.2 Analyze the validity and reliability of mental and emotional health products.

MEH3.8.3 Analyze the validity and reliability of mental and emotional health services.

MEH3.8.4 Describe situations that call for professional mental and emotional health services.

MEH3.8.5 Determine the availability of valid and reliable mental and emotional health products.

MEH3.8.6 Access valid and reliable mental and emotional health information from home, school, or community.

MEH3.8.7 Locate valid and reliable mental and emotional health products.

MEH3.8.8 Locate valid and reliable mental and emotional health services.

(continued)

NHES 4: Interpersonal Communication

MEH4.2.1 Demonstrate how to effectively communicate needs, wants, and feelings in healthy ways.

MEH4.2.2 Demonstrate effective active listening skills including paying attention, and verbal and nonverbal feedback.

MEH4.2.3 Demonstrate effective refusal skills to avoid participating in emotionally unhealthy behaviors.

MEH4.2.4 Demonstrate how to effectively tell a trusted adult when feeling threatened or harmed.

MEH4.2.5 Identify how to effectively communicate care and concern for others.

MEH4.5.1 Demonstrate effective verbal and nonverbal communication skills.

MEH4.5.2 Explain how to be empathetic and compassionate toward others.

MEH4.5.3 Demonstrate effective peer resistance skills to avoid or reduce mental and emotional health risk.

MEH4.5.4 Demonstrate healthy ways to manage or resolve interpersonal conflict.

MEH4.5.5 Demonstrate how to effectively ask for help to improve personal mental and emotional health.

MEH4.5.6 Demonstrate how to effectively communicate support for others.

MEH4.8.1 Demonstrate the effective use of verbal and nonverbal communication skills to enhance mental and emotional health.

MEH4.8.2 Demonstrate how to manage personal information in electronic communications and when using social media (e.g., chat groups, e-mail, texting, websites, phone and tablet applications) to prevent interpersonal conflict.

MEH4.8.3 Demonstrate effective peer resistance skills to avoid or reduce mental and emotional health risks.

MEH4.8.4 Demonstrate effective negotiation skills to avoid or reduce mental and emotional health risk.

MEH4.8.5 Demonstrate healthy ways to manage or resolve interpersonal conflict.

MEH4.8.6 Demonstrate how to effectively ask for assistance to improve personal mental and emotional health.

MEH4.8.7 Demonstrate how to effectively communicate empathy and support for others.

NHES 5: Decision Making

MEH5.2.1 Identify situations that need a decision related to mental and emotional health (e.g., dealing with interpersonal conflict, managing anger).

MEH5.2.2 Describe how family, peers, or media influence a decision related to mental and emotional health.

MEH5.5.1 Identify situations that need a decision related to mental and emotional health (e.g., dealing with interpersonal conflict, managing emotional stress).

MEH5.5.2 Decide when help is needed and when it is not needed to make a decision related to mental and emotional health (e.g., dealing with interpersonal conflict, managing emotional stress).

MEH5.8.1 Identify circumstances that help or hinder making a healthy decision related to mental and emotional health.

MEH5.8.2 Determine when situations require a decision related to mental and emotional health (e.g., dealing with interpersonal conflict, managing emotional stress).

MEH5.8.3 Distinguish when decisions about a mental or emotional health problem should be made individually or with the help of others.

MEH5.8.4 Explain how family, culture, media, peers, and personal beliefs affect a mental or emotional health-related decision (e.g., dealing with interpersonal conflict, acceptance of differences in others).

MEH5.2.3 Explain the potential positive and negative outcomes from decisions related to mental and emotional health (e.g., dealing with interpersonal conflict, managing anger).

MEH5.2.4 Describe when help is needed and when it is not needed to make a mentally and emotionally healthy decision (e.g., dealing with interpersonal conflict, managing anger).

MEH5.5.3 Explain how family, culture, peers, or media influence a decision related to mental and emotional health (e.g., dealing with interpersonal conflict, managing emotional stress).

MEH5.5.4 Identify options and their potential outcomes when making a decision related to mental and emotional health (e.g., dealing with interpersonal conflict, managing emotional stress).

MEH5.5.5 Choose a healthy option when making a decision related to mental and emotional health.

MEH5.5.6 Describe the final outcome of a decision related to mental and emotional health.

MEH5.8.5 Distinguish between healthy and unhealthy alternatives of a mental and emotional health-related decision.

MEH5.8.6 Predict the potential outcomes of healthy and unhealthy alternatives of a mental and emotional health-related decision (e.g., response when angry, dealing with interpersonal conflict).

MEH5.8.7 Choose a healthy alternative when making a decision related to mental and emotional health.

MEH5.8.8 Analyze the effectiveness of a final outcome of a mental and emotional health-related decision (e.g., response when angry, dealing with interpersonal conflict).

NHES 6: Goal Setting

MEH6.2.1 Identify a realistic personal short-term goal to improve or maintain positive mental and emotional health.

MEH6.5.1 Set a realistic goal to improve or maintain positive mental and emotional health.

MEH6.8.1 Assess personal mental and emotional health practices.

MEH6.8.2 Set a realistic goal to improve or maintain positive mental and emotional health.

MEH6.2.2 Track progress to achieve the goal to improve or maintain positive mental and emotional health.

MEH6.2.3 Identify people who can help achieve a goal to improve or maintain positive mental and emotional health.

NHES 7: Self-Management

MEH7.2.1 Identify mental and emotional health practices that reduce or prevent health risks.

MEH7.2.2 Demonstrate healthy mental and emotional health practices.

MEH7.2.3 Make a commitment to practice healthy mental and emotional-health behaviors.

NHES 8: Advocacy

MEH8.2.1 Make requests to others to promote personal mental and emotional health practices.

MEH8.2.2 Demonstrate how to encourage peers to make healthy mental and emotional health choices.

MEH6.5.2 Track progress to achieving the goal to improve or maintain positive mental and emotional health.

MEH6.5.3 Identify resources that can help achieve a goal to improve or maintain positive mental and emotional health.

MEH7.5.1 Describe mental and emotional practices and behaviors that reduce or prevent health risks.

MEH7.5.2 Demonstrate healthy mental and emotional health practices and behaviors.

MEH7.5.3 Make a commitment to practice healthy mental and emotional health behaviors.

MEH8.5.1 Give factual information to improve the mental and emotional health of others.

MEH8.5.2 State personal beliefs to improve the mental and emotional health of others.

MEH8.5.3 Demonstrate how to persuade others to make positive mental and emotional health choices

MEH6.8.3 Assess the barriers to achieving a goal to improve or maintain positive mental and emotional health.

MEH6.8.4 Apply strategies to overcome barriers to achieving a goal to improve or maintain positive mental and emotional health

MEH6.8.5 Use strategies and skills to achieve a goal to improve or maintain positive mental and emotional health.

MEH7.8.1 Explain the importance of being responsible for personal mental and emotional health behaviors.

MEH7.8.2 Analyze personal mental and emotional health practices and behaviors that reduce or prevent health risks.

MEH7.8.3 Demonstrate healthy mental and emotional health practices and behaviors to improve the health of oneself and others.

MEH7.8.4 Make a commitment to practice healthy mental and emotional health behaviors.

MEH8.8.1 State a health-enhancing position on a mental and emotional health topic, supported with accurate information, to improve the health of others.

MEH8.8.2 Persuade others to make positive mental and emotional health choices.

MEH8.8.3 Collaborate with others to advocate for improving mental and emotional health of individuals, families, and schools.

MEH8.8.4 Demonstrate how to adapt a positive mental and emotional health message for different audiences.

SOURCE: Centers for Disease Control and Prevention, *Health Education Curriculum Analysis Tool* (Atlanta, GA: Centers for Disease Control and Prevention, 2012). https://www.cdc.gov/healthyyouth/hecat/pdf/HECAT_Module_MEH.pdf

Developmentally Appropriate Knowledge and Skill Expectations

As with other health topics, teaching related to promoting mental and emotional health should be developmentally appropriate and be based on the physical, cognitive, social, emotional, and language characteristics of specific students. Teacher's Toolbox 5.1 contains a list of suggested developmentally appropriate knowledge and skill expectations to help teachers create lessons that will encourage students to practice the desired behavior outcomes by the time they graduate from high school. As with other health topics, teaching related to promoting mental and emotional health should be developmentally appropriate and be based on the physical, cognitive, social, emotional, and language characteristics of specific students.

Teacher's Toolbox 5.1 contains a list of suggested developmentally appropriate knowledge and skill expectations to help teachers create lessons that will encourage students to practice the desired behavior outcomes by the time they graduate from high school. Before each knowledge and skill expectation, the number represents topic abbreviation (MEH for Mental and Emotional Health), NHES standard number, grade group (last

grade in that group), and knowledge or skill expectation item number. For example, MEH 1.5.1 would represent Mental and Emotional Health, standard 1, grade group 3–5, knowledge expectation item 1. Note that these grade-level spans are aligned with the 2007 National Health Education Standards.

STRATEGIES FOR LEARNING AND ASSESSMENT

Promoting Mental and Emotional Health

This section provides an example of a standards-based learning and assessment strategy for each NHES standard. The examples in this chapter can be applied to any content area. Chapters 5 to 14 include content-specific learning and assessment strategies organized by standard and grade cluster (K–2, 3–5, and 6–8). Each set of strategies begins with a restatement of the standard and a reminder of the assessment criteria, drawn from the RMC Health rubrics in Appendix B. Strategies are written as directions for teachers and include applicable theory of planned behavior (TPB) constructs—intention to act in healthy ways, attitudes toward behavior, subjective norms, perceived behavioral control—in parentheses. These learning and assessment strategies provide building blocks for standards-based lessons and units that can be tailored to local needs. Assessment criteria are used with permission from the RMC Health. See Appendix B for Scoring Rubrics.

Many of the learning and assessment strategies in this first content chapter can be applied to other content areas. The strategies focus on actively engaging students in their own learning and having them take responsibility for it. Teachers should remember that almost all health education topics affect students' mental and emotional health. For example, a lesson that teaches no name-calling relates both to preventing violence and to promoting mental and emotional health.

NHES 1 | Core Concepts

Students will comprehend concepts related to health promotion and disease prevention to enhance health.

ASSESSMENT CRITERIA

- Connections—Describe relationships between behavior and health; draw logical conclusions about connections between behavior and health.
- Comprehensiveness—Thoroughly cover health topic, showing breadth and depth; give accurate information.

Grades K–2

Children's Literature for Mental and Emotional Health   The "Children's Literature" section at the end of the chapter lists a multitude of books that teachers can use to initiate discussions about mental and emotional health. The books describe situations or issues that impact the characters in ways that relate to their mental and emotional health. The stories help children see that others have problems and challenges similar to theirs—for example, a new baby in the family. Elementary teachers can expand their discussions of children's books to encompass health concepts and health skills in relation to a particular topic of interest to their students. Students might act out their ideas for an ending to the book before the teacher finishes the story, tell a story of their own about a similar situation and what they did about it, help create a class book about a particular topic (each student contributes a page), make puppets to dramatize a story, or make a shoebox display of how the characters felt inside and acted outside.

ASSESSMENT | Students can demonstrate their understanding of mental and emotional health concepts and skills in a wide variety of ways (see the list of sample assessment tasks in Chapter 3). For assessment criteria, students should provide accurate information about the mental and emotional health issue under discussion and make connections between behaviors and health. (Constructs: Perceived behavioral control, attitudes toward behavior.)

Read Aloud by Older Students   Teachers can work across grade levels to allow opportunities for older students to select and read to younger students books with mental and emotional health themes. For example, older students might select books about having and working toward a goal (links to NHES 6), using books such as those listed under "Goals and Decisions" at the end of the chapter. Teachers should work with older students before the lesson to help them plan questions for the younger students to discuss about the topic of interest and to make sure the older students provide health-enhancing messages.

ASSESSMENT | For an assessment task, younger students should be able to answer the questions the older students ask about meeting challenges

in ways that are mentally and emotionally healthy. For assessment criteria, younger students should be able to provide accurate information and make connections between behaviors and health. (Construct: Subjective norms.)

Is There Really a Human Race?   This book by Jamie Lee Curtis and Laura Cornell (see booklist at end of chapter) asks questions children can relate to about the way people live their lives and the importance of making good choices. In contrast to the rushing that children see all around them, this book reminds them to take their time, try their best, lend a helping hand, and speak up for those who can't speak for themselves—to make the world a better place. Teachers can use these messages to help build a positive learning environment and to talk with children about the "take cares" described earlier in this chapter: Take care of yourself, take care of each other, and take care of this place.

ASSESSMENT | For an assessment task, each child can identify special things they can do for the take cares. The class can make a take cares poster for the classroom to remind everyone of the way they want to work together. The actual examples children provide tell about their understanding of the take cares idea. For assessment criteria, children should explain how each of their ideas connects to creating a positive and healthy classroom. (Construct: Attitudes toward behavior.)

Grades 3–5

Emotions from A to Z: Feelings Alphabet   Students can work in small groups to brainstorm a list of as many "feeling words" as they can. To test whether a word is a feeling word, students can try filling in the blank: "I feel. . . ." If students find themselves saying "I feel *like* . . . " or "I feel *that* . . . ," they need to keep working to get to the actual feeling word or emotion. For example, students might say, "I feel like throwing up when we have a test." Throwing up isn't the feeling—scared, anxious, or agitated might be the emotion they are after. Students can put their group lists together to make a class list to post on the wall or bulletin board.

A feelings alphabet list is a great reference tool for lessons on mental and emotional health and discussions throughout the day. To add to the list, teachers can prepare strips of paper with new words (appropriate for the vocabulary level of learners) for students to "draw out of the hat," look up, and report back on to classmates. (*Note:* Teachers should remember that the purpose of this list is to help students identify strong feelings and act in healthy ways in response to them. Mental and emotional health means recognizing and dealing with feelings of all kinds, including those that aren't pleasant at the time.)

ASSESSMENT | For assessment criteria, students should provide an accurate description of a word drawn out of the hat in kid terms and make connections between behaviors and health related to the word. For example, when people feel quixotic, they might set goals that sound wonderful but are unrealistic. (Construct: Attitudes toward behavior.)

BAM! Your Life!   The Body and Mind (BAM!) website at www.cdc.gov/bam is provided by the Centers for Disease Control and Prevention (CDC). The "Your Life" link helps students explore topics such as getting along with others, dealing with bullies, and tips for managing stress. Teachers can have pairs of students choose and explore different parts of the website and report back to class members.

ASSESSMENT | For an assessment task, students can identify one source of stress they are facing and select three tips for managing their stress in healthy ways. Students can create a thirty-second video clip of strategies for dealing with that source of stress. For assessment criteria, students should make connections between their behaviors and health. (Constructs: Perceived behavioral control, attitudes toward behavior.)

Grades 6–8

Student-Generated Game Shows, PowerPoints, and Other Creative Ways to Learn Core Concepts Many educators will recall health education lessons that marched straight through a textbook—read the chapter, do the questions at the end, take a test on Wednesday. Middle school students are quite capable of researching mental and emotional health topics of interest and creating game shows, newsletters, dramatic presentations, PowerPoints, and other creative presentations. Class members can agree on topics of interest (see the previous two learning strategies for ideas) and work in small groups to present the content to class members in memorable and engaging ways. The students should literally run the show for this activity. Students can find game show templates online to use for their presentations.

ASSESSMENT | The creative presentation students make on their mental and emotional health topic of interest is the assessment task for this activity. For assessment criteria, students should provide accurate information and draw conclusions about connections between behaviors and health. (Construct: Perceived behavioral control.)

NHES 2 | Analyze Influences

Students will analyze the influence of family, peers, culture, media, technology, and other factors on health behaviors.

ASSESSMENT CRITERIA
- Identify both external and internal influences on health.
- Explain how external and internal influences interact to impact health choices and behaviors.
- Explain both positive and negative influences, as appropriate.

Grades K–2

Healthy Families Help Me Stay Strong The idea of this activity is to help students understand how family habits and practices help them stay mentally and emotionally healthy. Teachers can begin with the question "What kinds of things do you and your family do to stay healthy and strong?" Students might start with physical health practices, such as eating healthy, exercising, not smoking, and getting a good night's sleep. Teachers can help students dig deeper by asking "What do you and your family do to stay healthy and strong when you have a problem?" Students might say that they talk things out or watch a funny television show together. Students can draw from their family practices and habits to make a class book about healthy families. Teachers should know their students and families well before undertaking a lesson like this. If teachers know that several students are experiencing difficult times in their families, they might want to restructure this lesson to include healthy practices in general, rather than practices related directly to students' families. In addition, teachers should remind students not to use family members' names when talking about problems. The purpose of the activity is to help children understand how their families influence their health habits and practices, not to pry into what goes on in children's homes.

ASSESSMENT | The pages students create for a class book are the assessment task for this activity. For assessment criteria, students should explain at least one way their families influence them to stay healthy and strong. (Construct: Subjective norms.)

Grades 3–5

Admongo Students sometimes are surprised to learn that commercials and advertisements are targeted directly to kids their age. Teachers can find helpful information for talking about advertising with their students on the Common Sense Media website (www.commonsensemedia.org/blog/how-kids-can-resist-advertising-and-be-smart-consumers). Admongo (www.consumer.ftc.gov/Admongo/teachers.html) provides lesson ideas and support for teachers. Classroom activities should help students build critical thinking skills and media literacy—that is, the ability to access, evaluate, analyze, and produce print and electronic media by dissecting advertisements and other products of pop culture.

In terms of mental and emotional health, teachers can help students focus on aspects of advertising designed to make them want to buy products to make themselves feel better, feel cool, feel accepted, and feel good enough. Teachers can help students examine the veracity (a new vocabulary word) of such claims.

ASSESSMENT | Students can explore the Admongo website (www.consumer.ftc.gov/admongo) to discover how ads work, who is responsible for the ad, and the ad's aim. For an assessment task, students can view toy, soft drink, or cereal ads. Students can note what the product is, strategies used to sell it (see the advertising techniques in Chapter 3), how the product is pictured (what's around it, what the lighting is like), and whether the claims probably are truthful or not. For assessment criteria, students can take a screenshot of the ad and use a digital markup tool to identify at least three ways the advertiser is trying to influence them to buy products and the relation to mental and emotional health. How do advertisers promise consumers will feel if they buy the product? Are those claims true? Students also should discuss how advertisements are intended to make a person feel—not good enough, not attractive enough—and should refute those images. (Construct: Perceived behavioral control.)

The Lion & the Mouse Discuss with students the qualities desired in a friend, teammate, neighbor, or other. Discuss with students how the qualities of their peers can influence their personal choices and behaviors, such as doing the right thing, being kind, helping someone out when they are in a difficult situation, and the like. Access the book *The Lion & the Mouse* by Jerry Pinkney. This is a wordless adaptation of one Aesop's famous fables. Because of the wordless nature of the book, readers are allowed to individually interpret the story as they desire. Instead of reading aloud to students, show the pictures and allow students to "tell" the story. The first time through, have students write down what is being said on the pages the teacher designates. The second time you read the story, select different students to share their interpretation of each picture. Discuss the different ways students interpret and approach the same situation.

ASSESSMENT | For an assessment task, have students write a moral to the story. The moral should connect the discussion on qualities desired in a friend, teammate, or other, and how peers can influence us to do the right thing. For assessment criteria, students should be able to describe how peers influence choices related to mental/emotional health and related health practices and behaviors. (Constructs: Perceived behavioral control, attitudes toward behavior.)

Grades 6–8

Healthy Laughter—the Best Medicine Laughter helps boost mood and immunity, reduce stress and blood pressure, and connect people to each other. How can teachers use laughter in the classroom? Shannon Lowrey shared that she allowed her high school students to spend the first minute of homeroom each day telling jokes to get everyone off to a good start. Middle school teacher Georgia Goeas tells her students, "Your job is to entertain me—and you better be good. I have television, CDs, and DVDs!" Research indicates that students learn better when they feel safe, capable, and supported in their classrooms. Memes are a popular way to share humorous images and videos by Internet users.

ASSESSMENT | For an assessment task, students can use an online or app-based meme creator with an image of themselves laughing. The meme message should explain the benefits of healthy laughter or how hurtful humor and laughter can make others feel put down. For assessment criteria, students should explain how the created meme contributes to positive or negative feelings. (Constructs: Perceived behavioral control.)

My Family, My Culture, My Pride in Who I Am

An important aspect of analyzing influences is examining the roles family and cultural tradition play in people's lives. For this activity, students can identify traditions that are important in their lives, such as huge celebrations to mark a young person's sixteenth or twenty-first birthday. Religious traditions are important in many families and cultures, and include celebrations at specific times of the year. With parent or caregiver permission, students can share pictures, videotapes, or other keepsakes that mark their celebrations. Students should describe their traditions and answer two questions:

- How do my family and cultural traditions influence my pride in who I am?
- How do my family and cultural traditions influence my health?

In many instances, family and culture create a sense of belonging, which influences mental and emotional health in important ways. This activity can be a powerful one for dispelling misperceptions about people from different cultures and for inviting appreciation of diversity. Students might want to invite family members to visit the classroom to share more about their family and cultural traditions. As a follow-up activity, students can develop special traditions to celebrate their culture as a community of learners.

ASSESSMENT | The family and cultural traditions students share are the assessment task for this activity. For assessment criteria, students should describe how their family and cultural traditions influence their pride and sense of belonging and their mental and emotional health. (Construct: Subjective norms.)

Media Messages About Attractiveness—Says Who?

Students can dig into popular music, movies, television shows, and print advertising to look for messages about boys and girls and how they do/should express feelings, maintain relationships, express empathy, manage conflict and stress, and demonstrate impulse control. Students can display their findings as "media images and messages" versus their own "truth ads" to show what males and females are/should be like in the real world.

ASSESSMENT | Students can create poster or other visual displays to show the media messages and their own "truth" messages. For assessment criteria, students should contrast the media messages and internal/external influences with those they created in their "truth" messages about boys and girls and how they do/should foster mental and emotional health. (Construct: Perceived behavioral control, attitudes toward behavior.)

NHES 3 | Access Information, Products, and Services

Students will demonstrate the ability to access valid information and products and services to enhance health.

ASSESSMENT CRITERIA

- Access health information—Locate specific sources of health information, products, or services relevant to enhancing health in a given situation.
- Evaluate information sources—Explain the degree to which identified sources are valid, reliable, and appropriate as a result of evaluating each source.

Grades K–2

My Web of Caring

One of the most important things young children need to know is who the trusting adults in their lives are before there is a need to seek help from them. Have students brainstorm different adults the students could seek help from if there was a situation that caused them to feel nervous, worried, or upset. Discuss with students why these people would/would not be adults to seek help from and the characteristics of those they seek help from. Write the names of these different people, such as mother, babysitter, big brother, neighbor, and so forth, on slips of paper and have students play a game of charades to reinforce the different people in their lives from whom they could seek help.

ASSESSMENT | Students will create a word cloud to more specifically identify the adults from whom they could seek help. Using an online-based or web cloud app creator, students will add four to five adults by name whom they would seek help from if they felt nervous, worried, or upset about a situation. For assessment criteria, students should be able to explain why each of these individuals is an appropriate person from whom to seek help. (Constructs: Perceived behavioral control.)

Interview an Adult

As suggested in Chapter 4, students can interview a parent, a caregiver, another adult family member or friend, or a neighbor about mental and emotional health questions of interest. For example, students can interview three adults about questions such as these:

- What do you do to feel better when you are sad?
- What do you do to feel better when you are angry?
- What do you do to feel better when someone hurts your feelings?
- What do you say or do if someone is rude or mean to you?

Students can share their findings with the class. Teachers should remind students not to use anyone's real name when relating a personal story.

ASSESSMENT | The students' reports on their interviews are the assessment task for this activity. For assessment criteria, students can select three smart ways they found to deal with mental and emotional health issues and tell why their interviews were valid sources of information. (Constructs: Subjective norms, perceived behavioral control.)

Visits with School and Community Health Helpers

Teachers can help students write class letters of invitation, which they all sign, to invite health helpers from the school and community to visit their classroom. Teachers and students can discuss key health helpers for mental and emotional health issues and why these people are good sources of health information. Potential guests from the school might be the counselor or nurse. Community guests might include a mental health counselor or public health educator. Students can then prepare a list of questions related to some of the following topics for the guest and decide who will ask the questions: expressing feelings, controlling impulses, making and keeping friends, seeking help for troublesome feelings, or expressing empathy for others.

ASSESSMENT | For an assessment task, students should review the answers to their list of questions for the health helper. For assessment criteria, students explain why their interviews were valid sources of information and tell when and how they would contact these health helpers. (Construct: Perceived behavioral control.)

Grades 3–5

Ask the Experts: Broadcast News

Students can work in pairs to select and investigate a mental and emotional health topic for a class report. Students become the class experts on their topic and should be able to provide accurate information and answer questions about it.

The websites given in NHES 1 and NHES 3 are good places to start. Teachers and school librarians can help students locate additional information sources. Students can decide as a class on criteria for great presentations. Students could present their findings in a headline news format, complete with interviews and graphics. If the school has video cameras, students can record their news presentations and watch them in class.

ASSESSMENT | The news presentations students make are the assessment task for this activity. Teachers can allow students to select from a variety of formats, including PowerPoint or other computer-generated report formats or video-recording. For assessment criteria, students should provide accurate information and draw conclusions about connections between behavior and health (NHES 1) and should provide their information sources and explain why they are valid (NHES 3). (Construct: Perceived behavioral control.)

To Tell or Not To Tell—That Is the Question   One challenging experience that children struggle with at this age is the difference between privacy and secrecy. Internet users often are required to share personal information, establish a password, and interact with others. Knowing which information is appropriate to share, keep private, or tell an adult can become confusing. There are a number of websites developed specifically for kids that provide key information about staying safe on the Web. Before students begin surfing the Web, discuss some general rules about "safe surfing." Some basic tips to consider include:

- Talk with your parents first about sites you are visiting.
- Look at the site's "Privacy" link to see how it will use the information you give it.
- Keep your password, last name, phone number, and address to yourself.
- Stay away from chatting with people on the Web if you do not know them.
- Tell your parents, caregiver, or teacher if a site makes you feel uncomfortable in any way.

Demonstrate using some search engines or websites appropriate for students. See the websites listed in "Internet and Other Resources" at the end of the chapter.

ASSESSMENT | With a partner, students will create a list of safe surfing rules for the class. Have students share their list of rules with classmates. As a class, establish a list to be posted for the classroom. For assessment criteria, students should explain where they obtained their information, why their information is valid, and how they plan to stay safe while surfing the Web. (Construct: Perceived behavioral control.)

Interviewing Counselors and Administrators About Safe Schools   A safe school should be safe mentally, emotionally, socially, and physically. Teachers can assist their students in writing a letter of invitation to their school principal, vice principal, or counselors to learn more about policies and programs in place in their school to make sure everyone stays safe. For example, what are the rules about name-calling, bullying, or harassment? What happens if someone brings a weapon to school? What happens if there is a fight at school? How should students report a problem? What happens when students make a report? What if someone threatens to "get" students if they make a report? What should students do if they feel stressed out over an important test? Students should make a list of questions for their guest visitors. As an extension, students might also enjoy the books listed under "Safe and Healthy Classrooms and Schools" in the list of children's literature at the end of the chapter.

ASSESSMENT | For an assessment task, students should provide correct answers for all their questions after the interviews and tell where to go

for help in a safety situation of any kind. For assessment criteria, students should provide accurate information (NHES 1), explain why their interviews were valid sources of information (NHES 3), and tell what they can do to keep their school mentally and emotionally healthy. (Construct: Perceived behavioral control.)

Grades 6–8

Cover Stories: Health in the News   Teachers and students can start a class collection of magazine covers that deal with mental and emotional health issues such as depression, eating disorders, ADHD, and the science of happiness. Students can display the covers on a "Mental and Emotional Health in the News" bulletin board and use the accompanying stories as starting points for class reports and presentations on various mental and emotional health topics.

ASSESSMENT | The reports and presentations students make are the assessment task for this activity. For assessment criteria, students should provide accurate information and draw conclusions about connections between behaviors and health (NHES 1) and should provide their information sources and explain why they are valid (NHES 3). (Construct: Perceived behavioral control.)

Healthy Kids and Families Directory   Students can gather information to make a Healthy Kids and Families Directory. For each listing, the directory should include the name of the agency, a short description of services, contact information (phone, fax, e-mail), and hours of operation, if applicable. Students can work with their school technology specialist to locate appropriate resources and design an attractive cover for the directory and have it duplicated for students in their grade level or school. Students should create an attention-getting title for their directory that will appeal to middle school students.

ASSESSMENT | The directory students create is the assessment task for this activity. For assessment criteria, students should provide accurate information (NHES 1), tell why their resources are valid (NHES 3), and explain when and how to use the directory to promote good mental and emotional health. (Construct: Perceived behavioral control.)

NHES 4 | Interpersonal Communication

Students will demonstrate the ability to use interpersonal communication skills to enhance health and avoid or reduce health risks.

ASSESSMENT CRITERIA
- Use appropriate verbal/nonverbal communication strategies in an effective manner to enhance health or avoid/reduce health risks.
- Use appropriate skills (negotiation skills, refusal skills) and behaviors (eye contact, body language, attentive listening).

Grades K–2

Lilly's Purple Plastic Purse: **Children's Literature for Communication Skills**   Teachers and students will enjoy Kevin Henke's tale of Lilly and her purple plastic purse. Students will sympathize with Lilly when she makes an impulsive mistake, is nasty to a favorite teacher, and then has to find a way to make things right. This book and others listed under "Communication" at the end of the chapter can help children consider the dilemmas of communication. Sometimes people say things in the heat of the moment that they don't mean. How can they make it better? Sometimes people don't communicate clearly. How can they make their ideas make sense to others? Sometimes people don't tell the truth because they worry about what will happen if they do. What should they do? Teachers and students can use these books to spark discussions about being a good communicator—giving clear messages, being a good listener, and being mindful of body language and facial expression.

ASSESSMENT | For an assessment task, students can share and demonstrate a way they have learned to be better communicators. For assessment criteria, students should be able to identify and demonstrate at least one communication skill (listening, speaking clearly, facial expression, body language, I message, eye contact). (Construct: Perceived behavioral control.)

Punahele Bear: How Do We Talk to Each Other? This activity about the importance of using kind words, from family counselor Dr. Allana Coffee, can be tremendously successful with both younger and older children.[56] To begin the activity, children should sit in a circle. The teacher shows the children a stuffed animal, such as a teddy bear, and asks them to describe it (cuddly, friendly). Coffee calls her teddy bear "Punahele" (pronounced Poon-ah-hel-ay), which means "cherished" or "favorite" in Hawaiian. The teacher should place Punahele Bear in the middle of the circle. Next, the teacher tells the children a story about how excited Punahele Bear is to go to school and how much he is looking forward to it. However, sometimes things happen at school or people at school say things that make kids feel bad or ashamed. The teacher can ask students if they can think of things (without using real names) that kids or adults say or do that might make Punahele Bear feel bad or not want to come to school and should then ask students to volunteer things people say or do that might make others feel bad. As children volunteer ideas ("You can't play with us," "Your clothes are ugly," "You talk funny"), the teacher should have them place an old piece of cloth, a rag, or a paper towel over Punahele Bear. Children should go one at a time, be given plenty of time to think, and be allowed to volunteer their ideas. When the bear is covered up, the teacher should ask the children how they think he or she feels now (scared, in the dark, sad). Children can be asked to share instances when things have happened to them at school that might make them feel this way (remember, no names). As children share, everyone should listen carefully to understand how unkind words and actions can make classmates feel.

After the discussion, the teacher should ask students how they can help Punahele Bear feel better by using kind words to take off the rags, one at a time. Allow students to volunteer their kind words ("Come sit with us," "Thank you," "Let's go and play") and remove a rag, returning it to the teacher. This part of the activity often takes longer than saying the put-downs. Coffee shared that one kindergarten class told her not to take off all the rags. When she asked why, the children said, "Because even if you say sorry, it still hurts." Some teachers end this activity by leaving Punahele Bear in the classroom (on a bookshelf) to watch over class members and remind them to use kind words and actions. One lesson on kindness won't take care of all problems, of course, just as one reading lesson won't teach children to read. However, Punahele Bear provides a concrete reminder that teachers can refer to as situations arise during the school day.

Teachers can expect children to giggle or laugh when the activity starts; however, most students stop laughing as the activity goes on because the words so obviously are hurtful. Teachers also should note that some children will listen but not want to participate. Young children, in particular, may not want to say "mean words," even as an activity.

ASSESSMENT | For an assessment task, students should be able to explain, write about, or draw using kind words and actions with classmates and others. For assessment criteria, students should tell how kind words can help them be better communicators. (Construct: Perceived behavioral control.)

Tattling or Helping? Communicating So Adults Will Listen Anyone who has worked with young children is familiar with the phenomenon

of tattling. Weary teachers may routinely tell students "Settle it yourselves," but students sometimes genuinely need adult intervention. Teachers can help children think about their communication by making a two-column chart labeled "tattling" and "helping." Children should first define the terms in kids' words—tattling is telling to get someone in trouble, and helping is telling because someone is in danger, is upset, or might get hurt. Students can give examples of each, and teachers can help them link to the take cares discussed earlier in this chapter: Will telling help take care of yourself, others, and this place? One lesson won't solve the dilemma of tattling, because children are still learning about their world and about communication. However, the discussion gives teachers and students a reference point for future conversations that develop around real incidents. Allana Coffee recommends teaching children to ask adults for help in this way:

- Say "I need your help."
- In one sentence, tell what the person has done.
- In one sentence, explain what you have done to solve the problem yourself.
- Repeat "I need your help."[57]

For example, a student might say, "Mrs. Serna, I need your help. Lola and Lynn climbed up in the big tree on the playground when Kelvin was chasing them, and they don't know how to get down. I told them to hold on tight while I came to get you, and we need your help!"

ASSESSMENT | For an assessment task, students can work in pairs to dramatize a situation in which they tattle or ask for help from their teacher. Other students can guess which kind of communication, tattling or helping, they are demonstrating. For assessment criteria, students should be able to explain the difference between the two kinds of communication (telling to get someone in trouble versus telling because someone is in danger, is upset, or might get hurt) and give at least one communication tip on helping rather than tattling. (Construct: Perceived behavioral control.)

Grades 3–5

Same Words, Different Messages Joyce Fetro created this activity to help students try out different tones of voice, facial expressions, and body language.[58] Students can work in small groups to give different interpretations to the same sentences, either of their choosing or distributed by their teacher. Students should decide on (or draw from a hat) a different feeling or emotion to convey when they say the sentence. Following are some examples of sentences for students to interpret:

The coach says to stay and talk with her after practice.

We're getting our science test back today.

My teacher gave me a note for my parents.

I'm going to the mall with my sister after school.

My English teacher gave me a book to read over the holidays.

Jamie left a message for me to call back.

My Mom said we'll talk with my Dad about the party when he gets home today.

Students might express these statements with joy, disgust, exhaustion, worry, excitement, or some other emotion. Groups can have each person express a different feeling for their sentence with their tone of voice, facial expressions, and body language.

ASSESSMENT | The students' demonstrations are the assessment task for this activity. For assessment criteria, groups should be able to explain how differences in tone, facial expression, and body language changed the intended message of their sentence. (Construct: Perceived behavioral control.)

Pressure Lines: Making a Healthy Comeback Joyce Fetro recommended that students practice their peer refusal skills (see Chapter 3) by responding to a list of pressure lines.[59] Students can draw teacher-prepared slips of paper with pressure lines printed on them, or students can write pressure lines on index cards to exchange with other students. Examples of pressure lines include the following:

Hurry! Shana is holding the back door open so we don't have to pay for the movie.

Don't be a baby—we're all going to jump our bikes over the ditch.

Everyone is doing it. Drinking beer is cool, and no one will know.

You can't handle it? We all smoke, and we never get caught.

Nobody eats just one. Have some more chips!

We're cutting school at lunch—we're heading to the lake for a swim.

Students can work in small groups, with one student reading the pressure line and the others offering different peer resistance responses (repeat the refusal, use humor, suggest an alternative).

ASSESSMENT | For an assessment task, students should demonstrate their responses to the pressure lines for other class members. For assessment criteria, students should be able to identify and demonstrate at least three peer resistance strategies and tell how and when they would use them. (Construct: Perceived behavioral control.)

Grades 6–8

Communicating with the Good Thinker's Toolkit Students can use the "power tools" in the Good Thinker's Toolkit for class discussions. The seven tools (W, R, A, I, T, E, C), developed by Dr. Thomas Jackson as part of the Philosophy for Children (P4C) program at the University of Hawaii at Manoa, are

W = What do you mean?
- What do you mean by . . .?
- What is missing here?
- What have I forgotten to ask?
- What is going on here? What is the problem?
- What does this have to do with me?

R = Reasons
- What reasons are there that support what he/she said?
- Why do you say that?
- Can you give a reason? Is it a good reason?
- What makes a reason a good reason?

A = Assumptions
- What are we assuming (taking for granted as true)?
- What other assumptions might we make?
- How are our assumptions influencing what we are seeing/judging/thinking/saying?

I = Inferences; If . . . Then; Implications
- What inferences have we made from what was said?
- If what was said is true, then what?
- What are the implications of what is proposed?

T = Truth
- Is what is being said true?
- How do we know?
- How could we find out?

E = Examples; Evidence
- Can you think of an example to illustrate what you mean?
- What evidence can we find to support the claim being made?

Counterexamples
- Can you think of a counterexample to the claim being made?
- For example, suppose someone claims, "You have to go to be tall to be a good basketball player." Is this true? Can we think of a counterexample (i.e., someone who is not tall who is a good basketball player)?

Students can make their own tool kits by writing/drawing the seven power tools on index cards. Students then can select a topic for discussion in a community circle, using their seven power tools to question and respond to others. Dr. Jackson recommends making and passing a community ball (e.g., yarn ball) around the circle so that the only person speaking is the one holding the ball. Teachers can learn more at www.creighton.edu/ccas/philosophyforchildren/.

ASSESSMENT | Teachers can hold several health-related discussions on healthy versus unhealthy behaviors using the Good Thinker's Toolkit. For an assessment task, students then can take part in a fish bowl activity (a smaller circle of students are seated inside the larger community circle) where only the inner circle of students speak as they pass the community ball. For assessment criteria, each student should be able to use at least three power tools to question and respond to others about the health topic. (Constructs: Intention to act in healthy ways, attitudes toward behavior.)

Triple Your Resistance: The Power of Repeating Refusals Students might be interested to know that they often will need to repeat a refusal at least three times before people take them seriously and decide to stop pressuring them. Thus, students shouldn't be discouraged if they have to repeat a refusal. Students can work in small groups to practice their peer resistance skills, discussed in Chapter 3. Students can create scenarios to share with other groups and practice repeating a refusal three times or using three different kinds of refusals. Students can discuss how this strategy compares with saying something one time. Remind students to communicate a clear no message through their words, tone of voice, facial expressions, and body language.

ASSESSMENT | The repetition skills students demonstrate for their classmates are the assessment task for this activity. For assessment criteria, students should demonstrate three refusals, either by repeating the same refusal or by using different types of refusals, in a health-enhancing way. (Construct: Perceived behavioral control.)

Respecting Limits and Boundaries: No Pressuring Others Middle school students in health education classes often work on resisting pressure. However, sometimes middle-level students are the ones doing the pressuring. This activity involves looking at oneself and asking hard questions about communication and behavior toward others. Students should remember not to call anyone by name when giving examples. Students can start this discussion with the question "Why do people pressure and even bully other people to do things they don't want to do?" Students can first discuss this question in small groups and then share their answers with the class. From their list of possible reasons, students can go on to discuss responsible and respectful behaviors toward others, such as the following:

- Considering another person's point of view
- Respecting another person's physical and emotional comfort zone
- Using self-talk to think through words and actions, considering how they will affect another person
- Backing off when someone says, or acts in ways that say, no

Students might remember from their discussion of self-management that having a support group is a good strategy for resisting pressure. Students can commit to coming to each other's aid in pressure situations by being close by physically, helping a friend get out of a situation, or even saying "Don't pressure my friend."

ASSESSMENT | For an assessment task, students can designate words for the letters in the words *respect*, *limits*, or *support* or create a rap, slogan, poem, or song to communicate support for others and for the idea that pressuring others is wrong. For assessment criteria, students should communicate health-enhancing messages about respecting boundaries, not pressuring others, and coming to the support of friends. (Construct: Attitudes toward behavior.)

NHES 5 | Decision Making

Students will demonstrate the ability to use decision-making skills to enhance health.

■ **ASSESSMENT CRITERIA**

Reach a health-enhancing decision using a process consisting of the following steps:

- Identify a health-risk situation.
- Examine alternatives.
- Evaluate positive and negative consequences.
- Decide on a health-enhancing course of action.

Grades K–2

Helpful or Hurtful? At this age, children can begin the process of considering how their behavior impacts other people as well as evaluating whether the choices they make are helpful or hurtful. Create a list of situations, with the help of students if appropriate, that commonly occur among students where a student's feelings are hurt. Teach students a strategy such as STAR—stop, think, act, review. Practice the STAR strategy with a couple of scenarios as a class, demonstrating each step of the process. In the "review" process, students should focus on evaluating the effects of their actions on other people and determine whether their actions are helpful or hurtful. If the behavior is hurtful, students should determine a new helpful approach to the situation.

ASSESSMENT | In pairs, assign students a situation. Students will demonstrate a hurtful reaction to the situation, and then replay the situation with a helpful response. For assessment criteria, students will demonstrate the ability to examine alternatives, evaluate consequences, and take a helpful course of action. Additionally, students should be able to describe the importance of thinking about the effects of their actions on other people. (Constructs: Intention to act in healthy ways, perceived behavioral control, attitudes toward behavior.)

Children's Literature for Decision Making Many children's books focus on making a decision; see the list of appropriate books at the end of the chapter. Teachers and students can read these books and then talk about how people make good decisions (see Chapter 3). Young students don't need elaborate models. They do need to understand that they and other people make decisions every day that affect their health and well-being and to talk about how to make good decisions.

ASSESSMENT | For an assessment task, students can make pages for a class book about a good decision they made. For assessment criteria, students should identify health-enhancing decisions and write one or more sentences about how their decisions can help them stay strong and healthy. (Construct: Perceived behavioral control.)

Grades 3–5

Deciding About Ground Rules for Class Discussions Many teachers find it useful to set ground rules with students before engaging in conversations and discussions about health issues. Examples of ground rules include:

- Listen with your eyes, ears, and heart when others are talking.[60]
- Use encouraging words—no put-downs.
- Try to put yourself in someone else's situation.
- No gossiping about others or about class discussions outside the classroom.
- Don't ask personal questions about classmates or teachers.

Students can decide on the ground rules they want to follow for class discussions to keep everyone safe and willing to participate. For starters, teachers can go back to the take cares (take care of yourself, take care of others, take care of this place) and ask students to specify what these should look, sound, and feel like during class discussions.

ASSESSMENT | The ground rules students set are the assessment task for this activity. For assessment criteria, all rules should be health-enhancing and should have the take cares as a basis. (Construct: Intention to act in healthy ways.)

"What's Up?" Basket: Getting Help from Others About Issues and Decisions An important aspect of mental and emotional health is being able to ask others for help in decision making. This activity helps students put this idea into practice in a nonthreatening way. Students can write a question or an issue that they need help with on a piece of paper and put it in the teacher's "What's up?" basket or box. From time to time, the teacher can draw a piece of paper from the basket and read the question or issue aloud to the class. Teachers should screen the papers first, be careful not to read aloud anything that might upset a particular child or be so personal that a child would be identified, and follow up with individual children when a serious problem is revealed. When the teacher reads a question or an issue, students can volunteer their ideas and advice about how to handle the situation. For example, students might wonder what to do when a bully grabs their book bag and takes whatever he or she wants. Students might offer advice, such as hanging out with two or three good friends when the bully might be around or telling a parent or teacher about it. Sharing problems and questions in this way helps students realize that they are not alone and that others want to help them. Teachers also can get a good idea of the kinds of experiences students are having from the questions they write.

ASSESSMENT | For an assessment task, students can write a short story about a student who needs help and asks for it from friends, family members, or other caring adults. For assessment criteria, students should explain why the characters in their stories decided to ask for help and why that was a good decision. (Construct: Perceived behavioral control.)

Grades 6–8

Decision Trees: A Graphic Organizer for Decision Making Upper-elementary students tend to see their decisions as black and white—only two choices available. A graphic organizer such as a decision tree can help them see that often there are more than two options. In fact, many options may be available when they expand their thinking. Teachers can demonstrate making a decision tree by drawing a tree trunk and writing a problem or question about a decision across the trunk. The teacher then can draw three or more branches coming from the tree and ask students to name alternative methods for handling the problem or decision. Teachers can write the students' ideas on the branches, making sure the students suggest at least three alternatives. For example, students might want to attend a party on the weekend, but they've heard alcohol will be present and they don't want to drink. What can they do? Two obvious alternatives students will think of first are stay home or go to the party and drink. Other alternatives include go to the party with a couple of friends who also don't want to drink; go somewhere else, such as the movies, with other friends; and go to the party with a friend and be sure to take a cell phone to call for a ride home if things get out of hand.

Students then should identify the positive and negative consequences of each alternative. For example, going to a movie instead means that students miss the party (negative) but have a good time with their friends seeing the movie (positive). The decision tree can open students' eyes to the idea that more than two choices are available in most situations. To illustrate, a class was working on the problem of deciding whether to go to someone's house (the home of someone they really liked) when the parents weren't home, realizing there might be pressures to have sex. While students were naming alternatives (e.g., go, don't go), one student suddenly said, "Yeah, go—but take your sister with you!" The class laughed at the option that so clearly would remove the pressure to have sex.

ASSESSMENT | For an assessment task, students can work individually, in pairs, or in small groups to create a decision tree to share with the class. For assessment criteria, students should identify the problem or decision and at least three alternatives, name the positive and negative consequences of each alternative, select an action, and predict the outcome. (Constructs: Perceived behavioral control, attitudes toward behavior.)

Balloon Up for Decision Making Middle school health educator Lynn Shoji created this activity to help students learn the steps in a simple decision-making model (see Chapter 3).[61] Following is a step-by-step approach for teachers to use to implement the activity.

1. Before class, blow up and tie five or six large helium-quality balloons. Put them where students can see them.
2. Begin the health lesson by holding one balloon and telling students you have a problem for them to solve. The problem is to work together as a class to keep the balloon in the air for thirty seconds.
3. *Problem:* Write "problem" on the board and tell students the first step in making a decision is to state the problem. Ask the students, "What is the problem today?" To keep the balloon in the air for thirty seconds.
4. *Alternatives:* Write "alternatives" on the board. Tell students that the next step in making a decision is thinking of all the possible alternatives or choices they can make. Tell students that they can ask questions about alternatives, and you will let them know what is and is not allowed. (Rules: Students must stay in their seats with their bottoms in the chairs at all times, can hit the balloon with one hand at a time, can hit only once until another student hits and then can hit the balloon again, cannot move the chairs once the activity starts, can talk and call out to each other, and can move the chairs anywhere they want before the activity starts.)
5. *Consequences:* Write "consequences" on the board. Tell students that each alternative has a consequence, some positive and some negative. Students can ask questions about what consequences follow each alternative. (Examples: We have to stop and start over if the balloon touches the floor, the balloon comes to rest and stops moving, someone catches it or holds it, someone gets out of the chair or moves the chair, someone hits the balloon two times in a row. The class gets to be a "one-balloon class" if the balloon stays up for thirty seconds. Next the class can try to be a two-balloon class, a three-balloon class, and so on.)
6. *Action:* It's time to choose an action. Students should get into the position they want with their chairs before the activity starts (don't give advice; let students work out their own plan). When students are ready, say "Go," bat the balloon into the air, and time it for thirty seconds. Stop the action if any rules are broken, and start again. When the class keeps the balloon in the air for thirty seconds, stop the action and congratulate them for being a one-balloon class.

7. *Evaluate:* Whether or not the students kept the balloon up, ask them if what they did worked. Go back through the list of steps and ask if there's anything they want to change (new alternatives). Try the activity again, either with one balloon or, if they were successful, with two balloons.
8. Try the activity several more times, either repeating or going on to a greater number of balloons. Important: Each time, stop and go back over the steps (problem, alternatives, consequences, action, evaluation). Ask the students each time if they want to change anything to help them work together better.
9. Stop with four or five balloons the first day. Tell students what "number" their class is, and tell them they can try the activity again the next week. Go back over the steps a final time, asking students to apply them to a real-life problem.

ASSESSMENT | For an assessment task, have students write a one-page story about a real-life situation in which they are being pressured to do something they know their parents don't want them to do (cut class, go swimming unsupervised, let someone copy their homework, go with friends instead of coming straight home after school, smoke, drink, stay out past curfew). Students can choose their own pressure situation. For assessment criteria, students must state the problem in their story and then discuss each step in the decision-making process, ending with an action and an evaluation of how they think things will turn out. (Construct: Perceived behavioral control.)

Lilo and Stitch: Angels on My Shoulder Many middle-level students will have seen the movie *Lilo and Stitch* when they were younger. The characters provide students with a reference point: Lilo will try to get them to make the best decision, and Stitch will try his best to get them to engage in a risky behavior that could hurt them or others. Whether students use the Lilo and Stitch roles or the idea of "good angel/bad angel," this activity is one that middle-level students enjoy and learn from. Teachers should note that it can get very noisy! Be sure to do this activity in a location where other classes won't be disturbed.

Teachers can start this activity by having students work in groups of three. Each group has three roles for members:

- Decision maker
- Lilo ("good angel," or healthy influence)
- Stitch ("bad angel," or unhealthy influence)

If needed, some groups can have four students, with two decision makers, depending on the number of students in the class.

Teachers next should demonstrate the activity with two volunteers, who will play Lilo and Stitch. The teacher plays the decision maker in the demonstration and provides a scenario, such as the following:

> You worked hard on your math homework last night and finished all of it. You are feeling very good about your effort. When you get to school, however, a friend asks to copy your homework—he stayed up late playing computer games and didn't get his work done. What do you decide, and what do you say and do?

The decision maker's role in the first part of the activity is just to listen. Lilo and Stitch, however, will try with all their might to persuade the decision maker to follow their way of thinking. Lilo will try to convince the decision maker not to let the friend copy; Stitch will try to convince the decision maker to go ahead and let the friend copy. Teachers should give Lilo and Stitch a couple of minutes to think about their most persuasive arguments and then, on a signal, give them thirty seconds to argue their case, calling time at the end of the thirty seconds. What makes this activity noisy is that both Lilo and Stitch can talk at the same time.

When time is called, the teacher, as the decision maker, shares what he or she heard and which side was more persuasive. The teacher should then ask the class what they thought about the arguments and which side they thought was most persuasive. At this point, students should simply get the idea of how to do the activity. In the next round, the teacher will take the debriefing further.

When students have the idea, each group should designate roles (Lilo, Stitch, decision maker). Give a scenario; the persuaders have a couple of minutes to think about their arguments. Then signal "Go!" Following are some sample scenarios to get started:

- You've had a good morning at school, and you have a social studies test in the afternoon. During lunch, several students say that they are going to cut school in the afternoon to go skateboarding at the park when it's not crowded. They want you to come, too, and you have your board in your locker. What do you decide? What do you say and do?
- You and a friend are in a store at the mall. Your friend has been wanting to get a new DVD, but she doesn't have enough money to pay for it today, so she decides to shoplift it. She asks you to stand as a lookout to watch for the store manager and clerks to make sure she doesn't get caught. She doesn't want you to do the stealing—just to stand at the end of the aisle while she slips the DVD into her purse. What do you decide? What do you say and do?
- There's a new girl at school who wears a headscarf each day. Some of the kids in the class have been making fun of her behind her back. Someone passes you a slam book with really mean comments written about the girl and tells you to write in it, too. What do you decide? What do you say and do?
- You and your friends want to play basketball in the driveway, but your Dad's car is blocking the way. He took the subway into town today for a conference, and your Mom is at the grocery store in her car. You decide to move the car out of the way, but you wind up scraping it on the fence post, leaving a mark down the side. You can tell your parents what you did—or you can move the car back into place and act as if nothing happened. What do you decide? What do you say and do?

After the first role-play, stop the action and call on the decision maker in each group to tell what they heard from Lilo and Stitch, what was persuasive to them, and why. After hearing from every decision maker, use a "decision tree" to talk about alternatives and consequences. This debriefing is essential. Otherwise, the activity becomes mere entertainment and could even lead students to go away with the idea that dangerous and unhealthy behaviors are okay.

Teachers can have students work through several scenarios, giving each student the chance to play each of the three roles. Teachers and students should thoroughly debrief every scenario. If a student insists that an unsafe or unhealthy behavior is best, the teacher can ask, "What do others think? What could happen if this is what the decision maker does? Who would be affected? How?"

Teachers also can use this activity to discuss two other standards. Students can step back and examine communication style (NHES 4): What kind of communication—words, tone of voice, face, body language—makes a person want to listen to someone? Students also can analyze influences (NHES 2): How do students put pressure on one another? What is most persuasive? How can students deflect or resist that kind of pressure?

ASSESSMENT | For an assessment task, students can create and demonstrate an original Lilo and Stitch scenario for the class. For assessment criteria, students should perform the scenario and then lead the debriefing on decision making (NHES 5), communication style (NHES 4), and analyzing influences (NHES 2). (Construct: Perceived behavioral control.)

NHES 6 | Goal Setting

Students will demonstrate the ability to use goal-setting skills to enhance health.

ASSESSMENT CRITERIA

- Goal statement—Give goal statement that identifies health benefits; goal is achievable and will result in enhanced health.
- Goal setting plan—Show plan that is complete, logical, and sequential, and includes a process to assess progress.

Grades K–2

Children's Literature for Goal Setting   Many children's books tell stories of characters who have an important goal they work hard to reach. Teachers can use these books to talk with children about the importance of having achievable goals, making plans that include concrete steps to reach goals, overcoming obstacles, finding and building on sources of support, and monitoring progress. The resilience research says that learning to persist and work hard is important for children to grow to be healthy adults. See the list of books at the end of the chapter for stories about goal setting.

ASSESSMENT | For an assessment task, students can select a book and explain what various characters did to reach their goals. For assessment criteria, students should tell what the characters did in terms of (1) setting an achievable goal, (2) making a plan, (3) building on supports and dealing with obstacles, and (4) monitoring progress. Students also can tell alternative steps the characters could have taken. (Construct: Perceived behavioral control.)

Setting Behavioral and Academic Goals   Teachers will recall from earlier discussion in this chapter that building self-esteem, self-efficacy, and resilience hinges on helping students learn to achieve things for themselves. Former first grade teacher Diane Parker shared that she helped her students do this by setting an academic and a behavioral goal for each quarter of the school year. Although educators generally focus on helping young students set short-term goals (for a whole day washing their hands before they eat, using kind words all morning), Parker found that her first-grade students were able, with her help, to set achievable long-term goals and define steps toward reaching them. One of her students set the goal of not hitting others when she was upset or angry and to find other ways to let others know what she needed. When she and her teacher went over her goals at the end of the quarter, including the one about not hitting, she exclaimed with happiness, "I don't do that anymore!" Setting these kinds of goals means working with children one-on-one to find the

Learning to set goals and work toward achieving them builds self-esteem and self-efficac

specific issues that they feel their teachers—and their parents or caregivers—believe are important for their success. Students, with their teachers' help, choose the goals and set the steps for reaching them.

ASSESSMENT | The assessment task for this activity is for students to set, with their teachers' help, one academic and one behavioral goal to work on for a specified time period. For assessment criteria, the students' goals should be achievable and should include at least three concrete steps they will take to reach their goals. Students also should identify markers of success—that is, how they will know they have achieved their goals. (Constructs: Intention to act in healthy ways, perceived behavioral control.)

Grades 3–5

The Blue Ribbon Day: **We're All Good at Something!** Katie Couric's book *The Blue Ribbon Day* deals with the disappointment children and adults experience when a goal they care about doesn't work out for them. In this story, one sister makes the soccer team and the other does not. Teachers can use the book to help children think about ways to turn their disappointment into an opportunity to try new things. Children can discuss the importance of having strong sources of support (a parent) and of looking at challenges from new perspectives (submitting a project for the school science fair). This activity links to NHES 7, self-management.

ASSESSMENT | For an assessment task, children can trace the goal-setting steps throughout the story. What goals did the characters have? What steps did they take to reach their goals? What obstacles did they encounter, and how did they handle them? How did they find and build on supports? How did the characters monitor their progress? For assessment criteria, students should be able to identify at least two ideas for dealing with obstacles and two ideas for finding and building on supports. (Construct: Perceived behavioral control.)

Webbing It: Supports for and Barriers to Reaching Goals Upper-elementary students are ready to think about people and conditions that help them meet their goals and those that keep them from reaching their goals. For example, a student who attends a school and lives in a community with lots of opportunities for physical activity could count those opportunities as a "support" for reaching the goal of being more physically active. A student who lives in an area with little opportunity for participation in physical activity could count that lack of opportunity as a "barrier" to the goal of being physically active. Neither the support nor the barrier dictate what the student will be able to do. However, the student who has more opportunity might find it easier to be active, and the student with less opportunity might have to work harder to be active. Similarly, friends who say "Go ahead—you can do it, and we'll be there to watch you play" are a support. Friends who say "Why would you want to do that—let's go smoke" are a barrier. For this activity, students first identify several goals that are important to them, in both the short term and, if appropriate, the long term. Students then make a web of supports for and barriers to reaching their goals, using a different color for each. Around each support or barrier, students can write how they can take advantage of or overcome the supports and barriers, respectively.

ASSESSMENT | The web of supports and barriers students create is the assessment task for this activity. For assessment criteria, students should make a written plan for taking advantage of and overcoming each support and barrier. Students also can keep track of their experiences with the supports and barriers for a specified time period (one or two weeks). (Constructs: Intention to act in healthy ways, perceived behavioral control.)

Grades 6–8

Lōkahi for Mental and Emotional Health The Lōkahi Wheel, symbolizing balance, harmony, and unity (see the example in Chapter 1), provides an important visualization of mental and emotional health. If the parts of the wheel are in balance, students are likely to experience mental and emotional health, even in the face of challenges. For this activity, students can draw and decorate (linking to fine arts) their own Lōkahi Wheel, showing each of the six parts of the wheel: friends/family, feelings/emotions, thinking/mind, work/school, spiritual/soul, and physical/body. Teachers can review the parts of the wheel with students (spiritual/soul refers to the ways students renew themselves, which may or may not be related to faith-based practices) and have them answer two questions for each part:

1. How is it going?
2. How do I want it to go?

This very personal activity helps students look at the big picture of how things are going with their health and what issues they might like to work on for better health. Students show the six parts of their wheels as being of equal size or make the parts larger or smaller depending on how the parts apply to their lives. For example, many teacher education students show work/school taking up most of their wheel at this point in their lives. They often choose to work on improving the way they take care of themselves in physical/body (more sleep, regular exercise, better nutrition) and taking the time for more renewal in spiritual/soul.

ASSESSMENT | The Lōkahi Wheels students create are the assessment task for this activity. For assessment criteria, students should explain how things are going and how they want them to go in each part of the wheel and should set one goal and list steps to achieve it. (Construct: Intention to act in healthy ways.)

Building Your Support System in Middle School Building a support system in middle school is an important key to mental and emotional health, resilience, and reaching goals of all kinds. Teachers can use the book *Bully* by Patricia Polacco (see Children's Literature section at the end of Chapter 10) to bring the topic of support systems to life. After Lyla moves to a new middle school, she quickly makes friends with a boy named Jamie. She works hard at school and earns good grades and even a place on the cheerleading squad. *The Celebrities* (led by Gage) are the popular girls who have taken notice of Lyla and invite her into their clique. To fit in, Lyla needs a cell phone, a laptop, and a Facebook account. Her new popular friends help Lyla make changes to her appearance and encourage her to drop Jamie's friendship. After *The Celebrities* start posting cruel comments to other students' Facebook walls, Lyla begins to doubt the nature of their friendship. When a state exam is compromised and Lyla is blamed, it takes a true friend to come to her rescue and identify the actual culprit. Students can use this story to start a discussion on friendship. What is a real friend? In what ways did Jamie help Lyla when she first arrived at the new school? Would a friend behave in a hurtful way around other kids? How long should a person try to fit in, and how far should someone go to fit in? When does it make sense to look for new friends? How can a friend help another friend who is being singled out and picked on? What should Lyla have done, and why? What incidents in Gage's life led her to make the decisions she made? What healthy support systems could Gage have utilized to help her make different choices and build resilience? To dig more deeply, teachers can ask students to think about what they really want in friends—how to be that kind of friend and how to find those kinds of friends as a support system. Students can identify the kinds of friendships they want to develop and the kind of relationships they want to stay away from in middle school. After students have completed their discussion, they will be interested to know what Lyla actually decided to do.

Lyla used her support system—her family and a real friend—to work this problem out for herself, even when the going was really hard. Developing and maintaining a strong support system is an important aspect of middle school for students to consider.

ASSESSMENT | For an assessment task, students can write letters of response giving their best advice on how to deal with Lyla's situation. Students can exchange letters to discuss the similarities and differences in their approaches to dealing with problems that involve classmates. For assessment criteria, students should describe how they will find and keep friends who stand up for them throughout their middle school years and beyond. (Construct: Perceived behavioral control.)

Health Behavior Projects: Trying Out a Theory-to-Practice Approach
Sabo, Telljohann, and Kane published a helpful guide for working with students on health behavior change, titled *Improving Health Behaviors,* as part of the *HealthSmart* series for middle and high school students.[62] In these lessons, students learn to

- Identify unhealthy behaviors.
- Establish a goal to change an unhealthy behavior.
- Develop a plan and implement strategies for achieving a healthy goal.

The lessons are based on a modified version of the transtheoretical model (TTM), which many educators know as "stages of change." This model views behavior changes as a process over time, rather than as a one-time event. Sabo, Telljohann, and Kane explain the five stages of change as follows:

1. *Precontemplation:* People in this stage are not aware that their unhealthy behavior is a problem, or they may know it is a problem but don't intend to change.
2. *Contemplation:* People in this stage are aware that their unhealthy behavior is a problem and are thinking about changing it. They are more open to feedback and information from others.
3. *Preparation:* People in this stage are committed to changing their unhealthy behavior in the near future. They have been taking small steps to help them get ready to change the behavior.
4. *Action:* People in this stage are taking action to change their unhealthy behavior. They have put a plan in place and are making progress in practicing healthier behaviors.
5. *Maintenance:* People in this stage have followed their plan and have changed the unhealthy behavior. Their practice of healthier behaviors is becoming a habit.

Relapse may occur in the action or maintenance stage. Students can benefit from understanding the triggers or events that can bring on relapse and learn how to prepare for and successfully deal with them. Relapse should be seen not as a failure but as a temporary setback that can be overcome.[63] Middle-level students are ready to deal with unhealthy behaviors and are fascinated by working to change them with a "theory into action" approach. Teachers may find it helpful to explore the stages of change model more extensively through the ETR unit or other resources and provide their students with opportunities to try it for themselves.

ASSESSMENT | For an assessment task, students should select a health behavior they want to change, identify the stage they are in, establish a goal based on their stage of change, and develop and implement a plan. Students should keep records of their progress over time for class discussion and should summarize their experience in a health goal summary paper. For assessment criteria, students should be able to explain each step involved in working toward their goal. (Constructs: Intention to act in healthy ways, perceived behavioral control.)

NHES 7 | Self-Management

Students will demonstrate the ability to practice health-enhancing behaviors and avoid or reduce health risks.

ASSESSMENT CRITERIA
- Application (transfer)—Initiate health-enhancing behaviors; apply concepts and skills appropriate and effectively.
- Self-monitoring and reflection—Monitor actions and make adjustments; accept feedback and make adjustments; able to self-assess, reflect on, and take responsibility for actions.

Grades K–2

Relaxing with Angry Octopus Read the story "Angry Octopus: An Anger Management Story" by Lori Lite to the class. This story introduces students to the concept of progressive muscle relaxation, which is a relaxation technique that can be used by students when they are feeling stressed, angry, or having difficulty relaxing or falling asleep. Discuss with students the strategies the octopus uses to manage his feelings. Talk with students about other times, other than when they are angry, that using this relaxation skill might be useful. Using a progressive muscle relaxation technique prior to taking a standardized test, for example, might allow students the opportunity to relax and get focused on the task. Conducting an Internet search for children's progressive muscle relaxation can lead you to additional scripts that can be used with younger students—these tend to use analogies to which young people can relate, thus helping them tighten and relax different muscle groups.

ASSESSMENT | For an assessment task, have students create before, during, and after drawings of a time when they might be able to use a progressive muscle relaxation technique. The after drawing should focus on the benefits of using the technique, such as feeling more relaxed or performing better during a stressful event. For assessment criteria, students should be able to show health practices that reduce health risks (e.g., stress, anger) and demonstrate healthy mental/emotional health practices. (Constructs: Perceived behavioral control, attitudes toward behavior, intention to act in healthy ways.)

Controlling Myself Over a period of a few days, play a variety of games that encourage students to practice self-control. Modifying "I Spy" to "Silently I Spy" requires students to listen and think, but hold their responses until called upon. This gives younger students the awareness that they can keep their words under control. "Freeze Tag" can be modified as well. Play music and allow students to dance or move about. Silently hold up a card with a picture or word indicating a certain pose you want students to take when the music ends. Students can give the teacher a cue when they see the card (e.g., a wink, nod, bow). When the music stops, tag anyone who does not strike the pose when the music stops. This requires students to visualize the pose but wait to demonstrate it until the appropriate time, reinforcing that students can control their arms and legs at any time to do what is right.

ASSESSMENT | For an assessment task, students can draw or take a picture of a situation when they might need to practice using self-control— for some it is verbal, others physical. Then draw/take another picture of what it will look like when they are practicing self-control. Assessment criteria include being able to identify situations that require self-control and practice self-control in those situations. (Construct: Perceived behavioral control, attitudes toward behavior.)

Table Drumming: Go, Slow Down, and Stop Feelings Allana Coffee uses this activity to help children develop a sense of self-control and self-management with regard to how they handle strong feelings.[64] Teachers need three pieces of paper—green, yellow, and red—for this activity. Teachers also could create three stoplight pictures that feature the green, yellow, and red signals. Students can tell what these colors mean on a traffic light (go, slow down, stop). Some teachers have reported that their students say the yellow light means speed up. This can be a teachable moment! Teachers should tell students to drum on their desks with their

Self-management is an important skill for mental and emotional health. (Lawren, age 12)

not normally aware of. Finally, discuss as a class some of the things students observed and what they noticed about those things.

ASSESSMENT | After the class discussion, students should write down and describe at least two things they observed during the mindfulness exercise. They should also describe one or two specific things they noticed about the object, space, or sound. (Construct: Perceived behavioral control.)

Children's Literature on Taking Care of Family and Friends Maintaining relationships in families and friendships is an important aspect of mental and emotional health. Many children's books lend themselves to discussions about being good family members and friends and about dealing with problems and challenges in healthy ways. See especially the books listed under "Family and Friends" in the list of children's literature at the end of the chapter. Teachers can lead students in a discussion of their experiences about being good family members and friends and encourage them to identify ways they can be good family members and friends.

ASSESSMENT | For an assessment task, students can make a class list of self-management strategies for being good family members and friends. For assessment criteria, students should be able to give at least three concrete examples of how they will put their strategies into practice at home or school. (Construct: Intention to act in healthy ways.)

Grades 3–5

Mindful Breathing A simple yet effective strategy for calming down during a difficult situation is becoming aware of one's breathing. Ask students to find a comfortable position in their chairs. Students will first put one hand on their chest and one hand on their belly. Ask them to become aware of their breathing and how far into their bodies they are drawing their breath. Students should be breathing in such a way that brings the breath all the way into what feels like their bellies. Once students are able to notice this, ask them to put their hands on their thighs and focus their attention on their breathing. Have them draw their breath in for a five count, pause, and then breathe out for a five count. Encourage each student to keep their attention on their breathing and counting. If their attention wanders, instruct students to notice their attention has wandered, and direct it back to their breathing and counting. Students should repeat this activity for 3 to 5 minutes when first learning the technique. As a class, discuss what students experienced and how easy or difficult it was to focus on their breathing and counting.

ASSESSMENT | The assessment task for this strategy is the identification of situations that they have already experienced in which mindful breathing may be beneficial. Students should also describe why this technique would be helpful in these situations. (Construct: Perceived behavioral control.)

A Bad Case of Stripes: **Children's Literature on Being Okay with Being Unique** Many children's books deal with learning to accept and appreciate differences and unique attributes in oneself and others. Discussions on these kinds of issues can move well beyond the idea of tolerance to being actively interested in and open to learning about how human beings vary, in all kinds of ways. *A Bad Case of Stripes,* by David Shannon, is a wonderful example. Camilla Cream finds that she indeed has come

hands in response to the color being held up, drumming fast on green, slowing down on yellow, and stopping on red.

Teachers next can ask students to think of feeling words (referring to the feelings alphabet at the Online Learning Center) that apply to the different signals. What feeling words tell students it's okay to go, to slow down, and to stop altogether? Teachers can write these words on the board, or older students can make lists in small groups. For example, "go" words might include happy, calm, peaceful, excited, and rested; "slow down" words might include frustrated, irritated, tired, scared, and sad; and "stop" words could include furious, exhausted, stressed out, agitated, and terrified. Students might find it simpler to start by listing go and stop words, adding slow down words in between. This activity is a good vocabulary builder and helps students identify progressions of feelings (irritated, mad, furious, enraged). Table drumming provides a memorable way for students to think and talk about feelings. Teachers can use various scenarios to ask students what kinds of feelings might result—whether the person might be feeling "green," "yellow," or "red"—and what they should do about it. Coffee asks students what kind of day they are having, using the color words to help the children talk about situations and feelings in their lives.

ASSESSMENT | For an assessment task, students can describe green, yellow, and red feelings or draw a picture that shows them having a green, yellow, or red day, feeling, or experience. For assessment criteria, students should be able to explain what they do when they have that feeling or experience that helps them feel better and stay healthy. (Construct: Intention to act in healthy ways.)

Mindful Me Introduce the concept of mindfulness to students as a way of paying attention to and being aware of the things around you. The teacher should first ask students to, while seated quietly, notice their own breathing paying attention to the breath coming in and going out of their bodies. Next, students should be directed to look around and notice different objects and spaces throughout the classroom. First, ask students to observe an object that they normally do not interact with. Second, ask students to observe an area of the classroom that they do not spend much time in. Third, ask students to listen for a sound that they are down with a case of stripes—and the stripes are just the beginning of the changes Camilla experiences until she determines to be herself, rather than trying to be like others. Other books teachers can use are listed under "Diversity and Uniqueness" at the end of the chapter. Teachers can initiate the discussion by asking students what they noticed about the characters in the story. What was unique (a new vocabulary word for some students) about them? What was good, interesting, and valuable about the ways they were unique? How did other characters treat them with respect to the ways they were unique? How do students want to be treated with respect to their unique characteristics? How do they think it is best to treat others who are different from them?

ASSESSMENT | For an assessment task, students can describe unique characteristics of themselves and others and explain how they see those characteristics as valuable. For assessment criteria, students can explain a self-management strategy they use when they meet someone new for finding out and appreciating that person's unique characteristics. (Construct: Perceived behavioral control.)

Grades 6–8

Healthy Self-Talk: Reframing Doom and Gloom into Optimism Adults sometimes remark that early adolescents are hard on each other in terms of gossip and judgments. However, students in this age group may be even harder on themselves. At an age when their bodies are growing and changing in many ways, young adolescents often spend a great deal of time finding fault with themselves. Talking with students about practicing healthy self-talk can help them reframe what they say to themselves and others. For example: "My hips are getting huge!" might be replaced with "I'm beginning to look like a woman instead of a little girl, and that's a normal, healthy change—and it looks good, too!" "Everyone will notice this giant pimple on my chin!" might be replaced with "No one will notice if I don't call attention to it, and it will be gone in a few days. Besides, everyone is worrying about their own pimples." "I'm afraid to talk to that new girl in class" might be replaced with "She probably would like some of us to help her feel like she fits in here. I'll ask Sandy to go with me to ask her how she likes it here so far." "I'll never, ever get this work done—I'm doomed!" might be replaced with "I'll make a schedule and do one thing at a time until it's all done. I'll get my friends to help me stick to my schedule." Students will scoff at self-talk that is unrealistic or silly. However, with practice, they can learn to turn their thinking into positive action when their thoughts about themselves or others are unnecessarily negative.

Teachers can provide students with starting statements such as those above and ask students to work on turning them into healthy—and realistic—self-talk. Students can also make a list of doom-and-gloom statements and use them to create healthy self-talk statements.

ASSESSMENT | For an assessment task, students can work in small groups to combine their doom-and-gloom statements, along with their reframed self-talk statements, into a poster to share with class members. Working in groups helps take the focus off any one student. For assessment criteria, students should be able to tell how they used healthy self-talk as a self-management strategy for staying optimistic throughout the day. Students also can share which situations were easy to manage and which were more challenging. (Construct: Intention to act in healthy ways.)

Mindful Body Scan A helpful strategy for managing stress is becoming aware of an individual's body and how it responds in various situations. While students are seated quietly, ask them to become aware of their breathing. After a few moments, direct their attention to their feet. They should notice how they feel as they are planted on the floor. Next, students should direct their attention to their legs, noticing how they feel as they are seated at their desks. Direct their attention to their midsection as they draw

their breath deeply into their belly and out. What sensations do they notice? Lastly, ask students to bring their attention to their head, becoming aware of how the breath is coming in and out of either their mouth or their nostrils. Students should be encouraged to then become aware of their entire body as they focus on their breathing for the final few moments. Conclude with a partner and whole class discussion about areas of their body that they noticed as having pain or tension and those that were loose and relaxed.

ASSESSMENT | Students will reflect on the partner and whole class discussion by identifying the areas of their body where they feel tension and stress. They should also describe what they feel when experiencing their top two or three stressors. Lastly, students should indicate how using a mindful body scan could be useful in managing their top stressors. (Construct: Perceived behavioral control.)

Finding Your Courage: Standing Strong Even When It's Hard to Do An important and often difficult self-management task for middle-level students, and older people, is finding the courage to take a stand in the face of popular opinion or opposition. Teachers can use literature as a springboard to talk with students about this issue; see the books listed under "Courage" at the end of the chapter. To engage students in a discussion about courage, Dr. Nan Stein recommends that teachers ask students to consider "courage by degrees"—that is, addressing a list of scenarios by asking which take more or less courage.[65] A sample list might be as follows:

- Stand up for a friend whom other students are teasing.
- Stand up for a new student you don't know very well whom other students are teasing.
- Say no to a younger student who offers you a cigarette.
- Say no to an older student who offers you a cigarette.
- Walk away from a fight when you and one other student are involved.
- Walk away from a fight when lots of other kids are watching.
- Raise your hand to offer an answer you are very sure of in class.
- Raise your hand to offer an opinion that differs from what other students have said.
- Refuse to sign a slam book.
- Volunteer to head a committee for a school party.

Students should discuss why each scenario takes more or less courage and how students can find the courage to act in ways that are best for everyone. Students can add to the list of scenarios by reading a personal courage story about a teacher in American Samoa titled "Nina Rings the Tsunami Bell: A Story of Personal Courage" (see the Online Learning Center).

ASSESSMENT | For an assessment task, students can make a list of self-management strategies for finding courage when the going gets tough—for example, hanging out with friends who feel the same way about important issues (not drinking). For assessment criteria, students should explain how they will use three of the strategies in real situations. (Construct: Intention to act in healthy ways.)

NHES 8 | Advocacy

Students will demonstrate the ability to advocate for personal, family, and community health.

ASSESSMENT CRITERIA

- Health-enhancing position—Give clear, health-enhancing position.
- Support for position—Support position with facts, concepts, examples, and evidence.
- Audience awareness—Show awareness of target audience; choose words, tone, and examples to suit audience.
- Conviction—Display conviction for position.

Grades K–2

Sharing Time for Health   In this activity, students can share a way they keep themselves mentally healthy. For example, a student might describe listening to music, singing, or dancing to manage stress. Another student might share a strategy he or she uses to manage verbal conflicts with a sibling. Teachers can assign each child a particular day to share a practice they use for staying mentally healthy. Using the healthy behavior outcomes listed earlier in the chapter may help provide guidance for student sharing. By sharing, students advocate good mental health.

ASSESSMENT | The healthy practices students share are the assessment task for this activity. For assessment criteria, students should take a health-enhancing stand and explain their practice by giving reasons why it's healthy. (Construct: Subjective norms.)

Grades 3–5

Letter Writing for Health   Students should learn from an early age that they can make a difference. With their teacher's help, students can compose a letter to their principal or someone in their community about a mental and emotional health issue of interest to them. For example, students might want to ask the principal for permission to play music in the cafeteria during lunchtime to make it a more pleasant experience for students and faculty. In this case, students could offer to publicize the idea, soliciting agreement from students in all grades about acceptable behavior at lunch. Students can sign the letter after it is composed—with their teacher's help—to their satisfaction.

ASSESSMENT | The letter the students help compose is the assessment task for this activity. For assessment criteria, students should state a request, back it up with reasons, target their audience, and speak with conviction. (Constructs: Subjective norms, perceived behavioral control.)

No Name-Calling Week   Students might be interested in participating in an advocacy project called No Name-Calling Week, held in January. Teachers and students can find more information at www.glsen.org/no-name-calling-week. The website states, "Words hurt. More than that, they have the power to make students feel unsafe to the point where they are no longer able to perform in school or conduct normal lives." Through the website, teachers and students can learn how to conduct a no name-calling week in their school.

ASSESSMENT | Planning and implementing a no name-calling week, with the help of adults, is the assessment task for this activity. For assessment criteria, students should state a health-enhancing position, back it up with reasons, target their audience, and show strong conviction. Students also should explain how name-calling can affect mental and emotional health. (Constructs: Intention to act in healthy ways, subjective norms, attitudes toward behavior.)

Advocating for Being a Good Friend (and other healthy habits) Select, or have students select, a healthy behavior outcome from this unit, such as expressing feelings in healthy ways or managing stress and anxiety in healthy ways. With the selected behavior in mind, have pairs of students develop a digital advocacy message (e.g., iMovie, Keynote, PowerPoint, or other accessible tools) for their peers. The class should discuss what would make a message meaningful to their peers (e.g., use of pictures, simple words, type of message). Teams should then prepare a storyboard of their message that will be turned into a digital product.

ASSESSMENT | The digital advocacy message appropriate for peers will serve as the assessment task. The assessment criteria should persuade peers

to make positive mental and emotional health choices. (Constructs: Perceived behavioral control, subjective norms.)

Meet Our School Counselors   Upper-elementary students can plan a poster and speaking campaign to introduce their school counselors to all the students in the school. Students should help their classmates and schoolmates learn who the counselors are, how they can help, and how students can contact them for health concerns.

ASSESSMENT | The campaign students plan and carry out is the assessment task for this activity. For assessment criteria, students should specify how counselors can help and how students can contact them. (Constructs: Subjective norms, perceived behavioral control.)

Grades 6–8

Helping Others Be Mentally Healthy Middle school students can have a significant, positive influence on elementary students. Teachers can lead a discussion on the ways older students can influence the choices and behaviors of younger students in both positive and negative ways. Pairs of students can create advocacy messages geared at students in either grades K–2 or 3–5. Messages can focus on one of the following topics: expressing feelings in healthy ways, preventing or managing conflict and stress in healthy ways, using self-control, or seeking help for troublesome feelings. Students can be allowed to choose the format most fitting for their message, such as poster, morning announcement, or bulletin board.

ASSESSMENT | The advocacy message that students plan is the assessment task for this activity. For assessment criteria, students should provide accurate information; develop a strong, health-enhancing position; back it up with facts and reasons; target their audience; and present their message with conviction. This activity links with NHES 2—Analyzing Influences. (Constructs: Subjective norms, perceived behavioral control.)

Eating Disorders Are Illnesses, Not Choices   Students can learn more about eating disorders at websites such as those listed in "Internet and Other Resources" at the end of the chapter. Students can conduct research on eating disorders and develop a schoolwide campaign on recognizing and getting help for eating disorders. The campaign should help students know how to talk with friends they are concerned about and how to get help for their own personal concerns.

ASSESSMENT | The campaign students plan is the assessment task for this activity. For assessment criteria, students should develop a strong, health-enhancing position; back it up with facts and reasons; target their audience; and speak with conviction. (Constructs: Subjective norms, perceived behavioral control.)

More Than the Moody Blues: Teaching Classmates and Families About Depression   Another issue that middle school students might want to explore is depression. What is it? How can students recognize it? How can students get help for themselves and others? Many of the sites listed in "Internet and Other Resources" at the end of the chapter provide extensive information on depression. Students might want to plan an awareness campaign tailored for their school community.

ASSESSMENT | The campaign students plan is the assessment task for this activity. For assessment criteria, students should develop a strong, health-enhancing position; back it up with facts and reasons; target their audience; and speak with conviction. (Constructs: Subjective norms, perceived behavioral control.)

EVALUATED CURRICULA AND INSTRUCTIONAL MATERIALS

The Centers for Disease Control and Prevention provides Registries of Programs Effective in Reducing Youth Risk Behaviors at www.cdc.gov/healthyyouth/adolescenthealth/registries.htm. Various federal agencies have identified youth-related programs that they consider worthy of recommendation on the basis of expert opinion or a review of design and research evidence. These programs focus on different health topics, risk behaviors, and settings. Some, but not all, of these programs have shown evidence in reducing youth risk behaviors. Each agency has its own process and criteria for determining the programs that are worthy of recommendation. Users are encouraged to review each website to understand the inclusion criteria the registry used.

Registries related to mental and emotional health include:

- National Registry of Evidence-based Programs and Practices (NREPP) (http://nrepp.samhsa.gov/)
- Office of Juvenile Justice and Delinquency Prevention Model Programs Guide (www.ojjdp.gov/mpg/)
- What Works Clearinghouse (http://ies.ed.gov/ncee/wwc/)
- Child Trends LINKS (Lifecourse Interventions to Nurture Kids Successfully) Database (www.childtrends.org/what-works/)

INTERNET AND OTHER RESOURCES

WEBSITES

American Association of Suicidology
www.suicidology.org

American Psychiatric Association
www.psychiatry.org

American Psychological Association
www.apa.org

BAM! Body and Mind
www.cdc.gov/bam/

Get Your Angries Out
lynnenamka.com/

Health, Mental Health and Safety Guidelines for Schools
www.aap.org/en-us/about-the-aap/Committees-Councils-Sections/Council-on-School-Health/Pages/About-Us.aspx

HelpGuide
www.helpguide.org

KidsPeace
www.kidspeace.org

Mental Health America
www.mentalhealthamerica.net

National Association of Anorexia Nervosa and Related Disorders
www.anad.org/

National Association of School Psychologists
www.nasponline.org

National Eating Disorders Association
www.nationaleatingdisorders.org

National Education Association Health Information Network
www.neahin.org/

National Federation of Families for Children's Mental Health
www.ffcmh.org

National Institute of Mental Health
www.nimh.nih.gov/index.shtml

Southern Poverty Law Center: Teaching Tolerance
www.tolerance.org

Substance Abuse and Mental Health Services Administration (SAMHSA)
www.samhsa.gov/

CHILDREN'S LITERATURE

AGES 5–8

COMMUNICATION

Curtis, Jamie Lee, and Laura Cornell. *Big Words for Little People.* HarperCollins, 2008.

Henkes, Kevin. *Lilly's Purple Plastic Purse.* Greenwillow Books, 1996.

Lester, Helen. *Listen, Buddy.* Sandpiper, 1997.

McKissack, Patricia. *The Honest-to-Goodness Truth.* Atheneum Books for Young Readers, 2000.

Neal, Kate Jane. *Words and Your Heart.* Feiwel and Friends, 2017.

Sharmat, Marjorie Weinman. *A Big Fat Enormous Lie.* Puffin Books, 1978.

Turner, Jeffrey. *Who Broke the Vase?* Aladdin, 2017.

Verdick, Elizabeth. *Words Are Not for Hurting.* Free Spirit, 2004.

Willems, Mo. *Knuffle Bunny: A Cautionary Tale.* Hyperion Books for Children, 2004.

Willems, Mo. *Time to Say Please!* Hyperion Books for Children, 2005.

COURAGE

Angelou, Maya. *Life Doesn't Frighten Me.* Stewart, Tabori & Chang, 1993.

Castillo, Lauren. *Nana in the City.* Clarion Books, Houghton Mifflin Harcourt, 2014.

Cornwall, Gaia. *Jabari Jumps.* Candlewick Press, 2017.

Crist, James J. *What to Do When You're Scared and Worried: A Guide for Kids.* Free Spirit, 2004.

Demi. *The Empty Pot.* Henry Holt, 1990.

Lester, Helen. *Hooway for Wodney Wat.* Sandpiper, 2002.

Lester, Helen. *Something Might Happen.* Sandpiper, 2003.

McAnulty, Stacy. *Brave.* RP Kids, 2017.

Waber, Bernard. *Courage.* Houghton Mifflin/Walter Lorraine Books, 2002.

See also the books listed under "Dealing with Worries."

DIVERSITY AND UNIQUENESS

Appelt, Kathi. *Incredible Me!* HarperCollins, 2003.

Best, Cari. *My Three Best Friends and Me, Zulay.* Margaret Ferguson Books, Farrar Straus Giroux, 2015.

Britt, Paige. *Why Am I Me?* Scholastic Press, 2017.

Carlson, Nancy. *I Like Me!* Viking, 1988.

Corey, Shana. *Players in Pigtails.* Scholastic, 2003.

Couric, Katie. *The Brand New Kid.* Doubleday, 2000.

Curtis, Jamie Lee, and Laura Cornell. *Is There Really a Human Race?* Joanna Cotler Books, 2006.

Davol, Marguerite W. *Black, White, Just Right!* Albert Whitman, 1993.

Diggs, Taye. *Mixed Me!* Feiwel and Friends, 2015.

Fierstein, Harvey. *The Sissy Duckling.* Simon & Schuster Books for Young Readers, 2002.

Hamanaka, Sheila. *All the Colors of the Earth.* HarperTrophy, 1999.

Henkes, Kevin. *Chrysanthemum.* Greenwillow Books, 1991.

Hoffman, Mary. *Amazing Grace.* Scott, Foresman, 1991.

Johnson, Angela. *Violet's Music.* Dial Books for Young Readers, 2004.

Katz, Karen. *The Colors of Us.* Henry Holt, 1999.

Kotzwinkle, William, and Glenn Murray. *Walter the Farting Dog.* Frog, 2001.

Kraus, Robert. *Leo the Late Bloomer.* Windmill Books, 1971.

Lester, Helen. *Tacky the Penguin.* Sandpiper, 1990.

Lithgow, John. *The Remarkable Farkle McBride.* Simon & Schuster Books for Young Readers, 2000.

Lucado, Max. *You Are Special.* Crossway Books, 1997.

McAnulty, Stacy. *Beautiful.* RP Kids, 2016.

Munsch, Robert. *The Paper Bag Princess.* Annick, 2002.

Parr, Todd. *Be Who You Are.* Little, Brown and Company, 2016.

Parr, Todd. *It's Okay to Be Different.* Little, Brown, 2001.

Shannon, David. *A Bad Case of Stripes.* Blue Sky, 1998.

Swift, Keilly. *The Tigon and the Liger.* Lantana Publishing, 2017.

Tyler, Michael. *The Skin You Live In.* Chicago Children's Museum, 2005.

Wells, Rosemary. *Yoko.* Hyperion, 1998.

Whitcomb, Mary E. *Odd Velvet.* Chronicle Books, 1998.

Winters, Kari-Lynn. *French Toast.* Pajama Press, 2017.

Woodson, Jacqueline. *The Other Side.* GP Putnam's Sons, 2001.

FAMILY AND FRIENDS

Aliki. *We Are Best Friends.* Greenwillow Books, 1982.

Bansch, Helga. *Rosie the Raven.* Annick Press, 2016.

Blos, Joan. *Old Henry.* Scrbner's, 1987.

Beaumont, Karen. *Being Friends.* Dial Books for Young Readers, 2002.

Brown, Laura K., and Marc Brown. *How to Be a Friend.* Scholastic, 1998.

Carlson, Nancy. *My Best Friend Moved Away.* Penguin Putnam Books for Young Readers, 2001.

Collins, Suzanne. *Year of the Jungle.* Scholastic, 2013.

Dunklee, Annika. *Me, Me, Me.* Kids Can Press, 2017.

Dunklee, Annika. *Me, Too!* Kids Can Press, 2015.

Ferry, Beth. *Stick and Stone.* Houghton Mifflin Harcourt, 2015.

Lester, Helen. *Me First.* Sandpiper, 1995.

Lobel, Arnold. *Frog and Toad Are Friends.* HarperTrophy, 1970.

MacLachlan, Patricia. *Fly Away.* Margaret K. McElderry Books, 2015.

McAnulty, Stacy. *Excellent Ed.* Alfred A. Knopf, 2016.

Medina, Meg. *Mango, Abuela, and Me.* Candlewick Press, 2017.

Mellom, Robin. *Hannah Sparkles.* Harper, an imprint of HarperCollins Publishers, 2017.

Parr, Todd. *The Family Book.* Little, Brown, 2003.

Reynolds, Aaron. *Nerdy Birdy.* Roaring Brook Press, 2015.

Rodman, Mary Ann. *My Best Friend.* Viking, 2005.

Stead Philip Christian. *Lenny & Lucy.* Roaring Brook Press, 2015.

GOALS AND DECISIONS

Bridges, Shirin Yim. *Ruby's Wish.* Chronicle Books, 2002.

Climo, Shirley. *The Little Red Ant and the Great Big Crumb.* Houghton Mifflin, 2004.

Couric, Katie. *The Blue Ribbon Day.* Doubleday, 2004.

Dorfman, Craig. *I Knew You Could: A Book for All the Stops in Your Life.* Platt & Munk, 2003.

Ghigna, Charles. *First Times.* Orca Book Publishers, 2017.

Hamm, Mia. *Winners Never Quit!* HarperCollins, 2004.

Heide, Florence Parry. *Tales for the Perfect Child.* Atheneum Books for Young Readers, 2017

Henkes, Kevin. *Sheila Rae, The Brave.* Mulberry Books, 1987.

McGillivray, David J. *Dream Big: A True Story of Courage and Determination.* Nomad Press, 2018.

Newby, John. *Heart of the Game.* John Newby, 2002.

Pearson, Emily. *Ordinary Mary's Extraordinary Deed.* Gibbs Smith, 2002.

Piper, Watty. *The Little Engine That Could.* Platt & Munk, 1976, original edition, 1930.

Reynolds, Peter H. *Ish.* Candlewick, 2004.

Seuss, Dr. *Oh, The Places You'll Go!* Random House, 1990.

Troiano, Joe. *It's Your Cloud.* Barnes & Noble, 2004.

IALAC (I AM LOVABLE AND CAPABLE)

Andreae, Giles. *Giraffes Can't Dance.* Orchard Books, 1999.

Beaumont, Karen. *I Like Myself!* Harcourt, 2004.

Clanton, Ben. *Rot, The Cutest in the World.* Atheneum Books for Young Readers, 2017.

Curtis, Jamie Lee. *I'm Gonna Like Me: Letting Off a Little Self-Esteem.* Joanna Cotler Books, 2002.

Fierstein, Harvey. *The Sissy Duckling.* Simon & Schuster Books for Young Readers, 2002.

Gorin, Leslie. *Bertie Wings It!* Sterling Children's Books, 2016.

Ludwig, Trudy. *Better Than You.* Knopf Books for Young Readers, 2011.

Mandell, B. B. *Samanthasaurus Rex.* Balzer + Bray, an imprint of HarperCollins Publishers, 2016.

Merino, Gemma. *The Sheep Who Hatched an Egg.* Albert Whitman & Company, 2017.

Prelutsky, Jack. *Me I Am!* Farrar, Straus & Giroux, 2007.

Rosenthal, Amy Krouse. *Dear Girl.* Harper, an imprint of HarperCollins Publishers, 2017.

Seskin, Steve. *Don't Laugh at Me.* Tricycle, 2002.

Seuss, Dr. *The Sneetches and Other Stories.* Random House, 1989.

Shannon, David. *David Gets in Trouble.* Blue Sky, 2002.

Shannon, David. *No, David!* Blue Sky, 1998.

Viorst, Judith. *Alexander and the Terrible, Horrible, No Good, Very Bad Day.* Atheneum Books for Young Readers, 1972.

Other appropriate books include *Walter the Farting Dog* (Kotzwinkle/Murray); *Leo the Late Bloomer* (Kraus); *Lilly's Purple Plastic Purse* (Henkes); *The Meanest Thing to Say* (Cosby); and *The Sissy Duckling* (Fierstein).

MOODS AND STRONG FEELINGS

Bang, Molly. *When Sophie Gets Angry—Really, Really Angry....* Blue Sky, 1999.

Becker, Shelly. *Even Superheroes Have Bad Days.* Sterling Children's Books, 2016.

Bluthenthal, Diana Cain. *I'm Not Invited?* Atheneum Books for Young Readers, 2003.

Brown, Tameka Fryer. *My Cold Plum Lemon Pie Bluesy Mood.* Viking Juvenile, 2013.

Cain, Janan. *The Way I Feel.* Parenting, 2000.

Cocca-Leffler, Maryann. *Theo's Mood: A Book of Feelings.* Albert Whitman and Company, 2013.

Curtis, Jamie Lee. *Today I Feel Silly and Other Moods That Make My Day.* Joanna Cotler Books, 1998.

Curtis, Jamie Lee, and Laura Cornell. *It's Hard to Be Five: Learning How to Work My Control Panel.* Joanna Cotler Books, 2004.

Evans, Lezlie. *Sometimes I Feel Like a Storm Cloud.* Mondo, 1999.

Everitt, Betsy. *Mean Soup.* Harcourt Children's Books, 1992.

Freymann, Saxton, and Joost Elffers. *How Are You Peeling? Foods with Moods.* Arthur A. Levine Books, 1999.

Helquist, Shane. *Grumpy Goat.* HarperCollins, 2013.

Henkes, Kevin. *Julius the Baby of the World.* Greenwillow Books, 1990.

Henn, Sophy. *Pass It On.* Philomel Books, an imprint of Penguin Random House LLC, 2017.

Kim, Young-Ah. *Some Days Are Lonely*. Magination Press, 2013.

Lester, Helen. *Hurty Feelings*. Sandpiper, 2007.

Lichtenheld, Tom. *What Are You So Grumpy About?* Little, Brown, 2003.

Parr, Todd. *The Feel Good Book*. Little, Brown, 2002.

Radunsky, V. *What Does Peace Feel Like?* Atheneum Books for Young Readers, 2004.

Rubenstein, Lauren. *Visiting Feelings*. Magination Press, 2013.

Saltzman, David. *The Jester Has Lost His Jingle*. Jester, 1995.

Sanzo, Stephen. *Cranky Pants*. Cranky Pants, 2005.

Seuss, Dr., Steve Johnson, and Lou Fancher. *My Many Colored Days*. Knopf, 1998.

Shuman, Carol. *Jenny Is Scared! When Sad Things Happen in the World*. Magination Press, 2003.

Urban, Linda. *Mouse Was Mad*. Harcourt Children's Books, 2009.

Vail, Rachel. *Sometimes I'm Bombaloo*. Scholastic, 2002.

Willis, Jeanne, and Tony Ross. *Misery Moo*. Henry Holt, 2003.

Yolen, Jane. *How Do Dinosaurs Say I'm Mad?* The Blue Sky Press, an imprint of Scholastic, Inc., 2013.

Other appropriate books include *Lilly's Purple Plastic Purse* (Henkes); *Alexander and the Terrible, Horrible, No Good, Very Bad Day* (Viorst).

SAFE AND HEALTHY CLASSROOMS AND SCHOOLS

Catrow, David. *We the Kids*. Dial Books, 2002.

Creech, Sharon. *A Fine, Fine School*. Joanna Cotler Books, 2001.

Finchler, Judy. *Testing Miss Malarkey*. Walker & Company, 2000.

Kelley, Marty. *The Rules*. Zino Press Children's Books, 2000.

Mann, Jennifer K. *I Will Never Get a Star on Mrs. Benson's Blackboard*. Candlewick Press, 2017.

Pennypacker, Sara. *Stuart Goes to School*. Scholastic, 2003.

Polacco, Patricia. *The Junkyard Wonders*. Philomel Books, 2010.

Seuss, Dr. *Hooray for Diffendoofer Day!* Alfred A. Knopf, 1998.

Teague, Mark. *Dear Mrs. LaRue: Letters from Obedience School*. Scholastic, 2002.

Another appropriate book is *David Goes to School* (Shannon).

DEALING WITH WORRIES

Chiew, Suzanne. *The Worry Box*. Tiger Tales, 2018.

Cook, Julia. *Wilma Jean the Worry Machine*. National Center for Youth Issues, 2012.

Cuyler, Margery. *100th Day Worries*. Simon & Schuster Books for Young Readers, 2000.

Helakoski, Leslie. *Big Chickens*. Puffin Books, 2006.

Henkes, Kevin. *Wemberly Worried*. Greenwillow Books, 2000.

Hartt-Sussman, Heather. *Noni Is Nervous*. Tundra Books, 2013.

McKee, David. *Elmer*. Lothrop, Lee & Shepard Books, 1968.

Santat, Dan. *After the Fall: How Humpty Dumpty Got Back Up Again*. Roaring Books Press, 2017.

Viorst, Judith. *If I Were in Charge of the World and Other Worries: Poems for Children and Their Parents*. Aladdin, 1981.

Wolff, F., and H. Savitz. *Is A Worry Worrying You?* Tanglewood Press, 2005.

Zuppardi, Sam. *Jack's Worry*. Candlewick Press, 2016.

Other books about worries include *Mommy Doesn't Know My Name* (Williams); *It's Okay to Be Different* (Parr); *Leo the Late Bloomer* (Kraus); *The Brand New Kid* (Couric); *Yoko* (Wells); *Ish* (Reynolds); *Feeling Left Out* (Petty/Firmin); *Giraffes Can't Dance* (Andreae); *It's Hard to Be Five* (Curtis/Cornell); *I'm Not Invited?* (Bluthenthal); *What to Do When You're Scared and Worried* (Crist); and many of the books listed under "Courage."

OTHER BOOKS WITH AN EMOTIONAL HEALTH THEME

Coyle, Carmela LaVigna. *Do Princesses Wear Hiking Boots?* Rising Moon, 2003.

Fox, Mem. *Whoever You Are*. Voyager Books, 2001.

Hest, Amy. *The Purple Coat*. Macmillan, 1986.

Kirk, David. *Miss Spider's Tea Party*. Scholastic, 1994.

Krauss, Ruth. *The Carrot Seed*. HarperFestival, 1993.

Krosoczka, Jarrett J. *Baghead*. Alfred A. Knopf, 2002.

Lester, Helen. *All for Me and None for All*. Houghton Mifflin Harcourt, 2012.

Munsch, Robert. *We Share Everything!* Scholastic, 1999.

Munson, Derek. *Enemy Pie*. Chronicle Books, 2000.

Parr, Todd. *Reading Makes You Feel Good*. Little, Brown, 2005.

Penn, Audrey. *The Kissing Hand*. Child & Family, 1993.

Pfister, Marcus. *The Rainbow Fish*. North-South Books, 1992.

Rayner, Catherine. *The Bear Who Shared*. Dial Books for Young Readers, 2010.

Simms, Laura. *Rotten Teeth*. Houghton Mifflin, 1998.

Smith, Jada Pinkett. *Girls Hold Up This World*. Scholastic, 2005.

Spelman, Cornelia. *Your Body Belongs to You*. Albert Whitman, 1997.

Spires, Ashley. *The Most Magnificent Thing*. Kids Can Press, 2014.

Verdick, Elizabeth. *Feet Are Not for Kicking*. Free Spirit, 2004.

Verdick, Elizabeth. *Hands Are Not for Hitting*. Free Spirit, 2002.

Watkins, Rowboat. *Rude Cakes*. Chronicle Books, 2015.

Willems, Mo. *Should I Share My Ice Cream? (Elephant and Piggie)*. Hyperion Books for Children, 2011.

Wilson, Karma. *Hilda Must Be Dancing*. Margaret K. McElderry Books, 2004.

Wood, Douglas. *A Quiet Place*. Simon & Schuster Books for Young Readers, 2002.

AGES 8–12

Anderson, Laurie Halse. *Speak*. Puffin Books, 1999.

Anton, Carrie. *Digital World: How to Connect, Share, Play, and Keep Yourself Safe*. American Girl, 2017.

Applegate, Katherine. *Home of the Brave*. Feiwel & Friends, 2007. (multicultural)

Avi. *Nothing but the Truth*. Orchard Books, 1991. (Newbery Honor Book)

Blackstone, Margaret, and Elissa Haden Guest. *Girl Stuff: A Survival Guide to Growing Up*. Harcourt Paperbacks, 2006.

Blume, Judy. *Tales of a Fourth Grade Nothing*. Penguin Putnam Books for Young Readers, 2003.

Boynton, Sandra. *Yay, You! Moving Out, Moving Up, Moving On*. Simon & Schuster Children's Books, 2001.

Britt, Fanny. *Jane, The Fox and Me*. Groundwood Books/House of Anansi Press, 2013.

Brooks, Bruce. *The Moves Make the Man*. Harper & Row, 1984. (Newbery Honor Book)

Buyea, Rob. *Because of Mr. Terupt*. Delcorte Press, 2010.

Buyea, Rob. *The Perfect Score*. Delcorte Press, 2017.

Child, Lauren. *Clarice Bean Spells Trouble*. Orchard Books, 2004.

Choldenko, Gennifer. *Al Capone Does My Shirts*. Penguin Group, 2004. (Newbery Honor Book)

Creech, Sharon. *Ruby Holler*. HarperCollins, 2003. (Carnegie Medal winner)

Donoghue, Emma. *The Lotterys Plus One*. Arthur A. Levine Books, an imprint of Scholastic Inc., 2017

Estes, Eleanor. *The Hundred Dresses*. Harcourt, 1944.

Fletcher, Ralph. *Flying Solo*. Clarion Books, 1996.

Fonseca, Christine. *The Girl Guide: Finding Your Place in a Mixed-Up World*. Prufrock Press Inc., 2013.

Fry, Michael. *King Karl*. Disney/Hyperion Books, 2014.

Gaiman, Neil. *Instructions*. Harper/Harper Collins, 2010.

Giff, Patricia Reilly. *Winter Sky*. A Yearling Book, 2014.

Goebel, Jenny. *Fortune Falls*. Scholastic Inc., 2017.

Graff, Lisa. *Absolutely Almost*. Philomel Books, an imprint of Penguin Group (USA), 2014.

Graff, Lisa. *Lost in the Sun*. Puffin Books, 2016.

Graff, Lisa. *The Great Treehouse War*. Philomel Books, 2017.

Graff, Lisa. *The Thing About Georgie: A Novel*. Laura Geringer, 2006.

Hansen, Joyce. *The Gift Giver*. Clarion Books, 1980.

Henkes, Kevin. *The Year of Billy Miller*. Greenwillow Books/HarperCollins Publishers, 2013.

Herrera, Robin. *Hope Is a Ferris Wheel*. Amulet Books, 2014.

Holm, Jennifer. *Middle School Is Worse than Meatloaf: A Year Told Through Stuff*. Ginee Seo Books, 2007.

Kadohata, Cynthia. *Kira-Kira*. Simon & Schuster, 2004. (Newbery Medal winner)

Kelly, Erin Entrada. *Hello, Universe*. HarperCollins, 2018.

Korman, Gordon. *Slacker*. Scholastic Inc., 2017.

Krull, Kathleen. *Wilma Unlimited: How Wilma Rudolph Became the World's Fastest Woman*. Harcourt, 2000.

Lopez, Diana. *Ask My Mood Ring How I Feel*. Little Brown Books for Young Readers, 2013.

Lord, Cynthia. *Rules*. Scholastic Press, 2006. (Newbery Honor Book)

Lupika, Mike. *Travel Team*. Penguin, 2004.

Madison, Linda. *The Feelings Book: The Care and Keeping of Your Emotions*. Pleasant Company, 2002.

Madonna. *The English Roses*. Callaway, 2003.

McGovern, Cammie. *Just My Luck*. Harper, an imprint of HarperCollinsPublishers, 2016.

Moss, Peggy. *Say Something*. Tilbury House, 2004.

Naylor, Phyllis Reynolds. *Shiloh*. Atheneum, 1991. (Newbery Medal winner)

Paschen, Elise (ed.). *Poetry Speaks: Who I Am*. Sourcebooks, 2010.

Peterson, Stacey. *Friends: Making Them & Keeping Them*. American Girl, 2006.

Philbrick, Rodman. *Freak the Mighty*. Scholastic, 1993.

Polacco, Patricia. *Thank You, Mr. Falkner*. Philomel Books, 1998.

Schroeder, Lisa. *Keys to the City*. Scholastic Press, 2017.

Smith, Robert Kimmel. *The War with Grandpa*. Bantam Books, 1984.

Standiford, Natalie. *The Only Girl in School*. Scholastic Inc., 2018.

Stewart, Whitney. *Mindful Me Mindfulness and Meditation for Kids*. Albert Whitman & Company, 2018.

Tarshis, Lauren. *Emma Jean Lazarus Fell Out of a Tree*. Dial, 2007.

Urban, Linda. *A Crooked Kind of Perfect*. Harcourt Children's Books, 2007.

Van Leeuwen, Jean. *The Missing Pieces of Me*. Two Lions, 2014.

Vrabel, Beth. *A Blind Guide to Normal*. Sky Pony Press, 2016.

Winston, Sherri. *The Sweetest Sound*. Little, Brown and Company, 2018.

ENDNOTES

1. R. Kahakalau, "Every Child a Promise," *Keiki O Ka 'Aina*, Kanai'a Records, 1997.

2. M. E. P. Seligman and M. Csikszentmihalyi, "Positive Psychology: An Introduction," *American Psychologist* 55 (2000): 5–14.

3. M. Kitashima, conversation with author, June 2007.

4. M. L. Krovetz, *Fostering Resiliency: Expecting All Students to Use Their Minds and Hearts Well* (Thousand Oaks, CA: Corwin Press, 1999).

5. E. Werner and R. S. Smith, *Overcoming the Odds: High Risk Children from Birth to Adulthood* (Ithaca, NY: Cornell University Press, 1992).

6. R. C. Kessler et al., "Severity of 12-month DSM-IV disorders in the National Comorbidity Survey Replication Adolescent Supplement," *Archives of General Psychiatry* 69, no. 4 (2012): 381–389.

7. Krovetz, *Fostering Resiliency*.

8. U.S. Department of Health and Human Services, *Mental Health: A Report of the Surgeon General* (Rockville, MD: U.S. Department of Health and Human Services, Substance Abuse and Mental Health Services Administration, Center for Mental Health Services, National Institutes of Health, National Institute of Mental Health, 1999). https://profiles.nlm.nih.gov/ps/retrieve/ResourceMetadata/NNBBHS

9. K. R. Merikangas et al., "Lifetime Prevalence of Mental Disorders in U. S. Adolescents: Results from the National Comorbidity Study-Adolescent Supplement (NCS-A)," *Journal of the American Academy of Child and Adolescent Psychiatry* 49, no. 10 (2010): 980–989, doi:10.1016/j.jaac.2010.05.017.

10. National Institute of Mental Health, *Treatment of Children with Mental Illness* (www.nimh.nih.gov/health/publications/treatment-of-children-with-mental-illness-fact-sheet/index.shtml).

11. National Institutes of Health, *Mental Illness Exacts Heavy Toll, Beginning in Youth* (www.eurekalert.org/pub_releases/2005-06/niom-mie060105.php).

12. Centers for Disease Control and Prevention, *Children's Mental Health–New Report* (www.cdc.gov/Features/ChildrensMentalHealth).

13. National Mental Health Information Center, *Child Mental Health* (www.nlm.nih.gov/medlineplus/childmentalhealth.html).

14. https://www.cdc.gov/nchs/data/nvsr/nvsr66/nvsr66_06.pdf

15. National Institute of Mental Health, *Attention-Deficit/Hyperactivity Disorder (ADHD): The Basics* (https://www.nimh.nih.gov/health/publications/attention-deficit-hyperactivity-disorder-adhd-the-basics/index.shtml#pub12).

16. C. E. Basch, "Healthier Students Are Better Learners: A Missing Link in School Reforms to Close the Achievement Gap," *Equity Matters: Research Review*, no. 6 (2010): 51–60.

17. National Institute of Mental Health, *Majority of Youth with Mental Disorders May Not Be Receiving Sufficient Services* (https://www.nimh.nih.gov/news/science-news/2011/majority-of-youth-with-mental-disorders-may-not-be-receiving-sufficient-services.shtml).

18. Centers for Disease Control and Prevention, "Youth Risk Behavior Survey Data Summary & Trends Report 2007–2017" (https://www.cdc.gov/healthyyouth/data/yrbs/pdf/trendsreport.pdf).

19. U.S. Department of Health and Human Services, *Healthy People 2020* (www.healthypeople.gov/2020/default.aspx).

20. K. Kelleher, "Mental Health," in *About Children: An Authoritative Resource on the State of Childhood Today*, eds. A. G. Cosby, R.E. Greenberg, L. H. Southward, and M. Weitzman (Elk Grove Village, IL: American Academy of Pediatrics, 2005), 138–41.

21. H. Taras et al., *Health, Mental Health and Safety Guidelines for Schools* (American Academy of Pediatrics, 2005).

22. U.S. Department of Health and Human Services, *Report of the Surgeon General's Conference on Children's Mental Health: A National Action Agenda* (https://www.ncbi.nlm.nih.gov/books/NBK44233/).

23. National Association of School Psychologists, *School Psychologists: Providing Mental Health Services to Improve the Lives and Learning of Children and Youth* (http://www.wsasp.org/resources/Documents/GPR/School%20Psychologists%20Mental%20Health.pdf).

24. D. Viadero, "Social-Skills Programs Found to Yield Gains in Academic Subjects," *Education Week* 27, no. 16 (2007): 1, 15.

25. Basch, "Healthier Students Are Better Learners."

26. Society of State Directors of Health, Physical Education and Recreation (SSDHPER) and Association of State and Territorial Health Officials (ASTHO), *Making the Connection: Health and Student Achievement* (www.thesociety.org; September 2007).

27. J. Charvat, *Research on the Relationship Between Mental Health and Academic Achievement* (Bethesda, MD: National Association of School Psychologists, 2012). http://aps-legacy.materiell.com/cms/lib2/VA01000586/Centricity/Domain/29/SSAC%20Attachment%206_Research%20on%20the%20Relationship%20Between%20Mental%20Health%20and%20Academic%20Achievement_2.pdf

28. SSDHPER and ASTHO, *Making the Connection*.

29. Mental Health America, *What Every Child Needs for Good Mental Health* (http://www.mentalhealthamerica.net/every-child-needs; 2018).

30. Mental Health America, *Recognizing Mental Health Problems in Children* (www.mentalhealthamerica.net/recognizing-mental-health-problems-children).

31. Institute of Medicine, *Preventing Mental, Emotional, and Behavioral Disorders Among Young People: Progress and Possibilities* (https://www.ncbi.nlm.nih.gov/books/NBK32775).

32. Ibid.

33. Ibid.

34. Ibid.

35. Ibid.

36. Ibid.

37. Centers of Disease Control and Prevention, *Results from the School Health Policies and Practices Study 2016* (https://www.cdc.gov/healthyyouth/data/shpps/pdf/shpps-results_2016.pdf).

38. Centers of Disease Control and Prevention, School Health Policies and Practices Study (SHPPS) 2012 (www.cdc.gov/HealthyYouth/shpps/index.htm).

39. Taras et al., *Health, Mental Health and Safety Guidelines for Schools.*

40. J. Gibbs, *Tribes: A New Way of Learning and Being Together* (Windsor, CA: Center Source Systems, 2001).

41. B. M. Landau, *The Art of Classroom Management: Building Equitable Learning Communities* (Upper Saddle River, NJ: Pearson Education, 2004).

42. B. Sornson, *Mastering Classroom Management,* ASCD Express (www.ascd.org/ascd-express/vol5/524-sornson.aspx).

43. R. Reasoner, *The True Meaning of Self-Esteem* (http://healthyselfesteem.org/about-self-esteem/meaning-of-self-esteem).

44. M. E. P. Seligman, *The Optimistic Child* (New York: HarperPerennial, 1995).

45. M. Quakenbush, W. M. Kane, and S. K. Telljohann, *Teach and Reach: Emotional and Mental Health* (Santa Cruz, CA: ETR Associates, 2004).

46. Seligman, *The Optimistic Child*.

47. Krovetz, *Fostering Resiliency*.

48. B. Benard, "Fostering Resiliency in Kids," *Educational Leadership* 51, no. 3 (November 1993): 44–48.

49. Krovetz, *Fostering Resiliency*.

50. J. A. Deiro, *Teachers DO Make a Difference* (Thousand Oaks, CA: Corwin Press, 2005).

51. Ibid.

52. E. E. Werner and R. S. Smith, *Overcoming the Odds: High Risk Children from Birth to Adulthood* (Ithaca, NY: Cornell University Press, 1992).

53. Deiro, *Teachers DO Make a Difference*.

54. Quackenbush et al., *Teach and Reach*.

55. Deiro, *Teachers DO Make a Difference*.

56. A. W. Coffee, J. Coffee, and J. N. Elizalde, *Peace Signs: A Manual for Teaching School Children Anger Management and Communication Skills* (Honolulu: CoffeePress, 2000).

57. Ibid.

58. J. Fetro, *Personal and Social Skills* (Santa Cruz, CA: ETR Associates, 2000).

59. Ibid.

60. Gibbs, *Tribes*.

61. L. Shoji and B. Pateman, "Balloon Up! Engaging Early Adolescents in a Hands-on Decision-Making Process," *American Journal of Health Education* 34, no. 6 (2003): 49–51.

62. T. M. Sabo, S. K. Telljohann, and W. M. Kane, *Improving Health Behaviors* (Santa Cruz, CA: ETR Associates, 2004).

63. Ibid.

64. Coffee et al., *Peace Signs*.

65. N. Stein, E. Gaberman, and L. Sjostrom, *Bully Proof: A Teacher's Guide on Teasing and Bullying for Use with Fourth- and Fifth-Grade Students* (Wellesley, MA: Joint publication of the Wellesley College Center for Research on Women and the NEA Professional Library, 1996).

Design Elements: Books Icon: ©Amero/Shutterstock; Mouse Icon: ©abu/E+/Getty Images; Blocks Icon: ©2HotBrazil/E+/Getty Images; Magnifying Glass Icon: ©Thawat Tanhai/123RF; Light Bulb Icon: ©Comstock/PunchStock

6

(Lisa, age 12)

Promoting Healthy Eating

DESIRED LEARNER OUTCOMES

After reading this chapter, you will be able to . . .

- Describe the prevalence and cost of unhealthy eating among youth.

- Explain the relationship between unhealthy eating and compromised academic performance.

- Identify factors that influence healthy eating.

- Summarize current guidelines and practices related to healthy eating promotion for schools and teachers.

- Summarize developmentally appropriate healthy eating concepts and skills for K–8 students in the context of the National Health Education Standards and target healthy behavior outcomes.

- Demonstrate developmentally appropriate learning strategies and assessment techniques that incorporate concepts and skills shown to promote healthy eating among youth.

- Identify effective, evaluated commercial curricula on healthy eating.

- Identify websites and children's literature that can be used in cross-curricular instructional activities that promote healthy eating.

INTRODUCTION

Eating and physical activity patterns that are focused on consuming fewer calories, making informed food choices, and being physically active can help people attain and maintain a healthy weight, reduce their risk of chronic disease, and promote overall health. The 2015 Dietary Guidelines for Americans (DGAs) exemplify these strategies through recommendations that accommodate the food preferences, cultural traditions, and customs of the many and diverse groups of people who live in the United States.[1]

The 2015 DGAs reflect a rising concern about the health of Americans. Poor diet and physical inactivity are the most important factors contributing to an epidemic of overweight and obesity that affects adults and children in all segments of society. Even in the absence of overweight, poor diet and physical inactivity are associated with major causes of morbidity and mortality in the United States.[2]

The U.S. Department of Agriculture (USDA) and the U.S. Department of Health and Human Services (HHS) released the first edition of *Nutrition and Your Health: Dietary Guidelines for Americans* in 1980. Subsequent editions of the DGAs, published every five years, not only have been consistent in their recommendations for a health-promoting diet but also have changed to reflect an evolving body of evidence about nutrition, our food and physical activity environment, and health. The ultimate goal of the DGAs is to improve the health of current and future generations through a focus on healthy eating patterns.[3]

Prevalence and Cost of Unhealthy Eating

Poor diet and physical inactivity are the most important factors that contribute to an epidemic of overweight and obesity in the United States. Data indicate that 73 percent of men and 65 percent of women are overweight or obese, with about one-third of adults being obese. Poor diet and physical inactivity are associated with cardiovascular disease, hypertension, Type 2 diabetes, osteoporosis, and some types of cancer. Some racial and ethnic population groups are disproportionately affected by high rates of overweight, obesity, and associated chronic diseases.[4]

The DGAs focus particularly on children because of the vital role that nutrition plays throughout the life span. Too many children are consuming diets with too many calories and not enough nutrients and are not getting enough physical activity. Approximately one-third of children and adolescents aged 2 to 19 years are overweight or obese.[5] Approximately 17 percent of children and adolescents are obese. This rate has remained relatively stable for sometime. Recently, there have been significant declines in early childhood obesity (aged 2–5) from 13.9 percent in 2003 to 9.4 percent in 2014.[6]

Risk factors for adult chronic diseases increasingly are found in children and adolescents with excess body fat. For example, cardiovascular disease risk factors, such as high blood cholesterol and hypertension, and Type 2 diabetes are increasing in young people. These adverse effects tend to persist through the life span. Children and adolescents who are overweight and obese are at substantially increased risk of being overweight and obese as adults and developing weight-related chronic diseases later in life. Primary prevention of obesity, especially in childhood, is an important strategy for combating and reversing the obesity epidemic.[7]

The Centers for Disease Control and Prevention conducts the Youth Risk Behavior Survey (YRBS) in odd-numbered years to monitor priority health-risk behaviors among youth, including unhealthy dietary behaviors and overweight. See Table 6-1 for 2015 data.

In *Healthy People 2020,* the U.S. Department of Health and Human Services identifies objectives focused on nutritional risk reduction among school-age youth. Table 6-2 summarizes the major public health concerns related to healthy eating among children and adolescents.

Healthy Eating and Academic Performance

The link between learning, academic achievement, and nutrition is well established. Simply put, children who practice healthy eating habits on a regular basis do better in school. Unfortunately, many unhealthy eating patterns begin early in life and result in learning difficulties and health problems during the school years and into adulthood.

The Council of Chief State School Officers (CCSSO) recognized the enormous impact health status has on the academic achievement of young people.[8] CCSSO stated, "We believe that healthy kids make better students and that better students make healthy communities." CCSSO identified the nutrition-related conditions that threaten students' health and their ability to make academic progress as obesity, diabetes, and hunger. The council also identified behaviors and environments related to nutrition as important factors that can put the health of young people at risk.

Action for Healthy Kids (AFHK), a nonprofit organization, formed specifically to address the U.S. epidemic of undernourished, overweight, and sedentary youth by focusing on changes at school, summarized research from the many studies that show a direct link between nutritional intake and academic performance.[9] Evidence indicates that children who eat poorly or engage in too little physical activity do not perform as well as they could academically, whereas improvements in nutrition and physical activity can result in improved academic performance. Poor nutrition, physical inactivity, and the increasing prevalence of overweight among students, besides taking an economic toll on schools in terms of reduced state funding related to increased student absence, can have indirect costs such as physical and emotional problems among students.[10] AFHK's first report, *The Learning Connection: The Value of Improving Nutrition and Physical Activity in Our Schools,* identified cause-and-effect links between nutrition and learning as early as 2004. It provides examples such as the following:

- Well-nourished children tend to be better students than poorly nourished children, who tend to demonstrate weaker academic performance and score lower on standardized achievement tests.
- Increased participation in breakfast programs is associated with increased academic test scores, improved daily attendance, better class participation, and reduced tardiness.

AFHK's 2013 report, entitled *The Learning Connection: What You Need to Know to Ensure Your Kids Are Healthy and Ready to Learn,*[11] highlights that healthy children learn better and that good food and physical activity prepare kids for success.

AFHK identifies two important areas related to academic achievement: nutrition and weight.

TABLE 6-1

Youth Risk Behavior Survey Data Related to Healthy Eating, 2017

Risk Behavior	Percent Reporting Behavior		
	Total	Females	Males
Ate fruit or drank 100% fruit juices one or more times/day during the seven days before the survey	60.8	58.2	63.3
Ate fruit or drank 100% fruit juices two or more times per day	31.3	28.8	33.8
Ate fruit or drank 100% fruit juices three or more times per day	18.8	15.9	21.8
Ate vegetables one or more times a day during the seven days before the survey	59.4	59.3	59.4
Ate vegetables two or more times per day	26.6	24.5	28.7
Ate vegetables three or more times per day	13.9	12.1	15.9
Drank one or more glasses a day of milk during the seven days before the survey	31.3	22.5	40.4
Drank two or more glasses a day of milk	17.5	10.6	24.7
Drank three or more glasses a day of milk	7.9	4.1	11.8
Drank a can, bottle, or glass of soda or pop one or more times per day, not counting diet soda or diet pop, during the seven days before the survey	18.7	15.4	22.3
Drank soda or pop two or more times per day	12.5	10.0	15.0
Drank soda or pop three or more times per day	7.1	5.5	8.7
Did not eat breakfast during the seven days before the survey	14.1	14.5	13.6
Ate breakfast on all seven days during the seven days before the survey	35.3	31.0	39.9
Were overweight (≥85th percentile but <95th percentile for body mass index, based on sex- and age-specific reference data)	15.6	16.8	14.4
Were obese (≥95th percentile for body mass index, based on sex- and age-specific reference data)	14.8	12.1	17.5
Described themselves as slightly or very overweight	31.5	37.7	25.3
Were trying to lose weight	47.1	59.9	34.0

SOURCE: Centers for Disease Control and Prevention, "Youth Risk Behavior Surveillance—United States, 2017," *MMWR* vol. 67, no. SS-8, 2018, 1–114.

Nutrition

Nutrition and academic achievement are linked in a variety of ways. *The Learning Connection* reported:

- Children who don't eat healthy diets lack the essential vitamins, minerals, fats, and proteins for optimal cognitive functioning.
- Iron deficiency has been linked to shortened attention span, irritability, fatigue, and difficulty concentrating.
- Poor nutrition and hunger interfere with cognitive functions and are associated with lower academic achievement.
- Hungry children and those at risk for being hungry are twice as likely to have impaired functioning. Teachers report higher levels of hyperactivity, absenteeism, and tardiness among hungry and at-risk children than among their peers who were not hungry.

Even short-term hunger from missed meals and moderate undernutrition can compromise cognitive development and school performance. Chronically undernourished children not only attain lower scores on standardized achievement tests, are more irritable, have difficulty concentrating, and have lower energy levels but also have less ability to resist infection and thus are more likely to become sick and miss school.

School attendance is positively correlated with school completion and academic success.[12]

Taras and Potts-Datema examined the association between nutrition in school-age children and their performance in school and on tests of cognitive functioning. They reported that school breakfast programs seem to improve attendance rates and decrease tardiness. Among children who are severely undernourished, school breakfast programs appear to improve academic performance and cognitive functioning.[13] In the 2010 report "Healthier Students Are Better Learners," Basch also identified participation in the school breakfast program as a key strategy to improve dietary status and thereby influence readiness to learn.[14]

Weight

Many studies from the United States and other high-income countries indicate a correlation between weight and academic achievement in youth showing that students who are overweight and obese have inferior academic performance than their normal weight peers.[15] When looking at this relationship, it is important to keep in mind that there are many other possible contributing factors and that correlation does not indicate causation.

TABLE 6–2

Healthy People 2020: **National Health Promotion Objectives to Improve the Nutritional Health of American Youth**

AH-6	Increase the proportion of schools with a school breakfast program.
NWS-1	Increase the number of states with nutrition standards for foods and beverages provided to preschool-aged children in childcare.
NWS-2	Increase the proportion of schools that offer nutritious foods and beverages outside of school meals.
NWS-2.1	Increase the proportion of schools that do not sell or offer calorically sweetened beverages to students.
NWS-2.2	Increase the proportion of school districts that require schools to make fruits or vegetables available whenever other food is offered or sold.
NWS-5.2	Increase the proportion of primary care physicians who regularly assess body mass index (BMI) for age and sex in their child or adolescent patients.
NWS-6.3	Increase the proportion of physician visits made by all child or adult patients that include counseling about nutrition or diet.
NWS-10	Reduce the proportion of children and adolescents who are considered obese.
NWS-11	Prevent inappropriate weight gain in youth and adults.
NWS-12	Eliminate very low food security among children.
NWS-14	Increase the contribution of fruits to the diets of the population aged 2 years and older.
NWS-15	Increase the variety and contribution of vegetables to the diets of the population aged 2 years and older.
NWS-16	Increase the contribution of whole grains to the diets of the population aged 2 years and older.
NWS-17	Reduce consumption of calories from solid fats and added sugars in the population aged 2 years and older.
NWS-18	Reduce consumption of saturated fat in the population aged 2 years and older.
NWS-19	Reduce consumption of sodium in the population aged 2 years and older.
NWS-20	Increase consumption of calcium in the population aged 2 years and older.
NWS-21	Reduce iron deficiency among young children and females of childbearing age.

SOURCE: U.S. Department of Health and Human Services, Healthy People 2020, www.healthypeople.gov/2020/default.aspx.

More research of the correlation between childhood overweight and obesity and academic achievement is needed.[16,17]

Other studies indicate a link between childhood overweight and obesity and school absence.[18] This correlation is especially strong at the middle school level.[19] Being overweight may trigger or exacerbate certain kinds of health conditions (asthma, Type 2 diabetes, joint problems), resulting in school absences.[20]

In addition to missing schools, overweight children can face physical, psychological, and social problems related to their weight, which might lead to academic problems. Studies show that weight-based teasing was significantly associated with lower school performance for overweight and obese students.[21]

While more data is needed to definitively link weight and academic performance, the knowledge that obesity and overweight may be detrimental to academic performance could help tip the balance in administrator's decisions about school nutrition and physical activity policies and practices.

Factors That Influence Healthy Eating

Nutrition and dietary patterns influence academic achievement and health. This section focuses on three factors that influence students' eating practices: food insecurity, dietary and physical activity patterns that contribute to overweight and obesity, and healthy school food environments.

Food Insecurity

The 2016 report from the Economic Research Service at the United States Department of Agriculture (USDA) indicates that 12.3 percent of households are food insecure with 8 percent of those households including children. Although the magnitude of the problem is clear, national and even state estimates of food insecurity can mask the nuances that exist at the local level. Children are particularly vulnerable to the economic challenges facing families today, with food insecurity rates among households with children substantially higher than those found in the general population.[22]

Although food insecurity has the potential to lead to negative outcomes for individuals across the age spectrum, it can be particularly devastating among children because of their increased vulnerability and the potential for long-term consequences. The structural foundation for cognitive functioning is laid in early childhood, creating the underlying circuitry on which more complex processes are built. This foundation can be greatly affected by food insecurity. Inadequate nutrition can permanently alter a child's brain architecture and stunt his or her intellectual capacity, affecting the child's learning, social interaction, and productivity. Studies demonstrate that food insecurity impacts cognitive development among young children and is linked to poor school performance in older children.[23]

Federal nutrition programs and the charitable sector, with support from business, work to meet the nutritional needs of struggling families. Federal nutrition programs, including the Supplemental Nutritional Assistance Program (SNAP), The Emergency Food Assistance Program (TEFAP), and Community Supplemental Food Program (CSFP), target the poorest and most vulnerable households to provide them with critical nutrition assistance. Although SNAP is not a child nutrition program per se, the program continues to serve as the first line of defense against child hunger. In 2015, 44 percent of SNAP participants were children. The National School Lunch Program (NSLP), School Breakfast Program (SBP), Summer Food Service Program (SFSP), and Child and Adult Care Food Programs (CACFP) also address child food insecurity by serving children in school and daycare settings, after school, and during the summer. The Women, Infants, and Children (WIC) Food and Nutrition Service improves nutrition by targeting young, low-income children at nutritional risk. Together, these programs weave a comprehensive nutritional safety net that reach children where they live, learn, and play. Existing child nutrition programs could do much more to address food insecurity among children simply by improving participation rates among those underserved.[24]

Dietary and Physical Activity Patterns That Contribute to Overweight in Youth

Although some progress has been seen lately, childhood obesity is still a major public health problem. Children who are overweight or obese as preschoolers are more likely than normal weight children to be overweight or obese as adults and suffer lifelong physical and mental health problems. There is no single or simple solution to childhood obesity. The problem is influenced by many different factors, including for some children a lack of community places to get adequate physical activity or a lack of access to healthy foods such as fresh fruits and vegetables.[25]

Childhood obesity is the result of eating too many calories and not getting enough physical activity.[26] A variety of environmental factors determine whether the healthy choice is the easy choice for children and their parents. American society has become characterized by environments that promote increased consumption of less healthy food and physical inactivity. Making healthy food choices and getting enough physical activity can be difficult for children when they are exposed to environments in their home, childcare center, school, or community that are influenced by the following[27]:

- Sugary drinks and less healthy foods on school campuses. Many students have access to sugary drinks and less healthy foods at school from vending machines and school canteens throughout the day and at fundraising events, school parties, and sporting events.
- Advertising of less healthy foods. Foods high in total calories, sugars, salt, and fat, and low in nutrients are highly advertised and marketed through media targeted to children and adolescents, while advertising for healthier foods is almost nonexistent in comparison.
- Lack of daily, quality physical activity in all schools. Most adolescents fall short of the recommendation of at least sixty minutes of aerobic physical activity each day.

- No safe and appealing place, in many communities, to play or be active. Many communities are built in ways that make it difficult or unsafe to be physically active.
- Limited access to healthy affordable foods. Some people have less access to stores and supermarkets that sell healthy, affordable food such as fruits and vegetables, especially in rural, minority, and lower-income neighborhoods. Supermarket access is associated with a reduced risk for obesity.
- Greater availability of high-energy-dense foods and sugary drinks. High-energy-dense foods have a lot of calories in each bite. A recent study among children showed that a high-energy-dense diet is associated with a higher risk for excess body fat during childhood. Sugary drinks are the largest source of added sugar and an important contributor of calories in the diets of children in the United States.
- Increasing portion sizes. Portion sizes of less healthy foods and beverages have increased over time in restaurants, grocery stores, and vending machines. Research shows that children eat more without realizing it if they are served larger portions.
- Television and media. Children 8 to 18 years of age spend an average of 7.5 hours a day using entertainment media, including TV, computers, video games, cell phones, and movies.[28]

Healthy School Food Environments

Schools play a critical role in improving the dietary and physical activity behaviors of students. Schools can create an environment supportive of students' efforts to eat healthily and be active by implementing policies and practices that support healthy eating and regular physical activity and by providing opportunities for students to learn about and practice these behaviors. CDC's School Health Guidelines to Promote Healthy Eating and Physical Activity[29] call for schools to establish school environments that encourage all students to make healthy eating choices and be physically active throughout the school day. The nine guidelines include strategies such as:

- Provide access to healthy foods and physical activity opportunities and to safe spaces, facilities, and equipment for healthy eating and physical activity.
- Establish a climate that encourages and does not stigmatize healthy eating and physical activity.
- Create a school environment that encourages a healthy body image, shape, and size among all students and staff members, is accepting of diverse abilities, and does not tolerate weight-based teasing.[30]

With regard to healthy environments, the School Nutrition Association (SNA) is a good source of information on the National School Lunch Program (NSLP), the School Breakfast Program (SBP), and other food programs delivered through schools.[31] The NSLP was established officially in 1946 as a measure of national security, to safeguard the health and well-being of the nation's children, and to encourage the domestic consumption of nutritious agricultural commodities. The SBP, signed into law in 1966, is a federally assisted meal program that provides nutritionally balanced low-cost or free breakfasts to children in public and nonprofit private schools and residential childcare institutions. In 1998, Congress expanded the NSLP to reimburse participating schools for snacks served to youth in after-school educational and enrichment programs. Participants in the NSLP and SBP must provide meals that meet federal nutritional requirements.

Additional federal laws have been enacted to influence healthy school food environments. Section 204 of the Child Nutrition and WIC Reauthorization Act of 2004 required local education agencies (school districts) participating in the NSLP and SBP to establish a Local Wellness Policy by the beginning of the 2006–2007 school year. Federal law requires the Local Wellness Policy to have a minimum of eight specified components, including school nutrition guidelines for all food available on school grounds during the school day to promote student health and reduce childhood obesity.[32]

Federal regulations define "competitive foods" as those sold to children in competition with the NSLP and SBP in food service areas during lunch and breakfast periods. Federal law limits the sale of competitive foods in certain school locations at certain times by requiring state education agencies and school authorities to establish rules or regulations to control their sale. Schools cannot sell foods of "minimal nutritional value, such as sodas, chewing gum, candies, and candy-coated popcorn," in the food service area during lunch and breakfast periods.[33] In addition to federal, state, and local mandates, the food and beverage industries are getting involved in improving school nutrition. The Alliance for a Healthier Generation worked with beverage manufacturers to institute a self-imposed ban on the sale of sodas and other high-sugar drinks in most of the nation's public schools.

Some states are improving healthy school food environments through restrictions on food and beverage advertising to children in schools, and using zoning as a potential legal tool to encourage students to make healthier food choices during school and on their way to and from school. However, more work is needed to effectively challenge current marketing practices directed at school children and to restrict how close fast food restaurants can be to schools.[34]

In the report *Progress or Promises? What's Working For and Against Healthy Schools?*, Action for Healthy Kids stated that much of the attention and work in school wellness during the past several years has been focused on reducing or eliminating junk food, resulting in important progress. There is a growing focus on strategies to increase the actual nutritional quality of foods and beverages provided to students, and to genuinely engage students, parents, families, communities, teachers, administrators, and school staff in improving wellness at home and at school.[35]

GUIDELINES FOR SCHOOLS

State of the Practice

The Centers for Disease Control and Prevention (CDC) periodically conducts the School Health Policies and Practices Study (SHPPS) to assess current school health policies and programs at the district level.[36] The 2016 SHPPS showed that close to 80 percent of districts required teaching about nutrition and dietary behavior (70.6 percent of elementary, 76.9 percent of middle, and 84.6 percent of high schools). However, this is a decrease from 2012, especially at the elementary and middle school levels. Given the critically important role that dietary behaviors play in good health, this indicates area of improvement. In addition, more than half of the districts required teaching about food-borne illness prevention (34.6 percent of elementary, 47.9 percent of middle, and 59.6 percent of high schools). Table 6–3 looks at select SHPPS nutrition services in the school environment.

State of the Art

The *School Health Guidelines to Promote Healthy Eating and Physical Activity*, developed by the CDC, synthesize research and best practices related to promoting healthy eating and physical activity in schools, into nine guidelines.[37] These guidelines were informed by the *Dietary Guidelines for Americans*, the *Physical Activity Guidelines for Americans*, and the *Healthy People 2020* objectives related to healthy eating and physical activity among children and adolescents.

The guidelines serve as the foundation for developing, implementing, and evaluating school-based healthy eating and physical activity policies and practices for students. Each of the nine guidelines is accompanied by a set of implementation strategies developed to help schools work toward achieving each guideline. Although the ultimate goal is to implement all nine guidelines, not every strategy will be appropriate for every school, and some schools, due to resource limitations, might need to implement the guidelines incrementally.[38] More information on the guidelines is provided in Teacher's Toolbox 6.1.

©Ryan McVay/Getty Images

Eating breakfast, whether at home or at school, is associated with better school performance.

TABLE 6–3	SHPPS

School Health Policies and Practices Study 2016—Nutrition Services and the School Nutrition Environment

- 23.4% of districts required a newly hired district food service director to be certified, licensed, or endorsed by the state
- 15.5% of districts required and 28.9% recommended that schools offer a self-serve salad bar
- 51.4% of districts required and 17.4% recommended that schools prohibit advertisements for junk foods or fast food restaurants in school buildings

SOURCE: Centers for Disease Control and Prevention, School Health Policies and Practices Study (SHPPS) 2016, www.cdc.gov/healthyyouth/data/shpps/index.htm.

Teacher's Toolbox 6.1

School Health Guidelines to Promote Healthy Eating and Physical Activity

Implementing and sustaining school-based healthy eating and physical activity policies and programs will make a powerful contribution toward a healthy future for students in the United States. By adopting these nine guidelines, schools can help ensure that all students have the opportunity to attain their maximum educational potential and pursue a lifetime of good health.

1. Use a coordinated approach to develop, implement, and evaluate healthy eating and physical activity policies and practices.
2. Establish school environments that support healthy eating and physical activity.
3. Provide a quality school meal program and ensure that students have only appealing, healthy food and beverage choices offered outside of the school meal program.
4. Implement a comprehensive physical activity program with quality physical education as the cornerstone.

5. Implement health education that provides students with the knowledge, attitudes, skills, and experiences needed for healthy eating and physical activity.
6. Provide students with health, mental health, and social services to address healthy eating, physical activity, and related chronic disease prevention.
7. Partner with families and community members in the development and implementation of healthy eating and physical activity policies, practices, and programs.
8. Provide a school employee wellness program that includes healthy eating and physical activity services for all school staff members.
9. Employ qualified persons, and provide professional development opportunities for physical education, health education, nutrition services, and health, mental health, and social services staff members, as well as staff members who supervise recess, cafeteria time, and out-of-school-time programs.

SOURCE: Centers for Disease Control and Prevention, "School Health Guidelines to Promote Healthy Eating and Physical Activity," *MMWR*, vol. 60, no. RR-5, 2011, 1–76.

In 2009, the CDC published *Nutrition Standards for Foods in Schools,* publicizing the 2007 Institute of Medicine (IOM) report by the same name. These standards provide guidance for the nutritional content and availability of competitive foods, those sold separately from school meals (e.g., in school stores, snack bars, and vending machines) that are not subject to federal nutritional requirements. Teachers and students can find a summary of these standards in Figure 6-1.[39]

Exciting ideas are available from *Making It Happen! School Nutrition Success Stories,* developed by Team Nutrition (U.S. Department of Agriculture) and the Division of Adolescent and School Health (CDC).[40] *Making It Happen!* tells the stories of schools and districts across the United States that have implemented innovative strategies to improve the nutritional quality of food and beverages sold outside the federal school meal programs. One of the most important insights in *Making It Happen!* is that students will buy and consume healthful foods and beverages and schools can make money from selling healthful options.

GUIDELINES FOR CLASSROOM APPLICATIONS

Important Background for K–8 Teachers

Teachers will find a world of nutrition information at their fingertips with online sources listed at the end of this chapter. Accurate, up-to-date nutrition information has never been easier for teachers and their students to find. However, the sheer volume of information on nutrition and health can be overwhelming. This section focuses on key resources for teachers.

Team Nutrition

Becoming a Team Nutrition School helps focus attention on the important role nutritious school meals, nutrition education, and a health-promoting school environment play in helping students learn to enjoy healthy eating and physical activity. Team Nutrition provides the framework for coordinated efforts by school nutrition staff, teachers, parents, the media, and other community members. All program materials encourage students to make food and physical activity choices for a healthy lifestyle.

The HealthierUS Schools Challenge (HUSSC) is a component of the Team Nutrition program. It establishes rigorous criteria for schools' food quality, participation in meal programs, physical activity opportunities, and nutrition education—the key components that make for healthy and active kids—and recognizes schools that create healthier school environments through their promotion of good nutrition and physical activity.

School can learn more at www.fns.usda.gov/tn/join-team.[41]

Dietary Guidelines for Americans 2015

The U.S. Department of Agriculture (USDQ) and the U.S. Department of Health and Human Service (HHS) jointly publish the *Dietary Guidelines for Americans* (DGAs) every five years. The 2015 emphasizes establishing healthy eating patterns. The intent of the DGAs is to summarize and synthesize knowledge about individual nutrients and food components into an interrelated set of recommendations for healthy eating that can be adopted by the public. The DGAs recommendations can be summarized into five overarching concepts:

- Follow a healthy eating pattern across the lifespan.
- Focus on variety, nutrient density, and amount.
- Limit calories from added sugars and saturated fats, and reduce sodium intake.
- Shift to healthier food and beverage choices.
- Support healthy eating patterns for all.[42]

Foods and Beverages Recommended by the Institute of Medicine's

Nutrition Standards for Foods in Schools

For All Students at All Times of Day (Tier 1)	Examples

• Fruits, vegetables, whole grains, combination products, fat-free and low-fat milk and milk products, lactose-free and soy beverages, per portion as packaged:
  » ≤200 calories;
  » ≤35% of total calories from fat;
  » <10% of calories from saturated fats;
  » Zero trans fat (≤0.5 g per serving);
  » ≤35% of calories from total sugars; *and*
  » ≤200 mg sodium.
	• Individual fruits—apples, pears, oranges.
	• Fruit cups packed in juice or water.
	• Vegetables—baby carrots, broccoli, edamame.
	• Dried or dehydrated fruits—raisins, apricots, cherries.
	• 100% fruit juice or low-sodium 100% vegetable juice.
	• Low-fat, low-salt, whole-grain crackers or chips.
	• Whole-grain, low-sugar cereals.
	• 100% whole-grain mini bagels.
	• **8-oz servings of low-fat, fruit-flavored yogurt with ≤30 g** of total sugars.
	• 8-oz servings of low-fat or nonfat chocolate or strawberry milk with ≤22 g of total sugars.
	• **Low-sodium, whole-grain bars containing sunflower** seeds, almonds, or walnuts.

For High School Students, After School Only (Tier 2)	Examples

• Any foods or beverages from Tier 1.
• Snack foods that are ≤200 calories per portion as packaged, and
  » ≤35% of total calories from fat;
  » <10% of calories from saturated fats;
  » Zero trans fat (≤ 0.5 g per serving);
  » ≤35% of calories from total sugars; *and*
  » ≤200 mg sodium.
• Sugar-free, caffeine-free beverages with
  » Nonnutritive sweeteners;
  » **Not vitamin- or nutrient-fortified;** *and*
  » <5 calories per portion as packaged.
	• Low-salt baked potato chips (≤200 mg of sodium), crackers, and pretzels.
	• Animal crackers with ≤35% of calories from sugars.
	• Graham crackers with ≤35% of calories from sugars.
	• Ice cream bars low in sugar and fat.
	• **Caffeine-free, calorie-free, nonfortified soft drinks.**

Examples of Items That *Do Not Meet* the *Standards*	
• Potato chips or pretzels that have too much sugar or salt (i.e., exceeding the values listed above). • Cheese crackers that have too much fat or sodium. • Breakfast or granola bars that have too much fat or sugar. • Ice cream products that have too much fat or sugar.	• Cake, cupcakes, or cookies with too much sugar or salt. • **Fortified sports drinks or fortified water.** • Gum, licorice, or candy. • Fruit smoothies with added sugar. • Regular colas or sodas with sugar or caffeine.

Additional Standards for Foods and Beverages
• Make plain, drinkable water available throughout the school day at no cost to students. • Offer sports drinks only to student athletes engaged in school sport programs involving vigorous activity for more than 1 hour. • Foods and beverages should not be used as rewards or discipline for academic performance or behavior. • Reduce marketing of Tier 2 foods and beverages in high schools. • Encourage the use of Tier 1 foods and beverages for fundraising activities both during and after school at elementary and middle schools. Allow Tier 1 and 2 foods and beverages for fundraising activities at high schools. • Allow both Tier 1 and 2 foods and beverages for evening and community school activities involving adults.

FIGURE 6–1 | Foods and Beverages Recommended by the Institute of Medicine's Nutrition Standards for Foods in Schools

SOURCE: Institute of Medicine, *Nutrition Standards for Foods in Schools*, 2007.

A healthy eating pattern limits the intake of sodium, solid fats, added sugars, and refined grains. The DGAs recognize that a healthy eating pattern may vary slightly from person to person and includes recommendations for people following different diet plans. Overall, the DGAs emphasize that a healthy eating pattern includes nutrient-dense foods and beverages from all food groups. Food and beverages that are nutrient-dense provide vitamins, minerals, and other substances that contribute to adequate nutrient intakes or may have positive health effects, with little or no solid fats and added sugars, refined starches, and sodium.[43]

The DGAs also emphasize the importance of American's following the *Physical Activity Guidelines for Americans* (https://health.gov/paguidelines/guidelines/) in order to balance caloric intake and calories burned. By doing this, Americans will be able to manage their weight and curb the obesity epidemic.

Another key feature of the 2015 Dietary Guidelines is a focus on shifting the food intake patterns of Americans to healthier patterns.

Source: U.S. Department of Agriculture (USDA)

The USDA recommends eating a diet rich in fruits and vegetables. Students can increase their enjoyment of fruits and vegetables through gardening and learning where the food they eat comes from.

Replace

1. Solid fats with oils.

Increase

1. **Vegetables** from all vegetable subgroups including dark-green vegetable, red and orange vegetables, legumes (beans and peas), starchy vegetables, and all other vegetables.
2. **Fruits** in the form of whole fruits in nutrient-dense forms.
3. **Whole grains**, aiming to make half of all grains consumed to be whole grains.
4. **Dairy** in nutrient-dense forms such as fat-free and low-fat milk and yogurt over cheese products.
5. **Protein** sources that are nutrient-dense and high quality and striving to increase seafood and legume intake in place of meat several times a week.

Reduce

1. **Added sugars.** Target less than 10 percent of calories per day.
2. **Saturated fat.** Target less than 10 percent of calories per day.
3. **Sodium intake.** Target less than 2300 milligrams per day.[44]

Figure 6–2 shows the percentage of Americans currently meeting the dietary guidelines. More detail and additional information can be found at https://health.gov/dietaryguidelines/2015/

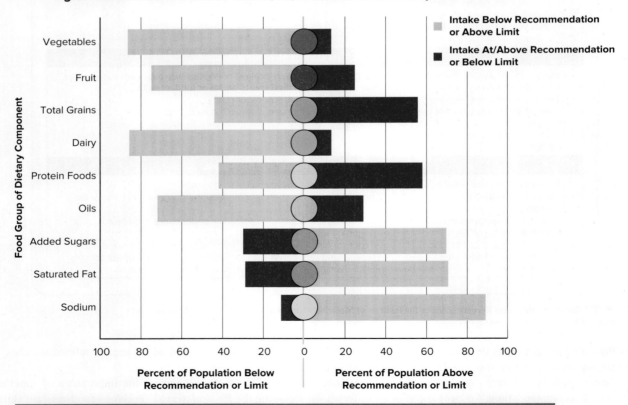

Dietary Intakes Compared to Recommendations. Percent of the U.S. Population Ages 1 Year & Older Who Are Below, At, or Above Each Dietary Goal or Limit

NOTE: The center (0) line is the goal or limit. For most, those represented by the orange sections of the bars, shifting toward the center line will improve their eating pattern.

DATA SOURCES: What We Eat in America, NHANES 2007-2010 for average intakes by age-sex froup. Healthy U.S.-Style Food Patterns, which vary based on age, sex, and activity level, for recommended intakes and limits.

FIGURE 6–2 | U.S. Department of Health and Human Services and U.S. Department of Agriculture. 2015–2020 Dietary Guidelines for Americans. 8th Edition. December 2015, p. 29, Figure 2.1. Available at http://health.gov/dietaryguidelines/2015/guidelines/.

Choose MyPlate.gov

MyPlate (Figure 6–3), released by the U.S. Department of Agriculture in 2011, is a tool to help consumers make better food choices.[45] MyPlate illustrates the five food groups, using the familiar mealtime visual of a place setting, and replaces the Food Guide Pyramid.

The website ChooseMyPlate.gov features practical information and tips to help Americans build healthier diets, focused on key behaviors.[46] Teachers will want to engage students in MyPlate Kids' Place at www.choosemyplate.gov/kids/index.html. The site provides games, activity sheets, videos and songs, a section called Move More, recipes, posters, and information for parents and educators. Parents and teachers are invited to use the MyPlate Kids' Place resources to deliver credible information and find "teachable moments" that will influence children's choices at home and at school. The site also includes Serving Up MyPlate: A Yummy Curriculum for grades 1–6.

Food Labeling and Nutrition

In 2016, the U.S Food and Drug Administration (FDA) announced updates to the Nutrition Facts label found on the back of packaged foods. Companies of different sizes have

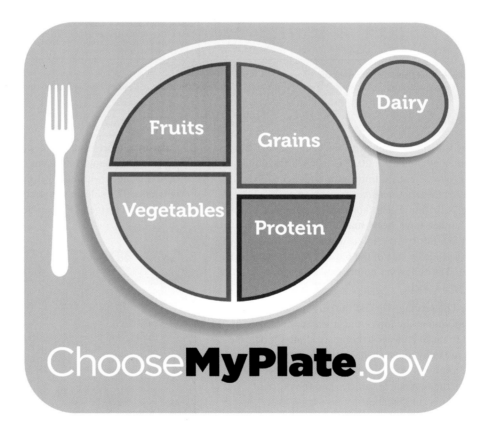

USDA is an equal opportunity provider and employer   USDA   June 2011

FIGURE 6–3 | MyPlate
SOURCE: U.S. Department of Agriculture, 2011.

Original label

Nutrition Facts

Serving Size 2/3 cup (55g)
Servings Per Container About 8

Amount Per Serving

Calories 230	Calories from Fat 72

	% Daily Value*
Total Fat 8g	**12%**
Saturated Fat 1g	**5%**
Trans Fat 0g	
Cholesterol 0mg	**0%**
Sodium 160mg	**7%**
Total Carbohydrate 37g	**12%**
Dietary Fiber 4g	**16%**
Sugars 1g	
Protein 3g	

Vitamin A	10%
Vitamin C	8%
Calcium	20%
Iron	45%

* Percent Daily Values are based on a 2,000 calorie diet. Your daily value may be higher or lower depending on your calorie needs.

		Calories:	2,000	2,500
Total Fat	Less than		65g	80g
Sat Fat	Less than		20g	25g
Cholesterol	Less than		300mg	300mg
Sodium	Less than		2,400mg	2,400mg
Total Carbohydrate			300g	375g
Dietary Fiber			25g	30g

New label

Nutrition Facts

8 servings per container

Serving size	**2/3 cup (55g)**

Amount per serving

Calories	**230**

	% Daily Value*
Total Fat 8g	**10%**
Saturated Fat 1g	**5%**
Trans Fat 0g	
Cholesterol 0mg	**0%**
Sodium 160mg	**7%**
Total Carbohydrate 37g	**13%**
Dietary Fiber 4g	**14%**
Total Sugars 12g	
Includes 10g Added Sugars	**20%**
Protein 3g	

Vitamin D 2mcg	10%
Calcium 260mg	20%
Iron 8mg	45%
Potassium 235mg	6%

* The % Daily Value (DV) tells you how much a nutrient in a serving of food contributes to a daily diet. 2,000 calories a day is used for general nutrition advice.

FIGURE 6–4 | **Sample Food Label for Macaroni and Cheese**

SOURCE: U.S. Food and Drug Administration, Original vs. New Format. https://www.fda.gov/downloads/food/guidanceregulation/guidancedocumentsregulatoryinformation/labelingnutrition/ucm501646.pdf

different dates by which to comply with the changes. All changes will be implemented by January 1, 2021. The new Nutrition Facts label aligns with new scientific information and the guidelines laid out in the *2015 Dietary Guidelines for Americans:*[47]

Much of the Nutrition Facts label has remained the same, however, key changes have been made to make it easier for consumers to make informed choices about their food intake. Figure 6–4 shows a side by side of the old and the updated Nutrition Facts Label. The following points explain how to read the new Nutrition Facts Label.

1. **Serving Size:** The serving size and the servings per container are found at the top of the label. Serving sizes are standardized to make it easier to compare similar foods and are provided in family units, such as cups or pieces, followed by the metric amounts (e.g., number of grams). The serving size influences the number of calories and the nutrient amounts listed later on the label.

   On the new Nutrition Facts label, for foods that are larger than one serving, but typically consumed in one sitting, such as a 20 oz bottle of a soft drink, the label will reflect one serving and adjust the remaining values accordingly. Another change consumers will notice is that some Nutrition Facts labels will contain two columns of information about calories and nutrients. If a container contains multiple servings, but is typically eaten in one or more sittings, the label will show both values for one serving and for the entire container.

2. **Calories:** Calories tell the amount of energy in a serving of this food. Many Americans consume more calories than they need without meeting recommended intakes for nutrients. The calorie section of the label can help with weight management. Remember that the number of servings

The Dietary Guidelines recommend that all Americans consume adequate amounts of fruits, vegetables, and whole grains.

consumed determines the number of calories eaten. Eating too many calories per day is linked to overweight and obesity. The new label removes "calories from fat" because newer research indicates that the type of fat is more important than the quantity of fat consumed.

3. **Nutrients and How Much:** The middle section of the label shows the nutrient content of the food. The nutrients listed first, fat (total, saturated, and trans), cholesterol, and sodium are nutrients that Americans generally eat in adequate amounts, or even too much. These nutrients may increase the risk of certain chronic diseases such as heart disease, certain cancers, and high blood pressure.

   Total carbohydrates are listed next. Underneath, the amount of dietary fiber is identified. Most Americans do not get enough dietary fiber. In addition to total sugar, the new label also identifies added sugars. This change is to help Americans meet nutrient needs and adhere to the Dietary Guidelines to limit added sugar to less than 10 percent of total calories. Values for vitamin D, potassium, calcium, and iron are required on the label and vitamins A and C are optional.

4. **Daily Values and Footnote:** There is an asterisk next to the Percent Daily Value (%DV) listed in the heading above the percentages by eat nutrient. This asterisk links to the footnote that reads, "*The %Daily Value tells you how much a nutrient in a serving of food contributes to a daily diet. 2,000 calories a day is used for general nutrition advice." The %DV is based on the Daily Value recommendations for key nutrients. It helps consumers determine whether a food serving is high or low in a nutrient. The label does the math to help interpret the numbers (grams and milligrams) by putting them all on the same scale for the day (0–100%DV). The %DV column does not add up vertically to 100 percent. Instead, each nutrient is based on 100 percent of the daily requirements for that nutrient for a 2,000-calorie diet.[48]

School Strategies to Promote Healthy Eating

The CDC *Guidelines for Schools to Promote Healthy Eating and Physical Activity* introduced in Teacher's Toolbox 6.1 provide practical strategies for creating school environments that make it possible for children to eat healthy and stay active.[49] With today's emphasis on high-stakes testing and test preparation, educational opportunities for healthy eating and activity can become low on the list of important school priorities. The strategies are designed to help schools make the healthy way the easy and accepted way. For example, strategies for establishing school environment include:

1. Provide access to healthy foods and physical activity opportunities and to safe spaces, facilities, and equipment for healthy eating and physical activity.
2. Establish a climate that encourages and does not stigmatize healthy eating and physical activity.
3. Create a school environment that encourages a healthy body image, shape, and size among all students and staff members, is accepting of diverse abilities, and does not tolerate weight-based teasing.

Teachers can find additional strategies at www.cdc.gov/healthyyouth/npao/strategies.htm.

Learning About Nutrition with Your Students

The authors of this book encourage educators to learn about nutrition with their students. Two classroom stories illustrate this point. In one, a fourth-grade teacher began her health lesson by saying to her students, "Who can give me an example of a carbohydrate? We talked about those last week." A student raised his hand and said, "An apple!" The teacher began to say yes, and then frowned to herself. "No-o-o," she said hesitantly, "carbohydrates are pasta, remember?" As the teacher went on with the lesson, the students (and the author who heard the interchange through the window) wondered what the teacher thought an apple was—a fat or a protein? The truth is that most adults don't know a great deal about nutrition, and information changes rapidly. Practicing the health education standard of accessing information is important for students and teachers. Teachers aren't the "answer machine," and shouldn't hesitate to say, "Hmm . . . how can we find out?"

In another example a parent reported that her kindergartener was eating an after-school snack (chips, unfortunately) on the drive home. During the ride, the mother realized that her daughter was talking to herself ("Well, that one is no good. Nope. That one's no good either.") and throwing her chips, one by one, out the car window, which was lowered a bit to catch the breeze. When she asked her daughter what she was doing, the little girl replied, "Well, my teacher said that if a food is bad, it will make a greasy spot on the napkin. So, all the ones I've tried are no good!" She was testing the chips, one after another, and throwing them out if they made a greasy spot on the napkin. However, rather than rejecting the bag outright, she was searching busily for a "good one" that she could eat. The teacher's lesson made an impression on this kindergarten student, but it stopped short of helping the child see the bigger picture. The child's age and development certainly were part of this story, but talking about health lessons with students and checking for understanding, rather than just telling information, can help correct these kinds of misperceptions, including that some foods are "bad."

The Strategies for Learning and Assessment, later in this chapter, provide opportunities for teachers to investigate topics with their students, including fast foods, portion sizes, fats and cholesterol, carbohydrates, body image and size, and fiber. Teachers should dive in and learn right along with their students because, hey—what's a cruciferous vegetable anyway?

Recommendations for Concepts and Practice
Healthy Behavior Outcomes

The goal of health education is to help students adopt or maintain health-enhancing behaviors. School districts and teachers should identify the health-enhancing behaviors they would like their students to maintain or adopt. The list found in Teacher's Toolbox 6.2 identifies possible healthy behavioral outcomes related to healthy eating. Though not all these suggestions are developmentally appropriate for students in grades K–8, this list can help teachers understand how the learning activities they plan for their students support both short- and long-term desired behavior outcomes.

Developmentally Appropriate Knowledge and Skill Expectations for Healthy Eating

HEALTHY BEHAVIOR OUTCOMES FOR HEALTHY EATING

HBO 1. Eat the appropriate number of servings from each food group every day.

HBO 2. Eat a variety of foods within each food group every day.

HBO 3. Eat an abundance of fruits and vegetables every day.

HBO 4. Choose to eat whole grain products and fat-free or low-fat milk or equivalent milk products regularly.

HBO 5. Drink plenty of water every day.

HBO 6. Limit foods and beverages high in added sugars, solid fat, and sodium.

HBO 7. Eat breakfast every day.

HBO 8. Eat healthy snacks.

HBO 9. Eat healthy foods when dining out.

HBO 10. Prepare food in healthful ways.

HBO 11. Balance caloric intake with caloric expenditure.

HBO 12. Follow an eating plan for healthy growth and development.

HBO 13. Support others to eat healthy.

Grades K–2 Knowledge Expectations	Grades 3–5 Knowledge Expectations	Grades 6–8 Knowledge Expectations
NHES 1: Core Concepts		
HE1.2.1 Explain the importance of trying new foods. (HBO 1 & 2)	HE1.5.1 Name the food groups and variety of nutritious food choices for each food group. (HBO 1 & 2)	HE1.8.1 Classify the amount of food from each food group that a person needs each day. (HBO 1 & 2)
HE1.2.2 Explain the importance of choosing healthy foods and beverages. (HBO 1, 2, 3, 4, 5, 6, 7, 8, 9 & 12)	HE1.5.2 Identify the amount of food from each food group that a child needs daily. (HBO 1 & 2)	HE1.8.2 Summarize a variety of nutritious food choices for each food group. (HBO 1, 2, 3, 4 & 13)
HE1.2.3 Identify a variety of healthy snacks. (HBO 2, 3, 4, 5, 8 & 12)	HE1.5.3 Describe the benefits of eating plenty of fruits and vegetables. (HBO 1, 2, 3, 12 & 13)	HE1.8.3 Describe the U.S. *Dietary Guidelines for Americans*. (HBO 1, 2, 3, 4, 5, 6, 11, 12 & 13)
HE1.2.4 Identify the benefits of drinking plenty of water. (HBO 5 & 12)	HE1.5.4 Explain the importance of eating a variety of foods from all the food groups. (HBO 1, 2 & 13)	HE1.8.4 Explain why the recommended amount of food a person needs each day may be different for each food group. (HBO 1, 2 & 13)
HE1.2.5 Describe the types of foods and beverages that should be limited. (HBO 6, 8, 9 & 12)	HE1.5.5 Identify nutritious and non-nutritious beverages. (HBO 5 & 6)	HE1.8.5 Summarize the benefits of eating plenty of fruits and vegetables. (HBO 1, 3 & 13)
HE1.2.6 Describe the benefits of eating breakfast every day. (HBO 7 & 12)	HE1.5.6 Describe the benefits of drinking plenty of water. (HBO 5, 12 & 13)	HE1.8.6 Describe the benefits of eating a variety of foods high in iron. (HBO 1 & 4)
HE1.2.7 Describe how to keep food safe from harmful germs. (HBO 10)	HE1.5.7 Identify foods that are high in fat and low in fat. (HBO 6 & 12)	HE1.8.7 Explain the similarities and differences among proteins, fats, and carbohydrates regarding nutritional value and food sources. (HBO 1 & 11)
HE1.2.8 Describe body signals that tell a person when they are hungry and when they are full. (HBO 12)	HE1.5.8 Identify alternate sources of fat (e.g., unsaturated fats and oils) (HBO 6)	HE1.8.8 Describe the benefits of consuming an adequate amount of calcium and a variety of foods high in calcium. (HBO 2 & 13)
HE1.2.9 Identify healthy eating patterns that provide energy and help the body grow and develop. (HBO 12)	HE1.5.9 Identify foods that are high in added sugars. (HBO 6 & 12)	HE1.8.9 Identify foods that are high in fiber. (HBO 3 & 4)
	HE1.5.10 Identify foods that are high in sodium. (HBO 6 & 12)	HE1.8.10 Identify examples of whole grain foods. (HBO 4)
	HE1.5.11 Describe the benefits of limiting the consumption of solid fat, added sugar, and sodium. (HBO 6, 12 & 13)	HE1.8.11 Summarize the benefits of drinking plenty of water. (HBO 5 & 13)
	HE1.5.12 Explain why breakfast should be eaten every day. (HBO 7 & 12)	HE1.8.12 Differentiate between nutritious and non-nutritious beverages. (HBO 5, 6 & 13)
	HE1.5.13 Describe methods to keep food safe from harmful germs. (HBO 10)	HE1.8.13 Summarize the benefits of limiting the consumption of solid fat, added sugar, and sodium. (HBO 6, 8, 9 & 13)
	HE1.5.14 Explain the concept of eating in moderation. (HBO 11 & 12)	HE1.8.14 Identify food preparation methods that add less fat to food and use unsaturated fats and oils to replace solid saturated fats. (HBO 6 & 10)
	HE1.5.15 Describe the benefits of healthy eating. (HBO 12 & 13)	HE1.8.15 Describe the importance of eating breakfast every day. (HBO 7)
		HE1.8.16 Explain the relationship between access to healthy foods and personal food choices. (HBO 8, 9, 11 & 12)
		HE1.8.17 Explain how to select healthy foods when dining out. (8, 9, 11 & 12)

HE1.5.16 Explain body signals that tell a person when they are hungry and when they are full. (HBO 11 & 12)	HE1.8.18 Explain various methods available to evaluate body weight. (HBO 11)
	HE1.8.19 Describe major chronic diseases and their relationship to what people eat and their physical activity level. (HBO 11 & 12)
	HE1.8.20 Analyze the benefits of healthy eating. (HBO 11 & 12)
	HE1.8.21 Identify healthy and risky approaches to weight management. (HBO 11 & 12)
	HE1.8.22 Describe the benefits of eating in moderation. (HBO 11, 12 & 13)

Grades K–2 Skill Expectations	Grades 3–5 Skill Expectations	Grades 6–8 Skill Expectations

NHES 2: Analyze Influences

HE2.2.1 Identify relevant influences of family on food choices and other eating practices and behaviors.	HE2.5.1 Identify relevant influences of culture on food choices and other eating practices and behaviors.	HE2.8.1 Explain the influence of school rules and community laws on food choices and other eating practices and behaviors.
HE2.2.2 Identify relevant influences of school personnel on food choices and other eating practices and behaviors.	HE2.5.2 Identify relevant influences of peers on food choices and other eating practices and behaviors.	HE2.8.2 Explain how perceptions of norms influence healthy and unhealthy food choices and other eating practices and behaviors.
HE2.2.3 Identify relevant influences of media and technology on food choices and other eating practices and behaviors.	HE2.5.3 Identify relevant influences of community on food choices and other eating practices and behaviors.	HE2.8.3 Explain how social expectations influence healthy and unhealthy food choices and other eating practices and behaviors.
HE2.2.4 Describe positive influences on personal food choices and other eating practices and behaviors.	HE2.5.4 Describe how relevant influences of family and culture affect personal food choices and other eating practices and behaviors.	HE2.8.4 Explain how personal values and beliefs influence food choices and other eating practices and behaviors.
HE2.2.5 Describe negative influences on personal food choices and other eating practices and behaviors.	HE2.5.5 Describe how relevant influences of school and community affect food choices and other eating practices and behaviors.	HE2.8.5 Describe how some health risk behaviors influence the likelihood of engaging in unhealthy eating practices and behaviors.
	HE2.5.6 Describe how relevant influences of media (e.g., advertising) and technology affect food choices and other eating practices and behaviors.	HE2.8.6 Analyze how relevant influences of family and culture affect personal food choices and other eating practices and behaviors.
	HE2.5.7 Describe how relevant influences of peers affect food choices and other eating practices and behaviors.	HE2.8.7 Analyze how relevant influences of school and community affect personal food choices and other eating practices and behaviors.
		HE2.8.8 Analyze how relevant influences of media (e.g., advertising) and technology affect personal food choices and other eating practices and behaviors.
		HE2.8.9 Analyze how relevant influences of peers affect personal food choices and other eating practices and behaviors.

NHES 3: Accessing Information, Products, and Services

HE3.2.1 Identify trusted adults at home who can help promote healthy eating.	HE3.5.1 Describe characteristics of accurate nutrition information.	HE3.8.1 Analyze the validity and reliability of nutrition information.
HE3.2.2 Identify trusted adults and professionals in school (e.g., food service director) who can help promote healthy eating.	HE3.5.2 Describe characteristics of appropriate and reliable nutrition products.	HE3.8.2 Analyze the validity and reliability of nutrition products.
HE3.2.3 Identify trusted adults and professionals in the community (e.g., registered dietitian, healthcare provider) who can help promote healthy eating.	HE3.5.3 Describe characteristics of appropriate and trustworthy nutrition services.	HE3.8.3 Analyze the validity and reliability of nutrition services.
	HE3.5.4 Demonstrate how to locate sources of accurate nutrition information.	HE3.8.4 Describe situations that call for professional nutrition services.
		HE3.8.5 Determine the availability of valid and reliable nutrition products.
		HE3.8.6 Access valid and reliable nutrition information from home, school, or community.
		HE3.8.7 Locate valid and reliable nutrition products.
		HE3.8.8 Locate valid and reliable nutrition services.

(*continued*)

Grades K–2 Skill Expectations	Grades 3–5 Skill Expectations	Grades 6–8 Skill Expectations

NHES 4: Interpersonal Communication

HE4.2.1 Demonstrate effective refusal skills to avoid unhealthy food choices and promote healthy eating.	HE4.5.1 Demonstrate effective verbal and nonverbal communication to avoid unhealthy food choices and promote healthy eating. HE4.5.2 Explain how to be empathetic and compassionate toward a family member who is trying to improve personal food choices and healthy eating. HE4.5.3 Demonstrate how to effectively ask for help to improve personal food choices and promote healthy eating.	HE4.8.1 Demonstrate the use of effective verbal and nonverbal communication to avoid unhealthy food choices and promote healthy food choices. HE4.8.2 Demonstrate effective peer resistance skills to avoid or reduce exposure to unhealthy food choices. HE4.8.3 Demonstrate effective negotiation skills to avoid or reduce unhealthy eating. HE4.8.4 Demonstrate how to effectively ask for assistance to improve personal food choices, eating behaviors, and weight management. HE4.8.5 Demonstrate how to effectively communicate empathy and support for others who are trying to improve personal food choices and healthy eating.

NHES 5: Decision Making

HE5.2.1 Identify situations that need a healthy eating-related decision. HE5.2.2 Identify how family, peers, or media influence a healthy eating-related decision. HE5.2.3 Explain the potential positive and negative outcomes from a nutrition-related decision. HE5.2.4 Describe when help is needed and when it is not needed to make a healthy nutrition decision.	HE5.5.1 Identify situations that need a decision related to healthy eating (e.g., when a peer offers a soft drink). HE5.5.2 Decide when help is needed and when it is not needed to make a decision related to healthy eating behaviors. HE5.5.3 Explain how family, culture, peers, or media influence a decision related to healthy eating behaviors. HE5.5.4 Identify options and their potential outcomes when making a decision related to healthy and safe eating behaviors. HE5.5.5 Choose a healthy food or beverage option when making a decision related to healthy eating behaviors. HE5.5.6 Describe the final outcome of a decision related to healthy eating behaviors.	HE5.8.1 Identify circumstances that help or hinder healthy decision making related to food and behavior choices. HE5.8.2 Determine when situations require a decision related to a healthy eating behavior. HE5.8.3 Distinguish when a decision related to food and beverage choices should be made individually or with the help of others. HE5.8.4 Explain how family, culture, media, peers, and personal beliefs affect a decision related to healthy eating behaviors. HE5.8.5 Distinguish between healthy and unhealthy alternatives of a decision related to eating behaviors. HE5.8.6 Predict the potential outcomes of healthy and unhealthy alternatives of a decision related to healthy eating behaviors. HE5.8.7 Choose a healthy food or beverage alternative when making a decision related to healthy eating behaviors. HE5.8.8 Analyze the effectiveness of a final outcome of a decision related to healthy eating behaviors.

NHES 6: Goal Setting

HE6.2.1 Identify a realistic personal short-term goal to improve healthy eating. HE6.2.2 Take steps to achieve a personal goal to improve healthy eating. HE6.2.3 Identify people who can help achieve a personal goal to improve healthy eating.	HE6.5.1 Set a realistic personal goal related to improve healthy eating behaviors. HE6.5.2 Track progress toward achieving a personal goal to improve healthy eating behaviors. HE6.5.3 Identify resources that can help achieve a personal goal to improve healthy eating behaviors.	HE6.8.1 Assess personal eating practices. HE6.8.2 Set a realistic personal goal to improve healthy eating behaviors. HE6.8.3 Assess the barriers to achieving a personal goal to improve healthy eating behaviors. HE6.8.4 Apply strategies to overcome barriers to achieving a personal goal to improve healthy eating behaviors. HE6.8.5 Use strategies and skills to achieve a personal goal to improve healthy eating behaviors.

NHES 7: Self-Management

HE7.2.1 Identify practices that reduce or prevent unhealthy eating behaviors. HE7.2.2 Demonstrate healthy eating practices. HE7.2.3 Make a commitment to practice healthy eating behaviors.	HE7.5.1 Describe practices and behaviors that reduce or prevent unhealthy eating behaviors. HE7.5.2 Demonstrate healthy eating practices and behaviors. HE7.5.3 Make a commitment to practice healthy eating behaviors.	HE7.8.1 Explain the importance of being responsible for personal healthy eating behaviors. HE7.8.2 Analyze personal practices, eating practices, and behaviors that reduce or prevent health risks. HE7.8.3 Demonstrate healthy eating practices and behaviors to improve the health of oneself and others. HE7.8.4 Make a commitment to practice healthy eating behaviors.

Grades K–2 Skill Expectations	Grades 3–5 Skill Expectations	Grades 6–8 Skill Expectations
NHES 8: Advocacy		
HE8.2.1 Make requests to others (e.g., family members) about preferences for healthy eating.	HE8.5.1 Give factual information to improve the food and beverage selections of others.	HE8.8.1 State a healthy eating position, supported with accurate information, to improve the health of others.
HE8.2.2 Demonstrate how to encourage peers to make healthy food and beverage choices.	HE8.5.2 State personal beliefs to improve the food and beverage selections of others.	HE8.8.2 Persuade and support others to make positive food and beverage choices.
	HE8.5.3 Demonstrate how to persuade others to make healthy food and beverage choices.	HE8.8.3 Collaborate with others to advocate for healthy eating at home, in school, or in the community.
		HE8.8.4 Demonstrate how to adapt healthy eating messages for different audiences.

SOURCE: Centers for Disease Control and Prevention, *Health Education Curriculum Analysis Tool* (Atlanta, GA: Centers for Disease Control and Prevention, 2011), www.cdc.gov.

Developmentally Appropriate Knowledge and Skill Expectations

As with other health topics, teaching related to healthy eating should be developmentally appropriate and be based on the physical, cognitive, social, emotional, and language characteristics of specific students. Teacher's Toolbox 6.2 contains a list of suggested developmentally appropriate knowledge and skill expectations to help teachers create lessons that will encourage students to practice the desired behavior outcomes by the time they graduate from high school. The numbers listed behind each knowledge expectation are aligned with and support the healthy behavior outcomes listed in the Teacher's Toolbox 6.2. Note that these grade-level spans are aligned with the 2007 National Health Education Standards.

STRATEGIES FOR LEARNING AND ASSESSMENT

Promoting Healthy Eating

This section provides an example of a standards-based learning and assessment strategy for each NHES standard. The examples in this chapter can be applied to any content area. Chapters 5 to 14 include content-specific learning and assessment strategies organized by standard and grade cluster (K–2, 3–5, and 6–8). Each set of strategies begins with a restatement of the standard and a reminder of the assessment criteria, drawn from the RMC Health rubrics in Appendix B. Strategies are written as directions for teachers and include applicable theory of planned behavior (TPB) (Constructs: Intention to act in healthy ways, attitudes toward behavior, subjective norms, perceived behavioral control). These learning and assessment strategies provide building blocks for standards-based lessons and units that can be tailored to local needs. Assessment criteria are used with permission from RMC Health. See Appendix B for Scoring Rubrics.

NHES 1 | Core Concepts

Students will comprehend concepts related to health promotion and disease prevention to enhance health.

ASSESSMENT CRITERIA

- Connections—Describe relationships between behavior and health; draw logical conclusions about connections between behavior and health.
- Comprehensiveness—Thoroughly cover health topic, showing breadth and depth; give accurate information.

Grades K–2

NHES 1, Grades K–2, Making Fruits and Vegetables Fun Teach an introductory lesson on the importance of eating a variety of foods within each food group. Visit www.choosemyplate.gov/ten-tips-kid-friendly-veggies-and-fruits. Select the link to the handout, "kid-friendly vegetables and fruits." If the school/classroom budget permits—or if parents/caregivers can help—prepare one of the fun creations identified on the handout. Allow students the opportunity to taste the food and talk about how making food fun can make it more enjoyable. Discuss different ways to make food fun referring to the handout for suggestions. Be sure to attend to food allergies.

ASSESSMENT | For an assessment task, students can work independently or in pairs to create their own fun food. Students could be assigned different categories, such as dippers, smoothies, kabobs, trail mix, or they can use their own creativity. The goal is to create a fun way to enjoy more fruits and vegetables in their diet. Students should create a poster including a picture and a brief description of the fun food. For assessment criteria, students should be able to identify one creative strategy for enjoying fruits and/or vegetables. (Constructs: Attitudes toward behavior, perceived behavioral control.)

Go, Slow, and Whoa Foods The National Heart, Lung, and Blood Institute (NHLBI) found that educating kids about good nutrition can help them develop smart eating habits. Providing kids with the knowledge and education they need to make healthier dietary choices is key. Of course, educating children about healthy eating and helping them apply that knowledge can be difficult. To help, the institute classified food into three groups (Teacher's Toolbox 6.3):

- The *Go* group includes heart-healthy foods that should be eaten every day because they are low in saturated fat and cholesterol (low-fat milk, whole-grain cereals).
- The *Slow* group includes foods that should be eaten only a few times a week (waffles, pancakes).
- The *Whoa* group includes foods that should be eaten only once in a while because they are high in saturated fat and cholesterol (French fries, doughnuts).

Healthy Eating with Go, Slow, and Whoa Foods

Food Group	GO (almost anytime)	SLOW (sometimes)	WHOA (once in a while)
Vegetables	Almost all fresh, frozen, and canned vegetables without added fat (such as butter) or sauces	All vegetables with added fat or salt Oven-baked fries Avocado	Any vegetable fried in oil, such as French fries or hash browns
Fruits	All fresh and frozen fruits Canned fruits packed in juice	100% fruit juice Fruits canned in light syrup Dried fruits	Fruits canned in heavy syrup
Breads and cereals	Whole-grain breads, pitas, and tortillas Whole-grain pasta Brown rice Hot and cold unsweetened whole-grain cereals	White bread and pasta that's not whole grain Taco shells French toast, waffles, and pancakes Biscuits Granola	Doughnuts, muffins, croissants, and sweet rolls Sweetened breakfast cereals Crackers that have hydrogenated oils (*trans* fats)
Milk and milk products	Skim and 1% milk Fat-free and low-fat yogurt Part-skim, reduced-fat, and fat-free cheese Low-fat and fat-free cottage cheese	2% milk Processed cheese spreads	Whole milk Full-fat cheese Cream cheese Yogurt made from whole milk
Meats and other sources of protein	Beef and pork that has been trimmed of its fat Extra-lean ground beef Chicken and turkey without skin Tuna canned in water Fish and shellfish that has been baked, broiled, steamed, or grilled Beans, split peas, and lentils Tofu Egg whites and substitutes	Lean ground beef Broiled hamburgers Ham Canadian bacon Chicken and turkey with the skin Low-fat hot dogs Tuna canned in oil Peanut butter Nuts Whole eggs cooked without added fat	Beef and pork that hasn't been trimmed of its fat Fried hamburgers Ribs Bacon Fried chicken Chicken nuggets Hot dogs Lunch meats Pepperoni Sausage Fried fish and shellfish Whole eggs cooked with fat
Sweets and snacks	Ice milk bars Frozen fruit-juice bars Low-fat frozen yogurt Low-fat ice cream Fig bars Ginger snaps Baked chips Low-fat microwave popcorn Pretzels		Cookies, cakes, and pies Cheesecake Ice creams Chocolate candy Chips Buttered microwave popcorn
Butter, ketchup, and other stuff that goes on food	Ketchup Mustard Fat-free creamy salad dressing Fat-free mayonnaise Fat-free sour cream Olive oil Vegetable oil Oil-based salad dressing Vinegar	Low-fat creamy salad dressing Low-fat mayonnaise Low-fat sour cream	Lard Salt pork Gravy Regular creamy salad dressing Mayonnaise Tartar sauce Sour cream Cheese sauce Cream sauce Cream cheese dips
Drinks	Water Fat-free and 1% milk Diet soda Diet and unsweetened iced teas and lemonade	2% milk 100% fruit juice Sports drinks	Whole milk Regular soda Drinks with added sugar Fruit drinks with less than 100% fruit juice

Source: U.S. National Heart, Lung, and Blood Institute, National Institutes of Health, www.nhlbi.nih.gov/health/public/heart/obesity/wecan/eat-right/choosing-foods.htm.

The trick is to teach children balance in selecting their diet. That means that the Whoa group isn't completely off limits but should be recognized as containing foods that aren't too healthy and should be eaten only every now and then. Parents and teachers can provide a good example by following the Go, Slow, and Whoa approach. The key is to give children choices and to stock plenty of Go group foods that they like. Remember, the Whoa group isn't entirely off-limits—make sure children know that foods from this group are occasional treats.

ASSESSMENT | For an assessment task, students can brainstorm a list of foods and then try categorizing them according to the Go, Slow, and Whoa chart. Teachers can share the NHLBI chart with students for comparison and discussion. For assessment criteria, students should explain how and why foods are categorized as they are in the chart, providing accurate information and drawing conclusions about connections between eating and health. (Construct: Attitudes toward behavior.)

Making Food Exciting   As students are beginning to develop their writing skills, they often are encouraged to use words that make their writing more interesting to the reader. First-grade teacher Melissa Hook challenges her students to use "exciting" words. For example, she challenges her students to think of more exciting words for *good*. Words such as *refreshing* or *crunchy* make food sound more exciting to try than *good*. Brainstorm with children common words used to describe food, such as *good, hot, yucky, yummy,* and so on. Then take one of those words and brainstorm exciting words that mean the same, but make the food sound more interesting, such as *delicious, gooey, colorful,* and so forth.

ASSESSMENT | The teacher provides the students with a paragraph about food that includes common describing words. Students are challenged to rewrite the paragraph making it more "exciting." Alternatively, students brainstorm five exciting words that describe food and use each of them in a sentence. The teacher can post the various exciting words around the room for the remainder of the unit. For assessment criteria, students can use the exciting words accurately to describe food and demonstrate their understanding of nutrition concepts with accurate sentences. (Construct: Attitudes toward behavior.)

Grades 3–5

What's Wrong with This Picture?   Teachers should instruct students on some or all of the following key nutrition concepts prior to this assessment: food groups, importance of eating plenty of fruits and vegetables, nutritious and nonnutritious beverages, foods high and low in fat, foods high in added sugars, and how to keep foods safe from harmful germs. Once students have a solid understanding of the key concept(s), teachers should present an example of a "what's wrong with this picture?" poster. The poster should include one key concept or theme using pictures cut out from magazines, hand drawings, computer clipart, and so on. The example can either have a variety of nonexamples (poor nutrition choices) or the majority of healthy choices with a few nonexamples. Students should discuss with a partner what they believe to be the concept being represented in the teacher example.

ASSESSMENT | With a partner, students create their own "What's Wrong with This Picture?" poster. The poster should represent one major concept or theme using pictures cut out from magazines, hand drawings, computer clipart, and so on. Students should then post their posters around the room for a gallery walk. The posters should be numbered and students should write down the nutrition concept being represented by their classmates' posters. For assessment criteria, students should be able to explain what concept is represented in their poster and why, as well as identify the concepts represented in the posters created by their classmates. Students should also be able to make connections between the behavior and health. (Construct: Attitudes toward behavior.)

Twenty Questions (or More) About Foods   Students can play a game of "twenty questions" to learn more about different kinds of foods. (Note: Any number of questions is allowed.) In preparation teachers can make index cards with the names or pictures of foods on them, one food per card (chicken, fish, apple, grape, cereal, yogurt, rice, tomato—including some combination foods, e.g., pizza, vegetable soup). Teachers should explain that students will have a card taped to their back, but they won't know what is on the card. Classmates will be able to read what is on each person's back. Students circulate around the room, asking yes or no questions (Is it eaten hot? Does it have a round shape? Is it green? Is it a breakfast food?). Students should talk to several different classmates to get information. Classmates can respond only with "Yes," "No," or "I don't know." Students cannot give any other information, no matter what the question, and students cannot tell classmates the names of the foods on their backs. Students who guess their foods correctly may take off their cards and then help other students.

Teachers can call time after five or ten minutes. When time is called, students should return to their seats. Students who haven't guessed their foods should continue to wear their cards on their backs without looking at them. Teachers should ask students who guessed their foods, what kinds of questions they asked, and what worked well in helping them find out the answer. Teachers also can suggest that students use the major food groups in MyPlate (fruits, vegetables, grains, milk, meat, and beans) to narrow their questions. Students who haven't yet guessed correctly can be given a few more minutes to try more questions. When time is called, all students should look at their cards. To end the activity, students should group their foods according to MyPlate. Foods like pizza and vegetable soup provide an opportunity to discuss combination foods that fit into more than one category.

ASSESSMENT | For an assessment task, play another round of the game, with students writing the food names and taping them to other students' backs. Students might enjoy trying a different configuration, such as a circle within a circle (outside circle facing in, inside circle facing out), moving around the circle to talk with different partners on a signal. Encourage students to write foods that are more difficult to guess this time (sweet potato, sushi, tamale, croissant). For assessment criteria, teachers can circulate and listen to students' questions to learn whether they have improved their skill at categorizing foods. For example, rather than asking, "Is it cookies, is it cake, is it candy?" students might ask, "Is it in the fruit group? Is it a bright color? Is it round? Is it orange?" (Construct: Attitudes toward behavior.)

Grades 6–8

Portion Distortion!   The National Heart, Lung, and Blood Institute (NHLBI) features an educational tool called "Portion Distortion" (www.nhlbi.nih .gov/health/educational/wecan/portion/index.htm) that middle school students should find interesting. The website includes slide shows that students can download to see how portion sizes of foods (bagels, cheeseburgers, French fries, soda) have changed during the past twenty years—and the changes in number of calories that have come with the distortions! Students also can download serving size cards to remind them of what a serving looks like (Figure 6–5). Teachers also can explore NHLBI's "We Can!" link on ways to enhance children's activity and nutrition.

ASSESSMENT | For an assessment task, students can collect various containers (clean, empty, washed) that they purchase foods in that often are thought of as a "serving" (popcorn box or bucket from the movies; other bags, boxes, bottles, cups, cans). Using the information on the serving size cards and the food labels, students can find "portion distortion" in their everyday lives. For assessment criteria, students should be able to show at least one portion distortion and contrast it with an actual serving size. Students should provide accurate information and draw conclusions about connections between behaviors and health. (Construct: Attitudes toward behavior.)

Serving Size Card:
Cut out and fold on the dotted line. Laminate for longtime use.

1 Serving Looks Like . . .	1 Serving Looks Like . . .
Grain Products	**Vegetables and Fruit**
1 cup of cereal flakes = fist	1/2 cup of fresh fruit = 1/2 baseball
1 pancake = compact disc	1 cup of salad greens = baseball
1/2 cup of cooked rice, pasta, or potato = 1/2 baseball	1 baked potato = fist
1 slice of bread = cassette tape	1 med. fruit = baseball
1 piece of cornbread = bar of soap	1/4 cup of raisins = large egg

1 Serving Looks Like . . .	1 Serving Looks Like . . .
Dairy and Cheese	**Meat and Alternatives**
1 1/2 oz. cheese = 4 stacked dice or 2 cheese slices	3 oz. meat, fish, and poultry = deck of cards
1/2 cup of ice cream = 1/2 baseball	3 oz. grilled/baked fish = checkbook
Fats	
1 tsp. margarine or spreads = 1 die	2 Tbsp. peanut butter = ping-pong ball

FIGURE 6–5 | **Portion Size Card**

SOURCE: National Heart, Lung, and Blood Institute, http://hin.nhlbi.nih.gov/portion/servingcard7.pdf.

Menu Planning Online Middle school students can work with the NHLBI online Menu Planner (www.nhlbi.nih.gov/health/educational/lose_wt/menuplanner.html), starting with a number of planned calories for a day and working through a series of food selections for different meals. The website keeps track of calories for the day as the students plan their meals.

ASSESSMENT | For an assessment task, students can work in pairs to plan menus for a day on the website and then share their work with others in the class. For assessment criteria, students should explain what they learned about healthy eating and menu planning, providing accurate information and drawing conclusions about connections between behaviors and health. (Construct: Attitudes toward behavior.)

NHES 2 | Analyze Influences

Students will analyze the influence of family, peers, culture, media, technology, and other factors on health behaviors.

ASSESSMENT CRITERIA
- Identify both external and internal influences on health.
- Explain how external and internal influences interact to impact health choices and behaviors.
- Explain both positive and negative influences, as appropriate.

Grades K–2

Pinkalicious—What Influences Our Food Choices? *Pinkalicious* (see book list at end of chapter), by Victoria Kann and Elizabeth Kann, provides a fanciful way to introduce the idea of influences on food choices. Pinkalicious eats so many pink cupcakes that she wakes up with pink hair and skin. Though the little girl is delighted with her new color, her mother takes her to the doctor, who describes a variety of healthy foods to help her return to normal. Teachers can pair this book with *A Bad Case of Stripes,* by David Shannon, which also involves food choices and appearance.

ASSESSMENT | *Pinkalicious* can lead to investigations of foods of many different colors. For an assessment task, students can categorize foods according to colors and select their favorites for a healthy eating plan. For assessment criteria, students can identify the factors that influence their selections of favorites (color, family or friends' preferences, taste). (Construct: Perceived behavioral control.)

Cultural and Family Celebrations with Food Foods play an integral role in cultural and family celebrations and traditions of all kinds. Students can write stories and draw pictures about the celebrations and traditions in their families and cultures. Students might want to talk with their families about the significance and preparation of the foods they share. Children can share their artwork and stories with classmates. Children can explain who gathers, who prepares the food, and how they and family members feel during the celebrations and traditions. What do students like best about these times together? Teachers can help students think about how their celebrations and traditions influence their feelings about family, food, and well-being.

ASSESSMENT | The students' artwork and stories are the assessment task for this activity. For assessment criteria, students should explain how the celebrations and traditions make them feel (how they are influenced). (Construct: Subjective norms.)

An Eye-Level Investigation Children are eager consumers and often have an important influence on what their parents and caregivers buy. Teachers can challenge children to investigate advertising aimed at them. With parental permission (send a letter home), students can investigate the products placed on low shelves on their next trip to the grocery store. Where are the sugary cereals? Where are the candies? Where are the snack foods and sodas? Students might find that certain kinds of products are placed at their height and eye level. Students can discuss whether they found healthy or less healthy products (go, slow, or whoa foods) at their eye level. What conclusions do they draw about marketing to kids? Who does the marketing and why? How do children feel about being targeted this way?

ASSESSMENT | For an assessment task, students can report their findings to class members. For assessment criteria, students should name at least two places in the grocery store where they found products they thought were being targeted to kids. Students also should tell whether the placement makes the products more noticeable or inviting to kids. (Construct: Perceived behavioral control.)

Grades 3–5

Moods and Foods Teachers can introduce this activity with the book *How Are You Peeling? Foods with Moods,* by Saxton Freymann and Joost

Elffers. Students can list ten of their favorite foods on one side of a paper or poster. On the other side, students can write people, places, or feelings they associate with those foods. Students can assess their favorites in terms of the go, slow, and whoa concept. Can students think of healthier replacements for any of their favorites? If so, what people, places, or feelings do they associate with the replacements? Can they still make positive connections? Students can discuss the associations people often make between favorite foods and good feelings. Students can list ways to keep those positive feelings while choosing healthier foods (more "go" foods).

ASSESSMENT | The students' associations between foods and moods, people, and places are the assessment task for this activity. For assessment criteria, students should select one healthy choice or improvement and explain how to keep a positive association with that food. (Construct: Perceived behavioral control.)

Food That Fools You! Students can view a number of fast food, cereal, soda, and snack ads (many can be found on YouTube.com) and evaluate them for the advertising techniques described in Chapter 3. Students can explore "Food That Fools You" at National Geographic Kids (kids.national-geographic.com/explore/food-that-fools-you). Students will learn about tricks used by food stylists to make food look more appetizing in advertisements.

ASSESSMENT | For an assessment task, students can utilize some of these tricks for a photo shoot emphasizing a healthy snack. The photographed snacks can be used to create print advertisements or video commercials that include messages from the junk food ads they watched to "sell" their product to classmates. For assessment criteria, students should identify the advertisement techniques they are using and their potential influence on middle school consumers of health-related products. (Construct: Perceived behavioral control.)

Grades 6–8

Advertising Bites With parents' or caregivers' permission (send a letter home), students can watch television for a specific period of time (half hour or one hour) to collect information about food and beverage commercials. Teachers should remind students to watch only one channel the entire time they are collecting data. Teachers and students can make a data collection log to record the time of each commercial, what's being sold, and the advertising techniques used to make the product attractive (see Chapter 3). Students can report their findings and compare them with those of other class members. What conclusions can students draw about advertising techniques that target kids their age? Did students find any exaggerations or misrepresentations? Teachers can extend this activity by having students create and perform commercials for nutritious products (or to tell the truth about products that are not nutritious).

ASSESSMENT | The students' analysis of the commercials they watch is the assessment task for this activity. If students make commercials, these also can be used as an assessment task. For assessment criteria, students should identify two or more advertising techniques used in television and in commercials and tell how they can refute false advertising. (Construct: Perceived behavioral control.)

NHES 3 | Access Information, Products, and Services

Students will demonstrate the ability to access valid information and products and services to enhance health.

ASSESSMENT CRITERIA
- Access health information—Locate specific sources of health information, products, or services relevant to enhancing health in a given situation.

- Evaluate information sources—Explain the degree to which identified sources are valid, reliable, and appropriate as a result of evaluating each source.

Grades K–2

Sorting Foods for Healthy Eating To reinforce the activity "Go, Slow, and Whoa Foods" in NHES 1, core concepts, teachers can ask students and their families (send a letter home to parents and caregivers) to bring in empty, clean, or washed food containers of all kinds. Students then can sort the collection of containers into three large boxes or bags labeled "Go," "Slow," and "Whoa." (Students might enjoy decorating boxes with pictures and words to illustrate the kinds of foods they have discussed.) For example, students could place a skim or 1 percent milk carton in the "Go" box, a 2 percent milk carton in the "Slow" box, and a whole-milk container in the "Whoa" box. This activity generates discussion about foods and what's in them, which is where the learning takes place. If students are stuck on how to categorize a food, they can access more information by reading labels with their teacher or investigating the food online or in books.

ASSESSMENT | The students' categorization of foods is the assessment task for this activity. For assessment criteria, students should be able to explain their reasoning, providing accurate information and telling where they got their information about the foods. (Construct: Attitudes toward behavior.)

Kids Only—Fight Bac! The Partnership for Food Safety Education offers an engaging website for young students called Fight Bac! (www.fightbac.org/kidsfoodsafety) to help them understand the causes and prevention of food-borne illness. Students also can become food detectives to fight bacteria at www.fooddetectives.com. Teachers can download information and activities from the sites for students to work on and discuss in class.

ASSESSMENT | Students can create a video to share proper hand washing techniques before handling food. For assessment criteria, students should provide accurate information and explain a valid source of food safety information. (Construct: Attitudes toward behavior.)

Grades 3–5

What's Up with Vitamins and Minerals? Going Live to the Micronutrients. One of the book's authors remembers the drudgery of memorizing charts about vitamins and minerals as part of health and home economics classes—boring! How can teachers make this important information come alive for today's students? One solution is to have pairs of students select a vitamin or mineral to investigate and report on as an action news team to the rest of the class. Students can find out

- Where do we find it?
- What does it do for us?
- What happens if we don't get enough—or too much?

Teachers can encourage students to use their creativity (props, costumes, visuals, camcorders) to make their investigative reporting come alive. Students might enjoy the opportunity to video their presentations in advance and show them to the class via television. The schools' technology specialists could be enlisted to teach students how to use recording equipment.

ASSESSMENT | The students' action reports are the assessment task for this activity. For assessment criteria, students should tell where they got their information and why their information sources are reliable and valid. (Construct: Attitudes toward behavior.)

To Get the Facts, Read the Label! The U.S. Food and Drug Administration provides excellent resources for learning to read and use food labels at www.fda.gov/Food/LabelingNutrition/ucm274593.htm (click on "How to Understand and Use the Nutrition Facts Label"). Students and teachers can download sample labels and educational information. Kids' Health also provides information at kidshealth.org/kid/stay_healthy/food/labels.html. Students can work in pairs or small groups to explain a particular part of a food label to class members. Students and teachers should try to collect many food containers (empty, washed, clean, and dry) to show how to comparison shop for good nutrition. As an extension activity, students can bring in advertisements they find for particular food products and compare the promises in the ads with the facts of the nutrition label. Students can access and print food labels for almost any kind of food at www.nutritiondata.com.

ASSESSMENT | For an assessment task, students can compare two or more products (different kinds of cereals, milk, or snack foods) and explain their nutrition analysis to the class. For assessment criteria, students should provide accurate information on the best choice and explain why the food label provides valid information. (Construct: Attitudes toward behavior.)

Kids' Health on Nutrition Students and teachers can access information on nutrition from the Kids' Health website (www.kidshealth.org). By clicking on the kids' site, "Staying Healthy," and then on "Fabulous Food," students can learn more about food allergies, food groups, snacking, labels, dieting, and many other nutrition topics. Using the topics discussed on the site, students can select a research project and teach one another. Students can prepare a poster presentation on their topic for a poster session, during which a certain number of class members present their posters as others circulate around the room to view the posters and ask questions. Teachers might want to work with parents or caregivers to provide healthy snacks during the poster sessions.

ASSESSMENT | The posters the students prepare and present are the assessment task for this activity. For assessment criteria, students should provide accurate information, draw conclusions about connections between behaviors and health, and provide valid sources for their information. Students also might like to set their own criteria for "great posters." (Construct: Attitudes toward behavior.)

Grades 6–8

Chew on This—Investigating What Goes into Your Food. The following books (see list at end of chapter) provide a great kick-off for middle school students to access information about fast food:

- *Chew On This: Everything You Don't Want to Know About Fast Food* by Eric Schlosser and Charles Wilson.
- *Fast Food Nation* by Eric Schlosser.
- *Processed Food (What's In Your Food? Recipe for Disaster)* by Paula Johanson.

Middle school students can work in teams to select a fast food topic that they want to research and report on to classmates. Students may want to write and film their own mini-documentaries, based on viewing recent movies such as *Supersize Me* and *Fast Food Nation 2006.* They can focus especially on the amount of fat, sugar, and salt in the fast foods they choose. Students should collaborate to decide what makes a great presentation and use those criteria to assess themselves and their classmates.

ASSESSMENT | The investigation and report that students generate is the assessment task for this activity. For assessment criteria, students should identify the components of a thorough investigation and top-notch report for their own classroom. (Construct: Attitudes toward behavior.)

Nutrients in a Nutshell Students can access information on the six essential nutrients at Kids' Health by logging onto www.kidshealth.org and visiting "Food and Fitness" in the teen link. Students should work in

six groups to investigate and report on the six nutrients. They should identify criteria in advance for "great presentations." During their presentations, students should be able to make links between the grain, vegetable, fruit, meat and bean, and milk groups in MyPlate and essential nutrients.

ASSESSMENT | The presentations students make are the assessment task for this activity. Teachers and students can use the criteria that students identify for great presentations as the assessment criteria. At a minimum, students should provide accurate information, draw conclusions about connections between behaviors and health, and explain their valid sources of information. (Construct: Attitudes toward behavior.)

See the Label with NutritionData.Com The NutritionData website (www.nutritiondata.com) provides a fantastic opportunity for students to learn about healthy eating by accessing Nutrition Facts labels for foods of all kinds. When students visit the Nutrition Facts and Calorie Counter home page, they can select among a tremendous number of foods for analysis, including brand-name foods, fresh fruits and vegetables, and restaurant foods. The site provides a Nutrition Facts label and other information that students can print to learn about foods of interest. Making food comparisons is a breeze with this Web tool.

ASSESSMENT | For an assessment task, students can access labels on a wide variety of favorite foods. For assessment criteria, students should summarize what they've learned about the nutritional value of their favorite foods and present their information to classmates, including where they found valid information. (Construct: Attitudes toward behavior.)

NHES 4 | Interpersonal Communication

Students will demonstrate the ability to use interpersonal communication skills to enhance health and avoid or reduce health risks.

ASSESSMENT CRITERIA

- Use appropriate verbal/nonverbal communication strategies in an effective manner to enhance health or avoid/reduce health risks.
- Use appropriate skills (negotiation skills, refusal skills) and behaviors (eye contact, body language, attentive listening).

Grades K–2

Green Eggs and Ham: **Food Poetry** Students can practice their communication skills to enhance their nutrition health by writing, illustrating, and reading couplets or poems to classmates. The focus of their writing should be on politely refusing less nutritious foods and/or politely requesting foods that are more nutritious. Children can write their poems individually or in small groups. Teachers can use the book *Green Eggs and Ham,* by Dr. Seuss, to introduce this activity. Children can read their poems and share their illustrations with classmates. Teachers can post the poems and illustrations in the classroom.

ASSESSMENT | Having students present their poems and illustrations to classmates is the assessment task for this activity. For assessment criteria, students should use verbal and nonverbal (illustrations) communication to creatively request or refuse foods. (Constructs: Perceived behavioral control, attitudes toward behavior.)

Grades 3–5

Is That All We Have for a Snack? Learning how to communicate with parents and other trusted adults about food choices becomes important for students as they develop preferences, understand nutrition, and desire to take greater control over their eating. Since parents and caregivers of students this age are typically doing the food shopping, learning to politely request foods that are more nutritious and refuse less nutritious foods becomes an important skill for students to develop. Brainstorm with students requests they might wish to make of their parents or caregivers regarding food and write them on slips of paper. Discuss strategies for communicating politely with adults. Have students draw one of the request slips and, with a partner, practice making polite requests of an adult.

ASSESSMENT | Have pairs of students select a different situation. Together they are to create a cartoon strip capturing the conversation between the student and the adult. Students can share their comic strips and the teacher can post them around the classroom. For assessment criteria, appropriate verbal and nonverbal communication strategies should be demonstrated. (Constructs: Perceived behavioral control, attitudes toward behavior.)

Grades 6–8

Bet You Can't Eat Just One! Responding to Pressures to Overeat Teachers can begin this activity by asking students to think of times they have been pressured to overeat by friends, family, or peers. Using these ideas, students and teachers can develop a list of pressure lines to overeat, for example:

"Go ahead and eat up! You can eat healthy tomorrow."

"One more won't hurt—you don't have a weight problem."

"Bet you can't eat just one—Cindy made these herself!"

"Stop being so silly. We're all having dessert!"

"Don't spoil the fun. Just have a bite!"

"I've been cooking all day for this dinner. You mean you aren't going to have more?"

"Now, Sherry, you know that children are starving in other parts of the world. Clean your plate like Susan did!"

Next, students can use different kinds of refusal skills (see Chapter 3) to eat only what they want to eat. The important idea is that students decide for themselves what they want to eat, rather than being pressured into poor choices by others.

ASSESSMENT | The pressure lines and refusal skills students demonstrate are the assessment task for this activity. For assessment criteria, students should be able to demonstrate refusals in at least three different ways. (Construct: Perceived behavioral control.)

NHES 5 | Decision Making

Students will demonstrate the ability to use decision-making skills to enhance health.

ASSESSMENT CRITERIA

Reach a health-enhancing decision using a process consisting of the following steps:
- Identify a health-risk situation.
- Examine alternatives.
- Evaluate positive and negative consequences.
- Decide on a health-enhancing course of action.

Grades K–2

The Peanut-Free Café—What Are Food Allergies? This picture book by Gloria Koster and Maryann Cocca-Leffler (see book list at end of chapter) provides a great opportunity to discuss food allergies. A new student who has a peanut allergy comes to Nutley Elementary. Principal Filbert makes a peanut-free lunch table, and anyone who has a

peanut-free lunch can eat there. At first, the student sits there alone, but other students join in to make a peanut-free café that features snacks, arts, and crafts. Children learn about the seriousness of food allergies and how they can support each other for good health.

ASSESSMENT | For an assessment, students can work in small groups to survey their friends, family members, and teachers to learn whether any of them have food allergies. Using the survey results, students can investigate the different types of food allergies identified. They should then work through the decision-making process to determine various strategies for helping safely manage the food allergies in the classroom and cafeteria. Groups should present their recommendations to the class. The class could then determine which options are reasonable for the situations and help classmates make health-enhancing decisions related to their food allergies. For assessment criteria, students give accurate information (NHES 1), identify a health-risk situation, examine alternatives, evaluate positive and negative consequences, and decide on a health-enhancing course of action. (Constructs: Attitudes toward behavior, perceived behavioral control, intention to act in healthful ways.)

Decision Making About Healthy Class Celebrations Children often want to celebrate birthdays or other special occasions at school by bringing treats. When children are invited to participate in the decision-making process, they often are more willing to try something new and will potentially consider healthy options. Teachers can engage students in a decision-making process to determine what types of food items can be brought in to celebrate birthdays or other special occasions to encourage healthy eating.

ASSESSMENT | In small groups, students can go through a simple decision-making process to determine healthy options when the class deserves a celebration. Groups can present their final decisions to the class. Teachers should facilitate a discussion to evaluate the decisions and determine which should be considered for celebration opportunities. For assessment criteria, students should examine alternatives, evaluate positive and negative consequences, and decide on a health-enhancing course of action. (Constructs: Perceived behavioral control, attitudes toward behavior.)

Milk Matters The National Institute of Child Health and Human Development initiated a Calcium Education Campaign, *Milk Matters,* to increase calcium consumption among children and teens. The simple message is "Calcium is critical to our health." Teachers can find more information at www.nichd.nih.gov/milk/. The Kids' Page (www.nichd.nih .gov/milk/kids/kidsteens.cfm) offers games and activities to engage children in learning about and increasing their calcium intake with the character "Bo Vine."

ASSESSMENT | For an assessment task, students can brainstorm ways to get more calcium into their diets. Students can decide on one idea to try and set a goal to follow their strategy for one week and report back to the class. For assessment criteria, students should be able to explain what their decision is (which strategy to try) and why they made that decision. Students also can name supports for and barriers to putting their decision into practice as a goal. (Note: If some students don't have access to a variety of foods, teachers can focus this activity on increasing calcium intake during the school meal programs.) (Construct: Intention to act in healthy ways.)

Grades 3–5

Fiber Up Your Cereal Decisions. Elementary and middle school students often eat cereal for breakfast. In addition to being high in sugar, some cereals that students commonly choose are quite low in fiber. Teachers can challenge students to collect nutrition information panels from cereal boxes from home and the web to help make decisions on

Planting a class garden can help students build decision-making and goal-setting skills as well as teach them more about the foods they eat.

©Simon Hadley/Alamy Stock Photo

One additional group of students can investigate cholesterol and its relation to saturated fat in the diet. Students should also note that "no cholesterol" claims on some food labels are misleading, because plant-based foods don't have cholesterol to begin with!

ASSESSMENT | The investigations and reports students create are the assessment task for this activity. For assessment criteria, students should provide accurate information that classmates need to make healthy choices about the fat in their diet.

"No White at Night" and Other Questionable Advice on Carbohydrates. Carbohydrates are in the news, too, and students wonder what they should eat for good health and healthy body weight. Popular advice abounds (such as no white at night, which means no white bread, pasta, or potatoes in the evening), but how can students and adults make sense of it? As with other nutrition topics, students enjoy investigating and learning from each other more than being lectured to by adults. For this topic, students might investigate

- Simple sugars
- Complex carbohydrates
- Starchy" carbs
- Sweeteners
- Fruits and fruit juices
- The glycemic index

Teachers and students can find a great resource in *The Complete Idiot's Guide to Total Nutrition* by Joy Bauer. This book, in its fourth edition, contains the basics about nutrition, written in an engaging format that everyone can understand.

ASSESSMENT | As with other similar activities, the investigations and reports the students complete are the assessment task. From a decision-making standpoint, students should provide accurate information that classmates need to make healthy choices. (Construct: Intention to act in healthy ways.)

NHES 6 | Goal Setting

Students will demonstrate the ability to use goal-setting skills to enhance health.

ASSESSMENT CRITERIA
- Goal statement—Give goal statement that identifies health benefits; goal is achievable and will result in enhanced health.
- Goal setting plan—Show plan that is complete, logical, and sequential, and includes a process to assess progress.

Grades K–2

Eat More of This, Less of That: Goal Setting for Healthy Eating Quackenbush, Telljohann, and Kane[50] recommend using the concept of "more of this, less of that" when encouraging children to eat nutritiously. While formal goal setting regarding nutrition may be more than students this age are capable of, mainly due to the lack of control over food options made available by adults, they are able to begin the process of charting food choices and be purposeful in increasing the amount of nutritious foods they are selecting and decreasing the foods that do not provide as

which cereals deliver the best taste and nutrition at the same time. As part of their research, students can investigate soluble (dissolves readily in water) and insoluble fiber and learn more about the foods in which these two types of fiber are found. Students might also want to conduct a taste test of different kinds of cereals and compare taste and nutrition value, including fiber, for each. Which of the cereals list whole grain as the first ingredient? Is there a lot of sugar? Is there partially hydrogenated or *trans* fat in the cereal? What cereal is most nutritious and most appealing at the same time?

ASSESSMENT | For an assessment task, students can work through the steps of a simple decision-making process to choose a nutritious, good tasting cereal.

- What's the problem?
- What are the alternatives?
- What are the consequences, positive and negative?
- What's the action the class recommends?
- What's their evaluation of their choices?

For assessment criteria, students should be able to work through all the steps to make a health-enhancing choice. (Construct: Intention to act in healthy ways.)

Grades 6–8

Getting the Scoop on Fats—Butter, Margarine, or Neither? Information about fats sometimes confuses adults as well as young people. As students prepare to investigate the topic of fat, teachers should remember that health education is not a chemistry class. Students need to know how different types of fats affect them, where the fats are found, and the amount that is recommended. Fat performs important functions in the body, but all fats are not created equal. Students can break into groups to find out more about and report to classmates on

- Triglycerides
- Monosaturated fats
- Polyunsaturated fats (check out the omega-3 fatty acids in fish)
- Saturated fats
- *Trans*-fatty acids

much nutritional value. Teachers can lead students in a brief assessment of the foods they eat over a two-day period. Based on the assessments students can make a goal to eat more of a certain food group, and less of another based on nutritional benefits. Students should brainstorm strategies that will help them meet their nutrition goal and identify things that might make it difficult to make this choice on a daily basis. Teachers should lead students in regularly assessing their progress toward eating "more of this, less of that."

ASSESSMENT | The student plan for eating "more of this, less of that" is the assessment for this activity. For assessment criteria, children should make a clear plan, identify potential obstacles and strategies to overcome them, and identify how to assess progress. (Constructs: Perceived behavioral control, intention to act in healthy ways.)

Plant a Garden Children can work on the goal of planning, planting, and harvesting a class garden. Children can brainstorm the kinds of foods they would like to grow and investigate (search the Internet, talk with an expert, consult gardening books) the kinds of foods that are feasible to grow for the time of year and soil in the community. The class can make their selections, design and draw out a plan for their garden, and decide on all the jobs class members will need to do to tend the garden (preparing the soil, planting, protecting the plants, watering, weeding, checking weather reports, and harvesting). Small groups of students can take responsibility for different sections of the garden and make a written plan for their work. Teachers can schedule a regular time in the week for garden work and have children keep a class journal about their garden. Children can celebrate the achievement of the class goal by preparing and eating the foods they have grown.

ASSESSMENT | Completing the class journal and garden are the assessment tasks for this activity. For assessment criteria, children should make a clear plan for their garden with achievable steps, identify potential obstacles (not enough rain, small-animal invasion) and strategies to overcome them, and specify a way to assess progress. (Construct: Perceived behavioral control.)

Grades 3–5

Healthy Habits for Families Students can talk in small groups about a healthy nutrition goal they would like to set with their families. Their goals should be clear, achievable, and measurable. Students should think about supports for and barriers to reaching their family goal. Students also should design a simple assessment plan for a given period of time. Students can take their goals home to get family input and to find out whether their families would be willing to try to reach the goal for a given period of time. Students can report back to the class on their progress.

ASSESSMENT | The students' plans and reports are the assessment task for this activity. For assessment criteria, students should be able to demonstrate the steps in goal setting (making a plan with specific steps, identifying supports and obstacles, assessing progress). (Constructs: Intention to act in healthy ways, subjective norms.)

Grades 6–8

Nutrition Behavior Change Project Students should identify one specific nutrition behavior they want to change or improve. For example, some students may routinely skip breakfast, have a soda every day after school, or eat no fruit on most days of the week. As part of their goal setting, students should write a clear, measurable goal for a specific amount of time (two weeks), specific steps to achieve their goal, plans to build support from others and overcome potential barriers, and a plan to assess progress. Students can keep a diary or journal for a specific period of time and report back to the class on their experiences.

ASSESSMENT | The goal-setting plan and food tracker are the assessment tasks for this activity. There are many food tracking apps and websites available. Students can choose an app to download or a website to track their food choices for a specific period of time. After tracking their food choices, students can evaluate their behaviors with the set goal. Discuss how the app or website helped the students make different choices and achieve their goals. For assessment criteria, students should demonstrate their ability to fulfill all the steps in goal setting (goal, steps, support, obstacles, plan to assess progress) over a specific period of time. (Constructs: Intention to act in healthy ways, perceived behavioral control.)

Building on Supports and Overcoming Barriers An important part of achieving a goal is identifying and making plans to deal with supports and barriers. Supports are those people, places, beliefs, conditions, circumstances, and cues that help people achieve a goal. For example, a friend who goes walking with you each day is a support. Barriers are those things that make achieving a goal more difficult—discouraging words from a family member, little personal belief that the goal can be achieved, conditions, and circumstances. For example, going out for a run in the southern United States is difficult in August because of the heat and humidity. Students can identify a healthy eating goal they would like to work toward and at least one support they can build on and one barrier they need to plan to overcome. Students can keep a journal during the course of working toward their goal to track their responses to supports and barriers.

ASSESSMENT | For an assessment task, students can report on their progress in terms of supports for and barriers to their goal periodically throughout the goal period. For assessment criteria, students should be able to tell at least two ways they've dealt with each support or barrier and describe the progress they've made as a result. (Construct: Intention to act in healthy ways.)

NHES 7 | Self-Management

Students will demonstrate the ability to practice health-enhancing behaviors and avoid or reduce health risks.

ASSESSMENT CRITERIA

- Application (transfer)—Initiate health-enhancing behaviors; apply concepts and skills appropriate and effectively.
- Self-monitoring and reflection—Monitor actions and make adjustments; accept feedback and make adjustments; able to self-assess, reflect on, and take responsibility for actions.

Grades K–2

Preparing Healthy Snacks Kids' Health (www.kidshealth.org) offers healthy snacks that kids can make or help make (with an adult assistant). The list includes peanut butter muffins, frozen yogurt pops, veggie bowls, smoothies, and many other kid-friendly snacks. Students and teachers can make healthy snacks in the classroom, with the help of parent assistants, if needed. Alternatively, students can download recipes to try at home or to bring from home for classmates to try. Be sure to check on student allergies.

ASSESSMENT | For an assessment task, students can describe their favorite choices for healthy snacks and what makes them healthy. For assessment criteria, students should explain the self-management skills they use to eat a healthy snack rather than a junk food snack. (Construct: Perceived behavioral control.)

Bread and Jam for Frances **and Other Picky Eaters** Helping students try new healthy foods and snacks is a big part of teaching self-management for healthy eating. Teachers can use popular children's books, like *Bread*

and Jam for Frances by Russell Hoban, to talk about trying different foods. In this story, Frances turns up her nose at any food other than bread and jam—so her mother gives her bread and jam at every meal. Frances soon realizes that variety is the spice of life. Other books with similar themes (see the book list at the end of the chapter) include

- *Gladys Goes Out to Lunch*, by Derek Anderson
- *I Will Never NOT EVER Eat a Tomato*, by Lauren Child
- *Little Pea*, by Amy Krouse Rosenthal
- *Picky Peggy*, by Jennifer Dussling
- *Princess Penelope Hates Peas: A Tale of Picky Eating and Avoiding Catastrophes*, by Susan D. Sweet
- *Sweet Tooth*, by Margie Palatini
- *Tales for Picky Eaters,* by Josh Schneider
- *Yoko*, by Rosemary Wells

ASSESSMENT | For an assessment task, students can sample and write about trying one new food during the week (in the cafeteria, during a classroom tasting party, at home). Teachers might want to have a tasting party at school because some children might not have access to a variety of foods at home. For assessment criteria, students should give at least two reasons why trying new foods can help them grow healthy. (Construct: Perceived behavioral control.)

Grades 3–5

Recipe Doctor: Update a Family Favorite   Students and teachers can bring in recipes from home to update for good health. Students can work in small groups of "Recipe Doctors" to examine the ingredients in recipes for possible substitutions to make foods healthier. The Mayo Clinic article "Healthy Recipes: A Guide to Ingredient Substitutions" is available by searching the title on the Internet. This article recommends strategies to reduce the amount of fat, sugar, and sodium. The site also contains substitution ideas, such as using extra-lean ground beef, chicken, or turkey in place of regular ground beef. If facilities permit, let students cook some of their improved recipes for a taste-testing party, or have students cook them at home with their families and bring the products to try in class.

ASSESSMENT | The students' improved recipes are the assessment task for this activity. For assessment criteria, students should explain the strategies they used and the reasons why the strategies make the recipes healthier. (Construct: Perceived behavioral control.)

Eating Breakfast—the Right Stuff   Students might have heard that breakfast is the most important meal of the day. Breakfast is the fuel that gets people going after a long night of sleep. Many students are in a hurry in the morning, but eating breakfast is important for everyone. Kids' Health (www.kidshealth.org) suggests a range of ideas for a healthy breakfast at the link "Ready, Set, Breakfast!" It includes traditional foods such as cereal, toast, and eggs as well as choices such as breakfast tacos, sandwiches, and banana dogs. Students can volunteer other ideas for breakfast that they eat at home or are interested in trying. Students can set a goal of eating breakfast every day for a week, whether at school or at home. For example, they might need to make sure they get up early enough to eat breakfast at home or get to school early enough to eat breakfast at school. This activity links to NHES 5 and 6, decision making and goal setting. Teachers might also work with parents to have a special "breakfast at school day," for which teachers, students, and parents or caregivers contribute different types of foods.

ASSESSMENT | For an assessment task, students can discuss various self-management steps they need to take to be sure they eat breakfast, whether at home or at school. For assessment criteria, students should select one self-management strategy to try for the week and report back to the class

on their progress. (Note: This activity is based on the assumption that all students have access to breakfast, at home or through the School Breakfast Program. If this is not the case, teachers should talk with school administrators about being certain that all students have access to breakfast.) (Construct: Perceived behavioral control.)

Smart Ways to Quench Your Thirst   *Dietary Guidelines for Americans* recommends that children consume beverages with few added sugars or caloric sweeteners (sugars and syrups added to foods at the table or during processing or preparation, such as high-fructose corn syrup). The National Heart, Lung, and Blood Institute recommends selecting beverages this way:

- *Almost anytime or "go" drinks:* water, fat-free and 1 percent milk, diet soda, diet and unsweetened iced teas and lemonade
- *Sometimes or "slow" drinks:* 2 percent milk, 100 percent fruit juice, sports drinks
- *Once in a while or "whoa" drinks:* whole milk, regular soda, drinks with added sugar, fruit drinks with less than 100 percent fruit juice

The best choices for children and adolescents are skim and 1 percent milk, water, and 100 percent fruit juice. (Note: 100 percent juice may not be appropriate for children who are diabetic.) Although artificial sweeteners are considered generally safe when consumed as part of a balanced diet, researchers disagree on their appropriateness for children. Students can set goals of drinking more healthy drinks—and less soda of any kind—to link self-management to NHES 5 and 6, decision making and goal setting. Teachers and parents will be interested to know that major soft drink companies (Coca-Cola and PepsiCo) recommend that schools not sell carbonated drinks in elementary schools during the school day. Further guidelines include making juices, water, and other products available where soft drinks are sold, at the same price.

ASSESSMENT | For an assessment task, students can keep track of everything they drink for five days (a school week). Students can combine their data to make a graph of class beverage consumption. Students can set individual or class goals to increase consumption of healthy drinks (water, skim or 1 percent milk, 100 percent juice) during the next week. For assessment criteria, students should report on the progress they made in increasing their consumption of healthy drinks and identify supports for and barriers to reaching their goals. Students also should identify at least two self-management strategies they used to increase healthy beverage consumption. (Construct: Perceived behavioral control.)

Grades 6–8

Eat This Not That!   Teachers should present a lesson on strategies for making eating out more nutritious. Concepts that might be addressed in the lesson include splitting a meal, ordering a smaller portion size, choosing a diet drink, or eliminating mayonnaise and other calorie-rich condiments. Use the "Fast Food Alert" lesson from Health Powered Kids (www.healthpoweredkids.org/lessons/fast-food-alert). This lesson provides information about making healthy choices and links to the nutritional information for common fast food chains. Doing an Internet search, students can find menus and the nutritional information for many restaurant chains. Have pairs of students use the nutritional concepts discussed throughout the unit and this lesson on eating out to create a blog post.

ASSESSMENT | The blog post that student pairs create is the assessment task. Students should create tips for making smart choices when eating at their top five favorite restaurants. Posts can be uploaded to the Internet or shared with classmates. Pairs can present their books to the class. Assessment criteria include applying nutrition concepts appropriately and effectively

Water, fat-free or 1 percent milk, and sometimes 100 percent fruit juice are the best beverage choices for children and adolescents.

©Creatas/PunchStock

to restaurant eating situations. (Constructs: Perceived behavioral control, intention to act in healthy ways.)

Kids' Health on Teen Dieting Adolescents often worry about their body size and weight. The Kids' Health website (www.kidshealth.org) has some helpful information for students who believe they need to lose weight. Topics include evaluating one's weight and different types of diets and dietary supplements. Students can work in pairs or small groups to learn more about a topic related to healthy body weight.

ASSESSMENT | For an assessment task, students can create a game show (*Jeopardy, Wheel of Fortune*) or another television show format (news, talk show) to teach classmates about their topic. For assessment criteria, students should provide accurate information about three or more self-management tips for safe and healthy ways to maintain healthy body weight. (Construct: Perceived behavioral control.)

Powerful Bones, Powerful Girls The National Bone Health Campaign has a website through the Centers for Disease Control and Prevention called "Powerful Girls Have Powerful Bones" (www.girlshealth.gov/nutrition/bonehealth/eating-for-strong-bones.html). At this site, girls (and boys) can learn about how to build strong bones through a healthy diet and weight-bearing physical activities. The site features games, quizzes, and a dictionary of key concepts. (Additional information is available at other girls' health websites; see the list at the end of this chapter.)

ASSESSMENT | For an assessment task, students can make a list of tips for bone health. For assessment criteria, students should explain how to practice at least three self-management strategies for healthy and strong bones. (Construct: Perceived behavioral control.)

NHES 8 | Advocacy

Students will demonstrate the ability to advocate for personal, family, and community health.

ASSESSMENT CRITERIA

- Health-enhancing position—Give clear, health-enhancing position.
- Support for position—Support position with facts, concepts, examples, and evidence.
- Audience awareness—Show awareness of target audience; choose words, tone, and examples to suit audience.
- Conviction—Display conviction for position.

Grades K–2

Building MyPlate: Trying New Foods Teachers can challenge students to try new healthy foods and share their experiences with classmates. Students can help create a large bulletin board of MyPlate (www.choosemyplate.gov). When students try a new food, they can cut out a picture or make a drawing of the food to add to the bulletin board in the appropriate category. In this way, students can make a public statement about their openness to trying new foods and have a positive influence on classmates. (Note: If some students don't have access to a variety of foods, teachers can make sure new foods are introduced during the school day as healthy snacks and for tasting parties.)

ASSESSMENT | The MyPlate students create is the assessment task for this activity. For assessment criteria, all students should try at least two new foods during the course of the activity and make a health-enhancing statement about trying new foods. (Constructs: Subjective norms, perceived behavioral control.)

Fruit and Vegetable School Is Now in Session The Produce for Better Health Foundation (pbhfoundation.org/pub_sec/edu) promotes fruit and vegetable consumption for adequate intake of vitamins, minerals, and phytochemicals. The site includes links both for educators and for kids. Teachers can teach healthy habits with "There's a Rainbow on My Plate," which includes lesson ideas and recipes. Students can participate in "Pack Assorted Colors for Kids," which encourages kids to eat more fruits and vegetables at home and school.

ASSESSMENT | For an assessment task, students can use the Five a Day tracker to monitor their fruit and vegetable intake. Teachers, cafeteria managers, administrators, and parents can help ensure that all students have the opportunity to eat and sample more fruits and vegetables during the campaign (and after). For assessment criteria, students should develop a health-enhancing message about eating fruits and vegetables. (Construct: Intention to act in healthy ways.)

Grades 3–5

Sharing My Opinion At the end of a nutrition unit, have students select a healthy behavior outcome (HBO) they feel strongly about, such as eating a variety of foods, drinking plenty of water, eating breakfast every day, or limiting foods and beverages high in added sugars, solid fat, and sodium. Discuss with students why this behavior is important to them and ask with whom they would like to share what they have learned—their parents, younger siblings, or classmates. Ask students to select a behavior and state their opinion in one sentence. As a class, discuss how writers support their arguments and opinions with reasons. Ask students to identify three to five reasons that support their opinion statement. Use questioning to help them develop their reasons, such as why do they feel a certain way? Encourage students to use credible sources to find additional information to support their ideas. Have students combine the sentences to write a persuasive text and share with the class.

ASSESSMENT | Once students have shared their ideas and received feedback from their peers, they can create an edited persuasive text for their target audience stating why the chosen behavior is important along with supporting evidence. The persuasive text is the assessment task. For assessment criteria, students should state a positive position, back it up with evidence, design the text to appeal to their target audience, and show strong conviction about the importance of the behavior. (Constructs: Intention to act in healthy ways, attitudes toward behavior, perceived behavioral control.)

Vitamin and Mineral Personalities Many teachers remember memorizing charts about vitamins and minerals. We may remember the memorizing itself more than what we learned. To learn about vitamins and minerals, students can make "sandwich boards" to wear at school on a given day. Students can choose the vitamin or mineral they want to portray and design their signs accordingly.

ASSESSMENT | The students' signs are the assessment task for this activity. For assessment criteria, students should design a clear message, back it up with facts, target their audience, and show strong conviction. (Constructs: Attitudes toward behavior, subjective norms.)

Grades 6–8

Healthy Nutrition Messages Select, or have students select, a healthy behavior outcome from this unit, such as eat breakfast every day or eat a variety of foods within each food group every day. With this behavior in mind, have pairs of students develop a digital advocacy message (e.g., iMovie, Keynote, PowerPoint, or other accessible tools) for younger students of an identified grade level. The class should discuss what would make a message meaningful to the grade level of students selected (e.g., use of pictures, simple words, type of message). Teams should then prepare a storyboard of their message that will be turned into a digital product.

ASSESSMENT | The digital advocacy message appropriate for a selected audience will serve as the assessment task. The assessment criteria should include the statement of a health-enhancing position and the message should be persuasive and meaningful to the target audience. (Construct: Subjective norms.)

Fight Bac! Campaign—Clean, Separate, Chill, and Cook Students and teachers can use materials from the Partnership for Food Safety Education (www.fightbac.org). Students can learn to keep foods safe from bacteria and advocate for others to do the same. Students can teach about the four steps (clean, separate, chill, and cook), safe produce handling, and food-borne illnesses. Students might want to put their performing arts and puppetry skills to work to help the Fight Bac! characters come alive at school. Students can meet Bac in Figure 6–6.

Keep Food Safe From Bacteria™

FIGURE 6–6 | **Food Safety** Children can be encouraged to take steps to prevent food-borne illness

SOURCE: Partnership for Food Safety Education, www.fightbac.org. Used with permission.

ASSESSMENT | The campaign students plan and carry out is the assessment task for this activity. For assessment criteria, students should have a clear, health-enhancing message, back it up with facts, target their audience, and show strong conviction. (Constructs: Intention to act in healthy ways, subjective norms.)

Raps for Nutrition Students can work in small groups to create a rap, poem, or song about a particular nutrient, one of the food groups in MyPlate, the *Dietary Guidelines for Americans*, food labels, or the importance of a healthy diet as part of a healthy lifestyle. Students should include factual information (NHES 1, core concepts) and a persuasive message for healthy dietary practices. To help get students thinking, show them some sample raps or songs found through a simple Internet search. One example is this Music Video from Hawaii 5210, a community organization dedicated to promoting healthy eating and active living to prevent childhood obesity (https://www.youtube.com/watch?v=qXu2XJUSedk).

ASSESSMENT | The raps, poems, or songs students create are the assessment task for this activity. For assessment criteria, students should provide a clear advocacy message, back it up with facts, target their audience, and perform with conviction. (Constructs: Intention to act in healthy ways, subjective norms.)

EVALUATED CURRICULA AND INSTRUCTIONAL MATERIALS

The Centers for Disease Control and Prevention provides Registries of Programs Effective in Reducing Youth Risk Behaviors at www.cdc.gov/healthyyouth/adolescenthealth/registries.htm. Various federal agencies have identified youth-related programs that they consider worthy of recommendation on the basis of expert opinion or a review of design and research evidence. These programs focus on different health topics, risk behaviors, and settings. Some, but not all, of these programs have shown evidence in reducing youth risk behaviors. Each agency has its own process and criteria for determining the programs that are worthy of recommendation. Users are encouraged to review each website to understand the inclusion criteria the registry used. Registries related to healthy eating include:

RTIPs (Research-Tested Intervention Programs, http://rtips.cancer.gov/rtips/index.do) is a searchable database of cancer control interventions and program materials and is designed to provide program planners and public health practitioners easy and immediate access to research-tested materials. Educators can select from fifteen intervention programs related to diet and nutrition, such as:

- Coordinated Approach to Child Health (CATCH)
- Eat Well and Keep Moving
- Five-A-Day Power Plus
- Middle School Physical Activity and Nutrition (MSPAN)

INTERNET AND OTHER RESOURCES

WEBSITES

Academy of Nutrition and Dietetics
www.eatright.org

CDC Healthy Youth: Nutrition, Physical Activity, and Obesity
www.cdc.gov/healthyyouth/npao/index.htm

Choose MyPlate.gov
www.choosemyplate.gov

Dietary Guidelines for Americans
www.health.gov/dietaryguidelines

Fast Food Nutrition Facts
www.fastfoodnutrition.org

Fruits and Veggies: More Matters
www.fruitsandveggiesmorematters.org

National Dairy Council
www.nationaldairycouncil.org

Nutrition Facts Label Programs & Materials
www.fda.gov/Food/LabelingNutrition/ucm20026097.htm

Partnership for Food Safety Education
www.fightbac.org

OTHER RESOURCES

Action for Healthy Kids. *The Learning Connection: The Value of Improving Nutrition and Physical Activity in Our Schools* (www.ActionForHealthyKids.org; 2004)

Action for Healthy Kids. *The Learning Connection: What You Need to Know to Ensure Your Kids Are Healthy and Ready to Learn* (www.actionforhealthykids.org/media-center/reports)

Action for Healthy Kids. *Progress or Promises? What's Working For and Against Healthy Schools* (www.ActionForHealthyKids.org; 2008)

Centers for Disease Control and Prevention. *School Nutrition* (www.cdc.gov/healthyschools/nutrition/schoolnutrition.htm)

Institute of Medicine. *Standards for Foods in Schools: Leading the Way Toward Healthier Youth* (www.nap.edu/catalog/11899/nutrition-standards-for-foods-in-schools-leading-the-way-toward)

U.S. Department of Agriculture. *Healthier U.S. School Challenge* (www.fns.usda.gov/tn/healthierus/index.html)

U.S. Department of Health and Human Services and U.S. Department of Agriculture. *2015–2020 Dietary Guidelines for Americans.* 8th Edition (health.gov/dietaryguidelines/2015/guidelines; December 2015)

CHILDREN'S LITERATURE

AGES 5–8

Allepuz, Anuska. *That Fruit Is Mine!* Albert Whitman & Company, 2018.

Aliki. *Milk: From Cow to Carton.* HarperTrophy, 1992.

Anderson, Derek. *Gladys Goes Out to Lunch.* Simon & Schuster Books for Young Readers, 2005.

Bellisario, Gina. *Choose Good Food!: My Eating Tips.* Millbrook Press, 2014.

Boothroyd, Jennier. *Taste Something New: Giving Different Foods a Try (Lightning Bolt Books: Healthy Eating).* Lerner Publications, 2016.

Brown, Marc. *D.W. the Picky Eater.* Little, Brown, 1997.

Brown, Marcia. *Stone Soup: An Old Tale.* Atheneum, 1947.

Bullard, Lisa. *My Food, Your Food.* Millbrook Press, 2015.

Burns, Marilyn. Spaghetti and Meatballs for All!: *A Mathematical Story.* Scholastic, 1997.

Carle, Eric. *Pancakes, Pancakes!* Aladdin, 1998.

Carle, Eric. *Today Is Monday.* Putnam, 1997.

Carle, Eric. *The Very Hungry Caterpillar.* Philomel, 1981.

Carle, Eric. *Walter the Baker.* Aladdin, 1998.

Child, Lauren. *I Will Never NOT EVER Eat a Tomato.* Candlewick, 2000.

Cleary, Brian P. *Apples, Cherries, Red Raspberries: What Is In the Fruit Group?* Millbrook Press, 2014.

Cooper, Helen. *Pumpkin Soup.* Farrar, Straus & Giroux (BYR), 1999.

Daley, Lashon. *Mr. Okra Sells Fresh Fruits and Vegetables.* Pelican Publishing Company, 2015.

Demi. *One Grain of Rice: A Mathematical Folktale.* Scholastic, 1997.

DePaola, Tomie. *Pancakes for Breakfast.* Voyager Books, 1990.

DePaola, Tomie. *Tony's Bread: An Italian Folktale.* Paperstar Book, 1996.

Dooley, Norah. *Everybody Bakes Bread.* Carolrhoda Books, 1995.

Dooley, Norah. *Everybody Cooks Rice.* Carolrhoda Books, 1992.

Dussinling, Jennifer. *Picky Peggy (Science Solves It (Kane)).* Kane Press 2004.

Ehlert, Lois. *Eating the Alphabet: Fruits and Vegetables from A to Z.* Voyager Books, 1993.

Ehlert, Lois. *Growing Vegetable Soup.* Voyager Books, 1990.

Ehlert, Lois. *Pie in the Sky.* Harcourt Children's Books, 2004.

Hoffmann, Mark. *Fruit Bowl.* Knopf Books for Young Readers, 2018.

Falwell, Cathryn. *Feast for 10.* Clarion Books, 1995.

Freymann, Saxton, and Joost Elffers. *How Are You Peeling? Foods with Moods.* Arthur A. Levine Books, 1999.

Galdone, Paul. *The Little Red Hen.* Clarion Books, 1985.

Gelman, Rita G. *Biggest Sandwich Ever.* Scholastic, 1981.

Gershator, David. *Bread Is for Eating.* Henry Holt, 1998.

Gibbons, Gail. *The Vegetables We Eat.* Dreamscape, 2007.

Greenfield, Eloise. *PAR-TAY!: A Dance of the Veggies (and Their Friends).* Alazar Press, 2018.

Hoban, Russell. *Bread and Jam for Frances.* HarperTrophy, 1993.

Hoberman, Mary Ann. *The Seven Silly Eaters.* Voyager Books, 2000.

Kann, Victoria, and Elizabeth Kann. *Pinkalicious.* HarperCollins, 2006.

Kasza, Keiko. *Badger's Fancy Meal.* Puffin Books, 2007.

Koster, Gloria, and Maryann Cocca-Leffler. *The Peanut-Free Café.* Albert Whitman & Company, 2006.

Kottke, Jan. *From Seed to Pumpkin.* Children's Press, 2000.

Kozlowski, Bryan. *Cook Me a Story: A Treasury of Stories and Recipes Inspired by Classic Fairy Tales.* Walter, Foster Jr., 2016.

Leedy, Loreen. *Jack and the Hungry Giant Eat Right with My Plate.* Holiday House, 2013.

Lin, Grace. *Our Food: A Healthy Serving of Science and Poems.* Charlesbridge, 2016.

Marisco, Katie. *Eat a Balanced Diet! (21st Century Junior Library: Your Healthy Body).* Cherry Lake Publishing, 2015.

Marlowe, Sara. *No Ordinary Apple: A Story About Eating Mindfully.* Wisdom Publications, 2013.

Murphy, Stuart J. *Just Enough Carrots: Comparing Amounts.* HarperTrophy, 1997.

Nolen, Jerdine. *In My Momma's Kitchen.* Amistad, 2001.

Palatini, Margie. *Sweet Tooth.* Simon & Schuster Children's Publishing, 2004.

Park, Linda Sue. *Bee-Bim Bop!* Sandpiper, 2005.

Peterson, Cris. *Harvest Year.* Boyds Mills Press, 1996.

Pollan, M. *The Omnivore's Dilemma for Kids: The Secrets Behind What You Eat.* Dial, 2009.

Pym, Christine. *Little Mouse's Big Breakfast.* Nosy Crow, an imprint of Candlewick Press, 2018.

Rabe, Tish. *Oh, the Things You Can Do That Are Good for You: All About Staying Healthy.* Random House Books for Young Readers, 2001.

Rath, Tom. *The Rechargeables: Eat Move Sleep.* Missionday, 2015.

Rattigan, Jama Kim. *Dumpling Soup.* Meagen Tingly, 1998.

Rockwell, Lizzy. *Good Enough to Eat: A Kid's Guide to Food and Nutrition.* HarperCollins, 2009.

Rosenthal, Amy Krouse. *Little Pea.* Chronicle Books, 2005.

Russ-Ayon, A. *We Eat Food That's Fresh!* Our Rainbow Press, 2009.

Sayre, April Pulley. *Go, Go, Grapes! A Fruit Chant.* Beach Lane Books, 2012.

Sayre, April Pulley. *Rah, Rah, Radishes! A Vegetable Chant.* Beach Lane Books, 2011.

Schneider, Josh. *Tales for Very Picky Eaters.* Clarion Books, 2011.

Seuss, Dr. *Green Eggs and Ham.* Random House Books for Young Readers, 1960.

Sharmat, Mitchell. *Gregory the Terrible Eater.* Scholastic, 1989.

Showers, Paul. *What Happens to a Hamburger?* HarperCollins, 1985.

Smallman, Steve. *Eat Your Veggies, Goldilocks (Fairytales Gone Wrong).* QEB Publishing, 2014.

Soto, Gary. *Too Many Tamales.* Paperstar Book, 1996.

Stevens, Janet. *Tops & Bottoms.* Farcourt Brace, 1995.

Stewart, Whitney. *What's On Your Plate?: Exploring the World of Food.* Sterling Children's Books, 2018.

Storper, B. *Janey Junkfood's Fresh Adventure.* Food Play Productions, 2008.

Sturges, Philemon. *The Little Red Hen Makes a Pizza.* Puffin Books, 1999.

Sweet, Susan D. *Princess Penelopea Hates Peas: A Tale of Picky Eating and Avoiding Catastropeas.* Magination Press, 2016.

Titherington, Jeanne. *Pumpkin Pumpkin.* Greenwillow Books, 1986.

Wellington, Monica. *Apple Farmer Annie.* Dutton Children's Books, 2001.

Wells, Rosemary. *Bunny Cakes.* Viking, 2000.

Wells, Rosemary. *Yoko.* Hyperion, 1998.

Wiesner, David. *June 29, 1999.* Clarion Books, 1995.

Willems, Mo. *A Busy Creature's Day Eating.* Hyperion Books for Children, an imprint of Disney Book Group, 2018.

Wilson, Karma. *Bear Wants More.* Margaret K. McElderry Books, 2003.

Eat Your Greens, Red, Yellow, and Purples. DK/Penguin Random House, 2016.

Food Like Mine. DK, 2017.

Zamorano, Ana. *Let's Eat.* Rebound by Sagebrush, 2001.

AGES 8–12

Archer, Joe. *Plant, Cook, Eat!: A Children's Cookbook.* Charlesbridge Publishing, Inc., 2018.

Are You What You Eat?: A Guide to What's On Your Plate and Why! DK, 2015.

Banyard Antonia. *Eat Up! An Infographic Exploration of Food (Visual Exploration).* Annick Press, 2017.

Crockett, Kyle A. *Nutrition and Your Future (Understanding Nutrition: A Gateway To Physical & Mental Health).* Mason Crest, 2014.

Elton, Sarah. *Meatless?: A Fresh Look At What You Eat.* Owlkids Books, 2017.

Etingoff, Kim. *Building a Healthy Diet With the 5 Food Groups (On My Plate).* Mason Crest, 2015.

Etingoff, Kim. *Diet Myths: Sorting Through the Hype (Understanding Nutrition: A Gateway to Physical & Mental Health).* Mason Crest, 2014.

Etingoff, Kim. *Healthy Alternatives to Sweets & Snacks (Understanding Nutrition: A Gateway to Physical & Mental Health).* Mason Crest, 2014.

Fulcher, Roz. *Be Good to Your Body: Healthy Eating and Fun Recipes.* Dover Publications, 2012.

Hengel, Katherine. *Garden to Table: A Kid's Guide to Planting, Growing, and Preparing Food.* Scarletta Junior Readers, 2014.

Johanson, Paula. *Processed Food (What's In Your Food? Recipe for Disaster).* Rosen Central, 2008.

Jukes, Mavis, and Lilian Wai-Yin. *Be Healthy! It's a Girl Thing: Food, Fitness, and Feeling Great.* Crown Books for Young Readers, 2003.

Mayo Clinic. *The Mayo Clinic's Kids' Cookbook: Favorite Recipes for Fun and Healthy Eating.* Good Books, 2012.

Priceman, Marjorie. *How to Make an Apple Pie and See the World.* Dragonfly Books, 1996.

Schlosser, Eric. *Chew On This: Everything You Don't Want to Know About Fast Food.* Houghton Mifflin, 2006.

Schlosser, Eric. *Fast Food Nation: The Dark Side of the All-American Meal.* Houghton Mifflin, 2001.

Schlosser, Eric, and Charles Wilson. *Chew On This: Everything You Don't Want to Know About Fast Food.* Houghton Mifflin, 2007.

Schuh, Mari C. *Healthy Snacks on MyPlate (Pebble Plus: What's On MyPlate?).* Capstone Press, 2013.

Shanley, Ellen, and Colleen Thompson. *Fueling the Teen Machine.* Bull, 2001.

Swanson, Diane. *Burp! The Most Interesting Book You'll Ever Read About Eating.* Kids Can Press, 2001.

Veness, Kimberley. *Let's Eat!: A Sustainable Food for a Hungry Planet (Orca Footprints).* Orca Book Publishers, 2017.

Ventura, Marne. *12 Tips for a Healthy Diet (Healthy Living (12 Story)).* 12-Story Library, 2017.

Woolf, Alex. *You Wouldn't Want to Live Without Vegetables.* Franklin Watts, an imprint of Scholastic Inc., 2016.

Zinczenko, David, and Goulding, Matt. *Eat This Not That! Restaurant Survival Guide: The No-Diet Weight Loss Solution.* Rodale Books, 2009.

ENDNOTES

1. U.S. Department of Health and Human Services and U.S. Department of Agriculture, *2015–2020 Dietary Guidelines for Americans,* 8th ed. (http://health.gov/dietaryguidelines/2015/guidelines/; December 2015).
2. Ibid.
3. Ibid.
4. Ibid.
5. Ibid.
6. Centers for Disease Control and Prevention, *Childhood Obesity Facts* (https://www.cdc.gov/obesity/data/childhood.html).
7. U.S. Department of Health and Human Services and U.S. Department of Agriculture, *2015–2020 Dietary Guidelines for Americans.* 8th Edition. December 2015. Available at http://health.gov/dietaryguidelines/2015/guidelines/
8. Council of chief State School Officers, *Policy Statement on School Health* (www.ccsso.org; 2004).
9. Action for Healthy Kids, *The Learning Connection: The Value of Improving Nutrition and Physical Activity in Our Schools* (www.actionforhealthykids.org/media-center/reports).
10. Ibid.
11. Action for Healthy Kids, *The Learning Connection: What You Need to Know to Ensure Your kids Are Healthy and Ready to Learn* (www.actionforhealthykids.org/media-center/reports).
12. Action for Healthy Kids, *The Learning Connection.*
13. H. Taras and W. Potts, "Obesity and Student Performance at School," *Journal of School Health* 75, no 8 (2005): 291–95.
14. C.E. Basch, "Healthier Students Are Better Learners: A Missing Link in School Reforms to Close the Achievement Gap," *Equity Matters, Research Review No. 6, A Research Initiative of the Campaign for Education Equity* (Teachers College, Columbia University, March 2010).
15. N. Black, D.W. Johnston, and A. Peeters, "Childhood Obesity and Cognitive Achievement," *Health Economics* 24, (2015): 1082–1100.
16. Ibid.

17. C.C.A. Santana et al., "The Association Between Obesity and Academic Performance in Youth: A Systematic Review," *Obesity Reviews* 18, (2017): 1191–1199.
18. R. An et al., "Childhood Obesity and School Absenteeism: A Systematic Review and Meta-analysis," *Obesity Reviews* 18, (2017): 1412–1424
19. H.I. Lanza and D.Y.C. Huang, "Is Obesity Associated with School Dropout? Key Developmental and Ethnic differences," *Journal of School Health* 85, (2015): 663–670.
20. R. An et al., "Childhood Obesity and School Absenteeism: A Systematic Review and Meta-analysis."
21. R.A. Krunkowski et al., "Overweight Children, Weight-Based Teasing and Academic Performance," *International Journal of Pediatric Obesity* 4, (2009): 274–80.
22. United States Department of Agriculture Economic Research Service, *Food Insecurity in the U.S.* (https://www.ers.usda.gov/topics/food-nutrition-assistance/food-security-in-the-us/key-statistics-graphics/).
23. Feeding America, *Child Food Insecurity* (http://www.feedingamerica.org/research/map-the-meal-gap/child-food-insecurity-executive-summary.html; 2017).
24. Ibid.
25. Centers for Disease Control and Prevention, *September is National Childhood Obesity Awareness Month* (www.cdc.gov/features/childhoodobesity/).
26. Ibid.
27. Ibid.
28. American Academy of Pediatrics, *Media and Children Communication Toolkit* (https://www.aap.org/en-us/advocacy-and-policy/aap-health-initiatives/Pages/Media-and-Children.aspx).
29. Centers for Disease Control and Prevention, *School Health Guidelines* (https://www.cdc.gov/healthyschools/npao/strategies.htm).
30. School Nutrition Association (www.schoolnutrition.org).
31. Centers for Disease Control and Prevention, *Local School Wellness Policy* (https://www.cdc.gov/healthyschools/npao/wellness.htm).

32. Centers for Disease Control and Prevention, *School Nutrition* (https://www.cdc.gov/healthyschools/nutrition/schoolnutrition.htm).
33. Ibid.
34. Ibid.
35. Ibid.
36. Centers for Disease Control and Prevention, *School Health Policy and Practices Study 2016* (https://www.cdc.gov/healthyyouth/data/shpps/results.htm).
37. Centers for Disease Control and Prevention, *School Health Guidelines.*
38. Ibid.
39. Centers for Disease Control and Prevention, *Nutrition Standards for Foods in Schools* (https://www.cdc.gov/healthyyouth/nutrition/pdf/nutrition_factsheet_service).
40. Centers for Disease Control and Prevention, *School Nutrition.*
41. Food and Nutrition Service, U.S. Department of Agriculture; Centers for Disease Control and Prevention, U.S. Department of Health and Human Services and U.S. Department of Education, *Making It Happen! School Nutrition Success Stories* (https://healthymeals.fns.usda.gov/local-wellness-policy-resources/school-nutrition-environment-and-wellness-resources/success).
42. U.S. Department of Agriculture, *Team Nutrition* (https://www.fns.usda.gov/tn/team-nutrition).
43. U.S. Department of Health and Human Services and U.S. Department of Agriculture, *2015–2020 Dietary Guidelines for Americans.*
44. Ibid.
45. Ibid.
46. U.S. Department of Agriculture, *My Plate* (www.choosemyplate.gov/MyPlate).
47. Ibid.
48. U.S. Food and Drug Administration, *Changes to the Nutrition Facts Label* (https://www.fda.gov/Food/GuidanceRegulation/GuidanceDocuments RegulatoryInformation/LabelingNutrition/ucm385663.htm#highlights).
49. Ibid.
50. Centers for Disease Control and Prevention, *School Health Guidelines.*

7

(Kalani, age 12)

Promoting Physical Activity

DESIRED LEARNER OUTCOMES

After reading this chapter, you will be able to . . .

- **Describe the prevalence and cost of inactivity among youth.**

- **Explain the relationship between physical inactivity and compromised academic performance.**

- **Identify factors that influence physical activity.**

- **Summarize current guidelines and practices for schools and teachers related to promotion of physical activity and the prevention of inactivity.**

- **Summarize developmentally appropriate physical activity concepts and skills for K–8 students in the context of the National Health Education Standards and target healthy behavior outcomes.**

- **Demonstrate developmentally appropriate learning strategies and assessment techniques that incorporate concepts and skills that have been shown to promote physical activity among youth.**

- **Identify characteristics of effective physical activity programming.**

- **Identify websites and children's literature that can be used in cross-curricular instructional activities promoting physical activity.**

INTRODUCTION

Although many reasons are offered for failure to participate in consistent patterns of physical activity, there is no question about the benefits of such pursuits for all age groups. Robust physical activity is important particularly for young people who are establishing personal health habits for a lifetime. Schools must organize a range of learning opportunities to meet the fitness needs of students of all abilities and interest levels. Such developmentally appropriate and well-designed instruction contributes to a sound foundation for maintaining health and promoting school success.

Prevalence and Cost

A growing body of literature has emerged that confirms the public health benefits of increasing physical activity as a way to reduce the effects of a sedentary lifestyle. A substantial amount of robust research has documented that for all age groups including people with disabilities, participation in some physical activity is better than no such engagement. To promote health, additional benefits are associated with increased intensity, frequency, and/or duration of periods of activity. While some health benefits seem to begin with as little as sixty minutes of physical activity a week, research has demonstrated that engaging in a total of 150 minutes (2 hours and 30 minutes) each week of such moderate-intensity aerobic activities as brisk walking reduces the risk of many chronic diseases and other negative health outcomes. Regular physical activity reduces the risk of many adverse health outcomes including

- Premature or early death
- Coronary heart disease and stroke
- High blood pressure (hypertension) and elevated cholesterol levels
- Type 2 diabetes
- Colon and breast cancer
- Unhealthy weight gain

In addition, participation in physical activity has been linked to the following positive health indicators:

- Weight maintenance and weight loss
- Improved cardiorespiratory and muscular fitness
- Increased bone density
- Improved sleep quality
- Better cognitive function among older adults[1]

In short, regular participation in moderate physical activity is an essential element of a healthy lifestyle for all Americans.[2]

Although further research is necessary to fully detail the relationship between physical activity and health among young people, evidence confirms that regular physical activity promotes health and fitness among youth. Compared to their inactive counterparts, youth who are physically active have higher levels of cardiorespiratory fitness, stronger muscles and tend to have lower levels of body fat and stronger bones. In addition, physical activity has been demonstrated to improve mental health among youth by decreasing and preventing anxiety and depression and improving mood.[3] Finally, youth who engage in regular activity have a better chance that they will live healthier adult lives.[4]

Consistent with these findings, the health benefits of physical activity have been confirmed for children and adolescents; young, middle-age, and older adults; women and men; people of all races and ethnicities; and those with disabilities and chronic conditions. In addition, the health benefits of physical activity generally are independent of body weight, shape, or size. While some people are concerned about the risk of injury or sudden heart attacks that might result from physical activity, research has demonstrated that the benefits far outweigh the possibility of adverse outcomes.[5]

Unfortunately, just over 50 percent of American adults meet the minimum recommendations for physical activity. This percent has been steadily increasing over the past ten years. However, 27 percent of American adults engage in zero-leisure-time physical activity.[6] Among adults, physical inactivity is more common among the following:

- Women
- African American and Hispanic adults (as opposed to their white counterparts)
- Those who are older rather than younger
- Adults who are less rather than more affluent[7]

Unfortunately, the data do not paint an optimistic picture of the physical activity patterns and associated consequences. The United States is facing a potentially devastating crisis related directly to overweight and obesity. In recent decades, the prevalence of overweight and obesity has increased dramatically among Americans of all ages. Today, more than one-third of adults are obese.[8] The percent of youth aged 6 to 19 who are obese has remained relatively stable at approximately 17 percent since 2011.[9] Today, more than one-third of all American children and adolescents are overweight or obese.[10]

Research has demonstrated that this epidemic is very complex and is influenced by changes in the environment, public policy, and economic, biomedical, and social factors. High-calorie and inexpensive foods are available widely and are advertised heavily through many media outlets. In addition, the widespread adoption of multiple technologies in homes, workplaces, and schools have reduced levels of daily physical activity. Communities have adopted car or other transportation-dependent designs that make it harder for children to find safe play spaces and safe and convenient routes for walking or biking to school.[11] Finally, due to changing priorities or budget constraints, many schools have begun to charge a fee for participation in extracurricular activities including sports and to eliminate other physical activity programs to which children once had access.[12]

Importantly, however, the obesity epidemic has been accelerated by specific behavioral changes among youth. Today, children drink more sugar-sweetened beverages while drinking less water than their counterparts in the past.[13]

Finally, there is no question that physical inactivity among youth has made a significant contribution to this epidemic. Although children and youth are more physically active than adults, activity levels decline as children approach adolescence and continue this trend throughout the teen years.[14] Table 7–1 contains Youth Risk

TABLE 7–1

Youth Risk Behavior Survey Data Related to Participation in Physical Activity, 2017

Risk Behavior	Percent Reporting Behavior		
	Total	Females	Males
Were physically active at least sixty minutes per day on five or more days	46.5	36.8	56.9
Did attend physical education class on all five days (in an average school week)	29.9	25.3	34.7
Played on at least one sport team (run by their school or community groups during the twelve months preceding the survey)	54.3	49.3	59.7
Watched TV three or more hours per day (on an average school day)	20.7	20.6	20.8
Played video or computer games or used a computer three or more hours per day	43	43.1	43

SOURCE: Centers for Disease Control and Prevention Division of Adolescent and School Health, *Youth Risk Behavior Surveillance System (YRBSS)* (https://www.cdc.gov/healthyyouth/data/yrbs/index.htm; 2015).

©Tatyana Vyc/Shutterstock

Regular physical activity promotes lifelong health and is associated with improved academic performance.

Behavior Survey data that confirm findings about the physical activity behaviors of students (grades 9–12) in 2015.[15] Clearly, these data signal an inactivity problem among older youth that could contribute to both short- and long-term negative health consequences.

Although the physical and emotional costs of excess weight strike the affected individual and his or her family most directly, the economic costs and consequences of this national health crisis have spread into every segment of society. The fact that America has become an overweight nation has come at a very high price. This is particularly true of the costs associated with overweight and obesity among American youth.

Schools bear avoidable or reducible costs related directly to the combined effects of poor nutrition and physical inactivity among enrolled students[16]. This economic burden is linked to losses in funding in states where daily student attendance influences the amount of money that local schools receive from state government. Severely overweight students miss on average more school than their peers of a healthy weight. Overweight- and

obesity-related absenteeism can cost a school approximately $1,392 per student per year in funding.[17]

In addition, businesses bear significant short- and long-term costs associated with childhood obesity since most children are included in the health insurance and medical care claims of their employed parents. Research has demonstrated that overweight children experience significantly more medical problems than their counterparts. In addition to greater use of their health insurance to cover the costs of treatment, the parents of such children have higher rates of absenteeism and lower productivity. The combined effects of these variables contribute to significant costs for employers.[18]

Healthy People 2020 specifies a number of national health promotion objectives specifying targets to encourage physical activity among youth. Upon reviewing Table 7–2, readers will note that many of these objectives specify a role for school communities in supporting physical activity among youth.[19]

Consistent with these national objectives, and based on the most current scientific evidence, the U.S. Department of Health

TABLE 7–2

Healthy People 2020 Objectives Related to Promoting Physical Activity Among Youth

Because physical activity is so important to promoting health and preventing disease, the 2020 National Health Objectives call for schools to collaborate with families and communities to increase activity opportunities for children and youth. The following specific objectives focus on such an agenda:

Objective PA-3	Increase the proportion of adolescents who meet the current federal physical activity guidelines for aerobic physical activity and for muscle-strengthening activity.
Objective PA-4	Increase the proportion of the nation's public and private schools that require daily physical education for all students.
Objective PA-5	Increase the proportion of adolescents who participate in daily school physical education.
Objective PA-6	Increase regularly scheduled elementary school recess in the United States.
Objective PA-7	Increase the proportion of school districts that require or recommend elementary school recess of an appropriate period of time.
Objective PA-8	Increase the proportion of children and adolescents who do not exceed recommended limits for screen time:
PA-8.2	Increase the proportion of children and adolescents aged 2 years through twelfth grade who view television, videos, or play video games for no more than two hours a day.
PA-8.3	Increase the proportion of children and adolescents aged 2 years through twelfth grade who use a computer or play computer games outside of school (for nonschool work) for no more than two hours a day.
Objective PA-10	Increase the proportion of the nation's public and private schools that provide access to their physical activity spaces and facilities for all persons outside of normal school hours (i.e., before and after the school day, on weekends, and during summer and other vacations).
Objective PA-13	Increase the proportion of trips made by walking.
PA-13.2	Children and adolescents aged 5 to 15 years, trips to school of one mile or less.
Objective PA-14	Increase the proportion of trips made by bicycling.
PA-14.2	Children and adolescents aged 5 to 15 years, trips to school of two miles or less.

SOURCE: U.S. Department of Health and Human Services, *Healthy People 2020* (www.healthypeople.gov/2020/topics-objectives/topic/physical-activity).

and Human Services has established Physical Activity Guidelines for all Americans. With a particular focus on youth, these guidelines specify that children and adolescents aged 6 to 17 should engage in sixty minutes (one hour) or more of various kinds of physical activity each day. To reach this daily goal, parents and all other adults who work with or care for children are encouraged to organize numerous and varied opportunities to help young people participate in physical activities that are developmentally appropriate and fun. There is no question that school-based professionals can play an important role in helping to reach this goal by establishing policies and practices that promote physical activity across the school day.[20]

Physical Activity and Academic Performance

Most educators who work with students in the elementary and middle grades understand that physical activity enriches the health of their students. Unfortunately, they are confronted by demands for academic accountability that make the integration of physical activity into the school day a challenge. In addition, many education stakeholders are skeptical about the extent to which physical activity supports or actually could threaten the academic mission of schools. In response to such common concerns, a growing body of research has documented the clear relationship between physical activity and improved academic outcomes among students.

Recently, the results of a landmark study were published by the Centers for Disease Control and Prevention. Researchers analyzed the impact of school-based physical education, recess, classroom-based physical activity, and extracurricular physical activity on a range of measures of school success. Findings revealed that none of these types of school-based physical activity exerted a negative impact on or intruded into time better spent on promoting academic achievement. In fact, such potential physical activity opportunities in schools were confirmed to be related to improved concentration, attention span, positive attitudes toward learning, on-task behavior, and scores on tests of math, reading, and other standardized measures of achievement.[21] Available evidence confirms that math and reading are the content areas most likely to be influenced positively by physical activity. In specific, analytical and reading skills depend on the engagement of efficient and effective executive functions. Importantly, such executive functions have been documented to be enriched by physical activity and fitness.[22]

In conclusion, this important study conducted by the CDC contained a summary of the substantial evidence that school-based physical activity, including physical education, can improve academic outcomes measured by grades and standardized test scores. In addition, CDC researchers confirmed the positive contribution that physical activity can make on cognitive skills, including concentration and attention to tasks, and on classroom behavior.[23]

In addition to physical activity, brain function is influenced by the development and refinement of motor skills. As motor skills are practiced, neurons in the brain form synapses (connections) that enable the brain to function better.[24] As a consequence, basic cognitive functions related to attention span and memory that facilitate learning are enriched by physical activity.[25]

Physical activity has also been demonstrated to reduce stress, improve mood, and promote a calming effect among students. These psychosocial benefits have been linked to evidence confirming that adolescents who are physically active are less likely to attempt suicide, adopt risk behaviors, and become pregnant. Clearly, such positive health outcomes are related to improved long-term academic prospects.[26]

©Arthur Tilley/Getty Images

Having fun at physical activities while young helps promote continuing patterns of physical activity throughout the life span.

- Incorporating role-plays into instruction to dramatize key concepts.
- Taking stand-and-stretch breaks every twenty minutes to energize the class.[28]

Such recommendations are based on brain research revealing that students learn best in time segments no longer than twenty minutes, followed by a two- to five-minute period of movement of some kind. For example, during a forty-minute lesson in which no opportunity for gross motor activity has been provided, retention is very high for the first eight to ten minutes and again during the last three to five minutes.[29]

In addition to increasing the number and variety of active learning strategies across the school day, teachers are encouraged to keep time parameters, particularly for younger students, as close to the twenty-minute ideal as possible. Such a time management strategy supports consistently high levels of retention at the beginning and end of lessons and minimizes downtime.[30]

Factors That Influence Physical Activity

Research has identified many factors associated with the patterns of physical activity among children and youth. Demographic variables, including sex and age, have been demonstrated to account for variations in exercise behaviors. For example, girls are less physically active than boys, and adolescents are less active than younger children.[31]

In addition, a number of individual characteristics have been shown to influence participation in physical activity. Students who perceive benefits from and believe in their capacity to participate in physical activity or sports (having fun, learning or refining new skills, staying in shape, improving appearance, and improving strength, endurance, or flexibility) are more likely to engage in a range of physical activities. Conversely, students who perceive barriers to participating in physical activities, particularly a lack of time, are less likely to engage in exercise behaviors.[32]

Physical activity patterns among children and adolescents also are influenced by interpersonal and environmental factors. Support for and engagement in physical activity among friends, siblings, and parents have been shown to influence the exercise behaviors of youth in positive ways.[33] Finally, convenient play spaces, access to well-functioning sports equipment, and transportation to sport or fitness activities also have been shown to have a positive effect on student exercise participation.[34]

In this regard, many young people are confronted with barriers to establishing and maintaining a physically active lifestyle. In particular, educators and other advocates would be wise to acknowledge and take steps to manage the following impediments:

1. In many communities, patterns of housing and urban development have centered on the use of the automobile. In such locales, walking and bicycling are discouraged, making it difficult for children to meet and participate in active play.
2. Increased concerns about safety have limited the time and locations in which children can play outside.
3. Appealing technology and electronic media (video and computer games, cable and satellite TV) encourage a sedentary lifestyle for many young people.

Finally, a growing body of research confirms that physical activity improves behavioral outcomes among children aged 5 to 12 diagnosed with attention deficit hyperactivity disorder (ADHD). Children with ADHD who exercised about forty minutes five days per week showed improved behavior in as few as three weeks.[27]

Given the national priority to improve outcomes on standardized tests, a broad change in school programming and policy to increase school-based physical activity participation among all students is warranted. Eric Jensen, an educator and scholar of note, suggests that active learning has advantages over sedentary learning. Benefits include outcomes that are longer lasting, better remembered, more fun, and age appropriate. This advocate urges classroom teachers to integrate a better blend of sitting and moving into daily classroom practice by the following:

- Engaging students in a greater variety of postures (walking, lying, moving, leaning, perching, or squatting) during classroom instruction.
- Engaging students in movement.
- Encouraging students to use their bodies to learn (demonstrate concepts, words, or rhythms).

4. Unfortunately, despite the evidence that active children learn better, many states and school districts have cut recess programs and reduced the requirements for participation in physical education classes. This problem is compounded in districts in which an unreasonable teacher–student ratio in physical education classes contributes to a risky or ineffective learning environment.

5. Due to budget constraints or other priorities, many communities have failed to invest in the development and maintenance of facilities, including parks and recreation centers, that are close to home for children and youth.[35]

In most cases, such circumstances are beyond the control of young people, but conspire against the physical activity pursuits of even those who are most highly motivated. Recognition of such issues is critical if communities, schools, and families are to develop and implement well-planned and collaborative solutions.

GUIDELINES FOR SCHOOLS

State of the Practice

As documented here and in Chapter 6, the majority of American youth are sedentary and do not eat well. These unhealthy practices are linked to academic difficulties and to health problems that carry into adulthood. As discussed, one of the most significant risks of poor eating and physical inactivity are overweight and obesity. Nearly 80 percent of youth who are overweight remain so, then become obese adults who have the potential to develop elevated cholesterol and blood pressure, gallbladder disease, joint problems, Type 2 diabetes, and depression.[36]

Unfortunately, many school communities have attempted to manage budget and time constraints by reducing or even eliminating school-based physical activity opportunities for students. Others have established policies that require students who want to participate in extracurricular activities, including sports, to pay a "pay to play" fee. Readers are reminded that the 2008 Physical Activity Guidelines recommend that all children and adolescents engage in a minimum of one hour of physical activity each day for best health. The Institutes of Medicine has recommended that this target be supported by policies and programs that enable students to participate in at least thirty minutes of physical activity during each school day.[37]

As a foundation for promoting physical activity for children, it is important to understand where and when they accumulate their activity time. During a school day, students have typical distinct opportunities to be active: in physical education classes, during recess or lunch periods, and either before or after school. Of these opportunities, schools can exercise the most control over the amount of activity embedded in physical education classes. As such, research has confirmed that students are more physically active on the days they have physical education class.[38]

High-quality physical education programs are defined to include three critical elements:

1. Instruction is delivered by certified/licensed physical education teachers.
2. Children in the elementary grades receive a minimum of 150 minutes per week (30 minutes per day) of formal

©Monkey Business Images/Shutterstock

Children should accumulate at least sixty minutes of physical activity each day. Such activity can be spread across the day including at recess, in physical education classes, during after-school play, and in formal practice sessions for organized or competitive sports. When done with family members, the value and fun of daily activity is reinforced.

physical education instruction. Their older counterparts in middle school participate in a minimum of 225 minutes per week (45 minutes per day).

3. Measurable standards for student achievement and for high school graduation have been established. While some experts question the importance of school-based physical education, research has demonstrated that quality programming enjoys strong support from parents and child health professionals.[39]

Unfortunately, few schools meet optimal targets for formal physical education programming. Although the majority of states mandate that students must participate in formal physical education of some kind, only about 77 percent of states require that local elementary schools provide such instruction for all students. Further, only about 73 percent of states require that students in the middle grades receive requisite physical education instruction. For both the elementary and middle school levels, fewer states are enforcing robust physical education requirements.[40] According to the 2016 Shape of the Nation report, only Oregon and the District of Columbia are meeting the national guidelines for weekly time in physical education for both elementary and middle school.[41]

The Centers for Disease Control and Prevention (CDC) conducts the periodic School Health Policies and Practices Study (SHPPS) to assess current guiding principles and school health activities across the United States. In 2016, the most recent SHPPS was conducted revealing insights about a range of policies and practices that guide physical activity in schools at the state and district levels. While state-level requirements for physical education are becoming more lax, over 92 percent of school districts require physical education at the elementary level. Additionally, at every level, about half of districts are implementing more formalized measures for assessments in physical education including Fitnessgram testing.[42]

State of the Art

Given the unfortunate reality about the amount and types of opportunities to promote physical activity among youth, parents, school professionals, and other significant adult caregivers are encouraged to examine the specific guidelines for physical activity for children and adolescents aged 6 to 17 contained in the 2008 Physical Activity Guidelines for Americans. In specific, while accumulating bouts of participation to meet the minimum activity target of sixty minutes per day, the Guidelines specify three types and amounts of each that contribute important health benefits for this age group: aerobic, muscle-strengthening, and bone strengthening.

- *Aerobic activities* include those in which youth move large muscle groups rhythmically. Examples of moderate-intensity aerobic activities for children include hiking, skateboarding, and brisk walking, while for adolescents, these activities can be supplemented with lawn mowing, baseball, or softball. More vigorous-intensity aerobic activities for all youth can include active games that involve running and chasing, bicycle riding, martial arts, and sports such as soccer, ice or field hockey, basketball, swimming, and tennis. Such activities increase cardiorespiratory fitness and should be done at least three days a week.
- *Muscle-strengthening activities* include those pursuits that make muscles do more work than what is usual in the course of daily living. This "overload" process strengthens muscles. Whether through unstructured play or in a structured context, examples of such activities include tug-of-war, push-ups, pull-ups; resistance exercises with body weights, bands, or weight machines; or climbing activities. Muscle-strengthening activities should be done a minimum of three days per week.
- *Bone-strengthening activities* also should be done at least three days per week and include pursuits that produce force on the bones that promote bone growth and strength. These activities are important particularly for children and young adolescents since the greatest gains in bone mass occur during the years just before puberty. In addition, the majority of peak bone mass is developed by the end of adolescence. Most commonly, the force that promotes bone health is produced most commonly by impact with the ground. As such, examples of bone-strengthening activities for youth include games such as hopscotch, jumping rope, running, and sports including gymnastics, basketball, volleyball, and tennis.[43]

Children and adolescents should meet these guidelines in developmentally appropriate ways because natural activity patterns differ across age groups. Children are naturally active in intermittent ways, particularly during unstructured active play. They engage in basic aerobic and bone-strengthening activities such as running, hopping, and skipping while practicing movement patterns and skills that are in development. In addition, it is common for children to alternate between bursts of vigorous and moderate-intensity activities and periods of rest. Most children increase their muscle strength during unstructured activities that require them to lift their body weight. As such, it is very unusual for them to need formal muscle-strengthening programs that involve weight lifting.

By contrast, it is common for adolescents to meet identified guidelines through free play, structured activities, or both. Structured programs can include organized sports that engage young people in all three types of activities. In addition, they can work with resistance bands or use their body weight for resistance through such activities as push-ups and pull-ups. Again, it is the combination of activity participation that helps older students meet the amount within each type and reach the target of one hour of activity per day.[44]

GUIDELINES FOR CLASSROOM APPLICATIONS

Schools and communities have the potential to increase the amount of healthy physical activity among students through the provision of instruction, programming, and services. As noted in Chapter 1, school-based efforts to promote physical activity among young people should be formalized as part of a Whole School, Whole Community, Whole Child (WSCC) approach to health-promoting practices in schools. In addition, community-based physical activity programs are essential since most physical activity among young people occurs during discretionary time away from the school setting.[45] In this context, schools and communities would be wise to coordinate efforts to make the best use of personnel and resources.

While the efforts of physical educators and classroom teachers are critical, in "Guidelines for School and Community Programs to Promote Lifelong Physical Activity Among Young People," the CDC published a comprehensive agenda for school and community programs to promote physical activity among young people. This agenda is based on four key principles that suggest physical activity programs for young people are more likely to be effective when they

- Emphasize enjoyable participation in physical activities that are easily done throughout life.
- Offer a range of diverse competitive and noncompetitive activities that are developmentally appropriate for different ages and abilities.
- Provide the skills and confidence that young people need to be physically active.
- Promote physical activity throughout all elements of Coordinated School Health and cultivate links between school and community programs.[46]

To support program development and coordination, the CDC in partnership with SHAPE America has updated this work in Comprehensive School Physical Activity Programs: A Guide for Schools. This document defines a Comprehensive School Physical Activity Program (CSPAP) as a "multi-component approach by which school districts and schools use all opportunities for students to be physically active, meet the nationally recommended sixty minutes of physical activity each day, and develop the knowledge, skills, and confidence to be physically active for a lifetime."[47] The goals of a CSPAP are as follows:

1. "To provide a variety of school-based physical activities to enable all students to participate in sixty minutes of moderate-to-vigorous physical activity each day, and

2. To provide coordination among the CSPAP components to maximize understanding, application, and practice of the knowledge and skills learned in physical education so that all students will be fully physically educated and well-equipped for a lifetime of physical activity."[48]

The important issue of lifetime physical activity was reinforced in a recent report released by the U.S. Department of Defense. In Still Too Fat to Fight, it was confirmed that approximately 25 percent of young Americans are too overweight to join the military. When combined with other disqualifying factors including the failure to graduate from high school (also potentially related to physical inactivity) and having a criminal record, a shocking 75 percent of youth between the ages of 17 and 24 years are ineligible to serve in the military if they wanted to. In response, more than 300 retired generals and admirals have joined with parents to offer strong support for new comprehensive efforts in schools to help students build stronger bodies with less excess fat.[49]

Consistent with this and other calls to address the crises of obesity and inactivity, a CSPAP reflects strong coordination between schools, communities, and governmental and nongovernmental agencies. In specific, a CSPAP mobilizes all resources of multiple programming and policy components to improve the physical activity prospects of youth. These include the following:

1. Quality physical education as the foundation.
2. Staff involvement.
3. Physical activity during school.
4. Physical activity before and after school.
5. Family and community engagement.[50]

Such collaborative initiatives are regarded as highly effective health promotion strategies and have shown promise in reducing the public health burden of chronic diseases associated with sedentary lifestyles. The attributes of the most successful programs include a focus on equipping students with knowledge, attitudes, motor and behavioral skills, and the confidence to be physically active during youth. With this foundation, lifelong physical activity patterns are likely to be established.[51]

Important Background for K–8 Teachers

As a foundation for advocacy and health promotion, teachers must be fluent in the basic science and the terminology of physical activity and fitness. A discussion of important concepts and issues follows.

Fundamental Concepts and Definitions

As a foundation for promoting student activity, understanding the scientific literature, and supporting their physical educator colleagues, elementary and middle school classroom teachers would be wise to review the distinctions among physical activity, exercise, and physical fitness. *Physical activity* is defined as any body movement that results in the expenditure of energy. *Physical activity* is a broad term that includes exercise, sport, dance, and movements as simple as walking or taking the stairs. In this context, *exercise* is a subset of physical activity and includes physical activities that are planned, structured, and repetitive done with the purpose of improving or maintaining one or more of the

components of fitness. Consistent with this definition, *health-related fitness* is a measure of a person's ability to perform physical activities requiring endurance, strength, and flexibility. The components of health-related fitness include cardiorespiratory endurance, muscular endurance, muscular strength, flexibility, and body composition.[52]

Comprehensive information about each of the elements of health-related fitness appears in Consider This 7.1.[53] To reinforce this discussion, it is very important and healthy for students to participate in a range of moderate (walking to school, bicycling, dancing, hopscotch, chores, or yardwork) and vigorous (active games, jumping rope, running, in-line or roller skating) physical activities. Students accumulate physical activity and exercise in a variety of settings, including their homes, schools, playgrounds, public parks and recreation centers, private clubs or sports facilities, hiking/biking trails, summer camps, dance studios, and religious facilities.[54]

Developmentally Appropriate Concepts and Skills

As with all health promotion content, administrators, teachers, and parents are reminded of the importance of organizing physical activity programming based on the developmental abilities and interests of learners.

The Society of Health and Physical Educators (SHAPE) has developed four overarching guidelines to help in the planning of physical activity programs for children. More detailed guidance is available on the SHAPE America website (www.shapeamerica.org).

1. Children should participate in at least sixty minutes of moderate to vigorous physical activity every day.
2. Children should engage in several periods of physical activity lasting at least fifteen minutes.
3. Children should participate in a variety of age-appropriate physical activities.
4. Children's daily routines should not have periods of inactivity lasting two hours or more.[55]

The Physical Activity Pyramid

As a foundation for reinforcing developmentally appropriate participation in a range of physical activities, scholars have developed MyActivity Pyramid (Figure 7-1). MyActivity Pyramid provides a visual representation of the recommended types and amounts of healthy exercise behavior. While there are several variations of physical activity pyramids available, they all share several key features. Five types of physical activities make up the bottom three levels of the pyramid:

- Base level—Lifestyle activities (to do as often as possible)
- Second level—Aerobic activities (to do every day)
- Third level—Muscle-strengthening activities (to do a minimum of three times a week).[56]

Within each level of the pyramid, activities are identified to help students evaluate their personal participation in physical activity. In addition, MyActivity Pyramid can serve as an excellent starting point for developing educational activities for students in elementary and middle schools. Not only does it provide direction for teachers, but Figure 7-1 also can help children identify the

Consider This 7.1

Elements of Health-Related Fitness

CARDIORESPIRATORY (AEROBIC) ENDURANCE

1. Aerobic endurance is the ability of the cardiovascular system (heart, blood, blood vessels, and lungs) to transport and utilize oxygen efficiently.
2. Aerobically healthy people can perform required tasks for extensive periods of time.
3. Inefficient cardiovascular fitness results in shortness of breath, fatigue, and the inability to work at normal tasks over time.
4. Long-term chronic diseases, such as diabetes, obesity, high blood pressure, and heart disease, are associated with poor cardiorespiratory fitness.
5. The process of cardiorespiratory disease starts in early childhood.
6. Aerobic endurance is enhanced by regular participation in such activities as running, bicycling, swimming, fast walking, and aerobic dance.

MUSCULAR STRENGTH AND ENDURANCE

1. Muscular strength is the amount of force one can exert to accomplish a task.
2. Endurance is the ability to use muscles over time without fatigue.
3. The likelihood of injury is reduced with increased muscle strength.
4. Muscular strength and endurance are developed through use of the muscles.
5. Although weight training may be appropriate for adolescents and adults, weight lifting is not recommended for students in elementary grades.

6. Younger children are encouraged to participate in activities such as push-ups (strengthen the triceps and chest muscles), chin-ups (biceps), and curl-ups (back and abdominal muscles).
7. Proper instruction is important to achieve the greatest benefit.

FLEXIBILITY

1. Flexibility is the range of movement of body joints and involves the ability to bend, stretch, and twist.
2. Inactivity can result in loss of flexibility, which is associated with risk for injury, poor posture, and discomfort.
3. Healthy levels of flexibility increase the ability to perform daily tasks and reduce injury risks.
4. Flexibility can be improved by slow, sustained stretching of the muscles and joints.
5. Quick, bouncing, or ballistic stretching exercises should be avoided.
6. Developmentally appropriate flexibility exercises include toe touches, sitting and curling of the back with the head between the knees, trunk-twists, and reach-and-stretch exercises.

BODY COMPOSITION

1. Body composition is the percentage of fat present in the body.
2. Risk factors associated with high body fat can be reduced by modifying body composition through diet and exercise.
3. School screening activities are helpful in early identification of children with potential weight problems (weight/growth charts and triceps skinfold thickness testing).

SOURCE: C. Caspersen, K. Powell, and G. Christenson, "Physical Activity, Exercise, and Physical Fitness: Definition and Distinctions for Health-Related Research," *Public Health Reports* 100, no. 2 (1985): 126–31.

kinds of activities necessary to maintain health, and develop activity plans that they can implement by themselves or with others.[57]

The base level of the MyActivity Pyramid identifies lifestyle activities in which students are encouraged to participate as often as possible. These activities form the foundation of the pyramid because research has confirmed the positive health benefits of daily participation in them. Children are encouraged to accumulate as many of their sixty minutes or more a day of any activity from this category. Activities done as part of a typical daily routine that require involvement of the large muscles of the body are considered to be everyday activities. Activities including playing outdoors, helping with chores, taking the stairs, picking up toys, and walking fit into this category. These are types of activities in which children commonly participate. Adults whose daily routine includes physical work, such as digging or lifting, are engaging in everyday activities.[58]

The second level of the MyActivity Pyramid includes active aerobics or those activities that can be done for long periods of time without stopping. Common and fun activities that fit into this

activity type include dancing, skateboarding, playing tag, bike riding, participating in martial arts such as karate, and playing sports including hockey, basketball, swimming, tennis, or soccer.[59]

The third level of the MyActivity Pyramid includes activities that helps strengthen muscles. These kinds of activities also help to strengthen bones to support short- and long-term fitness and health. Examples of such activities include tug-of-war, rope climbing, pull-ups, sit-ups, and push-ups.[60]

Finally, the tip of the pyramid highlights those activities in which children must minimize their participation or "cut down" on. These activities include completely sedentary (passive) activities and activities that require little large-muscle activity (playing computer games). It must be noted that activities such as reading and television viewing have been shown to have some health benefits in the areas of stress management and relaxation. It is not necessary for students to abstain from such activities unless they limit participation in other, more physical, activities. Rest and inactivity are valuable only as a supplement to participation in activities from the other three levels in the MyActivity Pyramid.[61]

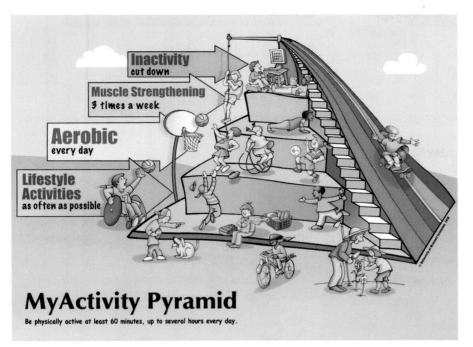

MyActivity Pyramid

Be physically active at least 60 minutes, up to several hours every day.

FIGURE 7–1 | MyActivity Pyramid For more information, visit http://extension.missouri.edu.

SOURCE: University of Missouri Extension, Department of Nutritional Sciences (Family Nutrition Education Programs), Adapted from USDA's MyPyramid and the 2008 Physical Activity Guidelines for Americans, Chapter 3. Funded in part by USDA's Food Stamp Program. *MyActivity Pyramid.* N386 Updated 2011 (http://extension.Missouri.edu/p/n386; June 2014).

Classroom teachers can promote physical activity in many ways, including integrating activity time into the daily classroom routine and using cross-curricular instructional strategies.

Promoting Physical Activity:
The Role of Physical Education

A high-quality physical education program is the cornerstone of a school's physical activity programming, and a well-written curriculum is the foundation for such a program.[62] As for other content areas, the Society of Health and Physical Educators (SHAPE) America has developed content standards to improve school-based physical education programs for students (Teacher's Toolbox 7.1).[63] Though a sound physical education program taught by qualified instructors whose practice is consistent with NASPE standards for professional practice is a critical foundational element of a school-based commitment to promoting physical activity, advocates of such a categorical approach are reminded of the complexity of promoting any health-enhancing behavior.

The ways in which fitness activities are taught and reinforced contribute to student attitudes about the value of being active for a lifetime. Because children spend a large percent of their waking hours at school, it is more educationally sound to develop a coordinated approach to promoting participation in physical activities. In a coordinated approach, a formalized physical education curriculum, planned recess, and short activity periods are supplemented by a range of opportunities for activity during the school day. Classroom teachers should integrate physical activities into cross-curricular instructional approaches. Through such an agenda, many professionals are sending a consistent message about the value of daily physical activity.[64]

As a foundation, researchers have identified the following guidelines for promoting physical activity in the physical education setting. However, classroom teachers are encouraged to examine ways they can collaborate with their physical education colleagues to extend this agenda beyond the confines of the gymnasium. In conclusion, all education professionals are encouraged to do the following:

1. Provide time for activity in the school setting.
2. Encourage self-monitoring of physical activity.
3. Provide opportunities in which activities can be individualized.
4. Expose students to a variety of activities.
5. During instruction, focus feedback on the value of regular participation and personal accomplishment, rather than on factors such as how fast, how many, or how difficult.
6. Reinforce physical skills.
7. Be an active role model.
8. Pay attention to student attitudes about the value of a lifetime of activity.

The physically literate individual:

Standard 1   Demonstrates competency in a variety of motor skills and movement patterns.

Standard 2   Applies knowledge of concepts, principles, strategies, and tactics related to movement and performance.

Standard 3   Demonstrates the knowledge and skills to achieve and maintain a health-enhancing level of physical activity and fitness.

Standard 4   Exhibits responsible personal and social behavior that respects self and others.

Standard 5   Recognizes the value of physical activity for health, enjoyment, challenge, self-expression, and/or social interaction.

SOURCE: SHAPE America, "Society of Health and Physical Education," *National Standards & Grade-Level Outcomes for K–12 Physical Education* (Reston, VA: SHAPE America, 2014), 12.

9. Reinforce successful accomplishment and minimize self-criticism.
10. Promote participation in activities outside the school environment.
11. Encourage participation in activities that can endure for a lifetime.[65]

Classroom teachers who are concerned that promoting such an agenda might require too much time and equipment are encouraged to review the suggestions in Teacher's Toolbox 7.2.

Recommendations for Concepts and Practice

Healthy Behavior Outcomes

The goal of health education is to help students adopt and maintain health-enhancing behaviors. School districts and teachers should identify the health-enhancing behaviors they would like their students to maintain or adopt. The list found in the Teacher's Toolbox 7.3 identifies possible healthy behavioral outcomes related to promoting a physically active lifestyle. Though not all these suggestions are developmentally appropriate for students in grades K–8, this list can help teachers understand how the learning activities they plan for their students support both short- and long-term desired behavior outcomes.

Developmentally Appropriate
Concepts and Skills

As with other health topics, teaching related to promoting a physically active lifestyle should be developmentally appropriate and be based on the physical, cognitive, social, emotional, and language characteristics of specific students. Teacher's Toolbox 7.3 contains a list of developmentally appropriate knowledge and skill expectations to help teachers create lessons that will

Teachers don't need a lot of complex or expensive equipment to promote physical activity among their students. Here are a few tips:

• Provide active brain breaks regularly throughout the day.
• Integrate physical activity into daily classroom practice. Think of physical activity in the same way you think about reading. Every child needs a book, and everyone needs to read—not just those students who are good at it or who enjoy it. Similarly, all children need lots of activity, not just the talented and/or interested students.
• Change the format of games in which children are "out" if they don't perform with success. Rather than sitting out for the rest of the game, children who would be considered "out" can create another group (perhaps called "lost and found") for the remainder of the ongoing round of activity.
• Look at games like "Duck-Duck Goose," "Drop the Handkerchief," and relays with new eyes. In all these games, only a few students are moving as many others stand and wait, rather than practicing, participating, and learning.
• Find new ways to move students into groups rather than having students pick teams. Often, the same students get picked last—no wonder they dislike activities for which they need the most practice.
• Play games with many smaller teams (e.g., lots of small games of volleyball like on the beach, or many smaller teams involved in kickball or softball games).
• Use many jump ropes (no more than three children per rope, two to turn the rope and one to jump) to avoid having children wait in lines.
• Use music and dance whenever possible to reinforce academic concepts and promote fun and activity.
• Set up activity learning centers in the classroom. A small amount of equipment can go a long way, and many children can rotate through many kinds of activities in very little time.
• Finally, just a few cautions concerning physical activity in the classroom:

Never use physical activity as punishment for poor academic performance or problem behavior!

Reinforce positive attitudes toward activity rather than cultivating negative or punishment associations about being active.

Never withhold recess as punishment for behavior problems, and never use recess, physical education, or other activity times as an opportunity for making up late or missed work.

encourage students to practice the desired behavior outcomes by the time they graduate from high school.[66] The numbers listed behind each knowledge expectation are aligned with and support the healthy behavior outcomes listed in the Teacher's Toolbox 7.3. Note that these grade-level spans are aligned with the National Health Education Standards.

Developmentally Appropriate Knowledge and Skill Expectations for Promoting Physical Activity

HEALTHY BEHAVIOR OUTCOMES (HBOS) FOR PROMOTING PHYSICAL ACTIVITY

HBO 1. Engage in moderate to vigorous physical activity for at least sixty minutes every day.

HBO 2. Regularly engage in physical activities that enhance cardiorespiratory endurance, flexibility, muscle endurance, and muscle strength.

HBO 3. Engage in warm-up and cool-down activities before and after structured exercise.

HBO 4. Drink plenty of water before, during, and after physical activity.

HBO 5. Follow a physical activity plan for healthy growth and development.

HBO 6. Avoid injury during physical activity.

HBO 7. Support others to be physically active.

Grades K–2 Knowledge Expectations	Grades 3–5 Knowledge Expectations	Grades 6–8 Knowledge Expectations
NHES 1: Core Concepts		
• Identify the recommended amount of physical activity for children. (HBO 1) • Explain ways to be active every day. (HBO 1) • Describe behaviors that are physically active and physically inactive. (HBO 1) • Describe how being physically active can help a person feel better. (HBO 1 & 2) • Describe the benefits of being physically active. (HBO 2) • Describe the benefits of drinking plenty of water before, during, and after physical activity. (HBO 4)	• Describe the recommended amount of physical activity for children. (HBO 1) • Identify ways to increase daily physical activity. (HBO 1) • Identify different types of physical activities. (HBO 1 & 2) • Describe the importance of choosing a variety of ways to be physically active. (HBO 1, 2 & 6) • Explain positive outcomes for being physically active. (HBO 1, 2, 6 & 7) • Identify short-term and long-term benefits of moderate and vigorous physical activity, such as improving cardiovascular health, strength, endurance, and flexibility and reducing the risks for chronic diseases. (HBO 1, 2, 6 & 7) • Identify warm-up activities to help prevent injury during physical activity. (HBO 3 & 6) • Describe the benefits of drinking water before, during, and after physical activity. (HBO 4) • Identify safety precautions for participating in various physical activities in different kinds of weather and climates. (HBO 4 & 6). • Explain how physical activity can contribute to maintaining a healthy body weight. (HBO 5 & 7). • Identify equipment needed for protection in sports and recreational activities, such as mouthpieces, pads, and helmets. (HBO 6)	• Describe the recommended amounts and types of moderate, vigorous, muscle strengthening, and bone strengthening physical activity for adolescents and adults. (HBO 1) • Explain how physical activity can be incorporated into daily life without special exercise equipment. (HBO 1, 5 & 7) • Describe ways to increase daily physical activity and decrease inactivity. (HBO 1 & 7) • Summarize the mental and social benefits of physical activity. (HBO 1 & 7) • Differentiate between physical activity, exercise, health-related fitness, and skill-related fitness (HBO 2) • Describe physical activities that contribute to maintaining or improving components of health-related fitness. (HBO 2 & 5) • Explain the short-term and long-term benefits of physical activity, including improving cardiovascular health, strength, endurance, and flexibility and reducing the risks for chronic diseases. (HBO 2 & 7) • Explain how an inactive lifestyle contributes to chronic disease. (HBO 2 & 7) • Explain the importance of warming up and cooling down after physical activity. (HBO 3) • Describe climate-related physical conditions that affect physical activity, such as heat exhaustion, sunburn, heat stroke, and hypothermia. (HBO 3, 4 & 6) • Summarize the benefits of drinking water before, during, and after physical activity (HBO 4, 6 & 7) • Summarize how physical activity can contribute to maintaining a healthy body weight. (HBO 5 & 7) • Describe the use of safety equipment for specific physical activities. (HBO 6 & 7) • Describe the ways to reduce risk of injuries from participation in sports and other physical activities. (HBO 6 & 7)

(continued)

Grades K–2 Skill Expectations	**Grades 3–5 Skill Expectations**	**Grades 6–8 Skill Expectations**

NHES 2: Analyze Influences

• Identify relevant influences of family on physical activity practices and behaviors. • Identify relevant influences of school on physical activity practices and behaviors. • Identify the influence of media and technology on physical activity practices and behaviors. • Describe positive influences on personal physical activity practices and behaviors. • Describe negative influences on personal physical activity practices and behaviors.	• Identify relevant influences of culture on physical activity practices and behaviors. • Identify relevant influences of peers on physical activity practices and behaviors. • Identify relevant influences of community on physical activity practices and behaviors. • Describe how relevant influences of family and culture affect personal physical activity practices and behaviors. • Describe how relevant influences of school and community affect personal physical activity practices and behaviors. • Describe how relevant influences of media (e.g., advertising, social networks) and technology (e.g., time playing video games) affect personal physical activity practices and behaviors. • Describe how relevant influences of peers affect personal physical activity practices and behaviors.	• Explain the influence of school rules and community laws (e.g., bicycling riding laws) on physical activity practices and behaviors. • Explain how perceptions of norms influence healthy and unhealthy physical activity practices and behaviors. • Explain how social expectations influence healthy and unhealthy behaviors related to physical activity practices and behaviors. • Explain how personal values and beliefs influence physical activity practices and behaviors. • Describe how some health risk behaviors influence the likelihood of engaging in physical inactivity practices and behaviors. • Analyze how relevant influences of family and culture affect personal physical activity practices and behaviors. • Analyze how relevant influences of school and community affect personal physical activity practices and behaviors. • Analyze how relevant influences of media (e.g., advertising, social networks) and technology (e.g., Internet shopping) affect personal physical activity practices and behaviors. • Analyze how relevant influences of peers affect personal physical activity practices and behaviors.

NHES 3: Accessing Information, Products, and Services

• Identify trusted adults at home who can help promote physical activity. • Identify trusted adults and professionals in school (e.g., physical education teacher) who can help promote physical activity. • Identify trusted adults and professionals in the community (e.g., recreation leader) who can help promote physical activity. • Explain how to locate school health helpers (e.g., teacher) who can help promote physical activity. • Explain how to locate school or community health helpers to promote physical activity.	• Describe characteristics of accurate physical activity information. • Describe characteristics of appropriate and reliable physical activity products. • Describe characteristics of appropriate and reliable physical activity services. • Demonstrate how to locate sources of accurate physical activity information.	• Analyze the validity and reliability of physical activity information. • Analyze the validity and reliability of physical activity products. • Analyze the validity and reliability of physical activity services. • Determine the availability of valid and reliable physical activity products. • Access valid and reliable physical activity information from home, school, or community. • Locate valid and reliable physical activity products. • Locate valid and reliable physical activity services.

Grades K–2 Skill Expectations	Grades 3–5 Skill Expectations	Grades 6–8 Skill Expectations

NHES 4: Interpersonal Communication

• Demonstrate effective refusal skills, including firmly saying "no," to avoid engaging in unsafe physical activities.	• Demonstrate effective verbal and nonverbal communication to avoid engaging in unsafe physical activities. • Explain how to be empathetic and compassionate toward others who are trying to maintain or increase physical activity. • Demonstrate effective peer resistance skills to avoid or reduce physical inactivity. • Demonstrate how to effectively ask for help to improve personal physical activity.	• Demonstrate the use of effective verbal and nonverbal communication to enhance physical activity. • Demonstrate effective peer resistance skills that avoid or reduce physical inactivity. • Demonstrate effective negotiation skills that avoid or reduce participation in unsafe physical activities. • Demonstrate how to effectively ask for assistance in accessing equipment necessary to safely engage in physical activities. • Demonstrate how to effectively ask for assistance to improve physical activity. • Demonstrate how to effectively communicate empathy and support to others who are trying to maintain or improve physical activity.

NHES 5: Decision Making

• Identify situations which need a decision related to physical activity. • Identify how family, peers, or media influence a decision related to physical activity. • Identify how family, peers, or media influence a decision to use proper equipment when engaging in physical activities. • Explain the potential positive and negative outcomes from a decision related to physical activity. • Describe when help is needed and when it is not needed to make a healthy decision related to physical activity.	• Identify situations which need a decision related to physical activity. • Decide when help is needed and when it is not needed to make a decision related to physical activity. • Explain how family, culture, peers, or media can influence a decision related to physical activity. • Identify options and their potential outcomes when making a decision related to physical activity. • Choose a safe and healthy option when making a decision related to physical activity. • Describe the final outcome of a decision related to physical activity.	• Identify circumstances that help or hinder making a decision to be physically active. • Determine when situations related to physical activity require a decision (e.g., when a peer suggests watching television, a friend suggests riding bikes without a helmet). • Distinguish when decisions related to physical activity can be made individually or with the help of others. • Explain how family, culture, media, peers, and personal beliefs affect a decision related to physical activity. • Distinguish between healthy and unhealthy alternatives to a decision related to physical activity. • Predict the potential healthy and unhealthy alternatives to a decision related to physical activity. • Choose a healthy alternative when making a decision related to physical activity. • Analyze the effectiveness of a final outcome of a decision related to physical activity.

NHES 6: Goal Setting

• Identify a realistic personal short-term goal to be physically active. • Take steps to achieve the personal goal to be physically active. • Identify people who can help achieve a personal goal to be physically active.	• Set a realistic personal goal to be physically active. • Track progress toward achieving a personal goal to be physically active. • Identify resources that can help to achieve a personal goal to be physically active.	• Assess personal physical activity practices. • Set a realistic personal goal to be physically active. • Assess the barriers to achieving a personal goal to be physically active. • Apply strategies to overcome barriers to achieving a personal goal to be physically active. • Use strategies and skills to achieve a personal goal to be physically active.

(continued)

Grades K–2 Skill Expectations	Grades 3–5 Skill Expectations	Grades 6–8 Skill Expectations
NHES 7: Self-Management		
• Identify practices that reduce inactivity and unsafe physical activity. • Demonstrate healthy and safe physical activity practices and behaviors. • Make a commitment to be physically active.	• Describe physical activity practices and behaviors that reduce or prevent health risks. • Demonstrate healthy physical activity practices and behaviors. • Make a commitment to be physically active.	• Explain the importance of being responsible for being physically active. • Analyze personal practices and behaviors that reduce or prevent physical inactivity. • Demonstrate healthy practices and behaviors to improve the physical activity of oneself and others. • Make a commitment to be physically active.
NHES 8: Advocacy		
• Make requests to others to promote being physically active. • Demonstrate how to encourage peers to be physically active.	• Give factual information to improve the physical activity of others. • State personal beliefs to improve the physical activity of others. • Demonstrate how to persuade others to make healthy physically active choices.	• State a health-enhancing position about being physically active, supported with accurate information, to improve the health of others. • Persuade others to make healthy and safe physical activity choices. • Collaborate with others to advocate for individuals, families, and schools to be physically active. • Demonstrate how to adapt a positive physical activity message for different audiences.

SOURCE: Centers for Disease Control and Prevention, *Health Education Curriculum Analysis Tool* (www.cdc.gov/healthyyouth/HECAT/index.htm, 2014): PA-3–PA-60.

STRATEGIES FOR LEARNING AND ASSESSMENT

Promoting Physical Activity

This section provides an example of a standards-based learning and assessment strategy for each NHES standard. The examples in this chapter can be applied to any content area. Chapters 5 to 14 include content-specific learning and assessment strategies organized by standard and grade cluster (K–2, 3–5, and 6–8). Each set of strategies begins with a restatement of the standard and a reminder of the assessment criteria, drawn from the RMC Health rubrics in Appendix B. Strategies are written as directions for teachers and include applicable theory of planned behavior (TPB) constructs (intention to act in healthy ways, attitudes toward behavior, subjective norms, perceived behavioral control). Additional strategies for learning and assessment for Chapter 7 can be found at the Online Learning Center. These learning and assessment strategies provide building blocks for standards-based lessons and units that can be tailored to local needs. Assessment criteria are used with permission from RMC Health. See Appendix B for Scoring Rubrics.

NHES 1 | Core Concepts

Students will comprehend concepts related to health promotion and disease prevention to enhance health.

ASSESSMENT CRITERIA

• Connections—Describe relationships between behavior and health; draw logical conclusions about connections between behavior and health.
• Comprehensiveness—Thoroughly cover health topic, showing breadth and depth; give accurate information.

Grades K–2

PE Central for Grades PreK–2   Lower-elementary teachers can find a wealth of ideas for teaching physical education and physical activity at PE Central (www.pecentral.org). The site includes lesson and assessment ideas, tips for creating a positive learning climate, and many other resources. Teachers also can find "activity cues" to help them teach specific skills in kid-friendly terms, for example, these cues about chasing:

• Definition: Chasing is moving quickly to catch up, tag, or overtake a moving object or person.
• Move quickly.
• Keep eye on the person's middle (waist) if chasing someone.
• Be ready to make quick changes of direction.

Many lower-elementary teachers are responsible for planning, implementing, and assessing their own physical education. PE Central offers one-stop shopping for tips on helping students get healthy through physical activity.

My Heart Is a Strong Muscle!   Ask children to give their ideas about what muscles are and where they are located. Children likely will indicate muscles in their arms and legs. Ask if they think their hearts might be muscles, too. Ask children to locate their hearts by pointing to the protective sternum in the center of the chest. Ask children if they know what a pulse is and where they can feel it. Have them try feeling for their carotid arteries on either side of their neck below the jaw line. Ask children what happens to the heart and pulse when we exercise. Ask them to stand and participate in an experiment. First, have children walk in place. Call time and ask them to feel for their pulse. What happened? Next, ask them to jog in place or in a small space. What happens to their pulse? Now ask them to run to a certain point and back. What happens? Children can check their pulse again in five or ten seconds to see if it has slowed. What's happening in there? How is exercise good for the heart? It makes it work and grow stronger, as it does any other muscle.

ASSESSMENT | Anyone who has worked with young children knows that asking them to count their pulse rate makes for wild and hilarious answers. Rather than having them count, simply ask them to feel the difference in pulse rates as they are more, or less, active. For an assessment task, children can describe the kinds of exercise that make their hearts strong. For assessment criteria, their information should be correct, and they should make a connection between exercise and healthy hearts. (Construct: Attitudes toward behavior.)

My Physical Activity Pyramid Introduce students to one of the many examples of children's physical activity pyramids available on the Internet. Select a pyramid model based on the developmental level of learners. Conduct a mini lesson with students about the importance of daily physical activity. Tell them that our bodies need to engage in different types of activities to strengthen muscles, to develop and maintain flexibility, and to make our hearts strong. Share with students the physical activity pyramid and discuss how the different activities help our bodies stay healthy. Have students identify what the different types of activities do to help our bodies be strong and healthy. Additionally, have students identify strategies they might use to remind themselves to get up and move when they have had thirty minutes of sitting time.

ASSESSMENT | For an assessment task, have students develop their own physical activity pyramid with activities they enjoy doing that correspond to each category of the pyramid. Additionally, have students identify what they like to do in their "down" time and identify two strategies they can use to encourage cutting down on sitting time. These ideas should be drawn to the outside of the pyramid. For assessment criteria, students should be able to provide correct information about different forms of physical activity that meet the pyramid categories (everyday, aerobic, etc.) and make connections through drawings included on the pyramid about the connections between physical activity and health. (Constructs: Attitudes toward behavior, perceived behavioral control.)

Active or Sedentary Teachers can ask students to define two words that might be new to them: *active* and *sedentary*. Students can consult dictionaries and talk to family members to help them define the words. Students will find that *sedentary* refers to a lot of sitting and little physical exercise. Students can brainstorm a list of things that are active (playing soccer, going for a walk, walking up the stairs) and sedentary (watching TV, sleeping on the couch, sitting at a desk). Students can also distinguish between activities that are somewhat or very active.

ASSESSMENT | For an assessment task, students can plan a variety of ways to get more physical activity into their day both at school and at home. For assessment criteria, students should identify at least five health-enhancing ways to increase physical activity. (Construct: Perceived behavioral control.)

Grades 3–5

PE Central for Grades 3–5 Upper-elementary teachers can find a wealth of ideas for teaching physical education and physical activity at PE Central (www.pecentral.org). The site includes lesson and assessment ideas, strategies for creating a positive learning environment, and many other resources. Teachers sometimes are hesitant about taking their students outdoors or to an indoor activity area for physical education. Following are some tips for successful physical education lessons:

- Use children's names, and notice and ask about what they are doing.
- Set clear boundaries for the lesson; for example, we will stay inside the area between the sidewalk and the cafeteria today.
- Post class rules clearly in all places in which you teach. A student can carry a laminated poster outside for physical activity lessons.
- When instructing, keep your "back to the wall" as much as possible. (Circulate outside of the group, with the children facing you.)

- While helping individual students with a task or skill, position yourself so you can see the rest of the class.
- Keep your eyes up and looking across the class so you can see what is going on with all the students, not just the students in front of you. Think of it as defensive driving—you don't look at the hood when driving but instead look out in front so you can anticipate and avoid potential problems.
- Have students practice and perfect the procedures and protocols you set for management tasks such as entering and leaving the classroom, lining up, getting out equipment, getting drinks, what to do on the "go" and "stop" signals, and so on.
- Enjoy the students! Physical activity lessons are a time to get to know students and learn about their talents, interests, and abilities in different ways. Let them know you see them.

Muscular Strength and Endurance Ask children how we make our muscles stronger. We can make our muscles stronger by exercising more (doing more push-ups or abdominal crunches) or longer (exercising for longer periods of time). Elementary children should not participate in weight training. Rather, young students become stronger through appropriate physical activity. Ask students whether they know the meaning of the word *endurance*. To try it out, have students place the back of one hand on their desks or a table top. Ask them to open and close their fist on a "go" signal as many times as they can, counting as they go, for a selected period of time (two to three minutes). When time is called, ask students to write down the number of fists they made and words to describe the feeling of muscle fatigue. Ask students to think of other activities that cause muscle fatigue in other parts of the body (arms, legs, abdominal muscles). Endurance activities make muscles stronger, but be sure students can explain why "no pain, no gain" is the wrong approach. Have students exercise until muscles feel mildly fatigued, but have them stop immediately if they feel any pain.

ASSESSMENT | The students' explanations of building muscle strength and endurance are the assessment task for this activity. For assessment criteria, students should provide correct information and make connections between building strength and endurance and good health. (Construct: Attitudes toward behavior.)

We Got the Beat! Taking Pulse Rates Teach students the correct technique for taking their carotid pulse. Working in pairs, have students take and record their resting heart rate in an electronic spreadsheet. Students can use the stopwatch feature on a tablet to count their heart beats for six seconds, stop, and multiply by ten (the equivalent of sixty seconds). Then have students participate in several kinds of aerobic activity (jumping rope, running in place, jogging to a certain point and back) and record postexercise pulse rates. *Aerobic* may be a new word for students. Have students record their pulse rates again in five or ten seconds to notice how quickly their heart rates return to resting rates. Emphasize the importance of a cooldown period after exercising hard.

ASSESSMENT | For an assessment task, have students record their resting, postexercise, and cooldown pulse rates. Students can use the recorded rates from the spreadsheet to create a graph. Have students include the graph in a document and type a paragraph to explain what is happening to their heart rates during each activity. Students can use the recorded rates from the spreadsheet to create a graph. Have students include the graph in a document and type a paragraph to explain what is happening to their heart rates during each activity. For assessment criteria, students should provide correct information and make connections between aerobic exercise and health. (Constructs: Attitudes toward behavior, perceived behavioral control.)

Why Exercise Is Cool!   Teachers and students can visit the Kids' Health website (www.kidshealth.org) to find out why exercise is cool and what counts as exercise. Students can investigate topics such as the following:

- Exercise makes your heart happy.
- Exercise strengthens muscles.
- Exercise makes you flexible.
- Exercise keeps the balance.
- Exercise makes you feel good.

Students can work in pairs or small groups to investigate these and other exercise-related topics on the Kids Health website. This activity links to NHES 3, access information, products, and services.

ASSESSMENT | For an assessment task, students can research and report on their topics to classmates. For assessment criteria, students should report accurate information and draw conclusions about the connections between behavior (being physically active) and good health. (Constructs: Perceived behavioral control, attitudes toward behavior, subjective norms.)

Fitness Spider Webs: Moderate and Vigorous Physical Activities with No Cost or Equipment   On a sheet of paper with two columns, students brainstorm a list of all moderate physical activities that they can do within walking or biking distance of their homes that have no associated cost and require no equipment (in column 1). In column 2, students repeat this task identifying all vigorous physical activities that meet the same criteria. Then the class is divided into teams of no more than eight students. One student from each team is given a ball of yarn. As this person verbalizes an example of a moderate physical activity from their list, they unroll and toss (or roll) the ball of yarn to a classmate in the circle. The activity is continued until all group members have contributed a unique activity. Students are asked to note the shape of the "spider web" that the yarn has created.

The process is reversed as the last person to have received the ball of yarn is asked to identify a vigorous physical activity from their written list. As they make their contribution they roll up the yarn and pass or carry it to the person from whom they received it. This reversing process is continued until all yarn is rolled back into balls. Students are asked to return to their desks and turn their sheets over to the blank back side. Here, they re-create two drawings of the spider web created by their group. On each line in the first drawing, they are asked to write an example of a moderate physical activity. They repeat this process on the second drawing, this time indicating vigorous physical activity examples on each line.

ASSESSMENT | The students' spider web drawings are the assessment task for this activity. For assessment criteria, students must have identified a minimum of eight examples of each type of activity that meet criteria identified for the original brainstorming phase of the activity. (Construct: Attitudes toward behavior.)

Grades 6–8

PE Central for Grades 6–8   Middle-level teachers can find a wealth of ideas for teaching physical education and physical activity at PE Central (www.pecentral.org). The site includes lesson and assessment ideas, strategies for creating a positive learning environment, and many other resources. The Best Practice link provides strategies such as "Building Fit Kids for Life—Fitness Portfolios." This strategy includes instructions for having students participate in a six- to eight-week unit for building fitness portfolios. Although many middle schools have physical education specialists, PE Central provides ideas for classroom teachers to help students dig deeper into connections between physical activity and health.

Graphic Organizer for Sports Skills   In *Children Moving*, Graham, Holt/Hale, and Parker organize children's physical education by generic skills themes: traveling; chasing, fleeing, and dodging; jumping and landing;

balancing; transferring weight and rolling; kicking and punting; throwing and catching; volleying and dribbling; striking with rackets and paddles; and striking with long-handled implements.[67] To begin this activity, have students use an online collaboration tool like Padlet (padlet.com) to generate a list of as many generic skills as they can. List them for the class, with the idea of adding to the list as needed. Next, have students add to the collaboration tool all the sports they can (track-and-field events, volleyball, soccer, gymnastics, softball, basketball, ice-skating, roller-blading, swimming, diving, water skiing, snow skiing, surfing, skateboarding, tennis, badminton, archery, golf, bowling, football, wrestling). Have students work in twos or threes to diagram the skills involved in one sport of their choosing. Students can use a graphic organizer app (like Inspiration, Popplet, iBrainstorm, and iCardSort) and name a sport as the main idea of the graphic organizer. Next, list the skills that are necessary for successful participation in the sport on the graphic organizer. Students can use the app to add photographs of themselves demonstrating each skill. Have students share their diagrams, demonstrations, and explanations with the class, adding more skills to the original class list, if needed. Ask class members to help out if they think of skills that groups didn't include for their sports. As an extension, students can categorize the skills according to health-related fitness categories (cardiorespiratory or aerobic endurance, muscular strength and endurance, flexibility, body composition).

ASSESSMENT | The students' graphic organizers are the assessment task for this activity. For assessment criteria, students should provide correct information and make connections between participating in regular physical activity and health. (Construct: Attitudes toward behavior.)

A Physical Activity Walkabout   This activity can focus on teaching any of the key essential concepts desired, particularly those where personal preference contributes to student engagement in physical activity. Create a handout asking students for information such as the following:

- Give an example of how to incorporate physical activity into your daily life without special exercise equipment.
- Identify one mental (or social) benefit of physical activity.
- Describe one short-term (or long-term) benefit of physical activity.
- Give an example of how physical inactivity can contribute to chronic disease.
- Give one example of how you reduce your chance of injury during physical activity.

Other questions can be generated from the HECAT Knowledge and Skill Expectations.

Have students individually complete each question giving their own preference or personal response in the first column (my answer). After students have answered the questions in their own words, they are to walk about the room interacting with other students and writing down their responses to the same questions in column 2 (and 3, if desired). This allows students to gain different perspectives on replies to the questions.

ASSESSMENT | For an assessment task, students are to select one question from the handout and create a photo journal, PowerPoint presentation, or poster (depending on resources available) identifying a minimum of three different approaches to the question. For assessment criteria, students must have identified a minimum number of examples of different ways to address the behavior. Student examples should be accurate and demonstrate an understanding of the connection between physical activity and health. (Constructs: Perceived behavioral control, attitudes toward behavior.)

NHES 2 | Analyze Influences

Students will analyze the influence of family, peers, culture, media, technology, and other factors on health behaviors.

ASSESSMENT CRITERIA

- Identify both external and internal influences on health.
- Explain how external and internal influences interact to impact health choices and behaviors.
- Explain both positive and negative influences, as appropriate.

Grades K–2

My Family's Favorite Activities Have students write and illustrate a page or short story about their families' favorite physical activities. As an alternative, have students write about physical activities they did while they were on vacation or visiting relatives. Have students share their pages or stories with the class. Students can bind pages into a class book about physical activity to share with other classes or to place in the library.

ASSESSMENT | The students' pages or short stories are the assessment task for this activity. For assessment criteria, students should write about how they feel about participating with their families. Does family involvement contribute to their enjoyment of physical activity and make them more likely to participate? (Construct: Subjective norms.)

My Personal Favorites Have students share their personal favorite physical activities. Make a class list on one side of a piece of chart paper or on the board. Students should explain what they like about particular activities and why. List the students' responses beside their activities. Ask students to consider how liking an activity makes them more likely to participate regularly.

ASSESSMENT | For an assessment task, students can describe a favorite physical activity and when and how often they participate in the activity. For assessment criteria, students should explain what they like about this activity and why and how this influences them to participate. (Construct: Subjective norms.)

You Can't Say You Can't Play Kindergarten teacher and author Vivian Paley wrote *You Can't Say You Can't Play* about her experiences working with children in kindergarten through grade 5.[68] Paley introduced this new rule to her kindergarten class and invited older children to share their opinions about the fairness of the rule. Teachers might introduce this rule to early elementary students and ask them to debate what it means and whether it's fair. What does it mean if some children are left out? How can everyone be included? How can children be sure everyone gets to play?

ASSESSMENT | For an assessment task, students can discuss ways they can practice the idea of you can't say "You can't play" for one week. For assessment criteria, students should identify three ways they can carry out the idea with their classmates. Students should assess their progress at the end of each day and at the end of the week. Students should explain how the new rule influenced their play time and their feelings about playing with others at school and in the community. (Constructs: Intention to act in healthy ways, subjective norms, attitudes toward behavior.)

Grades 3–5

Supports for and Barriers to Physical Activity Have students brainstorm a list of their favorite physical activities. Next, ask them to think about people, places, feelings, and conditions that help them participate more often (supports) and those that prevent their participation (barriers). Students should discuss ways to build their supports and overcome their barriers. Have students choose one strategy to put into practice during the coming week and report back to classmates. This activity links to NHES 5, decision making, and NHES 6, goal setting.

ASSESSMENT | For an assessment task, students can identify at least one personal support for and one personal barrier to physical activity. For assessment criteria, students should discuss or write about how these supports and barriers influence them and identify at least two strategies for building supports or overcoming barriers. (Construct: Subjective norms.)

Selling It! Students can collect advertisements for sports clothing, shoes, drinks, and equipment and keep a record of billboard, poster, and television commercial advertisements they see for sporting goods. Students can use the list of advertising techniques in Chapter 3 to identify the methods advertisers use to persuade young people to buy their products.

ASSESSMENT | For an assessment task, students can work individually, in pairs, or in small groups to analyze an advertisement for an activity- or sport-related product. For assessment criteria, students should identify the advertising techniques used and explain how they might influence young people. Students also should explain how the advertisements might be misleading. (Construct: Perceived behavioral control.)

Grades 6–8

Media Messages About Physical Activity and Gender Students can do an online image search of physical fitness media messages. Have students work in small groups to make a digital presentation that depicts media messages to males and females about physical activity. What conclusions do students draw from the media images they find? Do men and women get similar messages to be strong and active? Students should share their presentations and conclusions with classmates. How can students talk back to media images that they find false or misleading? Students might want to turn their talking back to media images into truth ads about physical activity for boys and girls.

ASSESSMENT | The students' presentations and conclusions are the assessment task for this activity. For assessment criteria, students should explain how media images might affect young people's impressions and decisions about physical activity and should provide at least two ways to talk back to false or misleading media messages. (Constructs: Perceived behavioral control, subjective norms.)

Puberty and Physical Activity Ask students to talk in same-gender groups about the changes males and females go through in puberty and how those changes can affect attitudes about and decisions to participate in physical activity. Then have the class "jigsaw" to form different mixed-gender groups. The new groups should share their previous discussions and ask for comments from new group members. What conclusions do students draw about how the onset of puberty might affect males' and females' attitudes about and decisions to participate in physical activity? What happens to early developers? What happens to late developers? How can students support and encourage their classmates to be physically active? What behaviors do students want stopped (teasing a girl about her developing breasts or hips, disparaging a boy who is small, making fun of students who are heavy or tall)?

ASSESSMENT | For an assessment task, students can make a two-column chart to show their analysis of how puberty can be a support for or a barrier to participating in physical activity for boys and for girls. For assessment criteria, students should identify at least three supports and three barriers and explain how to build on supports and overcome barriers. (Construct: Perceived behavioral control.)

NHES 3 | Access Information, Products, and Services

Students will demonstrate the ability to access valid information and products and services to enhance health.

- Access health information—Locate specific sources of health information, products, or services relevant to enhancing health in a given situation.
- Evaluate information sources—Explain the degree to which identified sources are valid, reliable, and appropriate as a result of evaluating each source.

Grades K–2

Health Helpers for Physical Activity   Children can name people in their homes, neighborhoods, schools, and communities who can help them learn more about fitness, physical activity, and safety (family member, athletic trainer, coach, athlete, teacher). Have students do an Internet search for outdoor activities for kids. Students can get new ideas from the search for a number of activities that can keep them active outdoors. The Outbound Collective (www.theoutbound.com) provides a search option for local outdoor recreation. Students can make a list of physical activities they can do at home and others they can do in the community.

ASSESSMENT | For an assessment task, students can create pages for a class book on physical activity for families. For assessment criteria, students should decide as a group what would make "great pages." Use these criteria to assess and help students assess their work. At a minimum, students should identify a safe place where families can be active. (Construct: Subjective norms.)

Places and Spaces for Family Physical Activity   Students can brainstorm a list of places they and their families can go to be physically active. Teachers can help students see everyday places in new ways. For example, families can be active right in their own backyards. Students can make a list of physical activities they can do at home and others they can do in the community.

ASSESSMENT | For an assessment task, students can create pages for a class book on physical activity for families. For assessment criteria, students should decide as a group what would make "great pages." Use these criteria to assess and help students assess their work. At a minimum, students should identify a safe place where families can be active. (Construct: Subjective norms.)

Grades 3–5

Collecting Information on Family Heart Rates   In class, have students take and record their resting heart rates (count their carotid pulse for six seconds and multiply by ten). As a homework activity, have students take and record the resting heart rates of at least six family members of different ages. Send home a note to parents or caregivers with a place to record data. Someone will need a watch with a second hand. When students return to class, have them graph their findings according to the ages of family members. What do they notice? Is there a connection between age and heart rate? What other factors influence heart rate (fitness, health status, weight)? As an extension, students might want to investigate the heart rates of different types of animals. They might be surprised at what they find.

ASSESSMENT | The graph or graphic organizer students make is the assessment task for this activity. For assessment criteria, students should explain their data and draw conclusions about the information they collected. (Construct: Attitudes toward behavior.)

Ask an Expert on Activity and Fitness   Help students write a letter of invitation to a local sports figure or sports medicine professional to come to class to talk about staying fit and healthy. Students can develop a list of interview questions for the visit. In particular, students can ask about

activities and practices that are *contraindicated* (a new vocabulary word), such as straight-legged sit-ups, ballistic stretching, and hard stretching while muscles are still cold.

ASSESSMENT | For an assessment task, students can work in small groups to make posters about recommendations for physical activity and safety. For assessment criteria, students should provide the sources of their information, including any research they do in addition to hearing the guest speaker. (Construct: Attitudes toward behavior.)

Use Your Head—Design a Helmet!   Teachers and students can visit the Bicycle Helmet Safety Institute website (www.bhsi.org) and Kids Health (kidshealth.org/en/kids/bike-safety.html) to learn more about bicycle helmet safety. Teachers and students can investigate topics such as how helmets work and how to fit them correctly; classroom materials are also available. Students also will find unusual topics that might pique their interest, such as whether helmets can be worn with braids or baseball caps.

Teachers should know that persuading students to wear bicycle helmets has been a difficult safety campaign, especially in low-income neighborhoods. In addition to helping students learn about bicycle helmets, teachers might have students take on the project of finding out what students in their school and community say about bicycle helmets and why. Based on their own school and community cultural findings (NHES 2), students can design their own bicycle helmets.

ASSESSMENT | For an assessment task, students can investigate the safety requirements for helmets and design their ideal bicycle helmet. For assessment criteria, students can explain the safety features of their design, where they obtained their information, and why their sources were valid ones. Helmet designs can be included with posters around the school to create an advocacy campaign for wearing helmets. (NHES 8). (Constructs: Attitudes toward behavior, subjective norms.)

Grades 6–8

Field Trips for Activity and Fitness   Help students arrange to visit a local sport or activity facility (fitness club, athletic arena, ball field). Have a staff member talk with the students about the training regimens and practices that individuals and team members follow. Students can prepare a list of questions in advance.

ASSESSMENT | Have students design a fitness plan for themselves, based on what they learned and other research. For assessment criteria, students should justify their plans and information sources. (Construct: Attitudes toward behavior.)

Designing a Fitness Course   This activity can range from the imaginary to the actual. Have students talk with experts and do their own research on designing a fitness course of some kind for their school or community. Students should determine the equipment needs, estimate costs, and provide a final diagram and budget. Students can work on their project as a whole class or in small groups and present their work to classmates, staff members, and parents or caregivers.

ASSESSMENT | The students' designs and accompanying explanations are the assessment task for this activity. For assessment criteria, students should provide and justify all information sources. (Construct: Perceived behavioral control.)

Bogus Claims and Scams for Physical Activity Products   Students and teachers will find that bogus and half-truth claims on "miracle products" abound in the area of physical activity. Students can participate in a scavenger hunt to find these products and claims in print media and on television. Students should note what the product is (a nutritional supplement, an exercise device, a diet pill), what claims are being made, the cost of the product, and the "fine print." In many cases, students will find that the fine print begins with the words "results not typical." Students also can investigate further to learn whether "miracle products" have caused harm to users.

ASSESSMENT | Students can work in pairs or small groups to investigate and report on the product of their choice. For assessment criteria, students should describe the product, state the claims, determine the cost, report the fine print or disclaimers, and determine whether the product has harmed anyone. Students also should explain where they obtained their information and why their sources are valid. (Construct: Perceived behavioral control.)

NHES 4 | Interpersonal Communication

Students will demonstrate the ability to use interpersonal communication skills to enhance health and avoid or reduce health risks.

ASSESSMENT CRITERIA
- Use appropriate verbal/nonverbal communication strategies in an effective manner to enhance health or avoid/reduce health risks.
- Use appropriate skills (negotiation skills, refusal skills) and behaviors (eye contact, body language, attentive listening).

Grades K–2

Let's Play More Adults dictate much of the physical activity in which young people engage. As children grow up it becomes important they develop the skills to be able to communicate with trusted adults about a variety of health topics, including physical activity. For this activity the goal is for children to be able to ask trusted adults to help children engage in more physical activity. Teachers should brainstorm with students times in the day when children are less active and begin feeling lazy, such as after a long school lesson or after school, or when students would like to increase their activity level, such as during recess. Engage students in a discussion of ways they could ask trusted adults to provide them more opportunities to be physically active during these times of the day and/or engage in more physical rather than sedentary activities.

ASSESSMENT | For an assessment task, students will take a half sheet of paper and fold it into three equal parts. In the first column students will identify a situation or time of the day during which they would like to increase their activity level. In the second column students will identify the appropriate trusted adult to seek assistance from. In the third column students will draw a picture or write the words they would use to ask the trusted adult to help them increase their activity level during the identified situation or time. For assessment criteria, students should demonstrate appropriate verbal and nonverbal communication and seek assistance respectfully. (Constructs: Attitudes toward behavior, perceived behavioral control.)

Let's Be Active and Safe Kids often challenge each other to take risks or engage in behaviors that could result in injury. Helping students begin to develop refusal skills is an important developmental task. Brainstorm with students for a list of physical activities they could be asked to engage in that might result in injury, create personal risk, or go against family safety rules (e.g., riding a bicycle without a helmet, swimming without an adult present, creating bike or skateboard jumps). Share with students strategies for saying no to such requests. There are a variety of different strategies students can use to say no. Identifying one that works for your students is important to increase the likelihood that they will apply the skill outside of the classroom setting. One strategy includes a three-step process: (1) State the problem; (2) State what could happen by engaging in the behavior (someone could get hurt, get in trouble, disappoint

someone); (3) Offer an alternative. Teach this or another refusal strategy to students and have them practice with partners with two or three scenarios you provide.

ASSESSMENT | For an assessment task, have students create a cartoon strip. Students are to identify a realistic physical activity situation of their own making that could put them at risk for depiction in the cartoon. Assessment criteria should include effective application of the refusal strategy taught during the lesson. Students should demonstrate clear verbal and nonverbal messages within their cartoon strip. (Construct: Perceived behavioral control.)

Communicating About Physical Activity with Children's Books Teachers can read a variety of children's books with students to get them talking about physical activity. The booklist at the end of the chapter includes books that address many themes related to physical activity, such as dealing with a bully on the playground, overcoming disappointment, and learning to work as a member of a team. Teachers can use these books to spark discussion about physical activity and the way students treat others and want to be treated in physical activity settings.

ASSESSMENT | For an assessment task, students can work in small groups to retell and act out the story, using verbal and nonverbal communication. For assessment criteria, students should demonstrate clear verbal and nonverbal communication to depict the story accurately. (Construct: Perceived behavioral control.)

Grades 3–5

Don't Be So Lazy Kids this age often choose free-time activities that tend to be sedentary, such as playing video games or talking with friends. As children establish patterns in how they spend time together it can become challenging to change the way friends interact or play together during free time. On individual slips of paper, have students write down three activities they do with their friends that are sedentary. Play a game of charades with students acting out these various situations. These situations create the context for which the communication skills can then be applied. In pairs, have students draw a different situation and through charades demonstrate how they might convince their friends to join them in a free-time activity that would require them to be physically active.

ASSESSMENT | For an assessment task, give pairs of students yet another situation from those written on the slips of paper. Pairs will now use verbal skills to influence their peer to participate in behaviors that are more physically active than that written on the slip of paper. For assessment criteria, students should demonstrate positive peer pressure through the use of appropriate verbal and nonverbal communication skills. (Constructs: Perceived behavioral control, subjective norms, intention to act in healthy ways.)

That's Not Safe! Kids often push the limits of safety when engaging in physical activity, such as riding bikes over jumps or leaping off playground equipment from unsafe heights. Learning how to continue to be physically active while also being safe is an important communication skill for students to develop. Prepare a carousel activity (see Chapter 4) with different forms of physical activity listed on each sheet of paper. Activities might include bike riding, swimming, rollerblading, soccer (or other team sports popular with students), recess games, and so on. Divide the class into equal groups of four or five students and assign each group one activity or poster. Give students about two minutes to brainstorm ways in which the listed activity could become unsafe when playing with friends. After two minutes, rotate students to the next activity/poster and allow them to brainstorm for one to two minutes. Repeat the process until brainstorming appears to be exhausted or as time permits. Following the carousel activity, assign groups their original poster topic. Have each group develop a set of communication strategies for avoiding the unsafe situations that were identified. Have groups share the strategies they identified.

ASSESSMENT | For an assessment task, individual students can create a short story, written scenario, or story board in which they take one of the unsafe physical activity situations and apply one of the communication strategies groups identified to the specific scenario. Students can share their work and the teacher can post them around the classroom. For assessment criteria, appropriate verbal and nonverbal communication strategies should be demonstrated, specifically negotiation skills to avoid unsafe physical activity. (Constructs: Perceived behavioral control, attitudes toward behavior.)

Reducing Physical Inactivity   Young people enjoy many activities that keep them from being physically active. Playing video games, watching television, or reading tend to be sedentary behaviors. Although we all need a little downtime, too much can be harmful to our health. Learning to communicate personal desires to be physically active can encourage others to be active, too. Engage students in a brainstorming session about why people engage in sedentary behaviors (e.g., they are tired, they enjoy the activity, they don't have a playmate, poor weather). Assign small groups of students one of the brainstormed responses. Have groups brainstorm a list of responses someone could use when given the response for not engaging in physical activity. Have groups share the different responses with the class.

ASSESSMENT | For an assessment task, students can select one of the reasons brainstormed and apply at least two of the different responses. Students can write a cartoon strip, role play, tell a story, or other to demonstrate their ability to apply the communication strategy to a situation. Assessment criteria include students applying the verbal and nonverbal communication skills effectively to encourage an individual to take a break from sedentary behavior and engage in physical activity. (Construct: Perceived behavioral control.)

Grades 6–8

Walk and Talk for Fitness   Have students walk or jog and talk with a buddy for a certain period of time during recess or physical education. The idea is to walk or jog and talk continuously—aerobic exercise should permit students to carry on a conversation. Afterward, have students discuss the pros and cons of exercising with someone else. Do students prefer exercising by themselves or with others?

ASSESSMENT | For an assessment task, students can make posters about exercising with a buddy. For assessment criteria, students should identify at least two ways that movement enhanced or detracted from their communication and enjoyment of exercise. (Construct: Perceived behavioral control.)

Physical Activity Pressure Lines   Review the techniques taught in previous lessons about refusing negative peer pressure. See Chapter 3 for peer resistance techniques that tend to be successful with middle school students. Model for students a situation in which someone is posing a negative influence to someone and their physical activity choices. Demonstrate for students a number of different approaches for dealing with the negative peer pressure, such as avoiding the situation or walking away, suggesting an alternative, or gaining support from a friend. As a class work through an additional scenario to determine that students have a solid grasp of how to apply the communication skills. Provide students with a note card and have each describe at least two situations where they have been pressured negatively regarding physical activity. Examples might be situations where the student was influenced to engage in unsafe physical activity behaviors or to choose inactivity over being active for long periods of time. In pairs, have students line up in two lines facing each other with partner A on one side, and partner B directly across about an arm's length away. Partner A describes the situation written on his or her card to Partner B. Partner B then pressures Partner A to engage in the situation described. Partner A uses appropriate verbal and nonverbal

communication strategies to resist the pressure. Partner A then moves one person to the right. Partner B then describes the situation written on his or her card to the new Partner A and the process is repeated. Repeat the process for at least four or five rotations so that students are given enough opportunities to practice their refusals. Students can alternate between the two situations they wrote down or use the same one for each rotation. After two or three rotations, briefly stop the activity to process how students are doing. Use some guided questions to determine how comfortable students are becoming using the refusals and how effective their refusals are.

ASSESSMENT | For an assessment task, students can be placed in groups of three. The trio then takes turns providing the pressure, refusing the pressure, and observing. The observer is responsible for providing the student refusing the pressure with feedback—two things he or she did well and two recommendations for improvement specifically as it relates to the refusal. After trios have served all three roles, students can write a brief reflection on what they learned about their communication skills from the pressure line activity as well as assessment scenarios. For assessment criteria, students should demonstrate appropriate verbal and nonverbal communication skills to reduce or avoid negative pressure related to physical activity. Additionally, students should be able to identify at least one strength and one area for improvement in relation to their ability to refuse negative peer pressure. (Constructs: Perceived behavioral control, attitudes toward behavior.)

Talk Back to Obstacles and Barriers   Ask students to name obstacles and barriers they have encountered that prevent their participation in physical activity. Their answers may range from unexpected rain to procrastination about doing homework (and thus not being able to go out to play). Students also might identify friends or family members who prefer to be inactive and want company. Students can demonstrate ways to talk back to obstacles and barriers to maximize opportunities for physical activity.

ASSESSMENT | Students can demonstrate talking back to obstacles and barriers to physical activity for an assessment task. For assessment criteria, students should be able to demonstrate at least two communication strategies to overcome barriers. (Construct: Perceived behavioral control.)

NHES 5 | Decision Making

Students will demonstrate the ability to use decision-making skills to enhance health.

ASSESSMENT CRITERIA | Reach a health-enhancing decision using a process consisting of the following steps:
- Identify a health-risk situation.
- Examine alternatives.
- Evaluate positive and negative consequences.
- Decide on a health-enhancing course of action.

Grades K–2

Playing Indoors or Outdoors   Have students brainstorm a list of physical activities they can do indoors and outdoors, at home and at school. Have them list the pros and cons of doing each activity (pro—out of the sun indoors, con—not enough room indoors). Have students make a decision about an indoor or outdoor activity they want to participate in during the coming week. Students should report back to the class on their decisions.

ASSESSMENT | For an assessment task, students can describe how their physical activity went. For assessment criteria, students should write or tell about why their decision did or did not work well and their plans for future activity, based on their experiences. (Construct: Perceived behavioral control.)

Grades 3–5

Make the Healthy Way the Easy Way   A European colleague shared the slogan "Make the healthy way the easy way." Students can work in pairs or small groups to identify ways to put this slogan into practice for students and their families. For example, students can list activities that don't require lots of equipment or special clothing. Students also might list environmental cues (the dog leash hanging over the kitchen doorknob to remind the family to go for a walk when the dog needs a walk). This activity links to NHES 7, self-management, and NHES 8, advocacy.

ASSESSMENT | For an assessment task, each student can decide on one strategy for making the healthy way the easy way and track progress for one week. For assessment criteria, students should report on their progress and identify supports for and barriers to making the healthy way the easy way. (Construct: Perceived behavioral control.)

Grades 6–8

The Best Activities for Me   Have students brainstorm a class list of all the kinds of physical activities they can name. Ask students to name the pros and cons of each activity (certain equipment is needed to play). Have each student choose three activities. Beside each activity, students should list the positive and negative consequences of participating in the activity. Have students choose one activity to participate in regularly for the next two weeks, keep a journal of progress, and report back to the class.

ASSESSMENT | The students' plans and reports are the assessment task for this activity. For assessment criteria, students should be able to work through a simple decision-making process, showing choices, consequences, decisions, and progress. (Construct: Perceived behavioral control.)

NHES 6 | Goal Setting

Students will demonstrate the ability to use goal-setting skills to enhance health.

ASSESSMENT CRITERIA
- Goal statement—Give goal statement that identifies health benefits; goal is achievable and will result in enhanced health.
- Goal setting plan—Show plan that is complete, logical, and sequential, and includes a process to assess progress.

Grades K–2

Recess Success   The lure of computers and other technology sometimes results in children wanting to stay indoors for recess rather than going out to play and be active. Ask students to talk about ways they can be active during recess, and have students set a simple goal for themselves ("During recess this week, I will walk around the play yard four times"). Have students draw and write their goal on a sheet of paper, making a note each day about what they did during recess to be active.

ASSESSMENT | The students' activity plans for recess are the assessment task. For assessment criteria, students should track their progress and identify at least one way to maintain or improve their activity during the following week. (Construct: Perceived behavioral control.)

Stress-Busting Through Physical Activity   Students can brainstorm a list of physical activities that help them feel better when they are stressed out. Students should list activities of all kinds and intensities (stretching, running, dancing). Each student can select a particular activity from the list to try as a stress-buster for the week. Students should report back to the class on how their stress-busting physical activity goal worked for them.

ASSESSMENT | The students' stress-buster reports are the assessment task for this activity. For assessment criteria, students should assess their progress and identify supports and barriers to practicing their stress-busters. (Construct: Perceived behavioral control.)

Grades 3–5

Going the Distance   Have students try this activity in a place where distance can be determined (at a track or in a play area that has distance markers). Have students walk at their own pace for ten minutes. At the end of that time, students should record on their own record sheets the distance they were able to walk in ten minutes. Repeat the ten-minute walks each day for one week, recording distance each day. Have students set a distance goal for the next week and record their distance each day. Repeat each week for a month. Have students graph their distance for each day or week to show progress and write a paragraph about increasing fitness.

ASSESSMENT | The students' graphs and paragraphs are the assessment task for this activity. For assessment criteria, students should identify a goal for each coming week, identify supports and barriers, and assess their progress over time. (Construct: Perceived behavioral control.)

Estimating for Activity   Correlate physical activity with mathematics by having students make individual estimates about how they will perform at various activity stations—for example, the number of free-throws out of twelve, the number of volleyball serves over the net out of seven, the distance of a standing broad jump, the distance of a running broad jump, the number of seconds balancing on one foot out of sixty seconds, and the number of soccer goals kicked out of eight. Have students record their estimates and their actual scores on an individual record sheet. Have older students convert their scores to percentages. Provide opportunities for students to practice the activities for a period of days and have them set goals and record their scores again. (Most people can jump a standing broad jump distance equal to their height. Have students test this idea.)

ASSESSMENT | The students' record sheets, complete with their plans to practice for improvement, are the assessment task for this activity. For assessment criteria, students should specify the goal they have set for each activity and their plans to practice and achieve it. (Construct: Intention to act in healthy ways.)

Environmental Cues   In a continuation of their discussion of supports for physical activity, have students identify environmental cues they can establish to help them stay active. For example, students might place their athletic shoes or sports equipment in a particular place (lightweight hand weights near the television set or computer) in their house so they'll see them and remember to exercise. Students also might want to establish environmental cues for their families.

ASSESSMENT | For an assessment task, students can identify and track the usefulness of an environmental cue for a week. For assessment criteria, students should write about how environmental cues did or did not influence their decisions to participate in physical activity. This activity links to NHES 5, decision making. (Constructs: Subjective norms, perceived behavioral control.)

Grades 6–8

Staying Active in Middle School   Students' lives tend to get busier in middle school—more responsibility, more opportunity, and more demands. Have students design a personal plan for staying active during the school year. Students should state their goal, name steps to achieve it, identify supports and barriers, and design a way to monitor progress. Have students share their progress with class members.

ASSESSMENT | The students' plans and progress reports are the assessment task for this activity. For assessment criteria, students should be able to demonstrate all parts of a simple goal-setting process. (Construct: Perceived behavioral control.)

My Own Activity Pyramid   After the previous activity (Staying Active in Middle School) has been completed, each student will develop a personal Activity Pyramid for each month of the school year. This activity should be completed in the first week of the month. Students' pyramids should be hung around the room as a reminder.

ASSESSMENT | The students' monthly pyramids are the assessment task for this activity. For assessment criteria, students must have completed all elements of their model and included a minimum of three examples of activities that they could do alone, three that they could do with their friends, and three that they could do with a family member. (Construct: Perceived behavioral control.)

NHES 7 | Self-Management

Students will demonstrate the ability to practice health-enhancing behaviors and avoid or reduce health risks.

ASSESSMENT CRITERIA

- Application (transfer)—Initiate health-enhancing behaviors; apply concepts and skills appropriate and effectively.
- Self-monitoring and reflection—Monitor actions and make adjustments; accept feedback and make adjustments; able to self-assess, reflect on, and take responsibility for actions.

Grades K–2

Keeping Active in All Kinds of Weather   Read the story *Before the Storm* by Jane Yolen (1995) to the class. The story takes place on a hot, lazy summer afternoon. Children pass the time reading and coloring, until one child brings out a hose. The children leap into the cool spray, escaping the heat of the day. An afternoon rainstorm sends the children scurrying inside. Following the story, discuss how different kinds of weather often determine the types of activity we like to participate in. Brainstorm with students some activities that can be done in all kinds of weather. Teachers should focus on weather that is typical in their region (hot and sticky weather, cold and snowy weather, rainy weather, etc.).

ASSESSMENT | For an assessment task, have students fold an 8½×11 piece of paper into four equal parts. In each section of the paper students should select a different weather condition and draw a picture of a way they could safely be physically active in that weather condition. For assessment criteria, students should identify four different weather conditions and appropriate physical activities for each condition. The pictures should demonstrate students' ability to maintain activity in a variety of weather conditions. (Construct: Perceived behavioral control.)

Get Moving! How Many Ways?   In a large space, challenge children to move in different ways without bumping anyone else. Designate a "go" signal and a "stop" (or "freeze") signal (drumbeat, claps, verbal signal) first; then have children practice with different locomotor movements (walking, jogging, galloping, sliding, skipping, leaping). Whenever children stop, or freeze, they should check to be sure that they have their own space, or "bubble," around them and are not standing close to anyone else. Then add levels of complexity. Have the children move at different speeds to a drumbeat, tambourine, or music. Have them move in different pathways (straight, curved, zigzag), at different levels (high, medium, low), and in different directions (forward, sideways, backward) as they try to perform a variety of locomotor movements. Have children try different

kinds of arm movements (fast, slow, smooth, strong). Ask children to think of other ways they can change how they move. (Here's an easy way to help young children learn to skip: Have them walk around a large space. As they continue to walk, ask them to make their walking "bouncy." Have them bounce more and more as they walk. With a little practice, most will find that their bouncy walking soon becomes skipping.)

ASSESSMENT | For an assessment task, students can demonstrate at least two kinds of movement. For assessment criteria, students should demonstrate that they can change from one type of movement to the next and back again smoothly, not stopping until the end of the pattern. (Construct: Perceived behavioral control.)

Drawing Playground Rules—What Safety Looks Like   Students are asked to fold a piece of paper in half and draw a line down the crease to divide it into two windows. Number each window. In window 1 students are asked to draw a picture of students violating the playground rule that they think makes the most important contribution to playground safety. In window 2, they are to draw students engaged in following this important playground safety rule. Drawings should be hung in the school cafeteria or hallway to the playground as a reminder for other students.

ASSESSMENT | The assessment task for this activity is students' drawings with contrasting depictions of playground rules. For assessment criteria, the drawings must contain a clear depiction of violation and compliance with playground rules. (Construct: Perceived behavioral control.)

Obstacle Course for Activity   In an area, lay out a simple obstacle course that includes many different types of activities. For example, students might jump over or climb under simple equipment (two milk crates and a bamboo pole), step or jump from hula hoop to hula hoop, run or dribble a ball in a zigzag pathway through plastic cones, jump across two jump ropes, and skip to end the course. Make simple posters to help children remember the activities. Have students try the course from the opposite direction, but remember that small children are concrete thinkers. For example, one kindergarten teacher asked her students to "go backward" through an obstacle course and was astounded when they began crawling backward. Incorporate natural features ("Run around the big tree") and constructed features ("Run and touch the fence and come back") of the school where appropriate. When students have the idea, they can help design portions of an obstacle course as a class effort. Have each group make a simple sign for its portion and then help lay out the course for participation.

ASSESSMENT | For an assessment task, children can work in pairs or small groups to draw and lay out a simple obstacle course for class participation. For assessment criteria, students should draw and write about how staying active can help them be healthy. (Construct: Perceived behavioral control.)

Grades 3–5

Physical Activity Learning Stations   Use cards or simple posters to number and label physical activity stations around a large space, indoors or out. Base stations on the generic skills identified by Graham et al. (chasing, fleeing, and dodging; jumping and landing; throwing and catching; kicking and volleying; striking with rackets and paddles; transferring weight and rolling) with a variety of soft, light equipment in different sizes (nerf balls, light plastic balls, balloons).[69] A "jumping and landing" station might include short and long jump ropes. A "throwing and catching" station might include nerf balls, plastic balls, Frisbees, and throwing rings. A "chasing, fleeing, and dodging" station might include playing a small-group dodgeball game with a nerf ball or chasing a partner to aim at a nerf ball. A "transferring weight and rolling" station might include trying cartwheels, walking on hands, and doing forward and backward rolls on the grass or a mat. A "dribbling and volleying" station might include volleying balloons or light plastic balls and dribbling basketballs or soccer balls. See www.pecentral.org for more ideas on children's physical activity. If possible, use recorded music as a cue to start and stop. Assign small groups to each station. When the music starts, begin. When the music stops, students should clean up the station and move on to the next. As students get the idea of the learning station, assign small groups a generic skill for designing a learning station for their classmates, complete with equipment selection and cards or posters. As a culminating activity, students can set up and explain their station and have the entire class participate.

ASSESSMENT | The students' designs for learning stations can serve as the assessment task for this activity. For assessment criteria, students should include a list of all equipment and steps to performing the activity on their station card or poster safely. (Construct: Perceived behavioral control.)

Shop Around for Fitness   Print a wide range of simple ideas for physical activity on strips of paper (toss and catch a beanbag ten times; jump rope for one minute; dribble a ball in and around legs; dribble two balls at once; serve a volleyball or plastic ball across a net or rope; dribble a soccer or playground ball around a set of cones; kick a goal through two cones; shoot a basketball ten times; throw a ball with a partner to play "one step," stepping back one step each time both partners make a catch). Scatter the strips of paper around a large play area, with needed equipment readily available. Students will participate in small groups of three or four. Have multiple strips of paper for each activity. To begin the activity, give each group a shopping or grocery bag. On the proper signal, students pick up slips of paper and complete the activity. When they finish, they put the slip of paper in their bag and choose another. If possible, play music while the students participate. At the end of a given period of time, ask groups to count the number of activities they have completed. There's no winner. Participation and fun are the goals for this activity. Have groups aim to complete more activities the next time. (This activity is not a relay with winners and losers. Relays often cause blame of team members, hurt feelings, and deterioration of skills as students hurry. Teachers can place the emphasis on being active and having personal and group goals rather than on beating others.)

ASSESSMENT | The students' graphs and paragraphs are the assessment task for this activity. For assessment criteria, students should identify a goal for each coming week, identify supports and barriers, and assess their progress over time. (Construct: Perceived behavioral control.)

Safe Physical Activity in All Kinds of Weather   Depending on the local climate, students can investigate safe practices for physical activity in various kinds of weather. For cold weather and rain, students can research frostbite and hypothermia. For hot weather, students can research heat stress, heat exhaustion, heatstroke, and sunburn. Students should learn about prevention, proper clothing, hydration, signs and symptoms, and how to get help. Students can learn about weather precautions during physical activity by talking with a physical educator or medical professional or by conducting a Web search.

ASSESSMENT | For an assessment task, students can demonstrate safety procedures for physical activity in different kinds of weather conditions. For assessment criteria, students should correctly explain and demonstrate the steps involved in their safety procedures. (Construct: Attitudes toward behavior.)

Grades 6–8

Fun Songs to Keep You Moving!   Many performing groups and sports teams have a signature song they play as their warm-up or when they want to get pumped up for a performance. One example of such a song is "We Will Rock You," by Queen. In pairs, have students select a signature song that could get a group pumped up and moving. Students

should then determine a thirty- to sixty-second segment of the song to play and then develop two or three different dance moves or physical activity movements to go along with the song that all their classmates could do. Pairs of students can then take turns presenting their music every day or two in order to energize the class. This activity could be further connected with determining target heart rate and warm-up and cool-down topics.

ASSESSMENT | For an assessment task, use the presentation of the thirty- to sixty-second song selection, including the activities that correspond with each song. Once students have made their presentation, they can write a short reflection on the song and activities they selected and whether they were able to energize and engage the class in a fun physical activity. For assessment criteria, students should be able to motivate peers to engage in physical activity, as well as reflect on the success of the implementation of their song selection and corresponding movements. (Construct: Perceived behavioral control.)

Fitness Apps   Technology can be a motivator for many individuals when it comes to physical activity: It can serve as our training partner, reinforcer, or instructor. Have students identify five different fitness apps that would support them in increasing their physical activity in some way based on personal needs or preferences. Have students do some research on the apps. For example, do they use recommended principles of fitness? come from a credible source? provide accurate information? and other relevant questions (NHES Standard 3). Then have students select one app to use over the next week.

ASSESSMENT | For an assessment task, students can write a reflection on how the fitness app supported or hindered their physical activity over the past week. Students can provide specific examples and make connections between the information gleaned from the fitness app and their personal health. For assessment criteria, students should provide accurate information, be able to apply fitness concepts, and monitor personal fitness behavior. (Constructs: Perceived behavioral control, attitudes toward behavior.)

NHES 8 | Advocacy

Students will demonstrate the ability to advocate for personal, family, and community health.

ASSESSMENT CRITERIA

- Health-enhancing position—Give clear, health-enhancing position.
- Support for position—Support position with facts, concepts, examples, and evidence.
- Audience awareness—Show awareness of target audience; choose words, tone, and examples to suit audience.
- Conviction—Display conviction for position.

Grades K–2

Physical Activity in Many Cultures: Games and Sports Around the World   Students can investigate the kinds of games and sports that children play in other countries and other cultures. Students can work with their school librarian or media specialist to access this information (NHES 3). Students can work in pairs or small groups to learn and teach a new activity to classmates. Learning about other cultures can help children expand their horizons, correct misperceptions, and become more educated world citizens. For example, one of the authors found while teaching summer school in American Samoa that a group of young boys were constantly pushing each other, shoulder to shoulder, during physical education class and recess. She redirected the boys to other activities several times before realizing that they were imitating the scrum movement in rugby, a popular sport in Samoan culture. The boys certainly must have wondered what was wrong with this visitor who didn't recognize a scrum when she saw one!

ASSESSMENT | For an assessment task, students can learn and teach a new type of physical activity to classmates. For assessment criteria, students should express a clear, health-enhancing position for learning about physical activity from cultures around the world. (Constructs: Intention to act in healthy ways, subjective norms.)

Equipment Drive for Recess   Many elementary classrooms don't have adequate or appropriate play equipment for recess. Students sometimes are inactive because they lack equipment to play with or because the equipment they have hurts their hands (hard, regulation-size balls). Have students brainstorm a list of inexpensive equipment they would like to have for their recess and physical education periods (short and long jump ropes, hula hoops, beanbags, nerf balls, lightweight plastic balls, plastic bats, wiffle balls, plastic scoops). Help students organize a drive for parents, community members, or Parent-Teacher-Student Associations (PTSAs) to collect equipment for classrooms. Be sure to list large, lightweight plastic barrels to transport and collect equipment before and after recess. Some schools don't make play equipment available for recess because they claim the children argue over it or misuse it. Use these situations as a teaching opportunity. Having plenty of equipment available will help with arguments. Who can blame children for not wanting to be "out" in a long jump rope activity when they have had to stand in a line of twenty-five children for a turn? The simple solution is to have plenty of long jump ropes—ideally, three children per rope, with two children turning while one jumps, changing places when someone misses. If children misuse equipment, use this as a time to teach them to use equipment properly—and do so with each new piece of equipment before it is introduced.

ASSESSMENT | The plan for the equipment drive is the assessment task for this activity. For assessment criteria, students should design a flyer or posters to appeal to parents, community members, or the PTSA. Flyers and posters should give a clear message, back it up with reasons, target a particular audience, and show strong conviction. (Constructs: Perceived behavioral control, subjective norms.)

How Many Ways to Be Active Campaign   Have students brainstorm a list of ways they and their families can be more active. Have students design flyers or posters to advocate for more physical activity at home and at school. Post students' work in the school and community.

ASSESSMENT | The students' flyers and posters are the assessment task for this activity. For assessment criteria, students should give a clear message, back it up with reasons, target a particular audience, and show strong conviction. (Construct: Subjective norms.)

Grades 3–5

Inclusive Physical Activity: Participation for All   Graham, Holt/Hale, and Parker[70] recommend this strategy for helping children develop acceptance and empathy for peers who have disabilities. Teachers can coordinate with special education teachers to help children learn about the nature of the disability, its correct name, any limitations it imposes, and the potential for activity. In addition, children should have opportunities to work and talk with children who have disabilities. To help children become more sensitive, Graham, Holt/Hale, and Parker suggest the following activities:

- Forming a circle, standing with legs shoulder-width apart, and rolling a playground ball across the circle with eyes closed

- Playing a simple game with no verbal sound—no verbal clues for directions, rules, or stopping the action
- Executing simple ball-handling skills with the students' nondominant hand

ASSESSMENT | For an assessment task, students can describe ways they can include children with disabilities in their physical activity at school. For assessment criteria, students should state a clear, health-enhancing position and back it up with reasons. (Construct: Subjective norms.)

Teach a Classmate   Have students share physical activity skills they have with the class. For example, some students might be experts at using a yo-yo, demonstrating hula hoop or fancy jump rope routines, or line-dancing. Have a certain number of students volunteer to be instructors on given days. Students can work with their teachers in small groups to learn a new skill.

ASSESSMENT | Having students teach others is the assessment task for this activity. For assessment criteria, students should make their explanations and demonstrations clear and encourage other students to keep trying. (Constructs: Perceived behavioral control, subjective norms.)

Get Your Family Moving   Have students brainstorm a list of activities they can participate in with their families. Students should design a plan for their families to get everyone active for at least three days per week. Have students implement their plans and report back to the class.

ASSESSMENT | Students' plans and reports are the assessment task for this activity. For assessment criteria, students should make a clear plan for their families, back it up with reasons, target their proposal to their family members, and show strong conviction. (Construct: Subjective norms.)

Grades 6–8

The H$_2$O Connection   Students can investigate the importance of drinking plenty of water during physical activity at Kids' Health (www.kidshealth.org) and other credible Internet sites. Topics include:

- Is it important to drink a lot of water?
- Dehydration
- Keeping your cool!

After students have the facts on physical activity and hydration, they can inspect their school to ensure that plenty of water (water fountains, bottled water) is available to students during physical activity times. If students find that water is in short supply, they can plan a presentation on the importance of hydration for their classmates, teachers, administrators, and parents or caregivers to try to increase water availability at school.

ASSESSMENT | The students' presentation is the assessment task for this activity. For assessment criteria, students should state a clear health-enhancing position, back it up with data, target their audience, and speak with conviction. (Constructs: Attitudes toward behavior, subjective norms.)

Paint It for Physical Activity   Have students design and sketch a layout for several types of physical activities that can be painted on sidewalks or other paved surfaces at school. Examples include Four-Square and Hop-Scotch. Have students determine measurements and supplies needed to paint these games for their own schools or for neighboring elementary schools. Game rules should be included as part of the plan. Help students arrange time and supplies to put their plan into action.

ASSESSMENT | The students' plans and calculations for measurements and supplies are the assessment task for this activity. For assessment criteria, students should present their plan to decision makers, including a clear message, reasons, a targeted audience, and conviction. (Construct: Perceived behavioral control.)

Teach Activity for Elementary Students   Have students brainstorm a list of activities they can teach to elementary-age students. Students should choose an activity and work together to design a lesson plan for teaching younger students to be active. Help students arrange visits to work with younger children.

ASSESSMENT | Students' lesson plans are the assessment task for this activity. For assessment criteria, students should be able to show all the steps they need to take to teach their lessons and justify their plans to decision makers. (Construct: Perceived behavioral control.)

EVALUATED CURRICULA AND INSTRUCTIONAL MATERIALS

In 2011, the National Prevention Council released The National Prevention Strategy: America's Plan for Better Health and Wellness. To achieve the goal of helping to increase the number of Americans who are healthy at every life stage, a network of stakeholders including health care systems, community organizations, families, and others were encouraged to collaborate in the development of health-promoting strategies. Among the priorities identified in this plan, is "Active Living."

With a particular focus on increasing physical activity among children, youth, and young adults, schools were encouraged to join with other educational institutions to:

- Provide daily physical education and recess that focuses on maximizing time physically active.
- Participate in fitness testing (e.g., the President's Challenge) and support individualized self-improvement plans.
- Support walk and bike to school programs (e.g., "Safe Routes to School") and work with local governments to make decisions about selecting school sites that can promote physical activity.
- Limit passive screen time.
- Make physical activity facilities available to the local community.[71]

This reinforces that physical activity participation among youth is a complex matter influenced by personal, family, community, and broader social and psychological variables.

While recognizing that the range and complexity of influential variables is important, advocates for evidence-based approaches to increasing physical activity in schools become frustrated with criteria that appear to be cumbersome or beyond their control. In response, Action for Healthy Kids, supported by a grant from the Robert Wood Johnson Foundation, has

identified ten essential criteria to help administrators, teachers, parents, and concerned others evaluate physical activity programs of interest. These criteria ask stakeholders to evaluate whether the school-based approach

1. Is based on professional theories and is consistent with professional and/or national standards of practice.
2. Is practical and realistic.
3. Has a goal or purpose that is clearly stated and easy to understand by interested audiences.
4. Has specific measurable objectives that address one or more of the following: knowledge, attitudes, skills, behaviors, policies, school environment.
5. Is age or developmentally appropriate and culturally relevant.
6. Is engaging to students, interactive, and skills based.
7. Can be adapted to a variety of situations and environments.
8. Can be assessed and monitored with an evaluation component.
9. Includes goals that are supported by evaluation data.
10. Supports easy implementation by providing clearly written and user-friendly instructions, training resources, contact information for technical support, and instructions and/or materials available in languages in addition to English.[72]

In addition to these criteria specifically related to curricular or program elements, the developers from Action for Healthy Kids recognized that school-based approaches need to be adoptable and usable. They developed "critical" evaluation criteria to help clarify the potential for users to implement the approach in a real-world context. These criteria focus on important attributes such as cost-effectiveness, potential fit with school mandates, support of student achievement, feasibility for implementation within the time constraints of the school day, potential to be supported by critical stakeholders, and potential sustainability.[73]

 ## INTERNET AND OTHER RESOURCES

WEBSITES

Alliance for a Healthier Generation
www.healthiergeneration.org

American Council on Exercise (ACE)
www.acefitness.org/education-and-resources/professional/expert-articles/5648/youth-fitness-games-for-kids

American Heart Association
www.heart.org

Building Our Kids' Success
www.bokskids.org

Cartoon Network—Move It Movement
www.cartoonnetwork.com/promos/mim/catch.index.html

Federal Highway Administration (Pedestrian and Bicycle Safety)
www.safety.fhwa.dot.gov/ped_bike

Fuel Up to Play 60
www.fueluptoplay60.com

GirlsHealth.gov
www.girlshealth.gov

GoNoodle
www.gonoodle.com

Kids' Health
www.kidshealth.org

NEA Healthy Futures—Healthy Steps for Healthy Lives
healthyfutures.nea.org/get-informed/student-physical-health
/healthy-steps-for-healthy-lives/

PE Central
www.pecentral.org

Playworks
www.playworks.org

President's Council on Fitness, Sports, & Nutrition
www.hhhs.gov/fitness.index.html

SPARK
www.sparkpe.org

OTHER RESOURCES

Basch, C. *Healthier Students Are Better Learners: A Missing Link in School Reforms to Close the Achievement Gap* (New York: Teachers College Press, Columbia University, March 2010).

Centers for Disease Control and Prevention. "School Health Guidelines to Promote Healthy Eating and Physical Activity." *MMWR* 60, no. 5 (September 16, 2011): 1–76.

Corbin, C. B. et al. "Youth Physical Fitness: Ten Key Concepts." *JOPERD* 85, no. 2 (February 2014): 24–31.

Finkelstein, E. A., W. C. Kang, and R. Malhotra. "Lifetime Direct Medical Costs of Childhood Obesity." *Pediatrics* 133, no. 5 (April 7, 2014): 1–9.

National Association of State Boards of Education. *Fit, Healthy, and Ready to Learn,* Chapter D: Policies to Promote Physical Activity and Physical Education, 2nd ed. (Arlington, VA: NASBE, 2012).

Trust for America's Health. *F as in Fat: How Obesity Threatens America's Future, 2011* (Washington, DC: Trust for America's Health, 2011).

U.S. Department of Health and Human Services. *Physical Activity Guidelines for Americans Midcourse Report: Strategies to Increase Physical Activity Among Youth* (Washington, DC: USDHHS, 2012).

CHILDREN'S LITERATURE

AGES 5–8

Ackerman, Karen. *Song and Dance Man.* Alfred A. Knopf, 1988. (Caldecott Medal)

Andreae, Giles. *Giraffes Can't Dance.* Orchard, 1999.

Bellisario, Gina. *Move Your Body!: My Exercise Tips.* Millbrook Press, 2014.

Bloom, Suzanne. *Bear Can Dance!* Boyds Mills Press, an imprint of Highlights, 2015.

Boelts, Maribeth. *Happy Like Soccer.* Candlewick Press, 2014.

Bolam, Emily, and Harriet Ziefert. *Murphy Meets the Treadmill.* Houghton Mifflin, 2001.

Bowes, Lisa. *Lucy Tries Soccer.* Orca Book Publishers, 2016.

Brown, Marc. *Arthur and the Race to Read.* Little, Brown, 2001.

Bugler, Beth. *My First Book of Soccer.* Liberty Street, an imprint of Time Inc. Books, 2017.

Carle, Eric. *From Head to Toe.* HarperCollins, 1999.

Carlson, Nancy. *Get Up and Go!* Puffin, 2008.

Cleary, Brian. *Run and Hike, Play and Bike: What is Physical Activity?* Millbrook Press, 2011.

Corey, Shana. *Players in Pigtails.* Scholastic, 2003.

Couric, Katie. *The Blue Ribbon Day.* Doubleday, 2004.

Fergus, Maureen. *The Day Dad Joined My Soccer Team.* Kids Can Press, 2018.

Gleisner, Jenna Lee. *My Body Needs Exercise (Healthy Me).* Amicus High Interest, 2015.

Hammond, Darell. *Go Out and Play!: Favorite Outdoor Games from Kaboom!.* Candlewick Press, 2012.

Hamm, Mia. *Winners Never Quit!* HarperCollins, 2004.

Krull, Kathleen. *Wilma Unlimited: How Wilma Rudolph Became the World's Fastest Woman.* Harcourt, 2000.

LaDeane, D. *E Is for Exercise.* Tate Publishing, 2009.

Long, Ethan. *Horse & Buggy: Dance, Dance, Dance!* Holiday House, 2018.

Martin, Bill, and Michael Sampson. *Swish.* Henry Holt, 1997.

Mayer, Mercer. *Little Critter: Good for Me and You.* HarperFestival, 2012.

Miller, Edward. *The Monster Health Book: A Guide to Eating Healthy, Being Active and Feeling Great for Monsters and Kids!* Holiday House, 2008.

O'Neill, Alexis. *The Recess Queen.* Scholastic, 2002.

Pfister, Marcus. *You Can't Win Them All, Rainbow Fish.* North/South, 2017.

Raschka, Chris. *Everyone Can Learn to Ride a Bicycle.* Schwartz & Wade, 2013.

Rockwell, Lizzy. *The Busy Body Book: A Kid's Guide to Fitness.* Dragonfly Books, 2008.

Rooyackers, Paul. *101 Circus Games for Children.* Hunter House, 2010.

Sif, Birgitta. *Frances Dean Who Loved to Dance and Dance.* Candlewick Press, 2014.

Singer, Mariyln. *Feel the Beat: Dance Poems That Zing from Salsa to Swing.* Dial Books for Young Readers, 2017.

Sjonger, Rebecca. *Do Your Bit To Be Physically Fit!* Crabtree Publishing Company, 2016.

Yoo, Tae-Eun. *You Are a Lion! And Other Fun Yoga Poses.* Nancy Paulson Books, 2012.

AGES 8–12

Adler, David. *A Picture Book of Jesse Owens.* Holiday House, 1994.

Adler, David. *Lou Gehrig: The Luckiest Man.* Harcourt Brace, 1997.

Freitas, Donna. *Gold Medal Winter.* Scholastic Inc., 2018.

Grimes, Nikki. *Garvey's Choice.* WordSong, an imprint of Highlights, 2016.

Guillian, Charlotte. *101 Ways to Get in Shape.* Raintree, 2011.

Holt, Kimberly Willis. *When Zachary Beaver Came to Town.* Bantam Doubleday Dell Books for Young Readers, 1999. (1999 National Book Award for Young People's Literature)

Hunt, Sara. *Stay Fit: Your Guide to Staying Active.* Capstone Press, 2012.

Kallio, Jamie. *12 Ways to Stay Active and Fit.* 12 Story Library, 2017.

Kortemeier, Todd. *12 Ways to Improve Athletic Performance.* 12 Story Library, 2017.

Kuskowski, Alex. *Cool Relaxing: Health & Fun Ways to Chill Out.* Checkerboard Library, 2012.

Levete, Sarah. *Maker Projects for Kids Who Love Sports.* Crabtree Publishing, 2017.

Lyon, Drew. *Against All Odds (Sports Illustrated Kids: Real Heroes of Sports).* Capstone Press, a Capstone Imprint, 2017.

Petersen, P. J. *White Water.* Simon & Schuster, 1997.

Prelutsky, Jack. *Good Sports.* Knopf Books for Young Readers, 2007.

Rissman, Rebecca. *Yoga for You.* Walter Foster Jr., an imprint of Quarto Publishing Group USA Inc., 2017.

Sackier, Shelley. *Dear Opl.* Sourcebooks Jabberwocky, 2015.

Spinelli, Jerry. *Maniac Magee.* HarperCollins, 1990. (Newbery Medal; Multicultural)

Strother, S. *The Adventurous Book of Outdoor Games: Classic Fun for Daring Boys and Girls.* Sourcebooks, Inc., 2008.

Tuminelly, Nancy. *Super Simple Exercise.* Super Sandcastle, 2011.

ENDNOTES

1. U.S. Department of Health and Human Services, *2008 Physical Activity Guidelines for Americans* (https://health.gov/paguidelines/guidelines/).

2. C. B. Corbin et al., *Physical Activity for Children: A Statement of Guidelines for Children Ages 5–12* (Reston, VA: SHAPE America, 2004).

3. Institute of Medicine (IOM), *Educating the Student Body: Taking Physical Activity and Physical Education to School* (Washington, DC: The National Academies Press, 2013).

4. U.S. Department of Health and Human Services, *2008 Physical Activity Guidelines for Americans.*

5. Ibid.

6. Centers for Disease Control and Prevention, *Physical Activity Recommendations and Guidelines: Trends in Meeting the 2008 Physical Activity Guidelines, 2008–2016* (https://www.cdc.gov/physicalactivity/downloads/trends-in-the-prevalence-of-physical-activity-508.pdf).

7. Centers for Disease Control and Prevention, *Exercise or Physical Activity: Early Release of Selected Estimates from the National Health Interview Survey* (https://www.cdc.gov/nchs/fastats/exercise.htm).

8. Centers for Disease Control and Prevention, *Adult Overweight and Obesity* (https://www.cdc.gov/obesity/adult/index.html).

9. Centers for Disease Control and Prevention, *Childhood Obesity Facts* (https://www.cdc.gov/obesity/data/childhood.html).

10. Child Trends, *Overweight Children and Youth* (https://www.childtrends.org/indicators/overweight-children-and-youth/; 2014).

11. S. B. Johnson, *The Nation's Childhood Obesity Epidemic: Health Disparities in the Making* (http://www.apa.org/pi/families/resources/newsletter/2012/07/childhood-obesity.aspx; 2012).

12. Communities in Schools, *2017 BackPack Index* (www.communitiesinschools.org/press-room/resource/huntington-bank-releases-2017-backpack-index-schools-costs-rise/).

13. S. B. Johnson, *The Nation's Childhood Obesity Epidemic: Health Disparities in the Making.*

14. P. Gordon-Larsen and M. C. Nelson, "Longitudinal Physical Activity and Sedentary Behavior Trends: Adolescence to Adulthood," *American Journal of Preventative Medicine* 27, no. 4 (2004): 277–83.

15. Centers for Disease Control and Prevention Division of Adolescent and School Health, *Youth Risk Behavior Surveillance System* (https://www.cdc.gov/healthyyouth/data/yrbs/index.htm; 2015).

16. National Dairy Council, *The Wellness Impact Enhancing Academic Success through Healthy School Environments* (https://www.nationaldairycouncil.org/content/2015/the-wellness-impact; 2014).

17. Ibid.

18. Ibid.

19. U.S. Department of Health and Human Services, *Healthy People 2020* (https://www.healthypeople.gov/).

20. U.S. Department of Health and Human Services, *2008 Physical Activity Guidelines for Americans.*

21. Centers for Disease Control and Prevention, *The Association Between School-based Physical Activity, Including Physical Education, and Academic Performance* (https://www.cdc.gov/healthyyouth/health_and_academics/pdf/pa-pe_paper.pdf; 2010).

22. Institute of Medicine (IOM), *Educating the Student Body: Taking Physical Activity and Physical Education to School.*

23. Centers for Disease Control and Prevention, *The Association Between School-based Physical Activity, Including Physical Education, and Academic Performance.*

24. B. McCraken, "Creating an Environment for Learning," *Education Standard,* (Autumn 2002): 46–51.

25. Institute of Medicine (IOM), *Educating the Student Body: Taking Physical Activity and Physical Education to School.*

26. H. Taras, "Physical Activity and Student Performance at School," *Journal of School Health* 75, no. 8 (2005).

27. B. McCraken, "Creating an Environment for Learning."

28. E. Jensen, "Moving with the Brain in Mind," *Educational Leadership* (November 2000).

29. B. McCraken, "Creating an Environment for Learning."

30. Ibid.

31. U.S. Department of Health and Human Services, *2008 Physical Activity Guidelines for Americans.*

32. E. M. Grant, D. R. Young, and T. T. Wu, "Predictors for Physical Activity in Adolescent Girls Using Statistical Shrinkage Techniques for Hierarchical Longitudinal Mixed Effects Models," *PLoS One* (2015), doi:org/10.1371/journal.pone.0125431.

33. Harvard T. H. Chan School of Public Health Obesity Prevention Source, *Environmental Barriers to Activity* (https://www.hsph.harvard.edu/obesity-prevention-source/obesity-causes/physical-activity-environment/).

34. Ibid.

35. U.S. Department of Health and Human Services and U.S. Department of Education, *Promoting Better Health for Young People Through Physical Activity and Sports* (https://usa.usembassy.de/etexts/sport/Promoting_better_health.pdf; 2000).

36. Action for Health Kids, *The Learning Connection: The Value of Improving Nutrition and Physical Activity in Our Schools* (http://www.actionforhealthykids.org/media-center/reports?start=10; 2004).

37. Institute of Medicine of the National Academies, *Preventing Childhood Obesity: Health in the Balance* (Washington, DC: The National Academies Press, 2004).

38. A. Beighle, C. F. Morgan, G. Le Masurier, and R. Pangrazi, "Children's Physical Activity During Recess and Outside of Schools," *Journal of School Health* 76, no. 10 (2006): 516.

39. Institute of Medicine (IOM), *Educating the Student Body: Taking Physical Activity and Physical Education to School.*

40. Society of Health and Physical Educators (SHAPE) America, *Shape of the Nation* (https://www.shapeamerica.org/advocacy/son/; 2016).

41. Ibid.

42. Centers for Disease Control and Prevention, *School Health Policy and Practices Study 2016* (https://www.cdc.gov/healthyyouth/data/shpps/results.htm).

43. U.S. Department of Health and Human Services, *2008 Physical Activity Guidelines for Americans.*

44. Ibid.

45. A. Beighle, C. F. Morgan, G. Le Masurier, and R. Pangrazi, "Children's Physical Activity During Recess and Outside of Schools."

46. Centers for Disease Control and Prevention, "Guidelines for School and Community Programs to Promote Lifelong Physical Activity Among Young People," *MMWR* 46, no. RR-6 (1997): 6–10.

47. Centers for Disease Control and Prevention, *Comprehensive School Physical Activity Program (CSPAP)* (https://www.cdc.gov/healthyschools/physicalactivity/cspap.htm; 2015).

48. Ibid.

49. Mission: Readiness-Military Leaders for Kids, *Still Too Fat to Fight* (https://www.strongnation.org/articles/16-still-too-fat-to-fight/ 2012)

50. Centers for Disease Control and Prevention, *Comprehensive School Physical Activity Program (CSPAP).*

51. Centers for Disease Control and Prevention, "Guidelines for School and Community Programs to Promote Lifelong Physical Activity Among Young People."

52. U.S. Department of Health and Human Services, *2008 Physical Activity Guidelines for Americans.*

53. C. Casperson, K. Powell, and G. Christenson, "Physical Activity, Exercise, and Physical Fitness: Definitions and Distinctions for Health-Related Research," *Public health Reports* 100, no. 2 (1985): 126–31.

54. Centers for Disease Control and Prevention, *Comprehensive School Physical Activity Program (CSPAP).*

55. C. B. Corbin et al., *Physical Activity for Children: A Statement of Guidelines for Children Ages 5–12.*

56. University of Missouri Extension, *My Activity Pyramid for Kids* (http://extension.missouri.edu/p/n386; 2014).

57. Ibid.

58. Ibid.

59. Ibid.

60. Ibid.

61. Ibid.

62. Centers for Disease Control and Prevention, *Physical Education Curriculum Analysis Tool* (https://www.cdc.gov/healthyschools/pecat/index.htm).

63. Society of Health and Physical Education (SHAPE) America, *National Standards and Grade Level Outcomes for K-12 Physical Education* (https://www.shapeamerica.org/standards/default.aspx).

64. C. B. Corbin et al., *Physical Activity for Children: A Statement of Guidelines for Children Ages 5–12.*

65. Ibid.

66. Centers for Disease Control and Prevention, *Health Education Curriculum Analysis Tool* (https://www.cdc.gov/healthyyouth/hecat/).

67. G. Graham, S. A. Holt/Hale, and M. Parker,. *Children Moving: A Reflective Approach to Teaching Physical Education* (Mountain View, CA: Mayfield, 2001).

68. V. Paley, *You Can't Say, You Can't Play* (Cambridge, MA: Harvard University Press, 1993).

69. G. Graham, S. A. Holt/Hale, and M. Parker, *Children Moving: A Reflective Approach to Teaching Physical Education.*

70. Ibid.

71. U.S. Department of Health and Human Services: National Prevention Council, *National Prevention Council Action Plan: Implementing the National Prevention Strategy* (https://www.surgeongeneral.gov/priorities/prevention/about/index.html; 2011).

72. Action for Health Kids, *An Action for Healthy Report: Criteria for Evaluating School-Based Approaches to Increase Good Nutrition and Physical Activity* (Skokie, IL: Action for Healthy Kids: Skokie, IL, 2004).

73. Ibid.

(Echo, age 12)

8

Promoting Safety and Preventing Unintentional Injury

DESIRED LEARNER OUTCOMES

After reading this chapter, you will be able to . . .

- **Describe the prevalence and cost of unintentional injuries among youth.**

- **Explain the relationship between unintentional injuries and compromised academic performance.**

- **Identify factors that influence unintentional injuries.**

- **Summarize current guidelines and practices for schools and teachers related to safety promotion and unintentional injury prevention.**

- **Summarize developmentally appropriate safety promotion and unintentional injury prevention concepts and skills for K–8 students in the context of the National Health Education Standards and target healthy behavior outcomes.**

- **Demonstrate developmentally appropriate learning strategies and assessment techniques that incorporate concepts and skills that have been shown to promote safety and prevent unintentional injury among youth.**

- **Identify websites and children's literature that can be used in cross-curricular instructional activities promoting safety and the prevention of unintentional injuries.**

INTRODUCTION

The Centers for Disease Control and Prevention's (CDC) *National Action Plan for Child Injury Prevention* opens with this important statement:

> Every day in the United States, two dozen children die from an injury that was not intended. Such tragedy often leaves families broken apart and changes the lives of those left behind. Injury deaths, however, are only part of the picture. Each year, millions of children in the United States are injured and live with the consequences of those injuries. These children may face disability and chronic pain that limit their ability to perform age-appropriate everyday activities over their lifetime. These deaths and injuries need not occur because they often result from predictable events. The good news is that we have solutions that work to prevent child injury. The challenge is to apply what we know and work together to prevent these unnecessary tragedies to children, families, and communities.[1]

Prevalence and Cost

The National Center for Injury Prevention and Control, Centers for Disease Control and Prevention, reported that unintentional injury is the leading cause of death among youth 0 to 19 years of age in the United States. Motor-vehicle crash injuries are the single leading cause of death for young people between the ages of 5 to 19.[2]

Unintentional injuries are those related to drowning, falls, fires or burns, poisoning, suffocation, road traffic, and sports. Each year, more than 8,000 young people aged 0 to 19 die from unintentional injuries, and nearly 9 million are treated in emergency departments for nonfatal injuries.[3]

According to CDC unintentional injury data, the injury rates for males are almost two times greater than for females in the 0 to 19 years' age group. The highest death rates are among occupants of motor vehicles in traffic.[4]

Injury death rates among children differ by age group. For children younger than 1 year of age, most injury deaths are due to suffocation. Drowning is the leading cause of injury death for ages 1 to 4 years. For ages 5 to 19 years, most injury deaths are due to motor-vehicle crashes.[5]

Males also have higher rates of nonfatal injuries than females among individuals 1 to 19 years of age. Injuries due to falls are the leading cause of nonfatal injury, with approximately 2.3 million children receiving treatment in hospital emergency departments. While nonfatal injuries vary by age group, falls are the leading cause of unintentional injury for children younger than 1 to 14 years of age. Nonfatal injury rates related to motor vehicles are highest in the 15 to 19 age group.[6]

Injury-related data from the 2017 Youth Risk Behavior Survey (YRBS) appear in Table 8–1.[7] Despite laws mandating seat-belt use, nearly 6 percent of high school students across the United States reported rarely or never wearing a seat belt while riding in a car driven by someone else. One in six students had ridden with a drinking driver during the past month, and more than 5 percent reported driving a car after drinking. More recently, concerns about the 13 percent of drivers who reported driving under the influence of marijuana and the nearly 40 percent of drivers reported texting or e-mailing while driving during the past 30 days, places themselves and others at significant risk for unintentional injuries. (YRBS data also are available by state and for many large cities at www.cdc.gov/healthyyouth/data/yrbs/index.htm.)

Injuries are among the most underrecognized public health problems facing the United States today. Preventable injuries claim the lives of approximately twenty-four children each day. These deaths are often due to predictable and preventable events. Injury treatment is the leading cause of medical spending for children. The estimated annual cost of hospitalization as a result of unintentional child injuries in the United States is nearly $87 billion in medical and societal costs.[8]

Table 8–2 describes the wide range of public health concerns related to unintentional injury prevention. This chapter addresses the ways families, schools, and communities can work together to promote safety and prevent and reduce injuries among children and adolescents.

Safety and Unintentional Injury and Academic Performance

Approximately 200,000 children are hospitalized annually due to unintentional injuries.[9] Young children are at greater risk for many injuries. This increased risk may be attributable to many factors. Children are curious and like to explore their environment. This characteristic may lead children to sample the pills in

TABLE 8–1			YRBS
Youth Risk Behavior Survey Data Related to Unintentional Injuries, 2017			

	Percent Reporting Behavior		
Risk Behavior	**Total**	**Females**	**Males**
Rarely or never wore seat belts when riding in a car driven by someone else	5.9	5.1	6.6
Rode with a driver who had been drinking alcohol during the past thirty days	16.5	17.1	15.7
Drove when drinking alcohol during the past thirty days	7.8	6.0	9.5
Drove when using marijuana during the past thirty days (among students who drove during the 30 days before the survey)	13.0	11.3	14.6
Texted or e-mailed while driving (among students who drove during the 30 days before the survey)	39.2	40.2	38.2

SOURCE: Centers for Disease Control and Prevention, "Youth Risk Behavior Surveillance—United States, 2015," *MMWR* 65, no. SS 6 (2016): 1–174.

TABLE 8–2

Healthy People 2020 Objectives Related to Unintentional Injury

AH-5.6	Decrease school absenteeism among adolescents due to illness or injury.
IVP-11	Reduce unintentional injury deaths.
IVP-12	Reduce nonfatal unintentional injuries.
IVP-13	Reduce motor vehicle crash-related deaths.
IVP-14	Reduce nonfatal motor vehicle crash-related injuries.
IVP-15	Increase use of safety belts.
IVP-16	Increase age-appropriate vehicle restraint system use in children.
IVP-18	Reduce pedestrian deaths on public roads.
IVP-19	Reduce nonfatal pedestrian injuries on public roads.
IVP-20	Reduce pedal cyclist deaths on public roads.
IVP-21	Increase the number of states and the District of Columbia with laws requiring bicycle helmets for bicycle riders.
IVP-22	Increase the proportion of motorcycle operators and passengers using helmets.
IVP-23	Prevent an increase in fall-related deaths.
IVP-24	Reduce unintentional suffocation deaths.
IVP-25	Reduce drowning deaths.
IVP-26	Reduce sports and recreation injuries.
IVP-27	Increase the proportion of public and private schools that require students to wear appropriate protective gear when engaged in school-sponsored physical activities.
IVP-28	Reduce residential fire deaths.

SOURCE: U.S. Department of Health and Human Services, *Healthy People 2020*, www.healthypeople.gov/2020/.

Helmets for bicycle safety should be a family habit.

the medicine cabinet, play with matches, or venture into a swimming pool. Young children have limited physical coordination and cognitive abilities. This can lead to a greater risk for falls from bicycles and playground equipment and make it difficult for them to escape from a fire. And their small size and developing bones and muscles may make them more susceptible to injury in motor-vehicle crashes if they are not properly restrained.[10] When childhood and adolescent injuries result in days missed from school, academic performance may be affected.

Factors That Influence Safety and Unintentional Injury

Several important factors play a role in unintentional injury morbidity and mortality. Rates of injuries among males are higher than among females, indicating risk-taking behavior by males and Western society's acceptance of it. Risk-taking behavior seems to begin early in the first decade of life and continues into adulthood, evidenced by behaviors such as drinking and driving, speeding, carrying a weapon, and using illicit drugs. All these behaviors can lead to an increased risk of injury.[11]

The science of injury prevention and control has moved away from a focus on "accident proneness" and parental supervision to an emphasis on the role of the environment as a modifiable risk or a protective factor for injury. Perhaps the most important environmental risk factor for injury among children is poverty.[12] Children living in poverty have a greater risk of almost every type of injury, including pedestrian–motor-vehicle collisions, fires and

burns, drowning, falls, and violence. Poor children often live in dilapidated housing, in tenements without heat or air conditioning, and in neighborhoods built for motor vehicles rather than for pedestrians or bicyclists. Poverty also can mean that children live in neighborhoods with high crime rates and easy access to guns. Lower levels of parental education make poor children less likely to use protective gear such as cycle helmets, child safety seats, and personal flotation devices.[13]

At times, children and adolescents are powerless over situations that lead to injury (e.g., a small child who is held in an adult's arms, rather than being properly restrained in a child safety seat, while riding in a motor vehicle). However, many children and teens willfully participate in behaviors that increase their risk of injury. These behaviors sometimes occur in combination. For example, among high school and college students, associations have been reported in relation to thinking about suicide, not using seat belts, driving after drinking alcohol, carrying weapons, and engaging in physical fights.[14]

William M. Kane and Marcia Quackenbush, authors of *Teach and Talk: Safety and Risk*, stated that taking risks is part of growing up. They explained:

> Children have a natural desire to grow up. They want to act like older kids. They want to feel like older kids. They like to look good in front of their peers, which often means looking more grown up. This is a normal, healthy developmental process, and every child does it to some degree. One of the places this process is played out is through risk taking.[15]

Despite these factors, serious child and adolescent injuries are not inevitable. Frederick P. Rivara, a world-renowned expert in the field of injury prevention, stated,

> One of the most important tasks for education and health professionals, parents, and community members to undertake is to implement fully the strategies that have been shown to reduce injuries to children and adolescents. As many as one-third of injury fatalities in this age group could be prevented through strategies such as motor vehicle occupant protection, traffic calming to

©Ariel Skelley/Getty Images

prevent pedestrian injuries, use of bicycle helmets, safe storage of guns, adequate pool fencing and use of personal flotation devices, and use of smoke detectors. . . . Some of these interventions require behavior change on the part of individuals, while others require behavior change at the level of communities and legislatures. . . . Perhaps the most important change is in attitudes. All injuries to children must be viewed as preventable if the United States is to reduce disparities and the toll of trauma.[16]

GUIDELINES FOR SCHOOLS

State of the Practice

The CDC's Division of Adolescent and School Health (DASH) conducts the School Health Policies and Practices Study (SHPPS) to monitor efforts to improve school health policies and programs. With regard to school health education, close to three-fourths of districts required schools to teach about injury prevention and safety (66.9 at the elementary, 71.3 at the middle, and 77.1 at the high school levels). In terms of a safe and healthy school environment, the majority of districts have developed, revised, or assisted in developing model policies, policy guidance, or other materials related to injury prevention and safety; however, the emphasis of the policy varies significantly across states and districts.[17] The 2016 report is available at www.cdc.gov/healthyyouth/data/shpps/index.htm.

State of the Art

Injury prevention efforts are most effective when schools and communities work in partnership. Students, teachers, parents and caregivers, school staff, and community members all play important roles.

The CDC's *School Health Guidelines to Prevent Unintentional Injuries and Violence* assist state and local education agencies and schools in promoting safety and help schools serve as safe places for students to learn.[18] The guidelines are based on extensive reviews of research, theory, and current practice in unintentional injury, violence, and suicide prevention; health education; and public health. There are eight major recommendations for preventing injuries:

1. A social environment that promotes safety.
2. A safe physical environment.
3. Health education curriculum and instruction.
4. Safe physical education, sports, and recreational activities.
5. Health, counseling, psychological, and social services for students.
6. Appropriate crisis and emergency response.
7. Involvement of families and communities.
8. Staff development to promote safety and prevent unintentional injuries, violence, and suicide.

Teacher's Toolbox 8.1 summarizes the guidelines related specifically to safety and unintentional injury prevention.

Kane and Quackenbush recommended three steps for keeping young people safe:

- Prevent injury events.
- Prevent injury when events occur.
- Prevent disability and promote healing when injury occurs.[19]

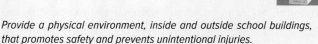

Teacher's Toolbox 8.1

Recommendations for the Prevention of Unintentional Injuries

Establish a social environment that promotes safety and prevents unintentional injuries.

- Ensure high academic standards and provide faculty, staff members, and students with the support and administrative leadership to promote the academic success, health, and safety of students.
- Encourage students' feelings of connectedness to school.
- Designate a person with responsibility for coordinating safety activities.
- Establish a climate that demonstrates respect, support, and caring.
- Develop and implement written policies regarding unintentional injury.
- Infuse unintentional injury prevention into multiple school activities and classes.
- Establish unambiguous disciplinary policies; communicate them to students, faculty, staff members, and families; and implement them consistently.
- Assess unintentional injury prevention strategies and policies at regular intervals.

Provide a physical environment, inside and outside school buildings, that promotes safety and prevents unintentional injuries.

- Conduct regular safety and hazard assessments; make repairs immediately following identification of hazards.
- Maintain structures, equipment grounds, and school buses and other vehicles.
- Actively supervise all student activities to promote safety and prevent unintentional injuries.
- Ensure that the school environment, including school buses, is weapon-free.

Implement health and safety education curricula and instruction that help students develop the knowledge, attitudes, behavioral skills, and confidence needed to adopt and maintain safe lifestyles and to advocate for health and safety.

- Choose prevention programs and curricula that are grounded in theory or that have scientific evidence of effectiveness.
- Implement unintentional injury prevention curricula consistent with national and state standards for health education.

(continued)

- Use active learning strategies, interactive teaching methods, and proactive classroom management to encourage student involvement in learning about unintentional injury prevention.
- Provide adequate staffing and resources, including budget, facilities, professional development, and class time to provide unintentional injury prevention education for all students.

Provide safe physical education and extracurricular physical activity programs.

- Develop, teach, implement, and enforce safety rules.
- Provide safe physical education and extracurricular physical activity programs.
- Ensure that spaces and facilities for physical activity meet or exceed safety standards for design, installation, and maintenance.
- Hire physical education teachers, coaches, athletic trainers, and other physical activity program staff members who are trained in injury prevention, first aid, and CPR and provide them with ongoing professional development.

Provide health, counseling, psychological, and social services to meet the physical, mental, emotional, and social health needs of students.

- Coordinate school-based counseling, psychological, social, and health services and the education curriculum.
- Establish strong links with community resources and identify providers to bring services into the schools.
- Identify and provide assistance to students who have been seriously injured.
- Assess the extent to which injuries occur on school property.

- Develop and implement emergency plans for assessing, managing, and referring injured students and staff members to appropriate levels of care.

Establish mechanisms for short- and long-term response to crises, disasters, and injuries that affect the school community.

- Establish a written response plan.
- Prepare to implement the school's plan in the event of a crisis.
- Have short-term and long-term responses and services established after a crisis.

Integrate school, family, and community efforts to prevent unintentional injuries.

- Involve parents, students, and other family members in all aspects of school life, including planning and implementing unintentional injury prevention programs and policies.
- Educate, support, and involve family members in prevention strategies.
- Coordinate school and community services.

For all school personnel, provide regular professional development opportunities that impart the knowledge, skills, and confidence to effectively promote safety and prevent unintentional injury; support students in their efforts to do the same.

- Ensure that staff members are knowledgeable about unintentional injury prevention and have the skills needed to prevent injuries at school, at home, and in the community.
- Train and support all personnel to be positive role models for a healthy and safe lifestyle.

SOURCE: Centers for Disease Control and Prevention, *Guidelines for School Health Programs to Prevent Unintentional Injuries and Violence* June 2006, stacks.cdc.gov.

These prevention principles occur at all levels—individual students, classrooms, schools, families, and communities. Thus, prevention efforts include teaching children to apply safety rules and skills and to assess risky situations as well as calling on adults to make the home, school, and community environments safer. Kane and Quackenbush assert:

> To help all kids be safe kids, injury prevention education must provide a foundation for children that enables them to make smart, safe choices when they face risky situations. Activities and projects that build a sense of community and belonging are among the most important. A connected community protects its own, speaks up to get help when needed, and knows that every individual in the community is important. This is a powerful perspective to have when assessing risky situations or thinking about ways to support friends.[20]

Similarly, the National Injury Prevention Foundation explains that children are at an impressionable stage of development, during which they enjoy learning new responsibilities and decision-making skills and attempting to influence their family members and peers. Teaching this age group has the potential to increase safety behaviors that will be maintained through the high-risk adolescent years and become lifelong habits.[21]

The CDC developed the Health Education Curriculum Analysis Tool (HECAT) to help educators consider state-of-the-art practice in health education. All HECAT modules were developed using the NHES and the CDC's Characteristics of an Effective Health Education Curriculum as the framework for guiding criteria and scoring rubrics to assist educators in analyzing the extent to which a curriculum is likely to enable students to master the essential knowledge and skills that promote safety. Module S includes needed guidance and appraisal tools intended to assist educators in a systematic assessment of curricula designed to promote safe and reduce unintentional injuries. The HECAT is available at the CDC Adolescent and School Health website (www.cdc.gov/HealthyYouth/HECAT/).

GUIDELINES FOR CLASSROOM APPLICATIONS

Important Background for K–8 Teachers

The events that lead to unintentional injuries often are referred to as accidents, although scientific evidence indicates that many of these events can be predicted and prevented. Students can learn to keep themselves safe by internalizing core concepts and practicing injury prevention skills such as self-management, communication, decision making, and peer resistance. Students need opportunities to determine solutions to a variety of safety scenarios and practice skills in a safe environment.[22]

Safety instruction should include active learning strategies, interactive teaching methods, and proactive classroom management techniques that encourage calm, orderly classrooms. Active learning strategies engage students in learning and help them develop the concepts, attitudes, and behavioral skills they need to act safely.[23]

Teachers should remember that young students often do not fully understand abstract concepts or different perspectives. For example, young children might assume that drivers can see them and will stop simply because the children see the car coming. Safety instruction for younger students must focus on concrete experiences, such as practicing—not just hearing about—skills such as crossing the street or feeling a door to find out whether it's hot or cold to the touch. More abstract associations among behaviors, environment, and injury risk become appropriate as students enter the upper-elementary and middle-level grades. Although families play an important role in children's safety decisions, peer pressure to engage in risky behaviors becomes a strong motivator as students grow older. By the time children enter middle school, they are far more capable of understanding and acting on the connection between behaviors and injury risks.[24]

Educational programs must be appropriate for the cultures in the community. Students within the same school and even within the same classroom have diverse experiences, knowledge, attitudes, abilities, and behaviors with respect to health and safety. Rather than adopting a one-size-fits-all approach to safety, educators should take this diversity into account to increase the likelihood of reaching students in meaningful ways. For example, if the streets in a particular community don't have street names or road signs, students must learn other ways to tell someone how to get to their house in an emergency (We live at the end of the road that runs by the creek).

In busy classrooms, teachers often want to know exactly what their students should be learning for their age or developmental level. In truth, teachers cannot know this without first getting to know their students, their students' families, and their students' communities. As an experienced teacher aptly put it to a group of preservice teachers, "Don't think of your students as one class of twenty-five—think of them as twenty-five classes of one." Teachers must take the time to find out what their students know and want to know about safety and unintentional injury topics as they plan instruction appropriate for the particular children in their classrooms.

The National Center for Injury Prevention and Control targets injuries related to transportation, home, and recreation activities. The types of unintentional injury that pose significant threat to American youth are motor-vehicle crashes, fireworks-related injuries, playground injuries, poisonings, residential fire-related injuries, traumatic brain injury, and drowning.[25] This section also includes information on pedestrian and bicycle safety, sports and recreation activities, and unsupervised children.

Child Passenger Safety

Motor-vehicle injuries, the leading cause of death and the greatest public health problem for today's children, often stem from the behavior of drivers rather than from the actions of children. Approximately one of six fatally injured children were riding with drinking drivers.[26] Use of restraints (car seats, seat belts) among young children often depends on the driver's seat-belt use. Almost 40 percent of children riding with unbelted drivers are themselves unrestrained. In addition, child-restraint systems often are used incorrectly.[27]

Recent research indicates that an estimated 6,18,000 children under the age of 13 rode unrestrained and more than 1 million children rode in the front seat of a vehicle at least once in the last thirty days. During that same period of time, close to 11 million children under 8 years of age reportedly used only adult seat belts. These research findings highlight the need for continued education and outreach to parents and children regarding optimal child-restraint use and rear seating position for children for every road trip.[28]

Most motor-vehicle injuries can be prevented. Children should be properly restrained in car seats or with seat belts, and children younger than 13 years should ride in the backseat of a car to avoid possible serious injury from airbag deployment. Every state has a child safety seat law in place, but specific requirements vary. Many laws do not offer full protection for children as they grow and their safety needs change. Child safety seat laws should be strengthened so that every time children ride, they are in federally approved child restraints that are appropriate for their age and size.[29]

At the classroom level, teachers can involve students and their families in education and awareness efforts to increase proper

Children under age 12 should ride in the backseat; younger children may need booster seats. Everyone in the vehicle should be secured with a seat belt.

child restraint in motor vehicles. At a minimum, students should know that they should:

- Always wear a seat belt or sit in a booster seat if appropriate for their size, every time they ride in a car.
- Ride in the backseat if they are younger than 13 years.

Fireworks-Related Injuries

Teachers may be surprised to see fireworks-related injuries on the list of priority prevention behaviors. However, depending on the community in which children live, fireworks can be a real danger. Of course, the safest way to prevent fireworks-related injuries is to leave fireworks displays to trained professionals. On the Fourth of July, in a typical year, fireworks account for nearly half (47%) of all reported fires. During the month surrounding the Fourth of July, more than one-third (35%) of people seen in emergency rooms for fireworks injuries were under 15 years of age, with nearly 10 percent being under age 5.[30]

The National Center for Injury Prevention and Control reports that despite federal regulations and varying state prohibitions, many types of fireworks are accessible to the public. Eighty-four percent of the firework injuries treated in hospital emergency departments in 2014 involved fireworks that federal regulations permit consumers to use.[31] It is not uncommon to find fireworks distributors near state borders, where residents of states with strict fireworks regulations can take advantage of more lenient state laws. Among the various types of fireworks, sold legally in some states, bottle rockets can fly into the face and cause eye injuries, sparklers can ignite clothing, and firecrackers can injure the hands or face if they explode at close range. Sparklers accounted for more firework-related injuries in 2014 than all of the reported injuries.[32]

Injuries can result from being too close to fireworks when they explode. Younger children often lack the physical coordination to handle fireworks safely. In addition, children are often excited and curious around fireworks, which can increase their chances of being injured. For example, they might reexamine a firecracker dud that initially failed to ignite. In particular, homemade fireworks can lead to dangerous explosions.[33]

If appropriate to the community, teachers can engage their students in discussions about safety around fireworks before holidays, such as New Year's Eve and the Fourth of July. Students can access information about fireworks danger—for example, sparklers can burn at more than 1,000 degrees Fahrenheit. Decision-making and self-management scenarios also make for lively discussion about fireworks safety.

Playground Injuries

Each year in the United States, emergency departments treat more than 2,00,000 children ages 14 and younger for playground-related injuries. About 10 percent of these children are treated for a traumatic brain injury, including concussion.[34] Although all children who use playgrounds are at risk for injury, boys sustain injuries slightly more often than girls. Children ages 5 to 9 have higher rates of emergency department visits for playground injuries than any other age group. Most of these injuries occur at school.[35]

Playground safety: Take care of yourself, take care of others, take care of this place.

Lack of supervision often is associated with playground injuries. In addition to providing close adult supervision, teachers can help students learn and apply the following basic information about fall prevention:

- Play safely by taking turns on equipment. Remind others not to push.
- Talk with parents, caregivers, and teachers about playground rules and safety.
- Ask adults if your playground has the right kind of safe, soft landing surface to prevent injuries.
- Be careful on stairs and ladders (e.g., on sliding boards). Take your time in order to stay safe and prevent falls.
- Ask for help from adults if you see an unsafe situation on the playground.

Poisonings

Every day, more than 300 children under the age of 19 in the United States are treated in an emergency department and two children die as a result of poisoning.[36] The National Center for Injury Prevention and Control defines poison as any substance that is harmful to the body when ingested (eaten), inhaled (breathed), injected, or absorbed through the skin. Any substance can be poisonous if enough is taken. For this reason, poisoning implies that too much of some substance has been taken. This definition does not include adverse reactions to medications taken correctly.

Poisonings are either intentional or unintentional. Intentional poisoning is the result of a person taking or giving a substance with the intention of causing harm. Suicide and assault by poisoning fall into this category. Unintentional poisoning includes the excessive use of drugs or chemicals for nonrecreational purposes, such as by a toddler. The National Poison Data System reported that children under the age of 6 accounted for approximately half of all human poison exposures in 2016. More male than female exposures were reported in children younger than 13; however, this gender distribution reversed in teenagers, with females accounting for more exposures than males.[37]

The American Association of Poison Control Centers recommends teaching students that poisoning can occur by eating, drinking, touching, or smelling something that can make them sick or hurt them. Some things, like medicine, can make them sick if they take the wrong kind or if they take too much. Children and adolescents should always ask a trusted adult before taking any medication. Young people should never put anything in their mouth if they are not sure if it is safe to eat.[38]

Teachers can help students learn and apply the following basic information about poison prevention:

- Call 9-1-1, the operator (dial 0), or the National Poison control Center (800-222-1222) in a poisoning emergency.
- Work with your family to be sure all poisonous materials are out of sight and out of the reach of young children.
- Check inside and outside the home for potential hazards, including poisonous plants, to protect small children and pets.
- Work with your family to be sure all medicines and toxic products are out of the reach of small children.
- Take medications only with adult supervision.
- Read the label and associated warnings and follow the directions.
- Don't keep medicines or toxic agents if you don't need them. Safely dispose of unused, unneeded, or expired prescription and over-the-counter drugs, vitamins, supplements, or toxic products.

Residential Fire-Related Injuries

Deaths from fires and burns are the third leading cause of fatal home injury in the United States. Small children and those living in substandard housing are at increased risk of fire-related injury and death.

At the classroom level, teachers can involve students and their families in education and awareness efforts to increase fire safety in the home. For example, the Centers for Disease Control and Prevention provides an online campaign called Protect the Ones You Love: Childhood Injuries Are Preventable (www.cdc.gov/safechild/). Teachers can help students learn strategies to prevent burns from fire and scalding:

- Check with their families to be sure they have a working smoke detector in the home and to test the batteries once every month.
- Plan a home fire escape route with their families.
- Use safe cooking practices such as keeping the handles of pots and pans turned toward the back of the stove, out of the reach of young children.
- Set the water heater thermostat to 120 degrees Fahrenheit or lower.[39]

Traumatic Brain Injury

A traumatic brain injury (TBI) is defined as a bump, blow, or jolt to the head or a penetrating head injury that disrupts the function of the brain. Not all blows or jolts to the head result in TBI. Severity may range from mild (a brief change in mental status or consciousness) to severe (an extended period of unconsciousness or amnesia after the injury). The majority of TBIs are concussions or other forms of mild TBI. The CDC provides online materials for schools, titled, Heads Up to Schools: Know Your Concussion ABCs as follows: A—Assess the situation; B—Be alert for signs and symptoms; C—Contact a health care professional.[40]

An excellent resource for teachers and students related to TBI prevention is the ThinkFirst National Injury Prevention Foundation (www.thinkfirst.org). The ThinkFirst for Kids Program was developed to increase knowledge and awareness among elementary school children about the causes and consequences of brain and spinal cord injury, injury prevention, and safety habits that reduce the risk of injury. ThinkFirst includes lessons on water, bicycle, vehicle, and playground safety intended for students in grades 1 through 3, and may also be adapted for kindergarten students. The site includes information for kids, youth, teens, parents, and teachers.[41]

Swimming and Water Safety

Swimming and other water-related activities are excellent examples of ways to get the physical activity for a healthy lifestyle. However, it's important to prevent water-related adverse health effects, such as sunburn and other injuries, drowning, and recreational water illnesses (e.g., diarrhea).[42]

Adult supervision is the key to water safety. Children can learn more about water safety at sites such as Kids' Health (www.kidshealth.org). The site offers information on staying safe in swimming pools, around lakes and ponds, at beaches, and at water parks, and on learning to swim.

Pedestrian and Bicycle Safety

Riding a bicycle is fun, an excellent source of exercise, and an environmentally friendly mode of transportation. However, children and teens must learn key safety measures to avoid serious injury when bicycling. Educators should emphasize the importance of finding the right helmet fit and wearing a helmet. Students can take the "Helmet Fit Test," shown in Teacher's Toolbox 8.2. Helmets are the most effective safety device for cyclists to reduce head injury and death.

Teacher's Toolbox 8.2

Steps in the Safe Kids Helmet Fit Test

Eyes check: Position the helmet on your head. Look up and you should see the bottom of the rim of the helmet. The rim should be one- to two-finger widths above the eyebrows.

Ears check: Make sure the straps of the helmet form a "V" under your ears when buckled. The strap should be snug but comfortable.

Mouth check: Open your mouth as wide as you can. Do you feel the helmet hug your head? If not, tighten the straps and make sure the buckle is flat against your skin.

SOURCE: Safe Kids Worldwide, "Helmet Fit Test", https://www.safekids.org/tip/helmet-fit-test-2013.

Children younger than age 10 should cross the street with an adult.

playground activities; and exercise and training activities, such as weight-lifting, aerobics, and jogging. Participation in sports and recreation activities contributes to health-related fitness. However, the risk of injury is inherent in any physical activity. Risk of injury varies depending on many factors, including the specific activity and the participant's age. Children might be at greater risk because of immature or undeveloped coordination, skills, and perception.[46]

Participation in sports and recreation activities varies widely across the country and by season and climate. Children in some parts of the United States participate in winter activities such as snow skiing and ice-skating. In other parts of the country, children surf, boogie-board, and swim in the open ocean. In many communities, children participate in activities such as skateboarding, in-line skating, and bicycling.

More information on sports and recreation activities safety can be found in Chapter 7, on promoting physical activity. Teachers and students also can access a number of websites with information on sports, recreation, and exercise safety. Students can conduct their own investigations into safety through websites.

Children Home Alone

Every day thousands of children arrive home from school to an empty house. The American Academy of Child and Adolescent Psychiatry estimates that more than 40 percent of children are left home alone at some time, though rarely overnight. In more extreme situations, some children spend so much time at home without their parents or caregivers that they are called "latchkey children," referring to the house or apartment key strung visibly around their neck.[47]

According to the U.S. Department of Health and Human Services Children's Bureau, only Illinois, Maryland, and Oregon currently have laws regarding a minimum age for leaving a child home alone. Even in those states, other factors, such as concern for a child's well-being and the amount of time the child is left alone, are considered. States that do not have laws may still offer guidelines for parents. Local Child Protective Service (CPS) agencies can provide information on laws and guidelines in their state. For help in contacting a local CPS agency, call Childhelp at 1-800-4-A-CHILD.[48]

Parents and caregivers should work with children to teach them about safety issues, such as not opening the door, staying in the house, answering the phone properly, practicing what to do if something goes wrong, knowing emergency numbers, and practicing what to say if they need to call 9-1-1.

Being home alone can be a frightening and stressful experience for children. In addition to the important teaching that parents and caregivers must do with their children to minimize

The Safe Kids Worldwide campaign (www.safekids.org) sponsors an annual Walk & Bike to School Day (www.walkbiketo-school.org/). The campaign creates community and global awareness about walking and biking to school safely. Policies that increase the number of people walking and bicycling appear to be an effective method for improving the safety of pedestrians and cyclists. Eighty percent of child pedestrian deaths occur at non-intersection locations. Developmentally, kids under the age of 10 cannot judge the speed and distance of approaching vehicles. Safe Kids Walk This Way is a program that works around the world to teach safe behavior to motors and pedestrians to create safer, more walkable communities. In 2005, the Safe, Accountable, Flexible, Efficient Transportation Equity Act: A Legacy for Users (SAFETEA-LU) was signed into law. It includes the establishment of Safe Routes to School, a program with the goal of making it safer for children to walk or bike to school, other than designated crosswalks.[43]

Teachers can find educational materials on International Walk to School Day in the United States at www.walkbiketoschool.org. The campaign is designed to increase safety as well as physical activity among children and their families.[44] The website contains a link to the National Center for Safe Routes to School, which enables community leaders, schools, and parents across the United States to improve safety and encourage more children, including children with disabilities, to safely walk and bicycle to school. Teachers can access the National Center for Safe Routes to School resources online to promote walking and biking to school.[45]

Sports and Recreation Activities

Participation in sports and recreation activities is an important part of a physically active lifestyle. Such activities include organized sports (school or club) and unorganized sports (backyard or pickup), such as basketball, football, and hockey; recreational activities, such as boating, biking, skiing, swimming, and danger and keep them safe, teachers can talk with students about safety issues after school. KidsHealth (www.kidshealth.org) provides an excellent overview for students, titled "When It's Just You After School." The site provides ideas for ground rules, staying safe, and strategies for dealing with feeling lonely.[49]

Other Safety Topics

Teacher may want to address other safety topics with their students, depending on the needs of the children and families of the local community. Example topics include:

- Safety around animals
- Holiday safety
- First aid
- CPR
- Safety around strangers
- Natural disasters
- School bus safety
- Field trip safety

- Internet safety
- Safety for children with special needs

Safe Kids USA (www.safekids.org/educators/) provides information and strategies on safety topics and is a useful resource for teachers and parents/caregivers.[50]

Recommendations for Concepts and Practice

Healthy Behavior Outcomes

The goal of health education is to help students adopt or maintain health-enhancing behaviors. School districts and teachers should identify the health-enhancing behaviors they would like their students to maintain or adopt. The list found in the Teacher's Toolbox 8.3 identifies possible healthy behavioral outcomes (HBOs) related to promoting safety and preventing unintentional injury. Though not all these suggestions are developmentally appropriate for students in grades K–8, this list can help teachers understand how the learning activities they plan for their students support both short- and long-term desired behavior outcomes.

Teacher's Toolbox 8.3

Developmentally Appropriate Knowledge and Skill Expectations for Promoting Safety and Preventing Unintentional Injury

HEALTHY BEHAVIOR OUTCOMES FOR PROMOTING SAFETY AND PREVENTING UNINTENTIONAL INJURY

HBO 1. Follow appropriate safety rules when riding in or on a motor vehicle.

HBO 2. Avoid driving a motor vehicle—or riding in a motor vehicle driven by someone—while under the influence of alcohol or other drugs.

HBO 3. Use safety equipment appropriately and correctly.

HBO 4. Apply safety rules and procedures to avoid risky behaviors and injury.

HBO 5. Avoid safety hazards in the home and community.

HBO 6. Recognize and avoid dangerous surroundings.

HBO 7. Get help for oneself or others when injured or suddenly ill.

HBO 8. Support others to avoid risky behaviors and be safe.

Grades K–2 Knowledge Expectations	Grades 3–5 Knowledge Expectations	Grades 6–8 Knowledge Expectations
NHES 1: Core Concepts		
S1.2.1 State the benefits of riding in the back seat when a passenger in a motor vehicle. (HBO 1)	S1.5.1 Identify ways to reduce risk of injuries while riding in a motor vehicle. (HBO 1, 2, 3 & 4)	S1.8.1 Describe ways to reduce risk of injuries while riding in or on a motor vehicle. (HBO 1, 2, 3 & 8)
S1.2.2 Describe the importance of using safety belts, child safety restraints, and motor-vehicle booster seats. (HBO 1 & 3)	S1.5.2 Explain how injuries can be prevented. (HBO 1, 2, 3, 4, 5, 6 & 8)	S1.8.2 Identify protective equipment needed for sports and recreational activities. (HBO 1 & 3)
S1.2.3 Identify safe behaviors when getting on and off and while riding on a bus. (HBO 1, 5 & 6)	S1.5.3 List examples of dangerous or risky behaviors that might lead to injuries. (HBO 2 & 4)	S1.8.3 Explain the importance of helmets and other safety gear for biking, riding a scooter, skateboarding, and inline skating. (HBO 1, 3 & 8)
S1.2.4 Identify safety rules for playing on playground, swimming, and playing sports. (HBO 3 & 4)	S1.5.4 Describe how to ride a bike, skateboard, ride a scooter, and/or inline skate safely. (HBO 3 & 4)	S1.8.4 Explain the risks associated with using alcohol or other drugs and driving a motor vehicle. (HBO 2, 4 & 8)
S1.2.5 Describe how injuries can be prevented. (HBO 3, 4, 5 & 6)	S1.5.5 Identify ways to reduce risk of injuries in case of a fire. (HBO 3, 4, 5 & 6)	S1.8.5 Describe the relationship between using alcohol and other drugs and injuries. (HBO 2, 4 & 8)
S1.2.6 Identify safety rules for being around fire. (HBO 4)	S1.5.6 Identify ways to reduce risk of injuries around water. (HBO 3, 4, 5 & 6)	S1.8.6 Identify actions to take to prevent injuries during severe weather. (HBO 3, 4, 5 & 6)
S1.2.7 Describe how to be a safe pedestrian. (HBO 4, 5 & 6)	S1.5.7 Identify ways to reduce injury from falls. (HBO 3, 4, 5 & 6)	S1.8.7 Describe ways to reduce risk of injuries from falls. (HBO 3, 4, 5 & 6)
	S1.5.8 Identify ways to protect vision or hearing from injury. (HBO 3, 4, 5 & 6)	S1.8.8 Describe ways to reduce risk of injuries around water. (HBO 3, 4, 5, 6 & 7)
		S1.8.9 Describe ways to reduce risk of injuries in case of fire. (HBO 3, 4, 5 & 7)

(continued)

Grades K–2 Knowledge Expectations (*continued*)	**Grades 3–5 Knowledge Expectations** (*continued*)	**Grades 6–8 Knowledge Expectations** (*continued*)
S1.2.8 Identify safety hazards in the home. (HBO 4 & 5)	S1.5.9 Identify ways to reduce injuries from firearms. (HBO 4, 5 & 6)	S1.8.10 Describe ways to reduce risk of injury when playing sports. (HBO 3, 4, 5, 6 & 7)
S1.2.9 Identify how household products are harmful if ingested or inhaled. (HBO 5)	S1.5.10 Identify ways to reduce injuries as a pedestrian. (HBO 4, 5 & 6)	S1.8.11 Describe how sharing or posting personal information electronically about self or others on social media sites (e.g., chat groups, e-mail, texting, websites, phone and tablet applications) can negatively impact personal safety of self or others. (HBO 4 & 8)
S1.2.10 Identify safety hazards in the community. (HBO 5 & 8)	S1.5.11 Identify safety precautions for playing and working outdoors in different kinds of weather and climates. (HBO 3, 4, 5, 6 & 8)	
S1.2.11 Identify people who can help when someone is injured or suddenly ill. (HBO 7)	S1.5.12 List ways to prevent injuries at home. (HBO 4, 5, 6 & 8)	S1.8.12 Explain climate-related physical conditions that affect personal safety, such as heat exhaustion, sunburn, heat stroke, and hypothermia. (HBO 4, 5 & 6)
	S1.5.13 List ways to prevent injuries in the community. (HBO 4, 5, 6 & 8)	S1.8.13 Describe ways to reduce risk of injuries as a pedestrian. (HBO 4, 5, 6 & 8)
	S1.5.14 Identify ways to reduce risk of injuries from animal and insect bites and stings. (HBO 4, 5, 6 & 8)	S1.8.14 Describe actions to change unsafe situations at home. (HBO 4, 5, 6 & 8)
	S1.5.15 List ways to prevent injuries at school. (HBO 4, 6 & 8)	S1.8.15 Describe actions to change unsafe situations at school. (HBO 4, 5, 6 & 8)
	S1.5.16 Explain why household products are harmful if ingested or inhaled. (HBO 5 & 6)	S1.8.16 Describe actions to change unsafe situations in the community. (HBO 4, 5, 6 & 8)
	S1.5.17 Explain what to do if someone is poisoned or injured and needs help. (HBO 7)	S1.8.17 Describe ways to reduce risk of injuries from firearms. (HBO 4, 5, 6 & 8)
		S1.8.18 Describe why household products are harmful if ingested or inhaled. (HBO 5, 6 & 8)
		S1.8.19 Describe potential risks associated with over-the-counter medicines. (HBO 5 & 8)
		S1.8.20 Describe first response procedures needed to treat injuries and other emergencies. (HBO 7)
		S1.8.21 Determine the benefits of reducing the risks for injury. (HBO 8)

Grades K–2 Skill Expectations	**Grades 3–5 Skill Expectations**	**Grades 6–8 Skill Expectations**
NHES 2: Analyze Influences		
S2.2.1 Identify relevant influences of family on safety and injury prevention practices and behaviors.	S2.5.1 Identify relevant influences of culture on safety and injury prevention practices and behaviors.	S2.8.1 Explain the influence of school rules and community laws on safety and injury prevention practices and behaviors.
S2.2.2 Identify relevant influences of school on safety and injury prevention practices and behaviors.	S2.5.2 Identify relevant influences of peers on safety and injury prevention practices and behaviors.	S2.8.2 Explain how perceptions of norms influence healthy and unhealthy safety and injury prevention practices and behaviors.
S2.2.3 Identify relevant influences of media and technology on safety and injury prevention practices and behaviors.	S2.5.3 Identify relevant influences of community on safety and injury prevention practices and behaviors.	S2.8.3 Explain how social expectations influence healthy and unhealthy safety and injury prevention practices and behaviors.
S2.2.4 Describe positive influences on safety and injury prevention practices and behaviors.	S2.5.4 Describe how relevant influences of family and culture affect personal safety and injury prevention practices and behaviors.	S2.8.4 Explain how personal values and beliefs influence personal safety and injury prevention practices and behaviors.
S2.2.5 Describe negative influences on safety and injury prevention practices and behaviors.	S2.5.5 Describe how relevant influences of school and community affect personal safety and injury prevention practices and behaviors.	S2.8.5 Describe how some health risk behaviors influence safety and injury prevention practices and behaviors (e.g., how alcohol and other drug use increased the risk of unintentional injury).
	S2.5.6 Describe how relevant influences of media and technology affect personal safety and injury prevention practices and behaviors.	S2.8.6 Analyze how relevant influences of family and culture affect personal safety and injury prevention practices and behaviors.
	S2.5.7 Describe how relevant influences of peers affect personal safety and injury prevention practices and behaviors.	S2.8.7 Analyze how relevant influences of school and community affect personal safety and injury prevention practices and behaviors.
		S2.8.8 Analyze how relevant influences of media and technology affect personal safety and injury prevention practices and behaviors.
		S2.8.9 Analyze how relevant influences of peers affect personal safety and injury prevention practices.

NHES 3: Accessing Information, Products, and Services

S3.2.1 Identify trusted adults at home who can help promote safety and injury prevention.

S3.2.2 Identify trusted adults and professionals in school who can help promote safety and injury prevention (e.g., school principal, facility and maintenance staff).

S3.2.3 Identify trusted adults and professionals in the community who can help promote safety and injury prevention (e.g., police, firefighter).

S3.2.4 Explain how to locate school health helpers who can help promote safety and injury prevention (e.g., school nurse, facility and maintenance staff).

S3.2.5 Explain how to locate community health helpers who can help promote safety and injury prevention (e.g., police officer, firefighter).

S3.2.6 Demonstrate how to locate school or community health helpers to enhance safety and injury prevention (e.g., police officer, firefighter).

S3.5.1 Describe characteristics of accurate safety and injury prevention information.

S3.5.2 Describe characteristics of appropriate and reliable safety and injury prevention products.

S3.5.3 Describe characteristics of appropriate and trustworthy safety and injury prevention services.

S3.5.4 Demonstrate how to locate sources of accurate safety and injury prevention information.

S3.8.1 Analyze the validity and reliability of safety and injury prevention information.

S3.8.2 Analyze the validity and reliability of safety and injury prevention products.

S3.8.3 Analyze the validity and reliability of safety and injury prevention services.

S3.8.4 Describe situations that call for professional safety and injury prevention services.

S3.8.5 Determine the availability of valid and reliable safety and injury prevention products.

S3.8.6 Access valid and reliable safety and injury prevention information from home, school or community.

S3.8.7 Locate valid and reliable safety and injury prevention products.

S3.8.8 Locate valid and reliable safety and injury prevention services.

Grades K–2 Skill Expectations	Grades 3–5 Skill Expectations	Grades 6–8 Skill Expectations

NHES 4: Interpersonal Communication

S4.2.1 Demonstrate how to effectively communicate needs, wants, and feelings in healthy ways to promote safety and prevent injury.

S4.2.2 Demonstrate effective active listening skills including paying attention, and verbal and nonverbal feedback to promote safety and avoid or reduce injury.

S4.2.3 Demonstrate effective refusal skills to avoid or reduce injury.

S4.2.4 Demonstrate how to effectively tell a trusted adult when feeling threatened or harmed.

S4.5.1 Demonstrate effective verbal and nonverbal communication skills to promote safety and avoid or reduce injury.

S4.5.2 Demonstrate effective peer resistance skills to avoid or reduce injury.

S4.5.3 Demonstrate healthy ways to manage or resolve conflict to avoid or reduce injury.

S4.5.4 Demonstrate how to effectively ask for help to avoid or reduce personal injury.

S4.8.1 Demonstrate the use of effective verbal and nonverbal communication skills to enhance safety and injury prevention.

S4.8.2 Demonstrate how to manage personal information in electronic communications and when using social media (e.g., chat groups, e-mail, texting, websites, phone and tablet applications) to protect the personal safety of oneself and others.

S4.8.3 Demonstrate effective peer resistance skills to avoid or reduce injury.

S4.8.4 Demonstrate effective negotiation skills to avoid or reduce injury.

S4.8.5 Demonstrate healthy ways to manage or resolve conflict to avoid or reduce injury.

S4.8.6 Demonstrate how to effectively ask for assistance to avoid or reduce personal injury.

NHES 5: Decision Making

S5.2.1 Identify situations that need a decision related to safety and injury prevention.

S5.2.2 Identify how family, peers, or media influence a decision related to safety and injury prevention.

S5.5.1 Identify situations that need a decision related to safety and injury prevention.

S5.5.2 Decide when help is needed and when it is not needed to make a decision related to safety and injury prevention.

S5.8.1 Identify circumstances that help or hinder healthy decision making related to safety and injury prevention.

S5.8.2 Determine when situations require a decision related to safety and injury prevention.

S5.8.3 Distinguish when safety and injury prevention decisions should be made individually or with the help of others.

(continued)

NHES 5: Decision Making (*continued*)

S5.2.3 Explain the potential positive and negative outcomes from a decision related to safety and injury prevention.

S5.2.4 Describe when help is needed and when it is not needed to make a decision related to safety and injury prevention.

S5.5.3 Explain how family, culture, peers, or media influence a decision related to safety and injury prevention.

S5.5.4 Identify options and their potential outcomes when making a decision related to safety and injury prevention.

S5.5.5 Choose a healthy option when making a decision related to safety and injury prevention.

S5.5.6 Describe the final outcome of a decision related to safety and injury prevention.

S5.8.4 Explain how family, culture, media, peers, and personal beliefs affect a decision related to safety and injury prevention.

S5.8.5 Distinguish between healthy and unhealthy alternatives to a decision related to safety and injury prevention.

S5.8.6 Predict the potential outcomes of healthy and unhealthy alternatives to a decision that could lead to injury.

S5.8.7 Choose a healthy alternative when making a decision related to safety and injury prevention.

S5.8.8 Analyze the effectiveness of a final outcome of a decision related to safety and injury prevention.

NHES 6: Goal Setting

S6.2.1 Identify a realistic personal short-term goal to avoid or reduce injury.

S6.2.2 Take steps to achieve a personal goal to avoid or reduce injury.

S6.2.3 Identify people who can help achieve a personal goal to avoid or reduce injury.

S6.5.1 Set a realistic personal goal to avoid or reduce injury.

S6.5.2 Track progress toward achieving a personal goal to avoid or reduce injury.

S6.5.3 Identify resources that can help achieve a personal goal to avoid or reduce injury.

S6.8.1 Assess personal safety and injury prevention practices.

S6.8.2 Set a realistic personal goal to avoid or reduce injury.

S6.8.3 Assess the barriers to achieving a personal goal to avoid or reduce injury.

S6.8.4 Apply strategies to overcome barriers to achieving a personal goal to avoid or reduce injuries.

S6.8.5 Use strategies and skills to achieve a personal goal to avoid or reduce injuries.

Grades K–2 Skill Expectations

NHES 7: Self-Management

S7.2.1 Identify practices that promote safety and reduce or prevent injuries.

S7.2.2 Demonstrate safety and injury prevention practices.

S7.2.3 Make a commitment to practice safety and injury prevention behaviors.

Grades 3–5 Skill Expectations

S7.5.1 Describe practices and behaviors that reduce or prevent injury.

S7.5.2 Demonstrate safety and injury prevention practices and behaviors.

S7.5.3 Make a commitment to practice safety and injury prevention.

Grades 6–8 Skill Expectations

S7.8.1 Explain the importance of being responsible for promoting safety and avoiding or reducing injury.

S7.8.2 Analyze practices and behaviors that reduce or prevent injuries.

S7.8.3 Demonstrate healthy practices and behaviors to improve safety and injury prevention of oneself and others.

S7.8.4 Make a commitment to practice safety and injury prevention.

NHES 8: Advocacy

S8.2.1 Make requests to others to promote safety and avoid or reduce injury.

S8.2.2 Demonstrate how to encourage peers to be safe and avoid or reduce injury.

S8.5.1 Give factual information to improve the safety and injury prevention of others.

S8.5.2 State personal beliefs to improve safety and injury prevention of others.

S8.5.3 Demonstrate how to persuade others to make choices to promote safety and avoid or reduce injury.

S8.8.1 State a health enhancing position, supported with accurate information, to improve the safety of others.

S8.8.2 Persuade others to make positive safety and injury prevention choices.

S8.8.3 Collaborate with others to advocate for individuals, families, and school safety and injury prevention.

S8.8.4 Demonstrate how to adapt safety and injury prevention messages for different audiences.

SOURCE: Centers for Disease Control and Prevention, *Health Education Curriculum Analysis Tool.* Atlanta, GA: CDC, 2012. www.cdc.gov.

Developmentally Appropriate Knowledge and Skill Expectations

As with other health topics, teaching related to promoting safety should be developmentally appropriate and be based on the physical, cognitive, social, emotional, and language characteristics of specific students. Teacher's Toolbox 8.3 contains a list of suggested developmentally appropriate knowledge and skill expectations to help teachers create lessons that will encourage students to practice the desired behavior outcomes by the time they graduate from high school. The numbers listed behind each knowledge expectation are aligned with and support the healthy behavior outcomes listed in the Teacher's Toolbox 8.3. Note that these grade-level spans are aligned with the NHES.

STRATEGIES FOR LEARNING AND ASSESSMENT

Promoting Safety and Preventing Unintentional Injury

This section provides an example of a standards-based learning and assessment strategy for each NHES standard. The examples in this chapter can be applied to any content area. Chapters 5 to 14 include content-specific learning and assessment strategies organized by standard and grade cluster (K–2, 3–5, and 6–8). Each set of strategies begins with a restatement of the standard and a reminder of the assessment criteria, drawn from the RMC Health rubrics in Appendix B. Strategies are written as directions for teachers and include applicable theory of planned behavior (TPB) constructs—intention to act in healthy ways, attitudes toward behavior, subjective norms, perceived behavioral control—in parentheses. These learning and assessment strategies provide building blocks for standards-based lessons and units that can be tailored to local needs. Assessment criteria are used with permission from the RMC Health. See Appendix B for Scoring Rubrics.

NHES 1 | Core Concepts

Students will comprehend concepts related to health promotion and disease prevention to enhance health.

ASSESSMENT CRITERIA
- Connections—Describe relationships between behavior and health; draw logical conclusions about connections between behavior and health.
- Comprehensiveness—Thoroughly cover health topic, showing breadth and depth; give accurate information.

Grades K–2

Talking Drawings About Safety   Locate a children's literature book (suggestions located at the end of the chapter) focused on children and safety (e.g., safety associated water, fire, household products, being a pedestrian, being a passenger). Prior to reading this book to the students, invite students to draw a picture on the topic. Ask students to show what they know about the topic through their picture. They can label items or phrases or just draw. Have students share their drawings upon completion. Now read the story to the class.

ASSESSMENT | Following the reading of the story on the topic, ask students to modify their drawings or, if it is easier, create an entirely new drawing on the topic based on the story that was shared. Encourage students to label parts of their illustrations and use any new technical terms they heard in the story. Have students share their drawings and discuss what they changed in their illustration after they listened to the text. For assessment criteria, students should present information that is accurate and shows connections between behaviors and safety. (Constructs: Attitudes toward behavior, perceived behavioral control.)

Creating Safety Word Shapes   As a final review for a safety unit, have students work in pairs to brainstorm vocabulary terms related to the unit. Encourage them to focus on identifying a few key terms that demonstrate priority concepts taught in the unit. Students need to be able to spell and explain the terms in their own words, or, if unable, access credible sources, such as picture dictionaries, to help spell correctly and determine the meaning. Terms students might consider include *risk*, *safety*, and *reduce risk*. Then have students go to the Tagxedo website at www.tagxedo.com/app.html. Students click on the "load" button and then type the words in the box next to where it says "enter text." They then click "submit." Students then click on the arrow button next to "shape" and select the shape that best connects to the topic they have chosen. For example, if they focused on sports safety they might choose the soccer ball; for weather safety, they might choose the umbrella. Students could select to use a word as a shape. Students can print their word shape to share with classmates. This activity is based on "Creating a Word Shape" by J. Altieri in her book *Powerful Content Connections*.

ASSESSMENT | The safety word shape is the assessment task. When students share their word shape with classmates they should focus on sharing information that is accurate and shows connections between behaviors and safety through the use of vocabulary. Posting the safety word shapes around the classroom will keep the safety messages and vocabulary visible to students. (Constructs: Attitudes toward behavior, perceived behavioral control.)

Please Play Safely on the Playground!   Bridget Heos's book *Be Safe on the Playground* (see the book list at the end of the chapter) is a child-friendly guide to playground behaviors. A young girl teaches the new student (an alien) about playground safety (choosing age-appropriate equipment, using the slide safely). Teachers can involve students right away in this story about how to act safely when they are playing with others. Students can work with a partner or group of three to develop scenarios for their own school playground, as well as going to and from the playground. Teachers might want to record the live action scenes to make a class movie about playing safely, or take pictures to make a class book.

ASSESSMENT | The scenarios from the book are the assessment task. For assessment criteria, students should demonstrate unsafe ways to act, followed by a demonstration of safe behaviors. Students should explain, in writing or for the camera, the connections between safe and unsafe behavior and health. (Construct: Attitudes toward behavior.)

Safety Rules and Practices   Provide opportunities for students to learn the most important facts and ideas relevant to early elementary students about these safety topics:

- Safety hazards in the home, school, and community
- Behaviors that can lead to injury
- Calling for and getting help in case of an injury or emergency
- Poisoning prevention (household products, medicines, help from adults)
- Fire safety
- Water safety
- Motor-vehicle safety (seat belts, booster seats, sitting in the backseat)
- School bus safety
- Pedestrian safety
- Insect bites and stings
- Safety around animals
- Playground safety
- Safety around firearms (tell an adult)
- Safety around fireworks (leave to professionals)
- Safety on bicycles, skateboards, scooters, and in-line skates
- Wearing protective equipment for sports and athletics
- Safety during physical activity (warm-up and cool-down)
- Safety in different kinds of weather

To begin, find out what students already know and can tell about safety rules and practices. Students may know a great deal that they've learned at home, in preschool, or in earlier grades. By sharing in the students' discussions, teachers have the opportunity to correct misperceptions. Other ideas are to (1) use Know-Wonder-Learn (KWL) charts, (2) have students work in small groups to list what they know about a particular safety topic and then share with the class, (3) invite guest speakers to talk about safety topics, (4) make field trips, such as to the fire department, and (5) have older students share with younger students about safety topics.

ASSESSMENT | For an assessment task, students can write, create drawings, or present skits to demonstrate their knowledge. For assessment criteria, students should present information that is accurate and show connections between behaviors and safety. (Construct: Attitudes toward behavior.)

Safe and Unsafe Behaviors and Situations

In the context of various safety topics, students can identify safe and unsafe behaviors and situations. Students enjoy acting out scenarios and using puppets to show what is safe and unsafe. Students can make connections between behaviors and safety.

ASSESSMENT | The students' dramatizations are the assessment task for this activity. For assessment criteria, students should provide correct information and make connections between behaviors and safety. (Construct: Attitudes toward behavior.)

Grades 3–5

Reducing My Risk!

Small groups of students can research strategies for reducing risks associated with one of the following suggested safety topics: fire, water, riding in a motor vehicle, firearms, pedestrian, animal and insect bites/stings, and injuries from falls. Examples of reducing risks in a motor vehicle might include always wearing a seat belt, sitting in the backseat, and using a booster seat. Once groups have developed a number of strategies for reducing risks for the assigned topic, they can develop a rap, lyrics to the tune of a familiar song (e.g., "Row, Row, Row Your Boat"), or some other musical format. Teachers may want to assess the risk reduction strategies prior to having students develop the musical message for accuracy. Student groups can present their musical message to the class.

ASSESSMENT | The student presentations are the assessment task for this activity. For assessment criteria, students should provide accurate information and draw conclusions between behaviors and health. (Constructs: Attitudes toward behavior, perceived behavioral control.)

Telling Fact from Fiction

Teachers can ask students to brainstorm a list of safety topics. Teachers should add to the list as needed. Students can work in small groups to investigate a safety issue of their choosing. Their assignment is to help classmates review and update their knowledge about safety by making fact-or-fiction statements for classmates to discuss and distinguish among. This activity links to NHES 3, access information, products, and services. Students can use the list of topics for the activity "Safety Rules and Practices" to help them choose a safety issue or topic.

ASSESSMENT | The students' fact-or-fiction statements and the students' responses are the assessment task for this activity. For assessment criteria, students should provide accurate information and make connections between behaviors and safety. (Construct: Attitudes toward behavior.)

Safe and Unsafe Behaviors in New Situations and Settings

As students grow older, their responsibilities for safe behavior grow as they encounter new situations and opportunities for autonomy (using public transportation, riding their bikes to a friend's house). Students can make a list of the kinds of recreational and other situations in which they are involved as third, fourth, and fifth graders and then identify and role-play safe and unsafe behaviors in these situations.

ASSESSMENT | The students' role-plays of safe and unsafe behaviors are the assessment task for this activity. For assessment criteria, students should provide accurate information, display appropriate depth and breadth of information, and make connections between behaviors and safety. (Construct: Attitudes toward behavior.)

Don't Touch That! Staying Clear of Icky Plants and Critters.

Jeff Day's book, *Don't Touch That! The Book of Gross, Poisonous, and Downright Icky Plants and Critters* (see the book list at the end of the chapter) offers helpful and humorous advice on avoiding bites, scratches, rashes, and more in the natural world around us. The book also helps students know what to do if the unexpected happens. Teachers can use this book to have small groups dig deeper into learning about the plants and critters in their own community. Students can work in small groups to investigate a plant or critter.

ASSESSMENT | For an assessment task, students can make a poster presentation about their investigation. Students should provide accurate information and make connections between safe behaviors and staying healthy. (Construct: Attitudes toward behavior.)

Grades 6–8

Staying Safe in All Kinds of Weather

With a partner, students can research (NHES 3) severe weather conditions relevant to the region (e.g., thunderstorms, tornados, blizzards, hurricanes) or climate-related physical conditions (e.g., heat exhaustion, sunburn, heat stroke, hypothermia). With the information learned, students can prepare informational posters with strategies for reducing risks/being safe in the given situation. Posters can be displayed throughout the school at the relevant time of the year.

ASSESSMENT | The posters students create are the assessment task for this activity. For assessment criteria, students should provide accurate information. For NHES 3, they also should cite their sources and explain why they are valid. (Constructs: Attitudes toward behavior, perceived behavioral control.)

Safety Presentations for Younger Students

Students can work in small groups to create dramatic presentations on various safety topics for younger students. Students must gather their own information and verify its accuracy (NHES 3). Teachers can help students make arrangements with teachers in other classes to present their work.

ASSESSMENT | The students' presentations are the assessment task for this activity. For assessment criteria, students should present accurate information, show appropriate depth and breadth of information, and make connections between behaviors and safety for their younger audiences. (Construct: Attitudes toward behavior.)

Expert Speakers on Safety Topics

Have students identify activities and issues that interest them from a safety perspective. Have students develop letters to invite expert guest speakers to the classroom. For example, students this age often are interested in skateboarding and extreme sports. What should they know about staying safe while participating in these activities? Students also might want to know about upkeep and repair of sports equipment. This activity links to NHES 3, access information, products, and services, in that students are accessing information from their expert speakers.

ASSESSMENT | For an assessment task, students can create graphic organizers, make posters about, or demonstrate what they learn from guest speakers. For assessment criteria, students should provide accurate information, show appropriate depth and breadth of information, and make connections between behaviors and safety. (Construct: Attitudes toward behavior.)

NHES 2 | Analyze Influences

Students will analyze the influence of family, peers, culture, media, technology, and other factors on health behaviors.

ASSESSMENT CRITERIA

- Identify both external and internal influences on health.
- Explain how external and internal influences interact to impact health choices and behaviors.
- Explain both positive and negative influences, as appropriate.

Grades K–2

Curiosity   Teachers can use stories from the *Curious George* books, by H. A. Rey, to introduce this discussion on curiosity. Students can define curiosity in their own words. Next, students can think about how to handle curiosity to stay safe in various unintentional injury prevention areas (fire, traffic, water). For example, students might be curious about fires and matches or lighters or about how deep the water is in a lake. What are safe and unsafe ways to handle this curiosity?

ASSESSMENT   Students can write and draw or use a digital storyboard/storybook generator tool to illustrate and describe ways to stay safe when they are curious. For assessment criteria, students should be able to explain how curiosity can affect behavior. (Construct: Perceived behavioral control.)

Family   Students can brainstorm family practices that help everyone stay safe at home (locking cabinets that contain cleaning products, regularly checking smoke detectors, developing an escape plan in case of a fire or emergency and practicing the plan). Teachers can read the book *At Home* by Claire Llewellyn (see book list at the end of the chapter) and ask students to make a list of safety tips for their homes (see the book list at the end of the chapter). Students can take their lists home to share with their families and create a book page about safety practices specific to the students' families. Each student will contribute the created page to a class book about home and family safety.

ASSESSMENT   The students' lists and book pages are the assessment tasks for this activity. For assessment criteria, students should explain and illustrate how families influence safety practices. (Construct: Perceived behavioral control.)

Grades 3–5

Likes and Dislikes   An important internal influence on injury prevention is what people like and dislike doing. For example, some students might like to go fast or climb to very high places. They might dislike having to ride in the back seat of a motor vehicle, wearing a protective helmet, or remain quiet during a fire drill. Teachers can have an open discussion with students about what they like and dislike related to safety issues at school, at home, and in the community and what they need to do regardless for the protection of everyone and why it is important. Students can list important reasons for safe behavior and plans to manage their likes and dislikes for personal safety and the safety of others. Some safety rules are nonnegotiable. No one would want to cause someone else to get hurt. This activity links to NHES 7, self-management.

ASSESSMENT   For an assessment task, children can create a page for a class book or a poster on likes, dislikes, and safety. For assessment criteria, students should identify criteria for "great" pages or posters. Teachers can use these criteria to assess and to help children assess their work. (Construct: Subjective norms.)

Friends and Peers   As students move into the upper-elementary grades, the influence of friends and peers becomes increasingly

important. Students can talk about the things they like to do with their friends (skateboarding, roller-blading, biking) and discuss safety issues in their activities. For example, do friends wear bicycle helmets? How do friends' decisions influence what they do? Do friends walk their bikes across intersections or do they ride in front of traffic? How can they do the courageous thing (wearing a bike helmet even if others don't) and influence their friends to act safely? To think more about peer pressure, students can visit the BAM! website (www.cdc.gov/bam/index.html) to check out "Grind Your Mind," an animated quiz on peer pressure. The site includes helpful tips for students, such as being aware of situations, trusting gut feelings, and respecting choices.

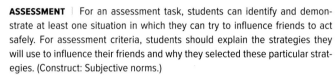

ASSESSMENT   For an assessment task, students can identify and demonstrate at least one situation in which they can try to influence friends to act safely. For assessment criteria, students should explain the strategies they will use to influence their friends and why they selected these particular strategies. (Construct: Subjective norms.)

Safe Friends   As young people begin to be highly influenced by their friends, it becomes important for them to develop the value for having safe friends. In the activity suggested by Kane and Quackenbush students identify the qualities of a safe friend, either through drawing a picture or making a list, or both.[51] The teacher then can tell a story about kids involved in an activity where a question about safety occurs, such as someone playing with matches or teasing a kid who is afraid to take a risk other friends are taking. The teacher can lead a discussion about what a safe friend would do in these situations.

ASSESSMENT   The class can identify a number of different situations where a question of safety occurs. With a partner, students can role-play how a friend would encourage another friend to act safely in the situation. Pairs of students can demonstrate their role-plays for the class or for small groups. Students then can write a brief exit slip responding to the prompt, "I am a safe friend because I . . ." For assessment criteria, students should identify and demonstrate at least one way in which they can influence a friend to act safely. (Constructs: Subjective norms, perceived behavioral control.)

Media Influences Safety   Movies, television shows, and commercials are filled with action heroes and extraordinary risk taking. What is real and what is simply media hype to increase product or ticket sales? Have students work in small groups to talk about media images they have seen that involve thrill seeking and over-the-top risk taking. How do students believe the media affect their decisions or the decisions of others? Teachers can provide examples in the news and in the community. What constitutes acceptable and unacceptable risk taking? How can students talk back to media images that promote unacceptable risk?

ASSESSMENT   For an assessment task, students can make posters, design a comic book, and use a technology tool such as Toondoo to illustrate their work, write stories, or create scripts about media influences on risk taking, examining what various individuals do. For assessment criteria, students should identify at least two influences on safety behaviors and explain how various influences can work together to influence behaviors. (Construct: Perceived behavioral control.)

Grades 6–8

Feelings   Middle grades students experience new and intense feelings as they go through puberty. Feelings are normal. However, the ways we behave in response to those feelings can influence our safety. For example, if Mary is angry with her best friend and storms away down the hall, she might run right into someone if she is not looking where she is going. Similarly, if Joe is daydreaming about a new student at school, he might not pay attention to what's around him while he rides his bike. At the most serious and damaging level, people sometimes deliberately hurt others when they are angry (violence in schools, homes, and communities). Students can work in small groups to brainstorm scenarios in which feelings might affect attention to safety and injury prevention. Students can rehearse and role-play their scenarios for classmates, with recommendations for managing feelings in safety situations and for helping others who are experiencing strong feelings. Students can find lots of information on dealing with feelings at www.kidshealth.org. This activity links to NHES 7, self-management.

ASSESSMENT | The students' role-plays are the assessment task for this activity. For assessment criteria, students should explain and demonstrate how feelings can influence behavior and how they can manage feelings for safety and well-being. (Construct: Perceived behavioral control.)

Celebrations and Fireworks-Related Injuries Many students live in communities where fireworks are a part of the culture of celebration. The Consumer Product Safety Commission (CPSC) (www.cpsc.gov) estimates there were more than 8,500 fireworks-related emergency department–treated injuries with children under 15 years accounting for approximately 40 percent of these injuries. Students can investigate the CPSC "Fireworks Information Center" located at www.cpsc.gov/en/safety-education/safety-education-centers/fireworks. Students can discuss how fireworks celebrations are conducted in their communities and the influences that might lead to injury among children and youth.

ASSESSMENT | For an assessment task, students can combine their discussion of influences with an advocacy newsletter (NHES 8) to families for fireworks safety in their communities, if appropriate. For assessment criteria, students should explain how fireworks celebrations can lead to injuries and advocate for safe holidays in the community by providing safety guidelines. (Construct: Subjective norms.)

NHES 3 | Access Information, Products, and Services

Students will demonstrate the ability to access valid information and products and services to enhance health.

ASSESSMENT CRITERIA

- Access health information—Locate specific sources of health information, products, or services relevant to enhancing health in a given situation.
- Evaluate information sources—Explain the degree to which identified sources are valid, reliable, and appropriate as a result of evaluating each source.

Grades K–2

Help Needed? As children become more independent, it becomes important for them to determine when adult help is needed and when a problem can be solved without consulting an adult. Teachers can use magazines and storybooks to present scenarios where a child is facing a problem. Some scenarios should be ones where children can manage on their own (e.g., cleaning up a scraped knee), and some that would need adult help (e.g., cleaning up broken glass). For each situation, have students decide whether the child can handle the situation on his/her own or should ask for help from an adult. If an adult is needed, students should suggest which adult's help is needed and why this adult is the most appropriate for the situation.

ASSESSMENT | After discussing a number of scenarios with the class, the teacher should present one final scenario to students. Students should draw a picture of how the situation should be handled—either manage on their own

or tell an adult. If telling an adult is appropriate, students should identify the adult. For assessment criteria, students should present accurate information and be able to identify a trusted adult appropriate for the circumstance. Students should be able to explain why the trusted adult is a safe person from whom to seek help. (Constructs: Perceived behavioral control.)

Getting Help in Emergencies Students can identify school and community helpers who can assist in emergency situations. Students can role-play the steps they would take to get the help they need. For example, children can use an old telephone to role-play calling the 9-1-1 operator (teacher or guest speaker). This activity links to NHES 7, self-management.

ASSESSMENT | The students' role-plays and demonstrations are the assessment task for this activity. For assessment criteria, students should explain why their school and community helpers are valid and reliable service providers. (Construct: Perceived behavioral control.)

Grades 3–5

Be Prepared for Disasters The website www.ready.gov/kids provides information on disaster preparedness. The site includes games, guidance for making a disaster plan, directions for building a safety kit, and facts about all kinds of weather-related conditions that could result in a disaster. Students can explore the website to play the games and become more knowledgeable. Based on the weather conditions affecting your part of the country, have students use this site and other credible information sources to prepare a family safety plan. Suggestions of key information to include in the plan can be found at this website.

ASSESSMENT | The family safety plan, developed from credible sources, is the assessment task. Students should present accurate information (NHES 1). They should also explain where they got their information and why their information sources are credible. (Constructs: Attitudes toward behavior, perceived behavioral control.)

Information Sources Students can work in small groups to investigate a variety of safety topics. Students might use resources in the school or public library, write or call safety organizations and agencies, e-mail an expert, and access Internet sites related to safety. Students can identify and document their sources, justify their selections, and make presentations to the class about their findings. See the list of websites at the end of the chapter for sources.

ASSESSMENT | The students' presentations are the assessment task for this activity. For assessment criteria, students should identify, document, and justify their sources. (Construct: Attitudes toward behavior.)

Products and Equipment for Safety Students can investigate various products and equipment that are important for injury prevention in activities of interest to them (bicycle helmets, sunscreen products, thermal clothing, mouth guards). Students can plan and make presentations to their classmates and to other classes. If students locate an expert in the community, teachers can assist them in writing a letter of invitation to have that person visit the classroom. Students can find information from the U.S. Consumer Product Safety Commission (www.cpsc.gov).

ASSESSMENT | The students' presentations are the assessment task for this activity. For assessment criteria, students should identify, document, and justify their sources. (Construct: Attitudes toward behavior.)

Learn About Chemicals Around Your Home Using the lesson "Toxic Chemicals: What's in Your Home?" (https://www.education.com/science-fair/article/toxic-chemicals/), students can study a list of chemicals and investigate common household cleaner labels to find which products contain them. Students will learn about the toxicity of the chemicals and identify alternative cleaning products. Students can create a digital presentation to share their findings and offer alternatives.

ASSESSMENT | The presentations students make are the assessment task for this activity. For assessment criteria, students should present accurate information and draw conclusions about the connections between safety and health (NHES 1). They also should explain where they got their information and why their information source is valid. (Construct: Attitudes toward behavior.)

Kidz Privacy: Surfing the Net   The Federal Trade Commission provides safety tips for kids and families on surfing the Web (www.onguardonline .gov). Important things to know about surfing, privacy, and personal information include

- Never give out your last or family name, your home address or your phone number in chat rooms, on bulletin boards, or to online pen pals.
- Don't tell other kids your screen name, user ID, or password.
- Look at a website's Privacy Policy to see how the site uses the information you give them.
- Surf the Internet with your parents. If they aren't available, talk to them about the sites you're visiting.
- Talk about the site's Privacy Policy with your parents so that you and your parents will know what information the site collects about you and what it does with the information.
- Websites must get your parent's permission before they collect many kinds of information from you.
- If a website has information about you that you and your parents don't want it to have, your parents can ask to see the information—and they can ask the website to delete or erase the information.
- Sites are not supposed to collect more information than they need about you for the activity you want to participate in. You should be able to participate in many activities online without having to give any information about yourself.
- If a site makes you uncomfortable or asks for more information than you want to share, leave the site.

Students can find additional information on safe Web surfing at these sites:

- jr.brainpop.com/health/besafe/internetsafety
- www.professorgarfield.org/pgf_safe_secure.html

ASSESSMENT | For an assessment task, students can create a list of safe surfing rules for their classroom. Students can take the list home for their parents or caregivers to read and sign. For assessment criteria, students should provide a list of rules that help promote safety and explain the valid sources of information they used to create the rules. (Construct: Attitudes toward behavior.)

Grades 6–8

WISQARS: Accessing Data About Injuries   Middle grades students can challenge their accessing information skills by visiting the WISQARS website (www.cdc.gov/injury/wisqars/index.html). WISQARS stands for Web-Based Injury Statistics Query and Reporting System. Students can access data on categories of fatal and nonfatal injuries. This activity links to mathematics—students might want to work with their mathematics teachers as they investigate the charts and tables. Students might be interested in the concept of "Potential Years of Life Lost" or premature death from injury.

ASSESSMENT | For an assessment task, students can work in small groups to investigate a category of interest and report to classmates. For assessment criteria, student should explain how they accessed their data and why their data source is a reliable one. (Construct: Attitudes toward behavior.)

Mapping Safe Walking and Biking Routes   Starting from their homes, students can map safe routes for walking or biking to places they go frequently (school, soccer practice). Students can use actual community maps or the interactive Google Earth application to mark the safest routes. Students should justify their choices and explain why they eliminated other routes, based on the information they gathered about their neighborhood or community. Students can access information on developing safe walking and biking routes to school at www.walkbiketoschool.org (International Walk to School Day).

ASSESSMENT | The students' routes are the assessment task for this activity. For assessment criteria, students should provide and justify the sources of information about their neighborhoods and communities. (Construct: Attitudes toward behavior.)

Using Youth Risk Behavior Survey (YRBS) Data   Students can go online (www.cdc.gov/HealthyYouth/yrbs/index.htm) to access information from the YRBS about unintentional injury–related behaviors among youth in their state or city and in the nation (the percentage of high school students who always or almost always wear seat belts while riding in cars, the percentage of students who did not ride with a drinking driver during the past thirty days). Alternatively, teachers can print tables from the website for students to use. Students can report the data from the healthy perspectives using a technology tool such as datagraphics or infographics to relay safety behaviors of teens in the United States (the percentage of students who practice the healthy behavior, such as wearing a bicycle helmet).

ASSESSMENT | The students' data reports are the assessment task for this activity. For assessment criteria, students should show how they used the data tables to find their information and explain why the YRBS is a valid and reliable source of data. (Construct: Subjective norms.)

How Are Your H$_2$O Smarts? BAM! on Water Safety   BAM!, the CDC Body and Mind website (www.cdc.gov/bam/index.html) for kids provides important tips on staying safe around water. BAM's top ten tips for kids are

- *DO* learn to swim.
- *DO* take a friend along.
- *DO* know your limits.
- *DO* swim in supervised (watched) areas only, and follow all signs and warnings.
- *DO* wear a life jacket when boating, jet skiing, water skiing, rafting, or fishing.
- *DO* stay alert to currents.
- *DO* keep an eye on the weather.
- *DON'T* engage in horseplay around and in the water.
- *DON'T* dive into shallow water.
- *DON'T* float where you can't swim.

Students also can access information on water pollution, water plants and animals, wearing sunscreen, water parks, personal flotation devices, currents, boating, jet skiing, swimming, white water rafting, surfing, and diving.

ASSESSMENT | For an assessment task, students can research, design, and prepare a presentation on water safety for other students in the school. The presentation might include skits, props, scenery, artwork, and costumes. For assessment criteria, students should provide accurate information and draw conclusions about connections between water safety and health (NHES 1).

They should explain where they found their information and why their sources are valid. (Construct: Perceived behavioral control.)

NHES 4 | Interpersonal Communication

Students will demonstrate the ability to use interpersonal communication skills to enhance health and avoid or reduce health risks.

ASSESSMENT CRITERIA
- Use appropriate verbal/nonverbal communication strategies in an effective manner to enhance health or avoid/reduce health risks.
- Use appropriate skills (negotiation skills, refusal skills) and behaviors (eye contact, body language, attentive listening).

Grades K–2

Communicating to Ask for Help   Young children can practice communicating clearly to get help from adults in a safety situation at home, at school, or in the community. Students can brainstorm a list of dangerous situations (a fallen electric wire) that might occur and practice asking an adult for help (say "I need your help," tell what happened and where, tell what you or others did, repeat "I need your help").

ASSESSMENT | Students can role-play asking for help as an assessment task for this activity. For assessment criteria, students should communicate information clearly and correctly. (Construct: Perceived behavioral control.)

Recognizing Signs and Signals for Safety   In addition to using verbal communication, people communicate through signs and signals. Students can identify and respond to traffic signs and signals, such as stop, yield, pedestrian or school crossing, railroad crossing, and traffic lights. Students can help make signs and signals for practice in the classroom. Students also should be able to identify symbols that indicate poison. Teachers can find a Traffic Sign Quiz for Kids and other safety information at the New York State Governor's Traffic Safety "Traffic Safety for Kids Page" (www.safeny.ny.gov/kids.htm).

ASSESSMENT | The students' correct responses to signs and signals are the assessment task for this activity. For assessment criteria, students should correctly identify safety signs and signals and respond to them appropriately. (Construct: Perceived behavioral control.)

Grades 3–5

Peer Resistance Skills in Safety Situations   Students can brainstorm a list of situations in which other students might dare or challenge them to try something dangerous (going into the ocean when danger flags are posted, jumping a bike over a very deep ditch). Students can work in pairs or small groups to demonstrate and compare effective and ineffective peer resistance skills, demonstrating a minimum of three skills. Teachers can find a list of peer resistance strategies for students to try in Chapter 3. Here is a sample scenario to get students started:

> Donna and Rich are meeting on Saturday morning to bicycle to the park with a group of classmates for a holiday picnic. As the group takes off, one of the riders says he knows a short-cut through a new housing development. The kids can get in through a gate that's been left open for deliveries, but there are big danger signs warning that the site is a hard-hat area and that only authorized personnel are allowed on the property. Donna thinks it's a good idea to save time and go through the construction site with the other kids. Rich knows that there are nails, loose pieces of board, deep ditches, and heavy machinery they would have to watch for on the ride. In addition, the developers might call their parents or even the police if the kids

trespass. Rich doesn't want to ride through. What examples of effective communication strategies can he use and still keep his friends? Contrast these with ineffective strategies.

ASSESSMENT | The students' demonstrations of peer resistance skills are the assessment task for this activity. For assessment criteria, students should be able to demonstrate a minimum of three peer resistance skills. (Construct: Perceived behavioral control.)

Positive Peer Pressure!   Teachers can lead a discussion with students to identify certain safety practices students follow and why they practice them, such as using seat belts when riding in a car, wearing a bike helmet when riding a bike or scooter, or waiting for the proper signal before crossing a street. The class can then discuss situations in which peers might not make the safest choice and how positive peer pressure might be used to encourage a friend to be safer.

ASSESSMENT | The students can create a storyboard or comic strip (consider using tools such as StoryBird [storybird.com/] and Toondoo [www.toondoo.com/]), demonstrating positive peer pressure with a friend to encourage him or her to do the safe behavior. For assessment criteria, students should use appropriate verbal and nonverbal communication strategies to help reduce risk and provide positive peer pressure. (Constructs: Subjective norms, perceived behavioral control, attitudes toward behavior.)

Grades 6–8

Communicating to Avoid Riding with Impaired Drivers   Unfortunately, young children often are not in a position to have a say about the adults, siblings, or family friends who drive them from place to place. However, as students reach middle school age, they can have more of a voice in refusing to ride with impaired drivers, whether they are adults or teenage friends with a new driver's license. Teachers can provide students with a variety of scenarios in which they are faced with the dangerous situation of riding with an impaired driver ("Your older sister's boyfriend offers you a ride, but you suspect he's been drinking"). Students can work in pairs or small groups to demonstrate a minimum of three refusal skills. For help in communicating in situations that involve drinking and driving, students might access the website for Students Against Destructive Decisions (SADD; www.sadd.org).

ASSESSMENT | The students' role-plays and demonstrations are the assessment task for this activity. For assessment criteria, students should demonstrate a minimum of three refusal skills. (Construct: Perceived behavioral control.)

Calling 9-1-1 and Designating a Bystander as a Helper   In first aid classes, students are taught to speak directly to a bystander in an emergency situation to ask for help—for example, "You in the purple shirt, please go and call 9-1-1!" Students can practice this important tip for getting help, explaining that when no one is designated everyone might assume that someone else will make the call. Students can learn more about calling 9-1-1 from Kids' Health (kidshealth.org/teen/safety/). Students will learn that when they call 9-1-1, the emergency dispatch operator might ask questions such as these:

- "*What* is the emergency?" or "*What* happened?"
- "*Where* are you?" or "*Where* do you live?"
- "*Who* needs help?" or "*Who* is with you?"

The operator needs to know the answers to these and other questions to determine what emergency workers should be sent and where to send them. Callers should give the operator all the relevant information they can about what the emergency is and how it happened. If the person is unconscious or has stopped breathing, the 9-1-1 operator might give instructions for providing immediate help, such as administering CPR or clearing the person's breathing passage. It's important to stay calm and to speak slowly and clearly so the 9-1-1 operator knows what kind of help is needed. Callers need to stay on the phone and *not hang up* until the operator says it's OK to do so—that way, the operator will have all the information needed to get help on the way fast.

ASSESSMENT | For an assessment task, students can write a short story about a scenario in which they appeal to a bystander for help in an emergency situation. For assessment criteria, students should clearly communicate their message to a specific individual. The story should include the bystander's calling 9-1-1 correctly. (Construct: Perceived behavioral control.)

NHES 5 | Decision Making

Students will demonstrate the ability to use decision-making skills to enhance health.

ASSESSMENT CRITERIA
- Reach a health-enhancing decision using a process consisting of the following steps:
- Identify a health-risk situation.
- Examine alternatives.
- Evaluate positive and negative consequences.
- Decide on a health-enhancing course of action.

Grades K–2

Children's Literature for Safety Decisions Many children's books contain decision-making themes for safety (*Sheila Rae, the Brave,* by Kevin Henkes). Teachers can read the story to students up to the point at which a character must make a decision. Teachers can stop and have the students discuss good decisions and why they are good. Teachers can finish the stories and compare the students' solutions with what happens in the story.

ASSESSMENT | The students' solutions for the story characters are the assessment task for this activity. For assessment criteria, students should explain why they recommended their decisions and how they compare with what the characters actually did. (Construct: Attitudes toward behavior.)

Officer Buckle and Gloria Safety Speech Teachers can read Peggy Rathmann's book *Officer Buckle and Gloria* to begin this activity. The students at Napville School never listen to Officer Buckle's safety tips until he brings his new buddy, Gloria, a police K9 to help. Gloria's interpretations of Officer Buckle's safety rules finally pique the students' interest. Pair students to create a safety tip as a video clip. While one student reads a scenario, the other student can act it out. Together, the students can offer advice on how to responsibly handle the situation. Put each safety tip clip together to create a safety speech video that can be shared with other students. Sample scenarios:

- You find a book of matches and a lighter in a cigarette case on the playground.
- You and your friend kick a ball that rolls out into the street.
- You get outside with your bicycle and realize you've forgotten your helmet.
- You are at your friend's house and find her father's gun cabinet unlocked.
- You are working on an art project in the classroom when you hear the fire alarm.
- You are upstairs at your friend's house when the smoke detector goes off.
- You go outside to the swimming pool before your older sister gets there.

ASSESSMENT | The students' solutions are the assessment task for this activity. For assessment criteria, students should act out a likely consequence of the scenario and offer a valid and healthy solution (Construct: Intention to act in healthy ways.)

Grades 3–5

The Courageous Thing to Do A recurring theme in personal and social skills for health is acting with courage, or doing the courageous thing, in the face of pressure to the contrary. Nan Stein's work in bullying prevention presents ideas for teaching about courage. As students grow up, peer pressures to act in certain ways to be popular increase. However, students of this age also can be quite idealistic and respond to the idea of acting courageously. Students can write individually about situations that require courage to prevent injury and share their scenarios in small groups. Groups can work through a decision-making process to act courageously. Groups can then share with the class. Students might also enjoy hearing the story *Courage,* by Bernard Waber, as an introduction to this activity.

ASSESSMENT | The students' sharing with the class is the assessment task for this activity. For assessment criteria, students should demonstrate all the steps in a decision-making process. (Constructs: Subjective norms, perceived behavioral control.)

Grades 6–8

Decisions About Alcohol and Other Drugs Alcohol and other drugs (AOD) play a tremendous role in unintentional injuries, especially motor-vehicle crashes. Students can work through a decision-making process about alcohol and other drug use related to various safety situations (drinking beer while boating). They can use their visual arts skills to create cartoon panels or posters illustrating the potential hazards of AOD use in various situations and their decisions to remain AOD-free, consider using tools such as StoryBird (https://storybird.com/) and Toondoo (toondoo .com/) to assist students in sharing their creative work with others. Students can find more information about making decisions about alcohol at websites listed at the end of this chapter and in Chapter 12.

ASSESSMENT | The students' cartoon panels are the assessment task for this activity. For assessment criteria, students should illustrate characters thinking through a decision-making process. (Constructs: Attitudes toward behavior, perceived behavioral control.)

NHES 6 | Goal Setting

Students will demonstrate the ability to use goal-setting skills to enhance health.

ASSESSMENT CRITERIA
- Goal statement—Give goal statement that identifies health benefits; goal is achievable and will result in enhanced health.
- Goal-setting plan—Show plan that is complete, logical, and sequential, and includes a process to assess progress.

Grades K–2

School Safety Goals Students can invite their principal, school nurse, or other school health care provider to the classroom to ask about the kinds of injuries that are most common at their school. If they find that a certain kind of injury occurs often (bloody noses, fingers caught in doors, falls), students can set a safety goal and steps to achieve the goal for students in their school. Students can assess the school's progress periodically. This activity links to NHES 8, advocacy.

Grades 3–5

Personal Goals to Prevent Athletic and Activity Injuries Children increasingly are involved in physical activity, such as dance and sports, as they reach the upper-elementary grades. Students can discuss the common injuries in the kinds of physical activities in which they are involved and prevention for those injuries. Teachers can invite an athletic trainer or a dancer from the local high school or community to talk with the students about injury prevention in physical activity and about practices that are helpful and harmful (hard stretching at the beginning of a workout is not recommended; instead, do a general body warm-up and stretch at the end of the workout). Teachers can assist the students in setting personal goals and listing the steps to achieve their goals to remain injury-free. Making a plan of this type links to NHES 7, self-management. Students can set goals and create their own fitness calendar at BAM! (Body and Mind) (http://www.cdc.gov/bam/index.html).

ASSESSMENT | For an assessment task, students can develop a goal and a plan to remain injury-free. For assessment criteria, students should identify an achievable goal, steps to reach it, plans to build support for it and to deal with obstacles, and a means for assessment. (Construct: Intention to act in healthy ways.)

Protective equipment helps everyone enjoy sports and activities safely.

©John Barry de Nicola/Shutterstock

Grades 6–8

New Responsibilities: Babysitting Basics Middle grades students might find themselves in a position to begin babysitting, a decision that carries a great deal of responsibility. The Kids' Health website (kidshealth. org) offers guidelines on babysitting for kids. Students can learn about important rules such as be prepared, know what to expect, and stay focused on the kids at all times. Students also can learn about babysitting basics and safety by contacting the local chapter of the American Red Cross or visiting www.redcross.org/take-a-class/babysitting-child-care.

ASSESSMENT | For students interested in becoming babysitters, making a plan for babysitting is an assessment task. For assessment criteria, students should explain all the decisions they need to make in advance and while carrying out their babysitting responsibilities. (Construct: Perceived behavioral control.)

NHES 7 | Self-Management

Students will demonstrate the ability to practice health-enhancing behaviors and avoid or reduce health risks.

ASSESSMENT CRITERIA

- Application (transfer)—Initiate health-enhancing behaviors; apply concepts and skills appropriate and effectively.
- Self-monitoring and reflection—Monitor actions and make adjustments; accept feedback and make adjustments; able to self-assess, reflect on, and take responsibility for actions.

Grades K–2

Children's Literature for Safety This chapter and the other content chapters include a list of children's books that can be used for health education lessons. Suggestions for children's books related to safety and self-management can be found in the book list at the end of the chapter. Teachers can read these books with students to spark discussions on self-management issues such as making and following safety rules and practices.

ASSESSMENT | Students can make and act out a list of class safety rules as an assessment task for reading children's literature. For assessment criteria, students should create rules that are health enhancing and should explain the correct steps for following the rules in various situations. (Construct: Perceived behavioral control.)

Safety Plans and Simulations Students can work individually or in small groups to make safety plans for various situations (home fire safety plan, safe biking plan, pool safety plan, home poisoning prevention plan). Researching topics by going to the library and talking to parents, teachers, and school health helpers links to NHES 3, access information, products, and services. To illustrate their self-management skills, students should identify and demonstrate the steps for safety. For example, students might arrange desks or chairs to simulate a "classroom bus" to show safe behaviors in planning for a field trip. Students need regular practice for school fire drills and weather emergency drills.

ASSESSMENT | Students' demonstrations are the assessment task for this activity. For assessment criteria, students should demonstrate safety steps correctly. (Construct: Perceived behavioral control.)

Safety Around Blood (Universal Precautions) Students in the early elementary grades frequently experience nosebleeds or minor cuts and scrapes. Other children often want to help. Have children demonstrate how to stop their own nosebleeds and bleeding from cuts or scrapes. In addition, have children demonstrate how to behave around the blood of others (don't touch blood, get help from the teacher or another adult). To stop nosebleeds, students should learn these tips:

- If you get a nosebleed, sit down and lean slightly forward. Keeping your head above your heart will make your nose bleed less. Lean forward so the blood will drain out of your nose instead of down the back of your throat. If you lean back, you might swallow the blood. This can cause nausea, vomiting, and diarrhea.
- Use your thumb and index finger to squeeze together the soft portion of your nose—the area located between the end of your nose and the hard, bony ridge that forms the bridge of your nose. Keep holding your nose until the bleeding stops. Hold it for at least five minutes. If it's still bleeding, hold it for another ten minutes straight.
- You can also place a cold compress or an ice pack across the bridge of your nose.
- Once the bleeding stops, don't do anything that might make it start again, such as bending over or blowing your nose.

ASSESSMENT | For an assessment task, students can demonstrate how to stop their own nosebleeds. For assessment criteria, students should follow all the steps correctly and in order. In addition, they should explain why it's not safe to touch the blood of others and how to get help from an adult if someone is bleeding. (Construct: Perceived behavioral control.)

Grades 3–5

Stress and Anger Management Stress and anger management skills are an important part of injury prevention. Students sometimes see adults behaving unsafely when they are angry (driving too fast, throwing things), rather than using self-management skills to calm themselves. Students can brainstorm a list of their favorite stress busters that they use to help themselves calm down. Students can make colorful stress buster posters as reminders for the classroom. Teachers might also want to use children's books to talk with students about ways to calm down when they are feeling angry or upset; see the books listed in Chapter 5 under "Moods and Strong Feelings" for ideas.

ASSESSMENT | The students' stress and anger management strategies and posters are the assessment tasks for this activity. For assessment criteria, students should be able to demonstrate specific steps for their strategies. (Construct: Perceived behavioral control.)

Grades 6–8

Simple First Aid Students can work in pairs or small groups to investigate and demonstrate simple first aid techniques for dealing with cuts, scrapes, burns, insect and animal bites, choking, and suspected broken bones. Students might want to invite a Red Cross instructor to class for more information. Students can develop a checklist of steps as a handout for their classmates. These checklists could be bound into a class book to duplicate and share with other classes. For more in-depth first aid instruction, teachers can help students arrange an evening course for interested students and families. Students can learn more about first aid by contacting their local chapter of the American Red Cross and by visiting www.redcross.org.

ASSESSMENT | The students' demonstrations and checklists are the assessment task for this activity. For assessment criteria, students should demonstrate first aid procedures accurately and in the correct order. (Construct: Perceived behavioral control.)

Role-Play Safety Skills Students can develop their language arts and health education skills by writing a script for a role-play or skit about a safety topic or issue. Students should present a scenario in which the

characters demonstrate their self-management skills by avoiding, leaving, or refusing risk situations (taking a dare, riding bicycles on a busy street, swimming when the ocean is too rough, taking someone else's moped for a joyride). Students can try new dramatic techniques, such as having the main character think things over while voices in the background speak aloud as if in his or her head. Students should emphasize doing the "courageous thing" in risk situations. This activity links to NHES 4, interpersonal communication.

ASSESSMENT | The students' role-plays and skits are the assessment task for this activity. For assessment criteria, students should present specific steps students can take for safety. (Construct: Perceived behavioral control.)

Motion Commotion—BAM! on Safety in Physical Activity CDC's BAM! (Body and Mind) website (www.cdc.gov/bam/activity/cards.html) features activity cards on how to play it safe while participating in diverse activities, including cycling, swimming, basketball, cheerleading, skating, fishing, football, martial arts, skiing, yoga, and many others. Students can work individually or with a partner to investigate and report on playing it safe in various kinds of activities.

ASSESSMENT | The reports and presentations students make are the assessment task for this activity. For assessment criteria, students should provide accurate information on self-management strategies for playing it safe in sports, recreation, and exercise. (Construct: Perceived behavioral control.)

NHES 8 | Advocacy

Students will demonstrate the ability to advocate for personal, family, and community health.

ASSESSMENT CRITERIA
- Health-enhancing position—Give clear, health-enhancing position.
- Support for position—Support position with facts, concepts, examples, and evidence.
- Audience awareness—Show awareness of target audience; choose words, tone, and examples to suit audience.
- Conviction—Display conviction for position.

Grades K–2

Getting the Safety Message Home Prior to beginning the unit, send a note home to parents/guardians explaining the purpose of the family message journal. Explain when the journal will be sent home, the type of response desired, and the importance of returning the journal. Explain to students that they will be sharing what they are learning about safety with their family in a family message journal. Remind students that their family members are not learning along with them, so the need to be detailed is important. As this is an advocacy opportunity, students need to make sure their message encourages others to practice or start healthy and safe behaviors. Any adult can read and respond: an older sibling, an aunt, a grandparent, or other. The following are types of journal entries that might be included (young students can draw pictures as part of their entry):

- An opinion entry on why wearing helmets is important when riding bikes/skateboards/scooters.
- A how-to entry that sequences what to do in severe weather or in a house fire.
- A descriptive entry about what has been learned in class that is important for their family to remember regarding safety.
- Remind students to consider their audience and what information is important to share. Modeling an entry for students is recommended to help establish expectations.

ASSESSMENT: | The journal entry serves as the assessment task. These entries can also provide evidence of students' writing skills. For assessment criteria, journal entries should include a clear safety message supported by accurate information with connections between behaviors and safety. Target audience (family members) should be considered. (Constructs: Subjective norms, attitudes toward behaviors.)

Smart Kids Stay Safe Campaign Students can make posters or banners for the school about the "Smart Kids Stay Safe" way to handle safety issues at home, at school, and in the community.

ASSESSMENT | The students' posters are the assessment task for this activity. For assessment criteria, posters should present a clear, health-enhancing message. (Construct: Subjective norms.)

Grades 3–5

Dumb Ways to Die (or Get Hurt) Show students the advocacy video message "Dumb Ways to Die" available on YouTube or at http://dumbwaystodie.com/. Discuss the messages shared in this video and the strategies used to appeal to the target audience. As a class decide on which key safety behaviors to focus as a result of community needs/concerns. Have teams of students create their own version of "Dumb Ways to Die (or Get Hurt)" in the form of a video, poster, PowerPoint visual, morning intercom announcement, or other creative approach.

ASSESSMENT | The safety message and artifact (video, poster, etc.) will serve as the assessment task. Students can share their projects around school. For assessment criteria, students should present a clear message, back it up with accurate information, target their audience, and demonstrate passion/conviction. (Constructs: Subjective norms, attitudes toward behavior.)

Safety in My Neighborhood Teachers can lead a discussion with students about the different types of neighborhoods that exist within their community. Some students will live on farms, some will live in populated city blocks, and others may live in apartment buildings. Students will pick one aspect of their neighborhood to research in terms of safety. For example, on a farm, students might research safety tips for using/riding all-terrain vehicles (ATVs). They can develop a safety campaign, including a slogan and a poster or public service announcement.

ASSESSMENT | The safety slogan and the poster or public service announcement will serve as the assessment task. Students can hang their posters around the school and present their public service announcements during school announcements. For assessment criteria, students should present a clear message, back it up, target their audience, and speak with conviction. (Constructs: Subjective norms, attitudes toward behavior.)

Grades 6–8

Think First! Voices for Injury Prevention (VIP) to Prevent Brain and Spinal Cord Injuries Middle-level students might be especially interested in the National Injury Prevention Foundation's ThinkFirst campaign to prevent brain and spinal cord injuries (thinkfirst.org/teens). Each year an estimated 5,00,000 persons in the United States sustain brain and spinal cord injuries. The most frequent causes of these injuries are motor-vehicle crashes; falls; sports and recreation accidents, especially diving accidents; and violence. Children and teens are at high risk for these devastating injuries, many of which are preventable. ThinkFirst, the National Injury Prevention Program's award-winning public education effort, targets this high-risk age group. The upbeat programs educate young people about personal vulnerability and risk taking. The message is that you can have a fun-filled, exciting life without hurting yourself if you "ThinkFirst" and use your mind to protect your body. More than 8 million young people have heard the ThinkFirst message. Teachers also can access curriculum materials through the website.

ASSESSMENT | For an assessment task, students can become VIPs (Voices for Injury Prevention) by designing and implementing a ThinkFirst campaign in their school. For assessment criteria, students should present a clear message, back it up, target their audience, and speak with conviction. (Construct: Subjective norms.)

Local Radio or Television Broadcast Students can create a public service announcement (PSA) for local radio or television. Students can work with technology specialists to develop a recording or videotape—or invite local radio or television personalities to work with them or their message.

ASSESSMENT | The students' PSAs are the assessment task for this activity. For assessment criteria, students should provide a clear, health-enhancing message; back it up with data or reasons; target a specific audience; and demonstrate conviction. (Construct: Attitudes toward behavior.)

Speak Out and Make NOYS: National Organizations for Youth Safety The mission of NOYS (www.noys.org), sponsored by the National Highway Traffic Safety Administration, is to promote youth empowerment and leadership and build partnerships that save lives, prevent injuries, and enhance safe and healthy lifestyles among all youth. Students can learn about youth projects such as "Global Youth Traffic Safety Month" or "Youth Turn." Toolkits are available to guide students in conducting a safety campaign.

ASSESSMENT | Students can plan a NOYS injury prevention project as an assessment task for this activity. For assessment criteria, students should present a clear message, back it up, target their audience, and speak with conviction. (Construct: Subjective norms.)

INTERNET AND OTHER RESOURCES

WEBSITES AND OTHER RESOURCES

American Academy of Pediatrics
   www.healthychildren.org/English/Pages/default.aspx (Healthy Children)

American Association of Poison Control Centers
   www.aapcc.org

American Red Cross
   www.redcross.org

BAM! (Body and Mind)
   www.cdc.gov/bam/index.html

California Department of Transportation Kids' Page
   www.dot.ca.gov/kids

Centers for Disease Control and Prevention
   www.cdc.gov/HealthyYouth (Adolescent and School Health)
   www.cdc.gov/injury/index.html (National Center for Injury Prevention and Control)
   www.cdc.gov/injury/wisqars/index.html (Web-Based Injury Statistics Query and Reporting System)

Children's Safety Network
   www.childrenssafetynetwork.org

Coastie's Homepage for Water Safety
www.coastie.auxpa.org

Federal Bureau of Investigation Safety Tips for Kids
www.fbi.gov/fun-games/kids/kids-safety

Federal Emergency Management Agency for Kids
www.ready.gov/kids
www.fema.gov/disaster/4086/updates/fema-kids

Federal Trade Commission
www.consumer.ftc.gov/features/feature-0038-onguardonline (On Guard Online Just for You Educators)

Kids' Health
www.kidshealth.org

McGruff (National Crime Prevention Council)
www.ncpc.org/about-ncpc/mcgruff

National Fire Protection Association
www.nfpa.org

National Highway Traffic Safety Administration
www.nhtsa.gov
www.nhtsa.gov/Bicycles (bicycle safety)

National Injury Prevention Foundation
www.thinkfirst.org

National Oceanic and Atmospheric Administration (weather safety, emergency preparedness)
www.education.noaa.gov

National Organization for Youth Safety
www.noys.org

National Program for Playground Safety
http://playgroundsafety.org/

National Safety Council
www.nsc.org

National School Safety Center
www.schoolsafety.us

Net Smartz Kids
www.netsmartzkids.org

Safe Kids Worldwide
www.safekids.org
www.safekids.org/home-safety-educators (Home Safety For Educators)

Safe Ride News
www.saferidenews.com

Smokey the Bear Smokey Kids
www.smokeybear.com/kids

STOP Sports Injuries
www.stopsportsinjuries.org

Traffic Safety Kids' Page (New York State Governor's Traffic Safety Committee)
www.safeny.ny.gov/kids.htm

U.S. Consumer Product Safety Commission
www.cpsc.gov/en/Safety-Education

U.S. Environmental Protection Agency
www.epa.gov/kidshometour (home chemical information)

WalkBike to School Day
www.walkbiketoschool.org

Youth Sport Safety Alliance
www.youthsportssafetyalliance.org

CHILDREN'S LITERATURE

AGES 5–8

Amstutz, Lisa J. *Bike Safety: A Crash Course.* Capstone Press, a Capstone imprint, 2014.

Bellisario, Gina. *Be Aware!: My Tips for Personal Safety.* Millbrook Press, 2014.

Bellisario, Gina. *Poison Alert!: My Tips to Avoid Danger Zones at Home.* Millbrook Press, 2014.

Berenstain, Stan, and Jan Berenstain. *The Berenstain Bears and No Guns Allowed.* Random House, 2000.

Bjorkman, Steve. *Dinosaurs Don't Dinosaurs Do (I Like to Read).* Holiday House, 2011.

Brown, Marc. *Arthur's Fire Drill.* Random House, 2000.

Cuyler, Margery. *Stop, Drop and Roll: A Book About Fire Safety.* Simon & Schuster, 2001.

Duncan, D. *Dude, Where's Your Helmet?* Rocky Mountain Books, 2009.

Feigh, Alison. *I Can Play It Safe.* Free Spirit Publishing, 2008.

Ghigna, Charles. *Plan and Prepare! (Fire Safety Books).* Cantata Learning, 2018.

Ghigna, Charles. *Stop, Drop, and Roll! (Fire Safety Books).* Cantata Learning, 2018.

Guard, Anara. *What If You Need to Call 911?.* Capstone Press, 2011.

Guard, Anara. *What If A Stranger Approaches You?* Capstone Press, 2011.

Harper, Jamie. *Miss Mingo and the Fire Drill.* Candlewick, 2012.

Henkes, Kevin. *Sheila Rae the Brave.* Greenwillow Books, 1987.

Heos, Bridget. *Be Safe on the Internet (Be Safe!).* Amicus Illustrated, 2015.

Heos, Bridget. *Be Safe on the Playground (Be Safe!).* Amicus Illustrated, 2015.

Hoffman, Dan. *Sparky The Fire Dog.* Imagine, a Charlesbridge Imprint, 2011.

Hubbard, Ben. *Staying Safe Online.* Capstone, 2017.

Jacobs, P. *Fire Drill.* Henry Holt and Co., 2010.

Joyce, Irma. *Never Talk to Strangers.* Random House Books, 2009.

Koski, Mary B. *Impatient Pamela Calls 911.* Trellis Publishing, 2005.

Kurtz, Jane. *Do Kangaroos Wear Seatbelts?* Dutton Children's Books, 2005.

Llewellyn, C. *Watch Out! Around Town.* Barron's Educational Series, 2006.

Llewellyn, C. *Watch Out! At Home.* Barron's Educational Series, 2006.

Llewellyn, C. *Watch Out! On the Road.* Barron's Educational Series, 2006.

Moore, Eva. *Franklin's Bicycle Helmet.* Scholastic, 2000.

Pendziwol, Jean. *No Dragons for Tea: Fire Safety for Kids (and Dragons).* Kids Can Press, 2001.

Pendziwol, Jean. *Once Upon a Dragon: Stranger Safety for Kids.* Kids Can Press, Ltd., 2007.

Prokos, Anna. *Not So Fast!* Red Chair Press, 2011.

Rothmann, Peggy. *Officer Buckle and Gloria.* Putnam & Grosset, 1995. (Caldecott Medal)

Rustad, Martha E. H. *Tanya Takes the School Bus.* Millbrook Press, 2018.

Safety Smarts (7-item Set). PowerKids Press, 2017.

Shaskan, Stephen. *Toad on the Road: A Cautionary Tale.* Harper, an imprint of HarperCollins Publishers, 2017.

Thomas, Pat. *I Can Be Safe: A First Look At Safety.* Barron's Educational Series, 2003.

Yolen, Jane. *How Do Dinosaurs Stay Safe?* The Blue Sky Press, an imprint of Scholastic Inc., 2015.

AGES 9–12

Cornwall, Phyllis. *Online Etiquette and Safety: Super Smart Information Strategies*. Cherry Lake Publishing, 2010.

Criswell, Patti Kelley. *Smart Girl's Guide to Staying Home Alone*. American Girl, 2011.

Day, Jeff. *Don't Touch That! The Book of Gross, Poisonous, and Downright Icky Plants and Critters*. Chicago Review Press, 2008.

DeFelice, Cynthia. *Weasel*. William Morrow, 1991.

Gemeinhart, Dan. *Scar Island*. Scholastic Press, 2017.

Hashimoto, Meika. *The Trail*. Scholastic Press, 2017.

Marsh Carole. *Who Ya Gonna Call?: The Kid's Directory for Self Help*. Bluffton Books, 2015.

O'Brien, Cynthia. *Innovations in Safety (Problem Solved! Your Turn to Think Big)*. Crabtree Publishing Company, 2017.

O'Dell, Scott. *Island of the Blue Dolphins*. Houghton Mifflin, 1960.

Osborne, Mary Pope. *Magic Tree House Survival Guide*. Random House, 2014.

Park, Barbara. *Mick Harte Was Here*. Alfred A. Knopf, 1995.

Paulsen, Gary. *Guts: The True Stories Behind Hatchet and the Brian Books*. Dell Laurel-Leaf, 2001.

Raymer, Dottie. *A Smart Girl's Guide: Staying Home Alone: A Girl's Guide to Feeling Safe and Having Fun*. American Girl, 2015.

Ridenour, Melissa Harker. *What Would You Do? A Kid's Guide to Staying Safe in a World of Strangers*. Headline Books, 2011.

Rissman, Rebecca. *No Running in the House: Safety Tips Every Babysitter Needs to Know*. Capstone Press a Capstone imprint, 2015.

Wise, Rachel. *Texting 1, 2, 3 (Dear Know-It-All)*. Simon Spotlight, 2013.

ENDNOTES

1. Centers for Disease Control and Prevention, *National Action Plan for Child Injury Prevention* (www.cdc.gov /safechild/NAP; 2012).

2. NCIPC: Web-based Injury Statistics Query and Reporting System (WISQARS), *Ten Leading Causes of Death and Injury* (www.cdc.gov/injury/wisqars/LeadingCauses .html; 2017).

3. Centers for Disease Control and Prevention, *Web-based Injury Statistics Query and Reporting System* (WISQARS). National Center for Injury Prevention and Control, Centers for Disease Control and Prevention (www.cdc.gov /injury/wisqars/index.html; 2017).

4. Ibid.

5. Ibid.

6. Ibid.

7. Centers for Disease Control and Prevention, "Youth Risk Behavior Surveillance—United States, 2015," *MMWR Surveillance Summaries* 65, no. 6 (June 10, 2016).

8. Centers for Disease Control and Prevention, *National Action Plan for Child Injury Prevention*.

9. Centers for Disease Control and Prevention, *Web-based Injury Statistics Query and Reporting System* (WISQARS).

10. National Center for Injury Prevention and Control, *CDC Childhood Injury Report*, 2008 (www.cdc.gov/safechild /child_injury_data.html).

11. F. P. Rivara, "Impact of Injuries," in *About Children: An Authoritative Resource on the State of Childhood Today*, eds. A. G. Cosby et al. (Elk Grove Village, IL: American Academy of Pediatrics, 2005).

12. Ibid.

13. Ibid.

14. Centers for Disease Control and Prevention, "School Health Guidelines to Prevent Unintentional Injury and Violence," *MMWR Recommendations and Reports* 50, no. RR22 (December 7, 2001): 1–46.

15. W. M. Kane and M. Quackenbush, *Teach and Talk: Safety and Risk* (Santa Cruz, CA: ETR Associates, 2001), 19.

16. Rivara, "Impact of Injuries," 125.

17. Centers for Disease Control and Prevention, *School Health Policies and Practices Study 2016* (www.cdc.gov /healthyyouth/data/shpps/results.htm).

18. Centers for Disease Control and Prevention, "School Health Guidelines to Prevent Unintentional Injury and Violence."

19. Kane and Quackenbush, *Teach and Talk*.

20. Ibid.

21. National Injury Prevention Foundation, *ThinkFirst for Kids* (www.thinkfirst.org/kids).

22. Centers for Disease Control and Prevention, "School Health Guidelines to Prevent Unintentional Injury and Violence."

23. Ibid.

24. Ibid.

25. Centers for Disease Control and Prevention, "Web-based Injury Statistics Query and Reporting System (WISQARS)." National Center for Injury Prevention and Control, Centers for Disease Control and Prevention (www.cdc.gov/injury/wisqars; 2018).

26. National Center for Statistics and Analysis, *Alcohol-impaired driving: 2016 data*. National Highway Traffic Safety Administration (crashstats.nhtsa.dot.gov/Api /Public/ViewPublication/812450).

27. B. E. Cody et al., *Child Passengers at Risk in America: A National Study of Restraint Use* (Washington, DC: National SAFE KIDS Campaign, 2002).

28. A. I. Greenspan, A. M. Dellinger, and J. Chen, "Restraint Use and Seating Position Among Children Less Than 13 Years of Age: Is It Still a Problem?" *Journal of Safety Research* 41, no. 2 (2010): 183–85.

29. American Academy of Pediatrics, *Car Safety Seats: A Guide for Families 2018* (www.healthychildren.org /English/safety-prevention/on-the-go/Pages/Car-Safety-Seats-Information-for-Families.aspx; 2018).

30. M. Ahrens, "Fireworks" (National Fire Protection Association, June 2016).

31. Ibid.

32. Ibid.

33. Centers for Disease Control and Prevention, "Brief Report: Injuries Associated with Homemade Fireworks—Selected States, 1993–2004," *MMWR* 53, no. 25 (July 2, 2004): 562–63.

34. Centers for Disease Control and Prevention, "Playground Safety" (www.cdc.gov/safechild/playground/index.html; 2016).

35. Ibid.

36. Centers for Disease Control and Prevention, "Poisoning Prevention" (www.cdc.gov/safechild/poisoning/index .html; 2016).

37. D. D. Gummin et al., "2016 Annual Report of the American Association of Poison Control Centers' National Poison Data System (NPDS): 34th Annual Report," *Clinical Toxicology* 55 (2017): 1072–1254.

38. American Association of Poison Control Centers, "Prevention: Children" (www.aapcc.org).

39. Centers for Disease Control and Prevention, "Protect the Ones You Love: Child Injuries Are Preventable: Burn Prevention" (www.cdc.gov/safechild/burns/index.html; 2016).

40. Centers for Disease Control and Prevention, National Center for Injury Prevention and Control, "Heads Up to Schools: Know Your Concussions ABCs" (www.cdc.gov /concussion/headsup/schools.html).

41. Think First National Injury Prevention Foundation, "Think First for Kids Program" (www.thinkfirst.org /kids).

42. Centers for Disease Control and Prevention, "Healthy Swimming" (www.cdc.gov/healthywater/swimming /index.html; 2018).

43. Safe Kids Worldwide, "Walk This Way" (www.safekids .org/walk-way).

44. National Center for Safe Routes to School, "Walk & Bike To School" (www.walkbiketoschool.org).

45. Ibid.

46. Centers for Disease Control and Prevention, "Child Safety and Injury Prevention: Sports Safety" (www.cdc .gov/safechild/sports_injuries/index.html; 2017).

47. American Academy of Child and Adolescent Psychiatry, "Home Alone Children," *Facts for Families* (www.aacap.org/AACAP/Families_and_Youth/Facts_ for_Families/FFF-Guide/Home-Alone-Children-046 .aspx; 2017).

48. Child Welfare Information Gateway, "Leaving Your Child Home Alone," U.S. Department of Health and Human Services Children's Bureau (www.childwelfare .gov/pubs/factsheets/homealone; 2013).

49. Kids Health, "When It's Just You After School" (http:// kidshealth.org/en/kids/homealone.html).

50. Safe Kids Worldwide, "Educator Portal" (www.safekids .org/educators).

51. Kane and Quackenbush, *Teach and Talk*.

Promoting Personal Health and Wellness

DESIRED LEARNER OUTCOMES

After reading this chapter, you will be able to . . .

- Describe the status of personal health and wellness among youth and the costs associated with poor personal health.

- Explain the relationship between personal health and wellness and compromised academic performance.

- Identify factors that influence personal health and wellness.

- Summarize current guidelines and practices for schools and teachers related to promotion of personal health and wellness.

- Summarize developmentally appropriate personal health and wellness promotion concepts and skills for K–8 students in the context of the National Health Education Standards and target healthy behavior outcomes.

- Demonstrate developmentally appropriate learning strategies and assessment techniques that incorporate concepts and skills that have been shown to promote personal health and wellness among youth.

- Identify effective, evaluated commercial personal health and wellness promotion curricula.

- Identify websites and children's literature that can be used in cross-curricular instructional activities promoting personal health and wellness.

INTRODUCTION

Scarcely one half of the children of our country continue in school much beyond the fifth grade. It is important, therefore, that so far as possible the knowledge which has most to do with human welfare should be presented in the early years of school life.... The health of a people influences the prosperity and happiness of a nation more than any other one thing. The highest patriotism is therefore the conservation of health.[1]

This quotation introduces the book *Health Lessons*, published in 1910. At that time, the author, Alvin Davison, was concerned with "infectious diseases and ... serious cases of sickness from contagious maladies, with all their attendant suffering, largely sacrifices on the altar of ignorance." In 1910, the leading cause of death in children age 11 and older was tuberculosis.

Health risks for children have changed tremendously during the period of more than one hundred years since *Health Lessons* was published. Many infectious diseases are well controlled with immunizations and other public health measures. In addition, chronic diseases, such as heart disease and cancer, and unintentional and intentional injuries now claim the greatest number of young lives. Efforts to prevent chronic disease and injury must include public and school health education.

When people think of school health education, they often think first of personal health habits—washing hands, bathing regularly, brushing and flossing teeth, eating nutritiously, exercising, and getting plenty of rest. Learning personal health care is extremely important. Many of today's communicable and chronic diseases could be largely prevented or controlled through just such simple, consistent measures. Illness from other conditions can be ameliorated through coordinated personal, family, school, and medical care. This chapter focuses on helping children learn basic personal health care skills and preventing and managing the common health problems school-age children experience.

Teachers will notice a departure from traditional personal health approaches that emphasize the body systems. Learning about body systems, one after another, outside a health context, more appropriately belongs in science or biology classes. To link learning about the body to health, teachers should help students apply their knowledge about priority health-risk behaviors to effects on body systems. For example, what are the effects of tobacco use on the respiratory and cardiovascular systems? What are the effects of healthy nutrition and regular physical activity on the muscular and skeletal systems? What are the effects of alcohol and other drug use on the nervous system? With these core concepts (NHES 1) in mind, students can practice the personal and social skills they need to promote health and prevent illness and injury.

In the content area of personal health, two of the National Health Education Standards are especially important. NHES 3, access information, products, and services, provides opportunities for students to investigate and find valid and reliable sources of information, products, and services to meet their health-related needs. For example, accessing information about the management of diabetes might mean searching the websites of the American Diabetes Association, the Centers for Disease Control and Prevention (CDC), and the National Institutes of Health (NIH). Accessing products and services might include selecting an appropriate sunscreen to wear during a softball game or talking to a school nurse about a health question.

NHES 7, self-management, also plays a major role in personal health. In the previous example, students who are good self-managers actually use the sunscreen and seek out the school nurse. In addition, they practice basic health habits, such as brushing and flossing teeth, washing hands, and managing stress. NHES 3 and 7 are a major focus in the learning and assessment strategies included in this chapter.

Prevalence and Cost

The Children's Defense Fund cites these moments in the life of America that pertain to the personal health and wellness of children:

Every forty-seven seconds in America, a child is confirmed as abused or neglected.

Every forty-nine seconds, a baby is born into poverty.

Every minute, a baby is born without health insurance.

Every three minutes, a baby is born to a teen mother.

Every two minutes, a baby is born at low birth weight.

Every twenty-three minutes, a baby dies before his or her first birthday.

Every one hour and six minutes, a child or teen dies from an accident.[2]

These sobering statistics point to an important fact: Although the health of Americans overall has improved dramatically during the past fifty years, children who are born into poverty—with its associated lower education, health care, and opportunity—are among those at highest risk for serious health problems.

Improvements in the health status of American children during the twentieth century were spectacular.[3] During this period, the life expectancy of Americans increased by 56 percent. The overall age-adjusted death rate declined by 74 percent, and the greatest single contribution to the increased longevity of Americans was the decline in infant and child death rates. Unfortunately, these impressive improvements in overall measures of child health obscure the confounding disparities associated with race, class, and geography and the continuing and emerging health problems of American children.[4]

The infant mortality rate (IMR), or death in the first year of life, declined greatly during the twentieth century. Many factors influenced this change, including improvements in the environment, a safe milk supply, parenting information, improved housing, medical advances, blood banks, modern family-planning methods, and neonatal intensive care.[5] The U.S. infant mortality rate declined 12 percent from 2005 to 2011 to a rate of 6.05 deaths per 1000 births. It has remained relatively the same since then with a rate of 5.9 deaths per 1000 births in 2016.[6] Over half of states have met the *Healthy People 2020* infant mortality goal of 6 deaths or fewer per 1000 births.[7] While progress is being made, the declines have not been equal. Infant mortality rates are also disproportionately high in the Black and African American community.[8]

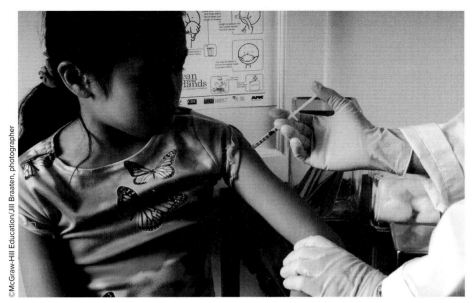

Regular medical checkups are an important part of personal health and wellness. Vaccinations have contributed to a significant decline in child mortality during the twentieth century.

For children older than 1 year, the decline in mortality during the twentieth century was tremendous. Today, fewer than two children die between their first and twentieth birthdays, compared with thirty in 1900. Child mortality rates from infectious diseases have declined 99 percent, even with the emergence of HIV/AIDS, while injuries have emerged as the leading cause of child deaths. These advances are due largely to improved sanitation and living standards during the first part of the century and to modern antibiotics, vaccines, and medications during the latter part.

At the beginning of the century, child injury deaths occurred mainly on farms, in factories, and from burns. Today, unintentional injuries are still the leading cause of death for school-age children and adolescents with motor-vehicle-related deaths accounting for more than half of all child injury deaths, with children as passengers or pedestrians. In addition to motor-vehicle-related deaths, child deaths from violence (homicide, suicide) increased by the end of the twentieth century.[9]

Approximately 20 million children live with a chronic health condition, with asthma among the most severe. On average, American children miss 14 million school days each year because of asthma,[10] which has become the second leading cause of hospitalization among children younger than 15.[11] Childhood obesity also affects many American children. The number of overweight children has more than doubled since 1980, and the number of overweight adolescents has tripled during that time. Being overweight increases the risk of suffering severe chronic diseases such as heart disease, Type 2 diabetes, high blood pressure, some cancers, stroke, and depression.[12]

Other personal health and wellness issues affect children. Millions of children today grow up completely free of the dental problems that their parents experienced.[13] These children are the beneficiaries of better understanding of the decay process, healthier diets, fluoride use, dental sealants, and preventive dental care. However, for too many other children, dental caries is a daily nightmare of pain, eating difficulties, unsightly smiles, and distraction from play and learning.[14]

In many ways, children today are better off than they have ever been, but new and emerging child health problems—such as asthma, obesity, ADHD, and HIV/AIDS—warrant special attention. Important disparities related to race and income continue to exist and in some cases have increased. To a large extent, these health disparities result from differences in access to health services and in the broader socioeconomic context in which many minority and low-income children live.[15]

Table 9–1 describes the wide range of public health issues related to children's personal health and wellness. The *Healthy People 2020* objectives call for an increase in the proportion of schools that provide school health education in the content areas presented in this text. School health programs can make an important contribution to the achievement of the national health objectives.

Personal Health and Wellness and Academic Performance

The academic success of America's youth is strongly linked with their health. Health-related factors such as hunger, physical and emotional abuse, and chronic illness can lead to poor school performance. Health-risk behaviors such as early sexual initiation, violence, and physical inactivity are consistently linked to poor grades and test scores and lower educational attainment. In turn, academic success is an excellent indicator for the overall well-being of youth and a primary predictor and determinant of adult health outcomes.[16]

Charles E. Basch, author of *Healthier Students Are Better Learners: A Missing Link in School Reforms to Close the Achievement Gap*,[17] identified seven educationally relevant health disparities as strategic priorities: (1) vision, (2) asthma, (3) teen pregnancy, (4) aggression and violence, (5) physical activity, (6) breakfast, and (7) inattention and hyperactivity. He stated:

> If children can't see well, if their eyes do not integrate properly with their brain and motor systems, they will have difficulty acquiring the basic and essential academic skills associated with reading, writing, spelling and mathematics. If their ability to concentrate, use memory, and make decisions is impeded by ill-nourishment or sedentary lifestyle, if they are distracted by negative feelings, it will be more difficult for them to learn and succeed in school. If their relationships at school with peers and teachers are negative, they will be less likely to be connected with and engaged in school, and therefore less motivated and able to learn. If they are not in school, because of uncontrolled asthma or because they are afraid to travel to or from school, they will miss teaching and learning opportunities. If they

TABLE 9–1

Healthy People 2020 Objectives Related to the Personal Health and Wellness of Children and Adolescents

EMC-1	Increase the proportion of children who are ready for school in all five domains of healthy development: physical development, social-emotional development, approaches to learning, language, and cognitive development.
EMC-3	Decrease the proportion of children who have poor quality of sleep.
EMC-4	Increase the proportion of elementary, middle, and senior high schools that require school health education.
AH-1	Increase the proportion of adolescents who have had a wellness checkup in the past twelve months.
AH-6	Increase the proportion of schools with a school breakfast program.
D-1	Reduce the annual number of new cases of diagnosed diabetes in the population.
HIV-1	Reduce the number of new HIV diagnoses among adolescents and adults.
HIV-4	Reduce the number of new AIDS cases among adolescents and adults.
ENT-VSL-2	Decrease otitis media in children and adolescents.
ENT-VSL-7	Reduce the proportion of adolescents who have elevated hearing thresholds, or audiometric notches, in high frequencies (3, 4, or 6 kHz) in both ears, signifying noise-induced hearing loss.
HDS-1	Increase overall cardiovascular health in the U.S. population.
IID-1	Reduce, eliminate, or maintain elimination of cases of vaccine-preventable diseases.
IID-7	Achieve and maintain effective vaccination coverage levels for universally recommended vaccines among young children.
IID-11	Increase routine vaccination coverage levels for adolescents.
IID-12	Increase the percentage of children and adults who are vaccinated annually against seasonal influenza.
OH-1	Reduce the proportion of children and adolescents who have dental caries experience in their primary or permanent teeth.
OH-2	Reduce the proportion of children and adolescents with untreated dental decay.
OH-7	Increase the proportion of children, adolescents, and adults who used the oral health care system in the past year.
OH-12	Increase the proportion of children and adolescents who have received dental sealants on their molar teeth.
SH-3	Increase the proportion of students in grades 9 through 12 who get sufficient sleep.
V-1	Increase the proportion of preschool children aged 5 years and under who receive vision screening.

SOURCE: U.S. Department of Health and Human Services, *Healthy People 2020*. www.healthypeople.gov.

drop out, perhaps because they are failing or faltering; or because they are socialized to believe that, even if they complete school, there will be no better opportunities; or because they associate with peers who do not value school; or because they become pregnant and there are no resources in place that enable them to complete school while pregnant and after they have a newborn, it is not likely that they can succeed. If they cannot focus attention and succeed socially, it is unlikely that they will succeed academically.[18]

Basch concluded with the reminder that "healthier students are better learners" and called for "a fundamental social change in the goals of schools, the way schools are financed, the personnel and services available and accessible, and the amount of time devoted to help youth learn social-emotional skills" if schools are to address health disparities that affect learning in a strategic and coordinated way.[19]

Factors That Influence Personal Health and Wellness

Healthy People 2020 describes five determinants of health—policymaking, social factors, health services, individual behavior, and biology and genetics—all of which contribute to levels of personal health and wellness. Poor health outcomes often are made worse by the interaction between individuals and their social and physical environment. For example, children's access to health services and the quality of those services impact health. Barriers to accessing health services include lack of availability, high cost, lack of insurance coverage, and limited language access.[20]

Biological and genetic factors affect specific populations more than others. Sickle-cell anemia, a common example of a genetic determinant of health, is a condition that people inherit when both parents carry the gene for sickle cell. Individual behavior also plays a role in health outcomes. Positive changes in individual behavior, such as diet, physical activity, tobacco and alcohol use, and hand washing, can reduce rates of disease.[21] However, children have little control over the health practices of the adults in their lives (e.g., decisions about immunization, drinking and driving, smoking) and the capacity of their caregivers to provide for them financially, physically, and emotionally.

The Annie E. Casey Foundation's 2017 *KIDS COUNT Data Book*[22] shows a mix of improvements and declines in the indicators measured for each of the four categories—economic well-being, education, health, and family and community—covered in the *KIDS COUNT Data Book*. At the national level:

Improvements: All four health indicators showed an improvement or no change from 2010 to 2015 with the largest improvement in children's health insurance coverage. Improvements were also seen across all four economic well-being indicators.

While this improvement is encouraging, it is still important to note that one in five children still lives in poverty.

Mixed picture: Whereas in the 2013 *Data Book*, improvements were seen in all four education indicators, in the 2017 *Data Book*, we see slight declines in two of the four categories and improvements in the other two. Declines were seen in the number of young children in school as well as eighth graders proficient in math. Improvements were seen in the number of fourth graders proficient in reading and the number of high school students graduating on time.

The indicators in the Family and Community category continued to have mixed results. There are more children living in single-parent families than in 2010. The number of children living in high poverty areas has been steadily increasing from 9 percent in 2000 to 14 percent in 2015. Improvements were seen in the number of children living in families where the household head lacks a high school diploma. The largest improvement was seen in number of births to teens with the teen birth rate declining from 34 births per 1,000 teens to 22 per 1,000.[23]

GUIDELINES FOR SCHOOLS

State of the Practice

The CDC conducts the School Health Policies and Practices Study (SHPPS) every six years to monitor efforts to improve school health policies and programs at the elementary, middle, and high school levels.[24] Overall, the percentage of school districts with district-level policies regarding specific areas of health education have been declining. Declines have been seen in areas related to personal health such as asthma, chronic disease prevention, allergies, HIV, infectious diseases (such as flu), and oral health. Over time, improvements in policies and practices have been seen in the areas of violence prevention and suicide prevention.[25] The 2016 report is available at https://www.cdc.gov /healthyyouth/data/shpps/results.htm.

State of the Art

Personal health and wellness efforts are most effective when schools and communities work in partnership. Students, teachers, parents, school staff, and community members all play important roles. To assist schools, the Division of Adolescent and School Health, Centers for Disease Control and Prevention (CDC), has published school health guidelines related to personal health and wellness promotion:

- *Guidelines for School Programs to Prevent Skin Cancer*[26]
- *Helping the Student with Diabetes Succeed: A Guide for School Personnel*[27]
- *Strategies for Addressing Asthma Within a Coordinated School Health Program*[28]

The CDC released the Health Education Curriculum Analysis Tool (HECAT) to help educators consider state-of-the-art practice in health education. The Personal Health and Wellness (PHW) module contains the tools to analyze and score curricula that are intended to promote personal health and wellness. The

Hand washing is an essential part of disease prevention.

module uses the National Health Education Standards as the framework for determining the extent to which the curriculum is likely to enable students to master the essential knowledge and skills that promote personal health and wellness. This chapter includes healthy behavior outcomes and developmentally appropriate concepts and skills for promoting personal health and wellness provided in the HECAT. The HECAT is available at www.cdc.gov/healthyyouth/hecat.

GUIDELINES FOR CLASSROOM APPLICATIONS

Important Background for K–8 Teachers

A range of topics falls under the heading of personal health and wellness. Background related to specific content areas, such as nutrition, physical activity, mental and emotional health, and injury prevention, are discussed in other topic-specific chapters. The background for teachers in this section focuses on the following:

- Hand washing and personal hygiene
- Dental and oral health
- Sleep and rest
- Skin cancer prevention and sun safety
- Communicable diseases
- Immunization
- Chronic diseases

Hand Washing and Personal Hygiene

Hand washing often is the first thing people think of when they hear the words *health* or *health education*. Indeed, thorough hand washing can prevent many communicable diseases. Children—and many adults—need instruction and practice in effective hand washing. Teachers can provide opportunities for children to wash their hands often and to demonstrate that they know how to do it well. Sometimes children and teachers report that their rest rooms are not stocked with soap and paper towels, either because of cost or because "the children make a mess." Teachers can use any mess making as a teaching opportunity to help children learn to wash their hands properly and to take care of their school rest rooms. Children can practice the take cares: take care of yourself, take care of others, and take care of this place.

Children should learn to wash their hands

- Before, during, and after preparing food.
- Before eating food.
- After using the toilet.
- After blowing their nose, coughing, or sneezing.
- After touching pets or pet treats.
- After touching garbage.
- Before and after treating a cut or wound.

The CDC provides these steps for hand washing:

- Wet your hands with clean, running water (warm or cold), turn off the tap, and apply soap.
- Lather your hands by rubbing them together with the soap; be sure to lather the backs of your hands, between your fingers, and under your nails.
- Scrub your hands for at least twenty seconds. Need a timer? Hum the "Happy Birthday" song from beginning to end twice.
- Rinse your hands well under clean running water.
- Dry your hands using a clean towel or air dry them.

If soap and water are not available, an alcohol-based hand sanitizer that contains at least 60 percent alcohol can be used. Alcohol-based hand sanitizers can quickly reduce the number of germs on hands in some situations, but sanitizers do not eliminate all types of germs. Hand sanitizers are not effective when hands are visibly dirty.[29]

Personal hygiene is an issue that teachers often want to address with students, especially with early adolescents. Teachers will find the KidsHealth website (www.kidshealth.org) especially helpful on hygiene issues (oily hair and skin, sweat and body odor). Teachers also must remember that poor hygiene on the part of some students may be linked to poor living conditions or to homelessness. A male middle school teacher related the story of being asked by female faculty members to talk with a student about his body odor and dirty clothes, even though he didn't have the student in any of his classes. As he got to know the young man and brought up the topic, the student began to cry. His family didn't have the soap, shampoo, laundry, and home conditions that most other students took for granted. The teacher and the school were able to help him get the products and clothes he needed, and access to the kinds of facilities he needed, without his classmates being the wiser.

Dental and Oral Health

The CDC states that oral health often is taken for granted, but it is an essential part of everyday life. Good oral health enhances the ability to speak, smile, smell, taste, touch, chew, swallow, and convey feelings and emotions through facial expressions. However, oral diseases, which range from cavities to oral cancer, cause pain and disability for millions of Americans each year.[30]

Tooth decay (cavities) is a common, preventable problem for people of all ages. For children, untreated cavities can cause pain, dysfunction, school absences, difficulty concentrating, and poor appearance—problems that greatly affect a child's quality of life and ability to succeed. Children from lower-income families often do not receive timely treatment for tooth decay and are more likely to suffer from cavities.[31]

Periodontal (gum) disease is an infection caused by bacteria that gets under the gum tissue and begins to destroy the gums and bone. Teeth become loose, chewing becomes difficult, and teeth may have to be extracted. Gum disease also may be connected to damage elsewhere in the body. Recent studies link oral infections with diabetes, heart disease, stroke, and premature, low-weight births. Further research is under way to examine these connections.[32]

Most oral diseases are preventable. However, many children and adults still go without simple measures that have been proven to be effective in preventing oral diseases and reducing dental care costs. An example is water fluoridation. Fluoride prevents tooth decay, and the most cost-effective way to deliver the benefits of fluoride to all residents of a community is through water fluoridation—that is, adjusting the fluoride in the public water

Regular visits to the dentist are an important part of good dental health.

supply to the appropriate level for decay prevention. Another safe, effective way to prevent cavities is through the use of dental sealants, which are plastic coatings applied to the chewing surfaces of the back teeth where most decay occurs. However, only about 40.5 percent of children aged 6 to 11 years have sealants. Although children from lower-income families are almost twice as likely to have decay as those from higher-income families, they are much less likely to have sealants.[33]

The American Dental Association (ADA) provides resources for educators and for children at Mouth Healthy Kids (www .mouthhealthykids.org/en/resources). The site contains videos, game and quizzes, activity sheets, information for preteens, and resources for educators, including a *Smile Smarts Dental Health Curriculum*.[34]

Sleep and Rest

The National Heart, Lung, and Blood Institute (NHLBI) reminds us that sleep is not just a time when we are not awake. While you sleep, your brain is hard at work forming the pathways necessary for learning and creating memories and new insights. Without enough sleep, you can't focus and pay attention or respond quickly. A lack of sleep may even cause mood problems. In addition, growing evidence shows that a chronic lack of sleep

©Fuse/Getty Images

Skin cancer prevention among students involves a coordinated effort between schools and families.

increases the risk for developing obesity, diabetes, cardiovascular disease, and infections.[35]

School-age children and adolescents need at least ten hours of sleep a night. The hormonal influences of puberty tend to shift adolescents' biological clocks. As a result, teenagers are more likely to go to bed later than younger children and adults, and they tend to want to sleep later in the morning.[36] This sleep–wake rhythm is contrary to the early-morning start times of many high schools and helps explain why 57.8 percent of middle school and 72.7 percent of high school students do not get enough sleep each night.[37]

Unlike adults, children who don't get enough sleep at night typically become hyperactive, irritable, and inattentive during the day. They also have increased risk of injury and more behavior problems, and their growth rate may be impaired. Sleep debt appears to be quite common during childhood and may be misdiagnosed as attention-deficit hyperactivity disorder.[38]

Teachers can help children learn about getting enough sleep by using a variety of children's books to prompt discussions on bedtime and going to sleep. Suggestions are included in "Children's Literature" at the end of the chapter.

Skin Cancer Prevention and Sun Safety

The CDC's *Guidelines for School Programs to Prevent Skin Cancer* state that skin cancer is the most common type of cancer in the United States. The two most common kinds of skin cancer—basal cell carcinoma and squamous cell carcinoma—are highly curable. Melanoma, the third most common type of skin cancer and one of the most common among young adults, is more dangerous. In the United States, diagnoses of new melanomas are increasing, whereas diagnoses of the majority of other cancers are decreasing.[39]

Exposure to ultraviolet (UV) radiation in childhood and adolescence plays an important role in the development of skin cancer. Thus, preventive health behaviors can play an important role in reducing skin cancer when the behaviors are initiated early and practiced consistently throughout life. Schools are in an important position to teach and model healthy behavior about sun safety and skin cancer prevention, including offering sun safety lessons that involve families. Skin cancer protective behaviors schools can teach include the following:

- Minimize exposure to the sun during peak hours (10:00 A.M.–4:00 P.M.).
- Seek shade from the midday sun (10:00 A.M.–4:00 P.M.).
- Wear clothing, hats, and sunglasses that protect the skin.
- Use a broad-spectrum sunscreen (UV-A and UV-B protection) with a sun protective factor (SPF) of 15 or higher.
- Avoid sunlamps and tanning beds.[40]

Sun safety measures should not reduce student participation in physical activity. If physical activity must be scheduled during the middle of the day, teachers and children can focus on sun safety measures such as wearing a hat, protective clothing, or sunscreen and seeking shade.[41]

Because UV radiation plays a role in the synthesis of vitamin D, teachers might have heard that limiting UV exposure might be cause for concern, perhaps leading to a decrease in levels of vitamin D. However, although the major source of vitamin D is skin exposure to sunlight, supplementing the diet with foods (fatty fish, vitamin D–fortified milk and breakfast cereal) can provide enough vitamin D to meet intake requirements.[42]

The CDC recognizes that skin cancer prevention measures vary in both their ease of adoption and their relevance. Schools should not allow an all-or-nothing approach to undermine the effectiveness of their skin cancer prevention efforts. For sun safety protection, a short-sleeve shirt and cap might be better than no hat and a sleeveless top. Flexibility is important while schools move in the direction of optimal skin cancer prevention environments, policies, and programs.[43] Teachers can find sun safety educational information from the American Cancer Society (www.cancer.org), the CDC (www.cdc.gov), and the National Safety Council (www.nsc.org/pages/home.aspx).

Communicable Diseases

Communicable diseases are infectious diseases caused by various types of microscopic organisms, including viruses, bacteria, parasites, and fungi. These organisms cause illnesses ranging from colds and flu to more serious long-term conditions such as HIV/AIDS. Infectious diseases vary in how they are spread. Some are spread through person-to-person contact, others are spread through the air, water, contaminated food, insects, and animals[44]. Teachers and students can learn about infectious diseases from CDC's Infectious Disease National Centers (www.cdc.gov/oid/centers.html) and the National Institute of Allergy and Infectious Diseases (NIAID) (www.niaid.nih.gov).

Many previously common childhood diseases now are controlled through immunization. Communicable diseases that teachers continue to encounter in school settings include chicken pox, colds and flu, eye and ear infections, scabies, ringworm, pediculosis (head lice), hepatitis, and human immunodeficiency virus (HIV). Children who become ill at school or return to school while they are still ill should be referred to the school nurse, a health aide, or a designated school staff member. Teachers can access information on infectious diseases as needed from government agencies such as the CDC and NIAID. This section includes a discussion of four communicable disease issues: immunization, colds and flu, head lice, and HIV.

Immunization

People are born with an immune system composed of cells, glands, organs, and fluids located throughout the body to fight invading bacteria and viruses. The immune system recognizes germs that enter the body as foreign invaders, or *antigens,* and produces protein substances called *antibodies* to fight them. A normal, healthy immune system has the ability to produce millions of these antibodies to defend against thousands of attacks every day, doing it so naturally that people are not even aware it is happening. Antibodies often disappear once they have destroyed the invading antigens, but the cells involved in antibody production remain and become *memory cells.* Memory cells remember the original antigen and then defend against it when the antigen attempts to reinfect a person, even after many decades. This protection is called *immunity.*[45]

Vaccines contain the same antigens or parts of antigens that cause diseases, but the antigens in vaccines are either killed or greatly weakened. Vaccine antigens are not strong enough to cause disease, but they are strong enough to make the immune system produce antibodies against them. Memory cells prevent reinfection when they encounter that disease again in the future. Through vaccination, children develop immunity without suffering the actual diseases that vaccines prevent.[46]

Children in the United States routinely get vaccines that protect them from more than a dozen diseases such as measles, polio, and tetanus. Most of these diseases are now at their lowest levels in history, thanks to years of immunization. Children must get at least some vaccines before they may attend school.[47]

Myths and misinformation about vaccine safety can confuse parents who are trying to make sound decisions about their children's health care. While some of the sickness or reactions that follow vaccination may be caused by the vaccine, many are unrelated events that occur by coincidence after vaccination. Therefore, the scientific research that attempts to distinguish true vaccine adverse events from unrelated, chance occurrence is important.[48]

Vaccines are held to the highest standard of safety. The United States currently has the safest, most effective vaccine supply in history. Years of testing are required before a vaccine can be licensed. Once in use, vaccines are monitored continually for safety and efficacy. However, vaccines, like any medication, can cause side effects. Any hint of a problem with a vaccine prompts further investigations by the CDC and FDA. If researchers find a vaccine may be causing a side effect, the CDC and FDA will initiate appropriate action that may include the changing of vaccine labels or packaging, distributing safety alerts, inspecting manufacturers' facilities and records, withdrawing recommendations for the use of the vaccine, or revoking the vaccine's license.[49] Educators and parents can learn more about specific vaccine safety through the CDC (www.cdc.gov), FDA (www.fda.gov), and NIH (www.nih.gov) by typing "vaccines" or "immunizations" into the search bar.

Colds and Flu The flu and the common cold are both respiratory illnesses, but they are caused by different viruses. Because these two types of illnesses have similar flulike symptoms, it can be difficult to tell the difference between them based on symptoms alone. In general, the flu is worse than the common cold, and symptoms such as fever, body aches, extreme tiredness, and dry cough are more common and intense. Colds are usually milder than the flu. People with colds are more likely to have a runny or stuffy nose. Colds generally do not result in serious health problems, such as pneumonia, bacterial infections, or hospitalizations.

In general, the flu is worse than the common cold, and symptoms such as fever, body aches, extreme tiredness, and dry cough are more common and intense. Colds are usually milder than the flu. People with colds are more likely to have a runny or stuffy nose. Colds generally do not result in serious health problems, such as pneumonia, bacterial infections, or hospitalization.[50]

People with the flu can spread it to others up to about six feet away. Most experts think that flu viruses are spread primarily by droplets that are sent airborne when people with the flu cough, sneeze, or talk. These droplets can land in the mouths or noses of people who are nearby or may be inhaled into the lungs. Less often, a person might also get the flu by touching a surface or object that has the flu virus on it and then touching his or her own mouth or nose.

To avoid this, people should stay away from those who are sick and stay home if sick. It also is important to wash hands often with soap and water. If soap and water are not available, one can use an alcohol-based hand rub. Linens, eating utensils, and dishes belonging to those who are sick should not be shared without being washed thoroughly first. Eating utensils can be washed either in a dishwasher or by hand with water and soap; they do not need to be cleaned separately. Further, frequently touched surfaces should be cleaned and disinfected at home, work, and school, especially if someone is ill.[51]

Head Lice Myths abound about the origin and treatment of head lice. Head lice are small, wingless insects about the size of a sesame seed that feed on human blood, do not live on pets, and survive only twenty-four hours off of their human host. Head lice leave an itchy feeling, like a mosquito bite. A head louse can lay up to ten nits (eggs) per day, and nits can be found anywhere on the head. Daily shampooing does not prevent head lice. Head lice can be spread through infested clothing or hats; infested combs, brushes, or towels; or infested bedding, couches, pillows, carpet, or stuffed animals that recently have been in contact with an infested person. Lice do not jump or fly—they crawl from place to place and person to person.[52]

Preschool and elementary school children become infested with head lice more often than older children. Lice typically are found on the scalp behind the ears and near the neckline at the back of the head. Parents should screen their children frequently for lice by looking closely through the hair and scalp for nits, baby lice, or adult lice. Finding lice can be difficult—they move quickly. Health care providers, school nurses, or local health department professionals can confirm an infestation.[53]

Teachers and school staff should be especially careful not to embarrass children or their families if an infestation occurs. Teasing by other children should not be permitted. Children typically are allowed to return to school after an approved treatment for head lice and when all lice and nits have been removed from the head. Families should contact a health care professional for advice on treating head lice. Many products designed for treating lice contain strong chemicals that can be dangerous to children.[54] Students and teachers can find more information about head lice from the National Pediculosis Association (www.headlice.org).

Human Immunodeficiency Virus (HIV) HIV stands for human immunodeficiency virus. It is the virus that can lead to acquired immunodeficiency syndrome, or AIDS. Unlike some other viruses, the human body cannot get rid of HIV. That means that once a person has HIV, he or she has it for life. HIV is a virus spread through body fluids that affects specific cells of the immune system, called CD4 cells, or T cells. Over time, HIV can destroy so many of these cells that the body can't fight off infections and disease. When this happens, HIV infection leads to AIDS.[55]

Youth in the United States account for a substantial number of HIV infections. Youth aged 13 to 24 accounted for an estimated 22 percent of all new HIV infections in the United States in 2010, and almost 60 percent of youth with HIV in the United States do not know they are infected. Gay, bisexual, and other men who have sex with men account for most new infections in the age group 13 to 24; black/African American or Hispanic/Latino gay and bisexual men are especially affected. Continual HIV prevention outreach and education efforts, including programs on abstinence, delaying the initiation of sex, and negotiating safer sex for the spectrum of sexuality and gender among youth—homosexual, bisexual, heterosexual, and transgender—are urgently needed for a new generation at risk.[56]

The risk for acquiring human immunodeficiency virus (HIV) infection during adolescence and early adulthood starts with initiation of sexual behavior or injection drug use, and initiation of contributing behaviors such as use of alcohol and other drugs. The prevalence of HIV in potential sex partners, the percentage of HIV-infected persons unaware of their status, and the frequency of risky sexual behaviors and injection drug use contribute to the level of risk. All persons need to understand the threat of HIV and how to prevent it.[57]

Youths, particularly those at highest risk, need effective school-based, school-linked, and community-based interventions that make them aware of their risk for HIV and help delay initiation of sexual activity, increase condom use for those who are sexually active, and decrease other behaviors, such as alcohol and drug use, that contribute to HIV risk.[58]

HIV prevention education provides an excellent opportunity to integrate health education with other subjects. For example, upper-elementary and middle school students might be especially interested in what scientists know about the origins of HIV and how the virus works in the body. However, knowing factual information about this retrovirus does not necessarily help students protect themselves against infection. Health education must address issues such as how the virus is and is not transmitted (Figure 9-1). In addition, health education must help students deal with issues such as setting personal boundaries and resisting pressure to participate in risk behaviors (using alcohol and other drugs and engaging in sexual activity).

Teachers must consider additional issues related to HIV infection. Educators must know local regulations regarding the confidentiality rights of children and staff members with regard to HIV status. Teachers potentially might deal with issues of gossip, discrimination, prejudice, misinformation, and mistreatment related to those who are infected or thought to be infected. Just as important, teachers must be aware of safety for themselves and for children when dealing with blood or other body fluid (urine, vomit, fecal matter) potentially containing blood.

The American Academy of Pediatrics calls for school staff to be educated on universal precautions for the safe handling of blood, vomit, urine, other body fluids, and fecal material. Ample and convenient supplies of gloves, containers for proper disposal of needles and other sharp objects, disinfectants (including bleach), and other equipment identified should be provided in predetermined locations, including classrooms. Good handwashing technique also is essential for preventing the spread of

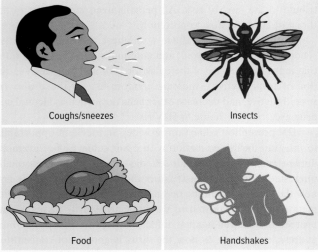

Ways HIV is spread

Through unsafe sexual contact

Through sharing needles

From mother to baby during pregnancy, birth, or breast feeding

Ways HIV is NOT spread (Casual Contact)

Coughs/sneezes

Insects

Food

Handshakes

FIGURE 9–1 | How HIV Is and Is Not Transmitted

disease and should be taught to all staff and students. Adequate facilities for hand washing should be available throughout all school facilities and include warm water, soap or detergent, towels, waste receptacles, and posted signs to instruct on hand-washing technique.[59]

Chronic Diseases

Chronic diseases such as heart disease, cancer, and diabetes are the leading causes of adult death and disability in the United States. Chronic diseases are not contagious, but they are very costly and highly preventable. Adopting healthy behaviors such as healthy eating, exercising regularly, and avoiding tobacco use can prevent or control many chronic diseases. Teachers and students can learn more about chronic diseases through the CDC's National Center for Chronic Disease Prevention and Health Promotion (www.cdc.gov/chronicdisease/index.htm). Information about conditions that affect children and adolescents is available through the CDC's Healthy Schools website

(www.cdc.gov/healthyschools/chronicconditions.htm). This section includes a discussion of four chronic diseases: asthma, allergies, diabetes, and epilepsy.

Asthma Asthma is a leading chronic illness among children and youth in the United States. On average, in a classroom of thirty children, about three are likely to have asthma. Asthma is one of the leading causes of school absenteeism. Low-income populations, minorities, and children living in inner cities experience more emergency department visits, hospitalizations, and deaths due to asthma than the general population.[60]

Asthma is a lung disease that makes breathing difficult for millions of Americans, both young and old. There is no cure for asthma, but it can be managed and treated so that young people can live a normal, healthy life. All students with asthma should have a written Asthma Action Plan, developed between parents and health care providers, that details personal information about the child's asthma symptoms, medications, and any physical activity limitations and provides specific instructions about what to do if an asthma attack does not improve with prescribed medication.[61]

The American Lung Association worked with partners to develop the National Asthma Public Policy Agenda to reduce the suffering and death from asthma. Two important policy recommendations are

1. All school systems should adopt and implement a comprehensive plan for the management of asthma that is based on current research and best practices. Schools are responsible for ensuring the health of all students while in school. Creating "asthma-friendly" environments is an essential step in preventing asthma emergencies, improving asthma management, and ensuring student learning.
2. All school systems should adopt and implement an environmental assessment and management plan. School environments can expose both children and staff to indoor and outdoor air pollutants that have harmful effects on health, including asthma. Cleaning up air pollution is important to make sure children are safe in school.[62]

The American Lung Association (www.lung.org) is an excellent resource for teachers and students. The Asthma-Friendly Schools Initiative is a comprehensive approach to asthma management in schools. By providing tools and resources, schools and communities are better able to create a sustainable, asthma management plan within their existing school structure. The goal of the Asthma-Friendly Schools Initiative is to keep children with asthma healthy, in school, and ready to learn. The Asthma-Friendly Schools Initiative Toolkit is a planning tool based on real-life activities that have been used in schools throughout the United States to create comprehensive asthma management systems. In addition, elementary school children can learn to manage their own asthma when they participate in the American Lung Association's award-winning Open Airways for Schools program. The program teaches children with asthma aged 8 to 11 how to detect the warning signs of asthma, avoid their triggers, and make decisions about their health.[63]

©Evgeniya Tiplyashina/123RF

Many students have allergies, and allergies account for many lost school days each year. Common allergens include pollen, dust mites, and animal dander.

Allergies In addition to dealing with asthma, colds, and flu, teachers often have students who suffer from various kinds of allergies. Any child may become allergic, but children from families with a history of allergy are more likely to be allergic. Children may inherit the tendency to become allergic from their parents, but only some of them will develop an active allergic disease.[64]

KidsHealth for Parents (www.kidshealth.org) explains that some of the most common allergies are related to food and to airborne allergens such as pollen, mold, dust mites, and animal dander. Allergies can be seasonal (pollen or certain molds) or year-round (dust mites). Regional differences also exist—different allergens are more prevalent in different parts of the country or the world. The type and severity of allergy symptoms vary from allergy to allergy and from child to child. Some children experience a combination of symptoms.[65]

Airborne allergens can cause allergic rhinitis, characterized by sneezing, itchy nose and/or throat, nasal congestion, and coughing. These symptoms often are accompanied by itchy, watery, and red eyes (allergic conjunctivitis) or dark circles around reddened eyes (allergic shiners). Allergic rhinitis and conjunctivitis can range from minor or major seasonal annoyances to year-round problems. If they occur with wheezing and shortness of breath, the allergy might have progressed to asthma.[66]

Common foods that can cause allergies include cow's milk, soy, egg, wheat, seafood, tree nuts (such as walnuts and pistachios), and peanuts. Peanuts are one of the most severe food allergens, often causing life-threatening reactions. In rare instances, if the sensitivity to an allergen is extreme, a child can develop a life-threatening condition called anaphylactic shock. Severe reactions to any allergen require immediate medical attention. Fortunately, severe or life-threatening allergies occur only

among a small percentage of children.[67]

All warm-blooded, furry animals, such as the average household pet, can cause allergic reactions, usually due to proteins in their saliva, dander, and urine. When the animal licks itself, the saliva is transferred to the fur. As the saliva dries, protein particles become airborne and work their way into fabrics in the home. Cats are the worst offenders, because their salivary protein is extremely tiny and cats tend to lick themselves as part of their grooming more than other animals.[68]

Teachers must be alert to signs and symptoms among their students of allergies related to pollens, animals, foods, and insect bites. Teachers should be informed about any known allergies their students have. If this information is not already available, teachers should be sure to obtain it from parents and caregivers. Teachers and students can learn more about allergies from NIAID (www.niaid.nih.gov) and from KidsHealth (www.kidshealth.org).

Diabetes Few other pediatric health problems have increased as rapidly or have posed such grave concerns as the epidemic of overweight among children and adolescents. The emergence of Type 2 (Figure 9-2) diabetes among children and adolescents represents a consequence of obesity that previously was thought to occur only in adults.[69]

Type 1 diabetes, which used to be called juvenile diabetes, is usually first diagnosed in children, teens, or young adults. In Type 1 diabetes, the body's immune system attacks and destroys beta cells in the pancreas, so that they no longer make insulin. People with Type 1 diabetes must take insulin every day.[70]

Type 2 diabetes, a disease usually diagnosed in adults aged 40 years or older, is now becoming more common among children and adolescents, particularly in American Indians, African Americans, and Hispanics/Latinos. Among youth, obesity, physical inactivity, and prenatal exposure to diabetes in the mother have become widespread, and may contribute to the increased development of Type 2 diabetes during childhood and adolescence.[71]

There is no single recipe to manage diabetes that fits all children. Each student with diabetes has different needs and must have an individualized care plan. Blood glucose targets; frequency of blood glucose testing; type, dose, and frequency of insulin; use of insulin injections with a syringe or a pen or pump; use of oral glucose-lowering medication; and details of nutrition management all may vary among individuals. The family and diabetes care team determine the regimen that best suits each child's individual characteristics and circumstances.[72]

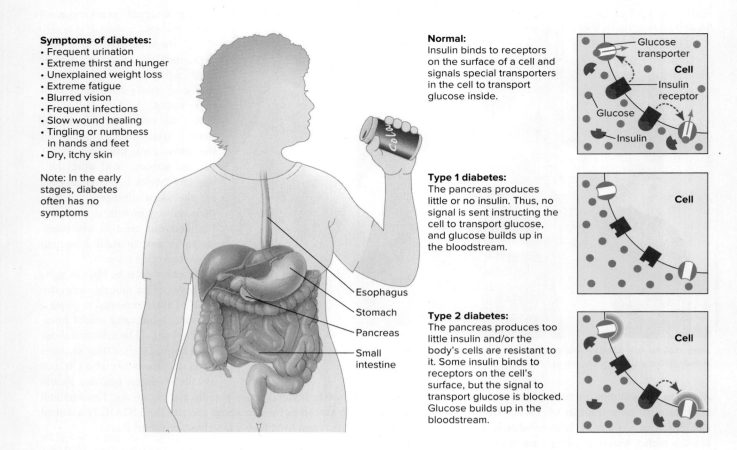

Symptoms of diabetes:
- Frequent urination
- Extreme thirst and hunger
- Unexplained weight loss
- Extreme fatigue
- Blurred vision
- Frequent infections
- Slow wound healing
- Tingling or numbness in hands and feet
- Dry, itchy skin

Note: In the early stages, diabetes often has no symptoms

Esophagus
Stomach
Pancreas
Small intestine

Normal:
Insulin binds to receptors on the surface of a cell and signals special transporters in the cell to transport glucose inside.

Glucose transporter
Cell
Insulin receptor
Glucose
Insulin

Type 1 diabetes:
The pancreas produces little or no insulin. Thus, no signal is sent instructing the cell to transport glucose, and glucose builds up in the bloodstream.

Cell

Type 2 diabetes:
The pancreas produces too little insulin and/or the body's cells are resistant to it. Some insulin binds to receptors on the cell's surface, but the signal to transport glucose is blocked. Glucose builds up in the bloodstream.

Cell

FIGURE 9–2 | **Diabetes** During digestion, carbohydrates are broken down in the small intestine into glucose, a simple sugar that enters the bloodstream. The presence of glucose signals the pancreas to release insulin, a hormone that helps cells take up glucose; once inside a cell, glucose can be converted to energy. In diabetes, this process is disrupted, resulting in a buildup of glucose in the bloodstream.

Diabetes care for children and teens should be provided by a team that can deal with these special medical, educational, nutritional, and behavioral issues. The team usually consists of a physician, diabetes educator, dietitian, social worker, or psychologist, along with the patient and family. Children should be seen by the team at diagnosis and in follow-up, as agreed on by the primary care provider and the diabetes team.[73] Teachers who have diabetic students in their classes can learn more from the American Diabetes Association (www.diabetes.org) and the National Diabetes Education Program (www.ndep.nih.gov). The American Diabetes Association Safe at School Campaign helps families of children with diabetes overcome barriers at school and ensure a safe learning environment.

Epilepsy About 3,00,000 American children under the age of 14 have epilepsy, and it affects children at different ages and in different ways. Early recognition and treatment are keys to the best possible outcome. For some, it will be a temporary problem, easily controlled with medication, outgrown after a few years. For others,

it may be a lifelong challenge affecting many areas of life. Epilepsy may be associated with serious, difficult-to-treat syndromes, including Lennox-Gastaut Syndrome, genetically related conditions and developmental disorders. Social impact in childhood is often severe, producing isolation and loss of self-esteem.[74]

Most children with epilepsy attend school and can participate in all activities. Some may need to take medicine at school, may need help with certain subjects, or require extra time on tests. They may sometimes have seizures at school. Teachers should start each school year by scheduling a meeting with the parents or caregivers of children who have epilepsy to discuss the child's condition, any learning issues, and how to respond if the child has a seizure. Teachers should ask if there are others at the school who should be informed, such as gym teachers, school nurses, librarian, cafeteria managers, and bus drivers. Teachers also can talk with parents about discussing epilepsy with the class in a way that is appropriate for the age level and that would be comfortable for the child. Having a seizure at school can be embarrassing for a child and frightening for others. Thus, the teacher's talking with students beforehand can help prevent teasing and correct inaccuracies children may have heard.[75]

The Epilepsy Foundation recommends developing a Seizure Response Plan for the child's classroom and school. The plan should include basic first-aid information,[76] such as:

- Stay calm and track time.
- Keep child safe.
- Do not restrain.
- Do not put anything in mouth.
- Stay with child until fully conscious.
- Record seizure in log.

The plan also should include a treatment protocol for school hours and an emergency response plan. More information is available at www.epilepsy.com/learn/managing-your-epilepsy/seizure-response-plans-101, including a sample Seizure Action Plan.[77]

Students might be interested to know that Napoleon, Vincent van Gogh, Danny Glover, and Theodore Roosevelt are among well-known people with epilepsy. Teachers and students can learn more about epilepsy at the Epilepsy Foundation (www.epilepsy.com).

Recommendations for Concepts and Practice

Healthy Behavior Outcomes

The goal of health education is to help students adopt or maintain health-enhancing behaviors. School districts and teachers should identify the health-enhancing behaviors they would like their students to maintain or adopt. The list found in the Teacher's Toolbox 9.1 identifies possible healthy behavioral outcomes related to personal health and wellness. Though not all these suggestions are developmentally appropriate for students in grades K–8, this list can help teachers understand how the learning activities they plan for their students support both short- and long-term desired behavior outcomes.

Developmentally Appropriate Knowledge and Skill Expectations

As with other health topics, teaching related to personal health and wellness should be developmentally appropriate and be based on the physical, cognitive, social, emotional, and language characteristics of specific students. Teacher's Toolbox 9.1 contains a list of suggested developmentally appropriate knowledge and skill expectations to help teachers create lessons that will encourage students to practice the desired behavior outcomes by the time they graduate from high school. Note that these grade-level spans are aligned with the 2007 National Health Education Standards.

STRATEGIES FOR LEARNING AND ASSESSMENT

Promoting Personal Health and Wellness

This section provides an example of a standards-based learning and assessment strategy for each NHES standard. The examples in this chapter can be applied to any content area. Chapters 5 to 14 include content-specific

learning and assessment strategies organized by standard and grade cluster (K–2, 3–5, and 6–8). Each set of strategies begins with a restatement of the standard and a reminder of the assessment criteria, drawn from the RMC Health rubrics in Appendix B. Strategies are written as directions for teachers and include applicable theory of planned behavior (TPB) constructs—intention to act in healthy ways, attitudes toward behavior, subjective norms, perceived behavioral control—in parentheses.

NHES 1 | Core Concepts

Students will comprehend concepts related to health promotion and disease prevention to enhance health.

ASSESSMENT CRITERIA

- Connections—Describe relationships between behavior and health; draw logical conclusions about connections between behavior and health.
- Comprehensiveness—Thoroughly cover health topic, showing breadth and depth; give accurate information.

Grades K–2

Sleep, Sleep, and More Sleep   The National Sleep Foundation (www.sleepfoundation.org/) recommends the following sleep tips for school age children in order to increase healthy sleep habits:

- Teach school-aged children about healthy sleep habits.
- Continue to emphasize need for regular and consistent sleep schedule and bedtime routine.
- Make child's bedroom conducive to sleep–dark, cool, and quiet.
- Keep TV and computers out of the bedroom.
- Avoid caffeine.

Teachers can share these tips with students along with the idea of the importance of establishing a bedtime routine. The story *Cornelius P. Mud, Are You Ready for Bed?* (see the Children's Literature section at the end of this chapter) can be read to students to create an opportunity to discuss the importance of a bedtime routine. In this story the spirited Cornelius, puts his own special twist on the bedtime routine. The class can discuss the different bedtime routines followed in their families. Students also can be encouraged to discuss what they have learned with their families.

ASSESSMENT | Students can create a door hanger out of construction paper. On one side of the door hanger they can create a quiet zone message, such as "Shhhh . . . sleeping." On the other side of the door hanger students can draw pictures of or write their bedtime routine. Taking this home can create an opportunity for students to discuss what has been learned in class. For assessment criteria, students should have accurate information and should be able to verbally explain the importance between sleep and health. (Constructs: Attitudes toward behavior.)

Join the Scrub Club!   Teacher and students can check out The Scrub Club at www.scrubclub.org. The Scrub Club program is the first of its kind—a fun, interactive, and educational website that teaches children the proper way to wash their hands. The site consists of a Webisode (*The Good, the BAC, and the Ugly*), interactive games, educational music, downloadable activities for kids, educational materials for teachers and program information for parents. Students can meet The Scrub Club and check out villains, such as E. Coli, Sal Monella, and Campy Lobactor. There's a Five Finger Alert for the Flu and a Hand-Washing Song. The Scrub Club Kids represent the six steps of the hand-washing process.

ASSESSMENT | For an assessment task, students can explore different parts of The Scrub Club website and report back to classmates. For assessment criteria, students should provide accurate information and make connections between hand-washing and health. (Construct: Attitudes toward behavior.)

Teacher's Toolbox 9.1

Developmentally Appropriate Knowledge and Skill Expectations for Personal Health and Wellness

HEALTHY BEHAVIOR OUTCOMES FOR PERSONAL HEALTH AND WELLNESS

HBO 1. Brush and floss teeth daily.
HBO 2. Practice appropriate hygiene habits.
HBO 3. Get an appropriate amount of sleep and rest.
HBO 4. Prevent vision and hearing loss.
HBO 5. Prevent damage from the sun.
HBO 6. Practice behaviors that prevent infectious diseases.
HBO 7. Practice behaviors that prevent chronic diseases.

HBO 8. Prevent serious health problems that result from common chronic diseases and conditions among youth, such as allergies, asthma, diabetes, and epilepsy.
HBO 9. Practice behaviors that prevent foodborne illnesses.
HBO 10. Seek out help for common infectious diseases and chronic diseases and conditions.
HBO 11. Seek out health care professionals for appropriate screenings and examinations.
HBO 12. Prevent health problems that result from fads or trends.

Grades K–2 Knowledge Expectations	Grades 3–5 Knowledge Expectations	Grades 6–8 Knowledge Expectations

NHES 1: Core Concepts

Grades K–2 Knowledge Expectations	Grades 3–5 Knowledge Expectations	Grades 6–8 Knowledge Expectations
PHW1.2.1 Identify the proper steps for daily brushing and flossing teeth. (HBO 1 & 2)	PHW1.5.1 Describe the benefits of personal health care practices such as tooth brushing and flossing, washing hair, and bathing regularly. (HBO 1 & 2)	PHW1.8.1 Summarize the benefits of good hygiene practices for promoting health and maintaining positive social relationships. (HBO 2)
PHW1.2.2 State why hygiene is important to good health. (HBO 1 & 2)	PHW1.5.2 Describe values that promote healthy behaviors. (HBO 2)	PHW1.8.2 Summarize the benefits of getting proper rest and sleep for healthy growth and development. (HBO 3)
PHW1.2.3 Identify the benefits of personal health care practices such as washing hair and bathing regularly. (HBO 1 & 2)	PHW1.5.3 Explain why sleep and rest are important for proper growth and good health. (HBO 3)	PHW1.8.3 Identify common causes of noise-induced hearing loss. (HBO 4)
PHW1.2.4 State the steps for proper hand washing. (HBO 2 & 6)	PHW1.5.4 Explain how hearing can be damaged by loud sounds. (HBO 4)	PHW1.8.4 Describe appropriate ways to protect vision and hearing. (HBO 4)
PHW1.2.5 Explain why sleep and rest are important for proper growth and good health. (HBO 3)	PHW1.5.5 Describe how vision can be damaged. (HBO 4)	PHW1.8.5 Summarize actions to take to protect oneself against potential damage from exposure to the sun. (HBO 5)
PHW1.2.6 Explain how hearing can be damaged by loud noise. (HBO 4)	PHW1.5.6 Describe ways to prevent vision or hearing damage. (HBO 4)	PHW1.8.6 Explain the difference between infectious, noninfectious, acute, and chronic diseases. (HBO 6 & 7)
PHW1.2.7 Identify ways to protect vision. (HBO 4)	PHW1.5.7 Describe ways to prevent harmful effects of the sun. (HBO 5)	PHW1.8.7 Summarize the symptoms of someone who is sick or getting sick. (HBO 6 & 7)
PHW1.2.8 Identify ways to protect hearing. (HBO 4)	PHW1.5.8 Explain the difference between infectious diseases and non-infectious diseases. (HBO 6 & 7)	PHW1.8.8 Summarize ways that common infectious diseases are transmitted. (HBO 6 & 9)
PHW1.2.9 List ways to prevent harmful effects of the sun. (HBO 5)	PHW1.5.9 Describe ways that common infectious diseases are transmitted. (HBO 6)	PHW1.8.9 Summarize health practices to prevent the spread of infectious diseases that are transmitted by food, air, indirect contact, and person-to-person contact. (HBO 6 & 9)
PHW1.2.10 Describe what it means to be healthy. (HBO 6)	PHW1.5.10 Describe ways to prevent the spread of germs that cause infectious diseases. (HBO 6)	PHW1.8.10 Describe food safety strategies that can control germs that cause foodborne illnesses. (HBO 6 & 9)
PHW1.2.11 Identify different ways that disease-causing germs are transmitted. (HBO 6)	PHW1.5.11 Describe symptoms that occur when a person is sick. (HBO 6 & 7)	PHW1.8.11 Explain ways to prevent the spread of germs that cause infectious diseases such as preventing the spread of HIV by not having sex, not touching blood, and not touching used hypodermic or tattoo needles. (HBO 6 & 12)
PHW1.2.12 Identify ways to prevent the spread of germs that cause common infectious diseases. (HBO 6)	PHW1.5.12 Explain how hand washing and covering your cough and sneeze are effective ways to prevent many infectious diseases. (HBO 6 & 9)	PHW1.8.12 Explain the behavioral and environmental factors that contribute to the major chronic diseases. (HBO 7 & 8)
PHW1.2.13 Identify foods and non-food triggers that are common causes of allergic reactions. (HBO 6)	PHW1.5.13 Describe how foodborne illnesses can spread at school or in the community. (HBO 6 & 9)	PHW1.8.13 Describe how an inactive lifestyle contributes to chronic disease. (HBO 7 & 8)
PHW1.2.14 Explain that foods can contain germs that can cause illness. (HBO 6)	PHW1.5.14 Describe how to keep food safe from harmful germs. (HBO 6 & 9)	PHW1.8.14 Describe the importance of seeking help and treatment for common infectious diseases and chronic diseases. (HBO 10)

Grades K–2 Knowledge Expectations	Grades 3–5 Knowledge Expectations	Grades 6–8 Knowledge Expectations

NHES 1: Core Concepts (*continued*)

PHW1.2.15 Identify food safety strategies that can control germs that causes foodborne illnesses. (HBO 6 & 9)

PHW1.2.16 Identify proper steps for treating a wound to reduce chances of infection. (HBO 6 & 10)

PHW1.5.15 Identify health problems associated with common childhood chronic diseases or conditions such as asthma, allergies, diabetes, and epilepsy. (HBO 7 & 8)

PHW1.5.16 Describe the importance of seeking help and treatment for common infectious diseases. (HBO 10)

PHW1.8.15 Describe the potential health and social consequences of popular fads or trends such as body piercing and tattooing. (HBO 12)

Grades K–2 Skill Expectations	Grades 3–5 Skill Expectations	Grades 6–8 Skill Expectations

NHES 2: Analyze Influences

PHW2.2.1 Identify relevant influences of family on personal health and wellness practices and behaviors.

PHW2.2.2 Identify relevant influences of school on personal health and wellness practices and behaviors.

PHW2.2.3 Identify relevant influences of media and technology on personal health and wellness practices and behaviors.

PHW2.2.4 Describe positive influences on personal health and wellness practices and behaviors.

PHW2.2.5 Describe negative influences on personal health and wellness practices and behaviors.

PHW2.5.1 Identify relevant influences of culture on personal health and wellness-related practices and behaviors.

PHW2.5.2 Identify relevant influences of peers on personal health and wellness-related practices and behaviors.

PHW2.5.3 Identify relevant influences of community on personal health and wellness-related practices and behaviors.

PHW2.5.4 Describe how relevant influences of family and culture affect personal health and wellness-related practices and behaviors.

PHW2.5.5 Describe how relevant influences of school and community affect personal health and wellness-related practices and behaviors.

PHW2.5.6 Describe how relevant influences of media and technology affect personal health and wellness-related practices and behaviors.

PHW2.5.7 Describe how relevant influences of peers affect personal health and wellness-related practices and behaviors.

PHW2.8.1 Explain the influence of school rules and community laws on personal health and wellness-related practices and behaviors.

PHW2.8.2 Explain how perceptions of norms influence healthy and unhealthy personal health and wellness-related practices and behaviors.

PHW2.8.3 Explain how social expectations influence healthy and unhealthy personal health and wellness-related practices and behaviors.

PHW2.8.4 Explain how personal values and beliefs influence personal health and wellness-related practices and behaviors.

PHW2.8.5 Describe how some personal health risk behaviors, such as using alcohol and other drugs, influence the likelihood of engaging in other unhealthy personal health and wellness-related behaviors.

PHW2.8.6 Analyze how relevant influences of family and culture affect personal health and wellness-related practices and behaviors.

PHW2.8.7 Analyze how relevant influences of school and community affect personal health and wellness-related practices and behaviors.

PHW2.8.8 Analyze how relevant influences of media and technology affect personal health and wellness-related practices and behaviors.

PHW2.8.9 Analyze how relevant influences of peers affect personal health and wellness-related practices and behaviors.

NHES 3: Accessing Information, Products, and Services

PHW3.2.1 Identify trusted adults at home who can help promote personal health and wellness.

PHW3.2.2 Identify trusted adults and professionals in school who can help promote personal health and wellness (e.g., school nurse, classroom teacher).

PHW3.5.1 Describe characteristics of accurate personal health and wellness information.

PHW3.5.2 Describe characteristics of appropriate and reliable personal health and wellness products.

PHW3.5.3 Describe characteristics of appropriate and trustworthy personal health and wellness services.

PHW3.5.4 Demonstrate how to locate sources of accurate personal health and wellness information.

PHW3.8.1 Analyze the validity and reliability of personal health and wellness information.

PHW3.8.2 Analyze the validity and reliability of personal health and wellness products.

PHW3.8.3 Analyze the validity and reliability of personal health and wellness services.

PHW3.8.4 Describe situations that call for professional personal health and wellness services.

PHW3.8.5 Determine the availability of valid and reliable personal health and wellness products.

(continued)

Grades K–2 Skill Expectations	**Grades 3–5 Skill Expectations**	**Grades 6–8 Skill Expectations**

NHES 3: Accessing Information, Products, and Services (*continued*)

PHW3.2.3 Identify trusted adults and professionals in the community who can help promote personal health and wellness (e.g., health care provider, police officer).		PHW3.8.6 Access valid and reliable personal health and wellness information from home, school or community.
PHW3.2.4 Explain how to locate school health helpers who can help promote personal health and wellness (e.g., school nurse).		PHW3.8.7 Locate valid and reliable personal health and wellness products.
PHW3.2.5 Explain how to locate community health helpers who can help promote personal health and wellness (e.g., health care provider, paramedic).		PHW3.8.8 Locate valid and reliable personal health and wellness services.
PHW3.2.6 Demonstrate how to locate school or community health helpers to enhance personal health and wellness (e.g., health care provider, paramedic).		

NHES 4: Interpersonal Communication

PHW4.2.1 Demonstrate how to effectively communicate needs, wants, and feelings in healthy ways to enhance personal health and wellness.	PHW4.5.1 Demonstrate effective verbal and nonverbal communication skills to enhance personal health and wellness.	PHW4.8.1 Demonstrate the use of effective verbal and nonverbal communication skills to enhance personal health and wellness.
PHW4.2.2 Demonstrate effective active listening skills including paying attention, and verbal and nonverbal feedback to enhance personal health and wellness.	PHW4.5.2 Explain how to be empathetic and compassionate toward others.	PHW4.8.2 Demonstrate effective peer resistance skills to avoid or reduce participating in behaviors that can negatively affect personal health and wellness.
PHW4.2.3 Demonstrate effective refusal skills, including verbally saying no, to avoid participating in behaviors that negatively affect personal health and wellness.	PHW4.5.3 Demonstrate effective peer resistance skills to avoid or reduce participating in behaviors that can negatively affect personal health and wellness.	PHW4.8.3 Demonstrate effective negotiation skills to avoid or reduce participating in behaviors that can negatively affect personal health and wellness.
PHW4.2.4 Identify how to communicate care and concern for others to enhance their personal health and wellness.	PHW4.5.4 Demonstrate healthy ways to manage to avoid or reduce participating in behaviors that can negatively affect personal health and wellness.	PHW4.8.4 Demonstrate how to effectively ask for assistance to improve personal health and wellness and the health of others.
	PHW4.5.5 Demonstrate how to effectively ask for help to improve personal health and wellness.	PHW4.8.5 Demonstrate how to effectively communicate empathy and support for others to improve their personal health and wellness.
	PHW4.5.6 Demonstrate how to effectively communicate support for others to improve their personal health and wellness.	

NHES 5: Decision Making

PHW5.2.1 Identify situations that need a decision related to personal health and wellness (e.g., washing hands before eating; wearing sun protection; brushing teeth daily).	PHW5.5.1 Identify situations that need a decision related to personal health and wellness	PHW5.8.1 Identify circumstances that help or hinder making a healthy decision related to personal health and wellness.
PHW5.2.2 Identify how family, peers, or media influence a personal health or wellness-related decision.	PHW5.5.2 Decide when help is needed and when it is not needed to make a personal health and wellness-related decision.	PHW5.8.2 Determine when personal health and wellness situations require a decision.
	PHW5.5.3 Explain how family, culture, peers, or media influence a personal health and wellness-related decision.	PHW5.8.3 Distinguish when decisions about personal health and wellness should be made individually or with the help of others.

Grades K–2 Skill Expectations	Grades 3–5 Skill Expectations	Grades 6–8 Skill Expectations

NHES 5: Decision Making (*continued*)

PHW5.2.3 Explain the potential positive and negative outcomes from personal health or wellness-related decisions.

PHW5.2.4 Describe when help is needed and when it is not needed to make a personal health or wellness-related decision.

PHW5.5.4 Identify options and their potential outcomes when making a personal health and wellness-related decision.

PHW5.5.5 Choose a healthy option when making a personal health and wellness-related decision.

PHW5.5.6 Describe the final outcome of a personal health and wellness-related decision.

PHW5.8.4 Explain how family, culture, media, peers, and personal beliefs affect a personal health and wellness-related decision.

PHW5.8.5 Distinguish between healthy and unhealthy alternatives of a personal health and wellness-related decision.

PHW5.8.6 Predict the potential outcomes of healthy and unhealthy alternatives to a personal health and wellness-related decision.

PHW5.8.7 Choose a healthy alternative when making a personal health and wellness-related decision.

PHW5.8.8 Analyze the effectiveness of a final outcome of a personal health and wellness-related decision.

NHES 6: Goal Setting

PHW6.2.1 Identify a realistic short-term goal to improve a personal health and wellness practice.

PHW6.2.2 Take steps to achieve the goal to improve personal health and wellness.

PHW6.2.3 Identify people who can help achieve a personal health and wellness goal.

PHW6.5.1 Set a realistic goal to improve a personal health and wellness practice.

PHW6.5.2 Track progress toward achieving a personal health and wellness goal.

PHW6.5.3 Identify resources that can help achieve a personal health and wellness goal.

PHW6.8.1 Assess personal health and wellness practices.

PHW6.8.2 Set a realistic goal to improve a positive personal health and wellness practice.

PHW6.8.3 Assess the barriers to achieving a personal health and wellness goal.

PHW6.8.4 Apply strategies to overcome barriers to achieving a personal health and wellness goal.

PHW6.8.5 Use strategies and skills to achieve a personal health and wellness goal.

NHES 7: Self-Management

PHW7.2.1 Identify personal health and wellness practices that reduce or prevent health risks.

PHW7.2.2 Demonstrate positive personal health and wellness practices.

PHW7.2.3 Make a commitment to practice positive personal health and wellness behaviors.

PHW7.5.1 Describe practices and behaviors that reduce or prevent personal health and wellness risks.

PHW7.5.2 Demonstrate positive personal health and wellness practices and behaviors.

PHW7.5.3 Make a commitment to practice positive personal health and wellness behaviors.

PHW7.8.1 Explain the importance of being responsible for personal health and wellness behaviors.

PHW7.8.2 Analyze personal health and wellness practices and behaviors that reduce or prevent health risks.

PHW7.8.3 Demonstrate healthy practices and behaviors to improve the personal health and wellness of oneself and others.

PHW7.8.4 Make a commitment to practice positive personal health and wellness behaviors.

NHES 8: Advocacy

PHW8.2.1 Make requests to others to promote positive personal health and wellness practices.

PHW8.2.2 Demonstrate how to encourage peers to make positive personal health and wellness choices.

PHW8.5.1 Give factual information to improve the personal health and wellness of others.

PHW8.5.2 State personal beliefs to improve the personal health and wellness of others.

PHW8.5.3 Demonstrate how to persuade others to make positive personal health and wellness choices.

PHW8.8.1 State a health-enhancing position, supported with accurate information, to improve the personal health and wellness of others.

PHW8.8.2 Persuade others to make positive personal health and wellness choices.

PHW8.8.3 Collaborate with others to advocate for individuals, families and schools to be healthy.

PHW8.8.4 Demonstrate how to adapt a personal health and wellness message for different audiences.

SOURCE: Centers for Disease Control and Prevention, *Health Education Curriculum Analysis Tool.* Atlanta, GA: CDC, 2012. www.cdc.gov.

HeadLice.Org for Kids   Children can visit the website www.headlice .org/kids/index.htm. The National Pediculosis Association displays news, FAQs, reports, projects, a catalog, and kids' head games and bug fun activities. Children can visit the site in the computer lab or at a learning station in the classroom. Children can discuss what they learned with classmates and write and draw about it.

ASSESSMENT | The children's discussions, drawings, and writing are the assessment task for this activity. For assessment criteria, students should provide correct information and describe at least two ways to prevent head lice infestation. (Construct: Attitudes toward behavior.)

Grades 3–5

Becoming a Food Detective   With the number of deadly cases of *E. Coli* in recent years, avoiding foodborne illness has become a priority for schools, government agencies, and others involved in food distribution and preparation. Children can begin the process of safe food preparation as soon as they begin sharing in the preparation process. Have students visit the Food Detectives website at www.fooddetectives.com. Students can learn about food safety and then solve cases to become food detectives.

ASSESSMENT | The interactive web cases serve as part of the assessment task for this activity. Students can demonstrate successfully solving the case and then share with the class what was learned on this website by completing a 4-3-2-1 exit slip. Exit slip questions can include questions such as: Identify four ways unsafe food handling can cause a person to become ill. List three ways to avoid food-borne illness when handling meat. State two tips for safely handling fruits and vegetables. Declare one practice you will observe to reduce your risk of foodborne illness. For assessment criteria, students should provide accurate information and be able to make connections between safe food handling and disease prevention. (Constructs: Attitude toward behavior, perceived behavioral control.)

Disease Detectives   Children can consult the CDC's BAM! (Body and Mind) website for kids (www.bam.gov) to investigate topics of interest. For example, students can check out Disease Detectives, The Immune Platoon, and Stalking SARS. Students can select a topic of interest from this or other sites (www.kidshealth.org or www.kids.gov) to research and report back to the class.

ASSESSMENT | The students' reports to the class are the assessment task for this activity. For assessment criteria, all information must be correct, and students should make at least two connections between behaviors and health. (Construct: Attitudes toward behavior.)

Grades 6–8

Protecting My Eyes and Ears   In pairs, have students select either eyes or ears, then have them research, using credible sources, five tips teens can follow for protecting their vision or hearing. Pairs will then create a visual (poster, video, PowerPoint, etc.) of the five tips for protecting vision or hearing.

ASSESSMENT | The visual students create is the assessment task. For assessment criteria, students should provide accurate information and be able to reflect on the importance of protecting vision and hearing as a young person to their overall health. A quick write or exit slip following the preparation of visuals would allow students to demonstrate their ability to express the connection between vision and hearing protection and health. Additionally, the ability to use credible sources can be connected to Standard 3. (Constructs: Attitudes toward behavior, perceived behavioral control.)

Fightbac!   Teachers can use the resources available at www.fightbac .org to turn their classroom into a science laboratory. Small groups of students can be assigned one of the various experiments available in the curriculum materials on the www.fightbac.org website to conduct. Once they have completed the experiment, groups can report their findings and food safety learning to the class.

ASSESSMENT | Students can create magnets with key messages learned from the various experiments. The magnets can then be taken home and posted on the refrigerator as reminders of safe practices when handling food. For assessment criteria, students should provide accurate information and make at least three connections between safe food handling practices and health. (Constructs: Attitude toward behavior, perceived behavioral control.)

NHES 2 | Analyze Influences

Students will analyze the influence of family, peers, culture, media, technology, and other factors on health behaviors.

ASSESSMENT CRITERIA
- Identify both external and internal influences on health.
- Explain how external and internal influences interact to impact health choices and behaviors.
- Explain both positive and negative influences, as appropriate.

Grades K–2

Bear Feels Sick: Getting Well in My Family   Students can identify and discuss things their families do when someone is sick. What practices or traditions do families have? For example, do family members eat or drink certain things when they have a cold (chicken soup)? Do family members lie down in a certain place when they are sick, such as on the sofa? Children can talk about how their families influence the health practices of family members. Teachers can read the book *Bear Gets Sick* by Karma Wilson and Jane Chapman (see the book list at the end of the chapter) to begin the discussion about how family members and friends take care of each other when someone gets sick.

ASSESSMENT | For an assessment task, students can write and draw about what their families do when someone doesn't feel well. For assessment criteria, students should identify at least one family practice they like when someone is sick (that person gets to lie on the sofa during the daytime). (Construct: Subjective norms.)

Sun Safety and Friends   Students can interview friends to find out what they do to stay safe in the sun and to avoid sunburn and skin damage. Students can report their findings to the class and answer the question "What do my friends do to stay safe in the sun?" Students can then make recommendations for sun safety that they want to share with friends who aren't being safe in the sun.

ASSESSMENT | For an assessment task, students can compare and contrast their own sun safety behaviors with those of their friends. For assessment criteria, students should identify how they and their friends influence each other. In a link to NHES 8, advocacy, students should explain how they can be a positive influence on their friends for sun safety. (Construct: Subjective norms.)

Grades 3–5

Personal Health Influences   Have students select one of the first five Healthy Behavior Outcomes (dental health, hygiene, rest/sleep, vision/hearing, or sun). Give students the task of observing family members related to the Healthy Behavior Outcome selected—the season of the year may impact which are easier to observe in practice. For example, if a student selects HBO 3, they are to observe (through watching or discussing) various family members' rest and sleep patterns—how many hours of sleep do they get a night, do they nap, their bedtime routine, and the like. Students can compare what they observe to their own health behaviors. Students should then research what recommendations credible sources suggest for their chosen behavior.

ASSESSMENT | For an assessment task, students can write a short story or a report that includes the following information: the health behavior observed and the specific health practices of the individuals (e.g., I observed my brother wear ear protection when mowing the lawn), how their family members impact their personal health by the choices made, how their family members' practices influence the student's own practices, and health practices they might want to maintain or start in order to protect their health based on what was learned from their research or from classmate observations. For assessment criteria, students should provide specific ways their family practices influence (either positively or negatively) their health practices, include accurate information, and suggest specific ways they will maintain or improve their personal health practice related to the chosen healthy behavior outcome. (Constructs: Attitudes toward behavior, perceived behavioral control, subjective norms.)

Personal Health Products in the Media Students can work in small groups to make posters or collages of all the personal health products and claims they can find in advertisements and on packaging. If they like, students can divide their posters into two sides—products and claims that are probably true and those that are probably not true. Students can show their posters to the class and discuss the claims they found that they think are exaggerated or untrue. Display the posters on a bulletin board or in the school hallways.

ASSESSMENT | Students can use the list of advertising strategies in Chapter 3 to identify techniques manufacturers and advertisers use to try to get people to purchase products. For assessment criteria, students should name at least two ways they can refute advertising claims. (Construct: Subjective norms.)

Grades 6–8

Investigating Family History for Health Middle school students might be interested in investigating the importance of family history and health. CDC states that family members share their genes, as well as their environment, lifestyles, and habits. Everyone can recognize traits that run in their family, such as curly hair, dimples, leanness, or athletic ability. Risks for diseases such as asthma, diabetes, cancer, and heart disease also run in families. Students can talk with their families about their own health history and investigate topics of most relevance.

ASSESSMENT | For an assessment task, students can investigate and report to class members on issues of most importance in their own families. For an assessment task, students should provide accurate information, make connections between family history and health, and verify the accuracy of their information resources. (Construct: Subjective norms.)

A Critical Take on Advertising Students can explore the influence of advertising in media by looking critically at how advertisements are constructed and disseminated. Using TV411's Tune in to Learning (www.tv411 .org/reading/understanding-what-you-read/truth-advertising), students will learn about and identify techniques used in advertising.

ASSESSMENT | The Duke University Libraries digital repository (https://repository.duke.edu/dc/adaccess?f%5Bactive_fedora_model _ssi%5D%5B%5D=Item) gives students access to over 7,000 advertisements from 1911 to 1955. Using the digital repository, students can choose a health product advertisement and rewrite the ad for today's audience

that will be delivered electronically (as a website ad or a post to social media). Students can use enticing photographs or videos and sell their products by using the advertising techniques in Chapter 3. Advertisements can be presented to the class. Students can evaluate each advertisement and identify the advertising techniques used. (Construct: Perceived behavioral control.)

NHES 3 | Access Information, Products, and Services

Students will demonstrate the ability to access valid information and products and services to enhance health.

ASSESSMENT CRITERIA
- Access health information—Locate specific sources of health information, products, or services relevant to enhancing health in a given situation.
- Evaluate information sources—Explain the degree to which identified sources are valid, reliable, and appropriate as a result of evaluating each source.

Grades K–2

Ask a School or Community Health Helper Children can create a Know-Wonder-Learn chart about personal health topics of interest to them. Children can invite (write a letter) to various school and community health helpers who can answer their questions.

ASSESSMENT | Students can write and draw about what they learned for an assessment task. For assessment criteria, students should explain where they got their information and why the information source is one they can trust. (Construct: Attitudes toward behavior.)

Is That Sound Safe? Introduce safe decibel levels using the National Institute on Deafness and Other Communication disorders (NIH) (www. noisyplanet.nidcd.nih.gov/kids-preteens/listen-up-infographic). Use the noise meter to demonstrate how different sounds reach different decibel levels that are considered safe or unsafe. Students will learn that safe sounds range from 0 to 70 decibels (like whispering or conversations), while those in the 80 decibel and higher range can cause permanent hearing loss, depending on the time exposed to the sound.

ASSESSMENT | Students can take a scavenger hunt around the school and playground to identify things that make sound. Using tablets, group students so that each group is using a different noise meter app to determine the safety levels of the sounds found and note the noise meter results. One group should make a video recording of the noise. After completing the scavenger hunt, students will compare the apps used and the sounds recorded to analyze the effectiveness and validity of each app. For assessment criteria, students should determine which app they felt was most effective and explain why this source is one they can trust. (Construct: Attitudes toward behavior.)

Android/iOS
- *Too Noisy* (toonoisyapp.com)
- *ClassDojo Noise Meter* (classdojo.com)
- *Quiet Classroom* (play.google.com/store/apps/details?id=com .eduapp.quietclass&hl=en) (itunes.apple.com/us/app/quiet-classroom /id825582891?mt=8)

Android
- *Sound Meter* (https://play.google.com/store/apps/details?id=com .gamebasic.decibel)
- *Decibel X-Sound Meter dBA, Noise Detector* (https://play.google.com /store/apps/details?id=com.skypaw.decibel&hl=en)

iOS
- *NIOSH Sound Level Meter* (https://itunes.apple.com/us/app/niosh-slm/id1096545820?mt=8)
- *Decibel X: dB, dBA Noise Meter* (https://itunes.apple.com/us/app/decibel-x-db-dba-noise-meter/id448155923?mt=8)

Internet Browser
- *Bouncy Balls* (https://bouncyballs.org)
- *Zero Noise Classroom* (https://chrome.google.com/webstore/detail/zero-noise-classroom/pgpkohbgbjmihckldcacljomfkkaogjd?hl=en)

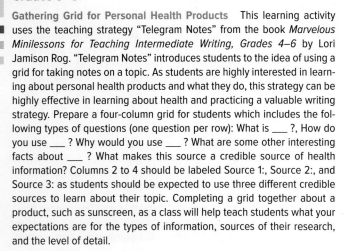

Grades 3–5

Gathering Grid for Personal Health Products   This learning activity uses the teaching strategy "Telegram Notes" from the book *Marvelous Minilessons for Teaching Intermediate Writing, Grades 4–6* by Lori Jamison Rog. "Telegram Notes" introduces students to the idea of using a grid for taking notes on a topic. As students are highly interested in learning about personal health products and what they do, this strategy can be highly effective in learning about health and practicing a valuable writing strategy. Prepare a four-column grid for students which includes the following types of questions (one question per row): What is ___ ?, How do you use ___ ? Why would you use ___ ? What are some other interesting facts about ___ ? What makes this source a credible source of health information? Columns 2 to 4 should be labeled Source 1:, Source 2:, and Source 3: as students should be expected to use three different credible sources to learn about their topic. Completing a grid together about a product, such as sunscreen, as a class will help teach students what your expectations are for the types of information, sources of their research, and the level of detail.

ASSESSMENT   The independent (or pair) completion of a grid for a personal health topic of their own choosing becomes the assessment task. For assessment criteria, students should include accurate information, responses from multiple sources, and be able to explain why the selected sources are credible sources of health information. (Constructs: Attitudes toward behavior, perceived behavioral control.)

What? Why? and How Do You Know?   Students have lots of hygiene and health questions at this age. This strategy allows them the opportunity to explore a personal interest topic using credible sources. Create a chart with three columns labeled: What? Why? How Do You Know? Determine how many reasons you expect students to provide as this will determine the number of rows needed. Have students brainstorm hygiene- and health-related questions they have, such as, "Should you squeeze/pop a pimple?" Complete one example as a class to model for students how to complete the chart and your expectations.

ASSESSMENT   Completing a "What? Why? How Do You Know? chart independently (or with a partner) is the assessment task. Students can then share their learnings in small groups or as a class so that others benefit from the research conducted. Assessment criteria include accurate information, use of credible sources, and the ability to make connections between health behaviors and health. (Constructs: Attitudes toward behavior, perceived behavioral control.)

Grades 6–8

Personal Health Products—To Use or Not To Use?   Middle school students are highly interested in hygiene products. Allow students to select a specific hygiene product commonly used by their peers (e.g., deodorant, soap, shampoo, body wash, pimple cream, toothpaste, etc.). Have students research the selected product using a minimum of three credible sources (in addition to the product website). Have students use their research to determine what the product is meant to do and what the product actually does (often this is not what is claimed). Additionally, have students determine if there are natural products that could be used as alternatives to sometimes expensive and highly advertised products. If no natural products exist, have the student compare two different forms of the health product.

ASSESSMENT   For an assessment task, students can prepare a small poster with a picture of their product and natural alternative (if one exists), key points about the benefit(s) and/or purposes of the product, and a determination of whether they would use or not use either of the products and why. For assessment criteria, students should gather their information from credible sources, provide accurate information, and make a determination of whether to use either product based on their research. (Constructs: Attitudes toward behavior, perceived behavioral control.)

Who You Gonna Call? Health Resource Guide for Kids and Families   Students can make a health resource guide to their community for classmates and families. Students should decide on the topics they want to include and work in small groups to investigate. Students can decide on a format for their guide and the information each group should collect. Teachers can make copies of the completed guide for students and families—and for other classes, if appropriate.

ASSESSMENT   The health resource guide the class produces is the assessment task for this activity. Students can set criteria for information gathering. Teachers can use these criteria to assess and help students assess their work. (Construct: Perceived behavioral control.)

Personal Health Newsletters   Teachers can have students design and create a personal health newsletter for students and families. Students can decide on the format and a list of topics for each month, with small groups assigned a particular month to produce the newsletter. Students must do their own research and artwork. Teachers can make copies for classmates and families.

ASSESSMENT   The newsletters are the assessment task for this activity. For assessment criteria, students can set the specifications for the appearance and level of information that should appear in the newsletter. Teachers can use these specifications to assess and help students assess their work. (Construct: Attitudes toward behavior.)

NHES 4 | Interpersonal Communication

Students will demonstrate the ability to use interpersonal communication skills to enhance health and avoid or reduce health risks.

ASSESSMENT CRITERIA
- Use appropriate verbal/nonverbal communication strategies in an effective manner to enhance health or avoid/reduce health risks.
- Use appropriate skills (negotiation skills, refusal skills) and behaviors (eye contact, body language, attentive listening).

Grades K–2

Shhhh, That's Too Loud   Teachers can work with students to brainstorm situations in which noise has made it difficult to hear someone talk or hurts their ears. A word web can be created for different locations, such as home, school, or the car. With the location in the center of the web, the class can web different types of noise that can be too loud in each location, such as brothers/sisters yelling in the car or big brother/sister playing music too loud in the car. The next layer of the web can focus on how to make a request to reduce the noise. Students can practice using these different strategies in various situations through role-plays with two other classmates. Students can share their role-plays with the class and the class can discuss which approaches were especially effective and why.

ASSESSMENT | Students can create a door sign for their bedroom using one of the messages used during the role-plays. Students can either draw a picture or use pictures, depending on their skills. Taking the door sign home will create an opportunity for students to share with others in their family what they have learned about noise. For assessment criteria, students should demonstrate a clear message (either verbally or nonverbally) in order to request noise to be reduced. (Construct: Perceived behavioral control.)

Grades 3–5

No, Thanks, I'm Allergic   As students become more independent they will find themselves able to make decisions about foods being offered by friends, parents of friends, relatives, teachers, or others. Children often find it difficult to refuse offers of adults, even when their health is at risk. Learning to refuse foods that may cause them to have an allergic reaction could be life saving. Practicing these sorts of refusals can add to the empathy other students have for those with allergies. If appropriate, students in the class with food allergies can share situations in which they have been offered a food they are allergic to otherwise the teacher can generate scenarios. Pairs of students can brainstorm different ways to respond to the scenario. Student responses can then be shared aloud and discussed as a class.

ASSESSMENT | Students can create a short story about a child being offered food he/she is allergic to and using appropriate communication skills to refuse respectfully. For assessment criteria, students should use appropriate verbal communication strategies to avoid food that cause allergic reactions. Students should also provide accurate information and make connections between behaviors and health (NHES 1). (Constructs: Perceived behavioral control, attitudes toward behavior.)

Medical Alert Jewelry   Teachers can ask a health care provider to visit the class, show children various kinds of medical alert jewelry, and explain how it can help when the person who wears it is ill. If a class member or staff member in the school wears medical alert jewelry, that person might be willing to share with class members. Children can talk about how the message on the jewelry can be used to communicate with health care providers when the wearer cannot communicate his or her needs.

ASSESSMENT | Students can create a drawing or short story about a situation in which health care providers are able to help someone because of medical alert jewelry. For assessment criteria, students should explain how such jewelry can be used to communicate.

Grades 6–8

Talking with Parents About Health and Hygiene   To get students talking with parents, classmates, and other adults about health and hygiene, students can research and design a questionnaire for other students, teachers, and parents or caregivers about the topic(s) determined by the class. Each student should interview an agreed-on number of students and adults and bring their findings back to class for collation and discussion. Teachers can ask students if their questionnaires led to any further discussions in their families and what they discussed. Students can identify the three leading misperceptions they found during their survey. Make copies of the students' final results for them to take home to their families.

ASSESSMENT | The students' final report on their findings is the assessment task for this activity. For assessment criteria, students should write a paragraph about how it felt to talk with their parents or caregivers about

health and hygiene and advice they have for other kids on talking with adults about the topic. (Construct: Subjective norms.)

NHES 5 | Decision Making

Students will demonstrate the ability to use decision-making skills to enhance health.

ASSESSMENT CRITERIA

Reach a health-enhancing decision using a process consisting of the following steps:

*   Identify a health-risk situation.
*   Examine alternatives.
*   Evaluate positive and negative consequences.
*   Decide on a health-enhancing course of action.

Grades K–2

Being a Friend   Sometimes people hesitate to be around someone with a chronic illness (diabetes, epilepsy, HIV) because they don't understand the condition. Chronic diseases are not contagious—people won't catch the illness from being around another person. Students can discuss ways they can be kind to a student or adult who has a chronic condition and list steps to making a decision to be a good friend.

ASSESSMENT | Identifying the steps to being a good friend is the assessment task for this activity. For younger children, teachers can use a simple model that includes stating a problem, identifying alternatives, naming positive and negative consequences of each alternative, choosing an action, and evaluating the action. For assessment criteria, students should be able to discuss each step in the decision process and how they could carry it out, as their teacher names the steps. (Construct: Perceived behavioral control.)

Grades 3–5

Choose a Path   Students can demonstrate the decision-making process about handling a situation of peer influence. As children are forming their own identities, they may be influenced by their peers to participate in negative behaviors. Provide students with several scenarios in which they could be influenced by their peers. Students can choose a scenario and create an infographic of the paths to making a decision about whether or not to participate in the activity and how to resist peer pressure.

ASSESSMENT | Students can use a graphic organizer app (such as *Inspiration* (http://www.inspiration.com)) to create a flowchart that outlines the decision-making process in Chapter 3. The graphic organizer should show potential outcomes with each decision made throughout the scenario leading to either a positive or negative outcome. (Constructs: Intention to act in healthy ways, attitude toward behavior.)

Grades 6–8

Decision Trees for Personal Health   Students in the middle-level grades are beginning to make personal health decisions for themselves. Students can identify a personal health issue of interest and make a decision tree about various alternatives, positive and negative consequences, and the decision that's best. Examples include what kind of drink to have after a soccer game (water, soda, juice, a nutrition drink), how to prepare for a big exam (go to bed on time, stay up late the night before to study, start studying several days ahead of the test), and what kind of deodorant to purchase (the expensive one with a designer name, the generic product at the drug store, the one that has the most impressive claims). Students can share their decision trees with the class. An important aspect of this activity is helping students realize that they often have more than two alternatives and should consider as many positive and negative consequences as possible.

ASSESSMENT | The students' decision trees are the assessment task for this activity. For assessment criteria, students should write a paragraph about three ways the decision tree helped them see their decisions in new ways. (Construct: Subjective norms.)

NHES 6 | Goal Setting

Students will demonstrate the ability to use goal-setting skills to enhance health.

ASSESSMENT CRITERIA

- Goal statement—Give goal statement that identifies health benefits; goal is achievable and will result in enhanced health.
- Goal-setting plan—Show plan that is complete, logical, and sequential, and includes a process to assess progress.

Grades K–2

Preventing Colds and Flu at School and at Home   Students can invite the school nurse or another health care provider to the classroom to talk about preventing colds and flu. Children can make a list of things they can do at school and at home to prevent colds and flu. Children can set a class goal of doing at least two of those things consistently (washing hands, not rubbing eyes) for a given period of time during cold and flu season.

ASSESSMENT | The students' goal for two practices to prevent colds and flu is the assessment task for this activity. For assessment criteria, children should list people, practices, and situations that will help them reach their goal (reminding each other to wash hands and cover sneezes) and those that might keep them from reaching their goal (being in too much of a hurry to wash hands). (Construct: Intention to act in healthy ways.)

Grades 3–5

Improving My Health   Once students have learned self-management skills related to personal health, they are ready to make a commitment to improve a personal health practice. Teachers can create a short self-assessment so students can rate their personal health practices. Personal health practices to consider include: brushing and flossing teeth daily, washing hands regularly, handling and storing food safely, getting adequate rest and sleep, wearing sun protection, and avoiding or minimizing exposure to loud sounds. Once students have completed the self-assessment, they can select one personal health practice to improve. Students can then set personal and/or class goals for improving a specific personal health practice for a certain period of time, such as two weeks. Students can report back to the class on their progress and conclusions about supports for and barriers to achieving their goal.

ASSESSMENT | For an assessment task, students can keep record of their personal health practice for the time period selected. They can record what they did, how they felt, and what helped or hindered their progress. For assessment criteria, students should identify at least two important supports for and barriers to achieving their goal and specify how improving this behavior can help keep them healthy. (Constructs: Perceived behavioral control, attitude toward behavior, intention to act in healthy ways.)

Grades 6–8

Identifying Supports and Barriers   Recognizing and managing supports for and barriers to achieving personal health goals is an important aspect of successful goal setting. Students can select a personal health goal of interest to them (being physically active for thirty minutes each day) and identify the supports they have in place to meet their goal. Students then can list ways they will use these supports to meet their goals. Examples of supports might be family members and friends who like to work out and living in a neighborhood conducive to regular physical activity. Next, students can identify potential barriers to meeting their goals and ways to manage them. Examples of barriers might be friends who don't want to be physically active and a neighborhood that doesn't have places for students to participate in physical activity.

ASSESSMENT | For an assessment task, students can explain or write a summary of their assessment of supports and barriers. For assessment criteria, students should name at least two potential supports and barriers and how they will use or manage them for reaching their goals. (Construct: Subjective norms.)

NHES 7 | Self-Management

Students will demonstrate the ability to practice health-enhancing behaviors and avoid or reduce health risks.

ASSESSMENT CRITERIA

- Application (transfer)—Initiate health-enhancing behaviors; apply concepts and skills appropriate and effectively.
- Self-monitoring and reflection—Monitor actions and make adjustments; accept feedback and make adjustments; able to self-assess, reflect on, and take responsibility for actions.

Grades K–2

Washing Hands   The importance of hand washing for people of all ages is key in preventing disease transmission. Teachers can provide a memorable experience for children as they practice their hand-washing skills. Children can rub a light coating of cooking oil or petroleum jelly on their hands. Next, teachers can sprinkle glitter lightly on the children's hands, using several different colors and sprinkling only one color on each child. Then, students can circulate to talk with others in the classroom, shaking hands as they do. Call the students back to their seats or to the circle after several minutes. Ask if they have glitter from other hands on their hands. Explain that, even though we can't see germs, they can rub off from one hand to another and from surfaces onto our hands. Next, children can conduct a hand-washing experiment. Some children can try washing off the oil and glitter using cold water only, while another group tries with warm water. Finally, another group tries with soap and water. Which worked best? All children can demonstrate their hand-washing skills with soap and water. Teachers can use children's books to extend this lesson, such as *Germs Make Me Sick,* by Melvin Berger, and *I Know How We Fight Germs,* by Kate Rowan.

ASSESSMENT | Students can write and draw in their journals or make pictures for a class bulletin board about hand washing. Students also can make posters about hand washing for school restrooms. For assessment criteria, students should name all the important steps learned in class for getting hands clean. (Construct: Perceived behavioral control.)

Going to the Dentist with Children's Literature   Teachers will find an extensive list of books at the end of this chapter that deal with children's health issues; for this activity, suggested books appear under "Dental Health." Teachers can ask students to discuss their experiences of going to the dentist to reassure students who might be anxious about dental visits. Students can write a class story about going to the dentist to help other children learn what to expect.

ASSESSMENT | The students' class book is the assessment task for this activity. For assessment criteria, students should provide accurate information about what happens at the dentist's office and how to take care of their own teeth at home. (Construct: Perceived behavioral control.)

Sick Simon   Teachers can read *Sick Simon* by Dan Krall to begin a discussion about getting sick and getting well. Additional books appear under "Getting Sick and Getting Well" at the end of the chapter. Students can identify Simon's symptoms, contagious behaviors, and precautions that he should have taken when he was not feeling well.

ASSESSMENT | Students can create their own public service announcement. Students should create a storyboard and script, then record either a video or podcast to share tips and practices for staying and getting well. For an assessment task, student recordings should have at least ten self-management strategies for staying and getting well. (Constructs: Attitude toward behavior, subjective norms.)

Grades 3–5

Preventing Droplet Spread: Stopping Germs at Home and School   The CDC states that the main way that colds and flu are spread is from person to person in respiratory droplets of coughs and sneezes, called droplet spread. This spread can happen when droplets from a cough or sneeze of an infected person move through the air and are deposited on the mouth or nose of people nearby. Sometimes germs also can be spread when a person touches respiratory droplets from another person on a surface such as a desk and then touches his or her own eyes, mouth, or nose before washing their hands. Some viruses and bacteria can live two hours or longer on surfaces such as cafeteria tables, doorknobs, and desks. To stop the spread of germs, students should remember to:

- Cover mouth and nose.
- Clean hands often.
- Remind others to practice healthy habits.

Students and teachers can learn more about self-management strategies at www.cdc.gov/flu/protect/stopgerms.htm.

ASSESSMENT | For an assessment task, students can design and illustrate posters or four-panel cartoons to help others learn to take steps to stop droplet spread. These can be placed around the school to help promote disease prevention during cold and flu season. For assessment criteria, students should provide accurate and specific steps for preventing droplet spread. (Construct: Intention to act in healthy ways.)

Slip! Slop! Slap! Wrap! for Sun Safety   Students can investigate How Can I Protect My Children from the Sun (www.cdc.gov/cancer/skin/basic _info/children.htm). Children can work in small groups to create a skit about going out in the sun for an activity of their choosing, demonstrating all the ways they can protect themselves from overexposure. Students can demonstrate their skits for classmates.

ASSESSMENT | The students' skits are the assessment task for this activity. For assessment criteria, students should correctly demonstrate at least three steps to protect themselves from sun exposure. (Construct: Perceived behavioral control.)

Achoo! Cold, Flu, or Allergies?   Students can work in groups to investigate colds, flu, and allergies and how to tell the difference. Students should explain self-management strategies for avoiding colds, flu, and allergies and tell what they should do to get better if they are ill. Students can find help at KidsHealth (www.kidshealth.org) "Illnesses and Injuries." They also can explore the website of the National Institute of Allergy and Infectious Diseases (www.niaid.nif.gov).

ASSESSMENT | For an assessment task, students can make a brochure or pamphlet for classmates and families about preventing and managing colds, flu, and allergies. For assessment criteria, students should provide health-enhancing self-management strategies. (Construct: Perceived behavioral control.)

Grades 6–8

Goldilocks Got the Flu and Other Fairy Tales   Remind students of various fables and fairy tales they have been familiar with from childhood. Invite students to use the information they have learned from their personal health and wellness unit by rewriting one of the favorite fables or fairy tales. Students should be able to explain the importance of being responsible about personal health and wellness-related behaviors, analyze the health-related behaviors of their main character, and suggest behaviors for improving the health of the main character.

ASSESSMENT | The story students write is the assessment task. For assessment criteria, students should explain the importance of being responsible about personal health and wellness-related behaviors, analyze the health-related behaviors of their main character, and suggest behaviors for improving the health of the main character. Additionally, accurate information and connections between behaviors and health should be expected. (Constructs: Perceived behavioral control, attitudes toward behavior.)

Why Don't We Do It in Our Sleeves?   Middle school students really will enjoy the five-minute video entitled, "Why Don't We Do It in Our Sleeves?" Available on the web from OtoRhinoLounsburgology Productions at www.coughsafe.com, the video states that its goal is to make coughing and sneezing into one's sleeve or other fabric "fashionable." The video features several individuals' coughing and sneezing behavior, which is evaluated by a panel of "international judges." The humor makes the video very memorable.

ASSESSMENT | After viewing the video, students can create their own skits or videos to illustrate these ideas for other students in their schools. For assessment criteria, students should show specific steps to take to prevent the spread of germs. (Construct: Attitudes toward behavior.)

Being a Friend: Asthma, Epilepsy, Diabetes   Teachers can help children learn the concept of a chronic health condition—one that is recurring but not contagious to others. Examples of chronic conditions are asthma, epilepsy, and diabetes. Students can investigate websites and talk to medical personnel to learn what people with various conditions need to do for themselves and what students need to do as supportive friends. If a student in the class has a chronic health condition, teachers can provide the opportunity (with the student's and parents' or caregivers' permission) for that child to talk openly with other students about managing the condition and what students can do to be supportive. Students can check out these websites:

American Diabetes Association (www.diabetes.org)

American Lung Association (www.lungusa.org)

Epilepsy Foundation (www.epilepsyfoundation.org)

National Diabetes Education Program (http://ndep.nih.gov)

ASSESSMENT | For an assessment task, students can write a short story about being a friend to someone who has a chronic health condition. For assessment criteria, students should include at least three ways they can act supportively to help a friend manage his or her condition. (Construct: Attitudes toward behavior.)

NHES 8 | Advocacy

Students will demonstrate the ability to advocate for personal, family, and community health.

ASSESSMENT CRITERIA
- Health-enhancing position—Give clear, health-enhancing position.
- Support for position—Support position with facts, concepts, examples, and evidence.
- Audience awareness—Show awareness of target audience; choose words, tone, and examples to suit audience.
- Conviction—Display conviction for position.

Grades K–2

Get Moving for Good Health   Students can brainstorm ways they, their classmates, their families, and their teachers can be more physically active at school and at home. Being physically active on a regular basis is tremendously important in preventing chronic disease. Students can make posters to display their ideas around school and make a class bulletin board of drawings to encourage physical activity.

ASSESSMENT | The students' posters and drawings are the assessment tasks for this activity. For assessment criteria, students should show a clear, health-enhancing message that is targeted to classmates, teachers, and families. (Construct: Subjective norms.)

Grades 3–5

Open Airways for Schools   Students can investigate the American Lung Association's Open Airways for Schools project (www.lungusa.org/lung -disease/asthma/in-schools/open-airways/open-airways-for-schools-1.html) and design an advocacy campaign to make their school asthma-friendly.

ASSESSMENT | The students' campaign is the assessment task for this activity. For assessment criteria, students should show a clear, health-enhancing message; back it up with facts; target their audience (other students, administrators, teachers); and demonstrate conviction about what they believe. (Construct: Subjective norms.)

Grades 6–8

Advocacy Ideas from Voluntary Health Organizations   Students can begin with websites to investigate the advocacy activities of various national and local voluntary health organizations. For example, the American Cancer Society sponsors the Great American Smokeout each November, and the American Diabetes Association sponsors the Walk for Diabetes. Students can select one of the advocacy activities or one of their own to organize for their school.

ASSESSMENT | The advocacy campaign the students design and carry out is the assessment task for this activity. For assessment criteria, students should show a clear, health-enhancing message, back it up with data and reasons, target their audience, and show conviction in their message. (Construct: Subjective norms.)

EVALUATED CURRICULA AND INSTRUCTIONAL MATERIALS

The Centers for Disease Control and Prevention provides Registries of Programs Effective in Reducing Youth Risk Behaviors at www.cdc.gov/healthyyouth/adolescenthealth/registries.htm. Various federal agencies have identified youth-related programs that they consider worthy of recommendation on the basis of expert opinion or a review of design and research evidence. These programs focus on different health topics, risk behaviors, and settings. Some, but not all, of these programs have shown evidence in reducing youth risk behaviors. Each agency has its own process and criteria for determining the programs that are worthy of recommendation. Users are encouraged to review each website to understand the inclusion criteria the registry used.

Registries related to mental and emotional health include:

- Child Trends LINKS (Lifecourse Interventions to Nurture Kids Successfully) Database (www.childtrends.org/ what-works/)
- National Registry of Evidence-based Programs and Practices (NREPP) (www.samhsa.gov/nrepp)
- Office of Juvenile Justice and Delinquency Prevention Model Programs Guide (www.ojjdp.gov/mpg)
- What Works Clearinghouse (http://ies.ed.gov/ncee/wwc)

INTERNET AND OTHER RESOURCES

WEBSITES

American Academy of Allergies, Asthma, and Immunology
   www.aaaai.org/home.aspx

American Academy of Pediatrics (Immunizations)
   https://www.healthychildren.org/English/safety-prevention/immunizations/Pages/default.aspx

American Cancer Society (Be Safe in the Sun)
   www.cancer.org/healthy/be-safe-in-sun.html

American Dental Association (Mouth Healthy)
   www.ada.org/en/public-programs/mouthhealthy/

American Diabetes Association
   www.diabetes.org

American Lung Association (Healthy Air at School)
   www.lung.org/our-initiatives/healthy-air/indoor/in-schools

Asthma and Allergy Foundation of American
   www.aafa.org

BAM! (Body and Mind) Teacher
   www.bam.gov/teachers/index.htm

Center for Health and Health Care in Schools
   www.healthinschools.org

Children's Defense Fund
   www.childrensdefense.org

Epilepsy Foundation
   www.epilepsy.com/

Healthy Youth (Adolescent and School Health, CDC)
www.cdc.gov/HealthyYouth

KidsHealth
kidshealth.org

Learning to Give Project
www.learningtogive.org

**National Center for Chronic Disease Prevention
and Health Promotion, CDC**
www.cdc.gov/chronicdisease/index.htm

National Heart, Lung, and Blood Institute
www.nhlbi.nih.gov/

National Institute of Allergy and Infectious Diseases
www.niaid.nih.gov

National Pediculosis Association
www.headlice.org/kids

National Sleep Foundation
sleepfoundation.org

The Scrub Club
www.scrubclub.org/home.aspx

Youth Learn
www.youthlearn.org

CHILDREN'S LITERATURE

AGES 5–8

BATHS AND BATHING

Boyd, Colin. *The Bath Monster*. Andersen Press USA, 2016.

Garton, Sam. *Otter: Oh No, Bath Time!* Balzer + Bray, an imprint of HarperCollins Publishers, 2016.

Mack, Jeff. *Who Needs a Bath?* Harper, an imprint of HarperCollins Publishers, 2015.

McAnulty, Stacy. *101 Reasons Why I'm Not Taking a Bath*. Random House, 2016.

Timberlake, Amy. *The Dirty Cowboy*. Farrar, Straus & Giroux, 2003.

Tucker, K. *Do Pirates Take Baths?* Albert Whitman, 1997.

Van Laan, Nancy. *Scrubba Dub*. Atheneum Books for Young Readers, 2003.

Willems, Mo. *The Pigeon Needs a Bath!* Hyperion Books for Children, an imprint of Disney Book Group, 2014.

Zion, Gene. *Harry the Dirty Dog*. HarperCollins, 1984.

DENTAL HEALTH

Brown, Marc. *Arthur's Tooth*. Little, Brown, 1985.

Dinmont, Kerry. *Pearl's New Tooth: A Book About Caring for Your Teeth*. The Child's World, 2018.

Jenkins, Pete. *Teeth (Ready Readers: I See, I Saw)*. Rourke Educational Media, 2018.

Keller, Laurie. *Open Wide!: Tooth School Inside*. H. Holt, 2003.

Laminack, Lester. *Trevor's Wiggly-Wobbly Tooth*. Peachtree, 1998.

Mayer, Mercer. *Just Going to the Dentist*. Western, 1990.

Miller, Edward. *The Tooth Book: A Guide to Healthy Teeth and Gums*. Holiday House, 2008.

Munsch, Robert. *Andrew's Loose Tooth*. Scholastic, 1998.

O'Connor, Jane. *Fancy Nancy and the Too-Loose Tooth*. Turtleback, 2012.

Palatini, Margie. *Sweet Tooth*. Simon & Schuster Books for Young Readers, 2004.

Simms, Laura. *Rotten Teeth*. Houghton Mifflin, 1998.

Troupe, Thomas Kingsley. *Kitanai and Cavity Croc Brush Their Teeth*. Picture Window Books, a Capstone imprint, 2015.

Vrombaut, An. *Clarabella's Teeth*. Clarion Books, 2003.

Willems, Mo. *I Lost My Tooth!* Disney-Hyperion, 2018.

Wilson, Karma. *Bear's Loose Tooth*. Margaret K. Elderberry Books, 2011.

Wright, Maureen. *Anna and the Tooth Fairy*. Two Lions, 2017.

Ziefert, Harriet. *ABC Dentist: Healthy Teeth from A to Z*. Blue Apple Books, 2008.

GETTING SICK AND GETTING WELL

Berger, Melvin. *Germs Make Me Sick*. HarperCollins, 1985.

Cline-Ransome, Lesa. *Germs: Fact and Fiction, Friends and Foes*. Henry Holt and Company, 2017.

Cyrus Kurt. *Be a Good Dragon*. Sleeping Bear Press, 2018.

Dealey, E. *Goldie Locks Has Chicken Pox*. Atheneum Books for Young Readers, 2002.

Erlich, Fred. *You Can't Take Your Body to a Car Mechanic: A Book About What Makes You Sick*. Blue Apple Books, 2014.

Krall, Dan. *Sick Simon*. Simon & Schuster Books for Young Readers, 2015.

Mathies, J. *Peter, the Knight with Asthma*. Albert Whitman, 2009.

McPhail, David. *Sick Day*. Holiday House, 2012.

Redmond, E.S. *Felicity Floo Visits the Zoo*. Candlewick Press, 2009.

Shannon, David. *A Bad Case of Stripes*. Blue Sky Press, 1998.

Stead, P. *A Sick Day for Amos McGee*. Roaring Books, 2010.

Wilson, Karma, and Jane Chapman. *Bear Feels Sick*. Margaret K. McElderry Books, 2007.

Yolen, Jane. *How Do Dinosaurs Get Well Soon?* Blue Sky, 2003.

SLEEP

Escoffier, Michael. *Sleep Tight, Charlie*. Princeton Architectural Press, 2017.

Fleming, Candace. *Go Sleep in Your Own Bed!* Schwartz & Wade Books, 2017.

Gay, Marie Louise. *Good Night, Sam*. Groundwood Books, 2003.

Krosoczka, Jarrett J. *Good Night, Monkey Boy*. Knopf Books for Young Readers, 2001.

McGee, Marni. *Bear Can't Sleep!* Tiger Tales, 2015.

Tarpley, Todd. *Beep! Beep! Go to Sleep!* Little, Brown and Company, 2015.

Wheeler, Lisa. *Even Monsters Need to Sleep*. Balzer + Bray, an imprint of HarperCollins Publishers, 2017.

Wood, Audrey. *The Full Moon at the Napping House*. Houghton Mifflin Harcourt, 2015.

Yolen, Jane, and Mark Teague. *How Do Dinosaurs Say Good Night?* Blue Sky, 2000.

OTHER PERSONAL HEALTH AND WELLNESS TOPICS

Adamson, Ged. *Douglas, You Need Glasses!* Schwartz & Wade Books, 2016.

Aliki. *My Five Senses*. HarperCollins, 1989.

Arnold, Tedd. *Even More Parts*. Dial Books for Young Readers, 2004.

Arnold, Tedd. *More Parts*. Dial Books for Young Readers, 2001.

Arnold, Tedd. *Parts*. Dial Books for Young Readers, 1997.

Barner, Bob. *Dem Bones*. Chronicle, 1996.

Bernheimer, Kate. *The Girl Who Wouldn't Brush Her Hair*. Schwartz & Wade Books, 2013.

Brown, Marc. *Arthur's Eyes*. Little, Brown, 1979.

Corn, Tori. *Dixie Wants an Allergy*. Sky Pony Press, 2014.

Hobbie, Holly. *Charming Opal*. Little, Brown, 2003.

Klise, Kate. *Stand Straight, Ella Kate-The True Story of a Real Giant*. Dial Books, 2010.

Koster, Gloria. *The Peanut Free Café*. Albert Whitman, 2006.

Kotzwinkle, William. *Walter, the Farting Dog*. Frog, 2001.

London, Jonathan. *The Lion Who Had Asthma*. Albert Whitman, 1992.

Miller, Margaret. *My Five Senses*. Simon & Schuster, 1994.

Parker, Nancy Winslow. *Organs!: How They Work, Fall Apart, and Can Be Replaced (Gasp!)*. Greenwillow Books, 2009.

Pirner, Connie White. *Even Little Kids Get Diabetes*. Albert Whitman, 1991.

Shannon, David. *Bugs In My Hair!* The Blue Sky Press/Scholastic, 2013.

Sorkin, Stephanie. *Nutley, the Nut-Free Squirrel*. Mascot Books, 2013.

Sweeney, Joan. *Me and My Amazing Body*. Crown, 1999.

AGES 9–12

Beevor, Lucy. *Understanding Our Skeleton (Brains, Body, Bones!)*. Capstone, 2017.

Bell, Cece. *El Deafo*. Amulet Books, 2014.

Blume, Judy. *Blubber*. Bradbury, 1974.

Braun, Eric. *Taking Action to Improve People's Health (Who's Changing the World?)*. Lerner Publications, 2017.

Carmichael, L.E. *Innovations in Health (Problem Solved! Your Turn to Think Big)*. Crabtree Publishing Company, 2017.

Cheung, Lilian. *Be Healthy! It's a Girl Thing: Food, Fitness and Feeling Great*. Crown, 2003.

Cottrell Boyce, Frank. *The Astounding Broccoli Boy*. Walden Pond Press, an imprint of HaperCollins Publishers, 2017.

Cronin, Doreen. *Cyclone*. A Caitlyn Dlouhy Book/Atheneum Books for Young Readers, 2017.

Dee, Barbara. *Halfway Normal*. Aladdin, 2017.

Dunham, K. *The Girl's Body Book: Everything You Need to Know for Growing Up YOU*. Applesauce Press, 2008.

Dunham, Kelli. *The Boy's Body Book: Everything You Need to Know for Growing Up YOU*. Applesauce Press, 2011.

Ehrlich, Esther. *Nest*. Wendy Lamb Books, 2014.

Haddix, Margaret Peterson. *Because of Anya*. Simon & Schuster Books for Young Readers, 2002.

Harrington, Karen. *Mayday*. Little, Brown and Company, 2018.

Hawkins, Frank C., and Greta Laube. *The Boy's Body Guide: A Health and Hygiene Book for Boys 8 and Older*. Boys Guide Books, 2007.

Korman, Gordon. *Restart*. Scholastic Inc., 2018.

Kyi, Tanya Lloyd. *50 Body Questions: A Book That Spills Its Guts (50 Questions)*. Annick Press, 2014.

MacLachlan, Patricia. *Edward's Eyes*. Aladdin Paperback, 2007.

Natterson, Cara. *The Care and Keeping of You 2: The Body Book for Older Girls*. American Girl, 2013.

Odhiambo, Eucabeth A. *Auma's Long Run*. Carolrhoda Books, 2017.

Palacio, R.J. *Wonder*. Knopf, 2012.

Rue, Nancy. *The Body Book (The Lily Series)*. Thomas Nelson, 2012.

Schwartz, J. *Short: Walking Tall When You're Not Tall at All*. Flash Point/ Roaring Book Press, 2010.

Stewart, Melissa. *How is My Brain Like a Supercomputer?: And Other Questions About . . . The Human Body*. Sterling, Children's Books, 2014.

Terry, Ellie. *Forget Me Not*. Square Fish, 2018.

Thompson, Lisa. *The Goldfish Boy*. Scholastic Press, 2017.

ENDNOTES

1. A. Davison, *Health Lessons: Book One* (New York: American Book Company, 1910), 5.
2. Children's Defense Fund, *State of America's Children*, (https://www.childrensdefense.org/reports/2017/the-state-of-americas-children-2017-report/3; December 2017).
3. B. Guyer and A. Wigton, "Child Health: An Evaluation of the Last Century," in *About Children: An Authoritative Resource on the State of Childhood Today*, eds. A. G. Cosby et al. (American Academy of Pediatrics, 2005), 102–5.
4. Ibid.
5. Centers for Disease Control and Prevention, *Infant Mortality* (www.cdc.gov/reproductivehealth/maternalinfanthealth/infantmortality.htm)
6. Centers for Disease Control and Prevention, *Recent Declines in Infant Mortality in the United States, 2005–2011*. (https://www.cdc.gov/nchs/data/databriefs/db120.htm#x2013;2011%3C/a%3E%20)
7. Centers for Disease Control and Prevention, *Infant Mortality* (https://www.cdc.gov/reproductivehealth/maternalinfanthealth/infantmortality.htm)
8. Ibid.
9. Centers for Disease Control and Prevention, *Ten Leading Causes of Death and Injury* (https://www.cdc.gov/injury/wisqars/LeadingCauses.html; 2017)
10. Centers for Disease Control and Prevention, *Asthma-related Missed School Days Among Children Aged 5–17 Years* (https://www.cdc.gov/asthma/asthma_stats/missing_days.htm; 2015)
11. B. Guyer and A. Wigton, "Child Health: An Evaluation of the Last Century."
12. Leyenaar, JK., Ralston, S.L., Shieh, M., Pekow, P.S., Mangione-Smith, R.M., and Lindenauer, P.K. 2016. *Epidemiology of pediatric hospitalizations at general hospitals and freestanding children's hospitals in the United States*. Journal of Hospital Medicine. 11(11): 743–749. (https://www.ncbi.nlm.nih.gov/pmc/articles/PMC5467435)
13. B. L. Edelstein, "Tooth Decay: The Best of Times, the Worst of Times," in *About Children: An Authoritative*

Resource on the State of Childhood Today, eds. A. G. Cosby et al. (American Academy of Pediatrics, 2005), 106–9.
14. Ibid.
15. Children's Defense Fund, *State of America's Children*, (https://www.childrensdefense.org/reports/2017/the-state-of-americas-children-2017-report/3; December 2017).
16. Centers for Disease Control and Prevention, Health and Academics (www.cdc.gov/healthyyouth/health_and_academics)
17. C. E. Basch, *Healthier Students Are Better Learners: A Missing Link in School Reforms to Close the Achievement Gap* (New York: Teachers College Press, Columbia University, March 2010).
18. Ibid.
19. Ibid.
20. U.S. Department of Health and Human Services, *Healthy People 2020* (www.healthypeople.gov/2020/default.aspx).
21. Ibid.
22. Annie E. Casey Foundation, 2017 *Kids Count Databook* (http://www.aecf.org/resources/2017-kids-count-data-book).
23. Ibid.
24. Centers for Disease Control and Prevention, *School Health Policies and Practices Study* (https://www.cdc.gov/healthyyouth/data/shpps/index.htm; 2016).
25. Centers for Disease Control and Prevention, 2016. *School Health Policies and Practices Study: Trends Over Time; 2000–2016*. (https://www.cdc.gov/healthyyouth/data/shpps/pdf/2016factsheets/Trends-SHPPS2016.pdf)
26. Centers for Disease Control and Prevention, *Guidelines for School Programs to Prevent Skin Cancer* (https://www.cdc.gov/cancer/skin/what_cdc_is_doing/guidelines.htm).
27. Centers for Disease Control and Prevention, *Helping the Student with Diabetes Succeed: A Guide for School Personnel* (https://www.niddk.nih.gov/health-information/communication-programs/ndep/health-professionals/helping-student-diabetes-succeed-guide-school-personnel)
28. Centers for Disease Control and Prevention, *Strategies for Addressing Asthma Within a Coordinated School Health*

Program (https://www.cdc.gov/healthyschools/asthma/strategies/asthmacsh.htm).
29. Centers for Disease Control and Prevention, *When and How to Wash Your Hands* (https://www.cdc.gov/handwashing/when-how-handwashing.html).
30. Centers for Disease Control and Prevention, *Oral Health: Preventing Cavities, Gum Disease, Tooth Loss, and Oral Cancers at a Glance 2016* (https://www.cdc.gov/chronicdisease/resources/publications/aag/oral-health.htm).
31. Ibid.
32. Ibid.
33. Centers for Disease Control and Prevention, *Working to Improve Oral Health for All Americans: At A Glance 2016* (https://www.cdc.gov/chronicdisease/resources/publications/aag/oral-health.htm).
34. American Dental Association, *Mouth Healthy Kids* (www.mouthhealthykids.org/en).
35. U.S. Department of Health and Human Services, *Your Guide to Healthy Sleep* (https://www.nhlbi.nih.gov/files/docs/public/sleep/healthy_sleep.pdf)
36. Ibid.
37. Centers for Disease Control and Prevention, *Sleep in Middle and High School Students* (https://www.cdc.gov/features/students-sleep).
38. U.S. Department of Health and Human Services, *Your Guide to Healthy Sleep* (https://www.nhlbi.nih.gov/files/docs/public/sleep/healthy_sleep.pdf).
39. Centers for Disease Control and Prevention, *Guidelines for School Programs to Prevent Skin Cancer* (https://www.cdc.gov/cancer/skin/what_cdc_is_doing/guidelines.htm).
40. Ibid.
41. Ibid.
42. Ibid.
43. Ibid.
44. American Public Health Association, *Communicable Disease* (https://www.apha.org/topics-and-issues/communicable-disease).
45. Centers for Disease Control and Prevention, *Vaccines and Immunizations* (https://www.cdc.gov/vaccines/vac-gen/howvpd.htm).

46. Ibid.
47. Centers for Disease Control and Prevention, *State Vaccination Requirements* (https://www.cdc.gov/vaccines/imz-managers/laws/state-reqs.html).
48. Centers for Disease Control and Prevention, *Vaccine Safety: Addressing Common Concerns* (www.cdc.gov/vaccinesafety/Concerns/Index.html).
49. Centers for Disease Control and Prevention, *Common Immunization Questions* (https://www.cdc.gov/vaccines/vac-gen/common-faqs.htm).
50. Centers for Disease Control and Prevention, *Cold Versus Flu* (https://www.cdc.gov/flu/about/qa/coldflu.htm).
51. Centers for Disease Control and Prevention, *How Flu Spreads* (https://www.cdc.gov/flu/about/disease/spread.htm).
52. National Pediculosis Association, *Frequently Asked Questions* (www.headlice.org).
53. Ibid.
54. Ibid.
55. Centers for Disease Control and Prevention, *About HIV/AIDS* (www.cdc.gov/hiv/basics/whatishiv.html).
56. Centers for Disease Control and Prevention, *HIV Among Youth* (www.cdc.gov/hiv/risk/age/youth).
57. Ibid
58. Ibid.

59. Centers for Disease Control and Prevention, *When and How to Wash Your Hands* (https://www.cdc.gov/handwashing/when-how-handwashing.html)
60. Centers for Disease Control and Prevention, *Asthma In Schools* (https://www.cdc.gov/healthyschools/asthma/index.htm).
61. American Lung Association, *Living with Asthma.* (http://www.lung.org/lung-health-and-diseases/lung-disease-lookup/asthma/living-with-asthma/managing-asthma/create-an-asthma-action-plan.html).
62. American Lung Association, *National Asthma Public Policy Agenda* (www.lung.org/lung-disease/asthma/becoming-an-advocate/national-asthmapublic-policy-agenda/schools.html).
63. American Lung Association, *Open Airways for Schools* (https://www.lung.org/lung-health-and-diseases/lung-disease-lookup/asthma/asthma-education-advocacy/open-airways-for-schools/).
64. American College of Asthma, Allergy, and Immunology, *Prevention of Allergies and Asthma in Children* (https://www.aaaai.org/conditions-and-treatments/library/allergy-library/prevention-of-allergies-and-asthma-in-children).
65. KidsHealth from Nemours, *All About Allergies* (http://kidshealth.org/en/parents/allergy.html)

66. Ibid.
67. Ibid.
68. Ibid.
69. Centers for Disease Control and Prevention, *Prevent Type 2 Diabetes in Kids* (https://www.cdc.gov/features/prevent-diabetes-kids/index.html).
70. American Diabetes Association, *Type 1 Diabetes* (http://www.diabetes.org/diabetes-basics/type-1).
71. Centers for Disease Control and Prevention, *Prevent Type 2 Diabetes in Kids* (https://www.cdc.gov/features/prevent-diabetes-kids/index.html).
72. National Institutes of Health, *Overview of Diabetes in Children and Adolescents* (www.ndep.nih.gov/resources/ResourceDetail.aspx?ResId=261).
73. Ibid.
74. Epilepsy Foundation, *About Kids* (https://www.epilepsy.com/living-epilepsy/parents-and-caregivers/about-kids).
75. Ibid.
76. Epilepsy Foundation, *Seizure First Aid* (https://www.epilepsy.com/start-here/seizure-first-aid).
77. Epilepsy Foundation, *Seizure Response Plans 101* (https://www.epilepsy.com/learn/managing-your-epilepsy/seizure-response-plans-101).

Design Elements: Books Icon: ©Amero/Shutterstock; Mouse Icon: ©abu/E+/Getty Images; Blocks Icon: ©2HotBrazil/E+/Getty Images; Magnifying Glass Icon: ©Thawat Tanhai/123RF; Light Bulb Icon: ©Comstock/PunchStock

Helping Students Translate Their Skills to Manage Health Risks

Section III focuses on the health risks students can avoid or reduce to help them live a healthy life. It contains the functional knowledge and essential personal and social skills that provide the foundation for the National Health Education Standards. Each chapter in this section has an introduction that provides the reader with information about the prevalence and cost of not practicing the positive health behavior, the relationship between the healthy behavior and academic performance, and the risk and protective factors related to the behavior. Information is examined concerning current school policy and practice contrasted with that which represents evidence-based "state of the art." Also each chapter in this section provides background information for the teacher, developmentally appropriate strategies for learning and assessment, sample student questions with suggested answers (Chapters 11–14), and children's literature, Internet, and other resources related to each content area.

10

(Colleen, age 12)

Preventing Intentional Injuries and Violence

DESIRED LEARNER OUTCOMES

After reading this chapter, you will be able to . . .

- **Describe the prevalence and cost of violence among youth.**

- **Explain the relationship between violence and compromised academic performance.**

- **Identify factors that influence violence.**

- **Summarize guidelines for schools and teachers related to violence prevention.**

- **Summarize developmentally appropriate violence prevention concepts and skills for K–8 students in the context of the National Health Education Standards and target healthy behavior outcomes.**

- **Demonstrate developmentally appropriate learning strategies and assessment techniques that incorporate concepts and skills that have been shown to prevent violence among youth.**

- **Identify effective, evaluated violence prevention curricula.**

- **Identify websites, print resources, and children's literature that can be used in cross-curricular instructional activities promoting violence prevention.**

- *Myth: Trying juvenile offenders in adult courts reduces the likelihood that they will commit more crimes.*
  Fact: Youth who are transferred to adult courts have significantly higher rates of reoffending and a greater likelihood of committing subsequent felonies than youth who remain in the juvenile justice system. Youth referred to the adult criminal justice system are more likely to be both physically and sexually victimized.
- *Myth: In the 1990s, school violence affected mostly white students or those who attended suburban or rural schools.*
  Fact: African American and Hispanic males attending large urban schools that serve poor neighborhoods faced and still face the greatest risk of becoming victims or perpetrators of school violence.
- *Myth: Weapon-related injuries in schools have increased dramatically over the past decade.*
  Fact: Incidence of such injuries has not changed significantly over the past twenty years. Compared to neighborhoods and homes, schools are safe places for students.
- *Myth: Most violent youth will be arrested for a violent crime.*
  Fact: Most youth who participate in violent behavior will never be arrested for a violent crime.[12]

Based on a review of the scientific literature, the *Report* concluded the following:

- Youth violence is not just a problem of the cities, isolated rural areas, or selected segments within society—it is our nation's problem.
- As a nation, we have access to credible knowledge that has been translated into programs documented to be effective at preventing youth violence.
- Intervention strategies exist that can be tailored to meet the needs of youth at every stage of development, from early childhood to late adolescence.[13]

To this end, *Healthy People 2020* has specified several national health promotion objectives targeting violence and abuse prevention for school-age children and youth (Table 10-2).[14] These objectives demonstrate the range and complexity of intentional injury risks to which children and youth in the United States are exposed. Although none of these objectives can be met by the isolated efforts of families, schools, or communities, this chapter contains suggestions for collaborative efforts focused on children in elementary and middle schools.

Intentional Injury Risks as a Threat to Academic Performance

Of particular interest to educators is research confirming exposure to violence and risk for intentional injuries threatens academic success. Research substantiates exposure to violence activates a set of threat responses in the brain. Extreme activation of the parts of the brain involved in responding to threatening circumstances can alter the developing brain of a child. These alterations can produce changes in the emotional, behavioral, and cognitive functioning of children forced to adapt to threats associated with violent experiences. Teachers must note that the specific changes in brain development and the ability of children

TABLE 10–2	HEALTHY PEOPLE

***Healthy People 2020* Objectives to Reduce Intentional Injuries (Violence and Abuse) Among Youth**

Objective AH-8	Increase the proportion of adolescents whose parents consider them to be safe at school.
Objective AH-9	Increase the proportion of middle and high schools that prohibit harassment based on a student's sexual orientation or gender identity.
Objective AH-10	Reduce the proportion of public schools with a serious violent incident.
Objective AH-11	Reduce adolescent and young adult perpetration of, and victimization by, crimes.
Objective IVP-29	Reduce homicides.
Objective IVP-34	Reduce physical fighting among adolescents.
Objective IVP-35	Reduce bullying among adolescents.
Objective IVP-36	Reduce weapon carrying by adolescents on school property.
Objective IVP-37	Reduce child maltreatment deaths.
Objective IVP-38	Reduce nonfatal child maltreatment.
Objective IVP-39	Reduce violence by current or former intimate partners.
Objective IVP-40	Reduce sexual violence.
Objective IVP-41	Reduce nonfatal intentional self-harm injuries.
Objective IVP-42	Reduce children's exposure to violence.

NOTE: IVP 5 Injury and Violence Prevention; AH = Adolescent Health
SOURCE: U.S. Department of Health and Human Services, *Healthy People 2020* (www.healthypeople.gov; May 2018).

exposed to violence to function depend on a number of factors, including the nature of the violent experiences, the child's response to the threat, and a host of family and community variables.[15]

Students who have experienced trauma are likely to exhibit attendance problems, frequent suspensions from school, failing grades in at least half their subjects, performance that is two or more grade levels below age level, and poor performance on standardized tests. While many students are compromised, others who are under threat can demonstrate temporary or subject-specific overachievement.[16]

Students who survive violence in their homes, communities, or schools, tend to lose interest in academic activities and are likely to manifest persistent behavior problems. Typically, these young people earn lower grades and have higher truancy and dropout rates than those who have not been exposed to violence.[17] Research also has shown that children who witness chronic violence tend to exhibit limited concentration and short attention spans.[18]

Abuse of children and youth by adult caregivers can cause children to be cautious and withdrawn. Abused children often manifest delayed language development, express feelings of powerlessness, and have a general inability to set goals or plan for meaningful futures.[19] Most compromised academic achievement among abused children is not due to general problems with intellectual development. Rather, academic problems among abused students commonly are related to the difficulty these children have in forming bonds with peers and teachers or to a common difficulty engaging in classroom learning activities.[20]

To reinforce the implications of such findings about younger learners, analyses of the 2017 Youth Risk Behavior Survey data (see Table 10-1) have confirmed an important connection between violent behavior and the class grades earned by high school students. Although these findings do not imply cause, students in grades 9 to 12 who earn higher grades are much less likely than other students to have engaged in such behaviors as:

- Be in a physical fight.
- Be in a physical fight on school grounds or property.
- Skip school because they feel unsafe either at school or on their way to or from school.[21]

Factors That Influence Violence

Risk factors for intentional injuries are evident in every area of the lives of students. These risk factors include internal attributes of the child and external variables within the family, school, social networks, and community. Some experts believe that violent images are so common in the media that children have become desensitized to their intense and devastating effects. Other experts suggest that violence can be linked to the complex social and economic changes that affect families and communities. They attribute youth violence to the actions of overworked and financially strapped parents who vent their frustrations at home. When frequent yelling or other aggressive or abusive acts become common in the home, children learn that such behaviors are acceptable or even necessary. Children who have not developed skills to control their impulses and behaviors might grow accustomed to using violence as a way to resolve conflicts or gain desired possessions. Students who have not learned that nonviolence is a better—or even possible—option view violence as an expedient and effective way to gain respect when confronted with frustrating circumstances.[22]

Research has increased our understanding of factors that make some youth more vulnerable to victimization and others to perpetration of violence. Although risk factors are not direct causes of youth violence, they increase the likelihood that a young person will become violent.[23]

Protective factors include variables demonstrated to buffer youth from risks of becoming violent, but rigorous research on protective factors has lagged behind that on risk factors. As a result, the CDC convened an Expert Panel on Protective Factors for Youth Violence.[24] Much less is known about protective than risk factors associated with youth violence. In a special issue of the *American Journal of Preventive Medicine,* the panel delineates the conceptual challenges with rigorously measuring protective factors.[25] Readers are encouraged to review available information about risk and protective factors for youth violence identified by the Centers for Disease Control and Prevention that can be found in Consider This 10.1.[26]

School staff should be prepared to recognize early warning signs of student violence. These can include social withdrawal, feelings of being picked on and persecuted, expression of violence in writings or drawings, patterns of impulsive, intimidating

and bullying behaviors, and intolerance for differences and prejudicial attitudes.[27] Examination of risk and protective factors will reinforce that it is the interaction among personal characteristics, other people, and environmental conditions that is important. The *Report of the Surgeon General on Youth Violence* confirmed that the developmental stages of childhood and adolescence are very influential for the development of risk and/or protective factors for violence. As children grow from infancy to adulthood, some risk factors become more influential while others become less so. For example, substance use among perpetrators is a greater risk factor for violence to children age 9 than to those age 14.[28]

It is rare that risk factors for violence operate in isolation. The more risk factors to which youth are exposed, the more likely it is that they will become violent. It is important to note, however, that no single risk factor or combination of factors can predict violence with complete accuracy. The majority of youth exposed to single or even multiple risk factors will not behave violently. Although no indicator is absolute, there is strong evidence that selected risk factors can point to the likelihood of youth violence. Attention to these risks can enable advocates to identify vulnerable young people. In this way, targets for intervention efforts can be identified and limited resources can be applied in the most effective ways.[29]

GUIDELINES FOR SCHOOLS CONCERNING PREVENTING VIOLENCE

It is clear that the kinds of violence to which children and youth are exposed are varied and involve girls and boys as both perpetrators and victims. Acts of aggression and violence range from bullying and verbal abuse to physical intimidation and assault and include acts of rape and other forms of sexual violence, homicide, and suicide. Though it must be noted that violence is relatively rare at the school site, bullying, weapon possession, gang activity, shootings, and other serious acts of youth violence have captured the attention of the national media and concerned citizens. The result has been a call for schools to assume a large share of the responsibility for developing and implementing violence prevention policies and programs.

State of the Practice

Recognizing that any act of violence, particularly one that occurs at school, is unconditionally unacceptable, states and school districts have done their best to develop and implement effective violence prevention policies and practices. Effective implementation requires knowledgeable and skilled school professionals. Tables 10-3 and 10-5 provide information from the School Health Policies and Programs Study (SHPPS) on the percentage of states and districts that provide support for or offer professional development on violence prevention. Table 10-4 highlights percentage of elementary and middle schools adopting policies requiring instruction on specific topics associated with violence prevention. Violence prevention topics and skills being addressed in the nation's elementary and middle schools.[30] The SHPPS data are encouraging but demonstrate the need for increased and more consistent school-based efforts to promote violence risk reduction across the school community.

Consider This 10.1

Risk and Protective Factors Associated with Youth Violence

INDIVIDUAL RISK FACTORS

History of violent victimization
History of early aggressive behavior
High emotional distress
Attention deficits or learning disorders
Antisocial beliefs and attitudes
Involvement with drugs, alcohol, or tobacco
Exposure to violence/conflict in the family

FAMILY RISK FACTORS

Authoritarian child-rearing attitudes
Harsh/lax/inconsistent discipline practices
Poor monitoring/supervision of children
Low attachment to parents/caregivers
Low parental involvement
Parental substance abuse/criminality

PEER/SCHOOL RISK FACTORS

Association with delinquent peers
Social rejection by peers
Low involvement in conventional activities
Low commitment to school
Poor academic performance

COMMUNITY RISK FACTORS

Diminished economic opportunities
High level of transience
High level of family disruption
Low levels of community participation
Socially disorganized neighborhoods

INDIVIDUAL PROTECTIVE FACTORS

Intolerant attitude toward deviance
High IQ/grade point average
Positive social orientation
Religiosity

FAMILY PROTECTIVE FACTORS

Connectedness to family/other adults
Ability to discuss problems with an adult
Frequent shared activities with parents
High parent expectations for academics

PEER/SCHOOL PROTECTIVE FACTORS

Commitment to school
Involvement in social activities
Consistent presence of parent/caregiver when awakening, after school, at evening mealtime, and/or at bedtime

SOURCE: Centers for Disease Control and Prevention, *Youth Violence: Risk and Protective Factors* (Atlanta, GA: CDC, 2017). (www.cdc.gov/ViolencePrevention/youthviolence /riskprotectivefactors.html; December, 2017).

SHPPS

TABLE 10–3

School Health Policies and Practices Study Data Related to Preventing Violence and Suicide

Percentage of States and Districts Who Provided Funding for or Offered Professional Development to Those Who Teach Health Education by Topic

	States (%) 2012	Districts (%) 2016
Emotional and mental health	64.0	63.6
Injury prevention and safety	54.0	61.0
Suicide prevention	64.7	68.8
Violence prevention	79.6	78.4

SOURCE: Centers for Disease Control and Prevention, *School Health Policies and Practices Study 2012, 2016.* (SHPPS) (Atlanta, GA: CDC, 2017). (www.cdc.gov/HealthyYouth/shpps).

TABLE 10–4

Percentage of Schools Adopting Policy Requiring Schools to Teach Specific Health Topics

Percentage of Schools in Which Students Are Required to Receive Instruction on Specific Health Topics

	Schools (%)	
	Elementary	Middle
Emotional and mental health	52.3	66.6
Injury prevention and safety	67.2	64.8
Suicide prevention	20.4	47.9
Violence prevention	75.5	76.0

SOURCE: Centers for Disease Control and Prevention, *School Health Policies and Practices Study 2014.* (SHPPS) (Atlanta, GA: CDC, 2015). (www.cdc.gov/HealthyYouth/shpps).

In addition to taking instructional approaches to violence prevention identified in SHPPS, many school communities have invested considerable time and money in broader policies and programs that have not been demonstrated to produce the desired outcomes. Many of these well-intentioned but ineffective practices persist because powerful stakeholders believe that "doing something is better than doing nothing." Research confirms that this often is not the case.

Although popular in many communities, peer counseling, peer mediation, and peer leader programs targeting all students have been demonstrated to be ineffective as primary prevention strategies. Administrators and other school leaders should note that no scientific evidence indicates that these activities reduce violence risks. While an unwise use of limited resources, such activities are not likely to harm younger learners. Importantly, however, research has demonstrated that such programming has the potential to harm high school students.

Some communities have applied a curious strategy in an attempt to reduce youth violence; specifically, some local boards of education have adopted a universal policy of restricting promotion to succeeding grades for violent students. Studies of this approach reveal very negative effects on achievement, attendance, behavior, and attitudes toward school.[31] However, research on the effects of zero tolerance policies, or mandated, predetermined punishments for specific offenses, reveals little association with safer schools.[32]

The widely implemented youth drug prevention program, Drug Abuse Resistance Education (DARE), has been extended in some communities to include violence prevention elements. Based on the conventional approach taken to implement DARE in grades 5 and 6, there is little evidence of its effectiveness in either substance use or violence risk reduction. Researchers suggest that the program's lack of effectiveness might be related to its lack of skill development. In addition, it is developmentally and culturally inappropriate to confront students with drug and violence situations that they have not encountered as part of daily living in their neighborhood or community.[33] Interestingly, despite such findings, DARE remains popular in many school communities. Readers can examine the evidence-based recommendations for violence risk reduction in this chapter, as well as review Chapter 12 for sound approaches to promoting an alcohol- and other drug-free lifestyle.

State of the Art

In light of the need to use finite resources in the most productive and evidence-based ways, an important body of literature has emerged that confirms attributes of school-based policies, programs, and practices with no or low potential to prevent violence. Although common in many school communities, the following activities should be avoided as they have been demonstrated to have very little potential to reduce youth violence. In addition, research has confirmed that some of these practices might actually increase the likelihood of aggression or violent acting-out behaviors among youth.[34]

1. *Using scare-tactic approaches based on pictures or videos depicting violent scenes or consequences.* There is a large body of research confirming that people who watch violence in the media are more likely than their counterparts to behave violently.

2. *Adding a violence prevention agenda to a school district that is overwhelmed with other activities.* It is important for schools to have an organizational structure and a climate that support violence prevention. Too often, school administrators try to add violence prevention programming to a school community that has not established intentional injury risk reduction as a priority. Although common, this practice can increase the burden on teachers, increase stress, and ultimately backfire for students, parents, and education professionals.

3. *Segregating aggressive or antisocial students into separate groups.* Integrating delinquent youth into a positive, nondelinquent peer group can have a positive effect. There is compelling evidence that efforts to separate or create groups composed exclusively of aggressive young people do not contribute to a reduction in problem behaviors. In fact, such a practice actually might contribute to an increase in criminal behaviors.

4. *Implementing brief instructional programs that are not reinforced by school climate variables.* Even instructional programs of sufficient duration to be educationally sound cannot sustain outcomes in a climate that is not supportive. More comprehensive approaches to prevention and intervention have proven to result in better outcomes.

5. *Focusing instructional programming exclusively on self-esteem enhancement.* Narrowly focused self-esteem programs have been determined to be largely ineffective. It is important to note that many gang-affiliated youth have a very highly developed sense of self-esteem. Those programs in which self-esteem enhancement is contextual to a broader agenda that promotes personal and social competency are more likely to produce desired outcomes.

6. *Focusing instructional programs only on knowledge acquisition.* Intentional injury programs focused on disseminating information, like those that have been evaluated in other health-risk content areas, do not succeed. Such programs do not teach functional knowledge or enable students to practice essential skills to avoid and manage conflicts.[35]

Evidence-based Youth Violence Prevention Strategies

Decades of research have resulted in an understanding of what is needed to strengthen youth violence prevention efforts. A combined focus on enhancing individual, community, and society strengths is needed to result in stronger and more sustainable improvements than a single strategy.[36] Educators, community leaders, and concerned parents are encouraged to review the following foundational elements of promising intentional injury risk reduction programs.

- *Build skills and competencies to choose non-violent, safe behaviors.* Fostering the development of protective factors decreases young people's risk for violence and their health and safety increases. Problem solving, communication, anger management, impulse control, and emotional regulation can be taught in a variety of settings including schools, after-school youth programs, and faith-based institutions.
- *Foster nurturing relationships between young people and their parents and caregivers.* Providing caregivers with support and knowledge about healthy child development, and building caregivers' skills related to communication, setting age-appropriate boundaries and rules, monitoring young people's activities and relationships, and using consistent and nonviolent behavior can contribute to reducing the risk of youth violence.
- *Build and maintain positive relationships between young people and caring adults in the community.* Healthy and safe relationships with adults who are not their primary caregivers can provide a buffer against young people's risk for violence.

Mentors, teachers, coaches, members of faith-based institutions, neighbors are among the many adults who can provide informal monitoring and guidance to youth and contribute to feelings of connectedness to caring adults, their school, and community.

- *Develop and implement school-wide activities and policies to foster social connectedness and a positive environment.* Students who believe that adults in their school care about their individual well-being as well as their learning are more likely to succeed academically and engage in nonviolent behaviors.
- *Improve and sustain a safe physical environment in communities and create spaces to strengthen social relationships.* Examination and potential modification of physical spaces in schools and the community to improve perceived and actual safety is an important strategy to reduce opportunities for crime and violence.
- *Facilitate the social cohesion and collective efficacy of the community.* When community members feel connected and are willing to help others, violence is less likely.
- *Change societal norms about the acceptability of violence and willingness to intervene.* Communities can encourage the belief that individuals have the power and responsibility to prevent violence.
- *Change the social and structural conditions that affect youth violence and lead to health inequity.* Activities such as improving early learning and educational opportunities, access to high-quality childcare, improving high school graduation rates, and increased access to mental health and social services can contribute to reducing social and structural conditions that affect youth violence.[37]

Teacher's Toolbox 10.1 offers specific guidelines to prepare school and community advocates to prevent and/or manage a range of risks for youth violence. These recommendations are excerpted from the CDC's *School Health Guidelines to Prevent Unintentional Injuries and Violence.* These recommendations and strategies clarify the elements of a comprehensive approach to preventing and intervening in youth violence.[38]

GUIDELINES FOR CLASSROOM APPLICATIONS

Important Background for K–8 Teachers

While many educators share a general concern about violent acts confronting children, few recognize the breadth of the kinds of violent acts and locations in which they occur. Teachers must be aware of the impact of violence in the world, homes, local communities, and schools on their students.

Violence in Their World: Helping Children Manage Trauma Associated with Catastrophic Events

In light of recent school shootings, terrorist acts and war, and natural disasters, educators need to update and refine skills to recognize and manage the effects of catastrophic events on students. Trauma occurs when an individual is exposed to an overwhelming event beyond the realm of normal human experience.

Exposure to such events results in excessive stress to the body, mind, and psyche. The National Institute of Mental Health has identified that trauma is characterized as more than simple loss. It is associated with exposure to or involvement in either of two kinds of events:

- Physical trauma can result from events that result in serious physical injuries or wounds.
- Psychological trauma can result from an emotionally painful, shocking, stressful, or life-threatening experience, including witnessing distressful events.[39]

Trauma can result from a broad range of conditions. Such events can include natural disasters, severe and constant criticism or bullying, divorce, car crashes, abuse or neglect, death of a family member or close friend, chronic exposure to violence, violent tragedies in communities, and terrorist acts or war.[40]

The impact of a catastrophe on children depends on a number of factors, including their physical proximity to the event and the support systems to which they have access. Importantly, trauma can pose particular challenges for younger learners. Children at early stages of development often are not cognitively prepared to understand either the impact or the magnitude of the situation. In addition, they might not be equipped to cope with the intensity of emotions associated with the event or its impact on their caregivers.[41]

Children react to trauma in a way that is unlike that of their adult counterparts. It is common for children to have immediate and instinctive reactions to danger or the threat of it. Limited in their physical strength and cognitive capacity, children often will use withdrawal skills, including hiding, running away, and fantasizing, when they feel threatened. As such it is not uncommon for firefighters to find a young child hiding in a cupboard or closet during a house fire. Or, a child who is being sexually abused might pretend to be asleep as a way not to provoke or stimulate the offender. Quite often, children freeze and/or become speechless in the face of danger. This reaction can be manifested in adults, but is an instinctive and primary coping mechanism among powerless children.[42]

Following their initial reaction, children often demonstrate a range of cognitive, emotional, behavioral, and physical responses to trauma. Although some are particularly resilient, it is common for parents and teachers to note fairly consistent manifestations of trauma among children. Specifically, teachers might observe the following in students confronted by a catastrophic event:

1. Avoidance: In the wake of trauma, children might:
   - Avoid feelings and memory of the trauma.
   - Become quiet around friends, family, and teachers.
   - Lie as a way to avoid a similarly traumatic situation.
2. An inability to build or maintain friendships or relationships with teachers that manifest as:
   - Inappropriate expressions of feelings (laughing or crying at unusual times).
   - Becoming irritable and disruptive or behaving destructively.
   - A tendency to develop physical symptoms or fears (stomachaches or frequent headaches).
   - Returning to behaviors common to being younger.[43]

School Health Recommendations to Prevent Violence and Suicide

RECOMMENDATION 1

Establish a social environment that prevents violence and suicide.

Guiding Principles
- Ensure high academic standards and provide faculty, staff members, and students with the support and administrative leadership to promote the academic success (achievement), health, and safety of all students.
- Encourage students' feelings of connectedness to school.
- Establish a climate that demonstrates respect, support, and caring and that does not tolerate harassment or bullying.
- Develop and implement written policies regarding violence and suicide prevention.
- Infuse violence and suicide prevention into multiple school activities and classes.
- Establish unambiguous disciplinary policies; communicate them to students, faculty, staff members, and families; and implement them consistently.
- Assess violence and suicide prevention strategies and policies at regular intervals.

RECOMMENDATION 2

Provide a physical environment, inside and outside school buildings, that prevents violence.

Guiding Principles
- Actively supervise all student activities to prevent violence.
- Ensure that the school environment, including school buses, is free from weapons.

RECOMMENDATION 3

Implement health education curricula and instruction that help students develop the knowledge, attitudes, behavioral skills, and confidence needed to adopt and maintain safe lifestyles and to advocate for health and safety.

Guiding Principles
- Choose prevention programs and curricula that are grounded in theory or that have scientific evidence of effectiveness.
- Implement violence prevention curricula consistent with national and state standards for health education.
- Use active learning strategies, interactive teaching methods, and proactive classroom management to encourage student involvement in learning about violence prevention.
- Provide adequate staffing and resources, including budget, facilities, staff development, and class time, to provide violence prevention education for all students.

RECOMMENDATION 4

Provide health, counseling, psychological, and social services to meet the physical, mental, emotional, and social health needs of students.

Guiding Principles
- Coordinate school-based counseling, psychological, social, and health services and the education curriculum.
- Establish strong links with community resources and identify providers to bring services into the schools.
- Identify and provide assistance to students who have witnessed violence and who have been victims of violence.

RECOMMENDATION 5

Establish mechanisms for short- and long-term responses to crises and disasters that affect the school community.

Guiding Principles
- Establish a written plan for responding to crises and disasters.
- Prepare to implement the school's plan in the event of a crisis.
- Have short-term responses and services established after a crisis.
- Have long-term responses and services established after a crisis.

RECOMMENDATION 6

Integrate school, family, and community efforts to prevent violence and suicide.

Guiding Principles
- Involve parents, students, and other family members in all aspects of school life, including planning and implementing violence and suicide prevention programs and policies.
- Educate, support, and involve family members in child and adolescent violence and suicide prevention.
- Coordinate school and community services.

RECOMMENDATION 7

For all school personnel, provide regular staff development opportunities that impart the knowledge, skills, and confidence to prevent violence and suicide and to support students in their efforts to do the same.

Guiding Principles
- Ensure that staff members are knowledgeable about violence and suicide prevention and have the skills needed to prevent violence at school, at home, and in the community.
- Train and support all personnel to be positive role models for a healthy and safe lifestyle.

SOURCE: U.S. Department of Health and Human Services, *School Health Guidelines to Prevent Unintentional Injuries and Violence* (Atlanta, GA: Centers for Disease Control and Prevention, December 7, 2001), 13–46.

A safe and stable classroom environment can help children cope with traumatic events.

Though the symptoms and manifestations of traumatic events vary a great deal from child to child, teachers play a critical role in helping students manage such events. Education professionals must recognize that their responses to a traumatic event can influence the reactions of their students. Children tend to react much more calmly if this is the reaction among the adults around them.

Unfortunately, while attending to the needs of children, many adult caregivers fail to make time to reflect and implement self-care strategies to help with their own management of the trauma. This can compromise the supportive quality of the interactions they have with their students.

Another problem occurs when well-meaning adult caregivers attempt to protect children by minimizing the impact of a catastrophic event. Some teachers in elementary and middle schools choose to proceed with typical classroom activities. Some teachers even extend this practice to the point that they fail to acknowledge that the event ever took place.

As a foundation for effective practice, education professionals and other caring adults are encouraged to continue to explore ways to help children work through their reactions to catastrophic events. Adult responses can strongly influence how children and adolescents react.[44]

In the school environment, teachers make a significant contribution by maintaining a safe, stable classroom environment. Many simple activities and support networks can be incorporated into classroom practice to promote a sense of security and ease among students. Following are general guidelines to help teachers prepare the learning environment:

1. From the beginning of the school year, encourage student participation in maintaining a positive and healthy classroom environment.
2. Teach nonviolent conflict resolution skills as an effective means of dealing with differences and problems.
3. Use life experiences and current events from children's lives as teaching resources.
4. Create a caring and nurturing learning environment for students.
5. Establish and maintain routines.
6. Cultivate peer mentorship among students.
7. Discuss academic problems and brainstorm solutions with the class.
8. Confront negative comments or actions that occur in the classroom.[45]

For further information, readers should review the additional information found in Chapter 14 on managing loss, death, and grief. Readers will find content that provides further clarification about the impact of catastrophic events on students and provides suggestions for educators.

Violence at the School Site

In an effort to present an accurate and comprehensive picture of the nature and scope of crime and violence on school property, the U.S. Departments of Education and Justice issue annual reports entitled Indicators of School Crime and Safety. The most recent of these reports confirmed that the percentage of public schools recording incidents of crime, student bullying, or verbal abuse of teachers has continued on a decline.[46] This report confirmed the following findings about the risks for intentional injury on school property:

- In general, schools are safe places.
- Despite the concerns of many, schools are not especially dangerous places in most communities. Most crimes at the school site involve theft and are not of a serious, violent nature (physical attacks, fights with a weapon, rape, robbery, murder, or suicide).
- Homicides are extremely rare events on school property.
- The concerns teachers have about their own safety are not without foundation. Secondary teachers are more likely to be threatened with injury, whereas those in elementary schools are more likely to have been physically attacked by a student.
- Since 1993, fewer students have been taking weapons to school. In addition, consequences for carrying weapons on school property have been formalized.
- Nearly all American schools have implemented some type of campus-security measures (security cameras; telephones in classrooms; required use of student and staff IDs; controlled access to buildings and grounds; required sign-in or escort policies for all guests; increase in school uniform policies).[47]

In response to particular concern about school shootings, a federal document provided a summary of findings from a study of school shootings that had occurred over time and in a number of states. This exhaustive research revealed the following:

- Incidents of targeted violence at schools rarely are impulsive. Such attacks are the culmination of an understandable and often traceable process of thinking and behavior, often in response to loss or failures.
- Prior to most incidents, the attacker(s) had told one or more people about the idea and the plan.

- Most attackers did not threaten targets directly prior to an attack.
- Many attackers had considered or attempted suicide at some time prior to attacks.
- Unfortunately, there is no useful profile of the "school shooter."
- Most attackers had experience using guns and had access to them.
- Most shooting incidents were not resolved by law enforcement action.
- In many cases, other students were involved in some capacity, including providing encouragement or participating in a cover-up.
- In a number of cases, retaliating for having been bullied by others was an important motivation for the attack.
- Most attackers engaged in some behavior prior to the incident that caused adults or other students to express concern or indicate that the student needed help.[48]

Though schools generally are very safe places, school violence can lead to a disruptive and threatening environment, physical injury, and emotional stress. All of these can threaten student achievement, the primary focus of educators. In response, school leaders have implemented a range of programs to prevent, deter, and respond to the potential for violence. Even though various kinds of policies and programs are implemented to reduce violence in schools, the three most common types include:

- Efforts to involve parents in preventing and reducing violence.
- Safety and security procedures (random metal detector checks, random dog sniffs to check for drugs, random sweeps for contraband, security cameras and guards).
- Disciplinary policies.

Teachers are encouraged to work with school leaders to merge classroom policies and practices with those implemented to prevent violence throughout the local school community.[49] The National Association of State Boards of Education identify major reasons to address violence prevention through effective policy development. Specifically, effective policies and practices:

- Improve student academic achievement.
- Reduce absences.
- Maintain a productive learning climate.
- Satisfy reasonable community expectations that schools ensure safety.
- Avoid economic consequences associated with violence.
- Prevent litigation.[50]

Violence in the Home: Recognizing and Managing Child Maltreatment

Child maltreatment is manifested in the form of physical, sexual, or emotional abuse or neglect. Though children might be the targets of a single form of maltreatment, it is common for a child to experience several types of abuse simultaneously. For example, for a physically abused child also to be neglected and/or emotionally victimized is not uncommon.

Child abuse is a growing problem in the United States. The number of cases of abuse reported each year has increased steadily since the 1970s. Evidence confirms that approximately one in four U.S. children experience some form of maltreatment at least once in their lifetime. Tragically, in 2017, about 1,750 children died as a result of abuse and neglect.[51] The effects of child abuse are evident in every aspect of development. Research has confirmed the following:

- Children who experience abuse and neglect are at increased risk for adverse health effects and chronic diseases as adults.
- Child abuse and neglect can have a negative effect on the ability of people to establish intimate relationships as adults.
- Youth who experienced abuse and neglect receive more medications for depression, anxiety, and other issues than other youth in psychiatric care.
- Abused and neglected children are at an increased risk for delinquency, teen pregnancy, and low academic achievement.[52]

Abuse is more likely to occur in families and communities enduring the stress of poverty and/or substance abuse. However, the maltreatment of adolescents and children can occur in any home on any street—it is a tragedy that crosses all cultures and socioeconomic levels.[53]

Perpetrators often attempt to convince children that they are to blame or in some way have contributed to their victimization. Because children are led to believe either that they are at fault for the abuse or that they will be punished further for revealing it, most young victims will not talk about abuse in their families. Thus, it is important that teachers and other adult caregivers not be misled by the silence of a child about such matters. Child advocates and educators must note the following characteristics that have been documented to be among the most common in young victims of maltreatment:

Sudden changes in behavior or school performance

Failure to receive help for physical or medical problems brought to the parents' attention

Learning problems that cannot be attributed to a specific physical or psychological cause

Lack of adult supervision

Overly compliant, passive, or withdrawn

Comes to school or other activities early, stays late, or does not want to go home[54]

The issue of child abuse is confounded by the fact that there is no universally accepted set of parenting rules or strategies. As a result, the boundaries of child abuse are blurred by cultural or community values. Among many Pacific Islanders, for example, it is regarded as cruel and dangerous to leave a young child in a separate bed for the night. Tolerance for the notion of "spare the rod, spoil the child" has contributed to debate over the legitimacy of corporal punishment for children in the United States. Regardless of other influential variables, *hurting children is never acceptable, even if it is delivered in the name of love, care, or discipline.*[55]

Child abuse, also referred to as acts of commission, is defined as words or overt actions that cause harm, potential harm, or threat of harm. Acts of commission are deliberate and intentional; however, harm to a child might not be the intended consequence, such as when a punishment results in the child having a concussion. Physical, sexual, and psychological abuse are considered acts of commission.[56]

Acts of omission, or child neglect, are the failure to provide for a child's basic physical, emotional, or educational needs or to protect a child from harm or potential harm. Harm to a child may not be the intended consequence. The following types of neglect involve acts of omission: physical neglect, emotional neglect, medical or dental neglect, educational neglect, inadequate supervision, or exposure to violent environments.[57] Teacher's Toolbox 10.2 provides detailed information about child abuse indicators.[58]

The Role of the "Mandated Reporter"   Detecting abuse or neglect is difficult because many children are too young or afraid to reveal what is happening to them. Maltreatment most often occurs behind closed doors or under circumstances in which no other adult or advocate is present. Also, many kinds of abuse leave no obvious sign of harm. In an effort to identify and help as many young victims as possible, each state has enacted laws requiring many kinds of professionals to act as "mandated reporters."

Specifically, these laws require certain individuals who suspect abuse or neglect to report their suspicions to state or county authorities. Reports can be made to the Childhelp National Child Abuse Hotline (800-4-A-CHILD or 800-422-4453) or to local child protection professionals or police. Though each state has its own laws governing mandated reporting protocol, in most cases any person who works with children on a regular basis is charged with the responsibility. In all states, this list of professionals includes counselors, lawyers, nurses, physicians, social workers, and teachers.[59]

If abuse is suspected, all concerned adults are encouraged to make a report to child protective service professionals, but mandated reporters are required to do so. It is important to note that such reports do not constitute an accusation. Rather, reports of such suspicions serve as a formal request for an investigation to be made on behalf of the child. In most states, reporters can remain anonymous and are immune from the legal actions of the unhappy parents or caregivers under investigation. However, teachers or other advocates who make reports are contributing significantly to the welfare of young people. In any case, teachers always should make a record of any abuse report, detailing to whom the report was made, the time and date of the report, and the information that was communicated. Although the most important thing for teachers to communicate is concern for the child, the following kinds of information might be helpful to the investigation process:

- The reporter's name, address, and relationship to the child.
- The name of and contact information for the child.
- Contact information for the parents, guardians, and/or siblings of the child.

- Details leading to the suspicion of maltreatment.
- Symptoms of abuse or neglect that have been observed.
- Other information that might expedite contact with parents or other custodial caregivers.[60]

The majority of teachers hope they will never have to manage a disclosure of any kind of maltreatment of a child. Unfortunately such revelations, although rare, are made to these trusted adults. Teachers must be equipped to respond as student advocates. In particular, when a child reveals an allegation of sexual abuse, the teacher must accept the disclosure at face value. Although it might be difficult for a teacher to believe that such an incident has occurred to a student in their class, educators must remember that most children do not have a frame of reference for describing sexual abuse unless it has happened to them.

After the child has revealed any information about abuse, it is important for teachers to respond in a calm manner. Education professionals are encouraged to thank the child for talking about this important matter. Teachers are cautioned not to react in an overtly emotional manner to the disclosure or ask questions such as "Are you telling the truth?" or "Did you see that on television?" Such inquiries indicate to students that their disclosure is not believed. Conversely, four important advocacy skills—observing, making referrals, gathering information, and following up—must be mastered by teachers and other professionals who have been designated as mandated reporters of suspected child abuse within their states.

1. *Observing Students—A Foundation for Advocacy.* As a foundation for advocacy on behalf of child and adolescent health, teachers and other concerned adults must train themselves to be critical observers of the students with whom they come into contact. Such professionals might be more able to notice the subtle signs or symptoms of abuse than nonabusive parents or other family members. Because teachers have the opportunity to observe students in the context of the child's age-cohort peers, any anomalies, changes, or injuries might be more conspicuous to them. In addition, teachers are charged with the responsibility of keeping records about a range of student performance measures. In this context, changes in student health, social interaction patterns, or academic performance could be noticeable over a period of time. Finally, teachers, physicians, and other mandated reporters often are better able than a child's relatives to maintain professional objectivity about potential problems.

In all cases in which teachers suspect that students are being abused or that violence is eminent, action must be taken. The best course of action is to make an immediate referral or report of these suspicions.

2. *Making Referrals—Reporting Abuse.* Children who are being abused need access to appropriate medical and social services. The principal agency that responds to child abuse in most communities is the child protective or children's service agency. Professional personnel, including social workers, are trained to provide the counsel, help, and legal advocacy needed by children who are being treated badly. Many agencies provide assistance to

Signs and Symptoms of Child Maltreatment

PHYSICAL ABUSE

1. A child who is being *physically abused* might have:
   a. Unexplained or unusually shaped injuries.
   b. Recurring physical marks or injuries.
   c. Bruises, welts, or adult-size bite marks.
   d. Injuries in various stages of healing.
   e. Lacerations or abrasions, particularly to the face, genitalia, arms, legs, or torso.
   f. Injuries to both sides of the face (injuries tend to affect only one side of the face).
   g. Grab marks on the arms or shoulders.
   h. Burns from cigarettes or cigars.
   i. Immersion burns from scalding water.
   j. Burns that resemble an object.
   k. Rope burns.
   l. Head and face injuries (hair loss from pulling).
   m. Broken bones or other internal injuries.
2. In the classroom, children being *physically abused* might:
   a. Complain of severe punishment at home.
   b. Exhibit behavioral extremes (aggression/withdrawal).
   c. Attempt to run away from home.
   d. Arrive early for school and/or be reluctant to go home.
   e. Show extreme anxiety or fear.
   f. Refuse to change clothes for physical education or athletic activities.
   g. Have a poor self-image.
   h. Self-mutilate and/or attempt suicide.

NEGLECT

1. A child who is *neglected* might exhibit signs such as:
   a. Delayed physical development.
   b. Constant hunger or the tendency to hoard food or overeat.
   c. Inappropriate dress for the season.
   d. Lack of medical care.
   e. Chronic or extreme fatigue.
   f. Lags in emotional and/or cognitive development.
   g. Speech disorders.
   h. Underweight.
   i. Untreated physical or dental problems.
   j. Poor hygiene, dirty skin, or matted hair.
   k. Frequent absences or late arrivals for school.
   l. Substance abuse.
   m. Flat affect (emotionally unresponsive).
   n. Listlessness or apathy.
   o. Parental behaviors toward younger siblings.
2. In the classroom, *neglected* children might:
   a. Have anxious or insecure attachments with caregivers.
   b. Interact less with peers.
   c. Appear helpless or passive.
   d. Be less attentive or involved in learning.
   e. Perform poorly on cognitive tasks and class assignments.
   f. Have poor grades and performance on standardized tests.
   g. Rarely express humor, laugh, or tell or understand jokes.

SEXUAL ABUSE

1. Children who are being *sexually abused* might have:
   a. Difficulty walking or sitting.
   b. Pain, itching, bleeding, or bruising in or around the genitalia.
   c. Torn, stained, or bloody underclothing.
   d. Pain during urination or bloody underclothing.
   e. Vaginal or penile discharge.
   f. Bruising to the oral cavity.
   g. Sexualized play.
   h. Sexually transmitted infections.
   i. Frequent touching or fondling of the genitals or masturbation.
   j. Pregnancy at a very young age.
   k. Inappropriate sexual expression with trusted adults.
   l. Developmentally age-inappropriate sexual knowledge or simulations of adult sexual behaviors.
   m. Significant social isolation.
   n. Fears and/or extreme avoidance of specific persons, places, or things.
   o. Statements suggesting sexual abuse.
2. Classroom manifestations of *sexual abuse* include:
   a. Withdrawn and often aggressive behaviors.
   b. Uncharacteristic attachment to the teacher.
   c. Extreme need for approval.

EMOTIONAL ABUSE

1. Children who are *emotionally abused* might behave:
   a. In a nice and pleasant manner or strive to be people pleasers.
   b. Very aggressively.
   c. In a "take-charge" manner as a way to define and control their environment.
   d. By rejecting praise or compliments.
   e. By acting out against conventional norms.
   f. In a socially isolated way.
   g. In a withdrawn or depressed manner.
2. Classroom manifestations of *emotional abuse* include:
   a. Demonstrations of little respect for the feelings or rights of others.
   b. Inconsistency, emotional instability, and/or impulse control problems.
   c. Speech disorders or other developmental delays.
   d. Academic performance below ability.
   e. Frequent physical health problems.
   f. Substance abuse, eating disorders, and/or self-mutilation.

SOURCE: CIVITAS, Right on Course: How Trauma and Maltreatment Impact Children in the Classroom and How You Can Help (Chicago, IL: CIVITAS, 2002), 31, 33, 37, 39, 43.

parents of abused children for the purpose of preventing further occurrences.

Schools have a significant role to play in the early identification of children who have been abused. Every state has a child abuse (including sexual abuse) reporting statute. Most of these laws mandate that teachers report any suspicions of abuse. This is not a particularly easy task for teachers. It is important to note that it is not the responsibility of the teacher to determine whether the child is actually being abused. Further, educators are not responsible for determining the identification of the perpetrator of the abuse. Instead, it is the job of teachers and other mandated reporters to report any suspicions of abuse. Teachers always have the concern that maybe their "hunch" is wrong. Also, many teachers are afraid that they can be sued by the parents or caregivers of the child for reporting their suspicions. However, in most states, the mandated reporter statutes provide legal immunity from liability for those who report suspected child abuse, neglect, or sexual abuse in the context of job responsibilities.

3. *Gathering Information.* Many teachers are of the opinion that, once they make a referral, they turn the responsibility for

Through interaction and careful observation, teachers can notice changes in students' health, social interactions, or academic performance that might be signs of abuse.

problematic issues confronting the child over to protective service professionals. In many cases, however, the child continues to attend the same school and work with the same teacher and classmates while the case is being investigated and resolved. Once teachers have reported their suspicions in a way that is consistent with current interpretations of state law, it is important that they gather information about ways to support the child and to continue to integrate the student into daily classroom practice. School counselors, psychologists, and social workers are good sources of such information. Teachers are encouraged to seek their support.

4. *Following Up.* Referral networks often move slowly, due in part to the fact that child protective service professionals often must interact with the legal system. In addition, many departments of child protective services are grossly understaffed and stretched beyond their capacity. Teachers who become frustrated with delays or with concerns that the system has abandoned a student are urged to pursue follow-up activities. Teachers are advised to avoid making contact with family members about such matters. Rather, information can be clarified and the best interests of the children and their families preserved through telephone contacts, updates, or follow-up contacts with caseworkers or other child protective service professionals to whom initial reports have been made.

Though teachers must be equipped to serve as advocates for all students, there are some actions that are not advised. Teachers who suspect abuse are encouraged *not* to:

- Call the parents or caregivers to discuss suspicions.
- Conduct an examination of unexposed areas of the child's body.
- Assert that the report is an emergency unless the danger appears to be immediate.
- Conduct an investigation.
- Wait to see if the situation improves.
- Discuss suspicions with colleagues, friends, or siblings of the child.
- Promise the child that the teacher will not share information that has been revealed.
- Ignore what the child reports about maltreatment and allow others to determine if reports should be made.[61]

Sexual Abuse Prevention and Education Developing meaningful prevention education strategies focused on sexual abuse is particularly challenging for most teachers. Often, educators feel uncomfortable with the topic or might be uninformed about developmentally appropriate approaches to managing instruction and/or questions about sexual matters. Many teachers believe that sexual issues are best managed within the family rather than in the academic environment. Increasingly, however, teachers are being called on to integrate sexual abuse risk reduction activities into classroom practice.

How should teachers teach the topic of sexual abuse to their students? It is important for teachers to examine their own feelings about teaching sexuality education and about reporting suspicions of sexual abuse. Educators must recognize that children who are empowered with information and skills are better equipped to tell an adult that they or a sibling is being sexually abused. Children are not to blame for being victimized and cannot defend themselves against adult perpetrators. They can only tell a concerned grown-up. Following are five main points that children should be taught regarding:[62]

1. Children should be taught about the meaning and implications of having a problem. The word *problem* should be defined, and children should be given the opportunity to share examples of problems they or their friends might be having. Typically, examples include fighting, teasing, homework, and sibling rivalries. Some children might bring up abuse or other problems that occur in their homes. If they do, teachers should thank them for sharing that information with the class and agree that abuse is a problem. The teacher should talk to individual students about any abuse in a one-on-one situation at a later time. Teachers then should ask the students how problems make them feel. Typical responses include "sad," "angry," "confused," and "mad." The next task is to discuss appropriate but specific strategies that will help children solve problems. Teachers should emphasize that children should always tell an adult when they have a problem and reinforce that, when problems are not revealed or managed, they tend to grow or get worse.

2. Children should be taught about the availability of support systems. Teachers should explain the concept and identify the two categories of support systems to which children have access: the community and the family. Because a high percentage of abusers are family members, teachers should emphasize community support systems. Teachers must emphasize that people in support systems can help when a problem exists, and that although other children might be part of a support system, it is best to tell an adult when there is a problem. It is also important for teachers to separate family and community support systems because of the high percentage of abusers who are family members. Students should be encouraged to identify specific adults in their personal support system to whom they can turn.

3. Children should be taught the concept of different touches. Teachers should define three different touches: safe, unsafe, and secret. Safe touches are those that make a person feel good. Teachers should ask students to give examples of some safe touches that make students feel comfortable and supported, including hugging, holding hands, a pat on the back, and giving a "high five."

Unsafe touches are those that make a person feel uncomfortable. Teachers should ask students for examples of unsafe touches, including kicking, hitting, pinching, and tripping. Some students might ask if sexual abuse is an unsafe touch. If this happens, teachers can simply tell students that sexual abuse is another type of touch called a secret touch. It is important that teachers define a secret touch in the following way: "A secret touch occurs when an adult or older person touches your genitals, or 'private body parts' (those covered by your bathing suit), or when they encourage or trick you into touching their genitals, or 'private body parts.'" Some school districts encourage

teachers to use correct anatomical terminology for body parts, whereas other districts are more comfortable using the term *private body parts.*

After discussing each type of touch, it is important to ask students how each of these touches would make a person feel. Most students respond that safe touches make them feel happy, and unsafe and secret touches might make them feel weird, confused, or mad. After the three types of touches have been defined and discussed, teachers should continue with a discussion of what to do if someone tries to give them a secret touch. Students should be taught the following rules: Say "no"; get away; and tell someone. It is important for teachers to emphasize that children can and should tell someone, because children might be too afraid to say no, or to get away, or to believe they can tell someone. The concept of support systems can be reinforced when discussing who can or should be told in the event that sexual abuse is occurring.

4. Children should be taught the concept of secrets. Teachers should emphasize that students should never keep a problem about any unsafe or secret touches a secret. It should be stressed that, even if students are afraid to tell, the problem will not go away unless they reveal the problem to a grown-up. Teachers can discuss the concept of secrets that are appropriate to keep, such as a surprise birthday party, versus secrets that are not appropriate to keep, including things that make the child uncomfortable or afraid.

5. Children should be taught the concept of blame or fault associated with sexual abuse. The concept of fault is often very difficult for students to understand. Teachers would be wise to devote adequate time to this topic. Teachers should stress that, as is the case with other forms of maltreatment, any sexual abuse problem is never a child's fault, even if he or she did not follow the rules, say no, get away, and tell someone. Students need to understand that sexual abuse is *always* the fault of the adult. Consequently, children should be supported in not feeling guilty if they have a problem that involves any form of sexual abuse.

In conclusion, the roles for teachers in managing abuse matters in general, and sexual abuse risk reduction in particular, can be challenging. Teachers and all school employees are encouraged to participate in pertinent staff development activities. Only in this way will they be prepared to act as effective advocates and be equipped to organize developmentally appropriate learning activities to meet the needs of the broadest range of learners.

Bullying

As a foundation for being able to thrive in their families, schools, and communities, children need to believe that they are socially, emotionally, and physically safe. Unfortunately many children are confronted by bullying in these important social contexts. Although bullying occurs at all developmental levels, including adulthood, incidence generally escalates in late elementary and reaches the greatest frequency in junior high/middle school. By high school, rates decline.[63] Although

Bullying behavior can lead to more serious acts of violence.

Modern, electronic technology such as computers, tablets, and cell phones provide a mechanism in which students can engage in bullying outside of physical school sites. This form of bullying is known as *cyberbullying*. It includes the use of e-mail, websites, virtual chat rooms, instant messaging, online games, social networking websites and apps, and text messages. Hiding behind relative or complete anonymity of the aforementioned types of communication technology, cyberbullies send or post mean messages, images, videos, or fake social media profiles that threaten, embarrass, and spread rumors.[67]

Electronic aggression or cyberbullying differs from other forms of aggression in that it can be:

bullying often is considered to be an inevitable part of growing up, it can be traumatic, depending on variables including the consistency and severity of the acts, the systems developed to support bullied children, and the internal capacity of a child to manage it.[64]

Bullying includes intentional acts of aggressive behavior that are characterized by an imbalance of power or strength. Although there are some variations in the definitions of bullying, in order to be considered bullying, the behavior must be aggressive and include:

- **An imbalance of power:** Kids who bully use their power to control or harm others. Power imbalances can change over time and in different situations, even if they involve the same people.
- **Repetition:** Bullying behaviors happen more than once or have the potential to happen more than once.[65]

Bullying generally manifests in three ways. Physical bullying includes open attacks such as hitting, kicking, pushing, or punching. Physical bullying can also include damage to or destruction of a person's possessions. Verbal bullying includes actions such as saying or writing mean things. Examples of verbal bullying include name calling, taunting, teasing, threatening, yelling, or making inappropriate sexual comments. Another form of bullying often is more difficult to detect. Social or relational bullying is characterized by manipulation of peer relationships, friendships, or reputation with intent. Perpetrators of social bullying spread rumors, to isolate victims from other students through purposeful social exclusion or public humiliation. Social bullying is also achieved when students exclude another student intentionally or tell others not to be a friend.[66]

- persistent—digital devices offer an ability to immediately and continuously communicate twenty-four hours a day, so it can be difficult for students experiencing cyberbullying to find relief.
- permanent—most information communicated electronically is permanent and public, if not reported and removed.
- hard to notice—because teachers and parents may not overhear or see cyberbullying taking place, it is harder to recognize.[68]

Research has confirmed that bullying is particularly common among students in the middle grades, whether carried out by an individual or by a group. Approximately 30 percent of young people admit to bullying others in surveys.[69] While it is no excuse, the behavior of many bullies is related to being bullied themselves or because of other forms of maltreatment by adults. A growing body of research has confirmed that bullying involves many more people than the bully and person being bullied. Since it is common for this form of violence to take place in public, often there are witnesses. Studies based on playground observations have revealed that in most cases there are at least four other peers that are part of the incident. Such students take on the role either of bystanders, assistants, or reinforcers of the bully, or defenders of the victim. Assistants participate in ridiculing or intimidating the victim and reinforcers provide encouragement for the bully by communicating their approval. Sadly, it is rare for students to come to the aid of the victim because many bystanders interpret that the victim is somehow responsible for or brought the situation on themselves.[70] It is important for teachers to know that students may take on different roles in bullying situations, so understanding the general categories is important.[71]

Teacher's Toolbox 10.3 shows the roles children may take on in bullying-related situations. Teachers also need to understand the risk factors for both perpetrators and those who are bullied.

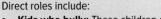

Teacher's Toolbox 10.3

Roles of Bullying

Direct roles include:

- **Kids who bully:** These children engage in bullying behavior toward their peers.
- **Kids who are bullied:** These children are the targets of bullying behavior.

Witnessing/contributing roles include:

- **Kids who assist:** These children may not start the bullying or lead in the bullying behavior, but serve as an "assistant" to children who are bullying. These children may encourage the bullying behavior and occasionally join in.
- **Kids who reinforce:** These children are not directly involved in the bullying behavior but they give the bullying an audience. They will often laugh or provide support for the children who are engaging in bullying. This may encourage the bullying to continue.
- **Outsiders:** These children remain separate from the bullying situation. They neither reinforce the bullying behavior nor defend the child being bullied. Some may watch what is going on but do not provide feedback about the situation to show they are on anyone's side. Even so, providing an audience may encourage the bullying behavior.
  - These kids often want to help, but don't know how. Learn how to be "more than a bystander."
- **Kids who defend:** These children actively comfort the child being bullied and may come to the child's defense when bullying occurs.

SOURCE: U.S. Department of Health and Human Services, *The Roles Kids Play* (www.stopbullying.gov/what-is-bullying/roles-kids-play/index.html; 2017).

Students who are perceived to be different from their peers, including lesbian, gay, bisexual, or transgendered (LGBT) youth, youth with disabilities or who are overweight or underweight, or socially isolated youth may be at an increased risk of being bullied. Students at risk to bully others may have social power and be overly concerned about their own popularity or perceived status among peers. Students who bully may also be easily frustrated, have trouble following rules, and have less parental involvement than their peers. Also, they might have friends who act like bullies. Conversely, some students who bully, are more isolated from peers, have low self-esteem, are less involved in school, or do not recognize or identify with the feelings of others.[72]

Consequences of bullying affect both perpetrators and those who are bullied, including, among others, absence from school, poor academic performance, lack of sleep, behavioral problems, and self-harming.[73] Most people recognize that bullying is a violation of the safety rights of students, and that unchecked it can generate serious and costly consequences for a school community. Bullying has been identified as a common thread in school shootings, student suicides, and costly litigation. In addition, visible incidents and ongoing patterns of more covert bullying can compromise the reputation of a school as a safe place conducive to learning.[74] The manipulation, intimidation, empowerment, and personal satisfaction experienced by many bullies can lead to more serious acts of violence. Many school bullies go on to engage in violent and other risky behaviors into adulthood.[75]

There is no question that bullying is a school safety issue. At its core, bullying is an act of violence. Whether it takes the form of physical or verbal aggression, bullying contributes to a hostile school environment and compromises school success among its victims.[76] Unfortunately, it is not uncommon for adults, including educators, to ignore such acts or to reflect attitudes that enable such violence to continue. These include:

- *Denial:* "We don't have a problem with violence in our community, but that other school district certainly does."
- *Minimization:* "Name-calling, pushing, and shoving are just normal behaviors for kids."
- *Rationalization:* "It is important for all kids to learn to stand up for themselves."
- *Justification:* "Our classes are just too big to do something about bullying."
- *Blame:* "Bullying and other forms of violence are the result of single-parent families and mothers who work outside of their homes."
- *Avoidance:* "My job is to teach; managing violence is an administrative responsibility."[77]

Teachers and other school staff have a tremendous responsibility to create a respectful school climate, yet many teachers and staff feel stressed and unsupported by administrators or peers to intervene in bullying situations. Such a scenario contributes to negative school climates where school professionals engage in disrespectful treatment of students, thereby creating an unsafe emotional context for learning.[78]

It is possible, however, for educational professionals to support each other in creating school climates that deter student bullying. Findings from a National Education Association study of teachers and educational support professionals revealed that teachers were more willing to intervene in bullying situations when they personally felt a sense of connectedness in their school. Teachers felt connected to their school when they believed they were valued as individuals and professionals involved in the learning process. Additionally, teachers felt more capable of intervening when they had effective strategies to do so and felt that others teachers would also intervene.[79] Important actions that teachers can take with each other to promote a culture of respect in their schools are as follows:

- Avoid consistent "student or school" problem-saturated conversation with other teachers.
- Be connected to as many teachers in the school as possible (avoiding exclusionary cliques).
- Remain reflective about the purpose of conversation with other adults about professional challenges and whether the intention is to momentarily vent or solve a problem.
- Foster appreciation on a regular basis by "catching others being successful" or by having special days or events.[80]

Finally, teachers can promote a culture of respect in their schools that prevents students from bullying one another by asking students about bullying so as to reinforce student communication with trusted adults. Teachers should also ask students about their relationships and connect with students who may be socially isolated. Teachers should create democratic learning classrooms that promote positive social norms and reject bullying behaviors, and they can seek professional development on the topic of bullying and promote antibullying values to their peers and students.[81]

Laws such as state education codes and "model" policies that provide examples for schools are addressed differently in each state. Common elements of state laws and policies include clarification of the impact of bullying and the purpose of the law or policy, the scope or breadth of school sites and events to which the law applies, prohibited "bullying" conduct, implementation of the law or policy, communication to all stakeholders about the law or policy, professional development for all school staff, and transparency and

monitoring of incidence about bullying. Examine state bullying laws and schools and districts' requirements at the U.S. Department of Health and Human Services StopBullying.gov website.[82]

What appears to work best in preventing or at least reducing bullying is to establish an evidence-based and comprehensive approach that incorporates the strategies and interventions of many levels and types of participants. All school staff share in the task of recognizing and intervening when they see it, implementing a consistent evidence-based plan to prevent school bullying. In this way, adults can participate in coordinated activities to address bullying and to improve young people's chances for academic and social growth. Review Teacher's Toolbox 10.4 for specific action steps to be taken by all stakeholders in the school community.

Administrators, teachers, law enforcement professionals, students, and parents must join together to reduce the incidences and

---

Teacher's Toolbox 10.4

A Coordinated Approach to Preventing and Managing Bullying

Recommendations for professional members of the school community:

- Treat all staff and students fairly and with respect.
- Come to consensus about a definition of bullying.
- Come to consensus about consequences for bullying behaviors.
- Encourage students to come forward when they or someone they know is being bullied. Reinforce that disclosing bullying is a courageous act that helps maintain a safe environment where everyone can learn.
- When bullying is observed, immediately bring it to a stop. Follow the school's policy for management of bullying with consistency.
- Collaborate to improve supervision at times and in locations where bullying is likely to occur (recess, lunch, in the gym, hallway transitions, on buses).[83]

Recommendations for administrators:

- Work on creating a safe and caring school where relationships between and among students and staff are supportive and civil and where an ethic of nonviolent conflict resolution is the norm. Reinforce all adults in the school for modeling civility and respect.
- Create a school-wide code of conduct that describes in concrete terms how students should and should not treat each other.
- Have clear and nonviolent consequences for bullying and other unacceptable behaviors.
- Ensure that students are supervised carefully.[84]

Recommendations for school counselors and other mental health providers:

- Offer direct and indirect support for students who have been the target of bullying.
- Do not have aggressors and victims work together in a mediated counseling context.
- Provide support and referrals for teachers to implement evidence-based bullying prevention strategies in their classrooms.

- When the victim of bullying needs help beyond the scope of school-based providers, refer the student and family to community mental health resources.[85]

Recommendations for school nurses:

- Be on the alert for overt and subtle signs of bullying (patterns of absences, complaints of nonspecific ailments, poorly explained wounds).
- Follow up with students who experience psychosomatic illnesses to determine if bullying or other child abuse might be involved.
- When bullying is suspected, communicate with school staff to ensure that school policies are implemented immediately and with consistency.
- Communicate and collaborate with counselors and teachers to identify and manage bullying before the onset of complex manifestations that could threaten academic success.[86]

Recommendations for school resource officers:

- Communicate to students and staff that any behavior intended to make someone feel unsafe is unacceptable and will not be allowed.
- When bullying occurs, inform the victim, the aggressor, and their parents or caregivers about school policies and consequences for such behavior.
- Intervene with participants in bullying incidents. Make sure to talk with the victim and the aggressor separately.
- Talk with students about what makes them feel unsafe in and around school.[87]

Recommendations for teachers:

- Work with students to develop classroom codes of behavior that communicate respect to all.
- Enforce classroom codes of conduct with consistency.
- Create developmentally and culturally appropriate instructional activities focused on bullying prevention.
- Following a bullying incident, do not use peer mediation or ask the aggressor and the target to meet and talk things out.[88]

effects of school bullying and its consequences. To this end, all concerned child advocates must take a stand against all forms of school violence, make a commitment to protect all students from emotional and physical injury, and promote school safety as a foundation for reaching the academic mission of the school community. Only in this way can the safety, dignity, and worth of all students be validated.[89]

Sexual Harassment: Acts of Violence, Not Humor or Attraction

Sexual harassment includes unwelcome sexual advances that affect a student's well-being and can compromise a student's ability to feel safe and to succeed in school.[90] Specific acts that constitute sexual harassment or violence include jokes, sexual text messages or e-mail comments, graffiti, sexually degrading skits or artistic depictions, bra snapping, pulling pants down, attempted sexual assault, and rape.[91]

Sexual harassment often happens in public and frequently is witnessed by teachers, coaches, or other adults in supervisory positions. Unfortunately, it is common for adults to fail to intervene or to respond with a wink or a nod upon observing acts that constitute sexual harassment. Such reactions communicate to victims, perpetrators, and any students who might have witnessed the behavior that sexual harassment is developmentally predictable, normal, and/or acceptable. In this way, young people are led to think that such behaviors must be equally acceptable in private.[92]

It is important to note that such behaviors, in addition to having unintended educational consequences, are illegal. Emerging from the civil rights movement of the 1960s and the equal employment rights movement of the 1960s and 1970s, federal law as promulgated in Title IX prohibits sexual discrimination and requires schools to provide equal access to all educational opportunities regardless of sex. Thus, schools have a legal responsibility to prevent and manage sexual harassment as one element of ensuring a safe and nurturing learning environment for all students.[93, 94] Though school communities commonly consider sexual harassment a form of bullying, bullying that is "sexual in nature—sexual harassment, in other words—is illegal."[95]

As for all activities that threaten the safety and potential for academic success of students, schools must develop prevention and intervention policies and practices that are consistently applied. Approaches that coordinate all the school's resources and expertise are most effective. Review Chapter 1 for a reminder of the elements of the *Whole School, Whole Community, Whole Child* model.

Conflict Resolution Education

All too often, small incidents and minor disagreements between young people escalate into destructive or violent acts. Individuals who have not cultivated the necessary skills to resolve conflicts efficiently and effectively will exchange harsh words, tempers will flare, the conflict will evolve, and violence can result.

In response, schools, churches, and community organizations offer training programs to help young people master a range of self-management and conflict resolution skills. In such programs, individuals practice how to:

- Figure out what strategies work best for them to control their anger and how to use them before they lose control.
- Identify adults (parents, teachers, counselors) with whom they can share anger, fears, and concerns.
- Anticipate consequences of potential responses to conflicts.
- Refuse to carry a gun or other weapon and avoid people who carry weapons.
- Avoid or use caution in places or situations in which conflict is common (cafeterias, crowded halls, bathrooms, unsupervised areas outside the school).
- "Reject the bait" for a fight.
- Treat others with respect.
- Weigh options to confront problems and manage conflicts that arise.[96]

Although there is great value in developing a range of self-management and interpersonal skills to resolve conflicts in nonviolent ways, extreme caution is urged when considering the adoption of peer-based approaches to mediate conflicts are questionable. In such programs, adopted in many school communities, students are selected and trained to mediate conflicts between and among students. Although popular, there is no evidence that conflict resolution or peer mediation is effective, particularly when it is applied to stopping bullying. Further, mediation that requires the target of bullying to confront the tormentor can be frightening for the victim and can cause perpetrators to escalate violent acts off school grounds or out of sight of adult supervisors.[97]

©LightField Studios/Shutterstock

Cooperation, respect, and conflict-resolution skills help students maintain positive peer relationships as well as reduce the risk of violence.

It is important to remember that bullying is a form of victimization, characterized by an imbalance of power in a relationship and not an example of peer conflict. Rather than communicating that bullying is a problem to be resolved between two individuals, school staff must take the lead in managing all bullying as a critical element of maintaining a safe environment for all students. School staff must be consistent in communicating that bullying must stop and that they will protect any student who is being victimized rather than delegate this responsibility to peers.

Youth Suicide

The transition from childhood to adolescence is a stressful developmental stage for many young people. In addition to dealing with predictable developmental challenges, many are confronted with mental health concerns, problematic relationships with adults and peers, and family discord. Educators and researchers have concluded that "growing-up today is an achievement rather than an expectation for many children."[98]

Though the pain experienced by youth is translated into news stories and movies, insufficient attention has been paid to strengthening the ability of significant adults to identify early risks and warning signs of mental health disorders and potential suicide. In addition, little is known about how to cultivate community foundations that optimize youth development and increase young people's resilience.[99]

Suicide refers to self-chosen behavior to end one's life that might reveal itself as expressed thoughts (ideation), suicidal gestures (attempts of suicide that do not result in death), and suicide (a death accomplished with intent).

Because suicide attempts that do not require medical attention are unlikely to be reported and a stigma is attached to suicide, it is difficult to get accurate estimates of the scope of the problem among American youth. The problems associated with underreporting are exaggerated because classification of a death as suicide requires others to draw conclusions about the intent of the student who has died.[100]

There is no simple answer to why youth commit suicide. Many adults conclude that youth suicide attempts are associated with attention seeking or motivations for revenge ("You'll be sorry when I'm gone"), but the research does not support this conclusion. Rather, evidence suggests that most adolescent suicides are associated with depression leading to the pursuit of escape or a desire to end painful life circumstances.[101] Additional identified risk factors for suicide include a history of previous attempts, family history, alcohol or other drug abuse, easy access to lethal means to commit suicide, isolation, barriers to accessing mental health treatment, and an unwillingness to seek help because of the stigma attached to mental health and substance abuse.[102]

To reduce and prevent suicide successfully, concerned adults must learn to recognize suicidal youth and refer them to professionals with specific expertise. In addition, parents, teachers, and community resource professionals must develop strategies to maximize protective factors and reduce risks for intentional injuries among youth.[103] Specific suggestions to support the work of administrators and teachers in this regard are discussed in Chapter 14.

Recommendations for Concepts and Practice

Healthy Behavior Outcomes

The goal of health education is to help students adopt or maintain health-enhancing behaviors. School districts and teachers should identify the health-enhancing behaviors they would like their students to maintain or adopt. The list found in the Teacher's Toolbox 10.4 identifies possible healthy behavioral outcomes related to preventing violence. Although not all of these suggestions are developmentally appropriate for students in grades K–8, the list can help teachers understand how the learning activities they plan for their students support both short- and long-term desired behavior outcomes.[104]

Developmentally Appropriate Concepts and Skills As with other health topics, teaching related to preventing violence should be developmentally appropriate and based on the physical, cognitive, social, emotional, and language characteristics of specific students. Teacher's Toolbox 10.5 contains a list of suggested developmentally appropriate knowledge and skill expectations to help teachers create lessons that will encourage students to practice the desired behavior outcomes by the time they graduate from high school.[105] Before each knowledge and skill expectation, the number represents topic abbreviation (V of Violence Prevention), *NHES* standard number, grade group (last grade in that group), and knowledge or skill expectation item number. For example, V1.5.1 would represent Violence, standard 1, grade group 3–5, knowledge expectation item 1.

STRATEGIES FOR LEARNING AND ASSESSMENT

Preventing Violence

This section provides examples of standards-based learning and assessment strategies for preventing violence. The strategies begin with a restatement of the standard and a reminder of the assessment criteria, drawn from the RMC Health rubrics in Appendix B. Strategies are written as directions

Teacher's Toolbox 10.5

Developmentally Appropriate Concepts and Skill Expectations for Preventing Violence

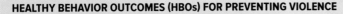

HEALTHY BEHAVIOR OUTCOMES (HBOs) FOR PREVENTING VIOLENCE

HBO 1. Manage interpersonal conflict in nonviolent ways.

HBO 2. Manage emotional distress in nonviolent ways.

HBO 3. Avoid bullying, being a bystander to bullying, or being a victim of bullying.

HBO 4. Avoid engaging in violence, including sexual harassment, coercion, exploitation, physical fighting, and rape.

HBO 5. Avoid situations where violence is likely to occur.

HBO 6. Avoid associating with others who are involved in or who encourage violence or criminal activity.

HBO 7. Get help to prevent or stop violence including harassment, abuse, bullying, hazing, fighting, and hate crimes.

HBO 8. Get help to prevent or stop inappropriate touching.

HBO 9. Get help to stop being subjected to violence or physical abuse.

HBO 10. Get help for oneself or others who are in danger of hurting themselves.

Grades K–2 Knowledge Expectations	Grades 3–5 Knowledge Expectations	Grades 6–8 Knowledge Expectations
NHES 1: Core Concepts		
V1.2.1 Describe the difference between bullying and teasing. (HBO 3)	V1.5.1 Identify nonviolent ways to manage anger. (HBO 2)	V1.12.1 Analyze why prosocial behaviors can help prevent violence. (HBO 1)
V1.2.2 Explain why it is wrong to tease or bully others. (HBO 3)	V1.5.2 Describe the benefits of using nonviolent means to solve interpersonal conflict. (HBO 1)	V1.12.2 Describe ways to express anger nonviolently. (HBO 1 & 2)
V1.2.3 Explain what to do if someone is being bullied. (HBO 3 & 9)	V1.5.3 Explain that anger is a normal emotion. (HBO 2)	V1.12.3 Summarize nonviolent ways to respond to stress when angry or upset. (HBO 2)
V1.2.4 Identify "appropriate" and "inappropriate" or "safe" and "unsafe" touches. (HBO 8)	V1.5.4 Identify examples of self-control. (HBO 2)	V1.12.4 Analyze why it is important to understand the perspectives of others in resolving a conflict situation. (HBO 2)
	V1.5.5 Describe the difference between bullying and teasing. (HBO 3)	V1.12.5 Summarize the qualities of a healthy dating relationship. (HBO 2)
V1.2.5 Explain why inappropriate touches should be reported to a trusted adult. (HBO 8)	V1.5.6 Define prejudice, discrimination, and bias. (HBO 3)	V1.12.6 Evaluate effective nonviolent strategies for dealing with difficult relationships with family members, peers, and boyfriends or girlfriends. (HBO 2)
V1.2.6 Explain that a child is not at fault if someone touches him or her in an inappropriate way. (HBO 8)	V1.5.7 Explain why it is wrong to tease or bully others based on personal characteristics (such as body type, gender, appearance, mannerisms, and the way one dresses or acts). (HBO 3)	V1.12.7 Summarize impulsive behaviors that can lead to violence and strategies for controlling them. (HBO 2 & 3)
	V1.5.8 Describe examples of prosocial behaviors that help prevent violence. (HBO 3 & 4)	V1.12.8 Analyze how power and control differences in relationships (peer, dating, or family relationships) can contribute to aggression and violence. (HBO 2 & 5)
V1.2.7 Explain why everyone has the right to tell others not to touch his or her body. (HBO 8)	V1.5.9 Identify short- and long-term consequences of violence to perpetrators, victims, and bystanders. (HBO 3 & 4)	V1.12.9 Analyze how mental and emotional health can affect violence-related related behaviors. (HBO 3)
	V1.5.10 Describe what to do if oneself or someone else is being bullied. (HBO 3 & 7)	V1.12.10 Analyze the negative consequences of violence to perpetrators, victims, and bystanders. (HBO 3)
	V1.5.11 Recognize techniques that are used to coerce or pressure someone to use violence. (HBO 4, 5 & 6)	V1.12.11 Explain how bystanders can help prevent violence by reporting dangerous situations or actions. (HBO 3 & 7)
	V1.5.12 Identify examples of dangerous or risky behaviors that might lead to injuries. (HBO 4, 5 & 6)	V1.12.12 Analyze the consequences of prejudice, discrimination, racism, sexism, and hate crimes. (HBO 3 & 7)
	V1.5.13 Identify situations that might lead to violence. (HBO 5)	V1.12.13 Explain why it is an individual's responsibility to verify that all sexual contact is consensual. (HBO 4)
	V1.5.14 Identify strategies to avoid physical fighting and violence. (HBO 5)	V1.12.14 Explain why it is wrong to trick, threaten, or coerce another person into having sex. (HBO 4)
	V1.5.15 Describe how participation in gangs can lead to violence. (HBO 6)	V1.12.15 Analyze techniques that are used to coerce or pressure someone to have sex. (HBO 4 & 8)
	V1.5.16 Explain the difference between tattling and reporting aggression, bullying, or violence. (HBO 7)	
	V1.5.17 Distinguish between "appropriate" and "inappropriate" touch. (HBO 8)	

Grades K–2 Knowledge Expectations	Grades 3–5 Knowledge Expectations	Grades 6–8 Knowledge Expectations

NHES 1: Core Concepts (*continued*)

	V1.5.18 Explain that inappropriate touches should be reported to a trusted adult. (HBO 8)	V1.12.16 Summarize why individuals have the right to refuse sexual contact. (HBO 4 & 8)
	V1.5.19 Explain why it is not the child's fault if someone touches him or her in an inappropriate way. (HBO 8)	V1.12.17 Analyze the relationship between using alcohol and other drugs and violence. (HBO 5)
	V1.5.20 Explain that everyone has the right to tell others not to touch his or her body. (HBO 8 & 9)	V1.12.18 Describe characteristics of the school or community that can increase or decrease the likelihood of violence. (HBO 5)
	V1.5.21 Explain the importance of telling an adult if someone is in danger of hurting themselves or others. (HBO 10)	V1.12.19 Analyze situations that could lead to different types of violence. (HBO 5)

Grades K–2 Skill Expectations	Grades 3–5 Skill Expectations	Grades 6–8 Skill Expectations

NHES 2: Analyze Influences

V2.2.1 Identify relevant influences of family on violence prevention practices and behaviors.	V2.5.1 Identify relevant influences of culture on violence prevention practices and behaviors.	V2.8.1 Explain the influence of school rules and community laws on violence prevention practices and behaviors.
V2.2.2 Identify relevant influences of school on violence prevention practices and behaviors.	V2.5.2 Identify relevant influences of peers on violence prevention practices and behaviors.	V2.8.2 Explain how perceptions of norms influence healthy and unhealthy violence and violence prevention practices and behaviors.
V2.2.3 Identify relevant influences of media and technology on violence prevention practices and behaviors.	V2.5.3 Identify relevant influences of community on violence prevention practices and behaviors.	V2.8.3 Explain how social expectations influence healthy and unhealthy violence and violence prevention practices and behaviors.
V2.2.4 Describe positive influences on violence prevention practices and behaviors.	V2.5.4 Describe how relevant influences of family and culture affect personal violence prevention practices and behaviors.	V2.8.4 Explain how personal values and beliefs influence personal violence prevention practices and behaviors.
V2.2.5 Describe negative influences on violence prevention practices and behaviors	V2.5.5 Describe how relevant influences of school and community affect personal violence prevention practices and behaviors.	V2.8.5 Describe how some health risk behaviors influence the likelihood of engaging in violent behaviors (e.g., how alcohol and other drug use influence violent behaviors).
	V2.5.6 Describe how relevant influences of media and technology affect personal violence prevention practices and behaviors.	V2.8.6 Analyze how relevant influences of family and culture affect personal violence practices and behaviors.
	V2.5.7 Describe how relevant influences of peers affect personal violence prevention practices and behaviors.	V2.8.7 Analyze how relevant influences of school and community affect personal violence practices and behaviors.
		V2.8.8 Analyze how relevant influences of media and technology affect personal violence practices and behaviors.
		V2.8.9 Analyze how relevant influences of peers affect personal violence prevention practices and behaviors.

NHES 3: Accessing Information, Products, and Services

V3.2.1 Identify trusted adults at home who can help prevent violence.	V3.5.1 Describe characteristics of accurate violence prevention information.	V3.8.1 Analyze the validity and reliability of violence prevention information.
V3.2.2 Identify trusted adults and professionals in school who can help prevent violence (e.g., school counselor, principal).		V3.8.2 Analyze the validity and reliability of violence prevention or intervention services.

(continued)

Teacher's Toolbox 10.5 (*continued*)

Grades K–2 Skill Expectations	Grades 3–5 Skill Expectations	Grades 6–8 Skill Expectations

NHES 3: Accessing Information, Products, and Services (*continued*)

V3.2.3 Identify trusted adults and professionals in the community who can help prevent violence (e.g., police officer).

V3.2.4 Explain how to locate school health helpers who can help reduce or avoid violence (e.g., school counselor, principal).

V3.2.5 Explain how to locate community health helpers who can help reduce or avoid violence (e.g., police officer).

V3.2.6 Demonstrate how to locate school or community health helpers who can help reduce or avoid violence (e.g., police officer, 911).

V3.5.2 Describe characteristics of appropriate and trustworthy health services that help reduce or avoid violence.

V3.5.3 Demonstrate how to locate sources of accurate violence prevention information.

V3.8.3 Describe situations that call for professional violence prevention or intervention services.

V3.8.4 Access valid and reliable violence prevention information from home, school, or community.

V3.8.5 Locate valid and reliable violence prevention or intervention services.

NHES 4: Interpersonal Communication

V4.2.1 Demonstrate how to effectively communicate needs, wants, and feelings in healthy ways to prevent violence.

V4.2.2 Demonstrate effective active listening skills including paying attention, and verbal and nonverbal feedback to prevent violence.

V4.2.3 Demonstrate effective refusal skills, including firmly saying "no" and getting away, to avoid or prevent violence.

V4.2.4 Demonstrate how to effectively tell a trusted adult when feeling threatened or harmed.

V4.2.5 Identify how to communicate care and concern for others to prevent violence.

V4.5.1 Demonstrate effective verbal and nonverbal communication skills to prevent violence.

V4.5.2 Explain how to be empathetic and compassionate toward others to prevent violence.

V4.5.3 Demonstrate effective peer-resistance skills to avoid or reduce violence.

V4.5.4 Demonstrate healthy ways to manage or resolve conflict to prevent violence.

V4.5.5 Demonstrate how to effectively ask for help to prevent violence.

V4.5.6 Demonstrate how to effectively communicate support for others to prevent violence.

V4.8.1 Demonstrate the use of effective verbal and nonverbal communication skills to prevent violence.

V4.8.2 Demonstrate effective peer-resistance skills to avoid or reduce violence.

V4.8.3 Demonstrate effective negotiation skills to avoid or reduce violence.

V4.8.4 Demonstrate healthy ways to manage or resolve conflict to prevent violence.

V4.8.5 Demonstrate how to effectively ask for assistance to prevent violence.

V4.8.6 Demonstrate how to communicate empathy and support for others to prevent violence.

NHES 5: Decision Making

V5.2.1 Identify situations that need a decision that could lead to violence.

V5.2.2 Describe how family, peers, or media influence a decision that could lead to violence.

V5.2.3 Explain the potential positive and negative outcomes from a decision that could lead to violence.

V5.2.4 Describe when help is needed and when it is not needed to make a decision related to violence prevention.

V5.5.1 Identify situations that need a decision to prevent violence.

V5.5.2 Decide when help is needed and when it is not needed to make a decision that could lead to violence.

V5.5.3 Explain how family, culture, peers, or media influence a decision that could lead to violence.

V5.5.4 Identify options and their potential outcomes when making a decision that could lead to violence.

V5.5.5 Choose a healthy option when making a decision that could lead to violence.

V5.5.6 Describe the final outcome of a decision related to violence prevention.

V5.8.1 Identify circumstances that help or hinder making a decision to prevent violence.

V5.8.2 Determine when potentially violent situations require a decision.

V5.8.3 Distinguish when decisions about potentially violent situations should be made individually or with others.

V5.8.4 Explain how family, culture, media, peers, and personal beliefs affect a decision that could lead to violence.

V5.8.5 Distinguish between healthy and unhealthy alternatives of a decision that could lead to violence.

V5.8.6 Predict the potential outcomes of healthy and unhealthy alternatives to a decision that could lead to violence.

V5.8.7 Choose a healthy alternative when making a decision that could lead to violence.

V5.8.8 Analyze the effectiveness of a final outcome of a decision that could lead to violence.

Grades K–2 Skill Expectations	Grades 3–5 Skill Expectations	Grades 6–8 Skill Expectations

NHES 6: Goal Setting

V6.2.1 Identify a realistic personal short-term goal to prevent violence.	V6.5.1 Set a realistic personal goal to prevent violence.	V6.8.1 Assess personal violent and nonviolent practices.
V6.2.2 Take steps to achieve the personal goal to prevent violence.	V6.5.2 Track progress to achieving a personal goal to prevent violence.	V6.8.2 Set a realistic personal goal to prevent violence.
V6.2.3 Identify people who can help achieve a personal goal to prevent violence.	V6.5.3 Identify resources that can help achieve a personal goal to prevent violence.	V6.8.3 Assess the barriers to achieving a personal goal to prevent violence.
		V6.8.4 Apply strategies to overcome barriers to achieving a personal goal to prevent violence.
		V6.8.5 Use strategies and skills to achieve a personal goal to prevent violence.

NHES 7: Self-Management

V7.2.1 Identify practices that reduce or prevent violence.	V7.5.1 Describe practices and behaviors that reduce or prevent violence.	V7.8.1 Explain the importance of being responsible for practicing violence prevention behaviors.
V7.2.2 Demonstrate violence prevention practices.	V7.5.2 Demonstrate violence prevention practices and behaviors.	V7.8.2 Analyze personal practices and behaviors that reduce or prevent violence.
V7.2.3 Make a commitment to practice violence prevention behaviors.	V7.5.3 Make a commitment to practice violence prevention behaviors.	V7.8.3 Demonstrate violence prevention practices and behaviors to improve the health of oneself and others.
		V7.8.4 Make a commitment to practice violence prevention behaviors.

NHES 8: Advocacy

V8.2.1 Make requests to others to prevent violence.	V8.5.1 Give factual information to others to prevent violence.	V8.8.1 State a health-enhancing position on a violence prevention topic, supported with accurate information, to improve the health of others.
V8.2.2 Demonstrate how to encourage peers to prevent violence.	V8.5.2 State personal beliefs to help others prevent violence.	V8.8.2 Persuade others to prevent violence.
	V8.5.3 Demonstrate how to persuade others to prevent violence.	V8.8.3 Collaborate with others to advocate for individuals, families, and schools to prevent violence.
		V8.8.4 Demonstrate how to adapt violence prevention messages for different audiences.

SOURCE: Centers for Disease Control and Prevention, *Health Education Curriculum Analysis Tool* (Atlanta, GA: Centers for Disease Control and Prevention, 2012).

for teachers and include applicable theory of planned behavior constructs in parentheses (intention to act in healthy ways, attitudes toward behavior, subjective norms, perceived behavioral control). These learning and assessment strategies provide building blocks for standards-based lessons and units that can be tailored to local needs. Assessment criteria are used with permission from the RMC Health. See Appendix B for Scoring Rubrics.

Additional strategies for learning and assessment for Chapter 10, including a complete list of all the strategies, is available at the Online Learning Center.

NHES 1 | Core Concepts

Students will comprehend concepts related to health promotion and disease prevention to enhance health.

ASSESSMENT CRITERIA

- Connections—Describe relationships between behavior and health; draw logical conclusions about connections between behavior and health.
- Comprehensiveness—Thoroughly cover health topic, showing breadth and depth; give accurate information.

Grades K–2

When I Feel This, My Body Feels That   One concept that is important for young students to learn is to be able to identify "appropriate" and "inappropriate" touches. Much of what makes a touch "appropriate" or "inappropriate" is how it makes a person feel, so exploring the relationship between physical sensations and feelings can be key in helping young students grasp this concept. Kane and Quackenbush recommend using stories, vignettes, or pictures that suggest different emotions.[106] Students can then be asked to think about the feelings a character might be having. Teachers can explain that a person's body will often tell him or her about feelings. They can ask students to explain how the character might feel in his or her body. Students can then identify what the emotion might be. Students can attempt to imagine some of their own body feelings in different situations, such as waiting in line to ride on a big roller coaster. Teachers can ask students, how does your body feel? How does your body react or respond? What is the emotion you are experiencing? Other situations that can be used to get students to imagine might be having a pet die, getting hugged too tight by a relative you don't know very well, or someone sitting too close to you on the couch to watch a movie. Teachers can discuss with students if there are people they would give a "high five" and/or a handshake to, but not others, and why that is. Do they get a feeling in advance of the touch that guides them in their interactions with others? These and other situations can be used to extend the conversation about how their body feels, the feelings being experienced, and touches that make a person feel comfortable and uncomfortable. Questions for teachers to explore with students include: What makes certain touches feel uncomfortable? How do you know you are feeling uncomfortable—what signs does your body give you? What should you do when touches make you feel uncomfortable?

ASSESSMENT | Teachers should provide students with one additional scenario or vignette. For the assessment task, students can draw a picture of how the situation makes them feel and select the appropriate feeling word from a word wall of feeling words. For assessment criteria, students should be able to explain their drawings, which should connect to the selected word wall word selected by the student. Students should be able to recognize the connection between how a person's body might feel and the corresponding emotion. (Construct: Attitudes toward behavior.)

Talking Drawings Locate a children's literature book focused on children telling a trusted adult when they are feeling sad and need to talk or effectively communicating needs, wants, and feelings related to bullying, teasing, or touching that feels unsafe or uncomfortable. Prior to reading this book to the students, invite students to draw a picture on the topic. Ask students to show what they know about the topic through their picture. They can label items or phrases or just draw. Have students share their drawings upon completion. Now read the story to the class.

ASSESSMENT | Following the reading of the story on the topic, ask students to modify their drawings or, if it is easier, create an entirely new drawing on the topic based on the story that was shared. Encourage students to label parts of their illustrations and use any new technical terms they heard in the story. Have students share their drawings and discuss what they changed in their illustration after they listened to the text.

Words, Hands, and Feet: Talking with Children About Pro-Social Behavior Teachers can read Elizabeth Verdick's books (*Feet Are Not for Kicking, Words Are Not for Hurting*) and Martine Agassi's *Hands Are Not for Hitting* with students to discuss behavior at school and at home. See Chapter 5 for information about these books and "Children's Literature" at the end of this chapter for other children's books about how students treat each other. After reading the books, students should be able to describe ways to use their words, hands, and feet to help others.

ASSESSMENT | For an assessment task, teachers can make a three-column chart that students complete by telling how they can use their words, hands, and feet in healthy ways. For assessment criteria, students should be able to identify at least three healthy ways each to use words, hands, and feet. (Construct: Attitudes toward behavior.)

Grades 3–5

Feeling Angry Is Normal: What We Do About It Can Keep Us Healthy An important core concept for violence prevention is that anger is a normal human feeling and feeling angry is okay. We must think about our responses to anger to determine whether we remain safe and healthy. Students can list some of the things that make them angry, without using anyone's name. Teachers can record the students' list on the left side of a piece of chart paper and then ask what they or others do when they feel angry. Students will give a range of responses. Students can go back to the list they made earlier in the lesson. For each item on the list, students can name a healthy way people can handle their anger. List

these healthy ways of managing anger on the chart. This activity links to NHES 7, self-management. Teachers might also want to read children's books, such as those suggested at the end of Chapter 5 and this chapter, in which characters experience and express strong negative feelings. Students can discuss the healthy ways the characters managed being angry or upset.

ASSESSMENT | The assessment task for this activity is the students' list of healthy ways to manage anger. For assessment criteria, students should be able to explain why the ways they have selected are healthy and to draw conclusions about connections between behaviors (healthy anger management) and good health. (Construct: Attitudes toward behavior.)

Snitching or Asking for Help? Many kids this age can relate to the younger child who tattles all the time, but may still find it challenging to separate tattling (or often referred to by upper-elementary students as snitching) from asking for help. Teachers can read the book *A Bad Case of Tattle Tongue* by Julia Cook, which is a humorous story about a boy that tattles too much, resulting in him having no friends and his tongue turning yellow. The story presents "tattle rules" for students to understand the difference between unnecessary tattling and the necessity of sharing with an adult about important matters. While this story is best suited for early-elementary students, the story can be used to humorously help upper-elementary students reconnect with the concept and come up with their own age-appropriate strategies for dealing with the issue. The teacher can lead a discussion following the story. Questions to ask include: What do your friends call tattling (this will help get students using the same language)? Is there a difference between tattling and snitching (or whatever the commonly used word is), and if so, what is it? Why do kids tattle/snitch? What is the consequence of regular tattling/snitching? If tattling/snitching is a problem with peers, how does a student know when to share with an adult?

ASSESSMENT | Pairs of students will create their own set of "snitch rules" (or whatever the agreed on commonly used word or phrase is). Each pair of students needs to create a poster identifying a few key rules about when it is critical for a young person to ask for help from an adult. Students can share their posters with the class. For assessment criteria, students should create at least three key rules related to student emotional or physical safety. Students should be able to explain why and how the rules they developed help students stay safe and draw conclusions between behavior and health. (Constructs: Perceived behavioral control, subjective norms, attitude toward behavior.)

Fact or Fiction Middle school students receive many mixed messages about violence, fighting, sexual assault, and child abuse. Students, individually or in pairs, are to select a specific violence topic to explore. Have students complete a KWL Chart, identifying what they currently know (K) to be true about the violence topic being researched in column one of the chart. In column two, students are to identify a minimum of three things they want to know (W) about their violence topic. In the final column, students will use credible sources (Standard 3) to determine if what they know (K) is fact or fiction. They will then identify on their KWL Chart which pieces of information they know are fact or fiction and find answers to the three things listed in the W column providing justification as to why the sources being used are credible.

ASSESSMENT | Students will write a Three-Minute Pause, which is a chance for students to reflect on the concepts and ideas they have learned and organize their thoughts, in which they answer all/some of the following questions:

- The health risks associated with (violence topic) are . . .
- I changed my attitude about . . .
- I became more aware of . . .
- I was surprised about . . .

- I still wonder . . .
- In conclusion, I believe violence (topic) . . .

Students should provide accurate information and draw conclusions about what they learned in their research and the connections between behavior and health. They also should be able to cite their resources and be able to state why their sources used in their KWL Chart are valid sources of information. (Construct: Attitudes toward behavior.)

Grades 6–8

No Name-Calling Week: No Sticks, No Stones, No Dissing Students and teachers can learn more about No Name-Calling Week at https://www.glsen.org/no-name-calling-week. No Name-Calling Week is an annual week of educational activities aimed at ending name-calling of all kinds and providing schools with the tools and inspiration to launch an ongoing dialogue about ways to eliminate bullying in their communities. Teachers and students can join the network, plan an event, and learn about resources. This activity links to NHES 8, advocacy. Lesson plans and other resources available at the site include posters, stickers, tips for creating classroom and school policies about bullying, and specific advice for students, parents, and teachers.

ASSESSMENT | For an assessment task, students can work in small groups to investigate one of the topics on the website. For assessment criteria, students should present their topics to the class, explaining how to implement "no name-calling" strategies and drawing conclusions about connections between behavior (no name-calling) and health. (Construct: Subjective norms.)

Targets, Perpetrators, Bystanders, and Problem Solvers This activity is based on a curriculum titled *Victims, Aggressors, and Bystanders,* developed as part of the Teenage Health Teaching Modules.[107] Teachers should begin by describing a conflict situation from literature, the news, or a fictional event. After students have heard the situation, they should try to identify these roles:

- *Target:* Who was the object of the conflict?
- *Perpetrator:* Who started, caused, or carried out the conflict?
- *Bystander:* Was anyone else present who didn't help?
- *Problem solver:* Who, if anyone, worked to solve the problem?

Students should discuss how the conflict could have been avoided. After students have identified the roles, they can work in small groups to describe true or fictional conflicts they have seen on television or in the movies, heard about, or created. Students should be careful not to use the name of anyone in the school or community. Teachers should encourage students to use the term *target* rather than *victim,* a word that can denote powerlessness. Students can identify the roles of target, perpetrator, bystander, and, if present, problem solver in their scenarios.

ASSESSMENT | Students' role identifications are the assessment task. For assessment criteria, students should explain why they assigned these roles based on behavior, tell how the characters could have avoided the conflict, and draw conclusions about the connections between behavior (avoiding or preventing conflict) and health. (Construct: Perceived behavioral control.)

What Does My School Say About Harassment? Students can investigate the definitions and consequences of harassment of any kind in their school system. In most cases, students can find this information on state or local education websites. A sample policy states,

Harassment means a person acts with intent to harass, bully, annoy, or alarm if he or she:

1. Strikes, shoves, kicks, or otherwise touches a person in an offensive manner or subjects another person to offensive physical contact.

2. Insults, taunts, or challenges another person in a manner likely to provoke a violent response.
3. Makes verbal or nonverbal expressions related to race, color, national origin, ancestry, sex, religion, disability, or sexual orientation, creating an intimidating, hostile or offensive school environment, or interfering with the education of a student, or otherwise adversely affecting the educational opportunity of a student.
4. Name calls, makes rude gestures, insults, or constantly teases another person who feels humiliated, intimidated, threatened, and/or embarrassed.
5. Makes a telephone call without purpose of legitimate communication.
6. Makes repeated communications anonymously, or at extremely inconvenient hours, or in offensively coarse language.
7. Causes fear as to prevent others from gaining legitimate access to or use of school buildings, facilities, or grounds such as, but not limited to, restroom facilities.
8. Causes others to feel uncomfortable, pressured, threatened, or in danger as a result of sexually related verbal or physical activity (sexual harassment).
9. Displays or possesses a "look-alike" gun or weapon.[108]

Students should note in item 4 that harassment occurs if another person "feels humiliated, intimidated, threatened and/or embarrassed." In other words, excuses such as "I was only kidding" or "I wasn't talking to him" provide no protection for perpetrators. Students should examine the antiharassment policies in their schools and districts carefully to understand how students are protected at school. They can invite an administrator to the classroom to help them understand the policies and the consequences of harassment. One school superintendent stated, "No student should feel threatened at school because of his or her race, color, national origin, ancestry, sex, religion, disability, or sexual orientation—or for any other reasons relating to personal identity or beliefs."[109] Teachers also can refer to the curriculum *Flirting or Hurting?* for more information on preventing or responding to harassment at school.[110] This activity links to NHES 3, access information, products, and services.

ASSESSMENT | For an assessment task, students can define and provide examples of the antiharassment policy at their school. For assessment criteria, students should provide accurate information and draw conclusions about connections between behaviors (a harassment-free campus) and good health. (Construct: Attitudes toward behavior.)

NHES 2 | Analyze Influences

Students will analyze the influence of family, peers, culture, media, technology, and other factors on health behaviors.

ASSESSMENT CRITERIA
- Identify both external and internal influences on health.
- Explain how external and internal influences interact to impact health choices and behaviors.
- Explain both positive and negative influences, as appropriate.

Grades K–2

Family and School Influences As a class use a mind or concept map to brainstorm different ways that family and school are positive influences for preventing violence. This brainstorming allows students to gain an understanding of the many different ways that rules, practices, and expectations help young people prevent violent practices and behaviors. This also allows students to understand how other families influence children to prevent violence.

ASSESSMENT | For an assessment task, have students create a word shape focused either on family or school. Inside the word shape, they should include words that emphasize how family or school positively influence them to prevent violence. For assessment criteria, students can share their word shapes and be able to express ways their family or school are positive influences for preventing violence. (Constructs: Subjective norms, perceived behavioral control.)

What Do Big Kids Do?   Teachers can ask children to think about what their older brothers, sisters, other relatives, friends, and students at school do when they get mad or stressed. Children might think of positive and negative examples of behavior. Invite several older students to talk with younger students about their stress and anger management strategies. Older students can role-play scenarios for younger students. This activity can be especially meaningful for older students, who see themselves as role models for younger children. This activity builds on the idea of positive models as an important influence in students' lives. Students can brainstorm positive and negative responses to stress or anger ("My grandpa says take a deep breath"; "My brother kicked the dog"). Teachers shouldn't express critical opinions of children's families but instead should focus on ways to handle stress and anger that don't hurt anyone. Having older students demonstrate various kinds of healthy anger or stress management strategies and explain why they chose them provides an excellent source of positive models for younger children.

ASSESSMENT | For an assessment task, younger students can describe or write about a healthy anger or stress management strategy that they saw modeled or heard discussed. For assessment criteria, students should explain how the older person they saw or individual influenced their selection. (Construct: Subjective norms.)

Grades 3–5

Personal Relationship Web   Students can draw a circle (about the size of a quarter) in the middle of a page and label the circle "Me." Depending on the age of the students, they should draw from five to ten other circles scattered around the "Me" circle and label these with the initials of the people with whom they have most regular contact (parents or caregivers, siblings, other relatives, classmates, teachers). Students should draw different kinds of lines from their circle to the circles of the other people to indicate the nature of their relationship. For example, a straight line might indicate a peaceful, solid relationship. A curvy line might indicate a relationship with ups and downs. A jagged line might indicate a relationship with conflicts or problems. For each of the relationships they identify, students can write a three-word description and one strategy they can use to maintain or improve the relationship. Students can reexamine their relationship page over time and write about ways their relationships are progressing.

ASSESSMENT | The relationship webs students create are the assessment task for this activity. For assessment criteria, students should explain how these relationships influence their feelings and behaviors and give strategies for maintaining or improving their relationships. (Construct: Perceived behavioral control.)

Television and Movie Conflict Analysis   Students can work in small groups to discuss television programs or movies, including animated features, they have seen that involve various types of conflict situations. Students also can watch a clip from a show or movie in class for discussion. Students should note the precipitating events (what led up to the conflict), the motivation of different characters, and the resolution (what happened). Students should be alert to depictions of alcohol and other drug use in relation to conflict and violence. Students can discuss how they

believe these types of media scenarios do and do not influence students. Students also might want to rewrite the endings for some of the situations.

ASSESSMENT | For an assessment task, students can discuss or write about the ways they think television and movie situations influence the behavior of students their age and other ages. For assessment criteria, students should explain at least two ways media could influence behavior and offer more health-enhancing resolutions, if needed. (Constructs: Attitudes toward behavior, subjective norms.)

Grades 6–8

Socialization Collages   Students can work in mixed-sex small groups to find magazine pictures that illustrate the different ways males and females are depicted as they communicate, solve problems, resolve conflicts, dress, and express themselves. Students can use the pictures to make a split-image collage of male and female socialization in the United States. Students can show their collages to the class, discuss the media messages, and respond to the media messages they find misleading or false. As students compare media images of what males and females do and how they "are," they likely will find stereotypes with which they disagree for both sexes. Additionally, students can explore and discuss media messages they observed that could lead to different types of violence.

ASSESSMENT | The collages students create are the assessment task for this activity. For assessment criteria, students should identify and explain stereotypes they encounter about males and females and respond to the stereotypes with alternative and health-enhancing ways males and females behave and respond to others. In particular, students should be alert for how alcohol and other drug use contributes to violence-related situations (e.g., fighting and sexual assault). (Construct: Subjective norms.)

Courage Continuum   This activity is based on a lesson titled "Courage by Degrees" from Nan Stein's *Bullyproof* curriculum.[111] It invites students to think deeply about the varying degrees of courage required to respond to different types of teasing and bullying. To analyze influences, students must scratch beneath the surface of what happens at school to understand those factors—particularly the perceived opinions as well as the responses of peers—that influence students' actions. Teachers can create a list of sentences that describe various teasing and bullying situations at school. (Teachers might need help from students if they have trouble making such a list.) The question to ask about each scenario is how hard would it be (or how much courage would it take) to

- Invite a new kid at school who has been left out all week to play a game at recess?
- Join a girl who is considered somewhat of an outcast at lunch?
- Run away from some mean older kids who yell for you to come there right now?
- Tell a teacher a fight is being planned for recess?

As teachers read each sentence, students should stand along a continuum or line labeled "very hard to do" at one end and "very easy to do" at the other. Students can discuss the factors that influence their choices (popularity, whether public or private, what friends do during the activity). Teachers might want to read Bernard Waber's book *Courage* and Maya Angelou's poem "Life Doesn't Frighten Me" to the class as part of this activity (see the books on courage in "Children's Literature" in Chapter 5).

ASSESSMENT | For an assessment task, students can discuss or write about the situation they thought took the very most and very least courage. For assessment criteria, students should explain at least two factors in each scenario that made it difficult or easy to deal with from their perspective. In particular, students should explain how other students influenced them during the activity. Being influenced by friends is normal, but sometimes students need to make decisions for themselves that differ from those of friends. Students also might want to make their own "Courage" class book. (Construct: Subjective norms.)

Photo Journaling About Violence Prevention Influences   Engage students in a lesson/discussion regarding the various influences they experience related to violence (e.g., media, parents, peers, school policies, culture, values, etc.). Explain to students that a photo journal is a series of photos that chronicles an experience, a person's day, or a special event. For this purpose, students will be capturing the influences of violence in their life. Assign students a minimum number of different influences, include both internal and external influences, they need to capture through a photograph. For each photo, students are to create a caption that explains the way in which the photo is or symbolizes an influence. Photo journals can be displayed in many ways depending on the technology available to students.

ASSESSMENT | The photo journal serves as the assessment task. Assessment criteria include students' ability to identify various internal and external influences, how the influences impact their health choices and behavior, and positive and negative influences. (Constructs: Attitudes toward behavior, subjective norms.)

Multicultural Approaches to Conflict Resolution   In some communities, students will have a strong sense of how conflicts are resolved in their cultures. For example, in Hawaiian culture, families practice "ho'oponopono," which means to set or make right, to correct and restore, and to maintain proper relationships among family members. Students can investigate conflict resolution practices in their own or other cultures. Students might find it helpful to interview older members of their families and communities to learn more.

ASSESSMENT | For an assessment task, students can report on the conflict resolution practices they learn about in the cultures they investigate. For assessment criteria, students should explain how these practices influence middle-level students' responses to conflict situations. (Construct: Subjective norms.)

NHES 3 | Access Information, Products, and Services

Students will demonstrate the ability to access valid information and products and services to enhance health.

ASSESSMENT CRITERIA
- Access health information—Locate specific sources of health information, products, or services relevant to enhancing health in a given situation.
- Evaluate information sources—Explain the degree to which identified sources are valid, reliable, and appropriate as a result of evaluating each source.

Grades K–2

Asking for and Getting Help   An important skill for young students across many of the priority content areas is learning how to get help from an adult or from emergency services. Students can participate in simulations of situations in which they need to get help from an adult or call 9-1-1 or other emergency numbers and provide appropriate information (e.g., feeling unsafe or scared, or actions to take when a hurtful situation occurring at home or school). Students should practice these skills so that they will know what to do when unexpected situations arise.

ASSESSMENT | For an assessment task, students can demonstrate how to get help in various situations (school, home, or community situations in which they or others are afraid or uncomfortable or need help). For assessment

criteria, students should explain how to contact helpers and tell why these are good choices. (Construct: Perceived behavioral control.)

My Secret Bully: Getting Help from Supportive Adults   Trudy Ludwig's book *My Secret Bully* (see "Children's Literature" at the end of this chapter) tells the story of Monica, who is bullied by a friend. This story about relational aggression explains the often hidden problem of emotional bullying within a network of friends. Instead of physical bullying, this story describes bullying that uses relationships, words, and gestures as weapons of attack. Name-calling, humiliation, exclusion, and manipulation are some of the bullying tactics Monica's friend Katie uses. Monica learns how to face her fears and reclaim her power with the help of a supportive adult, her mother, who helps her find ways to deal with Katie without acting like a bully herself. Teachers can read this book with students to talk about the importance of talking with a parent, caregiver, teacher, or other trusted adult when they need help. As contrast, teachers can read *The Recess Queen* by Alexis O'Neill. The main character in this story, Katie Sue, solves the problem by herself, without adult help, by making a friend of "Mean Jean." Students can discuss the similarities and differences between the two stories and tell when they need to get adult help.

ASSESSMENT | For an assessment task, students can describe times when children need help from adults and how they can go about getting it. For assessment criteria, students should identify at least three supportive adults who can help them and tell why they are good sources of help. (Constructs: Intention to act in healthy ways, perceived behavioral control.)

Grades 3–5

Finding Community Helpers for Violence Prevention or Response   Students can use the Internet to find the names and phone numbers of organizations and agencies that deal with problems related to violence prevention. Students can make a list of community helpers who can help with different kinds of violence prevention problems. Students also can visit the McGruff website (www.mcgruff.org) and click on "Advice" to access information on bullying, gun safety, staying home alone, community safety, Internet safety, and other topics.

ASSESSMENT | For an assessment task, students can make a directory of community helpers for class members and other students. For assessment criteria, students should provide contact information and explain why the helpers are good choices. (Construct: Perceived behavioral control.)

Collecting Data on Safe and Unsafe Places at School   The idea for this activity is based on a lesson in Dr. Nan Stein's *Bullyproof* curriculum called "On the Lookout."[112] In this data collection, students play the role of observers and researchers to look for safe and unsafe places at their school. Students might decide to make mental notes everywhere they go at school, or different students might take responsibility for observing certain areas (cafeteria). Students should write down their observations when they have a chance to do so without being noticed by others—they should not draw attention to themselves as observers. Students should not use real names in their notes but should describe the grade level of the students involved, the incident, and where it occurred. Students should watch for teasing, bullying, conflicts, name-calling, negative written words and drawings, and fighting. Students should collect their data for a certain period of time and then share their reports with the class.

ASSESSMENT | The students' analyses and reports are the assessment task for this activity. For assessment criteria, students should explain how they collected their data (NHES 3) and provide an analysis of who, what, where, when, why, and how for the incidents they observed. Students should make recommendations to their teachers and administrators for improving school safety, based on their findings (NHES 8). (Construct: Perceived behavioral control.)

How Would They Get Help?   Read the book *A Terrible Thing Happened* by Margaret Holmes to the class. A young raccoon named Sherman has seen something terrible (though the terrible thing is not defined). Sherman tries to go about the day ignoring his thoughts, but he continues to experience anxious feelings. It is finally through the help of a trusted adult at school that he is able to address his feelings and begin the healing process. This story is written for younger students but clearly identifies adults a child can turn to when they need help. This book can be read to create an opportunity for discussion on the types of help the child needs and whom he or she could get it from.

ASSESSMENT | Students can be provided with a scenario about children who need to make a choice about safety and comfort with an adult. Possible situations could be:

- A girl knows her uncle has been drinking and doesn't want to get in the car with him.
- A boy feels confused with the way his dad's friend keeps punching him on the shoulder as a joke. It hurts.
- A girl doesn't like the way her teenage sister's boyfriend keeps staring at her, teasing her, and touching her in a way that makes her feel uncomfortable.

For assessment criteria, students can create an infographic that illustrates the scenario and provides resources for the type of help the young person needs and from whom he or she should get the help. Students should be able to explain why the resources selected are appropriate for the situation and justify the type of help the young person needs. (Constructs: Perceived behavioral control, attitudes toward behavior.)

Grades 6–8

Accessing Information on Preventing Violence   Students can estimate and check the actual data for students' answers to violence-related questions on the Youth Risk Behavior Survey. These data are available online (www.cdc.gov/healthyyouth/yrbs/index.htm). Students can check data for the national high school survey and for state and local surveys. Alternatively, teachers can provide a printout of the data. Students can discuss the statistics and the kinds of violence-related problems some students face. In addition, teachers should be sure to point out that most students make healthy choices and are not involved in violent behaviors.

ASSESSMENT | For an assessment task, students can work in pairs or small groups to research the answers to various violence prevention Youth Risk Behavior Survey questions. For assessment criteria, students should present their findings, tell where they obtained their information (NHES 3), and explain how learning about what older students do can influence their own behavior choices (NHES 2). (Constructs: Subjective norms, perceived behavioral control.)

Love Doesn't Have to Hurt Teens: Accessing Information from the American Psychological Association   Students can access information on dating violence from the American Psychological Association (www.apa.org/pi/families/resources/) by scrolling down to the link to "Love Doesn't Have to Hurt Teens." This resource is a powerful one for early adolescents, who might know about or even be experiencing dating violence. During these discussions, teachers need to be especially open to the fact that some students might disclose problems to them. Teachers should thank the student for telling them and let the student know that they will help them find help. Teachers can't promise not to tell. If a student is in danger, students should know that the law requires teachers to get help for them.

ASSESSMENT | Students can work in pairs or small groups to research one of the topics on the website and report to the class. For assessment criteria, students should focus their reports on helping classmates identify abusive and

dangerous behaviors and getting help. (Constructs: Attitudes toward behavior, perceived behavioral control.)

NHES 4 | Interpersonal Communication

Students will demonstrate the ability to use interpersonal communication skills to enhance health and avoid or reduce health risks.

ASSESSMENT CRITERIA

- Use appropriate verbal/nonverbal communication strategies in an effective manner to enhance health or avoid/reduce health risks.
- Use appropriate skills (negotiation skills, refusal skills) and behaviors (eye contact, body language, attentive listening).

Grades K–2

Working Out Problems: The Classroom Peace Table   The film *Starting Small: Teaching Tolerance in Preschool and the Early Grades* (www.tolerance.org/classroom-resources/film-kits/starting-small) shows a classroom in Miami where the teacher has set up a "peace table" for the students to go and talk about their problems.[113] The table is placed close to the teacher's desk and has hand puppets for the children to use while they talk with each other. The children in this classroom have learned that they can ask to go to the peace table when they need to talk out a problem with a classmate. The videotape kit, available to schools at no cost from the Southern Poverty Law Center (www.tolerance.org/teach), contains a booklet with details on implementing the teaching strategies in the video. Teachers and students also could designate a mat, blanket, carpet, or other specified space for the classroom "peace place." Teachers can have students show their understanding of using a peace table or peace place by having pairs of students demonstrate resolving a conflict scenario (Marisa broke in line) for the rest of the class.

ASSESSMENT | The students' demonstrations are the assessment task. For assessment criteria, students should go to the peace table or peace place and use the puppets, if available, to talk about what's wrong to each other in just a few sentences. Each child listens to the other, and the two decide how to solve their problem. They agree and then leave the peace table or peace place as friends. (Construct: Perceived behavioral control.)

Communicating the "Take Cares"   Waikele Elementary and other schools have adopted an easy-to-remember set of school and classroom rules to help children get along: Take care of yourself, take care of each other, and take care of this place. Students can help make a three-column list for the classroom with examples of how they can practice the take cares. Teachers can encourage students to discuss how words and actions communicate the take cares. For example, standing up for oneself takes care of yourself. Using kind words helps take care of others. Keeping the classroom nice takes care of this place.

ASSESSMENT | The chart students help create is the assessment task for this activity. For assessment criteria, students should identify at least three ways to communicate the take cares through their words and actions. (Construct: Perceived behavioral control.)

Telling, Tattling, and Talking with Teachers   Teachers who work with young children can help students distinguish between telling (when someone is in danger or needs help) and tattling (getting someone in trouble) and learn to ask for help so adults will listen to them. Teachers can help students discuss the differences between telling and tattling by making a two-column class chart to display students' ideas. Teachers also can ask students to describe times when someone needed to tell or when someone was only tattling. Teachers should draw out as many concrete examples as possible to help students make the distinction. Teachers also can talk with students about ideas they have for solving problems themselves when they can and about asking for help from an adult when they can't. Family counselor Dr. Allana Coffee, in her book *Peace Signs,* recommends teaching this strategy to children:

Say "I need your help."
Tell what happened.
Tell what you did to try to make things better.
Say again "I need your help."[114]

Teachers can read scenarios to students and ask them to decide whether what the characters did was telling or tattling.

ASSESSMENT | For assessment criteria, students should be able to show how to ask an adult for help if someone is in danger or needs help. Teachers should note that one lesson won't take care of tattling for the year, but a lesson like this can be built on throughout the year as situations arise. (Construct: Perceived behavioral control.)

Grades 3–5

Nobody Teachers can read *Nobody!: A Story About Overcoming Bullying in Schools* by Erin Frankel. (Related books are listed under "Communication" in "Children's Literature" in Chapter 5.) Thomas does not want to go back to school because of a bully named Kyle who is a master at putting down all of the activities Thomas enjoys doing. Told in a comic-style format, Thomas' friends and some trusted adults help give him the courage to stand up to Kyle and realize that Kyle's bullying may have something to do with his own feelings of being a nobody.

ASSESSMENT | For an assessment task, students can use an online cartoon-generator such as ReadWriteThink's Comic Creator (www.readwritethink.org/classroom-resources/student-interactives/comic-creator-30021.html), Make Beliefs Comics (www.makebeliefscomix.com/Comix/), Professor Garfield Comic Lab (www.professorgarfield.org/pgf_comics_lab.html), or StripGenerator (http://stripgenerator.com/strip/create/) to show a situation that turns the tables on a bully and shows solutions that help everyone feel like a somebody. For assessment criteria, students should show at least two ways to use words and actions to resolve a conflict without hurting someone else. (Construct: Perceived behavioral control.)

Working Together to Solve Problems The Women's and Children's Health Network recommends using the following four steps when conflicts arise:

1. Understand
2. Avoid making things worse
3. Work together
4. Find a solution

Each of the steps is explained in detail on the Kids' Health page (navigate to "Your Feelings," then "Conflict Resolution") of the website www.cyh.com. Teachers can introduce students to these four steps (other conflict resolution steps exist and would work just as well). Students can brainstorm situations in which conflicts commonly arise with their friends, siblings, or other important people in their lives. Each pair of students can generate two or three scenarios. Scenarios can be exchanged between pairs of students and students can generate a role-play to demonstrate their ability to use the six steps.

ASSESSMENT | For the assessment task, pairs of students can create posters in which they identify their own steps for resolving conflicts. Acronyms (such as S.T.O.P.) or catchy titles (such as "Use Your Head") can be used to help students remember the conflict resolution strategy. Posters with conflict resolution steps can be posted around the room. Students can then find a strategy that will work best for them. Student-generated conflicts created in

the teaching of the previous steps should be rotated among groups. Pairs of students can apply the steps for conflict resolution that feels most comfortable to them to the scenario (their own or that of another student team). For assessment criteria, students should use appropriate verbal and nonverbal communication strategies effectively to reduce conflict. (Constructs: Perceived behavioral control, attitudes toward behavior.)

Grades 6–8

Wall of Words: Talking About Communication That Hurts or Helps A student teacher developed this activity after hearing the names and put-downs middle-level students directed at each other during school. One day when the students were out of the classroom at lunch, she wrote on the board all the name-calling and expressions she had heard students use on campus. As the students returned to the classroom, talking with one another as usual, they became quiet when they saw the wall of words on the board in the front of the room. The students began to ask questions about the words, which were shocking even to them when they saw them written together on the board. Their teacher responded that these were the words she had heard students use with each other. She then had the students work in small groups to discuss the words and names and how they affect the people who say them, hear them, and are the target of them. The students worked together to replace the name-calling and cruel expressions on the board with positive words and actions students can use with classmates.

ASSESSMENT | Rebuilding the wall of words into a positive and realistic set of words and actions is the assessment task for this activity. Students can work in groups on a particular section of the wall. For assessment criteria, students should explain their new wall of words in terms of health-enhancing verbal and nonverbal communication skills. (Constructs: Perceived behavioral control, subjective norms.)

Communicating Clear Messages About Boundaries Students can help prevent violence, including sexual and gender violence, when they understand and communicate a clear sense of personal boundaries. Nan Stein and Dominic Cappello, in the curriculum *Gender Violence, Gender Justice,* recommend first helping students define the word *boundaries.*[115] Students probably are familiar with the idea of boundaries or being out of bounds in sports. Students can discuss the penalties that result from playing out of bounds and how boundaries change from one type of game to the next. Students also will be familiar with the idea of the boundaries of their classroom, school grounds, town, county, and state. Nations also have boundaries that visitors must have permission to cross (passport, customs). Teachers should ensure that students grasp the concept that some boundaries are physical (marked by a fence) and others are legal, social, psychological, ethical, or cultural. Students can work in small groups to make a three-column chart of the boundaries that (1) are set for them by their parents or caregivers (come straight home after school), (2) are set by their school (stay on campus during recess and lunch), and (3) they set for themselves (no gossiping about classmates). After discussing these boundaries, students can determine what kinds of communication and self-management skills they need to communicate and maintain their own boundaries and to respect the boundaries of others. Students can use the peer resistance techniques in Chapter 3 to assist them.

ASSESSMENT | For an assessment task, students can identify communication (NHES 4) and self-management (NHES 7) skills that will help them communicate and maintain their own boundaries and respect the boundaries of others. For assessment criteria, students should identify a minimum of three skills and explain how they will use them. (Construct: Perceived behavioral control.)

NHES 5 | Decision Making

Students will demonstrate the ability to use decision-making skills to enhance health.

ASSESSMENT CRITERIA

Reach a health-enhancing decision using a process consisting of the following steps:

- Identify a health-risk situation.
- Examine alternatives.
- Evaluate positive and negative consequences.
- Decide on a health-enhancing course of action.

Grades K–2

What Is My Feeling Telling Me? What Needs to Change So I Will Feel Better? Read one of the following books (or another of your favorites with a similar theme) to the class: *The Way I Feel* by J. Cain, *Big Words for Little People* by J. Curtis, or *Today I Feel Silly & Other Moods That Make My Day* by J. Curtis. Other titles are recommended at the end of each chapter in the "Children's Literature" section. The purpose of this activity is to help students identify their feelings, what the feeling is "telling them," and what needs to change so they will feel better. Teachers should explore the feeling words used in the story with students and make sure students know what the different words mean. They should focus on words that are strongly associated with strong body feelings such as angry, frustrated, nervous, scared, and so on. Playing a game of charades with feeling words is one way to check for student understanding of the different words. Once confident the students understand the different words, the teacher can brainstorm with students using a word web much like a decision-making tree. For example, the teacher could present a scenario that would cause students to put *angry* in the center of the word web. The next layer of the word web should emphasize what the feeling is telling them—are they scared, nervous, and so forth. Often when someone acts out in anger, they are really feeling something else—frustrated, disappointed, nervous, and so on. The next layer of the word web should focus on what can be done so that the student will feel better (e.g., less scared or nervous). The teacher should focus on specific things that students can do or control themselves (e.g., leave the situation, play with someone else) rather than things that require someone else to change (e.g., Joe should stop calling me names or laughing at me) in order for students to gain control over their own feelings.

ASSESSMENT | For an assessment task, students can create their own word web either with words or pictures. Students should be presented with a situation that creates a strong feeling. They should determine the feeling generated from the situation and write that in the center of a new word web. What their body is telling them (maybe one thing, maybe more) should be the second layer of the web. For each feeling, students should generate at least two things they could do to feel better in this situation. For assessment criteria, students should present at least two alternatives and decide on a health-enhancing course of action in terms of what needs to happen to help them feel better. (Construct: Perceived behavioral control.)

Grades 3–5

Assessing Potential Danger Adults sometimes say of young people that they "just didn't think." Elementary school students don't have the experience and maturity level of adults. However, they certainly can think. Students can brainstorm potentially dangerous situations and how to decide when a situation is too dangerous for them. Students can categorize various situations on their list as green light (go ahead), yellow light (slow down and think more about it), and red (stop—don't go there!). Students can use a simple decision-making process to assess the positive

and negative consequences of various alternative actions. Upper-elementary and middle-level students' brains still are developing, so students won't necessarily make decisions that adults consider rational—especially in the presence of peers. However, inviting students to think through alternatives and consequences, both positive and negative, can heighten their awareness of possibilities. Another important aspect of decision making is support from peers.

ASSESSMENT | For an assessment task, students can brainstorm a list of potentially dangerous situations and categorize their finished list into traffic-light categories (green, yellow, red). For assessment criteria, students should identify at least three alternatives to each situation and explain the positive and negative consequences of each alternative. Students should then select an action in each case that they believe is realistic, doable, and health-enhancing. (Construct: Perceived behavioral control.)

Grades 6–8

Deciding to Seek Adult Help As students reach middle school, some become reluctant to ask adults for help. Students can discuss situations in which they might need adult help and go through a decision-making process to decide when and how to get help. What alternatives do they have? What are the positive and negative consequences of each alternative? What is the best decision in a particular situation? Students can examine the Kids' Health for Teens website (www.kidshealth.org) to explore topics such as going to a counselor or therapist, dealing with anger, talking with parents and other adults, and dealing with problems such as abusive relationships, date rape, cutting, and alcohol abuse. Students can select topics of interest to them to investigate and report on to the class.

ASSESSMENT | The reports students prepare are the assessment task for this activity. For assessment criteria, students should be able to list at least three alternatives for adults they can go to for help and explain the steps students can think through in deciding when to seek help from an adult. (Construct: Perceived behavioral control.)

Deciding: What Should I Do Now In preparation for this activity, the teacher develops unfinished scenarios that require students to make a decision about how to respond to a situation in which a younger child in their neighborhood is being bullied by another child that they don't know. Small groups of students are given the scenario and must apply a decision-making process to generate two different courses of action. When finished they must identify the best course of action to resolve the situation. When all groups are finished, groups take turns role-playing their two solutions. The class must identify the one that they think is the best, then the group members discuss the extent to which they agree with their classmates and why (in context of the steps of the decision-making process used).

ASSESSMENT | Student role-plays and discussions can serve as the assessment tasks. For assessment criteria, students must provide a clear depiction of the possible decisions and include all steps of the decision-making process in the discussion with their classmates. (Construct: Perceived behavioral control.)

NHES 6 | Goal Setting

Students will demonstrate the ability to use goal-setting skills to enhance health.

ASSESSMENT CRITERIA

- Goal statement—Give goal statement that identifies health benefits; goal is achievable and will result in enhanced health.
- Goal-setting plan—Show plan that is complete, logical, and sequential, and includes a process to assess progress.

Grades K–2

Goals for Kind Words   Young children understand the idea of kind and unkind words—the difference between words that help and words that hurt. See Chapter 5 for the activity "Punahele Bear: How Do We Talk to Each Other?" to help children think about the effects of kind and unkind words. Teachers can help students develop a written class goal for using kind words over a specified period of time (one day, three days, one week). To assist children's thinking, teachers can have them contribute to a three-column chart showing what kind words sound like, look like, and feel like in action. Teachers should have children assess their progress and offer the opportunity to continue their work on this goal.

ASSESSMENT | For assessment criteria, students should discuss or write about their progress periodically (twice a day or at the end of the day), assess their progress, and identify steps to help them reach their goal more successfully. (Constructs: Perceived behavioral control, subjective norms.)

Grades 3–5

We, the Kids: A Class Constitution   David Catrow's *We the Kids: The Preamble to the Constitution of the United States* is a great book for introducing the idea of a class constitution.[116] As Catrow says in the introduction to the book, "The first time I was forced to think about the Constitution was in the fifth grade. President's Day was coming up and my teacher, Mrs. Baldwin, wanted to talk about BIG IDEAS!: stuff like freedom, liberty, founding fathers, presidents. I remember thinking: Man, why couldn't the guys who wrote this just use regular English?" Catrow goes on to say that, as a grown-up, he figured out that the Constitution is simply a list of "rules and promises written down by people just like you and me." Teachers can use Catrow's book to help children create their own classroom constitution for how things will run in their domain.

ASSESSMENT | For an assessment task, students can draft, discuss, and finalize a constitution for their classroom. Students and teachers should work together to identify clear responsibilities and accountability for everyone. For assessment criteria, students should explain their constitution and the concrete steps they will take to achieve their goals. (Construct: Perceived behavioral control.)

Grades 6–8

Goals for a Peaceful Campus   Students can create and implement a campaign for a peaceful middle school campus. Students should collaborate to set a common goal, steps for achieving it, plans to overcome possible obstacles, and a means to assess progress. Students can set beginning and ending dates for their campaign and track progress over the course of the event. This activity links to NHES 8, advocacy. Students can find assistance for goal setting at websites such as www.stopbullying-now.com and https://www.glsen.org/no-name-calling-week. Teachers and parents can find helpful information from the National PTA, including information on cyber bullies, at https://www.pta.org/home/family-resources/safety/Digital-Safety/Parents-Can-Prevent-Cyberbullying.

ASSESSMENT | The peaceful school goal students set for their class, grade, or school is the assessment task for this activity. For assessment criteria, students should state an achievable goal, make a plan that includes sequential steps, identify and demonstrate ways to build on supports and deal with barriers, and decide on a process to assess achievement. (Constructs: Subjective norms, perceived behavioral control.)

NHES 7 | Self-Management

Students will demonstrate the ability to practice health-enhancing behaviors and avoid or reduce health risks.

ASSESSMENT CRITERIA

- Application (transfer)—Initiate health-enhancing behaviors; apply concepts and skills appropriate and effectively.
- Self-monitoring and reflection—Monitor actions and make adjustments; accept feedback and make adjustments; able to self-assess, reflect on, and take responsibility for actions.

Grades K–2

When I Feel Angry?   Talking about anger as a normal emotion and about healthy responses to anger is an important conversation for helping children become good self-managers of strong feelings. A book about anger that many teachers like to use is *When Sophie Gets Angry—Really, Really Angry,* by Molly Bang.[117] Students can brainstorm a list of things that make them angry at home, at school, on the playground, and during community activities (without using anyone's name). They can draw a simple picture of themselves, with arrows pointing to places they feel physical responses to anger (their stomach hurts, headaches, or heart beats fast). Then read the book about Sophie or another children's book in which the main character handles anger in healthy ways. Students can write their own responses to "When I feel angry, I feel . . ."; "The best way for me to behave when I get angry is to . . .; and "Ways that would not be best for me to act when I get angry are . . ." After students discuss their ideas, they can make a page for a class book about the healthy ways they handle angry feelings. "Children's Literature" in Chapter 5 and at the end of this chapter list more children's books with a similar self-management theme.

ASSESSMENT | For an assessment task, students can work individually or in pairs to create a page for a class book on healthy anger management strategies. For assessment criteria, students should report health-enhancing anger management strategies and demonstrate how they can carry them out successfully. (Construct: Perceived behavioral control.)

Quit It! Managing a Confrontation with "Bully Bob" or "Bully Betty"   The title for this activity is based on the K–3 bullying prevention curriculum *Quit It!* from the Wellesley College Center for Research on Women and the NEA Professional Library.[118] Students can use a picture collage app or drawing app (like PicStitch or Doodle Buddy) to import a picture of a bully. Nickname the character "Bully Bob" or "Bully Betty," or another name, being sure not to name a child in the class. Students can add characteristics to the bully, in things that he or she says or does, by adding these to the image using text boxes. As a math correlation activity, students can subtract a characteristic from the bully by crossing out or adding a prohibition sign over the negative characteristic and adding a way to safely manage a confrontation with a bully. Students also might enjoy the book *The Recess Queen,* by Alexis O'Neill and Laura Huliska-Beith, which deals with a new student's response to "Mean Jean," the school bully.[119] Students should know that good strategies for managing a bully include walking away, standing up to the person ("Don't do that!" "Leave my friend alone!"), and getting an adult.

ASSESSMENT | The image students label with safe strategies for managing a confrontation with a bully is the assessment task for this activity. For assessment criteria, students should name at least five strategies for dealing with bullies, including walking away, standing up to the person, and getting an adult. (Construct: Perceived behavioral control.)

Grades 3–5

A Handful of Strategies   Students can talk about the safe and effective ways they resolve conflicts (healthy self-management skills). Students also might want to talk about strategies that are tempting but unwise. After the discussion, students can trace their hands on a piece of construction paper and use each finger to list a strategy they have learned for handling conflicts and volatile situations. Teachers can post these pictures around the classroom as reminders of healthy self-management strategies. Students can learn more about healthy self-management strategies from Kids' Health (www.kidshealth.org) by clicking on Dealing with Feelings. Students can find advice for dealing with issues related to emotions and feelings such as peer pressure, anger, fear, respect, gossip, and prejudice.

ASSESSMENT | The handful of strategies students create for managing conflict is the assessment task for this activity. For assessment criteria, students should be able to explain how to carry out each strategy in a health-enhancing way. (Construct: Perceived behavioral control.)

Stop Bullying Teachers and students can learn more about bullying at the federal government bullying prevention website for kids (https://www.stopbullying.gov/kids/what-you-can-do/index.html). This website teaches students about interpersonal communication (NHES 4), decision making (NHES 5), self-management (NHES 7), and advocacy (NHES 8). Students can learn more about the causes and effects of bullying, how to recognize bullying behavior in themselves and others, and what to do when they experience or witness bullying. Students can work in pairs or small groups to investigate and report on self-management strategies to stop bullying. For example, students will learn that there are concrete things they can do if they are being bullied (always tell an adult, stay in a group, try to stand up to the person who is bullying you). The site also includes surveys, games, and "cool stuff," such as webisodes and cartoon characters.

ASSESSMENT | For assessment criteria, students should report health-enhancing strategies for stopping bullying and demonstrate how to carry them out successfully. (Construct: Perceived behavioral control.)

Enemy Pie Derek Munson's book *Enemy Pie* tells the story of a young boy who was looking forward to a perfect summer until his number one enemy moved into the neighborhood. His father assures him that he will make a pie to take care of enemies, but in the meantime the main character must spend the whole day with his enemy and even be nice to him. Annika Dunklee's book *Me, Me, Me* focuses on hurt feelings as three friends prepare an act for the school talent show. Teachers can read these and other stories with children to discuss things that come between friends and how friends can resolve their differences. The list of books on family and friends in "Children's Literature" in Chapter 5 includes other books appropriate for this activity.

ASSESSMENT | For an assessment task, students can create an interactive digital story about a real or imagined time when they had a disagreement with a friend and then made up. Students can use a browser-based creator like InkleWriter (https://writer.inklestudios.com/), a slideshow app (like Google Slides, PowerPoint, and Keynote), or a tablet app (like Book Creator) to write a story that shows a conflict between friends. Students can offer multiple choices for the story that develop into a positive and negative resolution. For assessment criteria, students should show the steps the friends took to work things out to become friends again. (Construct: Perceived behavioral control.)

What to Do When You're Scared and Worried: A Guide for Kids Teachers can read James Crist's book *What to Do When You're Scared and Worried: A Guide for Kids* (see "Children's Literature" in Chapter 5 for this and related titles) to talk about fears and worries and how to manage them. The book provides an example of ten "fear chasers and worry erasers" (self-management strategies) kids can use to feel safer, stronger, and calmer:

- "Get real" about your fears and worries.
- Flip the switch from negative to positive.

- Get your mind off your worries.
- Get active.
- Be aware of what you eat.
- Practice deep breathing and visualization.
- Relax those muscles.
- Write about your feelings.
- Be aware of your "red alerts."
- Tell others what you've learned.

Learning healthy self-management strategies can help students stop bullying and other violence-related behaviors. The authors would add to the list "Talk with trusted adults."

ASSESSMENT | For an assessment task, students can work in pairs or in small groups to investigate and discuss one of the fear chasers and worry erasers and report to classmates. For assessment criteria, students should demonstrate the self-management strategy in health-enhancing ways in at least two situations. (Construct: Perceived behavioral control.)

Grades 6–8

Sticks and Stones Can Break Your Bones, but Words Can Break Your Heart Middle-level students are very familiar with the rumor or gossip mill that goes on around them. Students can talk about the kinds of rumors and gossip that get spread by and about students their age, without mentioning anyone's name. Students can tell how this type of talk makes others feel and how it leads to misunderstandings, hurt feelings, and even fights. Teachers can ask students what they can do to prevent the problems associated with rumors and gossip, even when it's tempting to join in. Students can make a list of strategies for stopping this kind of hurtful talk as soon as they hear it. Students can find out more on the Kids' Health website page "The Scoop on Gossip" (http://kidshealth.org/en/kids/gossip.html).

ASSESSMENT | The list of strategies students make for stopping gossip is the assessment task for this activity. For assessment criteria, students should provide three or more concrete examples of using their strategies, including at least one situation in which students should tell an adult what is being said. (Constructs: Attitudes toward behavior, perceived behavioral control.)

Calming a Volatile Situation Teachers can ask students to discuss whether they have either seen or found themselves in situations in which students their age were so angry or upset that they thought there would be a physical fight. Unfortunately, middle-level students do find themselves in or around such situations. What kinds of words and behaviors help in such situations—and what kinds just make things worse? For example, has anyone ever seen students around the edge of a disagreement taunt two angry students to fight? These situations are difficult, and each calls for judgment on the part of those involved and bystanders. Students should talk frankly about how to help and their commitment to helping classmates stay out of violent situations. Students can work in small groups to write a detailed scenario and script of a conflict situation at school or in the community that could lead to a fight. The scenarios should include three or more characters and describe what they do and say. When the scenarios are complete, students can exchange them with other groups. Groups should respond by explaining what each character in the scenario could do to prevent a physical fight. Students also should talk about when adult help is needed and how to get it. The school counselor can be invited to join these discussions on solving problems nonviolently.

ASSESSMENT | For assessment criteria, students should explain how the strategies they propose can work and why the strategies are realistic ones for middle-level students to use. (Construct: Perceived behavioral control.)

Try to See It My Way: Walk a Mile in My Shoes Students might not be familiar with the old songs the title refers to, but they can try out the ideas. Teachers might want to start with an entertaining children's book, such as *The True Story of the Three Little Pigs* by Jon Scieszka. In this book, Alexander T. Wolf explains, from his perspective, how he was framed in the incident depicted in the famous children's story. The purpose of this activity is to invite students to realize that there are different perceptions and points of view in any situation, including some that could lead to fighting or violence. Students can practice taking other points of view by assuming the roles of characters in other well-known stories. When students understand the idea of looking at different points of view, they can apply their thinking skills to real-life scenarios that middle-level students face. Students can work in groups of three or more to write a real-life scenario that involves at least three characters. After reading the scenario to the class, each student should assume the role of one of the characters and explain what led up to the situation.

ASSESSMENT | For assessment criteria, students should explain how the characters can use health-enhancing self-management strategies, even when they are under stress or dealing with situations that others don't understand. (Construct: Perceived behavioral control.)

NHES 8 | Advocacy

Students will demonstrate the ability to advocate for personal, family, and community health.

ASSESSMENT CRITERIA
- Health-enhancing position—Give clear, health-enhancing position.
- Support for position—Support position with facts, concepts, examples, and evidence.
- Audience awareness—Show awareness of target audience; choose words, tone, and examples to suit audience.
- Conviction—Display conviction for position.

Grades K–2

My Opinion On . . . Talk with students about what it means to express an opinion. Share different advertising strategies used to try to convince young people to use a product or buy a toy. Explain how texts are commonly used to try get people to do things. Brainstorm words/phrases people use to make an idea interesting, exciting, or to convince someone of something. Work together on a topic such as, the best ways to resolve a conflict peacefully. Help students consider the following: who are they persuading; how do writers support their arguments/opinions with reasons; and how to create a topic sentence supported by three to five reasons which support their topic. Then combine the sentences into a persuasive text. Work through an example as a class to share expectations and ensure students understand the writing process.

ASSESSMENT | For an assessment task, students will write their own persuasive text. Consider topics such as, why it is wrong to tease or bully or what to do if someone is being bullied for the persuasive writing experience. For assessment criteria, students should be able to support their position with specific reasons, demonstrate conviction, and encourage others to engage in health-enhancing behaviors. (Constructs: Subjective norms, perceived behavioral control.)

Words of the Day Students can work on a campaign to put words or phrases of the day into action in their school. Words and phrases include *please, thank you, excuse me, why don't you go first?* and *I'm glad to see you.* Students can publicize their campaign and assess their efforts.

ASSESSMENT | The Word of the Day campaign students plan and carry out is the assessment task for this activity. For assessment criteria, students should

state a clear, health-enhancing message and target it to two audiences—students and adults in the school. (Construct: Subjective norms.)

Grades 3–5

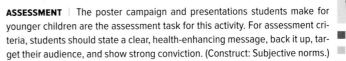

Posters for Younger Students Upper-elementary students can work in groups to make posters for lower-elementary students' classrooms to advocate for healthy problem solving and conflict resolution. Students can visit the younger students' classrooms to present the posters and provide in-person instructional time. Students also might want to display their posters at local businesses and elsewhere in the community.

ASSESSMENT | The poster campaign and presentations students make for younger children are the assessment task for this activity. For assessment criteria, students should state a clear, health-enhancing message, back it up, target their audience, and show strong conviction. (Construct: Subjective norms.)

Who Can Help at Our School? Students can make a list of the kinds of problems students might have in upper-elementary school and a corresponding list of school helpers and how to contact them. Students should advocate for the position "It's smart to get help when we need it."

ASSESSMENT | The students' presentation to other students of their list of school helpers is the assessment task for this activity. For assessment criteria, students should state a clear, health-enhancing message, back it up, target their audience, and show strong conviction. (Construct: Subjective norms.)

Grades 6–8

Anonymous Cards: What Can We Do to Help Keep Our School Safe? In Chapter 4, the anonymous cards strategy is discussed as a way to formalize and apply brainstorming to a specific problem or issue. Students are given 3 × 5 cards and asked to label one side "A" and the other side "B." The teacher presents a common problem that is a challenge to the safety in their school (lack of compliance with playground rules, disagreements between students, etc.) and asks students to identify and rank order three things that they could do to help solve the problem on side "A" and three things that they see students doing to contribute to the problem on side "B" of their card (students should be reminded to not place any identifying marks on the card). Teachers proceed by collecting all cards, shuffling them, and returning them to students (students should be reminded that although they might receive their own card by mistake, they should pretend that the responses that they share were provided by a classmate). As students share responses that appear on the card that they receive, a master list of contributors and helping strategies is generated on the board. The activity is concluded by having each student write a brief letter to the principal that identifies important ways that student behavior contributes to, but could intervene to solve, the identified problem. Finally, after the principal reads the letters, he or she is invited to the classroom to discuss implementation of student-generated advocacy strategies.

ASSESSMENT | The assessment task for this activity is student letters to the principal and the discussion with that school leader. For assessment criteria, the letters must contain a minimum of three contributors and interventions. During the conversation with the principal, the specifics of an action plan for the class should be finalized. (Construct: Perceived behavioral control).

No Name-Calling and No Bullying: Videos for Younger Students Middle-level students can work in teams to write and create a video about healthy problem-solving and conflict resolution scenarios for upper-elementary school students. As part of the scripts, students should show what led to the conflict and the deliberations someone involved might make about how to solve the problem. Students should stop the scripts at different points to allow younger students to decide what to do. Students should videotape different endings for various scenarios. Older and younger students can discuss the scenarios and resolution together, with the guidance of teachers from both classes. Students can use websites such as www.stopbullyingnow.com and https://www.glsen.org/no-name-calling-week to help with their planning.

ASSESSMENT | The videos or presentation students make to younger students are the assessment task for this activity. For assessment criteria, students should state a clear, health-enhancing message, back it up, target their audience, and show strong conviction. (Constructs: Subjective norms, perceived behavioral control.)

Youth Violence Prevention Week Students Against Violence Everywhere (SAVE) sponsors activities for Youth Violence Prevention Week. Visit their website (www.nationalsave.org) for ideas and activities for each day of youth violence prevention week. Students can either participate in specific activities suggested on the website or organize activities for the school.

ASSESSMENT | Following participation in youth violence prevention week activities, students can engage in a quick-write to share some of the lessons learned. Writing prompts, such as "Something that surprised me was . . .", "I changed my thinking about . . .", or "One thing I understand now is . . ." can be used to direct student sharing of lessons learned from engaging in youth violence prevention week activities. (Constructs: Subjective norms, perceived behavioral control.)

EVALUATED VIOLENCE PREVENTION CURRICULA

Regardless of the implementation of a well-planned and collaborative approach to violence risk reduction, many local school districts have established policies and implemented practices that dictate that specific violence risk reduction content be covered as part of the instructional program in the school district. In all school districts facing competing budget priorities and time limitations, educators must direct their energies and resources, implementing only those policies and programs documented to reduce risks for youth violence. The 2011 National Prevention Strategy: America's Plan for Better Health and Wellness specifies that such strategies include the implementation of ". . . policies, practices, and environmental design features to reduce school violence and crime (e.g., classroom management practices, cooperative learning techniques, student monitoring and supervision, limiting and monitoring access to buildings and grounds, performing timely maintenance).[120]

Various federal agencies have identified youth-related violence prevention programs demonstrated to be worthy of recommendation. Such recommendations are based on a number of criteria including expert opinion, a review of the design of the program, and/or research evidence. Agencies establish their own processes and standards for identifying programs that are worthy of recommendation to schools, communities, and families. As introduced in the "Internet and Other Resources" section of Chapter 2, two such federal agencies have established Web-based resources that contain recommended programs with a specific focus on various health topics including youth violence prevention. Interested readers are encouraged to examine the following:

- The National Registry of Evidence-Based Programs and Practices (www.nrepp.samhsa.gov/).
- What Works Clearinghouse (http://ies.ed.gov/ncee/wwc).

In response to the demand for recommendations about programs specifically focused on effective violence, drug, and crime prevention, the Center for the Study and Prevention of Violence at the University of Colorado has established Blueprints for Healthy Youth Development. This project has as its mission to identify those violence and drug prevention programs that meet the highest standard of excellence. Information about the availability and characteristics of such programs are important for two critical reasons:

1. Despite their good intentions, very few programs have evidence demonstrating effectiveness.
2. The implementation of ineffective programs is a waste of valuable and often limited resources.[121]

In addition to a number of programs based in the community or focused on family or therapeutic interventions, several programs focused on preventing violence among elementary and middle-grade students have met the rigorous criteria to be recognized as Model Programs by the Center for the Study and Prevention of Violence. The following is an example of a model program selected from a review of numerous prevention programs:

- *Life Skills Training* has been demonstrated to produce dramatic reductions in the use of tobacco, alcohol, and marijuana as well as reductions in delinquency and violence. This prevention program targets students in grades 6 and 7 and helps them develop:
  - General self-management skills.
  - Social skills.
  - Knowledge and skills particularly focused on preventing drug use.[122]

In addition to the identified model programs targeting violence prevention, the Center for the Study and Prevention of Violence at the University of Colorado has identified a number of Blueprints Promising Programs. Again, although these programs target a range of audiences and settings, several have a focus on students in elementary and middle grades. Interested readers are encouraged to review these promising programs at http://www.blueprintsprograms.com/.[123]

In summary, strategies that focus on building the capacity of the school to plan, implement, and sustain positive changes can reduce student delinquency and violence risk significantly. In addition, some classroom approaches have been demonstrated to reduce the risk of academic failure and promote violence risk reduction. Continuous progress is being made in developing programs designed to allow students to proceed through a hierarchy of skills shown to be particularly effective. As such, educators and other advocates must maintain a current knowledge base about evidence-based and state-of-the-art violence prevention policies, initiatives, and curricula.

INTERNET AND OTHER RESOURCES

WEBSITES

Adolescent Depression Awareness Program (ADAP)
www.hopkinsmedicine.org/psychiatry/specialty_areas/moods/ADAP/

American Association of Suicidology (AAS)
www.suicidology.org/

ASCD
www.ascd.org

Break the Cycle
www.breakthecycle.org/

Centers for Disease Control and Prevention
www.cdc.gov/injury

Centers for Effective Collaboration and Practice
https://www.air.org/project/center-effective-collaboration-and-practice-cecp

Child Welfare Information Gateway
www.childwelfare.gov

The Community Guide
www.thecommunityguide.org/violence/index.html

National Federal of Families for Children's Mental Health
www.ffcmh.org

Kentucky Center for School Safety
www.kysafeschools.org

Kids' Health
www.kidshealth.org

Minnesota Center Against Violence and Abuse
www.mincava.umn.edu

National Association for the Education of Young Children
www.naeyc.org

National Crime Prevention Council
www.ncpc.org

National Cyber Security Alliance
www.StaySafeOnline.org

National Data Archive on Child Abuse and Neglect
www.ndacan.cornell.edu/

National Education Association Health Information Network
www.neahin.org/

National PTA
www.pta.org

StopBullying.gov
www.stopbullying.gov/

Stop Cyberbullying
www.stopcyberbullying.org/

Striving To Reduce Youth Violence Everywhere (STRYVE)
vetoviolence.cdc.gov/STRYVE/

Teaching Tolerance
www.tolerance.org/

CHILDREN'S LITERATURE

Many relevant books are listed in "Children's Literature" at the end of Chapter 5; see especially the sections "Moods and Strong Feelings," "Communication," "Friends and Family," "Courage," and "Diversity and Uniqueness." Books with violence prevention themes are listed below.

AGES 5–8

Alexander, C. *Lucy and the Bully.* Albert Whitman, 2008.

Binkow, H. *Howard B. Wigglebottom Learns About Bullies.* Thunderbolt Publishing, 2008.

Cole, Henry. *Eddie the Bully.* Little Bee Books, 2016.

Cook, Julia. *A Bad Case of Tattle Tongue.* National Center for Youth Issues, 2006.

Cook, J. *Personal Space Camp.* National Center for Youth Issues, 2009.

Cook, Julia. *Soda Pop Head.* National Center for Youth Issues, 2011.

Cuyler, M. *Bullies Never Win.* Simon and Schuster, 2009.

Dewdney, Anna. *Llama Llama and the Bully Goat.* Viking, 2013.

Dinardo, Jerrey. *The Fable of the Bully Dragon.* Red Chair Press, 2016.

Fox, Mem. *Feathers and Fools.* Harcourt Brace, 1989.

Hansen, Diane. *These Are My Private Parts.* Empowerment Productions, 2007.

Holmes, Margaret M. *A Terrible Thing Happened.* Magination Press, 2000.

King, Kimberly and Zack King. *I Said No! A Kid-to-Kid Guide to Keeping Private Parts Private.* Boulden Publishing, 2016.

Kurtzman-Counter, Samantha. *Miles Is the Boss of His Body.* The Mother Company, 2014.

Levy, Janice. *Thomas the Toadily Terrible Bully.* Eerdmans Books for Young Readers, 2014.

Ludwig, Trudy. *My Secret Bully.* RiverWood Books, 2004.

O'Neill, Alexis. *The Recess Queen.* Scholastic, 2002.

Pearl, Michael. *Sara Sue Learns to Yell and Tell.* No Greater Joy Ministries, 2011.

Sanders, Jayneen. *Let's Talk About Body Boundaries, Consent and Respect: Teach Children About Body Ownership, Respect, Feelings, Choices and Recognizing Bullying Behaviors.* Educate2Empower Publishing, 2017.

Sanders, Jayneen. *My Body! What I Say Goes!: A Book to Empower and Teach Children About Personal Body Safety, Feelings, Safe and Unsafe Touch, Private Parts, Secrets and Surprises, Consent, and Respectful Relationships.* Educate2Empower Publishing, 2016.

Sanders, Jayneen. *Some Secrets Should Never Be Kept.* Educate2Empower Publishing, 2015.

Seeger, Laura Vaccaro. *Bully.* A Neal Porter Book/Roaring Book Press, 2013.

Spelman, Cornelia, M. *Your Body Belongs to You.* Albert Whitman, 2000.

Thomas, Shelly Moore. *Somewhere Today: A Book of Peace.* Albert Whitman, 1998.

AGES 9–12

Abbott, Tony. *The Summer of Owen Todd*. Farrar Straus Giroux, 2017.

Allman, Toney. *School Violence (Matters of Opinion)*. Norwood House Press, 2017.

Baskin, Nora Raleigh. *Runt*. Simon & Schuster, 2013.

Blevins, Wiley. *How to Deal With Bullies Superhero Style: Response to Bullying*. Red Chair Press, 2016.

Bunting, Eve. *Your Move*. Harcourt Brace, 1998.

Butler, D. *The Truth About Truman School*. Albert Whitman, 2009.

Cole, F. *The Adventures of Hashbrown Winters*. Bonneville Books, 2009.

Comen, Carolyn. *What Jamie Saw*. Front Street, 1995.

Cormier, Robert. *We All Fall Down*. Bantam, 1991.

Criswell, P. *Stand Up for Yourself and Your Friends: Dealing with Bullies and Bossiness and Finding a Better Way*. American Girl Press, 2009.

Ewing, Lynne. *Drive-By*. HarperCollins, 1998.

Foltz, Linda Lee. *Kids Helping Kids Break the Silence of Sexual Abuse*. Lighthouse Point Press, 2003.

Jakubiak, D. *A Smart Kid's Guide to Social Networking Online*. Power Kids Press, 2009.

Key, Watt. *Fourmile*. Square Fish, Farrar Straus Giroux, 2014.

Klass, David. *You Don't Know Me*. HarperCollins, 2002.

Krieg, J. *Griff Carver, Hallway Patrol*. Razorbill, 2010.

Ludwig, Trudy. *Confessions of a Former Bully*. Dragonfly Books, 2012.

Mayrock, Aija. *The Survival Guide to Bullying: Written By a Teen*. Scholastic, 2015.

McCormick, Patricia. *Cut*. Scholastic, 2000.

Myers, Walter Dean. *Scorpions*. HarperCollins, 1988. (Newbery Medal, American Library Association Notable Children's Book, American Library Association Best Book for Young Adults, American Library Association Recommended Book for Reluctant Readers)

Paulsen, Gary. *The Rifle*. Harcourt Brace, 1995.

Pettiford, Rebecca. *Resisting Bullying*. Bullfrog Books, 2018.

Polacco, Patricia. *Bully*. Putnam Juvenile, 2012.

Spinelli, Jerry. *Wringer*. HarperCollins, 1995. (Newbery Medal)

Spilsbury, Louise. *Say No to Bullying*. Barron's Educational Series, Inc., 2014.

Stasser, Todd. *If I Grow Up*. Simon & Schuster Books for Young Readers, 2009.

Stevens, E. Finn Reeder, *Flu Fighter: How I Survived a Worldwide Pandemic, the School Bully and the Craziest Game of Dodgeball Ever*. Arch Books, 2010.

Wittekind, Erika. *Violence as Entertainment: Why Aggression Sells (Exploring Media Literacy)*. Compass Point Books, 2012.

ENDNOTES

1. World Health Organization, "Definition and Typology of Violence" (http://www.who.int/violenceprevention /approach/definition/en/; 2018).

2. M. Forouzesh and D. Waetjen, "Youth Violence," in *Promoting Teen Health* (Thousand Oaks, CA: Sage, 1998), 166–68.

3. U.S. Department of Health and Human Services, *Healthy People 2020* (www.healthypeople.gov).

4. National Adolescent Health Information Center, *Fact Sheet on Violence: Adolescents & Young Adults* (San Francisco, CA: NAHIC, University of California, San Francisco, 2007).

5. Children's Defense Fund, *The State of America's Children 2017* (Washington, DC: CDF, 2017), 8.

6. Centers for Disease Control and Prevention, "Youth Risk Behavior Surveillance–United States, 2017," *MMWR Surveillance Summaries* 67, no. 8 (June 15, 2018).

7. P. S. Corso et al., "Medical Costs and Productivity Losses Due to Interpersonal Violence and Self-Directed Violence," *American Journal of Preventive Medicine* 32, no. 6 (2007): 474–82.

8. Centers for Disease Control and Prevention, *Youth Violence: Facts at a Glance, 2016* (www.cdc.gov /violenceprevention/pdf/yv-datasheet.pdf; 2017).

9. University of Colorado Boulder, *Center for the Study and Prevention of Violence–Facts* (www.colorado.edu/cspv; 2014).

10. Centers for Disease Control and Prevention, *Understanding Youth Violence, Fact Sheet, 2015* (www.cdc .gov/violenceprevention/pdf/youthviolence-factsheet. pdf; 2017).

11. Centers for Disease Control and Prevention, *Youth Violence: National Statistics*, (www.cdc.gov/injury/wisqars /index.html; 2014).

12. U.S. Department of Health and Human Services, *Youth Violence: A Report of the Surgeon General* (Rockville, MD: U.S. Department of Health and Human Services, 2001).

13. Ibid.

14. U.S. Department of Health and Human Services, *Healthy People 2020* (www.healthypeople.gov/2020/topics-objectives; 2018).

15. B. D. Perry, "The Neurodevelopmental Impact of Violence in Childhood," in *Textbook of Child and Adolescent Forensic Psychiatry*, eds. D. Schetky and E. Benedek (Washington, DC: American Psychiatric Press, 2001b), 221–38.

16. CIVITAS, *Right on Course: How Trauma and Maltreatment Impact Children in the Classroom and How You Can Help* (Chicago, IL: CIVITAS, 2002), 13.

17. A. T. Lockwood, *Preventing Violence in Our Schools* (Madison, WI: Wisconsin Center for Educational Research, 1993), 1–12.

18. R. S. Lorion and W. Saltzman, "Children Exposed to Community Violence: Following a Path from Concern to Research Action," *Psychiatry* 56, no. 1 (1993): 55–65.

19. D. Prothrow-Stith and S. Quaday, *Hidden Casualties: The Relationship Between Violence and Learning* (Washington, DC: National Consortium for African American Children, and the National Health Education Consortium, 1996).

20. CIVITAS, *Right on Course*, 23.

21. Centers for Disease Control and Prevention, *Making the Connection: Youth Violence and Academic Grades* (www.cdc.gov/healthyyouth/health_and_academics/pdf /DASHfactsheetViolence.pdf; 2017).

22. C. Remboldt, "Making Violence Unacceptable," *Educational Leadership* (September 1998): 32–38.

23. Centers for Disease Control and Prevention, *Youth Violence: Risk and Protective Factors* (www.cdc.gov /violenceprevention/youthviolence/riskprotectivefactors .html; 2017).

24. E. Hall et al., "Protective Factors for Youth Violence Perpetration: Issues, Evidence, and Public Health Implications," *American Journal of Preventive Medicine* 43, no. 2, Supplement 1 (2012), S1–S84.

25. Ibid.

26. Centers for Disease Control and Prevention, *Youth Violence: Risk and Protective Factors*.

27. K. Dwyer and D. Osher, *Safeguarding Our Children: An Action Guide* (Washington, DC: U.S. Departments of Education and Justice, American Institutes for Research, 2000). (www2.ed.gov/admins/lead/safety/actguide/ action_guide.pdf; 2018).

28. U.S. Department of Health and Human Services, *Youth Violence: A Report of the Surgeon General*.

29. Ibid.

30. Centers for Disease Control and Prevention, *School Health Policies and Programs Study 2014, 2016* (www.cdc .gov/healthyyouth/data/shpps/results.htm; 2017).

31. U.S. Department of Health and Human Services, *Youth Violence: A Report of the Surgeon General*.

32. S. C. Teske, "A Study of Zero Tolerance Policies in Schools: A Multi-Integrated Systems Approach to Improve Outcomes for Adolescents," *Journal of Child and Adolescent Psychiatric Nursing* 24 (2011): 88–97.

33. U.S. Department of Health and Human Services, *Youth Violence: A Report of the Surgeon General*.

34. L. Dusenbury et al., "Nine Critical Elements of Promising Violence Prevention Programs," *Journal of School Health* 67, no. 10 (December 1997): 409–14.

35. Ibid.

36. C. David-Ferdon and T. R. Simon, *Preventing Youth Violence: Opportunities for Action* (Atlanta, GA: National Center for Injury Prevention and Control, Centers for Disease Control and Prevention, 2014).

37. Ibid.

38. U.S. Department of Health and Human Services, *School Health Guidelines to Prevent Unintentional Injuries and Violence* (Atlanta, GA: Centers for Disease Control and Prevention, December 7, 2001), 13–46.

39. National Institute of Mental Health, *Helping Children and Adolescents Cope with Violence and Disasters: What Parents Can Do* (Bethesda, MD: NIMH, 2015).

40. Ibid.

41. CIVITAS, *Right on Course*, 6–7.

42. Ibid., 9.

43. National Institute of Mental health, *Health Children and Adolescents Cope with Violence and Disasters: What Community Members Can Do* (Bethesda, MD: NIMH, 2015).

44. National Institute of Mental Health, *Helping Children and Adolescents Cope with Violence and Disasters: What Parents Can Do*.

45. CIVITAS, *Right on Course*, 59.

46. National Center for Education Statistics, *Indicators of School Crime and Safety: 2017* (nces.ed.gov/pubs2018 /2018036.pdf; 2018).

47. Ibid.

48. B. Vossekuil et al., *The Final Report and Findings of the Safe School Initiative: Implications for the Prevention of School Attacks in the United States* (Washington, DC: U.S. Secret Service and U.S. Department of Education, 2004.

49. U.S. Department of Education, *Public School Practices for Violence Prevention and Reduction: 2003–2004 NCES 2007-010* (Jessup, MD: ED Pubs, September 2007).

50. L. Meyer and R. Johnson Chiang, "Chapter 1: Policies to Promote Safety and Prevent Violence," *Fit, Healthy, and Ready to Learn: A School Health Policy Guide* (Arlington, VA: National Association of State Boards of Education, 2012).

51. Centers for Disease Control and Prevention, *Child Abuse and Neglect: Consequences* (www.cdc.gov /violenceprevention/childabuseandneglect/consequences .html; 2018).

52. Ibid.

53. CIVITAS, *Right on Course*, 26.

54. Child Welfare Information Gateway, *What Is Child Abuse and Neglect? Recognizing the Signs and Symptoms* (Washington, DC: U.S. Department of Health and Human Services, Children's Bureau, 2013). (www .childwelfare.gov/pubPDFs/whatiscan.pdf; 2018).

55. CIVITAS, *Right on Course*, 26.

56. Centers for Disease Control and Prevention, *Child Abuse and Neglect: Definitions* (www.cdc.gov /violenceprevention/childabuseandneglect/definitions. html; 2018).
57. Ibid.
58. CIVITAS, *Right on Course*, 31, 33, 37, 39, 43.
59. Ibid., 90.
60. Ibid., 91.
61. Ibid., 93.
62. Building a Europe for and with children. *Protecting children from sexual violence: A comprehensive approach.* (Council of Europe Publishing, 2010).
63. National Association of School Nurses, *Position Statement: Bullying Prevention in Schools* (www.nasn.org /nasn/advocacy/professional-practice-documents /position-statements/ps-bullying 2014).
64. M. S. Stockdale et al., "Rural Elementary Students', Parents', and Teachers' Perceptions of Bullying," *American Journal of Health Behavior* 26, no. 4 (2002): 266.
65. U.S. Department of Health and Human Services, *Bullying Definition* (www.stopbullying.gov/what-is -bullying/definition/index.html; 2018).
66. U.S. Department of Health and Human Services, *What Is Cyberbullying?* (www.stopbullying.gov/cyberbullying /what-is-it/index.html; 2018).
67. Ibid.
68. Ibid.
69. Ibid.
70. S. Graham, "What Educators Need to About Bullying Behaviors," *Kappan* (September 2010): 66–69.
71. U.S. Department of Health and Human Services, *The Role Kids Play in Bullying* (www.stopbullying.gov/what-is -bullying/roles-kids-play/index.html; 2017).
72. U.S. Department of Health and Human Services, *Who Is at Risk* (www.stopbullying.gov/at-risk/index.html; 2018).
73. U.S. Department of Health and Human Services, *Effects of Bullying* (www.stopbullying.gov/at-risk/effects/index .html; 2017).
74. National School Safety Center, *Understanding, Preventing, and Responding to School Bullying* (Westlake Village, CA: National School Safety Center, December 2001), 5–6.
75. Ibid.
76. Ibid.
77. C. Remboldt, "Making Violence Unacceptable."
78. M. Beaudoin, "Respect—Where Do We Start?" *Educational Leadership* 69, no. 1 (2001): 41–44.
79. National Education Association, *Findings from the National Education Association's Nationwide Study of Bullying: Teachers' and Education Support Professionals' Perspectives* (2011) (www.nea.org/assets/docs/2010_ Survey.pdf; 2011).
80. Beaudoin, "Respect – Where Do We Start?"
81. P. C. Rodkin, "Bullying—And the Power of Peers," *Educational Leadership* 69, no. 1 (2011): 11–16.
82. U.S. Department of Health and Human Services, *Policies and Laws* (www.stopbullying.gov/laws/; 2014).
83. American School Health Association, "All Members of the School Community: Who Does What?" *Health in Action: Bullying in the School Community: Everyone Has a Role to Play in Preventing Bullying* 3, no. 4 (May/June 2005): 12.
84. M. J. Elias and D. I. Neft, "Administrators: Who Does What?" *Health in Action: Bullying in the School Community: Everyone Has a Role to Play in Preventing Bullying* 3, no. 4 (May/June 2005).
85. T. Feinberg, "School Counselors and Other Mental Health Providers: Who Does What?" *Health in Action: Bullying in the School Community: Everyone Has a Role to Play in Preventing Bullying* 3, no. 4 (May/June 2005): 12–13.
86. A. Cebulski, J. Vessey, and W. F. Connell, "School Nurses: Who Does What?" *Health in Action: Bullying in the School Community: Everyone Has a Role to Play in Preventing Bullying* 3, no. 4 (May/June 2005): 13.
87. L. Piculell, "School Resource Officers: Who Does What?" *Health in Action: Bullying in the School Community: Everyone Has a Role to Play in Preventing Bullying* 3, no. 4 (May/June 2005): 13.
88. American School Health Association, "All Members of the School Community," 13.
89. Ibid.
90. C. Blaber, "Sexual Harassment in Schools," *Health in Action: Bullying in the School Community: Everyone Has a Role to Play in Preventing Bullying* 3, no. 4 (May/ June 2005).
91. N. Stein, "Bullying or Sexual Harassment? The Missing Discourse of Rights in an Era of Zero Tolerance," *Arizona Law Review* 45, no. 783 (2003): 783–99.
92. Ibid.
93. Ibid.
94. Blaber, "Sexual Harassment in Schools."
95. N. Stein, *Harvard Education Letter* (January/ February 2000).
96. W. Schwartz, *How to Help Your Child Avoid Violent Conflicts* (ERIC Clearinghouse on Urban Education).
97. C. Blaber and L. F. Hergert, "Flash Points," *Health in Action: Bullying in the School Community: Everyone Has a Role to Play in Preventing Bullying* 3, no. 4 (May/June 2005).
98. A. Doucette, "Youth Suicide," in *About Children: An Authoritative Resource on the State of Childhood Today* (Elk Grove Village, IL: American Academy of Pediatrics, 2005), 146–49.
99. Ibid.
100. Ibid.
101. C. M. Kienhorst et al., "The Adolescents' Image of Their Suicide Attempt," *Journal of the American Academy of Child and Adolescent Psychiatry* 34, no. 5 (1995): 623–28.
102. Centers for Disease Control and Prevention, *Suicide: Risk and Protective Factors* (www.cdc.gov/violenceprevention /suicide/riskprotectivefactors.html; 2017).
103. Doucette, "Youth Suicide."
104. Centers for Disease Control and Prevention, *Health Education Curriculum Analysis Tool* (Atlanta, GA: CDC, 2012).
105. Ibid.
106. W. Kane and M. Quackenbush, *Teach & Talk: Safety & Risks* (Santa Cruz, CA: ETR Associates, 2001).
107. R. G. Slaby, R. Wilson-Brewer, and K. Dash, *Aggressors, Victims, and Bystanders: Thinking and Acting to Prevent Violence* (Newton, MA: Education Development Center, 1994), 28–29.
108. P. Hamamoto, "Letter to Editor Clarifies DOE's Rule on Harassment," *Honolulu Advertiser,* June 13, 2001,
109. Ibid.
110. N. D. Stein and L. Sjostrom, *Flirting or Hurting: A Teacher's Guide on Sexual Harassment in Schools, Grades 6-12* (Wellesley, MA: Wellesley College Center for Research on Women, 1994).
111. N. Stein, E. Gaberman, and L. Sjostrom, *Bullyproof: A Teacher's Guide on Teasing and Bullying for Use with Fourth and Fifth Grade Students* (Wellesley, MA: Wellesley College Center for Research on Women, 1996).
112. Ibid.
113. Teaching Tolerance, *Starting Small: Teaching Tolerance in Preschool and the Early Grades* (Montgomery, AL: Southern Poverty Law Center, 1997).
114. A. W. Coffee, J. Coffee, and J. N. Elizalde, *Peace Signs: A Manual for Teaching School Children Anger Management and Communication Skills* (Honolulu: CoffeePress, 2000).
115. N. Stein and D. Cappello, *Gender Violence, Gender Justice* (Wellesley, MA: Wellesley College Center for Research on Women, 1999).
116. D. Catrow, *We the Kids: The Preamble to the Constitution of the United States* (New York: Dial Books for Young Readers, 2002).
117. M. Bang, *When Sophie Gets Angry—Really, Really Angry* (New York: Blue Sky Press, 1999).
118. M. Froschl et al., *Quit It! A Teacher's Guide on Teasing and Bullying for Use with Students in Grades K–3* (Wellesley, MA: Wellesley College Center for Research on Women, 1999).
119. A. O'Neill and L. Luliska-Beith, *The Recess Queen Angry* (New York: Scholastic, 2002).
120. U.S. Department of Health and Human Services, *National Prevention Strategy: America's Plan for Better Health and Wellness* (Washington, DC: National Prevention, Health Promotion, and Public Health Council, 2011), 43.
121. Center for the Study and Prevention of Violence, *Blueprints for Healthy Youth Development* (www.blueprintsprograms.org; 2018).
122. Center for the Study and Prevention of Violence, *Life Skills Training (LST)* (http://www.blueprintsprograms .com/factsheet/lifeskills-training-lst; 2018.
123. Center for the Study and Prevention of Violence, *Blueprints for Healthy Youth Development* (http://www .blueprintsprograms.com/; 2018).

11

(Justin, age 12)

Tobacco Use and Electronic Nicotine Delivery Systems Prevention

DESIRED LEARNER OUTCOMES

After reading this chapter, you will be able to . . .

- **Describe the prevalence and cost of tobacco and electronic nicotine delivery systems (ENDS) use among youth.**

- **Explain the relationship between tobacco use and compromised academic performance.**

- **Identify factors that influence youth tobacco and ENDS use.**

- **Summarize current guidelines and practices for schools and teachers related to tobacco use prevention.**

- **Summarize developmentally appropriate tobacco prevention concepts and skills for K–8 students in the context of the National Health Education Standards and target healthy behavior outcomes.**

- **Demonstrate developmentally appropriate learning strategies and assessment techniques that incorporate concepts and skills that have been shown to reduce tobacco risks among youth.**

- **Identify effective, evaluated commercial tobacco use prevention curricula.**

- **Identify websites and children's literature that can be used in cross-curricular instructional activities promoting tobacco use prevention.**

INTRODUCTION

Tobacco use is an issue that young people will frequently face; many will be tempted to try tobacco products or other electronic nicotine delivery systems (ENDS) as they advance through late elementary and middle school. Teachers can help students avoid these products and ultimately prevent premature death. This section introduces teachers to the number of young people who use tobacco and ENDS, how much tobacco costs society, the relationship between tobacco and ENDS use and performance, and the factors that influence tobacco use.

Prevalence and Cost

Cigarette smoking and/or use of other tobacco products, including ENDS, is the single most preventable cause of death in the United States today. One in every five deaths in the United States is tobacco related. Each year, more than 4,80,000 people die of smoking-related illnesses (Figure 11-1).[1]

There is a definite need for tobacco use prevention programs in today's elementary and middle schools—virtually all adult smokers began smoking at or before the age of 18 (Figure 11-2).[2-3] Each day in the United States, 2,300 youth under 18 years of age try their first cigarette, and approximately 350 youth become regular smokers.[4] Although few data about cigarette use are collected for students under the age of 12, it appears that the peak years for first-time smoking is between the ages of 11 and 13. For example, one study found that 3 percent of eighth-grade students smoked their first cigarette by the fifth grade. Cigarette smoking has one of the lowest ages of initiation, although lifetime prevalence of cigarette smoking has declined. This suggests that late elementary school may be a strategic time to focus on smoking prevention efforts.[5-6] Even with all of the negative information about the health consequences of tobacco use documented through research, the number of adolescents who smoke is too high. Currently, 2.2 percent of ninth-grade students, 2.9 percent of tenth-grade students, 3.2 percent of eleventh-grade students, and 5.1 percent of twelfth-grade students are smokers (Table 11-1).[7] Total current cigarette use among middle school students (grades 6–8) is 2.3 percent with 2.4 percent of males and 2.2 percent of females reported as being current smokers.[8]

Many tobacco companies now produce and sell ENDS such as electronic cigarettes (e-cigarettes), vape pens, JUUL, and hookahs. These devices deliver nicotine through an aerosol that is inhaled into the lungs the same way cigarette smoke enters. So far there are no studies on the health effects of long-term use of ENDS or whether use of ENDS leads to cigarette smoking by youth.[9]

Students who had reported vaping anything in the last thirty days were 48.6 percent among twelfth-grade students, 41 percent among tenth-grade students, and 42.2 percent among eighth-grade students.[10]

Besides loss of life, there are economic costs related to smoking. Each pack of cigarettes sold in the United States costs the nation an estimated $19.16 in medical care and loss.[11, 12] Estimates indicate that smoking caused over $300 billion in annual health-related economic losses from 2006 to 2010, including $170 billion in direct medical costs, and $97 billion in lost productivity.[13]

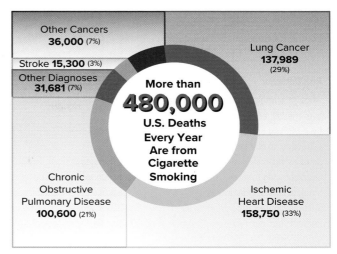

FIGURE 11-1 | **Annual Deaths Among Smokers Attributable to Smoking-Related Diseases**
SOURCE: Centers for Disease Control and Prevention, *2014 Surgeon General's Report*, Table 12.4, 660.

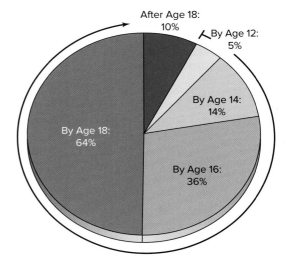

Age of smoking initiation among adult daily smokers: cumulative percent who began smoking by age 18

FIGURE 11-2 | **Tobacco Use Begins Early** Note that only 10 percent of adults who are daily smokers began smoking after age 18.
SOURCE: National Youth Tobacco Survey 2011–2012.

Because of the prevalence of diseases related to tobacco use in the United States, the 2010 national health objectives encourage schools to provide a Comprehensive Health Education Program to prevent tobacco use; several of the *Healthy People 2020* objectives are tobacco related (Table 11-2).

Tobacco Use and Academic Performance

The few research studies that have been conducted in the area of tobacco use and academic performance all show similar results. Preadolescents and adolescents who smoke tend to perform less well academically than their nonsmoking peers. For example, a longitudinal study, conducted with eighth-grade students found that high school failure was directly predicted by earlier

TABLE 11–1

Youth Risk Behavior Survey Data Related to Tobacco Use, 2018

	Percent Reporting Behavior		
Risk Behavior	Total	Females	Males
Smoked a whole cigarette for the first time before age 13	9.5	8.0	10.9
Ever tried cigarette smoking, even one or two puffs	28.9	27.3	30.7
Ever smoked one or more cigarettes every day for thirty days	2.0	2.0	2.0
Ever used an electronic vapor product	44.9	41.2	45.3
Smoked cigarettes on twenty or more of the past thirty days	2.6	2.6	2.7
Used chewing tobacco, snuff, dip, snus, or dissolvable tobacco products on more than one of the past thirty days	5.5	1.9	8.9
Smoked cigars, cigarillos, or little cigars on at least one of the past thirty days	8.0	5.4	10.5
Smoked cigarettes or cigars or used chewing tobacco, snuff, or dip on more than one of the past thirty days	14.0	10.7	17.3
Students had ever used an electronic vapor product (including e-cigarettes, e-cigars, e-pipes, vape pipes, vaping pens, e-hookahs, and hookah pens)	42.2	39.7	44.9
Students less than 18 years of age who were current electronic vapor product users and purchased products (including e-cigarettes, e-cigars, e-pipes, vape pipes, vaping pens, e-hookahs, and hookah pens) at a store or gas station during the past thirty days	13.6	10.8	15.6

SOURCE: Centers for Disease Control and Prevention, "Youth Risk Behavior Surveillance—United States, 2016," *Morbidity and Mortality Weekly Report* 65, no. 4 (June 10, 2016): 1–180.

TABLE 11–2

Healthy People 2020 Objectives Related to Tobacco Use Among Children and Adolescents

Objective ECBP-1	Increase the proportion of preschool Early Head Start and Head Start programs that provide health education to prevent health problems in tobacco use and addiction.
Objective ECBP-2	Increase the proportion of elementary, middle, and senior high schools that provide comprehensive school health education to prevent health problems in tobacco use and addiction.
Objective TU-2	Reduce tobacco use by adolescents.
Objective TU-3	Reduce the initiation of tobacco use among children and adolescents.
Objective TU-7	Increase smoking cessation attempts by adolescent smokers.
Objective TU-11	Reduce the proportion of children and adolescents exposed to secondhand smoke.
Objective TU-15	Increase tobacco-free environments in schools, including all school facilities, property, vehicles, and school events.
Objective TU-13	Establish laws in States, District of Columbia, Territories, and Tribes on smoke-free indoor air that prohibit smoking in public places and worksites.
Objective TU-18	Reduce the proportion of adolescents and young adults grades 6 through 12 who are exposed to tobacco advertising and promotion.
Objective TU-19	Reduce the illegal sales rate to minors through enforcement of laws prohibiting the sale of tobacco products to minors.
Objectives TU-0	Increase the number of States and the District of Columbia, Territories, and Tribes with sustainable and comprehensive evidence-based tobacco control programs.

SOURCE: U.S. Department of Health and Human Services, *Healthy People 2020* (www.healthypeople.gov/2020/default.aspx).

tobacco use.[14] A study with high school seniors found that those with a low grade-point average were more likely to smoke cigarettes.[15] Another study, conducted with fourth- to seventh-grade students, found that students reporting school difficulties were 1.4 to 5.6 times more likely to report a history of tobacco use than were students who did not report school difficulties.[16] Another study examining Mississippi high school students found that frequent smoking was identified as a significant factor associated with low academic performance.[17] These studies determine only that there is a relationship between tobacco use and poor academic performance. They do not determine whether students started using tobacco and then their academic performance declined *or* students' academic performance declined and then they started to use tobacco—or whether in some cases some third factor influenced both behaviors. Regardless, the relationship exists, and the results of these studies should motivate school administrators and teachers to include tobacco use prevention in their health education curriculum.

Factors That Influence Tobacco Use

Several factors differentiate those who use tobacco from those who do not. The factors associated with reduced potential for tobacco use are protective factors and those associated with greater potential for tobacco use are risk factors. A summary of the most common protective and risk factors for tobacco use is given in the following lists.[18-22]

Protective Factors

• *Parent and family connectedness.* Adolescents who experience a high degree of closeness, caring, and satisfaction with parents are less likely to use tobacco. Another protective factor for adolescents is feeling understood, loved, wanted, and paid attention to by family members.

• *Parental/adolescent activities.* Adolescents who participate in activities with their parents on a consistent basis are less likely to use tobacco products.

• *Parental academic expectations.* Adolescents whose parents expect them to graduate from high school or college are less likely to use tobacco products.

• *Behavioral and social skills.* Adolescents who can demonstrate and use effective refusal and stress management skills are less likely to use tobacco.

Risk Factors

• *Household access to tobacco.* Adolescents who live in households where there is easy access to tobacco are more likely to begin to use tobacco products than are adolescents who do not have easy access.

• *Family suicide or attempt of suicide.* Adolescents with a family member who has completed or attempted suicide in the past twelve months are at risk for tobacco use.

• *Low socioeconomic status.* Low socioeconomic adolescents are at increased risk for the initiation of tobacco use.

• *Tobacco availability.* When tobacco is easily accessible, adolescents are more likely to use tobacco. Unfortunately, most adolescents can easily access tobacco products. Nearly 12.6 percent of high school smokers usually buy their cigarettes directly from a store and 8.5 percent of high school students are buying tobacco products on the Internet.[23] However, it is clear that enforcement of youth access laws can reduce tobacco sales to minors. Numerous research studies have found that making obtaining cigarettes as inconvenient, difficult, and expensive as possible for kids reduces both the number of kids who try or regularly smoke cigarettes and the number of cigarettes consumed by kids who continue to smoke. Because youth purchases are a source of cigarettes smoked by kids, increasing cigarette prices and minimizing the number of retailers willing to illegally sell cigarettes to kids will reduce youth smoking.[24]

• *Tobacco acceptability.* There is an increased risk of tobacco use among adolescents with a perception of acceptance among family, peers, and the community. Acceptability is influenced by the tobacco industry through advertising and other promotional activities. The tobacco industry currently spends over $8.37 billion a year, or over $23 million a day, to advertise cigarettes, which equates to almost $27.00 a day for every person in the United States.[25] Tobacco companies claim they do not target their advertising toward youth, but the evidence does not support their claim. The federal government has found ample evidence that there is a causal relationship between tobacco company promotion and advertising and the initiation and continued use of tobacco among adolescents. This evidence shows that adolescents are exposed to cigarette advertising, they find the advertisements appealing, and the advertisements increase an adolescent's desire to smoke.[26]

• *Parental smoking.* Most research has shown a relationship between parental and adolescent smoking. Adolescents with one or both parents who smoke are more likely to also smoke. This relationship seems stronger for females than for males, and for whites than for African Americans, Hispanics, or Asians.

• *Sibling smoking.* A synthesis of most research shows that adolescents who have an older sibling who smokes were more likely to also smoke.

• *Peer smoking.* Almost all studies have shown a strong relationship between adolescent smoking and having friends who smoke. In a review of sixteen prospective studies, peer smoking was predictive of some phase of smoking in all but one study.

• *Perceived norms.* Perceived norms, defined as people's perceptions of others' beliefs and behaviors, often can be inaccurate. It has been found that when adolescents believe most of their peers smoke or overestimate the percentage of their peers who smoke, they are more likely to begin and continue to smoke.

• *Academic achievement.* As discussed in the previous section, a positive relationship has been found between low academic achievement and the onset of smoking among adolescents.

• *Risk taking, rebelliousness, and deviant behavior.* Several studies have found that when adolescents are considered to be risk takers, rebellious, or likely to participate in deviant behaviors (unconventional or antisocial behaviors) they are more likely to use tobacco.

• *Behavioral and social skills.* Adolescents who do not have effective refusal and stress management skills are more likely to use tobacco.

• *Self-esteem.* Most studies show that students with lower self-esteem are more likely to smoke than are adolescents with higher self-esteem.

• *Body image concerns.* Girls who are concerned about weight and weight gain are at increased risk to initiate tobacco use.

• *Aggressive behavior.* Adolescents who participate in aggressive behaviors such as fighting and weapon carrying are more likely to be tobacco users.

• *Nicotine sensitivity.* There is evidence that youth may be more sensitive to nicotine compared to adults, which may make them dependent on nicotine sooner than adults.

GUIDELINES FOR SCHOOLS

This section provides information about current tobacco prevention programs and policies for elementary and middle schools. The first part of this section includes data about the actual programs and policies in use in schools today. The second part provides information for teachers and administrators about what should be happening in schools to help children and adolescents stay tobacco-free.

State of the Practice

The Centers for Disease Control and Prevention (CDC) periodically conducts the School Health Policies and Practices Study

(SHPPS) to assess current school health policies and programs at the district level.[27] Because tobacco use contributes to the most preventable causes of death in the country today, it is important for school districts to have policies that reflect zero tolerance for tobacco use. The results of SHPPS 2016 found that 97.2 percent of school districts have a "tobacco-free policy," that is, a policy that prohibits tobacco use by students, faculty, staff, and visitors in school buildings, on school grounds, on school buses, or at off-campus school-sponsored events 77.6 percent of schools have this policy including any electronic nicotine delivery systems.[28]

School districts should also be supportive of tobacco prevention being taught in schools as a part of their comprehensive health education curriculum. SHPSS 2016 found that 65.9 percent of districts required tobacco use prevention be taught at the elementary school level and 80 percent at the middle school level.[29]

State of the Art

Even more important than the state of the practice in tobacco and ENDS prevention, however, is for elementary and middle school teachers to understand what should be included in a successful schoolwide tobacco prevention program. The Centers for Disease Control and Prevention examined all the current research about successful smoking prevention programs and developed seven recommendations for school health programs to prevent tobacco use and addiction[30]:

1. Develop and enforce a school policy on tobacco and ENDS use. The policy should:
   - Prohibit students, staff, parents, and visitors from using tobacco on school premises, in school vehicles, and at school functions.
   - Prohibit tobacco advertising (on T-shirts or caps or through sponsorship of school events) in school buildings, at school functions, and in school publications.
   - Require that all students receive instruction on avoiding tobacco use.
   - Provide access and referral to cessation programs for students and staff.
   - Help students who violate tobacco-free policies to quit using tobacco rather than just punishing them.
2. Provide instruction about the short- and long-term negative physiological and social consequences of tobacco use, about social influences on tobacco use, about peer norms regarding tobacco use, and about refusal skills. This instruction should:
   - Decrease the social acceptability of tobacco use and show that most young people do not smoke.
   - Help students understand why young people start to use tobacco, and identify more positive activities to meet their goals.
   - Develop students' skills in assertiveness, goal setting, problem solving, and resisting pressure from the media and their peers to use tobacco.
   - Programs that discuss only tobacco's harmful effects or attempt to instill fear do not prevent tobacco use.

3. Provide tobacco use prevention education in kindergarten through twelfth grade.
   - This instruction should be introduced in elementary school and intensified in middle or junior high school, when students are exposed to older students who typically use tobacco at higher rates.
   - Reinforcement throughout high school is essential to ensure that successes in preventing tobacco use do not dissipate over time.
4. Provide program-specific training for teachers.
   - The training should include reviewing the curriculum, modeling instructional activities, and providing opportunities to practice implementing the lessons. Well-trained peer leaders can be an important adjunct to teacher-led instruction.
5. Involve parents or families in support of school-based programs to prevent tobacco use. Schools should:
   - Promote discussions at home about tobacco use by assigning homework and projects that involve families.
   - Encourage parents to participate in community efforts to prevent tobacco use.
6. Support cessation efforts among students and all school staff who use tobacco.
   - Schools should provide access to cessation programs that help students and staff stop using tobacco rather than punishing them for violating tobacco use policies.
7. Assess the tobacco use prevention program at regular intervals. Schools can use CDC's "Guidelines for School Health Programs to Prevent Tobacco Use and Addiction" to assess whether they are providing effective policies, curricula, training, family involvement, and cessation programs.

As important as knowing what concepts to teach at each grade level is knowing what not to teach. Following are some guidelines for teachers to follow when teaching tobacco prevention:

1. Do not imply that people are "bad" if they smoke. Although this approach might work with some youth, it has been found to backfire, especially with high-risk students. The more smoking is labeled bad by authority figures, the more some high-risk students want to rebel.
2. Do not say that smoking is "dumb." Children need to maintain respect for their parents and other adults in their life, whether or not they smoke.
3. Do not encourage children, even indirectly, to denounce smoking at home. Smoking remains a personal choice. If the school is perceived as intruding in the home, parents might become alienated from the school's smoking prevention efforts.
4. Do not tell young children that smoking leads to deadly diseases. This approach can provoke anxiety in children whose parents or relatives smoke. This information should be taught in upper-elementary grades when children can understand that these risks generally are long term and that quitting can reverse the trend.
5. Do not warn older students that they will die an early death if they smoke. This "threat" approach is not effective. It is far more effective to focus on immediate consequences.

The vast majority of smokers began smoking as teenagers. In surveys, about 75 percent of teen smokers state that they wish they had never started smoking.

6. Do not give mixed messages. A teacher who smokes should not try to hide this fact from students but should indicate the intention to help them avoid similar unhealthy decisions. The concept of nicotine addiction can also be discussed.

GUIDELINES FOR CLASSROOM APPLICATIONS

Important Background for K–8 Teachers

Tobacco is addictive and is responsible for more than one out of every five deaths in the United States. Because the use of tobacco is related to so many health problems, preventing tobacco use has become a major focus over the past several years. *The Health Consequences of Smoking–50 Years of Progress* is the surgeon general's report that focuses on how to end the tobacco epidemic. Following are some of the major conclusions of that report:

- Tobacco use usually begins in early adolescence, typically by age 15.
- Most young people who smoke are addicted to nicotine and report that they want to quit but are unable to do so.
- Tobacco often is the first drug used by young people who use alcohol and illegal drugs.
- Among young people, those with poorer grades and lower self-images are most likely to begin using tobacco.
- Cigarette advertising appears to increase young people's risk of smoking by implying that smoking can satisfy adolescents' need to be popular, feel attractive, take risks, and avoid or manage stress.[31-32]

These conclusions highlight the importance of beginning tobacco use prevention education at a young age. Teachers must understand background information about tobacco before they can teach students about the dangers of tobacco use. Not all of this information is developmentally appropriate for all elementary and middle school students, but teachers should have a basic understanding of the negative side effects of tobacco use.

Smokeless or Spit Tobacco

The use of smokeless tobacco is common among many of today's youth. For example, the 2017 Youth Risk Behavior Survey found that 5.5 percent of high school students (8.9 percent of males and 1.9 percent of females) had used smokeless tobacco in the previous thirty days.[33] In addition, 2.2 percent of middle school students had used smokeless tobacco in the past thirty days.[34] Because some young people begin using smokeless tobacco at a young age, it is important for elementary and middle school teachers to focus on all forms of tobacco use.

There are three principal methods of using smokeless or spit tobacco: chewing, dipping snuff, and smoking. Chewing tobacco is made of tobacco leaves that are either dried and shredded and sold in a pouch or made into plugs or strands that are mixed with molasses, sugar, licorice, and other products. As the name "chewing tobacco" suggests, a portion of the loose leaf, plug, or strand is placed in the mouth and chewed, while excess juices periodically are spit out. Chewing tobacco is the least popular form of tobacco among today's youth. The dangers of chewing tobacco are similar to those of snuff.

Snuff is made from finely cut tobacco leaves and mixed with various products. There are two kinds of snuff: dry snuff and moist snuff. Dry snuff is made from finely ground, dried tobacco leaves and usually is sniffed through the nose. This type of snuff is not popular in most parts of the United States. Moist snuff also is made of finely ground tobacco leaves, but it is packaged while it is still damp. A small amount of moist snuff, known as a "pinch," is held between the lip or cheek and the gum and sucked, while excess juices periodically are spit out. This activity is commonly referred to as "dipping." Although many persons believe smokeless tobacco to be a safe form of tobacco, it has numerous dangerous side effects. Some of the more common negative side effects are

- *Nicotine addiction.* Nicotine is a powerful, addictive substance found in all tobacco products. Although nicotine is absorbed more slowly from smokeless tobacco than from cigarettes, the amount of nicotine absorbed from smokeless tobacco is three to four times the amount absorbed from a cigarette. Also, the nicotine stays in the bloodstream for a longer time. Nicotine may contribute to cardiovascular disease, high blood pressure, ulcers, and fetal problems. Like most users of stimulants, tobacco users build a tolerance for nicotine, resulting in a need to use more of the drug to get the same effect.[35] Unfortunately, adolescents who use smokeless tobacco are more likely to become cigarette smokers.[36]
- *Oral cancer.* Snuff tobacco contains twenty-eight carcinogens or cancer-causing agents. The most harmful carcinogens in smokeless tobacco are the tobacco-specific nitrosamines (TSNAs).[37] Because snuff stays in the mouth for a relatively long time, the nitrosamines may contribute to the high risk for oral cancer for tobacco snuff users. Many snuff users first experience a white, thick, hard patch of tissue in their mouths. Known as leukoplakia, this is considered to be a precancerous lesion. It has also been reported that smokeless tobacco users have a higher risk of developing oral, pancreatic, and esophageal cancers.[38] Oral cancer has a tendency to spread to the body's lymph system, where it becomes very difficult to treat.

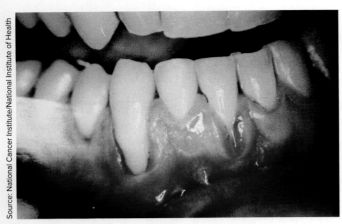

Receding gum lines are a common problem among smokeless tobacco users.

• *Gum and tooth problems.* Because sugar is added to smokeless tobacco and the tobacco is held in the mouth for long periods of time, users also tend to have more dental caries. One study found chewing tobacco users were four times more likely than nonusers to have decayed dental root surfaces. Spit tobacco also causes gingivitis, a gum disease that can lead to bone and tooth loss. Receding gums at the site of tobacco placement are common among smokeless tobacco users. Gum recession exposes the teeth to disease, and, because the gum will not grow back, this condition can be corrected only by surgery.[39]

Smoking Tobacco

There are three ways persons smoke tobacco: pipes, cigars, and cigarettes. Because cigarettes are the most popular way for adults and adolescents to smoke tobacco in the United States, the majority of tobacco information in this chapter focuses on cigarettes.

Young people who use tobacco are more likely to progress to using other drugs. For example, tobacco users are more than seven times more likely to start using marijuana than individuals who had never used tobacco.[40] This does not mean that cigarette smoking causes other drug use but rather that cigarette smokers are more likely to use other drugs, such as marijuana and cocaine. If the number of teenagers who begin smoking can be reduced through educational prevention programs, then the prevalence of smoking and other drug use among adults can be decreased.

When tobacco is burned or smoked, it produces hundreds of toxic chemicals. When these chemicals condense, they form a brown, sticky substance called tar. Some of the chemicals in tar are carcinogens. Nicotine, the main chemical or drug found in tobacco, is the addictive part of tobacco that causes increased heart rate, blood pressure, and breathing rate, as well as constriction (narrowing) of the blood vessels. Cigarette smoke also contains carbon monoxide, the deadly gas found in automobile exhaust. It is considered to be one of the most harmful components of tobacco smoke. When carbon monoxide is inhaled, it quickly bonds with hemoglobin and reduces red blood cells' ability to transport oxygen. Because of the reduced oxygen, smokers tend to experience shortness of breath. For youth, the short-term consequences of smoking include respiratory and nonrespiratory effects, decreased physical fitness, adverse changes in cholesterol, and reduced rates of lung growth and function. In addition, the younger people are when they begin to smoke, the more likely they are to become strongly addicted to nicotine. Individuals who begin smoking during adolescence are more likely to become addicted, to progress to daily smoking, to continue smoking into adulthood, and to become heavier tobacco users as adults.[41] Because of tar, nicotine, carbon monoxide, and many of the other chemicals and gases in tobacco, its use has many negative short-term consequences, including the following:

• *Increased heart rate.* After smoking just one cigarette, the heart rate increases by as many as thirty-three beats per minute. Although the heart rate will decrease over time, smokers generally have a higher resting heart rate than nonsmokers. This means that every day a smoker's heart has to work harder than does a nonsmoker's heart. This higher heart rate is attributed to the increased carbon monoxide levels and the constricted blood vessels caused by nicotine, which make it harder for the heart to pump blood throughout the body.[42] The resting heart rate for young adult smokers is two to three beats per minute faster than that of nonsmokers.[43]

• *Increased blood pressure.* After smoking just one cigarette, blood pressure increases. This increase is caused by the constricted blood vessels.[44]

• *Decreased skin temperature.* When persons smoke, their skin temperature quickly decreases. This is caused by nicotine, which reduces blood flow to the peripheral vessels.

• *Decreased hand steadiness.* Although some smokers believe that smoking relaxes them, it actually increases nervousness and tension and reduces hand steadiness. This is the result of the stimulant effect of nicotine. Decreased hand steadiness can affect athletic and art ability and other activities that require fine-motor skills.

• *Increased carbon monoxide levels.* Only about 5 percent of the smoke a person inhales is carbon monoxide; however, even this amount can be dangerous. When excess carbon monoxide is inhaled into the lungs, the oxygen-carrying capacity of the blood is reduced. The reduced amount of oxygen in the blood makes it more difficult for the body's organs, such as the heart and brain, to do their work. This is why many smokers get out of breath easily, which can affect athletic and musical performance.[45]

• *Bad breath.* Smoking causes bad breath. This is one short-term effect that should be stressed to students, especially when upper-elementary and middle-level students become more interested in social interactions with classmates.

• *Fires and burns.* Other short-term effects of smoking cigarettes are fires related to smoking. Smoking is the leading cause of fire-related deaths.[46] Each year, over 570 deaths and 1,140 injuries are associated with fires started by cigarettes. Most of these injuries and deaths are caused by smokers who are careless about how, when, and where they smoke.[47]

Though students should understand all of the effects associated with smoking cigarettes, attention to the short-term side effects of smoking is more developmentally appropriate for younger learners than are long-term consequences. However, because some students will be curious about the long-term effects of smoking, it is important for teachers to have some general knowledge about this topic. Although smoking has numerous long-term effects, only the most common are discussed next.

• *Lung cancer.* Lung cancer is the leading cancer killer for both men and women. Smoking is responsible for about 80 percent of all lung cancer cases, over 1,54,050 deaths each year.[48] The risk of developing lung cancer increases with the number of cigarettes smoked per day, the number of years of smoking, and the age at which the person started smoking. Smoking also increases the long-term risk of getting several types of cancers such as cancer of the larynx, bladder, esophagus, pancreas, uterus, kidney, cervix, stomach, pharynx, and mouth.[49]

• *Cardiovascular disease.* Smoking is the most important recognized, modifiable risk factor for cardiovascular disease. Smoking causes atherosclerosis (hardening and narrowing of the arteries), stroke, and coronary artery disease. Cigarette smokers are two to four times more likely to develop coronary artery disease than nonsmokers and are at twice the risk for strokes. Young people who smoke already show greater deposits of fat in the blood vessels leading to and from the heart. A person who quits smoking reduces the risk of cardiovascular disease by about 50 percent after 1 year. After 15 years, the risk of cardiovascular disease is similar to that of a person who has never smoked.[50]

• *Chronic obstructive lung disease.* Smoking accounts for at least 75 percent of all chronic obstructive lung disease deaths.[51] Chronic obstructive lung disease includes two related diseases: chronic bronchitis and emphysema. Both of these diseases are related to cigarettes because of the damage smoking does to the airways and the alveoli sacs, the sites of carbon monoxide and oxygen exchange in the lungs. Chronic bronchitis predisposes the smoker to emphysema, increasing risk. Chronic bronchitis is a persistent inflammation and infection of the smaller airways within the lungs. Emphysema is an irreversible disease in which the alveoli are destroyed. Even quitting smoking will not regenerate the alveoli. Healthy adults have about 100 square yards of interior lung surface, created by the lungs' thousands of alveoli sacs. When a person gets emphysema, the walls between the sacs break down, creating larger and fewer sacs and thus gradually diminishing the interior lung surface. Eventually, the lung surface is so small that people with emphysema spend most of their time gasping for air and carrying an oxygen tank along with them (Figure 11–3).

• *Secondhand smoke health effects.* Secondhand tobacco smoke has a long-term effect on children and adults who live in homes with smokers. Children exposed to secondhand smoke are at higher risk for sudden infant death syndrome (SIDS), acute lower respiratory tract infections, asthma induction and exacerbation, chronic respiratory symptoms, and middle ear infections.[52] In adults, secondhand smoke exposure increases the risk for lung cancer, respiratory problems, heart disease, and eye and nasal irritation.[53] Most exposure to secondhand smoke occurs in homes and workplaces. People are also exposed to secondhand smoke in public places such as restaurants, bars, and casinos, but also in cars or other vehicles.[54] It is important that teachers not scare children with this information but instead inform parents about the dangers of secondhand smoke.

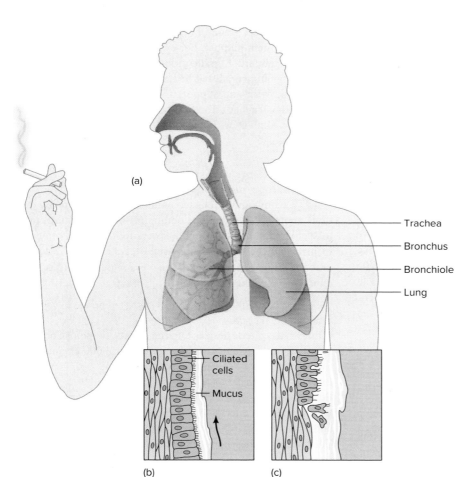

FIGURE 11–3 | **Damage to the Lungs Caused by Smoking** (a) The respiratory system. (b) The inside of a bronchiole of a nonsmoker. Foreign particles are collected by a thin layer of sticky mucus and transported out of the lungs, up toward the mouth, by the action of cilia. (c) The inside of a bronchiole of a smoker. Smoking irritates the lung tissue and causes increased mucus production, which can overwhelm the action of the cilia. A smoker develops a chronic cough as the lungs try to rid themselves of foreign particles and excess mucus. Eventually the cilia are destroyed, leaving the delicate lung tissue exposed to injury from foreign substances.

• *Thirdhand smoke health effects.* Thirdhand smoke is nicotine residue that remains on surfaces such as walls, drapery, carpet, clothes, and furniture. Seniors, children, and pets are most affected by this health hazard. Babies, toddlers, and children are at a greater risk of negative health effects because they inhale more than adults, they have greater hand/object/mouth contact so they absorb more through ingestion, and they have greater absorption through their skin. There is still much to be learned about thirdhand smoke.[55]

• *Aesthetic effects.* Numerous aesthetic effects are also associated with the long-term use of cigarettes. Smokers generally have bad breath and stains on their teeth and fingers. Smoking also destroys much of a person's sense of smell and taste, meaning that foods do not taste as good and flowers and other nice scents do not smell as good. Also, smoking causes the skin to wrinkle because of the constant constriction and relaxation of the surface blood vessels, which eventually makes people look much older.

Electronic Nicotine Delivery Systems

Nationwide, 44.9 percent of high school students had ever used electronic vapor products including but not limited to e-cigarettes, e-pipes, vaping pens, e-hookahs, and JUULs ("jewel"). Current electronic nicotine delivery systems (ENDS) are more prevalent among high school males at 25.6 percent and high school females are at 22.6 percent.[56]

Vaping is defined as the act of inhaling and exhaling the aerosol produced by ENDS. This is becoming much more popular among teens than regular cigarettes, especially given that the ENDS can be used with flavors such as mango, mint, and tutti frutti, or flavorings containing nicotine or THC, the chemical compound from marijuana. With many flavors for vaping liquids, it is clear that ENDS are marketed to teens. Vaping is also often sold as a "safer" alternative to cigarettes, and some teens are under the false assumption that because e-cigarettes don't contain tobacco they're safe.[57]

Of all the ENDS products, JUULs are the most popular among teens. Users of this product do not refer to such use as "e-cigarette use" or "vaping," but rather as "JUULing."[58] JUUL devices are sold online, in convenience stores, vape shops, and tobacco retailers. FDA law prohibits sales of such products to those under age 18 and some states and local laws have higher minimum age-of-sale laws.[59]

ENDS users can lead to more nicotine addiction. There is growing research suggesting these products could lead to negative health consequences, including brain, heart, and lung damage; cancerous tumor development; preterm deliveries and stillbirths in pregnant women; and harmful effects on brain and lung development in adolescence.[60]

ENDS can be a gateway to other drug usage. Teen ENDS users are more likely to start smoking tobacco than non users. Some evidence suggests that ENDS use is linked to alcohol use and other substances use, such as marijuana.[61]

Recommendations for Concepts and Practice

Healthy Behavior Outcomes

The goal of health education is to help students adopt or maintain health-enhancing behaviors. School districts and teachers should identify the health-enhancing behaviors they would like their students to maintain or adopt. The list found in the Teacher's Toolbox 11.1 identifies possible healthy behavioral outcomes related to tobacco use prevention.[62] Though not all these suggestions are developmentally appropriate for students in grades K–8, this list can help teachers understand how the learning activities they plan for their students support both short- and long-term desired behavior outcomes.

Developmentally Appropriate Knowledge and Skill Expectations

As with other health topics, teaching related to tobacco use prevention should be developmentally appropriate and be based on the physical, cognitive, social, emotional, and language characteristics of specific students. Teacher's Toolbox 11.1 contains a list of suggested developmentally appropriate knowledge and skill expectations to help teachers create lessons that will encourage students to practice the desired behavior outcomes by the time they graduate from high school.[63] Before each knowledge and skill expectation, the number represents topic abbreviation (T of Tobacco Use Prevention), *NHES* standard number, grade group (last grade in that group), and knowledge or skill expectation item number. For example, T1.5.1 would represent Tobacco, standard 1, grade group 3–5, knowledge expectation item 1. The numbers listed behind each knowledge expectation are aligned with and support the healthy behavior outcomes listed in the Teacher's Toolbox 11.1. Note that these grade-level spans are aligned with the 2007 Natural Health Education Standards.

Sample Students' Questions and Suggested Answers Regarding Tobacco

When learning about tobacco, students formulate many questions about the topic. Some commonly asked questions about tobacco and some suggested answers follow. It is not enough to just read the suggested answers—teachers should actually practice saying them aloud. Teachers should think of other questions students might ask and practice answering them as well.

1. *What's in a cigarette?*
A lot is in a cigarette besides tobacco. In fact, the smoke produced by a burning cigarette contains more than 4,000 chemicals. Of these 4,000 chemicals, 50 cause cancer.
2. *What do cigarettes do to the body?*
Besides causing cancer, lung disease, and heart disease, cigarettes have immediate effects. The carbon monoxide absorbed by the body from one cigarette stays in the blood for as long as six hours. This means the heart has to work harder to supply the body with enough oxygen.
3. *Most kids my age smoke, don't they?*
It might look that way, because tobacco companies pay lots of money to fill magazines and store windows with pictures of people smoking. But, according to the latest surveys, only 2 percent of middle school students have smoked in the past thirty days. That means most kids—98 percent—are smart enough to not smoke.

Developmentally Appropriate Knowledge and Skill Expectations for Tobacco Use Prevention

HEALTHY BEHAVIOR OUTCOMES (HBOs) FOR TOBACCO USE PREVENTION

HBO 1 Avoid using (or experimenting with) any form of tobacco.

HBO 2 Avoid secondhand smoke.

HBO 3 Support a tobacco-free environment.

HBO 4 Support others to be tobacco-free.

HBO 5 Quit using tobacco, if already using.

Grades K–2 Knowledge Expectations	Grades 3–5 Knowledge Expectations	Grades 6–8 Knowledge Expectations
NHES 1: Core Concepts		
T1.2.1 Identify a variety of tobacco products. (HBO 1)	T1.5.1 Identify short- and long-term physical effects of using tobacco. (HBO 1)	T1.8.1 Describe the short- and long-term physical effects of using tobacco. (HBO 1)
T1.2.2 Identify short-term effects of using tobacco. (HBO 1)	T1.5.2 Describe the benefits of abstaining from or discontinuing tobacco use. (HBO 1)	T1.8.2 Summarize the dangers of experimenting with tobacco products. (HBO 1)
T1.2.3 Describe the benefits of not using tobacco. (HBO 1)	T1.5.3 Explain the dangers of experimenting with tobacco. (HBO 1)	T1.8.3 Describe situations that could lead to tobacco use. (HBO 1)
T1.2.4 Describe the dangers of experimenting with tobacco. (HBO 1)	T1.5.4 Describe family rules about avoiding tobacco use. (HBO 2)	T1.8.4 Describe the relationship between using tobacco and alcohol or other drugs. (HBO 1)
T1.2.5 Identify family rules about avoiding tobacco use. (HBO 1)	T1.5.5 Explain the short- and long-term physical effects of being exposed to others' tobacco smoke. (HBO 2)	T1.8.5 Summarize the benefits of being tobacco-free. (HBO 1)
T1.2.6 Identify the short- and long-term physical effects of being exposed to tobacco smoke. (HBO 2)	T1.5.6 Identify the effects of tobacco use on social relationships. (HBO 1 & 4)	T1.8.6 Describe the social, economic, and cosmetic consequences of tobacco use. (HBO 1 & 2)
	T1.5.7 Explain that tobacco use is an addiction that can be treated. (HBO 4 & 5)	T1.8.7 Explain reasons most individuals do not use tobacco products. (HBO 1 & 3)
	T1.5.8 Describe how to support family and friends who are trying to stop using tobacco. (HBO 4)	T1.8.8 Explain school policies and community laws related to the sale and use of tobacco products (HBO 1, 3, & 4)
		T1.8.9 Summarize that tobacco use is an addiction that can be treated. (HBO 1 & 4)
		T1.8.10 Summarize the effects of secondhand smoke. (HBO 2)
		T1.8.11 Describe ways to support family and friends who are trying to stop using tobacco. (HBO 3 & 4)
		T1.8.12 Summarize how addiction to tobacco use can be treated. (HBO 4 & 5)
		T1.8.13 Summarize how smoking cessation programs can be successful. (HBO 4 & 5)

Grades K–2 Skill Expectations	Grades 3–5 Skill Expectations	Grades 6–8 Skill Expectations
NHES 2: Analyze Influences		
Skill expectations are not identified for this grade group.	T2.5.1 Identify relevant influences of culture on tobacco-related practices and behaviors.	T2.8.1 Explain the influence of school rules and community laws on tobacco-related practices and behaviors.
	T2.5.2 Identify relevant influences of peers on tobacco-related practices and behaviors.	T2.8.2 Explain how perceptions of norms influence behaviors related to tobacco use practices and behaviors.
	T2.5.3 Identify relevant influences of community on tobacco-related practices and behaviors.	T2.8.3 Explain how social expectations influence behaviors related to tobacco use practices and behaviors.
	T2.5.4 Describe how relevant influences of family and culture affect tobacco use practices and behaviors.	T2.8.4 Explain how personal values and beliefs influence tobacco use practices and behaviors.
	T2.5.5 Describe how relevant influences of school and community affect tobacco use practices and behaviors.	T2.8.5 Describe how some health-risk behaviors, such as alcohol use, influence the likelihood of engaging in tobacco use.
	T2.5.6 Describe how relevant influences of media (e.g., tobacco advertising) and technology affect tobacco use practices and behaviors.	T2.8.6 Analyze how relevant influences of family and culture affect tobacco use practices and behaviors.
	T2.5.7 Describe how relevant influences of peers affect tobacco use practices and behaviors.	T2.8.7 Analyze how relevant influences of school and community affect tobacco use practices and behaviors.
		T2.8.8 Analyze how relevant influences of media (e.g., tobacco advertising) and technology affect tobacco use practices and behaviors.
		T2.8.9 Analyze how relevant influences of peers affect tobacco use practices and behaviors.

(continued)

Grades K–2 Skill Expectations (*continued*)	Grades 3–5 Skill Expectations (*continued*)	Grades 6–8 Skill Expectations (*continued*)

NHES 3: Accessing Information, Products, and Services

T3.2.1 Identify trusted adults at home who can help prevent tobacco use.	T3.5.1 Describe characteristics of accurate tobacco use prevention information.	T3.8.1 Analyze the validity and reliability of tobacco use prevention information.
T3.2.2 Identify trusted adults and professionals in school (e.g., school nurse, school counselor) who can help prevent tobacco use.	T3.5.2 Demonstrate how to locate sources of accurate tobacco use prevention information.	T3.8.2 Analyze the validity and reliability of tobacco use cessation products.
		T3.8.3 Analyze the validity and reliability of tobacco use cessation services.
		T3.8.4 Describe situations that call for professional tobacco use cessation services.
T3.2.3 Explain how to locate school health helpers (e.g., school nurse) who can help prevent tobacco use.		T3.8.5 Determine the availability of valid and reliable tobacco use cessation products.
		T3.8.6 Access valid and reliable tobacco use prevention and cessation information from home, school, or community.
		T3.8.7 Locate valid and reliable tobacco use cessation products.
		T3.8.8 Locate valid and reliable tobacco use cessation services.

NHES 4: Interpersonal Communication

T4.2.1 Demonstrate how to effectively communicate needs, wants, and feelings that help avoid exposure to secondhand smoke.	T4.5.1 Demonstrate effective verbal and nonverbal communication to avoid exposure to secondhand smoke.	T4.8.1 Demonstrate the use of effective verbal and nonverbal communication to avoid exposure to secondhand smoke and tobacco use.
	T4.5.2 Explain how to be empathetic and compassionate towards others who are trying to quit using tobacco.	T4.8.2 Demonstrate effective peer resistance skills to avoid or reduce exposure to secondhand smoke and tobacco use.
	T4.5.3 Demonstrate effective peer resistance skills to prevent tobacco use.	T4.8.3 Demonstrate effective negotiation skills to avoid or reduce exposure to secondhand smoke and tobacco use.
	T4.5.4 Demonstrate how to effectively ask for help to avoid exposure to secondhand smoke.	T4.8.4 Demonstrate how to effectively ask for assistance to quit using tobacco.
		T4.8.5 Demonstrate how to effectively communicate empathy and support toward a family member who is trying to quit using tobacco.

NHES 5: Decision Making

T5.2.1 Identify how family, peers, or media influence a decision to not use tobacco.	T5.5.1 Identify situations which need a decision related to tobacco use.	T5.8.1 Identify circumstances that help or hinder making a decision to be tobacco free.
	T5.5.2 Decide when help is needed and when it is not needed to make a decision related to tobacco use.	T5.8.2 Determine when situations require a decision related to tobacco use (e.g., when offered a cigarette by a peer).
	T5.5.3 Explain how family, culture, peers, or media can influence a decision related to tobacco use.	T5.8.3 Distinguish when decisions related to tobacco use should be made individually or with the help of others.
	T5.5.4 Identify options and their potential outcomes when making a decision related to tobacco use.	T5.8.4 Explain how family, culture, media, peers, and personal beliefs affect a decision related to tobacco use.
	T5.5.5 Choose a healthy option when making a decision about tobacco use.	T5.8.5 Distinguish between healthy and unhealthy alternatives of a decision related to tobacco use.
	T5.5.6 Describe the final outcome of a decision related to tobacco use.	T5.8.6 Predict the potential outcomes of healthy and unhealthy alternatives to a decision related to tobacco use.
		T5.8.7 Choose a healthy alternative when making a decision related to tobacco use.
		T5.8.8 Analyze the effectiveness of a final outcome of a decision related to tobacco use.

NHES 6: Goal Setting

• Skill expectations are not identified for this grade group.	• Skill expectations are not identified for this grade group.	T6.8.1 Assess personal tobacco use practices.
		T6.8.2 Set a realistic personal goal to be tobacco free.
		T6.8.3 Assess the barriers to achieving a personal goal to be tobacco free.

Grades K–2 Skill Expectations (*continued*)	Grades 3–5 Skill Expectations (*continued*)	Grades 6–8 Skill Expectations (*continued*)
NHES 6: Goal Setting (*continued*)		
		T6.8.4 Apply strategies to overcome barriers to achieving a personal goal to be tobacco free.
		T6.8.5 Use strategies and skills to achieve a personal goal to be tobacco free.
NHES 7: Self-Management		
• Skill expectations are not identified for this grade group.	• Skill expectations are not identified for this grade group.	T7.8.1 Explain the importance of being responsible for being tobacco free.
		T7.8.2 Demonstrate tobacco prevention practices and behaviors to improve the health of oneself and others.
		T7.8.3 Analyze personal practices and behaviors that prevent tobacco use.
		T7.8.4 Make a commitment to be tobacco free.
NHES 8: Advocacy		
• Make requests to others to avoid secondhand smoke.	T8.5.1 Give factual information about the benefits of being tobacco free to improve the health of others.	T8.8.1 State a health-enhancing position about being tobacco free, supported with accurate information, to improve the health of others.
	T8.5.2 State personal beliefs about the dangers of behaviors related to tobacco use to improve the health of others.	T8.8.2 Demonstrate how to persuade others to be tobacco free.
	T8.5.3 Demonstrate how to persuade others to be tobacco free.	T8.8.3 Collaborate with others to advocate for individuals, families, and schools to be tobacco free.
		T8.8.4 Demonstrate ways to adapt a tobacco-free message for different audiences.

SOURCE: Centers for Disease Control and Prevention, *Health Education Curriculum Analysis Tool,* 2nd ed. (Atlanta, GA: CDC, 2012).

4. *We don't need to worry—smoking won't affect our health until we're a lot older, right?*

You already know that smoking can cause long-term problems such as cancer and heart disease over time, but symptoms start to develop as soon as you smoke your first cigarette—no matter how young you are. Symptoms include shortness of breath, coughing, nausea, dizziness, and phlegm production. Pretty gross, huh?

5. *But, if you smoke only a little bit, that can't hurt, can it?*

Symptoms such as wheezing and coughing have been found in kids who smoke just one cigarette a week.

6. *Kids who smoke think they're cool—are they?*

Only if by "cool" you mean kids who probably aren't doing well in school. Studies have found that students with the highest grades are less likely to smoke than those with the lowest grades. Kids who smoke have lower self-images. They smoke because they think it will give them a better image—cooler, maybe, or more attractive or more popular. And, because their self-image is low, they don't have the confidence to say no when someone urges them to use tobacco.

7. *Why do some kids smoke or use smokeless tobacco?*

There are no physical reasons to start smoking; people don't need tobacco the way they need food, water, and sleep. Most people say they start smoking because of social reasons. One common reason is to try to look older. Some kids may think that smoking or chewing tobacco makes them look more hip or glamorous,

like a movie star or a famous baseball player. Actually, smoking does make you appear older if stained teeth and wrinkled skin are the look you're going for. Some kids say that smoking helps them relax, but smoking actually raises your blood pressure and makes your heart beat faster. Other kids might think it's okay to smoke because other people in their family do. If you ask your mom, dad, uncle, or aunt about their tobacco use, chances are they will tell you not to start and that they wish very much that they could quit. It's always much easier to not start smoking than to quit.

8. *What happens when a kid first tries smoking or using smokeless tobacco?*

No one likes smoking or chew at first. Your body is smart, and it knows when it's being poisoned. When people try smoking, they often cough a lot and feel pain or burning in their throat and lungs. This is your lungs' way of trying to protect you and telling you to keep smoke out of them. Also, many people feel sick to their stomach or even throw up to try to get the poison out of their system. If chewing tobacco is accidentally swallowed, some kids are sick for hours.

9. *What can I do to help a friend who is smoking?*

If you know someone who is using tobacco, you should tell your friend that you don't want him or her to become addicted to cigarettes. Not only is nicotine a drug, but kids who smoke are more likely to become drinkers and use other drugs, such as

©RichLegg/E+/Getty Images

*More than 3,200 children become smokers every day. However, it is import-
ant to emphasize to students that most kids are smart enough to not smoke.*

marijuana or cocaine. You also can tell your friend that you avoid
smoking so that you can do your best on the sports field and earn
good grades.

10. *How can I get my mom to quit smoking?*

You might not be able to get your mom to quit smoking. Remember,
it is her choice and by now she may be very addicted. You can tell
her what you have learned about tobacco and that you would like
her to quit because you don't want her to get sick from smoking,
but the bottom line is that it is her choice.

STRATEGIES FOR LEARNING AND ASSESSMENT

Tobacco Use Prevention

This section provides examples of standards-based learning and
assessment strategies for promoting a tobacco-free lifestyle. The
sample strategies begin with a restatement of the standard and a
reminder of the assessment criteria, drawn from the RMC Health

rubrics in Appendix B. Strategies are written as directions for teachers and include applicable theory of planned behavior (TPB) constructs in parentheses (intention to act in healthy ways, attitudes
toward behavior, subjective norms, perceived behavioral control).
These learning and assessment strategies provide building blocks for
standards-based lessons and units that can be tailored to local needs.
Assessment criteria are used with permission from RMC Health. See
Appendix B for Scoring Rubrics.

Additional strategies for learning and assessment for Chapter 11 can
be found at the Online Learning Center.

NHES 1 | Core Concepts

*Students will comprehend concepts related to health promotion and dis-
ease prevention to enhance health.*

ASSESSMENT CRITERIA

- Connections—Describe relationships between behavior and health; draw
  logical conclusions about connections between behavior and health.
- Comprehensiveness—Thoroughly cover health topic, showing breadth
  and depth; give accurate information.

Grades K–2

KWL on Tobacco   Students can talk about their knowledge of tobacco
use by making a Know-Wonder-Learn (KWL; three-column) chart. Teachers
can use a large piece of chart paper to list all the things students say they
know (or think they know) about tobacco in a "Know" column, listing the
children's names beside the facts they provide. Next, ask students what
they wonder about tobacco (the "Wonder" column). Combine this activity
with NHES 3, access information, products, and services, to have children
check out their facts. Students might look up information in resource
books, surf the Internet, e-mail an expert, talk to family and community
members, or invite guest speakers to the classroom. When students have
confirmed their facts and answered their questions, they can list their new
knowledge in the "Learn" column.

ASSESSMENT | Following the completion of the "Learn" column of the KWL
chart, students should then draw a picture of how they are going to use what
was learned in the KWL on tobacco to help them stay healthy and avoid
tobacco. For assessment criteria, students should provide accurate information and demonstrate relationships between behaviors and health through
their drawing. (Constructs: Intention to act in healthy ways, attitudes toward
behavior, perceived behavioral control.)

Smoking Stinks—There's Nothing Good About Smoking!   Read the
book *Smoking Stinks* by Kim Gosseling to help students learn about the
detrimental effects of smoking and the seriousness of addiction (see
"Children's Literature" at the end of this chapter). Maddie and Alex prepare for their school health report about smoking and learn from Maddie's
grandfather why he started smoking and why he hasn't been able to quit.
The story stresses the importance of never using tobacco products and
the dangers of secondhand smoke, particularly for children with asthma
and allergies. This book has received positive reviews from the American
Cancer Society, the American Lung Association, and health care professionals. After reading to students, teachers can ask them to recall the
health effects of smoking discussed in the book, such as coughing and
trouble with allergies, and write them on a piece of newsprint as the children speak. The children should tell why they think Maddie's grandfather
says, "There's nothing good about smoking."

ASSESSMENT | The students' list of health effects of smoking is the assessment
task for this activity. For assessment criteria, the children should provide correct
information and be able to describe relationships between smoking and health

and draw conclusions about those connections. Each student should contribute one answer to the question of why Maddie's grandfather says, "There is nothing good about smoking." (Construct: Attitudes toward behavior.)

"S-M-O-K-I-N-G" Poetry   An acrostic poem uses the letters in a topic word to begin each line. All lines of the poem should relate to or describe the word. As a class develop an acrostic poem for the word H-E-A-L-T-H-Y.

ASSESSMENT | The students develop their own acrostic poem for the word S-M-O-K-I-N-G. For assessment criteria, the students should provide correct information and be able to make connections between smoking and health. (Constructs: Intention to act in healthy ways, attitudes toward behavior.)

Grades 3–5

Smoking Machine   The "smoking machine" is a popular teaching strategy for upper-elementary and middle-level students. Smoking machines help students see how tar accumulates in the lungs after smoking only a few cigarettes. *Because of school tobacco-free policies and the dangers of secondhand smoke, the authors recommend that teachers show and explain four unused smoking machines to students and then take the machines off campus to "smoke cigarettes" in them.* Bring the used smoking machines back to the classroom to allow students to compare the evidence of smoking one (machine 1), three (machine 2), six (machine 3), and ten (machine 4) cigarettes in the smoking machines. For their own safety, teachers should go outdoors to use cigarettes in the smoking machines. Teachers can purchase commercial smoking machines or make their own from simple materials. To make the machines, teachers need four clear plastic dish-soap bottles, cotton balls, clay or putty, one package of cigarettes, and a lighter or matches.

1. Thoroughly rinse and dry four clear plastic dish-soap bottles. Label the bottles 1: One cigarette, 2: Three cigarettes, 3: Six cigarettes, and 4: Ten cigarettes.
2. Insert loosely packed cotton balls into the bottles and replace the caps.
3. Remove the nozzles from the caps of the bottles.
4. Insert a cigarette into the opening of each cap and make an airtight seal around the cigarette with clay or putty.
5. The smoking machine is ready for use, outdoors and away from houses and other buildings.
6. Press firmly on the plastic bottle to force out the air before lighting the cigarettes. After lighting the cigarettes, proceed with a slow and regular pumping action. When the cigarette is completely smoked, remove the cigarette filter from the cap.
7. Use an entire package of twenty cigarettes. Smoke one cigarette in bottle 1, three cigarettes in bottle 2, six cigarettes in bottle 3, and the remaining ten cigarettes in bottle 4. (Note: To show students the result of smoking one pack of cigarettes per day, smoke twenty cigarettes in one additional smoking machine.)
8. Back in the classroom, show the students the four smoking machines, labeled with the number of cigarettes smoked. Explain to students that the cotton balls represent the lungs of a smoker. Ask the students what they notice has happened to the cotton balls after smoking one, three, six, and ten cigarettes. Students should compare the cotton balls in the bottles with clean cotton balls.
9. Unscrew the caps on the smoking machines to show students the tar buildup on the caps and the cotton balls. Emphasize the difference between the clean cotton balls and the tar-stained cotton balls in the bottles. Allow the students to smell the bottles and caps. Ask students what they think about the appearance and smell of the cap and the cotton balls. What connections can they make to what happens to people when they smoke?

10. To add to this activity, place clean cotton balls in a dish in a room where people smoke, and leave the dish there for one week. Have students compare these cotton balls, exposed to secondhand smoke, with the cotton balls from the smoking machine and with clean cotton balls.

ASSESSMENT | For an assessment task, students can draw a cartoon to show what happens to the lungs of a smoker, based on their observations of the cotton balls. Students should write a caption for their cartoons, with a warning label about smoking. For assessment criteria, the students' cartoons should show an accurate depiction of what happens to a smoker's lungs and the warning labels should describe a relationship between tobacco use and health. (Construct: Attitudes toward behavior.)

Forms of Tobacco—Is One Better than the Other?   Draw two three-circle Venn diagrams. Label one diagram "Physical effects" and the other one "Social effects." Use the following labels for the circles: "smoking tobacco or cigarettes," "smokeless tobacco," and "environmental tobacco smoke or secondhand smoke." In pairs, students can complete the Venn diagram identifying ways each of these forms of tobacco affect a person's physical and social health. In the overlapping portions of the three circles, students should identify the ways in which the three forms of tobacco affect one's physical and social health in similar ways. The Kids' Health website (www.kidshealth.org) can be used to locate core concepts information to support this activity.

ASSESSMENT | Following an oral sharing of the Venn diagrams, students can work with their partners to write a letter to one form of tobacco noting ways in which that form of tobacco is no better or worse than the other forms; for example, "Dear cigarettes" or "Dear secondhand smoke." Students should be sure that all their information is correct and should draw conclusions about connections between tobacco use and health. This activity could link to NHES 3, access information, products, and services. (Construct: Attitudes toward behavior.)

Grades 6–8

Cinquains: Reinforcing Tobacco Knowledge   Following a lesson on any of the knowledge expectations about tobacco (e.g., dangers of experimenting, short- and long-term effects, benefits of being tobacco free, effects of secondhand smoke), work as a class to create a short poem in a cinquain format to reinforce the lesson teachings. For a five-line cinquain, the criteria are as follows:

Line 1: A noun that is the topic of the poem. Example: *Expecting smokers*
Line 2: Two adjectives that describe the topic. Example: *abusive, damage*
Line 3: Three words that end in -ing. Example: *invading, impacting, lasting*
Line 4: A phrase related to the topic. Example: *cancerous intake for two*
Line 5: A synonym for the topic. Example: *child abuse*

ASSESSMENT | For an assessment task, each student can create his or her own five-line cinquain demonstrating key learnings from the lesson. For assessment criteria, each line of the cinquain should connect to the knowledge expectations taught in the lesson. (Construct: The construct will vary based on the knowledge expectations selected by the instructor: Intention to act in healthy ways, attitudes toward behavior, perceived behavioral control.)

Carousel Activity   After discussing the short-term physical, long-term physical, social, economic, and cosmetic effects of smoking, conduct a carousel activity with students. Divide students into five groups. Tape five large pieces of chart paper or newsprint around the room with the headings "Short-Term Physical," "Long-Term Physical," "Social," "Economic," and "Cosmetic." Have each group start at one of the papers to brainstorm the consequences of that type that could result from using tobacco. After a short time, students should rotate to the next piece of paper, read, and add new consequences. After each group returns to their original paper, have them decide on the five consequences they would least like to have.

ASSESSMENT | Students should write a paper indicating why they don't want to smoke. For assessment criteria, students should include at least five consequences in their paper from the carousel activity. (Construct: Attitudes toward behavior.)

■ NHES 2 | Analyze Influences

Students will analyze the influence of family, peers, culture, media, technology, and other factors on health behaviors.

ASSESSMENT CRITERIA
- Identify both external and internal influences on health.
- Explain how external and internal influences interact to impact health choices and behaviors.
- Explain both positive and negative influences, as appropriate.

Grades K–2

The Feel Good Book Read aloud Todd Parr's *The Feel Good Book* (see *"Moods & Strong Feelings"* in the Children's Literature section at the end of Chapter 5) to help students create a class book of activities that make them feel good inside. Examples in the Parr book include these:

> Giving a great, big hug feels good.
> Sharing your treats feels good.
> Making a new friend feels good.
> Saying "I love you" in sign language feels good.

Analyzing influences is an abstract idea for young children. Teachers can introduce this idea by having students identify caring things they do for others and for themselves that make them feel good inside. This activity builds on students' positive capabilities and links indirectly to tobacco use prevention. Students can share their ideas first with a partner and then with classmates. If students repeat the ideas in the Parr book at first, teachers can ask questions about things they have seen or heard students do to help them formulate their own ideas.

ASSESSMENT | For an assessment task, children can create individual pages for a class book about things that make them feel good inside. Students can draw a picture to express their idea and then write a sentence that explains their picture. Their pictures can be bound together into a book that they can read in the classroom and share with other classes. For assessment criteria, students should show ideas that are health-enhancing and that they can describe in words. (Construct: Attitudes toward behavior.)

What I Would Do? What Would My Parents Want Me to Do? Have students draw a picture of what they would do if friend or older sibling offered them a cigarette or smokeless tobacco. Then students should draw a picture of what they believe their parents would want them to do if they were offered a cigarette or smokeless tobacco by a friend or older sibling. Have students take their drawings home to share with their parents. Prepare a family letter explaining the in-class assignment and the at-home task. Encourage parents and students to discuss the drawings, including the similarities and differences of how students responded and how they thought their parents would want them to respond. Parents should be encouraged to share their hopes for their child regarding how to respond to any offer to use tobacco.

ASSESSMENT | Following the take-home activity, students can draw, write, or act out ways in which their parents and families encourage them to be healthy and avoid tobacco use. For assessment criteria, students should explain how the influence of their parents and families, as well as their personal beliefs, impacts their health choices and behaviors. (Constructs: Attitudes toward behavior, perceived behavioral control.)

Grades 3–5

Tobacco Advertising Approximately 1,200 smokers die each day in the United States. Thus, the tobacco industry needs to find 1,200 new smokers every day to replace them. Although the tobacco industry claims that tobacco advertising does not target young people, many of the advertising techniques are highly attractive to adolescents. Tobacco advertisements portray smoking as fun, sophisticated, cool, popular, attractive, and sexy. Help students analyze the external influence of tobacco advertising on the decisions and behaviors of young people.

1. Ask students to clip cigarette advertisements from magazines and bring them to class.
2. Have students examine the ads for techniques that make cigarette smoking seem attractive and appealing. (See Chapter 3 for a list of advertising techniques.)
3. Show students sample spoof ads to inspire creativity. Sample spoof ads can be found by searching the following phrase "spoof tobacco ads," which will allow teachers to find ads that are relevant to the student population.
4. Ask student to create new counter or "spoof" ads that depict more realistic outcomes of smoking. Students might want to use graphs of other data alongside their ads to emphasize their points.
5. Display students' work in the classroom and throughout the school.

ASSESSMENT | The spoof ads students create are the assessment task for this activity. For assessment criteria, students should identify the advertising techniques used in the real ads and the techniques they use in their spoof ads (see the list of advertising techniques in Chapter 3). (Construct: Subjective norms.)

Family Students can interview an adult family member about his or her feelings and attitudes toward youth smoking. Students can ask:

- How would you feel if I started smoking?
- What are our family rules and consequences about smoking?
- What advice can you give me about how to deal with pressures to smoke?

Knowing the attitudes and beliefs of their families is important for young people. Students can report on their interviews to the rest of the class and tell what their family attitudes and beliefs mean to them.

ASSESSMENT | The reports students make on their interviews are the assessment task for this activity. For assessment criteria, students should discuss how their family members' attitudes and beliefs influence their ideas about smoking. (Construct: Subjective norms.)

Grades 6–8

Truth Ads Students can create a digital video or image of an antitobacco commercial, popularly known as truth ads. One strategy is to portray the kinds of advertising techniques the tobacco industry uses in print ads (smoking is fun, sophisticated, and sexy) and deliver a truthful message to counter the claims. An alternative approach is for students to research different facts the tobacco industry used and create the "ugliest truth" poster or video. Examples can be viewed at www.thetruth.com. State and local health departments and YouTube also may have antitobacco spots appropriate for classroom use.

ASSESSMENT | The advertisements the students create are the assessment task for this activity. Students should base their ads on factual information about tobacco use to counteract the way smoking is portrayed. Link this activity to language arts and performing arts by inviting teachers in those content areas to get involved. For assessment criteria, students' advertisements should refute at least one misleading idea about how smoking is portrayed in advertisements or other media, include at least one fact from a credible source, and demonstrate an awareness of advertising techniques used to influence youth to use tobacco. This activity also links to Standard 3, accessing valid resources and Standard 8, advocacy. (Constructs: Attitudes toward behavior, subjective norms.)

Tobacco Warnings   Have students look at different warnings on tobacco products and ask them to discuss how effective they think the warnings are with young people and adults. Most students probably will say that they don't think the warnings are strong enough. Based on their knowledge of the short- and long-term effects of tobacco use, students can create and illustrate more effective warnings to deter youth smoking. Display these in the classroom and the hallways of the school. If possible, have students find examples of tobacco warnings that other countries use, which in some cases are more direct and graphic than American warnings. Students can conduct a general web search (www.google.com) of "tobacco warnings" or warnings for particular countries. For example, a Google search of "Australia tobacco warnings" reveals that Australia has some of the most graphic tobacco health warnings in the world on cigarette packets. Australia's tobacco industry must display warnings in color and text warnings that occupy 30 percent of the front and 90 percent of the back of cigarette packets. A set of fourteen health warnings ("Smoking causes mouth and throat cancer," "Smoking causes peripheral vascular disease," and "Smoking causes blindness") composed of graphic images and explanatory messages provide updated information on a range of adverse health effects of smoking. The more familiar warnings such as "Smoking kills" and "Smoking causes lung cancer and emphysema" are also included.

ASSESSMENT | For an assessment task, students can create posters that provide direct and graphic antitobacco warnings and display them on a drawing of tobacco products or as large print and picture ads. Showcase the students' work around the school. For assessment criteria, students should explain at least three ways tobacco warnings can influence young people's beliefs and attitudes about using tobacco. (Constructs: Attitudes toward behavior, subjective norms.)

Photo Journaling About Tobacco Influences   Engage students in a lesson and discussion regarding the various influences they experience related to tobacco (e.g., media, parents, peers, school policies, culture, values, religion, etc.). Explain to students that a photo journal is a series of photos that chronicles an experience, a person's day, or a special event. For this purpose, students will be capturing the influences of tobacco in their lives. Assign students a minimum number of different influences, include both internal and external influences, they need to capture through a photograph. For each photo, students are to create a caption that explains the way in which the photo is or symbolizes an influence. Photo journals can be displayed in many ways depending on the technology available to students.

ASSESSMENT | The photo journal serves as the assessment task. Assessment criteria include students' ability to identify various internal and external influences, how the influences impact their health choices and behavior, and positive and negative influences. (Constructs: Attitudes toward behavior, subjective norms.)

Looking at Tobacco Inside and Out   Students can really show the difference between the way tobacco use is portrayed in the media and the effects it has inside the body by making a shoebox or diorama display. Students can bring old shoeboxes from home and ask family, friends, and colleagues to donate old shoeboxes for this project. As students learn more about tobacco, they can design the inside of the shoebox to show tobacco's effects on the body, while designing the outside of the shoebox to show how advertising and other media glamorize tobacco use. Students can design the lid to give instructions to the user about viewing the inside and outside of the box. Display the boxes for other classes or in the school library.

ASSESSMENT | The shoebox display or diorama is the assessment task for this activity. Students should decide what would make a "great tobacco inside and out shoebox display." Use the students' criteria to assess and help them assess their work. (Constructs: Attitudes toward behavior, subjective norms.)

NHES 3 | Access Information, Products, and Services

Students will demonstrate the ability to access valid information and products and services to enhance health.

ASSESSMENT CRITERIA

- Access health information—Locate specific sources of health information, products, or services relevant to enhancing health in a given situation.
- Evaluate information sources—Explain the degree to which identified sources are valid, reliable, and appropriate as a result of evaluating each source.

Grades K–2

Interview Older Kids   Younger students often model their behavior after older siblings, friends, and students in their school. Arrange for a group of upper-elementary students to visit younger students for the purpose of being interviewed about their knowledge of and views on tobacco. The children can prepare a list of questions they want to ask. Younger students will learn that most of the older students don't smoke and don't like to be around smokers.

ASSESSMENT | For an assessment task, the younger students can provide their own answers to all the questions on their list after the older students have finished talking with them. For assessment criteria, the older students should make sure the younger students provide accurate answers and tell why the older students are a valid source of information. (Construct: Subjective norms.)

A Web of Trusted Adults   A critical skill for early elementary children to develop is being able to identify trusted adults who can help in preventing tobacco use. Recognizing who the trusted adults in one's life are is key to being able to reach out to them when challenging times are presented. Work together as a class to create a word relationship web. In the center circle write "Trusted Adults." To the left and right of the center circle attach another circle and write "School" in one and "Home" in another. From the "School" and "Home" circles add circles and identify key individuals at home and school who students can go to for help when feeling pressure about tobacco use (e.g., school = teacher, counselor, nurse; home = parent, older sibling, grandparent). Talk with students about how each person finds support from different trusted adults and the trusted adult we choose to get help from may change based on the situation.

ASSESSMENT | Have students create their own web of trusted adults similar to the one created by the class. Instead of using generic titles such as teacher, nurse, or grandparent, have students put specific names in the circle, such as Grammy Jane or Mrs. Smith. Students need to include "school" and "home," but also may include a third circle if there is another important place in their life, such as church, 4-H, or daycare, where there is a web of trusted adults. For assessment criteria, students should be able to identify trusted adults at home and school, and explain why they consider these individuals trusted adults. (Construct: Attitudes toward behavior.)

Grades 3–5

Finding Accurate Tobacco Facts on the Internet Introduce students to the concept of credible sources of information (see information on Standard 3). Give each student one 3 × 5 notecard. Have students write down a fact they believe to be true about tobacco *or* one question they have about tobacco on the notecard. Direct students to one or more of the following credible websites: www.kidshealth.org; www.tobaccofreekids. org; www.cyh.com/SubDefault.aspx?p=255 (navigate to "Topics," "Nearly Teens," and select "Smoking and its effects - info for kids"); www.freddyfit. co.uk/kids/articles/smoking.php. Have students search their website to locate information that appears to assist in confirming their fact or answering their question. Give students three to five more notecards. As the students are reading through the website, have them write down information that supports their question/fact. Once students have found supporting information, have them gather with students who had similar questions/facts. Have pairs or trios of students confirm their facts noting the different sources they used to gather the information.

ASSESSMENT | The assessment task for this assignment is for students to prepare an exit slip responding to the following statement: The website, _____, is a credible source/is not a credible source of tobacco information. I know this because _____ (have them identify at least two reasons the source is credible/not credible). Today I learned _____ about tobacco. (Constructs: Attitudes toward behavior, perceived behavioral control.)

Community Resources on Tobacco Students can use Internet searches to find community resources on tobacco use (American Lung Association, American Cancer Society, American Heart Association). By searching for "Tobacco Resources" and the state name, students can find state-specific resources for tobacco use and cessation. Small groups of students can write to or e-mail different agencies to request class materials on tobacco use prevention.

ASSESSMENT | For an assessment task, students can create an online directory of tobacco education and cessation resources. For assessment criteria, students should identify the sources of their information and explain why their sources are valid. (Construct: Perceived behavioral control.)

Grades 6–8

Accessing YRBS and GYTS Data on Youth Tobacco Use Teachers can use data from the CDC Youth Risk Behavior Survey (YRBS) and the Global Youth Tobacco Survey (GYTS) to help students get a true picture of tobacco use among school-age youth. These data are available on CDC websites at www.cdc.gov/healthyyouth/tobacco/data.htm and www.cdc.gov/ tobacco/global/. Have students estimate their answers to the survey questions on tobacco use. Then have students access the data online, or provide a printed summary for students to use. In most cases, students overestimate use among other young people. Learning the true prevalence of tobacco use among peers can be an important external influence (NHES 2) to support healthy behavior.

Students can compile their answers to make posters or charts to help other students learn about tobacco use among youth in the United States and around the world. Students should state their findings in a positive sense (the percentage of students who have remained tobacco free during the past thirty days, the number and percentage of students who have never used smokeless tobacco or smoked cigars). Students can show their findings with different kinds of graphics or graphic organizers.

For example, students could use small repeated symbols (♥ ♥ ♥) to show the number of students in a class of twenty-five who remained tobacco-free during the past thirty days.

ASSESSMENT | Students' posters are the assessment task. For assessment criteria, students should provide accurate information (NHES 1) and cite the sources of their data and tell why their sources are valid. (Construct: Subjective norms.)

Check Out TobaccoFreeKids.org Middle-level students can access all kinds of information on tobacco by visiting www.tobaccofreekids.org. The site contains reports on topics such as candy-flavored cigarettes, cigarette taxes, smoke-free laws, and Kick Butts Day. Students can click on links such as "The Problem" and "What We Do" to find youth-related information and initiatives. Students can use the website to launch a wide variety of standards-based tobacco prevention projects, including core concepts (NHES 1), analyze influences (NHES 2), and advocacy (NHES 8).

ASSESSMENT | For an assessment task, allow students to take charge of designing the different kinds of tobacco prevention projects they would like to complete using this website as a starting point. For assessment criteria, students should discuss and agree on a list of expectations for "great project presentations." Use the students' criteria to assess and help them assess their work. At a minimum, students should identify their information sources and explain why they are valid. (Constructs: Attitudes toward behavior, perceived behavioral control, subjective norms.)

The Toll of Tobacco Students can investigate the impact of tobacco in their state by going to the Campaign for Tobacco-Free Kids website (www. tobaccofreekids.org). In the section entitled "The Problem" students can explore fact sheets and the toll of tobacco. In the section entitled "The Toll of Tobacco in the United States" students should select their state and read the facts presented about the impact of the tobacco industry. Students can then select another state from a different region of the country (i.e., Midwest, West Coast, South, etc.) and compare and contrast the ways in which tobacco has influenced the two states.

ASSESSMENT | Students could each select a different state and research the toll of tobacco and the state's tobacco use prevention efforts. For assessment criteria, students should report the source of their information and tell why the information source is valid. Students can also include analysis of cultural/geographic influences on tobacco use behaviors (NHES 2). (Constructs: Attitudes toward behavior, subjective norms.)

NHES 4 | Interpersonal Communication

Students will demonstrate the ability to use interpersonal communication skills to enhance health and avoid or reduce health risks.

ASSESSMENT CRITERIA
- Use appropriate verbal/nonverbal communication strategies in an effective manner to enhance health or avoid/reduce health risks.
- Use appropriate skills (negotiation skills, refusal skills) and behaviors (eye contact, body language, attentive listening).

Grades K–2

Supporting Family Members Who Want to Stop Smoking Students shouldn't be told that people who smoke are bad or stupid, and students shouldn't be sent home to nag their parents or caregivers about smoking. These tactics usually backfire on the students and their teachers. However, sometimes students know that a family member is trying to stop smoking, and students can be supportive of these efforts. Ask students to imagine that their parents, caregivers, aunt, uncle, or grandparents have said they want to stop smoking. What can students say to let these relatives know that they are on their side? students can role-play supportive communication without nagging or scolding.

ASSESSMENT | For an assessment task, pairs or small groups of students can create short skits to show what they can say to support a particular family member who wants to stop smoking. For assessment criteria, students should demonstrate appropriate communication behaviors, such as eye contact, a respectful tone, attentive listening, and expressions of empathy, understanding, and support. (Construct: Subjective norms.)

Asking to Get Away from Secondhand Smoke   Young children learn that secondhand smoke is dangerous to them. However, they often have little control over what adults do around them. In this activity, students should brainstorm a list of things they can say and do to get away from secondhand smoke without being disrespectful to adults who are smoking. The list might include asking to go outside or into another room to play. Students might also consider saying to a smoker, "Tobacco smoke makes me cough and feel sick. Would you put your cigarette out for now or smoke outside?" Ask students what their experiences have been and what they have done to try to get away from secondhand smoke. Students can select the strategies they feel are best from their list. Remember that a brainstorm list includes everything students say, even if teachers think the ideas won't work very well.

ASSESSMENT | The students' list of strategies is the assessment task for this activity. For assessment criteria, the students' strategies should make a clear, respectful request to be excused from a place where there is smoking or for the smoker to put out the cigarette or go outside to smoke. Students should demonstrate their strategies in class. (Construct: Perceived behavioral control.)

Grades 3–5

Letters: Communicating with People We Care About   Although teachers don't teach students to nag or scold adults in their family who smoke, teachers often encounter the genuine concern many students feel about the health and well-being of smokers in their families. Some teachers and students have found a healthy compromise by having students who are concerned write a simple, caring letter to the smokers in their families. In the letter, students express their concern, support, and love. Writing a letter lets students express what they are feeling while recognizing that people make their own choices about smoking and no one else can control those choices.

ASSESSMENT | The letters students write are the assessment task for this activity. This activity can be a voluntary one that involves only some members of the class, or all students can choose to participate. Link this project to language arts by involving teachers who teach letter writing. For assessment criteria, students should express their own needs, wants, and feelings in a clear way while writing respectfully to the smoker. (Construct: Subjective norms.)

Resist the Pressure   This activity is good to use after discussing the negative consequences of tobacco. Educators should emphasize the addicting qualities of nicotine, so students understand the dangers of experimenting with tobacco. This activity gives students the opportunity to practice how they would get out of a peer pressure situation that encourages experimentation with tobacco.

1. Ask students to write a short, realistic scenario depicting being pressured to experiment with tobacco. Allow some students to read their scenario aloud and provide feedback.
2. Brainstorm with the class some ways they could respond to a peer who is pressuring them to use tobacco. List these responses on the board.
3. Place students into groups of four. Assign each student in the group a role: two students will apply pressure, one student will resist, and one student will judge the skills of the resistor. Have the two

students who will apply the pressure determine which scenario they will use.
4. The teacher should then tell students when to begin their role-play. The two students should apply pressure, and the resistor should use a variety of resistance skills to get out of the pressure situation.
5. After a few minutes, the teacher should provide time for the judges to give feedback to the resistor.
6. The students should rotate roles four times so that every student has the opportunity to practice the resistance skills one time.

ASSESSMENT | The feedback the judge gives the resistor is the assessment for this activity. For assessment criteria, students should use two resistance techniques to get out of the pressure situation. (Construct: Perceived behavioral control.)

Grades 6–8

Restaurant Manager   In this activity, students get the chance to project their communication skills beyond the classroom and beyond the world of peers and family. Have students imagine that they are the owner of a popular restaurant, and the state has repealed smoking bans. In pairs or small groups, students should take a stand on each side of the issue to determine if their restaurant should remain smoke-free. As a team, students should identify pros and cons, then communicate their argument to the opposing side. As an additional activity, students can post their conclusion to a class blog or in the style of a Facebook post and comment to each other about the decision while practicing good digital citizenship.

ASSESSMENT | For an assessment task, students can work in small groups or pairs to research the harmful effects of secondhand smoke and the rights of citizens in their state. Students can analyze their communication skills throughout the argument, posts, and comments. For assessment criteria, students should demonstrate appropriate verbal and nonverbal strategies for communicating the repeal and communication behaviors such as eye contact, clear "no" messages, repeated refusals, attentive listening to opponents, restatement of other points of view, and statements of needs, wants, and feelings (a nonsmoking restaurant protects the staff and other customers). (Constructs: Attitudes toward behavior, perceived behavioral control.)

Comparing Communication Skills   Like other content areas, communication skills are important—but they might vary for refusing tobacco compared to other content areas. Students can compare resistance skills for tobacco with the communication skills they would use in pressure situations for alcohol and other drugs, sexual involvement, or risk taking that could result in injury. How would they use the skills in similar and in different ways, depending on the context? Students can work in small groups to create pressure situations in three different content areas of their choice (safety, violence, tobacco, alcohol and other drugs, sexual health, nutrition, physical activity). Students should demonstrate one kind of communication skill (repeated refusal, suggest an alternative) across all three content areas. (See Chapter 3 for a list of peer pressure resistance skills.)

ASSESSMENT | Comparing communication across different content areas provides students with the chance to examine their skills in depth. For assessment criteria, students should be able to identify and demonstrate the communication skill of their choice and explain how they are using it similarly and differently in three pressure situations. (Construct: Perceived behavioral control.)

NHES 5 | Decision Making

Students will demonstrate the ability to use decision-making skills to enhance health.

ASSESSMENT CRITERIA

Reach a health-enhancing decision using a process consisting of the following steps:

- Identify a health-risk situation.
- Examine alternatives.
- Evaluate positive and negative consequences.
- Decide on a health-enhancing course of action.

Grades K–2

Decision Making for Safety   Use the following story to help children think about decisions to stay away from matches, lighters, and cigarettes. Read the story to students. You also might want to use puppets or role-playing.

Susan and Alex are visiting Tom at his house. Tom's dad is a smoker, and the children find his lighter and matches in the family room. They know they are not supposed to touch these items, but Susan picks up the lighter and begins to play with it.

- Ask students what they think Alex and Tom should do.
- Have students brainstorm and discuss all the possible solutions and then vote on the best way for the problem to be solved. Also ask the students to brainstorm different ways to avoid this situation.
- Have students draw pictures depicting what they should do when they find matches, lighters, or cigarettes. Display the pictures in the classroom and at open house sessions with parents.

ASSESSMENT | The discussions and pictures are the assessment task for this activity. At this grade level, students don't need to be able to name steps in a decision-making model. However, they should be able to discuss alternatives and explain a decision that they think is best. For assessment criteria, students should give two or more alternatives about what to do and choose and give a reason for their decision on how to act. (Construct: Perceived behavioral control.)

Reasons to Be Tobacco Free   Focus health education strategies on what students should do, rather than what they should not do. Students should brainstorm a list of reasons to be tobacco free and then list the positive and negative consequences of their reasons. Students can use their list and its consequences to counter the reasons people give for starting to smoke. Young children might not know the word *consequences*. Teachers can help them by asking, "What could happen if you . . . ?" In relation to a decision to be tobacco free, students might list as positive consequences that they could hang out and do things with other kids who don't smoke and that they could save money for other purchases. A negative consequence might be that students who are smokers could leave them out of their plans.

ASSESSMENT | For an assessment task, students can state a reason to be tobacco free and discuss the consequences of their decisions. For assessment criteria, students should identify two positive consequences of their decisions. (Construct: Attitudes toward behavior.)

Grades 3–5

Fortunately and Unfortunately: Thinking About Consequences   Students probably are accustomed to thinking about the short-term consequences of tobacco use in terms of physical outcomes. Have students expand their thinking about short-term consequences to social, emotional, financial, and family categories. Post five large pieces of paper, such as newsprint or chart paper, around the room. Label each with one category: "Physical," "Social," "Emotional," "Financial," "Family." Send a group of students to each of the papers to start.

First, ask students to write the words *Fortunately* or *Unfortunately* at the top of each of two columns on their paper. Students should tell what these words mean before starting the activity. Teachers can use examples

to be sure students understand the concept. Next, have students list "Fortunately" and "Unfortunately" things that might happen applicable to their category if they do or don't smoke. For example, under "Social, Fortunately," students might list "Fortunately, I will be with most of my friends if I don't smoke, because most students don't smoke." Under "Social, Unfortunately," students might list "Unfortunately, I might be unpopular with a small group of smokers—but people who pressure me aren't really my friends." On signal, students rotate to the next paper, read, and add to it. Continue until all groups have visited all papers. When the original groups gets back to their papers, the group members can read, discuss, and share with the larger group. This type of activity is called a carousel.

ASSESSMENT | The Fortunately/Unfortunately charts students make are the assessment task for this activity. Students should identify the three most important points on their charts when they get back to the place they started. For assessment criteria, students should explain how these three most important points would influence their decisions about tobacco use and share their answers with the class. (Constructs: Attitudes toward behavior, subjective norms.)

Grades 6–8

Cost of Smoking   Determining the cost of smoking serves as a good prevention technique. Students can calculate the cost of smoking for a week, a month, and a year, basing the calculations on the cost of one pack of cigarettes per day and then two packs per day. When students have their answers, ask them what they would rather do with that amount of money than spend it on tobacco. The potential cost of a smoking habit is a major insight and an important deterrent for some students.

Students can identify the cost of something they would like to purchase for the classroom (electronics or sports equipment) and calculate the number of packs of cigarettes that would equal the cost of the item they wish to purchase. How many days would it take to collectively accumulate the money if each member of the class saved the cost of one pack of cigarettes per day?

ASSESSMENT | This activity is a good link with mathematics. For assessment criteria, students should calculate how much money they would spend on cigarettes for one year if they smoked one pack per day. They could then write how they would spend that money. (Construct: Attitudes toward behavior.)

Laws, Rules, and Policies on Tobacco Use   Students can invite a school administrator and a community official, such as a police officer, to class to explain the laws, rules, and policies on tobacco use by minors in the school and in the community. The police officer also might be able to share information about tobacco sales compliance checks of community merchants. Have students prepare a list of questions in advance. Students can discuss the consequences of underage smoking from a school-rule and legal standpoint. How do these consequences affect their decision making about tobacco?

ASSESSMENT | For an assessment task, students can share their thinking about how tobacco laws, rules, and policies affect their decisions about tobacco use. For assessment criteria, students should describe the laws, rules, and policies in terms of alternatives and consequences that affect their decisions. (Construct: Subjective norms.)

NHES 6 | Goal Setting

Students will demonstrate goal-setting skills to enhance health.

ASSESSMENT CRITERIA

- Goal statement—Give goal statement that identifies health benefits; goal is achievable and will result in enhanced health.
- Goal-setting plan—Show plan that is complete, logical, and sequential, and includes a process to assess progress.

Grades 3–5

Class Goals Students can work together to set a class goal about smoking for their graduating group—for example, "By the time we graduate from middle school, all of us will still be tobacco-free." Students should list the steps they will need to take, ways to overcome barriers they might encounter, ways they can support each other, and a method for assessing their progress.

ASSESSMENT | Working through a simple goal-setting process is the assessment task for this activity (see Chapter 3 for goal-setting steps). For assessment criteria, students should (1) state their class goal in measurable terms (they will be able to tell whether they accomplished the goal), (2) make a plan for reaching their goal, stating specific steps they will carry out, (3) identify sources of support they can count on and barriers they will need to overcome and how, and (4) design a way to assess their progress along the way. (Construct: Subjective norms.)

Grades 6–8

Personal Commitment Making a public, personal commitment not to smoke is meaningful for some young people. Following are two ideas for students to make commitments:

1. Prepare a large piece of chart paper with the header "I promise not to use any tobacco products in middle and high school" at the top of the page. Invite students who want to make this commitment to sign the paper. Post the paper in a prominent place in the classroom so that students can see their classmates' commitments for the entire school year.
2. Students can also make commitments on individual pieces of paper. Have students write on their papers (or give the students preprinted papers) "I pledge to stay tobacco-free in middle and high school because _____." Signed: _____ Date: _____

Making commitments encourages students not to use tobacco and to think about why they won't use tobacco. The commitments also encourage peers not to use tobacco. Post the papers in the classroom or hallways, or send them home to parents and caregivers.

Remember from Chapter 3 that student pledges alone aren't necessarily sufficient to affect behavior. Teachers should bring the other components of the theory of planned behavior (intention to act in healthy ways, attitudes toward behavior, subjective norms, perceived behavioral control) into classroom discussions about making pledges. For example, students can discuss what their own attitudes toward tobacco use are, what they believe their families and friends think about tobacco use, and how successful they think they will be in remaining tobacco-free. Teachers also should assure students that signing pledges is voluntary. In fact, students might want to sign during a recess or break period rather than one by one in class. Students should not experience any pressure to sign from their teachers or classmates. Students might ask what would happen if a student breaks a pledge. Teachers can respond by saying that students can choose to take their name off the pledge poster at any time or sign it later. The reason for making the pledges "in middle and high school" is that most young people who remain tobacco-free during their school years do not begin smoking as adults. Limiting the pledges to middle and high school also provides a time frame that students can relate to realistically.

ASSESSMENT | This assessment is a bit more complicated than it might appear. Teachers assess students not on whether they sign a pledge but on their reasoning process. For an assessment task, students can write a short paper that answers these questions: (1) What are my plans about using tobacco in middle and high school? (2) What do I think about tobacco use? (3) What do my family and friends think about tobacco use? (4) How successful do I think I can be in remaining tobacco-free? Why? For assessment criteria, students should provide in-depth answers to all the questions. (Constructs: Intention to act in healthy ways, subjective norms, perceived behavioral control.)

NHES 7 | Self-Management

Students will demonstrate the ability to practice health-enhancing behaviors and avoid or reduce health risks.

ASSESSMENT CRITERIA
- Application (transfer)—Initiate health-enhancing behaviors; apply concepts and skills appropriate and affectively.
- Self-monitoring and reflection—Monitor actions and make adjustments; accept feedback and make adjustments; able to self-assess, reflect on, and take responsibility for actions.

Grades K–2

Keeping Away from Other People's Smoke Create a list of the different places where people smoke (e.g., home, car, restaurant, ball park, etc.). Have students brainstorm different strategies they can use for avoiding someone else's smoke in each of these settings. Help students focus on strategies that are within their control. Write the different settings on a slip of paper and place them in a container, enough for pairs of students to each draw one. With a partner, students draw a setting and then act out a situation where they demonstrate one of the strategies for keeping away from other people's smoke.

ASSESSMENT | Pairs of students draw another setting and each student acts out a different way of approaching the situation and keeping away from other people's smoke. For assessment criteria, students should demonstrate a health-enhancing behavior to reduce risk of tobacco smoke and be able to apply the strategies in a variety of situations. (Constructs: Attitudes toward behavior, perceived behavioral control.)

Growing Healthy and Strong Students can make a class list of things they do that help them grow healthy and strong. The students might list eating fruits and vegetables, exercising, getting enough sleep, spending time with their families, and brushing their teeth. Then ask students to make another list—things that could keep them from growing healthy and strong. Students probably will list tobacco use, among other detrimental habits. Help students emphasize the positive things they can do for their health. Ask them whether smoking might make it hard for them to do some of these things (running fast and for a long time to play a game).

ASSESSMENT | This and the preceding activity deal indirectly with tobacco use, which might or might not come up in the students' discussions. The emphasis is on positive self-management strategies for health rather than on what not to do. The two lists the students make are the assessment task for this activity. For assessment criteria, each student should describe or demonstrate a habit they practice for growing healthy and strong. (Construct: Attitudes toward behavior.)

Grades 3–5

Avoiding Risk Situations Sometimes students don't realize that they will be faced with a difficult situation, such as refusing tobacco. Other times there are warning signs that tobacco will be part of the scene. Students can give examples of how they might know that tobacco could be used in a particular situation (an invitation to go to someone's home when his or her parents, who are smokers, aren't there). Next, ask students to strategize about how to avoid these situations altogether, rather than having to maneuver to get out of them. These self-management skills involve communication and the physical act of going elsewhere.

ASSESSMENT | For an assessment task, students can illustrate "Don't Even Go There" posters showing strategies for avoiding risk situations that involve possible tobacco use. Students can make their posters individually or in small groups. For assessment criteria, students' posters should show a logical sequence of steps for avoiding tobacco risk situations. (Construct: Perceived behavioral control.)

A Bunch of Reasons Not to Smoke!   The American Heart Association website (www.heart.org/HEARTORG) provides tobacco-related activities for students in grades 3 to 5. In one activity, called "A Bunch of Reasons Not to Smoke," students brainstorm and make a list of reasons not to smoke. The students then use markers to carefully write their reasons on balloons. Students display the balloons in a large bunch in the classroom or on the school grounds. To go a step further, students could write alternatives to smoking (self-management strategies) on a different-color balloon and mix the two balloons together to make a larger bunch. This activity links to NHES 8, advocacy.

ASSESSMENT | For an assessment task, students write reasons to not smoke and alternatives to smoking on their balloons. For assessment criteria, students' alternatives to smoking, their self-management strategies, should be health-enhancing. (Constructs: Attitudes toward behavior, subjective norms.)

Grades 6–8

A Little Help from My Friends   Students might not be familiar with the old song about getting by with "a little help from my friends." However, the principle applies strongly to preventing and reducing risk behaviors. Students need a support group of family, friends, and other caring individuals in their lives. For this activity, students identify at least three people they can call on to help them stand their ground if they are pressured to smoke or engage in other risk behaviors. Students can make a drawing to show how they and their support group connect.

ASSESSMENT | For an assessment task, students can create a graphic organizer or illustration that shows their name and the names of at least three people they can count on to back them up in a pressure situation. For assessment criteria, students should write a short sentence next to each name saying why they can count on that person in their support system. Students should share their illustration with the people they named to reinforce their support. (Constructs: Subjective norms, perceived behavioral control.)

Bumper Stickers for Healthy Alternatives   Ask students whether they have seen the popular bumper stickers that begin with the phrase "I'd rather be . . . " Depending on the part of the country, the bumper stickers state that the driver would rather be skiing, surfing, skating, sailing, or fishing. Students can create a bumper sticker for their locker or notebook to remind them of things they would rather be doing than smoking. Students can use the Build a Sign website (www.buildasign.com/bumper-stickers/browse-id-rather-be) to create their stickers. Sticker proofs can be printed or purchased as a traditional bumper sticker. As an alternative, students can write a tweet using a hashtag message (#IdRatherBe). This activity links to NHES 8, advocacy.

ASSESSMENT | The stickers or tweets students create are the assessment task for this activity. For assessment criteria, students should share their stickers or tweets with classmates, explaining how and why their self-management strategies will help them resist pressure to engage in unwanted activities. (Construct: Subjective norms.)

NHES 8 | Advocacy

Students will demonstrate the ability to advocate for personal, family, and community health.

ASSESSMENT CRITERIA
- Health-enhancing position—Give clear, health-enhancing position.
- Support for position—Support position with facts, concepts, examples, and evidence.
- Audience awareness—Show awareness of target audience; choose words, tone, and examples to suit audience.
- Conviction—Display conviction for position.

Grades K–2

Letters of Appreciation   Help students write class thank-you letters to the Governor of their state for smoking restrictions. Specific state restrictions can be found on the American Lung Association website (www.lungusa2.org/slati/states.php). Have all students sign the letters, with parents' and caregivers' permission, and mail them to the Governor's office. Students will be excited to see if they receive reply letters. Students also can write a class thank-you letter to the local newspaper, recognizing the efforts of lawmakers to put restrictions in place. Student letters (with names redacted) can be shared to social media.

ASSESSMENT | The students' letters are the assessment task for this activity. For assessment criteria, students should express appreciation for the healthy decision lawmakers have made to go tobacco-free and show strong conviction for why they are appreciative. (Construct: Subjective norms.)

Rap to Be Tobacco-Free   Elementary students are fond of slogans, raps, and rhymes, especially those that have a strong beat. Small groups of students can create simple slogans, raps, or rhymes about staying tobacco-free and teach them to the class. For example, an elementary teacher found that her first graders liked the beat of the popular song "We Will Rock You." Her students used that beat to chant "No more, no more smoking!" with accompanying claps and beats on their desks.

ASSESSMENT | The rhyme or rap students create is the assessment task for this activity. For assessment criteria, the student should teach the rhyme or rap to other students their age or younger and should have a clear, antitobacco message that they state with conviction. (Construct: Subjective norms.)

Grades 3–5

Letter-Writing Campaign to Big Tobacco   Students can compose a class letter to a leading cigarette maker, indicating students' knowledge of tobacco advertising techniques that appeal to young people and of tobacco-related *morbidity* and *mortality* (new vocabulary words). Students should end their letter by stating their positions on tobacco advertising and marketing to youth and should ask the tobacco company for a reply letter. Have students sign the letter, with parents' and caregivers' permission, and mail it to the tobacco company. Students will be interested to see whether they receive a reply.

ASSESSMENT | The students' letter is the assessment task for this activity. For assessment criteria, students should state a clear, health-enhancing position, back it up with data, target their audience (a tobacco company), and write with conviction. (Construct: Subjective norms.)

Turning the Tables   Challenge students to use the same techniques the tobacco industry uses to make antitobacco banners to post in school and local businesses. Students might want to also make kites, buttons, or T-shirts to promote tobacco-free lives.

ASSESSMENT | Share the list of advertising techniques in Chapter 3 with students to help them turn the tables on tobacco advertising. The banners, kites, buttons, or T-shirts the students make are the assessment task for this activity. For assessment criteria, students should give a clear, health-enhancing message and communicate it with conviction by making a strong statement. (Construct: Subjective norms.)

I'm Glad I Don't Smoke   This is a good activity to do after reviewing the negative consequences of smoking. On a large sheet of chart paper or newsprint, write the heading "I'm Glad I Don't Smoke Because . . .". Give each student a marker and ask them to write down a response to the sentence stem. The newsprint should then be displayed in a prominent hallway in the school so that other students can read the responses.

ASSESSMENT | The student response to the sentence stem is the assessment task for this activity. For assessment criteria, the students should read their responses to the class and explain how it will help them remain tobacco-free. (Construct: Subjective norms.)

Grades 6–8

Healthy Messages   Select or have students select a healthy behavior outcome from this unit, such as avoid using tobacco or avoid secondhand smoke. With this behavior in mind, have pairs of students develop a digital (e.g., iMovie, Keynote, PowerPoint, or other accessible tools) advocacy message for younger students of an identified grade level. The class should discuss what would make a message meaningful to the grade level of students selected (e.g., use of pictures, simple words, type of message,

etc.). Teams should then prepare a storyboard of their message that will be turned into a digital product.

ASSESSMENT | The digital advocacy message appropriate for a selected audience will serve as the assessment task. The assessment criteria should include the statement of a health-enhancing position and the message should be persuasive and meaningful to the target audience. (Construct: Subjective norms.)

Tobacco-Free Advocacy Campaign   Begin class by asking students to sign a class pledge about not smoking. (Do not pressure students to sign if they do not want to.) Explain that one of the best ways they can help keep their peers tobacco-free is to become an advocate. Brainstorm ways to be an advocate (posters, computer screen saver messages, songs, announcements). Allow students to work in groups to determine the advocacy project they would like to do. Have students create a list of steps to complete their project. Allow one to two weeks to implement their advocacy project.

ASSESSMENT | The advocacy campaign that the students create is the assessment task for this activity. For assessment criteria, students should provide factual information about the benefits of being tobacco-free and the message should be convincing and appealing to same-age peers. (Construct: Subjective norms.)

EVALUATED CURRICULA AND INSTRUCTIONAL MATERIALS

Following are four middle-level, school-based tobacco prevention programs effective for reducing tobacco use among students who participate.

- *Life Skills Training.* The Life Skills Training (LST) program is ideally designed for students in sixth or seventh grade and focuses on tobacco, alcohol, and other drug prevention. The curriculum has an impact on social risk factors, including media influence and peer pressure, as well as personal risk factors, such as anxiety and low self-esteem. The curriculum teaches resistance skills, knowledge, attitudes, self-management skills, and general social skills. One study found that after more than five years of participating in the LST program, seventh-grade students had significantly lower overall tobacco initiation rates.[64] Teachers can purchase LST materials or arrange for training by calling (914-421-2525 or by visiting the website www.lifeskillstraining.com/.

- *Project ALERT.* Project ALERT is a drug prevention curriculum for middle school students (ages 11 to 14). The two-year, fourteen-lesson program focuses on the substances adolescents are most likely to use: alcohol, tobacco, marijuana, and inhalants. Project ALERT uses participatory activities and videos to help motivate adolescents against drug use, teach adolescents the skills and strategies they need to resist pro-drug pressures, and establish non-drug-using norms. Guided classroom discussions and small-group activities stimulate peer interaction and challenge students' beliefs and perceptions, while intensive role-playing activities help students learn and master resistance skills. Homework assignments that involve parents extend the learning process by facilitating parent–child discussions of drugs and how to resist using them. The lessons are reinforced through videos that model appropriate behavior. Evaluation

results show that fewer students from the Project ALERT group initiated smoking (26 percent of Project ALERT participants were new smokers compared to 32 percent of the control group) and there was a reduction in current and regular smoking (20 vs. 26 percent, and 13 vs. 17 percent, respectively). Teachers can find information on how to purchase the curriculum by contacting Project ALERT at (800) 253-7810 or www.project-alert.com.[65]

- *Project Towards No Tobacco Use (TNT).* TNT is a program designed to delay the initiation and reduce the use of tobacco by middle school students. The program consists of a comprehensive ten-day, classroom-based social influences program that examines media, celebrity, and peer portrayal of tobacco use; trains students in communication skills; and teaches about addiction. Studies have shown that students who participated in TNT reduced the initiation rate of cigarettes by 26 percent and weekly or more frequent smoking by 60 percent compared to control group students.[66] More information about the TNT program can be found at tnt.usc.edu or by calling 800-400-8461.

- *Keepin' It REAL.* Keepin' It REAL is a multicultural, school-based substance use prevention program for students aged 12 to 14 years. Keepin' It REAL uses a ten-lesson curriculum taught by trained classroom teachers in forty-five-minute sessions over ten weeks, with booster sessions delivered in the following school year. The curriculum is designed to help students assess the risks associated with substance abuse (including tobacco use), enhance decision-making and resistance strategies, improve antidrug normative beliefs and attitudes, and reduce substance use. The narrative and performance-based curriculum draws from communication competence theory and a culturally grounded resiliency model to incorporate traditional ethnic values and practices that protect against substance use. The curriculum places special emphasis on resistance strategies represented in the acronym "REAL" (Refuse offers to use substances,

Explain why you do not want to use substances, Avoid situations in which substances are used, and Leave situations in which substances are used). Study results found that curriculum participants reported significantly lower cigarette use than students who did not receive the program. Effects lasted up to eight months for cigarette use.[67] More information about the Keepin' It REAL curriculum can be found at real-prevention.com or at 814-883-6362.

INTERNET AND OTHER RESOURCES

WEBSITES

Action on Smoking and Health (ASH)
www.ash.org

Adbusters/Culture Jammers (Note: Teachers should download spoof ads for students rather than having students visit the site. Some of the language on the home page may be inappropriate for students.)
https://www.adbusters.org/spoof-ads

American Cancer Society
www.cancer.org

American Council on Science and Health
www.acsh.org

American Heart Association
www.heart.org/HEARTORG

American Legacy Foundation
www.legacyforhealth.org

American Lung Association
http://www.lung.org

BAM! Body and Mind
www.cdc.gov/bam/index.html

Campaign for Tobacco-Free Kids
www.tobaccofreekids.org

Centers for Disease Control and Prevention's Tobacco Information and Prevention Source
www.cdc.gov/tobacco

Foundation for a Smokefree America
www.tobaccofree.org and www.notobacco.org

Kick Butts Day
www.kickbuttsday.org

Kids' Health
www.kidshealth.org

National African American Tobacco Prevention Network (NAATPN)
www.naatpn.org

Tobacco Documents on Line
http://legacy.library.ucsf.edu

Tobacco News and Information
www.tobacco.org

Youth Risk Behavior Survey
www.cdc.gov/HealthyYouth/yrbs/index.htm

OTHER RESOURCES

American Lung Association, "Tobacco Product Advertising and Promotion Fact Sheet, September 2007" (www.lungusa.org/site/pp.asp?c=dvLUK9O0E&b=44462).

Centers for Disease and Control Prevention, "Cigarette Brand Preference Among Middle and High School Students Who Are Established Smokers—United States, 2004 and 2006," *Morbidity and Mortality Weekly Report* 58, no. 5 (November 9, 2010): 112–15.

Centers for Disease Control and Prevention, "Smoking-Attributable Mortality, Years of Potential Life Lost, and Productivity Losses—United States, 2000–2004," *Morbidity and Mortality Weekly Report* 57, no. 45 (November 14, 2008):1226–8.

Centers for Disease Control and Prevention, "Tobacco Product Use Among Middle and High School Students—United States, 2011 and 2012," *Morbidity and Mortality Weekly Report 62,* no. 45 (November 15, 2013): 893–7.

Centers for Disease Control and Prevention, "Guidelines for School Health Programs to Prevent Tobacco Use and Addiction," *Morbidity and Mortality Weekly Report* 43, no. RR-2 (1994).

Centers for Disease Control and Prevention, *Tobacco Industry Marketing* (www.cdc.gov/tobacco/data_statistics/fact_sheets/tobacco_industry/marketing/; July 2013).

Centers for Disease Control and Prevention, *Youth and Tobacco Use* (www.cdc.gov/tobacco/data_statistics/fact_sheets/youth_data/tobacco_use/; June 2013).

Centers for Disease Control and Prevention, "Youth Risk Behavior Surveillance—United States, 2011," *Morbidity and Mortality Weekly Report* 61, no. SS-05 (June 8, 2012): 1–162.

U.S. Department of Health and Human Services, *The Health Consequences of Smoking: A Report of the Surgeon General*, S/N 0-16-051576-2 (Washington, DC: U.S. Government Printing Office, 2004).

U.S. Department of Health and Human Services. *Preventing Tobacco Use Among Youth and Young Adults: A Report of the Surgeon General, 2012* (Washington, DC: Government Printing Office, 2012).

CHILDREN'S LITERATURE

AGES 5–8

Cosby, Eileen Tucker. *"N" Is for No Smoking . . . Please.* SWAK Pak, 2004.

Gosseling, K. *Smoking Stinks.* Jayjo Books, 2002.

McDaniel, Carren. *Fresh Air Friends: Stay Away from Secondhand Smoke.* Create Space Independent Publishing Platform, 2013.

Reimer, Jackie. *No Thanks, But I'd Love to Dance: Choosing to Live Smoke Free.* American Cancer Society, 2010.

AGES 9–12

Bass, Elissa. *E-Cigarettes: The Risks of Addictive Nicotine and Toxic Chemicals.* Cavendish Square, 2016.

Gleason, Carrie. *The Biography of Tobacco*. Crabtree Publishing Company, 2006.

Paris, Stephanie. *Smoking*. Teacher Created Materials, 2013.

Parks, Peggy J. *Smoking (Matters of Opinion)*. Norwood House Press, 2015.

Sharp, Katie John. *Teenagers and Tobacco: Nicotine and the Adolescent Brain*. Mason Crest, 2008.

Staffo, Deanna. *Let's Clear the Air: 10 Reasons Not to Start Smoking*. Lobster Press, 2007.

ENDNOTES

1. Centers for Disease Control and Prevention, *2014 Surgeon General's Report*, Table 12.4, 660.

2. Institute of Medicine, *Growing Up Tobacco-Free* (Washington, DC: National Academy Press, 1994).

3. National Youth Tobacco Survey 2011-2012 (https://www.surgeongeneral.gov/library/reports /50-years-of-progress/sgr50-chap-13.pdf).

4. Tobacco Free Kids (https://www.tobaccofreekids.org /assets/factsheets/0127.pdf; September 2018).

5. L. Johnston et al., *Monitoring the Future National Survey Results on Drug Use, 1975-2016: Volume 1, Secondary School Students, 2016* (Ann Arbor, MI: Institute for Social Research, The University of Michigan, 2017).

6. L. Johnston et al., *Monitoring the Future National Survey Results on Drug Use, 1975-2017* (Ann Arbor, MI: Institute for Social Research, The University of Michigan, 2017). (http://www.monitoringthefuture.org//pubs /monographs/mtf-vol1_2016.pdf).

7. Centers for Disease Control and Prevention, "Youth Risk Behavior Surveillance—United States, 2018," *Morbidity and Mortality Weekly Report* 67, no. 8 (June 15, 2018).

8. Centers for Disease Control and Prevention, "Current Tobacco Use Among Middle and High School Students—United States, 2017.

9. L. Johnston et al., *Monitoring the Future National Survey Results on Drug Use.*

10. Smoking and Youth, Fact Sheet (https://www.cdc.gov /tobacco/data_statistics/sgr/50th-anniversary/pdfs /fs_smoking_youth_508.pdf; 2014).

11. Centers for Disease Control and Prevention, *Sustaining State Programs for Tobacco Control* (Atlanta, GA: U.S. Department of Health and Human Services, Office on Smoking and Health, 2015).

12. Office on Smoking and Health, *National Center for Chronic-Disease Prevention and Health Promotion* (https://www.cdc.gov/tobacco/data_statistics/fact _sheets/economics/econ_facts/index.htm; 2017).

13. Ibid.

14. R. Abbott and R. Catalano, "Mediational and Deviance Theories of Late High School Failure: Process Roles and Structural Strains, Academic Competence, and General Versus Specific Problem Behaviors," *Journal of Counseling Psychology* 49, no. 2 (2002): 172-86.

15. M. Diego, T. Filed, and C. Sanders, "Academic Performance, Popularity, and Depression Predict Adolescent Substance Abuse," *Adolescence* 38, no. 149 (2003): 35-42.

16. D. Lee, E. Trapido, and R. Rodriguez, "Self-Reported School Difficulties and Tobacco Use Among Fourth- to Seventh-Grade Students," *Journal of School Health* 72, no. 9 (2002): 368-73.

17. R. Cox et al., "Academic Performance and Substance Use: Findings from a State Survey of Public High School Students," *Journal of School Health* 77, no. 3 (2007): 109-15.

18. M. Resnick et al., "Protecting Adolescents from Harm: Findings from the National Longitudinal Study on Adolescent Health," *Journal of the American Medical Association* 278, no. 10 (1997): 823-32.

19. U.S. Department of Health and Human Services, *Preventing Tobacco Use Among Young People: A Report of the Surgeon General* (Washington, DC: U.S. Government Printing Office, 2012).

20. U.S. Department of Health and Human Services, *Reducing Tobacco Use: A Report of the Surgeon General*, S/N 017-023-00204-0 (Washington, DC: U.S. Government Printing Office, 2000).

21. Centers for Disease Control and Prevention, *Youth and Tobacco Use* (www.cdc.gov/tobacco/data_statistics /fact_sheets/youth_data/tobacco_use/index.htm; 2018).

22. U.S. Department of Health and Human Services, *The Health Consequences of Smoking—50 Years of Progress: A Report of the Surgeon General* (Atlanta, GA: U.S. Department of Health and Human Services, Centers for Disease Control and Prevention, National Center for Chronic Disease Prevention and Health Promotion, Office on Smoking and Health, 2014).

23. Centers for Disease Control and Prevention, "Youth Risk Behavior Surveillance—United States, 2015," *Morbidity and Mortality Weekly Report* 65, no. 6 (June 10, 2016).

24. Campaign for Tobacco-Free Kids, *Where Do Youth Smokers Get Their Cigarettes?* (www.tobaccofreekids.org/ research/factsheets/pdf/0073.pdf; 2017).

25. Federal Trade Commission, *Cigarette Report for 2016, Exit Notification* (Washington, DC: Federal Trade Commission, 2018).

26. U.S. Department of Health and Human Services, *Preventing Tobacco Use Among Youth and Young Adults: A Report of the Surgeon General* (Atlanta, GA: U.S. Department of Health and Human Services, Centers for Disease Control and Prevention, National Center for Chronic Disease Prevention and Health Promotion, Office on Smoking and Health, 2012).

27. Centers for Disease Control and Prevention, *Results from the School Health Policies and Practices Study* (https://www.cdc.gov/healthyyouth/data/shpps/pdf /shpps-results_2016.pdf; 2017).

28. Ibid.

29. Ibid.

30. Centers for Disease Control and Prevention, *Tobacco Use Prevention Through Schools: Guidelines & Strategies* (https://www.cdc.gov/healthyschools/tobacco/strategies .htm; 2015).

31. U.S. Department of Health and Human Services, *The Health Consequences of Smoking—50 Years of Progress: A Report of the Surgeon General*, 2014.

32. Campaign for Tobacco-Free Kids, *Tobacco Company Marketing to Kids* (www.tobaccofreekids.org/assets /factsheets/0008.pdf; 2018).

33. Centers for Disease Control and Prevention, "Youth Risk Behavior Surveillance—United States, 2015."

34. Centers for Disease Control and Prevention, "Tobacco Use Among Middle and High School Students—United States, 2011-2016."

35. American Cancer Society, *Why People Start Smoking and Why It's Hard to Stop* (https://www.cancer.org/content /cancer/en/cancer/cancer-causes/tobacco-and-cancer /why-people-start-using-tobacco.html; 2015).

36. Center for Disease and Prevention, *Smokeless Tobacco (Dip, Chew, Snuff)* (https://www.cdc.gov /healthcommunication/toolstemplates/entertainment /tips/SmokelessTobacco.html; 2017).

37. National Cancer Institute, *Smokeless Tobacco and Cancer: Questions and Answers* (www.cancer.gov/cancertopics /factsheet/Tobacco/smokeless; 2010).

38. Campaign for Tobacco-Free Kids, *Smokeless Tobacco and Kids* (www.tobaccofreekids.org/research/factsheets /pdf/0003.pdf; 2018).

39. S. L. Tomar, "Chewing Tobacco Use and Dental Caries Among U.S. Men," *Journal of the American Dental Association* 130, no. 11 (1999): 1601-10.

40. K. Martin, "Youth's Opportunities to Experiment Influence Later Use of Illegal Drugs," *National Institute on Drug Abuse, Research Findings* 17, no. 5 (January 2003): 59-61.

41. D. Doubeni, G. Reed, and J. DiFranza, "Early Course of Nicotine Dependence in Adolescent Smokers," *Pediatrics* 125 (2010): 1127-33.

42. U.S. Department of Health and Human Services, *The Health Consequences of Smoking—50 Years of Progress: A Report of the Surgeon General* 2014.

43. Ibid.

44. Ibid.

45. Ibid.

46. J. Hall, *The Smoking-Material Fire Problem* (Quincy, MA: National Fire Protection Association, 2014).

47. Ibid.

48. American Cancer Society, *Cancer Facts and Figures* (https://www.cancer.org/research/cancer-facts-statistics .html; 2018).

49. Ibid.

50. American Lung Association, *Benefits of Quitting* (http:// www.lung.org/stop-smoking/i-want-to-quit /benefits-of-quitting.html; 2004).

51. Centers for Disease Control and Prevention, *COPD* (www.cdc.gov/dotw/copd; 2017).

52. Centers for Disease Control and Prevention, *Secondhand Smoke (SHS) Facts* (https://www.cdc.gov/tobacco /data_statistics/fact_sheets/secondhand_smoke /general_facts/index.htm; 2018).

53. Ibid.

54. Ibid.

55. National Environmental Health Association, *Third Hand Smoke* (https://neha.org/eh-topics/air-quality-0 /third-hand-smoke; 2018).

56. Centers for Disease Control and Prevention, "Youth Risk Behavior Surveillance—United States, 2017."

57. Partnership for Drug-Free Kids, *The Teen Vaping Trend – What Parents Need to Know* (https://drugfree.org /parent-blog/the-teen-vaping-trend-what-parents-need -to-know; 2017).

58. Tobacco Free Kids, *JUUL and Youth: Rising E-Cigarette Popularity* (https://www.tobaccofreekids.org/assets /factsheets/0394.pdf; 2018).

59. Ibid.

60. Center on Addiction, *10 Surprising Facts about E-Cigarettes* (https://www.centeronaddiction.org /e-cigarettes/about-e-cigarettes/10-surprising-facts -about-e-cigarettes; 2016).

61. National Institute on Drug Abuse, *E-Cigarettes: What You Need to Know* (https://teens.drugabuse.gov/blog/post /e-cigarettes-what-you-need-know; 2017).

62. Centers for Disease Control and Prevention, *Health Education Curriculum Analysis Tool*, 2nd ed. (Atlanta, GA: CDC, 2012).

63. Ibid.

64. R. Spoth et al., "Substance Use Outcomes 5½ Years Past Baseline for Partnership-Based, Family-School Preventive Interventions," *Drug and Alcohol Prevention* 96, no. 1-2 (2008): 57-68.

65. P. Ellickson et al., "New Inroads in Preventing Adolescent Drug Use: Results from a Large-Scale Trial of Project ALERT in Middle Schools," *American Journal of Public Health* 93, no. 11 (2003): 1830-6.

66. C. Dent et al. "Two-Year Behavior Outcomes of Project Towards No Tobacco Use," *Journal of Consulting and Clinical Psychology* 63, no. 4 (1995): 676-7.

67. S. Kulis et al., "Mexican/Mexican American Adolescents and Keepin' It REAL: An Evidence-Based, Substance Abuse Prevention Program," *Children and Schools* 27 (2005): 133-45.

12

(Keegan, age 13; Ryan, age 12)

Alcohol and Other Drug Use Prevention

DESIRED LEARNER OUTCOMES

After reading this chapter, you will be able to . . .

- **Describe the nature and prevalence and cost of alcohol and other drug use among youth.**

- **Explain the relationship between alcohol and other drug use and compromised academic performance.**

- **Identify factors that influence alcohol and other drug use.**

- **Summarize current guidelines and practices for schools and teachers related to prevention of alcohol and other drug use.**

- **Summarize developmentally appropriate alcohol and other drug prevention concepts and skills for K–8 students in the context of the National Health Education Standards and target healthy behavior outcomes.**

- **Demonstrate developmentally appropriate learning strategies and assessment techniques that incorporate concepts and skills that have been shown to reduce alcohol and other drug risks among youth.**

- **Identify effective, evaluated commercial alcohol and other drug prevention curricula.**

- **Identify websites and children's literature that can be used in cross-curricular instructional activities featuring alcohol and other drug prevention themes.**

INTRODUCTION

At some time in their life, all young people will have to make a decision about alcohol and other drug use. Teachers can play a significant role in helping students with this decision. Teachers need to understand why it is important to utilize class time to teach about alcohol and drug use prevention. This section introduces the percentage of students using alcohol and other drugs, the costs to society related to alcohol and other drug use, the risk factors associated with alcohol and other drug use, and, most important, how alcohol and other drugs can affect academic performance.

Nature, Prevalence, and Cost

Emerging knowledge about the drug use continuum and stages of substance use (i.e., No Use, Experimental Use, Social or Regular Use, Harmful and Compulsive Use, and Dependent Use)[1] and the characteristics of addiction as a chronic and progressive disease[2] have created greater awareness about the complex and dynamic factors related to substance abuse prevention, intervention, treatment, and recovery. Substance abuse occurs in a family and community context. These issues need to be addressed in a system of care that includes networks of organizations, agencies, and community members that coordinate a wide spectrum of services to prevent, intervene in, and treat substance use problems and disorders. In a system of care, the individual and family dwell in coordinated systems of community agencies, including schools. There is increasing recognition of the role of schools to promote well-being among students and staff by providing safe and healthy school environments that support the avoidance of tobacco, alcohol, and other illegal drugs, and to work closely with community agencies to develop coordinated and comprehensive approaches to addressing the continuum of use.[3]

Excessive alcohol consumption is the third-leading preventable cause of death in the United States today. It is associated with liver cirrhosis, various cancers, unintentional injuries, and violence.[4] Because of the many problems associated with alcohol and other drug use, there is a definite need for prevention programs in today's elementary and middle schools. The United States has the highest rate of teenage alcohol and other drug abuse among industrialized countries. In 2015, it was reported that 33.1 percent of 15-year-olds have had at least one drink in their lives; approximately 5.1 million people (about 13.4 percent) aged 12 to 20 years reported binge drinking in the past month.[5]

Further, in 2017 the Monitoring the Future study found that 8 percent of eighth graders drank alcohol in the thirty days prior to the survey and 4 percent of eighth graders reported binge drinking within the two weeks prior to the survey.[6] Seven teens ages 16 to 19 die every day from motor vehicle injuries.[7] Alcohol is responsible for more than 4,300 annual deaths among underage youth.[8]

Although the rate of youth alcohol and other drug use has decreased over the past decade, it is still too high. For example, a study by the Substance Abuse and Mental Health Services (SAMHSA) found that *every day* 7,540 youth between the ages of 12 and 17 have their first drink of alcohol.[9] Studies also show that students are more likely to use drugs and alcohol as they get older. The Parent's Resource Institute for Drug Education's (PRIDE) annual survey of a sample of students in grades 6 to 12 illustrates this trend (Table 12-2). (PRIDE, 2016) PRIDE National Survey. www.pridesurveys.com/customercenter/us15ns.pdf; November 04, 2016. For example, monthly consumption of alcohol is only 6.5 percent for students in grades 6 to 8 but 22.5 percent for students in grades 9 to 12. Monthly marijuana use also increases dramatically from middle school (3.8 percent) to high school (15.4 percent).[10, 11]

Young people give many reasons for using alcohol and other drugs, including the following:

- To help me relax.
- To have fun.
- Because being high feels good.
- To help forget my troubles.
- To deal with stress and pressures of school.
- My friends are using.
- To feel better about myself.
- To look cool.
- It's a habit; I can't stop.[12]

Media and other influences contribute to the idea young people have that "everybody's doing it." Research has shown that media does influence adolescent alcohol and other drug use. For example, one study found that 10- to 14-year-old youth who had viewed more movies with higher exposure to alcohol use were more likely to initiate alcohol use at a younger age. They also found depictions of alcohol use in 92 percent of over 600 contemporary films, including 54 percent of G-rated movies.[13]

Another media influence on young people is popular television. A study that examined four different episodes of the forty-two top-rated situation comedies and dramas on television found that alcohol was mentioned in 77 percent of the episodes, followed by tobacco (22 percent) and illicit drugs (20 percent). Forty-one percent of the episodes that showed or mentioned illicit drugs had at least one negative message about them. Alcohol was consumed in 71 percent of the episodes, including 65 percent of the top teen-rated episodes. Recent studies investigating whether children and young adults are exposed to advertising from major alcohol brands on social network sites found that some channels and brands did not have or use age restrictions.[14]

Alcohol advertising also has an effect on underage drinking. A recent study found that for each additional alcohol advertisement young people viewed (above the monthly youth average of 23 advertisements), they drank 1 percent more. That same study found that for each additional dollar per capita spent on alcohol advertising in a local market (above the national average of $6.80 per capita), young people drank 3 percent more.[15]

Why is alcohol and other drug use in our society a big deal? The cost of substance abuse to the U.S. economy is estimated at more than $740 billion annually. This cost includes those related to crime, lost work productivity, and health care. Tobacco use is the most costly estimated at $300 billion, followed by alcohol estimated at $249 billion, illicit drugs estimated at $193 billion, and prescription opioids estimated at $78.5 billion.[16] The costs associated with alcohol and illicit drugs are disproportionately

TABLE 12–1

Conceptual Framework of a Recovery-Oriented System of Care

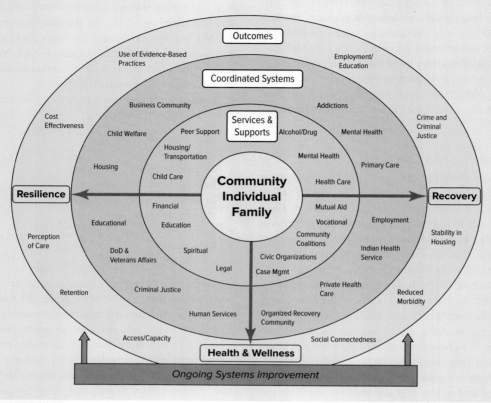

SOURCE: U.S. Department of Health and Human Services, *Guiding Principles and Elements of Recovery-Oriented Systems of Care*, 2009, 3, www.naadac.org/assets/1959/sheedyckwhitterm2009guiding_principles_and_elements.pdf.

TABLE 12–2

National Summary of the Parent's Resource Institute for Drug Education (PRIDE) Survey, Grades 6–12, 2015–2016

	Use of Selected Alcohol and Other Drugs			
	Grades 6–8		Grades 9–12	
Frequency of Use of Risk Behavior	**Annual Use %**	**Monthly Use %**	**Annual Use %**	**Monthly Use %**
Drank Alcohol	11.6	6.5	41.6	25.3
Used Marijuana	4.8	3.8	22.5	15.4
Tobacco	5.5	3.8	19.6	11.3

SOURCE: Pride Surveys Questionnaire for Grades 6 thru 12 Standard Report, 2015–2016 Pride National Summary (https://www.pridesurveys.com/customercenter/us15ns.pdf; November 4, 2016).

---

attributed to people between ages 15 and 44 because of higher prevalence rates and greater number of related deaths.[17] Because of the costs of alcohol and other drugs and the health problems related to their use, the federal government included several alcohol and other drug prevention objectives in *Healthy People 2020* (Table 12-3).[18]

Alcohol and Other Drug Use and Academic Performance

The education community has begun to recognize the relationship between drug use/abuse and learning and education. Results from the 2015 Youth Risk Behavior Survey show a negative association between alcohol and other drug use and academic achievement. Students with higher grades are significantly less likely to have engaged in behaviors such as:

- Current alcohol use.
- Current marijuana use.
- Ever used cocaine.
- Ever took prescription drugs without a doctor's prescription.[19]

Another study found that low academic performance (high school students with mostly Cs or below) during the twelve months preceding the survey was more prevalent among binge drinkers and marijuana users.[20] One study found that high school students who use alcohol or other drugs frequently are up to five times more likely than other students to drop out of school.[21]

TABLE 12–3

HEALTHY PEOPLE

Healthy People 2020 Alcohol and Other Drug Prevention Objectives

Objective ECBP-1	Increase the proportion of preschool Early Head Start and Head Start programs that provide health education to prevent health problems in alcohol and other drug use.
Objective ECBP-2	Increase the proportion of elementary, middle, and senior high schools that provide comprehensive school health education to prevent health problems in alcohol and other drug use.
Objective SA-1	Reduce the proportion of adolescents who report that they rode during the previous thirty days with a driver who had been drinking alcohol.
Objective SA-2	Increase the proportion of adolescents never using substances.
Objective SA-3	Increase the proportion of adolescents who disapprove of substance abuse.
Objective SA-4	Increase the proportion of adolescents who perceive great risk associated with substance abuse.
Objective SA-8	Increase the proportion of persons who need alcohol and/or illicit drug treatment and received specialty treatment for abuse or dependence in the past year.
Objective SA-13	Reduce past-month use of illicit substances.
Objective SA-14	Reduce the proportion of persons engaging in binge drinking of alcoholic beverages.
Objective SA-18	Reduce steroid use among adolescents.
Objective SA-19	Reduce the past-year nonmedical use of prescription drugs.
Objective SA-21	Reduce the proportion of adolescents who use inhalants.

SOURCE: U.S. Department of Health and Human Services, *Healthy People 2020* https://www.healthypeople.gov.

As a result of the many academic performance problems, economic costs, and health consequences related to alcohol and other drug use, Americans have consistently identified drug abuse as one of the leading problems facing our schools.[22]

Factors That Influence Alcohol and Other Drug Use

The factors associated with greater potential for drug use are called risk factors. Before teachers and school districts can decide on their alcohol and other drug use prevention program or curriculum, they first must understand the risk factors associated with alcohol and other drug use.

These risk factors should be interpreted in the same way as risk factors for heart disease. That is, if a child or family has one of these risk factors, the child's chance of developing a problem with alcohol or other drug use increases. Having one of these risk factors does not mean that a child will become a drug abuser—only that the risk is increased. Seventeen identified risk factors can be categorized as school, individual or peer, family, and community risk factors.[23-29] Teachers should pay special attention to

the school and the individual or peer risk factors. School risk factors include poor grades or academic achievement, problems or difficulties in school, and school transitions. Problems or difficulties in school include truancy and school safety, among other things. Related indicators can be found in the domains of Peer Interaction (bullying, association with deviant peers, peer rejection) and Community Involvement (participation in activities).

School Risk Factors

Academic Failure Beginning in Late Elementary School There is an increased risk for adolescent drug abuse when a child receives low or failing grades in fourth, fifth, and sixth grades. Poor school performance increases the likelihood of an early start of substance use as well as subsequent use. Academic failure can have many causes, including a lack of parental support, boredom, a learning disability, and a poor match between student and teacher. Whatever the cause, children who have poor school performance are more likely to turn to drugs than are students who succeed in school.

Little Commitment to School Students who are not committed to education are more likely to engage in drug use. Fundamentally, this means that the child does not perceive school as meaningful or rewarding. Regardless of the reason, students in grades 4 through 7 who lose interest in school have a greater risk of getting into trouble with drugs. By way of confirmation, students who expect to attend college have significantly lower usage rates of drugs such as cocaine, stimulants, and hallucinogens.

Individual or Peer Risk Factors

Rebelliousness In middle or junior high school, students who do not adhere to the dominant values of society and who have a low religious affiliation tend to be at higher risk for drug abuse than students who are bonded to societal institutions of family, school, and church. Students who rebel against authority, particularly parents and school officials, are also at increased risk for substance abuse.

Antisocial Behavior in Early Adolescence A consistent relationship has been found between adolescent drug abuse and male aggressiveness in kindergarten through second grade. The risk is especially significant when this aggressiveness is coupled with shyness and withdrawal. Hyperactivity, nervousness, inattentiveness, and impulsiveness are also characteristics of early antisocial behavior. Whatever the cause of the antisocial behavior and hyperactivity, students who exhibit these behaviors are at increased risk for abusing drugs as they get older. This risk factor includes a wide variety of behaviors, including school misbehavior and a low sense of social responsibility. Fighting, skipping school, and exhibiting general aggressiveness have been shown to be related to drug abuse. A consistent pattern of inappropriate classroom behaviors, including acting-out behaviors, is related to increased abuse of alcohol and other drugs.

Friends Who Use Drugs Association with drug-using friends during adolescence is one of the strongest predictors of adolescent drug use. Associating with friends who are involved in drug use

©Brand X Pictures/PunchStock

Aggressive or antisocial behavior is a risk factor for alcohol and other drug use.

operates independently of other risk factors. The evidence is clear that friends, rather than strangers, influence children to experiment with and continue to use drugs. This means that even children who grow up without other risk factors but who associate with children who use drugs are at an increased risk for drug use and/or abuse.

Gang Involvement   The influence of gang involvement on alcohol and other drug use is even more pronounced than that of simply having drug-using friends. Being a gang member is a significant risk factor for alcohol and other drug use.

Favorable Attitudes Toward Drug Use   Specific favorable attitudes toward drug use are a risk factor for initiation of use. Having negative attitudes toward the use of alcohol or other drugs inhibits initiation. When children are in elementary school, they may carry strong, adult-supported feelings against drugs, but by the time they reach middle school many have developed more favorable attitudes. This shift in attitude often comes just before children begin to experiment with tobacco, alcohol, and other drugs.

Early First Use of Drugs   Abusers of alcohol and other drugs tend to begin drinking or using at an early age. Generally, students begin using gateway drugs (tobacco and alcohol) and then progress to other, illegal, drugs. Early initiation into drug use increases the risk for extensive and persistent involvement in the use of more dangerous drugs. Children who begin to use tobacco, alcohol, or other drugs before age 15 are twice as likely to develop problems with drugs than are children who wait until they are older. Delaying first use until age 19 or older dramatically decreases the risk for subsequent abuse. In fact, young people

who have not used tobacco, alcohol, or other drugs by age 21 are unlikely to ever become addicted.

Family Risk Factors

Family History of Alcoholism or Addiction to Other Drugs   Current research continues to demonstrate a link between family drinking problems and adolescent alcohol and other drug abuse. Boys, in particular, have a high risk of abusing alcohol when they have alcoholic fathers. Alcoholics are more likely than nonalcoholics to have a history of parental or sibling alcoholism. In fact, 50 percent of today's alcoholics are the children of alcoholics.

Family Management Problems   Family management problems have been a consistent predictor of adolescent alcohol and other drug abuse. These problems include poorly defined rules for behavior, poor monitoring of children's behavior, inconsistent consequences for breaking rules, excessively severe discipline, negative communication patterns (including constant criticism), and absence of praise. In order to make good decisions about their own behavior, children need to be given clear guidelines for acceptable and unacceptable behavior by their families (Teacher's Toolbox 12.1). They need to be taught basic skills, and they need to be provided with consistent support and recognition for acceptable behaviors as well as consistent but appropriate punishment for unacceptable behaviors.

Favorable Parental Attitudes Toward Alcohol and Other Drug Use   Research confirms not only that child behaviors are related to family alcohol addiction but also that there is an increased risk that children will initiate drug use when their parents are users of alcohol and other drugs. If the parents involve their children in drug use, such as asking them to get a beer from the refrigerator, to light their cigarette, or to mix them a drink, the likelihood that the children will use drugs increases.

Family Conflict   Serious, persistent conflict between children and their caregivers increases the risk for alcohol and other drug use, regardless of the type of family structure.

Teacher's Toolbox **12.1**

Advice for Parents

There are many steps parents can take to help prevent their children from using alcohol and other drugs:

- Get involved in your child's life.
- Maintain positive communication with your child.
- Establish rules and consequences about using alcohol and other drugs. Make sure your child knows the rules and believes you will follow through on the consequences.
- Be a positive role model. If you drink, drink responsibly and in moderation.
- Teach your child to choose his or her friends wisely. Make sure you meet the parents of your child's friends.
- Monitor your child's activities.

Community Risk Factors

Economic and Social Deprivation Children from families who experience social isolation, extreme poverty, and poor living conditions are at elevated risk for delinquency. When extreme poverty accompanies childhood behavior problems, there is an increased risk for drug problems and alcoholism.

Transitions and Mobility Transitions, such as residential moves and the move from elementary to middle school, are associated with increased rates of drug use and abuse. This is important for teachers who teach in transitional grades. For example, if a middle school begins at grade 5, fifth-grade teachers should focus more attention on drug abuse prevention. If a new child enters a class during the middle of the year, teachers should make sure that he or she has positive support from classmates.

Community Laws and Norms Favorable Toward Drug Use Communities with laws that are favorable toward drug use, such as low taxes on alcohol, have higher rates of alcohol consumption and alcohol-related traffic fatalities. Greater availability of drugs in schools, combined with inadequate policies against alcohol and other drug use, leads to a higher use of drugs among students.

Availability of Alcohol and Other Drugs When alcohol and other drugs are easily available in the community, the risk of use increases among youth. Risk is increased even when teens only perceive that alcohol and other drugs are easily available.

Low Neighborhood Attachment and Community Disorganization There are higher rates of drug problems when people have little attachment to their neighborhood and community. Low neighborhood attachment can be present when people do not feel that they can make a difference in their community, when there is little involvement in area schools, and when voter turnout is low.

GUIDELINES FOR SCHOOLS

This section provides information about current approaches to alcohol and other drug prevention programs and policies in elementary and middle schools. The first part of the section includes data about the actual programs and policies in schools today; the second part provides ideas for teachers and administrators about what should be happening in schools to help children and adolescents stay drug free.

State of the Practice

The CDC periodically conducts the School Health Policies and Practices Study (SHPPS) to assess current school health policies and programs at the state, district, school, and classroom levels.[30] This study is important to determine the progress toward reaching the _Healthy People 2020_ objectives; to help states determine technical assistance, funding needs, and priorities among their districts and schools; and to help school personnel determine how their school health policies and programs compare to those of other schools. Because alcohol and other drug use contributes to many deaths and injuries among young people, it is important that states and school districts have policies that reflect zero tolerance for alcohol and other drug use among students. Throughout the first decade of the new millennium school districts prioritized environmental approaches to alcohol and other drug prevention by developing and implementing policies that restricted substance use on school grounds and requiring drug prevention programs. For example, in 2016, 81.8 percent of school districts had a policy prohibiting the use of electronic vapor products (e.g., e-cigarettes, e-cigars, e-pipes, vape pipes, vaping pens, e-hookahs, and hookah pens) by students, and 77.3 percent prohibit their use among faculty and staff during any school-related activity.[31]

With regard to mandating alcohol and other drug prevention programs, 63.9 percent of school districts required alcohol and other drug use prevention education at the elementary level. Approximately 58.9 percent of school districts provided funding for professional development or offered professional development for school faculty and staff on how to implement school-wide policies and programs related to alcohol use prevention.[32]

State of the Art

It is important for elementary and middle school teachers to understand what should be included in a successful, comprehensive alcohol and other drug prevention program. Before teachers can decide what to do in their classrooms to help prevent substance abuse, they must first understand what does and doesn't work in preventing young people from using alcohol and other drugs. To clarify what doesn't work, it is important to examine historical drug prevention programs that have not been successful.

History of Unsuccessful Drug Use Prevention Programs

Over the years, educators and health professionals have learned how to be more effective in promoting health-enhancing behaviors with students. Consequently, many changes in teaching strategies have occurred. This is especially true for drug prevention programs. It is important, however, to learn from past mistakes and to understand why some drug prevention strategies have been unsuccessful. Consistently incorporating successful drug prevention strategies into our schools and communities will likely result in a decrease in the rates of drug use by students.

In the 1960s, when there was a tremendous increase in drug usage, many teachers used scare tactics to try to deter their students from using drugs.[33] For instance, they taught their classes that, if students took LSD, they would experience a bad trip and either jump off a building or feel as though spiders were crawling all over them. Although this technique might have scared some students at first, it took only one student in the class to have a brother or sister who experienced a "good" LSD trip to make that teacher lose all credibility. Other inquisitive students might have read credible information on LSD and learned that bad trips did not always occur. Other teachers tried to scare their students by telling them they would become hooked on drugs after the first time they used them or that, if they were drinking and driving, they would be involved in a car crash. It is important for teachers to be truthful to students to maintain their credibility. Once teachers lose their credibility, students become skeptical of anything the teachers say. Another problem with scare tactics is that they tend to have short-lived outcomes. In other words, the effects of scare tactics might last for a few weeks, but then students return to their prior belief system.

In the early 1970s, a very popular component of a drug prevention program was to invite recovering addicts to class to discuss the problems they experienced with their addiction. Although this technique is still commonly used and might sound effective, many times students internalize messages that are different from those intended by the speaker. The intended message from the recovering addicts is not to get involved with drugs. Some students, however, conclude, "If I do get involved with drugs, I can get off of them, just as the speaker did." Another misinterpretation is "I am stronger than the speaker, and I won't get hooked on drugs."[34] Yet another problem with this strategy is that, if the recovering addicts are significantly older than the students, the students have difficulty relating to the intended message. Many athletes, actors, actresses, and musicians who are recovering addicts are used in antidrug commercials. These commercials give students the message that, if they use drugs and quit, they can recapture their original goals or become popular.

Later in the 1970s, many health professionals started using a different strategy for drug prevention. They believed that if the students were taught all of the facts about drugs, they would certainly choose not to try them or use them. These programs did increase knowledge about drugs; however, students' behavior was unaffected.[35] Individuals do not base their decisions about how to behave on information alone but also on their feelings, values, beliefs, and skills. Even adults do not make decisions based on information alone, even when that information is reinforced by law. This is shown by the number of adults who are involved in drinking and driving incidents and who do not wear seat belts. Information is the foundation for health-enhancing decisions, but other topics need to be included in effective drug prevention programs.

Another popular initiative is the "Just Say No" campaign. The "Just Say No" public service announcement campaign is not developmentally appropriate for many upper-elementary and middle-level students and is an ineffective way to deal with the drug problem in our country. In these public service announcements, children and adolescents are told to "Just Say No" but are not told how or why to say no to drugs. There are, however, "Just Say No" clubs in many school systems that have components of effective substance use prevention programs. These encourage students to say no to drug use and allow students to practice getting out of negative peer-pressure situations by using various peer resistance techniques. "Just Say No" clubs also provide social support for kids who do not use drugs and a positive alternative way to meet and make friends.

Another popular, though unsuccessful, program that is still being used is the "one-shot approach." In this model, schools organize a schoolwide assembly in which an expert addresses all students about the dangers of drugs and the wisdom of abstinence. Drug use, abuse, and refusal are very complex behaviors. Therefore, even the most entertaining or spectacular one-shot program cannot begin to have an impact on the use of tobacco, alcohol, and other drugs.[36]

Another popular elementary drug prevention program is the DARE program (Drug Abuse Resistance Education). DARE is

A father and son work together on a drug use prevention homework assignment.

the most widely used school-based drug prevention program in the United States. However, the results from multiple studies that have been conducted to determine the DARE program's effectiveness are disappointing. In fact, a recent meta-analysis reviewed twenty research studies that have been conducted on the DARE program. The conclusion of the authors was that the DARE program had no statistically significant long-term effect on preventing youth illicit drug use. However, the DARE program has recently been redesigned and future research may result in more positive effects.[37]

The substance abuse prevention methods of the 1960s and 1970s were unsuccessful because they did not focus on the causes of drug use and abuse. Unfortunately, many teachers are still using these outdated methods. Every profession makes mistakes, but the key is to learn from those mistakes and make the necessary changes to be successful.

Key Alcohol and Other Drug Principles for Schools and Communities

The U.S. Department of Health and Human Services has identified a comprehensive list of principles that schools and communities should apply to help prevent alcohol and other drug use among youth (Teacher's Toolbox 12.2). These sixteen principles are intended to help parents, educators, and community leaders think about, plan for, and deliver research-based drug abuse prevention programs at the community level. The principles are divided into three categories: risk and protective factors, prevention planning (family, school, and community programs), and prevention program delivery.[38]

Principles for Preventing Alcohol and Other Drug Use Among Youth

RISK AND PROTECTIVE FACTORS

Principle 1: Alcohol and other drug prevention programs should enhance protective factors and reverse or reduce risk factors because the risk of becoming a drug abuser increases as the number of risk factors (e.g., deviant attitudes and behaviors) increases, and decreases as the number of protective factors (e.g., parental support) decreases. The possible impact of specific risk and protective factors changes with age. For example, risk factors within the family have greater impact on a younger child, whereas association with drug-abusing peers may be a more significant risk factor for an adolescent. Early intervention with risk factors (aggressive behavior and poor self-control) often has a greater impact than later intervention, by changing a child's life path (trajectory) away from problems and toward positive behaviors.

Principle 2: Prevention programs should address all forms of drug abuse, alone or in combination. These forms include the underage use of legal drugs (tobacco or alcohol); the use of illegal drugs (marijuana or heroin); and the inappropriate use of legally obtained substances (inhalants), prescription medications, or over-the-counter drugs.

Principle 3: Prevention programs should address the type of drug abuse problem in the local community, target modifiable risk factors, and strengthen identified protective factors.

Principle 4: Prevention programs should be tailored to address risks specific to population or audience characteristics, such as age, gender, and ethnicity, to improve program effectiveness.

PREVENTION PLANNING

Family Programs

Principle 5: Family-based prevention programs should enhance family bonding and relationships and include parenting skills; practice in developing, discussing, and enforcing family policies on substance abuse; and training in drug education and information. Family bonding is the foundation of the relationship between parents and children. Bonding can be strengthened through skills training on parent supportiveness of children, parent–child communication, and parental involvement.

    Parental monitoring and supervision are critical for drug abuse prevention. These parenting skills can be enhanced with training on rule setting; techniques for monitoring activities; praise for appropriate behavior; and moderate, consistent discipline that enforces defined family rules.

    Drug education and information for parents or caregivers reinforce what children are learning about the harmful effects of drugs and open opportunities for family discussions about the abuse of legal and illegal substances.

School Programs

Principle 6: Prevention programs can be designed to intervene as early as preschool to address risk factors for drug abuse, such as aggressive behavior, poor social skills, and academic difficulties.

Principle 7: Prevention programs for elementary school children should target improving academic and social-emotional learning to address risk factors for drug abuse, such as early aggression, academic failure, and school dropout. Education should focus on the following skills:

- Self-control
- Emotional awareness
- Communication
- Social problem solving
- Academic support, especially in reading

Principle 8: Prevention programs for middle or junior high and high school students should increase academic and social competence in the following skills:

- Study habits and academic support
- Communication
- Peer relationships
- Self-efficacy and assertiveness
- Drug resistance skills
- Reinforcement of antidrug attitudes
- Strengthening of personal commitments against drug abuse

Community Programs

Principle 9: Prevention programs aimed at general populations at key transition points, such as the transition to middle school, can produce beneficial effects even among high-risk families and children. Such interventions do not single out risk populations and therefore reduce labeling and promote bonding to school and community.

Principle 10: Community prevention programs that combine two or more effective programs, such as family-based and school-based programs, can be more effective than a single program alone.

Principle 11: Community prevention programs reaching populations in multiple settings (schools, clubs, faith-based organizations, and the media) are most effective when they present consistent, community-wide messages in each setting.

PREVENTION PROGRAM DELIVERY

Principle 12: When communities adapt programs to match their needs, community norms, or differing cultural requirements, they should retain core elements of the original research-based intervention, including

- Structure (how the program is organized and constructed)
- Content (the information, skills, and strategies of the program)
- Delivery (how the program is adapted, implemented, and evaluated)

Principle 13: Prevention programs should be long-term with repeated interventions (booster programs) to reinforce the original prevention goals. Research shows that the benefits from middle school prevention programs diminish without follow-up programs in high school.

Principle 14: Prevention programs should include teacher training in good classroom management practices, such as rewarding appropriate student behavior. Such techniques help to foster students' positive behavior, achievement, academic motivation, and school bonding.

Principle 15: Prevention programs are most effective when they employ interactive techniques, such as peer discussion groups and parent role-playing, that allow for active involvement in learning about drug abuse and reinforcing skills.

Principle 16: Research-based prevention programs can be cost-effective. Like earlier research, recent research shows that each dollar invested in prevention can result in a savings of up to $10 in treatment for alcohol or other substance abuse.

SOURCE: National Institute on Drug Abuse, *Preventing Drug Use Among Children and Adolescents: A Research-Based Guide For Parents, Educators, and Community Leaders*, 2nd ed., Bethesda, MD: U.S. Department of Health and Human Services, 2003.

GUIDELINES FOR CLASSROOM APPLICATIONS

Important Background for K–8 Teachers

This section presents basic information about alcohol, marijuana, inhalants, and prescription and over-the-counter drugs, the drugs that elementary and middle school students are most likely to use and abuse. There are too many drugs to discuss every one, and the majority of students do not use the other illicit drugs. Teacher's Toolbox 12.3 lists the most common drugs, along with their trade or slang names, the likelihood of physical and psychological dependence, their effects, and how long the drugs' effects last. Most of the information about illicit drugs in Teacher's Toolbox 12.4 is not developmentally appropriate for elementary and middle school children (see the section "Developmentally Appropriate Concepts and Skills"). However, teachers should possess basic literacy about these drugs, because students might ask questions about them. The common terms used in drug education and their definitions are listed in Teacher's Toolbox 12.5.

Teacher's Toolbox 12.3

Commonly Abused Drugs

Substances: Category and Name	Examples of *Commercial* and Street Names	DEA Schedule*/How Administered**	*Acute Effects*/Health Risks
Tobacco			*Increased blood pressure and heart rate*/chronic lung disease; cardiovascular disease; stroke; cancers of the mouth, pharynx, larynx, esophagus, stomach, pancreas, cervix, kidney, bladder, and acute myeloid leukemia; adverse pregnancy outcomes; addiction
Nicotine	Found in cigarettes, cigars, bidis, and smokeless tobacco (snuff, spit tobacco, chew)	Not scheduled/smoked, snorted, chewed	
Alcohol			*In low doses, euphoria, mild stimulation, relaxation, lowered inhibitions; in higher doses, drowsiness, slurred speech, nausea, emotional volatility, loss of coordination, visual distortions, impaired memory, sexual dysfunction, loss of consciousness/* increased risk of injuries, violence, fetal damage (in pregnant women); depression; neurologic deficits; hypertension; liver and heart disease; addiction; fatal overdose
Alcohol (ethyl alcohol)	Found in liquor, beer, and wine	Not scheduled/swallowed	
Cannabinoids			*Euphoria; relaxation; slowed reaction time; distorted sensory perception; impaired balance and coordination; increased heart rate and appetite; impaired learning, memory; anxiety; panic attacks; psychosis/*cough; frequent respiratory infections; possible mental health decline; addiction
Marijuana	Blunt, dope, ganja, grass, herb, joint, bud, Mary Jane, pot, reefer, green, trees, smoke, sinsemilla, skunk, weed	I/smoked, swallowed	
Hashish	Boom, gangster, hash, hash oil, hemp	I/smoked, swallowed	
Opioids			*Euphoria; drowsiness; impaired coordination; dizziness; confusion; nausea; sedation; feeling of heaviness in the body; slowed or arrested breathing/*constipation; endocarditis; hepatitis; HIV; addiction; fatal overdose
Heroin	*Diacetylmorphine:* smack, horse, brown sugar, dope, H, junk, skag, skunk, white horse, China white; cheese (with OTC cold medicine and antihistamine)	I/injected, smoked, snorted	
Opium	*Laudanum, paregoric:* big O, black stuff, block, gum, hop	II, III, V/swallowed, smoked	
Stimulants			*Increased heart rate, blood pressure, body temperature, metabolism; feelings of exhilaration; increased energy, mental alertness; tremors; reduced appetite; irritability; anxiety; panic; paranoia; violent behavior; psychosis/*weight loss; insomnia; cardiac or cardiovascular complications; stroke; seizures; addiction **Also, for cocaine**—nasal damage from snorting **Also, for methamphetamine**—severe dental problems
Cocaine	*Cocaine hydrochloride:* blow, bump, C, candy, Charlie, coke, crack, fake, rock, snow, toot	II/snorted, smoked, injected	
Amphetamine	*Biphetamine, Dexedrine:* bennies, black beauties, crosses, hearts, LA turnaround, speed, truck drivers, uppers	II/swallowed, snorted, smoked, injected	
Methamphetamine	*Desoxyn:* meth, ice, crank, chalk, crystal, fire, glass, go fast, speed	II/swallowed, snorted, smoked, injected	

Substances: Category and Name	Examples of *Commercial* and Street Names	DEA Schedule*/How Administered**	*Acute Effects*/Health Risks
Club Drugs			***MDMA**—mild hallucinogenic effects; increased tactile sensitivity, empathic feelings; lowered inhibition; anxiety; chills; sweating; teeth clenching; muscle cramping/sleep disturbances; depression; impaired memory; hyperthermia; addiction*
MDMA (methylene-dioxymethamphetamine)	Ecstasy, Adam, clarity, Eve, lover's speed, peace, uppers	I/swallowed, snorted, injected	
Flunitrazepam***	*Rohypnol:* forget-me pill, Mexican Valium, R2, roach, Roche, roofes, roofnol, rope, rophies	IV/swallowed, snorted	***Flunitrazepam**—sedation; muscle relaxation; confusion; memory loss; dizziness; impaired coordination/addiction*
GHB***	*Gamma-hydroxybutyrate:* G, Georgia home boy, grievous bodily harm, liquid ecstasy, soap, scoop, goop, liquid X	I/swallowed	***GHB**—drowsiness; nausea; headache; disorientation; loss of coordination; memory loss/unconsciousness; seizures; coma*
Dissociative Drugs			*Feelings of being separate from one's body and environment; impaired motor function/anxiety; tremors; numbness; memory loss; nausea*
Ketamine	*Ketalar SV:* cat Valium, K, Special K, vitamin K	III/injected, snorted, smoked	
PCP and analogs	*Phencyclidine:* angel dust, boat, hog, love boat, peace pill	I, II/swallowed, smoked, injected	***Also, for ketamine**—analgesia; impaired memory; delirium; respiratory depression and arrest; death*
Salvia divinorum	Salvia, Shepherdess's Herb, Maria Pastora, magic mint, Sally-D	Not scheduled/chewed, swallowed, smoked	***Also, for PCP and analogs**—analgesia; psychosis; aggression; violence; slurred speech; loss of coordination; hallucinations*
Dextromethorphan (DXM)	Found in some cough and cold medications: Robotripping, Robo, Triple C	Not scheduled/ swallowed	***Also, for DXM**—euphoria; slurred speech; confusion; dizziness; distorted visual perceptions*
Hallucinogens			*Altered states of perception and feeling; hallucinations; nausea*
LSD	*Lysergic acid diethylamide:* acid, blotter, cubes, microdot, yellow sunshine, blue heaven	I/swallowed, absorbed through mouth tissues	***Also, for LSD and mescaline**—increased body temperature, heart rate, blood pressure; loss of appetite; sweating; sleeplessness; numbness; dizziness; weakness; tremors; impulsive behavior; rapid shifts in emotion*
Mescaline	Buttons, cactus, mesc, peyote	I/swallowed, smoked	***Also, for LSD**—Flashbacks, Hallucinogen Persisting Perception Disorder*
Psilocybin	Magic mushrooms, purple passion, shrooms, little smoke	I/swallowed	***Also, for psilocybin**—nervousness; paranoia; panic*
Other Compounds			***Steroids**—no intoxication effects/hypertension; blood clotting and cholesterol changes; liver cysts; hostility and aggression; acne; in adolescents—premature stoppage of growth; in males—prostate cancer, reduced sperm production, shrunken testicles, breast enlargement; in females—menstrual irregularities, development of beard and other masculine characteristics*
Anabolic steroids	*Anadrol, Oxandrin, Durabolin, Depo-Testosterone, Equipoise:* roids, juice, gym candy, pumpers	III/injected, swallowed, applied to skin	
Inhalants	*Solvents (paint thinners, gasoline, glues); gases (butane, propane, aerosol propellants, nitrous oxide); nitrites (isoamyl, isobutyl, cyclohexyl):* laughing gas, poppers, snappers, whippets	Not scheduled/inhaled through nose or mouth	***Inhalants** (varies by chemical)—stimulation; loss of inhibition; headache; nausea or vomiting; slurred speech; loss of motor coordination; wheezing/cramps; muscle weakness; depression; memory impairment; damage to cardiovascular and nervous systems; unconsciousness; sudden death*
Prescription Medications			
CNS Depressants	For more information on prescription medications, please visit www.drugabuse.gov/drugs-abuse/commonly-abused-drugs-charts#prescription-opioids and www.drugabuse.gov/drugs-abuse/commonly-abused-drugs-charts#prescription-stimulants.		
Stimulants			
Opioid Pain Relievers			

*Schedule I and II drugs have a high potential for abuse. They require greater storage security and have a quota on manufacturing, among other restrictions. Schedule I drugs are available for research only and have no approved medical use; Schedule II drugs are available only by prescription (unrefillable) and require a form for ordering. Schedule III and IV drugs are available by prescription, may have five refills in 6 months, and may be ordered orally. Some Schedule V drugs are available over the counter.

**Some of the health risks are directly related to the route of drug administration. For example, injection drug use can increase the risk of infection through needle contamination with staphylococci, HIV, hepatitis, and other organisms.

***Associated with sexual assaults.

SOURCE: Commonly Abused Drugs Chart, National Institutes of Health, U.S. Department of Health and Human Services, April 2012, https://www.drugabuse.gov/drugs-abuse

Commonly Abused Prescription Drugs

Substances: Category and Name	Examples of *Commercial* and Street Names	DEA Schedule*/How Administered	*Intoxication Effects*/Health Risks
Depressants			*Sedation/drowsiness, reduced anxiety, feelings of well-being, lowered inhibitions, slurred speech, poor concentration, confusion, dizziness, impaired coordination and memory/slowed pulse, lowered blood pressure, slowed breathing, tolerance, withdrawal, addiction; increased risk of respiratory distress and death when combined with alcohol*
Barbiturates	*Amytal, Nembutal, Seconal, Phenobarbital:* barbs, reds, red birds, phennies, tooies, yellows, yellow jackets	II, III, IV/injected, swallowed	
Benzodiazepines	*Ativan, Halcion, Librium, Valium, Xanax, Klonopin:* candy, downers, sleeping pills, tranks	IV/swallowed	
Sleep Medications	*Ambien (zolpidem), Sonata (zaleplon), Lunesta (eszopiclone)*	IV/swallowed	*for barbiturates—euphoria, unusual excitement, fever, irritability*/life-threatening withdrawal in chronic users
Opioids and Morphine Derivatives**			*Pain relief, euphoria, drowsiness, sedation, weakness, dizziness, nausea, impaired coordination, confusion, dry mouth, itching, sweating, clammy skin, constipation/slowed or arrested breathing, lowered pulse and blood pressure, tolerance, addiction, unconsciousness, coma, death; risk of death increased when combined with alcohol or other CNS depressants*
Codeine	*Empirin with Codeine, Fiorinal with Codeine, Robitussin A-C, Tylenol with Codeine:* Captain Cody, Cody, schoolboy; (with glutethimide: doors & fours, loads, pancakes, and syrup)	II, III, IV/injected, swallowed	
Morphine	*Roxanol, Duramorph:* M, Miss Emma, monkey, white stuff	II, III/injected, swallowed, smoked	*for fentanyl—80–100 times more potent analgesic than morphine*
Methadone	*Methadose, Dolophine:* fizzies, amidone, (with MDMA: chocolate chip cookies)	II/swallowed, injected	
Fentanyl and analogs	*Actiq, Duragesic, Sublimaze:* Apache, China girl, dance fever, friend, goodfella, jackpot, murder 8, TNT, Tango and Cash	II/injected, smoked, snorted	*for oxycodone—muscle relaxation/twice as potent analgesic as morphine; high abuse potential*
Other Opioid Pain Relievers: Oxycodone HCL Hydrocodone Bitartrate Hydromorphone Oxymorphone Meperidine Propoxyphene	*Tylox, Oxycontin, Percodan, Percocet:* Oxy, O.C., oxycotton, oxycet, hillbilly heroin, percs *Vicodin, Lortab, Lorcet:* vike, Watson-387 *Dilaudid:* juice, smack, D, footballs, dillies *Opana, Numorphan, Numorphone:* biscuits, blue heaven, blues, Mrs. O, octagons, stop signs, O Bomb *Demerol, meperidine hydrochloride:* demmies, pain killer *Darvon, Darvocet*	II, III, IV/chewed, swallowed, snorted, injected, suppositories	*for codeine—less analgesia, sedation, and respiratory depression than morphine* *for methadone—used to treat opioid addiction and pain; significant overdose risk when used improperly*
Stimulants			*Feelings of exhilaration, increased energy, mental alertness/increased heart rate, blood pressure, and metabolism, reduced appetite, weight loss, nervousness, insomnia, seizures, heart attack, stroke*
Amphetamines	*Biphetamine, Dexedrine, Adderall:* bennies, black beauties, crosses, hearts, LA turnaround, speed, truck drivers, uppers	II/injected, swallowed, smoked, snorted	
Methylphenidate	*Concerta, Ritalin:* JIF, MPH, R-ball, Skippy, the smart drug, vitamin R	II/injected, swallowed, snorted	*for amphetamines—rapid breathing, tremor, loss of coordination, irritability, anxiousness, restlessness/delirium, panic, paranoia, hallucinations, impulsive behavior, aggressiveness, tolerance, addiction* *for methylphenidate—increase or decrease in blood pressure, digestive problems, loss of appetite, weight loss*
Other Compounds			*Euphoria, slurred speech/increased heart rate and blood pressure, dizziness, nausea, vomiting, confusion, paranoia, distorted visual perceptions, impaired motor function*
Dextromethorphan (DXM)	*Found in some cough and cold medications:* Robotripping, Robo, Triple C	not scheduled/swallowed	

*Schedule I and II drugs have a high potential for abuse. They require greater storage security and have a quota on manufacturing, among other restrictions. Schedule I drugs are available for research only and have no approved medical use. Schedule II drugs are available only by prescription and require a new prescription for each refill. Schedule III and IV drugs are available by prescription, may have five refills in 6 months, and may be ordered orally. Most Schedule V drugs are available over the counter.

**Taking drugs by injection can increase the risk of infection through needle contamination with staphylococci, HIV, hepatitis, and other organisms. Injection is a more common practice for opioids, but risks apply to any medication taken by injection.

SOURCE: Commonly Abused Prescription Drugs Chart, National Institutes of Health, U.S. Department of Health and Human Services, October 2011, https://www.drugabuse.gov/drugs-abuse/commonly-abused-drugs-charts#prescription-opioids and https://www.drugabuse.gov/drugs-abuse/commonly-abused-drugs-charts#prescription-stimulants

Teacher's Toolbox 12.5

Common Terms Used in Drug Prevention Education

Club drug One of a variety of psychoactive drugs typically used at raves, bars, and dance clubs.

Dependence The compulsive use of a drug, which results in adverse social consequences and the neglect of constructive activities.

Drug Any substance, natural or artificial (other than food), that by its chemical or physical nature alters structure or function in the living organism.

Drug abuse Any use of a legal or illegal drug in a way that is detrimental to a person's health.

Gateway drugs A legal or illegal drug that represents a user's first experience with a mind-altering drug and can serve as the "gateway" or path to the use of other drugs.

Intoxication The state of being mentally affected by a chemical.

Misuse The inappropriate use of legal drugs intended to be medications.

Synergism The ability of one drug to enhance the effect of another.

Tolerance Lower sensitivity to a drug such that a given dose no longer has the usual effect and a larger dose is needed.

Withdrawal Physical and psychological symptoms, which can be mild or life-threatening, that follow the interrupted use of a drug on which a user is physically dependent.

Alcohol

Alcoholic drinks contain ethyl alcohol, which is a depressant. Ethyl alcohol is not the same as isopropyl alcohol (rubbing alcohol) or methyl alcohol (wood alcohol). Methyl alcohol, even in small amounts, is dangerous. Isopropyl alcohol is found in antifreeze and some cosmetics and can be dangerous if ingested. Every year a small number of people die from drinking methyl alcohol, thinking it is the same as ethyl alcohol.

There are three main types of ethyl alcohol: beer, wine, and distilled spirits. Although some people believe beer is a less dangerous type of ethyl alcohol, all forms of ethyl alcohol are dangerous if misused. It is important to note that there is the same amount of ethyl alcohol in a 12-ounce beer, a 5-ounce glass of table wine, and a 1.5-ounce shot of 80 proof distilled spirits (Figure 12-1).[39]

Alcohol, along with tobacco, is a gateway drug. That is, although those children who use tobacco and alcohol will not all go on to use other drugs, they do increase the likelihood that they will go on to use "hard"

drugs later. It is important to delay the onset of alcohol use because it has been found that the younger the age of the beginning drinker, the more likely he or she will later turn to illegal drugs.[40] Unfortunately, 60.4 percent of high school students have had at least one drink of alcohol in their life and 29.8 percent have had at least one drink of alcohol in the past month. More disturbing, however, is that 13.5 percent of high school students have participated in heavy episodic drinking (five drinks in a row) in the past month.[41] When young people drink, they typically drink a lot at one time. For example, young people consume more than 90 percent of their alcohol through binge drinking.[42]

Alcohol is the most commonly abused substance during adolescence.[43] Drinking has acute effects on the body, especially on the body of an adolescent who is not used to drinking alcohol. Researchers are beginning to recognize the significant negative consequences of drinking on the adolescent brain. One area of the brain that is vulnerable to alcohol-related damage is the cerebral cortex, the region largely responsible for our higher brain functioning such as problem solving and decision making. Other areas of the brain negatively affected by alcohol are the hippocampus, which is important for memory and learning, and the cerebellum, which is important for coordination.[44] Heavy use of alcohol by adolescents may interfere with brain activity and brain development, leading to memory loss and the diminishment of other skills.[45] Magnetic resonance imaging (MRI) of brains shows that adolescents who abuse alcohol or are alcohol dependent have smaller memory areas in the brain than do same-age nondrinking adolescents.[46]

Alcohol use can also alter judgment, vision, coordination, and speech, and its use often leads to dangerous risk-taking behavior. Because young people have lower body weight than adults, they absorb alcohol into their blood system faster and exhibit greater impairment for a longer time. Alcohol use not only increases the likelihood of being involved in a motor-vehicle crash but also increases the risk of serious injury in a crash because of its

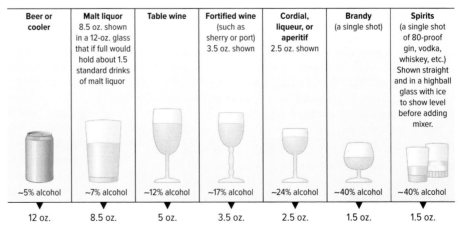

Beer or cooler	Malt liquor 8.5 oz. shown in a 12-oz. glass that if full would hold about 1.5 standard drinks of malt liquor	Table wine	Fortified wine (such as sherry or port) 3.5 oz. shown	Cordial, liqueur, or aperitif 2.5 oz. shown	Brandy (a single shot)	Spirits (a single shot of 80-proof gin, vodka, whiskey, etc.) Shown straight and in a highball glass with ice to show level before adding mixer.
~5% alcohol	~7% alcohol	~12% alcohol	~17% alcohol	~24% alcohol	~40% alcohol	~40% alcohol
12 oz.	8.5 oz.	5 oz.	3.5 oz.	2.5 oz.	1.5 oz.	1.5 oz.

A standard drink is any drink that contains about 14 grams of pure alcohol (about 0.6 fluid ounces or 1.2 tablespoons). Above are standard drink equivalents. These are approximate, as different brands and types of beverages vary in their actual alcohol content.

FIGURE 12-1 | **How Much Is One Drink?**

SOURCE: U.S. Department of Health and Human Services, *The Surgeon General's Call to Action to Prevent and Reduce Underage Drinking,* Bethesda, MD: U.S. Department of Health and Human Services, 2007.

harmful effects on numerous parts of the body. Motor-vehicle crashes are the leading cause of death for 15- to 20-year-olds, and one-third of these crashes involve alcohol.[47] Alcohol use among young people is also associated with fighting, crime, risky sexual behavior, depression, and suicide. Each year, approximately 5,000 people under the age of 21 die as a result of underage drinking. This includes 1,900 deaths from motor vehicle crashes, 1,600 as a result of homicide, 300 from suicide, and hundreds of others from injuries such as falls, burns, and drownings.[48]

When a person drinks alcohol, it takes time for the body to oxidize it. Alcohol always takes the same pathway in the body (Figure 12-2). First, alcohol travels through the esophagus to the stomach. The stomach is able to absorb about 20 percent of the alcohol, depending on how much and what kind of food is in the stomach. The rest of the alcohol, about 80 percent, travels to the small intestine and is absorbed into the bloodstream. The bloodstream then carries alcohol to all parts of the body, and it continues to circulate through the body until it is broken down and excreted. The brain is one of the organs influenced by alcohol. The more a person drinks, the more the control centers of the brain become depressed. In the short term, alcohol depresses the following functions sequentially: judgment, inhibitions, reaction time, coordination, vision, speech, balance, walking, standing, consciousness, breathing, and heartbeat—all affecting life itself. Alcohol is also transported to the liver, where it undergoes oxidation. The liver is able to oxidize about 0.5 ounce, or one drink, of alcohol per hour. If there is more than 0.5 ounce of alcohol in the body, the remainder circulates throughout the body until the liver can oxidize more alcohol. The amount of alcohol that circulates in the body and blood is known as the blood alcohol concentration, or BAC. As the BAC rises in the blood and reaches the brain, predictable changes occur (Table 12-4). The last organs to be affected by alcohol are the lungs and the kidneys, where about 10 percent of the alcohol is eliminated by breath and urine.[49]

Eight factors influence the absorption of alcohol into the bloodstream:

1. *Concentration of the alcoholic beverage.* The stronger the concentration of alcohol in the beverage, the faster the rate of absorption. If one person drinks 5 ounces of beer and another person drinks 5 ounces of wine, the person who drinks 5 ounces of wine will have a higher BAC, because wine has a higher concentration of alcohol (review Figure 12-1).

2. *Number of alcoholic beverages consumed.* The more alcoholic beverages a person consumes, the more alcohol there is in the body to absorb. There is a direct relationship between the amount of alcohol consumed and the BAC.

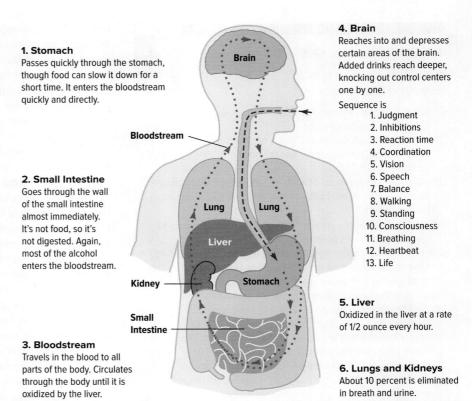

1. Stomach
Passes quickly through the stomach, though food can slow it down for a short time. It enters the bloodstream quickly and directly.

2. Small Intestine
Goes through the wall of the small intestine almost immediately. It's not food, so it's not digested. Again, most of the alcohol enters the bloodstream.

3. Bloodstream
Travels in the blood to all parts of the body. Circulates through the body until it is oxidized by the liver.

4. Brain
Reaches into and depresses certain areas of the brain. Added drinks reach deeper, knocking out control centers one by one.
Sequence is
1. Judgment
2. Inhibitions
3. Reaction time
4. Coordination
5. Vision
6. Speech
7. Balance
8. Walking
9. Standing
10. Consciousness
11. Breathing
12. Heartbeat
13. Life

5. Liver
Oxidized in the liver at a rate of 1/2 ounce every hour.

6. Lungs and Kidneys
About 10 percent is eliminated in breath and urine.

FIGURE 12-2 | **Pathways of Alcohol How does alcohol work? This diagram shows what happens to that drink after it's swallowed**

3. *Rate of consumption.* The faster alcohol is consumed, the higher the BAC. It is important to remember that the liver can oxidize only about 0.5 ounce of alcohol per hour; any additional alcohol stays in the blood and other organs in the body.

4. *Amount of food in the stomach.* The more food in the stomach, especially fatty foods, meat, and dairy products, the slower the absorption rate of alcohol.

5. *Drinking history.* People who have been heavy drinkers for an extended period of time build a tolerance to alcohol, which means they have to drink more alcohol than before to get the same desired effects.

6. *Type of alcoholic drink.* Carbonated alcoholic beverages, such as champagne, and alcohol mixed in warm drinks, such as a hot rum toddy, are absorbed faster than other kinds of alcoholic beverages.

7. *Body weight and build.* Greater body weight allows a higher volume in which alcohol can be distributed. This means that a person who weighs more will be less affected by the same amount of alcohol ingested by a smaller person. Also, the greater the person's muscle mass, the lower the BAC.[50]

8. *Gender.* On average, females weigh less and have a higher proportion of body fat than do males. This means that females generally have a lower proportion of body water in which to distribute alcohol.

Alcohol has several negative short-term side effects.[51] Because students deal with the present, it is important to stress these negative short-term side effects. Students will identify better with the immediate consequences.

Alcohol Intoxication: Progressive States of Impairment with Increasing Blood Alcohol Concentration (BAC)

BAC (%)	Possible Effects of Alcohol
0.01	Usually mild effects, if any; slight changes in feeling; heightening of moods.
0.03	Feelings of relaxation and slight exhilaration; minimal impairment of mental function.
0.06	Mild sedation; exaggeration of emotion; slight impairment of fine-motor skills; increase in reaction time; poor muscle control; slurred speech.
0.08	Legal evidence of driving under the influence of alcohol in many states.
0.09	Visual and hearing acuity reduced; inhibitions and self-restraint lessened; increased difficulty in performing motor skills; clouded judgment.
0.10	Legal evidence of driving under the influence of alcohol in many states.
0.12	Difficulty in performing gross-motor skills; blurred vision; unclear speech; definite impairment of mental function.
0.15	Major impairment of physical and mental functions; irresponsible behavior; general feeling of euphoria; difficulty in standing, walking, talking; distorted perception and judgment.
0.20	Mental confusion; decreased inhibitions; gross-body movements can be made only with assistance; inability to maintain upright position; difficulty in staying awake.
0.30	Severe mental confusion; minimum of perception and comprehension; difficulty in responding to stimuli; general suspension of sensibility.
0.40	Almost complete anesthesia; depressed reflexes; likely state of unconsciousness or coma.
0.50	Complete unconsciousness or deep coma, if not death.
0.60	Death most likely now, if it has not already occurred at somewhat lower BACs, following depression of nerve centers that control heartbeat and breathing; person is "dead drunk."

SOURCE: Charles Carroll and Dean Miller, *Health: The Science of Human Adaptation*, 4th ed. (Dubuque, IA: Wm. C. Brown Publishers, 1986).

1. *Perception and motor skills.* As indicated in Table 12-4, even a BAC of 0.06 percent (one or two drinks) begins to impair fine-motor skills, reaction time, speech, and muscle control. These perception and motor skills are important in many sport, art, and music skills, as well as in riding a bike or driving a car. Over 50 percent of the motor-vehicle deaths that occur each year are related to alcohol use. At higher BAC levels, there is a decrease in visual and hearing acuity, balance, and estimation of time.

2. *Heart and blood vessels.* Alcohol temporarily increases both heart rate and blood pressure. Alcohol also constricts the arteries that supply the heart. Although persons who drink alcohol feel warm, they are actually losing body heat, because alcohol causes the peripheral blood vessels to dilate, or expand. This can be extremely dangerous in cold weather and can lead to hypothermia, the extreme loss of body heat.

3. *Sleepiness.* Because alcohol is a depressant, it causes a person to become tired. Many persons believe alcohol is a stimulant because of the way alcohol users act; however, those actions result from alcohol initially depressing the part of the brain that controls inhibitions. Alcohol might help a person fall asleep more quickly, but the sleep is often light, making the person feel tired and unrefreshed even after eight hours of sleep.

4. *Emotions.* Alcohol depresses the prefrontal lobe of the brain, which controls judgment. With lack of judgment, persons under the influence of alcohol tend to have poor decision-making skills. This tends to increase risk taking and reduce inhibitions, temporarily decrease fears, and increase feelings of relaxation. Increased risk taking, combined with decreased motor skills and perception, causes many motor-vehicle crashes each year.

5. *Hangovers.* Hangovers can have many signs and symptoms, including headache, nausea, stomach distress, and generalized discomfort. These symptoms are caused by drinking too much alcohol, and only time can take away the unpleasant feelings.

Theories attribute hangovers to an accumulation of acetaldehyde (a toxic chemical), dehydration, the depletion of important enzymes, and the metabolism of congeners (toxins) in the alcohol. Vodka tends to be low in congeners, whereas red wine and bourbon are high. The higher the concentration of congeners, the greater the probability of a hangover.

6. *Overdose.* Alcohol can depress the central nervous system to the point at which the heart and lungs quit functioning, resulting in cardiac or respiratory arrest. This occurs when large amounts of alcohol have been consumed over a short period of time. Approximately 4,500 people under the age of 21 die from alcohol poisoning or an alcohol overdose each year.[52]

Source: U.S. Air Force photo illustration by Senior Airman Mike Meares

The combination of drinking and driving accounts for over 50 percent of the motor-vehicle deaths that occur each year.

7. *Lack of nutritional value.* Alcohol provides only empty calories, which means it does not have any nutritional value. Alcohol has a high caloric content—9 calories per gram. Persons who are trying to watch their weight should avoid alcohol.

Although many young students have a difficult time dealing with future outcomes, they should know that prolonged, heavy use of alcohol has several negative long-term side effects. For instance, longtime alcohol abusers shorten their life span by ten to twelve years. Other, more common, long-term side effects include the follow[53, 54]:

• Cirrhosis of the liver is commonly associated with alcohol consumption. With a person's continued use of alcohol, liver cells are damaged and gradually destroyed. The destroyed cells often are replaced by fibrous scar tissue, a condition known as cirrhosis of the liver. This disease is the leading cause of death among alcoholics and is the twelfth leading cause of death in the United States.

• Heavy drinkers also can experience gastrointestinal system disorders, which cause irritation and inflammation of the esophagus, stomach, small intestine, and pancreas. Alcohol use and cancer also have been correlated. Clinical and epidemiological studies have implicated excessive use of alcohol in the development of cancers of the mouth, pharynx, esophagus, and pancreas.

• Another problem for heavy drinkers is that they fulfill their caloric intake from alcoholic beverages instead of from food. Even though alcohol is high in calories, it has little nutritional value, such as vitamins and minerals. Decreased appetite, vomiting, and diarrhea contribute to nutritional imbalances. The diuretic properties of alcohol also cause a loss of water-soluble vitamins.

• Hypoglycemia is another problem associated with heavy alcohol use. Hypoglycemia is a condition in which blood sugar levels are lower than normal. Because heavy drinkers put such stress on the liver, it has a difficult time producing glucose and storing it as glycogen.

• Long-term, heavy use of alcohol can lead to cardiovascular disease. Long-term use of alcohol damages the heart muscle, leading to a condition known as cardiomyopathy, which can be fatal. It also can lead to premature heartbeats or total loss of rhythm in the heartbeat.

• Long-term heavy drinking increases the risk of developing high blood pressure, some kinds of stroke, and some types of cancer.

• Alcohol abuse is an additional long-term consequence of using alcohol. Alcohol abuse is a pattern of drinking that is linked to problems such as the inability to meet work, school, or family responsibilities; involvement in drunk-driving arrests; car crashes related to alcohol use; and relationship difficulties.[55]

• Alcoholism or alcohol dependence can be another negative consequence of long-term alcohol use. Alcoholism is a disease that has formal diagnostic criteria, with four symptoms:

1. Craving alcohol—a craving sometimes as strong as the need for food or water
2. Not being able to stop drinking once it has started
3. Physical addiction, characterized by withdrawal symptoms such as sweating, shakiness, nausea, and anxiety
4. Tolerance, or the need to drink greater amounts of alcohol to feel high, or intoxicated

Research shows that the risk for developing alcoholism runs in families. In fact, studies show that children of alcoholics are about four times more likely than the general population to develop problems related to alcohol. However, that does not mean that a child of an alcoholic will also become an alcoholic—50 percent of children of alcoholics do not become alcoholics themselves. It is also important for students to understand that some people develop alcoholism in the absence of any associated family history.[56-58]

An estimated 22.2 million persons aged 12 or older were classified with substance dependence or abuse in the past year (8.5 percent of the population aged 12 or older).[59] Because teachers will be dealing with children of alcoholics (COAs), it is important that they have factual information regarding these children. Alcoholism affects the entire family. Living with a nonrecovering alcoholic can contribute to stress for all family members, including children.

A child in such a family may have a variety of problems:

• *Guilt.* The child may see himself or herself as the main cause of the parent's drinking.

• *Anxiety.* The child may worry constantly about the situation at home. He or she may fear fights and violence between the parents or that the alcoholic parent will become sick or injured.

• *Embarrassment.* Parents may give the child the message that there is a terrible secret at home. The ashamed child does not invite friends home and is afraid to ask anyone for help.

• *Inability to have close relationships.* Because the child has been disappointed by the drinking parent many times, he or she often does not trust others. In addition, because the child may not invite friends home, it may be difficult to develop friendships with others.

• *Confusion.* The alcoholic parent will change suddenly from being very loving to being angry, regardless of the child's behavior. Additional confusion exists because there is no regular daily schedule in the child's life (bedtimes and mealtimes). A routine is very important for a child.

• *Anger.* The child feels anger at the alcoholic parent for drinking, and may be angry at the nonalcoholic parent for lack of support and protection.

• *Depression.* The child feels lonely and helpless to change the situation.

Although the child tries to keep the alcoholism a secret, teachers may sense that something is wrong. Mental health professionals advise that the following behaviors may signal a drinking or other problem at home:

• Failure in school; truancy.
• Lack of friends; withdrawal from classmates.
• Delinquent behavior, such as stealing or violence.
• Frequent physical complaints, such as headaches or stomach aches.

- Abuse of drugs or alcohol.
- Aggression toward other children.
- Risk-taking behaviors.
- Depression or suicidal thoughts or behavior.[60]

These children deserve special attention, because they most likely come from a home that lacks warmth, security, and even physical care. COAs can benefit when teachers help these students to:

- Develop autonomy and independence.
- Develop a strong social orientation and social skills.
- Engage in acts of "required helpfulness."
- Develop a close bond with teachers.
- Gain positive attention from others.
- Maintain a positive vision of life.
- Perceive their experiences constructively.
- Develop coping strategies for emotionally hazardous experiences.[61]

The American Academy of Child and Adolescent Psychiatry has prepared "Facts for Families-Children of Alcoholics," available at www.aacap.org/App_Themes/AACAP/docs/facts_for_families /17_children_of_alcoholics.pdf.[62]

Marijuana

Marijuana is most likely to be the first illicit drug young people will use. It is a drug that is easy for many young people to get. In fact, 21 percent of students surveyed thought they could get marijuana within a day.[63] Three out of four of these students indicated that they would be able to get marijuana from a friend or classmate. Access to marijuana is becoming increasingly easy, in part, due to legalization. As of March 2018, nine states and the District of Columbia have legalized marijuana for adult recreational use, and twenty states have legalized marijuana for medicinal purposes.[64] Some research has indicated that legalization has led to increased use among youth due to a change in perceived norms; however, more research is needed.[65]

Young people believe that marijuana is not very harmful. They think that it is natural, has a medical use, is harmless, and is not addictive.[66] Therefore, it is important that teachers understand the dangers associated with marijuana so that they can counteract their students' beliefs about the drug.

Marijuana is a green or gray mixture of dried and shredded flowers and leaves of the hemp plant *Cannabis sativa*. The marijuana plant contains over 400 chemicals, but the main active chemical in marijuana is delta-9-tetrahydrocannabinol (THC). When smoked, THC passes from the lungs and is quickly absorbed into the bloodstream and then transported to the brain. It is redistributed to the rest of the body, so that within thirty minutes much of the THC is gone from the brain. All forms of marijuana have immediate and negative physical and mental effects.

The immediate short-term effects of smoking marijuana include:

- Impaired short-term memory (memory of recent events)— making it hard to learn and retain information, particularly complex tasks.

- Slowed reaction time and impaired motor coordination— throwing off athletic performance, impairing driving skills, and increasing the risk of injuries.
- Altered judgment and decision making—possibly leading to high-risk sexual behaviors that could lead to the spread of sexually transmitted diseases.
- Increased heart rate by 20 to 100 percent—possibly increasing the risk of heart attack, especially in otherwise vulnerable individuals.
- Altered mood—creating euphoria or calmness in low doses, and anxiety or paranoia in high doses.[67]

Because several of these short-term consequences are related to driving ability, marijuana use makes it difficult to judge distances and react to signals and sounds on the road. Marijuana is the most commonly identified illicit drug in fatal accidents (approximately 14 percent of drivers), sometimes in combination with alcohol or other drugs.[68] For more on the signs of drug use, see Teacher's Toolbox 12.6.

Smoking marijuana also has long-term negative effects. Research shows that marijuana use increases users' difficulty in trying to quit smoking cigarettes. In addition, memory and learning skills are affected longer than with intoxication. Marijuana affects the brain, especially a young person's developing brain[69] and some research suggests that it may impact a person's IQ if they began using marijuana during the teen years and continue into adulthood.[70]

The adverse effects can last for days or weeks, even after the drug has worn off. Long-term marijuana use also can increase the risk of chronic cough, bronchitis, and emphysema. The risk of head, neck, and lung cancer also increases with long-term use, because marijuana smoke contains 50 to 70 percent more carcinogenic hydrocarbons than tobacco smoke. Marijuana users usually inhale more deeply and hold their breath longer than do tobacco smokers, which increases users' risk of lung cancer. Finally, long-term marijuana use can lead to addiction in some people. It is estimated that 9 percent of people who use marijuana will become dependent on it, with this number increasing from one to six for those who start using in their teens.[71] Marijuana accounts for 4.3 million of the estimated 7.5 million Americans dependent on or abusing illicit drugs. Eighteen percent of people aged 12 and older entering drug abuse treatment programs reported marijuana as their primary drug of abuse.[72]

Inhalants

Inhalants are legal, everyday products that have a useful purpose, but can be misused. Inhalant abuse is the intentional inhalation of a volatile substance for the purpose of achieving a mind-altering effect or a euphoric state. Inhalant use is unlike most other classes of drugs in that their use is most common among younger adolescents while declining as youth grow older. Inhalant use at an early age may reflect the fact that most are cheap, readily available (typically in the home), and legal to possess and purchase. For example, in the Monitoring the Future study, an annual National Institute of Drug Abuse study supported a survey of the nation's secondary school students,

Teacher's Toolbox 12.6

Signs and Symptoms of Drug Use

Changing patterns of performance, appearance, and behavior might signal the use of drugs. The items in the first category provide direct evidence of drug use; the items in the other categories may indicate drug use. Adults should watch for extreme changes in children's behavior, changes that together form a pattern associated with drug use.

SIGNS OF DRUGS AND DRUG PARAPHERNALIA

- Possession of drug-related paraphernalia, such as pipes, rolling papers, small decongestant bottles, eye drops, or small butane torches.
- Possession of drugs or evidence of drugs, such as pills, white powder, small glass vials, or hypodermic needles; peculiar plants or butts, seeds, or leaves in ashtrays or in clothing pockets.
- Odor of drugs, incense, or other cover-up scents.

IDENTIFICATION WITH DRUG CULTURE

- Drug-related magazines, drug-related slogans on clothing.
- Conversation and jokes that are preoccupied with drugs.
- Hostility in discussing drugs.
- Collection of beer cans.

SIGNS OF PHYSICAL DETERIORATION

- Memory lapses, short attention span, difficulty in concentration.
- Poor physical coordination, slurred or incoherent speech.
- Unhealthy appearance, indifference to hygiene and grooming.
- Bloodshot eyes, dilated pupils.

DRAMATIC CHANGES IN SCHOOL PERFORMANCE

- Marked downturn in student's grades—not just from Cs to Fs but from As to Bs and Cs; assignments not completed.
- Increased absenteeism or tardiness.

CHANGES IN BEHAVIOR

- Chronic dishonesty (lying, stealing, cheating), trouble with the police.
- Changes in friends, evasiveness in talking about new ones.
- Possession of large amounts of money.
- Increasing and inappropriate anger, hostility, irritability, secretiveness.
- Reduced motivation, energy, self-discipline, self-esteem.
- Diminished interest in extracurricular activities and hobbies.

eighth graders regularly report the highest rate of current, past-year, and lifetime inhalant abuse compared to tenth and twelfth graders. In 2017, use of inhalants significantly increased among eighth graders. The percentage of eighth graders who had ever used inhalants in their lifetime increased 7 percent, a significant increase; use in the past twelve months increased almost 4 percent, also a significant increase. The increase in use may mark the end of a decline over a ten-year period. The increase

in use may be due to perceptions of risk from using inhalants among eighth graders steadily declining since 2010. Lowered perception of risk is often a leading indicator in increased usage. Young teens may not understand the risks of inhalant use as well as they should.[73] Inhalants can be divided into four categories:

- *Volatile solvents* are liquids that vaporize at room temperature. They are found in a multitude of inexpensive, easily available products used for common household and industrial purposes. These include paint thinners and removers, dry-cleaning fluids, degreasers, gasoline, glues, correction fluids, and felt-tip marker fluids.
- *Aerosols* are sprays that contain propellants and solvents. They include spray paints, deodorant and hair sprays, vegetable oil sprays for cooking, and fabric protector sprays.
- *Gases* include medical anesthetics, as well as gases used in household and commercial products. Medical anesthetic gases include ether, chloroform, halothane, and nitrous oxide, commonly called laughing gas. Nitrous oxide, the most abused of these gases, can be found in whipped cream dispensers and products that boost octane levels in racing cars. Household and commercial products containing gases include butane lighters, propane tanks, whipped cream dispensers, and refrigerants.
- *Nitrites* often are considered a special class of inhalants. Unlike most other inhalants, which act directly on the central nervous system (CNS), nitrites act primarily to dilate blood vessels and relax the muscles. Other inhalants are used to alter mood, but nitrites are used primarily as sexual enhancers. Nitrites include cyclohexyl nitrite, isoamyl (amyl) nitrite, and isobutyl (butyl) nitrite. Cyclohexyl nitrite is found in room odorizers. Amyl nitrite is used in certain diagnostic procedures and is prescribed to some patients for heart pain. Illegally diverted ampules of amyl nitrite are called "poppers" or "snappers" on the street. Butyl nitrite is an illegal substance that is often packaged and sold in small bottles[74]

Inhalants can be breathed in through the mouth or the nose in the following ways:

- Sniffing or snorting fumes from containers.
- Spraying aerosols directly into the mouth or nose.
- Sniffing or inhaling fumes from substances sprayed or deposited inside a plastic or paper bag (known as "bagging").
- "Huffing" from an inhalant-soaked rag stuffed in the mouth.
- Inhaling from balloons filled with nitrous oxide.[75]

Nearly all abused inhalant products produce effects similar to those of anesthetics, which slow down the body's functions. When inhaled via the nose or mouth into the lungs in sufficient concentrations, inhalants can cause intoxicating effects. Intoxication can last only a few minutes or up to several hours if the inhalant is taken repeatedly. Initially, users might feel slightly stimulated; with successive inhalations, they might feel less inhibited and less in control. Ultimately, a user can lose consciousness. A strong need to continue using inhalants has been reported among some individuals, particularly those who have used inhalants for prolonged periods over several days.[76]

Sniffing highly concentrated amounts of the chemicals in solvents or aerosol sprays can directly induce heart failure and death, known as sudden sniffing death syndrome. Other irreversible effects caused by inhaling specific solvents are:

- Hearing loss—from paint sprays, glues, dewaxers, cleaning fluids, and correction fluids.
- Limb spasms—from glues, gasoline, whipped cream dispensers, and gas cylinders.
- Central nervous system or brain damage—from paint sprays, glues, and dewaxers.
- Bone marrow damage—from gasoline.
- Short-term memory loss—from a variety of inhalants.

Serious but potentially reversible effects include:

- Liver and kidney damage—from correction fluids and dry-cleaning fluids.
- Blood oxygen depletion—from organic nitrites, such as poppers, rush, varnish removers, and paint thinners.[77]

Many teachers include the topic of inhalants when teaching about alcohol and other drugs. Most experts, however, believe that the topic should be included in teaching about safety and label reading. The following concepts about inhalants, developed by Isabel Burk, a drug prevention consultant, should be taught for the specified age groups.[78]

Ages 4–7

- Teach about oxygen's importance to life and body functioning.
- Discuss the need for parental supervision and adequate room ventilation for cleaning products, solvents, glues, and other products.
- Be a good role model; let students see you reading labels and following instructions.

Ages 7–10

- Define and discuss the term *toxic;* students can practice reading labels and following instructions.
- Teach about oxygen's importance to life and body functioning, with emphasis on body systems and brain functions.
- Discuss the need for parental supervision, following directions, and adequate room ventilation.
- Discuss and discourage "body pollution" and introducing poisons into the body.
- Be a good role model; let students see you reading labels and following instructions.

Ages 10–14

- Discuss negative effects of oxygen deprivation.
- Teach or reinforce peer resistance skills.
- Discuss environmental toxins and personal safety issues.

Over-the-Counter and Prescription Drugs

Medicines, or legal drugs, are used to cure illness, relieve pain, prevent the spread of disease, and prolong life. They can be prescription drugs or over-the-counter (OTC) drugs. Prescription drugs can be obtained only through a licensed professional practitioner, whereas OTC drugs can be bought in a store without a prescription. Medicines can cause harm if misused. Drug misuse is the use of a legal drug in an improper way, such as taking more than the recommended dosage, taking a medicine longer than needed or prescribed, not taking the medication long enough, or using someone else's prescribed medication. Students need to be taught that all medicines should be taken under adult supervision and that the directions should be read and followed.

The United States has seen an alarmingly large rise in the use of a particular type of prescription drug known as opioids or pain killers.[79] Despite the rise in opioid and overdose deaths and opioid misuse among adults, lifetime, past-year, and past-month misuse of prescription opioids dropped dramatically over the past five years in twelfth graders (the only grade surveyed in this category) according to the Monitoring the Future study. Specifically, Vicodin use dropped by 51 percent in eighth graders, 67 percent in tenth graders, and 74 percent in twelfth graders. A possible contributor to this decline could be that teens also think these drugs are not as easy to get as they used to be. Approximately 36 percent of twelfth graders said they were easily available in the 2017 survey, compared to more than 54 percent in 2010.[80] Despite this promising trend, one of the big concerns with the abuse of prescription drugs is that adolescents are more likely than young adults to become dependent on prescription medication.[81]

Over-the-counter drugs are also problematic. For example, it has been reported that some young people are abusing OTC cough medicines containing dextromethorphan (DXM), an effective and safe cough-suppressant ingredient. If the directions are followed, products containing DXM produce few side effects and have a long history of safety and effectiveness. Some teens, however, are attempting to get high by taking much larger than recommended doses of DXM in OTC cough syrups, tablets, and gel caps. In high doses, DXM can have hallucinogenic and dissociative effects.[82] The most recent Monitoring the Future survey found that the percentage of teens using cough medicine containing DXM to get high remains at just 3 percent, the lowest level recorded for teen abuse since 2015.[83] Regardless of the type of legal drug, teachers should stress the importance of reading and following the directions on both OTC and prescription medications.

Recommendations for Concepts and Practice

Healthy Behavior Outcomes

The goal of health education is to help students adopt or maintain health-enhancing behaviors. School districts and teachers should identify the health-enhancing behaviors they would like their students to maintain or adopt. The list found in the Teacher's Toolbox 12.7 identifies some possible healthy behavior outcomes related to promoting an alcohol- and other drug-free lifestyle. Though not all of the suggestions are developmentally appropriate for students in grades K–8, this list can help teachers understand how the learning activities they plan for their students support both short- and long-term desired behavior outcomes.

Developmentally Appropriate Knowledge and Skill Expectations for Promoting an Alcohol- and Other Drug-Free Lifestyle

HEALTHY BEHAVIOR OUTCOMES (HBOs) FOR AN ALCOHOL-FREE AND OTHER DRUG-FREE LIFESTYLE

HBO 1. Avoid misuse and abuse of over-the-counter and prescription drugs.

HBO 2. Avoid experimentation with alcohol and other drugs.

HBO 3. Avoid the use of alcohol.

HBO 4. Avoid the use of illegal drugs.

HBO 5. Avoid driving while under the influence of alcohol and other drugs.

HBO 6. Avoid riding in a motor vehicle with a driver who is under the influence of alcohol or other drugs.

HBO 7. Quit using alcohol and other drugs if already using.

HBO 8. Support others to be alcohol and other drug free.

Grades K–2 Knowledge Expectations	Grades 3–5 Knowledge Expectations	Grades 6–8 Knowledge Expectations
NHES 1: Core Concepts		
AOD1.2.1 Identify how household products are harmful if intentionally inhaled or absorbed. (HBO 1)	AOD1.5.1 Explain why household products are harmful if intentionally absorbed or inhaled. (HBO 1)	AOD1.8.1 Distinguish between proper use and abuse of over-the-counter medicines. (HBO 1)
AOD1.2.2 Explain the harmful effects of medicines when used incorrectly. (HBO 1)	AOD1.5.2 Explain the benefits of medicines when used correctly. (HBO 1)	AOD1.8.2 Differentiate between proper use and abuse of prescription medicines. (HBO 1)
AOD1.2.3 Describe the potential risks associated with use of over-the-counter medicines. (HBO 1)	AOD1.5.3 Explain how to use medicines correctly. (HBO 1)	AOD1.8.3 Describe the health risks of using weight loss drugs. (HBO 1)
AOD1.2.4 Identify family rules about medicine use. (HBO 1)	AOD1.5.4 Describe potential risks associated with inappropriate use of over-the-counter medicines. (HBO 1)	AOD1.8.4 Describe the health risks of using performance-enhancing drugs. (HBO 1)
AOD1.2.5 Identify school rules about use of medicines. (HBO 1)	AOD1.5.5 Explain the potential risks associated with inappropriate use and abuse of prescription medicines. (HBO 1)	AOD1.8.5 Summarize the negative consequences of using alcohol and other drugs. (HBO 2, 3 & 4)
AOD1.2.6 Describe how to use medicines correctly. (HBO 1)	AOD1.5.6 Identify short- and long-term effects of alcohol use. (HBO 2 & 3)	AOD1.8.6 Determine reasons why people choose to use or not to use alcohol and other drugs. (HBO 2, 3 & 4)
	AOD1.5.7 Identify family and school rules about alcohol use. (HBO 2 & 3)	AOD1.8.7 Describe situations that could lead to the use of alcohol and other drugs. (HBO 2, 3 & 4)
	AOD1.5.8 Explain the difference between medicines and illicit drugs. (HBO 2 & 4)	AOD1.8.8 Explain why using alcohol or other drugs is an unhealthy way to manage stress. (HBO 2, 3 & 4)
		AOD1.8.9 Explain school policies and community laws about alcohol and other drugs. (HBO 2, 3 & 4)
		AOD1.8.10 Describe the relationship between using alcohol and other drugs and other health risks, such as unintentional injuries, violence, suicide, sexual risk behaviors, and tobacco use. (HBO 2, 3, 4, 5 & 6)
		AOD1.8.11 Determine the benefits of being alcohol- and other drug-free. (HBO 2, 3, 4 & 8)
		AOD1.8.12 Describe positive alternatives to using alcohol and other drugs. (HBO 2, 3, 4 & 8)
		AOD1.8.13 Explain the relationship between intravenous drug use and transmission of blood-borne diseases, such as HIV and hepatitis. (HBO 2 & 4)
		AOD1.8.14 Explain the risks associated with using alcohol or other drugs and driving a motor vehicle. (HBO 5 & 6)

Grades K–2 Skill Expectations	Grades 3–5 Skill Expectations	Grades 6–8 Skill Expectations
NHES 2: Analyze Influences		
AOD2.2.1 Identify relevant influences of family on taking medicines safely.	AOD2.5.1 Identify relevant influences of culture on practices and behaviors related to alcohol use.	AOD2.8.1 Explain the influence of school rules and community laws on alcohol- and other drug-related practices and behaviors.
AOD2.2.2 Identify relevant influences of school personnel on taking medicines safely.	AOD2.5.2 Identify relevant influences of peers on practices and behaviors related to alcohol use.	AOD2.8.2 Explain how perceptions of norms influence healthy and unhealthy alcohol- and other drug-use practices and behaviors.
	AOD2.5.3 Identify relevant influences of community on practices and behaviors related to alcohol use.	AOD2.8.3 Explain how social expectations influence healthy and unhealthy alcohol- and other drug-use practices and behaviors.

Grades K–2 Skill Expectations	Grades 3–5 Skill Expectations	Grades 6–8 Skill Expectations

NHES 2: Analyze Influences (*continued*)

	AOD2.5.4 Describe how relevant influences of family and culture affect practices and behaviors related to alcohol use.	AOD2.8.4 Explain how personal values and beliefs influence alcohol- and other drug-use practices and behaviors.
	AOD2.5.5 Describe how relevant influences of school and community affect practices and behaviors related to alcohol use.	AOD2.8.5 Describe how alcohol and other drug use can influence the likelihood of engaging in other unhealthy behaviors.
	AOD2.5.6 Describe how relevant influences of media (e.g., alcohol advertising) and technology affect practices and behaviors related to alcohol use.	AOD2.8.6 Analyze how relevant influences of family and culture affect alcohol- and other drug-use practices and behaviors.
	AOD2.5.7 Describe how relevant influences of peers affect practices and behaviors related to alcohol use.	AOD2.8.7 Analyze how relevant influences of school and community affect alcohol- and other drug-use practices and behaviors.
		AOD2.8.8 Analyze how relevant influences of media (e.g., alcohol advertising) and technology affect alcohol- and other drug-use practices and behaviors.

NHES 3: Accessing Information, Products, and Services

AOD3.2.1 Identify trusted adults at home who can help with taking prescriptions and over-the-counter medicines.

AOD3.2.2 Identify trusted adults and professionals in school (e.g., school nurse) who can help with taking prescriptions and over-the-counter medicines.

AOD3.2.3 Explain how to locate school health helpers (e.g., school nurse) who can help with information about prescriptions and over-the-counter medicines.

AOD3.5.1 Describe characteristics of accurate information for over-the-counter and prescription medicines.

AOD3.5.2 Describe characteristics of accurate alcohol-use prevention information.

AOD3.5.3 Describe characteristics of appropriate and reliable over-the-counter and prescription medicines.

AOD3.5.4 Describe characteristics of appropriate and trustworthy alcohol-use prevention services.

AOD3.5.5 Demonstrate how to locate sources of accurate information for over-the-counter and prescription medicines.

AOD3.5.6 Describe how to locate sources of accurate information for alcohol-use prevention.

AOD3.8.1 Analyze the validity and reliability of information for over-the-counter and prescription medicines.

AOD3.8.2 Analyze the validity and reliability of information for alcohol- and other drug-use prevention.

AOD3.8.3 Analyze the validity and reliability of alcohol- and other drug-use prevention and treatment services.

AOD3.8.4 Describe situations that call for professional alcohol- and other drug-use treatment services.

AOD3.8.5 Determine the availability of valid and reliable alcohol- and other drug-use cessation products.

AOD3.8.6 Access valid and reliable alcohol- and other drug-use prevention information from home, school, or community.

AOD3.8.7 Locate valid and reliable alcohol- and other drug-use treatment services.

NHES 4: Interpersonal Communication

AOD4.2.1 Demonstrate effective refusal skills, including firmly saying "no" and getting away, when offered medicine or other drugs by someone other than a trusted adult.

AOD4.2.2 Demonstrate how to effectively tell a trusted adult when feeling threatened or harmed when offered medicine other drugs by someone other than a trusted adult.

AOD4.5.1 Demonstrate effective verbal and nonverbal communication skills to avoid taking another's prescription medication.

AOD4.5.2 Demonstrate effective verbal and nonverbal communication skills to avoid alcohol and other drug use.

AOD4.5.3 Demonstrate effective verbal and nonverbal communication to avoid riding in a motor vehicle with a driver who has been drinking alcohol.

AOD4.5.4 Explain how to be empathetic and compassionate toward a family member who is trying to quit alcohol or other drug use.

AOD4.5.5 Demonstrate how to effectively ask for help to avoid exposure to others who use alcohol or drugs.

AOD4.8.1 Demonstrate the use of effective verbal and nonverbal communication to avoid taking another's prescription medication.

AOD4.8.2 Demonstrate the use of effective verbal and nonverbal communication to avoid alcohol and other drug use.

AOD4.8.3 Demonstrate the use of effective verbal and nonverbal communication to avoid riding in a motor vehicle with a driver who is under the influence of alcohol or other drugs.

AOD4.8.4 Demonstrate effective peer resistance skills to avoid or reduce alcohol and other drug use.

AOD4.8.5 Demonstrate effective negotiation skills to avoid or reduce exposure to alcohol and other drug use.

AOD4.8.6 Demonstrate how to effectively ask for assistance to quit using alcohol or other drugs.

AOD4.8.7 Demonstrate how to effectively communicate empathy.

(*continued*)

Grades K–2 Skill Expectations (*continued*)	**Grades 3–5 Skill Expectations** (*continued*)	**Grades 6–8 Skill Expectations** (*continued*)

NHES 5: Decision Making

AOD5.2.1 Identify how family, peers, or media influence a decision to not use over-the-counter and prescription medicines in unsafe ways.	AOD5.5.1 Identify situations which need a decision related to alcohol- and other drug-use prevention. AOD5.5.2 Decide when help is needed and when it is not needed to make a decision to not use alcohol or other drugs. AOD5.5.3 Explain how family, culture, peers, or media influence a decision related to alcohol and other drug use. AOD5.5.4 Identify options and their potential outcomes when making a decision related to alcohol and other drug use. AOD5.5.5 Choose a healthy option when making a decision about alcohol and other drug prevention. AOD5.5.6 Describe the final outcome of a decision related to alcohol and other drug use.	AOD5.8.1 Identify circumstances that help or hinder making a decision to be alcohol- and other drug-free. AOD5.8.2 Determine when situations related to alcohol and other drug use require a decision (e.g., when a peer offers an alcoholic drink, deciding about getting into a motor vehicle with a driver who has been using alcohol and other drugs). AOD5.8.3 Distinguish when decisions related to alcohol and other drug use should be made individually or with the help of others. AOD5.8.4 Explain how family, culture, media, peers, and personal beliefs affect a decision related to alcohol and other drug use. AOD5.8.5 Distinguish between healthy and unhealthy alternatives of a decision related to alcohol and other drug use. AOD5.8.6 Predict the potential outcomes of healthy and unhealthy alternatives to a decision related to alcohol and other drug use. AOD5.8.7 Choose a healthy alternative when making a decision related to alcohol and other drug use. AOD5.8.8 Analyze the effectiveness of a final outcome of a decision related to alcohol and other drug use.

NHES 6: Goal Setting

NA Skill expectations are not identified for this grade group.	AOD6.5.1 Set a realistic goal to be alcohol-free. AOD6.5.2 Track progress to achieving a personal goal to be alcohol-free. AOD6.5.3 Identify resources that can help achieve a personal goal to be alcohol-free.	AOD6.8.1 Assess personal practices related to alcohol and other drug use. AOD6.8.2 Set a realistic personal goal to be alcohol- and other drug-free. AOD6.8.3 Assess the barriers to achieving a personal goal to be alcohol- and other drug-free. AOD6.8.4 Apply strategies to overcome barriers to achieving a personal goal to be alcohol- and other drug-free. AOD6.8.5 Use strategies and skills to achieve a personal goal to be alcohol- and other drug-free. AOD6.8.6 Set a realistic personal goal to be alcohol- and drug-free or to avoid riding in a motor vehicle with a driver who is under the influence of alcohol or other drugs. AOD6.8.7 Assess the barriers to achieving a personal goal to be alcohol- and drug-free or to avoid riding in a motor vehicle with a driver who is under the influence of alcohol or other drugs. AOD6.8.8 Apply strategies to overcome barriers to achieving a personal goal to be alcohol- and drug-free or to avoid riding in a motor vehicle with a driver who is under the influence of alcohol or other drugs. AOD6.8.9 Use strategies and skills to achieve a personal goal to be alcohol- and drug-free or to avoid riding in a motor vehicle with a driver who is under the influence of alcohol or other drugs.

Grades K–2 Skill Expectations	Grades 3–5 Skill Expectations	Grades 6–8 Skill Expectations

NHES 7: Self-Management

NA Skill expectations are not identified for this grade group.	AOD7.5.1 Describe practices and behaviors that prevent alcohol use, avoid taking others' prescription medications, or avoid riding in a motor vehicle with a driver who is under the influence of alcohol or other drugs. AOD7.5.2 Demonstrate healthy alcohol- and other drug-use prevention practices and behaviors. AOD7.5.3 Make a commitment to practice healthy alcohol- and other drug-use prevention behaviors.	AOD7.8.1 Explain the importance of being responsible for being alcohol- and other drug-free. AOD7.8.2 Analyze personal practices and behaviors that reduce or prevent alcohol and other drug use. AOD7.8.3 Demonstrate alcohol- and other drug-use prevention practices and behaviors to improve the health of oneself and others. AOD7.8.4 Make a commitment to practice healthy alcohol- and other drug-use prevention behaviors. AOD7.8.5 Make a commitment to avoid riding in a motor vehicle with a driver who is under the influence of alcohol or other drugs.

NHES 8: Advocacy

AOD8.2.1 Make requests to others to avoid driving while under the influence of alcohol or other drugs.	AOD8.5.1 Give factual information about the benefits of being alcohol- and other drug-free. AOD8.5.2 State personal beliefs about the dangers related to alcohol and other drug use. AOD8.5.3 Demonstrate how to persuade others to be alcohol- and other drug-free. AOD8.5.4 Demonstrate how to persuade others to avoid driving while under the influence of alcohol or other drugs. AOD8.5.5 Demonstrate how to persuade others to avoid riding in a motor vehicle with a driver who is under the influence of alcohol or other drugs.	AOD8.8.1 State a health-enhancing position about being alcohol- and other drug-free, supported with accurate information, to improve the health of others. AOD8.8.2 Persuade others to be alcohol- and other drug-free. AOD8.8.3 Persuade others to avoid driving while under the influence of alcohol or other drugs. AOD8.8.4 Persuade others to avoid riding in a motor vehicle with a driver who is under the influence of alcohol or other drugs. AOD8.8.5 Collaborate with others to advocate for individuals, families, and schools to be alcohol- and other drug-free. AOD8.8.6 Demonstrate how to adapt alcohol- or other drug-free messages for different audiences.

SOURCE: Centers for Disease Control and Prevention, *Health Education Curriculum Analysis Tool*, Atlanta, GA, CDC, 2012, www.cdc.gov.

Developmentally Appropriate Knowledge and Skill Expectations

As with other health topics, teaching related to promoting an alcohol- and other drug-free lifestyle should be developmentally appropriate and be based on the physical, cognitive, social, emotional, and language characteristics of specific students. Teacher's Toolbox 12.7 contains a list of suggested developmentally appropriate knowledge and skill expectations to help teachers create lessons that encourage students to practice the desired behavior outcomes by the time they graduate from high school. The numbers listed behind each knowledge expectation are aligned with and support the healthy behavior outcomes listed in the Teacher's Toolbox 12.7.[84] These grade-level spans are aligned with the 2007 National Health Education Standards. Note that some of these knowledge and skill expectations are reinforced in other content areas (the concept "explain why household products are harmful" also applies to safety and unintentional injury). Note that these grade-level spans are aligned with the 2007 Natural Health Education Standards.

©Hill Street Studios/Getty Images

Caregivers should always assist children with prescription and OTC medications.

Sample Students' Questions and Suggested Answers Regarding Alcohol and Other Drugs

A list of some commonly asked questions about alcohol and other drugs and some suggested answers follows. It is not enough to just read the suggested answer—teachers should actually practice saying them aloud. Teachers are encouraged to think of other questions students might ask and to practice answering them as well.

1. *Why do people take illegal drugs?*

There are lots of reasons. They might not know how dangerous they are. They also might not know how to handle their problems, so they take drugs to forget about them. Many times, young people take drugs because of outside pressure from peers or from what they see in the media. None of these are good reasons to take drugs.

2. *Why are some drugs good for you and some drugs bad for you?*

When you get sick, the drugs the doctor gives you will help you get better. But if you take these drugs when you're healthy, they can make you sick. Also, some drugs, such as LSD, are never good for you. To be safe, never take any drugs unless your parent, your caregiver, or the doctor says it's okay.

3. *Is alcohol addictive?*

A person who drinks alcohol on a regular basis can become addicted. This usually happens to people who have been drinking for several years and who drink almost every day. However, some people can become addicted much faster—even after just a few months of regular drinking. It is important to wait until you are 21 to begin drinking alcohol, because people who wait until that age almost never become addicted.

4. *Can you get hooked on marijuana?*

Long-term marijuana abuse can lead to addiction in some people. They abuse the drug even though it interferes with family, school, and recreational activities. Long-term marijuana users can experience cravings and withdrawal symptoms when they try to quit.[81]

5. *What does it mean to get high?*

Being high is the feeling a person gets when taking a drug. It is usually a good feeling, followed by a complete letdown, or crash. These temporary highs are not worth it, because a person will want to feel that way always and usually will have to take more and more of a drug to get that high feeling.

6. *Why do people sell drugs?*

People sell drugs for many reasons. Some people sell drugs just to make money; others sell drugs so they have enough money to buy drugs for themselves. Regardless of the reason, it is against the law and hurts many young people.

7. *Are drugs really that bad for you?*

Yes. People who use drugs usually say they feel great at first, but that feeling doesn't last long. Over time, they need more and more of the drug to get the same high. This really increases the risk for addiction and, in some cases, overdose. Drugs can ruin people's health, make them drop out of school, cause them to lose friends, and hurt their judgment so that they do some really dangerous things.

8. *What should I do if I have a friend who wants to start sneaking his or her parent's beer?*

This is a difficult situation, but you do have influence over other people. First, don't agree to join your friend. Second, try to convince your friend not to do it by explaining some of the health and legal problems related to alcohol and pointing out that, if your friend gets caught, he or she will lose his or her parents' trust. Ask other friends to help you convince your friend that this is a bad idea.

9. *Can I make an alcoholic in my family stop drinking?*

No. It is important to know that an alcoholic needs help to stop drinking, but no one can be forced to accept the help, no matter how hard you try or what you do. It is also important to know that you cannot provide the help that an alcoholic needs. An alcoholic needs the help of people trained to treat the disease. Also, it is important to remember that it is not your fault that someone in your family is an alcoholic. If you want to talk to someone about the problem, remember that you can talk to the school counselor.

10. *Why can't kids drink if their parents can?*

Kids' bodies and brains are still developing, and alcohol has a greater effect on their physical and mental well-being, compared with its effect on adults. For example, people who begin drinking before age 15 are four times more likely to develop alcoholism than those who begin at age 21.

11. *Aren't beer and wine safer than liquor?*

No. One 12-ounce bottle of beer or 5-ounce glass of wine has as much alcohol as 1.5 ounces of liquor. Regardless of the type of drink, alcohol can cause you problems.

12. *Why is the legal drinking age set at 21?*

The government has set the legal drinking age at 21 for several reasons. First, young and growing bodies are more negatively affected by alcohol. Second, adults have lived longer and should be better at making decisions, such as whether they have had too much to drink. Third, adults should be better at dealing with the emotional effects of alcohol.

STRATEGIES FOR LEARNING AND ASSESSMENT

Promoting an Alcohol- and Other Drug-Free Lifestyle

This section provides an example of a standards-based learning an assessment strategy for each NHES standard. The examples in this chapter can be applied to any content area. Chapters 5 to 14 include content-specific learning and assessment strategies organized by standard and grade cluster (K–2, 3–5, and 6–8). Each set of strategies begins with a restatement of the standard and a reminder of the assessment criteria, drawn from the RMC Health rubrics in Appendix B. Strategies are written as directions for teachers and include applicable theory of planned behavior (TPB) constructs in parentheses (intention to act in healthy ways, attitudes toward behavior, subjective norms, perceived behavioral control). These learning and assessment strategies provide building blocks for standards-based lessons and units that can be tailored to local needs. Assessment criteria are used with permission from the RMC Health (rmc.org). See Appendix B for Scoring Rubrics.

NHES 1 | Core Concepts

Students will comprehend concepts related to health promotion and disease prevention to enhance health.

ASSESSMENT CRITERIA

- Connections—Describe relationships between behavior and health; draw logical conclusions about connections between behavior and health.
- Comprehensiveness—Thoroughly cover health topic, showing breadth and depth; give accurate information.

Grades K–2

Medicine Cabinet Safety   Students can draw pictures of places in the home where storing medicines is safe and appropriate. Students can add words or pictures to illustrate rules about taking medicines at home and at school ("Take only your own medicine" and "Take medicine under the supervision of an adult, such as a parent, nurse, or doctor"). Students should tell why the proper use and storage of medicines is important.

ASSESSMENT | For an assessment task, students can draw a picture about using medicine safely and write a sentence to explain their picture. For assessment criteria, students should give correct information and describe a relationship between behavior (safe use of medication) and health. Meeting this criterion requires that students' sentences have a "because" statement to explain the relationship (Take your medicine the way the doctor says, because too much can make you sick). (Construct: Attitudes toward behavior.)

Safe and Unsafe Products   Ask students to explain their ideas about the words *safe* and *unsafe*. Students can make a class list of safe or unsafe products found in and around homes. Ask students to think about products that would or would not harm them if they swallowed them or got them on their skin. Safe items include milk, orange juice, water, coffee, and tea. Unsafe items include gasoline, bleach, bathroom cleaners, insecticides, and pills from a medicine cabinet. Ask students to think a little harder about products such as sunscreen, which would be safe on the skin but unsafe to swallow. Next, have students classify pictures or empty, clean containers of safe or unsafe items by placing them in one of two large boxes labeled "safe" and "unsafe." Students might want to draw on, color, or decorate the boxes to illustrate their ideas about safe or unsafe products. Provide enough product containers and pictures so that every child has a turn to place an item in one of the boxes.

ASSESSMENT | The assessment task for this activity is the students' categorization (placing products in a box or bag) of products as safe or unsafe. For assessment criteria, students should make correct decisions and be able to explain their decisions accurately. Students should explain why the unsafe products would be dangerous if used incorrectly. (Construct: Attitudes toward behavior.)

Grades 3–5

Short-Term Effects of Alcohol Use   Students can make a class list of things they like to do that require good balance (walking, running, playing tag games, dancing, doing gymnastics, playing sports, riding a bicycle, skateboarding, and in-line skating). Next, ask for a volunteer to demonstrate walking a straight line. Tape down a long piece of masking tape (15 feet) to guide the student. After the demonstration, spin the student around several times and ask him or her to try to walk the straight line again. The student will not be able to succeed at the task this time because of the balance difficulties that result from spinning. Identify loss of balance as one of the short-term effects of alcohol use. Students should discuss how loss of balance from alcohol use would affect the things they like to do now (riding a bicycle) and want to do in the future (driving a car). Help students think about this activity. While it's fun to spin around and even feel dizzy when students are playing, they wouldn't choose to feel dizzy while they are doing something that requires good balance. Make

the distinction between spinning around for fun in a safe situation and being off-balance in a situation that could cause someone to get hurt.

ASSESSMENT | For an assessment task, students can identify activities they like to do that require good balance and explain how alcohol use could keep them from doing the activities well or could cause them or others to get hurt. For assessment criteria, each child should identify at least one activity and draw a conclusion about connections between alcohol use and health. (Construct: Attitudes toward behavior.)

Drawing the Line   Bring old magazines to class for this activity. (Ask others to save magazines for you. Also check with your librarian, doctor, or dentist to get the old magazines they discard.) Students can look through the magazines and cut out pictures of products and activities that are healthful and products and activities that are harmful. Students can display their selections by gluing them onto a piece of paper or a poster, with one side of the sheet labeled "healthy for me" and the other labeled "harmful to me." Students are "drawing the line" between these concepts. Create a gallery around the room, so that students can see and discuss each other's pictures. Students should tell why they made selections for both sides of their poster. Students probably will choose pictures of people using tobacco and alcohol for the harmful side.

ASSESSMENT | For an assessment task, students can work in pairs or small groups to make their healthy/harmful posters. For assessment criteria, students should categorize correctly and explain their decisions, drawing conclusions about connections between behaviors and health. (Constructs: Attitudes toward behavior, subjective norms.)

Remaining Drug Free   Ask students to brainstorm a list of why adolescents use drugs. Answers may include

- To feel grown-up.
- Out of boredom.
- Everyone else is doing it.
- Curiosity.
- To feel good.

Divide students into small groups and assign one of the reasons to each group. Instruct students to create a poster that counteracts their assigned reason to use drugs. For example, the group who is assigned "out of boredom" could create a list of fun or constructive activities that they can do in their free time that will help them feel better emotionally and physically.

ASSESSMENT | The group poster is the assessment task for this activity. For assessment criteria, students should present their posters to the class and explain how their ideas successfully counteract the reason to use drugs. (Construct: Attitudes toward behavior.)

Grades 6–8

Fact or Fiction   Middle school students receive many mixed messages about the use of alcohol and other drugs, particularly as they explore weight loss and performance-enhancing drugs. Students, individually or in pairs, are to select a specific weight-loss or performance-enhancing drug to explore. Have students complete a KWL Chart, identifying what they currently know (K) to be true about the drug being researched in column one of the chart. In column two, students are to identify a minimum of three things they want to know (W) about the drug. In the final column, students will use credible sources (Standard 3) to determine if what they know (K) is fact or fiction. They will then identify on their KWL Chart which pieces of information they know are fact or fiction and find answers to the three things listed in the W column providing justification as to why the sources being used are credible.

ASSESSMENT | Students will write a Three-Minute Pause, which is a chance for students to reflect on the concepts and ideas they have learned and organize their thoughts, in which they answer all or some of the following questions:

- The health risks of using weight-loss or performance-enhancing drugs . . .
- I changed my attitude about . . .
- I became more aware of . . .
- I was surprised about . . .
- I still wonder . . .
- In conclusion, I believe weight-loss or performance enhancing drugs . . .

Students should provide accurate information and draw conclusions about what they learned in their research and the connections between behavior and health. They also should be able to cite their resources and be able to state why their sources used in their KWL Chart are valid sources of information. (Construct: Attitudes toward behavior.)

Help Us Learn What We Want to Know: Real AOD Questions from a Real Seventh-Grade Classroom Seventh-grade health education teacher Donna Rodenhurst shared this learning strategy for alcohol and other drugs from her standards-based classroom in Kaneohe, Hawaii. Rodenhurst asked her students to put their heads together to decide exactly what *they* wanted to know about various kinds of alcohol and other drugs. After class discussions, the students compiled the following list of questions:

When was it made? How long has it been around?

Where did it come from?

Who created it?

What are the effects on the body? What happens when you take it?

Why do people use it?

What are other names (street names) for the drug?

Who uses it? What percentage of people use it?

How much does it cost?

How is it taken?

What may have influenced people to take the drug?

What age are most people who take it?

What form does it come in?

Why do people need it?

How do they get it?

What's its *real* purpose?

How can you tell users from others?

The students worked together in groups of four or five to access information (NHES 3) to learn core concepts (links to NHES 1) about the drug name they pulled from a bowl (Rodenhurst prepared slips of paper in advance). By working this way, no drugs were repeated, and the students were able to learn about a wide variety of AOD topics of interest to them. The students were excited to see which drug their group would draw. Rodenhurst arranged for the students to work with the school librarian to find resources and websites to answer their questions. The students created posters and presented their information orally to the class. Each group chose eight to ten questions to answer with their poster and presentation. The students said that they enjoyed this project because they had a say in what they wanted to learn.

ASSESSMENT | For an assessment task, teachers and students can work together to identify the kind of end products students could prepare to demonstrate their learning. The students in this class created posters and prepared oral presentations. For assessment criteria, students should decide what would make a "great presentation" (answering eight to ten questions in

the class list). Students should provide accurate information, draw conclusions about the connections between behavior and health, cite their resources, and explain why their resources are valid sources of information. (Constructs: Attitudes toward behavior, perceived behavioral control.)

NHES 2 | Analyze Influences

Students will analyze the influence of family, peers, culture, media, technology, and other factors on health behaviors.

ASSESSMENT CRITERIA

- Identify both external and internal influences on health.
- Explain how external and internal influences interact to impact health choices and behaviors.
- Explain both positive and negative influences, as appropriate.

Grades K–2

Nonmedicinal Alternatives to Medicine A common learning standard for young learners is to participate in shared research and writing projects. For this learning strategy, the class will conduct research on different approaches to taking care of oneself using nonmedicinal alternatives and natural remedies, such as getting plenty of rest, drinking plenty of clear fluids (such as water, juice, and broth), use of a humidifier, and so forth.

ASSESSMENT | As many of these alternatives are influenced by family values, students can create a list of nonmedicinal alternatives to treating the symptoms of cold, influenza, respiratory, or digestive issues based on the class research. Each student can then take their list home to discuss with their parents or caregivers in terms of choices their family would make. Once students have family confirmation, each student can create a digital photo collage including nonmedicinal alternatives and natural remedies that their family might use if experiencing symptoms. For assessment criteria, students should include three to four remedies their family uses as nonmedicinal alternatives and label the collage with the illness and alternatives. Nonmedicinal alternatives should reflect accurate research conducted by the class. (Construct: Attitudes toward behavior.)

What Does Stress Have to Do with Alcohol? As in other content areas, help students realize that some people use alcohol to cope with stress and problems. However, using alcohol doesn't make the stress or problem go away—it is still there. Students can give examples of stress or problems people might try to solve with alcohol and come up with healthy ways people can cope that do not involve using alcohol. This activity links to NHES 7, self-management.

ASSESSMENT | For an assessment task, students can describe the ways they know they are feeling stress or having a problem (nervous, headache, scared, frustrated, heart beats fast). For assessment criteria, students should identify three ways they know they are experiencing stress or a problem and three healthy ways to cope. (Construct: Perceived behavioral control.)

Grades 3–5

Counting Commercials With their parents' or caregivers' permission, students can watch television for one hour or a half hour and count the number of alcohol or drug commercials they see, writing down the theme or idea of each commercial. When the students return to school, ask them to discuss and identify different techniques that were used in the commercials to try to influence people to buy alcohol or drugs. Have students identify unrealistic claims and suggest alternative claims that are more truthful. Students might want to make and perform new versions of the commercials to reveal a more truthful message. Teachers can make or have students make an Observation Sheet to use while they watch commercials. The Observation Sheet can include columns for the date, the time, the program they were watching, the products advertised, and the content of the commercial. Students should have parents' or caregivers' permission to complete this activity. Remind students that commercials for over-the-counter (pain relievers) and prescription (blood pressure medication) drugs should be included in their observations, as well as advertisements for alcoholic beverages.

ASSESSMENT | The assessment task for this activity is reporting on the number and kind of commercials the students observed, as well as who they believe was the target audience (e.g., parents, doctors, teens, males, females). The list of advertising techniques in Chapter 3 can help students analyze influences. For assessment criteria, students should draw conclusions about the amount of advertising they documented for alcohol and other drugs and their response to the advertising. (Construct: Attitudes toward behavior.)

Why Are All the People in the Alcohol Ads So Good-Looking? Collect or have students collect color alcohol advertisements from magazines. Students can work in small groups to discuss what the people portrayed in the ads seem to have in common. The students might say that the people all seem to be relaxed and having fun—and they all are very attractive. Students can use the list of advertising techniques in Chapter 3 to spot the kinds of strategies alcohol makers use to make their products appear inviting. Students might note techniques such as bandwagon, snob appeal, fun and friendship, and romance. Ask students their opinions on whether the advertisements are telling the whole story of alcohol use. What kinds of problems do real people have with alcohol (alcoholism, losing a job for not showing up for work, not having enough money for food because of spending on alcohol, violent behavior in families)? What are the ads leaving out? Having students examine misleading portrayals of alcohol use is especially important, because some students might mistakenly believe that alcohol is safer than the drugs they see antiuse commercials about on television.

ASSESSMENT | As with tobacco advertising, for an assessment task students can make truth ads that mock the original alcohol ads and provide a more truthful depiction of alcohol use. Students can explain and display their advertisements in the classroom and around the school. For assessment criteria, students should point out the false claims of the original ads and how they have counteracted them with their advertisements. This activity links to NHES 8, advocacy. (Construct: Perceived behavioral control.)

Getting Support Have a discussion about the influences that encourage use of alcohol (media, friends, older siblings). Ask students to create their list of five people who will help them stay alcohol free. Next to each person's name, students should write how that person can help them stay alcohol free. Encourage students to share the list with each person they wrote down.

ASSESSMENT | The list of people is the assessment task. For assessment criteria, students should indicate how the people will help them stay drug free. (Construct: Subjective norms.)

Grades 6–8

Carousel Divide students into five groups. Tape five large pieces of chart paper or newsprint around the room with the headings "Social," "Family," "Educational," "Financial," and "Emotional." Have each group start at one of the papers to brainstorm the consequences of that type that could result from getting caught drinking alcohol or smoking marijuana. After a certain amount of time, students can rotate to the next piece of paper, read, and add new ideas. Have a class discussion about

students' perspectives on the consequences they named. Is AOD use worth it? Why or why not?

ASSESSMENT | After students get back to their original chart, they should read everything their classmates have written. For an assessment task, each group can select three important consequences that could result from being caught using alcohol or marijuana. For assessment criteria, students should share their consequences with the class and discuss how those potential consequences influence their attitudes and intentions toward using alcohol. (Construct: Attitudes toward behavior.)

Estimating AOD Use by Peers Use national, state, or local Youth Risk Behavior Survey (YRBS) data from the Centers for Disease Control and Prevention (CDC) to have students investigate the choices high school students make related to alcohol and other drug use. First, have students work in pairs or small groups to estimate the percentage of high school (or middle school, if local data are available) students who participate in the alcohol and other drug use behaviors identified in the YRBS. Next, have students examine the actual YRBS data. Students can access YRBS data at the CDC website (www .cdc.gov/HealthyYouth/YRBS/index.htm), or teachers can provide a summary of the data. Have students discuss the discrepancies between their estimates and the actual data. Also have students calculate the positive side of the data (the percentage of students who were alcohol free). Many middle school students believe that "everyone is doing it." Use YRBS data to help establish the fact that most of their peers choose healthy behaviors.

ASSESSMENT | For an assessment task, students can work in small groups to research various alcohol and other drug use data reported for the YRBS and plan a presentation on their findings to classmates. For assessment criteria, students should discuss how their findings might influence their own attitudes toward alcohol and other drug use and compare the influence of the YRBS data to other influences in their lives. (Construct: Subjective norms.)

Multicultural Sources of Resiliency Students can investigate the meaning of the word *resiliency*, which is used often in speaking about healthy influences and protective factors. Students will learn that resiliency is the ability to bounce back or recover when life is challenging. Another way to explain resiliency is as the ability of people to spring back into shape after being bent or stretched by the things that happen to them. Students can discuss how their cultural and family traditions and beliefs serve as sources of resiliency for them when the going gets tough. This kind of inquiry might be a new idea for students. Encourage them to stick with this question to explore how their cultures and families can help them bounce back during difficult times.

ASSESSMENT | For an assessment task, students can apply their ideas about resiliency from culture and family to the area of alcohol and other drug use. How do their cultures and families influence their decisions and behaviors (In my culture and family, we believe . . .)? For assessment criteria, students should identify at least three sources of resiliency they draw on from their cultures and families and explain how these sources influence their decisions and behaviors. (Construct: Subjective norms.)

What's the True Message? This is a good activity to conduct with students prior to discussing the dangers of alcohol. Place students into groups of four and electronically distribute multiple alcohol advertisements to each group. Students can use a digital markup tool to identify techniques (see "Advertising Techniques" in Chapter 3) advertisers are using to encourage people to drink the product and write a caption that depicts what they believe to be the message portrayed. Students can share the new image with the class and explain the rationale for their markups and caption. After each group has shared, direct students to count how many people in their advertisements are under the age of 25 and are attractive. Record the responses from each group. Next, have a discussion regarding the alcohol industry and alcohol advertising utilizing the following questions:

- Why would alcohol distributors want to target young people as consumers?
- What recurring themes and images do you see in alcohol advertising? Why would these appeal to young people?
- What are some of the differences in advertising for various types of alcohol (wine, beer, liquor, wine coolers.)
- Which advertisements in these collages are more effective than others? Why would you choose one product over another based on its advertisements?
- Which TV, radio, and print alcohol advertising campaigns do you remember best, perhaps even talk about the most? What elements contribute to this (humor, celebrities, music, or characters)?

After completing this discussion, continue the lesson by discussing the short-term and long-term problems associated with alcohol use. Students can use the marked-up images and class discussion to create a Facebook post or Twitter-style message that could be posted to advocate for truth in advertising.

ASSESSMENT | The edited image and advocacy message is the assessment task for this activity. For assessment criteria, the student should present their image to the class and use the advocacy message to explain how the alcohol industry targets youth to use alcohol. (Construct: Subjective norms.)

NHES 3 | Access Information, Products, and Services

Students will demonstrate the ability to access valid information and products and services to enhance health.

ASSESSMENT CRITERIA

- Access health information—Locate specific sources of health information, products, or services relevant to enhancing health in a given situation.
- Evaluate information sources—Explain the degree to which identified sources are valid, reliable, and appropriate as a result of evaluating each source.

Grades K–2

Reading Medicine Labels—Who Can Help? Identifying trusted adults who can help read and follow directions on medicine labels is a key skill that children should develop. While children should never be left to make decisions about medicine on their own, learning how to read labels, follow directions, and get help from trusted adults does help ensure safe medicine use. As a class, show students some different medicine bottles with childproof lids. Discuss the purpose of these types of lids as it relates to safety. Brainstorm with students the potential consequences of someone taking medicine that is not meant for him or her or in the proper doses. Have students share situations when a trusted adult has helped them with medicine safety, and identify who those trusted adults were. Discuss with students how they identify who a trusted adult is and have them name some examples of potential trusted adults.

ASSESSMENT | Provide students with the first frame of a comic strip. The first frame should include a picture of a child coming across a medicine bottle. In no more than four more frames, children can finish the comic strip. The comic strip should emphasize finding a trusted adult for help with what to do with the medicine bottle. For assessment criteria, students should be able to tell whom they sought out for help and why they chose that person in this situation. (Construct: Perceived behavioral control.)

Grades 3–5

Investigate School Rules Students can invite a school administrator to class to be interviewed about school rules related to alcohol and other drug use. Have students prepare questions in advance about the reasons for the rules. After the interview, students can discuss the consequences of AOD use at school and what they should do if they see AOD use at school. Students should write a thank-you letter to the administrator for spending time with them.

ASSESSMENT | For an assessment task, after the interview students can go back and answer all the questions they posed to the administrator. For assessment criteria, students should provide correct information (links to NHES 1) and explain why the administrator was a valid source of information. (Construct: Attitudes toward behavior.)

Grades 6–8

Locating Community Support Systems Locating community support systems is an important skill for students. Students can work in small groups to use online resources that locate agencies and recovery centers that could help them if they or a family member had an alcohol or other drug problem. Examples of online resources include Alcoholics Anonymous (www.aa.org), Drug Rehab.com (www.drugrehab.com/addiction/alcohol/resources), SAMHSA (www.findtreatment.samhsa.gov), Alcohol Rehab Guide (www.alcoholrehabguide.org/resources), and Recovery.org (www.recovery.org).

ASSESSMENT | For an assessment task, students can create a directory of community resources and contact information for other students and families. For assessment criteria, students should be able to explain why they selected the community resources and what services these provide. (Construct: Perceived behavioral control.)

Interviewing Adults in My Family Knowing how the important adults in their lives feel about alcohol and other drug use is important for young people. As a homework assignment, have students interview parents or caregivers about their stance on alcohol and other drug use by adolescents. Include the following questions in the interview (students can write the questions, or teachers can provide copies of the list):

- How would you feel if I started drinking alcohol at my age?
- What are the rules and consequences in our family about drinking alcohol?
- What advice do you have for me about how to deal with pressures to drink?

Students can share the results of their interviews with classmates. Ask students to reflect on what family attitudes toward AOD mean to them. In doing this activity, teachers must consider the fact that the adults in some students' families drink alcohol occasionally or often. The questions the students ask are about family beliefs and attitudes about alcohol use for young people. However, if students know that adult family members drink, they might want to ask them why the rules are different (if they are) for young people. If some adult family members express the opinion that it's okay for young people to drink alcohol, teachers should be careful not to criticize those family members. Instead, teachers can ask students what they think the best decisions are for them, and why, as they grow from teenagers to adults. Ask other students to express their support. This activity links to NHES 2, analyze influences, such as family attitudes and beliefs.

ASSESSMENT | The students' reports on their interviews are the assessment task for this activity. This activity combines NHES 3 and NHES 2. Students collect information and analyze how their families' beliefs and attitudes influence their behavior and intentions to behave. For assessment criteria, students should explain why the adults in their family are valid sources of information and how the information influences their decisions about alcohol and other drug use. (Construct: Subjective norms.)

NHES 4 | Interpersonal Communication

Students will demonstrate the ability to use interpersonal communication skills to enhance health and avoid or reduce health risks.

ASSESSMENT CRITERIA
- Use appropriate verbal or nonverbal communication strategies in an effective manner to enhance health or avoid or reduce health risks.
- Use appropriate skills (negotiation skills, refusal skills) and behaviors (eye contact, body language, attentive listening).

Grades K–2

Asking Adults for Help Health educators recommend teaching peer resistance and/or refusal skills in upper-elementary and middle-level grades. In lower-elementary grades, students should practice skills for clear communication to get the help they need. Students can practice telling a trusted adult when feeling uncomfortable about a situation that involves medicines or other drugs and someone other than a trusted adult. Students can practice in small groups their communication skills using requests for help from a trusted adult and help each other determine words or phrases that are effective requests.

ASSESSMENT | For an assessment task, give students various scenarios in which they need to ask for help. Ask the following types of questions of students related to the scenarios: How would you ask for help? How would you ask a teacher for help? How would you ask the nurse for help? How would you ask your parent or guardian for help? Students can work in pairs to demonstrate how they would ask for help for their given scenario. For assessment criteria, students should give a clear message about needing help. (Construct: Perceived behavioral control.)

Nonverbal Communication Skills Small children understand and enjoy the idea of nonverbal communication—body language. Students can demonstrate different messages without saying anything aloud ("Stop," "No," and "I'm sad"). Students can stand and practice as a group. They also might enjoy portraying a particular idea they have chosen and having their classmates guess what they are saying. Although this activity is not specific to alcohol and other drug use, learning to use nonverbal communication is a building block for communicating clear refusal skills as children grow older.

ASSESSMENT | For an assessment task, students can work in pairs to demonstrate a nonverbal message to their classmates. Classmates can try to guess the message that is being communicated. Teachers can write different messages on slips of paper for students to pick (We need you to come with us, We're confused, We're so tired), or students can decide on their own messages. For assessment criteria, students should communicate their message clearly to others without using any words. (Construct: Perceived behavioral control.)

Grades 3–5

Effective and Ineffective Refusals Students might have learned and practiced peer resistance and/or refusal skills in other content areas. Now they can apply their skills to alcohol and other drug use. Students can work in groups to write scenarios in which they are pressured to try alcohol or other drugs. Have them exchange their scenarios with other groups, who

will rehearse and demonstrate effective and ineffective refusals for dealing with the situations. Each group can read their scenario to the class and then demonstrate both effective and ineffective peer pressure resistance techniques. For example, repeated refusals (no, not interested . . . no thanks . . . no, not for me . . .) can be an effective technique, while giving a mixed message (well, okay . . . no, stop . . . well, maybe . . .) can be ineffective.

ASSESSMENT | Students can use the peer pressure resistance techniques in Chapter 3 in their demonstrations of communication strategies. For assessment criteria, students should demonstrate and explain the difference between effective and ineffective techniques. (Construct: Perceived behavioral control.)

Talking with Friends About AOD Decisions Students might find themselves in situations in which they want to talk with friends about decisions their friends are about to make. How can students help their friends make a healthy decision without turning them off? Create or have students create scenarios in which a friend is considering alcohol or other drug use or is going to a location where AOD likely will be used. Students can work in pairs to write a scenario in which they know that a friend will be making a decision about using alcohol or other drugs (being invited to ride with a group of students who smoke pot on the way to and from school). As a class, students can discuss ways of communicating that are agreeable, as well as ways of communicating that turn them off. With this discussion in mind, students should decide on a way to talk to their friends about making a healthy decision in a way they think their friends will hear and consider tuning out. Students can explain their scenarios and communication plans to the class and ask for feedback.

ASSESSMENT | For assessment criteria, students should demonstrate a clear message and appropriate communication behaviors (eye contact, a respectful tone, attentive listening, restatement of friends' points of view, alternatives, and expression of needs, wants, and feelings). (Constructs: Subjective norms, perceived behavioral control.)

Grades 6–8

Saving Face One of the important aspects of communication and resistance skills is staying safe while maintaining relationships—saving face for oneself and for others. Middle-level students do not want to call attention to themselves as being different. Resistance skills should allow them to take healthy actions without appearing foolish or uncool to their friends and peers. Students can brainstorm situations they want to avoid or get out of while still appearing to be just like other kids. For example, a new student at school gets offered a drink of alcohol at the first party he or she attends. How can the student maintain new relationships and still say no? Teachers need to express their understanding that saving face is important for adolescents. Ask students what "saving face" means to them, and ask them to talk about verbal and nonverbal communications that do and do not help save face. What kind of communication works with kids their age? What turns them off or makes them potential targets of ridicule?

ASSESSMENT | For an assessment task, small groups of students can demonstrate a scenario that shows different ways to avoid or get out of a difficult situation. For assessment criteria, students should demonstrate communication that saves face and communication that does not, explain the difference, and make recommendations on communication to classmates. (Construct: Perceived behavioral control.)

Compare and Contrast Communication Skills Middle-level students enjoy the challenge of comparing and contrasting the use of communication and resistance skills in different risk areas. For example, students might politely say to a favorite aunt that they are just too full to eat another piece of pie. However, that particular resistance statement would hardly work for refusing alcohol or tobacco. In that case, students might say "Nah, not right now. Let's go shoot some hoops." That statement might work well for refusing substances, but what would work best for refusing sexual pressures or not wanting to gossip about or fight with another student? Students can try communication statements from one scenario in another. Do they still work? How can communication be changed and targeted to be most effective?

ASSESSMENT | For an assessment task, students can select one of the peer pressure resistance skills (give an excuse or reason, strength in numbers, suggest alternatives) from Chapter 3 and plan a demonstration of the skill in three different pressure situations (pressure to try marijuana, to shun another student, to shoplift). For assessment criteria, students should compare and contrast the use of the skill across the three situations. How was the skill the same or different in the way they used it in each situation? (Construct: Perceived behavioral control.)

NHES 5 | Decision Making

Students will demonstrate the ability to use decision-making skills to enhance health.

ASSESSMENT CRITERIA

Reach a health-enhancing decision using a process consisting of the following steps:

- Identify a health-risk situation.
- Examine alternatives.
- Evaluate positive and negative consequences.
- Decide on a health-enhancing course of action.

Grades K–2

Everyday Decisions Young children need to see themselves as being able to make a difference in what happens in their lives—to have some responsibility and power to make decisions and act on them. Introduce the idea of decision making by asking students to name decisions they make each day. Many decisions are made for children (what to eat, where to go). However, children should be able to think of decisions they make for themselves, such as choosing the clothes they wear to school, the books they read for pleasure, the colors and paints they use in a picture, and the games they play at recess and after school. Provide young children with various opportunities to make decisions for themselves, such as deciding which of two tasks to do first, with the understanding that both must be completed, and choosing between joining a game of tag, playing catch with different-size balls, or jumping rope during recess. Although this activity isn't related specifically to alcohol and other drugs, children should begin acquiring the skill and responsibility of decision making at an early age.

ASSESSMENT | For an assessment task, students can make a class list of decisions they are allowed to make at home and at school. Teachers might need to help students realize that they make more decisions than they think they do. For assessment criteria, students should describe what they think makes a smart decision or a not-so-smart decision. Students also should describe healthy and not-so-healthy decisions and explain the difference. Students should be able to describe at least two smart or healthy decisions they make on a daily basis and explain how they know their decisions are smart or healthy. (Construct: Perceived behavioral control.)

Grades 3–5

The Decision Is Yours Read the first part of the book (or a similar type of choose-your-own-ending book) *Under Whose Influence?: A Decision Is Yours Book* by Judy Laik (see the Children's Literature

section) to the class following a lesson on the steps in the decision-making process (see Chapter 3). Allow students to use the question presented at the first decision point to explore the situation personally. In a written response, have students make a decision of what he or she will do while demonstrating the ability to apply the formal decision making process to the situation.

ASSESSMENT | The student-written response to the decision posed is the assessment criteria. For assessment criteria, students should identify the decision to be made, determine if help is needed in making the decision, explain how family and peers may influence the decision, identify options and their potential outcomes related to the decision, choose an option and provide justification as to why that choice will lead to a health-enhancing outcome, and describe the final outcome of the decision. (Constructs: Attitudes toward behavior, perceived behavioral control.)

Ask My Parent/Guardian Parents and guardians can be excellent resources for advice regarding decisions. Students should ask their parents what steps they take when making important decisions in life. Then, students should ask parents what is important to consider when making decision about what to put in their bodies (food, drugs, etc.). Together, parents and their child can create a checklist for making decisions like these. When students bring these in to school, they should discuss their checklist items with a partner and why they chose these items. The teacher should then facilitate a class discussion and see what items were similar across students' checklists.

ASSESSMENT | The assessment task for this strategy is the items students identified and wrote down with their parents. Next to each item, students should indicate why they chose these items with their parents for a decision-making process. (Construct: Intention to act in healthy ways)

Grades 6–8

VICTORE-E Decision-Making[85] During the middle school years, it is helpful for students to begin learning about decision-making processes. A simple strategy for making decisions about various health-related decisions, especially those around drug use, is the VICTOR-E model. The letters meant the following: V-Vision, I-Identify the decision, C-Consider the effects of the decision on your vision, O-Oppose or Defend your decision, R-Reflect on your choice, E-Evaluate the decision. The steps begin with students describing the vision they have for their future (who do they want to be and what do they want to do?). The teacher should then describe a scenario involving a drug that middle school students may be exposed to. Students should then look up the effects of this particular drug using the National Institute of Drug Abuse (NIDA) drug chart found at: https://www.drugabuse.gov/drugs-abuse/commonly-abused-drugs-charts. Then students can consider what effect the drug may have on their vision. Finally, students should complete the rest of the steps from the VICTOR-E model.

ASSESSMENT | The assessment is how well students were able to "consider the effects of the decision on their vision," which should include information gathered from the NIDA website. Each step of the model should be clearly articulated and described. (Constructs: Intention to act in healthy ways, perceived behavioral control.)

Decisions Puzzle—How Do the Pieces Fit? The Centers for Disease Control and Prevention—Division of Adolescent and School Health prepared a series of reports looking at the association between certain health-risk behaviors and academic grades. For example, a graph is presented showing the percentage of students who drank alcohol for the first time prior to age 13 and the type of grades earned (mostly As, Bs, Cs, etc.).

Data are reported for five major risk behaviors. Go to www.cdc.gov/healthyyouth/health_and_academics/ to access these reports. Teachers can share the data with students to begin a discussion on how alcohol and other drug use might be associated with other risk behaviors (content of Chapters 5 to 14) and the various potential consequences, including grades. Write on poster paper the different risk behaviors such as those associated with Chapters 5 to 14 (e.g., violence [fighting], tobacco use, early or unsafe sexual behaviors). Assign small groups one of the risk behaviors and have students discuss how decisions about alcohol and other drug use might be connected to the risk behavior or across risk behaviors. Students can share their possible connections with the class.

ASSESSMENT | For an assessment task, students can design a graphic of some kind to illustrate the possible connections they have made between decisions to use alcohol and other drugs and behaviors in other content areas. For an extension, students can conduct a Web search to find out whether any of their hypotheses have been documented in studies on alcohol and other drug use. For assessment criteria, students should work through the decision-making model in Chapter 3 to discuss how alternatives and consequences related to one decision (alcohol and other drug use) can affect alternatives and consequences in other content areas. (Construct: Attitudes toward behavior.)

NHES 6 | Goal Setting

Students will demonstrate the ability to use goal-setting skills to enhance health.

ASSESSMENT CRITERIA

- Goal statement—Give goal statement that identifies health benefits; goal is achievable and will result in enhanced health.
- Goal-setting plan—Show plan that is complete, logical, and sequential, and includes a process to assess progress.

Grades K–2

Healthy Goals   Begin building the idea of setting and reaching goals over a short period of time. During the morning, have children choose a goal for the day. The goals can be individual or group goals. For example, the entire class might set a goal of using kind words for the entire day. Have children assess their progress at the end of the day. For a whole week, individual children might choose brushing their teeth each day before school or eating breakfast every morning. Have children assess their progress at the end of the week and talk about how they feel about how things went for them. How did they feel when they did or didn't reach their goal? What would they do next time? Although this activity isn't related specifically to alcohol and other drugs, setting and reaching goals that children select for themselves can help build healthy habits.

ASSESSMENT | For an assessment task, students can select a class goal for the day. Students should state the goal in clear terms (so they will know whether they've achieved it) and identify steps they will take during the day to reach their goal, people who can help them meet their goal (supports), and people or situations that might make it hard for them to meet their goal (barriers). At the end of the day, students should reflect on how they did in meeting their goal. For assessment criteria, students should be able to answer questions about steps they took to meet their goal, supports and barriers, and how they did. (Construct: Perceived behavioral control.)

Grades 3–5

In the News   Students can monitor current national or local news stories online for two weeks and bookmark stories related to alcohol and other drug use. Alternatively, teachers can provide newspapers for students to search for articles in class, or can clip articles for students to review in class. Teachers should be mindful of students' family and community connections and omit articles that could affect class members personally. Students can share their articles with class members by creating a blog post that links to the articles. Students likely will find articles related to motor-vehicle crashes, pedestrian injuries, violence, and arrests. Ask students how the consequences they found in the articles could affect their short-term goals (playing in a soccer match this week).

ASSESSMENT | For assessment criteria, students should use the blog post to identify the consequences of alcohol and other drug use in the articles and explain how the articles affect their decision making about alcohol and other drug use. In addition, students should describe how their important goals (playing sports, becoming an artist) could be adversely affected by the outcomes in the articles if they were involved in the situations under discussion. Students can practice their digital citizenship skills by commenting to each post and including their own goals that would also be adversely affected. (Construct: Attitudes toward behavior.)

Grades 6–8

Overcoming Barriers to Being Drug Free   Teachers can invite, or have students write a letter to invite, a police officer or judge to class to discuss the laws related to alcohol and other drug use, including issues such as underage drinking, fake identification use, and riding in the car with a driver under the influence. Students should be allowed to ask questions they really want to ask. Students can then reflect on how these legal consequences might impact their personal goals. Following the discussion and reflection, ask students to set personal goals associated with staying drug free throughout their school years. Goal setting can include participating in activities that require a young person to remain drug free to participate, such as athletic teams and other performing or school-associated clubs. A discussion on barriers and strategies to overcome barriers to achieving goals should follow the setting of goals. The information gleaned from the guest speaker can provide context for the discussion on barriers to goal setting and overcoming these barriers.

ASSESSMENT | For an assessment, students will determine a minimum of three barriers to achieving their goal (see Chapter 3 for information on barriers). They will then need to generate at least two strategies for overcoming each barrier. Students can present their barriers and strategies for overcoming the barriers through a photo journal including one introductory photo of their goal. For each picture, students can create a caption to describe the photo. Assessment criteria should focus on a goal that is health enhancing and associated with living a drug-free lifestyle, barriers that are realistic and relevant to the goal, and strategies that are realistic for overcoming barriers. The photo journal should demonstrate the ability to set a health-enhancing goal and strategies for achieving it. (Constructs: Attitudes toward behavior, perceived behavioral control.)

AOD and Families   Students can talk in small groups about how alcohol and other drug use can affect family life. Teachers should make an agreement with students that no one will identify individuals or families by name. Students can share their group discussion with the rest of the class. Have students reflect on how the consequences of AOD use on families might affect their decisions about AOD use. Ask students to set personal goals about staying alcohol free throughout their school years.

Students can work in small Two groups to complete a Lōkahi Wheel (see Chapter 1) showing how alcohol and other drug use can affect families in terms of the following areas: physical/body, friends/family, thinking/mind, spiritual/soul, work/school, and feelings/emotions. Students can share and compare their wheels with other groups. Alternatively, the six parts of the wheel can be used in a carousel activity in which students rotate to different posters on signal.

ASSESSMENT | Some students will have experienced problems in their families or in families close to them related to alcohol and other drug use. Be sure to set ground rules that no one will refer to a family member or other individual by name. For an assessment criteria, students should discuss each component of the Lōkahi Wheel in relation to how it would affect their decisions about using alcohol and other drugs and the possibility of reaching important goals in the future. (Constructs: Attitudes toward behavior, perceived behavioral control.)

NHES 7 | Self-Management

Students will demonstrate the ability to practice health-enhancing behaviors and avoid or reduce health risks.

ASSESSMENT CRITERIA

- Application (transfer)—Initiate health-enhancing behaviors; apply concepts and skills appropriate and effectively.
- Self-monitoring and reflection—Monitor actions and make adjustments; accept feedback and make adjustments; able to self-assess, reflect on, and take responsibility for actions.

Grades K–2

Poison-Proof Your Home   As a homework assignment, have students take home a checklist (Figure 12–3) to complete with their parents or caregivers. This activity provides an opportunity for parents and caregivers to reinforce medicine and product safety at home and to take corrective action as needed. Students can report back to classmates on the results of this activity.

ASSESSMENT | The Poison-Proof Your Home checklist is the assessment task for this activity. For assessment criteria, students should explain the safety precautions that were and were not in place in their homes and the actions their families will take to make improvements. (Construct: Perceived behavioral control.)

It's Okay to Ask for Help   As children grow up and gain independence, they often want to do things for themselves. While some things are okay to do independently, others need adult supervision. Brainstorm with students different health-related situations in which help from adults is not necessarily required (e.g., getting a snack, brushing teeth, putting on a seatbelt). Then have students generate a list of situations that do require adult supervision and discuss why these situations should be supervised by an adult (e.g., taking medicine, preparing a meal).

ASSESSMENT | Write the different scenarios generated that do require adult supervision on separate slips of paper (enough for pairs of students to draw at least one). Students role-play asking a parent or trusted adult for help (links to NHES 4). Feedback can be provided to pairs of students on how to improve their requests for help. For assessment criteria, students should apply communication skills effectively as well as be able to receive feedback and adjust their action based on the feedback. (Construct: Perceived behavioral control.)

Grades 3–5

Avoiding or Getting Out of Pressure Situations   In upper-elementary school, some students begin to experience pressures to use alcohol and other drugs. Students find themselves in situations they perhaps could have avoided or gotten out of by thinking through various scenarios in a safe classroom environment. Dealing with pressure situations often

involves NHES 4, interpersonal communication. However, avoiding and getting away from risky situations also involves actions, such as going elsewhere or getting a ride home with someone who isn't drinking. Ask students to describe AOD pressure situations that students their age might encounter. For each pressure situation, students can brainstorm and discuss various self-management strategies they could plan in advance and use in situations that arise. Students should talk about what they believe will work in real situations. Teachers should acknowledge that sometimes adults have ideas about what works and students have other ideas. Teachers should listen to students' ideas about what is real and relevant to them.

ASSESSMENT | For an assessment task, students can work in small groups to participate in a behavioral rehearsal. Each group should identify a realistic situation that might occur related to alcohol and other drug use. Students should script and rehearse the self-management strategies they choose (carry money for a phone call or a cell phone). Students can perform their behavioral rehearsals up until the point at which a self-management strategy is needed and then freeze the action (some performing arts educators call this a tableau) while classmates give advice on what to do. After classmates have given advice, the group should finish their dramatization to demonstrate the self-management strategy they chose during rehearsal. For assessment criteria, the performing students should explain which self-management strategy they think would work best for them and why. (Construct: Perceived behavioral control.)

Preventing Inhalant Use: Reading Labels and Following Instructions   The National Inhalant Prevention Coalition (www.inhalants.org/teacher.htm) offers a link called "Tips for Teachers," designed to help educators talk with different age groups about inhalant use. The site recommends starting prevention efforts by age 5 and linking inhalants to safety and environmental issues. Teachers must be especially careful not to give details on "how to use" or trendy products being abused. For grades 3 to 5, teachers are encouraged to try strategies such as discussing the term *toxic,* teaching about the importance of oxygen to life, and reading labels and following instructions. For this activity, bring a variety of empty, and clean, product containers to class for students to practice reading labels and to discuss how to follow instructions. Students should note the warnings the labels include and discuss why these are important to follow for their own health and a healthy environment.

ASSESSMENT | Students are learning self-management skills when they read labels and follow directions. They also are accessing information (NHES 3) from labels in this activity. For an assessment task, students can work in pairs to explain a label to the class. For assessment criteria, students should tell their classmates the correct steps for using the product and any warnings they should be aware of about harm to their health or the environment. (Construct: Perceived behavioral control.)

Grades 6–8

Changing a Habit   To help students understand how difficult it is to change a behavior, such as drinking alcohol, have students start by defining the word *habit*. Then have students choose a current habit that they want to change, such as nail biting, procrastinating in doing homework, or drinking soda each day after school. Teachers should be sure that the habits students choose are appropriate targets for change. Have students design a daily log sheet to record the steps they take and their progress. Link this activity to NHES 5 and 6, decision making and goal setting, in setting clear and measurable steps for achieving their goals. Students can record their progress for a given period of time (two weeks) and report back to the class on what helped (supports) and what hindered (barriers) their progress. Although stopping alcohol use is much more difficult for an alcoholic than students' projects will be for them,

Note to Parents

Name _____ Date _____

Dear Parent or Guardian,

Today in my class we learned about SAFE things and UNSAFE things. I have several "SAFE" and "UNSAFE" labels for us to properly label various substances in our home. I also have a checklist to help us keep our home safe.

Please help me complete the checklist and sign this form so I can return them both to school tomorrow.

Thank you very much.

_____
signature of parent or guardian

WE'RE PUSHING FOR A DRUG-FREE STATE
TEXAS EDUCATION AGENCY

Name _____ Date _____

Poison Proof Your Home

With your parents' help, check your house for unsafe areas.

☐ Keep drugs, poisons, and other dangerous substances (such as paint, charcoal lighter fluid, gasoline, and cleaning supplies) out of reach of children and pets. If possible, store these items in locked cabinets.

☐ Read all labels carefully.

☐ Clearly label all poisonous substances.

☐ Store poisonous substances away from food or food containers.

☐ Protect utensils and food when spraying chemicals such as bug spray and cleaning solutions.

☐ Date all drug supplies when you buy them.

☐ Keep medicines in original labeled bottles; do not transfer them into unlabeled bottles.

☐ Clean out the medicine cabinet regularly to remove outdated medicines and prescriptions.

☐ When you throw away drugs and medicines, flush them down the toilet or discard them in containers that cannot be reached by children or pets.

☐ Keep a poison control kit in the house in case an accidental poisoning happens.

☐ Make sure that all family members know what to do in case of a poisoning emergency.

WE'RE PUSHING FOR A DRUG-FREE STATE
TEXAS EDUCATION AGENCY

FIGURE 12–3 | **A Homework Assignment to Be Done by Parents and Children Together to Teach Medicine and Product Safety**

SOURCE: Texas Education Agency

their experiences can help students grasp the idea that preventing a negative behavior is easier than trying to change a behavior that has become a habit.

ASSESSMENT | The records students keep and their reflection on their experiences are the assessment task for this activity. Ask students to share with each other throughout the designated time period and offer support for each other. For assessment criteria, students should reflect on and write about (1) the habit they chose and why; (2) the plan they made, with specific steps; (3) the supports and barriers they prepared for and those they encountered unexpectedly; and (4) an assessment of their progress, including any next steps. (Construct: Perceived behavioral control.)

■ **Real-World Strategies for Staying Safe** Middle school students can consider more complex scenarios involving alcohol and other drug use that they might have to manage. For example, what if they get to a party and unexpectedly find alcohol on the scene? What if the person they are supposed to ride home with is drinking? Students can plan ahead by visualizing scenarios that might put them at risk and taking actions to stay safe. Students can make agreements with parents, caregivers, or other adult family friends to come and get them if they are stranded. To do this, students need to carry money for a phone call at all times or carry a cell phone. Students also might say that they should carry money for bus or cab fare. Enlisting the support of friends who don't drink or use drugs is another self-management strategy students might use (using strength in numbers).

ASSESSMENT | An important aspect of this activity is allowing students to explain situations that have happened to them or that they know have happened to others. The idea is to try to think ahead to envision tough situations they might have to manage. For an assessment task, students can work in pairs to draw a cartoon of a situation and a self-management strategy for getting out of the situation safely. For assessment criteria, students should illustrate all the steps they would take to put their self-management strategy into action. (Constructs: Subjective norms, perceived behavioral control.)

NHES 8 | Advocacy

Students will demonstrate the ability to advocate for personal, family, and community health.

ASSESSMENT CRITERIA
- Health-enhancing position—Give clear, health-enhancing position.
- Support for position—Support position with facts, concepts, examples, and evidence.
- Audience awareness—Show awareness of target audience; choose words, tone, and examples to suit audience.
- Conviction—Display conviction for position.

Grades K–2

Please Be Safe! Young children are very aware of the health habits of trusted adults and other important people in their lives. Young people can begin learning the skill of advocacy by selecting a health behavior a loved one is involved in that they are concerned about (e.g., riding in the car with friends who have been drinking, driving after drinking, not following medicine safety) and creating an advocacy message especially for that individual. Students can brainstorm different ways to share their message—a card, poster, song, and so on.

ASSESSMENT | The advocacy message students create (song, poster, card, etc.) is the assessment task for this activity. For assessment criteria, students should communicate a clear message, back it up with accurate information, target their audience, and show conviction. (Constructs: Subjective norms, perceived behavioral control.)

Safe Home Week Campaign As a homework assignment, students can inspect their homes, inside and out, with their parents or caregivers to make sure that all medicine, poisons, cleaners, and automobile products are locked away or out of the reach of small children and pets. Students can report back to classmates on any changes they made at home as a result of their advocacy campaign for safety.

ASSESSMENT | For an assessment task, students can make posters for their grade or school about Safe Home Week. Students can help design a checklist for other students to use with their families to check around their homes. For assessment criteria, students should communicate a clear message about what they want other students to do and target their message to their schoolmates. (Construct: Perceived behavioral control.)

Grades 3–5

Drug-Free Posters Upper-elementary children can practice their advocacy skills specifically in relation to alcohol and other drugs. Students can work in pairs to design posters for the classroom and school that illustrate a drug-free message. Students can show healthy alternatives to AOD use and the consequences of AOD use. Arrange to have the posters displayed around the school.

ASSESSMENT | The posters the students make are the assessment task for this activity. For assessment criteria, students should communicate a clear message, back it up with accurate information, target their audience, and show conviction. (Construct: Subjective norms.)

Ready—Action! Students can work as individuals, pairs, or small groups to design a drug-free message through some type of performing art: raps, songs, poems, dance, skits, commercials, game shows, public service announcements. Provide ample time for students to rehearse before their performances. For example, students might work on this project for a certain amount of time each day for a week. Having students take the time to plan and rehearse will result in better performances than having students perform on the spur of the moment. They can make and select props or scenery that they think will add to their performance. Videotape their performances, if possible, to share with families and other classes. (Some students might be hesitant to perform in front of others. Provide alternative formats for their presentations, or work with them to find a performance format that is comfortable for them.)

ASSESSMENT | The drug-free message students present is the assessment task for this activity. For assessment criteria, students should communicate a clear message, back it up with accurate information, target their audience, and show conviction. (Construct: Subjective norms.)

Grades 6–8

Reality Check Middle-level students need to feel accepted and part of a group. Thus, if they believe that everyone is drinking alcohol, they are inclined to want to be like their friends and the students they admire. Early adolescents tend to overestimate the prevalence and acceptability of alcohol use among their peers. This activity provides an important reality check. Give each student a small slip of paper (make sure that all papers look alike) and ask students simply to write "yes" or "no" in answer to the question of whether they currently drink alcohol. Collect the pieces of paper and ask the class to predict the response (how many "yes," how many "no"). A couple of students can count the actual responses. In most cases, students' predictions will be an overestimate. Students can discuss the reasons middle-level students overestimate drinking and other risk behaviors. Teachers can ask students how they can share with other students what they learned in their reality check.

ASSESSMENT | Students might have made similar estimates when they discussed tobacco use among peers. These kinds of reality checks are important in all the content areas. For an assessment task, students can use their results to make a slogan about refusing alcohol or other drugs, including the social norm for nonuse in their class or grade. For assessment criteria, students should communicate a clear message, back it up with accurate information, target their audience, and show conviction. (Construct: Subjective norms.)

Advocating Healthy Behaviors Select, or have students select, a healthy behavior outcome from this unit, such as avoid the use of alcohol, avoid riding in a motor vehicle with a driver who is under the influence, or support others to be alcohol and other drug free. With this behavior in mind, have pairs of students develop an advocacy message for other middle school students. The class should discuss what would make a message meaningful to the middle school students (e.g., use of pictures, simple words, type of message) and the type of medium most fitting for their message and the target audience (e.g., digital, posters, public service announcement over the morning announcements). Teams should then prepare a storyboard of their message that will be turned into the final product.

ASSESSMENT | The final advocacy message appropriate for the target audience (middle school) will serve as the assessment task. The assessment criteria should include the statement of a health-enhancing position and the message should be persuasive and meaningful to the target audience. (Construct: Subjective norms.)

EVALUATED CURRICULA AND INSTRUCTIONAL MATERIALS

Several evaluated commercial alcohol and drug prevention programs are available to school districts. These curricula should complement, not replace, a Comprehensive School Health Education curriculum. The evaluation results of these curricula have been reviewed by many organizations (e.g., Substance Abuse and Mental Health Services Administration [SAMHSA]) and have been shown to be effective in reducing the number of students who use alcohol and other drugs or in reducing the number of students who intend to use alcohol and other drugs. Effective, research-based prevention programs can be cost effective: each $1 invested in prevention can result in a $10 savings in alcohol and other drug treatment[86]. This section does not provide information about commercial programs that target high-risk youth; instead, it provides information on selected commercial curricula targeted toward all elementary and/or middle school youth and a summary of the evaluation results.

The National Registry of Evidence-based Programs and Practices (NREPP) is a searchable online database of mental health and substance abuse interventions. All interventions in the registry have met NREPP's minimum requirements for review and have been independently assessed and rated for Quality of Research and Readiness for Dissemination.

The purpose of NREPP is to help the public learn more about available evidence-based programs and practices and determine which of these may best meet their needs. NREPP is one way that SAMHSA is working to improve access to information on evaluated interventions and reduce the lag time between the creation of scientific knowledge and its practical application in the field.

NREPP is a voluntary, self-nominating system in which intervention developers elect to participate. There will always be some interventions that are not submitted to NREPP, and not all that are submitted are reviewed. In addition, new intervention summaries are continually being added, so the registry is always growing. Be sure to check back regularly to access the latest updates at www.samhsa.gov/nrepp

- *All Stars*. All Stars is a multiyear school-based program for middle school students (11 to 14 years old) designed to prevent

or delay the onset of high-risk behaviors such as tobacco use, drug use, violence, and premature sexual activity. The program focuses on five topics important to preventing high-risk behaviors: (1) developing positive ideals that do not fit with high-risk behavior; (2) creating a belief in conventional norms; (3) building strong personal commitments; (4) bonding with school, pro-social institutions, and family; and (5) increasing positive parental attentiveness. The All Stars curriculum includes highly interactive group activities, games and art projects, small group discussions, one-on-one sessions, a parent component, and a celebration ceremony. The All Stars Core program consists of thirteen 45-minute class sessions delivered on a weekly basis by teachers, prevention specialists, or social workers. The All Stars Booster program is designed to be delivered one year after the core program and includes nine 45-minute sessions reinforcing lessons learned in the previous year. Multiple program packages are available to support implementation by either regular teachers or prevention specialists. All Stars participants reported significantly lower average levels of inhalant use and alcohol use at post test compared with students who did not receive the program[87]. Approximately 1,750 sites are currently implementing the All Stars program, according to the program developer. The number of students who have participated in All Stars has consistently grown each year from an estimated 20,000 in 1999 to more than 1 million in 2010.

- *Good Behavior Game*. Developed in 1969 as a classroom behavior management strategy, GBG was first evaluated as a preventive intervention in a population-based randomized field trial in the mid-1980s. Since 2003, an estimated 4,000 children in the United States and internationally have received GBG through implementations led by Johns Hopkins Bloomberg School of Public Health and the American Institutes for Research (AIR). In 2010, SAMHSA awarded five-year grants to twenty-two local educational agencies in economically disadvantaged communities across the country, including tribal communities, to implement GBG. Outside the United States, GBG has been implemented and evaluated as part of randomized field trials in the Netherlands and Belgium, and it is currently being piloted in England[88].

- *Guiding Good Choices.* The Guiding Good Choices (GGC) curriculum was field-tested over two years in ten public schools in Seattle, Washington, under the name "Preparing for the Drug Free Years" before being made into a video-assisted program for wider distribution in 1987. A multicultural population of Hispanic, African American, Samoan, American Indian, and white families was represented in that initial trial. Since 1987, GGC workshops have been delivered to urban, suburban, and rural families in all fifty states and the District of Columbia, Puerto Rico, and the U.S. Virgin Islands, as well as in Canada, Cyprus, the Netherlands, Spain, Sweden, and the United Kingdom. In 1993, GGC was implemented as part of an experimental, longitudinal study in rural Midwest communities. The curriculum developer estimates that more than 313,820 families have been served by GGC since 1987.[89]

- *Life Skills Training.* The Life Skills Training (LST) curriculum focuses on resistance skills training within the context of broader personal and social skills. There are fifteen core sessions in sixth or seventh grade, with ten booster sessions the second year and five booster sessions the third year. The program focuses primarily on drug resistance skills and information, self-management skills, and general social skills. It has more published evaluations than any other curriculum.

Broad dissemination of LST began in 1995. Since then, an estimated 50,000 teachers have implemented the curriculum, but implementation varies: some sites have implemented LST for five years or longer. LST has been extensively evaluated in more than thirty scientific studies involving more than 330 schools or school sites and 26,000 students in suburban, urban, and rural settings. Most of these studies were conducted by Dr. Gil Botvin and colleagues at Weill Medical College of Cornell University. To date, at least seven independent evaluation studies have been conducted by external research groups.

School-level analyses showed that annual prevalence rate was 61 percent lower for smoking and 25 percent lower for alcohol use at the posttest assessment in schools that received the prevention program when compared with control schools. In addition, mean self-esteem scores were higher in intervention schools at the posttest assessment relative to control schools. Findings indicate that a school-based substance-abuse prevention approach previously found to be effective among middle school students is also effective for elementary school students.

The evaluations of the program showed a reduction in tobacco, alcohol, and marijuana use by 50 to 87 percent. Long-term evaluation found significantly lower smoking, alcohol, and marijuana use six years after the initial baseline assessment. The prevalence of cigarette smoking, alcohol use, and marijuana use for students who received the program was 44 percent lower than for control students, and their weekly use of multiple drugs was 66 percent lower (www.blueprintsprograms.com/factsheet/lifeskills-training-lst).[90, 91]

- *Michigan Model for Health.* Michigan Model for Health was first implemented in 1985 when multiple Michigan State agencies collaborated to create a coordinated program providing school-age children with information and skills related to health promotion and disease prevention. According to the results of a 2008 survey of schools, approximately 80 percent of Michigan schools implement the Michigan Model for Health, and 72 percent of all Michigan students (1.2 million) receive the lessons annually. Michigan has a network of regional school health coordinators who conduct required teacher trainings on the intervention and provide ongoing technical assistance in their respective school districts. Including Michigan, the Michigan Model for Health has been implemented in forty states.

A two-year, randomized control study of the effectiveness of the Michigan Model for Health curriculum was conducted in the 2006/2007 and 2007/2008 school years. It involved over 2,500 students and 300 teachers in grades 4 and 5 across over 50 schools in Michigan and Indiana.

Results showed that students who received the Michigan Model for Health curriculum showed significant, positive changes compared to a randomized control group of students who did not receive the program. Specifically, students who received the Michigan Model had better interpersonal communication skills, social emotional skills, and self-management skills; improved pro-safety attitudes; stronger drug and tobacco refusal skills; less reported alcohol and tobacco use in the past thirty days; and enhanced knowledge and skills in physical activity and nutrition.[92]

- *Project ALERT.* The Project ALERT curriculum is a two-year curriculum for grades 6 through 8 that covers information on alcohol, tobacco, marijuana, and inhalants. Consisting of eleven sessions the first year and three sessions the second year, this program emphasizes the development of resistance skills (both perceived or internal pressure and overt peer pressure) and helps establish nondrug-using norms.

Two major evaluations of Project ALERT have been undertaken, both by Dr. Phyllis Ellickson and colleagues at RAND Corporation. The first major evaluation involved thirty middle schools in eight urban, suburban, and rural communities in California and Oregon. The schools were randomly assigned to two treatment conditions (teacher-led, teacher plus teen leaders) and one control condition. The second major evaluation involved fifty-five middle schools in South Dakota, representing a wide variety of Midwestern communities. These schools were randomly assigned to one treatment and one control condition.

Results indicate that Project ALERT had statistically significant effects on all the targeted risk factors associated with cigarette and marijuana use and more modest gains with the pro-alcohol risk factors. The program helped adolescents at low, moderate, and high risk for future use, with the effect sizes typically stronger for the low- and moderate-risk groups. Thus, school-based drug prevention programs can lower risk factors that correlate with drug use, help low- to high-risk adolescents, and be effective in diverse school environments.

Broad dissemination of Project ALERT began in 1995. Since then, more than 50,000 teachers have been trained to deliver the intervention in an estimated 3,500 U.S. school districts.

The evaluation of this program showed a reduction in marijuana use initiation by 30 percent, a decrease in current and heavy smoking by participants of 33 to 55 percent, a 60 percent decrease in current marijuana use, and a reduction in pro-drug attitudes and beliefs; the curriculum also helped current smokers quit.[93, 94]

INTERNET AND OTHER RESOURCES

WEBSITES

Children's Safety Network Community Anti-Drug Coalitions of America
www.cadca.org

Delivering the Scientific Facts About Drug Abuse to Teens
https://www.childrenssafetynetwork.org/webinar/delivering-scientific-facts-about-drug-abuse-teens

Indiana Prevention Resource Center
www.drugs.indiana.edu

Just One Night
www.pbs.org/justone

Kids' Health—Teens
www.kidshealth.org/teen

National Center on Addiction and Substance Abuse at Columbia University
www.casacolumbia.org

National Clearinghouse for Alcohol and Drug Information
www.samhsa.gov

National Inhalant Prevention Coalition
www.inhalants.org

National Institute on Alcohol Abuse and Alcoholism
www.niaaa.nih.gov

National Institute on Drug Abuse
www.nida.nih.gov

Office of National Drug Control Policy
www.whitehousedrugpolicy.gov/index.html

Partnership for a Drug-Free America—Kids and Teens
www.drugfree.org

Pride Surveys
www.pridesurveys.com

Stop Underage Drinking: Portal of Federal Resources
www.stopalcoholabuse.gov

Substance Abuse and Mental Health Services Administration Center for the Application of Prevention Technologies Online Training
www.captonline.edc.org

Teen Health and the Media
http://depts.washington.edu/thmedia

OTHER RESOURCES

Center on Alcohol Marketing and Youth. *Underage Drinking in the United States: A Status Report, 2005* (Washington, DC: Center on Alcohol Marketing and Youth, 2005). (http://www.camy.org/_archive2015/research/Underage_Drinking_in_the_United_States_A_Status_Report_2005/_includes/status0306.pdf).

National Institute on Drug Abuse. *Drugs, Brains and Behaviors—The Science of Addiction* (Washington, DC: National Institutes of Health, 2014) (https://d14rmgtrwzf5a.cloudfront.net/sites/default/files/soa_2014.pdf).

National Institute on Drug Abuse. *Research Report Series: Marijuana* (Washington DC: NIDA, 2014) (https://www.drugabuse.gov/publications/research-reports/marijuana/letter-director).

National Research Council and Institute of Medicine. *Reducing Underage Drinking: A Collective Responsibility,* eds. R. Bonnie and M. O'Connell (Washington, DC: National Academies Press, 2014).

Office of National Drug Control Policy. *Teens and Prescription Drugs: An Analysis of Recent Trends on the Emerging Drug Threat* (Washington, DC: Office of National Drug Control Policy, 2009). (https://files.eric.ed.gov/fulltext/ED495769.pdf).

The National Academies of Sciences, Engineering, and Medicine, Health and Medicine Division, Board on Population Health and Public Health Practice, Committee on the Health Effects of Marijuana: An Evidence Review and Research Agenda. *The Health Effects of Cannabis and Cannabinoids: The Current State of Evidence and Recommendations for Research* (http://nationalacademies.org/hmd/Reports/2017/health-effects-of-cannabis-and-cannabinoids.aspx).

U.S. Department of Health and Human Services. *The Surgeon General's Call to Action to Prevent and Reduce Underage Drinking* (Rockville, MD: Office of the Surgeon General, 2007) (http://www.camy.org/_docs/resources/fact-sheets/Call_To_Action.pdf).

U.S. Department of Health and Human Services. *The Surgeon General's Call to Action to Prevent and Reduce Underage Drinking: A Guide to Actions for Educators* (Rockville, MD: Office of the Surgeon General, 2009).

CHILDREN'S LITERATURE

AGES 5–8

Birdseye, T. *Tucker.* Holiday, 1990. (ebook only)

Crosson, Denis. *Mommy's Coming Home from Treatment.* Central Recovery Press, 2009.

Palmore, Elaine Mitchell. *The Dragon Who Lives at Our House: A Story of What It Feels Like to Lose Control of Your Life.* Rising Star Studios, 2011.

Rudebjer, Lars. *Wishes and Worries: Coping with a Parent Who Drinks Too Much Alcohol.* Tundra Books, 2011.

Vigna, J. *I Wish Daddy Didn't Drink So Much.* Albert Whitman, 1988.

AGES 9–12

Black, Claudia. *My Dad Loves Me, My Dad Has a Disease.* Central Recovery Press, 2018.

Bunting, Eve. *A Sudden Silence*. Harcourt, 1990.

Byars, Betsy. *The Pinballs*. HarperTrophy, 1977.

Connor, Leslie. *Waiting for Normal*. Katherine Tegen Books, 2008.

DiCamillo, Kate. *Because of Winn-Dixie*. Candlewick Press, 2000.

Fogelin, Adrian. *The Sorta Sisters*. Peachtree, 2011.

Gantos, J. *Joey Pigza Loses Control*. First HarperTrophy, 2004.

Haydu, Corey Ann. *Rules for Stealing Stars*. Katherine Tegen Books, an imprint of HarperCollins Publishers, 2017.

Kehret, P. *Cages*. Puffin, 2001.

KidsPeace. *I've Got This Friend Who: Advice for Teens and Their Friends on Alcohol, Drugs, Eating Disorders, Risky Behavior and More*. Hazelden, 2007.

Klein, Robin. *Came Back to Show You I Could Fly*. Text Publishing, 2017.

Laik, Judy. *Under Whose Influence?* Parenting Press, 1994.

Lamb, Jody. *Easter Ann Peters' Operation Cool*. Scribe Publishing Company, 2012.

Mead, Alice. *Junebug*. Square Fish, 2009.

Paratore, Coleen. *Dreamsleeves*. Scholastic Press, 2012.

Roberts, Willo Davis. *The Old House*. Aladdin, 2016.

Voigt, C. *Izzy, Willy-Nilly*. Ballantine, 1986.

Zindel, P. *The Pigman*. Harper and Row, 1968.

ENDNOTES

1. University of Rochester Medical Center (www.urmc .rochester.edu/encyclopedia/content.aspx?Content TypeID=1&ContentID=3060; 2014).

2. Office on Child Abuse and Neglect, Children's Bureau, ICF International, "Protecting Children in Families Affected by Substance Use Disorders," 2009.

3. U.S. Department of Health and Human Services, *Guiding Principles and Elements of Recovery-Oriented Systems of Care* (https://www.naadac.org/assets/2416/sheedyck whitterm2009_guiding_principles_and_elements.pdf).

4. Alcohol Related Harm in the United States, Copyright © Alcohol Justice (https://alcoholjustice.org/images /factsheets/AlcoholRelatedHarm2014.pdf; January 2014).

5. Substance Abuse and Mental Health Services Administration (SAMHSA), 2015 National Survey on Drug Use and Health (NSDUH) (www.samhsa.gov/data /sites/default/files/NSDUH-DetTabs-2015/NSDUH-DetTabs-2015/NSDUH-DetTabs-2015.htm#tab2-19b).

6. L. D. Johnston et al., "Monitoring the Future national survey results on drug use, 1975–2017: Overview, key findings on adolescent drug use" (Ann Arbor: Institute for Social Research, The University of Michigan, 2018), 116.

7. Centers for Disease Control and Prevention, Alcohol-Related Disease Impact (ARDI) Application (https:// nccd.cdc.gov/DPH_ARDI/default/default.aspx).

8. Ibid.

9. Substance Abuse and Mental Health Services Administration, *The OAS Report: A Day in the Life of American Adolescents: Substance Use Facts Update* (Rockville, MD: Office of Applied Studies, April 29, 2010).

10. PRIDE Surveys, *Pride Surveys Questionnaire for Grades 6 thru 12 Standard Report, 2015–2016 Pride National Summary* (https://www.pridesurveys.com/customercenter /us15ns.pdf; November 14, 2016).

11. Ibid.

12. 2012 Partnership Attitude Tracking Study, MetLife Foundation (www.drugfree.org/wp-content/uploads/2013/04 /PATS-2012-FULL-REPORT2.pdf; April 23, 2013).

13. P. Anderson et al., "Impact of Alcohol Advertising and Media Exposure on Adolescent Alcohol Use: A Systematic Review of Longitudinal Studies," *Alcohol* 44 (2009): 229–43.

14. J. D. Sargent et al., "Alcohol Use in Motion Pictures and Its Relation with Early-Onset Teen Drinking," *Journal of Studies on Alcohol* 67 (2006): 54–65.

15. L. B. Snyder et al., "Effects of Alcohol Advertising Exposure on Drinking Among Youth," *Archives of Pediatrics and Adolescent Medicine* 160 (2006): 18–24.

16. National Institute on Drug Abuse (NIDA), "Trends and Statistics" (https://www.drugabuse.gov/related-topics /trends-statistics#supplemental-references-for-economic-costs).

17. T. Miller and D. Hendrie, *Substance Abuse Prevention Dollars and Cents: A Cost-Benefit Analysis* (Rockville, MD: DHHS Pub. No. SMA 07-4298, Center for Substance Abuse Prevention, Substance Abuse and Mental Health services Administration, 2008).

18. U.S. Department of Health and Human Services, *Healthy People 2020 Online Documents* (www.cdc.gov/nchs /healthy_people/hp2020).

19. C. N. Rasberry, G. F. Tiu, L. Kann, et al., "Health-Related Behaviors and Academic Achievement Among High School Students – United States, 2015," *MMWR* 66 (2017):921–27, doi: dx.doi.org/10.15585/mmwr .mm6635a1.

20. R. Cox et al., "Academic Performance and Substance Use: Findings from a State Survey of Public High School Students," *Journal of School Health* 77, no. 3 (2007): 109–15.

21. The National Center on Addiction and Substance Abuse at Columbia University, *Malignant Neglect: Substance Abuse and America's Schools* (New York: Columbia University, 2001).

22. W. Bushaw and S. Lopez, *The 39th Annual Phi Delta Kappa/Gallop Poll of the Public's Attitude Towards Public Schools* (http://journals.sagepub.com/doi/abs/10.1177 /003172170708900107).

23. National Institute on Alcohol Abuse and Alcoholism, "Why Do Adolescents Drink, What Are the Results, and How Can Underage Drinking Be Prevented?" *Alcohol Alert* 67 (2006): 1–10.

24. J. Hawkins, R. Catalano, and R. Miller, "Risk and Protective Factors for Early Alcohol and Other Drug Problems in Adolescence and Early Adulthood," *Psychological Bulletin* 112, no. 1 (1992): 64–105.

25. U.S. Department of Health and Human Services, *The Surgeon General's Call to Action to Prevent and Reduce Underage Drinking: A Guide to Actions for Educators* (Rockville, MD: Office of the Surgeon General, 2007).

26. M. Cleveland et al., "The Role of Risk and Protective Factors in Substance Use Across Adolescence," *Journal of Adolescent Health* 43 (2008): 157–64.

27. M. E. O'Connell, T. Boat, and K. E. Warner, *Preventing Mental, Emotional, and Behavioral Disorders Among Young People: Progress and Possibilities* (Washington, DC: The National Academies Press, 2009); and U.S. Department of Health and Human Services, Substance Abuse and Mental Health Services Administration.

28. S. Oesterle et al., "A Cross-National Comparison of Risk and Protective Factors for Adolescent Drug Use and Delinquency in the United States and the Netherlands," *Journal of Drug Issues* 42, October (2012): 337. (http:// jod.sagepub.com/content/42/4/337).

29. P. L. Benson, P. C. Scales, and A. K. Syvertsen, "The Contribution of the Developmental Assets Framework to Positive Youth Development Theory and Practice," in *Advances in Child Development and Behavior*, eds. R. M. Lerner, J. V. Lerner, and J. B. Benson, vol. 41 (Burlington, NJ: Academic Press, 2011), 197–230.

30. Centers for Disease Control, Division of Adolescent and School Health, *School Health Policies and Practices Study 2016* (https://www.cdc.gov/healthyyouth/data/shpps /pdf/2016factsheets/Overview-SHPPS2016.pdf).

31. School Health Policies and Practices Study (SHPPS) 2016, "2016 Overview" (https://www.cdc.gov /healthyyouth/data/shpps/pdf/2016factsheets/Overview-SHPPS2016.pdf).

32. SHPPS 2016, "Trends over Time: 2000–2016" (https:// www.cdc.gov/healthyyouth/data/shpps/pdf /2016factsheets/Trends-SHPPS2016.pdf).

33. R. Towers, *How Schools Can Help Combat Student Drug and Alcohol Abuse* (Washington, DC: National Education Association, 1987).

34. U.S. Department of Education, *Drug Prevention Curricula: A Guide to Selection and Implementation* (Washington, DC: U.S. Government Printing Office, 1988).

35. R. E. Glasgow and K. D. McCaul, "Life Skills Training Programs for Smoking Prevention: Critique and Directions for Future Research," in *Prevention Research: Deterring Drug Abuse Among Children and Adolescents*, eds. C. Bell and R. Battjes (Washington, DC: NIDA Research Monograph no. 63, DHHS publication number [ADM] 85-1334, 1985).

36. M. Goodstadt, "School-Based Drug Education in North America: What Is Wrong? What Can Be Done?" *Journal of School Health* 56, no. 7 (1986): 278.

37. W. Pan and B. Haiyan, "A Multivariate Approach to a Meta-Analytic Review of the Effectiveness of the D.A.R.E Program," *International Journal of Environmental Research and Public Health* 6, no. 1 (2009): 267–77.

38. National Institute on Drug Abuse, *Preventing Drug Use Among Children and Adolescents: A Research-Based Guide For Parents, Educators, and Community Leaders*, 2nd ed. (Bethesda, MD: U.S. Department of Health and Human Services, 2003).

39. U.S. Department of Health and Human Services, *The Surgeon General's Call to Action to Prevent and Reduce Underage Drinking* (Rockville, MD: Office of the Surgeon General, 2007).

40. L. Degenhardt et al., "Does the 'Gateway' Matter? Associations Between the Order of Drug Use Initiation and the Development of Drug Dependence in the National Comorbidity Study Replication," *Psychological Medicine* 39, no. 1 (2009): 157–67.

41. Centers for Disease Control and Prevention, "Youth Risk Behavior Survey Data Summary and Trends Report 2007–2017" (https://www.cdc.gov/healthyyouth/data /yrbs/pdf/trendsreport.pdf).

42. National Institute on Alcohol Abuse and Alcoholism (NIAAA), "Underage Drinking" (https://pubs.niaaa.nih .gov/publications/UnderageDrinking/Underage_Fact.pdf).

43. Ibid.

44. National Institute on Drug Abuse, *Drugs, Brains and Behaviors–The Science of Addiction* (Washington, DC: National Institutes of Health, 2007).

45. National Research Council and Institute of Medicine, in *Reducing Underage Drinking: A Collective Responsibility*, eds. R. Bonnie and M. O'Connell (Washington, DC: National Academies Press, 2004).

46. M. Bellis et al., "Hippocampal Volume in Adolescent-Onset Alcohol Use Disorders," *American Journal of Psychiatry* 157, no. 5 (2000): 737–44.

47. National Highway Traffic Safety Administration, *Traffic Safety Facts 2008* (Washington, DC: National Center for Statistics and Analysis, U.S. Department of Transportation, 2009).

48. U.S. Department of Health and Human Services, *The Surgeon General's Call to Action to Prevent and Reduce Underage Drinking: A Guide to Actions for Educators* (Rockville, MD: Office of the Surgeon General, 2007).

49. J. Kinney, *Loosening the Grip: A Handbook of Alcohol Information* (New York: McGraw-Hill, 2010).

50. Ibid.

51. P. Insel and W. Roth, *Core Concepts in Health*, 11th ed. (New York: McGraw-Hill, 2010).

52. L. T. Midanik et al., "Alcohol-Attributable Deaths and Years of Potential Life Lost–United States, 2001," *Morbidity and Mortality Weekly Report* 53, no. 37 (2004): 866–70.

53. P. Insel and W. Roth, *Core Concepts in Health.*

54. Kinney, J. (2015). Loosening the Grip: A Handbook on Alcohol Information. McGraw Hill.

55. Ibid.

56. National Institute on Alcohol Abuse and Alcoholism, Alcohol and Your Health. (www.niaaa.nih.gov /alcohol-health)

57. Centers for Disease Control and Prevention, *Alcohol and Public Health* (https://www.cdc.gov/alcohol/index .htm).

58. Substance Abuse and Mental Health Services Administration, *Results from the 2012 National Survey on Drug Use and Health: Summary of National Findings.* NSDUH Series H-46, HHS Publication No. (SMA) 13-4795 (Rockville, MD: Substance Abuse and Mental Health Services Administration, 2013).

59. American Academy of Child and Adolescent Psychiatry, *Children of Alcoholics*, no. 17 (http://www.aacap.org /AACAP/Families_and_Youth/Facts_for_Families /Facts_for_Families_Pages/Children_Of_Alcoholics_17 .aspx; 2011).

60. Kit for Parents, National Association for Children of Alcoholics (NACoA) (https://moyerfoundation.org /resources/family-addiction-book/).

61. Ibid.

62. M. Quackenbush, W. Kane, and S. Telljohann, American Academy of Child and Adolescent Psychiatry, *Children of Alcoholics*.

63. National Conference of State Legislatures, State Medical Marijuana Laws (http://www.ncsl.org/research/health /state-medical-marijuana-laws.aspx).

64. M. J. Paschall, J. W. Grube, and A. Biglan, "Medical Marijuana Legalization and Marijuana Use Among Youth in Oregon," *The Journal of Primary Prevention* 38, no. 3 (2017): 329–41. (https://doi.org/10.1007 /s10935-017-0476-5).

65. National Institute on Drug Abuse, *Topics in Brief: Marijuana* (https://www.drugabuse.gov/drugs-abuse /marijuana).

66. National Institutes of Health, National Institute on Drug Abuse, *Marijuana: Facts Parents Need to Know*, Revised (www.drugabuse.gov/sites/default/files/parents_mj_ brochure_2016.pdf; 2011), 62.

67. W. Hall and L. Degenhardt, "Adverse Health Effects of Nonmedical Cannabis Use," *Lancet* 374 (2009): 1383–91.

68. National Institute on Drug Abuse, *Research Report Series: Marijuana Abuse* (www.drugabuse.gov/publications /research-reports/marijuana/letter-director; 2010).

69. Ibid.

70. M. H. Meier et al., "Persistent Cannabis Users Show Neuropsychological Decline from Childhood to Midlife," *Proceedings of the National Academy of Sciences of the United States of America* 109, no. 40 (2012):E2657–E2664, doi:10.1073/pnas.1206820109.

71. Lopez-Quintero C, Pérez de los Cobos J, Hasin DS, et al. Probability and predictors of transition from first use to dependence on nicotine, alcohol, cannabis, and cocaine: results of the National Epidemiologic Survey on Alcohol and Related Conditions (NESARC). *Drug Alcohol Depend*. 2011;115(1–2):120–130. doi:10.1016/j .drugalcdep.2010.11.004.

72. Anthony JC. The epidemiology of cannabis dependence. In: Roffman RA, Stephens RS, eds. *Cannabis Dependence: Its Nature, Consequences and Treatment.* Cambridge, UK: Cambridge University Press; 2006:58–105.

73. Michigan Institute for Social Research, "National Adolescent Drug Trends in 2017: Findings Released" (http://monitoringthefuture.org/pressreleases/17drugpr .pdf).

74. National Institute on Drug Abuse, "Inhalants: What Are Inhalants?" (https://www.drugabuse.gov/publications /drugfacts/inhalants).

75. Ibid.

76. Ibid.

77. Ibid.

78. I. Burk, National Inhalant Prevention Coalition, "The Health Network," *Tips for Teachers* (www.inhalants.org /teacher.htm; 2010).

79. C. S. Florence et al., The Economic Burden of Prescription Opioid Overdose, Abuse, and Dependence in the United States, 2013, *Med Care* 54, no. 10 (2016):901–906, doi:10.1097/MLR.0000000000000625.

80. National Institute on Drug Abuse (NIDA), "Monitoring the Future Survey: High School and Youth Trends" (https://www.drugabuse.gov/publications/drugfacts /monitoring-future-survey-high-school-youth-trends).

81. Ibid.

82. Partnership for a Drug-Free America, *What Every Parent Needs to Know About Cough Medicine Abuse.*

83. L. D. Johnston et al., "Monitoring the Future National Survey Results on Drug Use, 1975–2017: Overview, Key Findings on Adolescent Drug Use" (Ann Arbor: Institute for Social Research, The University of Michigan, 2018), 116.

84. Centers for Disease Control and Prevention, *Health Education Curriculum Analysis Tool,* 2nd ed. (Atlanta, GA: CDC, 2011).

85. Erbe, R. G. (2014). Puzzle Vision. *Journal of Health Education Teaching Techniques, 1*(1), 1–12.

86. National Institute on Drug Abuse, Preventing Drug Use Among Children and Adolescents: A Research-Based Guide for Parents, Educators, and Community Leaders, 2nd ed. (Washington, DC: U.S. Department of Health and Human Services, 2003).

87. N. Harrington et al., "Evaluation of the All Stars Character Education and Problem Behavior Prevention Program: Effects on Mediator and Outcome Variables for Middle School Students," *Health Education and Behavior* 28, no. 5 (2001): 533–46.

88. S. Mihalic, D. Huizinga, and A. Ladika, *An Evaluation of the Good Behavior Game Intervention* (Princeton, NJ: Robert Wood Johnson Foundation, 2011).

89. W. A. Mason et al., "Reducing Adolescents' Growth in Substance Use and Delinquency: Randomized Trial Effects of a Parent-Training Prevention Intervention," *Prevention Science* 4, no. 3 (2003): 203–12.

90. G. Botvin et al., "School-Based Drug Abuse Prevention with Inner City Minority Youth," *Journal of Child and Adolescent Substance Abuse* 6, no. 5 (1997): 5–19.

91. G. Botvin et al., "Preventing Tobacco and Alcohol Use Among School Students Through Life Skills Training," *Journal of Child and Adolescent Substance Abuse* 12, no. 4 (2003): 1–18.

92. Michigan Model for Health Improves Student Health Knowledge, Skills, Attitudes and Behaviorsm, Educational Materials Center, Michigan State University (www.michiganmodel.org/; April 2013).

93. B Ghosh-Dastidar et al., "Modifying Pro-Drug Risk Factors in Adolescents: Results from Project Alert," *Health Education Behavior* 31, no. 3 (June 2004): 318–34.

94. Substance Abuse and Mental Health Services Administration, *Project Alert* (https://nrepp.samhsa.gov /ProgramProfile.aspx?id=155).

13

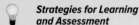

(Nicolette, age 12; Marlo, age 12)

Promoting Sexual Health

DESIRED LEARNER OUTCOMES

After reading this chapter, you will be able to ...

- **Describe the prevalence and cost of early sexual involvement and sexual risk-taking behaviors among youth.**

- **Explain the relationship between early sexual involvement and sexual risk-taking behaviors and compromised academic performance.**

- **Describe how to deal with individuals and groups who oppose sexuality education.**

- **Identify factors that influence early sexual involvement and sexual risk-taking behaviors.**

- **Summarize current guidelines and practices for schools and teachers related to sexuality education.**

- **Summarize developmentally appropriate sexuality education concepts and skills for K–8 students in the context of the National Health Education Standards and target healthy behavior outcomes.**

- **Demonstrate developmentally appropriate learning strategies and assessment techniques that incorporate concepts and skills that have been shown to reduce early sexual involvement and sexual risk-taking behaviors among youth.**

- **Identify effective, evaluated commercial sexuality education curricula.**

- **Identify websites and children's literature that can be used in cross-curricular instructional activities promoting healthy sexuality.**

INTRODUCTION

Teaching sexuality education can be interesting, exciting, and sometimes anxiety producing for teachers. It is important that teachers have a good grasp of why sexuality education is an important subject to include as part of a comprehensive health education curriculum. This introduction provides teachers with an understanding of the prevalence and cost of risky sexual behavior, how teen pregnancy can affect academic performance, the risk and protective factors associated with early risk-taking sexual activity, opposition to sexuality education, and reasons to include sexuality education at the elementary and middle levels.

Prevalence and Cost

Today's children and adolescents are faced with many serious issues and decisions regarding their sexuality. Unfortunately, they often receive mixed messages from families, peers, and the media about sexuality, which can contribute to confusion about their sexual development and related behaviors. Youth between the ages of 8 and 18 spend an average of seven hours and thirty minutes consuming media each day[1]. Types of media include TV, music, computer, video games, texting, social media use, and movies. Many of these media include messages related to sexuality. For example, a Kaiser Family Foundation study found that 68 percent of all network primetime television shows contained either talk about sexuality or sexual behavior. Those programs with sexual content averaged more than five scenes per hour with a reference to a sexuality-related topic.[2]

Research has found that heavy exposure to sexual content on television related strongly to teens' initiation of intercourse or their progression to more advanced behaviors such as "making out" or oral sex. Teens who viewed the greatest amounts of sexual content were twice as likely as those who viewed the smallest amount to initiate sexual intercourse during the following year or to progress to more advanced levels of other sexual activity.[3]

Although sexual intercourse rates among youth have declined in the past decade, a high number of preadolescents and adolescents participate in sexual intercourse and other risky sexual behaviors at a young age (Table 13–1).

Just as is true for sexually active adults, young people engaging in risky sexual behavior are at risk for pregnancy, HIV, and other sexually transmitted diseases (STDs).

The teen pregnancy rate in the United States has reached a historic low since peaking in 1990 declining from a rate of 118 per 1,000 to 26 per 1,000 in 2013 for teens 15 to 19 years old.[4] This dramatic decline is promising, however, the United States still has one of the highest rates of teen pregnancy compared to other high-income countries and pronounced disparities still exist between racial and ethnic groups in the United States.[5] Equally encouraging, the pregnancy rate for teens 14 years old declined from 17.7 to 4.8 per 1,000 from 1990 to 2011.[6]

These significant declines can be attributed to many factors including increases in the number of schools providing health education with comprehensive sexuality education as a component, increased use of contraception including birth control medications by sexually active teens, and higher numbers of teens choosing to be sexually abstinent.[7]

YRBS

TABLE 13–1

Youth Risk Behavior Survey (YRBS) Data Related to Risky Sexual Behaviors, 2017

In 2017, high school students in the United States reported the following health-risk behaviors related to risky sexual behavior.

Sexual Risk Behavior	Percent Reporting Behavior		
	Total	Females	Males
Students who have ever had sexual intercourse	39.5	37.7	41.4
Students who are currently sexually active	28.7	28.8	28.6
Had sexual intercourse before age 13	3.4	2	4.8
Had four or more sexual partners during their lifetime	9.7	7.9	11.6
Used a condom during last sexual intercourse	53.8	46.9	61.3
Used alcohol or other drugs before their last sexual intercourse	18.8	15.9	21.6

SOURCE: Centers for Disease Control and Prevention, "Youth Risk Behavior Surveillance—United States, 2017," *MMWR*, vol. 67 no. SS-8, 2017, 1–172.

It is a critical work to continue to decrease the teen pregnancy rate as it entails a considerable financial cost, with teen pregnancy costing society over $9.4 billion annually. In other words, the average annual cost associated with a child born to a teen mother is $1,682. Most of these costs are associated with negative consequences for the children of teen mothers including increased costs for health care, foster care, reliance on child welfare, and lower lifetime earnings.[8] While teen pregnancy primarily impacts partners who are engaging in vaginal intercourse, STDs are a risk for any teen of any gender engaging in any type of sexual intercourse including vaginal, oral, and anal sex. Every year, young people aged 15 to 24 acquire half of all new STDs even though teens account for only 25 percent of the sexually active population.[9] Two out of every five sexually active adolescent females have had an STD many of which have potential lifelong consequences.[10] Additionally, the cost to society for STDs is also very high. It is estimated that STDs cost the U.S. health care system $17 billion annually.[11]

Because of the high cost of teen pregnancy and STDs and the associated health problems, the federal government included the following specific-related objectives in *Healthy People 2020*:

ECBP-2. Increase the proportion of elementary and middle high schools that provide comprehensive school health education to prevent unintended pregnancy, HIV/AIDS, and STD infection.[12]

Sexual Health and Academic Performance

Teen pregnancy also creates academic problems. Parenthood is a leading cause of high school dropout among teen girls. Only about 40 percent of teens who begin families before age 18 ever complete high school.[13] Early parenting also limits young mothers' chances of getting a postsecondary education, which increases the chances that they will live in poverty. Less than

2 percent of teen mothers attain a college degree by age 30.[14] Numerous challenges also face the children of teen parents. For example, children of teen parents are 50 percent more likely to repeat a grade and to perform worse on standardized tests. They also are less likely to complete high school, compared to children with parents who delayed childbearing.[15]

Factors That Influence Sexual Health

Factors have been identified that differentiate those who participate in early risky sexual behaviors from those who do not. The factors associated with greater potential for engaging in early risky sexual behaviors, pregnancy, and STDs are called risk factors; the factors associated with a reduced potential for such activity are called protective factors. Some protective factors against early risky sexual behaviors include youth who

1. Live in a community where there is a high proportion of foreign-born residents.
2. Live with two parents.
3. Live with parents who have a high level of education.
4. Live in a home where there is a high quality of family interactions, connectedness, and satisfaction with relationships.
5. Live in a household where there is adequate parental supervision and monitoring.
6. Have parents who disapprove of premarital sex or teen sex.
7. Have parents who accept and support contraceptive use for sexually active teens.
8. Have good parent–child communication about sex and condoms or contraception, especially before the teen initiates sex.
9. Have peers who use condoms or have positive norms or support for condom or contraceptive use.
10. Have a partner who is supportive of condom or contraceptive use.
11. Are connected to school, as demonstrated by their positive attendance rates, good grades, and participation in extracurricular activities, and plan to go to college.
12. Are involved in the community.
13. Have a religious affiliation.
14. Are involved in sports (girls only).
15. Have a higher level of cognitive development.
16. Have a higher internal locus of control.
17. Take a virginity pledge.
18. Have a greater perceived male responsibility for pregnancy prevention.
19. Have a belief that condoms do not reduce sexual pleasure.
20. Believe that there are benefits to using condoms and are motivated to use condoms or other contraceptives.
21. Have confidence in the ability to demand condom use and use condoms or other contraceptives.
22. Have an intention to use condoms.
23. Perceive negative consequences of pregnancy.
24. Are motivated to avoid pregnancy and STD.
25. Are older at first voluntary sex.
26. Discuss sexual risks, pregnancy, and STD prevention with their sexual partner.[16]

Some risk factors for early risky sexual behaviors, pregnancy, and STDs include youth who

1. Live in a community where there is community disorganization (violence, substance abuse).
2. Live in a family that has experienced disruption (divorce, change to a single-parent household).
3. Live in a household where there is substance abuse.
4. Live in a household where there is physical abuse and general maltreatment.
5. Have a mother who first had sex at an early age or gave birth at an early age.
6. Have peers and close friends who are older.
7. Have an older sibling who has had sex or a sister who has given birth as an adolescent.
8. Have peers who drink alcohol, are sexually active, or have a permissive attitude toward premarital sex.
9. Have a romantic relationship with an older person.
10. Are black or Hispanic.
11. Are behind in school or having problems in school.
12. Are involved in delinquent behaviors including alcohol and drug use, being part of a gang, or carrying weapons.
13. Work in a paid job more than twenty hours a week.
14. Have depression or thoughts of suicide.
15. Have permissive attitudes toward premarital sex.
16. Date frequently.
17. Have a romantic relationship with a boyfriend or girlfriend.
18. Have a high number of sexual partners.
19. Have a history of prior sexual coercion or abuse.[17]

Opposition to Sexuality Education

Although problems regarding risky sexual behavior are well documented, not nearly enough students receive comprehensive K–12 sexuality education. Currently, at the district level, 52 percent of elementary schools, 75 percent of middle schools, and 80 percent of high schools have adopted a policy stating schools will teach human sexuality.[18] Most states and school districts teach one unit of sexuality education during a one-semester ninth- or tenth-grade health class. Studies show that sexuality education begun before youth are sexually active helps them stay abstinent and use protection when they do become sexually active.[19]

With all the sexuality issues and decisions facing young people today, why don't school districts mandate a K–12 sexuality education program? There is one main obstacle to such programming: controversy regarding sexuality education. A handful of vocal parents opposed to such instructional activities often have succeeded at keeping developmentally appropriate, quality, comprehensive sexuality education out of many school districts. Yet a variety of studies show that the majority of parents overwhelmingly support comprehensive sexuality education. One national survey found that 93 percent of junior high parents believe it is very important or somewhat important to have sexuality education as a part of the school curriculum. The same study found that 95 percent of parents of junior high students believe that birth control and other methods of preventing pregnancy are appropriate topics to teach in school.[20] Another study found that 93 percent of parents support school-based sexuality education, and 80 percent feel it should begin in middle school or earlier.[21] If the majority of parents are supportive of sexuality education in the schools, why are quality, comprehensive programs reaching only a small percentage of students? The main issue is that many administrators are nervous about the political and practical implications of teaching such a sensitive topic.

Sexuality education, or family life education, encompasses a broad scope of concepts and skills, including acquiring information about sexual development, reproductive health, interpersonal relationships, affection, body image, and gender roles and identity. It also includes skill development in areas such as communication, decision making, refusal techniques, and goal setting. Sexual health promotion programming is grounded in the premise that sexuality is a natural, ongoing process that begins in infancy and continues through life. From the moment of birth, children are learning about themselves as sexual people through the unintentional and informal messages of parents and caregivers. As children grow and explore more of their environment, they can learn about sexuality through television, friends, books, and newspapers. Given the speed of communication networks and information transfer, it is unrealistic to presume that students can be shielded from all information about sexuality until they reach adulthood. Parents and teachers cannot control a child's curiosity and desire to learn about sexuality. They can, however, empower children with formal, developmentally appropriate sexuality education experiences in the classroom environment that give students accurate, quality, and comprehensive information. Sexuality education should be a planned, intentional, and specific program of instruction that encourages parents and educators to identify the kinds of information, skills, and attitudes that are developmentally appropriate for children of different ages.

If school districts in the United States continue to be held captive by a few vocal minority groups who oppose such instruction, students likely will be forced to make sexual decisions without the benefit of the best information, skills, and support available to them. There will continue to be high rates of teenage pregnancy, STD, and HIV resulting from a lack of information, healthy attitudes, and appropriate skills regarding sexuality. Research shows that sexuality education programs do not hasten the onset of intercourse, nor do they increase the frequency of intercourse or the number of sexual partners. In fact, effective skill-based programs have been shown to delay significantly the onset of sexual intercourse and to increase contraceptive and condom use among sexually experienced adolescents.[22]

Concrete steps can be taken to minimize controversy and garner support for implementing a comprehensive sexuality education curriculum. First, determine the goals of the sexuality curriculum. For example, if the goal of the curriculum is to prevent teen pregnancies and sexually transmitted diseases, most parents would support that goal. It is important for school districts to focus the discussion around these common goals. Second, school districts should base their curriculum on sound research. Knowing current research can help support a well-written curriculum. Third, when writing a curriculum, form a broad-based, knowledgeable, and inclusive committee. This will help assure that people feel they have a voice in determining what will be included in the curriculum.[23, 24]

Reasons to Include Sexuality Education in Elementary and Middle Schools

It is important for teachers to have a solid understanding of why sexuality education is important to include in an elementary and middle school health education curriculum. It is not uncommon for parents to contact teachers about their concerns on this topic. The following reasons should help teachers formulate their own rationale for teaching sexuality education.

1. Attitudes regarding sexuality are formulated early in life, which makes them difficult to change once a person has internalized them. Children begin forming opinions about their bodies, their gender identity, and their feelings about sexuality at a young age. If parents and teachers provide children with negative messages about their sexuality when children are young, these messages generally stay with them through adulthood. For instance, if a 6-year-old girl is taught to use slang terms for body parts and functions, such as *boobs* and *pee pee,* she will probably continue to use that terminology as she gets older. Some parents and teachers feel this is not a problem, but it gives children a message that something is wrong with those body parts.

When children ask adults questions about sexuality and the adults respond, "I never want to hear you talk like that again," or "Wait until you get older," children quickly get the message that there must be something wrong with their concerns or questions about their sexuality. In contrast, when children grow up in an open and honest environment regarding sexuality and are reinforced for seeking information from significant adults rather than from peers, they have a better chance of developing healthy attitudes and appropriate sexual communication skills as they get older.

2. If factual information and skills are presented in a positive manner throughout the elementary and middle grades, negative attitudes, apprehensions, and fears about sexuality can be reduced and superseded by a positive understanding that people live as sexual beings. Unfortunately, many school districts limit sexuality education to discussing puberty and the menstrual cycle through a one- or two-day presentation during the fifth or sixth grade. Outside experts sometimes give the presentation, with the girls and boys in separate classrooms. At this age, many students have already begun going through puberty, making the presentation developmentally inappropriate. Also, students might feel uncomfortable with an outsider, might not have a question concerning puberty on that day, or might be more curious about what is happening in the opposite gender's presentation. Again, the message that students get from this type of presentation is that there is something wrong or embarrassing about sexuality because the classroom teacher is too embarrassed to talk about puberty. Further, such a strategy sends messages about communication between girls and boys on sexual issues. How are mutual respect and appropriate sexual communication to be

reinforced if boys and girls are not allowed to listen to the same presentation?

If student questions are not answered by trained professionals during that one- or two-day presentation in the fifth or sixth grade, students typically have to wait until sexuality is again formally discussed during a high school health class. Again, that gives students the message that sexuality is not important enough to discuss or that there is something wrong with developmentally appropriate curiosity and concern about the topic.

3. Information and skill development are the greatest defenses against the negative aspects of sexuality, such as promiscuity, teen pregnancy, sexually transmitted diseases, and sexual abuse. Sexuality knowledge increases when students are instructed on the topic. Also, skill-based programs can significantly delay the onset of sexual intercourse and increase contraceptive and condom use among sexually experienced youth. No studies have revealed evidence that sexuality education leads to earlier or increased sexual experience, and several indicate that it is associated with the delay of sexual intercourse.[25]

4. Schools can provide a unique opportunity for students to exchange ideas and thoughts about sexuality with their peers, under the guidance of a trained teacher. Sexuality education should take place at home, because parents can add love, security, and values to the factual information and skills being taught. Without usurping this pivotal role of the family, school-based programs can formalize student interaction with their peers about sexuality issues. Many students talk about sexuality with their friends, but in an unsupervised arena. Encouraging students to share thoughts, feelings, and questions about sexuality with their peers and a trained teacher complements the learning taking place at home.

5. Students receive a distorted view of sexuality through the mass media (see the section "Prevalence and Cost").

6. Many parents do a wonderful job of teaching formal sexuality education to their children, but some parents are so uncomfortable talking to their children about sexuality that they ignore or avoid the topic. Every student is entitled to formal sexuality education as a means of learning correct information and developing health-enhancing attitudes and skills.

GUIDELINES FOR SCHOOLS

This section provides information about current sexuality education programs and policies in elementary and middle schools. The first portion includes information about where to learn more about programs and policies in place in schools today, while the second part provides information for teachers and administrators about what should be happening in schools to help prevent risky sexual behaviors and to promote healthy sexuality among children and adolescents.

State of the Practice

The CDC conducts the School Health Policies and Practices Study (SHPPS) to assess current school health policies and programs at the state and district levels. Because pregnancy, STDs, and HIV cause so many problems for young people, it is important for states and school districts to have policies that require

prevention education in these areas. The number of states and districts requiring such policies has been documented in the current SHPPS report.[26] SHPPS also provides important data related to the pregnancy, HIV, and STD prevention education topics and skills being taught at the elementary and middle school levels.

State of the Art

Several guidelines are important to consider when teaching sexuality education. These guidelines can help school districts make decisions about their sexuality education and help teachers not be defensive with parents and students when teaching sexuality education.

School districts should establish sexuality education guidelines and policies with the input of parents, teachers, administrators, community members, and support staff. Policies might include topics such as the omission of specific students from sexuality education classes, how teachers should respond to questions about specific sexuality topics, and what teachers should do if a student questions his or her own sexual orientation. Without established guidelines and policies in place, teachers will have a difficult time determining how to manage these situations.

After creating a K–12 sexuality curriculum, it is important to determine whether it includes the information and skills that will help children and adolescents make positive sexual choices. The following ten characteristics of effective sexuality education programs can help school districts create their curriculum[27, 28]:

1. Effective programs focus on reducing one or more sexual behaviors that lead to unintended pregnancy or HIV/STD infection.
2. Effective programs are based on theoretical approaches that have been demonstrated to influence other health-related behavior and identify specific important sex antecedents to be targeted.
3. Effective programs deliver and consistently reinforce a clear message about abstaining from sexual activity and/or using condoms or other forms of contraception. This appears to be one of the most important characteristics that distinguish effective from ineffective programs.
4. Effective programs provide basic, accurate information about the risks of teen sexual activity and about ways to avoid intercourse or use methods of protection against pregnancy and STDs.
5. Effective programs include activities that address social pressures that influence sexual behavior.
6. Effective programs provide examples of and practice with communication, negotiation, and refusal skills.
7. Effective programs use teaching methods designed to involve participants and have them personalize the information.
8. Effective programs incorporate behavioral goals, teaching methods, and materials that are appropriate to the age, sexual experience, and culture of the students.
9. Effective programs last a sufficient length of time (more than a few hours).
10. Effective programs select teachers or peer leaders who believe in the program and then provide them with adequate training.

Some states and school districts have ignored these ten characteristics and have adopted abstinence-only curricula. States and school districts have opted for these programs because of pressure from minority groups and legislation at the federal level. Government funding of abstinence-only-until-marriage programs has been provided for much of the past thirty years. Funding for these programs peaked in the mid-2000s and then declined in favor of comprehensive programs. In 2016, funding for abstinence-only-until-marriage programs rose again to about $85 million.[29] At best, these programs are ineffective. Research shows that they do not result in young people delaying sexual intercourse.[30] At their worst, they can be misleading and dangerous to young people. Many of the previously funded abstinence-only programs contain false, misleading, or distorted information. In fact, an investigation reviewing thirteen commonly used abstinence-only curricula taught to millions of school-age youth concluded that two of the curricula were accurate but that eleven others blurred religion and science, and contained unproven claims and subjective conclusions or outright falsehoods regarding the effectiveness of contraceptives, gender traits, and when life begins.[31]

For their part, teachers should encourage proper terminology in the classroom. Beginning in kindergarten, students should learn the proper terms for their external body parts, including their reproductive organs. At that age, it is not important for students to know the names of their internal body parts (such as *fallopian tube* or *epididymis*), because they are concrete thinkers and have difficulty imagining what the inside of their body is like. However, as students get older, they should learn the proper terminology for internal reproductive body parts. If students are taught proper terminology at an early age, they will not be as embarrassed to say words such as *penis, testes, vulva,* and *vagina* when they get older. This will allow students to communicate about sexuality in a more comfortable manner.

Teachers do not have to know all the answers to every sexuality-related question. Students are capable of asking a variety of questions about sexuality. Because most elementary and middle school teachers do not receive adequate training in this area, they cannot be expected to know all the answers about this subject. It is appropriate for teachers to respond "I don't know" to a question, as long as they find out the answer and relay that information to the student as soon as possible. The teacher also can ask students to find the answer to the question. Perhaps a student can volunteer to find the correct answer.

Although teachers cannot be prepared for all questions asked by children, it is important for them to understand that students are capable of asking unexpected questions. If teachers act shocked when students ask questions about sexuality, the students will be less likely to ask another question in the future. A good way to overcome a shocked look is to practice answering common questions that children ask about sexuality. A sample list of questions with suggested answers can be found in the section "Recommendations for Concepts and Practice."

Teachers should teach only those topics in sexuality education that have been approved as part of their course of study by their board of education and administrators. Many teachers have felt so strongly about teaching all aspects of sexuality education that

they have jeopardized their jobs because they did not have administrative support for teaching certain sexuality topics. Such a practice can jeopardize the credibility of the entire health education program. If teachers feel that more sexuality education should be included in their curriculum, they should seek the support of their administrators, boards of education, and parents in the community.

Teachers should not use handmade drawings of the reproductive system. Students have a difficult time imagining what the internal male and female reproductive systems look like. When teachers use handmade drawings, there is a better chance that the proportions or specific organs will be incorrect. There are enough good professional drawings of the male and female reproductive systems that handmade drawings are not necessary.

Activities should be structured to include parents or caregivers whenever possible. When teaching sexuality education topics, teachers should encourage students to discuss the information taught that day with parents. This will help bridge the gap among children, parents, and schools. Teachers might even want to have specific questions written out on a handout for parents and children to discuss.

GUIDELINES FOR CLASSROOM APPLICATIONS

Important Background for K–8 Teachers

Depending on the grade level, not all of the information presented in this section is relevant to all elementary and middle school students, but teachers should have background knowledge about relationships, families, the male and female reproductive systems, and puberty.

Relationships

Students develop many relationships throughout their elementary and middle school years. Relationships with family members, same-age friends, relatives, and teachers change as children continue through elementary and middle school. It is vital that teachers have a basic understanding of the importance children place on friends as they advance through elementary and middle school.

When children first enter school at age 5, they are very self-centered and more concerned about their own needs and identity than about the needs or characteristics of others. As they progress through kindergarten, they begin to develop an increasing awareness of others. They start to understand that other people have needs and rights, too. This recognition might conflict with their early attitudes of self-gratification and might be displayed by their throwing temper tantrums and not wanting to share. Friends, and their behaviors, are not that important to students at this age.[32]

Children from age 6 to 8 begin to redirect their personal concerns to intellectual concerns and group activities. They begin to expend more energy on friendships and the community around them. Children in this age group also become less dependent on their parents, although their parents are still important to them. Most 9- and 10-year-old children accept sexuality education as they do other subjects. Many children of this age do not yet feel self-conscious about their bodies, making it an ideal time to discuss the reproductive system. At this age, boys and girls begin to regard the opinions of their friends as more important than those of their parents. Although same-sex friendships are more popular in this age group, children begin to become interested in the opposite sex. This interest typically is exhibited in the forms of teasing and aggressive behavior.[33]

Between ages 11 and 13, children become even more independent of their parents. Their friendships are increasingly more important as they try to emancipate themselves from their parents and other adult authority figures. This is a means of exploring the parameters of their own unique identities. Peer pressure becomes a major issue during this time because children are struggling with developing their own codes of morals and ethics. Preadolescents also are beginning to become more self-conscious about the physical changes to their bodies. Teachers might find it more difficult to discuss sexual issues with students of this age because of their self-consciousness. They also become more interested in the opposite sex as they get older.[34]

As sexual feelings begin to develop during puberty, it is not uncommon for students to have an increased interest in learning about romantic relationships including same-sex or gender relationships. Teachers are sometimes nervous about addressing this topic because of fear of how parents and students will react, or they may be uncomfortable with this subject themselves. As with all areas of sexuality, it is important that the teachers know what is in the course of study or curriculum before teaching about a specific topic. If the issue of gays and lesbians is included in the curriculum, teachers should have some background information on the topic.

Students should understand that people who have a sexual and/or emotional relationship with others of the same sex or gender often consider themselves to be gay. They should learn that the term *gay* can refer to two males or two females and the term *lesbian* refers to two females. It is important for young people to understand that being lesbian, gay, bisexual, transgender, or questioning/queer (LGBTQ) is normal. LGBTQ adolescents need to feel that they are okay and it is important to help prevent violence against them. It is important teachers also explain that preadolescents sometimes have attractions toward individuals of the same sex, and that this may mean that their sexual orientation is gay or these feelings may be transitory. According to the 2017 YRBS, 2.4 percent of youth identify as gay or lesbian, 8 percent identify as bisexual, and 4.2 percent are not sure of their sexual orientation.[35] If a student has concerns about his or her sexual orientation, teachers should be supportive and refer the student to an LGBTQ-friendly counselor within the school district. In addition, students should be encouraged to discuss their feelings with supportive family members. Teachers should feel secure in knowing that discussions about sexual orientation will not suddenly make someone change who they are attracted to.

Families

When discussing the family structure and the role of the family during sexuality education, the teacher should not be judgmental about different types of families and the way they function. Today's

Boys and girls should be encouraged to participate in play with a variety of toys not just those that are often considered gender-specific like tools or dolls.

families are quite different from the families of fifty to one hundred years ago. For example, in the past, extended families were common. This meant that parents, children, grandparents, and other relatives lived in the same house or in close proximity. Children had several adult role models they could depend on for love, support, understanding, and protection. Various factors have contributed to the changing structure of the family. For example, the increased mobility of families has made it difficult to maintain extended families. It was once common to grow up in a town, marry someone from that town, and raise a family in that town. Today, many people move often because of career changes and no longer live close to the town in which they were raised.

Some people believe that the "typical" or "normal" family of today is the nuclear family. A nuclear family consists of children living with both of their biological parents. Of course, many nuclear families exist, but there are many other types of families as well. People can no longer assume that the nuclear family is the norm.

Today's families are more diverse than in the past. Types of families include different sex or gender parents, same sex or gender parents, single-parent families, and families with stepparents and half-siblings. There are many single-parent families because of the high divorce rate, teenagers who become pregnant and decide not to marry, and never-married single people who are raising children. It is important that elementary and middle school teachers not assume that all students are being raised in a nuclear family and recognize that some students might have special needs because of their family situation. Students also should be taught that members of a family might not be blood-related, such as in an adoption or a remarriage. It is important that children believe they belong to a family regardless of its structure.

Children also should be taught that family members have responsibilities to one another and to the overall functioning of the family unit. For example, certain tasks need to be accomplished by a family, such as buying groceries, cooking, cleaning, and helping each other. Teachers should discuss the concept of family roles and responsibilities with their students. It is important that students understand what is most important is that each person must contribute if the family is to be nurturing, mutually supportive, and happy.

Some families still establish and reinforce clear gender roles for boys and girls—for example, the boys mow the lawn, and the girls wash the dishes.

It is not the teacher's role to judge the ways different families function. Teachers can, however, try to eliminate gender-role stereotyping in their classrooms. For example, certain chores should not be identified as being for boys or for girls. Textbooks also should be reviewed with gender-role stereotyping in mind. These activities can help balance students' attitudes about gender-roles. Allowing students to participate in all types of activities also allows them to explore interests and talents without fear of negative judgment.

The Male and Female Reproductive Systems

A general understanding of the male and female reproductive systems is an important part of sexuality education. The reproductive system is the only system in the body that has different organs for the male and the female. The following information should provide enough background for the elementary and middle school teacher about the male and female anatomy and physiology of the reproductive system. As teachers begin teaching about puberty and the reproductive system, it is important to be sensitive to students who may be experiencing gender incongruence. Gender incongruence is when a person's lived gender experience does not align with their assigned sex.[36]

The Male Reproductive System The function of the male reproductive system is to produce sperm cells, which are the male cells that can unite with female eggs to form fertilized eggs and ultimately lead to pregnancy. Both external and internal organs make up the male reproductive system (Figure 13–1).

The external part of the male sex organs, called the genitalia, is composed of the penis and the scrotum. The penis is a tubelike organ composed mainly of erectile tissue and skin. Some males are circumcised and others are not. In circumcision the foreskin of the penis is removed. Approximately 58 percent of newborn males in the United States are circumcised (see Figure 13–1a).[37] When a male becomes sexually excited, the erectile tissue in the penis becomes filled with blood, which makes it become enlarged and erect. The scrotum is the pouch-like structure hanging behind and slightly below the penis.

The major internal organs of the male reproductive system are the testes (testicles), vasa deferentia, seminal vesicles, prostate gland, Cowper's glands, and urethra.

The scrotum contains the testes and acts as a thermometer. Because the scrotum keeps the testes at a constant temperature, they can produce viable sperm. For example, if the body temperature rises, muscles in the scrotum relax to lower the testes away from the body, cooling the scrotum. Sperm are produced in a section of the testes called the seminiferous tubules. These tubules produce about 500 million sperm a day and can produce billions of sperm throughout a lifetime. After the sperm are produced, they are stored in the epididymis. After about sixty-four days, the sperm reach maturity and are capable of uniting with a female egg.

The vasa deferentia, two tubes connected to the epididymis, are used to store and transfer sperm to the seminal vesicles during ejaculation. The seminal vesicles are two small pouches near the prostate gland. Their function is to secrete a fluid, which mixes with the sperm. This fluid contains nutrients for the sperm, helps make the sperm mobile, and provides protection for them.

The prostate gland is about the size of a chestnut and is located near the bladder. It produces a thin, milky, alkaline fluid, which mixes with sperm to make semen. The alkaline fluid acts as an acid neutralizer and a coagulant.

The two Cowper's glands are about pea-size and open up into the urethra. These glands secrete a clear fluid, prior to ejaculation, that helps neutralize the urethra. This fluid can contain some sperm, and its release is not felt by the male.

The urethra is a tube that runs the length of the penis. The urethra allows both urine and semen to leave the body, but not at the same time. When semen enters the urethra, the internal and external urethral sphincters close the connection between the bladder and the urethra.

The Female Reproductive System The function of the female reproductive system is to release a mature egg, which can unite with a sperm to make a fertilized egg and ultimately create a pregnancy. Both external and internal organs make up the female reproductive system.

The external part of the female sex organs, called the vulva, is composed of the clitoris, vaginal opening, hymen, and labia (Figure 13–2a).

The clitoris is a knob of tissue located in front of the vaginal opening. It contains many nerve endings and blood vessels. When the female gets sexually excited, the clitoris becomes engorged with blood and enlarges. The clitoris is the only part of the female sexual anatomy that does not have a reproductive function, but it does produce sexual arousal.

The hymen is a flexible membrane that partially covers the vaginal opening. It has no known function and is different in every female. For example, some females have a hymen that covers a large portion of the vaginal opening, some have a hymen that is barely visible. A common myth about the hymen is that an intact hymen is a sign of virginity. This is not true, because every female's hymen is unique and, in fact, some females do not have a hymen at birth.

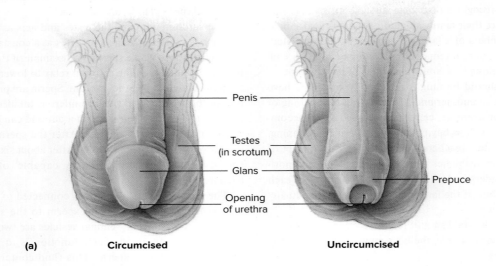

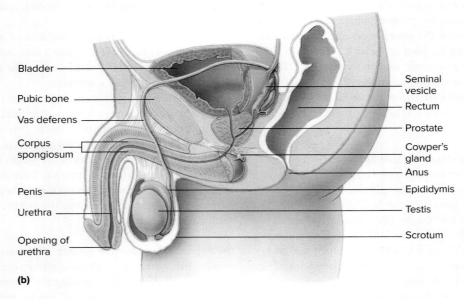

FIGURE 13–1 | **The Male Sex Organs** (a) External structures. (b) Internal structures.

The labia are folds of skin that protect the female genitals from germs entering the body. There are two labia: the labia majora and the labia minora. The labia majora are large folds of skin that surround the opening of the vagina. The labia minora are smaller folds of skin located between the labia majora.

The internal reproductive organs in the female are the vagina, uterus, fallopian tubes, and ovaries (Figure 13–2b). The vagina is a muscular tube that goes from the outside of the body to the uterus. It has three main functions: It receives the penis during vaginal sex, it is the opening for menstrual flow to exit the body, and it serves as the birth canal. It is called the birth canal because, during birth, the baby is pushed from the uterus through the vagina and out of the mother's body.

The uterus is an elastic muscle the size of a fist and the shape of a pear. The tip of the uterus, which leads to the vagina, is called the cervix. The role of the cervix is to help keep the baby inside the uterus until the time of delivery. The lining of the uterus is composed of many blood vessels. About once every month, this lining thickens and turns into a nourishing place for a fertilized egg to develop into a baby. If an egg is not fertilized, the thickening material disintegrates because it is no longer needed. The fluid and membrane then leave the body through the vagina; this process is called menstruation or having a period.

There are two fallopian tubes, which curl around the ovaries and connect to the uterus. The fallopian tubes are narrow and are

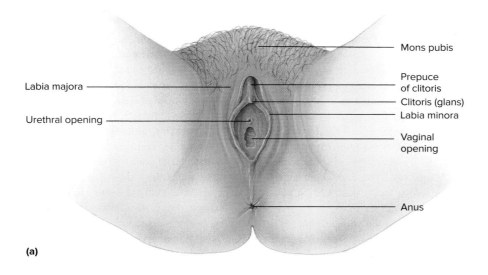

(a)

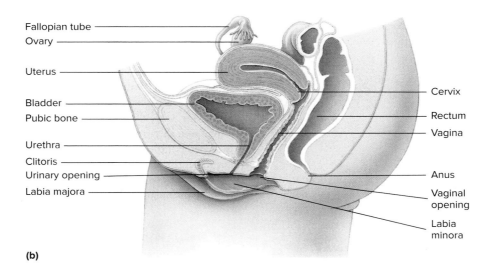

(b)

FIGURE 13-2 | **The Female Sex Organs**   (a) External structures. (b) Internal structures.

lined with tiny, hairlike projections called cilia. After an egg is released from an ovary, it travels through a fallopian tube for a few days, where it waits to be fertilized. If the egg is fertilized, it travels to the uterus, where it attaches itself. If the egg is not fertilized while it is in the fallopian tube, it disintegrates.

There are two ovaries, located on each side of the uterus and next to the fallopian tubes. The functions of the ovaries are to house the egg cells for maturation and to produce the hormones estrogen and progesterone. Though males manufacture sperm following puberty, females are born with all the egg cells they will ever have.

Puberty

Puberty is not a single event but rather a long process that includes many physical and emotional changes. Regardless of the age at which puberty begins, it takes four to five years for boys and three to four years for girls to complete.

Teachers should remember that not all students reach puberty at the same time. That is why some upper-elementary and middle-level students might seem both physically and emotionally mature for their age but others might seem very immature. Puberty changes can occur as early as age 7 and as late as age 18. However, about 50 percent of boys and girls reach puberty before age 13.

When teaching students about the changes that accompany puberty, it is important to emphasize that these changes can begin anytime from age 7 to 18. When teachers say "The average age of puberty is 13," students tend to remember the number 13 and not the word *average*. It should be emphasized that there is no best time to go through puberty and that everyone will experience these changes when his or her body is ready.

The emotional changes that preadolescents experience are diverse because of their changing hormone levels and the developmentally consistent feeling of wanting to be independent. Shifts in certain hormones can trigger feelings of irritability, restlessness, anxiety, happiness, excitement, and frustration. For instance, students going through puberty might be happy and sensible one day but depressed and irrational the next. These mood swings are normal and should be expected throughout puberty. Whatever emotion students express, teachers should be patient and understanding when interacting with them.

Boys and girls also are curious about the physical changes that are happening to them during puberty. The physical changes that occur throughout puberty are called secondary sex characteristics. These changes occur because different hormones are being released in males and females.

Female Changes During Puberty   For girls, the secondary sex characteristics, produced by the release of estrogen, include (Figure 13-3):

- A gain in height and weight
- Breast enlargement
- Growth of pubic and underarm hair
- Onset of menstruation
- Widening of hips
- Deepening of the voice
- Vaginal discharge

Females will notice the external changes that happen throughout puberty gradually, such as breast enlargement and pubic hair

growth. During this time, internal changes also occur, which the female cannot see. The reproductive organs develop so that a female is able to bear children. Part of this internal process is menstruation. Menarche, which is the first period, or menstruation, is a sign that a female's reproductive system is beginning to function so that she can become pregnant.

The menstrual cycle begins at puberty and continues until a woman is in her middle to late forties. Before the cycle has begun and after it has ended, a woman is usually unable to bear children.

The number of days for the complete menstrual cycle varies from female to female. For adolescents, it is usually twenty-six to thirty-two days, although it can be anywhere from twenty to forty-two days. Teenagers generally have an irregular cycle during the first year of menstruation.

The purpose of the menstrual cycle is to produce a mature egg and to develop the lining of the uterus so that it is ready to receive and nourish a fertilized egg. The menstrual cycle is complex, because many hormonal and physical changes occur each month. It is not necessary for the elementary or middle school teacher to understand every detail in the menstrual cycle; a general knowledge of the changes that occur is sufficient (Figure 13-4). The cycle begins when one egg in one of the ovaries develops, becomes larger, and is mature enough to produce a pregnancy if it is joined by a sperm. This mature egg is called an ovum. An ovum is produced every month, usually in alternating ovaries. While the egg is growing, the lining of the uterus becomes thick with blood and other materials in preparation for a fertilized egg. As the uterine lining continues to thicken, the egg breaks through the wall of the ovary (called ovulation) into the fallopian tube, where it travels toward the uterus for a few days. If the egg is to be fertilized, it must be joined by a sperm while it is in the fallopian tube. While the egg is traveling through the fallopian tube, the uterine lining continues to get thicker and be filled with blood.

If the egg does not meet the sperm while it is in the fallopian tube, it disintegrates. The buildup in the uterus is no longer needed, so it begins to shed. The shedding of the uterine lining (menstruation) lasts for three to seven days. The cycle then continues with the maturing of another egg and the buildup of the lining of the uterus.

Male Changes During Puberty   Males also go through many physical changes during puberty. Their secondary sex characteristics, produced by the release of the hormone testosterone, that teachers and peers might observe include the following (see Figure 13-3):

- A gain in height and weight
- Growth and added muscle strength
- Growth of body hair around the penis and scrotum, under the arms, and on the face, arms, legs, and chest

©George Rudy/Shutterstock

Children grow at different rates while going through puberty.

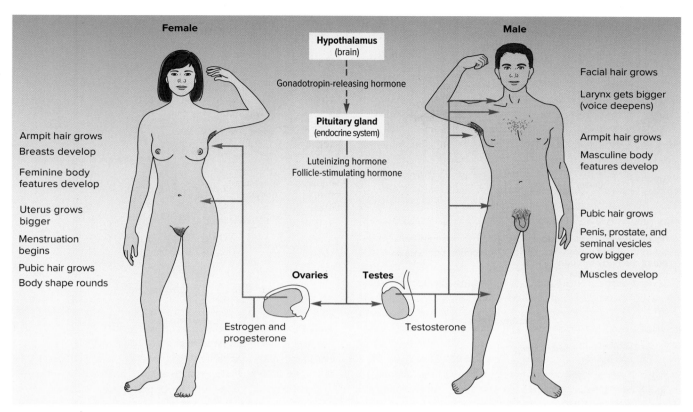

FIGURE 13–3 | Female and Male Secondary Sex Characteristics Hormones secreted by the brain and endocrine system trigger the production of sex hormones by the ovaries and testes; these hormones in turn trigger the physical changes of puberty.

- An increase in the size of the penis and scrotum
- Broadening of the shoulders
- Deepening of the voice
- Possible nocturnal emissions (wet dreams)
- Possible breast swelling

As with girls, boys will notice some of the physical changes occurring gradually in their bodies throughout puberty. During this time, internal changes also are happening, which the male cannot see. Hormones are being released, making it possible for the male to produce sperm in the testes (testicles).

Before sperm are being produced, males can become sexually excited and have orgasms; however, no semen is ejaculated. Once a male is able to produce sperm, he ejaculates semen. When males go through puberty, many times they experience ejaculation while sleeping. This is called a nocturnal emission, or wet dream. There is no warning when this will occur, and it cannot be prevented. Wet dreams are natural, and boys should be informed about wet dreams before they go through puberty so that they are not frightened by them.

Sexually Transmitted Diseases

Although most middle school students do not get sexually transmitted diseases (STDs), students will ask questions about them. In addition, some middle school health curricula include sexually transmitted disease prevention, so it is important for middle school health teachers to have basic understanding of the most common STDs, how to prevent them, and issues regarding treatment. STDs are infections that a person can get from having sex with someone who has the infection. The causes of STDs are bacteria, parasites, and viruses. These infections can be passed through vaginal, oral, and anal sex. They can also be passed through sexual skin to skin contact with the genitals. There are more than twenty types of STDs including chlamydia, gonorrhea, herpes simplex, human immunodeficiency virus (HIV), human papillomavirus (HPV), syphilis, and trichomoniasis (Table 13–2).[38]

The only sure way to prevent STDs is by not having sex. If a person is sexually active, the risk for getting an STD can be lowered by only having sex with someone who isn't having sex with anyone else (monogamy) and who does not have an STD. Some STDs, including certain strains of the human papillomavirus (HPV), have vaccines to help prevent contracting the STD. Another way to reduce the risk of getting an STD is to use a male condom correctly and consistently. Condoms, however, are not 100 percent safe and they can't protect a person from coming into contact with sores that can occur with some STDs including herpes simplex or warts. Other ways to reduce the risk of getting an STD are to limit the number of sex partners, get tested for STDs on a regular basis if sexually active, and to discuss STD testing with a sex partner.[39]

It is not important for middle school students to memorize every STD and their signs and symptoms. However, it is important to have an understanding of the common signs/symptoms of STDs. They include:

- Itching around the vagina and/or unusual discharge from the vagina.
- Discharge from the penis.

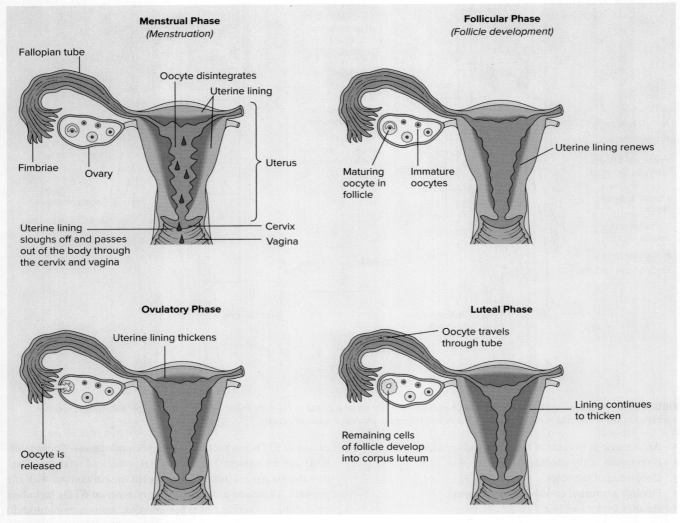

Menstrual Phase
(Menstruation)

Fallopian tube

Oocyte disintegrates

Uterine lining

Fimbriae

Ovary

Uterus

Uterine lining sloughs off and passes out of the body through the cervix and vagina

Cervix

Vagina

Follicular Phase
(Follicle development)

Uterine lining renews

Maturing oocyte in follicle

Immature oocytes

Ovulatory Phase

Uterine lining thickens

Oocyte is released

Luteal Phase

Oocyte travels through tube

Remaining cells of follicle develop into corpus luteum

Lining continues to thicken

FIGURE 13–4 | The Stages of Menstruation

- Pain during sex.
- Pain during urination.
- Pain in the pelvic area.
- Sore throats in people who have oral sex.
- Pain in or around the anus for people who have anal sex.
- Chancre sores (painless red sores) on the genital area, anus, tongue and/or throat.
- A scaly rash on the palms of the hands or soles of the feet.
- Dark urine, loose, light-colored stools, and yellow eyes and skin.
- Small blisters that turn into scabs on the genital area.
- Swollen glands, fever, and body aches.
- Unusual infections, unexplained fatigue, night sweats, and weight loss.
- Soft, flesh-colored warts around the genital area.[40]

Treatment for an STD depends on the specific type. For some STDs, treatment may involve taking medicine or getting a shot. For other STDs that can't be cured, such as herpes, there is treatment to relieve the symptoms. STD research is continually advancing. While HIV is not curable, treatments have improved and many HIV-infected individuals are successfully reaching an undetectable viral load. As long as they maintain this level, the chance of them passing HIV on to a sexual partner is near zero.

Recommendations for Concepts and Practice

Healthy Behavior Outcomes

The goal of health education is to help students adopt or maintain health-enhancing behaviors. School districts and teachers should identify the health-enhancing behaviors they would like their students to maintain or adopt. The list found in the Teacher's Toolbox 13.1 identifies some possible behavior outcomes related to promoting sexual health. Though not all of the suggestions are developmentally appropriate for students in grades K–8, this list can help teachers understand how the learning activities they plan for their students support both short- and long-term desired behavior outcomes

Developmentally Appropriate Knowledge and Skill Expectations

As with other health topics, teaching related to promoting sexual health should be developmentally appropriate and be

TABLE 13-2

Common Sexually Transmitted Diseases (STDs) Symptoms and Treatment

STD	Common Symptoms	Treatment
Chlamydia	Chlamydia can be dangerous because symptoms may not be noticed. Males: • A discharge from the penis • Burning or itching around the opening of the penis during urination Females: • An unusual discharge from the vagina • Burning during urination	Chlamydia can be treated and cured with antibiotics. It is important to finish all of the medication to make sure the disease is cured.
Gonorrhea	Gonorrhea is one of the most reported STDs. It can be dangerous because symptoms may not be noticed, especially in females. Males: • A discharge from the penis • Pain or burning when urinating • Painful or swollen testicles Females: • Vaginal bleeding between periods • Pain or burning during urination • Increased vaginal discharge	Gonorrhea can be treated and cured with antibiotics. It is important to finish all of the medication to make sure the disease is cured.
Genital Human Papillomavirus (HPV)	HPV is the most common STD. Nearly all unvaccinated sexually active people will have genital HPV at some time in their lives. Individuals with HPV may not have any symptoms. Certain strains of HPV can lead to various cancers including cervical, penile, oral, and anal cancers. The most common symptom is genital warts around the sex organs.	Because HPV is a virus, there is no cure. There are treatments for the health problems that some types of HPV can cause, like genital warts. The CDC recommends all youth aged 11 or 12 get vaccinated. The vaccine is also recommended for older youth and young adults up to age 26 for women and 21 for men who were not vaccinated at age 11 or 12.
Genital Herpes	Most people who have genital herpes don't know it. The most common symptoms are painful blisters and sores around the sex organs. Some people might have flu symptoms when sores are present. Sores can disappear and then come back several times within a year.	There is no cure for genital herpes, but there are treatments for its symptoms. Some medications can prevent blisters or make them go away faster.
Human Immunodeficiency Virus (HIV)	There typically are no symptoms for HIV. HIV causes AIDS, which can cause the immune system to fail.	There is no cure for HIV. There are treatments that can help an individual to live longer. A newer medication, pre-exposure prophylaxis (or PrEP), is available to help reduce the risk of contracting HIV by 90 percent when taken as prescribed[41].
Syphilis	Many people infected with syphilis have no symptoms for years. The first symptom a person may see is a single sore (chancre) where syphilis entered the body. It is usually painless. If left untreated, more severe symptoms can appear later. Without treatment, individuals with syphilis can die.	Syphilis is easy to treat in its early stages with an antibiotic.
Trichomoniasis	Some people may not have symptoms, especially men. Males: • A burning feeling or irritation inside the penis • A discharge from the penis Females: • An unusual discharge from the vagina, which will have a strong odor • Discomfort during urination or sex • Irritation or itching around the genitals	Trichomoniasis can be treated and cured with antibiotics. It is important to finish all of the medication to make sure the disease is cured.

SOURCES: Centers for Disease Control and Prevention, *Sexually Transmitted Diseases, The Facts*, www.cdc.gov/std/healthcomm/the-facts.htm, 2013; Centers for Disease Control and Prevention, *About HIV/AIDS*, www.cdc.gov/hiv/basics/whatishiv.html, 2014.

Developmentally Appropriate Knowledge and Skill Expectations for Promoting Sexual Health

HEALTHY BEHAVIOR OUTCOMES (HBOs) FOR PROMOTING SEXUAL HEALTH

HBO 1. Establish and maintain healthy relationships.

HBO 2. Be sexually abstinent.

HBO 3. Engage in behaviors that prevent or reduce sexually transmitted diseases (STDs), including HIV infection.

HBO 4. Engage in behaviors that prevent or reduce unintended pregnancy.

HBO 5. Avoid pressuring others to engage in sexual behaviors.

HBO 6. Support others to avoid or reduce sexual-risk behaviors.

HBO 7. Treat others with courtesy and respect without regard to sexual status.

HBO 8. Utilize appropriate health services to promote sexual health.

Grades K–2 Knowledge Expectations	Grades 3–5 Knowledge Expectations	Grades 6–8 Knowledge Expectations

NHES 1: Core Concepts

Grades K–2 Knowledge Expectations	Grades 3–5 Knowledge Expectations	Grades 6–8 Knowledge Expectations
• Identify the benefits of healthy family relationships. (HBO 1) • Identify the benefits of healthy peer relationships. (HBO 1) • Identify different ways that disease-causing germs are transmitted. (HBO 3) • Identify ways to prevent the spread of germs that cause common infectious diseases. (HBO 3) • Explain why it is wrong to tease or bully others based on gender identity and roles. (HBO 7)	• List healthy ways to express affection, love, and friendship. (HBO 1) • Identify characteristics of healthy relationships. (HBO 1) • Describe the benefits of healthy family relationships. (HBO 1) • Describe the benefits of healthy peer relationships. (HBO 1) • Identify characteristics of a responsible family member. (HBO 1) • Describe common ways infectious diseases are transmitted. (HBO 3) • Explain that HIV is not easily transmitted like other common infectious diseases. (HBO 3) • Describe ways to prevent the spread of germs that cause infectious diseases. (HBO 3) • Describe basic male and female reproductive body parts and their functions. (HBO 3, 4 & 8) • Describe the physical, social, and emotional changes that occur during puberty. (HBO 3, 4 & 8) • Explain how puberty and development can vary considerably and still be normal. (HBO 3, 4 & 8) • Describe personal characteristics related to sexual identity, orientation, and gender that make people different from one another. (HBO 7) • Summarize why it is wrong to tease or bully others based on gender identity and roles. (HBO 7)	• Describe characteristics of healthy relationships. (HBO 1) • Explain the qualities of a healthy dating relationship. (HBO 1) • Differentiate healthy and unhealthy relationships. (HBO 1) • Describe healthy ways to express affection, love, and friendship. (HBO 1) • Explain the importance of talking with parents and other trusted adults about issues related to relationships, growth and development and sexual health. (HBO 1, 2, 3, 4, 7 & 8) • Determine the benefits of being sexually abstinent. (HBO 2) • Explain why individuals have the right to refuse sexual contact. (HBO 2) • Describe why sexual abstinence is the safest, most effective risk avoidance method of protection from HIV, other STDs, and pregnancy. (HBO 2) • Describe the factors that contribute to engaging in sexual risk behaviors. (HBO 2, 3 & 4) • Describe the factors that protect against engaging in sexual risk behaviors. (HBO 2, 3 & 4) • Explain the importance of setting personal limits to avoid sexual risk behaviors. (HBO 2, 3, 4, 5, 6 & 7) • Describe the relationship between using alcohol and other drugs and sexual risk behavior. (HBO 2, 3, 4, 5, 6 & 7) • Describe techniques that are used to coerce or pressure someone to engage in sexual behaviors. (HBO 2, 5 & 6) • Analyze ways common infectious diseases are transmitted. (HBO 3) • Explain how the most common STDs are transmitted. (HBO 3) • Explain how HIV is transmitted. (HBO 3) • Describe usual signs and symptoms of common STDs. (HBO 3) • Describe usual signs and symptoms of HIV. (HBO 3) • Explain that some STDs and HIV are asymptomatic. (HBO 3) • Explain the short- and long-term consequences of common STDs. (HBO 3) • Explain the short- and long-term consequences of HIV. (HBO 3) • Summarize which STDs can be cured and which can be treated. (HBO 3)

NHES 1: Core Concepts (*continued*)

		• Summarize ways to decrease the spread of STDs and HIV by not having sex, using condoms consistently and correctly when having sex, not touching blood, and not touching used hypodermic needles. (HBO 3)
		• Describe how the effectiveness of condoms can reduce the risk of HIV, and other STDs including HPV (Human Papillomavirus). (HBO 3)
		• Describe ways sexually active people can reduce the risk of HIV, and other STDs including HPV (Human Papillomavirus). (HBO 3)
		• Summarize basic male and female reproductive body parts and their functions. (HBO 3, 4 & 8)
		• Describe conception and its relationship to the menstrual cycle. (HBO 4)
		• Identify the emotional, social, physical and financial effects of being a teen parent. (HBO 4)
		• Summarize ways to prevent pregnancy, including not having sex and effective use of contraceptives. (HBO 4)
		• Describe how the effectiveness of condoms can reduce the risk of pregnancy. (HBO 4)
		• Describe ways sexually active people can reduce the risk of pregnancy. (HBO 4)
		• Explain the benefits of respecting individual differences in growth and development, physical appearance and sexual status. (HBO 7)
		• Explain why it is wrong to tease or bully others based on their sexual status, such as sexual activity, sexual abstinence, sexual orientation, gender, or gender identity. (HBO 7)
		• Describe how intolerance of differences in sexual status (such as sexual activity, sexual abstinence, sexual orientation, gender, or gender identity) can affect others. (HBO 7)
		• Describe ways to show courtesy and respect for others whose sexual status (such as sexual activity, sexual abstinence, sexual orientation, gender, or gender identity) is different from one's own. (HBO 7)

Grades K–2 Skill Expectations	Grades 3–5 Skill Expectations	Grades 6–8 Skill Expectations

NHES 2: Analyze Influences

• Skill expectations are not identified for this grade group.	• Identify relevant influences of peers on relationships. • Identify relevant influences of culture on relationships. • Describe how relevant influences of media and technology affect personal relationships.	• Explain how perceptions of norms influence healthy and unhealthy sexual practices, behaviors, and relationships. • Explain how social expectations influence healthy and unhealthy sexual practices, behaviors, and relationships. • Explain how personal values and beliefs influence sexual health practices, behaviors, and relationships. • Describe how some health risk behaviors influence the likelihood of engaging in sexual risk behaviors (e.g., how alcohol use influences sexual risk behavior). • Analyze how relevant influences of family and culture affect sexual health practices, behaviors, and relationships. • Analyze how relevant influences of school and community affect sexual health practices, behaviors, and relationships. • Analyze how relevant influences of media and technology affect sexual health practices, behaviors, and relationships. • Analyze how relevant influences of peers affect sexual health practices, behaviors, and relationships.

(continued)

Grades K–2 Skill Expectations (*continued*)	Grades 3–5 Skill Expectations (*continued*)	Grades 6–8 Skill Expectations (*continued*)

NHES 3: Accessing Information, Products, and Services

• Skill expectations are not identified for this grade group.	• Skill expectations are not identified for this grade group.	• Analyze the validity and reliability of sexual health information. • Analyze the validity and reliability of sexual health care products. • Analyze the validity and reliability of sexual health care services. • Describe situations that call for professional sexual health care services. • Determine the availability of valid and reliable sexual health care products. • Access valid and reliable sexual health information from home, school, or community. • Locate valid and reliable sexual health care products. • Locate valid and reliable sexual health care services.

NHES 4: Interpersonal Communication

• Demonstrate how to effectively communicate needs, wants, and feelings in healthy ways to promote healthy family and peer relationships. • Demonstrate how to effectively communicate care and concern for others to promote healthy family and peer relationships.	• Demonstrate effective communication skills to promote healthy family and peer relationships. • Explain how to be empathetic and compassionate toward others who are at a different stage of puberty from oneself. • Demonstrate how to effectively ask for help to deal with physical and emotional changes that occur during puberty. • Demonstrate how to effectively communicate support for peers who are progressing through puberty.	• Demonstrate effective communication skills to promote sexual health and healthy relationships. • Demonstrate how to manage personal information in electronic communications and when using social media to protect the sexual health of oneself and others. • Demonstrate effective peer resistance and negotiation skills to avoid or reduce sexual risk behaviors. • Demonstrate how to effectively ask for assistance to improve and/or maintain sexual health and healthy relationships. • Demonstrate how to effectively communicate support for peers when aspects of their sexuality are different from one's own.

NHES 5: Decision Making

• Skill expectations are not identified for this grade group.	• Skill expectations are not identified for this grade group.	• Identify circumstances that help or hinder making a decision related to a potentially risky sexual situation. • Determine when potentially risky sexual health-related situations require a decision. • Distinguish when decisions about potentially risky sexual health-related situations should be made individually or with others. • Explain how family, culture, media, peers, and personal beliefs affect a sexual health-related decision. • Distinguish between healthy and unhealthy alternatives to a sexual health-related decision. • Predict the potential outcomes of healthy and unhealthy alternatives to a sexual health-related decision. • Choose a healthy alternative when making a sexual health-related decision. • Analyze the effectiveness of a sexual health-related decision.

NHES 6: Goal Setting

• Skill expectations are not identified for this grade group.	• Skill expectations are not identified for this grade group.	• Assess sexual health practices. • Set a personal goal to reduce the risk of pregnancy and transmission of HIV and avoid or reduce the risk of other STDs. • Assess the barriers to achieving a personal goal to reduce the risk of pregnancy and transmission of HIV and avoid other STDs.

Grades K–2 Skill Expectations	Grades 3–5 Skill Expectations	Grades 6–8 Skill Expectations
NHES 6: Goal Setting (*continued*)		
		• Apply strategies to overcome barriers to achieving a personal goal to reduce the risk of pregnancy and transmission of HIV and avoid other STDs.
		• Use strategies to achieve a personal goal to reduce the risk of pregnancy and transmission of HIV and avoid other STDs.
NHES 7: Self-Management		
• Skill expectations are not identified for this grade group.	• Skill expectations are not identified for this grade group.	• Explain the importance of being responsible for practicing sexual abstinence.
		• Analyze personal practices and behaviors that reduce or prevent sexual risk behaviors.
		• Demonstrate practices and behaviors to improve the sexual health of oneself and others.
		• Make a commitment to practice healthy sexual behaviors.
NHES 8: Advocacy		
• Skill expectations are not identified for this grade group.	• Demonstrate how to persuade others that it is wrong to tease or bully others based on differences in gender or other personal characteristics.	• State a health-enhancing position on a sexual health-related topic, supported with accurate information, to improve the health of others.
		• Persuade others to avoid or reduce risky sexual behaviors.
		• Persuade others to avoid teasing, bullying, or stigmatizing others based on their personal characteristics and perceived sexual status.
		• Collaborate with others to advocate for safe, respectful, and responsible relationships.
		• Collaborate with others to advocate for opportunities to avoid or reduce risky sexual behaviors.
		• Demonstrate how to adapt positive sexual health-related messages for different audiences.

SOURCE: Centers for Disease Control and Prevention. *Health Education Curriculum Analysis Tool*, 2nd ed. Atlanta, GA: CDC, 2012.

based on the physical, cognitive, social, emotional, and language characteristics of specific students. Teacher's Toolbox 13.1 contains a list of suggested developmentally appropriate knowledge and skill expectations to help teachers create lessons that encourage students to practice the desired behavior outcomes by the time they graduate from high school. The numbers listed behind each knowledge expectation are aligned with and support the healthy behavior outcomes listed in the Teacher's Toolbox 13.1. These grade-level spans are aligned with the National Health Education Standards. Note that some of these knowledge and skill expectations are reinforced in other content areas (the concept "identify the benefits of healthy family relationships" also applies to mental and emotional health). Additional information on developmentally appropriate sexual health knowledge and skills can be located in the National Sexuality Education Standards: Core Content and Skills, K–12 available at www.futureofsexed.org/nationalstandards.html.

Sample Student Questions and Suggested Answers About Sexuality

A list of some commonly asked questions about sexuality and some suggested answers follows. It is not enough just to read the suggested answers—teachers should practice saying them out loud. Teachers are encouraged to think of other questions children might ask and to practice answering them as well.

There are several frameworks and models for answering challenging questions posed by students. While organized slightly differently, they contain the same key guidance. Often students will ask values-based questions that can be more challenging to answer than fact-based questions. When answering questions about sexuality, it is important to stick with medically accurate information. If a teacher is going to discuss values with a student, it is important to present a range of possible values and beliefs. Most importantly, teachers should practice answering difficult questions without strong negative reactions. Students need to feel safe and comfortable approaching adults with questions.

Sample Questions Lower-Elementary Students Commonly Ask

1. *Where do babies come from?*

Babies come from their mothers' bodies. The baby grows inside the mother's body in a place called the uterus. [Do not tell the child that a seed has been planted in the mother's body, because the child might imagine a plant starting to grow.]

2. *How does a baby eat and breathe before it is born?*

Before a baby is born, it gets food and air from its mother's blood through a long tube, called the umbilical cord. One end of the cord is attached to the inside of the mother's uterus, and the other end is attached to the baby's navel, or belly button.

3. *Why do grown-ups have hair on their bodies, but I don't?*

When children grow up and go through puberty, many changes happen in their bodies. One of these changes is for hair to grow in different places on the body. As you get older, hair will grow on you, too.

4. *How long does a baby grow inside the mother?*

A baby grows for about nine months inside the mother.

5. *How does a baby get in a mother's body?*

A man and a woman make a baby. [If this answer does not satisfy the child, the teacher might have to give more detail.] When a man and woman want to have a baby, they put their bodies very close together. This feels good to both of them. When they are close, the man's penis becomes hard and is put into the woman's vagina. This is called sexual intercourse. In time, a fluid called semen comes out of the man's body. The semen has sperm cells in it. When one sperm meets with a woman's egg, the egg becomes fertilized. The egg can then stick inside the uterus and the woman is now pregnant.

6. *What is gay?*

Gay is a term used to describe people of the same sex or gender who are attracted to each other. They may have a sexual and/or emotional relationship.

7. *When is a boy old enough to make a baby?*

A boy is able to make a baby when he starts producing sperm cells and is able to release them in a process called ejaculation. Ejaculation becomes possible sometime during puberty that usually takes place between the ages of 9 and 15. Just because a boy can physically make a baby at this age does not mean he is responsible enough to take care of a baby.

8. *When is a girl old enough to make a baby?*

Girls are able to make babies when they begin to have their menstrual cycle. This usually happens when girls are around age 9 to 16. A girl may be physically ready to have a baby when she begins to menstruate, but she is probably not emotionally ready to care for it.

9. *Why do boys stand up to pee, but girls don't?*

Boys stand up to pee or urinate through an opening in the penis called the urethra. Girls sit down to pee or urinate through an opening between their legs called the urethra. These are the easiest and neatest ways for boys and girls to urinate.

10. *How does a baby get out of a mother?*

When the baby is big enough and is ready, the baby usually comes out of an opening between the mother's legs called the vagina.

Sample Questions Upper-Elementary and Middle-Level Students Commonly Ask

1. *What is a rubber?*

Rubber is a slang term for condom. A condom is a covering made out of a rubber-like material. It is worn over the penis and helps keep sexual fluids from entering another person's body during sex.

2. *What makes puberty happen?*

Glands in the body become more active and begin making different hormones. Hormones are natural chemicals in the body. These hormones have specific functions, which make the body change and develop.

3. *Can urine and semen come out at the same time?*

No; when semen comes out of the urethra, muscular contractions shut off the valve that allows urine to leave the body.

4. *How does a girl know when she will start her period?*

Nobody knows exactly when a girl will have her first period. She can watch for changes in her body such as pubic hair growth, breast development, and vaginal discharge as clue that her period is going to start soon. When it happens, she may feel dampness in the vaginal area. When she goes to the bathroom, she will notice some menstrual blood in her panties. This means menstruation has begun.

5. *Does a penis have to be a certain size to work?*

No; there are different sizes to all body parts, including the penis; however, most erect penises are about the same size.

6. *Do boys have menstrual periods?*

No; when a boy goes through puberty, he does not have a menstrual cycle. Instead, he begins to produce sperm cells in the testicles. Sperm can be released from the body at any time. Sometimes his body builds up sperm and it needs to be released. One way his body releases the built up sperm is when he is in deep sleep, usually at night, his penis becomes erect and then the sperm and semen exit the body through the penis (ejaculation). When this happens, it is called a wet dream, or a nocturnal emission. Most of the time, it has nothing to do with what he is dreaming about.

7. *Can a woman have a baby without being married?*

Yes; a woman can have a baby when she is able to produce an egg and that egg meets with a sperm. Sometimes you might hear people talk about getting married before having a baby. This is because it can be challenging for a person, especially a young person, to take care of a baby without a partner.

8. *Is wet dream another term for masturbation?*

No; masturbation is when someone touches their own private area of the body in a sexual way while they are awake. A wet dream happens involuntarily while a person is asleep.

9. *How do the sperm and egg get together?*

When a man puts his penis into a woman's vagina, some fluid, called semen, is released through the penis. There are many sperm in the semen. If one of them finds and fertilizes an egg in the woman's fallopian tube, a new life can begin to grow. This is called vaginal sex.

10. *What is semen?*

Semen is a white, sticky fluid produced in the male reproductive system. It helps to carry sperm cells out of the body.

11. *What does it mean to be transgender?*

People who are transgender feel as if they are living inside a body that's wrong for them. They often feel that their experienced gender does not match the sex they were assigned at birth.

STRATEGIES FOR LEARNING AND ASSESSMENT

Promoting Sexual Health

This section provides examples of standards-based learning and assessment strategies for promoting sexual health. The sample strategies begin with a restatement of the standard and a reminder of the assessment criteria, drawn from the RMC Health rubrics in Appendix B. Strategies are written as directions for teachers and include applicable theory of planned behavior (TPB) constructs in parentheses (intention to act in healthy ways, attitudes toward behavior, subjective norms, perceived behavioral control). These learning and assessment strategies provide building blocks for standards-based lessons and units that can be tailored to local needs. Assessment criteria are used with permission from RMC Health. See Appendix B for Scoring Rubrics.

Additional strategies for learning and assessment for Chapter 13 can be found at the Online Learning Center.

NHES 1 | Core Concepts

Students will comprehend concepts related to health promotion and disease prevention to enhance health.

ASSESSMENT CRITERIA

- Connections—Describe relationships between behavior and health; draw logical conclusions about connections between behavior and health.
- Comprehensiveness—Thoroughly cover health topic, showing breadth and depth; give accurate information.

Grades K–2

Family Members Talking about family similarities and differences and the roles and responsibilities of family members is an important concept in sexual and family health for early elementary children. Teachers should be sure classmates treat each other with respect—no teasing or put-downs. Start a discussion by asking children to volunteer to tell how many people are in their family and who they are. As they tell who is in their family, have other children stand up, if they like, to represent each of the family members. Note that some families are larger and some are smaller—but all are families. Next, ask children to draw and color a picture of one of their family members. As a summary, children can volunteer to tell a story about the person they drew and how that person helps the family.

ASSESSMENT | For an assessment task, children can draw a picture of a family member (or all their family members) and share a story with classmates about how that person helps the family stay healthy and safe. Children also can write a sentence to go with their picture about how the person helps the family. For assessment criteria, students should be able to express the concept of family members helping one another stay healthy and safe. (Construct: Attitudes toward behavior.)

Families in Many Cultures Books about families are listed at the end of this chapter. In addition to reading children's books, students can investigate family traditions around the world through library and Internet searches. Children can talk about what they learn about family traditions in different places and cultures, including the families represented in their own classroom.

ASSESSMENT | For an assessment task, students can work in small groups to plan and present a puppet show about family traditions they've investigated. Students can design paper-bag or sock puppets as a link to performing arts. For assessment criteria, students should explain how family traditions help keep families safe and healthy. (Construct: Attitudes toward behavior.)

Preventing the Spreading of Germs Learning how disease-causing germs are spread is age-appropriate content for K–2 students. To help them begin making connections between germs and disease, select a children's literature book appropriate for your class focusing on how germs are spread. *It's Catching: The Infectious World of Germs and Microbes* by Jennifer Gardy is one example. Read the book to the class. Introduce key vocabulary to students such as germs, infectious, prevention, contagious, transmission, disease, and others. Then discuss the different ways that germs can cause disease and what students can do to prevent the spread of germs that cause common infectious diseases.

ASSESSMENT | For an assessment task, have students draw a cartoon strip identifying specific strategies they can practice to prevent the spread of germs that cause common infectious diseases. For assessment criteria, students should be able to demonstrate accurate information about the spread of germs through their cartoon strip drawings. (Constructs: Attitudes toward behavior, perceived behavioral control).

Grades 3–5

Qualities of a Good Friend Teachers present a lesson on friendship—help students generate a list of qualities of a good friend. Then discuss with students how friends can demonstrate these qualities and how these qualities can be symbolized in a picture. Provide students with materials to make paper bag puppets including lunch-sack-size paper bags, yarn, felt, construction paper, crayons, buttons, and so forth. Students should create a puppet that symbolizes at least three qualities of a good friend. Examples of symbols that relate to qualities of a friend might be a heart for caring, a fishing pole for friends who like to fish together (other symbols representing other personal interests), an athletic shirt for being a team player, and so on.

ASSESSMENT | The puppet symbolizing three qualities of a good friend is the assessment task. Along with the puppet, students should write a brief paragraph describing the puppet including the puppet's name and a description of how the symbols demonstrate qualities of a good friend. For assessment criteria, students should be able to identify at least three qualities of a good friend and symbolize that in the puppet they create. (Constructs: Attitudes toward behavior, subjective norms.)

Grades 6–8

Matching Game for the Reproductive System After teaching upper-elementary students the names and functions of the reproductive organs, teachers can use this activity to reinforce that information. Write the name of one reproductive organ on an index card, and write its function on another card. For example, one index card might have "fallopian tube" written on it, and another card might have "a tubelike structure connected to the uterus where fertilization takes place" written on it. Make matching cards for every reproductive organ discussed in class. Give one index card to each student. Tell students that half of the cards contain the names of the reproductive organs and the other half contain the functions of the reproductive organs. Tell students to find the person who has the index card that matches the correct organ to its function. This activity allows students to say the reproductive organ names aloud and encourages students to interact with a variety of classmates. Repeat the activity several times so that students receive a different organ or function each time.

ASSESSMENT | For an assessment task, students can complete the activity several times, starting with a different card each time. For assessment criteria, students should match the cards correctly and consistently. (Construct: Attitudes toward behavior.)

A Wheel of Healthy Relationships Middle-level students have a growing interest in relationships and what dating is all about. Ask students to describe the qualities of a healthy relationship, using the Lōkahi Wheel from Chapter 1. Students should think about healthy relationships in terms of these dimensions:

- Physical/body
- Friends/family
- Thinking/mind
- Spiritual/soul
- Work/school
- Feelings/emotions

Students might say that people in a healthy relationship respect the physical boundaries and limits of others and think in similar ways about important ideas. Help students dig beneath the surface to discuss what would (expressing enthusiasm for another person's success) and would not (behaving jealously and putting down another person's success) be part of a healthy relationship. In the physical and feelings areas, students should identify hitting or belittling as unhealthy behaviors in relationships.

ASSESSMENT | For an assessment task, students can work in small groups to complete one section of a large Lōkahi Wheel, identifying characteristics and examples of healthy and unhealthy relationships. Alternatively, students can rotate to different posters in a carousel activity. For assessment criteria, students should contrast healthy and unhealthy relationship qualities in each of the six Lōkahi areas. (Construct: Attitudes toward behavior.)

Preventing STDs After providing an overview to students about STDS, divide students into groups of three or four. Assign each group a common STD. Instruct them to create a poster about their assigned STD. The poster should contain the following information:

- How the STD is transmitted
- The symptoms of the STD
- The treatment of the STD
- How to prevent the STD
- The responsibility of someone who has the STD

After the students have finished making their posters, allow time for them to present them. Process the presentations by asking students to identify the common concepts presented.

ASSESSMENT | The completed poster and presentation is the assessment task for this activity. For assessment criteria, students should provide accurate information about their assigned STD and communicate that information to the class. (Construct: Attitudes toward behavior).

NHES 2 | Analyze Influences

Students will analyze the influence of family, peers, culture, media, technology, and other factors on health behaviors.

ASSESSMENT CRITERIA
- Identify both external and internal influences on health.
- Explain how external and internal influences interact to impact health choices and behaviors.
- Explain both positive and negative influences, as appropriate.

Grades K–2

How We Do Things in My Family Families are an important influence on how we do things (NHES 7, self-management skills) of all kinds—from brushing our teeth to handling our feelings when we are upset or angry. Students can write about the "way we do things to stay healthy in my family." Ask students to think about how the decisions they make and the things they do are influenced by family habits and self-management strategies. Students can make a list of the ways their families influence them to behave in healthy ways. Students can think through a typical day in their lives, from getting up to going to bed, to help them consider family habits and their influence on family members. Over time students internalize these habits.

ASSESSMENT | For an assessment task, students can draw a picture and write a sentence about "how my family helps me stay healthy." For assessment criteria, students should explain at least one healthy preference or habit they have developed (internalized) because of the way their family does things. (Construct: Subjective norms.)

Friendship Stories Use a writing or drawing activity to help students think about friendship. Ask students to write or draw a short story titled "Making Friends With the New Kid." Have students write or draw a story showing chronological order of at least three things they could do to make friends with a student new to the class. As showing chronological order is one of the early essay-writing skills students are expected to demonstrate, this writing task allows them a practice opportunity. Adjust the instructions to meet your specific writing expectations in your state. Ask students to share their stories with the rest of the class. After the students read their stories, they can discuss ways they can help everyone have friends. This activity focuses on the importance of having and maintaining friendships. Friends influence the health behaviors of other friends. This activity asks students to think about helping everyone have friends.

ASSESSMENT | The short stories students write are the assessment task for this activity. For assessment criteria, students can explain the importance of having friends and how friends are important positive influences to our health and safety. (Constructs: Attitudes toward behavior, subjective norms.)

Grades 3–5

All Kinds of Families Teachers can create a handout to go home with students inviting parents/trusted adults to watch an episode of a TV show that involves a family. Families can then discuss what they learned about the family they observed. Questions for families to consider are: What was learned about the way the family communicates with each other? How do the children show responsibility? How do the family members show respect for each other? What do you like/dislike about the way this family interacts? How is this family similar to/different from your family? Teachers can include acknowledgment in the letter sent home to families that not all TV families are positive examples of family relationships, thus creating additional opportunities for discussion among the student and their family members.

ASSESSMENT | The assessment task is students writing a short compare and contrast paragraph of their family and the family observed on the TV show that was watched. For assessment criteria, students should be able to identify similarities/differences between their family and the TV family as well as explain how watching such shows can influence the way people interact with others. (Constructs: Subjective norms, attitudes toward behavior.)

Being a Good Friend in the Online World: Changing Stereotypes Have students access and play the online game *CyberSense and Nonsense: The Second Adventure of the Three CyberPigs* available from Canada's Centre for Digital Media and Literacy (available at mediasmarts.ca/game/cybersense-and-nonsense-second-adventure-three-cyberpigs).

The teacher's guide explains how to play the game; provides background information regarding online safety, stereotyping, and cyberbullying; and suggests additional learning experiences to enhance the learnings from the online game. The game focuses on the importance of authenticating online information, observing rules of online communication, and recognizing bias and stereotyping in online content. This online gaming experience also can be used to reinforce Standard 3 and the importance of accessing valid sources of information, as well as personal safety content.

ASSESSMENT | For an assessment task use one of the extension activities from the teacher's guide—*Stories from a Different Point of View*. Read *The True Story of the Three Little Pigs* by Jon Scieszka to the class. Following the reading of the story, engage students in a discussion about other stories or fairy tales that feature stereotypical villains (e.g., evil witches, cruel giants, wicked stepmothers). Allow students the opportunity to rewrite a familiar story from a new perspective emphasizing how different stereotypes might be viewed from alternative points of view. Encourage students to include points about the negative impact stereotypes can have on relationships with family and friends. For assessment criteria, students should be able to describe how stereotypes can influence relationships and what can be done to positively change common stereotypes. (Constructs: Attitudes toward behavior, perceived behavioral control.)

Grades 6–8

Messages in the Media About "Ideal" Men and Women Ideas about sexual attractiveness are reflected in and come from images in the media. Middle-level students enjoy this assignment of finding magazine pictures of what men and women are "supposed" to look like, according to media images—the "ideals." Students can make posters or collages. The images for males and females, side by side, are especially revealing. Women are encouraged to be thin (perhaps strong, but always thin). Men are encouraged to be strong and muscular. What do these images mean in terms of health? How realistic are the images? Are the pictures altered (air-brushed, touched up)? Share with students that a famous model answered a question about whether she dieted before a photo shoot by saying "No, I don't diet. That's what air-brushing is for!"

ASSESSMENT | For an assessment task, students can explain their media messages about men and women in terms of myths and misperceptions. For example, girls might say that it's a myth that women are attracted to men who have overdeveloped muscles. Boys might say that it's a misperception that men are attracted to women who are skinny. Students also might say that, in terms of health, the images portrayed in the media could lead to problems—eating disorders, steroid use, unbalanced nutrition, obsession with exercise and dieting, and obsession with appearance. For assessment criteria, students should identify at least five myths and misperceptions about media images of "ideal" men and women and provide healthy alternatives to the images. (Construct: Subjective norms.)

Coming of Age in Different Cultures Students might be interested to learn that many cultures celebrate the time in young people's lives when they go through adolescence, marking their growth to become an adult woman or man. Students can work with librarians or media specialists to access books and other information on how different cultures celebrate adolescence or coming of age. For example, in Australian Aboriginal culture, boys are sent on "walkabout" to test the tracking and survival skills they've learned while growing up. In some African tribes, young boys bring back a particular animal that they have hunted alone. In some Native American cultures, boys go away and survive special night adventures.[42] Judaism celebrates bar mitzvah for a boy when he turns thirteen and is recognized as a man and bat mitzvah for a girl when she turns twelve and is recognized as a woman. In Australia,

New Zealand, and numerous other countries, a party known as the "Twenty First" has long celebrated coming of age. On their twenty-first birthdays, young people and their families and friends traditionally gather for parties where gifts are presented to the birthday young man and woman. The Quinceañera (Fifteenth Birthday) for a young Latina is a rite of passage signifying that she has reached adulthood; the event is marked by a large celebration and a candle-lighting ceremony that acts as a spiritual mark of the young woman's achievement.[43] Coming-of-age ceremonies have been held for centuries in Japan. In the past, boys marked their transition to adulthood when they were around 15, and girls celebrated their coming of age around 13. During the Edo period (1603–1868), boys had their forelocks cropped off and girls had their teeth dyed black. It wasn't until 1876 that 20 became the legal age of adulthood in Japan.[44] Many cultures celebrate a girl's first menstrual period, although other cultures isolate girls during this time.

ASSESSMENT | For an assessment task, students can work in pairs or small groups to investigate the coming-of-age traditions in different cultures or parts of the world. Students also can interview their own families about how they mark adolescence in their family or culture. For assessment criteria, students should reflect, orally or in writing, on how coming-of-age traditions might influence a young person's beliefs and attitudes about becoming a man or woman. For example, would a young person feel pride or shame? How could these feelings influence a young person's behaviors with regard to sexual health? (Construct: Attitudes toward behavior.)

NHES 3 | Access Information, Products, and Services

Students will demonstrate the ability to access valid information and products and services to enhance health.

ASSESSMENT CRITERIA

- Access health information—Locate specific sources of health information, products, or services relevant to enhancing health in a given situation.
- Evaluate information sources—Explain the degree to which identified sources are valid, reliable, and appropriate as a result of evaluating each source.

Grades K–2

Finding Out About Growth and Development A popular classroom activity for discussing growth and development with young children is hatching chicken eggs in an incubator. Watching the chicks grow and change lets children access information for themselves about growth and development. However, teachers should realize that sometimes the eggs don't hatch or the chicks die, and the children might raise questions about death and dying. Teachers must be prepared to explain this to children. Chapter 14 includes helpful ideas for discussing these topics with children. Teachers also can have guppies or small animals for classroom pets. If they reproduce, use the teachable moment to discuss reproduction, growth, and development with students. It is important that teachers think about a permanent home for any classroom animals.

ASSESSMENT | Learning about growth and development with classroom pets is a good link to science education. For an assessment task, students can keep journals to draw and describe the changes they observe each day or week. First grade teacher Diane Parker shared that one of her students said he was sad when their class butterfly emerged from its cocoon and flew away, saying "I miss the old Blackie!" For assessment criteria, students should report their findings accurately (links to NHES 1) and explain why their observations are a valid source of information. (Construct: Attitudes toward behavior.)

Adults I Can Count On Identifying trusted adults is an important skill for early elementary students. Students need to know they can count on adults if they have questions or need help with a problem. In particular, students need to identify adults they could turn to if they experience unwanted touching or other situations that make them feel scared or uncomfortable. Have students trace the outline of one hand and label each finger with the name of an adult at home, at school, or in the community that they can go to if they have a question or need help.

ASSESSMENT | The students' hand tracings are the assessment task for this activity. For assessment criteria, students should be able to identify five people they can count on in at least three different locations (home, school, community). (Construct: Perceived behavior control.)

Grades 3–5

Puberty and Growing Up Students this age have lots of questions about their changing bodies. Allow them the opportunity to research, using a credible online resource, to find out more about what changes they will experience during puberty. Have students access the *Puberty & Growing Up* page at http://kidshealth.org/kid/grow/. In pairs, have students select a topic. Before they begin researching, have students frame the topic in the form of a question that kids their age wonder about. Have students research their question on the kidshealth.org website and explain three key points to help answer their selected question.

ASSESSMENT | For an assessment task, have pairs of students write a column for a classroom newsletter titled *What Is Happening to Me: Puberty & Growing Up*. They should use the newsletter column to answer the question they selected and support the response with a minimum of three facts from their credible online source. (Constructs: Perceived behavioral control, attitudes toward behavior.)

Finding Out About How Families Work Together Students can interview their parents or caregivers to find out what their families say "makes a caring and helpful family member" and "what kinds of jobs various family members do to help our family." Children can brainstorm a list of questions they want to ask and share their answers with classmates.

ASSESSMENT | The students' reports on their family interviews (what makes a caring family member, what jobs family members do to help the family) are the assessment task for this activity. For assessment criteria, students should report their information sources and tell why the sources are valid. (Construct: Perceived behavioral control.)

Grades 6–8

Interviews About Dating Parents and caregivers sometimes are uncomfortable about initiating conversation with their early adolescents about dating and relationships. Students can begin the conversation by creating a Google form or other online survey and send it to important adults in their lives. Survey questions might include the following:

- How old were you the first time you went out on a date?
- How did you feel about going on your first date?
- Where did you go and what did you do on your first date (go to a movie, eat out)?
- What kind of curfew did you have?
- What advice do you have for me to make dating safe and fun?

After receiving responses from the survey, students can analyze the survey results to determine norms about dating and relationships in their families, then put all of the survey results together to determine norms in families as a class. With the norms in mind, encourage students to complete a homework assignment to interview one of the people surveyed.

Students can point to specific responses and ask the adult for anecdotal evidence.

ASSESSMENT | For an assessment task, students can analyze survey results and share their findings with their classmates. After completing the interviews, students can choose to share some of their anecdotal evidence with the class. Students can create a poster of best advice from their parents and caregivers on dating. For assessment criteria, students should provide advice that is health enhancing (links to NHES 1) and explain why their surveys are valid sources of information. (Constructs: Subjective norms, perceived behavioral control.)

Ask the Expert Students can be given a variety of questions related to sexual decision making that have been asked by students their age or younger (these can be questions formulated by the teacher or ones that have been generated by real students). Students are to act as "experts" and apply their knowledge regarding STDs and pregnancy to help answer each question. Some examples include

- I heard that you can't get pregnant if you have sex just once. Is that true? Signed, Confused
- Is it OK to have sex with my boyfriend if I really love him? Signed, In True Love
- All of my friends are having sex. What is wrong with me? Signed, Left Out

ASSESSMENT | The answer students write is the assessment task for this activity. For assessment criteria, students should provide factual information in their answer and encourage the person asking the question to act in a healthy way. (Constructs: Attitudes towards behavior, perceived behavioral control.)

Products and Services—Which Should I Use? There are many products and services available to young people going through the changes of adolescence: Some come from credible sources others do not. Allowing the students the opportunity to access credible information about sexual health products and services can give them the confidence they need to make decisions about their sexual health as they grow up and are faced with more questions and challenges. Students can access information about HIV or other STD-testing resources in the community, typical clinical exams boys and girls should expect to experience, information on various hygiene products, and more. Have individuals or pairs of students generate a question of interest. Using sites such as www.kidshealth.org and other teacher-approved credible sites, students can research the topic.

ASSESSMENT | For an assessment task, students can prepare a poster to inform other adolescents about their topic of research. Students should prepare a visually appealing poster with facts and guidance from credible sources. For assessment criteria, students should provide accurate information, use credible sources of information, and be able to provide a brief statement as to why each source is valid and reliable. (Constructs: Attitudes toward behavior, perceived behavioral control.)

NHES 4 | Interpersonal Communication

Students will demonstrate the ability to use interpersonal communication skills to enhance health and avoid or reduce health risks.

ASSESSMENT CRITERIA
- Use appropriate verbal/nonverbal communication strategies in an effective manner to enhance health or avoid/reduce health risks.
- Use appropriate skills (negotiation skills, refusal skills) and behaviors (eye contact, body language, attentive listening).

Grades K–2

Your Body Belongs to You: Communicating About Your Body Children often participate in games and songs to name their exterior body

Discussing the parts of the body covered by a swimsuit is a good way to introduce students to the concept of the parts of their bodies that are private.

parts by touching their head, eyes, ears, nose, cheeks, mouth, neck, chest, arms, elbows, hands, wrists, fingers, abdomen, hips, legs, knees, feet, ankles, and toes. Thus, children can communicate easily about these body parts ("I fell and hurt my knee"). Teachers can use Cornelia Spelman's book *Your Body Belongs to You* to talk with children about the "private parts of their bodies or those covered by their bathing suits." By reading and discussing the book with students, teachers can help children understand that their bodies belong to them and that the only other people allowed to touch their private parts are (1) parents or other adults, such as teachers, who are helping them go to the bathroom or (2) doctors or nurses when they visit the doctor's office. Children should always tell a trusted adult if someone touches or tries to touch them in a way that makes them feel scared or uncomfortable. Children should say "Stop it!," get away as soon as they can, and tell a trusted adult as soon as possible, no matter who the person is or what the person doing the touching says to them about telling.

ASSESSMENT | For an assessment task, students can tell what they would say and do if someone touched or tried to touch them in a way that made them feel scared or uncomfortable. For assessment criteria, students should be able to list saying "Stop it!," getting away as soon as they can, and telling a trusted adult as soon as possible that someone touched or tried to touch them on their private parts. (Construct: Perceived behavioral control.)

Asking for Help   Be sure that young children know how to ask for help from adults so that adults will listen. Family counselor Allana Coffee recommends that children take the following steps:

1. Say "I need your help."
2. Tell what happened.
3. Tell what you did to try to make the situation better.
4. Say again "I need your help."[45]

Have children demonstrate asking for help in different kinds of situations. Asking adults for help in ways that make adults stop and listen to them is an important communication skill for children. Teachers, in particular, sometimes become frustrated with what they perceive as tattling and tell children to "solve it yourself," even when children genuinely need help. Practicing the steps in asking for help can assist children in communicating more clearly when someone needs help or is in danger.

ASSESSMENT | For an assessment task, students can work in pairs to demonstrate their skills. One student can play the role of an adult (parent, teacher, crossing guard), and the other can play the student role. For assessment criteria, students should be able to communicate the four steps in this activity (saying "I need your help," telling what happened, telling what the student did to try to help, and saying again "I need your help." (Construct: Perceived behavioral control.)

Grades 3–5

Talking About Privacy   Wilson, Quackenbush, and Kane state that discussions and questions about sexuality often can be handled more easily when children understand the concept of "privacy."[46] The examples the authors provide include teaching students that it's inappropriate to go through someone else's desk or to keep asking questions when someone has declined to answer. Teachers can ask students for other examples of "wanting privacy" or wanting to "keep things private." Students can communicate with their teachers through notes if they have questions or concerns they don't want to voice in front of the class. Teachers should be sure to respond to these questions. However, teachers must communicate clearly to students that teachers are required to get help for students if they are in danger or might endanger someone else. Teachers can't promise "not to tell," because they have to keep students safe. Students also can discuss when they should or shouldn't keep something private and ways to protect privacy. For example, first-grade students in Diane Parker's classroom devised an interesting solution to protect the privacy of their desks. Each student designed and decorated a paper cover ("lock") to fit across the opening in his or her desk. These locks, which were the students' own idea, ended "borrowing" from other people's desks.

ASSESSMENT | For an assessment task, students can make a "Respecting Privacy" list that tells ways they can respect the privacy of others (knocking on my sister's closed bedroom door before entering) and ways they want others to respect their privacy (not looking in my book bag while I'm away from my desk). For assessment criteria, students should explain when they should and shouldn't tell a trusted adult about "private" concerns a friend or family member might have. Students should always tell a trusted adult when they feel that they or others are unsafe or in danger. (Construct: Perceived behavioral control.)

Communicating About Boundaries and Limits   Setting and respecting *limits* and *boundaries* is an important concept for upper-elementary students. Start by asking students how they would define these terms. The students might need to access information by looking in a dictionary or asking older students or adults about these words. Students can discuss the kinds of boundaries and limits their families set on various activities (watching television, eating snacks, letting someone know where they are and where they are going). Students also can discuss personal limits and boundaries they set for themselves. What's okay and what's not okay for them? Students can discuss effective and ineffective ways to communicate their limits and boundaries to others. What kind of communication is clear? What kind of communication might give a mixed message? Teachers can link this activity to various risk areas, including sexual health and responsibility.

Students can write anonymous blog posts to ask advice about communicating boundaries and limits. Teachers can provide an example to start, such as a post from a boy asking for help in telling a girl he likes that he wants to be friends but doesn't feel right about going to her house while her parents aren't at home. Students can discuss their communication advice in this example before writing their own posts about situations of their choosing.

ASSESSMENT | For assessment criteria, students should write a comment on another person's post giving advice on health-enhancing communication. Students can share their answers by reading the posts and comments of others and engaging in a class discussion about them. Students should recommend at least two effective communication strategies (see examples in Chapter 3). (Construct: Perceived behavioral control.)

Grades 6–8

Talking Back to Pressure Lines: Which Part of "No" Don't You Understand?
In the safe environment of the classroom, students enjoy developing assertive things to say to pressure lines. Teachers can write pressure lines (one-sentence lines to pressure someone into doing something) and/or have students write them. Examples of pressure lines include "Everyone is doing it," "If you loved me you would," "No one will find out." Students can work in small groups to come up with replies to pressure lines, demonstrating different types of peer resistance/refusal skills (repeat the refusal, suggest an alternative, make an excuse, give a reason). Students can demonstrate different kinds of refusal skills to the same pressure line. Some of the refusal skills should deal with pressures to have sex. Teachers should remind students that their goal in communication is to give a clear message and to maintain relationships. Students can use the "Right to Resist" page of The Cool Spot website (www.thecoolspot.gov/right_to_resist.aspx) to learn about assertive refusal skills and resisting peer pressure.

ASSESSMENT | For an assessment task, students can work in small groups to demonstrate passive, aggressive, and assertive responses to pressure lines that they create or draw from a bowl (teachers can prepare slips of paper or have students write pressure lines and put them in a bowl). (See Chapter 3 for more information on these three types of responses.) Students can create short videos demonstrating the three types of responses, including body language that validates the verbal responses. The videos can be presented to the class to identify the type of response and evaluate the success of each. Students can discuss their own experiences in similar situations and develop a plan for future pressures. For assessment criteria, students should explain why passive and aggressive responses usually are ineffective and how the assertive response, coupled with appropriate body language, can be most effective. (Construct: Perceived behavioral control.)

Communicating to Abstain Distribute index cards to each student. Instruct students to use a pencil (so that they will not be identified by ink color on their card) and write down what a person might say to a partner if they were being pressured to have sex. Collect the cards, read each one for appropriateness, and then distribute one to each student. Have students create two circles—an inner circle and an outer circle—where students are facing each other. Tell students to take turns reading their refusal statement to their partner. Have students pass their cards to the person on their right and repeat the process. After students have read all of the resistance statements, ask them to write the three statements that would work best for them.

ASSESSMENT | Writing the three resistance statements that will work best for them is the assessment task. For assessment criteria, students should explain why those statements would work best for them. (Construct: Perceived behavioral control).

R-E-S-P-E-C-T Teachers can use a recording of the song "R-E-S-P-E-C-T," by Aretha Franklin, to introduce the idea of respecting oneself and others.

Begin the discussion by having students share their ideas about respect—for example, "When is a person respecting me?" "When is a person disrespecting me?" "What in my behavior could show respect or disrespect for others?" Students might be surprised to learn that they have different ideas about being respectful and disrespectful. Then turn the conversation to pressures on young people to have sex. What kind of communication shows respect? Disrespect? How do students respond to both kinds of communication in ways that give a clear message?

ASSESSMENT | For an assessment task, students can create their own version of an R-E-S-P-E-C-T song, a rap, or some other kind of reminder. For assessment criteria, students should list at least three examples of the respect they want ("R-E-S-P-E-C-T, find out what it means to me!") (Construct: Perceived behavioral control.)

NHES 5 | Decision Making

Students will demonstrate the ability to use decision-making skills to enhance health.

ASSESSMENT CRITERIA
Reach a health-enhancing decision using a process consisting of the following steps:

- Identify a health-risk situation.
- Examine alternatives.
- Evaluate positive and negative consequences.
- Decide on a health-enhancing course of action.

Grades K–2

What Do You Do, Dear? As recommended in the standards-based learning strategies in Chapter 3, children's literature can be used to discuss the concept of decision making. Characters in children's books often are faced with a problem or decision. What do they decide, and do students agree or disagree with that decision? Children can predict what might happen if other decisions were made. A book that examines decision making in a fun and fanciful way is Joslin and Sendak's *What Do You Do, Dear? Proper Conduct for All Occasions.*[47] For example, what do you do if

- A lady polar bear walks into your igloo in a white fur coat?
- You meet someone coming the other way on a circus tightrope?

Children can provide their own decisions about what to do and how to decide and then compare their answers with those in the book.

ASSESSMENT | For an assessment task, students can make up their own "What do you do, Dear?" questions and answers. For assessment criteria, students should explain what to do and why they chose to do it. All answers should be health enhancing. (Construct: Perceived behavioral control.)

Grades 3–5

Deciding for Me Students can think about decisions that other people make for them, along with decisions they get to make for themselves. In elementary school and at home, many decisions are made for children (what assignments to do, what time to go to bed). However, children do make some decisions for themselves (what book to read, what shirt to wear). Children can list decisions in two columns—decisions others make and those they make for themselves. Emphasize the importance of making good decisions in those areas where students get to decide for themselves. If feasible, follow this discussion with an activity in which the children get to make a decision (which assignment to do first, what to do for a class celebration).

ASSESSMENT For an assessment task, students can make their two-column list of decisions that others make and that they make and explain how they can make good decisions. If the activity includes making individual or class decisions, students can explain how they make their decisions. For assessment criteria, students should explain three alternatives for a specific decision, name positive and negative consequences, choose a decision, and tell how they will know whether it was a good one. (Construct: Perceived behavioral control.)

Grades 6–8

Making the Hard Decisions: What if We Don't Want to Say NO? The idea for this discussion with middle-level students came from the classroom experiences of health educator Lynn Shoji. When she was working with her health education classes on refusal skills, a group of boys asked very honestly, "But, Mrs. Shoji—what if we don't want to say no?" That was a teachable moment and a time for conversation that was relevant and current in students' lives. In the area of sexual health and responsibility, students naturally become curious as they reach adolescence. In the area of sexuality, students get many messages, from parents, the school, friends, and the media. What are they to do with their curiosity and new feelings? These questions present an ideal opportunity to look honestly at alternatives and the positive and negative consequences of those alternatives: "How will my decisions affect my health and safety?" "How will they affect my family?" "How will they affect my friends or other people who are involved in my decisions?" "How will my decisions affect my goals for the future and the kind of person I want to be—and to be known as?" Providing an open forum for discussion helps students think through the short- and long-term outcomes of the decisions they are beginning to face.

Facilitating a discussion like this one requires a skillful teacher—one who can listen and help students think deeply without scolding or demanding that students say they think a certain way (even if they don't). Teachers can facilitate and guide the discussion by listening carefully, respecting what students say, and asking questions to help them scratch beneath the surface of short- and long-term outcomes.

ASSESSMENT For an assessment task, students can work through the steps of a decision-making model (see Chapter 3). (To review the decision-making model, students can participate in a short session of "Balloon Up" from Chapter 5.) Students can state a problem or decision they are interested in related to sexual health, name three or more alternatives, identify positive and negative consequences for each alternative, choose a decision, and then evaluate how they think this decision would work for them. For assessment criteria, students should work through all five steps of decision making and arrive at a health-enhancing conclusion. If students have difficulty arriving at a health-enhancing conclusion, teachers can continue to ask other students to talk about what they think and ask about consequences. (Constructs: Attitudes toward behavior, perceived behavioral control.)

Deciding on Abstinence Introduce the activity by emphasizing that not making a good decision about sex is one of the reasons teens can become pregnant or infected with HIV or other STDs. Explain that one decision teens can make about sex is to abstain until they are older. Post two pieces of newsprint with the word "Abstinence" on one piece and "Reasons to Remain Abstinent" on the other piece. Ask the class to define the word abstinence. Some possible responses might include avoiding something such as sweets, alcohol, meat, or sex. Emphasize that people choose to abstain from something for many reasons including health, religion, fear, or lack of interest.

Next, divide the class into groups of four or five students. Ask students to create a list of reasons why teens might decide not to have sex. Once they have created their list, create a master list on the second piece of newsprint. Some ideas might include fear of pregnancy, fear of an STD,

want to graduate from high school, personal beliefs, or religious beliefs. After each reason is listed, discuss it with the class.

ASSESSMENT For an assessment task, students can write down the reasons to remain abstinent that have the most meaning to them. For assessment criteria, students should be able to explain why their reasons have the most meaning and why those reasons would help them remain abstinent. (Construct: Attitudes towards behavior)

NHES 6 | Goal Setting

Students will demonstrate the ability to use goal-setting skills to enhance health.

ASSESSMENT CRITERIA
- Goal statement—Give goal statement that identifies health benefits; goal is achievable and will result in enhanced health.
- Goal-setting plan—Show plan that is complete, logical, and sequential, and includes a process to assess progress.

Grades K–2

Goals for Being a Good Friend Students can work in small groups to brainstorm the qualities of a good friend. The importance of friendship increases as children get older, and their responses will change through time. Ask the groups to share their responses with the rest of the class. Students should identify one way they could improve on being a good friend. Teachers can help them set a goal and make a plan to try to improve that quality.

ASSESSMENT For an assessment task, students can set an individual or class goal for being a good friend or a better friend for one week. Students should discuss their progress day by day during the week. For assessment criteria, students should state a clear goal (I will be a better friend by using kind words at school), make a plan (I will listen to what I say and what others say), plan for supports and barriers (I will hang out with friends who use kind words; I will be especially careful of what I say if someone makes me mad), and evaluate results (I will check on how I'm doing at lunch and at the end of school each day). (Constructs: Subjective norms, perceived behavioral control.)

Grades 3–5

Goals to Help My Family Students can discuss ways they can be of help in their families without being asked. Students can set a personal goal to help in a certain way in their families for a week, without publicizing their goal at home. Ask students to keep a journal about their progress during the week and about the response of family members at their volunteering to help without being asked.

ASSESSMENT The goals students set are the assessment task for this activity. For assessment criteria, students should set a clear goal, tell what steps they will take to achieve it, identify supports and barriers and ways to deal with barriers, and plan a way to assess their progress. (Construct: Perceived behavioral control.)

Grades 6–8

Teen Parenting—Not One of My Goals Conduct this activity after discussing that one of the negative outcomes of becoming sexually active is becoming a teen parent. This carousel activity is a way to get students to think about how becoming a teen parent would affect them. Students can work in small groups to brainstorm on a sheet of newsprint about how their lives would change in each of five categories—financial, family, social, educational, and emotional—if they became a teen parent. After each group returns to its original sheet of newsprint, students should circle the three answers that would be the most persuasive reasons to not become a teen parent.

ASSESSMENT | For an assessment task, students can share with the class the three most persuasive reasons to not become a teen parent. During their presentation, students should share personal goals that would be affected if they became teen parents. For assessment criteria, students should list at least three goals that would be affected and explain how these goals affect their decisions related to sexual health. (Construct: Attitudes toward behavior.)

NHES 7 | Self-Management

Students will demonstrate the ability to practice health-enhancing behaviors and avoid or reduce health risks.

ASSESSMENT CRITERIA
- Application (transfer)—Initiate health-enhancing behaviors; apply concepts and skills appropriate and effectively.
- Self-monitoring and reflection—Monitor actions and make adjustments; accept feedback and make adjustments; able to self-assess, reflect on, and take responsibility for actions.

Grades K–2

My Family, My Support System Children can draw and color pictures of their families and then share their pictures with the class and tell how their family members help each other. Sharing about families helps children understand that there are many different types of families and that all families are important. Counting on families as support systems helps students with healthy self-management in knowing where they can go for help and support.

ASSESSMENT | For an assessment task, students can explain or write about how the family members in their pictures help them—how family members make up a support system for them. For assessment criteria, students should name of least three family or extended family members who make up their special support system. (Construct: Attitudes toward behavior.)

***Julius, the Baby of the World:* A New Brother or Sister in the Family** Kevin Henkes's book *Julius, the Baby of the World* (Greenwillow, 1990) is a favorite for talking with young students about what it's like to have a new baby brother or sister in the house. Big sister Lilly is excited about having a new baby in the family; however, her enthusiasm cools when her parents admire the baby rather more than she expected. The book allows new older brothers and sisters to identify with Lilly's rejection campaign ("If you were a number, you would be zero," she tells the baby) in the safe environment of the classroom. Children also will find that when a visiting relative insults the baby, Lilly displays tremendous loyalty to Julius. Teachers can ask students to share their experiences about having new siblings at home.

ASSESSMENT | For an assessment task, students might want to make new pages to add to *Julius, the Baby of the World:* A New Brother or Sister in the Family based on their own experiences. Students should report their feelings honestly, but they also should discuss healthy ways to deal with their feelings. For assessment criteria, students should be able to describe at least one feeling and explain a healthy way to manage it. (Construct: Attitudes toward behavior.)

Grades 3–5

Let's Talk Some children are naturally good at conversing with peers and adults, while others avoid the opportunity for a conversation at all costs. Developing comfort with initiating a conversation will benefit students throughout their lives. Brainstorm situations in which students would initiate a conversation with peers, such as meeting a new student, and adults. Discuss various strategies for starting a conversation. Write these conversation starters on the board for student reference. Place students in two circles (one within the other) so that each student is facing a partner from the other circle. Begin with the outside circle initiating the conversation. Provide this group with one of the topics brainstormed by the group and give students the opportunity to practice initiating a conversation. After a minute or so, stop the group and have the inner circle move one to the left. Then give the inner circle a topic and repeat the process. After a couple of rounds, discuss what was easy/difficult about initiating a conversation. Have students share phrases and strategies that were helpful. Repeat the process a few more times, with students role-playing initiating conversations with an adult. Again, discuss phrases and strategies that were helpful.

ASSESSMENT | For an assessment task, students can create a 3-2-1 slip identifying the following information:
- Three statements that can be used to initiate a conversation with peers or adults.
- Two reasons it is important to be able to initiate conversations with adults.
- One person they would like to initiate a conversation with and how they will go about it.

For assessment criteria, students should specify specific ways for initiating a conversation and suggest how they will do so within a specific situation. (Constructs: Attitudes toward behavior, perceived behavioral control.)

Getting Help For all priority content areas, students need to know how to get help when they need it. Getting help might include telling a safe adult about a problem, or it might mean calling 9-1-1 in an emergency. Students should know how to get the help they need should an uncomfortable, threatening, or emergency situation arise. Students need to know that it's important for them to tell an adult if someone bothers or hurts them, no matter what that person tells them. Similarly, it's important for adults to believe children who come to them for help and see that they get the assistance they need. Read more about preventing and reporting sexual assault in Chapter 10 on preventing violence.

ASSESSMENT | For an assessment task, students can describe and discuss situations in which they might feel uncomfortable or unsafe. Students can work in pairs or small groups to write a scenario in which they feel the need to get help and then share the scenario with the class. For assessment criteria, students should specify at least two ways to get help in the scenario they describe. (Construct: Perceived behavioral control.)

Hugs and Kisses: Expressing Feelings Appropriately Teachers should lead students in a word web activity. The web should have a person (or category of person, such as parents, aunts/uncles, friends) and one feeling, such as affection, love, friendship, or concern, in the web center. The teacher should lead a word web brainstorm session to identify appropriate and inappropriate ways to express the designated feeling to the identified person/group of persons. Students can then be assigned a different person/group of persons and a feeling to create their own word web identifying appropriate and inappropriate ways to express that feeling to the identified person/group of persons.

ASSESSMENT | For an assessment task, students can create a storyboard demonstrating appropriate ways to express a teacher identified feeling to a person/group of persons. For assessment criteria, students should identify ways to appropriately express feelings of affection, love, friendship, or concern to the identified person/group of persons. Students should be able to explain why this form of expression is appropriate for the relationship/situation they created in the storyboard. (Constructs: Attitudes toward behavior, perceived behavioral control, intention to act in healthy ways.)

Grades 6–8

Role-Plays for Self-Management Students can work in small groups to brainstorm challenging or risky situations they know that students their age face or might face in the future. Students can choose one of the situations and show a strong or courageous way to handle the situation, as well as a less decisive way that could lead to problems. Have students volunteer to demonstrate their two role-plays for the class. Classmates should identify the two strategies and discuss how difficult or easy they would be to carry out. Students might role-play pressures to smoke, use drugs, have sex, or brag about doing these things.

ASSESSMENT | For an assessment task, students can work in small groups to demonstrate a challenging situation with two self-management outcomes—one effective and one ineffective. Students can follow their demonstration by asking classmates which techniques were effective or ineffective and why. For assessment criteria, students should compare and contrast at least one effective and one ineffective self-management strategy for responding to the challenging situation they demonstrate for the class. (Construct: Perceived behavioral control.)

Healthy Ways to Handle New and Normal Feelings Ask students to talk about some of the feelings they have as they become adolescents and go through puberty. Students might say that they feel anxious or scared, different from one day to the next, stressed, or just plain weird. Help students understand that their feelings are normal and a natural part of growing up. Ask students to talk about healthy ways to manage new feelings. The class might want to make a "tip sheet" or "survival sheet" of their favorite self-management strategies. Students can visit the BAM! (Body and Mind) website for kids (www.cdc.gov/bam/life/frazzled.html) and click on "Your Life," and then "Feelin Frazzled … ?" to learn ten tips to help stay cool, calm, and collected: put your body in motion, fuel up, lots of laughing, have fun with friends, spill to someone you trust, take time to chill, catch some Zs, keep a journal, get it together, lend a hand.

ASSESSMENT | For an assessment task, students can create their own class list of adolescent survival tips, using the BAM website to get them started. For assessment criteria, the students' list should expand the website ideas of healthy self-management strategies. Students also might want to list "dead end" strategies, such as tobacco or alcohol use and overeating. (Constructs: Attitudes toward behavior, perceived behavioral control, subjective norms.)

Sexual Abstinence: What Does It Mean and How Does It Work? Middle-level students often hear that they should be "sexually abstinent." What does that mean, and how does it work? Why is abstinence a smart self-management strategy for middle-level students? To answer these and other questions, students can visit the Kids' Health website (www.kidshealth.org) and click on "For Teens" and type "abstinence" into the search bar to learn

- What is it?
- How does it work?
- How well does it work?
- How does it protect against STDs?
- How do you do it?

Students will learn that abstinence is the simplest form of birth control—if two people don't have sex, then sperm can't fertilize an egg and pregnancy can't occur. Students also learn that although abstinence protects

against sexually transmitted diseases (STDs), some STDs spread through oral-genital sex or skin-to-skin contact without actual penetration. Thus, only complete and consistent abstinence protects against pregnancy and STDs. HIV and hepatitis B can be transmitted through nonsexual activities such as using contaminated needles for drugs or tattooing. With regard to decisions about abstinence, the website talks about media messages, peer pressure, and other influences. When students are clear on what abstinence is and how it can protect them, they can discuss how and why it can be a smart self-management strategy for middle-level students.

ASSESSMENT | For an assessment task, students can work in small groups to make a list of pros and cons of practicing abstinence as a self-management strategy during their middle school years. Students can share and compare their lists with classmates. For assessment criteria, students should describe at least three reasons why abstinence is a smart self-management strategy for middle-level students and three ideas for helping students remain abstinent (hang out with other kids who have decided to remain abstinent in middle school, avoid situations where there could be pressure to have sex, express intentions to remain abstinent in middle school). (Construct: Attitudes toward behavior.)

NHES 8 | Advocacy

Students will demonstrate the ability to advocate for personal, family, and community health.

ASSESSMENT CRITERIA
- Health-enhancing position—Give clear, health-enhancing position.
- Support for position—Support position with facts, concepts, examples, and evidence.
- Audience awareness—Show awareness of target audience; choose words, tone, and examples to suit audience.
- Conviction—Display conviction for position.

Grades K–2

It's Okay to Be Different: **Treating Others with Friendliness and Compassion** Todd Parr's book *It's Okay to Be Different* (see "Children's Literature" in Chapter 5) is a good one for helping children think about the issues in this activity. After reading the book, teachers can ask students to define the words *friendliness* and *compassion*. Students might want to look in their dictionaries and check with parents and caregivers to learn what these words mean. Teachers then can ask students whom they treat with kindness and compassion in their everyday lives. Children might name their family members, classmates, and teachers. Teachers can ask students to think about other people who need their kindness and compassion, such as people who are sick with diseases like cancer or HIV or people they perceive to be different in some way. Teachers can help students understand that they don't need to be afraid of people who seem different in some way and that they can treat all people with friendliness and compassion.

ASSESSMENT | For an assessment task, students can make a list of ways they can treat others with friendliness and compassion (smile and say hello, ask other kids to come and play). For assessment criteria, students should explain why they would "take a stand" by doing these things. (Construct: Subjective norms.)

Grades 3–5

Growing Up Is Great! Teachers can put students in pairs to discuss and brainstorm a list of advantages and disadvantages of growing up.

Teachers can read the book *Diary of a Wimpy Kid (Book 1)* by Jeff Kinney or have students read it with their partner. This popular series follows the everyday life of sixth-grader Greg and his best friend, Rowley. As the boys enter middle school, they find themselves experiencing the challenges of growing up. While many students may have read this book, encourage them to read it from a new perspective. Have students identify the changes Greg is experiencing and how he handles those changes, noting fails and successes. Following the reading of the story, students should pair up again with their book end, discuss and compare their reactions to the story, and compare and contrast their list of advantages and disadvantages of growing up based on their reactions to the story and the lessons learned.

ASSESSMENT | For an assessment task, students can create #TBT (Throwback Thursday) messages. Students can create Instagram-like posts sharing images of their favorite memories of growing up. In their messages, students can identify what made the memory positive and point out why that experience was only possible at the age in which it occurred. Students can then create #StepForwardSaturday messages to indicate experiences that would only be possible as the students grow older and to advocate for the advantages of growing up. For assessment criteria, students should provide accurate information (NHES 1), and show the characteristics of a good advocate—stating a strong position, providing accurate information, targeting an audience, and displaying conviction for the message. (Constructs: Subjective norms, attitudes toward behavior.)

Grades 6–8

Easing the Teasing: Supporting Classmates Who Choose Abstinence In middle school, students are ready to discuss the pressures they encounter or expect to encounter for risky behaviors, such as sexual involvement. Students can think about ways they will support the healthy decisions of their classmates, such as remaining abstinent throughout school. One of the most daunting aspects of making a decision is the fear that others will make fun of it. Ask students to talk openly about how they can support each other and prevent or deflect the teasing or taunting of other students. Teachers can help students with concrete strategies to deal with teasing from the "Easing the Teasing" website (www.easingtheteasing.com). The site provides ten strategies, including using humor, responding to the teaser with a compliment, ignoring the teasing, and asking for help. In addition to thinking about their own experiences, students can identify how they can adapt the strategies to support and advocate for others who choose abstinence and other healthy behaviors in middle school. This activity links to NHES 4, interpersonal communication, and NHES 7, self-management.

ASSESSMENT | For an assessment task, students can work in small groups to demonstrate one of the ten strategies adapted for supporting friends who choose abstinence. Students can divide into at least ten groups to be sure all strategies are covered. For assessment criteria, students should show the characteristics of a good advocate—stating a strong position, backing it up, targeting the audience, and speaking with conviction. (Constructs: Subjective norms, perceived behavioral control.)

Spreading the Word: Most Kids Make the Healthy Choice   As with the other priority content areas, high school (and, in some locales, middle school) data are available on the sexual behaviors of young people. Students can review and publicize their findings from the Youth Risk Behavior Survey (YRBS) to other classes within their school. The bottom line is that most kids make the healthy choice. YRBS data are available at www.cdc.gov/HealthyYouth/yrbs/index.htm.

ASSESSMENT | For an assessment task, students can prepare pamphlets or PowerPoint presentations on what they learn about the sexual behavior of high school students. Students should present their data from the positive perspective (the percentage of students who are abstinent in high school). For assessment criteria, students should state a strong position, back it up, target the audience, and speak with conviction. (Construct: Subjective norms.)

EVALUATED CURRICULA AND INSTRUCTIONAL MATERIALS

There are many high school and a few evaluated middle school commercial pregnancy, STD, and HIV prevention programs available to school districts. These curricula should complement, not replace, a comprehensive school health education curriculum. The evaluation results of these curricula have been reviewed by many professionals and have been shown to be effective in reducing the number of students who engage in sexual intercourse or in increasing the number of students who use condoms or other contraceptives. As with any curricular material, it is important that teachers review programs to ascertain if the selected program meets the requirements set forth by their district or state. Following are commercial curricula targeted toward all middle school youth:

- *Draw the Line–Respect the Line.* This middle school sexuality education program has multiple sessions spanning grades six through eight. five in the sixth grade, seven in the seventh grade, and seven in the eighth grade. It includes instruction on the consequences of unplanned sex, personal sexual limit setting, and refusal skills. The evaluation showed that it had significant effects in reducing the initiation of intercourse for seventh- and eighth-grade boys, but no significant differences for girls.
- Making a Difference! This is an eight-module program targeting middle school students. It follows an abstinence approach to reduce STDs including HIV and teen pregnancy. The evaluation of this program showed that it decreased the number of youth engaging in sexual activity three months after the program ended.

There are many commercially available programs that, while not as rigorously studied as some teen pregnancy and STD prevention programs are, have shown promise in addressing puberty and sexual health for older elementary and middle school students. Some of these programs include:

- *Puberty: The Wonder Years* https://pubertycurriculum.com/
- *Puberty Workshop and Curriculum* https://www.hrmvideo.com/catalog/puberty-workshop-and-curriculum
- *Rights, Respect, Responsibility: A K-12 Sexuality Education Curriculum* 3rs.org/3rs-curriculum

INTERNET AND OTHER RESOURCES

WEBSITES

Advocates for Youth
advocatesforyouth.org

Alan Guttmacher Institute
www.guttmacher.org

Amaze
amaze.org

Averting HIV and AIDS (Avert)
www.avert.org/

Center for Sex Education
http://www.sexedcenter.org/

Centers for Disease Control and Prevention
www.cdc.gov/HealthyYouth

Office of Adolescent Health
https://www.hhs.gov/ash/oah/

Planned Parenthood
www.plannedparenthood.org

Power to Decide
powertodecide.org/

Procter and Gamble School Programs
https://www.pgschoolprograms.com/

Resource Center for Adolescent Pregnancy Prevention (ReCAPP)
recapp.etr.org/recapp/

Sex, etc.
www.sexetc.org

Sexuality Information and Education Council of the United States (SIECUS)
siecus.org

OTHER RESOURCES

Averting HIV and AIDS (Avert). *Sex Education That Works* (www.avert .org/sex-education.htm; 2014).

Future of Sex Education. *National Sexuality Education Standards: Core Content and Skills, K-12* (www.futureofsexed.org/documents /josh-fose-standards-web.pdf; 2012).

Future of Sex Education. *National Teacher Preparation Standards for Sexuality Education* (www.futureofsexed.org/documents /teacher-standards.pdf; 2014).

Kirby, D. *Emerging Answers 2007: Research Findings on Programs to Reduce Teen Pregnancy and Sexually Transmitted Diseases* (Washington, DC: The National Campaign to Prevent Teen and Unplanned Pregnancy, 2007).

Kirby, D., and G. LePore. *Sexual Risk and Protective Factors—Factors Affecting Teen Sexual Behavior, Pregnancy, Childbearing and Sexually Transmitted Disease: Which Are Important? Which Can You Change?* (Washington, DC: The National Campaign to Prevent Teen and Unplanned Pregnancy, 2007).

Sexuality Information and Education Council of the United States. *Guidelines for Comprehensive Sexuality Education,* 3rd ed. (New York: Sexuality Information and Education Council of the United States, 2004).

Sexuality Information and Education Council of the United States. *Sexuality Education Questions and Answers* (www.siecus.org/index.cfm?fuseaction=page. viewpage&pageid=521&grandparentID=477&parentID=514; 2014).

Suellentrop, K. *What Works: Curriculum-Based Programs That Prevent Teen Pregnancy* (Washington, DC: The National Campaign to Prevent Teen and Unplanned Pregnancy, 2011).

CHILDREN'S LITERATURE

AGES 5–8

Brown, Laurene Krasny. *What's the Big Secret?: Talking About Sex With Girls and Boys.* Little, Brown, and Co., 1997.

Curtis, Jamie Lee. *Tell Me Again About the Day I Was Born.* HarperCollins, 1996.

Davis, Jennifer. *Before You Were Born.* Workman, 1997.

Harris, Robie. *It's Not the Stork: A Book About Girls, Boys, Babies, Bodies, Families and Friends.* Candlewick, 2008.

Harris, Robie. *It's So Amazing! A Book About Eggs, Sperm, Birth, Babies, and Families.* Candlewick, 2004.

Henkes, Kevin. *Julius, the Baby of the World: A New Brother or Sister in the Family.* Mulberry, 1990.

Hoberman, Mary Ann. *All Kinds of Families!* Little Brown Books for Young Readers, 2009.

Hoberman, Mary Ann. *Fathers, Mothers, Sisters, Brothers.* Puffin, 1991.

Hoffman, Mary. *Boundless Grace.* Penguin, 1995.

King, Zack. *I Said No!: A Kid-To-Kid Guide to Keeping Private Parts Private.* Boulden Pub., 2010.

Mayle, Peter. *Where Did I Come From? A Guide for Children and Parents.* Kensington, 1999. (Multicultural)

Murkoff, Heidi Eisenberg. *What to Expect When Mommy's Having a Baby.* Harper Festival, 2004.

Nemiroff, Marc. *All About Adoption: How Families Are Made and How Kids Feel About It.* American Psychological Association, 2003.

Newman, Leslea. *Heather Has Two Mommies.* Candlewick Press, 2016.

Newman, Leslea. *Mommy, Mama, and Me.* Tricycle Press, 2009.

Numeroff, Laura. *What Mommies Do Best/What Daddies Do Best.* Simon & Schuster, 1998.

Oelschlager, Vanita. *A Tale of Two Mommies.* VanitaBooks, 2011.

Parr, Todd. *The Family Book.* Little Brown Books for Young Readers, 2010.

Pitman, Gayle. *This Day in June.* Magination Press, 2014.

Polacco, Patricia. *In Our Mother's House.* Philomel, 2009.

Richardson, Justin. *And Tango Makes Three.* Simon & Schuster Books for Young Readers, 2015.

Saltz, Gail. *Amazing You: Getting Smart About Your Private Parts.* Dutton Juvenile, 2008.

Saunders, Catherine. *Children Just Like Me.* DK/Penguin Random House, 2016.

Schiffer, Miriam B. *Stella Brings the Family.* Chronicle Books, 2015.

Silverberg, Cory. *What Makes a Baby.* Triangle Square, 2013.

Spelman, Cornelia. *Your Body Belongs to You.* Albert Whitman, 2000.

AGES 9–12

American Medical Association. *American Medical Association Boy's Guide to Becoming a Teen.* Jossey-Bass, 2006.

American Medical Association. *American Medical Association Girl's Guide to Becoming a Teen.* Jossey-Bass, 2006.

Anderson, Laurie Halse. *Speak.* Puffin, 1999.

Atwood, Sarah. *Making Sense of Sex: A Forthright Guide to Puberty, Sex and Relationships for People with Asperger's Syndrome*. Jessica Kingsley Publishers, 2008.

Blackstone, Margaret, and Elissa Haden Guest. *Girl Stuff: A Survival Guide to Growing Up*. Harcourt Paperbacks, 2006.

Blake, Ashley Herring. *Ivy Aberdeen's Letter to the World*. Little, Brown and Company, 2018.

Bloom, Naama. *Helloflo: The Guide, Period*. Dutton Children's Books, 2017.

Callender, Kheryn. *Hurricane Child*. Scholastic Press, 2018.

Cole, Joanna., and Thomas, Bill. *Asking About Sex and Growing Up (revised edition): A Question-and-Answer Book for Kids*. Collins, 2009.

Dunham, Kelli. *Girl's Body Book*. Applesauce Press, 2013.

Dunham, Kelli. *The Boy's Body Book: Everything You Need to Know for Growing Up You*. Applesauce Press, 2007.

Frost, Helen. *When My Sister Started Kissing*. Farrar, Straus, Giroux, 2017.

Gephart, Donna. *Lily and Dunkin*. Delacorte Press, 2016.

Gerhardt, Jake. *My Future Ex-Girlfriend*. Viking, 2017.

Gravelle, Karen. *The Period Book: A Girl's Guide to Growing Up*. Bloomsbury, 2017.

Harris, R. *It's Perfectly Normal: Changing Bodies, Growing Up, Sex and Sexual Health*. Candlewick, 2009.

Hitchcock, Shannon. *One True Way*. Scholastic Press, 2018.

Howe, James. *Totally Joe*. Atheneum Books for Young Readers, 2007.

Ibrahim, Marawa. *The Girl Guide: 50 Ways to Learn to Love Your Changing Body*. HarperCollins, 2018.

Kinney, Jeff. *Diary of a Wimpy Kid*. Amulet, 2007.

Korman, Gordon. *Supergifted*. Balzer + Bray, an imprint of HarperCollinsPublishers, 2018.

Madaras, Lynda. *The "What's Happening to My Body?" Book for Boys*. Newmarket, 2007.

Madaras, Lynda. *The "What's Happening to My Body?" Book for Girls*. Newmarket, 2007.

Madaras, Lynda. *My Body, My Self for Boys, Revised Third Edition*. Newmarket, 2007.

Madaras, Lynda. *My Body, My Self for Girls, Revised Third Edition*. Newmarket, 2007.

Mar, Jonathan. *The Body Book for Boys*. Scholastic Paperbacks, 2010.

Metzger, Julie. *Will Puberty Last My Whole Life? REAL Answers to REAL Questions from Preteens about Body Changes, Sex, and Other Growing-up Stuff*. Sasquatch, 2012.

Moss, Marissa. *Amelia's Boy Survival Guide*. Simon & Schuster Books for Young Readers, 2015.

Natterson, Cara Familian. *Guy Stuff: The Body Book for Boys*. American Girl Publishing, 2017.

Nuchi, Adah. *Bunk 9's Guide to Growing Up: Secrets, Tips, and Expert Advice on the Good, the Bad & the Awkward*. Workman Publishing, 2017.

Paschen, Elise. *Poetry Speaks: Who I Am*. Sourcebooks, 2010.

Peck, Richard. *The Best Man*. Dial Books for Young Readers, 2016.

Petro-Roy, Jen. *P.S. I Miss You*. Feiwel and Friends, 2018.

Saltz, Gail. *Changing You!: A Guide to Body Changes and Sexuality*. Puffin, 2009.

Silverberg, Cory. *Sex Is a Funny Word: A Book About Bodies, Feelings, and You*. Seven Stories Press, 2015.

Telgemeier, Raina. *Smile*. Graphix/Scholastic, 2010.

Tolan, Stephanie. *Applewhites Coast to Coast*. Harper, an imprint of HarperCollinsPublishers, 2017.

Vail, Rachel. *Well, That Was Awkward*. Viking, 2017.

ENDNOTES

1. American Academy of Pediatrics, *Media and Children Communication Toolkit* (https://www.aap.org/en-us/advocacy-and-policy/aap-health-initiatives/Pages/Media-and-Children.aspx).

2. Ibid.

3. Ibid.

4. R. Wind, *Birth and Abortion Among Adolescents and Young Adults Continue to Decline* (https://www.guttmacher.org/news-release/2017/us-rates-pregnancy-birth-and-abortion-among-adolescents-and-young-adults-continue; 2017).

5. Child Trends, *Data Bank Indicator: Teen Pregnancy* (https://www.childtrends.org/indicators/teen-pregnancy; 2016).

6. Ibid.

7. J. Manlove et al., "Linking Changes in Contraceptive Use to Decline in Teen Pregnancy Rates," *Societies* 6, no. 1 (2016). (http://www.mdpi.com/2075-4698/6/1/1/htm).

8. Centers for Disease Control and Prevention, *About Teen Pregnancy* (https://www.cdc.gov/teenpregnancy/about/index.htm; 2018).

9. Centers for Disease Control and Prevention, *STD Trends in the United States: 2010 National Data for Gonorrhea, Chlamydia, and Syphilis* (https://www.cdc.gov/std/stats/; 2011).

10. Office of Adolescent Health, *Adolescent Development and STDs* (https://www.hhs.gov/ash/oah/adolescent-development/reproductive-health-and-teen-pregnancy/stds/index.html; 2016).

11. Centers for Disease Control and Prevention, *STD Trends in the United States: 2010 National Data for Gonorrhea, Chlamydia, and Syphilis*.

12. U.S. Department of Health and Human Services, *Healthy People 2020* (www.healthypeople.gov/2020/default.aspx).

13. Power to Decide, *Why it Matters* (https://powertodecide.org/what-we-do/information/why-it-matters).

14. Ibid.

15. G. Ehrlich and C. Vega-Matos, *The impact of Adolescent Pregnancy and Parenthood on Educational Achievement: A Blueprint for Education Policymaker's Involvement in Prevention Efforts* (Alexandria, VA: National Association of State Boards of Education, 2000).

16. D. Kirby and G. LePore, *Sexual Risk and Protective Factors - Factors Affecting Teen Sexual Behavior Pregnancy, Childbearing and Sexually Transmitted Disease: Which Are important? What Can You Change?* (ETR Associates, 2007).

17. Ibid.

18. Centers for Disease Control and Prevention, *School Health Policy and Practices Study 2016* (https://www.cdc.gov/healthyyouth/data/shpps/results.htm).

19. D. Kirby and G. LePore, *Sexual Risk and Protective Factors - Factors Affecting Teen Sexual Behavior Pregnancy, Childbearing and Sexually Transmitted Disease: Which Are important? What Can You Change?*.

20. Kaiser Family Foundation, *Sex Education in America: General Public/Parents Survey* (Washington, DC: Kaiser Family Foundation, 2004).

21. M. Eisenberg et al., Support for Comprehensive Sexuality Education: Perspectives from Parents of School-Age Youth, *Journal of Adolescent Health* 42, (2008):352–59.

22. H. B. Chin et al., The Effectiveness of Group-Based Comprehensive Risk-Reduction and Abstinence Education Interventions to Prevent or Reduce the Risk of Adolescent Pregnancy, Human Immunodeficiency Virus, and Sexually Transmitted Infections: Two Systematic Reviews for the Guide to Community Preventive Services, *American Journal of Preventative Medicine* 42, no. 3 (2012):272–294.

23. Future of Sex Education. *Youth Health and Rights in Sex Education*. (http://www.futureofsexed.org/youthhealth-rights.html)

24. Eisenstein, Z. *Survey Says (Again): People Overwhelmingly Support Sex Ed*. Sexuality Information and Education Council of the United States. (https://siecus.org/survey-says-people-support-sex-ed; 2018)

25. D. Kirby, *Emerging Answers 2007: Research Findings on Programs to Reduce Teen Pregnancy and Sexually Transmitted Diseases* (https://powertodecide.org/sites/default/files/resources/primary-download/emerging-answers.pdf; 2007).

26. Centers for Disease Control and Prevention, *School Health Policy and Practices Study 2016*.

27. D. Kirby, *Emerging Answers 2007: Research Findings on Programs to Reduce Teen Pregnancy and Sexually Transmitted Diseases*.

28. ETR, *10 Characteristics of Effective Sex and HIV Education Programs* (http://recapp.etr.org/recapp/documents/theories/tenCharAssess.pdf; 2004).

29. M. K. Donavan, *The Looming Threat to Sex Education: A Resurgence of Federal Funding for Abstinence-Only Programs?* (https://www.guttmacher.org/gpr/2017/03/looming-threat-sex-education-resurgence-federal-funding-abstinence-only-programs; 2017).

30. H. B. Chin et al., "The Effectiveness of Group-Based Comprehensive Risk-Reduction and Abstinence Education Interventions to Prevent or Reduce the Risk of Adolescent Pregnancy, Human Immunodeficiency Virus, and Sexually Transmitted Infections: Two Systematic Reviews for the Guide to Community Preventive Services."

31. U.S. House of Representative Committee on Government Reform—Minority Staff Special Investigations Division, *The Content of Federally Funded Abstinence-Only Education Programs* (Washington, DC: Prepared for Representative Henry A. Waxman, 2004).

32. Levine, A. *What is Normal Childhood Sexual Development?* Sexuality Information and Education Council of the United States. https://siecus.org/wp-content/uploads/2015/07/FAT_Newsletter_V3N4-Normal-Childhood-Sexual-Development.pdf

33. Ibid.

34. Ibid.

35. Centers for Disease Control and Prevention, "Youth Risk Behavior Surveillance System, 2017," *MMWR* 67, no. 8 (2017).

36. World Health Organization, "Revision of ICD-11 (gender incongruence/transgender) – questions

and answers (Q&A)," [video recording], June 18, 2018, https://www.youtube.com/watch?v=kyCgz0z05Ik.

37. National Center for Health Statistics, *Trends in Circumcision for Male Newborns in U.S. Hospitals: 1979–2010* (https://www.cdc.gov/nchs/data/hestat /circumcision_2013/circumcision_2013.htm; 2015).

38. Medline Plus, *Sexually Transmitted Diseases* (www.nlm .nih.gov/medlineplus/sexuallytransmitteddiseases.html; 2014).

39. American Academy of Family Physicians, *STIs: Common Symptoms and Tips on Prevention* (http://familydoctor .org/online/famdocen/home/common/sexinfections /sti/165.html; 2010).

40. Ibid.

41. Avert, *What Does Undetectable Mean?* (https://www.avert .org/living-with-hiv/antiretroviral-treatment/what-does -undetectable-mean; 2018).

42. The Jewish Agency for Israel, *Adolescent Issues and Coming of Age Ceremonies* (2014).

43. Answers.com, *Coming-of-Age* (www.answers.com/topic /coming-of-age; 2014).

44. Kids Web Japan, *Coming-of-Age Day* (http://web-japan.org /kidsweb/explore/calendar/January/seijinshiki.html; 2014).

45. W. Coffee, J. Coffee, and J. N. Elizalde, *Peace Signs: A Manual for Teaching School Children Anger Management and Communication Skills* (Honolulu: Coffee Press Publications, 2000).

46. P. M. Wilson, M. Quackenbush, and W. M. Kame, *Teach and Talk: The Subject Is Sex* (Santa Cruz, CA: ETR Associates, 2011).

47. S. Joslin and M. Sendak, *What Do You Do Dear? Proper Conduct for All Occasions* (HarperTrophy: New York, NY, 1986).

(Tracy, age 12)

Managing Loss, Death, and Grief

DESIRED LEARNER OUTCOMES

After reading this chapter, you will be able to . . .

- **Describe the reasons to include loss, death, and grief education in elementary and middle schools.**

- **Describe the developmental stages of understanding death.**

- **Explain the stages of grief.**

- **Explain the stages of dying.**

- **Summarize the current teacher's role when a student or a student's relative dies.**

- **Summarize the school's and teacher's role when dealing with a disaster or traumatic event.**

- **Explain the school's role when handling a suicide.**

- **Demonstrate developmentally appropriate learning strategies incorporating concepts and skills that help students deal with loss, death, and grief.**

- **Demonstrate developmentally appropriate loss, death, and grief assessment techniques that can be used with K–8 students.**

- **Use loss, death, and grief Internet and other resources.**

- **Provide examples of children's literature featuring loss, death, and grief themes that can be used in cross-curricular instructional activities.**

INTRODUCTION

Loss, death, and grief affect everyone, regardless of race, gender, or age, yet they remain taboo topics of discussion in our society. To change this attitude, formalized instruction and informal discussion, particularly of critical incidents and events related to loss, death, and grief, need to be included in the elementary and middle school health education curriculum. The tendency is to try to protect children and preadolescents from these topics. This prevents those young people from obtaining accurate information, which in turn can exacerbate their fears and anxieties about these natural life processes.

Teaching about loss, death, and grief helps students deal effectively with their feelings when a loved one dies, but many adults find it difficult to discuss these things, particularly with children. For example, parents sometimes find it easier to evade the issue or even lie about a death because they want to protect their children from any uncomfortable feelings. Although parents who react to a death in this way are trying to help their children, in the long run avoidance can cause problems. Some parents use euphemistic language with their children, such as "Grandma is taking a long vacation" or "Grandpa is sleeping." Although the parents' intention is to ease the pain of loss, children at a more concrete developmental level might be frightened to take a vacation or go to sleep because they are confused about what happened to Grandma or Grandpa. Parents also might immediately replace a dead pet with a new one. Children typically do not want their pet replaced, but parents sometimes feel it will help the children forget the loss and get over the death.

Teachers who have researched the subject and have been trained in the various aspects of death and grief are able to satisfy the natural and developmentally consistent curiosities of young children. They can help children understand that their feelings about death are normal and even healthy. Teachers also can deal professionally and truthfully with other important issues of death and grief.

At the elementary and middle grades, professional instruction is important, because this is the time when many students first experience a loss, for example, when they move away from a best friend, when their parents divorce, or when an older brother or sister goes to college. Many elementary children experience a death, whether seen on television or experienced with a pet or a family member. It is estimated that one in twenty or 5 percent children will lose a parent by death by age 16; two-thirds of children experience the death of a friend, sibling, parent, or grandparent by age 10; and almost every child will experience the death of a pet, a friend, or a relative.[1, 2] Children need to know the facts and issues surrounding death, dying, and loss so that any false impressions they have formed can be dispelled and so that they can deal with death in a healthy manner.

Readers might notice that this chapter is organized differently than the previous content-related chapters (Chapters 5–13). Unlike behaviors such as tobacco use or inactivity, loss and grief cannot be prevented. These are feelings and experiences that all children have, and teachers should be equipped to help students through the process. This chapter presents information about loss, death, and grief and ideas on teaching these topics to elementary and middle school students. Even with accurate information and suggested teaching activities in hand, teachers need to explore their own attitudes about loss, death, and grief before trying to teach the subject. Pronounced death anxiety or fears on the part of teachers might be conveyed to their students. Such well-meaning professionals can do more harm than good.

REASONS TO INCLUDE LOSS, DEATH, AND GRIEF EDUCATION IN ELEMENTARY AND MIDDLE SCHOOLS

Some administrators and teachers feel overwhelmed by the number of subjects and topics they are asked to teach their students during the school year. Loss, death, and grief education is an important topic to include within the elementary and middle school health education curriculum. Seventy to 100 years ago, loss, death, and grief would not have been an important topic to teach children, because families, churches, and the health care delivery system were different than they are today. During that time, it was common for children to experience the death of a sibling, parent, neighbor, or grandparent. Not only did deaths occur at a younger age, but the families were responsible for preparing the body and making all the funeral arrangements. There were no funeral homes as we know them today, and undertakers did not take care of all of the arrangements. Today, the living are isolated from the dying because the terminally ill typically are in hospitals, hospices, and nursing homes, whereas in the past dying people stayed at home. When a person dies, the funeral home takes care of all the details, from the preparation of the body for the funeral to the burial. Many parents totally isolate their children from the dying person and the funeral because they want to shelter them from pain. The changes have made death mysterious and, for some, more fearful. Many children do not have any real experiences with death and are only educated by the media. Because children are removed from death and do not understand what it is all about, teachers and other adults need to talk with them about death.

Although death is portrayed in the media, the portrayals are often misleading and confusing. According to Elisabeth Kübler-Ross, the media present "death in a two-dimensional aspect that tends to make it unreal and devoid of significant emotions."[3] A person is alive and then dead, and the emotions surrounding the death often are ignored. Because of these misleading portrayals, children once again are protected from the very real emotions that are connected with death. Children also might get confused about death when watching television because they might see a character get killed on one show and two days later see the same actor as a different character on another show.

Children, even those younger than age 6, are curious about death and typically have many questions about the topic.[4-6] Many parents do not feel comfortable talking about death, so they ignore the questions or lie to the child. For example, if a child asks what *dead* means, the parent might tell the child that he or she is too young to understand. The teacher can be an objective resource for answers to many of these sensitive questions.

Another reason to include loss, death, and grief education in the elementary and middle school curriculum is to allow students to express their feelings. Students should be taught about grief so that, if they do experience a loss, they will know that they are not alone in how they feel. Students also might have a relative going through the dying process and, if allowed to discuss the stages of dying and the feelings associated with those stages, might feel less isolated.

It is healthy for children to gain an understanding of what people do for those who are grieving. Teachers should explain to children that loss or death is a topic that is out-of-bounds for teasing. Students should be taught how to respond to the grieving process. It should be explained to them that loss and grief might be a long process and a challenge for their classmates. Sending sympathy cards and acknowledging another student who is grieving are important skills for students to master.

In the upper-elementary and middle-level grades, students might become more interested in death-related issues as a result of technology, such as euthanasia. Students will hear those issues being discussed on television, and they might need a forum in which to discuss them openly.

Some people might argue that the home or the church is the place to discuss the issues of loss, death, and dying. It would be wonderful if all children could discuss this topic openly with their parents; however, it just does not happen. As stated previously, many parents do not talk to their children about death because they are uncomfortable with the topic.[7] All children deserve the opportunity to discuss this relevant issue openly, which leaves the schools as the most practical place to teach about issues of loss, death, and grief.

IMPORTANT BACKGROUND FOR K–8 TEACHERS

There are a variety of topics about loss, death, and grief with which teachers should be both familiar and comfortable. These topics include the developmental stages of understanding death, the stages of grief, and the stages of dying. Depending on the grade level, not all of this information is developmentally appropriate; however, all teachers should have a basic understanding of these concepts.

Developmental Stages of Understanding Death

Several studies have been conducted with children to determine the developmental stages of understanding death. Perhaps the most widely cited study was published in 1948 by Maria Nagy.[8] Nagy maintained that children's ideas about death develop in three age-related stages. Although her work has been the standard for this topic, more current research suggests that the age of a child is not the best predictor of the

child's understanding of death. There are several factors in children's environments that affect their understanding of death. Unfortunately, findings from studies regarding this issue are inconsistent. Researchers tend to agree that age, cognitive ability, teachings by parents and significant others, input from the media, and death experience influence a child's understanding of death. However, there is no agreement on the age or level of cognitive development needed to have a mature understanding of death.[9, 10] Although there are disagreements about Nagy's age-graded developmental model of understanding death, it still provides a foundation for elementary and middle school teachers as they work with their students.

- *Stage one (ages 3 to 5).* During this developmental stage, children do not understand the finality of death. They see death as a sleeplike, reversible state because their conceptions of time are concrete. They view the dead person as still being able to eat, work, laugh, and cry as if alive. Because of this view, children often seem matter of fact or callous about death. This is often demonstrated at funerals, when children in stage one show no signs of grief and, in fact, enjoy themselves with other stage one cousins and relatives. Parents are sometimes embarrassed when this type of behavior occurs; however, because these children believe the dead person will eventually return and continue to function, they see no reason to grieve. Children might also act this way if the person who died is not in their immediate circle of contact or support. It is not uncommon for children in this stage to ask questions such as "When is Daddy coming back?" It is especially important for adults *not* to explain death in terms of sleep or a vacation, because doing so reinforces some inaccurate beliefs. Although young children do not understand the finality of death, that lack of understanding does not negate the sense of grief that children might experience with any type of separation. Depending on experiences and maturity, many children in kindergarten through second grade will still view death as not final.
- *Stage two (ages 5 to 9).* Nagy found that children in stage two have an understanding of finality; however, they believe that an outside source, such as the "bogeyman" or "death man," causes death. Children often communicate with the bogeyman by asking him to leave their family alone or to go away. Many guilt feelings are associated with death during this stage, because stage two children believe the bogeyman is watching their actions. For instance, if a 7-year-old boy asks his grandfather to buy him a toy and the grandfather refuses, the boy might think negative thoughts about the grandfather. If the grandfather then dies, the boy might think that the bogeyman heard his negative thoughts about his grandfather and therefore he caused his grandfather's death. During this stage, it is important for teachers to be aware of potential guilt feelings and to try to alleviate them.
- *Stage three (age 9 and older).* During stage three, children fully understand the finality of death and know that it is something that happens within the body, not something strictly external. They are more likely to understand that death is universal and an inevitable end to everyone's life, including their own. Children in stage three do not associate

© Tatyana Tomsickova/123RF

It is appropriate for children to attend funerals and visit graves.

death with themselves, however, but rather associate death with other, "old" people. During this stage, middle school students may experience a variety of feelings and emotions, expressed in ways such as acting out, crying, anger, or self-injurious behavior.[11]

Although these stages have been identified, it is important to remember that they are not prescriptive but instead should serve as guidelines. Children's behavior, depending on their personal experiences with death, might not conform to the suggested age parameters.

Stages of Grief

Grief is the psychological and sometimes physical response to the death of a loved one or to the loss or longing of someone due to transition (divorce of parents, a move). It consists of the feelings of sorrow, anger, depression, guilt, confusion, shock, and despair that occur after someone dies. For most children, death is a new experience and can be confusing. Children's reaction to loss and grief are influenced by their understanding of the permanence of death (see previous section). Their grief is also influenced by how well their family deals with loss. For example, if a child experiences the death of one parent, it may be difficult for the surviving parent to be supportive because of the grief he or she is facing. Other factors that may affect the way children respond to loss or death include their age, personality, coping skills, history of other losses or death, available support systems, type of death, and the relationship with the person who died.[12]

For many years, professionals believed that children went through stages of grief, similar to the stages a person might go through when dying (see Stages of Dying section in this chapter). Today, most experts in this field believe that children do not grieve in sequential stages, but instead experience many feelings, either simultaneously or independent of one another. It is

important for teachers to understand common feelings and behaviors a young person may display after a loss or death. It is also important for teachers to understand problem behaviors and reactions to a loss and know when to refer the student to a mental health professional.

Common and normal childhood reactions to a death or loss in which teachers should be aware include[13-17]:

1. *Shock.* This is a typical reaction to death or loss, and it can help the child detach from the pain he or she is experiencing.
2. *Sadness.* Children may exhibit their feelings of sadness through crying, isolating themselves from others, or being very quiet or introverted.
3. *Regressive behaviors.* Some children may begin to regress to behaviors they exhibited when they were younger. For example, children who were beginning to act independently may instead begin to act childishly and be clingy.
4. *Guilt.* Because children are very egocentric, they commonly feel like they are the cause of the death, regardless of the situation. They may believe their thoughts, wishes, or actions were the cause of a death. For example, a child may believe a person died because he or she wished the person were dead after a fight.
5. *Anxiety or fear.* Children may feel anxious or fearful, especially after the death of a parent. The child may wonder who would take care of them if the other parent dies. In addition, if a sibling dies, the surviving child may wonder if he or she is next.
6. *Isolation.* Children who experience a loss or death may feel isolated for a variety of reasons. For example, they may not have an adequate support system at home, if the adults in their life are having a difficult time with the death. In addition, classmates may not know how to respond to a student who has experienced a death, so they may ignore or exclude that student. The classmates aren't trying to be mean, but they may not know appropriate ways to talk or act around the grieving student. Another cause for isolation may happen because the adults in the child's life avoid talking about the deceased person in fear that it might upset the child. The child might get the message that it is not acceptable to talk about his or her feelings associated with the death.
7. *Explosive emotions or acting out.* Children and pre adolescents who think they are not supposed to cry or act sad, sometimes express their grief through explosive emotions or negative behaviors because they don't know any other way to express their feelings of grief.

When children express grief, the most important things for adults to remember are to allow them to grieve and to provide them with as much support as possible. There are three things that are of primary importance to grieving children:

1. They need to feel safe. Teachers can make the classroom feel safe by listening to students' concerns and not ignoring their grief.

Children need to understand that grief is a normal and healthy response to loss.

2. They need teachers and other significant adults to acknowledge their pain. Just by saying to a student "You seem sad today" acknowledges their feelings of pain and lets them know that their feelings are okay.

3. They need to know that there is no time limit on their grief. Children and preadolescents will express their grief differently. Some students will seem okay for an extended period and then go through a time of sadness. Anniversaries, birthdays, and other special events can trigger these feelings of sadness. Don't expect students to "get over" a death in a set time period.[18]

Many times, teachers are concerned about what is normal or abnormal grieving. The distinction is not easy to determine. It is not so much the emotions or behaviors that stand out, but their intensity and duration. What should be of concern is the continued denial or avoidance of reality, prolonged bodily distress, persistent panic, extended guilt, enduring anxiety, and unceasing hostility. If there is any doubt about whether a child needs professional attention, it is best to ask the school counselor for advice.[19]

Stages of Dying

It is important for teachers and students to understand the stages of dying. Some students might have a relative who is dying, and it would be helpful for those students to understand why their relative acts the way he or she does. Elisabeth Kübler-Ross is the person most associated with research on the emotions of the dying. She interviewed about 200 terminally ill patients and found that most of them went through five psychological stages.[20] Not everyone with a terminal illness will experience all these stages, and not everyone progresses through these stages in the stated order. Some people fluctuate between two stages at the same time, whereas others skip various stages. These stages should not be valued as being good or bad but rather should be seen as guidelines to help a person interact with the dying. The stages are denial, anger, bargaining, depression, and acceptance.

• *Denial.* The first emotion that most persons experience when they are told they have a terminal illness is denial. This is a healthy response to a stressful situation, and it acts as a temporary buffer to help protect the individual. It is not uncommon for the terminally ill to return periodically to the denial stage, even after progressing to other stages. This stage becomes dangerous only when the terminally ill person seeks third and fourth opinions about an illness or spends money on quack cures.

• *Anger.* After terminally ill persons can no longer deny their approaching death, they typically become angry, resentful, and hostile. This is perhaps the most difficult stage for loved ones to deal with because the anger sometimes is directed at them. Anger might be expressed through shouting, complaining, and bitterness. For instance, the person might say, "I don't want to see anyone—go away." These emotions are understandable but not always easy to deal with. This is an especially important stage for children to understand, because a terminally ill grandparent might yell or express meanness to a child while in this stage. Children need to understand that the grandparent is angry not at them but at the situation.

• *Bargaining.* Bargaining typically occurs throughout most of the dying process. This stage is characterized by the terminally ill person's bargaining with someone in power, such as the physician or God, to prolong life. For instance, a terminally ill person might think, "If you let me live until my next birthday, I promise I will always be a kind person." An outsider might not be aware of this stage, because many patients keep these bargains a secret.

• *Depression.* Many terminally ill people bounce back and forth among the bargaining stage, the depression stage, and the anger stage. After they determine that the bargaining has not worked, they become depressed. They begin to understand that death is certain, and feelings of sadness and depression become overwhelming. Although it might be frightening for a child to visit a terminally ill person, children should not be discouraged from doing so. Many times, children can help the patient deal with or temporarily forget about death. When visiting a terminally ill relative, children should be encouraged to take a small present, such as an art project from school. This can give the patient and the child something to talk about. The opportunity to bring some happiness to a dying person might also help children feel useful and helpful.

• *Acceptance.* The last stage of the dying process occurs when the person accepts the outcome of death. It does not mean that the person is happy; rather, there is a lack of feelings. During this stage, the dying person wants to make psychological and practical arrangements, such as funeral arrangements or the writing of a will. Those arrangements become difficult and frustrating if the relatives still deny the death; however, it is important to accommodate the dying person as much as possible.

Children should understand that one of the biggest fears of dying people is the fear of being alone. If children understand this and the stages of dying, they might be more inclined to make frequent visits or contacts with a terminally ill relative.

GUIDELINES FOR TEACHERS

When teaching about loss, death, and grief, it is important not only to identify activities that are useful for elementary teachers but also to understand the guidelines for teaching about loss and death, dealing with a grieving student, handling a traumatic event, and facing the aftermath of a student suicide. What follows are guidelines for teachers in dealing with all of these events. These guidelines can help teachers and administrators avoid becoming defensive with parents and students when teaching a controversial topic such as loss, death, and grief.

Teaching About Loss, Death, and Grief

Teachers must be honest with students—many times, parents and other adults try to shield children from any loss- or death-related experiences or emotions. Although shielding children might delay their pain, it will emerge at some point. For instance, while discussing death-related issues in college classes, some students express their anger about not being able to go to their grandparent's funeral when they were younger or not being told about a pet's or a relative's death. When children are not allowed to attend funerals or memorials, they often create images in their minds that are far worse than the actual event.[21] Following are some guidelines for talking with students about loss, death, and grief.

- *It is important for teachers to be honest and open when answering children's questions about death.* If children are capable of asking a question, then they are capable of understanding an answer offered at the same level. Sometimes, teachers might not know the answer to a child's question. Instead of making up an answer, teachers should not hesitate to say "I don't know, but I will try to find an answer for you." As soon as the teacher obtains the answer, it should be relayed to the student.
- *When teachers are answering students' questions, it is important to be as factual as possible.* For instance, if a student asks, "What makes people die?" an appropriate response is "A person's heart stops beating." Although this seems concrete and simple, it is important to remember that most elementary students are concrete thinkers.

If a teacher does not understand a question, he or she can refer the question back to the child. For instance, if a child asks, "Do children die?" it might be a good idea to find out what the child thinks and why he or she has asked the question. The teacher might respond by asking, "Do you think children die?" or "What made you ask that question?" The responses to these questions can give the teacher more information and provide a framework to best answer the original question.

- *Teachers should avoid providing personal values and beliefs on controversial issues related to death.* Parents become uncomfortable when teachers voice their views on controversial issues related to death. For instance, a teacher should not suggest that dead people go to heaven, that euthanasia should be legalized, or that reincarnation is possible. These beliefs should be discussed within the family unit. Death and grief education should focus on the facts and feelings surrounding grief and death. Children, however, will ask teachers their opinions about value-related issues, such as "What happens to people when they die?" The safest way for a teacher to respond to that question is to simply state, "There are many ideas about what happens to people when they die, and the best thing to do is to ask your parents or caregivers what their beliefs are about this question." Because there are numerous religious viewpoints about death, it is important for teachers not to promote any one viewpoint. Remember, teachers should not impose their philosophy of death on children, no matter how comforting they think it might be.[22]
- *Teachers should be especially good and supportive listeners when children are discussing their feelings about death.*[23] Many children already will have experienced the death of a pet or a relative by the time they reach elementary school, but they might not have been given the opportunity to express their feelings about death. While discussing death or teaching a lesson about grief, many children want the opportunity to express their feelings about the death of someone they knew. It is important for teachers to listen and encourage the sharing of feelings so that students understand that other classmates have felt the same way in similar situations. It is also acceptable for teachers to share the feelings of grief they have experienced.
- *Teachers should ask children to explain what they have learned about death during class.* Although the developmental attributes of young children are consistent with concrete thinking, adults tend to use metaphorical explanations about death. Many teachers do not realize they are using metaphors or euphemistic language and can innocently confuse children. For example, if a euphemism such as *gone away* is used instead of *died,* children might view death as a person leaving for a while. Sentence stems can be offered at the end of a lesson to summarize what each student has learned:

I learned . . .

I was surprised . . .

I feel . . .

The Teacher's Role When a Student or a Student's Relative Is Dying or Dies

If a person teaches long enough, he or she probably will experience the death of a student or the death of a student's close relative, such as a parent or sibling. Although it is best to discuss death before it occurs, sometimes this is not possible. Regardless of whether dying, death, and grief have been formally taught before a death occurs, several guidelines should be remembered when discussing the death of a classmate or the

Children can be encouraged to write sympathy cards.

death of a classmate's relative with elementary and middle school students[24-29]:

1. Teachers should be prepared to deal with a child in the class who is dying. For example, there might be frequent absences or hair loss due to therapeutic regimens. Children should participate in discussions of their feelings about dying as well as death. The class might vote to get a special hat for the child who has lost his or her hair and to wear hats also.

2. Teachers should feel comfortable in expressing their grief openly after the death of a child. When teachers share their grief with the class, students are able to see that it is acceptable to cry or feel sad. Many teachers are afraid they will say something wrong or act inappropriately, but the most important thing to children is the sincere care and concern their teachers show toward them.

3. If possible, talk with the grieving child before he or she returns to school. Ask the child what he or she wants the class to know about the death.

4. Talk to the class about how grief affects people. Discuss how difficult it may be for their classmates to return to school.

5. Teachers should acknowledge and discuss guilt feelings. Guilt is commonly felt by survivors of a loved one. A teacher can help by acknowledging the guilt and helping children understand that the death was not their fault. It might be helpful for upper-elementary and middle-level students to write about their feelings if they are having a difficult time discussing them.

6. Teachers should encourage students to write personal sympathy cards to the parents or to a student who has had someone close die. This helps students deal with their grief, and the survivors appreciate it. Teachers can instruct students to emphasize their fond memories of the deceased and their sorrow. Teachers also can ask students how they want to commemorate a student who has died. They might create a memorial book,

collect money for a charitable donation, or plant a tree to help them remember their friend.

7. Teachers should allow children to express their grief and sadness. Because grief always surfaces at some point, it is important for children to be allowed to grieve. Many times, adults tell children to be brave and be strong, but this causes students to repress their grief. Because the school might be the only place where children are allowed to express their sadness, teachers should give the students time to openly express their feelings.

8. If a classmate dies, teachers should not force a typical day on grieving students. It is important to have structured and planned activities; however, part of the day should revolve around sharing feelings and discussing death. For example, students should help decide what to do with the empty desk and possessions of a classmate who dies. Some daily routines should be maintained, because children can become agitated and disoriented when boundaries disappear in times of crisis.

9. Teachers should expect unusual behavior from students for several weeks or months after the death of a classmate or relative. Students might become aggressive, exhibit a lack of concentration, be withdrawn, have mood swings, become nervous, or experience headaches and nausea. These are normal behaviors for persons who are experiencing grief. If a teacher is concerned about a student's excessive behavior, it is important that the teacher refer the student to the school counselor. Teachers also should reassure children that feelings of sadness, loneliness, anger, and anxiety are normal reactions to a death. Sometimes, just knowing that these reactions are normal is helpful to children.

10. Teachers should not focus on the details of death. For example, it is not important to describe an automobile crash or a deteriorating disease to students. This may frighten them needlessly and cause unwarranted stress.

11. In talking with students, teachers should use the words *dead* and *death,* avoiding phrases meant to soften the blow, such as "she went away" or "God took him." These phrases can be confusing and scary.

12. A touch sometimes can communicate more comfort than words can to children who are experiencing grief. If it is appropriate, a teacher can ask permission to give a child a hug.

13. Teachers should plan nonverbal activities to allow expressions of grief. For example, listening to music, drawing pictures, and writing journal entries allow nonverbal students an opportunity to express grief.

14. Teachers should not try to tell children how they feel. Teachers should ask them how they feel but should not say "I know how you must feel."

15. Teachers should encourage social interactions with peers. Children who are grieving need social interaction. Teachers can plan activities in which all students are required to interact with one another.

16. Teachers should have resources available in the classroom about death and grief or offer to read a book to children that helps explain grief.

17. Teachers should allow a distraught child to call home if necessary. A child who has experienced the death of a parent, sibling, or grandparent might need reassurance that a parent is still at home, waiting.

These guidelines can help teachers who are faced with the death of a student or of a student's relative. If teachers have other concerns, funeral directors and school counselors are good resources on how to deal with children after a death has occurred.

The School's and Teacher's Roles When Dealing with Disasters or Traumatic Events

It is not uncommon for children to witness or experience a disaster or traumatic event. For example, past generations of children have witnessed or lived through the shooting of national leaders (J. F. Kennedy, Martin Luther King, Jr.), school shootings (Columbine, Sandy Hook), and the destruction of buildings (the Oklahoma City bombing and World Trade Center) and have experienced tornadoes, hurricanes (Katrina), fires, earthquakes, and other natural disasters.

It is important for school personnel to understand how to help children deal with disasters and traumatic events. For example, most children react in the following ways:

- They feel a loss of control—disasters and traumatic events are something over which we have little or no control. This feeling of loss of control can be overwhelming to children and adults alike.
- They experience a loss of stability—disasters and traumatic events threaten a child's routine and structure. They get scared that, if this event could happen once, it could happen again.
- They are very self-centered—these events can make children worry about their own safety and well-being, to an extent that some adults may think is unreasonable. Children need ongoing messages of comfort regarding their safety.[30]

Traumatic events can lead to painful emotions in children. Studies show that following disasters and traumatic events many children experience academic failure, post-traumatic stress disorder (PTSD), depression, anxiety, bereavement, delinquency, and substance abuse.[31-34] If these signs and symptoms persist, it is advisable for teachers to refer students to a school counselor or another mental health professional. Some common stress symptoms that elementary teachers might observe or hear about include:

Clinginess

Aggressiveness

Withdrawal from activities and friends

Increased fighting with friends

School avoidance

Loss of interest and poor concentration in school

Regressive behavior (acting much younger than their age—e.g., asking for help to be fed or dressed)

Headaches or other physical complaints

Depression

Fear about safety

Irritability

Difficulty sleeping because of nightmares[35, 36]

Some common stress symptoms that middle school teachers might observe or hear about include:

Poor school performance

School problems (fighting, attention-seeking behaviors)

Physical complaints such as headaches and stomachaches

Withdrawal from friends

Agitation

Sleep disturbances

Loss of appetite

Rebellion at home (refusal to do chores, not obeying parents)[37, 38]

There are many things school districts and teachers can do after students have experienced a natural disaster or a traumatic event:

1. School districts should have a plan in place as to how they will handle a natural disaster or traumatic event. For example, counselors should be available to help students and teachers handle the event. Administrators should prepare a uniform announcement that teachers can use to tell children about an event if it happens while they are in school. Administrators should also prepare a typed message that can be sent home with students to communicate with parents about how the school dealt with the situation.

2. Teachers should provide opportunities for children to talk about the event and to ask questions. If the natural disaster or traumatic event is something that they are continually seeing on television, they might ask questions for several days or weeks. If teachers don't know the answer to their questions, they should not be afraid to admit it.

3. When a teacher does know the answers to students' questions, the teacher should answer them at an appropriate developmental level.

4. Teachers should practice emergency procedures at school so that children are confident they know what to do in case of an emergency (shelter-in-place, lockdown, evacuation). Also, teachers should encourage children to practice emergency procedures at home with their families (fire escape routes, earthquake procedures).

5. Teachers should promote positive coping and problem-solving skills.

6. Teachers should assure children that there is a wide range of emotions that are appropriate, normal, and healthy and should encourage them to express their emotions.

7. Teachers should try to focus on some positive events that surround the natural disaster or traumatic event (identifying heroes and discussing organizations and people who have been helpful during and after these events).

8. Teachers should try to maintain a routine for children. Children need structure and routine to help them understand that not everything in the world has changed.[39, 40]

The School's Role When Handling a Suicide

Dealing with student suicide is a difficult situation that might occur in some middle schools. Suicide is the third leading cause of death in 10- to 14-year-olds, with 267 deaths among children in this age group.[41] Although it is not common for middle school students to commit suicide, it can happen, and school districts and teachers should be prepared.

It is first important for teachers to understand the risk and protective factors associated with youth suicide. As with other risk factors for various health problems, the more risk factors that are present, the more likely a person is to participate in the risky behavior. The more protective factors that are present, the less likely a person is to participate in the risky behavior. The risk and protective factors for suicide include the following.

Biopsychosocial Risk Factors

- Mental disorders, particularly mood disorders, schizophrenia, anxiety disorders, and certain personality disorders
- Alcohol and other substance use disorders
- Hopelessness
- Impulsive and/or aggressive tendencies
- History of trauma or abuse
- Some major physical illnesses
- Previous suicide attempt
- Family history of suicide

Environmental Risk Factors

- Job or financial loss
- Relational or social loss
- Easy access to lethal means
- Local clusters of suicide that have a contagious influence

Sociocultural Risk Factors

- Lack of social support and sense of isolation
- Stigma associated with help-seeking behavior
- Barriers to accessing health care, especially mental health and substance abuse treatment
- Certain cultural and religious beliefs (for instance, the belief that suicide is a noble resolution of a personal dilemma)
- Exposure to, including through the media, and influence of others who have died by suicide[42]

Protective Factors

- Effective clinical care for mental, physical, and substance use disorders

- Easy access to a variety of clinical interventions and support for help-seeking
- Strong connections to family and community support
- Support through ongoing medical and mental health care relationships
- Skills in problem solving, conflict resolution, and nonviolent handling of disputes
- Cultural and religious beliefs that discourage suicide and support self-preservation[43]

Teachers should be aware of these risk and protective factors and know the warning signs for suicide, which appear in Teacher's Toolbox 14.1. If teachers notice these warning signs in a student, they should refer that student to the school counselor. No one should keep a secret about suspected suicidal behavior. The parents of the suicidal student must be notified.

If an elementary or middle school child does commit suicide, it is important that schools have a plan in place to deal with the suicide and help prevent suicide contagion or copycat suicides. The principal of the school should try to get as much information as soon as possible. The suicide should first be verified by the principal, and permission from the family to discuss the suicide should be obtained. He or she should then meet with teachers and staff to inform them of the proper way to announce the death, support the reactions of their students, and identify and refer close friends of the victim and other high-risk students for counseling. The teachers then should inform each class of students about the suicide. It is important that all the students hear the same thing. After they have been informed, they should have the opportunity to discuss their feelings. The school should have extra counselors available for students and staff who need to talk. Students who appear to be the most severely affected might need parental notification and outside mental health referrals.[44]

Schools also should be very careful not to glorify the victim and sensationalize the suicide. For example, school memorial services at which the victim is held in high esteem should be avoided. Schools should announce when and where the funeral is to be held but should not organize a memorial service.[45] By not glorifying the victim, schools can help prevent further suicides by students who have thought about committing suicide and see the positive attention paid to the victim. Teacher's Toolbox 14.2 summarizes the steps a school should and should not take when a suicide happens.

EVALUATED CURRICULA AND INSTRUCTIONAL MATERIAL

There are two evaluated middle school suicide prevention programs available to school districts. This curriculum should complement, not replace, a comprehensive school health education curriculum. The evaluation results of this curriculum have been reviewed by many professionals and have been shown to be effective.

- *Lifelines Curriculum.* This schoolwide middle school suicide prevention curriculum has as its goals to promote a caring, competent school community in which help seeking is encouraged and modeled and suicidal behavior is recognized as an issue that cannot be kept a secret. The Lifelines includes resources to help a school district establish guidelines and procedures for responding to a student at risk, training for faculty to enhance suicide awareness and skills in identifying and responding to a student with suicidal behavior, and four forty-five-minute lessons for students. The evaluation showed it had significant effects in increasing knowledge about suicide, improving attitudes about suicide intervention, and seeking adult help and not keeping a friend's suicide thoughts a secret.[46]

- *STEP UP.* This schoolwide middle school suicide prevention curriculum is aimed to promote positive mental health, build emotional competence, and create a safe school climate. STEP UP incorporates components of the social-ecological model, social learning/social cognitive theory, and positive psychology in its curriculum implementation and instruction. Resources are included that provide parents or caregivers follow-up strategies and suggestions to reinforce program skills at home. The evaluation showed the program enhances social-emotional skills, promotes pro-social attitudes, established lifelong positive coping skills, and builds skills and strategies to safely and effectively deal with social and emotional challenges.[47]

Recommendations for Concepts and Practice

Sample Students' Questions and Suggested Answers About Loss, Death, and Grief

A list of some commonly asked questions about loss, death, and grief and some suggested answers follows. It is not enough to just read the suggested answers—teachers should practice saying them aloud and adjust their answers to the age of the child asking the question. Teachers are encouraged to think of other questions students might ask and to practice answering them as well.

1. *Why do people die?*

It is sad, but dying is a very natural thing. All things that live will die one day. People, plants, insects, and animals all will die one day.

2. *Is dying like going to sleep?*

No, it's different. When someone dies, the person's body is no longer working. The heart stops beating, the person no longer needs to eat or sleep, and he or she no longer feels any pain. The person doesn't need the body any longer. That means we will never see that person again as we could before.

3. *Does dying hurt?*

Not normally; many people who are old just quietly die. Sometimes, people involved in accidents die so quickly they don't even know it has happened. Even when someone dies after being ill for a long time, the doctor gives him or her special medicine to stop any pain while the person is alive.

4. *Where do dead people go when they die?*

Well, different people believe different things. This is a very important question to ask your parent or caregiver to see what they think.

5. *Why did my grandma die and leave me?*

Your grandma didn't choose to leave you, and I know it doesn't seem fair. She loved you very much and would be with you if she could.

6. *Why didn't someone else die instead of my brother?*

All over the world, living things die every day. Someone else dying would not have prevented your brother from dying.

7. *When someone dies, is she being punished for being bad?*

No; people die because their bodies stop working, either because they have worn out or they have been damaged. Most people live for a long time, but sometimes younger people die because of an accident or a bad illness. Their death has nothing to do with being bad.

8. *Why can't the doctor stop people from dying?*

Doctors often can stop someone from dying, and most people who are ill do not die. Sometimes, though, when there are lots of things wrong with the body or it just wears out, the doctor cannot stop the person from dying.

9. *Why do we have funerals?*

A funeral is a chance for people to comfort each other and remember all the good things about the person who has died.

10. *What causes death?*

Many things can cause death. Injuries, illness, and disease can cause the body to stop working and die. Sometimes, growing very old results in death. Some things never cause death—wishes or thoughts will never cause death. Sometimes, we might not be sure why someone we love has died, and that can confuse us and leave us with many unanswered questions.

11. *My grandpa just died. What can I do when I feel really sad?*

After someone we love dies, it is natural to feel sad, scared, or angry. The best way to take care of yourself is to find a grown-up you trust and let him or her know how you are feeling. Sometimes, just letting someone know how we are feeling reminds us that we are not alone, and this can really help.

12. *What is death?*

Death is the end of living. All things that live eventually die. Just as flowers and animals die, so do people. When people die, they don't breathe, their heart stops beating, and they don't need to eat or drink. Death is not like sleeping. When someone dies, his or her body stops working forever.

STRATEGIES FOR LEARNING AND ASSESSMENT

Managing Loss, Death, and Grief

Learning strategies dealing with managing loss, death, and grief can be used successfully with a range of age groups. Some of the strategies in this section link to science education, as students discuss the characteristics of living and nonliving things. Teachers should be certain that children have opportunities to discuss and understand the range of normal emotions people are likely to experience when someone dies. Teachers should vary the topics and level of discussion to suit the needs and interests of their students. Teachers must know what is going on in their students' lives before initiating lessons related to loss, death, and grief. For example, lessons such as these would be inappropriate if a child has experienced a family death and is back in school for the first time. However, teachers might conduct lessons to help class members demonstrate understanding and empathy when the child returns to school. The anniversary of the September 11, 2001, attacks on the United States often brings up discussions about death, tragedy, and commemorations of people's lives. Teachers will want to know if any children in their classes lost relatives or loved ones during that time.

This section provides examples of standards-based learning and assessment strategies for managing loss, death, and grief. The strategies begin with a restatement of the standard and a reminder of the assessment criteria, drawn from the RMC Health rubrics in Appendix B. Strategies are written as directions for teachers. These learning and assessment strategies provide building blocks for standards-based lessons and units that can be tailored to local needs. Assessment criteria are used with permission from RMC Health. See Appendix B for Scoring Rubrics.

NHES 1 | Core Concepts

Students will comprehend concepts related to health promotion and disease prevention to enhance health.

ASSESSMENT CRITERIA

- Connections—Describe relationships between behavior and health; draw logical conclusions about connections between behavior and health.
- Comprehensiveness—Thoroughly cover health topic, showing breadth and depth; give accurate information.

Grades K–2

Living or Nonliving?   Early elementary students might have difficulty distinguishing the ideas of *living* and *nonliving*. They also might be unsure about what will and will not die. Discuss examples and characteristics of living and nonliving things with students. Make a two-column list. Next, ask them to work in groups of two or three to make a collage of pictures (have magazines on hand or a variety of precut pictures) and drawings of things that live and die and things that do not. Children should explain their categorizations, and teachers should help answer their questions. Experiment with "planting" various kinds of objects—such as seeds of various kinds, flower bulbs, lightbulbs, rocks, chalk—and compare the results. Students also might enjoy breathing or coughing on a piece of bread and sealing it in a plastic bag to see if anything "living" will grow. These experiments help clarify students' ideas about things that are and are not living (and thus cannot grow and cannot die).

ASSESSMENT | The students' categorization of items as living or nonliving is the assessment task for this activity. For assessment criteria, students should be able to categorize accurately and explain their categorizations. This activity links to science education. (Construct: Attitudes toward behavior.)

Water Bugs and Dragonflies: **Explaining Death to Young Children**   In this story D. Stickney (Pilgrim Press) adapts the fable about a water bug that changes into a dragonfly to illustrate the notion of someone going beyond our sight. This story can be used when someone in the class has experienced a death to help young children begin to understand that people and things that die cannot come back. Teachers should read the story to students and discuss how the water bugs are changed into dragonflies. Additionally, considering community and school values/standards, teachers should discuss some of the other key concepts identified in the book. Children should be encouraged to talk with their parents about what they learned from the story and about what their family members believe happens when someone or something dies.

ASSESSMENT | For an assessment task, students can describe in their own words or through drawings the transformation experienced by the water bugs. For assessment criteria, students should accurately explain the transformation and the main concepts of the story. Students should provide accurate information and draw logical conclusions about life cycles. (Construct: Attitudes toward behavior.)

ABC+ Brainstorming   Engage students in ABC Brainstorming, where they try to think of a word (or short phrase) beginning with each letter of the alphabet that ties to the topic of loss, death, and grief. The brainstorm can be completed as a whole-class activity on the board, or older students can complete individually or in small groups. Students may not be able to think of a word for every letter, but they should think of as many as possible. Following the initial brainstorm, students can share their responses, and additional words can be generated for each letter. Bring the class back together and discuss the words students thought of during their brainstorming. This activity will allow students to share what they know about loss, death, and grief, as well as allow the teacher to clarify or correct any misconceptions young students have.

ASSESSMENT | Following the brainstorming and discussion or clarification of the meaning of words, have students select three words that are new to them and use those words in a simple paragraph to demonstrate their understanding of the words or for students who are not yet writers, create a picture demonstrating their understanding of the word. The assessment criterion is the student's ability to demonstrate understanding of loss, death, and grief concepts. (Construct: Attitudes toward behavior.)

The Many Meanings of Loss Brainstorm with students the different word forms of *loss,* such as lost, lose, and examples of different things that can be lost. For example, divorce can feel like the loss of a family, we can lose our favorite bracelet that was given to us by someone special, or fire can bring about the loss of all of our important things and our home. Engage students in exploring different feelings that can be experienced as a result of the different ways we can experience *loss.* Students will begin to gain empathy for the different kinds of loss their friends and family members may experience and be able to have patience with themselves when they have strong feelings associated with losses in their life.

ASSESSMENT | For an assessment, invite students to create a picture of a loss they have experienced and capture the feeling associated with that loss. Students can create a short caption (1 or 2 sentences) to help explain their drawing and the feelings associated with the loss. The assessment criteria include the student's ability to demonstrate their understanding of loss and the emotion that may be felt by the loss. (Constructs: Perceived behavioral control, attitudes toward behavior, social norms.)

Grades 3–5

How Do You Feel? Teachers can begin the lesson by facilitating a discussion about famous people who have died both recently and in the more distant past. Next, have students brainstorm and discuss various ways of remembering someone who has died. Some possibilities include planting a tree or shrub, writing a poem, or composing a song. Then ask students to think of a person who was close to them, or a pet who has died. (If students do not have anyone in mind, allow them to complete this activity about a famous person who has died.) Tell the students that they will write a letter to a person or a pet who has died. The following is a list of things you might ask students to include in the letter:

- How you feel?
- What you miss about the pet or the person?
- What would you want to say to the pet or the person?
- How will you remember the person or pet?

Tell students to indicate on the back of their letter if they are willing to have their letter read aloud to the class. Collect the letters, and choose some to share with the class.

ASSESSMENT | The letter that the students write is the assessment task for this activity. For assessment criteria, students should explain how writing the letter helps them remember the person or pet and deal with their feelings in healthy ways. (Construct: Perceived behavioral control.)

Grades 6–8

Lots of Ways to Cope Conduct a mini-lesson on the various reactions young people have to loss, death, and grief. Include the stages of grief and dying and the various types of reactions young people will have during each

stage of grief or dying. Talk with students about the importance of having a variety of coping skills during difficult times as we are sometimes surprised by the different ways we may react. Share with students three rules for dealing with the feelings that may result when dealing with loss, death, and grief: (1) You can't hurt yourself, (2) you can't hurt others, and (3) you can't damage property. Work with students to further clarify these three rules and to reinforce that the rules apply to both physical and emotional hurt. For example, discuss activities like throwing rocks or screaming: Do those behaviors fit the three rules? Often the situation will depend on the circumstances.

ASSESSMENT | Following the mini-lesson, students can create a four-week "uncalendar." The premise of an uncalendar is that it is undated so you can start at any time. For each day of their uncalendar, students identify a different way they can cope with loss, death, and grief while adhering to the three rules of not hurting oneself, not hurting others, and not damaging property. Students can draw pictures, cut and paste from magazines, or use words. Limiting the number of times a week a student can use playing sports will force students to think of alternative ways to cope when sports are not an option. Students can share their uncalendars and post them around the classroom for other students to learn new strategies for coping. For assessment criteria, students should be able to identify nearly twenty-eight different coping strategies when faced with feelings associated with loss, death, and grief. (Constructs: Attitudes toward behavior, perceived behavioral control, subjective norms.)

NHES 2 | Analyze Influences

Students will analyze the influence of family, peers, culture, media, technology, and other factors on health behaviors.

ASSESSMENT CRITERIA
- Identify both external and internal influences on health.
- Explain how external and internal influences interact to impact health choices and behaviors.
- Explain both positive and negative influences, as appropriate.

Grades K–2

Personal Life Interviews Whether students are grieving because of illness, death, or divorce, personal stories can carry positive lasting memories. Students can interview an ailing loved one or other family members about their memories and life lessons.

ASSESSMENT | For an assessment task, students can conduct personal life story interviews using a smartphone or other video recording device. Story Corps (storycorps.org/participate/great-questions) provides examples for conversation starters and questions to get students started. Students can include healthy ways that family members have dealt with the loss and their own memories. (Constructs: Attitudes toward behavior, subjective norms.)

Grades 3–5

Sentence Stems Teachers can use sentence stems to begin a discussion of dying and death with upper-elementary students. Some examples of sentence stems are:

- Death is like . . .
- A good thing about death is . . .
- The scariest thing about death is . . .
- When someone dies, I feel . . .
- A bad thing about death is . . .
- An important thing to remember about death is . . .

After students complete their sentences, they can share with each other in small groups and then with the rest of the class. These statements can act as a springboard for discussing some of the issues and feelings related to death.

ASSESSMENT Students can use the completion of the sentence stems to initiate a conversation about where people learn their ideas about death and loss. For an assessment task, students can analyze whether their sentence completions come from internal (feelings, moods, curiosity, fear, likes, dislikes) or external influences (family, peers, culture, media) or both. For example, when students share their ideas about good, bad, or scary things about death, they can analyze how they might have learned these responses. For assessment criteria, students should specify and explain at least three influences on their and others' ideas about loss and death. (Construct: Attitudes toward behavior.)

Grades 6–8

Dealing with Loss, Death, and Grief in Different Cultures Teachers can ask students what they know about how different cultures deal with issues related to loss, death, and grief. Students can work in pairs or small groups to find out more about the culture of their family or a culture they want to know more about. For example, Mexicans observe the Day of the Dead (Dia de los Muertos) to remember members of their families who have died and to celebrate the continuity of life. The focus of students' research is how different cultures help their members deal with loss, death, and grief in healthy ways. To illustrate, the Day of the Dead is not a day of mourning but a festive time. Many other cultures honor their ancestors with ceremonies of respect.

ASSESSMENT For an assessment task, students can investigate the culture of their families or a culture of interest to learn how traditions related to loss, death, and grief are observed. Students can create a digital presentation to share their findings. For assessment criteria, students should explain how the traditions help members of the culture deal with loss, death, and grief in healthy ways. This activity links to social studies. (Construct: Attitudes toward behavior.)

Portrayals of Death in the Media Middle school students can brainstorm about the ways they have seen death portrayed in movies, television shows, news, and commercials. Students can work as a class or in small groups to add to a brainstorm list with four columns (movies, television shows, news, commercials), saying all the things that pop into their minds, without editing. Students then can analyze their lists for themes and ideas that come up repeatedly. For example, students might say that movies often portray violent death or strong emotions about death. They might notice television commercials about buying life insurance for family members. Television shows might include jokes about or make fun of death (a weekly cartoon in which the same character is killed each week). Students can draw conclusions about the influences portrayed in the media related to ideas about loss, death, and grief.

ASSESSMENT For an assessment task, students can identify themes or ideas they notice in their brainstorm list. For assessment criteria, students should explain how these themes or ideas might influence a young person's ideas about loss, death, and grief. (Construct: Attitudes toward behavior.)

NHES 3 | Access Information, Products, and Services

Students will demonstrate the ability to access valid information and products and services to enhance health.

ASSESSMENT CRITERIA

- Access health information—Locate specific sources of health information, products, or services relevant to enhancing health in a given situation.
- Evaluate information sources—Explain the degree to which identified sources are valid, reliable, and appropriate as a result of evaluating each source.

Grades K–2

Talking Things Out One of the most important health education skills for children of all ages is knowing where to go for help and to ask for help when they need it. Children can talk about who can help them when they feel sad, angry, or depressed. Students can draw a support tree to show the people they can go to when they need to talk things out. Children should include at least two adults on their support tree.

ASSESSMENT The support tree or other graphic (helping hand) students draw to illustrate the people in their support system is the assessment task for this activity. For assessment criteria, students should include at least two adults in their support system and explain how each person can help them if they need to talk to someone about questions or problems. (Construct: Perceived behavioral control.)

Grades 3–5

Answering My Questions About Death, Loss, and Grief As students grow, the questions they will have about these topics will change. Students need to identify credible sources for answering questions that may arise. Have students write down two or three questions they have about death, loss, and grief. Giving students sentence starters can help, such as: What happens when . . .?; How do people . . .?; Why do I feel . . .?, and so on. Then have students visit www.kidshealth.org to see if they can locate a response to some of their questions. Kidshealth.org is organized for kids, teens, and adults. The kids' section should provide students with thoughtful ways to think about the questions they raised. Have students read the answers to their questions and continue clicking on links within the short articles to learn more. This is an independent opportunity for students to explore a credible source and get answers to questions they may have.

ASSESSMENT Following exploration of responses on the website, have students engage in a 4-3-2-1 write. Have students identify four new things they learned from reviewing the information on the web page; three things they want to learn more about and where they might go to find the answer; two ways they can tell this is a credible website for information; and one question they have for their parents or guardian about their family beliefs about death, loss, and grief. Allow students to share their responses with the class. For assessment criteria, students' responses should reflect accurate information, students should be able to identify what makes the website a credible source of information, and they should recognize their parents or guardians as credible sources for understanding family beliefs. (Construct: Perceived behavioral control.)

Grades 6–8

Helping a Friend or Family Member Students need to know how to help or get help for a friend or family member who is experiencing sadness, anger, or other difficult emotions. Teachers can make a list of school and community health helpers with younger students. Older students can use phone books to identify community helpers and organizations.

ASSESSMENT The list of school and community helpers students make for helping a family member or friend is the assessment task for this activity. For assessment criteria, students should explain how to contact the school and community helpers and tell why they are good sources of assistance. (Construct: Perceived behavioral control.)

The Hopeline Network Students can learn about suicide prevention lifelines at www.suicidepreventionlifeline.org. At this site, students can use the crisis center locater to find a Lifeline network crisis center in their area, identify strategies to help themselves or someone else in a crisis situation, as well as access suicide prevention information.

ASSESSMENT | For an assessment task, students can explain how to get help through a suicide hotline. For assessment criteria, students should explain how to determine whether a hotline is a valid source of assistance (has trained professional counselors). (Construct: Perceived behavioral control.)

NHES 4 | Interpersonal Communication

Students will demonstrate the ability to use interpersonal communication skills to enhance health and avoid or reduce health risks.

ASSESSMENT CRITERIA
- Use appropriate verbal/nonverbal communication strategies in an effective manner to enhance health or avoid/reduce health risks.
- Use appropriate skills (negotiation skills, refusal skills) and behaviors (eye contact, body language, attentive listening).

Grades K–2

Expressing My Feelings   This is an activity that can be used with very young children who might have a difficult time expressing their feelings. It can be used with one child who is grieving or for a whole class who is grieving. Provide grieving students with a paper bag. Tell students to make a paper mask that shows how they are feeling.

ASSESSMENT | The paper mask is the assessment task for this activity. For assessment criteria, students should be able to describe the feeling that they drew on their mask. (Construct: Perceived behavioral control.)

Expressing Concern for Others   Young children are often unsure about what to say to a friend who has experienced a loss. This learning strategy can follow NHES 1, The Many Meanings of Loss lesson. Using the pictures that students created about the different loss experiences they have experienced and the feelings each experienced, students can discuss thoughtful and helpful ways to respond to a friend or family member who has experienced loss. The class can brainstorm on the board helpful or harmful responses and discuss ways individuals might react or feel about different responses and why. This discussion will continue to increase student empathy for others who are experiencing loss.

ASSESSMENT | Have pairs of students switch drawings from NHES 1, The Many Meanings of Loss. Have each student write two different ways he or she could respond to the situation of his or her classmate. Then have the pairs come back together and discuss their responses. Ask students to determine if the response would provide comfort and demonstrate concern, or if the statement may need to be revised to avoid being accidentally unthoughtful through words. Students can revise their statements so that in the end all have created statements that demonstrate how to thoughtfully express concern to someone experiencing loss. For assessment criteria, students will be able to effectively communicate concern for others as well as to provide feedback to a peer as to how to improve a concern statement. (Constructs: Perceived behavioral control, attitudes toward behavior.)

Grades 6–8

Helpful vs. Hurtful Statements   Begin the lesson by asking students to think about their own experiences with grief. Ask them to think about helpful and hurtful things that were said to them after the death of someone close to them. Write the following statements on an individual card and then mix them up. Give one card to each student and ask them to read the statement. Have a discussion about whether the statement is helpful or hurtful.

Examples of Helpful Statements

"How can I be of help?"

"Tell me how you are feeling."

"It must be hard to accept."

"That must be very painful."

"I'm sorry."

"I wish I could take the pain away."

Examples of Hurtful Statements

"I know how you feel."

"Time heals all things."

"She/he led a full life."

"Don't worry, you will get over it."

"Don't be such a baby."

"Just try to forget about it."

ASSESSMENT | The response to each statement is the assessment task for this activity. For assessment criteria, students should be able to explain why the statement is either helpful or hurtful to a grieving person. (Construct: Perceived behavioral control.)

Expressing Care and Concern   Young people often have a difficult time communicating with someone who is terminally ill or dying or experiencing the loss of a loved one. Discuss with students why it is important to continue to express care and concern for loved ones who are grieving, ill, or dying. Brainstorm ways for expressing care and concern for these individuals, as well as different situations in which this might be important and beneficial. In groups of three, have one student be the ill or dying individual, one be an observer, and the third be the young person wishing to express care and concern. Allow students to role-play a minimum of three different scenarios so that each person has the opportunity to play each role.

ASSESSMENT | For an assessment task, provide students one additional situation and in either a written dialogue, storyboard, oral role-play, or other appropriate format of students' choice, students should demonstrate their ability to express care and concern appropriately for the situation. For assessment criteria, students should be able to express appropriate verbal and nonverbal communication strategies for the situation and be able to explain how their communication skills demonstrate their ability to communicate in a health-enhancing way. (Constructs: Perceived behavioral control, attitude toward behavior.)

NHES 5 | Decision Making

Students will demonstrate the ability to use decision-making skills to enhance health.

ASSESSMENT CRITERIA
Reach a health-enhancing decision using a process consisting of the following steps:
- Identify a health-risk situation.
- Examine alternatives.
- Evaluate positive and negative consequences.
- Decide on a health-enhancing course of action.

Grades K–5

Planning a Funeral or Memorial   Many students have questions about funerals, wakes, and other types of services associated with death. Teachers can discuss the idea of remembering and honoring the life of a person as the reasons for these services, allowing students to discuss their experiences of these services with the rest of the class. If a class pet dies, students might want to plan a funeral for it, but it should be a generic service without any specific religious affiliations. An appropriate focus for the service is to allow students to share memories of the class pet with one another. For example, the students might plan a program that includes a song performed by a group of students, memory sharing, the burial, and another music selection.

ASSESSMENT | For an assessment task, students can use this activity to make decisions about planning a funeral or remembrance for a class pet (or a community member, if appropriate). For assessment criteria, students should decide how they will carry out their funeral or remembrance. Students can use the decision-making model described in Chapter 3 to help them work through the process (state the problem, identify alternatives, consider consequences, choose their action, evaluate how it went). (Construct: Perceived behavioral control.)

Grades 6–8

Decision Making About Living Wills Students might have heard about "living wills" or "advanced health care directives" on the news during the past several years. These documents tell family members and medical personnel whether a person wants to be kept on artificial life support if he or she is ever permanently unconscious or otherwise dying and unable to speak for himself or herself. Living wills are created differently across the fifty states. Students can investigate living wills in various states through a Web search and report to class members on the kinds of decisions that must be made in establishing a living will.

ASSESSMENT | The reports students make on living wills are the assessment task for this activity. For assessment criteria, students should explain the decisions required for making a living will and discuss their ideas about establishing such a document. (Constructs: Attitudes toward behavior, perceived behavioral control.)

NHES 6 | Goal Setting

Students will demonstrate the ability to use goal-setting skills to enhance health.

ASSESSMENT CRITERIA
- Goal statement—Give goal statement that identifies health benefits; goal is achievable and will result in enhanced health.
- Goal-setting plan—Show plan that is complete, logical, and sequential, and includes a process to assess progress.

Grades 6–8

How Will Others Remember Me? Joyce Fetro uses a teaching activity called "Writing My Own Epitaph" to have students think about what they want to accomplish in life.[48] In this activity, students write their own epitaph—an inscription on a gravestone that contains a brief statement about the dead person. Students should consider what they want to accomplish before they die and what they want to be remembered for doing. Dr. Fetro has students draw a tombstone and write their epitaph. This activity truly is an example of "beginning with the end in mind" as students consider the kind of life they want to lead and how they want to be remembered.

ASSESSMENT | The epitaphs students write are the assessment task for this activity. For assessment criteria, students should identify three short- or long-term goals they would like to accomplish that would lead toward their being remembered in the way they write. (Construct: Perceived behavioral control.)

NHES 7 | Self-Management

Students will demonstrate the ability to practice health-enhancing behaviors and avoid or reduce health risks.

ASSESSMENT CRITERIA
- Application (transfer)—Initiate health-enhancing behaviors; apply concepts and skills appropriately and effectively.
- Self-monitoring and reflection—Monitor actions and make adjustments; accept feedback and make adjustments; able to self-assess, reflect on, and take responsibility for actions.

Grades K–2

Jenny Is Scared! When Sad Things Happen in the World Teachers can read Carol Shuman's book *Jenny Is Scared! When Sad Things Happen in the World* to talk with young children about managing their fears related to terrorism, war, and other violent events. In this story, Jenny and her brother Sam know that something sad is on the news that has adults upset. There's no school, and Jenny and Sam want to know what's going on and how not to be scared. The book provides concrete suggestions for helping children feel safer and offers families and educators ideas for making the world a better place. This book is published by the American Psychological Association's Magination Press (Special Books for Children's Special Concerns; www.maginationpress.com).

ASSESSMENT | For an assessment task, teachers can help students make a list on chart paper of the ways the story recommends to help children feel better and not be scared (ask questions, talk about how I feel, send loving thoughts to other people). Each student can select a way to feel better to draw and write about. For assessment criteria, students should explain at least one way to feel better and less scared. (Construct: Perceived behavioral control.)

The Memory Box: A Book About Grief Joanna Rowland, author of *The Memory Box: A Book About Grief,* tells the story of a young girl who has lost a loved one and uses memories to help in the grieving process. She worries that she might forget the person and creates a memory box filled with tokens that will help sustain her memories. Rowland has created an instructional video (www.youtube.com/watch?v=Doz2FsyqTVE) to share her ideas for making a memory box.

ASSESSMENT | For an assessment task, students can illustrate, create a digital "memory box," or describe the things they would put into their memory boxes of special relatives, friends, or pets. Students can create a digital slide show that showcases images, photographs, and sayings that remind them of their loved one. For assessment criteria, students should explain how making a memory box can help them deal with changes in healthy and positive ways. (Construct: Perceived behavioral control.)

Grades 3–5

Magic Circle Teachers can prepare discussion questions for this activity in advance to use in that all-important teachable moment—instances such as the death of a class pet, the death of a student's pet (with the student's permission), or the death of a public figure. The class should sit in a circle, in chairs, desks, or on the floor, so that children are face to face and can make eye contact with each other. Questions should be appropriate for the age of the students and the degree of feeling they have about the pet or person who died. The idea of the Magic Circle is to allow children to express their feelings, rather than to dwell on the details of the death. The teacher might simply say, "We want to spend some time talking about and remembering [name]. What do you remember?" As children contribute, the teacher might ask how students feel about the memory they shared. Diane Parker, a first-grade teacher, had her class watch a caterpillar ("Blackie") spin a cocoon and, over time, emerge from the cocoon and fly away.[49] As the children discussed these events, one student said with sadness, "I just miss the old Blackie!" Even though Blackie didn't die, the caterpillar the children had come to regard as part of their class was no longer with them, and they had feelings about that. The children talked about Blackie and shared their memories of watching Blackie change and grow.

After a loss, students need opportunities to express their feelings, ask questions, and clarify misconceptions about death. Teachers sometimes hesitate to conduct an activity such as this one, fearing that children will not want to share their feelings or that they will be overcome with grief. Teachers who build trust, respect, and a sense of community in their classrooms throughout the school year will find that students generally welcome the opportunity to talk about how they feel and what they remember. Teachers need to ask students' permission to talk about anything that involves them personally. Teachers might need to seek parental permission, too. Invite the school counselor to sit in with the circle to help answer questions and respond to children's feelings.

ASSESSMENT | The focus of this activity is talking things out to help students deal with strong feelings, an important self-management strategy. Contributions are voluntary; students can skip their turn at any time. For an assessment task, students can write a paragraph or draw a picture with a sentence about the person or pet they are remembering. For assessment criteria, students should indicate how they use their memories to keep the person or pet in a special place in their minds and hearts. (Constructs: Subjective norms, attitude toward behavior.)

Memory Book   Children can make a memory book if a class pet dies. This activity can also be used if a classmate dies or if a friend of the class or school dies. Adults and children can find comfort and sometimes even pleasure in sharing memories of the deceased. Memories reaffirm that loved people and pets go on living in our minds and will always be an important part of us now and as we grow older. Students can make their own memory book from a stapled, construction paper booklet, or they might contribute a page to a class book. Students can write notes and draw pictures that remind them of the deceased. Students can share their memory books with the rest of the class. If students make a class book, they might want to give it to the family of the deceased. Students can complete a memory book as an individual project for children who have lost a pet or a loved one.

ASSESSMENT | The memory book students create is the assessment task for this activity. For assessment criteria, students should explain how creating the book helps them remember the person or pet and deal with their feelings in healthy ways. (Constructs: Subjective norms, attitude toward behavior.)

Grades 6–8

Healthy Strategies for Dealing with Loss   The Kids' Health website for teens (www.kidshealth.org/teen) provides information on a variety of topics young people might be dealing with regarding loss or grief. Some of the topics students can investigate include:

- Coping with the death of a family member.
- Dealing with divorce, moving, or a breakup.
- Coping with death and grief.
- Talking with a friend about suicide.
- Coping with the death of a pet.

Students can investigate one of the topics that is of interest to them or relevant to the class.

ASSESSMENT | For an assessment task, students can work in pairs or small groups to research and report on these and other related topics, and develop a list of healthy self-management strategies for their topic. For assessment criteria, students should be able to identify how the information presented comes from a credible source (NHES 3) and identify healthy self-management strategies appropriate for their topic. (Constructs: Attitudes toward behavior, perceived behavioral control.)

NHES 8 | Advocacy

Students will demonstrate the ability to advocate for personal, family, and community health.

ASSESSMENT CRITERIA
- Health-enhancing position—Give clear, health-enhancing position.
- Support for position—Support position with facts, concepts, examples, and evidence.
- Audience awareness—Show awareness of target audience; choose words, tone, and examples to suit audience.
- Conviction—Display conviction for position.

Grades K–2

Ida Always   Teachers can use Caron Levis's book *Ida, Always* to talk with children about their reactions to people who are ill or dying. Loosely based on real-life polar bears Ida and Gus at New York's Central Park Zoo, this story tells how Gus discovers that Ida is terminally ill and how he handles this revelation. He goes through anger and denial as he does not want to imagine life without Ida. In the days that follow, the two bears go through the stages of grief together. Some days they play and some days they need to be alone to process their feelings. Students can discuss how they might feel in Gus's place, but they can discuss other feelings as well. This activity provides a good opportunity to talk with children about expressing caring and compassion for those who are ill and remembering that a loved one can stay with them in spirit and memories.

ASSESSMENT | For an assessment task, students can identify the ways that Gus felt, cared for, and spent time with Ida in her final days. Students can draw a picture of themselves feeling similar emotions from personal experience and write a message expressing how they would want someone to care for them. For assessment criteria, students should identify a stage of grief and a positive support system to help them cope. (Construct: Subjective norms.)

Grades 3–5

The AIDS Memorial Quilt (The NAMES Project)   Students can learn more about the AIDS Memorial Quilt at www.aidsquilt.org/. The mission of this advocacy project is to preserve, care for, and use the AIDS Memorial Quilt to foster healing, heighten awareness, and inspire action in the struggle against HIV and AIDS. The goals of the AIDS Memorial Quilt are to:

- Provide a creative means for remembrance and healing.
- Effectively illustrate the enormity of the AIDS epidemic.
- Increase the general public's awareness of HIV and AIDS.
- Assist others with education on preventing HIV infection.
- Raise funds for community-based AIDS service organizations.

Students can learn about making panels for the quilt, view the quilt, and learn about the quilt's history.

ASSESSMENT | For an assessment task, students can discuss how the AIDS Memorial Quilt meets the expectations for an advocacy project. For assessment criteria, students should be able to explain the message, the background, the target audience, and the conviction of the project. (Construct: Subjective norms.)

Grades 6–8

It's Okay to Ask for Help   First, have students identify different community resources that are available for students and family members who have experienced a loss or who are grieving. Next, guide the students in creating table tents, wall posters, public service announcements to be read on the morning announcements, or other appropriate advocacy formats. The advocacy messages should give a message that it is okay to ask for help and some credible resources available to seek help from.

ASSESSMENT | The advocacy messages are the assessment task. For assessment criteria, students should be able to justify how the resources identified in their message are credible sources (NHES 3) as well as show the characteristics of a good advocate—state a strong position, back it up, target the audience, and speak with conviction. (Constructs: Subjective norms, perceived behavioral control.)

INTERNET AND OTHER RESOURCES

WEBSITES

American Academy of Child and Adolescent Psychiatry
www.aacap.org

Comfort Zone Camp
www.comfortzonecamp.org

Compassionate Friends
www.compassionatefriends.org

Dougy Center for Grieving Children and Families
www.dougy.org

Fernside
www.fernside.org

GriefNet
www.griefnet.org

National Alliance for Grieving Children
www.childrengrieve.org

National Association of School Psychologists
www.naspcenter.org

National Center for School Crisis and Bereavement
www.cincinnatichildrens.org/svc/alpha/s/school-crisis

Parents Trauma Resource Center
www.tlcinstitute.org

Public Broadcast Service
www.pbs.org

Substance Abuse and Mental Health Services Administration
www.samhsa.gov

Suicide Hotlines
www.suicidehotlines.com

OTHER RESOURCES

American Foundation for Suicide Prevention. *After a Suicide: A Toolkit for Schools* (afsp.org/our-work/education/after-a-suicide-a-toolkit-for-schools/; 2011).

Burns, G. *When Kids Are Grieving: Addressing Grief and Loss in School* (Thousand Oaks, CA: Corwin Publishing, 2010).

Children's Safety Network. *Suicide Prevention Resource Guide 2012* (www.childrenssafetynetwork.org/sites/childrenssafetynetwork.org/files/YouthSuicidePrevention_ResourceGuide2012.pdf; 2012).

Corr, C., and D. Balk, *Children's Encounters with Death, Bereavement, and Coping* (New York: Springer Publishing Company, 2010).

Goldman, L. *Great Answers to Difficult Questions About Death* (London, England: Jessica Kingsley Publishers, 2009).

National Commission on Children and Disasters. *2010 Report to the President and Congress,* AHRQ Publication No. 100M037 (Rockville, MD: Agency for Healthcare Research and Quality, 2010).

Schonfeld, David, and Marcia Quackenbush. *The Grieving Student: A Teacher's Guide* (Baltimore, MD: Brookes Publisher, 2010).

U.S. Department of Health and Human Services. *The Courage to Remember: Childhood Traumatic Grief Curriculum* (Rockville, MD: Center for Mental Health Services, 2007).

CHILDREN'S LITERATURE

AGES 5–8

Aliki. *The Two of Them.* Greenwillow Books, 1979.

Barber, Elke. *Is Daddy Coming Back in a Minute?: Explaining (Sudden) Death to Very Young Children in Words They Can Understand.* Jessica Kingsley Publishers, 2016.

Beck, Carolyn. *That Squeak.* Fitzhenry & Whiteside, 2015.

Buscaglia, Leo. *The Fall of Freddie the Leaf.* Henry Holt, 1982.

Clifton, L. *Everett Anderson's Goodbye.* Holt, Rinehart & Winston, 1973. (Multicultural)

Cohen, M. *Jim's Dog Muffins.* Greenwillow Books, 1984.

Cook, Julia. *Grief Is Like a Snowflake.* National Center for Youth Issues, 2011.

Davies, Benji. *Grandad's Island.* Candlewick Press, 2016.

Davies, Nicola. *The Pond.* Graffeg, 2017.

Demas, C. *Saying Goodbye to Lulu.* Little, Brown Books for Young Readers, 2009.

Fox, Mem. *Tough Boris.* Harcourt Brace, 1994.

Hayes, Geoffrey. *Benny and Penny in How to Say Goodbye.* Toon Books, an imprint of Raw Junior, 2016.

Hest, Amy. *My Old Pal, Oscar.* Abrams Book for Young Readers, 2016.

Innes, Shona. *Life Is Like the Wind (Big Hug).* Barron's Educational Series, 2014.

Kerner, Susan. *Always By My Side.* Star Bright Books, 2013.

Larsen, Elisabeth Helland. *I Am Life.* Little Gestalten, 2017.

Levis, Caron. *Ida, Always.* Atheneum Books for Young Readers, 2016.

Loewen, Nancy. *Saying Good-bye to Uncle Joe: What to Expect When Someone You Love Dies.* Picture Window Books, 2011.

Lowry, Lois. *Gooney Bird Is So Absurd.* HMH Books for Young Readers, 2009.

MacLachlan, Patricia. *Snowflakes Fall.* Random House Books for Young Readers, 2013.

Maier, Inger M. *Ben's Flying Flowers.* Magination Press, 2012.

Marcero, Deborah. *Rosie and Crayon.* Peter Pauper Press, Inc., 2017.

Mathers, Petra. *When Aunt Mattie Got Her Wings.* Beach Lane Books, 2014.

Meng, Cece. *Always Remember*. Philomel Books, 2016.

Parr, Todd. *The Goodbye Book*. Little, Brown and Company, 2015.

Penn, A. *Chester Raccoon and the Acorn Full of Memories*. Tanglewood Press, 2009.

Rowland, Joanna. *The Memory Box: A Book About Grief*. Sparkhouse Family, 2017.

Salerno, Steven. *Tim's Goodbye*. Farrar, Straus and Grioux, 2018.

Shuman, Carol. *Jenny Is Scared!* Magination Press, 2003.

Smith, Patricia. *Janna and the Kings*. Lee & Low Books Inc., 2016.

Stickney, Doris. *Water Bugs and Dragonflies: Explaining Death to Young Children*. Pilgrim Press, 2014.

Thompson, Holly. *One Wave at a Time: A Story About Grief and Healing*. Albert Whitman & Company, 2018.

Viorst, Judith. *The Tenth Good Thing About Barney*. Atheneum, 1971.

Weninger, Brigitte. *Aunt Fanny's Star: Children and the Loved Ones They Lose*. Minedition, 2017.

White, E. B. *Charlotte's Web*. Harper Junior Books, 1952.

Willems, M. *City Dog, Country Frog*. Hyperion Books for Children/ Disney, 2010.

AGES 8–12

Anderson, John David. *Ms. Bixby's Last Day*. Walden Pond Press, an imprint of HarperCollins Publishers, 2017.

Avery, Tom. *My Brother's Shadow*. Schwartz & Wade Books, 2014.

Benjamin, Ali. *The Thing About Jellyfish*. Little, Brown and Company, 2017.

Bishop, Jenn. *The Distance to Home*. A Yearling Book, 2017.

Carestio, M. *Black Jack Jetty: A Boy's Journey Through Grief*. Magination Press, 2010.

Chan, Crystal. *Bird*. Atheneum Books for Young Readers, 2015.

Cochrane, M. *The Girl Who Threw Butterflies*. Yearling, 2010.

Creech, S. *Walk Two Moons*. HarperCollins, 1998. (Newbery Medal) (Multicultural)

Cuevas, Michelle. *The Care and Feeding of a Pet Black Hole*. Puffin Books, 2018.

Erskine, Kathryn. *Mockingbird*. Puffin, 2010. (National Book Award Winner)

Frost, Helen. *Applesauce Weather*. Candlewick Press, 2016.

Gemeinhart, Dan. *Some Kind of Courage*. Scholastic Press, 2016.

Geringer Bass, Laura. *The Girl with More Than One Heart*. Amulet Books, 2018.

Graff, Lisa. *Umbrella Summer*. HarperCollins, 2011.

Grimes, Nikki. *What Is Goodbye?* Hyperion, 2004.

Hesse, K. *Out of the Dust*. Scholastic, 1997. (Multicultural)

LaFleur, S. *Love, Aubrey*. Wendy Lamb Books, 2009.

Laso, Maria D. *Otherwise Known as Possum*. Scholastic Press, 2017.

Lean, Sarah. *A Dog Called Homeless*. Katherine Tegen Books, an imprint of HarperCollins Publishers, 2014.

Magnin, Joyce. *Jelly Bean Summer*. Sourcebooks Jabberwocky, 2017.

Martinez, C. *The Smell of Old Lady Perfume*. Cinco Puntos Press, 2008.

Maschari, Jennifer. *The Remarkable Journey of Charlie Price*. Balzer + Bray, and imprint of HarperCollins Publishers, 2016.

Mass, Wendy. *Jeremy Fink and the Meaning of Life*. Little, Brown Young Readers, 2006.

McGhee, Holly M. *Matylda, Bright & Tender*. Candlewick, 2017.

Moranville, Sharelle Byars. *27 Magic Words*. Holiday House, 2016.

O'Reilly, Jane H. *The Notations of Cooper Cameron*. Carolrhoda Books, 2017.

Oechsle, Michael. *The Lost Cipher*. Albert Whitman & Company, 2017.

Patron, Susan. *The Higher Power of Lucky*. Atheneum/Richard Jackson Books, 2006. (Newbery Award, 2007)

Patterson, James. *The Worst Years of My Life*. Little, Brown and Company, 2014.

Patterson, K. *Bridge to Terabithia*. Avon Books, 1972.

Rylant, C. *Missing May*. Orchard Books, 1992.

Schroder, Monika. *Be Light Like a Bird*. Capstone Young Readers, a Capstone imprint, 2016.

Scott, Lisa Ann. *School of Charm*. Katherine Tegen Books, an imprint of HarperCollins Publishers, 2014.

Scrimger, Richard. *Downside Up*. Tundra Books, 2016.

Silberberg, Alan. *Milo: Sticky Notes and Brain Freeze*. Aladdin, 2011.

Sloan, Holly Goldberg. *Counting by 7s*. Dial, 2013.

Smith, Doris. *A Taste of Blackberries*. Crowell, 1972.

Smith, Tamara Ellis. *Another Kind of Hurricane*. Schwartz & Wade Books, 2015.

Spinelli, J. *Eggs*. Little, Brown Books for Young Readers, 2008.

Ventrella, Kim. *Skeleton Tree*. Scholastic Press, 2017.

Williams-Garcia, Rita. *Clayton Byrd Goes Underground*. Amistad, an imprint of HarperCollins Publishers, 2017.

ENDNOTES

1. R. McCarthy and J. Jessop, *Young People, Bereavement and Loss: Disruptive Transitions?* (London: National Children's Bureau for Joseph Rowntree Foundation, 2005).

2. D. Brunk, "Expert Shares Tips on Supporting Children's Grief: Ask the Families of Patients to Keep You Informed About All Important Events That Affect Their Children," *Pediatric News* 41, no. 4 (2007): 37.

3. E. Kübler-Ross, *On Death and Dying* (New York: Macmillan, 1969).

4. C. Willis, "The Grieving Process in Children: Strategies for Understanding, Educating, and Reconciling Children's Perceptions of Death," *Early Childhood Education Journal* 29, no. 4 (2002): 221–26.

5. T. Granot, *Without You: Children and Young People Growing Up with Loss and Its Effects* (Philadelphia, PA: Jessica Kingsley, 2005).

6. Brown University Child and Behavior Letter, "Helping a Child Deal with Death," *Brown University Child and Behavior* (2011).

7. D. Seibert, J. Drolet, and J. Fetro, *Helping Children Live with Death and Loss* (Carbondale, IL: Southern Illinois University Press, 2003).

8. M. Nagy, "The Child's Theories Concerning Death," *Journal of Genetic Psychology* 73 (1948): 3–27.

9. S. Hunter and D. Smith, "Predictors of Children's Understandings of Death: Age, Cognitive Ability, Death Experience and Maternal Communicative Competence," *Omega* 57, no. 2 (2008): 143–62.

10. National Association of School Psychologists, *Helping Children Cope with Loss, Death, and Grief: Tips for Teachers and Parents* (www.nasponline.org/assets /documents/Resources%20and%20Publications /Handouts/Safety%20and%20Crisis/CopeGrief.pdf; 2003).

11. Ibid.

12. D. Schonfeld and M. Quackenbush, *The Grieving Student: A Teacher's Guide* (Baltimore, MD: Paul H. Brookes Publishing Co., 2010).

13. Ibid.

14. M. Heath and B. Cole, "Strengthening Classroom Emotional Support for Children Following a Family Member's Death," *School Psychology International* 33, no. 3 (2012): 243–62.

15. American Academy of Child and Adolescent Psychiatry, *Children and Grief*, no. 8 (https://www.aacap.org /AACAP/Families_and_Youth/Facts_for_Families/FFF -Guide/Children-And-Grief-008.aspx; 2013).

16. The Dougy Center: The National Center for Grieving Children and Families, *Developmental Responses to Grief* (elunanetwork.org/assets/files/Developmental_ Responses_2017.pdf)

17. National Association of School Psychologists, *Helping Children Cope with Loss, Death, and Grief: Tips for Teachers and Parents* (www.nasponline.org/resources /crisis_safety/griefwar.pdf; 2003).

18. Fernside, *How to Help a Grieving Child* (www.fernside .org/grief-resources/how-to-help-a-grieving-child; 2010).

19. M. Heath et al., "Coping with Grief: Guidelines and Resources for Assisting Children," *Intervention in School and Clinic* 43, no. 5 (2008): 259–69.

20. Kübler-Ross, *On Death and Dying*.

21. D. Schonfeld and M. Quackenbush, *After a Loved One Dies: How Children Grieve and How Parents and Other Adults Can Support Them* (New York: New York Life Foundation, 2009).

22. American Hospice Foundation, *Grief at School: A Guide for Teachers and Counselors* (Washington, DC: American Hospice Foundation, 2014).

23. The Dougy Center: The National Center for Grieving Children and Families, *How to Help a Grieving Child* (www. dougy.org/grief-resources/how-to-help-a-grieving-child/; 2018).

24. National Association of School Psychologists, *Helping Children Cope with Loss, Death, and Grief: Tips for Teachers and Parents*.

25. J. Holland, "How Schools Can Support Children Who Experience Loss and Death," *British Journal of Guidance and Counseling* 36, no. 4 (2008): 411–24.

26. D. Seibert, J. Drolet, and J. Fetro, *Helping Children Live with Death and Loss.*

27. M. Jellinek, J. Bostic, and S. Schlozman, "When a Student Dies," *Educational Leadership* 65, no. 7 (2007): 78–82.

28. Heath et al., "Coping with Grief."

29. J. Milton, "Helping Primary School Children Manage Loss and Grief: Ways the Classroom Teacher Can Help," *Education and Health* 22, no. 4 (2004): 58–60.

30. The National Child Traumatic Stress Network, *Age-Related Reactions to a Traumatic Event* (https://www.nctsn.org/sites/default/files/resources//age_related_reactions_to_traumatic_events.pdf; 2010).

31. A. Masten and J. Osofsky (eds.), "Disasters and Their Impact on Child Development [Special Section]," *Child Development* 81, no. 4 (2010): 1029–1286.

32. Annette M. LaGreca et al. (eds.), *Helping Children Cope with Disasters and Terrorism* (Washington, DC: American Psychological Association, 2002).

33. The National Child Traumatic Stress Network, *Child Trauma Toolkit for Educators* (www.nctsn.org/sites/default/files/resources//child_trauma_toolkit_educators.pdf; 2008).

34. D. Abramson et al., *Impact on Children and Families of the Deepwater Horizon Oil Spill: Preliminary Findings of the Coastal Population Impact Study*, Research Brief 2010-8 (New York: National Center for Disaster Preparedness, Columbia University Mailman School of Public Health, 2010).

35. The National Child Traumatic Stress Network, *Child Trauma Toolkit for Educators.*

36. P. Lazarus, S. Jimerson, and S. Brock, *Responding to Natural Disasters: Helping Children and Families* (http://www.psychology.org.nz/wp-content/uploads/2014/04/4-Responding-to-Natural-Disasters-Helping-Children-and-Families-Information-for-School-Crisis-teams1.pdf; 2014).

37. The National Child Traumatic Stress Network, *Child Trauma Toolkit for Educators.*

38. P. Lazarus, S. Jimerson, and S. Brock, *Responding to Natural Disasters: Helping Children and Families.*

39. Ibid.

40. The National Child Traumatic Stress Network, *Child Trauma Toolkit for Educators.*

41. Centers for Disease Control and Prevention, *Five Leading Causes of Deaths Among Person Ages 10–14, United States, 2010* (www.cdc.gov/injury/images/lc-charts/leading_causes_of_death_by_age_group_2017_1100w850h.jpg; 2017).

42. U.S. Department of Health and Human Services, *National Strategy for Suicide Prevention* (Rockville, MD: U.S. Department of Health and Human Services, 2001).

43. Ibid.

44. American Foundation for Suicide Prevention, *After a Suicide: A Toolkit for Schools* (afsp.org/our-work/education/after-a-suicide-a-toolkit-for-schools/; 2011).

45. Ibid.

46. M. Madden, D. Haley, and C. Saliwanchik-Brown, "Maine Youth Suicide Prevention Program Garrett Lee Smith Memorial Project Evaluation Report," *Report for SAMHSA, 2009* (www.maine.gov/suicide/docs/samhsa-ll-proj-eval.pdf).

47. STEP UP (Strategies and Tools Embrace Prevention with Upstream Programs) (https://nrepp.samhsa.gov/ProgramProfile.aspx?id=97; 2013)

48. J. Fetro, *Personal and Social Skills, Level 1* (Santa Cruz, CA: ETR Associates, 2000), 211–12.

49. D. Parker, conversation with author, Honolulu, HI, January 1997.

APPENDIX

RMC Health Rubrics for the National Health Education Standards

Scoring Rubric for Core Concepts

NHES #1: Students will comprehend concepts related to health promotion and disease prevention to enhance health.

Connections	Score	Comprehensiveness	Score
Completely and accurately describes relationships between behavior and health. Draws logical conclusion(s) about the connection between behavior and health.	4	Thoroughly covers health topic, showing both breadth (wide *range* of facts and ideas) and depth (*details* about facts and ideas). Response is completely accurate.	4
Describes relationships between behavior and health with some minor inaccuracies or omissions. Draws a plausible conclusion(s) about the connection between behavior and health.	3	Mostly covers health topic, showing breadth and depth, but one or both less fully. Response is mostly accurate, but may have minor inaccuracies.	3
Description of relationship(s) between behavior and health is incomplete and/or contains significant inaccuracies. Attempts to draw a conclusion about the connection between behavior and health, but conclusion is incomplete or flawed.	2	Minimal coverage of health topic, showing some breadth but little or no depth. Response may show some inaccuracies.	2
Inaccurate or no description of relationship(s) between behavior and health. Inaccurate OR no conclusion drawn about the connection between behavior and health.	1	No coverage of health topic information. Little or no accurate information.	1

Goals or Action: _____

Core Concepts Score: _____

Scoring Rubric for Analyzing Influences

NHES #2: Students will analyze the influence of family, peers, culture, media, technology, and other factors on health behaviors.

	Score
Accurately identifies both external and internal influences. Effectively explains how external and internal influences interact to impact health choices and behaviors of individuals, families, and communities. The explanation may include both positive and negative influences.	4
Accurately identifies influences and explains how these influences impact health choices and behaviors of individuals, families, and communities. The explanation may distinguish between external and internal influences, but does not clarify how external and internal factors interact to impact health choices and behaviors.	3
Identifies one or more relevant influences, but does not provide an effective explanation of how the influence(s) impact(s) health choices and behaviors of individuals, families, and communities.	2
Does not identify relevant influences, OR offers no explanation, OR the explanation reveals a flawed analysis of the influences' impact on health choices and behaviors of individuals, families, and communities.	1

Goals or Action: _____

Analyzing Influences Score: _____

Scoring Rubric for Accessing Information

NHES #3: Students will demonstrate the ability to access valid information and products and services to enhance health.

Accessing Health Information	Score	Evaluating Information Sources	Score
Locates very specific sources of health information, products, or services especially relevant for enhancing health in a given situation.	4	Clearly and accurately explains the degree to which identified sources are valid, reliable, and appropriate as a result of a thorough evaluation of each source. The explanation includes specific and extensive evaluative criteria for determining validity, reliability, and appropriateness.	4
Locates general sources of health information, products, or services that may enhance health in a given situation.	3	Explains the degree to which identified sources are valid, reliable, and appropriate as a result of an evaluation of each source. However, the explanation does not include extensive or specific evaluative criteria used in determining validity, reliability, and appropriateness of the sources.	3
Locates general sources of health information, products, or services; however, the information does not specifically support health-enhancing behaviors in a given situation.	2	Attempts to explain whether identified sources are valid, reliable, and appropriate; however, the evaluation is incomplete or flawed, OR the explanation is ineffective.	2
No sources located OR the information does not support health-enhancing behaviors in a given situation.	1	Does not attempt to evaluate sources to determine validity, reliability, and appropriateness to the given health situation. No explanation is provided.	1

Goals or Action: _____

_____

Accessing Information Score: _____

SOURCE: RMCHealth, *Health Education Sample Rubrics: Accessing Information,* Copyright © 2011. Reprinted with permission. For information call 303-239-6494 or access the RMC website (http://rmc.org/health-education-skills-models/).

Scoring Rubric for Interpersonal Communication

NHES #4: Students will demonstrate the ability to use interpersonal communication skills to enhance health and avoid or reduce health risks.

Communication Strategies*	Score
Uses appropriate verbal/nonverbal communication strategies in a highly effective manner (in a given situation with a particular audience) to enhance health or avoid/reduce risk for the health of self and others.	4
Uses appropriate verbal/nonverbal communication strategies in a generally effective manner (in a given situation with a particular audience) to enhance health or avoid/reduce risk for the health of self and others.	3
Uses verbal/nonverbal communication strategies effectively, but the strategies may be inappropriate for a given situation or a particular audience, OR the use of the selected strategy may be ineffective. In either case, the effect may not enhance health or avoid/reduce risk for the health of self and others.	2
Uses inappropriate verbal/nonverbal communication strategies to the given situation and particular audience, OR the communication strategies are used ineffectively. In either case, the effect will not enhance health or avoid/reduce risk for the health of self and others.	1

*This rubric can be used to assess a variety of communication skills and strategies, including:

Skill Sets
- Negotiation skills
- Refusal skills
- Conflict management skills
- Advocacy skills

Behaviors
- Eye contact
- Body language
- Respectful tone
- Clear message
- "I" messages

- Expressing needs, wants, and feelings
- Attentive listening
- Restating other points of view
- Suggesting an alternative

Goals or Action: _____

_____

Interpersonal Communication Score: _____

SOURCE: RMCHealth, *Health Education Sample Rubrics: Interpersonal Communication,* Copyright © 2011. Reprinted with permission. For information call 303-239-6494 or access the RMC website (http://rmc.org/health-education-skills-models/).

Scoring Rubric for Decision-Making **DM**

NHES #5: Students will demonstrate the ability to use decision-making skills to enhance health.	
Use of a Decision-Making Process	**Score**
Reaches a health-enhancing decision using a decision-making process consisting of the following steps: • Identifies a situation poses a health risk. • Examines a comprehensive set of alternative courses of action. • Effectively evaluates the positive and negative health consequences of each alternative course of action. • Decides on a health-enhancing course of action.	**4**
Reaches a health-enhancing decision using a decision-making process consisting of the following steps: • Identifies a situation that poses a health risk. • Examines some alternative courses of action. • Evaluates some of the positive and negative health consequences of each alternative course of action. • Decides on a health-enhancing course of action.	**3**
The decision-making process is incomplete or contains flaws. *For example:* • May not identify a situation that poses a health risk. • Does not examine alternative courses of action. • Fails to fully or effectively evaluate the positive and negative health consequences of alternative courses of action. • Presents a course of action that is vague, incomplete, or unlikely to enhance health.	**2**
Does not reach a health-enhancing decision due to an ineffective decision-making process. Steps of the decision-making process are ineffectively used or not evident.	**1**

Goals or Action: _____

Decision-Making Score: _____

SOURCE: RMCHealth, *Health Education Sample Rubrics: Decision Making,* Copyright © 2011. Reprinted with permission. For information call 303-239-6494 or access the RMC website (http://rmc.org/health-education-skills-models/).

Scoring Rubric for Goal Setting **GS**

NHES #6: Students will demonstrate the ability to use goal-setting skills to enhance health.

Goal Statement	Score	Goal-Setting Plan	Score
Clear and complete goal statement that explicitly states health benefits. The goal is achievable and will result in enhanced health.	**4**	The goal-setting plan: • Is complete—all important steps are included. • Follows a logical, sequential process. • Includes a process for assessing progress.	**4**
Goal statement that suggests or implies health benefits. The goal is achievable and will result in enhanced health.	**3**	The goal-setting plan: • Is complete—all important steps are included. • Follows a sequential process but may contain minor flaws. • Includes a process for assessing progress but could be incomplete.	**3**
Goal statement, but with no reference to health benefits. The goal may be unrealistic or unlikely to lead to health benefits.	**2**	The goal-setting plan may be incomplete or difficult to implement because of one or more of the following: • Does not include all important steps. • Does not follow a logical, sequential process. • Does not include a process for assessing progress.	**2**
No clear goal statement, OR the goal will not enhance health.	**1**	No goal-setting plan is stated, OR the plan is vague, illogical, or unrealistic.	**1**

Goals or Action: _____

Goal-Setting Score: _____

SOURCE: RMCHealth, *Health Education Sample Rubrics: Goal Setting,* Copyright © 2011. Reprinted with permission. For information call 303-239-6494 or access the RMC website (http://rmc.org/health-education-skills-models/).

NHES #7: Students will demonstrate the ability to practice health-enhancing behaviors and avoid or reduce health risks.

Application (Transfer)	Score	Self-Monitoring and Reflection	Score
• Consistently initiates health-enhancing behaviors to avoid or reduce risks without prompts or cues. • Applies learned concepts and skills appropriately and effectively in new situations to enhance health and avoid or reduce risks.	4	• Consistently monitors actions and makes adjustments as needed. • Openly accepts feedback and makes adjustments as needed. • Consistently able to self-assess, reflect on, and take responsibility for one's actions.	4
• Usually initiates health-enhancing behaviors to avoid or reduce risks without prompts or cues. • Applies learned concepts and skills appropriately and effectively in most new situations to enhance health and avoid or reduce risks.	3	• Usually monitors actions and makes adjustments as needed. • Is open to feedback and willing to make adjustments as needed. • Usually self-assesses, reflects on, or takes responsibility for one's actions.	3
• Rarely initiates health-enhancing behaviors to avoid or reduce risks without prompts or cues, OR requires prompts, cues, and reminders to initiate health-enhancing behaviors. • Seldom applies learned concepts and skills appropriately and/or effectively in new situations.	2	• Rarely monitors actions and makes needed adjustments. • Rarely accepts feedback and makes needed adjustments. • Rarely self-assesses, reflects on, or takes responsibility for one's actions.	2
• Never initiates health-enhancing behaviors to avoid or reduce risks without prompts or cues, OR requires prompts, cues, and reminders to initiate health-enhancing behaviors. • Unable to, or does not, apply learned concepts and skills to new situations.	1	• Does not monitor actions. • Fails to accept feedback and does not make adjustments. • Does not self-assess, reflect on, or take responsibility for one's actions.	1

Goals or Action: _____

_____

_____

_____

_____

Self-Management Score: _____

SOURCE: RMCHealth, *Health Education Sample Rubrics: Self-Management,* Copyright © 2011. Reprinted with permission. For information call 303-239-6494 or access the RMC website (http://rmc.org/health-education-skills-models/).

NHES #8: Students will demonstrate the ability to advocate for personal, family, and community health.

Health-Enhancing Position	Score	Support for Position	Score	Audience Awareness	Score	Conviction	Score
Extremely clear, health-enhancing position.	4	Thoroughly supports position using relevant and accurate facts, concepts, examples, and evidence.	4	• Strong awareness of the target audience (e.g., their background, perspective, interests). • Word choice, tone, examples, graphics, etc., are well suited for the target audience.	4	Displays strong and passionate conviction for position.	4
Generally clear, health-enhancing position.	3	Adequately supports position using facts, concepts, examples, and evidence; support may be incomplete and/or contain minor inaccuracies.	3	• Awareness of audience is evident. • Word choice, tone, examples, graphics, etc., are appropriate for the target audience.	3	Displays conviction for position.	3
Unclear or conflicting positions.	2	Inadequately supports position. Facts, concepts, examples, or evidence used contain significant inaccuracies and/or have little relevance.	2	• Some awareness of audience may be evident, however, word choice, tone, examples, graphics, etc., are not always appropriate for target audience.	2	Displays minimal conviction for position.	2
No position stated, OR position is not health-enhancing.	1	No accurate or relevant support for position is provided.	1	• No evidence of audience awareness. • Word choice, tone, examples, graphics, etc., are not appropriate for the audience.	1	No conviction for position is evident.	1

Goals or Action: _____

_____

_____

_____

_____

Advocacy Score: _____